Recent Research in Management, Accounting and Economics (RRMAE)

Edited by:

Dr. Hafinaz

Hariharan R

R. Senthil Kumar

Recent Research in Management, Accounting and Economics (RRMAE)

A case study on Recent Research in Management, Accounting and Economics

Edited by:

Dr. Hafinaz

Senior Lecturer and Academic Leader at the School of Accounting and Finance, Asia Pacific University of Technology & Innovation, Technology Park Malaysia

Hariharan R

Faculty School of Business and Management CHRIST(Deemed to be University) Bangalore, India

R. Senthil Kumar

Associate Professor, Department of Science & Humanities, AAA College of engineering & Technology, Sivakasi,Tamilnadu, India

Routledge
Taylor & Francis Group

First published 2025
by Routledge
4 Park Square, Milton Park, Abingdon, Oxon OX14 4RN

and by Routledge
605 Third Avenue, New York, NY 10158

Routledge is an imprint of the Taylor & Francis Group, an informa business

British Library Cataloguing-in-Publication Data
A catalogue record for this book is available from the British Library

ISBN: 9781032999029 (hbk)
ISBN: 9781032999036 (pbk)
ISBN: 9781003606642 (ebk)

DOI: 10.1201/9781003606642

Typeset in Sabon LT Std
by HBK Digital

Contents

About Conference

INTERNATIONAL CONFERENCE ON RECENT RESEARCH INMANAGEMENT, ACCOUNTING AND ECONOMICS -2024 (RRMAC-2024) will take place in the Pasumpon Muthuramalinga Thevar College, Usilampatti and Collaborated with Sri Sai Foundation, Madurai is to bring together innovative academics and industrial experts in the field of presenting novel contributions related to all real-world aspects of ECONOMICS, MANAGEMENT and ACCOUNTING. Theoretical papers must make a convincing case for the relevance of their results to practice. Authors are encouraged to write the abstract and introduction of their paper in a way that makes the results accessible and compelling to a general Management-Economics researcher. In particular, authors should bear in mind that anyone on the programme committee may be asked to review any paper.

The primary goal of the conference is to promote research and developmental activities in Management, Economics and Accounting. Another goal is to promote scientific information interchange between researchers, developers, engineers, students, and practitioners working in and around the world. The conference will be held every year to make it an ideal platform for people to share views and experiences in INTERNATIONAL CONFERENCE ON RECENT RESEARCH IN MANAGEMENT, ACCOUNTING AND ECONOMICS -2024 related areas.

About the Editors

Dr. Hafinaz

Dr. Hafinaz is a Senior Lecturer and Academic Leader at the School of Accounting and Finance, Asia Pacific University of Technology and Innovation, specializing in Banking and Finance. She earned her Ph.D. from the University of Technology Malaysia, where she gained expertise in secondary data analysis. Her research interests include analyzing mutual fund performance and testing the relationship between cryptocurrencies and macroeconomic variables. Dr. Hafinaz also holds a Master of Business Administration in Islamic Finance and received the University's Book Prize from the Open University Malaysia. She graduated with a Bachelor of Accounting with Honors from Tenaga National University, winning a full scholarship from MARA. Dr. Hafinaz is a Certified Retail Credit Practitioner and an Associate Member of the Asian Institute of Chartered Bankers. She has over a decade of academic and practical experience in the financial advisory field of the banking industry. She serves as an External Examiner for Financial Management professional papers for the Malaysian Association of Company Secretaries.

Hariharan R

Hariharan R currently working as an Assistant Professor in School of Business and Management, CHRIST (Deemed to be University), Yeshwanthpur campus, Bangalore. He has 9 years 2 months of teaching and 12 years of research experience. He holds Ph.D. degree in Finance (Banking Technology) from Department of Banking Technology, Pondicherry Central University, Puducherry. He has published almost 46 research papers include in Scopus, Web of Science, Thomas Returners, UGC care list and peer viewed Journals. He has authored 13 books and 11 chapters in edited volume books in International and National publishers. He also holds 4 copy rights from Indian Copyright office, India and one Patent published in India Patent office. He has done his certification from Microsoft on Certified Business Management Specialist, module (finance & warehouse) and NSE on Financial Markets in AMFI (Mutual Fund Advisor) module of NCFM. He has been resource person and delivered guest lecturer for MBA Schools and Universities on topic of Data Analysis using Excel and other statistical software. His area of interest is Finance, Banking, Enterprise Resource Planning, Analytics, Information Technology and Statistical Packages.

Senthil kumar

Senthil kumar is a Associate Professor in Science & humanities, AAA College of Engineering & Technology, Sivakasi, Tamil Nadu, India. He has more than teaching 12 years of teaching experience. He holds Ph.D. degree in General Topology (Mathematics) from Department of Mathematics, Bharathiar University, Coimbatore. He has published almost 56 research papers include in Scopus, Web of Science, Thomas Returners, UGC care list and peer viewed Journals.. He has conducted International conference more times particularly get TNSCST sponsored Two times. He has been resource person and delivered guest lecturer for many times and also act as Guest editor in IOP,AIP and few Scopus indexed journals. His area of interest is Mathematics, Network Theory, Enterprise Resource Planning, Analytics, Information Technology and Statistical Packages.

List of Figures

List of Tables

1 A study on impact of material delivery for metal products with reference to Chitra metals

P. S. Sumithra[a] and G. Meena Suguanthi[b]

Karpagam Academy of Higher Education, Coimbatore, Tamil Nadu, India

Abstract

In this investigation, the intricate realm of material handling and delivery, specifically focusing on the delivery of metal products, is meticulously examined. The study delves into the efficiency of this process, acknowledging its intricacies and the pivotal role played by labour-intensive tasks and robust logistics management. A comprehensive analysis is conducted through interviews with key stakeholders actively engaged in the delivery process. The study encompasses a sample size of 150 individuals, incorporating managers responsible for purchase, sales, and logistics handling. Through these interviews, a nuanced understanding of the challenges and intricacies within the metal product delivery process is sought, aiming to shed light on potential areas for improvement and optimization in this critical facet of logistics management.

Keywords: Raw materials, NEFT, Logistics, Transaction

Introduction

This investigation focuses on scrutinizing the ramifications of material delivery within Chitra Metals. Material delivery, the seamless movement of goods from their origin to the end user, stands as a pivotal process in the realm of logistics. In the context of Chitra Metals, the delivery of goods involves the transfer of ownership, facilitated through diverse transactions such as cash and carry, NEFT, and online fund transfers. The delivered materials encompass both finished goods and raw materials, with a significant emphasis on the latter, constituting 90% of the merchandise. Remarkably, the majority of transactions manifest as business-to-business exchanges, where these materials function as raw inputs for subsequent processes in other enterprises. This study aims to comprehensively explore and comprehend the intricate dynamics of material delivery within Chitra Metals, shedding light on its operational intricacies and implications Table 1.1.

Review of Literature

Table 1.1 Overview of key studies in iron and steel industry – authors, years, and focus areas.

Author name	Year	Study
Burange and Yammi	2010	Performance analysis of iron and steel industries, focusing on competitiveness from 1971 to 2008, utilizing secondary data from SAIL report, exploring variables like production, export, and import.
Saikia and Rajput	2018	Qualitative study on material handling and storage in the steel industry, emphasizing hazard management for workers, proposing mitigating measures to reduce daily workplace risks.
Wang and Zhang	2013	Analysis of scrap metals using Eddy current separation technology, detailing the unique process that separates metals and non-metals, discussing technology advancements, pros and cons, and its industry applications.
Kanhar and Wang	2020	Examination of fly ash and its treatment in the metal industry to reduce solid wastages, emphasizing effective waste management with an environmentally friendly approach.
Bhattacharya	2003	Exploration of government policies promoting growth opportunities in the Indian iron and steel industry, including investment opportunities, future prospects, industry analysis, and the study of existing and new plants.
Tripathy	2003	Intensive study of the Indian steel industry, analyzing the support provided by state and central governments, with a focus on promotion and industry sustenance.

[a]sumithrasakthivel2@gmail.com, [b]meenasuganthi.govindaraj@kahedu.edu.in

Author name	Year	Study
Sen Gupta	2005	Highlighting Indian steel industry policies post-economic liberalization, studying the global market, and providing suggestions for modernizing the industry.
Goyal and Acharya	2017	Exploration of advanced technology in the steel industry, assessing the availability of raw materials in domestic and international markets, and reviewing previous research articles related to the subject.
Dalvadi and Tagariaya	2019	Study of shareholder returns in the iron and steel industry, utilizing secondary data from 2017 to 2018, employing statistical tools like ANOVA for analysis .

Source: Author

Problem Statement

The purchasing process at Chitra Metals is marred by challenges, including the delivery of defective products, insufficient product availability, discrepancies in ordered volumes and delivered items, and seasonal shortages of high-demand goods, posing significant problems for both the organization and its customers.

Objective of the Study

- To study how much time customer spends on placing orders.
- To study the payment preference of customer.
- To understand the unique service provided by Chitra Metals.
- To evaluate the polices like order placing, return polices, delivery of goods.

Hypothesis of the Study

- 1Hypothesis: There is no significant association between no of experience in this field and how long you are using the product purchasing from Chitra Metals.
- 2Hypothesis: There is no significant association between no of experience in this field and Chitra Metals had a reasonable return and exchange policy.
- 3Hypothesis: There is no significant association between annual turnover of the company and how much time you spend on placing order in Chitra Metals.
- 4Hypothesis: There is no relationship between order and satisfaction.

Research Methodology

This study is conducted for the first time and so primary data is collected with the help of the questionnaire, the secondary data is also used for the study and most of it is collected from sales and purchase reports, customer database financial statement of the company and the feedback which is already collected from the customers & other distributors.

Analysis and Findings

The analysis and interpretation section unveils a comprehensive examination of the survey conducted on Chitra Metals' clientele, delving into their profiles, purchasing preferences, and satisfaction levels. Through detailed statistical analyses, the study explores the associations between variables such as experience and duration of purchase, experience and return policies, annual turnover and order placement duration, and the correlation between order frequency and customer satisfaction. The findings aim to shed light on the intricate dynamics of customer behaviour, offering valuable insights for Chitra Metals to enhance customer relations and optimize its business strategies.

I. Respondent profile
- **Experience in the field:**
  - Less than 1 year: 19.3%
  - 1 - 2 years: 22.0%
  - 2 - 3 years: 14.7%
  - 3 - 4 years: 16.7%
  - More than 4 years: 27.3%
- **Profession:**
  - Sole proprietor: 62.0%
  - Partnership: 15.3%
  - Wholesaler: 4.0%
  - Retailer: 18.7%
- **Annual turnover:**
  - Less than 1 crore: 40.7%
  - 1 - 2 crores: 38.7%
  - 2 - 3 crores: 20.7%
- **Duration of using Chitra Metals products:**
  - 1 month: 1.3%
  - Less than 1 month: 8.0%
  - 1 year: 12.7%
  - Less than 1 year: 49.3%
  - More than 1 year: 28.7%
- **Time spent on placing orders:**

- Every day: 1.3%
- Weekly once: 9.3%
- Once a month: 23.3%
- Twice a month: 36.0%
- Every 2 or 3 months: 30.0%

II. Purchasing preferences
- **Reasons for choosing Chitra Metals:**
    - Less price: 13.3%
    - Good quality: 37.3%
    - Fast delivery: 16.0%
    - Standard: 33.3%
- **Expenditure per Order:**
    - Under 1,00,000: 4.0%
    - 1,00,000 - 2,00,000: 12.0%
    - 2,00,000 - 3,00,000: 38.0%
    - 3,00,000 - 4,00,000: 39.3%
    - Above 4,00,000: 6.7%
- **Factors influencing placing an order:**
    - Discounts and offer: 19.3%
    - Product quality: 22.0%
    - Availability: 14.7%
    - Fast delivery: 16.7%
    - Fair deal: 27.3%
- **Preferred mode of payment:**
    - Credit card: 55.3%
    - Debit card: 1.3%
    - Net banking: 43.3%
- **Reasons for choosing Chitra Metals over others:**
    - Saves time: 26.7%
    - Wide choices: 28.0%
    - Ease to find product: 45.3%
- **Unique services satisfying customers:**
    - Reasonable return and exchange policy: 33.3%
    - Quality product: 26.0%
    - Fast delivery: 18.0%
    - Transaction security: 22.7%
- **Sources influencing product orders:**
    - Family and friends: 40.7%
    - Budget-friendly: 28.0%
    - Transaction security: 29.3%
    - Others: 2.0%
- **Factors contributing to overall satisfaction:**
    - Less price: 10.7%
    - Discounts & Offer: 19.3%
    - Fast delivery: 14.7%
    - Transaction security: 14.0%
    - Quality product: 41.3%

III. Statistical Analysis
- **Association between experience and duration of purchase:**
    - Chi-Square Tests:
        - Pearson Chi-Square: 38.70

- Asymptotic Sig. (2-tailed): 0.001
- Result: A significant relationship between experience and duration of purchase.

- **Association between experience and return and exchange policy:**
    - Chi-Square Tests:
        - Pearson Chi-square: 16.62
        - Asymptotic sig. (2-tailed): 0.002
        - Result: No significant association between experience and return & exchange policy.
- **Association between annual turnover and time spent on placing orders:**
    - Chi-square tests:
        - Pearson Chi-square: 17.17
        - Asymptotic Sig. (2-tailed): 0.028
        - Result: Significant association between turnover and time spent on placing orders.
- **Correlation between order and satisfaction:**
    - Correlations:
        - Pearson correlation: 0.086
        - Sig. (2-tailed): 0.297
        - Result: No significant relationship between order and satisfaction.

IV. Findings
- The majority of respondents have over 4 years of experience in the field (27.3%) and are sole proprietors (62.0%).
- Most companies have an annual turnover of less than 1 crore (40.7%).
- Preferences include good quality products (37.3%), spending 2,00,000 - 3,00,000 per order (38.0%), and placing orders twice a month (36.0%).
- Key reasons for choosing Chitra Metals are standard products (33.3%) and ease of finding products (45.3%).
- Major modes of payment are credit cards (55.3%).
- Respondents highly value ease of finding products (45.3%) and product quality (41.3%).
- Statistical analysis reveals a significant association between experience and duration of purchase, turnover, and time spent on placing orders.
- No significant correlation exists between order and satisfaction.

In conclusion, the study provides insights into the purchasing preferences and satisfaction levels of Chitra Metals customers, indicating areas for improvement and potential strategies for enhancing customer satisfaction.

The findings reveal that a majority of respondents have over four years of experience, with sole proprietorship being the predominant profession. The study highlights a significant association between annual turnover and the time spent on placing orders. However, there's no conclusive relationship between experience and the duration of purchasing or the satisfaction with return policies. Customer preferences lean towards quality products, fair deals, and the ease of finding items. Credit cards are the preferred mode of payment, and overall satisfaction is heavily influenced by product quality. These insights offer Chitra Metals actionable data to refine strategies, enhance service quality, and strengthen customer satisfaction.

Conclusion

In conclusion, the internship experience has provided a profound understanding of the significance of metals in human life and their integral role in various business operations. The exposure to different types of metals, their diverse applications, and adherence to governmental regulations has enriched my knowledge base. The internship emphasized the vast potential of the metal scraps business, which can be pursued on both small and large scales, accommodating varying financial capacities. The insights gained extend beyond the business intricacies, encompassing the nuances of import-export procedures in compliance with legal norms. Moreover, the experience has been instrumental in developing a comprehensive understanding of materials reproduction, along with basic knowledge in GST filing and IT procedures. This holistic learning journey has been made possible through the invaluable guidance and support of Chitra Metals, contributing significantly to the acquisition of both fundamental and practical business knowledge in the realm of metals.

References

Bhattacharya, K. (2003). Government policy and FDI triggering growth opportunities of iron steel in India. *Indian Journal of Research*, 7(4), 148–151.

Burang, L. G., and Yamini, S. (2010). The performance of iron and steel industries in India. *International Journal of Geology, Agriculture and Environmental Science*, 7(2), 1–3.

Dalvadi, Y. M., and Tagariya, M. B. (2019). Performance analysis on iron and steel companies in India depending on financial status and efficiency using PBT margin ratio. *Journal of Business Management*, 1, 1–12.

Goyal, A., and Acharya, V. (2017). Automation impact on Indian steel industry. *International Journal of Theoretical and Applied Machines*, 12(1), 13–20.

Kanhar, A. H., and Wang, F. (2020). Incineration fly ash and its treatment to possible utilization. *Energies*, 13(668), 1–35.

Saikia, P. P., and Rajput, S. (2018). Material handling and storage in steel industry: a qualitative study. *International Journal of Creative Research Thoughts*, 6(1), 536–541.

Sen Gupta, N. (2005). Government policy and FDI triggering growth opportunities of iron steel in India. *Indian Journal of Research*, 7(4), 148–151.

Tripathy, B. K. (2003). Government policy and FDI triggering growth opportunities of iron steel in India. *Indian Journal of Research*, 7(4), 148–151.

Wang, D., and Zhang, S. (2013). Research review of scrap metals eddy current separation technology. *Sensors and Transducers*, 158(11), 242–248.

2 A study on employee work life management in knitwear with reference to Coimbatore

A. Swetha[a], S. Mathankumar[b] and K. Srivignesh Kumar[c]

Karpagam Academy of Higher Education, Coimbatore, Tamil Nadu, India

Abstract

Ensuring a harmonious equilibrium between work and personal life is pivotal for managing stress and fostering success, both for employees and the company they serve. The ramifications of an imbalanced lifestyle are not only costly due to heightened stress, which undermines productivity, but also pose substantial health risks for individuals. Those adept at navigating the delicate balance between professional commitments and personal responsibilities tend to exhibit greater contentment, better health, and heightened efficiency. Notably, younger generations increasingly prioritize work-life balance, making it a pivotal consideration for potential employees. Organisations that embed this balance within their corporate ethos are better poised to attract and retain skilled candidates. Extensive research underscores that structured goal-setting significantly enhances learning outcomes. The concept of "work-life management" offers a methodology enabling employees to strike a balance between their personal and professional spheres. By prioritising tasks and allocating time to family, health, leisure, and career, this approach fosters a holistic life equilibrium, enhancing motivation and overall well-being.

Keywords: Employees, knit wear, work-life management

Introduction

Knitting, a craft involving interlocking yarn loops to create fabric, yields materials with superior stretch compared to woven fabrics. These loops, or stitches, form the basis of this textile creation process. In labour-intensive garment industries, both human and machine labour play crucial roles, with women largely constituting the workforce, often migrating from rural areas near Bengaluru. Despite their significant contributions, these workers, typically with lower educational backgrounds than their male counterparts, seek better opportunities, posing a challenge of high turnover. The apparel industry grapples with recruitment and retention issues due to these factors, leading to increased costs for hiring and training new staff. Quality of Work Life (QWL) initiatives prove pivotal in retaining skilled workers, addressing challenges such as turnover, absenteeism, and employee retention. This study aims to evaluate the QWL of employees within the apparel sector to devise strategies fostering retention and enhancing employee satisfaction, thus mitigating industry-wide talent shortages.

Literature Review

Problem Statement

The study aims to analyse work-life management's impact on female employees' productivity and well-being within the Coimbatore knitwear industry, addressing absenteeism and job dissatisfaction. Focusing on factors like scheduling, leave allocation, and production, it explores how effective work-life balance influences employee morale and organisational success. With HR's pivotal role in maintaining this balance, the investigation seeks to provide actionable recommendations for enhancing work-life management, aiming to improve workers' satisfaction and performance.

Objective of the Study

The study aims to investigate and enhance employee work-life management within the Coimbatore knitwear industry.

Hypothesis

H0: There is no significance relationship between monthly income and Job allows you to productive in all situations.

Research Methodology

- Employed simple random sampling, surveying 120 employees from 250 industry units, focusing on work-life balance management.
- Limited the study's scope to assess employee work-life balance across 120 respondents.

[a]swethaayyappan19@gmail.com, [b]mathanyuva33@gmail.com, [c]Ksvk2007@gmail.com

Table 2.1 Insights into work-life management: diverse perspectives and findings from academic studies.

Author	Study/findings/interpretation	Reference
Glasier (2016)	Emphasizes work-life management encompassing job stability, fair conditions, compensation, and equal opportunities. Identified employee dissatisfaction with aspects like occupational health, managers, income, work-family balance, and job interest.	Ramani (2016)
Tausig and Fenwick (2016)	Highlighted the positive effects of successful work-life balance strategies on stress reduction, job satisfaction, productivity, and reduced healthcare costs. Industries adopting accommodating policies due to work-life balance concerns.	Goldstein and Ford (2017)
Luthans (2016)	Explored WLB's impact on workplace environments, considering physical and mental demands, work timings, and their implications, especially in clothing manufacturing amidst globalization.	Aswathappa (2019)
Katzell et al. (2017)	Defined work-life management through worker perceptions, linking high quality of working life to job satisfaction, motivation, and compatibility between personal and work lives. Identified eight key domains.	Gupta (2020)
Kavoussi et al. (2017)	Explored poor working conditions' contribution to high absenteeism in Iranian textile firms, advocating for better environments to reduce absenteeism's widespread effects.	Nair (2021)
Kalaiselvi et al. (2017)	Examined work-life balance of clothing factory managers in Tamil Nadu, highlighting challenges like increased workload, job insecurity, and rising costs. Recommended tactics like scheduling actions and eliminating discrimination.	Murthy and Bhojanna (2022)
Runcie (2018)	Stressed the link between positive employee perceptions of work and increased productivity. Advocated for specific roles, structures, and support systems to sustain work-life management programs. Noted the potential of better work-life balance in improving productivity and reducing complaints, turnover, and accidents.	Moorthy (Year)
Aggarwal (2018)	Investigated work-life balance among Indian Oil Corporation Limited refinery employees, focusing on stressors, organizational structure, and the impact on personal and professional lives.	Thayumanavar and Srivignesh Kumar (2017)
Meenakshisundaram and Panchanatham (2018)	Explored the impact of task allocation on garment industry employees' work-life balance, stressing the need for manageable workloads.	Thayumanavar and Srivignesh Kumar (2018)

Source: Author

- Invested 3 months in conducting interviews, primarily using an interview schedule to gather primary data.
- The interview schedule functioned as a tool, collecting information and opinions from respondents.
- Utilized secondary data from corporate documents, the internet, and observational data gathered by the researcher.

Analysis and Interpretation

The analysis and interpretation section provides a comprehensive insight into the demographic profile of respondents in the study Table 2.1. Through detailed charts and a socio-economic profile table, it delineates key aspects such as age, marital status, educational qualifications, designation, experience, and monthly income distribution among the participants. This segment delves into the nuanced characteristics and distributions within the surveyed group, offering a comprehensive understanding of the workforce's diversity. Additionally, it explores the outcomes of hypothesis testing via Chi-square tests, seeking to establish potential relationships between monthly income and job productivity among the respondents.

Demographic profile of respondents:
Age distribution: Among the respondents, the age distribution showcased a varied range.

- 28.3% were under 20, 21.5% between 21-30, 20.8% between 31-40, 17.5% between 41-50, and 11.7% over 50.

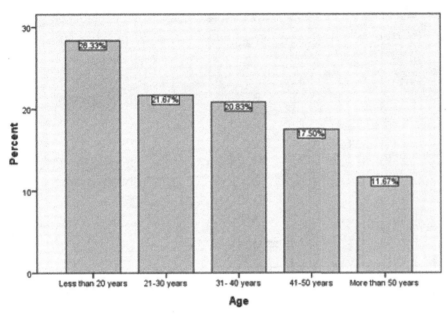

Figure 2.1 Depicts the age range distribution among the respondents
Source: Author

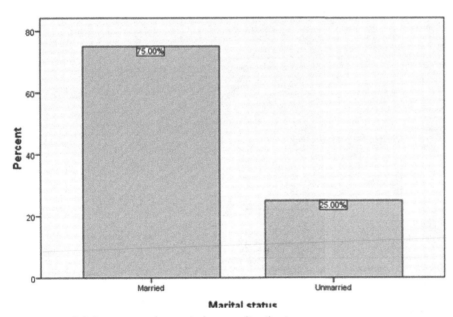

Figure 2.2 Represents the marital status distribution
Source: Author

This broad distribution signifies a diverse demographic, crucial for understanding the workforce composition and preferences.

Marital status: The marital status of respondents sheds light on their personal life situations.

- A total of 75% of respondents were married, while 25% were unmarried.

This insight into marital status aids in comprehending potential responsibilities and family-related demands impacting work-life balance Figure 2.1 and 2.2.

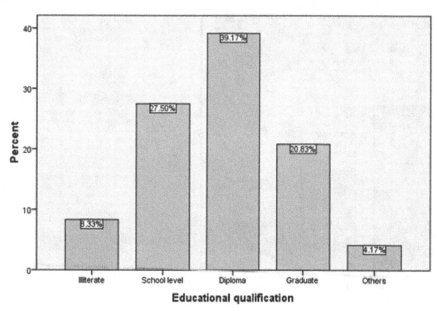

Figure 2.3 Illustrates the educational qualifications
Source: Author

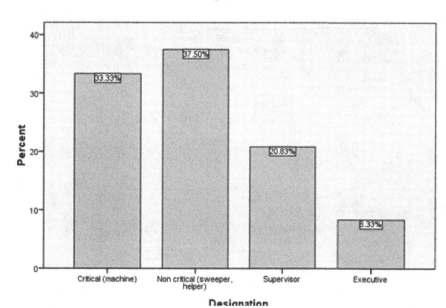

Figure 2.4 Shows the distribution of designations
Source: Author

Educational qualification: Understanding the educational qualifications gives insight into the respondents' academic background.

- 8.3% were literate, 27.5% had school-level education, 39.2% held diplomas, and 20.8% possessed degrees.

Designation and experience:

- A total of 33.3% were in critical roles, 37.5% in non-critical positions, 20.8% were supervisors, and 8.3% were executives.
Chart 2.5: .

Experience

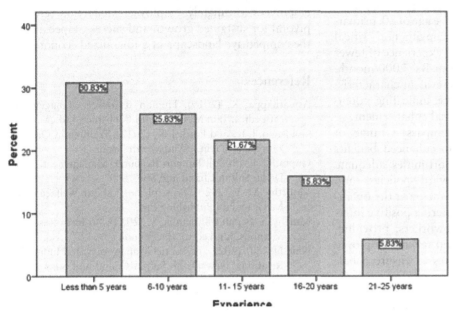

Figure 2.5 Presents respondents' work experience
Source: Author

- 30.8% had 0-2 years, 25.8% had 2-5 years, 21.7% had 5-8 years, 15.8% had 8-10 years, and 5.8% had over 10 years of experience.

Monthly income distribution: Evaluating monthly income categories showcases the financial diversity among respondents.

- 31.7% earned below 5000, 25% between 5000-10000, 21.7% between 10000-15000, 15% between 15000-20000, and 6.7% above 20000.

Hypothesis testing (Chi-square test): Hypothesis testing aimed to establish a relationship between income and productivity.

- **Null hypothesis (H0):** No connection exists between monthly salary and productivity at work.
- **Alternative hypothesis (H1):** A significant relationship exists between monthly income and job productivity.
- All 120 cases were valid for analysis.

The Chi-square test reveals a potential connection between monthly income and job productivity based on respondents' perceptions.

Cross tabulation results:
- The cross-tabulation reveals responses based on monthly income and perceived job productivity.

- Among those earning below 7000, 37 strongly agreed and one agreed to being productive, while other income brackets showed varied responses.

Chi-square test outcome:
- Pearson Chi-square value was 3.313E2 with a significance of .000, rejecting the null hypothesis.
- The likelihood ratio was 304.559 with a significance of .000, indicating a significant relationship between income and productivity.
- Despite some cells with expected counts below 5, the minimum expected count was .67.

Result interpretation:
- Acceptance of the null hypothesis was based on the significance level of less than 0.05.
- The analysis concludes that there's no significant difference between monthly income and work productivity based on the data collected.

Upon scrutinizing the data, the analysis suggests a significant relationship between monthly income and work productivity. However, nuances in interpretation remain due to certain cells with expected counts below five in the Chi-square test.

The interpretation based on demographic factors and statistical analysis shows a meaningful correlation between income and job productivity among the respondents

Conclusion

The findings of this study unveil a demographic profile dominated by respondents under the age of 20, primarily married, holding diplomas, occupying non-critical positions, possessing limited work experience of fewer than 5 years, and earning less than Rs 7,000/month. These insights shed light on the prevalent characteristics within the surveyed workforce, indicating potential areas of focus for organizational enhancement.

The suggestions outlined encompass a range of improvements, advocating for an enhanced benefits package, career advancement opportunities, adequate training provisions, refined reward policies, and implementation of a promotion strategy at the operational level. Stress is placed on fostering positive interpersonal relationships among coworkers, providing specialized on-the-job training, and seeking employee input in decision-making processes to ensure a balanced workload.

In conclusion, human resources stand as a crucial asset influencing an organization's productivity, reputation, and overall quality. Emphasizing employees' work-life balance becomes pivotal in motivating them to perform efficiently and accurately. The responsibility lies with the employer to cultivate a healthy and supportive workplace environment that safeguards employees' physical and emotional well-being. This study serves as a pointer to minor disparities in perceptions within the Wipro engineering sector, emphasizing the company's commitment to nurturing robust organizational practices and fostering harmonious workplace dynamics between management and employees. Ultimately, employee satisfaction remains pivotal for sustained growth and success, especially in the competitive landscape of a liberalized economy.

References

Aswathappa, K. (2019). Human Resource Management, (5th edn.). Tata McGraw Hill Publishing Ltd.

Goldstein, I. L., and Ford, J. K. (2017). Training in Organizations, (4th edn.). Wadsworth Group.

Gupta, C. B. (2020). Human Resource Management. New Delhi: Sultan Chand and Sons.

Moorthy, M. V. (2020). Principles of Labour Welfare. Tata McGraw Hill Publishing Ltd.

Murthy, S. N., and Bhojanna, V. (2022). Business Research Methods, (2nd edn.). Excel Books.

Nair, N. G. L. (2021). Personnel Management and Industrial Relations. New Delhi: Sultan Chand and Sons Company Ltd.

Ramani, V. V. (Ed.). (2016). Training and Development. ICFAI Publications.

Thayumanavar, B., and Srivignesh Kumar, K. (2017). A study on quality of work life of teachers employed in private arts and science colleges with special reference to Tirupur district. *International Journal of Multidisciplinary Research and Modern Education*, 3(1), 130–135.

Thayumanavar, B., and Srivignesh Kumar, K. (2018). A quality of work life of teachers in private arts and science college at Tirupur district. *Shanlax International Journal of Arts, Science and Humanities*, 5, 49–59.

3 A study on financial performance analysis in iron and steel industries in Tamil Nadu

Balasubramaniyan G and S. Venkatachalam[a]

Karpagam Academy of Higher Education, Coimbatore, Tamil Nadu, India

Abstract

This study explores the pivotal role of the steel and iron industry in bolstering economic development, particularly in Tamil Nadu. The author meticulously analyses the financial performance of companies in this sector using statistical tools, with a focus on ratios and ANOVA for data scrutiny. The research aims to provide insights into the economic contributions of these companies to both regional and national growth. Through rigorous statistical methodologies, this investigation informs stakeholders, policymakers, and industry players about the financial dynamics within the sector, enhancing our understanding of its impact on economic stability and development.

Keywords: Steel industry, Iron industry, raw materials

Introduction

With a population exceeding 1.4 billion in 2023, India presents substantial opportunities for investors and proprietors in the civil and construction projects, given its immense construction needs. As steel and iron form the fundamental raw materials for these projects, India emerges as a major global consumer of iron scrap. This study delves into the steel and iron industry in Tamil Nadu, recognizing its pivotal role in driving both the nation's economic growth and the individual logistics sector. The researcher focuses on comprehensively analyzing the financial performance of companies, emphasizing aspects such as working capital management and stakeholder engagement. The objectives encompass studying the growth of steel industries, assessing the profitability, liquidity, and solvency of selected companies, and conducting a comparative financial analysis using ratios. The problem statement underscores the criticality of financial management in navigating the competitive business landscape, emphasizing the need for sound financial analysis to monitor company performance in an era of heightened competition.

Review of Literature

- Ali Hasanbeigi's (2018) exploration of the steel industry underscores its intricate nature, characterized by fragmentation and dominance of small and medium enterprises (SMEs). Despite abundant energy-efficiency prospects in steel plants, these opportunities often go unrealized due to a lack of information on implementation methods. To enhance energy efficiency, there is a pressing need to compile and disseminate knowledge on relevant technologies and practices within the steel sector.

- In Zahid and Nanik's (2018) investigation, a comprehensive analysis of a company's financial and inventory statements, reveals commendable production and cash flow. Recognizing the pivotal role of maintaining liquid cash, especially for companies in the iron and steel industry, becomes imperative for effective financial crisis management and debt control.

- Rakesh and Kulkarni's (2018) research, encompassing five companies over an 11-year period, employs statistical tools to scrutinize financial statements. The outcomes highlight the effectiveness of these firms, emphasizing positive results in terms of financial position, current and fixed assets, concluding that their overall performance is robust.

- Marimuthu (2018) delves into the financial performance of the steel industry, focusing on listed companies in Tamil Nadu, renowned as the "Manchester of South India." Erode and Tirupur emerge as significant contributors to India's steel market and knitwear exports, respectively. Marimuthu suggests companies base their investments on a comparative analysis of current performance vis-à-vis the previous year or other firms.

- Chris et al.'s (2019) exploration underscores the growing importance of environmental management for fashion and steel manufacturers in re-

[a]venkatachalam.s@kahedu.edu.in

sponse to rising environmental concerns. The production processes of fashion and steel-related products, characterized by high energy and water consumption and significant pollutant emissions, necessitate a heightened responsibility toward environmental sustainability.

Analysis and Interpretation

Embarking on a meticulous exploration of the steel industry's financial intricacies, this study employs an analytical research design and delves into comprehensive secondary data. Spanning five companies from 2017-2018 to 2021-2022, the investigation utilizes ratio analysis and analysis of variance for robust data interpretation. The subsequent sections dissect key financial ratios—current, liquidity, debt equity, gross profit, and net profit—unveiling trends, statistical nuances, and industry variations. Through rigorous scrutiny, this analysis aims to offer a profound understanding of financial landscapes, paving the way for nuanced decision-making and strategic insights within the dynamic steel sector.

Research methodology and data interpretation: a comprehensive analysis
Research methodology: In employing an analytical research design, the study utilized secondary data encompassing company profiles, financial statements, and inventory statements.

Data interpretation: current ratio
- **Current ratio trends:** The study spanned from 2017-2018 to 2021-2022, revealing a fluctuating current ratio for the companies.
- **Analysis techniques:** Statistical tools, specifically ratio analysis and analysis of variance (ANOVA), were applied for data interpretation.

Interpretation highlights:
- High standard deviation observed in Ahmedabad Steel Industries.
- Skewness varied among companies, indicating asymmetry in current ratios.
- Kurtosis values suggested both leptokurtic and platykurtic trends.

Data interpretation: liquidity ratio
- **Liquidity ratio trends:** Examining the same companies from 2017-2018 to 2021-2022, a diverse pattern in liquidity ratios emerged.
- **Analysis techniques:** Similar statistical tools, ratio analysis and ANOVA, facilitated robust data interpretation.

Interpretation highlights:
- Good Luck Steel Industries exhibited a low standard deviation.
- Skewness and kurtosis patterns were noted, portraying diverse characteristics among companies.

Data interpretation: debt equity ratio
- **Debt equity ratio trends:** Focusing on the period from 2017-2018 to 2021-2022, the research unveiled fluctuations in debt equity ratios.
- **Analysis techniques:** The study employed the same statistical tools, ratio analysis and ANOVA, for thorough interpretation.

Interpretation highlights:
- Oil Country Industries showcased a high standard deviation.
- Skewness and kurtosis observations hinted at distinct characteristics across companies.

Data interpretation: gross profit ratio
- **Gross profit ratio trends:** Spanning from 2017-2018 to 2021-2022, the gross profit ratios demonstrated a diverse trajectory.
- **Analysis techniques:** Utilizing Ratio analysis and ANOVA facilitated nuanced insights.

Interpretation highlights:
- Good Luck Steel Industries portrayed a low standard deviation.
- Skewness and kurtosis patterns offered insights into the gross profit dynamics.

Data interpretation: net profit ratio
- **Net profit ratio trends:** Covering the same period, 2017-2018 to 2021-2022, the net profit ratios exhibited varied trends.
- **Analysis techniques:** Ratio analysis and ANOVA were instrumental in extracting meaningful conclusions.

Interpretation highlights:
- Oil Country Industries displayed a high standard deviation.
- Skewness and kurtosis unveiled unique features in net profit ratios.

Analysis of variances:
- **Current ratio:** Significantly varied among the companies ($p < 0.05$), indicating industry-specific differences.
- **Liquidity ratio:** Significant variation ($p < 0.05$) reinforced the presence of diverse balance sheet characteristics.

- **Debt equity ratio:** Though not significant (p > 0.05), the study recognized industry-specific variations.
- **Gross profit ratio:** No significant difference (p > 0.05) in balance sheet characteristics among companies.
- **Net profit ratio:** No significant variance (p > 0.05) suggested uniformity in industry performance.

Interpretation of variances: The significant variations in current and liquidity ratios imply distinct financial management strategies among companies. Although debt equity ratios showed no significant difference, peculiar trends still emerged. The absence of significant variance in gross and net profit ratios suggests a consistent industry-wide financial performance, emphasizing the need for nuanced interpretation based on specific financial indicators.

The research unfolds a fluctuating trend in the current ratio, reaching 2.07 in 2021-2022, indicating a nuanced control over stock positions. Liquidity ratio displays variability, from 0.014 in 2017-2018 to 0.007 in 2021-2022. The debt equity ratio reveals a decreasing trend in fixed asset ratios. Gross and net profit ratios demonstrate industry variations, with notable fluctuations. Findings underscore the imperative of vigilance in managing financial dynamics, guiding stakeholders towards informed decisions. Interpretation of variance analyses substantiates these observations, offering a comprehensive comprehension of the steel industry's financial nuances.

Conclusion

In conclusion, the study underscores the paramount importance of maintaining a robust working capital in the steel and iron industry. The essence lies in safeguarding against capital loss inherent in current assets and ensuring liquidity. Efficient liquidity not only facilitates smooth operations but also acts as a protective shield against potential financial crises. Moreover, in the realm of material management, the 'make or buy' decision emerges as a pivotal consideration for prudent financial performance. The study recommends a strategic adoption of the 'buy' policy, allowing the company to optimize its spending on raw materials, particularly steel and iron. The implementation of the first-in-first-out method in inventory management is advocated to curb excess purchases, aligning operational efficiency with financial prudence.

In the dynamic landscape of the steel and iron industry, companies must adapt to economic fluctuations. Recent price hikes, influenced by both national and international factors, necessitate a judicious approach. Building a general reserve from profits emerges as a proactive measure, providing a financial safety net amid the sector's economic and price volatility. This comprehensive approach ensures not only sustained financial well-being but also resilience in the face of evolving industry dynamics.

References

Andersen, T. J. (2016). *Information and Management, 39*(2), 85–100.

Chris K. Y. Lo et al.'s. (2019). Human Resource Management, (5th edn.). Tata McGraw Hill Publishing Ltd.

Hasanbeigi, A. (2018). A review of energy use and energy efficiency technologies for the textile industry. *Renewable and Sustainable Energy Reviews, 16*(6), 3648–3665.

Lin, H. L., et al. (2017). Agglomeration and productivity: firm-level evidence from China's textile industry. *China Economic Review, 22*(3), 313–329.

Lo, C. K. Y., et al. (2021). *International Journal of Production Economics, 135*(2), 561–567.

Marimuthu. (2018). Principles of Labour Welfare. Tata McGraw Hill Publishing Ltd.

Rakesh and Kulkarni's. (2018). Human Resource Management. New Delhi: Sultan Chand and Sons.

Yalcin, N., et al. (2019). Expert systems with applications. 39(5), 5872–5880.

Yalcin, N., et al. (2020). Expert systems with applications. 39(1), 350–364.

Zahid and Nanik's. (2018). Performance analysis on iron and steel companies in India depending on financial status and efficiency using PBT margin ratio. Journal of Business Management, 1, 1–12.

4 Green logistics challenges and benefits: examining practices in Chennai-based companies for enhanced environmental management

Kalai Mathi and S. Venkatachalam[a]

Karpagam Academy of Higher Education, Coimbatore, Tamil Nadu, India

Abstract

In the realm of logistics, one of the world's oldest industries, the traditional focus has been on safely transporting products from origin to end customer. However, the contemporary paradigm shift towards green logistics management introduces a crucial aspect—environmental consciousness. This research delves into the analysis of the awareness and adoption of green logistics management practices among employees and customers within organizations. The study, situated in Chennai district, scrutinizes the challenges encountered and the benefits derived from implementing green logistics practices in companies. With a sample size of 150, the research sheds light on the intricate interplay between environmental responsibility and logistical efficiency, providing valuable insights for companies navigating the complex landscape of sustainable business practices.

Keywords: Data risk, green logistics management, pollution, supply chain management

Introduction

Migration, an age-old phenomenon, has been the catalyst for evolutionary processes for thousands of years. Despite its historical roots, contemporary migration is facilitated by advanced transportation, giving rise to logistics—a pivotal system ensuring safe and damage-free delivery of goods. However, the surge in commercial vehicles has significantly contributed to environmental pollution, prompting the evolution of green logistics management (GLM). GLM, while not novel, embodies an eco-friendly approach to logistics, involving loading, transporting, and safe delivery of goods. This study focuses on analyzing the challenges and benefits encountered by GLM companies in Chennai districts. The advantages of GLM include resource sustainability, enhanced efficiency, product differentiation, regulatory compliance, and improved product quality. Conversely, challenges encompass cost implications, data security risks, and potential increases in product prices. Objectives of the study aim to discern the benefits, effectiveness, and challenges faced by logistics and supply chain companies implementing GLM in Chennai district.

Problem Statement

The study addresses the critical issue of environmental sustainability by examining the challenges and advantages associated with the implementation of GLM practices in companies, emphasizing the pressing need to mitigate the environmental impact of transportation activities in the face of global changes, affecting both humans and wildlife.

Review of Literature

Cagno et al. (2020) highlights that over the past decade, companies in the logistics sector have become increasingly aware of the challenges facing the industry. The author notes a lack of emphasis on research and development in this field, and some third-party logistics companies exhibit reluctance to adopt GLM. The primary barriers identified in GLM implementation include cost-effectiveness, as substantial financial investments are required for research endeavors.

Haleem et al. (2020) observe that in India, nearly all vehicle manufacturing companies maintain their own production plants. Despite the presence of hurdles in the GLM process, mainly due to a reliance on paper formats, there is ongoing support from industry experts. Successful GLM implementation in the vehicle manufacturing industry could herald a new era for the sector.

Bhattacharjee (2020) focuses on the current trend of green-oriented concepts. In today's competitive world, companies are prioritizing environmental protection. GLM aims to deliver products to end customers safely through eco-friendly systems. Given the pressing issues of pollution and global warming resulting from increased CO_2 emissions, governments, including in

[a]venkatachalam.s@kahedu.edu.in

the automobile industry, are taking steps to address these concerns.

Luthra et al. (2016) discuss the successful implementation of GLM in the Indian automobile industry, attributing its triumph to the country's large population and robust automotive sector. The focus on eco-friendly practices and corporate social responsibility (CSR) has contributed to increased efficiency. The paper primarily examines the performance and outcomes of companies in this context.

Analysis and Interpretation

In exploring the dynamics of GLM, this study delves into critical aspects such as the demographic profile of workers, income distribution, work experience, and the level of consciousness regarding GLM implementation. By scrutinizing these factors, the research aims to unveil key patterns and correlations that influence GLM practices within the workforce Braithwaite and Hall (1999). As the logistics industry grapples with environmental concerns, understanding the awareness, experiences, and perceptions of employees becomes imperative. This introductory section sets the stage for a comprehensive analysis, shedding light on the workforce's characteristics and their implications for successful GLM implementation Bowersox and Closs (1996).

Analysis design: Descriptive analysis
Sample design: Random sampling
Sample size: 150
Method of data collection: Questionnaire
Origin of information: Primary and secondary information

Interpretation

Table 4.1: Age of the workers
- Age distribution:
  - 20-30: 20.0%
  - 30-40: 51.3%
  - 40-50: 20.0%
  - Above 50: 8.7%
- Inference: The majority (51.3%) of workers fall within the 30-40 age range.

Table 4.2: Income of workers
- Income Distribution:
  - Below Rs.10,000: 20.0%
  - Rs.10,000-15,000: 20.0%
  - Rs.15,000-Rs.20,000: 47.3%
  - Above Rs. 20,000: 12.7%
- Inference: Nearly half (47.3%) earn between Rs. 15,000-20,000.

Table 4.3: Workers' experience in the company
- Experience distribution:
  - Below 5 years: 24.7%
  - 5-10 years: 48.7%
  - 10-20 years: 13.3%
  - Above 20 years: 13.3%
- Inference: A significant portion (48.7%) has 5-10 years of experience.

Table 4.4: Level of consciousness in GLM implementing
- Awareness levels:
  - Highly aware: 52.7%
  - Partly aware: 30.7%
  - No awareness: 16.7%
- Inference: A majority (52.7%) are highly conscious of GLM.

Correlation analysis
- Relationship between income and GLM benefits:
  - Pearson correlation: 0.151
  - Sig. (2-tailed): 0.066
- Inference: A positive relationship exists between income and GLM benefits.

Findings and suggestions

Findings:
- Age distribution: The majority (51.3%) of workers fall within the 30-40 age range.
- Income: Nearly half (47.3%) earn between Rs. 15,000-20,000.
- Experience: A significant portion (48.7%) has 5-10 years of experience.
- GLM awareness: A majority (52.7%) are highly conscious of GLM.
- Correlation: There is a positive relationship between income and GLM benefits.

Suggestions:
1. Awareness campaigns:
   - Implement GLM awareness programs for both customers and employees.
   - Provide knowledge, experience, and training to personnel for successful GLM implementation.
2. Leadership involvement:
   - Top-level officials should actively participate in implementing GLM.
   - Regular monitoring of implementation costs is crucial to prevent profit shortages.
3. Government support:
   - Encourage government initiatives for eco-friendly systems in society.
   - Advocate for flexible rules supporting GLM implementation in organizations.

These findings and suggestions highlight the importance of fostering awareness, leadership involvement, and government support for successful GLM implementation in companies Zailani 2009.

The study reveals notable findings, showcasing that a majority of workers fall within the 31-40 age group, with 47.3% earning between Rs. 15,000-20,000. Additionally, 48.7% possess 5-10 years of work experience, while 52.7% exhibit high awareness of GLM. A positive correlation between income and the benefits of GLM implementation is established. These insights underline the importance of targeted awareness campaigns, training initiatives, and top-level commitment for successful GLM integration Beamon (1999). The study's findings provide valuable direction for fostering eco-friendly logistics practices within organizations in pursuit of sustainability and environmental responsibility.

Conclusion

In conclusion, the study underscores the critical need for green logistics management (GLM) initiatives to counteract the pervasive impact of pollution on human and environmental well-being. Acknowledging that a single mistake can have widespread consequences, GLM emerges as a crucial pathway for industries to transition toward eco-friendly business practices. The study illuminates the cooperative role of both private enterprises and governmental support in cultivating a pollution-free logistics sector. While companies express a readiness for this transformative change, the significant impediment lies in the financial investment required for GLM implementation.

However, it is imperative to recognize that the cost hurdle should not overshadow the long-term benefits of fostering environmentally sustainable practices. Efforts should be directed towards developing cost-effective strategies and garnering financial support mechanisms to facilitate a seamless transition toward a green, eco-friendly future for logistics industries. The study underscores the urgency of overcoming financial challenges to pave the way for a more sustainable, ecologically responsible business landscape.

References

AlKhidir, T., and Zailani, S. (2009). Going green in the supply chain towards environmental sustainability. *Global Journal of Environmental Research,* 3(3), 246–251.

Beamon, B. M. (1999). Designing the green supply chain. *Logistics Information Management,* 12(4), 332–342.

Bhattacharjee, K. (2020). Green supply chain management - challenges and opportunities. *Asian Journal of Technology and Management Research,* 5(1), ISSN: 2249–0892.

Borade, A. B., and Bansod, S. V. (2007). Domain of supply chain management – a state of art. *Journal of Technology Management and Innovation,* 2(4), 109–121. ISSN: 0718-2724 (http://www.jotmi.org).

Bowersox, D. J., and Closs, D. J. (1996). Logistical Management: The Integrated Supply Chain Process. New York, NY: The McGraw-Hill Company, Inc.

Braithwaite, A., and Hall, D. (1999). Risky Business: Critical Decisions in Supply Chain Management. Logistics Consulting Partners. Hertfordshire, United Kingdom: LCP Ltd.

Cagno, E., Perotti, S., and Micheli, G. J. L. (2020). Motivations and barriers to the adoption of green supply chain practices among 3PLs. *International Journal of Logistics Systems and Management,* 20(2), 179–198.

Haleem, A., Luthra, S., Kumar, V., and Kumar, S. (2020). Barriers to implement green supply chain management in the automobile industry using interpretive structural modelling technique - an Indian perspective. *Journal of Industrial Engineering and Management,* 4(2), 231–257.

Luthra, S., Garg, D., and Haleem, A. (2016). The impacts of critical success factors for implementing green supply chain management towards sustainability: an empirical investigation of the Indian automobile industry. *Journal of Cleaner Production,* 121, 142–158.

5 Women's preference, satisfaction, and problems with the free bus travel scheme in Coimbatore

B. Athira[a], M. Prema[b], O. Udisha[c], R. Velmurugan[d] and J. Sudarvel[e]

Karpagam Academy of Higher Education, Coimbatore, Tamil Nadu, India

Abstract

The Government of Tamil Nadu's Zero Ticket Bus Travel Scheme aims to provide accessible transit for women while empowering them. Using a mixed-methods strategy, including surveys, interviews, and focus group discussions, this study researches into women's preferences, satisfaction levels, and challenges with the free bus service. It seeks to understand the degree of preference for the scheme, assess passenger satisfaction, and identify service-related issues. The research captures insights into women's awareness, usage patterns, and factors influencing decisions, considering demographic variations in preferences. Opinions on timeliness, regularity, cleanliness, comfort, and safety will be gauged through surveys and interviews. The study aspires to reveal women's choices, satisfaction, and challenges in using the free bus service, offering insights for policymakers to refine the program for diverse needs. Ultimately, this research contributes to the formulation of gender-responsive transport policies, promoting the empowerment and well-being of women in Tamil Nadu.

Keywords: Challenges, free bus travel scheme, government of Tamil Nadu and transportation, passenger, preference, problems, satisfaction level, service, women

Introduction

The Tamil Nadu government's introduction of a free bus travel program for women represents a significant stride towards gender equity and socio-economic empowerment. This policy aims to enhance women's mobility, addressing disparities and fostering a sense of autonomy. Evaluating its effectiveness necessitates understanding women's preferences, satisfaction levels, and challenges in using the free bus service. Mobility is a cornerstone for women's socio-economic advancement, impacting their access to employment, healthcare, and education. By eliminating financial barriers, the government seeks to elevate the overall well-being of women.

Examining women's preferences for the free bus travel program is crucial in comprehending its acceptance and utility. Policymakers can enhance the program's alignment with women's needs by leveraging preference data. Evaluating the satisfaction of female passengers, influenced by factors like timeliness, cleanliness, and safety, is vital for gauging its effectiveness. Recognizing and addressing challenges such as overcrowding and safety concerns are imperative to ensure a positive travel experience for women. This research contributes to ongoing gender-responsive transport policy efforts, providing insights for policymakers to refine the program and empower women in Tamil Nadu.

Review of Literature

Table 5.1 Insights into public transport: a comprehensive overview of studies and findings.

Author	Study	Findings
Carreira et al. (2013)	Vehicle design and service management's importance in effective transportation policy	Physical amenities, such as waiting rooms and sleeping facilities, impact overall passenger comfort.
Freitas (2017)	Delays in bus departure attributed to factors like boarding and luggage placement	Drivers' responsibility and adherence to traffic laws crucial for safety and avoiding delays.
Naveen (2019)	Examination of passenger patterns and preferences in intercity bus transportation	Demographic and mobility factors significantly influence service quality perception and overall satisfaction.

[a]babujessy991@gmail.com, [b]mpremasundar2@gmail.com, [c]Udishaomanakuttan@gmail.com, [d]drvelsngm@gmail.com, [e]j.sudarvel@gmail.com

Author	Study	Findings
De Palma et al. (2015)	Development of crowd and discomfort functions in public transport	Time's crucial role in public transport, categorized by scenarios of available seats and crowded standing passengers.
Robert Berezny and Vladimir Konecny (2017)	Measuring the influence of transportation service quality on suburban bus demand	Findings contribute to stabilizing and improving suburban bus transportation services.
Kamaruddin et al. (2012)	Evaluation of user expectations and satisfaction with public transport	Preferences for LRT and monorail, with safety concerns driving expectations and loyalty.
Rohani et al. (2013)	Importance of bus services tailored to local requirements	Adaptations like air conditioning in Asia and bike carriers in the UK cater to diverse user groups.
Salini (2018)	Impact analysis of factors on traffic flow in urban and suburban areas	Identifying side friction factors, such as buses stopping and pedestrian interference, affecting traffic flow.
Singh (2016)	Assessment of passenger satisfaction with public bus transport services	Dissatisfaction prevalent, with comfort and safety having the most significant impact on satisfaction.
Soloviev (2015)	Emphasis on bus safety in European roads	Bus service providers upgrading equipment for safety and adherence to transportation laws.
Sudarkodi and Balasubramani (2021);	Analysis of an innovative free bus transit plan in Tamil Nadu	The scheme empowers women and serves as a model for similar initiatives in India.
Imrea and Celebia (2016)	Importance of comfort in public transportation	Novel index developed based on qualitative and quantitative factors for evaluating comfort.
Sumaedi et al. (2016)	Aspects related to passenger satisfaction	Factors such as dependability, responsiveness, and security impact public transportation users' pleasure.
Joewono et al. (2016)	Relationship between road-based public transport users' preferences and expectations	Disparities in influence of determinants on support for policy improvement scenarios across different urban areas.

Source: Author

Problem Statement

The execution of Tamil Nadu's free bus travel program for women raises critical concerns necessitating investigation. The primary issues revolve around understanding women's preferences, exploring the factors influencing their choice, and evaluating the program's efficacy. Examining female passengers' satisfaction is vital, considering elements such as timeliness, cleanliness, safety, and overall experience. Identifying potential challenges, including crowded buses and safety concerns, is imperative to enhance the service's safety and convenience. This study aims to uncover women's preferences, assess satisfaction levels, and identify challenges in utilizing the free bus service, providing insights for policymakers to improve the program and ensure equitable, reliable, and safe transportation for women in Tamil Nadu.

Objectives of the Study

- To know the preference of women towards free bus scheme.
- To study the satisfaction level of passenger using free bus service.
- To ascertain problems on using free bus service.

Research Methodology

- **Data collection:** Data for the study were gathered using an Interview Schedule, focusing on the profile, preferences, satisfaction, and issues of women utilizing the free bus travel scheme.
- **Source of data:** Primary data were obtained through a well-structured questionnaire distributed both in hard copy and soft copy formats to the respondents.
- **Sampling design:** Convenience sampling was employed, collecting data from 300 respondents in Coimbatore city.
- **Area of study:** The study focused on Coimbatore city, encompassing 55 towns. Data were collected from 26 towns, including Madhukarai, Peelamedu, Sai Baba colony, Thondamuthur, and others.
- **Framework of analysis:** Analytical methods include:
    - Simple percentage analysis,
    - Weighted average rank,
    - Factor analysis.

Significance of the Study

This study's findings on women's preferences, satisfaction, and challenges with the Coimbatore free bus transit plan have far-reaching implications for various stakeholders. It offers valuable insights into the program's efficiency and its alignment with women's preferences, aiding policymakers in evaluating strengths and addressing weaknesses. By understanding women's experiences, the research contributes to gender-responsive transport policy, highlighting the need for services tailored to women's unique requirements. The study's outcomes empower women in Tamil Nadu, informing the development of inclusive transportation networks that enhance safety, mobility, and overall well-being. Additionally, the research guides transportation planners in making informed decisions, improving services, and promoting societal equality through better mobility options for women. Ultimately, the study has the potential to influence policy, foster gender equality, and empower women in Tamil Nadu, making it a significant contribution to societal development.

Analysis and Interpretation

In exploring the dynamics of women's experiences with the free bus travel scheme in Coimbatore, this study delves into demographic characteristics, preferences, satisfaction levels, and challenges faced by female passengers. From age distribution to preferences towards the scheme and levels of satisfaction and problems encountered, this comprehensive analysis sheds light on crucial aspects of women's interaction with public transportation. The findings not only offer insights for policymakers to refine the program but also contribute to the broader discourse on gender-responsive transport policies, aiming to create safer, more efficient, and gender-inclusive public transportation networks.

Demographic characteristics:
- **Age:** The majority of passengers fall within the 21-30 age group.
- **Educational qualification:** Predominantly, passengers have an under-graduate educational background.
- **Marital status:** Most passengers are unmarried.
- **Occupation:** A significant portion of passengers work in the private sector.
- **Monthly income:** The majority of passengers earn between Rs. 10,000-20,000/month.
- **Area of residence:** The urban population constitutes the majority of passengers.

- **Usage of free bus scheme:** A significant portion of passengers regularly utilizes the free bus facility.
- **Amount spent for traveling:** Most passengers spend up to Rs. 1000/month for bus travel.
- **Amount of savings:** The majority of passengers save up to Rs. 1000/month.

Preferences toward women free bus travel scheme:
- **Free of cost for travel:** The most preferred aspect of the scheme.
- **Money saving:** High preference for financial savings.
- **Availability of buses in location:** Ranked lower in preference.
- **No kilometers limits:** Considered significant in preference.
- **Availability of seats:** Receives a lower preference ranking.
- **Reducing dependence on family:** Significant preference for reduced dependence.
- **Upliftment of status of women:** Considered moderately important.
- **Increasing female ridership:** Second-highest preference.
- **Better safety for women:** A significant concern, ranked moderately.
- **Increasing female participation in workforce:** Moderate preference.

Level of satisfaction with women free bus travel scheme:
- **Bus timing:** Moderately satisfied.
- **Bus arrival on correct time:** Among the least satisfying aspects.
- **Bus reaches destination on correct Time:** Moderately satisfying.
- **Seat availability:** Among the least satisfying aspects.
- **Bus condition:** Generally satisfied.
- **Cleanliness of bus:** High satisfaction levels.
- **Driver's behavior:** Generally satisfied.
- **Conductor's behavior:** Moderately satisfying.
- **Satisfaction of ZTBT (Zero Ticket Bus Travel):** The highest level of satisfaction.
- **Satisfaction of money saving through the scheme:** The second-highest level of satisfaction.

Level of problems with women free bus service:
- **Unsafety for women:** A significant problem.
- **Overloaded/overcrowded:** A significant problem.
- **Ill-treatment by conductor/driver:** A significant problem.
- **Buses did not stop at correct bus stop:** A moderate problem.
- **Poor seat condition:** A moderate problem.

- **Non-availability of seats:** A significant problem.
- **Quality of bus/working condition:** A significant problem.
- **Poor hygienic condition:** A significant problem.
- **Travel by standing of overcrowd:** A moderate problem.
- **Inadequate bus facility on work timing:** A significant problem.
- **Delay in travel timing:** A significant problem.

In conclusion, the study highlights demographic patterns, preferences, satisfaction levels, and challenges faced by women using the free bus travel scheme. The findings provide valuable insights for policymakers, enabling them to enhance the scheme's effectiveness, address specific issues, and create a more inclusive and satisfactory transportation experience for women.

The study reveals that a majority of women utilizing the free bus travel scheme in Coimbatore are aged 21-30, predominantly possess an undergraduate educational qualification, and are unmarried. Most passengers reside in urban areas, demonstrating the scheme's urban-centric impact. Additionally, a significant number regularly use the free bus service, spending up to Rs. 1000 per month. Preferences highlight the high appeal of free travel, safety, and enhanced female ridership. Women are notably satisfied with the ZTBT and perceive safety and cleanliness as strengths. Factor analysis identifies key problems, including safety concerns, overcrowding, and ill-treatment by staff.

Conclusion

In conclusion, the study illuminates key insights into women's preferences, satisfaction, and challenges with Tamil Nadu's free bus travel program. It underscores the scheme's popularity due to affordability and convenience but highlights critical issues like punctuality, overcrowding, and employee conduct. The proposed recommendations encompass safety enhancements, improved staff training, route adherence, and better bus conditions, aiming to address these concerns. Implementing these suggestions could create a safer, more reliable, and comfortable public transport system, meeting the unique needs of women and fostering gender empowerment. Continuous evaluation and collaboration with law enforcement, other transportation modes, and private partners are essential for sustained success. Policymakers and stakeholders can leverage this study to enhance women's access to secure and efficient public transit, contributing to the overall development of Tamil Nadu. Through ongoing assessment and strategic adjustments, the government can ensure the free bus travel program's positive impact on women's lives, advancing gender equality and bolstering the state's progress.

References

Berezny and Konecny (2017). Employability of Iranian engineering graduates: influential factors, consequences and strategies, Journal of Teaching and Learning for Graduate Employability, 11(1), 110–130.

Carreira , R., Patrício, L., Jorge, R. N., Magee, C., and Hommes, Q. V. E. (2013). Towards a holistic approach to the travel experience: a qualitative study of bus transportation. *Transport Policy*, 25, 233–243.

De Palma, A., Kilani, M., and Proost, S. (2015). Discomfort in mass transit and its implication for scheduling and pricing. *Transportation Research Part B: Methodological*, 71, 1–18.

Doepke, M., and Tertilt, M. (2011). Female empowerment promotes economic development. IZA Discussion Paper No. 5637.

Freitas, A. L. P. (2017). Service quality in the context of competitive. *Producao on Line*, 5(1), 1–24.

Kamaruddin, R., Osman, I., and Pei, C. A. C. (2012). Employees' health and safety requirements. *Journal of Asian Behavioral Studies*, 2(5), 219–236.

Naveen (2019). Identification of key employability attributes and evaluation of university graduates' performance. Higher Education, Skills and Work Based Learning, 10(3), 449–466.

Rohani, M. M., Wijeyesekera, D. C., and Karim, A. T. A. (2013). Bus operation, quality service, and the role of bus provider and driver. *Procedia Engineering*, 53, 167–178.

Sayulu, K., Sardar, G., and Sridevi, B. (2005). Impact of self-help groups on women empowerment: an empirical study. *Management Researcher,* XI(3 & 4), 22.

Salini (2018). Challenging the primacy of lectures: The dissonance between theory and practice in university teaching. Journal of University Teaching and Learning Practice, volume 12(1), 1–3.

Sanjay Kumar Singh(2016). Employability Skills -A Study on the Perception of the Engineering Students and their Prospective Employers. Global Journal of Management and Business Studies. ISSN 2248-9878. 3, 5.

Sudarkodi and Balasubramani (2021). Graduate employability, 'soft skills' versus 'hard' business knowledge. A European Study Special Issue: Employability, Mobility and the Labour Market, 33(4), 411–42.

Sedamkar, H., and Ashappa, C. (2011). Women empowerment and rural development: policies and programs in Gulbarga district. *Indian Streams Research Journal*, 1, 1–13.

Shiralashetti, A. S. (2013). Awareness level towards government schemes: a study of women entrepreneurs of north Karnataka districts. *Summer Internship Society*, 5, 24–33.

Soloviev, A. (2015). Bus and coach transportation: buses can compete with air and rail transportation.

6 A study on employee performance on Unique Shell Mould India Private Limited, Coimbatore

T. Saranya[a] and S. Deva[b]

Karpagam Academy of Higher Education, Coimbatore, Tamil Nadu, India

Abstract

Employee performance is pivotal to how effectively individuals fulfil their roles. It profoundly influences a company's overall success in today's competitive landscape. This study delves into the performance analysis of employees at the Shell Mould India Private Limited at Coimbatore. The focus is on identifying factors impacting employee performance, including education, work environment, skills, management support, and compensation. Results reveal that compensation significantly and positively affects performance. The broader work environment, skills, education, and management support also interconnect, collectively influencing employee performance. Employing the weighted average method and regression analysis, this research sheds light on the intricate dynamics shaping employee performance, offering valuable insights for organizations aiming to enhance their workforce's effectiveness.

Keywords: Employee, knowledge, performance, training

Introduction

Employee performance is a multifaceted process encompassing actions, skills, development, and results, crucial for an organization's success. Defined by work-related activities, it gauges how effectively employees fulfill their roles. In the organizational realm, various resources contribute to smooth operations, with human capital standing out as the only dynamic component. While organizations can procure materials, funds, and machinery, acquiring the right human capital remains pivotal for competitiveness.

Employee performance is paramount in the 21st-century business landscape, enabling organizations to navigate evolving environments and stay competitive. Assessing and understanding the factors influencing employee performance is vital for organizational success. A well-functioning organization relies on skilled employees, emphasizing the integral role of human resources in achieving optimal performance and competitiveness. Recognizing the significance of employee performance in this dynamic era ensures organizations can effectively compete and thrive.

Table 6.1 Exploring perspectives: unveiling influences on employee performance and motivation across diverse studies.

Author name	Study	Findings
Matlala (2022)	Examined employee perceptions of aesthetics in performance evaluation systems.	Employees within a company hold a negative impression of the fairness of the systems they use. Distributive, procedural, and interactive justice significantly influence employees' fairness judgments. The study explores the cognitive complexity of executive appraisal and its impact on executive alienation during performance reviews.
Boachie-Mensah et al. (2022)	Investigated employee perceptions of employee performance approach at an educational institution in Ghana.	Employee views on an organization's performance system vary due to individual perceptions, influencing thoughts and behaviors. Findings reveal that employees are affected by performance systems and prone to critical mistakes, analyzed using methods such as descriptive statistics.
Aslam (2022)	Explored the cross-industry relationship between employee performance reactions and motivation.	Employee reactions to performance significantly impact motivation, with perceived satisfaction, acceptability, usefulness, fairness, and accuracy playing crucial roles in job motivation.

[a]Saranya2720001@gmail.com, [b]deva.seliyan@kahedu.edu.in

Rajput et al. (2021)	Investigated the multifaceted nature of employee performance systems, noting variations in evaluation frequency.	Employee performance is annually evaluated for existing employees but quarterly for trainees and new hires. Nursing managers assess different jobs in the nursing process, leading to varied ratings influenced by competition and reviewers' leniency.
Usman (2021)	Explored the effects of rewards and assessments on job satisfaction and motivation.	Found a close relationship between job motivation and satisfaction, emphasizing employee awareness and participation in decision-making for increased motivation. Focus was primarily on economic motivation within the company.
Sultana and Mohd Nazri (2020)	Addressed factors affecting employee performance in the Shah Alam retail market.	Aimed to identify key factors impacting retail employee performance, leading to positive and negative effects. The study relied on empirical evidence and questionnaire surveys to empower retail executives and employees for enhanced performance.

Source: Author

Problem Statement

In the pursuit of organizational development and survival amidst constant change, business leaders emphasize the crucial role of employee performance as a management tool, relying on competencies to optimize contributions; however, specific issues in the mentoring phase of performance appraisal systems warrant attention for effective talent management and sustained progress towards organizational goals.

Objectives of the Study

- To investigate the various factors impacting employee performance at unique shell company.
- To examine employee's perception on facilities and opportunities offered at workplace.

Hypotheses of the Study: H0: Training, work environment, skills and knowledge, management support and rewards and compensation factors not influenced employee performance.

Research Methodology

- Research methodology systematically addresses research problems.
- It serves as a source for understanding the scientific process of research.
- Researchers employed various procedures aligned with the project "Study of Different Factors Affecting Employee Performance."
- The study collected data from 120 respondents using simple random sampling in Unique Shell Mould India Private Limited, Coimbatore.

Analysis and Interpretation

This section provides a detailed examination of the factors influencing employee performance, encompassing aspects like training, work environment, skills, knowledge, management support, rewards, and compensation Table 6.1. Through methods such as weighted average analyses and regression modelling, we assess employees' viewpoints within Unique Shell Mould India Private Limited. The results offer valuable insights into workforce sentiments, highlighting areas of consensus and divergence. The ensuing interpretation succinctly captures the essence of each factor, revealing trends and attitudes essential for comprehending and improving organizational dynamics.

Interpretation: weighted average method
1. **Training factor:**
   - Employees generally agree that training improves skills, knowledge, attitude, and capabilities.
   - Majority prioritize the effectiveness of training methods used by the organization.
   - Weighted average rank indicates overall agreement with the training factor.
2. **Work environment factor:**
   - Employees feel they can easily communicate across all levels.
   - A good working environment is emphasized, especially with provided equipment and resources.
   - Weighted average rank highlights agreement with the work environment factor.
3. **Skill and knowledge factor:**
   - Employees agree that their jobs allow the use of abilities and skills.
   - Learning goals for continuous improvement are acknowledged.
   - Jobs are seen as a continuous lifelong endeavor.
   - Weighted average rank emphasizes agreement with the skills and knowledge factor.

4.   **Management support factor:**
   - Clear work assignment explanations and detailed performance reviews are well-received.
   - Majority feel they receive the right amount of support and guidance from supervisors.
   - Opportunities for promotion are considered positively.
   - Weighted average rank signifies overall agreement with the management support factor.

5.   **Rewards and compensation factor:**
   - Employees generally agree that they receive the right amount of salary for their work.
   - Readiness to increase work effort for rewards and compensation is acknowledged.
   - Positive effects of rewards on the work atmosphere are recognized.
   - Weighted average rank demonstrates overall agreement with the rewards and compensation factor.

6.   **Employee performance:**
   - Employees prioritize seeking new challenges and coming up with creative solutions.
   - Overall, employees agree on the importance of planning, achieving results, and taking on responsibilities.
   - Weighted average rank indicates a positive attitude towards employee performance.

Regression analysis:
- **Hypothesis testing:**
   - Null hypothesis is rejected for rewards and compensation, indicating a significant impact on employee performance.
   - Work environment, skills and knowledge, and management support do not show a significant impact on employee performance.
- **Regression model summary:**
   - E-value is 18.2290, and the adjusted R square-value is 0.046.
   - Significant values for work environment, skills and knowledge, and management support are above 0.05, suggesting no significant impact.
   - Rewards and compensation have a significant impact on employee performance.

The study reveals a positive perception of training, work environment, skills and knowledge, management support, rewards, and compensation. Rewards and compensation significantly impact employee performance. Recommendations could focus on strengthening areas with less significant impact, aligning policies with employee perceptions.

From the weighted average rank test, it is founded that majority of the employee has agreed with the training factor and the statement that the training improves their skills, knowledge, attitude change and new capabilities followed by the training increase them ability of the work and majority of the employee has agreed with the work environment factor and the statement that the departments provide all the equipment's supplies and resource necessary to perform my duties followed by the general working environments favours my performance and productivity ad majority of the employee has agreed with the skills and knowledge factor and the statement that the jobs allows me to use my abilities and skills followed by the statement that the knowledge has a direct influence on work performance.

Conclusion

In conclusion, this thesis has successfully addressed the primary objective of scrutinizing the factors influencing employee performance at Unique Shell Mould India Private Limited. The meticulous examination of five key factors—training, work environment, skills and knowledge, management support, and rewards and compensation—revealed nuanced interactions and impact on employee performance. Notably, rewards and compensation emerged as a pivotal factor, demonstrating a direct, positive, and statistically significant influence on employee performance. Additionally, the interplay among work environment, skills and knowledge, training, and management support exhibited a noteworthy collective influence on employee performance. These findings underscore the multi-faceted nature of factors shaping employee performance within the company.

In essence, this study contributes valuable insights for both academics and practitioners, shedding light on the intricate dynamics that contribute to or impede employee performance. Recognizing the significance of rewards and compensation, along with the interconnectedness of other factors, provides a foundation for devising strategic interventions and policies aimed at enhancing overall employee performance at Unique Shell Mould India Private Limited.

References

Aslam, S. (2022). Employee's reactions towards employee performance. 24 (3), 367–379.

Boachie-Mensah, et al. (2022). Employee/staff perceptions on employee performance method. 24(3), 367–379.

Matlala (2022). Employees at the organization have a negative perception. 35(10), 1779–1795.

Rajput, et al. (2021). Annual basis for existing. 54, 73–82.
   Received 13 November 2014, Revised 9 April, Accepted 9 May 2016, Available online 21 May.

Sultana, U. S., and Mohd Nazri, A. A. B. (2020). Factors affecting employees' performance in the retail sector. *Psychology and Education, 57(9),* 2564–2570. ISSN: 00333077. Article Received: 10 August 2020, Revised: 25 October 2020, Accepted: 18 November 2020.

Usman, A. A. (2021). Dimensions of work motivation. *55,* 25–34. Received 2 February, Revised 30 March, Accepted 8 April, Available online 15 April.

7 Production and marketing practices of flame lily in Dindigul district (Oddanchatram-Tk)

Selva Kumar D[a] and M. Pavithra[b]

Karpagam Academy of Higher Education, Coimbatore, Tamil Nadu, India

Abstract

Cultivating medicinal plants, like glory lily, in Dindigul, Tamil Nadu, offers multifaceted benefits. These plants serve as sources for traditional remedies, supporting local healthcare. Their active compounds aid various ailments, enhancing community well-being. Local farmers can diversify and earn from these plants, boosting income through cultivation and sales. Exporting these plants and derivatives can generate foreign exchange income, meeting global demand. Crucially, this cultivation maintains biodiversity and safeguards local ecosystems while curbing wild plant overexploitation. Properly managed, it significantly bolsters rural economies, creating jobs, advancing infrastructure, and enriching socio-economic conditions. A Dindigul study, focusing on glory lily across four villages, assessed cultivation practices, economic impact, and local benefits comprehensively. Overall, cultivating medicinal plants, notably glory lily, in Dindigul holds promise for bolstering local healthcare, income, foreign exchange, biodiversity, and rural economic growth.

Keywords: Flame lily, marketing, medicinal plants, production

Introduction

Flame lily (*Gloriosa superba*), named for its glorious and superb nature, has a rich history as a medicinal plant and an ornamental beauty. Thriving in tropical climates, its vibrant flowers bloom from June to August, captivating gardeners since its introduction in 1875. While flame lily cultivation holds promise for rural economic development, the focus on the Dindigul district in Tamil Nadu reveals India's stature as a key supplier of medicinal plants globally. However, challenges in marketing and trade practices persist, impacting sustainability and fair distribution of benefits. Addressing these issues is crucial for sustainable and equitable cultivation, benefiting local communities and biodiversity. Beyond its aesthetic allure, flame lily holds cultural significance, serving as national emblems and featuring in various ceremonies. Its use in traditional medicine, speculated to treat various ailments, attracts scientific interest for potential therapeutic applications. Scientists explore its biology, genetics, and ecological roles, while breeders aim to enhance its traits for better blooms and disease resistance. Harnessing the flame lily's potential requires not just cultivation but also addressing trade challenges, ensuring its sustainable growth and equitable benefits for all stakeholders.

Literature Review

Several studies have investigated various aspects of Gloriosa superba, shedding light on its medicinal potential, toxic properties, and cultivation traits. Arunkumar and Elangaimannan (2017) employed High-performance liquid chromatography (HPLC) to assess colchicine levels in different genotypes of *Gloriosa superba*, identifying the Thirnalvalli genotype as having the highest colchicine concentration. However, comprehensive details were not provided. Rathnayaka et al. (2017) studied about *Gloriosa superba* poisoning, highlighting its impact on multiple organ systems and emphasizing the need for early recognition and management. Udengwu and Nwafor (2018) explored the genotoxic and cytotoxic effects of *Gloriosa superba* tuber extract, suggesting its potential as an alternative to pure colchicine in research settings. Sreelatha and Sugumar (2018) analyzed quantitative elements in *Gloriosa superba*, proposing specific plant sections for treating particular ailments. Vaishnavi et al. (2019) emphasized the pharmacological characteristics and endangered status of the plant. Additionally, studies by Megala and Elango (2019), Jothi Uchimahali et al. (2019), Sellamuthu et al. (2020), Mishra and Sharma (2021), Iyer and Quadri (2021), and Uddin et al. (2021) further explored various facets of *Gloriosa superba*, encompassing phytochemical analysis, antibacterial properties, cultivation practices, propagation challenges, ethnomedicinal uses, and morphophysiological traits related to growth and flowering.

[a]selvakumardurai16121@gmail.com, [b]rmpavithra96@gmail.com

Problem Statement

Farmers in Dindigul lack vital information and resources for effective flame lily cultivation and marketing. They face challenges in accessing quality seeds, fertilizers, and expert guidance on pest control and irrigation. Poor market connections hinder sales and product development, limiting their ability to gauge demand and set competitive prices. Access to market data is scarce, hampering decision-making. Addressing these issues requires education, improved resources, better market links, and collaborative efforts among agricultural entities and local farmers for sustainable flame lily production and marketing in Dindigul. Objectives of the study are as follows: (a) to ascertain marketing practices on flame lily. (b) to identify the problems of production and marketing practices on flame lily. The study is restricted to the respondents of Oddanchatramtaluk. Hence the result arrived from this study may not be applicable or generalized to other geographical location. Perception of general public varies time to time. The option expressed by the respondents might have biased answer for reason.

Methodology

Data was gathered via an Interview Schedule focusing on flame lily cultivators' profiles, production, marketing practices, and production issues. Using a well-structured questionnaire circulated in hard copy, primary data was collected through convenience sampling of 130 respondents in Oddanchatramtaluk, specifically targeting five villages within KallimanthayamTaluk: Aranmanaivalasu (25), Thoppakavalasu (64), Velyuthampalayampudur (25), Thumbichipalayam (12), and Mandavadi (4).

Table 7.1 Simple percentage analysis.

sandy soil. All farmers engage in flame lily cultivation from June to November, planting below 500 kg within a six-month period, utilizing drip irrigation. They follow a rotation period for cultivation every 10 to 15 days in dry land conditions. Most of these farmers sell their produce through wholesale channels, experiencing hurdles due to market unavailability and often negotiating prices. They register profits ranging from Rs. 1,00,000-5,00,000 but encounter significant losses due to intermediaries. Their cultivation of flame lily primarily occurs from August to February. To identify the prominent reasons that induce a person to choose flame lily, Weighted Average, Rank Test is employed. The following table 4.47 discloses the result of the study.

Percentage analysis categorized respondents by demographic and socio-economic profiles in-depth. The majority of cultivators, predominantly in rural areas, are males with an age range between 44 and 68 years and an educational qualification of SSLC. They typically earn monthly incomes ranging from Rs. 50,001- 94,000, while their monthly expenditures fall between Rs. 20,001 and Rs. 44,000. These cultivators tend to have small families, with up to two members, residing in terrace-style houses, owning less than 1 acre of flame lily on	Numbers (n = 130)	Percentage
Area of residence		
Rural	118	90.8
Urban	12	9.2
Age		
Up to 44 years	21	16.2
44 to 68 years	83	63.8
Above 68 years	26	20.0
Gender		
Male	112	86.2
Female	18	13.8
Educational qualification		
Illiterate	41	31.5
SSLC	42	32.3
HSC	35	26.9
Under graduate	5	3.8
Post graduate	7	5.4
Monthly income		
Up to 50000	11	8.5
50001 to 94000	100	76.9
Above 94001	19	14.6
Monthly expenditure		
Up to 20000	5	3.8
20001 to 44000	106	81.5
Above 44001	19	14.6
Members in family		
Up to 2 members	111	85.4
3 to 5 members	18	13.8
Above 5 members	1	.8

Type of family		
Joint family	11	8.5
Nuclear family	119	91.5
Type of house		
Hut	21	16.2
Rent	7	5.4
Terrace	102	78.5
Acres of flame lily		
Below 1 acres	93	71.5
Between 1 to 2 acres	37	28.5
Nature of soil		
Sandy soil	97	74.6
Red soil	33	25.4
Seasonal month		
June to November	130	100.0
Yielding time		
6 month	130	100.0
Flame lily planted per acre		
Below 500 kg	70	53.8
500 to 750 kg	35	26.9
750 to 1000kg	21	16.2
Above 1000kg	4	3.1
Nature of irrigation		
Drip irrigation	130	100.0
Duration of harvesting		
6 months once	130	100.0
Rotation period		

10 to 15 days	60	46.2
16 to 20 days	48	36.9
Above 20 days	22	16.9
Types of land		
Dry land	130	100.0
Selling pattern		
Wholesale	72	55.4
Mixed sale	58	44.6
Availability of separate market		
Non available	130	100.0
Fixation of flame lily		
Bargaining price	74	56.9
Rate fixed by Government	56	43.1
Profits of flame lily		
Below 1,00,000	31	23.8
1,00,000 to 5,00,000	64	49.2
Above 5,00,000	35	26.9
Loss incurred by middle man		
High	68	52.3
Moderate	59	45.4
Low	3	2.3
Seasonal month		
August to February	67	51.5
September to March	63	48.5
Suggestion for marketing problems		
Farmers association	130	100.0

Source: Author

Table 7.2 Showing marketing problems among flame lily.

Marketing problems	SA	A	N0	DA	SDA	Total	Mean score	Rank
	5	4	3	2	1			
Problems in storing seeds	53	28	36	9	4	130	3.9000	7
	265	112	108	18	4	507		
Multiple channels of distribution	66	29	19	15	1	130	4.1077	5
	330	116	57	30	1	534		
Variation of price	82	36	6	4	2	130	4.4769	1
	410	144	18	8	2	582		
Problems in exports	0	54	39	20	17	130	3.0000	10
	0	216	117	40	17	390		
Limited market information	52	37	30	8	3	130	3.9769	6
	260	148	90	16	3	517		
Absence of stabilized price	65	39	13	12	1	130	4.1923	4
	325	156	39	24	1	545		
Increased cost of marketing	70	42	15	2	1	130	4.3692	2
	350	168	45	4	1	568		

Marketing problems	SA	A	N0	DA	SDA	Total	Mean score	Rank
Absence of standardization and grading	71	34	16	8	1	130	4.2769	3
	355	136	48	16	1	556		
Less facilities for flame lily seeds processing	0	67	37	25	1	130	3.3077	8
	0	268	111	50	1	430		
Ineffective institutional organization	0	68	37	18	7	130	3.2769	9
	0	272	111	36	7	426		
Forced sale	0	54	13	52	11	130	2.8462	11
	0	216	39	104	11	370		

Source: Author

The result of weighted average ranks illustrates that majority of marketing problems on flame lily is variation of price followed by increased cost of marketing, absence of standardization and grading etc Table 7.1 and 7.2.

KMO and Bartlett's test

Kaiser-Meyer-Olkin measure of sampling adequacy.		.712
Bartlett's test of sphericity	Approx. Chi-square	247.288
	df	55
	Sig.	.000

To identify the prominent factor that influence a level of production problem in flame lily, factor analysis is employed. Kaiser-Meyer-Olkin (KMO) and Bartlett's test of sphericity has been used as pre-analysis testing for suitability of the entire sample for factor analysis. The result of KMO and Bartlett's Test is found greater than 0.70. Hence the collected data is fit for employing factor analysis. Further the large value of Bartlett's test of sphericity (2002.522, df: 276, Sig .. . 000) indicated the appropriateness of factor analysis i.e., the sample was adequate.

Rotated component matrixa

	Component			
	1	2	3	4
Low germination seeds	.751	.033	-.022	
Government Subsidy	.631		.255	.152
Unskilled labors	.626	.104	.039	.173
Demand for seed	.583	.156	.399	
Climate change	.047	.794		.271
Fungal disease		.788	.214	
Insufficient labor	.286	.695	.045	
Fertilizer limited	.046	.068	.827	.033

Rotated component matrixa

	Component			
	1	2	3	4
Suitability of soil	.228	.098	.789	
Providing government loan	.285	.214	.140	.749
Financial problem	.287	.332	.231	

Eigen values above unity identify significant factors. Component loadings of 0.5+ indicate issues for flame lily: low germination, government subsidy, unskilled labor, demand, climate change, insufficient labor, fertilizer limitations, soil suitability, loans, and financial problems. These variables form distinct factors based on their loadings, revealing key problems.

Recommendations

The outlined recommendations encompass a wide spectrum, spanning cultivation, finance, marketing, infrastructure, and quality control, intending to enhance flame lily production's efficiency, profitability, and sustainability. Suggestions advocate meticulous soil testing for optimal cultivation sites and urge financial institutions and governmental bodies to stabilize seed prices and support financially vulnerable farmers. Emphasizing skill development among younger farmers, fostering equitable resource distribution, and ensuring timely financial aid are highlighted to bolster agricultural output and bridge income gaps. Market-oriented strategies, like crop diversification and direct selling programs, are proposed to empower farmers and reduce reliance on intermediaries. Moreover, encouraging collaboration, technology adoption, and quality enhancement measures are suggested to fortify competitiveness and standardization. Mitigating challenges such as low productivity, seed quality, labor expertise, and infrastructure issues remains pivotal. Overall, these suggestions, demanding collective efforts from stakeholders, offer a holistic framework to overcome constraints in flame lily production and marketing, aiming for sustainable and profitable outcomes in the agricultural sector.

Conclusion

Government assistance is crucial for small farmers, offering financial aid, infrastructure development, and access to essential inputs like seeds and fertilizers. These measures can notably enhance flame lily cultivation productivity. Implementing standardized tissue culture methods can address propagation issues, creating genetically superior, resilient plants with increased colchicine production. Conservation measures are vital to preserve its medicinal potential. PCR-based approaches aid in identifying superior clones for quick conservation. Resolving marketing, labor, and natural challenges, along with providing agricultural finance, can bolster sector profitability. Government attention and support are pivotal for agriculture sector growth, emphasizing intervention, infrastructure, cultivation, conservation, and resolving challenges for flame lily's sustainable success and farmer well-being.

References

Arunkumar, P., and Elangaimannan, R. (2017). Quantification of colchicine golrisa lily (golrisasuperba). In UGC SAP National Seminar on Emerging Trends in Crop Improvement, (pp. 9–12).

Biswas, A., Muntaha, S. N., and Rahman, M. M. (2014). Comparative karyotype analysis in two lifeforms of Gloriosa superba L. *Journal of Pharmaceutical Biology*, 4(2), 77–80.

Elangaimannan, R. (2017). Evaluation of golrisasuperba for quantitative. Medicinal and Aromatic Plant Science and Biotechnology. 27–31.

George, P. (2010). Death related to herbal therapy for joint pains – A rare case of gloriossa superba poisoning. *Journal of Clinical and Diagnostic Research*, 5(2), 379–380.

Khandel, A. K., Ganguly, S., and Bajaj, A. (2012). Gloriosa superba L. (Glory lily) spotted for the first time in vegetation of pachmarhi biosphere reserve. (Hoshangabad district), central India. *International Journal of Pharmacy and Life Sciences*, 3(6), ISSN: 0976-7126.

Mishra, T., and Sharma, P. (2020). A critical review of golry lily: a rare medical plant. *World Journal of Pharmacy and Pharmaceutical Sciences*, 9(10), 1123–1133, ISSN 2278 – 4357.

Mishra, T., and Sharma, P. (2021). Vegetative propagation of golry lily. *Suraj Punj Journal for Multidisciplinary Research*, 11(1), 168–173, ISSN NO: 2394–2886.

Padmapriya, S., Rajamani, K., and Sathiyamurthy, V. A. (2015). Glory lily (gloriosa superba L.) - a review. *International Journal of Current Pharmaceutical Review and Research*, 7(1), 43–49, ISSN: 0976 822X.

Selvarasu, A., and Kandhasamy, K. (2013). Reproductive biology gloriosa rothschildaina. *Medicinal and Aromatic Plant Science and Biotechnology*, 7(1), 45–49.

Uddin, A. F. M. J., Rakibuzzaman, M., Dina, A., Raisa, I., and Husna, M. A. (2021). Morpho-physiological characterization and petal color analysis of gloriosa as a potential cut flower. *Bangladesh Journal of Agriculture*, (44–46), 1–7.

Vaishnavi, B. A., Khanm, H., and Bhoomika, H. R. (2019). Review on pharmacological properties of glory lily (Gloriosa superba Linn.): an endangered medicinal plant. *International Journal of Current Microbiology and Applied Sciences*, 8(2), 1359–1364, ISSN: 2319–7706.

8 Obstacles faced by fishermen in Karaikal

P., Babu^a, D. Mary Prema^b, M. Anandan^c, J. Sudarvel^d and R. Velmurugan^e

Karpagam Academy of Higher Education, Coimbatore, Tamil Nadu, India

Abstract

This study investigates the multifaceted challenges faced by fishermen in Karaikal, India, offering a comprehensive exploration of both operational and marketing obstacles unique to this coastal community. Utilizing surveys, interviews, and data analysis, the research identifies a range of significant issues, including difficulties in ocean fishing, product perishability, financial constraints, high operational costs, limited family time, overfishing, monsoon variability, catch fluctuations, regulatory concerns, income inconsistencies, and vessel damage. Marketing challenges encompass insufficient cold storage, storage issues, price volatility, auctioneer commissions, market knowledge gaps, payment delays, competition, traditional sales slumps, transportation costs, and low product demand. The study is crucial for informing policymakers, fishing communities, and stakeholders about these distinctive challenges, with the aim of shaping targeted interventions and regulations to enhance the long-term sustainability and profitability of Karaikal's fishing sector. The research proposes recommendations such as collaborative stakeholder efforts, financial support, credit accessibility, improved storage facilities, enhanced market education, fair payment systems, and sustainable fishing practices to address and mitigate these challenges. Ultimately, this research seeks to uplift the fishing community in Karaikal, mitigate their challenges, and foster the sustainable growth of the local fishing industry by proposing practical solutions.

Keywords: Fishermen, fishing industry, general problems and marketing issues, Karaikal, obstacles

Introduction

The fishing industry holds paramount importance in global coastal economies, notably impacting livelihoods. In the Karaikal coastal region of India, fishermen contend with various challenges affecting their fishing operations and overall well-being. Understanding and surmounting these challenges are imperative for fostering sustainable growth in Karaikal's fishing sector. This introduction provides a comprehensive overview of the obstacles confronting Karaikal's fishermen, encompassing both operational and marketing concerns. It underscores the significance of addressing these issues and the potential outcomes of implementing solutions.

Numerous general challenges impede the productivity and profitability of Karaika's fishing sector, including oceanic fishing difficulties, perishable harvests, funding constraints, high costs, limited family time, overfishing, adverse monsoons, seasonal catch variations, regulatory issues, income inconsistency, and boat damage. Beyond these, fishermen in Karaikal encounter distinctive marketing challenges impacting the sale and distribution of their fish products. Inadequate cold storage, market knowledge gaps, slow payment procedures, competition, low sales on ceremonial days, high transportation costs, and insufficient demand exacerbate their difficulties. Policymakers, fishing groups, and stakeholders can enhance fishermen's livelihoods and overall well-being by recognizing and addressing these challenges, promoting sustainable development in the fishing sector. This study investigates these challenges, aiming to uncover their root causes and propose effective remedies through comprehensive research methods such as surveys, interviews, and data analysis. The ultimate goal is to contribute to the sustainable development of the fishing sector, the conservation of fish populations and ecosystems, and the enhancement of the socio-economic conditions of Karaikal's fishing community.

^a deybabu249@gmail.com, ^b dmprema280@gmail.com, ^c nmcanandan@gmail.com, ^d j.sudarvel@gmail.com, ^e drvelsngm@gmail.com

Review of Literature

Table 8.1 Studies on fisheries: authors, focus, and key findings.

Author name	Study	Findings
Muringai et al. (2020)	Lake Kariba, Zimbabwe	Small-scale fishing groups face challenges influenced by environmental, social, political, and economic factors, negatively impacting fish output.
Kinseng et al. (2019)	Weather impact on fishing	Majority of fishermen are affected by uncertain weather, leading to smaller catches and high fuel expenses.
Jahan et al. (2018)	Belia Bael	Study reveals 27 fish species in Belia Bael, with 23 indigenous and 4 alien. Emphasizes the need to educate fishing communities on biodiversity.
Jarin (2018)	Dagupan city tributaries	Young adult males from large families, with minimal education, dominate fishermen near Dagupan City's tributaries.
Kotni (2017)	Challenges in fisheries	Identifies challenges in infrastructure, export restrictions, environmental concerns, economics, finance, marketing, technology, research, and services.
Salim et al. (2017)	Healthcare and education	Improved healthcare and education positively impact the lifestyle of fishing communities, providing prospects for future advancement.
Patilkhede et al. (2018)	Artisanal fishing barriers	Study uncovers poverty, food crisis, and vulnerability among artisanal fishing populations, highlighting social, financial, and commercial barriers.

Source: Author

Problem Statement

The fishing sector faces multifaceted challenges encompassing operational hindrances such as inadequate catch, high costs, overfishing, and environmental impacts, as well as marketing issues including storage limitations, price fluctuations, and insufficient market awareness. To address these challenges and promote overall profitability and sustainability, collaborative efforts among fishermen, governmental bodies, fishing groups, and stakeholders are essential, necessitating practical solutions like sustainable fishing practices, financial support, technological advancements, improved storage facilities, enhanced market knowledge, diversified marketing channels, and fair payment procedures.

Scope of the Study

This study on the fishing business delves into various critical aspects. It considers geographical factors, allowing for focused analysis based on climate, fishing methods, and specific regions. Stakeholders, including fishermen, groups, government bodies, intermediaries, and consumers, are examined to understand diverse perspectives. The study explores fishermen's challenges, such as catch limitations, financial constraints, and marketing issues. Root causes, effects, and solutions are scrutinized. Sustainable fishing methods, financial support, technological advancements, and market strategies are proposed solutions. Socioeconomic and environmental impacts are assessed, and governance and policy aspects are examined for sustainable industry growth, with the study's scope flexible based on research goals, resources, and time constraints.

Objectives of the Study

To identify the obstacles faced by fishermen in Karaikal.

Research Methodology

Data: The primary data is collected through a well framed and structured questionnaire. The questionnaire was circulated by hard copy and soft copy to the fishermen's.

Sampling design: Data collected by convenience sampling method from 160 fishermen in Karaikal Frame work of analysis

- Simple percentage analysis
- Weighted average test

Significance of the Study

The study enhances understanding of challenges faced by fishermen, aiding stakeholders and policymakers in identifying root causes. Policymakers can craft effective policies based on the study's insights, offering empirical solutions for improved fishing sector efficiency. By addressing these challenges, the research seeks to elevate fishermen's living standards, enhance economic conditions, and contribute to the overall well-being of coastal communities Brahmane et al. (2016). It emphasizes sustainable fishing methods and resource management for preserving ecosystems and supporting economic resilience. The study promotes market access and competitiveness for fishermen through measures like improved market knowledge and storage facilities, fostering collaboration among industry players for long-term solutions. Overall, it contributes to the fishing sector's growth, influencing positive change, policy decisions, and fishermen's lives.

Analysis and Interpretation

Socio-economic profile of fishermen in Karaikal:
- **Age:** Majority of fishermen are above 40 years old. Distribution: 18 to 25 years (20.0%), 26 to 30 years (15.0%), 31 to 36 years (26.3%), Above 40 years (38.8%).
- **Education qualification:** Majority have an H.SC. degree. Distribution: SSLC (32.5%), H.SC (40.0%), non-educated (27.5%).
- **Type of family:** Majority belong to nuclear families. Distribution: Joint (26.2%), nuclear (73.8%).
- **Monthly income:** Majority earn between 20201 to 49000. Distribution: Below 20200 (26.2%), between 20201 to 49000 (53.8%), above 49001 (20.0%).
- **Years of work experience:** Majority have 5 to 12 years of experience. Distribution: Below 4 years (23.8%), between 5 to 12 years (56.3%), above 13 years (20.0%).

Marketing problems faced by fishermen:
- **Price fluctuation:** Weighted average score: 3.11 which is ranked 2nd among marketing problems.
- **Inadequate demand:** Weighted average score is 2.48 and ranked 10th among marketing problems.
- **Storage problem:** Weighted average score: 3.91 and ranked 1st among marketing problems.
- **Inadequate market knowledge:** Weighted average score: 2.79 and ranked 5th among marketing problems.
- **Competition from other sellers:** Weighted average score is 2.66 and ranked 7th among marketing problems.

- **High expenses of transport:** Weighted average score is 2.56 and ranked 9th among marketing problems.
- **Delay in payment:** Weighted average score is 2.76 and ranked 6th among marketing problems.
- **Low sale on ritual days:** Weighted average score is 2.64 and ranked 8th among marketing problems.
- **Auctioneer's commission:** Weighted average scoreis 3.06 and ranked 3rd among marketing problems.
- **Cold storage facilities:** Weighted average score is 2.84 and ranked 4th among marketing problems.

General problems faced by fishermen:
- **Unable to capture fish all over the sea:** Weighted average score is 4.40 and ranked 1st among general problems.
- **Perishable nature of product:** Weighted average score is 4.34 and ranked 2nd among general problems.
- **Lack of finance:** Weighted average score is 4.28 and ranked 3rd among general problems.
- **High petrol/diesel expenses:** Weighted average score is 4.18 and ranked 4th among general problems.
- **Unable to spend time with family:** Weighted average score is 4.09 and ranked 5th among general problems.
- **Overfishing:** Weighted average score is 3.90 and ranked 6th among general problems.
- **Poor monsoon:** Weighted average score is 3.66 and ranked 7th among general problems.
- **Unable to capture fish all over the year:** Weighted average score: 3.61. Ranked 8th among general problems.
- **Trouble from other country officials:** Weighted average score: 3.30. Ranked 9th among general problems.
- **No regular income:** Weighted average score: 3.30. Ranked 9th among general problems.
- **Damage of boat:** Weighted average score: 3.05. Ranked 11th among general problems.

Suggestions:
- Encourage adoption of advanced fishing techniques and technology (GPS, fish finding equipment).
- Offer financial aid or microcredit programs for essential infrastructure and equipment.
- Promote sustainable fishing methods through fishing quotas and laws.
- Explore alternate revenue streams during non-fishing seasons (aquaculture, fish processing, tourism).

- Invest in developing or upgrading cold storage facilities near fishing locations.
- Provide market information, training, and seminars on market trends and pricing.
- Explore direct marketing methods like farmers' markets or online platforms.
- Investigate new markets locally and abroad to reduce price swings and insufficient demand.
- Form cooperatives or associations to enhance market access, bargaining power, and quality standards

The findings reveal a majority of fishermen in Karaikal are aged above 40, hold H.SC qualifications, and belong to nuclear families. Most earn between INR 20,201 to 49,000 monthly, with 5 to 12 years of work experience. Marketing challenges include storage problems, price fluctuations, and inadequate market knowledge. General problems involve overfishing, high fuel costs, irregular income, and the perishable nature of the catch. The study identifies 'Unable to capture fish all over the sea' as the primary general issue and 'Storage problem' as the major marketing problem. Recommendations encompass technology adoption, financial aid, sustainable fishing practices, and market-oriented strategies.

Conclusion

The multifaceted challenges faced by fishermen impact both the marketing dynamics of fish products and the overarching facets of fishing operations. From the general issues of overfishing to the complexities of marketing-related problems like price fluctuations and inadequate market knowledge, the study highlights the intricacies of the fishing sector. The plethora of obstacles, spanning from the environmental to economic, necessitates a comprehensive approach for resolution.

To address these challenges, proposed strategies involve embracing modern fishing technologies, diversifying income streams, enhancing market awareness through training initiatives, exploring direct marketing channels, and fostering cooperative marketing efforts. Transparent payment systems and thorough market research also emerge as vital components of the proposed solutions. For these strategies to materialize and foster a conducive environment for sustainable fishing practices, improved market access, and enhanced profitability, collaboration among fishermen, government entities, fishing organizations, and other stakeholders is imperative. This collective effort can propel the fishing sector towards heightened profitability, increased market competitiveness, and enduring sustainability.

References

Brahmane , V. T., Solanki, V. M., Patel, M. R., and Baraiya, K. G. (2016). Socio-economic status and scope for improvement of navi bandar fishing village of Saurashtra. *Advances in Life Sciences*, 5(10), 4039–4042.

Jahan, M. I., Alam, M. S., Karim, M. S., Sultana, N., Mamun, M., and Rafiquzzaman, S. (2018). Assessment of fish diversity and socio-economic condition of fishermen in Bangladesh. *Asian Journal of Medical and Biological Research*, 4(1), 69. doi:10.3329/ajmbr.v4i1.36824.

Jarin, S. A. (2018). Socio-economic status and environmental problems affecting the fishermen along the river tributaries of Dagupan City. *Asia Pacific Journal of Multidisciplinary Research*, 6(1), 82–87.

Kinseng, R. A., Mahmud, A., Hamdani, A., and Hidayati, H. N. (2019). Challenges to the sustainability of small-scale fishers' livelihood in Banyuwangi regency, East Java, Indonesia. *IOP Conference Series: Earth and Environmental Science*, 352, 1–13.

Kotni (2017). Management and socio-economic conditions of fishermen in Andhra Pradesh. *Journal of Fisheries*, 1(1), 30–36.

Muringai, R. T., Naidoo, D., and Mafongoya, P. (2020). The challenges experienced by small-scale fishing communities of Lake Kariba, Zimbabwe. *Journal for Transdisciplinary Research in Southern Africa*, 16(1), 1–16.

Patilkhede et al. (2018). Review on pharmacological properties of glory lily (Gloriosa superba Linn.): an endangered medicinal plant. International Journal of Current Microbiology and Applied Sciences, 8(2), 1359–1364, ISSN: 2319– 7706.

Salim, S. S., Narayanakumar, R., Sathiadhas, R., Antony, B., and Manjusha, U. (2017). Assessment of socio-economic status of fishers across different sectors in Tamil Nadu. *Fishery Technology*, 54(4), 291–293.

9 A study on non-performing assets of Indian scheduled commercial banks

R. Shalini[a], P. Soni Pawar[b], P. Praseeja[c], R. Velmurugan[d] and J. Sudarvel[e]

Karpagam Academy of Higher Education, Coimbatore, Tamil Nadu, India

Abstract

Scheduled Commercial Banks in India experience a substantial impact from non-performing assets (NPAs). The financial stability and profitability of banks are impacted by the existence of NPAs. As loans become NPAs, banks experience a decline in interest revenue and profitability. Profitability and capital adequacy are further impacted by the requirement to put aside provisions to offset anticipated losses on NPAs. The quantity of money available for lending and other business operations decreases as a result of capital erosion. Concerns concerning credit risk management procedures are raised by high numbers of NPAs. Stakeholders may lose trust in it, and it may draw regulatory attention. Banks with a large percentage of NPAs may become more risk-averse, cautious about lending, and tighten credit requirements. This might limit loan availability to profitable industries, which would have an effect on economic development and growth. Thus, an effort has been undertaken in this study to quantify the amount of non-performing assets in India's scheduled commercial banks and to make recommendations for reducing NPA.

Keywords: Asset quality, bad loans, loan defaults, non-performing assets, NPA ratio

Introduction

The banking sector's growth has spurred non-performing assets (NPAs) in Indian banks, posing challenges like disrupted credit cycles and financial instability. This study delves into NPA levels across Scheduled Commercial Banks (SCBs), stressing the importance of effective NPA management for stability and improved asset quality. Factors contributing to NPAs, like recovery inefficiencies and economic fluctuations, are dissected. Public sector banks (PSBs) tend to face higher NPAs due to diverse borrower profiles, while small finance banks (SFBs) dealing with smaller entities display lower NPA percentages. Understanding these differences is crucial for formulating policies and enhancing trust in banking. However, this study has limitations, relying solely on secondary data and having a restricted scope and timeframe. PSBs struggle with governance issues, while SFBs maintain cautious lending, impacting their NPA levels. Foreign banks also show lower NPAs due to proactive risk management and targeted lending strategies. The diverse performance among banks highlights varied risk approaches and regulatory influences affecting NPA levels.

Table 9.1 Gross non-performing assets.

Year	PSBs	Private	Foreign	SFBs	Average	SD	CV
2018	895601	129335	13849	0	259696.25	427883.13	164.76
2019	739541	183604	12242	1087	234118.50	347148.61	148.28
2020	678317	209568	10208	1709	224950.50	317137.67	140.98
2021	616616	197508	15044	5971	208784.75	285845.17	136.91
2022	542174	180782	13786	6911	185913.25	250743.99	134.87
Average	694449.80	180159.40	13025.80	3135.60			
SD	134165.30	30664.36	1863.00	3096.65			
CV	19.32	17.02	14.30	98.76			

Source: Author

[a]shaliniramesh38@gmail.com, [b]sonipawar2008@gmail.com, [c]praseeja.ponmala@kahedu.edu.in, [d]drvelsngm@gmail.com, [e]j.sudarvel@gmail.com

Net Non-Performing Assets

Net non-performing assets (NNPAs) depict bad loans adjusted for provisions, highlighting PSBs' higher risk exposure compared to SFBs' cautious lending practices Table 9.1.

Sub-standard Assets

Financial assets undergo classifications, such as "substandard" before hitting "non-performing" level.

These assets pose increased default risk, affecting banks differently.

Doubtful assets

The term "doubtful assets" refers to a class of assets held by banks and other financial institutions that are more unsure about their chances of being repaid and are more likely to become non-performing assets (NPAs). Compared to substandard assets, these assets

Table 9.2 Net non-performing assets.

Year	PSBs	Private	Foreign	SFBs	Average	SD	CV
2018	454473	64380	1548	0	130100.25	218318.26	167.81
2019	285122	67309	2051	586	88767.00	134550.22	151.58
2020	230918	55683	2005	765	72342.75	108772.59	150.36
2021	196451	55377	3241	2981	64512.50	91344.67	141.59
2022	154745	43733	3023	2725	51056.50	71759.06	140.55
Average	264341.80	57296.40	2373.60	1411.40			
SD	116532.68	9228.79	723.82	1349.11			
CV	44.08	16.11	30.49	95.59			

Source: Author

Table 9.3 Substandard assets in Scheduled Commercial Banks.

Year	PSBs	Private	Foreign	SFBs	Average	SD	CV
2018	205340	27203	3831	0	59093.50	98236.16	166.24
2019	137377	42440	3190	719	45931.50	63889.16	139.10
2020	132530	56588	3273	1023	48353.50	61714.17	127.63
2021	103744	65363	3648	4965	44430.00	48911.48	110.09
2022	75843	41251	3649	5039	31445.50	34337.71	109.20
Average	130966.80	46569.00	3518.20	2349.20			
SD	48359.65	14781.46	273.70	2450.13			
CV	36.93	31.74	7.78	104.30			

Source: Author

Table 9.4 Doubtful assets of Scheduled Commercial Banks.

Year	PSBs	Private	Foreign	SFBs	Average	SD	CV
2018	593615	69978	8364	0	167989.25	285461.08	169.93
2019	506492	104696	8019	360	154891.75	239161.04	154.41
2020	404724	92396	5775	648	125885.75	190598.55	151.41
2021	351014	90228	5566	841	111912.25	164606.81	147.09
2022	329264	77394	7953	1908	104129.75	153947.48	147.84
Average	437021.80	86938.40	7135.40	751.40			
SD	111130.30	13552.58	1348.37	720.11			
CV	25.43	15.59	18.90	95.84			

Source: Author

have more flaws and are more likely to default or delay repayment.

Loss Assets

In Indian SCBs, the term "loss assets" refers to a class of assets that have been designated as non-performing and are seen as either irrecoverable or having slim chances of recovery. The banks have recorded a complete write-off of these assets as losses on their balance sheets.

Priority Sector NPA

PSBs face higher NPAs in RBI-designated priority sectors compared to foreign banks due to mandatory lending and differing business strategies.

Non Priority Sector NPA

Non-priority sector NPAs exclude RBI-designated priority sectors like agriculture, MSMEs, education, housing, and export credit from NPAs.

NPA Recovery Mechanism

NPA recovery methods encompass varied strategies employed by financial institutions to reclaim unpaid debts. In India, strategies like Lok Adalat offer informal dispute resolution, while Debt Recovery Tribunals specialize in resolving loan conflicts. The SARFAESI Act empowers banks to enforce security interests for debt recovery, and the Insolvency and Bankruptcy Code aims for efficient insolvency resolution.

The Insolvency and Bankruptcy Code (IBC) shows higher NPA recovery rates than Lok Adalat. The IBC ensures efficient insolvency handling, employing experts and involving creditors. Conversely, Lok Adalats focus on compromise, potentially limiting their effectiveness with complex financial disputes like NPAs in commercial banks. Their reliance on negotiation methods might not suit intricate financial issues requiring specialized knowledge, leading to lower recovery rates compared to the IBC.

Table 9.5 Loss assets of Scheduled Commercial Banks.

Year	PSBs	Private	Foreign	SFBs	Average	SD	CV
2018	46521	5243	1635	0	13349.75	22222.38	166.46
2019	66239	9576	1034	44	19223.25	31634.59	164.56
2020	107163	34986	1161	39	35837.25	50239.57	140.19
2021	122217	31350	986	165	38679.50	57551.14	148.79
2022	102400	50616	2184	39	38809.75	48400.15	124.71
Average	88908.00	26354.20	1400.00	57.40			
SD	31366.02	18810.18	508.02	62.71			
CV	35.28	71.37	36.29	109.25			

Source: Author

Table 9.6 Priority sector NPA.

Year	PSBs	Private	Foreign	SFBs	Average	SD	CV
2018	187511	18426	1184	0	51780.25	90878.16	175.51
2019	212315	29721	1103	893	61008.00	101776.07	166.82
2020	236212	36219	1692	1376	68874.75	112750.10	163.70
2021	257858	50557	1802	4974	78797.75	121433.66	154.11
2022	243283	48588	2555	6111	75134.25	114033.13	151.77
Average	227435.80	36702.20	1667.20	2670.80			
SD	27732.17	13381.12	582.83	2697.68			
CV	12.19	36.46	34.96	101.01			

Source: Author

Table 9.7 Non priority sector NPA.

Year	PSBs	Private	Foreign	SFBs	Average	SD	CV
2018	657964	83998	12645	0	188651.75	315052.51	167.00
2019	497794	126991	11139	230	159038.50	233006.96	146.51
2020	408205	147751	8516	333	141201.25	190423.34	134.86
2021	319116	136684	8397	996	116298.25	148871.21	128.01
2022	264225	120676	11231	874	99251.50	122611.86	123.54
Average	429460.80	123220.00	10385.60	486.60			
SD	155574.57	24197.66	1859.91	428.89			
CV	36.23	19.64	17.91	88.14			

Source: Author

Table 9.8 NPA recovery mechanism.

Year	Lokadalat	DRT	Sarfaesi	IBC	Average	SD	CV
2018	1811	7235	26380	4926	10088.00	11086.39	109.90
2019	2750	10552	38905	66440	29661.75	29025.86	97.86
2020	4211	9986	34283	104177	38164.25	45896.93	120.26
2021	1119	8113	27686	27311	16057.25	13517.11	84.18
2022	2777	12114	27349	47421	22415.25	19505.61	87.02
Average	2533.60	9600.00	30920.60	50055.00			
SD	1166.51	1948.07	5451.89	37942.43			
CV	46.04	20.29	17.63	75.80			

Source: Author

Recommendations

Addressing NPAs in Indian Scheduled Commercial Banks requires a multifaceted approach: strengthening credit appraisal, risk management, monitoring, recovery mechanisms, risk-based supervision, financial literacy, stringent NPA classification, corporate governance, Asset Quality Reviews (AQRs), industry-specific reforms, technological advancements, and collaboration among stakeholders. These strategies aim to improve credit assessment, risk identification, timely monitoring, effective recovery, regulatory oversight, borrower education, transparent reporting, governance practices, sector-specific reforms, technological innovation, and collaborative efforts. Customization to bank-specific needs, continuous evaluation, and adaptation of these measures are crucial for effective NPA containment and sustained efficacy.

Conclusion

The study on non-performing assets (NPAs) in Indian Scheduled Commercial Banks provides crucial insights into NPA status, administration, and implications. It delves into gross and net NPA levels, loan classification, sector-wise NPAs, and recovery processes, spanning 2018 to 2022. Its significance lies in understanding NPAs' impact on banking stability, the economy, and policy formulation. The study stresses robust credit appraisal, risk management, and vigilant monitoring to curb NPAs. It emphasizes strong recovery processes, transparent reporting, and sector-specific alterations. Further research opportunities include longitudinal analysis for deeper trends, comparative studies, macroeconomic analysis, qualitative approaches, regulatory impact assessments, regional differences, technological interventions, societal and environmental impacts, policy effectiveness, investor perceptions, and governance influences. Extensive research in these domains can inform policy and enhance NPA management in Indian banks.

References

Agarwal, R. B., Goyal, M., and Srivastava, P. (2021). Exploring factors affecting non-performing assets of banks with reference to small and marginal farmers in Rajasthan. In Proceedings of the International Conference on Advances in Management Practices (ICAMP 2021).

Desai, R. (2017). Impact of sectorial advances on priority sector NPA – case of BSE bankex. *Amity Journal of Management Research*, 2(2), 13–21.

Gaur, D., and Mohapatra, D. R. (2019). Non-performing assets in India: priority vs non- priority sector lending. *NMIMS Management Review*, 37(3), 53–65.

Gopi, E., and Paulraj, J. (2015). Causes and remedies of non performing assets towards Indian public sectors bank. *Indian Journal of Research*, 4(7), 144–146.

Kulkarni, P., Pimplapure, V. U., and Pachpor, M. P. (2020), Effect of lending pattern on NPA in Indian banks. *Palarchs' Journal of Archaelogy of Egypt / Egyptology*, 17(8), 1223–1230.

Mahlawat, S. (2015). Analysis of the factors causing non performing assets and reduction strategies for PSB in India. *International Journal of Business Quantitative Economics and Applied Management Research*, 2(3), 39–55.

Mishra, B. (2021). An analysis of factors affecting non-performing assets in Indian banking sector. *EPRA International Journal of Economic and Business Review*, 9(11), 24–29.

Prasanth, S., Nivetha, P., Ramapriya, M., and Sudhamathi, S. (2020), Factors affecting non performing loan in India. *International Journal of Scientific and Technology Research*, 9(1), 1654–1657.

Rathore, D. S., Malpani, S., and Sharma, S. (2016). Non-performing assets of Indian banking system and its impact on economy. *IOSR Journal of Economics and Finance*, 7(6), 21–26.

Shabbir, N., and Mujoo, R. (2014). Problem of non performing assets in priority sector advances in india. *Journal of Economics and Development Studies*, 2(1), 241–275.

Sikdar, P., and Makkad, M. (2013). Role of non performing assets in the risk framework of commercial banks – a study of select Indian commercial banks. *AIMA Journal of Management & Research*, 7(4), 1–19.

Sudha, B., and Alamelu Mangai, R. (2020), Non-performing assets: reasons and remedies. *International Journal of Scientific and Technology Research*, 9(3), 1125–1127.

Susena, K. C., Huda, M., Maseleno, A., Sahoo, B. P., and Kaur, K. (2021). A study on impact of PSL on gross NPAS of nationalised banks: an empirical approach. *Linguistics and Culture Review*, 5(3), 81–96.

Throve, H. A. (2015). Analytical study of priority & non –priority sector lending with reference to nationalized banks in India. *Paridnya - The MIBM Research Journal*, 3(1), 97–100.

10 A case study on investors awareness and preference toward mutual fund at ARA security Pvt. Ltd

Arun Kumar, P.[a], Ramyaprabha, N.[b] and Hemamalini, P. H.[c]

Karpagam Academy of Higher Education, Coimbatore, Tamil Nadu, India

Abstract

Investments in mutual funds are funded by investors with predetermined financial objectives. It is a trust that collects money from numerous investors and invests it in various programs in accordance with their goals. SEBI (Security and Exchange Board of India) regulates mutual funds, which are set up as trusts with a sponsor, trustee, asset management company (AMC), and custodian. With a focus on the district of Palakkad, the current study examines the connections between investor awareness, preference, and perception of mutual funds, as well as information sources, income levels, educational attainment levels, factors considered when selecting mutual funds to invest in, and investment types. Convenience sampling and structured questionnaires were employed by the researcher.

Keywords: AMC, mutual fund, security and exchange board of India

Introduction

Mutual funds pool money from various individuals to invest in securities like stocks, bonds, and more. Managed by professionals, these funds aim to increase profits or generate income for investors, offering access to diversified portfolios. The trustees oversee unit holders' interests, ensuring compliance with SEBI regulations. Compared to direct investments, mutual funds offer scale economies, diversification, liquidity, and expert management. Despite their advantages, lack of awareness among investors leads to favoring short-term investments over mutual funds. This research aims to explore investors' awareness, preferences, and reasons behind their choices in mutual funds within India's growing market. With varying financial capabilities and investment knowledge, investors face confusion in selecting strategies. This study intends to fill knowledge gaps, emphasizing the importance of understanding mutual funds as a viable investment option amidst diverse investment choices and financial considerations.

Literature Review

Researchers have extensively examined investor behavior in the selection of mutual funds and life insurance, as indicated by Hassan Qamar's research (2020). Dr. Bhagaban Das, Ms. Sangeeta Mohanty, and Mr. Nikhil Chandra Shil conducted around 100 interviews to gather both qualitative and quantitative data, analyzed statistically to test insurance-related hypotheses, detailed in their study published in the International Journal of Business Management. Aadish's findings (2019) suggest that consumers favor certain brands or companies based on age, education, gender, and career while choosing between mutual funds and life insurance products. However, their study lacked specifics on the data, casting doubt on the validity of their conclusions. Meanwhile, Ramdenial's comprehensive poll (2019) involving AMC houses analyzed fund performance based on geographical regions and distribution methods. Wen Ke's study (2019) highlighted the rationale behind closing funds to maintain performance, emphasizing spillover effects as a significant factor. Vasudevan (2018) emphasized the challenge of choosing mutual funds due to varied attributes like asset size and fee structures. Gorex's study (2016) introduced a novel visual tool, the density-based distribution map, to understand the link between fund features and returns. Additionally, study (2018) aimed to assess fund performance using data envelopment analysis before selecting investment objectives.

Research Methodology

The study's primary focus is on descriptive elements. The researcher utilized a carefully constructed questionnaire to get the data. Secondary information was gathered from books, periodicals, newspapers, internet, etc. For primary data collection, the researcher employed the convenience sampling method. 100 mutual fund investors at ARA Security Pvt. Ltd. were chosen by the researcher.

[a]havocarun2001@gmail.com, [b]ramyameena1990@gmail.com. [c]hemamalini2007ster@gmail.com

Hypotheses

H0: There is no significant relation between experience and overall stock management performance.

H1: There is a significant correlation between experience and overall stock management performance.

Data analysis procedures
- Weighted average
- ANOVA analysis
- Chi-square analysis

The weighted average rank result reveals that equities funds, dividend yield funds, and large cap funds are the most common types of mutual fund schemes.

The null hypothesis is upheld across multiple instances as the significant values—0.298, 0.165, and 0.635—exceed the accepted threshold of 0.05, leading to its acceptance in each scenario.

Hypothesis Testing

Hypothesis 1
H0: There is no association between gender and the quantity of safety
H1: There is a connection between gender and the quantity of safety
Hypothesis 2
H0: There is no connection between gender and the quantity of liquidity.
H1: There is a connection between gender and the amount of liquidity.
Hypothesis 3
H0: There is no correlation between the quantity of Capital admirations and gender.
H1: There is no association between capital admiration rates and gender.
Hypothesis 4
H0: There is no correlation between professional management numbers and gender
H1: There is a connection between professional management numbers and gender.

Table 10.1 Data analysis and interpretation weighted average.

	SDA	DA	N	A	SA			
	1	2	3	4	5			
Equity fund	15	27	18	28	12	100		
	15	54	54	112	60	295	2.95	2
Large cap fund	16	26	17	28	13	100		
	16	52	51	112	65	296	2.96	1
Mid cap fund	25	48	13	11	3	100		
	25	96	39	44	15	219	2.19	8
Small cap fund	25	48	12	11	4	100		
	25	96	36	44	20	221	2.21	6
Multi cap fund	26	47	12	11	4	100		
	26	94	36	44	20	220	2.2	7
ELSS fund	23	44	12	14	7	100		
	23	88	36	56	35	238	2.38	5
Dividend yield fund	16	26	18	28	12	100		
	16	52	54	112	60	294	2.94	3
Focused fund	22	44	12	14	8	100		
	22	88	36	56	40	242	2.42	4

Source: Author

Table 10.2 ANOVA.

		Sum of squares	Df	Mean square	F	Sig.
Safety	Between groups	1.830	1	1.830	1.095	.298
	Within groups	163.810	98	1.672		
	Total	165.640	99			
Liquidity	Between groups	1.830	1	1.830	1.095	.298
	Within groups	163.810	98	1.672		
	Total	165.640	99			
Capital admiration	Between groups	2.138	1	2.138	1.953	.165
	Within groups	107.252	98	1.094		
	Total	109.390	99			
Professional management	Between groups	1.830	1	1.830	1.095	.298
	Within groups	163.810	98	1.672		
	Total	165.640	99			
Flexibility	Between groups	1.830	1	1.830	1.095	.298
	Within groups	163.810	98	1.672		
	Total	165.640	99			
Regular income	Between groups	2.138	1	2.138	1.953	.165
	Within groups	107.252	98	1.094		
	Total	109.390	99			
Diversification benefits	Between groups	1.830	1	1.830	1.095	.298
	Within groups	163.810	98	1.672		
	Total	165.640	99			
Loan facility	Between groups	.322	1	.322	.227	.635
	Within groups	139.238	98	1.421		
	Total	139.560	99			
Tax benefit	Between groups	.322	1	.322	.227	.635
	Within groups	139.238	98	1.421		
	Total	139.560	99			

Source: Author

Hypothesis 5
H0: There is no connection between gender and the quantity of flexibility.
H1: There is a connection between gender and flexibility.
Hypothesis 6
H0: There is no correlation between the number of Regular earners and their gender.
H1: The amount of Regular income earners and their gender are related.
Hypothesis 7
H0: There is no association between gender and the volume of gains from diversification.
H1: There is a correlation between gender and the amount of gains from diversification.
Hypothesis 8
H0: There is no association between gender and the availability of loan facilities.
H1: There is a connection between the quantity of loan facilities and gender.
Hypothesis 9
H0: There is no association between gender and the quantity of tax benefits.
H1: There is a connection between gender and the amount of tax benefits.

Chi-square test
The table shows an examination of the relationship between Returns from Mutual Funds and Very Low Growth in Unit Value.

Hypothesis

H0: There is no correlation between returns from mutual funds being lower than anticipated and the very slow growth in unit value Table 10.1 and 10.2.
H1: There is no correlation between Returns from Mutual Funds have been less than anticipated and Very Little Growth in Unit Value.

Mutual fund performance has performed worse than anticipated.
Chi-square tests

	Value	Df	A symp. Sig. (2-sided)
Pearson Chi-Square	25.943[a]	20	.168
Likelihood ratio	26.492	20	.150
Linear-by-linear association	1.029	1	.310
No. of valid cases	100		

23 cells (76.7%) have an expected count of fewer than 5. The predicted count must be at least.12.

Hypothesis

HO: It makes no difference. Professionally accomplished experts in management have underperformed * There has been very little unit value growth
   H1: There is no correlation between professionally expert managers' underperformance and the very slow growth in unit value.
Mutual fund returns haven't performed as well as anticipated.

Chi-square tests

	Value	df	A symp. Sig. (2-sided)
Pearson Chi-square	23.748[a]	20	.254
Likelihood ratio	26.009	20	.166
Linear-by-linear association	1.024	1	.311
No. of valid cases	100		

24 cells (80.0%) have an expected count of fewer than 5. The predicted count must be at least.03.

Findings

Between ages 31 and 50, 30.0% of respondents lie; 70.0% are men. 42.0% graduated high school, 80.0% are married, and 53.0% earn Rs. 30,000 to Rs. 40,000, while 66.0% make over Rs. 40,000. 42.0% are from banks and share the image of a fund manager; 39.0% are aged 3 to 5 years old, and 28.0% belong to the public.

Weighted Average

The weighted average rank demonstrates that major mutual fund schemes include large cap funds, equity funds, and dividend yield funds. The ANOVA test indicates a strong relationship between respondents' gender and storage upkeep in the organization, with a significant F-value of 109.080 (p < 0.05). Similarly, the Chi-square test supports H1, revealing a significant association between respondents' gender and storage upkeep (F-value: 109.080, p < 0.05).

Conclusions

To engage younger generations, educational institutions should introduce mutual fund education. ARA Security Private Limited needs to engage investors for feedback, offer investment updates, and align fund managers' actions with investors' goals. Mutual fund marketing stands as a vital information source; therefore, businesses must use advertising to disseminate necessary details for public awareness. Knowledgeable managers providing timely updates are crucial, considering investors' potential unfamiliarity with mutual fund schemes. The study delves into connections between mutual fund knowledge, information sources, income, education levels, investor considerations, and investment preferences. The survey highlights the appeal of superior return policies in attracting investors. Introducing new schemes can enhance investor confidence and expand the mutual fund industry overall.

References

Anbukarasi, M., and S, P. J. (2022). A study on level of awareness and perceived usefulness of block chain technology in boosting financial inclusion. *International Journal for Research in Engineering Application and Management (IJREAM)*, 07(10), 168–173. doi:10.35291/2454-9150.2022.0028.

Balamurugan, S., Selvalakshmi, M., and Vasundhara, S. (2021). an empirical study of behavioural finance perspectives of mutual fund .

Kaur, S. J., and Bharucha, J. (2021). The emerging mutual fund industry in india: an impact analyis of investors awareness on investment behaviuor. *International Journal of Business and Globalisation*, 27(1), 51–69.

Khemka, A. (2021). A study of invetors awareness and perception aboout invetsment in mutual funds. *Journal of Management and Technology* .

Kwon, S., Lowry, M., and Qian, Y. (2020). Mutual fund investment in private firms. *Journal of Financial Economics*, 136(2), 407-443.

Manjare, S. O. (2021). Critical analysis of the factors affecting mutual fund investment and retail investors. *International Journal of Research and Analysis in Commerce and Management* .

Shaneeb, P., and Sumathy, M. (2021a). Impact of intellectual capital on financial performance in Indian textile industries. *Academy of Accounting and Financial Studies Journal*, 25(4), 1–14.

Shaneeb, P., and Sumathy, M. (2021b). Impact of intellectual capital on firm performance in Indian it companies. Journal of Contemporary Issues in Business and Government, 27(02), 4335–4340. https://doi.org/10.47750/cibg.2021.27.02.459.

Sujith, T. S. (2016). A study on economic benefits of goods and services tax on Indian tax scenario. *International Journal of Current Research in Multidisciplinary*, 2(17), 10–13.

Sujith, T. S. (2017). Awareness of green marketing and its influence on buying behavior of consumers in Kerala. *International Journal of Scientific Research and Management*, 5(7), 6156–6164.

Sujith, T. S., and Julie, C. D. (2017). Opportunities and challenges of e- payment system in India. *International Journal of Scientific Research and Management (IJSRM)*, 5(9), 6935–6943.

Sujith, T. S., and Sumathy, M. (2019). Customer or member satisfaction of primary agricultural credit societies in Kerala. *International Journal of Scientific and Technology Research*, 8(12), 2665–2670.

Sujith, T. S., Sumathy, D. M., and Anisha, T. (2019). Customer perception towards mobile wallet among Youth with special reference to Thrissur city. *International Journal of Scientific and Engineering Research*, 10(3).

Sumathy, M., and Sujith, T. S. (2018a). Effect of brand on customer loyalty among sbi banking customers. *International Journal of Scientific Engineering and Research*, 6(9), 2015–2018.

Sumathy, M., and S, T. S. (2018b). A comparative study on perception of customers towards service quality of Canara and ICICI bank. research review. *International Journal of Multidisciplinary*, 3085(Special Issue), 187–190.

11 A study on non-monetary benefits influencing employee productivity

Mohammed Razick, A.[a], Dr. R Manju Shree and N. Nagalakshmi[b]
Karpagam Academy of Higher Education, Coimbatore, Tamil Nadu, India

Abstract

Non-monetary benefits encompass rewards not quantifiable in monetary terms, such as the contentment derived from specific work-life aspects, like enjoying company-provided family holidays. Employee satisfaction, a positive emotional state stemming from job, recognition (Locke et al., 1969), influences employees' dedication and contribution to their work (Ellickson and Logsdon, 2002). This study delves into assessing employee perspectives on non-monetary benefits and their influence on job satisfaction, engagement, and loyalty. It aims to understand how these benefits impact employees' perceptions and emotional commitment to their roles.

Keywords: Engagement, loyalty, non-monetary, productivity

Introduction

Various scholars present multifaceted perspectives on employee incentives and productivity enhancement. Deci and Ryan categorize rewards into monetary (extrinsic) and non-monetary (intrinsic), both impacting employee performance. Financial compensation, bonuses, and promotions affect productivity, while job satisfaction and engagement also play vital roles. Phadtare (2022) emphasizes the significance of motivation, recognition, and favorable work conditions, proposing rewards aligned with employee performance. Kumawat (2022) suggests a balanced approach encompassing motivation, opportunity, culture, and leadership factors to enhance performance. Azad et al. (2022), highlight effective stress management's impact on productivity, showing stable results for workplace stress training. Kiran (2021) delves into employee productivity's components, including motivation, teamwork, and recognition, underscoring their role in total quality management. Rajgarhia (2020) emphasizes non-financial incentives fostering commitment and a sense of ownership toward organizational goals. However, the challenge lies in organizations struggling to leverage non-monetary incentives effectively, leading to absenteeism, delays, and decreased productivity, raising questions about their true impact on employee commitment and organizational productivity (Locke et al., 1969). Two primary objectives of the study are to assess the employee perception on non-monetary benefits, and to measure the impact of non-monetary benefits on employee job satisfaction, engagement and loyalty.

Hypotheses of the Study

H1: There is significant impact on employee satisfaction due to the welfare facilities.

H0: There is no significant impact on employee loyalty due to the welfare facilities

Research Methodology

A research methodology is a systematic way of solving a research question. It includes various steps from design to implementation of statistical tools to conclusions, which are usually considered when considering the problem and the logic behind it. This study addresses non-monetary benefits that affect employee productivity (Ellickson and Logsdon, 2002). The total number of samples collected for the study is 150 respondents. A random sampling method was used in the study. The most commonly used statistical tools for analyzing collected data are factor analysis and regression.

Analysis and Interpretations

Factor analysis involves grouping similar variables into dimensions. This process is used to identify latent variables or constructs.

In the above table, KMO measure of sampling adequacy shows the value as 0.861 which means the factor analysis of the selected variable is found to be appropriate or good to the data. The p-value from Bartlett's test of sphericity is 0.000 which is lower than 0.05 significance level Hanaysha (2020). Hence alternative hypothesis is accepted stating that variables are correlated enough.

[a]razick.anees@gmail.com, [b]nagalakshmi.nagendran@kahedu.edu.in

Extraction method: principal component analysis

The table shows three factors in employee perception with Eigenvalues over 1.0, representing variance explained by principal components. Eigen values greater than zero indicate significance, and those ≥ 1 explain more variance than a single observed variable. Before rotation, the variance explained by the first, second, and third factors is 54.1%, 18.9%, 16.1%, while after rotation it's 31.9%, 30.1%, 27.3% respectively. These factors influence employee perception regarding non-monetary benefits from the organization, detailed in the following table.

Table 11.1 KMO and Bartlett's test.

Kaiser-Meyer-Olkin measure of sampling adequacy.		.861
Bartlett's test of sphericity	Approx. Chi-Square	2465.351
	Df	66
	Sig.	.000

Source: Author

Extraction Method: Principal Component Analysis. Rotation Method: Varimax with Kaiser Normalization

The factor extraction table showcases three distinct factors. The first, "perception of commitment," comprises

Table 11.2 Total variance explained.

Component	Initial Eigenvalues			Loadings			Loadings		
	Total	% Of Variance	Cumulative %	Total	% Of Variance	Cumulative %	Total	% Of Variance	Cumulative %
1	6.51	54.3	54.3	6.51	54.3	54.3	3.8	31.9	31.9
2	2.28	18.9	73.3	2.28	18.9	73.3	3.6	30.1	62.1
3	1.93	16.1	89.3	1.93	16.1	89.3	3.3	27.3	89.3
4	.338	2.8	92.1						
5	.283	2.4	94.5						
6	.182	1.52	95.9						
7	.164	1.37	97.4						
8	.128	1.07	98.4						
9	.066	.552	98.9						
10	.058	.486	99.5						
11	.042	.349	99.8						
12	.022	.185	100						

Source: Author

Table 11.3 Rotated component matrix.

Factors	Components		
	1	2	3
The company introduces non-monetary schemes for its employees with a view to increase the earnings of its employees for an improved work performance	.941		
The firm's non-monetary incentive schemes tend to match its employee's desired intentions	.935		
The basic idea of introducing non-monetary incentive schemes is only to bring about an increase in output	.916		
The rate of labor turnover can be reduced by introducing attractive non-monetary incentives	.891		
Employees can accomplish their defined targets without assistance		.931	
Rewarding incentives has increased the quality of work over time		.924	
Do you feel you are supported to balance your role and responsibilities without pressure		.918	

Factors	Components		
	1	2	3
Employees can Identify and give innovative ideas to become more productive		.870	
Labor has trust and confidence in the non-monetary incentive schemes offered by the management			.908
Non -monetary incentive schemes offered in the organization do not show favoritism and it is unbiased			.878
The non-monetary incentive plans of the company are easy to understand and it is simple to calculate			.855
Employees views and suggestions are sought after by management while evolving non-monetary schemes			.854

a. Rotation converged in five iterations.
Source: Author

Table 11.4 Factor extraction table.

Factors	Cumulative %	Loading
Perception of commitment	31.942	
The company introduces non-monetary schemes for its employees with a view to increase the earnings of its employees for an improved work performance		.941
The firm's non-monetary incentive schemes tend to match its employee's desired intentions		.935
The basic idea of introducing non-monetary incentive schemes is only to bring about an increase in output		.916
The rate of labor turnover can be reduced by introducing attractive non-monetary incentives		.891
Perception of support	62.060	
Employees can accomplish their defined targets without assistance		.931
Rewarding incentives has increased the quality of work over time		.924
Do you feel you are supported to balance your role and responsibilities without pressure		.918
Employees can identify and give innovative ideas to become more productive		.870
Perception of transparency	89.310	
Labor has trust and confidence in the non-monetary incentive schemes offered by the management		.908
Non -monetary incentive schemes offered in the organization do not show favoritism and it is unbiased		.878
The non-monetary incentive plans of the company are easy to understand and it is simple to calculate		.855
Employees views and suggestions are sought after by management while evolving non-monetary schemes		.854

Source: Author

items related to company objectives and strategies for non-monetary benefits, demonstrating loadings from 0.891 to 0.941. The second, "perception of support," includes items linked to the support employees receive due to these benefits, with loadings from 0.870 to 0.931. Lastly, the third, "perception of transparency," encompasses items indicating employees' transparency in non-monetary schemes, reflected in loadings from 0.854 to 0.908. These factors delineate employee perceptions in commitment, support, and transparency regarding non-monetary benefits provided by the organization. The Regression technique determines the relationship strength between dependent and independent variables, aiding in predicting variance in the dependent variable accounted for by a set of independent variables. Regression coefficients range from -0 to +1, with values closer to +1 signifying a stronger impact of the independent variable on the study variable.

Table 11.5 Descriptive statistics.

Factors	Mean	St. deviation	N
Overall impact on Emp satisfaction due to non-monetary benefits	71.23	14.39	150
Non-monetary benefits related to management culture within the organization	69.11	18.69	150
Non-monetary benefits related to the labor welfare facilities provided within the organization	76.48	14.74	150
Non-monetary benefits related to the job working conditions of the employee	63.12	20.34	150
Non-monetary benefits related to the training and development activities in the organization	75.29	16.43	150
Non-monetary benefits related to the rewards and recognitions provided to employees for good performance	76.67	17.33	150

Source: Author

Model summary

Model	R	R Square	Adjusted R Square	Std. Error of Estimate
1	.924	853	.848	5.61280

Coefficients

Model	Unstandardized coefficients		Standardized coefficients	t	Sig.	95.0% Confidence interval for B	
	B	Std. Error	Beta			Lower Bound	Upper Bound
(Constant)	1.47	3.27		.448	.655	-5.00	7.93
Non-monetary benefits related to management culture within the organization	.102	.027	.133	3.797	.000	.049	.156
Non-monetary benefits related to the labour welfare facilities provided within the organization	.099	.039	.102	2.546	.012	.022	.177
Non-monetary benefits related to the job working conditions of the employee	.372	.031	.526	11.975	.000	.311	.434
Non-monetary benefits related to the training and development activities in the organization	.262	.035	.300	7.574	.000	.194	.331
Non-monetary benefits related to the rewards and recognitions provided to employees for good performance	.154	.028	.186	5.520	.000	.099	.210

a. Dependent variable: Overall impact on Emp satisfaction due to non-monetary benefits

The Beta values (.133, .102, .526, .300, and .186) are positive but not close to +1.0. The regression significance, below 0.05, rejects the null hypothesis, supporting the alternate for all non-monetary independent variables. Among the impactful factors, job conditions (Beta .526) and training and development (Beta .300) stand out. With an adjusted R-squared of 0.848, these benefits contribute significantly (84.8%) to employee satisfaction. To evaluate their impact on employee engagement, factors like management culture, welfare facilities, job conditions, training and development, and rewards and recognition are analyzed Pellegrino et al. (2021).

The beta values (.144, .105, .505, .312, .186) are positive but not close to +1.0. The regression significance below 0.05 leads to rejecting the null hypothesis, accepting the alternate for non-monetary variables. Among the five impactful benefits, job conditions (.505) and training and development (.312) stand out for employee engagement. The test aims to determine

Table 11.6 Descriptive statistics.

Factors	Mean	St. deviation	N
Overall impact on Emp satisfaction due to non-monetary benefits	71.38	14.34	150
Non-monetary benefits related to management culture within the organization	69.11	18.69	150
Non-monetary benefits related to the labour welfare facilities provided within the organization	76.48	14.75	150
Non-monetary benefits related to the job working conditions of the employee	63.12	20.34	150
Non-monetary benefits related to the training and development activities in the organization	75.29	16.43	150
Non-monetary benefits related to the rewards and recognitions provided to employees for good performance	76.67	17.33	150

Source: Author

Model summary

Model	R	R Square	Adjusted R square	Std. Error of estimate
1	.922	.849	.844	5.66217

Coefficient

Model	Unstandardized coefficients		Standardized coefficients	t	Sig.	95.0% Confidence interval for B	
	B	Std. Error	Beta			Lower Bound	Upper Bound
(Constant)	1.09	3.301		.330	.742	-5.435	7.61
Non-monetary benefits related to management culture within the organization	.111	.027	.144	4.069	.000	.057	.164
Non-monetary benefits related to the labour welfare facilities provided within the organization	.102	.039	.105	2.593	.010	.024	.180
Non-monetary benefits related to the job working conditions of the employee	.356	.031	.505	11.351	.000	.294	.418
Non-monetary benefits related to the training and development activities in the organization	.273	.035	.312	7.803	.000	.204	.342
Non-monetary benefits related to the rewards and recognitions provided to employees for good performance	.154	.028	.186	5.469	.000	.098	.210

a. Dependent variable: overall impact on Emp engagement due to non-monetary benefits

which benefit significantly impacts employee loyalty among management culture, welfare facilities, job conditions, training and development, and rewards and recognition.

Table 11.7 Descriptive statistics.

Factors	Mean	St. deviation	N
Overall impact on Emp satisfaction due to non-monetary benefits	71.18	17.37	150
Non-monetary benefits related to management culture within the organization	69.11	18.69	150
Non-monetary benefits related to the labor welfare facilities provided within the organization	76.48	14.74	150

Factors	Mean	St. deviation	N
Non-monetary benefits related to the job working conditions of the employee	63.12	20.34	150
Non-monetary benefits related to the training and development activities in the organization	75.29	16.43	150
Non-monetary benefits related to the rewards and recognitions provided to employees for good performance	76.67	17.33	150

Source: Author

Model summary

Model	R	R Square	Adjusted R square	Std. error of estimate
1	.910	.828	.822	7.32284

Coefficient

Model	Unstandardized coefficients		Standardized coefficients	T	Sig.	95.0% confidence interval for B	
	B	Std. error	Beta			Lower bound	Upper bound
(Constant)	4.22	4.27		.988	.325	4.22	12.7
Non-monetary benefits related to management culture within the organization	.046	.035	.049	1.31	.194	.024	.115
Non-monetary benefits related to the labour welfare facilities provided within the organization	.009	.051	.008	.183	.855	-.091	.110
Non-monetary benefits related to the job working conditions of the employee	.627	.041	.734	15.3	.000	.547	.707
Non-monetary benefits related to the training and development activities in the organization	.181	.045	.171	3.99	.000	.091	.270
Non-monetary benefits related to the rewards and recognitions provided to employees for good performance	.129	.036	.129	3.54	.001	.057	.201

a. Dependent variable: overall impact on Emp loyalty due to non-monetary benefits.

The beta values of .049, .008, .734, .171, and .129, while positive, aren't notably close to +1.0, indicating significance for most non-monetary independent variables except management culture and welfare facilities, with significance values of .194 and 0.855 respectively. Of the three impactful non-monetary benefits on employee engagement, job conditions (beta value of .734) and training and development (beta value of .171) stand out. The R squared value of .822 illustrates that 82.2% of employee loyalty

Table 11.8 Impact of non-monetary benefits on employee satisfaction.

Sl. No	Dimension (factor)	Regression significance value	Accepted hypothesis	Remarks
1	Management culture	.000	Alternate	There is significant impact on employee satisfaction due to the management culture
2	Welfare facilities	.012	Alternate	There is significant impact on employee satisfaction due to the welfare facilities"

Sl. No	Dimension (factor)	Regression significance value	Accepted hypothesis	Remarks
3	Job conditions	.000	Alternate	There is significant impact on employee satisfaction due to the job conditions
4	Training and development	.000	Alternate	There is significant impact on employee satisfaction due to the training and development programs
5	Rewards and recognitions	.000	Alternate	There is significant impact on employee satisfaction due to the rewards and recognition activities

Source: Author

variance is explained by these benefits collectively. Through Factor analysis, perceptions of non-monetary benefits cluster into commitment, support, and transparency dimensions. commitment refers to genuine management efforts to enhance productivity and match employee aspirations. Support involves mechanisms aiding employees to achieve these benefits, fostering self-reliance and innovation Mani and Mishra (2021). Transparency concerns the inclusive and unbiased nature of evolving such schemes, nurturing trust and confidence among employees.

Table 11.9 Impact of non-monetary benefits on employee engagement.

Sl. no	Dimension (factor)	Regression significance value	Accepted hypothesis	Remarks
1	Management culture	.000	Alternate	There is significant impact on employee engagement due to the management culture
2	Welfare facilities	.010	Alternate	There is significant impact on employee engagement due to the welfare facilities
3	Job conditions	.000	Alternate	There is significant impact on employee engagement due to the job conditions
4	Training and development	.000	Alternate	There is significant impact on employee engagement due to the training and development programs
5	Rewards and recognitions	.000	Alternate	There is significant impact on employee engagement due to the rewards and recognition activities

Source: Author

Impact of non-monetary benefits on employee loyalty

Sl. no	Dimension (factor)	Regression significance value	Accepted hypothesis	Remarks
1	Management culture	.194	Null	There is no significant impact on employee loyalty due to the management culture
2	Welfare facilities	.855	Null	There is no significant impact on employee loyalty due to the welfare facilities
3	Job conditions	.000	Alternate	There is significant impact on employee loyalty due to the job conditions
4	Training and development	.000	Alternate	There is significant impact on employee loyalty due to the training and development programmes
5	Rewards and recognitions	.001	Alternate	There is significant impact on employee loyalty due to the rewards and recognition activities"

Conclusions

The study highlights job rotation, autonomy, and work flexibility as crucial aspects requiring consistent management attention to influence employee mindset positively. Management perception among employees needs improvement, urging initiatives like town halls and one-on-one interactions. Welfare facilities receive good feedback, aligning with competitors. Junior employees lack emotional attachment and commitment, possibly due to monetary measures. Management is advised to revise compensation policies for juniors. In conclusion, employee satisfaction and engagement significantly impact morale, productivity, and retention. Organizations leverage non-monetary benefits to engage employees strategically in today's dynamic business landscape.

References

Azad, E., Hassanvand, B., and Eskandar, M. (2022). Effectiveness of a training program based on stress management on NEDSA staff and line staff. *Saf Health Work*, 13(2), 235–239, and Published online 2022 Mar 3. doi: 10.1016/j.shaw.2022.02.003.

Hanaysha, J. (2020). Testing the effects of employee engagement, work environment, and organizational learning on organizational commitment. *Procedia - Social and Behavioral Sciences*, 229, 289–297.

Kiran, D. R. (2021). Chapter 11–total employee involvement total quality management key concepts and case studies 2017. 143–162.

Kumawat, K. S. (2022). A study of non monetary factors impacting employees performance in selected automobile manufacturing industry.

Mani, S., and Mishra, M. (2021). Employee engagement constructs: "CARE" model of engagement – need to look beyond the obvious. *Leadership and Organization Development Journal*, 42(3), 453–466, (ISSN: 01437739).

Pellegrino, R., Crandall, P. G., O'Bryan, C. A., and Seo, H. S. (2021). A review of motivational models for improving hand hygiene among an increasingly diverse food service workforce. *Food Control*, 50, 446–456.

Phadtare, S. D. (2022). Employee engagement practices during the COVID19 lockdown: human resource management challenges and a roadmap. *Journal Press India*, 10(4), 75–83.

Rajgarhia, C. (2020). Monetary and non – monetary incentives - effect on job satisfaction of the employees at work place. *IJCRT International Journal of Creative Research Thoughts*, 8(11), 3367–3375, ISSN: 2320-2882.

12 Financial performance analysis of listed companies in food industry

K. Hari Haran and M. Nandhini[a]

Karpagam Academy of Higher Education, Coimbatore, Tamil Nadu, India

Abstract

The research titled "financial performance analysis of selected food industry enterprises" focuses on assessing the financial standing of companies within the food industry by comparing their current performance with data from the past five years. Utilizing secondary data from annual reports, the study underlines the necessity for these corporations to bolster their current assets, given that, on average, their current liabilities tend to surpass available assets. Through comprehensive analyses such as the comparative balance sheet, common size balance sheet, and comparative balance sheet analysis, it becomes evident that enhancing current assets can substantially fortify the financial position of these entities. The study endeavors to scrutinize the financial outcomes of a specific cohort of food industry enterprises, aiming to offer insights into how these businesses can enhance their financial standing.

Keywords: Financial analysis, ratio analysis, working capital and profitability

Introduction

Financial performance analysis involves scrutinizing a company's financial strengths and weaknesses by establishing precise relationships between items on the balance sheet and profit and loss account. This analysis is crucial for identifying growth opportunities and making both short- and long-term projections. Essentially, "analysis" means breaking something down to understand its parts and how they connect to the whole and other elements. In the realm of financial statements, it entails examining how the different sections interrelate to comprehend the company's status and performance.

Similar to a doctor assessing various vital signs before diagnosing a patient, a financial analyst evaluates financial statements using diverse analytical tools to gauge an organization's profitability and stability. Financial analysis is the means through which this evaluation occurs, determining an organization's financial strengths and weaknesses before conclusions are drawn. Financial performance encapsulates a company's monetary activities, depicting the extent to which financial objectives have been met. Ultimately, this process involves quantifying the value derived from a company's strategies and operations.

Problem Statement

The absence of a comprehensive understanding of a company's status and performance due to limited examination of fundamental financial statement elements impedes creditors and investors from accurately evaluating past, present, and future performance, financial situation, profitability, and stability, thereby undermining informed financial decision-making and investment support.

Objectives of the Study

- To determine the listed company's situation with regard to liquidity and long-term solvency position in the food sector.
- To evaluate the food industry profitability position of the chosen listed company.

Research methodology
- **Research design:** Employed an analytical research design.
- **Sources of data:** Utilized information extracted from annual reports, manuals, and accounts of selected food industry listed businesses.
- **Period of the study:** Collected data spanning a five-year period from 20172018 to 20212022.
- **Area of study:** Focused on examining ten specific listed companies within the food industry, including ADF Foods, LT Foods, Hindustan Foods, Godrej, Zydus Wellness, Hatsun Agro Product Limited, Jubilant Food Works Limited, Tirupati Starch & Chemicals Limited, Milk food Limited, and MSR India.
- **Tools of analysis:** Applied Ratio analysis, Analysis of Variance, and correlation analysis to derive research findings and draw conclusions for the present study.

[a]nandhini1817@gmail.com

Literature Review

Table 12.1 Exploring diverse studies in the food industry: insights from academic research.

Author name	Reference	Study
Rosenbusch	(Year)	Explored VC's impact on food firms, showing slight initial benefits that disappear with industry considerations. Noted gains in business expansion but no impact on profitability. Used 76 samples, 36,567 businesses.
Rakshit	(2007)	Examined Indian food industry decentralization and its role in meeting production needs. Emphasized handloom clusters' shift to power-driven looms for increased output and profits.
Pintea	(Year)	Explored link between company environmental practices and financial success in Romania. Studied environmental impact on packaging industry profits over 2005-2010 with Romanian enterprises.
Simpson and Shetty	(Year)	Analyzed post-MFA Indian food industry, highlighting structural issues, market barriers, and government initiatives. Conducted in-depth interviews with government representatives.
Reddy	(Year)	Investigated Andhra Pradesh's Food Industry (1989-1999) regarding investment patterns, capital, and profit performance. Emphasized need for resource influx and modernization.
Meenakshi	(2022)	Explored WTO's potential impact on Indian food industry, suggesting strategies for effective competition. Highlighted rising domestic consumption and income trends.
Diabat	(2020)	Discussed pressures on industries, especially in India, to adopt sustainable practices due to global demands. Explored ethical supply chain systems and enabling factors in Indian industries.
Singh and Kathuria	(2022)	Explored challenges faced by Indian garment exporters post-quota. Focused on Delhi- and Ludhiana-based exporters, highlighting export obstacles and issues faced by women in the sector.

Source: Author

Results and Discussion

Table 12.2 Financial analysis summary: ANOVA results and correlation analysis of selected consumer food companies' ratios.

Analysis type	Null hypothesis	SS	df	MS	F	Sig	Result
ANOVA - current ratio	Significant difference in current ratio	171.003	9	19	10.987	0	Reject H0, accept h1; significant differences among current ratio of selected consumer food companies
ANOVA - quick ratio	Significant difference in quick ratio	748.102	9	83.122	22.315	0	Reject H0, accept h1; significant differences among quick ratio of selected consumer food companies
ANOVA - proprietary ratio	No significant difference in proprietary ratio	15.371	9	1.708	1.081	0.398	Fail to reject H0; no appreciable distinction among proprietary ratio of selected consumer food companies
ANOVA - gross profit ratio	Significant difference in gross profit ratio	139895504.2	9	15543944.91	75.848	0	Reject H0, accept h1; important differences among gross profit ratio of selected consumer food companies
ANOVA - net profit ratio	Significant difference in net profit ratio	139904679.8	9	15544964.42	75.645	0	Reject H0, accept h1; significant difference among net profit ratio of selected consumer food companies

Analysis type	Null hypothesis	SS	df	MS	F	Sig	Result
Correlation analysis	Pearson correlation coefficients among various ratios	--	-	-	-	-	A table showing correlations between different financial ratios used for analysis.

Source: Author

Table 12.3 Correlation analysis of financial ratios in selected companies.

Ratio	Positive correlation	Correlation value	Negative correlation	Correlation value
Current ratio	Quick ratio, proprietary ratio, payable turnover ratio	0.883, 0.096, 0.156	Debt ratio, gross profit ratio, net profit ratio, receivable turnover ratio	(-)0.003, (-)0.338, (-)0.334, (-)0.018
Quick ratio	Current ratio, proprietary ratio, payable turnover ratio	0.883, 0.003, 0.238	Debt ratio, gross profit ratio, net profit ratio, receivable turnover ratio	0.011, (-)0.322, (-)0.317, (-)0.137
Proprietary ratio	Current ratio, quick ratio, receivable turnover ratio	0.096, 0.003, 0.264	Debt ratio, gross profit ratio, net profit ratio, payable turnover ratio	(-)0.117, (-)0.160, (-)0.147, (-)0.091
Debt ratio	Quick ratio, gross profit ratio, net profit ratio	0.011, 0.053, 0.034	Current ratio, proprietary ratio, receivable turnover ratio, payable turnover ratio	(-)0.003, (-)0.117, (-)0.161, (-)0.020
Gross profit ratio	Debt ratio, net profit ratio, payable turnover ratio	0.053, 0.903, 0.017	Current ratio, quick ratio, proprietary ratio, receivable turnover ratio	(-)0.338, (-)0.322, (-)0.160, (-)0.509
Net profit ratio	Debt ratio, gross profit ratio, payable turnover ratio	0.034, 0.903, 0.057	Current ratio, quick ratio, proprietary ratio, receivable turnover ratio	(-)0.334, (-)0.317, (-)0.147, (-)0.438
Receivable turnover ratio	Proprietary ratio	0.264	Current ratio, quick ratio, debt ratio, gross profit ratio, net profit ratio, payable turnover ratio	(-)0.018, (-)0.137, (-)0.161, (-)0.509, (-)0.438, (-)0.319
Payable turnover ratio	Current ratio, quick ratio, gross profit ratio, net profit ratio	0.156, 0.238, 0.017, 0.057	Proprietary ratio, receivable turnover ratio	(-)0.091, (-)0.391

Source: Author

Findings and Inferences

This correlation analysis showcases relationships between various financial ratios in selected companies. Positive correlations (values >0) indicate mutual movement, while negative correlations (values <0) signify opposite movements. For instance, Current Ratio positively relates to quick ratio, proprietary ratio, and payable turnover ratio, but negatively relates to debt ratio, gross profit ratio, net profit ratio, and receivable turnover ratio.

The findings reveal consistent patterns across multiple financial ratios within the Consumer Food Companies sector. Notably, Zydus Wellness, LT Foods, Godrej, ADF Foods, and Hindustan Foods showcase high standard deviations, positive skewness, and increased leptokurtic tendencies across diverse ratios like current, quick, cash, net working capital, debt-equity, debt, proprietary, gross profit, and net profit ratios. These statistical traits shed light on the interrelationships among these financial metrics,

offering insights into the sector's financial dynamics and unique variances.

Conclusion

The study's suggestions emphasize critical areas for enhancement within the selected steel companies. Enhanced return on equity can be achieved by bolstering current ratios, quick ratios, and inventory turnover ratios across the sector. Prioritizing return on capital employed stands as pivotal for illustrating profitability-based performance and necessitates a focus on low-risk investments, potentially reducing both risk and stock market valuation.

The research indicates the prudent use of resources by the chosen Indian steel businesses during the study period. It underscores the imperative for these companies to optimize their resource utilization further. Financial performance analysis isn't just a project-specific responsibility in production; it's a fundamental skill. The analysis reveals insights into the food industry's financial health, indicating areas where profitability may have been compromised during their study period. Looking ahead, the focus should pivot towards attaining profitability while navigating internal and external challenges. The business's adept resource management and inventory management serve as commendable aspects needing continued attention and refinement.

References

Diabat, A. (2020). Journal article title. *Journal of Cleaner Production*, 83, 391–403.

Meenakshi (2022). Future Sustainability of Products and Foods in the United Kingdom: Addressing Environmental Issues. University of Ca.

Pintea, M. O. (2011). Financial performance analysis: a case study. *Current Research Journal of Social Science.*

Rakshit, A. K. (2007). Powerloom sector in India. *Foods Review*, 2(6).

Reddy, S. (2016). A study of financial performance analysis of Force Motors Limited. *International Journal for Innovative Research in Science and Technology.*

Rosenbusch, N. (2014). Financial statement analysis, measurement of performance and profitability: Applied study of Baghdad Soft Drink Industry. *Research Journal of Finance.*

Simpson, A., and Shetty, B. (2021). Identification of dyes on single food fibers by HPLC-DAD-MS. *Analytical Chemistry*, 85(23), 11335–11343.

Singh, A., and Kathuria, B. (2022). Addressing environmental issues. *Asian Foods Business*, 13.

13 Occupational satisfaction of auto drivers in Coimbatore district

Abdul Rihaskhan, A.[a] and Rathnapriya, B.[b]

Karpagam Academy of Higher Education, Coimbatore, Tamil Nadu, India

Abstract

Auto drivers, crucial in urban and semi-urban transport, face demanding work, engaging with diverse passengers impacting job satisfaction. Using a convenience approach, interviews with a driver sample explored their perspectives and factors influencing job contentment. A wider survey assessed various aspects like pay, hours, conditions, and overall happiness. Focusing on Coimbatore district drivers, the study delves into their satisfaction, exploring income, hours, passenger behavior, safety, and support from relevant agencies. Recommendations target policymakers, urging improvements in driver conditions to elevate job contentment, ultimately enhancing transportation services in the region. Identifying key variables affecting satisfaction can lead to better working conditions, fostering increased happiness among auto drivers, thus uplifting Coimbatore's transportation standards.

Keywords: Auto drivers, job satisfaction, occupational satisfaction, transportation services, working conditions

Introduction

The Coimbatore district's transport system greatly benefits from the work of car drivers. Auto drivers provide seamless flow of people and commodities by providing crucial last-mile connections, especially in urban and semi-urban settings. But the nature of their profession frequently involves long hours, difficult working conditions, and encounters with a wide range of people. Their level of job satisfaction may be significantly impacted by these variables. Occupational satisfaction is a term used to describe how happy and fulfilled people feel in their jobs. It includes a variety of factors, including pay, working conditions, hours, and job security, in addition to social contacts and overall job satisfaction. In order to enhance auto drivers' performance, well-being, and the caliber of the transportation services they offer, it is essential to comprehend the aspects affecting their occupational happiness in the Coimbatore district. Numerous research have looked into the job happiness of different occupational groups, but little is known about the precise variables influencing the satisfaction levels of vehicle drivers in the Coimbatore district.

Literature Review

In Coimbatore district, auto drivers serve a crucial role in local transportation, yet little is known about their job satisfaction. This study aims to delve into their occupational happiness, pinpointing factors shaping it—pay, hours, conditions, passenger behavior, safety concerns, social contacts, and support from authorities. Understanding these elements is key to tailoring effective solutions. Challenges like long hours, traffic, job insecurity, and passenger issues hinder satisfaction, but understanding these can drive impactful solutions. By addressing these issues, this study aims to shed light on Coimbatore district auto drivers' occupational happiness, adding to transportation job satisfaction knowledge. The findings can guide policymakers, authorities, and stakeholders in improving working conditions, ultimately enhancing transportation services.

Objectives of the Study

Assess factors influencing auto drivers' job satisfaction.

Research Methodology

Data were collected via a structured questionnaire from 150 respondents in Coimbatore using a convenience sampling method. Analysis involved simple percentage analysis and weighted average rank.

Significance of Study

Understanding factors affecting auto drivers' satisfaction can enhance their well-being, aiding in retention and recruitment. It impacts driver turnover rates, service quality, and the local economy. Satisfied drivers offer better services, boosting customer satisfaction and benefiting the transportation system.

[a]abdulrihaskhan2k1@gmail.com, [b]priyamidhun2014@gmail.com

Table 13.1 Socio economic profile of the respondents.

Particulars		Numbers (N = 150)	Percentage
Age	18-25 Years	21	14.0
	26-35 Years	54	36.0
	36-45 Years	49	32.7
	Above 45 years	26	17.3
Gender	Male	146	97.3
	Female	4	2.7
Educational qualification	Illiterate	45	30.0
	SSLC	61	40.7
	HSC	29	19.3
	Diploma	14	9.3
	Degree	1	.7
Marital status	Married	114	76.0
	Unmarried	36	24.0
Family type	Nuclear	121	80.7
	Joint	29	19.3
Nature of house	Owned	55	36.7
	Rented	95	63.3
Nature of vehicle	Owned	78	52.0
	Rented	72	48.0
Monthly income	Below 8000	10	6.7
	8001-15000	78	52.0
	15001-25000	62	41.3
Experience	Less than 1 year	6	4.0
	2-5 Years	27	18.0
	5-10 Years	45	30.0
	More than 10 years	72	48.0
Hours of driving in a day	Below 8 hours	12	8.0
	8-10 Hours	48	32.0
	11-12 Hours	50	33.3
	More than 12 hours	40	26.7
Earnings per day	Upto Rs. 500	22	14.7
	Rs. 500-750	50	33.3
	Rs. 750-1000	51	34.0
	Rs. 1000 and above	27	18.0

Source: Author

Limitations of the Study

- Limited sample size and representativeness might impact result generalizability.
- Self-reporting by drivers may introduce response bias.
- Social desirability might influence responses.
- Static data collection may not capture changing satisfaction levels.
- Contextual factors unique to Coimbatore could affect the findings' applicability.

In essence, studying Coimbatore's auto drivers' job satisfaction offers insights to improve their well-being, tackle industry challenges, and elevate the transportation system and community development. However, acknowledging and addressing the study's limitations is essential for a comprehensive understanding of auto drivers' occupational satisfaction in the region. The following table discloses the socio-economic profile of Auto-drivers. Based on socio-economic profile, majority of auto drivers ages range from 26 to 35years. Majority of auto drivers are male. Most auto drivers are at the SSLC educational level. Most auto drivers are married. Most auto drivers belong to the nuclear family type. Most auto drivers rent houses. Most auto drivers own a vehicle. Majority of auto drivers' monthly income ranges between Rs. 8001 and Rs. 15,000. Most auto drivers have more than 10 years in the field. The majority of auto drivers' earnings range between Rs. 750 and Rs. 1000 and above.

Occupational satisfaction of auto-drivers

KMO and Bartlett's test		
Kaiser-Meyer-Olkin measure of sampling adequacy.		.698
Bartlett's test of sphericity	Approx. Chi-square	817.624
	Df	78
	Sig.	.000

Factor analysis is used to determine the most important aspects that influence a person's happiness level. Kaiser-Meyer-Olkin (KMO) and Bartlett's test of sphericity were employed as pre-analysis tests to determine the overall adequacy of the sample for factor analysis. The result of KMO and Bartlett's test is greater than 0.50. Thus, the acquired data is suitable for factor analysis. Furthermore, the large value of Bartlett's test of Sphericity (817.624, Df: 78, Sig..000) revealed that factor analysis was reasonable, implying that the sample size was enough. Rotated component matrix.

Four factors are identified by locating Eigen values greater than one. Factors with component loadings of 0.5 or above are considered significant. The rotated components matrix shows that income, road tax, insurance premium, petrol price, support from government officials, spare parts price, passenger cooperation, minimum auto fare fixed, family support, entry of online companies, social status (respect from the public), road condition, and traffic condition all have component loadings of 0.5 or higher. Hence, these thirteen variables comprise the first factor. In the

second element, road tax, insurance premium, petrol price, support from government officials, spare parts price, fixed minimum auto fare, entry of internet companies, social status (public respect), and road quality were determined to be important. In the third factor, road tax and insurance premium, Petrol price, spare parts price, minimum auto fare fixed, Family support, the entry of online companies, road conditions, and traffic conditions have all been identified as significant. In the fourth factor, road taxes, Petrol price, passenger cooperation, fixed minimum vehicle fare, social status (public respect), and road condition have all been identified as significant.

Conclusion

The study on auto drivers' occupational satisfaction in Coimbatore district underscores factors impacting their job contentment and overall welfare. Valuable insights emerged, guiding policymakers, industry stakeholders, and driver associations in enhancing auto drivers' experiences. Key suggestions include implementing clear and fair tariff structures accounting for trip details, which can alleviate income concerns crucial for job happiness. Improving driver environments with safety measures, comfortable seating, and rest areas can mitigate fatigue and enhance well-being amid long work hours. Furthermore, driver skill development initiatives emphasizing communication, road safety, and customer service can elevate their job satisfaction and service quality.

Establishing and maintaining a reliable transport system, encompassing clean roads, proper signage, and designated parking, can reduce stress and enhance productivity for drivers and passengers alike. Introducing social security programs and tailored insurance plans can address worries about health, accidents, and retirement benefits, ensuring financial protection. Recognizing drivers' contributions through events, awards, or incentives can boost morale, fostering a positive work atmosphere and pride in their job.

Granting drivers access to tools like traffic updates, route planning apps, and customer service best practices can enhance productivity and job satisfaction. Efficient procedures for handling complaints and disputes can create a stress-free workplace environment. Overall, by ensuring fair remuneration, transparent fare structures, and addressing income stability concerns, policymakers can significantly impact auto drivers' financial security and job satisfaction. Enhancing working conditions through comfortable seating, proper ventilation, and rest areas also contributes to their overall well-being.

References

Chougule, P. S., Kurane, T., Patil, S. V., Kamble, D., Kumbhare, B., and Waghamare, S. (2020). A study the problems of auto rickshaw drivers in Kolhapur city using statistical tools and techniques. *EPRA International Journal of Multidisciplinary Research (IJMR)- Peer Reviewed Journal*, 6(11).

Jain, S., and Barthwal, V. (2021). Health impact assessment of auto rickshaw and cab drivers due to exposure to vehicular pollution in Delhi: an integrated approach. *Research Square* , https://doi.org/10.21203/rs.3.rs-685838/v1.

Sarannya, Sivasankaran, and Poornima (2022). A study on job satisfaction of auto drivers with special reference to Coimbatore district. *International Journal of Innovative Research in Technology*, 9(1), ISSN: 2349-6002.

Vesvikar, M., and Watambale, K. (2023). Female auto drivers: an exploratory study of the opportunities and challenges of the non-traditional livelihood in Thane district. *International Journal of Research* , ISSN:2350-0530.

Waghmare, N., and Chaudhari, S. V. (2022) Awareness of physiotherapy amongst auto-rickshaw drivers in Nagpur city. *International Journal of Medical Dental and Allied Health*, 1(1), 1–9.

14 A study on quality of work life of firecracker workers in Sivakasi

R. Ramanan[a], J. Smruthymol[b], M. Anandan[c], J. Sudarvel[d] and R. Velmurugan[e]

Karpagam Academy of Higher Education, Coimbatore, Tamil Nadu, India

Abstract

The present study has been carried out to investigate the quality of work life (QWL) of firecracker workers in Sivakasi, Tamil Nadu, India. The fireworks business has a considerable presence in Sivakasi, which employs a sizable workforce. But there have been concerns about the working conditions in this sector, creating issues regarding the workers' quality of life. The results of this study will add to the amount of knowledge already known about the quality of life for workers in the firecracker sector. The study intends to pinpoint areas that require interventions in order to raise workers' QWL, such as boosting safety precautions, improving working conditions, and resolving work-life balance difficulties. The research aims to create positive changes in the sector by highlighting the significance of worker well-being and encouraging discourse among stakeholders.

Keywords: firecracker workers, job satisfaction, quality of work life, Sivakasi, occupational health and safety, work environment, work-life balance

Introduction

The fireworks industry in Sivakasi, Tamil Nadu, India, provides a significant number of job opportunities, exerting a tremendous impact on the local economy. Sivakasi, known as the "Fireworks Capital of India," supplies the majority of the nation's firecrackers. However, issues persist concerning the working environment and conditions in this field, raising concerns about the quality of work life (QWL) for firework employees. QWL encompasses factors such as job satisfaction, work-life balance, the work environment, social support, and occupational health and safety. Evaluating employees' QWL is crucial to maintaining their overall welfare, job satisfaction, and productivity, irrespective of the industry. The manufacturing process of firecrackers involves handling hazardous chemicals, intricate procedures, and exposure to potentially dangerous working environments. Workers engage in tasks that jeopardize their health and safety, including chemical mixing, explosives handling, and machinery operation. Additionally, excessive working hours, low wages, insufficient facilities, and a lack of social support may further impact the QWL of firework employees.

Previous research has stressed the need to examine the QWL of workers in the fireworks sector to identify areas for improvement and drive positive changes. However, there exists a dearth of dedicated studies focusing on the QWL of firework workers in Sivakasi. To bridge this research gap, the current study aims to explore the QWL of firecracker employees in Sivakasi, Tamil Nadu. Through this study, we aim to enhance our understanding of the QWL of industrial employees and illuminate the unique challenges faced by Sivakasi's firecracker workers. The findings from this study could influence governmental reforms, support workers' rights, and advance programs aimed at enhancing the QWL of firework employees, ultimately fostering a safer and more conducive workplace.

Literature Review

Table 14.1 Cumulative insights from studies on work life quality across industries and regions.

Authors	Study focus	Key findings
Ashifa and Ramya (2019)	Health problems among female employees in fireworks sector	- Health initiatives needed - encourage interest and enjoyment at work - consider female employees' career development - Increase pay in compliance with legal requirements

[a]ramanan2804@gmail.com, [b]jayalalsmruthy@gmail.com, [c]nmcanandan@gmail.com, [d]j.sudarvel@gmail.com, [e]drvelsngm@gmail.com

Authors	Study focus	Key findings
		- Awareness programs by management - establish primary healthcare facilities
Chandrasekar and Kanagasabapathi (2019)	Quality of work life (QWL) among cracker workers	- QWL linked to job awareness, health measures, workplace atmosphere, wages
Padmaja (2018)	Quality of life for workers in fireworks and match works business in Sivakasi	- QOL linked to relationships, income, bonuses, working hours, welfare programs
Jegatheesan et al. (2017)	Factors influencing QWL	- Workplace conditions crucial - Improve with hand gloves, face masks, first aid supplies - enhance work culture through job rotation, self-evaluation tools, adherence to principles - Foster self-development via training, education, career development - Enable independent work through target-oriented systems, flexible schedules
Jnaneswar (2016)	Level of quality of work life in Kerala public sector units	- Male and female employees share similar QWL experiences
t	TRACK quality of work-life model in terms of transparency, relationship, autonomy, collaboration, knowledge	- The TRACK model focuses on shared commitment, employer-worker relations, and an environment nurturing this commitment
Ferdous (2015)	Factors enhancing job happiness among ready-to-wear (RMG) workers in Bangladesh	- Ensure decent income, prompt payment, admissible benefits
		- consider supervisor behavior, working atmosphere, cafeteria, and medical facilities for worker satisfaction
Nanjundeswara-swamy, and Swamy (2015)	Link between organizational leadership, business ethics, and quality of organizational life	- Leadership, ethics contribute to organizational quality - positive impact on members and wider community

Source: Author

Research Gaps

The investigation into the QWL among firecracker employees in Sivakasi, Tamil Nadu, reveals a significant research gap in understanding their unique challenges. Despite the acknowledged importance of studying QWL in the fireworks industry, limited attention has been given to the specific issues faced by workers in Sivakasi, a pivotal hub for firecracker production. Previous studies in the fireworks sector rarely focused on Sivakasi, resulting in a lack of comprehensive understanding regarding QWL challenges specific to this workforce. The production process for firecrackers involves hazardous substances, explosions, and intricate procedures, demanding a concentrated assessment of occupational health and safety measures in Sivakasi. While earlier research highlighted the dangers faced by fireworks workers, the impact of these risks on their QWL remains inadequately explored. Moreover, the impact of long workweeks on their work-life balance has received limited attention, hindering interventions aimed at improving this aspect of QWL. Understanding the distinct work patterns and the ability of firecracker workers in Sivakasi to manage personal responsibilities is crucial for interventions enhancing their work-life balance. Furthermore, there is a lack of research on the accessibility and effectiveness of social support networks and welfare programs for these workers, which could significantly contribute to their social well-being and QWL. Addressing these research gaps is crucial to gain deeper insights into the QWL of Sivakasi's firecracker employees. Utilizing this knowledge, targeted interventions, policies, and programs can be developed to improve their working environment, safety measures, work-life balance, and overall well-being. Moreover, bridging these gaps will facilitate better communication among industry stakeholders and decision-makers, fostering positive changes in the fireworks sector and raising awareness about the specific challenges faced by this workforce.

Problem Statement

The fireworks industry in Sivakasi, Tamil Nadu, employs a substantial workforce in firecracker manufacturing. However, there's a glaring research gap concerning the QWL specifically for these workers in Sivakasi. This gap impedes a full grasp of their unique challenges, crucial for enhancing their conditions. Current literature lacks comprehensive exploration despite the dangers, long hours, low pay, inadequate facilities, and lacking support these workers face. This dearth of research hampers targeted interventions to improve the QWL of firecracker employees. The problem statement underscores the necessity for detailed investigation into their specific challenges, workplace hazards, balancing work-family dynamics, and limited social support. Examining workplace variables, job satisfaction, and occupational health is essential to address these issues. This study aims to fill this gap by providing insights into the QWL of Sivakasi's firecracker workers. It seeks to inform strategies and interventions enhancing their working conditions, safety measures, work-life balance, and support networks. Ultimately, this research aims to uplift their QWL and overall quality of life.

Scope of the Study

The study aims to comprehend how workers perceive the quality of their work life.

This study delves into the QWL among firecracker workers in Sivakasi, aiming for a comprehensive grasp of various vital aspects related to their work environment and overall welfare. It focuses on multiple dimensions: firstly, examining job satisfaction levels and the factors influencing them, including wages, working hours, security, career growth, and recognition. Secondly, assessing the work environment's elements like safety, cleanliness, ventilation, noise, lighting, and ergonomics to understand their impact on workers' QWL. Thirdly, scrutinizing the occupational health and safety measures adopted in Sivakasi's firecracker industry, evaluating protocols, equipment availability, training, and workers' safety perception. Identifying areas for enhancements to ensure worker well-being is a primary goal.

Additionally, this research delves into the challenges of achieving a healthy work-life balance for firecracker workers, considering factors like extended work hours, shift patterns, leisure time, and how work demands affect personal and family life. Furthermore, it investigates available social support systems, including organizational roles, unions, and welfare initiatives, examining their effectiveness in addressing workers' social and emotional needs. The insights and recommendations drawn from this study are transferrable to similar contexts, potentially aiding in enhancing the QWL of firecracker workers in Sivakasi and comparable regions.

Table 14.2 Demographic details of participants in various categories such as age, gender, education qualification, status in family, type of family, and monthly income.

Category	Frequency	Percentage
Age		
Up to 34 years	30	17.6
Between 35 to 56 years	116	68.2
Above 57	24	14.1
Gender		
Male	74	43.5
Female	96	56.5
Education qualification		
SSLC	58	34.1
HSC	16	9.4
Illiterate	96	56.5
Status in family		
Head	66	38.8
Member	104	61.2
Type of family		
Joint	6	3.5
Nuclear	164	96.5
Monthly income		
Up to 8000	30	17.6
Between 8001 and 12000	114	67.1
Above 12001	26	15.3

Source: Author

Interpretation

After analyzing the rotated component matrix, it's evident that several key factors significantly impact the QWL among firecracker workers in Sivakasi. These influential factors, with component loadings above 0.5, are numerous and encompass a broad spectrum of workplace-related aspects Thilagaraj (2020). The prominent contributors to QWL identified through the analysis of the component matrix include the company's concern for employees' needs, the satisfaction derived from financial services such as Provident Fund, Group Insurance, and miscellaneous loans, support for career planning and growth within the organization, satisfactory maternity benefits for women employees, the sense of pride in being associated with the company, provision of children's educational schemes, training opportunities for skill enhancement and career development, periodic medical check-ups, prioritization of workers' rights, assistance in personal aspirations, prompt response to employee emergencies, encouragement to engage in cultural and community activities, fair promotion policies, healthy relationships with colleagues, reliable colleague support during job difficulties, availability of comfortable housing and amenities, hygienic canteen facilities, statutory welfare provisions, equal respect in the workplace, sick leave benefits, market-aligned salaries and allowances, respectful treatment from superiors, satisfactory leave encashment benefits, manageable work-life balance, committed teamwork, acknowledgment for maintaining a conducive work environment, a robust grievance redressal system, adequate workspace and facilities including sanitation, noise control initiatives, job rotation policies, the positive impact of job security on creativity, productivity, and morale, sufficient family time, organizational support for personal aspirations, rotational weekly offs, quality medical facilities, favorable wage payment practices, and a supportive work environment with freedom. Among these factors, the first contributes significantly with 29.966%, followed by others contributing 6.937%, 3.197%, 1.910%, 1.593%, and 1.230% respectively, cumulatively amounting to 71.164% impact on the QWL of firecracker workers in Sivakasi. These dimensions comprehensively depict the elements that influence the QWL among these workers, showcasing their multifaceted and interconnected nature in shaping a positive work environment and employee well-being.

Conclusion

The study outlined numerous strategies aimed at improving the quality of work life (QWL) among firecracker industry workers in Sivakasi, Tamil Nadu. Recommendations included focusing on workplace safety by maintaining safety equipment and conducting regular safety training. Providing incentives for innovative ideas, ensuring ample first aid resources, and fostering open communication through suggestion boxes were highlighted. Suggestions also encompassed improving ventilation systems, establishing counselling programs, offering career development opportunities, and emphasizing job security. Strategies involving employee assistance, maternity benefits, child education, career planning, and cooperative work relationships were proposed to enhance overall QWL. Ensuring statutory welfare, grievance resolution mechanisms, promoting work-life balance, sharing career information, establishing transparent HR policies, and providing adequate workplace amenities were emphasized. The study concludes by emphasizing the significance of these strategies in enhancing the QWL of firecracker industry workers, aiming to improve workplace safety, employee acknowledgment, well-being, and job security, ultimately enhancing working conditions for these employees in Sivakasi. The rotational component matrix highlighted essential factors influencing the QWL, including work-life balance, job security, professional growth, work environment, employee rights, and welfare, underscoring the need for suitable support, development opportunities, positive work environments, and job stability.

References

Chandrasekar, T., and Kanagasabapathi, J. R. (2019). Employee expectation and its impact on quality of work life of employees in Indian crackers industry. *International Journal of Recent Technology and Engineering (IJRTE)*, 8(4S2), ISSN: 2277–3878.

Jegatheesan, K., Selvakumar, M., and Kalaivani, K. (2017). Quality of work life of workers in fireworks industry – a study with reference to Tamil Nadu. *International Journal of Science Technology and Management*, 6(2), 282–297. http://data.conferenceworld.in/SRNM/80.pdf.

Padmaja, R. (2018). Quality of work life of women employees in fireworks and match industries in Sivakasi, Tamil Nadu. *Asian Review of Social Sciences*, 7(2), 50–56, ISSN: 2249–6319.

Thilagaraj, A. (2020). Analytical study on employee's job satisfaction in standard fireworks at Sivakasi, Tamil Nadu. *PalArch's Journal of Archaeology of Egypt/Egyptology*, 1, 2896–2906.

15 Customer perception toward Chinese products in Coimbatore district

Miruthula, S.[a], Rajeswari, E.[b], Aiswarya, S.[c], Sudarvel, J.[d] and Velmurugan, R.[e]

Karpagam Academy of Higher Education, Coimbatore, Tamil Nadu, India

Abstract

This study investigates the nuanced landscape of customer perceptions toward Chinese products in Coimbatore District, recognizing the pivotal role such insights play in the current global trade scenario. Focused on a region marked by a thriving industrial and retail sector, the research delves into customer perspectives on crucial aspects, such as quality, pricing, brand reputation, perceived value, and trustworthiness of Chinese items. Employing a comprehensive approach to data analysis, including descriptive statistics, factor analysis, and weighted average tests, the study reveals diverse consumer opinions. While some appreciate the accessibility and affordability of Chinese goods, others express concerns about their quality, durability, and impact on the domestic market. The research enhances the understanding of how consumers in the Coimbatore District perceive Chinese products, offering valuable insights for policymakers, businesses, and merchants to navigate customer preferences and decisions.0

Keywords: Chinese products, Coimbatore district, customer perception

Introduction

The global influence of China, particularly in the distribution of its products, has significantly impacted consumer behaviors, notably in India. Coimbatore District in Tamil Nadu emerges as a vital industrial and commercial hub, renowned for its manufacturing expertise and historical trade connections with China. Investigating consumer perceptions towards Chinese goods in this dynamic region gains particular significance due to its unique economic and cultural attributes. As consumer preferences evolve with the increased availability of Chinese products, understanding these sentiments becomes paramount for policymakers and industry participants. Coimbatore's rich industrial landscape, spanning engineering, equipment, and textiles, offers an intriguing backdrop for probing consumer attitudes, contributing valuable insights for trade regulations and industry growth strategies. Employing a mixed-method approach, combining qualitative interviews and quantitative surveys, this research aims to comprehensively explore how consumers in Coimbatore perceive Chinese goods, delving into aspects like quality, pricing, brand reputation, perceived value, and trustworthiness. By shedding light on the nuanced dynamics of consumer behavior, the study aims to bridge existing research gaps and equip policymakers, businesses, and retailers with informed strategies tailored to evolving market expectations.

Review of Literature

Uyar's (2018) survey revealed a prevailing negative sentiment among consumers towards Chinese products, manifesting in a reluctance to purchase and a notable influence of the product's nation of origin on their buying decisions.

Khan and Ahmed (2016) utilized the concepts of felt life and perceived value to evaluate the effectiveness of price and quality. While Chinese goods are perceived as cost-effective, the study emphasizes the urgent need to address concerns about product quality, as they are often perceived as inferior.

Dr. Chandan Thakur, Divyanshu Kumar, Soumya Vyas (2020) highlight India's 'vocal for local' campaign, encouraging domestic production and consumption, particularly in response to the COVID-19 pandemic. This shift is evidenced by consumers avoiding Chinese products, leading to decreased demand in the market.

Suvija et al. (2021) study underscores widespread dissatisfaction with the perceived quality of Chinese items, with only a small percentage expressing satisfaction. Quality and price emerge as pivotal factors shaping customer perceptions of Chinese products.

[a]miruthu0801@gmail.com, [b]rajiguna84@gmail.com, [c]aiswaryaselva11@gmail.com, [d]j.sudarvel@gmail.com, [e]drvelsngm@gmail.com

Sengupta (2020) reveals that young Indians prioritize quality and price over the country of origin (COO) when purchasing products, with concerns about Chinese dominance in the Indian market influencing those who oppose Chinese goods. Conversely, those favoring Chinese items show less susceptibility to Indo-China rivalry impacting their buying decisions.

Problem Statement

The study aims to understand consumer perceptions of Chinese products in Coimbatore district, addressing the knowledge gap on factors such as quality, pricing, brand reputation, perceived value, and trustworthiness. The findings will guide informed decision-making for government, business, and retail stakeholders in the region.

Scope of the Study

This study explores how consumers in the Coimbatore district perceive Chinese goods, leveraging the region's diverse consumer base and thriving industries. Using a mixed-methods approach, it combines qualitative interviews with key stakeholders and quantitative data from standardized questionnaires. Focusing on factors like quality, price, brand reputation, perceived value, and trustworthiness, the research aims to uncover nuances in consumer perception. However, it is limited to the Coimbatore district, and results may not generalize to other Indian regions. Additionally, the study does not delve into specific product categories or analyze market trends but contributes valuable insights into consumer attitudes, aiding local decision-makers.

Objective of the Study

To examine the perception of users toward Chinese products.

To identify the reason for perceived Chinese products.

Research Methodology

Data: Data required for the study is primary in nature. Collecting primary data through interviews can be an effective method for gathering detailed and specific information directly from the participants. By using an interview schedule, you can ensure consistency in the questions asked and obtain standardized responses, making the data collection process more reliable.

Sampling and sample size: Convenient sampling can be a useful approach when it is difficult to access or reach the entire population of interest. It allows researchers to collect data quickly and easily from individuals who are readily available or accessible. Thus, by employing convenient sampling technique, data have gathered from 200 customers at Coimbatore district.

Framework of analysis: The collected have been analyzed by employing simple percentage and factor analysis.

Significance of the Study

This study on consumer perception of Chinese products in Coimbatore district holds significant implications for policymakers, manufacturers, retailers, and consumers. Policymakers can use the findings to inform trade policies, legislation, and industry growth strategies, considering consumer attitudes. For retailers and manufacturers, the conclusions provide insights for product development, pricing, branding, and marketing tactics, enhancing competitiveness. Consumers benefit by making informed purchase decisions based on factors like quality, pricing, and trustworthiness. The study contributes to understanding how Chinese goods impact the local market, aiding stakeholders in strategic decision-making for a competitive and sustainable industrial environment. The research also fills a knowledge gap, serving as a guide for future studies on global commerce, consumer behavior, and market dynamics. Overall, its significance lies in supporting business growth, enhancing consumer education, and advancing academic understanding.

Analysis and Interpretation

In this comprehensive socio-economic analysis, we delve into the demographic landscape of consumers in the Coimbatore district, exploring key factors such as gender, age, educational qualifications, occupation, monthly income, family type, and the duration of using Chinese products. The nuanced findings provide a detailed understanding of the consumer base. Additionally, we examine major findings, shedding light on the dominant trends among consumers. The subsequent sections delve into the reasons for purchasing Chinese products, problems faced by customers, and their satisfaction levels. This multifaceted examination aims to offer valuable insights for policymakers, manufacturers, retailers, and academics alike.

Socio-economic profile

Gender:
- Male: 127 (63.5%)
- Female: 73 (36.5%)
- Total: 200 (100.0%)

Age:
- Below 20 years: 30 (15.0%)
- 21 to 30 years: 95 (47.5%)
- 31 to 40 years: 46 (23.0%)
- Above 40 years: 29 (14.5%)
- Total: 200 (100.0%)

Educational qualification:
- School level: 54 (27.0%)
- UG: 69 (34.5%)
- PG: 59 (29.5%)
- Ph.D.: 18 (9.0%)
- Total: 200 (100.0%)

Occupation:
- Students: 37 (18.5%)
- Professional: 70 (35.0%)
- Employees: 70 (35.0%)
- Businessman: 23 (11.5%)
- Total: 200 (100.0%)

Monthly income:
- Below Rs. 20,000: 45 (22.5%)
- Rs. 20,000 to Rs. 30,000: 87 (43.5%)
- Rs. 30,000 to Rs. 40,000: 41 (20.5%)
- Above Rs. 40,000: 27 (13.5%)
- Total: 200 (100.0%)

Type of family:
- Joint: 92 (46.0%)
- Nuclear: 108 (54.0%)
- Total: 200 (100.0%)

Years of using China product:
- 1-2 Years: 44 (22.0%)
- 2-3 Years: 69 (34.5%)
- 3-4 Years: 52 (26.0%)
- 4-5 Years: 35 (17.5%)
- Total: 200 (100.0%)

Major findings
- Majority of customers are male.
- Majority of customers' age ranges from 21 to 30 years.
- Majority of customers have an educational qualification at the UG level.
- Majority of customers are professionals and employees.
- Majority of customers fall into the income group of Rs. 20,000- 30,000.
- Majority of customers belong to nuclear families.
- Majority of customers have used Chinese products for 2-3 years.

Reasons for purchasing Chinese products:
- Less price
- Wide product range
- Product availability
- Technological advancements
- Supply chain efficiency
- Replacement
- Usage of the products
- Value for money
- Customer reviews
- Product quality
- Brand reputation
- After sales service

Problems faced by customers on Chinese products:
- Poor product quality
- Counterfeit products
- Difficulty in finding spare parts or accessories
- Customer service and warranty support
- Challenges in returns and refunds
- Product safety concerns

Customer satisfaction toward Chinese products:
- Price
- Replacement facility
- Guarantee/warranty offered
- After sales service
- Quality of the product

The study reveals a predominant male consumer base (63.5%), with a significant portion aged 21 to 30 years (47.5%). Most customers hold UG qualifications, are professionals or employees, and fall within the income range of Rs. 20,0000-30,000. Nuclear families are prevalent, and a majority of users have employed Chinese products for 2-3 years. Findings suggest a strong inclination towards Chinese products due to factors like affordability, wide product range, and technological advancements. The noteworthy problems include concerns about poor product quality and counterfeit items. However, customers express satisfaction with pricing, replacement facilities, and offered guarantees/warranties.

Conclusion

In conclusion, this study delved into the consumer perceptions of Chinese goods in Coimbatore District, India, revealing a strong inclination towards these products due to their affordability, diverse offerings, accessibility, technological advancements, and perceived value for money. The research unveiled crucial determinants of customer satisfaction, emphasizing the significance of competitive pricing, effective customer service, robust warranties, and high-quality products.

However, notable challenges were identified, including concerns about poor product quality, counterfeit items, difficulties in finding spare parts, and issues with customer service and warranty support. To address these issues, manufacturers and policymakers should implement stringent quality control, anti-counterfeiting measures, improved customer service, simplified returns processes, adherence to safety standards, and consumer education initiatives.

In conclusion, this study provides valuable insights for stakeholders to adapt strategies, enhance customer satisfaction, and address challenges associated with Chinese goods in Coimbatore District. By implementing the outlined recommendations, stakeholders can foster consumer confidence, cultivate a positive market environment, and ensure customer satisfaction in the context of Chinese products.

References

Anonymous (n.d.). [Title of the article]. *Online Library*. doi:10.1002/pa.2388.

Khan, L. M., and Ahmed, R. (2016). A comparative study of consumer perception of product quality: Chinese versus non-Chinese products. *Pakistan Journal of Engineering, Technology and Science*, 2. doi:10.22555/pjets.v2i2.698.

Suvija, S., et al. (2021). Consumer attitude and satisfaction towards Chinese products in India. *International Journal of Advanced Research in Science, Communication and Technology (IJARSCT)*, 11(1).

Uyar, A. (2018). A study on consumers' perception about Chinese products and their willingness to buy.

Watung, E. C. (2014). The analysis of consumer perception towards Chinese products in Manado. *Jurnal Riset Ekonomi, Manajemen, Bisnis dan Akuntansi*, 2(3).

16 A study on students skill sets requirement for employability

J. T. Deepika[a] and S. Swathi Newashini[b]

Karpagam Academy of Higher Education, Coimbatore, Tamil Nadu, India

Abstract

This study explores essential skill sets crucial for student employability in today's evolving job market. Employers increasingly seek diverse skills beyond academics. Pinpointing these skills guides institutions and students in comprehensive career preparation. Using mixed-methods (interviews, surveys), the research gathers employer and student data. Insights gained highlight valued skills and potential student-employer skill gaps. Outcomes aid policymakers, educators, and students in aligning curricula with industry needs, improving employability. The research aims to contribute to understanding required skill sets, offering actionable recommendations to bridge the education-industry gap. Ultimately, this research enhances students' career readiness and job market prospects.

Keywords: ANOVA, Chi-square, employability, simple percentage

Introduction

In modern business, management education faces a challenge: enhancing employability skills. Academic institutions recognize the demand for diverse managerial expertise, now emphasizing job-specific performance. Excelling academically falls short; students need interpersonal and teamwork skills. Understanding employability skills is key, combining technical prowess with soft skills like communication and problem-solving. The gap between academia and industry calls for reform in management education, favoring hands-on learning. Integrating real-world experiences like case studies, internships, and industry projects into the curriculum builds practical skills. Career guidance services and industry ties add value. Institutions must update curricula, blending theory with practical skills, ensuring graduates meet employer expectations. Bridging this gap greatly enhances graduate employability in the dynamic business world.

Table 16.1 Literature review.

Authors	Study focus
Rudrama (2021)	English proficiency's role in job market opportunities
Ramlan and Ngah (2020)	Soft skills deficit among engineering students in Malaysia
Van Dalen and Henkens (2019)	Integration of employability skills in academics
Abbas and Sagsan (2019)	Challenges in developing problem-solving skills among graduates in Australia
Esa et al. (2018)	Employability skills in human resource management graduates
Bhagwath et al. (2018)	Employability skills of MBA students in Delhi's National Capital Region
Pandey (2018)	Awareness of life skills and their impact on employability among management students
Bremner (2018)	Evaluation and enhancement of degree program focusing on soft skills and digital skills
Aida et al. (2017)	Contextual approach in graduate employability training
Shamsuri et al. (2016)	Key skills highly valued by employers in Malaysian universities
Shukla (2012)	Employability skills among engineering graduates in Bhopal, India
Mason et al. (2009)	Effects of employability skill initiatives in higher education on graduate labor market outcomes
Padmini (2012)	Skill gap among engineering and management graduates in Andhra Pradesh, India

Source: Author

[a]jtdeepika2000@gmail.com, [b]swathinivashini@gmail.com

Research Scope and Objectives

The research aims to fill the gap in understanding the specific employability skills required by students. This study analyzes current literature to identify these skills, benefiting educators, policymakers, and employers interested in enhancing students' job readiness Table 16.1. The challenges in technical education leading to unemployment stem from curriculum flaws and a lack of practical exposure. Graduates face employability issues due to curriculum-industry mismatch. To tackle this, students must seek practical skill development. This study seeks to define crucial skills and ways to acquire them, bridging the gap between education and industry demands for better job preparedness..

Scope, Research Methodology, and Analysis

The study in Coimbatore and Pollachi uses questionnaires to gauge respondents' social, economic profiles, and employability skills. Its focus is identifying skill gaps and aligning education with job market needs. Targeting improvement areas and refining teaching methods can better equip students for employment. Data was gathered via structured interviews and questionnaires distributed to 200 randomly selected individuals. Analytical techniques like percentage, Chi-square, and factor analysis were used. This study is crucial as it informs tailored programs, aligning education with job needs, boosting graduates' employability, and closing the skills gap. It emphasizes vital skills like communication, leadership, teamwork, and problem-solving, vital for graduates' job market success.

Table 16.2 Simple percentage analysis.

Particulars	Frequency	Percentage
Gender		
Male	110	55.0
Female	90	45.0
Area of nativity		
Urban	38	19.0
Semi-urban	34	17.0
Rural	128	64.0
Location of college		
Urban	26	13.0
Semi-urban	25	12.5
Rural	149	74.5
Course of study		
Arts	129	64.0

Particulars	Frequency	Percentage
Science	36	18.0
Technical	35	17.5
Nature of admission		
Merit	61	30.5
Non merit	139	69.5
Medium of instruction at School		
Tamil	26	13.0
English	174	87.0
Nature of institution		
Government	6	3.0
Private	17	8.5
Aided	40	20.0
University	137	68.5
NAAC accredited at institution		
Yes	15	7.5
No	185	92.5
Placement training is offered		
Yes	110	55.0
No	90	45.0
Syllabus is regularly updated		
Yes	139	69.5
No	61	30.5
Internship program		
Yes	128	64.0
No	72	36.0
Extracurricular activities		
Yes	125	62.5
No	75	37.5
Studying additional part from Ug and Pg		
Yes	110	55.0
No	90	45.0

Source: Author

The data showcases various aspects predominantly favoring male students residing in rural areas pursuing higher education in arts programs on a non-merit basis. Most attend English-medium schools and study at universities, often in institutions lacking NAAC accreditation. However, a majority receives placement training and benefit from regularly updated curricula, internships, and participation in extracurricular activities. Additionally, a significant number pursue additional courses beyond their undergraduate or postgraduate studies. These statistics reflect the substantial impact of factors like nativity, college location, chosen course, and language of instruction on students' experiences and academic paths.

Table 16.3 KMO and Bartlett's test.

Kaiser-Meyer-Olkin		Measure of Sampling		
Adequacy.				.731
Bartlett's	Test	of	Approx. Chi-square	972.786
Sphericity			Df	190
			Sig.	.000

Factor analysis assessed the essential skills for employability. Pre-analysis with KMO and Bartlett's test showed suitable data (KMO > 0.70).

	Rotated component matrix[a]									
	Component									
	1	2	3	4	5	6	7	8	9	10
Help classmates and volunteering as peer	.746									
Able to communicate ideas to justify position, motivate and convince others, and responsibly challenge existing procedures and policies.	.726									
Able to exert a high level effort and continue toward goal attainment with my colleagues	.692									
Learning is the habit	.657									
Believe in self-worth and maintain a positive view of my self	.653									
Able to work with different aged people, irrespective of gender, race, religion or political persuasion	.649									
Identity, analyses and resolve a problem	.631									
Able to set personal goals, monitor progress, exhibit self-control and take responsibility for my actions	.623									
Able to draft emails and letters	.609									
Knowledge on how social, organizational, and technological organize work	.523									
I raise doubt to the speaker during the presentation	.522									
Able to answer the queries	.504									

Conclusion

This study highlights essential factors pivotal for student employability, encompassing diverse skills like communication, teamwork, problem-solving, and adaptability. Collaboration between educational institutions and businesses remains crucial, requiring active student engagement. Postgraduates face distinct job market challenges, demanding institutions to equip them with contemporary workplace skills. Graduates must balance academic excellence with vital competencies like collaboration and adaptability. Academia's role involves curriculum revisions, technological integration, and faculty development to meet industry needs. Soft skills' incorporation into the curriculum is vital, alongside students seeking career coaching. Future research avenues include longitudinal studies and industry perceptions of educational curricula. This study bridges academia-industry gaps while advocating for ongoing employability exploration.

References

Abbas, J., and Sagsan, M. (2019). Identification of key employability attributes and evaluation of university graduates' performance. *Higher Education, Skills and Work Based Learning*, 10(3), 449–466.

Adriana, E. (2012). Employability of iranian engineering graduates: influential factors, consequences and strategies. *Journal of Teaching and Learning for Graduate Employability*, 11(1), 110–130.

Ahmad, K. (2012). Relationship between employability and graduates' skill. *International Business Management*, 6(4), 440–445, 2012.ISSN-1993-5250 med well journals 2012.

Aida, N., et al. (2017). Graduate employability, 'soft skills' versus 'hard' business knowledge. *A European Study Special Issue: Employability, Mobility and the Labour Market*, 33(4), 411–422.

Chadha, R., and Mishra, A. (2014). Challenging the primacy of lectures: the dissonance between theory and practice in university teaching. *Journal of University Teaching and Learning Practice*, 12(1), 1–3.

Chithra, R. (2013). Employability skills -a study on the perception of the engineering students and their prospec-tive employers. *Global Journal of Management and Business Studies*, 3(5), 525–534, ISSN 2248-9878.

Esa, A., Padil, S., Selamat, A., and Idris, M. T. M. (2018). Perceptions of employability skills necessary to enhance human resource management graduates" prospects of securing a relevant place in the labor market. *European Scientific Journal*, 20, 129–143.

Green, S., and Mc Intosh, S (2002). Is there a genuine under-utillisation of skill amongst the over qualified?. SKOPE Research paper No.30.ESRC Center on skill, Knowledge and Organisational performance, Oxford and Warwick University.

Heavey, A., and Morey, A. (2003). Enhanching Employability, Recognizing Diversity. London: Universit UK and Higher Education Careers Services Unit.

Shukla, D. (2012). Employability skill among professionals – chagrin of HR executives in Indian labor market : a study on engineering graduates of Bhopal City. *VSRD International Journal of Business and Management Research*, 2(8).

17 A study on job satisfaction among tea plantation workers in Valparai Taluk, Coimbatore district

V. Ajay Raj[a], D. Vishnu Vardhan[b], R. Velmurugan[c] and J. Sudarvel[d]

Karpagam Academy of Higher Education, Coimbatore, Tamil Nadu, India

Abstract

The study delves into job satisfaction among ValparaiTaluk's tea workers in Coimbatore district. Job satisfaction significantly impacts employee well-being and productivity, especially in labor-intensive sectors like tea plantations. Understanding the factors influencing job satisfaction among these workers is vital to enhance their work environment and overall business performance. Preliminary findings highlight key factors affecting job satisfaction: pay, working hours, job security, conditions, supervisor support, interpersonal relations, and career prospects. Challenges faced, such as low pay and limited access to healthcare and education, were also identified. These insights aim to drive interventions, aiding unions, governments, and plantation owners in creating strategies for better conditions, improved pay, and meeting workers' social and economic needs.

Keywords: Career development, Coimbatore district, job satisfaction, labor-intensive industries, tea workers, ValparaiTaluk, wages, working conditions, working hours

Introduction

The ValparaiTaluk in Coimbatore district, known for its significant tea plantations, relies heavily on its workforce for industry growth. Understanding the job satisfaction of these tea workers is crucial for their well-being and the industry's development. Job satisfaction, encompassing aspects like pay, work environment, and advancement opportunities, influences employee engagement, performance, and turnover rates. Investigating factors affecting job satisfaction among tea workers offers insights into their challenges, allowing targeted improvements and focused interventions by plantation owners and authorities. This study employs a mixed-methods approach, combining surveys and interviews, to delve into tea workers' job satisfaction in ValparaiTaluk. The findings aim to drive initiatives enhancing pay, benefits, and overall satisfaction for tea workers. This research intends to contribute to the knowledge base of job satisfaction within the tea plantation sector and aims to improve workers' lives while sustaining the industry's long-term viability.

Table 17.1 Literature review.

Study	Approach	Sample size	Analysis methods	Findings
Rodrigo et al. (2022)	Deductive, quantitative	66	Correlation, regression	Positive correlation between job performance and satisfaction; Improved performance linked to income, supervisor relations, training, recognition.
Abdul Rafeeque and Sumathy (2020)	Qualitative	Not specified	Not specified	Employees disagree with adequate working conditions.
Priyadarshan (2020)	Not specified	Not specified	Not specified	Job qualities impact satisfaction; safety, incentives, advancement opportunities affect contentment.
Santhosh Kumar (2019)	Not specified	Not specified	Not specified	Job dissatisfaction increases grievances, negative behavior, health issues, absenteeism.
Santhosh (2019)	Not specified	Not specified	Not specified	Lack of enthusiasm, stress, irregular leaves linked to low productivity and job dissatisfaction.
Anton et. al (2018)	Not specified	Not specified	Not specified	Job satisfaction considerably influences productivity positively.

[a]ajaysanjay93444@gmail.com, [b]vishnuvardhanvvn@gmail.com, [c]drvelsngm@gmail.com, [d]j.sudarvel@gmail.com

Study	Approach	Sample size	Analysis methods	Findings
Latif et al. (2015)	Not specified	Not specified	Not specified	Strong relationship found between organizational effectiveness and job satisfaction.
Yvonne et al. (2014)	Quantitative	77	Correlation, descriptive statistics	Weak positive connection between job satisfaction and performance.
Gupta (2014)	Not specified	Not specified	Not specified	Job satisfaction significantly impacts work output.

Source: Author

Research Statement, Gaps and Method

The exploration into the job satisfaction of ValparaiTaluk's tea workers is a crucial endeavor due to its impact on their well-being and the local economy Ozturk and Hancer (2011). Understanding the intricate factors influencing their contentment becomes imperative considering the challenges these workers often face, encompassing long hours, low pay, limited access to healthcare, and constrained educational opportunities. This study delves into these issues to grasp the nuanced elements shaping the job satisfaction levels within this sector Banerjee (2015).

Primarily, this research aims to assess the job satisfaction among Valparai's tea workers, recognizing its direct correlation to employees' overall quality of life, stress levels, and mental health Perera et al. (2018). Addressing these aspects holds the potential to enhance the work-life balance of tea workers and contribute to improved productivity and reduced turnover rates, Jaganathan and Palanichamy (2017). Discontentment among employees can lead to a loss of skilled labor, raising training costs and impacting the industry's competitiveness.

Given the labor-intensive nature of the tea plantation sector, this study's insights into job satisfaction are crucial. They shed light on the challenges these workers endure and provide a platform to initiate changes aimed at rectifying their concerns Linz (2003). A satisfied and motivated workforce is pivotal for the industry's growth and sustainability Oroni et al. (2014). Thus, by identifying and addressing job satisfaction aspects, this research aims to not only improve the working conditions and contentment levels of Valparai's tea workers but also bolster their overall health Karatepe et al. (2003).

The objectives of this study revolve around pinpointing the job satisfaction of Valparai's tea plantation workers. Utilizing primary data collection methods such as interviews ensures the acquisition of detailed and standardized responses, enhancing the reliability of the data Perera (2018). The convenient sampling

Table 17.2 Demographic factors and job satisfaction metrics among tea plantation workers in Valparai Taluk, Coimbatore district.

Demographic factors	Frequency	Percentage
Age		
Up to 26	26	17.3
Between 27 - 50	92	61.3
Above 50	32	21.3
Gender		
Male	67	44.7
Female	83	55.3
Education qualification		
Illiterate	34	22.7
SSLC	37	24.7
HSC	28	18.7
Under graduate	17	11.3
Post graduate	34	22.7
Type of family		
Joint	79	52.7
Nuclear	71	47.3
Monthly income		
Up to 8000	6	4
8001 – 19000	26	17.3
Above 19000	118	78.7
Job Satisfaction metrics	Mean Score	Rank
Job security	2.707	10
Salary	2.58	11
Promotion policy	3.553	5
Recognition	3.627	4
Relation with colleague	3.753	1
Working condition	3.087	8
Infrastructure facilities	3.547	6
Technology facilities	3.72	2
Leave facilities	3.093	7
Safety measures	2.76	9

Demographic factors	Frequency	Percentage
Compensation to employees	2.52	12
Retirement benefits	3.647	3
Social securities	2.58	11
Training policy	3.087	8

Source: Author

technique, considering the challenging accessibility to the entire worker population, yielded insights from 150 tea plantation employees Savur (1973).

Analyzing this data was executed through simple percentage calculations and factor analysis Sinha (2022). These methodologies were chosen for their ability to distill comprehensive insights from the collected information, providing a robust framework for interpreting the job satisfaction dynamics within this specific sector. This research endeavors to bridge the gap between job contentment and the challenges faced by tea workers, offering pathways to elevate their satisfaction and well-being.

Conclusion

The comprehensive analysis of tea workers' job satisfaction reveals a notable affinity for aspects like colleague relationships, technology facilities, retirement benefits, and recognition, underlining several focal areas where contentment is high. However, the analysis also uncovers areas requiring immediate attention, predominantly health-related issues and specific job factors that exhibit lower satisfaction scores. This extensive review reflects the multifaceted interplay of elements influencing tea workers' contentment within ValparaiTaluk's tea plantation industry. Addressing these facets demands a multi-pronged approach. Encouraging open and transparent communication channels and implementing robust employee engagement initiatives will cultivate an environment conducive to feedback and active participation. Providing avenues for continuous professional development aligned with personal career trajectories is crucial, promoting skill enhancement and knowledge enrichment. Prioritizing a healthy work-life balance through flexible schedules and family-friendly policies can significantly enhance the well-being of tea workers. Structuring fair and transparent performance evaluations and recognition programs can empower employees, reinforcing their sense of value within the organization. Furthermore, fostering a culture of inclusive decision-making empowers tea workers, providing a sense of ownership and responsibility that positively impacts job satisfaction. Initiating wellness programs encompassing healthcare access, health screenings, and mental health support demonstrates commitment toward the overall well-being of tea workers. Transparent communication regarding organizational policies, updates, and benefits is essential for building trust and ensuring informed decisions. Establishing regular feedback mechanisms and adapting measures based on tea workers' input ensures relevance and efficacy of implemented strategies. Guaranteeing fair compensation aligned with industry standards, inclusive pay discussions, and linking career growth to rewards and promotions form pivotal elements in ensuring equity and motivation among tea workers. The collaborative efforts of stakeholders, including tea plantation owners, policymakers, governmental bodies, and non-governmental organizations, are crucial in implementing these strategies effectively. Consistent monitoring, evaluation, and feedback mechanisms are imperative to gauge the impact of these measures and facilitate necessary adjustments. These strategies, when implemented collectively and collaboratively, hold the potential to significantly elevate tea workers' satisfaction, foster a productive work environment, and fortify the long-term viability of ValparaiTaluk's tea plantation industry. Ultimately, a harmonious blend of various initiatives aimed at addressing the nuanced layers of job satisfaction can pave the way for a thriving, contented, and sustainable tea workforce in ValparaiTaluk.

References

Abdul Rafeeque, A. K., and Sumathy, N. (2020). A study on the job satisfaction among tea plantation women workers in wayanad district. *Journal of University of Shanghai for Science and Technology*, 22(11), 638–644.

Banerjee, S. (2015). Job satisfaction and burnout: a study on the executives of tea industy. *International Journal of Business Quantitative Economics and Applied Management Research*, 1(8), 50–65.

Gupta, I. (2014). Impact of job satisfaction on employee's performance. *Scholarly Research Journal for Interdisciplinary Studies*, II/XV, 2307–2316.

Jaganathan, A., and Palanichamy, K. (2017). A study on small tea growers satisfaction level and and problems with special reference to the Nilgiris District of Tamil Nadu. *International Journal of Science and Research*, 6(6).

Karatepe, O. M., Avci, T., Karatepe, T., and Canozer, S. (2003). The measurement of job satisfaction. *International Journal of Hospitality and Tourism Administration*, 4(1), 69–85.

Latif, M. S., Ahmad, M., Qasim, M., Mushtaq, M., Ferdoos, A., and Naeem, H. (2015). Impact of worker's job satisfaction on organizational performance. *European Journal of Business and Management*, 7, 166–171.

Linz, S. J. (2003). Job satisfaction among russian workers. William Davidson Working Paper Number 46.

Oroni, R. O., Iravo, M., and Elijah, C. M. (2014). Influence of motivation on tea factory worker performance in Kenya. a case of Kisii County, Kenya. *Journal of Business and Management*, 16(4), 36–41.

Ozturk, A. B., and Hancer, M. (2011). The effect of demographics on job satisfaction: a study of hotel managers in Turkey. *International Journal of Hospitality and Tourism Administration*, 12(3), 189–201.

Perera, K. A. R. C. (2018). Job satisfaction and productivity of the factory offices of the tea plantation sector in Sri Lanka. *European Journal of Business and Management*, 10(2), 49–53.

Perera, K. A. R. C., Khatibi, A., Silva, S., and Dharmarathna, I. (2018). Job satisfaction and productivity of the factory offices of the tea plantation sector in Sri Lanka European. *Journal of Business and Management*, 10(2), 49–53.

Priyadarshan, S. (2020). Workers satisfaction on the facilities provided by the tea plantation companies –with special reference to Kerala State. *Journal of Management (JOM)*, 6(3), 157–178.

Rodrigo, J. A. H. N., Kuruppu, C. L., and Pathirana, G. Y. (2022). The impact of job satisfaction on employee performance: a case at ABC manufacturing company. *Asian Journal of Economics, Business and Accounting*, 22(2), 1–9.

Santhosh Kumar, R. (2019). A study on job satisfaction related issues in tea industry with special reference to Idukki District, Kerala, India. *International Journal of Current Advanced Research*, 8(4), 18163–18167.

Savur, M. (1973). Labour and productivity in the tea industry. *Economic and Political Weekly*, 8(11), 551–559.

Sinha, S. (2022). Impact analysis of skill development on the performance of small tea growers of Assam. *Pacific Business Review (International)*, 14(7), 97–108.

Yvonne, W., Rahman, R. H. A., and Long, C. S. (2014). Employee job satisfaction and job performance: a case study in a franchised retail chain organization. *Research Journal of Applied Sciences, Engineering and Technology*, 8(17), 1875–1883.

Problems with Special Reference to the Nilgiris District of Tamil Nadu. *International Journal of Science and Research*, 6(6), 809–812.

18 Consumer preference toward health insurance in Coimbatore district

Shree Hari, L[a], N. Ananathakumar[b], R. Velmurugan[c] and J. Sudarvel[d]
Karpagam Academy of Higher Education, Coimbatore, Tamil Nadu, India

Abstract

This study investigates health insurance preferences among consumers in Coimbatore district. Recognizing the pivotal role health insurance plays in accessing quality healthcare and covering medical expenses, understanding consumer preferences is crucial for insurers to tailor offerings effectively. Employing a mixed-methods approach, a quantitative survey will collect data on current health insurance coverage and factors influencing choices among randomly sampled Coimbatore residents. A structured questionnaire will gather demographic details and insights on insurance options, premiums, benefits, and service quality. Statistical analysis, including factor analysis and descriptive statistics, will uncover key choice influencers from quantitative data, while thematic analysis will identify patterns in qualitative data. These findings will illuminate factors influencing consumer preferences, aiding insurers in crafting specialized policies and improved customer experiences. Policymakers can also use these insights to enhance health insurance accessibility and affordability in the district.

Keywords: Accessibility, affordability, Coimbatore district, consumer preference, customer service, health insurance, insurance coverage, premium costs, satisfaction levels

Introduction

A robust healthcare system hinges on health insurance, safeguarding individuals against medical expenses and ensuring access to quality care. In India, the demand for health insurance has steadily risen due to a growing emphasis on personal health, escalating healthcare costs, and increased awareness of insurance benefits. Coimbatore district in Tamil Nadu, a thriving economic hub, necessitates an understanding of local health insurance preferences amid its economic growth and urbanization. This study delves into consumer choices regarding health insurance, aiming to inform regulators, insurers, and policymakers. Understanding the drivers of consumer decisions is pivotal for tailoring insurance services to meet local needs and expectations.

Employing a mixed-methods approach, the study will merge quantitative surveys and qualitative interviews. While surveys offer a broad overview of the health insurance landscape, qualitative interviews provide deeper insights into motives and perspectives. The study aims to identify primary influencers like benefits, premiums, coverage options, and customer service, alongside demographic factors and prior insurance experiences affecting decision-making.

Results from this research will contribute to existing knowledge on health insurance preferences in India, specifically in Coimbatore. These findings will aid in crafting personalized insurance policies, marketing strategies, and client engagement initiatives. Moreover, insights gained can inform regulatory measures, fostering improved accessibility and affordability of health insurance. Ultimately, understanding consumer preferences is pivotal for adapting insurance offerings to meet evolving demands, benefitting both consumers and insurance providers alike.

Table 18.1 Literature review.

Study and author (Year)	Main findings
Sodani (2001)	Identified cost and service quality as the pivotal factors influencing enrollment in health insurance plans; suggested the integration of provider and insurer systems and recommended hospitalization and maternity services coverage.
Namasivayam et al. (2006)	Found age, education, and gender insignificance but highlighted family size, income, and occupation's impact on life insurance policy purchases.

[a]shreeharishreehari426@gmail.com, [b]ananthares@gmail.com, [c]drvelsngm@gmail.com, [d]j.sudarvel@gmail.com

Study and author (Year)	Main findings
Vellakal (2007)	Explored India's health insurance programs, favoring Micro Health Insurance (MHI) for equity in low- and middle-income households; indicated gaps in current programs regarding client preferences and low coverage.
Devi and Sarkar (2007)	Analyzed personal characteristics impacting consumer decisions in buying insurance, emphasizing factors like education, profession, locality, age, income, marital status, family structure, and health issues.
Khurana (2008)	Revealed consumer preferences for insurance plans, highlighting the public sector's favor over private ones, with most purchases driven by protection needs; showed satisfaction and willingness for repeat purchases.
Debasish (2008)	Identified five key factors influencing Indian consumers' preference for health insurance, gathering data from insurance agents and consumers; emphasized the need for product design alignment with consumer preferences.
Powell and Goldman (2014)	Analyzed a manufacturing firm's claims data in the U.S. to study the impact of different health insurance plans on medical expenditures; highlighted the significant influence of Adverse Selection in explaining preferences for plan generosity.
Jothi and Sitaram (2014)	Used PLS-SEM analysis to understand consumer preferences for life insurance; found that the product and the marketing mix significantly influenced consumer attitudes and purchase intentions.

Source: Author

Table 18.2 Analysis and interpretation.

Gender	Frequency	Percentage
Male	101	85.0
Female	19	15.0
Total	120	100.0
Age	Frequency	Percentage
Up to 25 Years	18	15.0
26 – 40 Years	82	68.3
Above 40 years	20	16.7
Total	120	100.0
Education qualification	Frequency	Percentage
SSLC	16	13.3
HSC	44	36.7
Diploma	16	15.0
UG	10	8.3
PG	14	10.0
Professional	20	16.7
Total	120	100.0
Occupation	Frequency	Percentage
Agriculturist	32	26.7
Businessman	42	35.0
Employee	30	25.0
Student	4	3.3
Others	12	10.0
Total	120	100.0
Status in family	Frequency	Percentage
Joint	16	13.3

Gender	Frequency	Percentage
Head	104	71.7
Total	120	100.0
Income	Frequency	Percentage
Up to 18000	18	15.0
18001-90000	84	70.0
Above 90000	18	15.0
Total	120	100.0
Medical claim insurance	Frequency	Percentage
Public	16	13.3
Private	104	85.0
Total	120	100.0

Source: Author

The survey reveals that the predominant respondents are predominantly male, aged between 26 to 40 years, with a higher secondary education level, engaged in business, heading their families, having over three earning members in their households, earning between Rs. 18,001-90,000, and primarily holding health insurance from the private sector. The investigation of customer preferences for health insurance in the Coimbatore district is the focal point of this study. Its primary research question revolves around understanding the determinants that influence health insurance choices in the district. By addressing this, the study aims to offer an extensive comprehension of consumer preferences and the factors shaping decision-making in health insurance selection, contributing valuable insights for insurance companies, decision-makers, and regulatory agencies to enhance the design, delivery, and accessibility of health insurance products and services. The study's objective is to identify the factors influencing consumer preference for health insurance in the Coimbatore district. Its scope is confined to the Coimbatore area of Tamil Nadu, India, analyzing consumer perceptions, experiences, and decision-making processes regarding various health insurance types. It delves into factors like coverage availability, premium costs, features, customer service quality, and past insurance experiences impacting preferences. Employing a mixed-methods approach combining quantitative surveys and qualitative interviews, the study aims to gather comprehensive data. Quantitative surveys will offer an overview of consumer preferences, while qualitative interviews will provide nuanced insights. The research methodology entails primary data collection through interviews, employing convenient sampling, and analyzing the gathered data using simple percentage and factor analysis. The study's significance lies in several aspects. It can assist health insurance companies in tailoring policies to meet local population needs, potentially increasing consumer satisfaction and market competition. Additionally, the findings can guide regulators in formulating evidence-based policies to enhance insurance availability, affordability, and quality in the district Hoyt and Powell (2006). By understanding consumer preferences, insurance firms can develop targeted marketing strategies, boosting public awareness and adoption rates. Moreover, empowering consumers with knowledge about health insurance options aids in informed decision-making, potentially influencing access and affordability barriers. Overall, this research endeavors to contribute to existing knowledge on Indian consumer behavior related to health insurance, specifically focusing on the Coimbatore district. By influencing stakeholders and consumers, it aspires to improve health insurance

KMO and Bartlett's test		
Kaiser-Meyer-Olkin measure of sampling adequacy.		.903
Bartlett's test of Sphericity	Approx. Chi-square	4699.385
	df	561
	Sig.	.000

Rotated component Matrix[a]

	Component						
	1	2	3	4	5	6	7
Flexibility in provider choice	.815						
Rising healthcare costs and affordability	.698						
Mental health coverage	.678						
Availability of additional benefits	.672						
Personalized coverage options	.653						
Coverage for prescription medications	.641						
Tax benefits and savings	.634						
Protection against Catastrophic events	.613						
Financial protection against medical expenses		.836					
Quality of customer service		.757					
Effectiveness of grievance handling		.755					
Coverage for pre-existing conditions		.755					
Access to quality healthcare services		.715					
Speedy settlement of claim		.708					
Peace of mind and security		.569					
Cost of the treatment			.771				
Yearly premium payable			.770				
Speedy and transparent approval process			.647				

	Component						
	1	2	3	4	5	6	7
Considerations for Different life stages			.570				
Emergency and hospitalization Coverage			.517				
Network of preferred providers			.511				
Employer-sponsored health insurance				.766			
Government mandates and subsidies				.715			
Life stage considerations				.686			
Importance of preventive care and wellness				.606			
Insurance reputation and trustworthiness					.799		
Timely access to medical care					.799		
Importance of Preventive Care and Wellness					.629		
Family Coverage and Protection					.048	.781	
Financial Planning and Budgeting						.754	
Employer-sponsored Health Insurance Benefits						.672	
Compliance with Government Requirements						.650	
Coverage for pre-existing conditions							.677
Access to quality healthcare providers							.642
Total	11.222	4.942	2.272	1.640	1.389	1.211	1.038
% of Variance	33.007	14.534	6.681	4.825	4.086	3.562	3.052
Cumulative %	33.007	47.541	54.222	59.047	63.133	66.695	69.748

Extraction Method: Principal Component Analysis.

Rotation Method: Varimax with Kaiser Normalization.

a. Rotation converged in 17 iterations.

options, customer satisfaction, and healthcare outcomes in the region Dror et al. (2007).

The data collected seems suitable for factor analysis based on Kaiser-Meyer-Olkin (KMO) and Bartlett's test of Sphericity results. The KMO measure, indicating sampling adequacy for factor analysis, exceeds the acceptable threshold at 0.903. Bartlett's Test, evaluating the correlation matrix of variables, yields a high statistic (4699.385) and a low associated p-value (0.000), suggesting the data's suitability for factor analysis. Both tests affirm that the data is apt for identifying influential factors impacting consumer preferences in health insurance through factor analysis.

Conclusion

The Conclusion must be clearly marked as shown. When referring to other Sections in the Letter, please use the Section heading, or describe the relevant Section as the 'following' or 'preceding' Section in relation to the current Section in the text.

The analysis of the rotated component matrix identified numerous factors, each with component loadings of 0.5 or higher, significantly contributing to consumer preferences toward Health Insurance. These factors encompass diverse elements such as flexibility in provider choice, rising healthcare costs and affordability, mental health coverage, and more, collectively explaining 69.748% of the migration workers problem. Recommendations following this study's scope include collaborative efforts with local health insurance companies, ensuring representative sampling strategies for the quantitative survey, incorporating the insights from uninsured populations, adhering to ethical standards, and considering longitudinal studies to gauge changing preferences. Additionally, contrasting findings with other regions, disseminating findings widely, and sharing results with pertinent stakeholders are suggested. This comprehensive approach can foster cooperation, improve policy suggestions, and influence better healthcare outcomes in the Coimbatore district, ultimately enriching consumer satisfaction and shaping the health insurance landscape positively. Overall, this study aims to offer substantial insights to insurance providers, policymakers, consumers, and the academic community, augmenting understanding and catalyzing enhancements in healthcare access, policy, and consumer satisfaction in the Coimbatore district.

References

Debasish, S. S. (2008). ³Exploring customer preference for health insurance in India. *Journal of Management XI MB*, 1(1).

Dror, D. M., Koren, R., Ost, A., Binnendijk, E., Vellakal, S., and Danis, M. (2007). Health insurance benefit packages prioritized by low-income clients in India: three criteria to estimate effectiveness of choice. *Social Science and Medicine*, 64, 884–896.

Hoyt, R. E., and Powell, L. S. (2006). Assessing financial performance in medical professional liability insurance. *Journal of Insurance Regulation*, 25(1), 3–13.

Jothi, A. L., and Sitaram, G. (2014). A comprehensive study on product preferences and purchase decision making of life insurance customers. *International Journal of Applied Business and Economic Research*, 12(4), 1407–1418.

Namasivayam, N., Ganesan, S., and Rajendran, S. (2006). Socioeconomic factors influencing the decision in taking life insurance policies. Insurance Chronicle. The ICFAI University Press (pp. 65–70).

Powell, D., and Goldman, D. (2021). Disentangling moral hazard and adverse selection in private health insurance. *Journal of Econometrics*, 222(1, Part A), 141–160.

Sodani, P. R. (2001). Potential of Health Insurance for Informal Sector-A Pilot Study from Jaipur, Rajasthan. Jaipur: Indian Institute of Health Management Research.

Vellakal, S. (2007). Health Insurance Schemes in India: An economic analysis of demand and management under risk pooling and adverse selection. PhD thesis in Economics-(Mangalore University)-p10-13, 172-174.

19 Relationship among motivational factors and job satisfaction in ceramics industry

M. Dharani and A. Martin Jayaraj[a]

Karpagam Academy of Higher Education, Coimbatore, Tamil Nadu, India

Abstract

This study delves into the ceramics industry's workforce dynamics, seeking to understand the motivational factors influencing job satisfaction. A comprehensive literature review highlights historical motivators associated with job satisfaction, encompassing both extrinsic factors like pay and job stability and intrinsic factors like recognition and opportunities for career progression. Empirical data were collected through surveys administered to employees in various roles within the ceramics sector. Preliminary findings suggest a significant impact of intrinsic and extrinsic motivational factors on job satisfaction, with positive associations noted for challenging work, advancement opportunities, and fair compensation. Moreover, a positive organizational culture, effective communication, and a balanced work-life environment were identified as additional contributors to job satisfaction. This study's insights contribute to an enhanced understanding of motivational elements crucial for job satisfaction in the ceramics industry, offering organizations valuable guidance to formulate effective strategies, thereby fostering employee motivation, satisfaction, and overall organizational performance.

Keywords: Ceramics industry, employee engagement, extrinsic motivation, intrinsic motivation, job satisfaction, motivational factors, organizational culture

Introduction

Job satisfaction is integral to employee productivity and organizational success, particularly in sectors like ceramics reliant on skilled labor. This introduction highlights the diverse operations within the ceramics sector, producing items crucial for industries like construction, automotive, aerospace, electronics, and healthcare. The significance of motivated and satisfied workers for maintaining product quality, achieving production goals, and fostering innovation is emphasized. However, the ceramics industry poses unique challenges, such as repetitive tasks, exposure to hazardous materials, and the need for ongoing skill development, potentially impacting job satisfaction. The distinction between intrinsic and extrinsic motivational factors, linked to personal fulfillment and external rewards, is discussed. Understanding these factors is pivotal for employers to implement effective reward systems, cultivate positive organizational cultures, and provide opportunities for career advancement. Moreover, individuals can leverage this knowledge for informed career decisions, seeking fulfilling work environments and advocating for themselves within their organizations.

Review of Literature

Table 19.1 Exploring motivational dynamics: unveiling influences on job satisfaction and organizational success in diverse studies

Author name	Study	Findings
Commeiras et al. (2018)	Traineeship's impact on job satisfaction	Traineeship is vital for enhancing skills and aligning individuals with organizational goals, fostering motivation.
Eguchi (2018)	Benefits of job rotation	Job rotation reduces monotony, prevents health issues, enhances morale, and provides diverse perspectives, contributing to efficient learning.
Wickramasinghe (2018)	Influence of tenure and gender on job satisfaction	Job satisfaction is affected by factors like workplace culture and working conditions, influencing overall productivity.

[a]martin.a@kahedu.edu.in

Author name	Study	Findings
Zhang and Wu (2018)	Job security and employee motivation	Job security enhances confidence, reduces stress, and motivates employees, leading to increased dedication and profit maximization.
Mescib (2019)	Social opportunities and employee motivation	Providing social chances boosts motivation, aiding organizations in achieving their goals.
Kunz and Pfaff (2018)	Extrinsic rewards and intrinsic drive	Extrinsic rewards don't undermine intrinsic drive; good strategic alignment increases motivation and performance.
Baldwin et al. (2018)	Motivation's impact on learning outcomes	Motivated employees show better learning outcomes, making training essential for skill enhancement and organizational success.
Hunter et al. (2019)	Achievement as a key to organizational success	Achievement-oriented employees enhance job output, contributing significantly to organizational success.
Ghulam Salma (2019)	Leadership's influence on student motivation	Leadership impacts student motivation; hiring based on merit and reducing political pressure enhance workforce motivation.

Source: Author

Problem Statement

In the ceramics sector, well-documented challenges such as physically demanding work, repetitive tasks, and exposure to hazardous materials may potentially impede workers' motivation and job satisfaction, yet there is a paucity of research on the specific relationship between motivational elements and job satisfaction in this context. This study aims to fill this gap by exploring and analyzing the interplay between motivating factors and job satisfaction among ceramics industry workers. The insights gained will enable organizations in the ceramics sector to devise effective strategies for enhancing employee motivation and satisfaction. By uncovering the unique motivational factors influencing job satisfaction in this industry, this research contributes valuable knowledge to the broader understanding of motivational dynamics and job satisfaction in the workplace.

Objectives of the Study

- To examine the demographic profile of the employees working in ceramic industries.
- To analyze perception of employees towards motivational factors affecting the Ceramics industry.

　　To assess the relationship among motivational factors and job satisfaction and employee performance.

Research methodology

In context of this study's objectives, the researcher has employed the descriptive design. The research consists of both primary and secondary data. Data is collected from the employees of ceramics industry in Coimbatore District. 120 respondents' details were collected by using simple random sampling method. This study applied statistical tools like ANOVA, correlation analysis and weighted average rank test to examine the data.

Analysis and Interpretations

This section delves into a comprehensive analysis of factors influencing motivation in the ceramic Industry, scrutinizing demographic variations and their impact on employee perspectives Hurley (2019). Utilizing ANOVA tests, correlation analysis, and weighted average rank tests, the study explores gender, age, education, experience, residence, and income disparities McCarthy (2020). Findings illuminate the nuanced relationships between these variables and motivational elements Qin (2021). Additionally, a detailed examination of non-monetary benefits and job satisfaction correlation, as well as a ranking of motivational factors, provides valuable insights into the dynamics shaping employee engagement in the ceramic industry Wensveen (2022).

Analysis and interpretations:
1. **Demographic variation in motivational factors:**
    - **Gender:**
        - Between groups: Significant difference ($p < 0.001$).
        - Within groups: Inconclusive.
        - Conclusion: No difference in opinion based on gender Wylie (2018).
    - **Age:**
        - Between groups: Significant difference ($p < 0.001$).

- Within groups: Inconclusive.
- Conclusion: No consensus across age groups.
- **Educational qualification:**
  - Between groups: No significant difference (p = 0.105).
  - Within groups: Inconclusive.
  - Conclusion: No impact based on education.
- **Years of experience:**
  - Between groups: Significant difference (p < 0.001).
  - Within groups: Inconclusive.
  - Conclusion: Varied opinions with experience.
- **Area of residence:**
  - Between groups: Significant difference (p = 0.001).
  - Within groups: Inconclusive.
  - Conclusion: Location affects opinions.
- **Income per month:**
  - Between groups: Significant difference (p < 0.001).
  - Within groups: Inconclusive.
  - Conclusion: Income influences motivational factors.

2. **Correlation analysis:**
   - **Non-monetary benefits and job satisfaction:**
   - Pearson correlation: Strong positive correlation (0.736).
   - Conclusion: Direct relation observed.

3. **Weighted average rank test:**
   Motivational factors ranking:
   1. Hygiene restrooms (mean score: 1.95)
   2. Pleasant working conditions (Mean score: 1.91)
   3. Quality work equipment (mean score: 1.89)
   4. Effective cooperation with co-workers (mean score: 1.82)
   5. Proper hygiene condition at the workplace (mean score: 1.77)

- **Conclusion:**
  - Hygiene-related factors and pleasant working conditions are most motivating.
  - Cooperation with co-workers and hygiene conditions at the workplace rank lower.

Findings:

4. **Demographics impact:** No significant variation in motivational factors based on gender, age, education, experience, residence, and income.

5. **Correlation analysis:** Strong positive correlation observed between non-monetary benefits and job satisfaction.

6. **Motivational factors ranking:**
   - Top contributors: Hygiene restrooms and pleasant working conditions.
   - Least contributors: Cooperation with co-workers and hygiene conditions at the workplace.

In conclusion, while demographics play a minimal role, hygiene-related factors and a positive work environment significantly influence motivation and job satisfaction in the ceramic industry. These insights can aid in tailoring strategies to enhance employee motivation and satisfaction in this sector.

The study reveals no significant demographic-based differences in opinions regarding motivational factors in the ceramic industry. A robust positive correlation exists between non-monetary benefits and job satisfaction. Weighted average rank analysis identifies hygiene and pleasant working conditions as prominent motivators, while cooperation with co-workers and workplace hygiene are comparatively less influential. These insights signify the need for targeted motivational strategies in the industry.

Inferences: Demographic factors minimally impact motivational perceptions, emphasizing a universal approach. Prioritizing hygiene and workplace comfort is vital for employee motivation, while fostering cooperation and enhancing workplace hygiene warrants attention. This nuanced understanding aids in crafting effective motivation strategies tailored to the ceramic industry's unique dynamics.

Conclusion

The culmination of this research offers valuable suggestions for enhancing employee motivation within the ceramics sector. Emphasizing the pivotal role of promotion and incentives, organizations should maintain and further extend educational and training benefits. Ensuring job and social security, alongside implementing safety measures, can significantly contribute to a motivated and satisfied workforce. Tailoring workload to the specific demands of the ceramic industry emerges as a targeted strategy. These recommendations, rooted in research findings and personal observations, form a blueprint for fostering a supportive work environment that prioritizes job satisfaction, employee well-being, and overall productivity within the ceramics sector.

The study underscores the indispensable relationship between motivating variables and job satisfaction in the ceramics industry. While contributing to the existing body of evidence on motivational factors, it sheds light on the sector-specific challenges and opportunities. Recognizing the study's limitations, notably its specific setting and sample, future research endeavors should aim for broader and more diverse samples to validate and expand upon these insights. In essence, the research advocates for a holistic understanding of motivational dynamics, emphasizing their profound impact on job satisfaction, employee well-being, and organizational success within the ceramics industry.

References

Commeiras, et al. (2018). The motivation of ceramics firm staff members: an implementation in antalya province. *The International Journal of Social Sciences,* 8(1), 64–75.

Eguchi (2018). Motivation of medical employees. (pp. 44–48). ISBN 978-83-62182-33-6.

Hurley, S. F. (2019). An investigation of the relationship between global manufacturing practices and outcomes in machine tools and textile industries. 16(2–3), 291–299.

McCarthy, B. J. (2020). An overview of the technical spinning mills sector. In Handbook of Technical Spinning mills (2nd edn), (Vol. 1), Technical Textile Processes (pp. 1–20). Woodhead Publishing.

Mescib (2019). The motivation of tiles firm staff members: An implementation in Antalya Province. *The International Journal of Social Sciences,* 8(1), 64–75.

Qin, Y. (2021). A brief description of the manufacturing processes for medical textile materials. In Woodhead Publishing Series in Spinning mills (pp. 43–54).

Wensveen, S. (2022). Designing ultra-personalized embodied smart textile services for well-being. In Woodhead Publishing Series in Spinning mills. (pp. 155–175).

Wickramasinghe (2018). Motivation of employees and behavior modification in Health Care Organizations. *Acta Medica Medianae,* 46(2), 53–62.

Wylie (2018). The impact of nurses' motivation to work, job satisfaction, and socio-demographic characteristics on the intention to quit their current job: an empirical study in Turkey. *Applied Nursing Research,* 22(2), 113–118.

Zhang and Wu (2018). Motivation of employees and behavior modification in Health Care Organizations. *Acta Medica Medianae,* 46(2), 53–62.

20 A study on employee job satisfaction among roasted gram mills in Tamil Nadu

Raghul R, Smruthymol[a] and J. P. Chitra[b]

Karpagam Academy of Higher Education, Coimbatore, India

Abstract

This research delves into job satisfaction among roasted gram mill employees in Tamil Nadu, India, recognizing its pivotal role in productivity and employee welfare. By employing a comparative approach, it surveyed workers across various mills, collecting data on factors like compensation, work-life balance, security, and interpersonal relationships using structured questionnaires. Through descriptive statistics and factor analysis, the study unveiled the key determinants influencing job satisfaction in this industry. These findings are invaluable for mill management, aiding in tailored strategies to enhance employee satisfaction and engagement. Yet, it's essential to note the study's focus on this specific sector and region, urging caution in applying these insights universally across diverse economic sectors or geographic regions. Nonetheless, this research is poised to provide meaningful guidance for improving the work environment and overall satisfaction among roasted gram mill workers in Tamil Nadu.

Keywords: Employee engagement, employee satisfaction, job satisfaction, roasted gram mills, Tamil Nadu, work environment

Introduction

Job satisfaction plays a pivotal role in employee well-being and directly influences their dedication, productivity, and motivation, thereby affecting organizational effectiveness. Understanding the factors impacting job satisfaction is crucial for creating a harmonious work environment. In Tamil Nadu, the roasted gram milling industry, contributing significantly to the region's economy, faces challenges in retaining competent and motivated staff. This study aims to assess job satisfaction levels among employees in these mills, employing comparative research to identify potential variations based on demographics.

Insights gained from this research will empower management and stakeholders, aiding in decision-making to enhance workplace dynamics. The study aims to expand the understanding of job satisfaction specifically in the roasted gram milling sector, offering valuable information for improving human resource policies and practices to bolster employee engagement and organizational performance. Subsequent sections will detail the methods, data, and analyses, concluding with recommendations to elevate job satisfaction in the industry. The study's ultimate goal is to enhance the performance, well-being of employees, and overall socioeconomic development of Tamil Nadu's roasted gram milling industry.

Table 20.1 Literature review.

Author (Year)	Research focus
Hochheiser (1998)	Hochheiser revises the approach to workplace success, emphasizing positive relationships and meeting the ego needs of superiors, peers, and subordinates to achieve personal objectives at work.
Esen (2007)	Examines over 20 job satisfaction markers concerning industry, staff size, age, and gender of employees, including career advancement, benefits, work-life balance, and salary.
Rowan (2008)	Provides realistic advice on enhancing job happiness and navigating workplace challenges without changing careers.
Stride et al. (2008)	Offers benchmarking data and measurement tools for organizational commitment, mental health, well-being, and job satisfaction from a broad sample across various industries, professions, age, and gender.
Buhler and Scott (2009)	Advocates for a culture prioritizing employee well-being and presents a case study illustrating the financial benefits of this strategy.

[a]ragulvjleonel@gmail.com, [b]jayalalsmruthy@gmail.com

Author (Year)	Research focus
Halkos and Bousinakis (2017)	Explores the impact of job stress and dissatisfaction during crises using cluster sampling from Greece's private and public sectors, analyzing contributing factors and their effects through logistic regressions.
Ozturkoglu et al. (2018)	Investigates the link between workplace conditions, ergonomics, and job satisfaction, proposing a model involving 34 factors and emphasizing the importance of ergonomics in worker happiness, particularly in the Turkish automotive industry.
Abraham Pizam (2020)	Compares job characteristics, demographics, and lifestyle of U.S. hospitality employees with other industry groups, revealing distinct traits in the hospitality workforce, including lower social class identification and less satisfaction with work and life.

Source: Author

Problem Statement

This study delves into job satisfaction among Tamil Nadu's roasted gram mill workers, aiming to uncover key factors influencing their contentment. It addresses workers' overall job satisfaction, elements impacting it (like compensation, work-life balance), and their engagement. The study seeks to comprehend how job satisfaction affects employee commitment. Addressing these questions will illuminate job satisfaction levels, aiding in strategic improvements, boosting morale, and fostering a positive workplace. Furthermore, this research could serve as a foundational study, enriching the understanding of employee satisfaction in manufacturing, guiding future research in related fields or regions.

The objective of the study is to identify the employee Job satisfaction among roasted gram mills in Tamil Nadu.

Scope of the Study

The study delves into job satisfaction exclusively within Tamil Nadu's roasted gram milling industry, narrowing its focus to employee experiences in compensation, work-life balance, and career prospects. Its comparative approach aims to identify job satisfaction variations across different mills in the state. Data collection relies solely on systematic questionnaires from mill workers, lacking a long-term job satisfaction trend analysis Spector (1997). While valuable within this sector, caution is advised in applying the findings beyond these mills Scheuring Leipold (2008). The study does not delve into implementing suggested improvements or their feasibility, focusing solely on job satisfaction insights within the industry Cranny et al. (1992). Primary data collected mainly through interviews ensures detailed insights Boucher (2004). Convenient sampling facilitated access to 240 employees, and the analysis framework comprises simple percentages and Factor analysis, providing a structured approach for interpretation Penn (2008).

Significance-wise, the study holds immense value for mill management, offering critical insights into factors shaping employee job satisfaction. This knowledge could aid in tailoring strategies, fostering engagement, and enhancing productivity Cammann et al. (1983). Improved job satisfaction relates to higher retention rates, ensuring a stable workforce and reduced recruitment costs. Addressing dissatisfaction could positively impact employee well-being and mental health, fostering a nurturing workplace. Prioritizing job satisfaction provides a competitive edge, enhancing motivation, innovation, and customer focus, benefiting the industry overall. Policymakers can leverage these findings to craft worker welfare-centric guidelines. The study enriches the understanding of job satisfaction, potentially influencing future research and organizational discourse. A contented workforce can uplift regional economies, improving living conditions. By focusing on job satisfaction factors, organizations can build inclusive, socially responsible work environments, fostering better management-employee relations. The study's conclusions could guide interventions, aiding data-driven decisions to enhance employee contentment and organizational performance, potentially transforming the socio-economic landscape of roasted gram milling in Tamil Nadu.

The data analysis reveals key demographics: predominantly male respondents (61.7%), mostly aged 2535 (39.2%), with nearly equal marital distribution (51.7% married, 48.3% unmarried), and smaller family sizes (below 3 members - 35.0%). Educational distribution was even among school, higher secondary, and graduate levels (25.0%, 30.8%, 30.8% respectively). Predominant departments were maintenance (40.8%) and production (30.0%). Majority had below 4 years of experience (40.0%) and favored half-shifts (43.3%). Motivations centered on salary increase (54.2%) and loans mostly included house

Table 20.2 Socio economic profile.

Sl. no.			No of respondents	Percentage
1	Gender	Male	148	61.7
		Female	92	38.3
2	Age	Below 25 years	50	20.8
		25-35 years	94	39.2
		36- 45 years	58	24.2
		Above 45 years	38	15.8
3	Marital status	Married	124	51.7
		Unmarried	116	48.3
4	Size of the family members	Below 3 members	84	35.0
		3-4 members	66	27.5
		4-5 members	60	25.0
		Above 5 members	30	12.5
5	Educational qualification	School level	60	25.0
		Higher secondary	74	30.8
		Graduate	74	30.8
		Post Graduate	18	7.5
		Others	14	5.8
6	Department of respondents	Production	72	30.0
		Maintenance	98	40.8
		Commercial	48	20.0
		Others	22	9.2
7	Working experience	Below 4 Year	96	40.0
		4-8 year	64	26.7
		8-12 year	58	24.2
		Above 12 years	22	9.2
8	Shift mostly working	Day shift	86	35.8
		Half shift	104	43.3
		Day & night	34	14.2
		Full night	16	6.7
9	Motivational factor to be in the organization	Salary Increase	130	54.2
		Promotion	64	26.7
		Leave	18	7.5
		Motivational	16	6.7
		Recognition	12	5.0
10	Kinds of loans provided	Educational	88	36.7
		Medical	58	24.2
		House loan	86	35.8
		other loans	8	3.3

Source: Author

and educational options (35.8%, 36.7% respectively). The collected data meets criteria for factor analysis based on KMO (0.789) and Bartlett's Test (8546.314, p-value 0.000), indicating suitability for investigating factors affecting job satisfaction in roasted gram mills.

KMO and Bartlett's test		
Kaiser-Meyer-Olkin measure of sampling adequacy.		.866
Bartlett's test of sphericity	Approx. Chi-Square	8991.776
	df	780
	Sig.	.000

Rotated component matrix[a]

	Component							
	1	2	3	4	5	6	7	8
Employee appreciation events	.797							
Continuous learning culture	.740							
Work-life integration	.735							
Collaborative decision-making	.729							
Task variety	.719							
Technological advancements	.674							
Employee satisfaction surveys	.599							
Training and development	.584							
Work environment aesthetics	.564							
Autonomy and responsibility	.558							
Supportive management	.557							
Team collaboration	.543							
Employee motivation strategies		.791						
Safe working conditions		.751						
Opportunities for growth		.744						
Work-life balance		.680						
Employee benefits		.597						
Competitive compensation		.589						
Job security		.567						
Positive work culture		.556						
Recognition and appreciation		.556						
Stress management			.748					
Workload management			.706					
Social connection			.684					
Career advancement opportunities			.583					
Job stability				.527				
Transparent communication				.809				
Incentive programs				.747				
Employee empowerment				.652				
Work schedule flexibility				.629				
Skill utilization				.574				
Recognition programs					.808			
Grievance resolution mechanisms					.764			
Performance feedback					.512			

	Component							
	1	2	3	4	5	6	7	8
Inclusive workplace culture					.571			
Performance recognition						.650		
Professional development opportunities						.602		
Workforce diversity and inclusion							.616	
Health and wellness programs								.553
Employee input and decision-making								.524
Total	18.684	2.781	2.288	1.712	1.398	1.280	1.030	1.011
% of variance	46.709	6.953	5.720	4.279	3.496	3.199	2.574	2.528
Cumulative %	46.709	53.663	59.383	63.661	67.157	70.356	72.931	75.459

Conclusion

The findings unveil significant factors influencing job satisfaction in roasted gram mills, such as employee events, learning culture, work-life balance, and recognition. These components, evident in the rotated component matrix, contribute significantly to job satisfaction, totaling 75.459%. Recommendations aim to enhance employee well-being and satisfaction, emphasizing work-life balance, career growth, recognition, safety, inclusive culture, feedback mechanisms, and community engagement. Implementing these suggestions could foster a motivated workforce, boosting productivity and camaraderie. The study highlights demographic insights and motivators like salary increments and loan provisions, aiding companies in aligning rewards with workforce demands. By prioritizing employee happiness, employers can create a positive work culture and sustainable growth in the roasted gram milling sector in Tamil Nadu.

References

Boucher, J. (2004). How to Love the Job You Hate: Job Satisfaction for the 21st Century. Beagle Bay Books.

Buhler, P., and Scott, J. (2009). The Employee Satisfaction Revolution: Understanding and Unleashing the Power of a Satisfied Workforce. Prestwick House, Inc.

Cammann, C., Fichman, M., Jenkins, Jr. D., and Klesh, J. R. (1983). Assessing the Attitudes and Perceptions of Organizational Members. John Wiley and Sons, Inc.

Cranny, C. J., Smith, P. C., and Stone, E. F. (1992). Job Satisfaction: How People Feel About their Jobs and How it Affects their Performance. Lexington Books.

Esen, E. (2007). Job Satisfaction. Society for Human Resource Management.

Hochheiser, R. M. (1998). Its a Job Not a Jail: How to Break Your Shackles When You Can't Afford to Quit. Simon & Schuster.

Ozturkoglu, O., Saygılı, E. E., and Ozturkoglu, Y. (2018). A manufacturing-oriented modelfor evaluating the satisfaction of workers – evidence from Turkey. *International Journal of Industrial Ergonomics*, 54, 73–82, Received 13.

Penn, J. (2008). How to Enjoy Your Job. Lulu Publishers.

Rowan, S. (2008). Happy at Work: Ten Steps to Ultimate Job Satisfaction. Pearson Education Limited.

Scheuring-Leipold, M. A. (2008). Job Satisfaction. VDM Verlag.

Spector, P. E. (1997). Job Satisfaction : Application, Assessment, Causes, and Consequences'. Sage Publications.

Stride, C., Wall, T. D., and Catley, N. (2008). Measures of Job Satisfaction, Organisational Commitment, Mental Health and Job Related Well-Being. John Wiley and Sons.

21 An empirical study on working capital management with special reference to steel industry in India

Ranjith Kumar L[a] and M. Nandhini[b]

Department of Management, Karpagam Academy of Higher Education, Coimbatore, Tamil Nadu, India

Abstract

During the aftermath of the 2008 financial crisis, businesses pivoted from boosting sales to managing working capital. This abstract delves into the correlation between working capital and business performance. Research reveals a divergence between perceived and actual impacts of working capital management on revenue growth. While companies assert harmony between managing working capital and sales growth, empirical evidence across analyzed industries suggests otherwise. Specifically, in the steel industry, where ten companies were scrutinized for liquidity and profitability, findings indicate a discrepancy: the increase in net working capital doesn't consistently align with justifiable revenue growth. This discrepancy challenges the presumed relationship between working capital management and sales expansion. The study underscores the need for businesses to reevaluate their strategies, considering the nuanced interplay between managing working capital and achieving sustainable revenue growth.

Keywords: Cash conversion cycle, current assets, current liabilities, management attention, revenue growth, working capital, working capital management

Introduction

Effective management of working capital plays a pivotal role in the steel industry, directly influencing the financial robustness and operational efficiency of steel companies Coase (1937). Given the capital-intensive nature of this sector, substantial investments in raw materials, equipment, and operations underscore the significance of efficient working capital management. Its optimization facilitates cash flow, sustains liquidity, and bolsters day-to-day operations Dash and Ravipati (2009). The scope of working capital encompasses a range of components relating to short-term asset and liability management. It includes current assets like cash, bank balances, stocks, and accounts receivable, juxtaposed with current liabilities such as credit, bills payable, and short-term loans Deloof (2003). Balancing current assets to adequately cover working capital elements without excess or insufficiency is the primary objective. However, discrepancies arise where seemingly satisfactory current and quick ratios fail to accurately reflect a firm's liquidity position Vataliya (2009). The methodologies employed by managers often lack grounding in financial principles, relying more on experiential approaches. This can lead to overcapitalization or undercapitalization, hindering effective working capital management. The study examines the relationship between working capital management and firm performance, highlighting significant empirical evidence. However, managerial decisions often deviate from financial principles, potentially causing mismatches in working capital features Eljelly (2004). To evaluate performance and identify risk, financial statements serve as crucial data sources, necessitating further financial analysis and interpretation. Using five years' financial statements, this study employs simple percentage methods and graphical representation for data analysis, ultimately enhancing understanding of company performance and profitability.

Table 21.1 Literature review.

Author	Summary
Imran (2008)	Demonstrates using financial statement analysis to forecast a company's future plans and assess its financial status. Findings are based on secondary data, highlighting strong financial situations. Helps economists assess economic power concentration and risks in financial policies, influencing legislative actions.

[a]ranjithalk66@gmail.com, [b]nandhini1817@gmail.com

Author	Summary
Yazdi (2013)	Highlights the labor-intensive decline in steel and apparel industries due to low-value products and high resource inputs. Notes the industries' significance in consumer goods with a long supply chain. Discusses challenges, like raw material costs, prompting a shift towards high-tech steel production.
Khatri (2013)	Explores factors influencing the fast-moving consumer goods (FMCG) industry, including income rise and changing consumer preferences. Highlights FMCGs' advantages in profit generation but notes threats from multinational companies. Employs regression analysis on secondary data to assess liquidity factors. Indicates satisfactory overall financial health due to diversification.

Source: Author

The objective of this study is to analyze the working capital position of selected steel companies, and to examine the liquidity and profitability, solvency position of selected steel companies. The research methodology employed in this study adheres to a systematic approach for problem-solving, encompassing data collection, statistical analysis, interpretation, and drawing conclusions from the research data. The research design focuses on analyzing annual financial statements of various organizations within the steel industry. Ratios derived from these financial reports, including balance sheets, income statements, cash flow statements, and statements of shareholder equity, are instrumental in assessing financial efficiency. The chosen analytical research design aligns with the study's aim of predicting financial efficiency. The study covers a period from 20172018 to 20212022, ensuring a comprehensive analysis of trends and patterns over multiple fiscal years. To ensure accuracy and reliability, data collection involves both primary and secondary sources. Primary data is obtained through personal discussions with financial executives, providing firsthand insights. Secondary data, derived from annual reports of the selected companies, supplements and validates the primary findings. Ten companies within the steel industry, including Ankit Metal, AryavanEnterorise, Bloom Ind, Inducto Steel, National Steel, Pradhin Steel, RemiEdelstahl, RishabhDisha, SathavahanaIspat, and Supremex, were selected for this analysis. The employed tools and techniques comprise ratio analysis, variance analysis, and trend analysis. These analytical methodologies facilitate a comprehensive evaluation of financial performance, allowing for insights into trends, comparisons, and variance assessments across the selected companies during the study period.

Data Analysis

Table 21.2 Current ratio.

Years (2017-2022)	Ankit Metal	Aryavan Enterprise	Bloom Ind	Inducto Steel	National Steel	Pradhin Steel	Remi-Edelstahl	Rishabh-Digha	Sathava-hanaIspat	Supremex
17-18	0.24	31.51	8.89	1.28	0.03	8.84	1.44	5.7	0.02	37.62
18-19	0.33	22.46	38.67	0.39	0.05	8.54	1.51	29.46	0.03	2.09
19-20	0.35	5.52	7.39	21.55	0.07	4.5	1.7	6.1	0.05	1.61
20-21	0.42	7.08	5.19	1.79	0.12	1.44	1.47	5.23	0.1	2.76
21-22	0.45	4.01	2	13.76	0.4	6.66	1.29	7	0.17	2.17
Total	1.79	70.58	62.14	38.77	0.67	29.98	7.41	53.49	0.37	46.25
Average Ratio	0.358	14.11	12.42	7.754	0.13	5.99	1.48	10.69	0.074	9.25
Standard Deviation	0.08228001	12.22	14.89	9.46	0.15	3.08	0.14	10.50	0.061	15.86
Coefficient Of Variance	22.98324294	86.59	119.86	122.02	113.74	51.4	9.95	98.22	83.63	171.5
Skewness	-0.485067683	0.87	2.06	0.96	1.98	-0.82	0.41	2.21	1.13	2.23
Kurtosis	-0.338686838	-1.57	4.42	-1.2	4.02	-0.47	1.55	4.92	0.34	4.98

Negative skewness noticed on Ankit Metal and Pradhin Steel other companies' current ratio noticed on positive skewness. Leptokurtic noticed on Bloom Ind, National Steel, RishabhDisha and Supremex since kurtosis value greater than 3 and other companies current ratio noticed on playkurtic since kurtosis value less than 3.

Source: Author

Table 21.3 Financial performance analysis of steel companies (20172022): ratios, trends, and statistical indicators.

Years	Ankit Metal	Aryavan Enterprise	Bloom Ind	Inducto Steel	National Steel	Pradhin Steel	RemiEdel-stahl	Rishabh-Disha	Sathava-hanaIspat	Supremex
2017-2018	0.375	31	12.415	1.373	0.035	8.354	2.295	0.375	0.038	37.444
2018-2019	0.401	22.176	37	0.178	0.08	8.077	2.594	9.538	0.045	2.083
2019-2020	0.436	5.554	7.348	16.214	0.121	4.315	2.545	15.344	0.067	1.606
2020-2021	0.528	6.307	5.214	1.71	0.918	1.399	1.883	2.59	0.15	2.759
2021-2022	0.592	3.476	2	15.906	0.463	6.7	1.82	3.009	0.2	2.166
Total	2.332	68.513	63.977	35.381	1.617	28.845	11.137	30.856	0.5	46.058
Avg. Ratio	0.4664	13.7026	12.7954	7.0762	0.3234	5.769	2.2274	6.1712	0.1	9.2116
Std. Dev.	0.091	12.213	14.051	8.222	0.373	2.919	0.362	6.162	0.072	15.788
CoV	19.512	89.133	109.811	116.185	115.327	50.601	16.256	99.856	71.516	171.389
Skewness	0.632	0.862	1.851	0.587	1.335	-0.941	-0.236	0.957	0.78	2.232
Kurtosis	-1.581	-1.651	3.577	-3.294	0.881	-0.376	-2.919	-0.544	-1.723	4.987
Years	Ankit Metal	Aryavan Enterprise	Bloom Ind	Inducto Steel	National Steel	Pradhin Steel	RemiEdel-stahl	Rishabh-Disha	Sathava-hanaIspat	Supremex
2017-2018	-6.82	-1.43	3.32	3.93	-26.36	1.74	0.6	0	-435.09	0
2018-2019	-18.11	0	-4.35	-47.37	-14.4	-0.94	0.26	-63.65	-1,218.21	2.53
2019-2020	-13.68	2.65	-4.58	0.38	-22.21	0.42	0.13	15.88	-113.87	0.99
2020-2021	-22.55	20.23	-5.27	0.56	-22.22	-5.08	0.09	35.39	-45.68	3.18
2021-2022	-97.29	4.73	-7.31	1.07	-3.39	0.17	-3.17	37.74	-125.66	1.77
Total	-158.45	26.18	-18.19	-41.43	-88.58	-3.69	-2.09	25.36	-1938.51	8.47
Avg. Ratio	-31.69	5.236	-3.638	-8.286	-17.716	-0.738	-0.418	5.072	-387.702	1.694
Std. Dev.	37.129	8.712	4.061	21.896	9.103	2.608	1.551	41.387	488.011	1.253
CoV	-117.163	166.392	-111.617	-264.249	-51.381	-353.342	-371.158	815.995	-125.873	73.956
Skewness	-2.099	1.836	1.754	-2.212	1.187	-1.512	-2.14	-		

Source: Author

Table 21.4 Financial performance comparison of companies over time: percentage variations in key metrics.

Years	Ankit Metal	Ankit Metal (%)	Aryavan Enterprise	Aryavan Enterprise (%)	Bloom Ind	Bloom Ind (%)	Inducto Steel	Inducto Steel (%)	National Steel
2017-2018	-1207.27	100	3.6	100	8.79	100	14.91	100	-1894.86
2018-2019	-1062.62	88.01	3.6	100	2.52	28.66	-3.78	-25.35	-1642.25
2019-2020	-933.47	77.32	3.78	105	2.73	31.05	2.13	14.28	-1439.09
2020-2021	-738.93	61.2	3.45	95.83	2.95	33.56	8.13	54.52	-1254.09
2021-2022	-576.47	47.74	2.65	73.61	3.18	36.17	4.77	31.99	-973.68
2017-2018	-6.82	100	-1.43	100	3.32	100	3.93	100	-26.36
2018-2019	-18.11	265.54	0	0	-4.35	-131.02	-47.37	-1205.34	-14.4
2019-2020	-13.68	200.58	2.65	-185.31	-4.58	-137.95	0.38	9.66	-22.21
2020-2021	-22.55	330.64	20.23	-1414.68	-5.27	-158.73	0.56	14.24	-22.22
2021-2022	-97.29	1426.5	4.73	-330.76	-7.31	-220.18	1.07	27.22	-3.39

Source: Author

Table 21.5 Percentage changes in company performance metrics over time: a comparative analysis.

National Steel (%)	Pradhin Steel	Pradhin Steel (%)	RemiEdel-stahl	RemiEdel-stahl (%)	Rishabh-Digha	Rishabh-Digha (%)	Sathava-hanaIspat	Sathava-hanaIspat (%)	Supremex	Supremex (%)
100	5.81	100	36.02	100	-0.35	100	-1778.82	100	3.28	100
86.66	5.45	93.8	35.36	98.16	1.11	-317.14	-1695.86	95.33	0.26	7.92
75.94	5.67	97.59	32.47	90.14	4.16	-1188.57	-1362.96	76.61	3.5	106.7
66.18	5.01	86.23	30.38	84.34	2.56	-731.42	-1023.25	57.52	3.36	102.43
51.38	5.7	98.1	19.88	55.19	2.07	-591.42	-760.94	42.77	3.23	98.47
100	1.74	100	0.6	100	-435.09	100	0	100	0	0
54.62	-0.94	-54.02	0.26	43.33	-63.65	0	-1218.21	279.99	2.53	0
84.25	0.42	24.13	0.13	21.66	15.88	0	-113.87	26.17	0.99	0
84.29	-5.08	-291.95	0.09	15	35.39	0	-45.68	10.49	3.18	0
12.86	0.17	9.77	-3.17	-528.33	37.74	0	-125.66	28.88	1.77	0

Source: Author

Conclusions

The extensive analysis conducted between 2017 and 2022 across various financial ratios of steel companies unravels a dynamic financial landscape characterized by noteworthy fluctuations and discernible trends. These findings offer insights into the operational and financial intricacies that impacted the companies' liquidity, profitability, and operational efficiency over the study period. The working capital turnover exhibited a volatile trajectory, ranging from 3.03 to -13.20. This fluctuation signifies the companies' inconsistent ability to efficiently utilize their working capital, leading to irregular operational cycles and potential inefficiencies in managing short-term assets and liabilities. Inventory turnover revealed a declining trend from 10.12 to 6.17, hinting at potential challenges in managing and utilizing inventory effectively. This decrease suggests a potential lag in sales relative to the available inventory, possibly signaling inefficiencies or shifts in consumer demand. Debtors turnover displayed considerable variations, ranging between 9.04 and 39.01, without a defined standard norm. This inconsistency in collecting debts might indicate diverse credit policies or challenges in managing outstanding receivables. Profitability ratios, including net profit ratio, witnessed fluctuations, declining from 7.53 to -4.66. These variations underscore the challenges in generating profits relative to revenue and highlight potential inefficiencies or increased costs affecting the companies' bottom line. The current ratio, while fluctuating between 0.99 and -0.36, consistently maintained levels above the industry standard. Despite the decline, these ratios remained above one, indicating the companies' capacity to meet short-term obligations with their current assets. Quick ratios decreased to 0.53, remaining compliant with standard norms despite the decrease. This ratio emphasizes the companies' ability to meet immediate financial demands with their most liquid assets, providing a glimpse into their financial robustness. Operating profit ratios saw a significant decline from 16.77 to 2.09, signaling potential challenges in generating profits from core operations. This decrease underscores operational inefficiencies or increased costs impacting profitability. The findings underscore the critical need for resource optimization among Indian steel companies to bolster their liquidity and profitability. A balanced financial approach, delineating long-term funding for permanent assets and short-term financing for temporary assets, emerges as a strategic imperative. This comprehensive approach aims to navigate the complexities of managing working capital, facilitating sustained growth, and mitigating the challenges posed by fluctuating financial performances across the steel industry. It offers a roadmap for these companies to address inefficiencies and challenges, fostering resilience and agility in an ever-evolving economic landscape.

References

Coase, R. H. (1937). The nature of the firm. *Economica*, 4, 386–405.

Dash, M., and Ravipati, R. (2009). Liquidity-profitability trade-off model for working capital management. Working Paper, Alliance Business School. http://papers.ssrn.com/sol3/papers.cfm?abstract_id=1408722.

Deloof, M. (2003). Does working capital management affect profitability of Belgian firms? *Journal of Business Finance and Accounting*, 30, 573–588.

Eljelly, A. M. A. (2004). Liquidity-profitability trade off: An empirical investigation in an emerging market. *International Journal Commerce and Management*, 14, 48–61.

Imran, M. A. (2008). Working capital management policies of firms: empirical evidence 2. 2.

Khatri, A. (2013). Working capital management and profitability: evidence from Ghanaian listed manufacturing firms. *Journal of Economics and International Finance*, 5(9), 373–379.

Vataliya, K. S. (2009). Practical Financial Accounting (Advance Methods, Techniques & Practices).

Yazdi, M. (2013). The relationship between working capital management and profitability: evidence from Saudi cement companies. *British Journal of Economics, Management and Trade*, 4(1), 3.

22 User preferences toward online shopping in Coimbatore district

B. Prabhu[a], S. Jegadeeswari[b], J. Sudarvel[c] and R. Velmurugan[d]

Karpagam Academy of Higher Education, Coimbatore, India

Abstract

This study delves into user preferences for online shopping in Coimbatore district, a prominent commercial hub in southern India. With the escalating prominence of e-commerce, understanding consumer choices becomes imperative. Employing a mix of quantitative and qualitative methods, a survey questionnaire explores user motivations and concerns in online purchasing decisions. Initial findings underscore convenience and time savings as primary drivers for online shopping, with product variety, competitive pricing, and easy return processes significantly shaping decision-making. Notably, electronics, clothing, and home appliances emerge as leading online sales categories. Customer feedback and vendor reliability emerge as pivotal factors influencing purchasing behavior. The study aims to furnish valuable insights for e-commerce entities, merchants, and policymakers in Coimbatore, facilitating a nuanced comprehension of consumer preferences to enhance customer satisfaction and foster increased adoption of online shopping platforms.

Keywords: Coimbatore district, consumer behavior, e-commerce, online shopping, user preferences

Introduction

The surge in global online shopping owes its momentum to the evolution of the internet and technological advancements. This phenomenon has been embraced worldwide, particularly in India, attributing to the populace's inclination towards the accessibility and convenience offered by online platforms. Coimbatore district, nestled in Tamil Nadu, follows this trend, presenting a fertile ground for e-commerce given its thriving textile industry, manufacturing sector, and educational institutions, attracting a diverse population engaged in various economic activities.

Understanding user preferences for online shopping in Coimbatore is crucial for e-commerce entities, retailers, and policymakers. This study aims to decipher what prompts consumers in the district to opt for online purchases, their preferred product categories, satisfaction levels, and potential concerns. By employing both quantitative and qualitative research methods, the study seeks to contribute to the existing knowledge on e-commerce, providing valuable insights for businesses to refine marketing strategies, enhance customer satisfaction, and cultivate brand loyalty. Policymakers can leverage these findings to formulate regulations fostering e-commerce growth while safeguarding consumer rights.

In essence, this study addresses the imperative need for comprehending Coimbatore residents' online shopping preferences, offering a knowledge foundation to inform decision-making processes and catalyze the expansion of e-commerce in the region.

Review of Literature

Table 22.1 Unlocking the digital marketplace: exploring consumer trends in online shopping for a seamless retail experience.

Author name	Study
Kavitha and Inbalakshmi (2018)	Found that with technological advancements, people increasingly prefer online shopping for its convenience. Emphasized the importance of factors like price, product quality, comparison, payment mode, and security in customer decisions. Online retailers need to be mindful of these factors for success.
Thandauthapani et al. (2021)	Highlighted the significant impact of online shopping on customers, emphasizing quick responses to inquiries and the positive effect of discounts on happiness.
Kuester (2012)	Explored consumer behavior, emphasizing the influence of psychology, sociology, and behavioral trends on purchasing decisions. Discussed how individuals, groups, and society affect decision-making in buying goods. Examined external influences beyond personal perception.

[a]prabhu4898@gmail.com, [b]sjegadeeswari15@gmail.com, cj.sudarvel@gmail.com, [d]drvelsngm@gmail.com

Author name	Study
Jigyasha and Kaur (2017)	Explored customer preferences for online shopping, highlighting advantages like low prices, time savings, and convenience. Acknowledged risks to transactional security and privacy. Contrasted with traditional shopping, this allows physical inspection and interaction but has limitations.
Raj (2016)	Found that consumers prefer online shopping due to extensive selection, significant discounts, and easy product comparison. Emphasized the importance of emphasizing cash on delivery as the respondents' preferred payment method.
Mishra and Saha (2021)	Identified primary elements driving online shopping, including Convenience, Usability, Product Availability, Price Comparison, Mode of Payment, and Advertising. Discussed popular categories for online purchases and top websites preferred by Guwahati shoppers.
Pankaj (2015)	Explored three factors—convenience, credibility, and risk—impacting online product purchases. Found that convenience and credibility positively influence consumer acceptance, while the risk factor has a negative impact.
Banu et al. (2014)	Examined factors influencing consumers' intention to make online purchases. Found no significant relationship between preferred products, general buying preferences, and gender. Concluded that key elements influencing online shopping decisions are delivery time, company reputation, accurate product descriptions, and security.

Source: Author

Problem Statement

In the backdrop of Coimbatore district's burgeoning e-commerce landscape, this study addresses the critical need to comprehend customer preferences and influencing factors in the online shopping domain. It seeks to understand the specific reasons driving residents to opt for online purchases over traditional retail, aiding businesses in tailoring strategies for customer attraction and retention. The study further delves into the preferred product categories for online purchases, enabling businesses to optimize inventory, pricing, and promotions. Exploring user satisfaction and challenges in the online shopping experience, the research aims to enhance overall satisfaction and build consumer trust. Recognizing the significance of trust and security in online decisions, the study helps businesses establish a reliable online presence. With a focus on the Coimbatore district, this region-specific research contributes unique insights, allowing businesses to cater specifically to local preferences, behaviors, and challenges. Addressing these issues provides valuable knowledge for policymakers, retailers, and e-commerce entities, fostering targeted strategies, enhanced consumer satisfaction, issue resolution, and the continued growth of the local online retail market.

Objective of the study
To identify the user preferences toward online shopping in Coimbatore district

Scope of the Study

This study aims to comprehend Coimbatore district residents' online shopping preferences, delving into drivers, product categories, happiness levels, and concerns. Focused on a diverse sample, the research combines quantitative surveys and qualitative methods like interviews and focus groups. The investigation scrutinizes decision-making processes, preferred product categories, satisfaction, and trust levels. Unique to the Coimbatore district, the study will provide tailored recommendations for e-commerce entities, merchants, and policymakers, fostering satisfaction, issue resolution, and market growth. While region-specific, the findings may offer insights applicable to similar contexts.

Research Methodology

- Primary data, vital for the study, is collected through interviews to gather detailed and specific information directly from participants, ensuring reliability using an interview schedule.
- Convenient sampling is employed when accessing the entire population is challenging, allowing quick data collection from readily available individuals. In this study, 310 online shoppers in the Coimbatore district are included.
- Analysis involves simple percentage and weighted average methods for the collected data, providing a structured framework for meaningful interpretation and conclusions.

Analysis and Interpretation

In this comprehensive analysis of online shopping preferences in the Coimbatore District, we delve into the socio-economic profile of 310 participants, examining their age, gender, education, occupation, residence, income, and online shopping habits Deepa et al. (2021). The subsequent exploration of user preferences provides a nuanced understanding of the factors influencing online shopping choices. With a focus on convenience, accessibility, and varied product categories, the study employs weighted average rank analysis to distil key insights. These findings not only offer a snapshot of consumer behavior but also furnish valuable guidance for businesses seeking to tailor their strategies to meet the unique preferences of Coimbatore's online shoppers.

- **Socio-economic profile:**
  - Majority aged between 25 and 35.
  - Predominantly female.
  - Most have undergraduate education.
  - Primarily employed in the private sector.
  - Majority reside in rural areas.
  - Mainly earn between 15001 and 40000.
  - Majority prefer shopping on Amazon.
  - Most log in to social networks daily.
  - Majority spend around 1 hour online.
  - Prefer to shop online occasionally.
  - Most have been shopping online for up to 2 years.
- **User preferences for online shopping:**
  - Convenience ranks highest in user preferences.
  - 24/7 availability is valued for online shopping.
  - Wider selection is considered a significant factor.
  - Competitive prices play a crucial role.
  - Reviews and ratings are influential.
  - Easy price comparison is appreciated.
  - Discreet purchases are valued.
  - Home delivery is essential.
  - Time-saving is a key consideration.
  - Easy payment options matter.
  - Avoiding crowds is a factor.
  - Global access is moderately important.
  - Access to exclusive products is appreciated.
  - Gift shopping made easy is considered.
  - Access to deals and discounts is valued.
  - Environmentally friendly practices matter.
  - Easier returns and refunds are crucial.
  - Comparison websites play a role.
- **Weighted average rank analysis:**
  - Convenience, time-saving, and home delivery are the top-ranked preferences.
  - Easy price comparison and easier returns and refunds are also significant.
  - Environmentally friendly practices and easy payment options are valued.

- Comparison websites and 24/7 availability play a role.
- Reviews and ratings are influential in user preferences.
- **Conclusion:**
  - User preferences for online shopping are diverse, with convenience and time-saving being the top priorities.
  - Factors like home delivery, easy price comparison, and environmentally friendly practices also influence preferences.

These insights can guide e-commerce strategies to align with user expectations, enhancing the overall online shopping experience for consumers in the Coimbatore District.

Conclusion

In light of the findings, several recommendations emerge to enhance the online shopping experience in the Coimbatore District. Firstly, a focus on convenience should guide the optimization of online platforms, emphasizing streamlined navigation, improved mobile apps, and user-friendly interfaces. Providing accessible customer service and FAQs will contribute to a positive online shopping environment. Additionally, the study underscores the importance of prompt and reliable delivery services, transparent return and refund policies, and tools for easy price comparison.

Furthermore, the research recommends offering a range of secure payment options, encouraging customer feedback, maintaining accessibility 24/7, and promoting eco-friendly practices. Customizing marketing strategies to align with the local culture and prioritizing cyber security are crucial. Lastly, forming partnerships with local businesses can contribute to community engagement.

In conclusion, this study sheds light on Coimbatore District users' preferences for online shopping, emphasizing the significance of convenience. The insights gathered provide a valuable resource for e-commerce businesses, merchants, and policymakers to tailor their approaches, fostering customer satisfaction and contributing to the growth of the online retail sector in the region. While the study is geographically specific, its findings offer universal principles adaptable to diverse online shopping landscapes. As the digital realm evolves, understanding and responding to consumer preferences will remain pivotal for sustained success in the e-commerce industry.

References

Banu, A. M., Rani, M. U., Malini, R., Idhayajothi, R., and Pavithra, G. (2014). A study on customer preference towards online shopping with special reference to Tiruchirappall district. *International Journal of Advanced Research in Management and Social Sciences,* 3(5), 205–214.

Deepa, S., Suguna, R., Sathishkumar, P., Jamunadevi, C., and Vidhya, E. N. (2021). Consumer product preference prediction towards online. *IOP Conference Series: Materials Science and Engineering,* 1055(1), 012092.

Jigyasha, D., and Kaur, J. (2017). A study on consumer preference towards online shopping and traditional shopping. *South Asian Journal of Marketing and Management Research,* 7, 5. doi:10.5958/2249-877X.2017.00017.0.

Kavitha, R., and Inbalakshmi (2018). Customers preference towards online shopping. *International Journal of Creative Research Thoughts,* 6(2).

Mishra, A. K., and Saha, A. (2021). Consumer preference and satisfaction towards online shopping in Guwahati. *Pacific Business Review (International),* 14(4).

Pankaj, Y. (2015). Acceptance of online buying in Himachal Pradesh. *International Journal of Research in Computer Application and Management,* 5(01), 106–110.

Raj, L. (2016). Customer Preferences towards Online Shopping. *Asian Journal of Advanced Basic Sciences.*

Thandauthapani, A., Karthikeyan, T., and Venkatesh, S. (2021). A study on customer preference towards online shopping platforms with special reference to Tamilnadu. *International Journal of Innovative Science and Research Technology,* 6(10).

23 Relationship among safety, health and job satisfaction in textile mills

B. Krishna Kumari and A. Martin Jayaraj[a]

Karpagam Academy of Higher Education, Coimbatore, India

Abstract

In the realm of global manufacturing, the textile industry stands as a crucial player, employing a substantial workforce. This abstract delineates the pivotal strategies implemented within textile mills to ensure the safety and well-being of employees, thereby cultivating a salubrious working atmosphere. Central to health and hygiene practices in textile mills is the meticulous upkeep of clean and sanitized working environments. Initiatives encompass routine cleaning, effective waste management, optimal ventilation, and the provision of clean water and sanitary facilities, collectively bolstering the overall welfare of employees and mitigating the risk of occupational health challenges. Emphasizing the cultivation of a positive work culture that prioritizes safety and health, the abstract underscores its far-reaching impacts, including heightened job satisfaction, augmented productivity, diminished turnover rates, and the fostering of a sustainable workforce. The study, in essence, scrutinizes the intricate interplay between safety, health, and job satisfaction within the distinctive context of textile mills.

Keywords: Coimbatore district, employee health and safety, job satisfaction, textile mills

Introduction

The labor-intensive textile industry poses challenges in worker health, safety, and job satisfaction, demanding a focus on creating secure and healthy work environments in mills. This is especially crucial due to the physical risks involved. Addressing health factors includes proper ventilation, managing chemical exposure risks, and promoting staff wellness programs to enhance physical health, reduce job-related stress, and elevate job satisfaction. Factors like work-life balance, employment autonomy, growth opportunities, and supportive management contribute significantly to employee contentment, interacting with safety and health measures. The intricate relationship between safety, health, and job happiness is evident as employee satisfaction rises with a safe workplace, fostering a positive atmosphere, trust, and loyalty. Conversely, poor safety and health conditions lead to stress, dissatisfaction, increased turnover, and reduced productivity. Recognizing this connection is vital for organizations to improve employee well-being, creating a positive work environment that safeguards welfare and cultivates a motivated and content workforce.

Review of Literature

Table 23.1 Exploring workforce well-being: insights from diverse studies on health, safety, and job satisfaction in different labour environments.

Author name	Reference	Study
Ragin (2017)	Employee health and safety in SMEs	Prioritizing employee health and safety in small and medium-sized businesses (SMEs) is crucial, especially in Africa where it is often overlooked, leading to increased incidents. Lack of managerial support in SMEs prioritizing profit over working conditions compromises worker safety.
Rumchev and Dhaliwal (2000)	Cultural differences in labour safety	Examines the impact of cultural differences on labor safety in Taiwan and Japan, highlighting distinct leadership approaches. Taiwanese practices adopt a "top-down directive" strategy, while Japanese practices focus on a "bottom-up participative" approach, encouraging employee participation in safety programs.

[a]martin.a@kahedu.edu.in

Author name	Reference	Study
Jane et al. (2014)	Job loss and health impact	Investigates the health impact of job loss due to privatization, revealing increased general practitioner visits and minor mental discomfort for those facing unstable re-employment or unemployment. Factors like financial stress, psychosocial issues, and health-related behaviors contribute to these outcomes.
Joseph. et al. (2013)	Safety practices in small enterprises	Explores how employees in small- and medium-sized businesses perceive actions to enhance workplace health and safety. Inadequate safety measures can result in serious and minor injuries, negatively impacting both organizational function and the workforce's well-being.
Upadhyay and Gupta (2021)	Employee satisfaction and welfare measures	Stresses the importance of communication in organizational welfare measures to raise employee satisfaction. Recommends prioritizing factors like motivational features, employee empowerment, and effective communication to foster a productive work environment, promoting job satisfaction and overall well-being.
Iosifidi (2016)	Environmental consciousness and labor supply	Assesses the impact of environmental consciousness on households' consumption choices and labor supply using American household survey data. Environmental awareness negatively influences labor supply, suggesting that individuals more conscious of the environment tend to employ fewer people. The study also explores the impact on consumption of pollution-causing commodities.
Godoy and Triches (2016)	Physical exercise and wages in Brazil	Investigates the relationship between physical exercise and wages in the Brazilian labor market, revealing that individuals frequently engaging in physical activity generally have better social and economic circumstances. Sedentary behavior is more prevalent among female employees, influencing wage disparities in the labor market.
Ramachandran et al. (2016)	Awareness of coronary heart disease in Singapore	Examines awareness, knowledge, and healthy lifestyle behaviors related to coronary heart disease (CHD) among Singapore's labor force. Highlights the higher susceptibility of women to CHD due to less awareness of the ailment and associated risk factors. Aims to bridge the knowledge gap and promote healthier living in the Singaporean labor force.
Laose et al. (2015)	Obesity and labour market outcomes in Canada	Investigates the association between obesity and labor market outcomes in Canada using longitudinal data. Despite the established negative link between obesity and labor results, the study aims to uncover the specific causes behind this association by analyzing comprehensive data from the National Population Health Survey in Canada over a decade.

Source: Author

Problem Statement

The inadequacy of comprehensive studies on health and safety measurement in the context of selected employees and textile firms within the British English framework poses a persistent challenge, hindering the establishment of effective safety and health measures crucial for achieving workers' safety objectives and understanding a hospital's capacity to address health and safety concerns.

Objectives of the Study

- To ascertain safety and health practices in textile mills.
- To determine the perception of demographic profile and safety and health practices.
- To examine the various safety and health factors contributing to job satisfaction.

Research Methodology

In context of this study's objectives, the researcher has employed the descriptive design. The research consists of both primary and secondary data. Data is collected from the employees of Textile Spinning Mills in Coimbatore District. 120 respondents' details were collected by using simple Random sampling method. This study applied statistical tools like ANOVA, correlation analysis and weighted average rank test to examine the data.

Analysis and Interpretations

This study investigates the nuanced perspectives of respondents on health and safety practices in firms, examining demographic influences and job satisfaction factors Alexander and Michael (2011). Utilizing ANOVA tests, correlation analyses, and weighted average rank tests, we dissect opinions based on age, gender, marital status, income, experience, education, and area of residence. Additionally, we explore the correlation between years of experience and safety climate. The weighted average rank test scrutinizes job satisfaction factors related to health and safety. These multifaceted analyses uncover intricate patterns, guiding firms towards tailored strategies to enhance health and safety practices and prioritize job satisfaction factors for a holistic approach to employee well-being.

Opinion variation in health and safety practices: an in-depth analysis

ANOVA test insights

- **Age:** No significant difference in opinion based on age groups.
- **Gender:** Opinion is consistent across genders.
- **Marital status:** Significant differences in opinion, suggesting marital status influences perceptions.
- **Income per month:** No significant variance in opinion based on income.
- **Number of years of experience:** Consistent opinion across experience levels.
- **Educational qualification:** Educational background does not lead to significant differences in opinion.
- **Area of residence:** No significant differences based on the location of residence, indicating a uniform perspective.

Conclusion: Except for marital status, demographic variables like age, gender, income, experience, education, and area of residence do not significantly impact opinions on health and safety practices in firms.

Correlation analysis on years of experience and safety climate:

- **Pearson correlation:** A positive correlation (0.245) between years of experience and safety climate opinion.
- **Significance:** The correlation is statistically significant (p = 0.007), implying a relationship.

Interpretation: Respondents with more years of experience tend to have a more positive opinion about the prevailing safety climate in firms.

Weighted average rank test on job satisfaction factors

1. **Ventilation and noise at work:** Highest ranked job satisfaction factor.
2. **Recreation facilities:** Second-highest ranked factor.
3. **Lighting and cleanliness:** Third-highest ranked factor.

4. **Shift system:** Lowest contributing factor.
5. **Promptness in payment of accident compensation:** Second-lowest contributing factor.

Insight: Job satisfaction factors related to health and safety vary, with ventilation and noise at work being the most crucial, and promptness in payment of accident compensation and shift systems being less significant.

Overall implications: This comprehensive analysis indicates that while demographic factors have limited influence on opinions regarding health and safety practices, certain job satisfaction factors carry more weight than others. Prioritizing aspects like ventilation, noise reduction, and recreation facilities can significantly enhance employee satisfaction, contributing to a healthier and safer workplace. These insights are crucial for firms aiming to optimize their health and safety strategies and improve overall employee well-being.

The study reveals that, except for marital status, demographic variables like age, gender, income, experience, education, and area of residence don't significantly influence opinions on health and safety practices. A positive correlation is identified between years of experience and the perceived safety climate in firms. Job satisfaction factors, assessed through a weighted average rank test, indicate that ventilation and noise at work, followed by recreation facilities and lighting/cleanliness, are top contributors, while promptness in payment of accident compensation and shift systems are less influential. These findings offer nuanced insights for firms aiming to enhance employee well-being and safety practices.

Findings: The findings of the study are summarized as follows. There is no difference of opinion of respondents based on all demographic variables of age, gender, income, experience, education qualification and area of residence on Safety and Health practices in firms except marital status. There is a positive correlation relation between number of years of experience of respondents and opinion on safety climate prevailing in the firms. The results of the weighted average rank discloses that the majority of the job satisfaction factors related to health and safety are ventilation and noise at work followed by Recreation facilities, lighting and cleanliness at working place. The least contributing factors are Promptness in payment of accident compensation and Shift system.

Conclusion

The study recommends that firms in the textile industry should prioritize ongoing training programs focusing on health and safety to prevent injuries and enhance overall efficiency. Creating awareness through worker training, especially for new recruits, is crucial. Specialized training on hazard identification and risk assessment can empower workers with knowledge about safety and environmental requirements. The implementation of improved 5S techniques is suggested for fostering safer and healthier organizational practices.

In conclusion, organizations are urged to prioritize comprehensive safety measures and health initiatives, including training programs, risk assessments, and the provision of necessary safety equipment. A concentrated effort on promoting employee health, ergonomic designs, and wellness initiatives is vital. By investing in safety, health, and job satisfaction, textile mills can cultivate a positive work culture that positively impacts employee well-being, engagement, and loyalty. This holistic approach leads to enhanced productivity, lower turnover rates, and a more sustainable workforce, ensuring the long-term success and resilience of textile mills in the industry.

References

Alexander and Michael (2011). Safety practices in small & medium-sized enterprises. *E3 Journal of Business Management and Economics.* ISSN 2141-7482.

Godoy, M. R., and Triches, D. (2016). Effects of physical activity on earnings in the Brazilian labor market. *EconomiA*, 18(2), 180-191. Available online 2 August 2016, In Press, Accepted Manuscript.

Iosifidi, M. (2016). Environmental awareness, consumption, and labor supply: Empirical evidence from household survey data. *Ecological Economics*, 129, 1–11.

Jane, et al. (2014). A research on employees' welfare facilities and its impact on employees' efficiency. *Journal of Research in Management and Technology*, Online ISSN-2320-0073.

Joseph, et al. (2013). A study on employees' satisfaction & safety measures. *Indian Journal of Applied Research*, 33(33), ISSN - 2249.

Larose, S. L., Kpelitse, K. A., Campbell, M. K., Zaric, G. S., and Sarma, S. (2015). Does obesity influence labour market outcomes among working-age adults? evidence from Canadian longitudinal data. *Economics and Human Biology*, 20, 26–41.

Ragin (2017). Safety management practices and safety behaviour: assessing the mediating role of safety knowledge and motivation. *Accident Analysis and Prevention*, 42, 2082–2093.

Ramachandran, H. J., Wu, V. X., He, H. G., Jiang, Y., and Wang, W. (2016). Awareness, knowledge, healthy lifestyle behaviors, and their correlates to coronary heart disease among Labour in Singapore. *Heart and Lung*, 45(4), 341–349. Alice Lee Centre for Nursing Studies, Yong Loo Lin School of Medicine, National University of Singapore, Singapore.

Rumchev and Dhaliwal (2000). Employment status and health after privatization in white collar civil. *BMJ*, 322.

Upadhyay, & Gupta (2021). Assessing occupational safety & health training. D.H.H.S [NIOSH] publication number-98-145.

and their correlates to coronary heart disease among Labour in Singapore. *Heart and Lung*, 45(4), 341–349. Alice Lee Centre for Nursing Studies, Yong Loo Lin School of Medicine, National University of Singapore, Singapore.

Rumchev, and Dhaliwal (2000). Employment status and health after privatization in white collar civil. *BMJ*, 322.

Upadhyay, & Gupta (2021). Assessing occupational safety & health training. D.H.H.S [NIOSH] publication number-98-145.

24 Impact of sales promotion techniques on consumer purchase intentions in FMCG products in Coimbatore

Dinesh Raj, K.[a], Renuka Devi, S.[b], Sudarvel, J.[c] and Velmurugan, R.[d]

Karpagam Academy of Higher Education, Coimbatore, Tamil Nadu, India

Abstract

The study investigates the impact of sales promotion strategies on consumer purchase intentions within the fast-moving consumer goods (FMCG) sector in Coimbatore. This industry, known for its rapid turnover and high demand, requires insight into consumer behavior. Findings highlight the significant influence of sales promotions on purchasing decisions. Discounts and free samples notably impact prompt purchases among consumers in Coimbatore. The research delves into mediating variables like perceived value, product necessity, and brand loyalty, offering insights into how promotions affect consumer choices. This study informs FMCG companies on tailoring strategies to meet consumer preferences, fostering deeper engagement and brand loyalty. By aligning sales promotions with consumer behavior, organizations can enhance customer engagement and drive sales in the competitive Coimbatore market.

Keywords: Employees, knit wear, work-life management

Introduction

The fast-moving consumer goods (FMCG) sector in Coimbatore relies on rapid sales and high demand, driving businesses to employ diverse promotional strategies. Coimbatore's status as a hub for FMCG products in Tamil Nadu attracts both local and global enterprises, emphasizing the need to grasp consumer behavior for effective marketing. This study dissects sales promotion tactics, such as discounts and loyalty programs, crucial for boosting sales and brand loyalty. Investigating their impact on purchasing decisions aids FMCG firms in customizing strategies for Coimbatore's competitive market, fostering enduring consumer connections and sustainable growth.

Literature Review

Table 24.1 Literature review.

Researchers	Findings
Abdelkhair et al. (2023)	Merchants found purchase intention to mediate between sales promotions and impulsive purchases, aiding in designing strategies encouraging impulse buying and enhancing retail success.
Khan et al. (2019)	Bonus packs associate with negative perceptions, often seen as lower quality goods, specifically chosen for less popular items or to counter strong competition selling higher-quality products.
Bhatti (2018)	Social media and sales promotions influence buying intentions, while discounts have minimal impact. Social media moderates the relationship between promotions and buying inclination.
Chang (2017)	Sales promotions significantly impact consumer participation and purchase intent, especially among highly involved consumers, influencing brand sentiment and increasing purchase probability. Sales promotion success hinges on consumer involvement and brand attitude, fostering engagement to boost purchase intent.
Qazi et al. (2021)	Price discounts and premiums hold the most influence on customer purchasing, surpassing other promotional techniques. All seven hypotheses' path coefficients have been verified.
Rizwan et al. (2013)	Attitudes toward price discounts and free samples significantly associate with purchase intention variations. Price discounts and free samples contribute 25% and 16%, respectively, to purchase intention. This study aids in identifying influential promotions for marketers, aiding in strategic development and competition enhancement.
Neha and Manoj (2013)	Sales promotion tools greatly affect consumer purchasing decisions, with offers having the most impact, followed by premiums and contests. Price packs and rebates show minimal influence, suggesting a need to reposition these tools to drive purchase decisions.

Source: Author

[a]dineshraj7227@gmail.com, [b]renudeepak005@gmail.com, [c]j.sudarvel@gmail.com, [d]drvelsngm@gmail.com

Table 24.2 Socio economic profile.

Age		
Up to 25 Years	96	30.19
26 – 35 Years	128	40.25
36 – 45 Years	62	19.50
Above 45 Years	32	10.06
Total	318	100
Gender		
Male	188	59.12
Female	130	40.88
Total	318	100
Educational qualification		
SSLC	18	5.66
HSC	42	13.21
UG	180	56.60
PG	78	24.53
Total	318	100
Marital Status		
Married	196	61.64
Unmarried	122	38.36
Total	318	100
Monthly income (Rs.)		
Up to 20,000	34	10.69
20,000 - 30,000	120	37.74
30,000 – 50,000	96	30.19
Above 50,000	68	21.38
Total	318	100
Profession		
Government employee	12	3.77
Private employee	124	38.99
Business	94	29.56
Professional	28	8.81
Home maker	20	6.29
Others	40	12.58
Total	318	100
Area of residence		
Urban	140	44.03
Semi urban	92	28.93
Rural	86	27.04
Total	318	100

Source: Author

Table 24.3 KMO and Bartlett's test.

Kaiser-Meyer-Olkin measure of sampling adequacy.		.867
Bartlett's test of sphericity	Approx. Chi-square	5013.398
	Df	496
	Sig.	.000

Source: Author

Problem Statement

The focus within Coimbatore's FMCG sector lies in leveraging sales promotions to influence consumer purchase intentions effectively. While these promotions drive rapid sales and brand loyalty, understanding their impact on consumer behavior is crucial. This study aims to uncover consumers' perceptions of different sales strategies and their influence on FMCG purchases in Coimbatore. It explores which promotions garner positivity, skepticism, or indifference and how these strategies shape quick buying decisions. By addressing these questions, it aims to guide FMCG companies in tailoring more impactful sales programs. This insight will align marketing efforts with consumer preferences, bolster engagement, and fortify brand loyalty in this competitive market. The study's outcomes promise to enhance understanding of consumer behavior and sales promotions, benefiting both academia and business.

Objective of this study is to discern how sales promotion techniques affect customers' purchase intentions.

Scope

The study explored how sales promotions impact FMCG purchase intentions in Coimbatore. Focusing on various FMCG categories and tactics like rebates and free samples, it examined consumer perceptions across demographics. Insights into brand loyalty's influence on purchase decisions and its effect on brand perception were highlighted. Providing actionable strategies for Coimbatore's FMCG firms, the study aimed to bolster customer engagement and refine promotions. While specific to Coimbatore, its broader applicability requires further investigation. Nonetheless, it serves as a valuable guide for marketers and businesses, enriching our understanding of consumer behavior and sales promotions in Coimbatore's FMCG domain.

Methodology

The research method primarily involves collecting firsthand data through interviews, ensuring

Table 24.4 Principal components analysis (PCA).

Rotated component matrix[a]

	Component						
	1	2	3	4	5	6	7
I don't take sales promotion schemes into consideration when purchasing products	.765						
I'm not particularly interested in sales promotion schemes	.728						
I believe that sales promotion schemes shape the product's image	.705						
I am usually aware of the sales promotion schemes of the products I purchase	.601						
I usually don't bother being aware of sales promotion schemes	.588						
Sales promotion schemes are beneficial to me	.	.695					
I think customers should not pay too much attention to sales promotion schemes while purchasing products		.642					
Sales promotion schemes mislead customers into purchasing lower-quality products		.614					
Products with sales promotion schemes are often of good quality		.565					
I don't give much thought to sales promotion schemes		.514					
I enjoy trying products with sales promotion schemes		.508					
If I see people purchasing products with sales promotion schemes, I consider them rational			.703				
Companies often offer sales promotion schemes when they are unable to sell products			.688				
I have often found that sales promotion schemes are available for not-so-good products			.668				
Sales promotion schemes are designed with consideration for customers' needs			.636				
I prefer to purchase products with sales promotion schemes			.556				
I have found that knowing about sales promotion schemes doesn't make a difference in my purchase decisions				.741			
I usually judge products based on their merits rather than considering sales promotion schemes				.627			
I believe it is essential to be aware of the sales promotion schemes				.573			
A sales promotion scheme can make a product more popular				.573			
Good products tend to have more frequent sales promotions				.507			
Price-based sales promotions can have a negative impact on our brand image				.503			
Regularly using sales promotions is likely to have a long-term positive effect on consumer perceptions					.771		
Utilizing sales promotions helps us build a more secure distribution network					.759		

Rotated component matrix[a]

	Component						
	1	2	3	4	5	6	7
Price-based promotions might affect the perceived quality of our product					.721		
Consumers show significant involvement when purchasing our product					.611		
Sales promotion has a positive effect on our brand image					.142	.773	
Overusing price-based promotions may harm our brand equity						.769	
Price-based sales promotions make our customers more deal-prone						.553	
Regularly using price-based sales promotions could have a long-term negative effect on consumers' perceptions						.544	
Utilizing sales promotion helps us increase awareness						.415	.596
Generally, people are aware of sales promotion schemes for popular products							.582
Total	10.376	2.3189	1.8748	1.7811	1.3037	1.1645	1.0983
% of Variance	32.425	7.246	5.858	5.566	4.074	3.639	3.432
Cumulative %	32.425	39.672	45.531	51.097	55.171	58.810	62.242

Source: Author

consistency and reliability in responses. Employing convenient sampling, data were gathered from 316 customers in Coimbatore Table 24.4. Analysis was conducted using simple percentages and factor analysis. The study's significance lies in revealing insights into customer preferences and behaviors towards FMCG sales promotions, aiding businesses in crafting targeted marketing campaigns. It provides fact-based insights for Coimbatore's FMCG firms to enhance promotional planning, build brand loyalty, and gain a competitive edge. Ultimately, this research advances consumer behavior and marketing knowledge, benefiting both businesses and consumers in Coimbatore's FMCG market.

The impact of sales promotion techniques on customers' purchase intentions was analyzed based on the socio-economic profile of respondents. Most respondents were aged 26-35 (40.25%), followed by those under 25 (30.19%), 36-45 (19.50%), and over 45 (10.06%). Males dominated (59.12%) over females (40.88%). The educational breakdown was undergraduates (56.60%), postgraduates (24.53%), HSC holders (13.21%), and SSLC graduates (5.66%). Married respondents prevailed (61.64%) compared to unmarried (38.36%). Income-wise, the range of 20,000 - 30,000 Rs. had the highest respondents (37.74%). Predominantly, private employees (38.99%) participated. Urban residents constituted

44.03%, followed by semi-urban (28.93%) and rural (27.04%) residents. Analyzing the Kaiser-Meyer-Olkin statistic (0.867) and Bartlett's test of sphericity (p-value 0.000, statistic 5013.398), the collected data is deemed suitable for factor analysis, demonstrating the impact of sales promotions on customer purchase intentions.

Conclusion

The component analysis identified factors strongly influencing purchase intention due to sales promotion techniques in the Coimbatore district. Key aspects included customers' varying attitudes toward promotions, impacts on brand equity, and perceived product quality. Factor one held a significant 32.425% contribution, followed by others at 7.246% to 3.432%, totaling 62.242% across seven factors. Suggestions for businesses encompass tailoring promotions to diverse customer segments, emphasizing product quality, and employing a balanced mix of promotions, especially avoiding overuse of price-based strategies. Additionally, vigilance on competitor promotions, ethical practices, and clear communication were advised. Implementing these could elevate brand loyalty, enhance market competitiveness, and foster growth in the Coimbatore FMCG sector. The study's implications revealed consumer preferences, encouraging transparent promotions and underscoring product value. Businesses should navigate carefully when utilizing price-based promotions to avoid diluting brand equity. Segmenting customers, understanding long-term promotion impacts, and staying updated on consumer trends were recommended for sustained success.

This research, illuminating consumer behavior nuances, serves as a valuable resource for FMCG firms and marketers, providing insights for effective promotional campaigns and fostering consumer relationships in Coimbatore. The study suggests potential avenues for future research, including longitudinal studies, qualitative assessments, and investigations into online and culturally sensitive marketing's impact on consumer behavior.

References

Abdelkhair, F. Y., Babekir, M. Y., Mudawi, S. S., and Abiad, A. B. A. A. (2023). Sales promotion and impulse buying behavior towards consumer goods: the mediating role of purchase intention. *Indian Journal of Marketing*, 53(2), 26–42.

Bhatti, A. (2018). Sales promotion and price discount effect on consumer purchase intention with the moderating role of social media in Pakistan, science arena publications. *International Journal of Business Management*, 3(4), 50–58.

Chang, A. Y. P. (2017). A Study on the effects of sales promotion on consumer involvement and purchase intention in tourism industry. *EURASIA Journal of Mathematics, Science and Technology Education*, 13(12), 8323–8330.

Khan, M., Tanveer, A., and Zubair, D. S. S. (2019). Impact of sales promotion on consumer buying behavior: a case of modern trade, Pakistan (June 30, 2019). Impact of sales promotion on consumer buying behavior: a case of modern trade, Pakistan. *Governance and Management Review*, 4(1), 38–53. Available at SSRN: https://ssrn.com/abstract=3441058.

Neha, S., and Manoj, V. (2013). Impact of sales promotion tools on consumer's purchase decision towards white good (refrigerator) at Durg and Bhilai region of CG, India. *Research Journal of Management Sciences*, 2(7), 10–14.

Qazi, E. F., Muzaffar, S., Khan, A. A., and Basit, A. (2021). Offer to buy: the effectiveness of sales promotional tools towards purchase intention. *Bulletin of Business and Economics*, 10(3), 33–42.

Rizwan, M., Irshad, Q., Ali, K., Nadir, M., and Ejaz, M. (2013). Impact of sales promotional tools on purchase intention. *International Journal of Management Sciences and Business Research*, 2(1), 36–49.

25 Employee attrition toward textile industries in Karur district

S. Navaneshwaran[a], J. Sudarvel[b], Shrie Bhubaneswari[c] and R. Velmurugan[d]
Karpagam Academy of Higher Education, Coimbatore, Tamil Nadu, India

Abstract

This study investigates employee attrition in Karur's textile sector, a significant manufacturing hub in Tamil Nadu, India. Utilizing mixed methods, including surveys, interviews, and data analysis, the research explores the intricate factors behind employee turnover. Economic fluctuations, work conditions, career prospects, and organizational culture are among the aspects scrutinized. Findings stress the need for targeted strategies to enhance talent retention and highlight the role of proactive human resource management. The study underscores the impact of attrition on productivity, employee well-being, and industry growth. It advocates collaborative efforts involving businesses, government, and industry associations for an inclusive and supportive environment. The study aims to provide actionable insights for stakeholders, aiding the development of interventions to mitigate attrition and nurture a stable workforce in Karur's textile industry.

Keywords: Employee attrition, Karur and turnover, textile industries

Introduction

Karur's textile industry, a cornerstone of Tamil Nadu's economy, grapples with a pressing concern—high employee attrition. This phenomenon, characterized by the frequent departure of workers in pursuit of better opportunities, poses challenges such as reduced productivity and heightened training expenses. In the context of Karur's cyclical textile demand and evolving market dynamics, comprehending the intricate reasons behind employee turnover becomes paramount.

This study delves into the multifaceted factors influencing attrition, considering economic shifts, technological advancements, and the physical demands of the sector. Beyond mere identification, the research aspires to propose targeted solutions, offering a valuable resource for stakeholders, including employers, policymakers, and industry associations. By addressing the root causes, this study aims to provide actionable insights that contribute to employee satisfaction, retention, and the sustained growth of Karur's vital textile industry.

Review of Literature

Table 25.1 Unveiling the tapestry: insights into employee attrition in Karur's textile industry comprehensive exploration of causes and solutions.

Author	Study	Findings
Mohan (2023)	Research on attrition factors	Identifies primary elements contributing to attrition, emphasizing organizational culture, job performance, workload, environment, and welfare programs. Recommends fostering a work atmosphere that supports career growth, recognition, rewards, and a warm working environment.
Harini and Anandan (2023)	Study on attrition reasons	Attributes attrition to increased job pressure, discrimination, and lower pay. Suggests retention methods such as fair performance evaluation, welfare policies, wage increases, awards, and recognition.
Sultana and Poala (2020)	Investigation on perceived criteria in textile business	Reveals a significant gap in mean rankings related to perceived criteria influencing employee retention in the textile industry.
Krishnamoorthy et al. (2020)	Survey on employee attrition	Identifies discontent with pay, poor working conditions, improper management behavior, lack of career advancement as leading causes of employee attrition.

[a]21MBAP035@kahedu.edu.in, [b]j.sudarvel@gmail.com, [c]shrie.bhubaneswari@gmail.com, [d]drvelsngm@gmail.com

Author	Study	Findings
Banerjee (2019)	Analysis on employee satisfaction	Highlights dissatisfaction with compensation schemes as a major concern. Recommends thorough planning, improved communication, and initiatives to enhance working conditions, pay, benefits, and social security.
Delphenraj (2019)	Research on attrition reasons	Points out money and career advancement prospects as the main reasons for employee turnover.
Umamaheswari et al. (2017)	Study on employee motivation	Notes that employees are motivated by the firm but are uneasy with the compensation packages. Some express dissatisfaction with TTL or TGL.
Hayes (2016)	Investigation on turnover intentions	Establishes a substantial correlation between age, income, and turnover intentions. Recommends pay-for-performance initiatives to reduce turnover, decrease work stress, promote family well-being, and increase engagement in social and civic activities.

Source: Author

Problem Statement

High employee attrition rates pose a significant challenge to Karur's textile industry, impacting productivity, operational efficiency, and overall competitiveness. The complex interplay of factors such as economic fluctuations, cyclical demand patterns, physically demanding work conditions, and limited opportunities for career advancement contribute to this urgent concern. The industry's instability and job insecurity during uncertain periods, coupled with poor working conditions, insufficient safety measures, and the absence of opportunities for professional growth, further exacerbate attrition.

Additionally, uncompetitive compensation packages, inadequate work-life balance, a lack of organizational flexibility, and poor leadership contribute to discontent and employee turnover. The study aims to thoroughly investigate and comprehend these multifaceted issues, proposing evidence-based strategies to address the root causes of attrition and foster a supportive and engaging work environment. The ultimate goal is to enhance employee satisfaction, establish a stable and motivated workforce, and promote the sustained growth of Karur's textile industry.

Objective of the Study

To identify the reasons for employee attrition

Scope of the Study

The study on employee attrition in Karur's textile industry is sharply focused, aiming to explore factors influencing attrition. Encompassing various textile production units and employee levels, it includes perspectives from entry-level workers to senior executives, employers, and HR specialists. The study evaluates economic conditions, work environment, career opportunities, compensation, work-life balance, organizational culture, job insecurity, and technological impacts. Ethically conducted, the research will propose evidence-based recommendations to reduce attrition in the Karur textile industry, staying within realistic scope and resource constraints while generating valuable insights on this pervasive issue.

Research Methodology

- Data collection: The study primarily relies on gathering firsthand information through interviews, ensuring detailed insights directly from participants.
- Interview schedule: A structured interview schedule promotes consistency in questioning, yielding standardized responses and enhancing the reliability of collected data.

Sampling and sample size:

- Convenient sampling: When accessing the entire population is challenging, this approach proves useful. It facilitates swift data collection from readily available individuals.
- Sample size: Employing convenient sampling, data from 450 employees in the Karur's textile industry are included in the study.

Framework of Analysis

The collected have been analyzed by employing simple percentage and factor analysis.

Significance of the Study

The study on employee attrition in Karur's textile sector is crucial for stakeholders, offering insights and practical applications. Understanding attrition's causes can enhance industry competitiveness and stability, reducing recruitment costs and fostering a dedicated workforce. It sheds light on worker preferences, enabling tailored retention strategies to improve job satisfaction. This knowledge informs industry groups and policymakers about challenges, guiding efforts for talent retention. High attrition rates hinder the textile sector's long-term viability, impacting the local economy. Discovering effective retention practices can serve as industry benchmarks, fostering progress and knowledge exchange. The study enriches HRM and attrition knowledge, benefiting academics and supporting regional development goals by addressing attrition challenges. Its significance lies in fostering a stable, engaged, and sustainable textile industry for the well-being of stakeholders and the local economy.

Analysis and Interpretation

In exploring the intricate landscape of employee attrition in Karur's textile sector, a comprehensive socioeconomic profile lays the foundation. Analyzing demographic factors such as gender, age, marital status, educational background, monthly income, and work experience provides a nuanced understanding of the workforce. Additionally, employing factor analysis to uncover the reasons behind attrition unveils a myriad of influential factors. The data's suitability for this analysis, indicated by the Kaiser-Meyer-Olkin measure and Bartlett's Test, strengthens the study's credibility. This section delves into the profound insights gleaned from both the socioeconomic profile and factor analysis, unravelling the complexities of employee attrition in the Karur's textile industry.

Socioeconomic Profile:

Gender: Male: 276 respondents (61.3%)
Female: 174 respondents (38.7%)
Total: 450 respondents (100%)

Age: Up to 25 years: 66 respondents (14.7%)
25 - 30 years: 198 respondents (44%)
31 - 35 years: 111 respondents (24.7%)
36 - 40 years: 45 respondents (10%)
Above 40 years: 30 respondents (6.7%)
Total: 450 respondents (100)

Marital status: Married: 240 respondents (53.3%)
Unmarried: 210 respondents (46.7%)
Total: 450 respondents (100%)

Educational qualification: Illiterate: 72 respondents (16%)
HSC: 228 respondents (50.7%)
UG (Undergraduate): 72 respondents (16%)

PG (Postgraduate): 21 respondents (4.7%)
Others: 57 respondents (12.7%)
Total: 450 respondents (100)

Monthly income: Below Rs.10,000: 33 respondents (7.3%)
Rs. 10,00115,000: 156 respondents (34.7%)
Rs. 15,00120,000: 204 respondents (45.3%)
Above Rs. 20,000: 57 respondents (12.7%)
Total: 450 respondents (100)

Experience: Below 5 years: 138 respondents (30.7%)
6 years10 years: 213 respondents (47.3%)
11 years15 years: 57 respondents (12.7%)
16 years20 years: 27 respondents (6%)
Above 20 years: 15 respondents (3.3%)
Total: 450 respondents (100)

Reasons for employee attrition: The collected data is suitable for factor analysis based on the Kaiser-Meyer-Olkin (KMO) measure (0.781) and Bartlett's test of sphericity (Chi-square: 23194.497, Sig: 0.000). This indicates the data's appropriateness for identifying reasons for employee attrition.

Factors contributing to attrition:
- Burnout and stress
- Poor communication within the organization
- job insecurity
- Inadequate training and development opportunities
- Office Politics and Favoritism
- Discrimination and harassment
- Inflexible work hours or schedules
- Relocation of family
- Commute and transportation issues
- Lack of challenging or meaningful work
- Company mergers or acquisitions
- Lack of recognition and rewards
- Boredom or monotony in job role
- Limited opportunities for advancement
- Lack of social support at work
- Job dissatisfaction among peers
- Inadequate employee benefits
- Unresolved grievances and complaints
- Demographic and generational differences
- High employee turnover in the organization
- Lack of diversity and inclusion initiatives
- Inadequate work equipment and resources
- Better job opportunities elsewhere
- Layoffs and downsizing
- Work-life balance
- Leadership and management
- Workload and overburdening

- Company reputation and image
- Unfair performance evaluations
- Limited flexibility for remote work
- Perceived job insecurity
- Lack of autonomy and decision-making power
- Inadequate work-life balance policies
- Retirement
- Insufficient work-life integration
- Employee engagement
- Career growth and development
- Personal health or medical concerns
- Unhealthy workplace relationships
- Dissatisfaction with job stability
- Lack of trust in leadership
- Ineffective conflict resolution
- Work environment and physical conditions
- Lack of team collaboration and support
- Job dissatisfaction
- Job fit and role clarity
- Compensation and benefits
- Salary
- Personal problems of employees
- Organizational culture
- Lack of ethical practices within the organization

Factor analysis results:
Factor 1: Contributes 37.225%
Factor 2 to factor 13: Contribute cumulatively to 76.114%

The identified factors significantly contribute to the reason for employee attrition. Addressing these factors can lead to a more stable and engaged workforce, positively impacting the textile industry in Karur. The findings reveal a demographic tapestry of the textile workforce in Karur, illustrating factors like gender distribution, age demographics, marital status, educational qualifications, income levels, and work experience. Factor analysis identifies significant contributors to employee attrition, encompassing issues like burnout, poor communication, job insecurity, and more. The cumulative impact of these factors highlights their substantial role, explaining 76.114% of the variance in attrition. These insights substantiate the multifaceted nature of attrition, guiding interventions for a more stable, engaged, and sustainable textile industry in Karur. The study offers a nuanced understanding, equipping stakeholders with actionable data for informed decision-making.

Conclusion

In conclusion, this study on employee attrition in Karur's textile industries uncovers crucial insights into the multifaceted challenges faced by the sector. The findings underscore the intricate interplay of demographic factors, workplace dynamics, and personal issues contributing to attrition. Addressing this issue requires a comprehensive approach, as suggested by the extensive list of recommendations. Implementing employee engagement programs, fostering work-life balance, providing career development opportunities, and nurturing a supportive organizational culture emerge as key strategies to combat attrition. The study not only serves as a guide for textile businesses in Karur but also holds relevance for academics, industry stakeholders, and policymakers aiming to fortify the textile industry's foundation in the region.

Furthermore, the research suggests promising avenues for future exploration. Longitudinal studies, qualitative analyses, and a deeper understanding of technological impacts on turnover provide exciting prospects. The study's comprehensive nature offers a roadmap for targeted interventions, setting the stage for ongoing efforts to enhance employee satisfaction, retention, and the sustained growth of Karur's textile sector.

References

Banerjee, A. (2019). Failure of employee retention and its consequences on organization through content analysis. *International Journal of Research Granthaalyah-Knowledge Repository,* 7(3), 200–207.

Delphenraj, R. (2019). A study on employee attrition in natura tex pvt ltd Tirupur. *Think India Journal,* 22(14), 1628–1634.

Harini, M., and Christi Anandan, C. R. (2023). Factors influencing attrition and retention: an empirical analysis in a textile industry. *Journal of Academia and Industrial Research (JAIR),* 11(3), 60–64.

Hayes, T. M. (2016). Demographic characteristics predicting employee turnover intentions. Doctoral Thesis submitted to Walden University, Minneapolis, United States of America.

Krishnamoorthy, P., and Ramprathap, K. (2020). A study on employee attrition and retention techniques at the textile industry with reference to Karur District, Tamilnadu. *International Journals of Creative Research Thoughts,* 8(7), 2748–2752, ISSN:2320-2882.

Mohan, K. (2023). A study one employees attrition level of textile industry in Coimbatore district. *International Journal of Current Science (IJCSPUB),* 13(3), 418–429.

Nishath Sultana, A., and Poala, J. I. (2020). A study on employee retention strategies in textile industry. *International Research Journal of Modernization in Engineering Technology and Science,* 2(10).

Umamaheswari, S., Thirumalai Kumar, R., and Saranya Jegajothi, S. (2017). Early attrition and retention strategies of apparel industries with special reference to North Chennai. *International Journal of Science and Technology and Management,* 6(2), 6–16.

26 A study on consumer brand awareness toward branded Dhall products with reference to Salem

D. Sundharamoorthi[a], P. Easwaran[b] and N. Sivakrithika[c]

Karpagam Academy of Higher Education, Coimbatore, Tamil Nadu, India

Abstract

In today's global market, brand awareness stands as a pivotal factor determining a brand's success. Companies employ diverse metrics to gauge brand awareness, recognizing its profound influence on consumer purchasing behavior. This research delved into consumer perceptions of the brand 'Dhall' through a targeted survey. Most Dhall mills are strategically positioned near populous cities like Kolkata, Chennai, Mumbai, Hyderabad, and Delhi, as well as in pulse-rich regions like Indore, Jalgaon, Akola, and Nagpur across India. The lack of effective branding poses a significant challenge in marketing and selling Dhall products for these mills. To address this issue, the study gathered data from 120 respondents, using statistical tools such as simple percentage analysis, Chi-square, and Anova. The investigation aimed to understand Consumer Brand Awareness and suggests actionable recommendations to bolster awareness for branded Dhall.

Keywords: Brand, consumer awareness and preference, Dhall

Introduction

Consumer brand awareness gauges the extent to which individuals can recall or recognize a brand across different scenarios. It's a blend of knowledge about a brand comprising two aspects, impacted by consumer behavior, advertising strategies, and brand management. Purchasing decisions heavily rely on consumers' ability to identify or recall a brand, requiring familiarity with both the product category and the brand itself. Increased brand awareness often predicts brand success.

Consumer information gathering isn't solely from advertisements; it encompasses multiple sources shaping purchase decisions. As consumers explore a category, they expand their awareness of various brands, leading to alterations in their awareness sets. Empirical research suggests contemplation sets are usually three times larger than the evoked sets.

The Dhall milling industry is a significant sector in India's agricultural processing. Nearly 75% of the country's 13.19 million tons of pulses annually undergo processing in Dall mills. From roughly 2000 mills in 1972, the count steadily increased to 14,000 by 1999-2000. India boasts around 125 Dhall mill associations, with notable concentrations in Chennai, Maharashtra, and Delhi.

The objective of this study explores how familiarity influences initial purchases in a new culture and its impact on buying behavior.

Table 26.1 Literature review.

Author	Key points
Hans van (2017)	Demonstrates variation in customer product awareness. Factors like aspirations, communication methods, and education significantly influence ingredient awareness.
Percy et al. (2017)	Brand awareness arises from presenting brands that stimulate recognition, recall, and familiarity among consumers.
Chen and Wang (2018)	Defines brand loyalty as an ongoing ethical purchase process. It influences consumer preference, purchase intent, and financial success for the business.
Srinvasan, Park (2018)	Brand awareness includes knowledge of attributes, benefits, thoughts, and experiences tied to a brand. These inform ongoing interactions and consumer understanding.
Lee and Wu (2019)	Brand identity reflects a brand's distinct traits setting it apart from competitors.
Engel et al. (2020)	Brand image is the amalgamation of tangible and intangible associations of a brand, impacting equity, loyalty, buying behavior, and brand performance.

[a]21mbap056@kahedu.edu.in, [b]easwar83@gmail.com, [c]sivakrithika.nellaiappan@kahedu.edu.in

Author	Key points
Geetha (2021)	Explores brand perception, awareness, and factors influencing brand loyalty among consumers of various food brands. Suggests price reduction to attract consumers.
Kalaiselvi (2021)	Examines perception and preferences of branded household food items, highlighting gender-specific differences. Emphasizes advertising for increasing consumer awareness.
Aaker (2021)	Divides loyalty into various categories and links it to consumer-based brand value, showcasing how brand perception is shaped by underlying values.
Keller (2022)	Brand awareness is the ability to recognize a brand in different scenarios. Customer experiences and familiarity shape brand retention in consumers' minds.

Source: Author

Table 26.2 ANOVA: Research Methodology.

Basic	Particulars	No. of respondents	Percentage (%)
Gender	Male	49	40.8%
	Female	71	59.2%
Age	18-20	3	2.5%
	21-30years	81	67.5%
	31-40years	24	20.0%
	41 –50 years	9	7.5%
	Above 51	3	2.5%
Marital status	Single	57	47.5%
	Married	63	52.5%
Educational qualification	Higher secondary	6	5.0%
	High school	16	13.3%
	Under graduate	59	49.2%
	Post graduate	39	32.5%
Occupation	Business man	7	5.8%
	Professional	40	24.2%
	Unemployment	43	28.3%
	Others	30	41.7%
Monthly income	Below \Rs.10000	7	5.8%
	Rs.1000019000	40	33.3%
	Rs.2000029000	43	35.8%
	Rs. 3500039000	30	25.0%

Source: Author

Research Methodology

A research technique is a systematic method for addressing research problems. This study involved several steps in analyzing the research problem, along with the rationale. To explore the issue, a descriptive study was conducted, focusing on the nature of the investigation. Both primary and secondary information were utilized in this study, involving a sample of 120 respondents. Statistical tools such as simple percentage analysis, chi-square analysis, and ANOVA were employed in this study.

Interpretation

The F-value of 916.187 confirms acceptance of H1, indicating a significant relationship between

Table 26.3 Chi-square test results for various demographic factors vs. preferences.

Hypothesis	Test type	Value	df	Asymp. Sig. (2-sided)
Gender vs. preference	Pearson Chi-square	2.491	2	0.288
	Likelihood ratio	2.641	2	0.267
	Linear-by-linear	1.658	1	0.198
Age vs. preference	Pearson Chi-square	4.885	8	0.77
	Likelihood ratio	6.793	8	0.559
	Linear-by-linear	2.773	1	0.096
Marital status vs. preference	Pearson Chi-square	4.201	2	0.122
	Likelihood ratio	4.28	2	0.118
	Linear-by-linear	4.166	1	0.041
Education vs. preference	Pearson Chi-sSquare	22.84	6	0.001
	Likelihood ratio	18.895	6	0.004
	Linear-by-linear	0.782	1	0.377
Occupation vs. preference	Pearson Chi-square	6.39	6	0.381
	Likelihood ratio	7.089	6	0.313
	Linear-by-linear	0.048	1	0.827
Monthly income vs. preference	Pearson Chi-square	9.328	6	0.156
	Likelihood ratio	8.364	6	0.213
	Linear-by-linear	3.983	1	0.046

Source: Author

respondents' monthly income and their perception of the product's brand ($p < 0.05$). The study finds no correlation between branded Dhall awareness and age, marital status, education, occupation, or monthly income Betteman and Park, Boyland and Whalen (2015), Ustjanauskas et al. (2014), Nyilasy et al. (2016). ANOVA analysis links respondents' income to brand preference Jones and Kervin (2011), Remar et al. (2016). Recommendations include enhancing promotional techniques, adapting pricing strategies, product enhancement, impactful advertising, introducing new detergent varieties, involving a VIP as a brand ambassador, and employing compelling logos or taglines for advertising and promotion Vassalos and Lim (2016).

Conclusion

Food companies facing fierce competition must enhance their products and focus on innovative sales promotion techniques to boost sales. Developing effective marketing strategies will aid in retaining current markets and expanding into new ones. Maintaining quality, competitive pricing, diverse offerings, and strong brand awareness among customers are critical factors for sustained success in the food industry.

References

Aaker (2021). The measurement and dimensionality of brand association. *Journal of Product and Brand Management*, 9(6), 350–368.

Betteman and Park. Branding and brand equity. 130–161.

Boyland, E. J., and Whalen, R. (2015). Food advertising to children and its e_ects on diet: review of recent prevalence and impact data. *Pediatric Diabetes*, 16, 331–337.

Chen and Wang (2018). Decline and variability in brand boyalty. *International Journal of Research in Marketing*, 14(5), 405–420.

Engel, Blackwell and Miniard (2020). Brand image strategy affects brand equity after M&A. *European Journal of Marketing*, 45(7/8), 1091–1111.

Geetha (2021). Brand awareness in the business to business market. *Industrial Marketing Management*, 33, 371–380.

Hans van (2017). Understanding brand equity for successful brand awareness. *Journal of Consumer Marketing*, 12(4), 51.

Jones, S. C., and Kervin, L. (2011). An experimental study on the e_ects of exposure to magazine advertising on children's food choices. *Public Health Nutrition*, 14, 1337–1344.

Kalaiselvi (2021). Measuring brand awareness across products and markets. *California Management Review*, 38(3), 102–120, 174.

Keller (2022). Brand Awareness of packed food-a study of urban consumers. *International Journal of Enhanced Research in Management and Computer Applications*, 4(6), 29–35.

Lee and Wu (2019). Effects of brand awareness on choice for a common, repeat-purchase product. 17(September), 141–148.

Nyilasy, G., Lei, J., Nagpal, A., and Tan, J. (2016). Colour correct: the interactive e_ects of food label nutrition colouring schemes and food category healthiness on health perceptions. *Public Health Nutrition*, 19, 2122–2127.

Percy et al. (2017). Managing Brand Equity Capitalizing on the Value of a Brand Name. New York: Free Press.

Remar, D., Campbell, J., and DiPietro, R. B. (2016). The impact of local food marketing on purchase decision and willingness to pay in a foodservice setting. *Journal of Foodservice Business Research*, 19, 89–108.

Srinvasan Park (2018). Awareness, image, branding & benchmarking marketing research studies.

Ustjanauskas, A. E., Harris, J. L., and Schwartz, M. B. (2014). Food and beverage advertising on children's web sites. *Pediatric Obesity*, 9, 362–372.

Vassalos, M., and Lim, K. H. (2016). Farmers' willingness to pay for various features of electronic food marketing platforms. *International Food and Agribusiness Management Review*, 19, 131–149.

27 Employee perception toward green logistics and sustainability

P.T. Sriram, II[a], M. Dhivya Dharshini and Arul Kumar, M[b]

Karpagam Academy of Higher Education, Coimbatore, Tamil Nadu, India

Abstract

In this comprehensive investigation, we inquire into the perceptions of employees regarding green logistics, a pivotal strategy in addressing contemporary environmental challenges within the logistics sector. The study employs a mixed-methods approach to scrutinize the intricate dynamics of employee attitudes, behaviors, and involvement in green logistics across diverse industries and organizational contexts. By combining quantitative surveys and qualitative interviews, the research elucidates how employee comprehension of sustainable practices is shaped by awareness and education. It also examines the impact of tangible rewards on employee impressions, highlighting the role of individual and group incentives. Furthermore, the study explores the factors influencing employee engagement in green logistics, including perceptions of reduced environmental impact, financial savings, and enhanced corporate reputation. The research meticulously addresses the obstacles and challenges faced by employees during the adoption of eco-friendly practices, elucidating the difficulties associated with the transition to sustainability. Ultimately, the findings furnish valuable insights for businesses seeking to align employee engagement with organizational goals, fostering a culture of sustainability in the logistics sector.

Keywords: Employee perception, green logistics and sustainability

Introduction

In recent years, the global community has increasingly acknowledged the imperative of sustainable practices, particularly in the domain of logistics, to address environmental concerns. Even in Coimbatore, a prominent industrial city in India, similar environmental challenges persist. Balancing economic growth with ecological preservation is vital, necessitating the integration of green logistics and sustainability as local businesses and industries continue to thrive. This analytical study focuses on comprehensively examining employee perceptions of sustainable practices and green logistics specific to the Coimbatore context. Encompassing diverse industries like manufacturing, textiles, engineering, and services, Coimbatore's economic strength significantly impacts its local ecology. To grasp how employees engage with sustainability, the study employs a mixed-methods approach, combining quantitative surveys and qualitative interviews. It aims to reveal the intricacies of employee attitudes, awareness, and challenges in adopting green logistics practices. By exploring social dynamics and leadership influence, the research seeks to provide actionable insights for academia and the local business community, fostering sustainable practices in Coimbatore that align with both traditional values and modernization efforts. The ultimate aim is to identify variables shaping employee perceptions and pave the way for a prosperous and environmentally conscious future in the city.

Problem Statement

The logistics sector faces challenges in aligning its workforce's diverse views on green initiatives. Ranging from support to skepticism, influenced by environmental awareness and operational concerns, these varied perspectives hinder coordinated efforts. The absence of a standardized approach exacerbates the issue, requiring effective management to transition smoothly to eco-friendly practices. This study aims to understand and mitigate employee perceptions, enhancing the industry's capacity for sustainable practices.

Objectives

- To identify the employee perception toward green logistics.

Scope of the Study

This study extensively investigates employee perspectives on green logistics in the logistics industry, considering factors like leadership commitment, operational concerns, financial implications, and environmental awareness. It aims to analyze both

---

[a]saikutti1997@gmail.com, [b]rmarul1992@gmail.com

positive and negative aspects, offering insights into practical strategies for overcoming obstacles and fostering favorable impressions. The research explores a spectrum of employee views, emphasizing the impact of environmental awareness, communication, and training in shaping perceptions. It evaluates the influence of organizational culture and leadership commitment, providing insights for enhancing sustainable supply chain management practices in the logistics industry.

Research Methodology

- Primary data is essential for this study, gathered through interviews to obtain detailed information directly from participants using standardized questions for reliability.
- Convenient sampling is employed, especially when accessing the entire population is challenging, allowing for quick data collection from readily available individuals.
- Utilizing a convenient sampling technique, data from 132 workers in logistics companies were gathered for analysis.
- Analysis involved employing simple percentages and the Factor analysis method to scrutinize the collected data effectively.

Significance of Study

This study is pivotal for the logistics industry, offering insights and guidance for sustainable development and green logistics. Findings empower decision-making, strategic planning, and policy formulation, fostering positive change and eco-friendly operations. Understanding and addressing employee perceptions enhance engagement and the successful adoption of sustainable practices. The study highlights transparent communication, strong leadership, and organizational culture for sustainability. Its conclusions guide effective supply chain management, contributing to global environmental conservation goals by reducing carbon emissions and waste in the logistics industry.

Analysis and Interpretation

In exploring employee perceptions towards green logistics, this study probes into the socio-economic profile of 132 respondents in the logistics industry. The demographic snapshot reveals gender distribution, age brackets, educational qualifications, monthly income, and professional experience. Concurrently, the study employs factor analysis, validated by the Kaiser-Meyer-Olkin measure and Bartlett's test, to discern key factors significantly influencing employee

Table 27.1 Literature review: overview of green logistics studies and key findings.

Author name	Study	Findings (Insights/interpretation)
Osman et al. (2023)	Customers demand greener freight, accepting higher costs. Green logistics driven by corporate initiatives, marginal impact from regulations.	Growing customer preference for eco-friendly freight, corporate-driven green logistics, and limited impact from governmental regulations.
Visamitanan and Assarut (2021)	Green education, marketing, and warehousing positively impact engagement and commitment. Green manufacturing negatively affects performance, mediated by social and operating factors.	Positive influences on employee engagement from green education, marketing, and warehousing. The negative impact of green manufacturing on performance is mediated by social and operating factors.
Ren et al. (2020)	A comprehensive evaluation of 306 G&SL contributions over 20 years reveals growth trends and knowledge taxonomy.	The evaluation highlights G&SL research trends, academic landscape, and knowledge taxonomy with five major alignments and 50 sub-branches.
Amin et al. (2020)	Environmental training and supervisory support correlate with perceived organizational support. Rewards lack significant correlation. Organizational support influences employee participation.	Positive links between environmental training, supervisory support, and perceived organizational support. Rewards lack significant correlation. Organizational support influences employee participation.
Seroka-Stolka (2014)	Customer pressure on environmental behavior varies, influenced by supply chain position. Organizational considerations are pivotal; logistics managers anticipate future technological challenges.	The impact of customer pressure on green logistics varies with supply chain position. Organizational considerations are crucial; logistics managers prepare for future technological challenges. Managerial environmental knowledge is crucial for long-term goals.

Source: Author

perspectives on green logistics. The ensuing analysis identifies pivotal factors and gauges their cumulative contribution, offering valuable insights for strategic decision-making in fostering sustainable practices within the logistics sector.

Socio-economic profile:
- **Gender distribution:** Out of 132 respondents, 99 (66.67%) identified as male, and 33 (33.33%) as female.
- **Age distribution:**
  - Up to 25 years: 31 respondents (23.1%)
  - 26–35 years: 48 respondents (35.8%)
  - 36–45 years: 41 respondents (30.6%)
  - Above 45 years: 14 respondents (10.4%)
- **Educational qualification:**
  - Up to SSLC: 41 respondents (31.1%)
  - HSC: 50 respondents (37.0%)
  - Bachelor's degree: 23 respondents (17.0%)
  - Master's degree: 14 respondents (10.4%)
  - Others: 6 respondents (4.4%)
- **Monthly income distribution:**
  - Below Rs. 20,000: 44 respondents (33.33%)
  - Rs. 20,000–30,000: 64 respondents (48.48%)
  - Rs. 30,000–40,000: 17 respondents (12.88%)
  - Above Rs. 40,000: Seven respondents (5.30%)
- **Experience distribution:**
  - Below 2 years: 24 respondents (18.18%)
  - 2–5 years: 56 respondents (42.42%)
  - 5–10 years: 36 respondents (27.27%)
  - Above 10 years: 16 respondents (12.12%)

Employee perception toward green logistics:
- **KMO and Bartlett's test:**
  - Kaiser-Meyer-Olkin measure of sampling adequacy: 0.926 (acceptable)
  - Bartlett's test of sphericity: Chi-square = 3431.321, df = 378, p = 0.000 (suitable for factor analysis)
- **Rotated component matrix (factors identified):**
  - Factor 1 (standardization of trucks, wireless technologies, long term environmental objectives, etc.): 55.01%
  - Factor 2: 5.94%
  - Factor 3: 4.92%
  - Factor 4: 4.16%
- **Factors significantly contributing to employee perception toward green logistics:**
  - Standardization of trucks
  - Wireless technologies
  - Long term environmental objectives
  - Process optimization
  - ISO certification
  - Clean material handling
  - Top management involvement

- Low carbon storage
- Clean vehicles
- Minimizing inventories
- Freight consolidation
- Carbon footprint reduction
- Fuel efficiency
- Reconditioning and reuse of pallets
- Innovative handling
- Scheduling
- Recycle, reuse of packaging
- Backhauling
- System monitoring devices,
- Optimization, restrict excess packaging,
- Environmental reports
- ISO suppliers
- Ecological material
- Environmental messages on packaging
- Staff training
- Energy saving
- Less disasters.
- **Cumulative contribution of factors:** 70.03%

This study on employee perception towards green logistics reveals key socio-economic characteristics, with the majority being male, aged 26–35, holding an HSC qualification, earning between Rs. 20,000–30,000, and having 2–5 years of experience. Factor analysis identifies crucial factors significantly contributing to employee perception towards green logistics. The study's insights can aid the logistics industry in informed decision-making, strategic planning, and policy formulation to enhance sustainability efforts.

Conclusion

In conclusion, prioritizing activities aligned with crucial characteristics, such as deploying wireless technologies, standardizing trucks, and establishing precise long-term environmental goals, significantly impacts employee perceptions of green logistics. Emphasizing effective communication, extensive training, and senior management involvement fosters a culture of sustainability. Recognition and rewards for supporting green initiatives, cooperation across departments, and monitoring tools contribute to the overall success of green logistics practices. Environmental messages, regular evaluation, and encouraging employee insights ensure ongoing progress. Addressing these recommendations can enhance employee attitudes, cultivate sustainability, and drive more effective implementation of green practices in the logistics industry.

In a rapidly evolving global environment focused on environmental issues, the logistics industry acknowledges the imperative adoption of green logistics practices. This study underlines the crucial role of employee perceptions in the success of sustainability measures. Examining influential factors like wireless technologies and long-term environmental goals highlights the diverse components shaping a sustainable supply chain. Effective communication, thorough training, leadership commitment, and a dynamic approach are essential for aligning employee attitudes with the goals of green logistics. The study further emphasizes on the significance of addressing employee perceptions to propel the logistics industry toward a more sustainable future, balancing economic growth with environmental preservation.

References

Amin, I., Zailani, S., and Rahman, M. K. (2020). Predicting employees' engagement in environmental behaviours with supply chain firms. *Management Research Review*, 44(6), 825–848. © Emerald Publishing Limited. ISSN 2040-8269. DOI: 10.1108/MRR-05-2020-0280.

Osman, M. C., Huge-Brodin, M., Ammenberg, J., and Karlsson, J. (2023). Exploring green logistics practices in freight transport and logistics: a study of biomethane use in Sweden. *International Journal of Logistics Research and Applications*, 26(5), 548–567. DOI: 10.1080/13675567.2022.2100332.

Seroka-Stolka, O. (2014). The development of green logistics for implementation sustainable development strategy in companies. *Procedia - Social and Behavioral Sciences*, 151, 302–309.

Visamitanan, K., and Assarut, N. (2021). Impact of green supply chain management practices on employee engagement and organizational commitment: mediating role of firm performance. *Global Business Review*.

28 A study on impact of IT on supply chain management

A. Karthikeyan[a], S. Swathi Newashini[b], T. Y. Ebenezer Paul Rajan[c], and S. Jegadeeswari[d]

Karpagam Academy of Higher Education, Coimbatore, Tamil Nadu, India

Abstract

Supply chain management technology offers production managers comprehensive insights into intricate supply chain operations, fostering confidence in their ability to secure crucial resources precisely when required. Beyond accelerating corporate processes, this advancement minimizes bottleneck risks. Companies are notably advancing toward goals such as punctual procurement, streamlined inventory, and enhanced operational efficiency, especially in manufacturing. Information technology serves as a key support for supply chain organizations to adeptly meet evolving client demands. A study with 120 respondents, representing a defined sample, concentrated exclusively on customer expectations and perspectives. Employing convenience sampling, the research amalgamated primary and secondary data sources, resulting in meaningful conclusions that provide valuable insights.

Keywords: Information technology, management, practices, supply chain

Introduction

The primary aim of supply chain management is to gain or strengthen a competitive edge, involving the strategic coordination and supervision of supply chain operations. This intricate discipline encompasses the entire manufacturing spectrum, from procuring raw materials to finalizing the product. Positioned at the heart of organizational functions, supply chain management entails strategic planning, conception, regulation, and execution of all operational processes tied to procurement, manufacturing, distribution, and fulfillment.

Essentially, supply chain management involves various tasks like aligning supply with demand, sourcing raw materials, intricate manufacturing, detailed inventory tracking, efficient order handling, seamless multi-channel distribution, and delivering goods to customers. It forms a complex network that interconnects businesses, from primary suppliers to end users, facilitating information exchange and providing goods and services. This comprehensive concept encapsulates the essence of supply chain management, serving as the backbone for achieving competitive advantages.

Object of the Study

The study aims to assess the influence of information technology (IT) on three critical aspects within supply chain management. Firstly, it seeks to measure how IT impacts the flexibility of supply chain management, examining how technological integration affects the adaptability and responsiveness of supply chains to changing demands and scenarios. Secondly, the research intends to evaluate the role of IT in enhancing the comprehensiveness of decision-making processes within supply chain management, focusing on how technology influences the breadth and depth of information considered in strategic choices. Lastly, the study aims to analyze the impact of IT on customer relationship practices within supply chains, exploring how technological advancements shape and optimize interactions, communication, and service delivery to customers, ultimately affecting the quality and depth of these relationships. Through these focal points, the study endeavors to provide insights into the multifaceted impact of IT on key facets of supply chain management.

Research Methodology

The research methodology adopted a descriptive research design to explore the specified objectives. Convenience sampling was utilized to select a sample size of 120 respondents from six specific organizations involved in the study. Primary data, primarily acquired through individual interviews and structured questionnaires, formed the bulk of the newly obtained information. Statistical analysis incorporated various tools such as simple percentage analysis, correlation analysis, and chi-square analysis to comprehensively analyze the collected data, enabling a thorough examination of the relationships and patterns relevant to the research objectives.

[a]karthikeyan4735@gmail.com, [b]swathinivashini@gmail.com, [c]ebepaulraj@gmail.com, [d]sjegadeeswari15@gmail.com

Table 28.1 Literature review.

Authors	Publication year	Summary
Ameri and Patil (2019)	2019	The tradable good in the manufacturing market is manufacturing process capability. A market allows for the purchase of capacity units, which are represented by manufacturing services, as and when they are required, improving the ability of supply chains to adapt to changes in supply and demand. Manufacturing Market can be built physically as a spot market, but more benefits can be realized with a web-based architecture. The online version, digital manufacturing market (DMM), faces barriers like standard representation of manufacturing needs and capabilities, intelligent provider search and assessment, and automation of the supply chain configuration process.
Wieteska (2020)	2020	This article presents a theoretical model that offers a generalized representation of the problem area in supply chain management (SCM), exploring various theoretical models encompassing moderators, mediators, moderated mediation, and mediated moderation. The study analyzes 97 papers, comprising theoretical models used in SCM research from 2014 to 2019. Models with mediators and moderators gain significant interest in SCM research, notably those with moderated mediation, displaying an increasing trend. The research sheds light on the complex dynamics in SCM studies.
Liao and Widowati (2021)	2021	The work focuses on SCM involving suppliers, manufacturers, warehouses, distribution centers, and distributors aiming to minimize supply chain costs while maintaining service quality standards. It explores theoretical models' impact on supply chain management's investigation, emphasizing their role in the study's framework development. The research methodology involves an extensive examination of supply chain management through databases like ScienceDirect, Wiley Online Library, Sage Online Journals, etc., covering 2014 to 2019. It delves into variables like moderators, mediators, moderated mediations, and mediated moderations, aiming to understand complex SCM dynamics.

Source: Author

Table 28.2 Reduction of cost of operational process.

Particulars	No. of the respondents	Percent
Strongly agree	17	14.2
Agree	45	37.5
Neither agree nor disagree	28	23.3
Disagree	22	18.3
Strongly disagree	8	6.7
Total	120	100.0

Source: Author

Table 28.3 Speeding up the transfer of information between organizations.

Particulars	No. of the respondents	Percent
Strongly agree	34	28.3
Agree	47	39.2
Neither agree nor disagree	11	9.2
Disagree	9	7.5
Strongly disagree	19	15.8
Total	120	100.0

Source: Author

Respondents' views on reducing operational expenses are detailed in the table. 14.2% strongly agreed, 37.5% agreed, 23.3% held a neutral stance, while 18.3% rejected and 6.7% strongly disagreed. Overall, the majority favored cost reduction in operational processes AlMudimigh et al. (2020).

Respondents' opinions on enhancing information flow between organizations are illustrated in the table. 39.2% agreed, 28.3% strongly agreed, 9.2% remained neutral, while 7.5% disagreed, and 15.8% strongly disagreed Gu et al. (2021). Overall, most favored accelerating information transfer between organizations.

The table summarizes respondents' views on tools for tracking market changes. 35.8% rated them "excellent," 58.3% as "good," 3.3% as "average," 1.7% as "bad," and 0.8% as "poor." Overall, most respondents viewed the tools positively for monitoring market changes.

The respondents' viewpoints on various aspects are diverse Prasad (2020). A notable 37.5% agree on reducing operational costs, while 39.2% agree on accelerating inter-organizational information transfer. Moreover, 58.3% acknowledge tools for monitoring market changes as good. Conversely, only 29.2% consider these tools poor for adapting to market shifts. Interestingly, 47.5% strongly agree that these tools aid in decision-making support, while 48.3% find them

Table 28.4 Aids to monitor the changes in the market condition.

Particulars	No. of the respondents	Percent
Excellent	43	35.8
Good	70	58.3
Average	4	3.3
Bad	2	1.7
Poor	1	.8
Total	120	100.0

Source: Author

Table 28.5 Chi-square test.

	Value	df	Asymp. Sig. (2-sided)
Pearson Chi-square	16.707[a]	20	.672
Likelihood ratio	21.001	20	.397
Linear-by-linear association	1.854	1	.173
N of valid cases	120		

Source: Author

Table 28.6 Correlation analysis relationship between age of the respondents and it in economic impact.

		Age of the respondents	ECON
Age of the respondents	Pearson correlation	1	-.261[**]
	Sig. (2-tailed)		.004
	N	120	120
IT in economic impact	Pearson correlation	-.261[**]	1
	Sig. (2-tailed)	.004	
	N	120	120

Source: Author

excellent for altering product designs. Additionally, 49.2% see them as excellent for assessing customer satisfaction, while 51.7% find them good for enhancing customer service at lower costs. Overall, respondents acknowledge the tools' varied effectiveness in streamlining operations, decision-making support, and improving customer interactions, albeit with diverse perspectives on their specific functionalities.

Recommendations

To optimize resource utilization, the organization should leverage efficient IT tools that prioritize time-saving measures and reduce HR expenses. Specifically, within supply chain management, streamlining administrative tasks is vital to enhance operational efficiency. Additionally, the integration of information technology should aim to minimize operational costs and expedite communication flow for smoother supply chain operations. Moreover, the IT system should facilitate the market introduction of new products and services while effectively tracking and responding to market changes. These recommendations underscore the importance of IT tools in simplifying processes, reducing costs, and fostering agility within the organization's supply chain and market strategies.

Conclusions

In the realm of supply chain management, information technology emerges as an indispensable asset, affording businesses a distinct competitive edge through its advanced capabilities and integration. This integration not only fortifies competitiveness but also fosters an environment conducive to innovation in product and service development. Notably, the infusion of information technology yields multiple benefits within supply chain management, notably the reduction of operating costs and the enhancement of process efficiency. The strategic implementation of technology optimizes the production process, effectively reducing operational expenses and elevating overall process efficiency. This optimization plays a pivotal role in shaping the supply curve, driving it toward an upward trajectory fueled by heightened efficiency attributed to technological advancements. Consequently, the reduction in production costs coupled with burgeoning customer interest amplifies product demand, steering the business towards expansion. Looking ahead, there lies a promising journey of continuous growth and innovation propelled by the sustained adoption and utilization of technology across supply chain and logistics domains. The trajectory is marked by an upward trend, showcasing the persistent evolution and widespread integration of technology as an integral force propelling the efficacy and dynamism of supply chain management. This ongoing evolution promises not just efficiency gains but also sets the stage for further innovation and competitive advantage in the ever-evolving landscape of supply chain operations.

References

Al-Mudimigh, A. S., Zairi, M., and Ahmed, A. M. M. (2020). Extending the concept of supply chain: the effective management of value chains. *International Journal of Production Economics*, 87(3), 309–320.

Ameri, F., and Patil, L. (2019). Digital manufacturing market: a semantic web-based framework for agile supply chain deployment. *Journal of Intelligent Manufacturing*, 23, 1817–1832.

Gu, M., Yang, L., and Huo, B. (2021). The impact of information technology usage on supply chain resilience and performance: an ambidexterous view. *International Journal of Production Economics*, (17)7, 778–781.

Liao, S. H., and Widowati, R. (2021). A supply chain management study: a review of theoretical models from 2014 to 2019. *Operations and Supply Chain Management*, 14(2), 173–188.

Prasad, R. (2020). IT enabled supply chain management. *Serbian Journal of Management*, 2(1), 47–56.

Wieteska, G. (2020). The impact of supplier involvement in product development on supply chain risks and supply chain resilience. *Operations and Supply Chain Management*, 13(4), 359–374.

29 Employees organization commitment as a strategic role in logistic management

V. Balu[a], G. Sumathi[b] and V. Simi[c]

Karpagam Academy of Higher Education, Coimbatore, Tamil Nadu, India

Abstract

Logistics management's day-to-day operations encompass overseeing third-party logistics providers, managing inventory, forecasting supply and demand, handling goods' supply and distribution, as well as warehousing, handling, and fulfillment. This study aims to explore how employees are perceived in logistics management and their level of involvement. The study involved a sample size of 120 individuals and employed a descriptive research plan using convenience sampling. Primary information was gathered through a questionnaire. Statistical tools like simple percentage analysis, one-way ANOVA, and correlation were utilized to draw conclusions. The findings revealed no significant correlation between respondents' educational qualifications and their commitment to the organization in a strategic capacity. It is recommended that employees remain adaptable to organizational changes. Businesses are advised to facilitate the setup of suggestion and complaint boxes where necessary. Moreover, the study affirms that strategic management, external partnerships, and outsourcing tactics in procurement, supply chain, inventory management, and transportation can synergize to enhance logistical efficiency.

Keywords: Logistics, warehousing and service providers

Introduction

Logistics encompasses the art and science of procuring, producing, and disseminating goods and materials in the right quantities and locations. It involves transporting commercial goods to customers, managing order fulfillment, storage, shipping, handling, and packaging—all synchronized within a network of locations. Some advocate for a definition emphasizing the importance of obtaining the correct product, in the right condition, quantity, place, and time, at the appropriate price for the customer.

This process includes acquiring, storing, and delivering resources efficiently. Logistics management involves identifying potential distributors and suppliers, assessing their efficiency, and determining their accessibility. It falls under the broader umbrella of supply chain management, essential for efficiently planning, executing, and supervising the smooth movement and storage of data, goods, and services from their origin to destination. Employing logistics management can lower costs and enhance customer service, as it aids in strategizing, managing, and executing the movement and storage of goods.

In today's digital era, logistics is vital for optimizing supply chain operations and enhancing customer experiences. Recognizing its value, businesses prioritize logistics management, understanding its crucial role in product procurement, storage, and delivery to end consumers. Effective logistics management is imperative in navigating the complexities of supply chain management and staying abreast of industry trends. Embracing reliable logistics strategies becomes pivotal for business expansion, as it allows for process optimization and fosters sustainable growth.

Literature Review

Since logistics plays a role in a company's overall strategic planning, e-business and IT applications help implement strategic planning efficiently and successfully Olah et al. (2019) (Kamariotou et al., 2021). This viewpoint contends that earlier researchers disregarded the significance of planning for information systems (IS), involving the selection and implementation of the best IS for the circumstance at hand Tang and Veelenturf (2019). This study examines the information systems planning (ISP) stages influencing the process's outcome Izzah et al. (2018). Methods: 73 IT managers from Greek SMEs in the logistics industry gathered data and used regression analysis for examination Maemunah and Syakbani (2021). Results: The analysis findings indicate that executives should be aware of how IS planning strategically enhances spirited benefit Haglund and Rudberg (2022). Managers must select suitable IT infrastructure aligning with business strategy and organizational structure Liu et al. (2018). Conclusions: These findings assist managers in focusing on logistical tasks and understanding ISP's significance in logistics Anca (2019). Choosing

[a]21mbap072@kahedu.edu.in, [b]sumathiganesh18@gmail.com, [c]simigvg2020@gmail.com

the right IS offers enhanced spirited benefit, faster communication, cost reductions, improved customer value, and more accurate data storage and retrieval Akdogan and Demirtas (2019). Their study addresses whether a company's size affects the perceived importance of organizational aspects in logistic workers' knowledge (Komanda and Klosa, 2021). It defines current challenges in executing employees' data management within company logistics. The literature analysis reveals principles governing the placement of individual capital concept concerning facts management. It gives examples of how organizational conditions impact logistics effectiveness and business participation in the supply chain. Conducting a survey among logistics experts justified by the importance of employees' tacit knowledge for company growth (non-probability sampling, PSAQs, n = 197). Analysis shows that as company size (measured by employee count) increases, recognition of employees adhering to organizational procedures and their familiarity with those procedures also rises. This paper broadens the problem of organizational procedures, offering a fresh perspective focusing on employees and their job satisfaction levels in relation to organizational practices. Their article explores trends in HR management amidst global logistification, highlighting logistics competencies, investment flows, practical knowledge, and increased internationalization. It describes a novel logistics HR management model and aims to link how a firm's human function design affects logistics management efficiency (Gołembska and Gołembski, 2020). Talent and competence management, handling people risks, and employer branding are key personnel function facets. Investigating various HR practices identifies personnel function characteristics and challenges in proactive HR management in logistics. The article presents empirical findings from 20172018 on 236 major, medium-sized, and small Polish businesses using diagnostic assessment, questionnaires, and factor analysis. It proposes a unique perspective on the human role in logistics organizations tailored to Polish business characteristics. Conclusions discuss the current and future state of HR management in logistics, noting the impact of logistification on knowledge transfer in supply chains and the decentralization of HR management in larger businesses, impacting recruitment functions differently among different business sizes.

Study: Objectives Scope, Research Methodology

The study aims to achieve two primary objectives: firstly, to evaluate employees' organizational commitment as a strategic element within logistics management, and secondly, to gather suggestions from respondents aimed at enhancing strategies implemented in logistics management. Employing an empirical approach, the study relied predominantly on field surveys to collect pertinent information on this issue. Sources such as books, journals, newspapers, and reports were used to gather additional data. The study conducted personal interviews to obtain specific insights from a selected group of respondents, constituting a sample size of 120 employees chosen through convenience sampling. Statistical tools including Simple Percentage, one-way ANOVA, and correlation analysis were utilized for primary data analysis.

Table 29.1 Demographic profile of the respondents.

Particulars	Variables	Respondents	Percentage
Gender	Male	83	70
	Female	37	30
	Total	120	100
Age	Below 20	16	13
	21-30	61	51
	31-40	18	15
	41-50	16	13
	Above 50	9	8
	Total	120	100
Education	Higher secondary	17	12
	Graduate	47	39
	Post graduate	26	22
	Diploma	6	5
	Others	24	20
	Total	120	100
Marital sStatus	Married	86	72
	Single	34	28
	Total	120	100
Type of family	Nuclear	53	44
	Joint	67	56
	Total	120	100
Salary	Below 10,000	37	31
	10,000-20,000	49	41
	20,001-30,000	26	22
	Above 30,000	8	7
	Total	120	100

Source: Author

Table 29.2 Relationship between educational qualification of the respondents and organization commitment as strategic role.

		Education al qualifications of the respondent ts	Organizational committee as strategic role
Educational qualification of the respondents	Pearson correlation	1	-.247**
	Sig. (2-tailed)		.007
	N	120	120
Organisation commitment as strategic role	Pearson correlation	-.247**	1
	Sig. (2-tailed)	.007	
	N	120	120

Source: Author

Table 29.3 Employees knowledge as strategic role.

Employees Knowledge As Strategic Role					
	Sum Of Squares	Df	Mean Square	F	Sig.
Between Groups	810.854	4	202.713	19.390	.000
Within Groups	1202.271	115	10.455		
Total	2013.125	119			

Source: Author

Regarding the research design, it aimed to address investigative questions while aligning with the financial system of method. This design encompasses the plan, structure, and strategy guiding the inquiry process, acting as the conceptual framework for research, data collection, measurement, and analysis. The study combined descriptive and analytical methods to achieve its goals. However, it's important to note the study's limitations, primarily stemming from the sample selection, which may introduce biases in the respondents' opinions. Consequently, caution should be exercised before generalizing the study's results.

Conclusion

Ensuring employees have a comprehensive understanding of how their workload is distributed is crucial. This necessitates effective electronic data interchange (EDI) to expedite tasks and disseminate essential information across all departments seamlessly. Additionally, an efficient web portal system becomes imperative, guaranteeing seamless information sharing among teams. Cultivating a culture of mutual respect among employees is vital, complemented by adequate training to enhance departmental proficiency. Flexibility and readiness to embrace

organizational changes are essential attributes for employees. Facilitating the establishment of suggestion and complaint boxes in relevant areas enables the prompt handling of diverse issues, ensuring swift resolutions tailored to each concern. A robust strategic management approach is pivotal for optimizing a company's supply chain system. This involves meticulous planning and oversight of quality, operations, and services across both public and private sectors within the operational industry. Leveraging effective strategic management significantly enhances the overall performance of a company's supply chain system, fostering efficiency and synergy among its various facets. By implementing strategic management practices, companies can ensure smoother operations and better alignment with evolving industry standards, driving overall improvement in the supply chain's efficacy and service delivery.

References

Akdogan, A., and Demirtas, O. (2019). Managerial role in strategic supply chain management. In 10th International Strategic Management Conference. ScienceDirect. *Procedia - Social and Behavioral Sciences*, 150, 1020–1029.

Anca, V. (2019). Logistics and supply chain management: an overview. *Studies in Business and Economics*, 14(2), 209–215. https://doi.org/10.2478/sbe-2019-0035.

Gołembska, E., and Gołembski, M. (2020). A new model of the personnel function delivery in the logistics of polish firms. *Logistics*, 4(3), 15.

Haglund, P., and Rudberg, M. (2022), A longitudinal study on logistics strategy: the case of a building contractor. *The International Journal of Logistics Management*, 34(7), 1–8.

Izzah, N., Liu Yao, and Cheng Jack, K. (2018). A review of logistics management related knowledge management. *Science International (Lahore)*, 29(2), 527–531.

Liu, S. M., Chen, H., and Hu, Z. (2018). Research on logistics time management decision based on supply chain.

IOP Publishing. *IOP Conference Series: Materials Science and Engineering*, 394(3), 032088.

Maemunah, S., and Syakbani, B. (2021). Conceptual framework related to the logistics strategy of halal products on customer loyalty.

Olah, J., Karmazin, G., Peto, K., and Popp, J. (2019). Information technology developments of logistics service providers in Hungary. *International Journal of Logistics Research and Applications*, 21(3), 332–344.

Tang, C. S., and Veelenturf, L. P. (2019). The strategic role of logistics in the industry 0 era. *Transportation Research Part E Logistics and Transportation Review*, 129(4), 1–11.

30 A study on working capital management in the selected textile companies

M., Sakhtivel[a], R. Sarojadevi[b], G. Meena Suguanthi[c] and J. Smruthymol
Karpagam Academy of Higher Education, Coimbatore, Tamil Nadu, India

Abstract

Working capital, the difference between a company's current assets and liabilities, signifies its short-term financial stability and ability to manage ongoing expenses. Recognized as pivotal in corporate management, this study investigates the impact of working capital regulations on profitability measured by return on assets (ROA). Utilizing ratios like current assets to total assets and current liabilities to total assets, alongside metrics such as quick ratio, debt-to-equity ratio, and firm size, the study computes strategies for working capital management. Emphasizing prudent asset and liability management, the research aims to offer valuable insights to industry leaders responsible for this sector, aiding in informed decision-making and effective management practices.

Keywords: Crisis, ownership, variables

Introduction

Working capital embodies the circulation of capital within day-to-day business operations. This encompasses a spectrum of elements, encompassing raw materials, warehouse stock, semi-finished and finished goods, cash reserves, and the aggregate of various creditors outlined in annual industry surveys. Managing working capital involves navigating current assets and obligations, aiming to strike a balance between excessive and deficient levels that could detrimentally impact any firm. Effective management entails optimizing the levels of current assets and liabilities to ensure operational efficiency. Ideally, a company operates without financial constraints impeding its activities. The management of working capital significantly influences a company's solvency, liquidity, and overall structural robustness. It involves crafting strategies that consider profitability, liquidity, and risk, focusing on decisions regarding the types and quantities of current assets and the selection of appropriate sizes and compositions of current liabilities. In India, working capital typically consists of two main segments: current assets and current liabilities. Current assets encompass assets available for immediate utilization or sale, including cash, receivables, inventory, and short-term investments. On the other hand, current liabilities constitute debts with a repayment window within one year, covering accrued expenses, short-term loans, and accounts payable. These components delineate the core elements within the framework of working capital management, crucial for sustaining operational fluidity and financial stability in businesses.

Problem Statement

The Crown's investment in a department includes working capital, incurring an opportunity cost as a consequence. Investment opportunities in other areas might incur a "cost" due to capital tied up in one area. If a department utilizes more working capital than necessary, the Crown faces overcharging in this scenario.

Objectives

The study has several objectives. Firstly, it aims to scrutinize the working capital management practices employed by the company. Additionally, it seeks to evaluate the effectiveness and efficiency of these working capital management strategies adopted by the organization. Furthermore, the study endeavors to assess the overall financial standing of the organization by utilizing ratio analysis as a tool for measurement and evaluation. Through these objectives, the study aims to gain insights into the company's financial health and the efficacy of its working capital management approaches.

Literature Review

Juan Gallegos Mardones (2021) conducted a study delving into the influence of working capital investments on the financial performance of businesses listed in Chile, Mexico, Peru, and Brazil between 2000 and 2018. Despite the dearth of empirical data concerning emerging economies, the research

[a]21mbap045@kahedu.edu.in, [b]rajendransaro@gmail.com, [c]meenasuganthi.govindaraj@kahedu.edu.in

highlighted a positive and significant yet non-linear relationship between working capital investments and company performance. The panel data technique employed revealed contrasting results across different countries and industries, potentially attributed to varying macroeconomic conditions facilitating easier access to financing for such endeavors.

In another study by Tarkom A. (2022), the focus was on exploring the impact of the COVID-19 pandemic on working capital management (WCM) within 2,542 publicly traded US corporations from 2019 Q1 to 2021 Q2. The research indicated that firms exposed to COVID-19 tended to exhibit higher levels of Cash Conversion Cycle (CCC), serving as a proxy for WCM. It was highlighted that enterprises with more investment opportunities and those benefiting from government incentives, such as deferred taxes and investment tax credits (DT_ITC), operated with elevated CCC levels. The study underscored the detrimental effect of COVID-19 on WCM and proposed that increasing investment opportunities and government incentives could alleviate this impact. The findings contribute to ongoing discussions regarding the pandemic's influence on business decisions and outcomes, prompting suggestions for future research to explore additional public grants that could aid impacted businesses in optimizing their WCM. The study's novelty lies in revealing that enterprises exposed to COVID-19 operated with higher CCC levels while suggesting that companies with more DT_ITC and greater investment prospects could potentially manage smaller CCC levels.

Research Methodology

The research design employed for investigating the working capital management of Namakkal-based KKP Textiles Private Limited is analytical, often utilized in projects requiring problem computation or formula-based computations. Essential to any research study is the meticulousness of data collection, as inaccurate data could significantly impact the study's outcomes, potentially leading to erroneous results. The spectrum of data collection methods varies for impact evaluation, spanning quantitative techniques at one end and qualitative approaches at the other. In this investigation, secondary data served as the primary source, drawn from the company's annual reports spanning 2017–18 through 2020–22, forming the basis for statistical analysis. Secondary data, derived from previously published sources, encompass a range of origins such as prior research, published or unpublished materials within or outside the organization, library records, online databases, and internet sources. For this study, secondary data collection involved sourcing information from the internet, publications, web articles, and annual reports. The researchers extensively utilized ratio analysis methodologies in their analysis.

Working Capital Turnover Ratio

The working capital turnover ratio gauges a company's ability to generate revenue from its operational budget. To calculate this ratio, a company divides its net annual sales by its working capital. Meanwhile, the net working capital ratio indicates how effectively a business's current assets can cover its immediate

Table 30.1 Comparative financial ratios analysis for select textile companies (Years 2017-2022).

S. No	Company	Year	Current ratio	Cash ratio	Net working capital	Debt equity ratio	Working capital turn over ratio	Inventory turn over ratio
1	Arvind Ltd	2022-2021	0.88	0.02	92.88	0.28	46.44	3.54
		2021-2020	0.91	0.03	125.07	0.21	62.54	3.58
		2020-2019	0.83	0.04	77.78	0.26	38.89	2.61
		2019-2018	0.98	0.02	138.03	0.16	69.02	3
		2018-2017	0.86	0.02	152.01	0.22	76.01	3.22
		Average	0.892	0.026	117.154	0.226	58.58	3.19
2	Vardhman Textiles Ltd	2022-2021	1.93	0.05	-3.68	2.44	-1.84	1.99
		2021-2020	0.37	0.01	-135.42	0.5	-67.71	3.01
		2020-2019	0.23	0.01	-165.72	22.76	-82.86	2.72
		2019-2018	1.7	0.11	-44.54	0	-22.27	2.39

S. No	Company	Year	Current ratio	Cash ratio	Net working capital	Debt equity ratio	Working capital turn over ratio	Inventory turn over ratio
		2018-2017	0.76	0.05	-165.56	0	-82.78	0.31
		Average	0.998	0.046	-102.984	5.14	-51.492	2.084
3	WelspunIndis Ltd	2022-2021	1.08	0.26	-30.48	0.11	-15.24	9.64
		2021-2020	0.91	0.28	-17.86	0.18	-8.93	7.54
		2020-2019	1.76	0.82	63.56	0	31.78	7.24
		2019-2018	1.96	1.19	115.58	0	57.79	6.71
		2018-2017	1.73	0.69	110.8	0	55.4	4.97
		Average	1.488	0.648	48.32	0.058	24.16	7.22
4	Raymond Ltd	2022-2021	0.56	0	-119.11	3.08	-59.55	9.99
		2021-2020	0.54	0	-173.93	2.71	-86.96	14.3
		2020-2019	0.45	0	-240.8	1.82	-120.4	10.13
		2019-2018	0.75	0.07	-1.29	2.12	-0.65	14.5
		2018-2017	0.48	0.41	-135.95	3.2	-67.97	9.76
		Average	0.556	0.096	-134.216	2.586	-67.106	11.736
5	Trident Ltd	2022-2021	0.76	0.08	3.67	0.47	1.84	11.5
		2021-2020	0.71	0.07	2.31	0.53	1.16	11.58
		2020-2019	0.63	0.05	-21.34	0.54	-10.67	8.55
		2019-2018	0.98	0.23	34.47	0.4	17.23	13.16
		2018-2017	1.03	0.03	74.48	0.43	37.24	12.68
		Average	0.822	0.092	18.718	0.474	9.36	11.494
6	Kpr Mill Ltd	2022-2021	0.6	0.05	-95	0.54	-47.5	10.06
		2021-2020	0.66	0.03	-63.88	0.81	-31.94	10.29
		2020-2019	0.73	0.15	-9.5	0.86	-4.75	7.48
		2019-2018	0.84	0.28	188.65	0.77	94.32	6.24
		2018-2017	0.62	0.23	25.69	0.84	12.84	7.7
		Average	0.69	0.148	9.192	0.764	4.594	8.354
7	Nitin Spinners Ltd	2022-2021	1.18	0.07	128.87	0.47	64.43	4.31
		2021-2020	1.02	0.06	163.88	0.45	81.94	4.17
		2020-2019	1.04	0.06	175.3	0.48	87.65	3.46
		2019-2018	2.06	0.5	270.81	0.16	135.4	4.6
		2018-2017	1.34	0.09	234.11	0.23	117.05	4.83
		Average	1.328	0.156	194.594	0.358	97.294	4.274
8	Rupa Company Ltd	2022-2021	1.11	1.13	113.39	0.1	56.69	10.09
		2021-2020	1.19	1.46	149.16	0.13	74.58	10
		2020-2019	1.26	0.84	118.13	0.2	59.06	8.29
		2019-2018	1.45	1.38	189.08	0.15	94.54	11
		2018-2017	1.24	1.26	187.8	0.26	93.9	9.93
		Average	1.25	1.214	151.512	0.168	75.754	9.862

S. No	Company	Year	Current ratio	Cash ratio	Net working capital	Debt equity ratio	Working capital turn over ratio	Inventory turn over ratio
9	Himatsingka Seide Ltd	2022-2021	0.69	0.11	-3.97	0.03	-1.98	11.94
		2021-2020	1.05	0.3	31.87	0	15.93	11.97
		2020-2019	1.44	0.85	87.76	0	43.88	10.23
		2019-2018	2.2	2.04	166.06	0	83.03	14.68
		2018-2017	0.26	0.04	-142.5	1.18	-71.25	16.7
		Average	1.128	0.668	27.844	0.242	13.922	13.104
10	Jct Ltd	2022-2021	1.12	0.57	29.84	0.04	14.92	10.52
		2021-2020	0.98	0.47	8.99	0.07	4.49	7.92
		2020-2019	1.21	0.55	58.15	0.06	29.07	6.1
		2019-2018	1.49	1.12	119.8	0.03	59.54	12.04
		2018-2017	0.96	0.58	48.25	0.12	24.12	7.9
		Average	1.152	0.658	53.006	0.064	26.428	8.896

Source: Author

Table 30.2 Correlation relationship between various ratio.

Ratio	Cash ratio	Cash ratio	Liquidity ratio	Net working capital ratio	Working capital turnover ratio	Inventory turnover ratio	Total assets turnover ratio
Cash ratio	Pearson correlation	1.000	.605	.465	.465	.299	.294
	Sig. (2-tailed)		.000	.001	.001	.035	.038
	N	50	50	50	50	50	50
Liquidity ratio	Pearson correlation	.605	1.000	.517	.516	-.140	.016
	Sig. (2-tailed)	.000		.000	.000	.331	.910
	N	50	50	50	50	50	50
Net working capital ratio	Pearson correlation	.465	.517	1.000	1.000	-.175	.448
	Sig. (2-tailed)	.001	.000		.000	.224	.001
	N	50	50	50	50	50	50
Working capital turnover ratio	Pearson correlation	.465	.516	1.000	1.000	-.175	.448
	Sig. (2-tailed)	.001	.000	.000		.224	.001
	N	50	50	50	50	50	50
Inventory turnover ratio	Pearson correlation	.299	-.140	-.175	-.175	1.000	.277
	Sig. (2-tailed)	.035	.331	.224	.224		.052
	N	50	50	50	50	50	50
Total assets turnover ratio	Pearson correlation	.294	.016	.448	.448	.277	1.000
	Sig. (2-tailed)	.038	.910	.001	.001	.052	
	N	50	50	50	50	50	50

Source: Author

liabilities. This ratio serves as a measure of a company's ability to fulfil imminent financial obligations.

Recommendations

KKP Textiles Private Limited has achieved remarkable progress within a short timeframe, witnessing its trademark achieving its highest-ever turnover Palombini and Nakamura (2018). This progress is further underscored by increased plant capacity utilization and multiple operational efficiency achievements, all pointing toward significant organizational growth P Ansari and Keyvani (2019). Based on the study conducted, several recommendations can be implemented by the company Yousaf et al. (2021). The liquidity ratio, gauging the company's ability to meet current obligations, was assessed and indicated sufficient liquidity Upreti and Venkata (2021). Similarly, the turnover ratio, reflecting turnover status, demonstrates a consistently high rate over a five-year average, a positive indicator Marco Della Porta and Nowak (2021). Strong financial performance has resulted in substantial market share and overall business growth. To further enhance operations, a collaborative effort among production, sales, inventory, and credit collection is crucial, supported by an efficient information system. Proper allocation of funds between current and fixed assets will ensure smooth business operations.

Conclusions

The efficacy of a company in adeptly managing its working capital is pivotal for ensuring its success. The analysis indicates commendable working capital management in Namakkal, with KKP Textiles Private Limited noting a rising profit trend. However, there's a suggestion to adopt a more systematic approach in maintaining working capital to exhibit superior commercial outcomes. Prior to any modifications in credit policy variables, thorough research on potential sales level increments should be conducted. Credit policies serve as a tool for retaining existing customers and enticing new ones, potentially diverting them from

competitors. Enhanced coordination among departments such as sales, production, and procurement play a critical role in mitigating credit risks and reducing debt recovery timeframes.

References

Ansari, M. N. A., and Keyvani, S. M. A. (2019). Management of liquidity in public sector petrochemicals industry. *Indian Journal of Accounting*, XXVI, 59–65.

Marco Della Porta, and Nowak, B. (2021). Working capital management and profitability: empirical evidence. *Journal of Business Management and Economic Research*, 12(4), 1953–1959.

Palombini, N. V. N., and Nakamura, W. T. (2018). Key factors in working capital management in the Brazilian market. *Revista de Administração de Empresas Sao Paulo*, 52(1), 55–69.

Upreti, D., and Venkata, V. (2021). Working capital management strategies in nepalese institutional schools. *Open Journal of Business and Management*, 9, 2522–2529. doi: 10.4236/ojbm.2021.95138.

Yousaf, M., Bris, P., and McMillan, D. (2021). Effects of working capital management on firm performance: Evidence from the EFQM certified firms. *Cogent Economics and Finance*, 9(1).

31 A study on impact of GST on FMCG goods

Arunkumar, B.[a], Jayalakshmi, R.[b] and Hemamalini[c]

Karpagam Academy of Higher Education, Coimbatore, Tamil Nadu, India

Abstract

Fast moving consumer goods (FMCG) refers to fast-moving, often low-cost products in the market, falling under consumer packaged goods (CPG). Distribution costs for FMCG currently stand at 2-7% but are expected to be reduced to 1.5% post-GST software implementation. This study examines GST's impact on FMCG, focusing solely on consumer opinions. With 100 respondents chosen through convenience sampling, primary and secondary data were used, analyzed through percentage, chi-square, and correlation analyses. Findings show a notable link between factors like respondents' income levels and GST awareness. It's recommended that governments enhance GST awareness through various media channels. While GST stands as a crucial post-independence tax reform in India, its full economic impact is anticipated gradually, given its early implementation stage.

Keywords: Buyer, FMCG, GST, perception

Introduction

Goods and Services Tax (GST) replaced numerous earlier indirect taxes in India and was enacted on March 29, 2017, operational from July 1, 2017. It's a comprehensive, multi-stage, destination-oriented tax on each value addition in the provision of goods and services.

The fast moving consumer goods (FMCG) sector is crucial for India's economy, employing about 3 million individuals and representing the fourth largest segment. FMCG products are consumed widely across demographics due to low market entry barriers, a robust distribution network, minimal operational costs, modest per capita consumption, and simple manufacturing processes requiring low investments.

This industry is fiercely competitive, featuring global corporations, domestic firms, and an unorganized sector selling unbranded goods, claiming significant market share. Over 50% of FMCG revenues come from products priced at Rs 10 or less, fostering local brands distributed freely in rural areas. In recent years, domestic companies have rivaled and even outperformed multinational corporations, with domestic profits surging by 24% between 2005 and 2014, outstripping the 14% growth of international firms. These trends signify the sector's robustness and its significance in India's economic landscape.

Problem Statement

In the era of globalization, India needed a robust tax system to compete globally. The GST implementation promises transparency and streamlined business operations. Globally, GST has proven to boost government revenue, influencing its adoption in India. This unified taxation mechanism stands as a pivotal tax reform in the nation, affecting all sectors. The transition impacts businesses, government entities, and consumers, shaping perceptions about GST's influence on FMCG purchases. This study aims to analyze GST's impact on FMCG goods amidst changing consumer behavior, reflecting diverse perceptions about this tax reform.

Objectives of the Study

The objectives of this study encompass several key aspects. Firstly, it aims to thoroughly examine the influence of GST on FMCG products and comprehensively assess its impact on this specific industry. Secondly, it seeks to gauge and evaluate the extent of GST awareness prevailing within the FMCG sector, considering its implications and effects. Finally, the study endeavors to delve into and understand the perspectives of buyers regarding FMCG items, particularly within the context of the GST framework. Through these objectives, the study aims to unravel the multifaceted dimensions and the varying impacts of GST on the FMCG sector, encompassing both industry perceptions and buyer behavior.

Research Methodology

The research design employed in this study is descriptive in nature, aiming to provide a detailed account of the subject under investigation. Utilizing a convenience sampling design, the study involves a sample

[a]arunak1700@gmail.com, [b]thizisjaya@gmail.com, [c]hemamalini2007ster@gmail.com

size of 100 individuals, chosen based on their accessibility to the researcher. The data collection sources include both primary and secondary data. The primary data collection techniques encompass quantitative and qualitative methods. Quantitative data collection relies on mathematical computations through closed-ended surveys, correlation and regression methods, mean, mode, and median calculations. This approach ensures a standardized process and facilitates rapid and cost-effective data gathering. The study utilizes tools such as Simple Percentage Analysis, Chi-Square Test, and Correlation Analysis to analyze the collected data and draw meaningful conclusions.

Literature Review

Sheela et al. (2021) conducted an empirical examination of retailers focusing on the supply chain from production to distribution to the end user, along with tax collection. The government's introduction of various slab rates aimed to facilitate international investments for retailers. Employing empirical research methods, the study gathered insights through direct or indirect observations and experiences with retailers. A sample size of 100 individuals was used with basic random sampling to gauge people's perceptions of retailers. Utilizing ANOVA, the study presented how retailers perceive the GST. Primary data collection methods were employed to acquire information directly and indirectly from merchants. The study highlighted how GST increased taxpayers while preventing cascade effects in the supply chain.

Yadav and Kumar (2021) focused on the GST, a value-added tax imposed on both products and services by federal and state governments, consolidating all indirect taxes in India. The study emphasized the GST's inauguration on July 1, 2017, marking a significant tax overhaul in Indian history. It highlighted GST as a consumption-based tax on the production, sale, and consumption of products and services aiming to integrate the nation's markets. Relying on secondary data sources like periodicals, newspapers, journals, and articles, the study aimed to comprehend the core and implications of GST across various sectors. Employing both quantitative and qualitative data, the research aimed to provide a comprehensive understanding of GST concepts and explore its positive impact on the Indian economy post-implementation.

Vashistha et al. (2022), emphasized GST's primary goal of simplifying the nation's tax framework and establishing an easily implementable taxation system. The study highlighted the prevalent standardized tax collection approach globally, where basic necessities and essential foods attract lower tax rates, while luxury goods bear higher taxation. The research aimed to gather data from 100 FMCG consumers to understand the impact of GST on their purchasing behavior, using appropriate statistical tools for analysis. Predominantly relying on secondary data sources without primary data collection, the study used online financial statements of companies for sample selection. While encompassing 100 FMCG product traders in Varanasi, the study acknowledged the potential limitation in wholly representing the trader population in the region. Emphasizing inferential statistics, the study aimed to probe into how GST influenced consumer buying patterns within the FMCG sector, examining trends before and after GST implementation.

The above table shows that 22.0% of the respondents said that they were fully aware, 61.0% of the respondents said that partly aware and 17.0% of the respondents said that no aware towards awareness in GST impact on price of the FMCG goods. Thus, the majority of the

Table 31.1 Awareness in GST impact on price of the FMCG goods.

Particulars	Frequency	Percent
Fully aware	22	22.0
Partly aware	61	61.0
No aware	17	17.0
Total	100	100.0

Source: Author

Table 31.2 Awareness on various GST Rates on FMCG.

Particulars	Frequency	Percent
Fully aware	34	34.0
Partly aware	23	23.0
No aware	43	43.0
Total	100	100.0

Source: Author

Table 31.3 Chi-square.

	Value	df	Asymp. sig. (2-sided)
Pearson Chi-square	12.15	13	0.51
Likelihood ratio	14.16	13	0.36
Linea-by-linear association	3.71	1	0.05
No. of valid cases	100		

Source: Author

respondents said that partly aware towards awareness in GST impact on price of the FMCG goods.

Null Hypothesis

There is no significant relationship between the marital status of the respondents and buyer's perception towards FMCG with GST.

Findings and Recommendations

The respondents' viewpoints on various aspects related to GST reveal significant insights: 47.0% are fully aware of GST's influence on each purchase, while 34.0% strongly agree that GST affects buying patterns and increases FMCG prices. Furthermore, 27.0% neither agree nor disagree that GST decreases disposable

Table 31.4 Correlation analysis - age and consumer behavior toward the FMCG goods after implementation of GST.

	Correlations	Age of the respondents	Consumer behavior towards the FMCG goods after implementation of GST
Age of the respondents	Pearson correlation	1	.205*
	Sig. (2-tailed)		.041
	N	100	100
Consumer behavior towards the FMCG goods after implementation of GST	Pearson correlation	.205*	1
	Sig. (2-tailed)	.041	
	N	100	100

*. Correlation is significant at the 0.05 level (2-tailed).

Source: Author

Table 31.5 Independent *T*-test relationship between income level of the respondents with awarenesslevel toward GST.

Income level of the respondents		N	Mean	Std. deviation	Std. error mean
Awareness level	Below Rs. 1,00,000	12	5.0000	.00000	.00000
Towards GST	Rs. 1,00,000- 2,00,000	25	6.8000	2.44949	.48990

Independent samples test

	Levene's test for equality of variances		T-Test for equality of means					95% Confidence interval of the difference	
	F	Sig.	t	df	Sig. (2-tailed)	Mean difference e	Std. error differe nce	Lower	Upper
Equal variances Awareness assumed level	27.20 6	.000	-2.527	35	.016	-1.80000	.71234	-3.24613	-.35387
toward Equal GST variances not assumed			-3.674	24.0	.001	-1.80000	.48990	-2.81110	-.78890

Source: Author

income, and 32.0% disagree that it reduces FMCG purchasing frequency. Additionally, 36.0% are neutral about GST prompting a shift to unbranded products for price reduction. On the government's preparation for GST, 48.0% strongly agree, and 35.0% are neutral about products becoming cheaper post-GST. Notably, 49.0% strongly agree that GST isn't essential for FMCG's survival, and 37.0% believe it increases the tax burden. Moreover, 49.0% agree that GST escalates living costs and inflation, with 34.0% strongly agreeing on increased expenses. Besides, 34.0% believe there are significant short-term cash flow issues. Additionally, 27.0% neither agree nor disagree about payment issues with sellers, while 32.0% disagree that GST leads to misleading product pricing. Recommendations arising from these findings include adjusting GST rates based on consumer convenience, ensuring lower product prices post-GST, ongoing monitoring of consumer behavior, and maintaining clarity on diverse GST rates for different products.

Conclusion

The research on Goods and Service Tax (GST) has revealed crucial insights that underscore the importance of consumer perception and understanding. It's evident that the government needs to invest more effort in ensuring consumers grasp the nuances of GST, fostering a positive viewpoint and widespread acceptance. Consumer comprehension plays a pivotal role in shaping perceptions about this taxation policy. To achieve this, the customs department could initiate extensive publicity campaigns, aimed at enhancing awareness and fostering a positive outlook among consumers. Such initiatives would contribute significantly to enlightening consumers about the rationale and significance of GST within the Indian context. Ultimately, this concerted effort could lead to a more favorable reception and wider acceptance of GST among the populace.

References

Ahamed, E., and Podder, S. (2009). Goods and service tax reforms and intergovernmental consideration in India. *Asia Research Center LSE*.

Garg. G. (2014). Basic concepts and features of goods and service tax in India. *International Journal of Scientific Research and Management*, 2(2).

Keshap, P. K. (2015). GST-goods and service tax in India. *Journal of Global Economics*, 3(4), 159.

Kumar, N. (2014). Goods and service tax in India a way forward. *Global Journal of Multidisciplinary Studies*, 3(6), 216–225.

Sheela, D., Murugesan, R., and Subangini Devi, A. (2021). A empirical research on retailer perception on GST in Vellore district. *International Journal of Innovative Technology and Exploring Engineering (IJITEE)*, 9(2S3), 419–421, ISSN: 2278-3075.

Vashistha, V., Jain, S., and Garg, G. (2022). *International Research Journal of Modernization in Engineering Technology and Science*, 04(05), 4871–4877, ISSN: 2582-5208.

Yadav, P., and Kumar, M. (2021). Impact of GST on various sector of Indian economy. 6(1), 602–606, ISSN 2348 –1269.

32 A study on cargo handling procedure in logistics organization

Abishvaran, P.[a], Sujitha, S.[b], R. Gayathri Chitra[c], Sujith, B.[d] and Reshmi, S.[e]

Karpagam Academy of Higher Education, Coimbatore, Tamil Nadu, India

Abstract

This paper delineates the functionality of the cargo handling system and evaluates the most effective method for energy conservation within this system. It specifically scrutinizes the viability of batteries as an energy-saving mechanism, delving into their merits and demerits. Cargo handling encompasses the intricate processes involved in managing cargo movement between waterborne vessels and shores—facilitating imports, exports, or transit. These operations encompass various tasks such as processing, lashing, unlashing, stowing, transporting, and temporarily storing cargo within the relevant handling terminal. However, it excludes supplementary procedures like warehousing, stripping, repackaging, or other optional operations, unless determined otherwise by the Member State. Furthermore, cargo handling also encompasses the provisioning or arrangement of warehouse facilities and services catering to the storage and handling of shipments transported by air.

Keywords: Cargo handling, energy saving, hybrid system

Introduction

The term "cargo handling" has now expanded to encompass various types of freight, whether transported by train, van, truck, or intermodal container. It specifically pertains to goods or produce conveyed for commercial purposes via ship, boat, or aircraft. Even perishable inventory stored in cold storage or similar climate-controlled facilities remains in transit to its final end-use, hence the term "cargo" extends to goods within the cold-chain system. Consequently, this research delves into issues that transcend site-specific concerns, encompassing challenges beyond cargo handling and transportation. To unravel the significance, usage, and procedures involved in handling cargo within large-scale projects, extensive literature was thoroughly examined and analyzed.

Ensuring the safe and timely delivery of supplies or finished goods to customers stands as a paramount concern. The effectiveness of cargo transportation significantly hinges on its safety measures. Consequently, delving into proper cargo handling practices becomes imperative. Neglecting this aspect could result in a decline in the quality of materials being transported. Therefore, undertaking research on cargo handling procedures becomes crucial.

The objective of the study is (a) to examine cargo handling procedures within the logistics industry. (b) to assess the measures of care implemented in cargo handling.

Research Methodology

The research design for this study is primarily descriptive, focusing on collecting and analyzing data to systematically describe a phenomenon, situation, or population. It aims to address the questions of what, when, where, and how. Employing a simple random sampling method, three logistics companies were selected for the study, distributing questionnaires to 150 employees to gather responses, ultimately receiving 137 completed responses after accounting for a non-response rate. Both primary and secondary data sources were utilized in this research. The statistical tools applied included simple percentage analysis and the Pearson correlation coefficient.

Literature Review

Nair (2020) highlights the transformative impact of an e-commerce company on handloom sales, particularly in the Western market's growing interest in saris. The company observes a significant rise in sari sales from overseas customers, particularly from the US, UK, Singapore, and the UAE. Despite this increase, the demand for traditional weaves and festive wear remains consistent. The data also reveals a predominant interest among younger Indian women aged 25 to 44 in adopting saris, both in traditional and modern styles.

Bergheim et al. (2021) delve into the correlation between psychological capital (PsyCap), work

[a]eapcas@gmail.com, [b]Nandhini.aruchamy@kahedu.edu.in, [c]rajendransaro@gmail.com

environment perceptions, and job satisfaction among maritime employees from Norwegian shipping companies. Their study indicates PsyCap's influence on variations in safety climate perception, particularly highlighting that higher PsyCap levels among officers lead to a more positive safety climate perception than non-officers with similar high PsyCap levels. Moreover, cross-national differences were noted, primarily affecting workers from Europe and not Filipinos, emphasizing the relevance of PsyCap in safety-focused interventions.

Karahalios (2022) delves into ship operators' strategies for business growth within a competitive and regulated sector. They propose employing management systems to mitigate risks to ship crews and cargoes, particularly focusing on risk management principles related to monetary losses from ship collisions. The paper suggests employing a performance management system to gauge anticipated costs and benefits in case of a ship collision. Utilizing fuzzy sets and analytic hierarchy process (AHP), the study develops design scorecards, essential in accident prevention strategies aboard ships. The results offer insights to ship operators in assessing their management approaches while considering the financial implications of potential incidents.

The table indicates that 38.3% of the respondents rated the firm's handling method of cargo goods and service as excellent, while 43.3% considered it good. Additionally, 10.0% rated it as moderate, 5.0% as poor, and 3.3% as very poor. The majority, comprising 43.3% of the respondents, considered the handling method of cargo goods and service as good for the firm.

Table 32.2 shows that mode of the shipment follows in firm, 35.0% of the respondents said they follow air freight follows in firm and 65.0% of the respondents said they follow sea freight follows in firm.

Table shows that type of cargo handled in firm, 28.3% of the respondents said they handle garments, 31.7% of the respondents are said they handle plastics, 14.2% of the respondents said they handle chemicals, and 25.8% of the respondents are said they handle electronics. The majority 31.7% of the respondents said they handle plastics.

Table shows that favorable for company trust, 62.5% of the respondents said the network are good, 70.0% of the respondents said the security system are better, 55.0% of the respondents said the communication are better, and 44.2% of the respondents said the

Table 32.1 Handling method of cargo goods and service.

Handling method	Respondents	Percentage
Excellent	46	38.3%
Good	52	43.3%
Moderate	12	10.0%
Poor	6	5.0%
Very poor	4	3.3%
Total	120	100.0%

Source: Author

Table 32.2 Mode of the shipment.

Mode of shipment	Respondents	Percentage
Air freight	42	35.0%
Sea freight	78	65.0%
Total	120	100.0%

Source: Author

Table 32.3 Type of cargo.

Type of cargo	Respondents	Percentage
Garments	34	28.3%
Plastics	38	31.7%
Chemicals	17	14.2%
Electronics	31	25.8%
Total	120	100.0%

Source: Author

Table 32.4 Favorable for company trust.

Opinion/ commitment	Good		Better		Moderate		Poor		Very poor	
	Res	%	Res	%	Res	%	Res	%	Res	%
Network	75	62.5%	25	20.8%	8	6.7%	6	5.0%	6	5.0%
Security	84	70.0%	20	16.7%	6	5.0%	5	4.2%	5	4.2%
Communication	29	24.2%	66	55.0%	11	9.2%	7	5.8%	7	5.8%
Tracking	53	44.2%	38	31.7%	12	10.0%	11	9.2%	6	5.0%

Source: Author

Table 32.5 Correlation analysis.

H0 there is no significant relationship between educational qualification of the respondents and the packing of cargo handling in the firm.

		Educational qualification of the respondents	The packing of cargo handling in the firm
Educational qualification of the respondents	Pearson correlation	1	.931**
	Sig. (2-tailed)		.000
	N	120	120
The packing of cargo handling in the firm	Pearson correlation	.931**	1
	Sig. (2-tailed)	.000	
	N	120	120

**Correlation is significant at the 0.01 level (2-tailed).

			Educational qualification of the respondents	The packing of cargo handling in the firm
Kendall's tau_b	Educational qualification of the respondents	Correlation coefficient	1.000	.867**
		Sig. (2-tailed)	.	.000
		N	120	120
	The packing of cargo handling in the firm	Correlation coefficient	.867**	1.000
		Sig. (2-tailed)	.000	.
		N	120	120
Spearman's rho	Educational qualification of the respondents	Correlation coefficient	1.000	.897**
		Sig. (2-tailed)	.	.000
		N	120	120
	The packing of cargo handling in the firm	Correlation coefficient	.897**	1.000
		Sig. (2-tailed)	.000	.
		N	120	120

**. Correlation is significant at the 0.01 level (2-tailed).

Source: Author

tracking are good. The majority 62.5% of the respondents said the network is good position.

Conclusion

The Conclusion must be clearly marked as shown. When referring to other Sections in the Letter, please use the Section heading, or describe the relevant Section as the 'following' or 'preceding' Section in relation to the current Section in the text.

Findings

The responses gathered indicated various opinions and perceptions among the respondents regarding different aspects of cargo handling within the firm. A significant majority, around 43.3% of the respondents, considered the firm's handling method of cargo goods and service to be good. Additionally, other aspects like following sea freight (65.0%), handling plastics (31.7%), accuracy concerning commitments (31.7%), cargo commitment communication (41.7%), network and security facility sufficiency (60.0%), global management (35.8%), training and safety roles (34.2%), firm tracking for globalization (89.2%), cargo packing handling satisfaction (39.2%), reasons for goods damages (59.2%), insurance for unexpected incidences (47.5%), custom duty offers (37.5%), service quality of cargo agencies (43.3%), network quality (62.5%), and the relationship between respondents' age, educational qualifications, experience, and their opinions on global management, cargo packing, and cargo agency services, were found to have varying levels of significance or relationships based on the survey responses.

Recommendations

There is a pressing need for rigorous technological advancements in cargo handling processes Taplin (2021). This includes the availability of more screening equipment and increased personnel at the cargo complex to ensure enhanced efficiency. Implementing modern machinery with adequate screen space capable of handling large volumes of cargo can significantly diminish queue wait times, consequently reducing the prolonged dwell time of import cargo Kannan (2019). Furthermore, the introduction of electronic shipping bill filing within the business complex would substantially minimize paperwork, leading to more streamlined transactions and a reduction in overall transaction time.

Conclusions

The Indian ship cargo industry, a significant sector of the economy, has seen expansion due to trade policy liberalization and globalization. Yet, within this globalized landscape, cost management stands as a pivotal aspect for competitive advantage. This study aims to assess the efficiency of logistics management in cargo handling specifically within Madurai. Effective logistics management not only reduces transportation expenses but also enhances ship cargo traffic. The study endeavors to provide recommendations aimed at refining the current logistics management practices employed by international ship cargo for heightened effectiveness.

References

Bergheim, K., Nielsen, M. B., Mearns, K., and Eid, J. (2021). The relationship between psychological capital, job satisfaction, and safety perceptions in the maritime industry. *Safety Science*, 74, 27–36.

Kannan (2019). Network assignment model of integrating maritime and hinterland container shipping: application to Central America. *Maritime Economics and Logistics*, 19, 234–273.

Karahalios, H. (2022). The contribution of risk management in ship management. *Safety Science*, 63, 104–114.

Nair, (2020). A study on materials handling in spinning mills. *The Indian Textile Journal*, http://www.indiantextilejournal.com/articles/FAdetails.asp?id=1308.

Taplin, I. M. (2021). ICMESE: intelligent consultant system for material handling equipment selection and evaluation. *Journal of Manufacturing Systems*, 15, 325–336.

33 A study on efficiency and effectiveness of warehouse management system

Priyanga, S.[a], K. Kannan[b], S. Deva[c] and Thamodiran, R.[d]

Karpagam Academy of Higher Education, Coimbatore, Tamil Nadu, India

Abstract

A network of facilities, known as supply chain management, processes raw materials into intermediate products and eventually into finished goods, which are then distributed to customers. The way this supply chain operates and the roles performed vary across sectors and companies. Consequently, supply chain management (SCM) has emerged as a critical concern for businesses, professionals, and researchers. Success in supply chain management is believed to hinge upon a comprehensive understanding of the entire supply chain structure. This essay aims to furnish readers with an in-depth comprehension of supply chain management by meticulously analyzing existing literature. It presents an overview of the primary tasks within the supply chain.

Keywords: Implementation plan, performance measurement, supply chain management, supply chain operations

Introduction

In today's landscape, the Internet stands as a ubiquitous and favored means of communication for both businesses and individuals. There's a prevailing trend dictating that the internet is pivotal for enhancing profit margins, prompting both established and emerging businesses to sporadically create websites. The rationale behind stores having websites is manifold; these platforms serve informational and transactional purposes, facilitate advertising and direct marketing, aid in public relations, drive sales, and enhance customer service. Over the past decade, B2C e-commerce has made significant strides since its inception. Consequently, scholars and practitioners in electronic commerce continually strive to deepen their understanding of online consumer behavior. The advent of the internet has noticeably altered the way people shop for and purchase goods and services.

Problem statement: When we initially embraced online shopping, we encountered numerous issues. Another widely recognized online retailer is Flipkart, accessible to millions today. Several problems plague customers, including the unease caused by receiving defective products and the disruption caused by delivery delays. Moreover, customers may receive an item incorrectly, either in a different color or design than expected. Additionally, there might be instances where customers are unable to acquire the desired goods or services.

Conclusion

The conclusion must be clearly marked as shown. When referring to other Sections in the Letter, please use the Section heading, or describe the relevant Section as the 'following' or 'preceding' Section in relation to the current Section in the text.

The objectives of this study encompass several key aspects related to warehouse management. Firstly, the research aims to delve into the current Warehouse Management System that the organization has adopted. It seeks to comprehensively understand its structure and functionality. Additionally, the study intends to evaluate the effectiveness of this system in terms of its impact on cost control and reduction within the organization. This assessment includes scrutinizing how well the system manages and curtails costs. Furthermore, the research strives to identify and analyze the challenges encountered by the organization concerning Warehouse Management. This exploration aims to highlight the hurdles and difficulties faced in effectively managing warehouses and their operations.

Research Methodology

The research design employed for this study is descriptive, aiming to systematically describe and analyze the phenomenon under investigation. To gather the sample for the study, a simple random sampling design was adopted from the larger population. In total,

---

[a]priyanga082000@gmail.com, [b]kannank.svm@gmail.com, [c]devasezhiyan@gmail.com, [d]thamodiran93@gmail.com

the study involved five logistics companies, and the sample size comprised 120 participants. The primary method for data collection centered on using a questionnaire designed specifically for this purpose, which was distributed among the respondents to gather relevant data. As for the statistical analysis, the study utilized tools such as Simple Percentage Analysis and Correlation Analysis to interpret and derive insights from the collected data.

Literature Review

Randall and Ulrich (2020) examine the relationship between commercial performance, supply chain structure, and product diversity. When a company decides to place production outside its target market, there's a trade-off between these costs and the expense of market reconciliation. These findings suggest that a company's selection of a variant type can be influenced and guided by its current supply chain capabilities. This behavior is logical as supply chain decisions are often made concerning product flow choices. The link

between diversity, market reconciliation, and production costs is either diminished or aggravated by outsourcing. Companies are encouraged to expand to offer a dominant production variety.

Geoffrey et al. (2021) emphasize that determining the environmental protection strategy of the chain is a crucial initial step in selecting the life cycle analysis (LCA) type. The outcome and feasibility of LCA implementation are determined by specific requirements. Understanding the relationship between LCA types and chain structure is vital to ensure the successful implementation of LCA and to fulfill the environmental objectives of the chain strategy.

Bechtel and Handfield (2022) assert that managers must seek ways to foster new types of relationships based more on trust to shorten cycle times between supply chain units. A proposed model suggests that suppliers invest in site-specific human and resource resources, while buyers use contracts cautiously to manage interdependencies effectively within a trust-based relationship.

Table 33.1 Warehousing system provides safety and maintenance.

		Frequency	Percent	Valid percent	Cumulative percent
Valid	Yes	21	17.5	17.5	17.5
	No	42	35.0	35.0	52.5
	3	36	30.0	30.0	82.5
	4	21	17.5	17.5	100.0
	Total	120	100.0	100.0	

Source: Author

Table 33.2 Transportation management helps in load balancing.

	Frequency	Percent	Valid percent	Cumulative percent
Strongly disagree	32	26.7	26.7	26.7
Disagree	48	40.0	40.0	66.7
Neutral	35	29.2	29.2	95.8
Agree	5	4.2	4.2	100.0
Total	120	100.0	100.0	

Source: Author

Table 33.3 Distribution of goods economically.

Warehousing planning helps in distribution of goods economically					
		Frequency	Percent	Valid percent	Cumulative percent
Valid	strongly disagree	120	100.0	100.0	100.0

Source: Author

Table 33.4 Inflow and outflow of goods.

		Frequency	Percent	Valid percent	Cumulative percent
Valid	Strongly disagree	16	13.3	13.3	13.3
	Disagree	104	86.7	86.7	100.0
	Total	120	100.0	100.0	

Source: Author

Table 33.5 Effective warehousing enhances profitability.

Effective warehousing enhances profitability					
		Frequency	Percent	Valid percent	Cumulative percent
Valid	Strongly disagree	16	13.3	13.3	13.3
	Disagree	1	.8	.8	14.2
	Neutral	103	85.8	85.8	100.0
	Total	120	100.0	100.0	

Source: Author

Table 33.6 Correlation analysis.

		Warehousing control ensures smooth inflow and outflow of goods	Warehousing management avoids unnecessary waiting time	Warehouse control can handle multi-stock room inventories	Effective warehousing enhances profitability	Warehousing control provides ready availability of stocks
Warehousing control ensures smooth inflow and outflow of goods	Pearson correlation	1	.424**	.073	.740**	.235**
	Sig. (2-tailed)		.000	.429	.000	.010
Warehousing management avoids unnecessary waiting time	Pearson correlation	.424**	1	.073	.477**	.184*
	Sig. (2-tailed)	.000		.428	.000	.044
Warehouse control can handle multi-stock room inventories	Pearson correlation	.073	.073	1	.075	-.097
	Sig. (2-tailed)	.429	.428		.417	.292
Effective warehousing enhances profitability	Pearson correlation	.740**	.477**	.075	1	.226*
	Sig. (2-tailed)	.000	.000	.417		.013
Warehousing control provides ready availability of stocks	Pearson correlation	.235**	.184*	-.097	.226*	1
	Sig. (2-tailed)	.010	.044	.292	.013	

**. Correlation is significant at the 0.01 level (2-tailed).

*. Correlation is significant at the 0.05 level (2-tailed).

Source: Author

The above table shows that warehouse safety and maintenance of the respondents, 17.5% of the respondents are yes, 35% of the respondents are no, 30% of the respondents are 3, 17.5% of the respondents are 4.

Findings and Recommendations

The responses indicate various viewpoints among the respondents regarding different aspects of warehouse management Bartholdi and Hackman (2019). A majority of 50.8% favor a separate warehouse management system, while 35% express disagreement concerning safety and maintenance. Additionally, 41.7% oppose the involvement of third-party logistics. Interestingly, a substantial majority of 60% strongly disagree with the notion that warehouse management minimizes losses, and 40% express disagreement toward transportation management. Conversely, 72.5% agree that effective warehouse management assists in handling goods economically Caplice and Sheffi (1995). However, respondents unanimously disagree (100%) that it ensures smooth inflow and outflow processes and 86.7% disagree that it avoids unnecessary waiting times. Similarly, respondents' express disagreement (43.3%) in handling multitask room inventories and strongly disagree (96.7%) that it enhances profitability. Additionally, 85.8% maintain a neutral stance on the provision of ready availability of stocks, and 48.3% agree that it provides security for products. Views are varied regarding keeping goods properly (26.7% agree) and opinions on transportation (64.2%) and storage (50%) remain mostly neutral. Furthermore, the majority are neutral about unloading products (73%) and supplier scheduling (42.5%).

Warehouse management stands as a crucial function in the success of tire manufacturing enterprises, playing a pivotal role in ensuring their efficiency. A well-executed inventory system holds the potential to significantly enhance overall business operations. Utilizing contemporary warehouse management practices incorporates advanced techniques, facilitating dynamic inventory optimization. This approach aims to elevate customer service standards by maintaining optimal inventory levels and reducing operational costs. It's important to note that the pursuit of superior warehouse management isn't about achieving perfection but about ongoing enhancement. Introducing a proposed transportation system could notably enhance the relationship between management and employees, fostering better internal and external communication channels and potentially curbing employee turnover rates. Implementing the right manufacturing methodology, particularly in the context of a tire company, offers a means to effectively control escalating costs.

Conclusions

To maintain competitiveness, meeting customer requirements is imperative. This achievement involves various aspects, including enhancing process flexibility through the implementation of radio frequency technology, expanding delivery coverage to offer same-day and faster delivery, especially via air freight, improving customer satisfaction by reducing complaints, ensuring better inventory visibility with higher accuracy, and cutting costs through enhanced labor productivity and minimized inventory investments. Protocols have been established to monitor and evaluate warehouse management system (WMS) activities. This ongoing effort will significantly benefit paint manufacturers intending to broaden their business interests. Embracing the framework set by transportation operators is essential, along with imparting the fundamental principles and philosophies to all associated providers. This approach aims to illustrate the benefits and importance of adopting these practices.

References

Bartholdi, J. J., and Hackman, S. T. (2019). Warehouse and distribution science. Retrieved from https://www.warehouse-science.com/.

Bechtel and Handfield (2022). Organizing warehouse management. *International Journal of Operation and Production Management*, 33(9), 12–40. doi: 10.1108/IJOPM-12-2011-0471.

Caplice, C., and Sheffi, Y. (1995). A review and evaluation of logistics performance measurement systems. *The International journal of Logistics Management*, 6(1), 61–74.

Geoffrey, et al. (2021). The impact of effective inventory control management on organisational performance: a study of 7up bottling company nile mile Enugu, Nigeria. *Mediterranean Journal of Social Sciences*, 5(10), 109–118.

Randall, T., and Ulrich, K. (2020). Design and application of internet of thing-based warehouse management system for smart logistic. *International Journal of Production Research*, 1(4), 190–206.

34 Explanatory study on impact of emotional intelligence and quality of work life among the employees of automobile industry

Kalki, B.[a], Kannan, K.[b], Nagalakshmi, N.[c] and Thamodiran, R.[d]

Karpagam Academy of Higher Education, Coimbatore, Tamil Nadu, India

Abstract

The survey examines the perceptions of work life quality among employees in automotive companies. A well-designed survey served as the measurement method. Randomizer.org, a random sample tool, was utilized to select 100 respondents randomly for gathering primary data. Both chi-square analysis and factor analysis were employed in the study. It was revealed that self-awareness and self-management are interlinked with drive, self-awareness, and overall emotional intelligence, constituting essential elements in enhancing work life quality. The study also unveiled a strong correlation between emotional intelligence and happiness in work life, suggesting that higher emotional intelligence positively impacts one's level of contentment in work-life balance.

Keywords: Emotional intelligence, human capital, quality of work life

Introduction

The crux of managing individuals lies in their emotional intelligence, crucial for career progression. The pervasive performance pressure in the sector invariably affects employees' workplace well-being. High emotional intelligence fosters more democratic labor relations and a humane work environment. This study aimed to identify mediating factors influencing both emotional intelligence (EI) and quality of work life (QWL). Understanding the EI-QWL link demands scrutiny of both the individual and their environment—EI pertains to individuals, while QWL pertains to organizations and their interaction. Work-life balance has gained considerable attention due to its associated business benefits. Achieving this balance requires dedication to tasks and seizing life's varied experiences. Health—impacted by diet, activity, emotional, and spiritual contentment—shapes our approach. Attaining work-life balance entails finding happiness and success across life domains. Fulfilling personal expectations within a company ensures QWL. Factors like creativity, respect for individual rights, secure work conditions, safety, and growth opportunities affect QWL. Addressing transitions, work schedules, and fieldwork impacts employee emotional intelligence.

Problem statement: The study aimed to explore the relationship between occupational quality of life and emotional intelligence, intending to showcase facets like self-awareness, empathy, and optimistic, driven thinking. I selected these dimensions based on the significance of self-awareness in managing employees' emotions, the role of empathy in understanding employee issues, the importance of motivation to self-motivate in challenging situations while managing employees, and the necessity of a positive mindset in employee management.

Scope and Objective of the Study

This study demonstrates how EQ and work-life balance collectively foster competitive workplaces and organizational success. By developing one's emotional intelligence abilities, individuals can gain a better grasp of and manage others' emotions, thereby creating a healthy work-life balance. Work-life balance and emotional intelligence exhibit a positive correlation. The primary objectives of this research are twofold: first, to investigate the correlation between EI and work-life balance in corporate settings, and second, to analyze the degree of interdependence between EI and work-life balance. The study aims to delve into the intricate relationship between these two factors within the corporate world, seeking to understand how EI impacts and relates to the attainment of a harmonious work-life balance among employees. Through this exploration, the study intends to shed light on the

[a]kalki.priyan2000@gmail.com, [b]kannank.svm@gmail.com, [c]lavanyaa2302@gmail.com, [d]thamodiran93@gmail.com

extent of reliance and mutual influence that EI and work-life balance exert on each other in professional environments.

The research methodology section outlines the framework used for data collection and analysis. A crucial component of any study, the research design, aims to balance procedural efficiency while staying pertinent to the research focus. In this study, a descriptive research design was adopted to fulfill these objectives effectively. Sampling methods play a pivotal role in selecting a representative portion of the population under study. In this research, convenient sampling was employed, enabling the selection of participants based on the researcher's preferences. The study involved two automobile manufacturing companies, constituting a sample size of 100 respondents. Primary data, unique in nature as it's gathered from scratch, was acquired through a questionnaire designed to obtain firsthand information. Statistical tools utilized in the study encompassed several methods, including the independent sample T-Test, ANOVA, multiple regression analysis, and factor analysis. These tools were instrumental in analyzing and interpreting the collected data for comprehensive insights into the relationship between EI and work-life balance within the corporate sector.

Literature Review

Srivastava and Parihar (2011) assessed EI among married, educated, employed, and unemployed women in the Rewa district. The study delved into 15 dimensions of emotional intelligence categorized for working and non-working women. These dimensions encompassed assertiveness, emotional self-awareness, self-regard, interpersonal relationships, empathy, independence, social responsibility, problem-solving, reality testing, adaptability, impulse control, happiness, optimism, and stress tolerance.

Khurram et al. (2011) focused on self-awareness, self-management, social awareness, and relationship management as integral facets of emotional intelligence and their impact on employee performance. The study highlighted that social awareness and relationship management significantly influence employee performance compared to self-awareness and self-management. Thus, emphasizing emotional intelligence in recruitment and enhancing employees' performance is crucial.

Ashkan (2012) argued for the emphasis on relationship management in EI within human resource strategies and employee training programs. The study assessed EI behaviors through a 28-item performance-based emotional intelligence appraisal based on Goleman's (2002) four-factor taxonomy, covering self-awareness, self-management, social awareness, and relationship management. Interestingly, the research revealed no substantial gender differences in self-awareness, self-management, and social awareness competencies. However, it identified considerable distinctions in relationship management skills between genders.

Table 34.1 Multiple regression analysis.

Model	R	R Square	Adjusted R square	Std. error of the estimate	Change statistics		Durbin-watson
					R Square change	F Change	
1	0.437	0.191	0.183	0.876	0.191	23.127	
2	0.512	0.262	0.246	0.841	0.071	9.297	.825
3	0.547	0.3	0.278	0.824	0.038	5.206	

Source: Author

Table 34.2 Independent sample *T*-test.

		T-Test for equality of means		
		t	df	Sig. (2-tailed)
Degree of influence doesyour work environment	Equal variancesassumed	1.054	98	0.295
	Equal variances not assumed	1.055	94.576	

Source: Author

Table 34.3 ANOVA: Factor Groups analysis.

	SS	df	MS	F	Sig.
Between Groups	2.740	4	.685	.721	.580
Within groups	90.260	95	.950		
Total	93	99			

Source: Made by Author

Table 34.4 ANOVA.

	Sum of squares	df	Mean square	F	Sig.
Between groups	16.297	4	4.074	5.046	0.001
Within groups	76.703	95	0.807		
Total	93	99			

Source: Author

Table 34.5 Factor analysis.

Component	Initial Eigen values			Extraction sums of squared loadings		
	Total	% of Variance	Cumulative %	Total	% of Variance	Cumulative %
1	5.385	28.34	28.34	5.385	28.34	28.34
2	2.194	11.548	39.888	2.194	11.548	39.888
3	1.661	8.744	48.632	1.661	8.744	48.632

Source: Author

Table 34.6 Rotated component matrix.

	Components		
	1	2	3
I work, I am treated with respect	0.717	0.209	0.065
working conditions	0.71	0.097	0.064
Best of my skills and abilities	0.682	0.015	0.039
Relationship with the employer	0.622	0.012	0.042
Perception with the leaves	0.655	0.439	0.299
I take initiative to meet people in social situation	0.558	0.396	0.349
I mobilize other though unusual, enterprising effort.	0.487	0.375	0.266
I try to understand and meet the expectations of people.	0.502	0.234	0.472
I seek information about people's need	0.456	0.46	0.396
I can relate well with people	0.623	0.279	0.119
Enthusiastically interact	0.062	0.131	0.291
I can quickly reorient my thinking	0.08	0.122	0.706
Overall impression	0.089	0.042	0.511

Extraction method: Principal component analysis.

Source: Author

The predictors listed, such as the ability to swiftly change thinking when problem-solving strategies fail, are examined in relation to the overall satisfaction, perceived working environment, and leave policies within the organization Lowe et al. (2003). These predictors serve as potential factors influencing the dependent variable, overall pleasure Table 34.3. The regression model demonstrates the highest R Square value, indicating a strong fit for the model. The R Square value in the table represents the correlation, reinforcing the suitability of the model in depicting the relationship between these predictors and the overall satisfaction level Ramezani (2004).

The study aimed to compare the means between gender and the work environment, considering the null hypothesis (H0) that there's no significant difference between these variables. With a significance value of 0.295, indicating a p-value greater than 0.05, the study failed to reject the null hypothesis. This suggests that there isn't a notable difference observed between gender and the perceived work environment Reyan (1995). Additionally, the ANOVA table regarding overall satisfaction and enterprising effort also supports the null hypothesis, indicating no significant distinction among respondents concerning overall satisfaction in terms of enterprising effort Shahrashob (2006).

Findings and Recommendations

The findings from the study reveal several key points about the respondents' perceptions within the company. Around 34% expressed a neutral sentiment regarding their satisfaction with the provided working conditions, while 43% agreed that their skills aligned well with the job requirements. Moreover, 39% indicated a neutral view about the bond among employees within the organization, and a similar 46% had a neutral perception regarding the leaves provided by the company. About 41% of respondents agreed with initiatives to meet people in social situations, and 39% expressed a neutral stance toward gathering information about people's needs to provide assistance. Additionally, 54% felt neutral about relating well with influential individuals within the organizational structure, and 48% responded neutrally regarding the atmosphere promoting enthusiastic interaction and teamwork. Furthermore, 65% indicated a neutral stance regarding the ability to swiftly reorient thinking. The study also highlighted that there's no significant difference in overall satisfaction based on gender.

Moving forward, it's recommended that management fosters internal brainstorming sessions to gather innovative ideas from employees, thereby enhancing performance in areas requiring innovation. Encouraging regular performance feedback can aid employees in identifying areas for improvement, motivating them through better communication, suitable rewards, and reinforcement. Establishing strong and positive relationships between management and staff through ongoing communication, fair treatment, a welcoming work environment, and task completion encouragement is crucial to address performance issues. Lastly, providing appropriate training can significantly enhance employee performance, addressing concerns of poor performance within the company.

Conclusion

Emotional intelligence encompasses self-awareness, self-knowledge, and self-management, crucial in enhancing employee performance within organizations navigating today's competitive market. This study aims to dissect empathy's components across various organizational frameworks. Effective communication proves vital in aiding employees to comprehend their roles and perform optimally, reducing errors and enhancing efficiency. Leadership that coaches, empowers, or fosters participation significantly bolsters employee performance. Commitment to tasks is the desired outcome for any company, achievable by encouraging and motivating workers to excel. A motivated workforce invariably operates more effectively, where rewards play an inadvertent yet powerful role in inspiring and driving performance.

References

Ashkan (2012). The academic work environment in australian universities: a motivating place to work? *Higher Education Research and Development*, 21(3), 241–258.

Khurram , et al., (2011). Working with Emotional Intelligence. New York: Bantam Books.

Lowe, G. S., Schellenburg, G., and Shannon, H. S. (2003). Correlates of employees' perceptions of a healthy work environment. *American Journal of Health Promotion*, 17(6), 390–399.

Ramezani, F. M. (2004). Evaluation of quality of working life with normal practice managers girls and boys high school city of Hamedan. MA Thesis for management training course, Tehran: A Allameh Tabatabai University, Faculty of Science of Educational Psychology.

Reyan, G. M. (1995). Theoretical basic for the QWL concept. University of Siena: quality (esprit project 8162) (9 working paper).

Shahrashob, T. (2006). Relationship between quality of working life and organizational commitment in Gonbade Kavus city high school teachers. Education Management MA thesis, Tehran: Allameh Tabatabai University, School of Psychology and Educational Sciences.

Srivastava, A., and Parihar, N. S. (2011). Emotional Intelligence: Why it Can Matter than IQ. New York: Bantam Books.

35 An explanatory study on inventory management system adopted in manufacturing industry

Rooba Shri, C[a], Thamodiran, R.[b], S. Deva[c], and K. Kannan[d]

Karpagam Academy of Higher Education, Coimbatore, Tamil Nadu, India

Abstract

The study aimed to scrutinize the inventory management process, highlighting the benefits derived from pinpointing inventory control issues. The research methods involved unstructured interviews, on-site investigations, and an analysis of the annual report. Inventory management stands as a pivotal facet within the manufacturing sector. Failure to effectively manage inventory can lead to significant setbacks for businesses. Maintaining an optimal inventory level poses a challenge, but various techniques exist to address this issue. The primary objective of this article was to explore inventory management techniques prevalent in the manufacturing industry, identifying avenues for enhancing the company's inventory management processes. While the current inventory management system demonstrates adequacy, there's room for enhancement. Implementing additional inventory management techniques could substantially bolster the company's existing system.

Keywords: Challenges, inventory, management and techniques

Introduction

Inventory management, synonymous with inventory control, is pivotal in overseeing materials and goods reserved for future use following production or subsequent governmental commercial activities. Its primary aim involves rectifying conflicting financial aspects arising from a reluctance to retain excessive stocks. A retailer's ability to fulfil customer needs is crucial; failure to do so may result in customer loss for that item and potentially future purchases. Committing to effective inventory management holds equal importance to maximizing profits from available resources. Managing the financial aspects of shareholding is denoted as share management, crucial for organizational interests. Inventory management's significance lies in its representation on the asset statement's resources side for many organizations. It serves as a tool to document, forecast, and regulate stock growth, encompassing the harmonious coordination of responsibilities and authorities governing the production and completion of essential documents (Kotler, 2002).

Editorial organizations have encountered the challenge of soaring creative expenses lately. A significant portion of these costs can be attributed to inventory management issues, stemming from management's struggle to effectively control them. Many production associations diligently procure resources to fuel their creativity and ensure their sustainability. Essentially, inventory management, as highlighted previously, involves both organization and control.

The objectives of this study are twofold: first, to examine the efficiency of the inventory management system; and second, to identify and understand the issues that the organization encounters concerning the tracking of stock management.

Research Methodology

The study operates within an exploratory framework, serving as the blueprint for data collection and analysis. The design of the study is both explanatory and systematic. Simple random sampling was employed to select the sample from a pool of nine manufacturing companies, totaling a sample size of 120. Primary data was the primary source, collected through diverse survey methods including open-ended surveys, closed surveys, and buyer questionnaires. These surveys aimed to gather essential information vital to the study. The statistical tools utilized in the analysis encompassed simple percentage analysis, chi-square test, correlation analysis, and ANOVA.

Literature Review

Chow and Larson (2020) underscore the paramount importance of inventory management, recognizing it as a top asset listed on every balance sheet. They advocate for effective inventory control strategies to reduce stocking and storage costs, addressing challenges that may arise. A case study in marketing illustrates that corrective actions through such strategies can swiftly tackle these challenges.

[a]roobashrichandrasekar2000@gmail.com, [b]thamodiran93@gmail.com, [c]devasezhiyan@gmail.com, [d]kannank.svm@gmail.com

Tom Jose et al. (2021) identified discrepancies between inventory and purchased quantities, revealing the organization's inefficiency in utilizing stock for raw material procurement. Consequently, their inventory management appears to be inadequate. The Health Stock Meter allows organizations to determine their annual inventory retention.

Lavely (2022) perceives inventory as a tangible accumulation of capital on shelves and a source of profit for businesses. However, his findings suggest that up to 30% of a retail store's inventory remained unsold. Lavely argues that inventory control aids in-store operations by reducing wait times and subsequently boosting transaction margins. Additionally, it offers distinct inventory calculations to ascertain the necessary inventory levels for trading margins.

H0: There is no significant association between inventory control and overall performance of stock management

Table 35.1 Warehousing provide time utility and place utility.

Options	No. of respondents	Percentage
Strongly agree	89	74.2
Agree	31	25.8
Total	120	100.0

Source: Author

Table 35.2 Warehousing control reduces overall lead time.

Option	No. of respondent	Percentage
Strongly agree	44	36.7
Agree	73	60.8
Disagree	3	2.5
Total	120	100.0

Source: Author

Table 35.3 Problems faced in logistics and supply chain management system.

Statement	Mean score	Rank
Resistance to change from employees	417	3
Resource shortage	425	2
Skill shortage	456	1
Insufficient vendor support	401	4
Hidden cost	383	6
Integration with existing system	397	5

Source: Author

Null hypothesis is accepted. Hence there is no significant association between inventory control and overall performance of stock management

The survey results indicate significant trends among respondents. A majority—ranging from 48.3% to 74.2%—pointed out critical aspects within the organizational structure. Over 60% of the respondents identified skill shortages, insufficient vendor support, hidden costs, and integration issues with existing systems as prevalent challenges. Moreover, the survey highlighted concerns about the organization's efficacy in producing products cost-efficiently, reliability of the production system, utilization of production capacity, waste management, and supporting orders. Additionally, an overwhelming majority, above 70%, expressed strong agreement concerning warehousing's utility in providing time and place utility to products, offering protection, reducing overall lead time, and aiding in inventory control, production distribution, transportation sufficiency, and quality control. These findings underscore the significance of these factors within the organizational framework.

Recommendations

The inventory balancing process is more suitable for managing inventory without frustrating buyers, unlike the "keep full" approach that might overwhelm retail customers by displaying a complete absence of the item they intend to purchase Shen et al. (2016). This method avoids stocking old, unwanted, or outdated items, unlike the "trigger points" system that rearranges inventory when specific thresholds are reached. It efficiently utilizes inventory ratios, preventing redundant assembly processes and maintaining a clear view of items in retail settings. The process involves a straightforward desktop application connected to a live distribution center to update in-store information for validation Sunitha (2012). It ensures data security and confidentiality, preventing any leaks from the system. Furthermore, it assists in organizing sales data, providing a comprehensive overview of monthly transactions.

Table 35.4 Chi-square test.

	Value	Df	Asymp. Sig. (2-sided)
Pearson Chi-Square	3.977[a]	2	.137
Likelihood Ratio	4.374	2	.112
Linear-by-Linear Association	3.898	1	.048
N of Valid Cases	120		

Source: Author

Table 35.5 Correlation analysis the table shows that the relationship between store department is facing problem and equipment and spares.

		Inventory control	Warehousing	Production distribution	Sufficient transportation	Quality control
Inventory control	Pearson correlation	1	.181*	.036	.181*	.303**
	Sig. (2-tailed)		.048	.699	.048	.001
	N	120	120	120	120	120
Warehousing	Pearson correlation	.181*	1	.726**	.744**	.774**
	Sig. (2-tailed)	.048		.000	.000	.000
	N	120	120	120	120	120
Production distribution	Pearson correlation	.036	.726**	1	.676**	.653**
	Sig. (2-tailed)	.699	.000		.000	.000
	N	120	120	120	120	120
Sufficient transportation	Pearson correlation	.181*	.744**	.676**	1	.890**
	Sig. (2-tailed)	.048	.000	.000		.000
	N	120	120	120	120	120
Quality control	Pearson correlation	.303**	.774**	.653**	.890**	1
	Sig. (2-tailed)	.001	.000	.000	.000	
	N	120	120	120	120	120

**. Correlation is significant at the 0.01 level (2-tailed).

Source: Author

Conclusions

Inventory management entails maintaining precise records of finished goods ready for shipment. This process commonly includes tallying recently completed products within the overall inventory and processing the final dispatch of finished items to buyers. When an organization establishes an exchange, the finished goods inventory often includes a subgroup to account for rebranded or class 2 quality returned goods. Maintaining accurate tracking of finished goods inventory allows for swift transmission of data to the business faculty, providing real-time information on available stock ready for shipment.

References

Chow and Larson (2020). The impact of inventory management practice on firms' competitiveness and organizational performance: empirical evidence from micro and small enterprises in Ethiopia. *Cogent Business and Management*, 5(1), 1503219.

Lavely, R. (2022). Case study on inventory management improvement. *Information Technology and Management Science*, 18(1), 91–96.

Shen, H., Deng, Q., Lao, R., and Wu, S. (2016). A case study of inventory management in a manufacturing company in China. *Nang Yan Business Journal*, 5(1), 20–40.

Sunitha, K. V. (2012). A Study on Inventory Management in Sujana Metal Products Limited. (Master's Report, Jawaharlal Nehru Technological University, Hyderabad).

Tom Jose, V., Akhilesh, J. K., and Sijo, M. T. (2021). Analysis of inventory control techniques- a comparative study. *International Journal of Scientific and Research Publications*, 3(3), 520–530.

36 Impact of training and development on employee retention with special reference to textile industry

Vishnu Prasath, T.[a], Thamodiran, R.[b], Nandhini, A.[c] and Kannan, K.[d]

Karpagam Academy of Higher Education Coimbatore, Tamil Nadu, India

Abstract

The objective of this study was to investigate how training initiatives affect employees' inclination to stay or leave the organization. Research has identified the importance of training activities' impact in employee retention. Data was collected from 153 employees of the textile industry using a convenience sampling technique. The data was evaluated using descriptive, correlation, and regression statistical analyses. According to the findings, there is a positive correlation between training and employee retention, which suggests that training practices may be instrumental in motivating employees to extend their tenure within the organization.

Keywords: Employee motivation, employee retention, training and development

Introduction

Training is a simple idea in developing useful human resources. It's about developing a particular skill in a fancy style using training and exercise. Training serves as an immensely valuable resource that directly empowers employees to execute their tasks with proficiency, efficacy, and a strong sense of responsibility. It encompasses the process of enhancing an employee's expertise and competencies required for executing a specific role. Training encompasses instruction and cultivation of the comprehensive skill set and knowledge relevant to beneficial competencies, whether for oneself or others.

In addition to the basic learning required for a work-study student, careers or career-trackers in the market are striving to realize as early as 2008 the desire to pursue learning beyond the prerequisites:

Maintain, improve and update their capabilities throughout their professional life. People in many professions and occupations can also consider this type of learning as professional development.

Problem Statement

A high turnover rate of staff negatively impacts the organization, leading to increased expenses for recruitment and selection, delays in service delivery, and decreased employee morale. This situation hampers the organization's ability to flourish in today's competitive economy, mainly due to its struggle in retaining high-quality employees. Furthermore, the relationship between training, development, and employee retention remains somewhat ambiguous, with many studies on their interplay yielding inconclusive outcomes.

Another noteworthy factor is the dearth of empirical research focused on training and development's effects within higher education institutions, particularly in areas like organizational commitment and employee retention. This knowledge gap is particularly evident in administrative staff within companies.

Scope of the Study

Irrespective of an organization's size, productivity, economic nature, or establishment timeline, it is imperative for every entity to offer training to all its employees, regardless of their qualifications, skills, or suitability for their roles. This research employs a questionnaire-based approach for data collection, targeting a sample audience of 153 employees. Investigating retention strategies holds significant value for organizations, shedding new light on comprehending and addressing attrition challenges. The issue of attrition has broadened the horizon of employee retention, accentuating its influence on organizational effectiveness. Ensuring the retention of hardworking, indispensable employees becomes a paramount concern, underscoring their crucial role within the system.

Objective of the study is to measure the impact of training on employee productivity, and determination of factors affecting employee retention.

[a]prasathappus@gmail.com, [b]thamodiran93@gmail.com, [c]nandhini.aruchamy@kahedu.edu.in, [d]kannank.svm@gmail.com

Literature Review

The training process molds the employee's perspective, fostering a culture of high-quality performance (Kulkarni). Its nature is both ongoing and enduring. For survival and the attainment of shared objectives, organizations and individuals must evolve harmoniously. Hence, contemporary managers are tasked with advancing their organizations through human resource development, particularly via training and developmental initiatives. Employee training constitutes a vital component within the broader framework of human resource development, representing a specialized function and fundamental operational aspect of human resource management.

Training optimizes the utilization of human resources by facilitating the alignment of employees' efforts with both organizational and personal objectives (Lin). It not only furnishes a comprehensive framework for nurturing technical and behavioral proficiencies across an organization's workforce but also cultivates a holistic viewpoint. Additionally, training empowers employees across all tiers to cultivate their expertise and proficiencies, fostering personal advancement. In essence, training serves as a catalyst for expanding the intellectual capacities and holistic character of the workforce.

Training also helps increase employee productivity, helping the organization achieve its sustainability goals (Wright). The training course inculcates a sense of teamwork, teamwork and cooperation between groups. Training and development helps develop leadership skills, motivation, loyalty, better attitudes and other aspects that successful workers and managers often exhibit. Training and development demonstrates a commitment to keeping employees up to date with the latest knowledge and best practices. This helps build employees' enthusiasm for learning new things. It helps build awareness and positive feelings about the organization. Overall, training channels have improved workforce morale and created a better company

Noe () States that whenever an employee participates in training initiatives, ample opportunities for learning and skill application should be provided to enhance outcomes. Training programs should encompass comprehensive, pertinent, and insightful instructional materials, aligning with the anticipated training program objectives. Ensuring a seamless training experience and effective transference of acquired competencies to employees necessitates the fulfillment of fundamental prerequisites. Through training programs, employees can refine their abilities and address deficiencies, ultimately leading to improved outcomes.

Table 36.1 Training enhanced to become more productive and efficient management.

Particulars	No. of the respondents	Percent
Highly satisfied	29	19.0
Satisfied	42	27.5
Neutral	53	34.6
Dissatisfied	22	14.4
Highly dissatisfied	7	4.6
Total	153	100.0

Source: Author

Table 36.2 Chi-square test - gender and adoption of training and retention of employee.

	Value	df	Asymp. sig. (2-sided)
Pearson Chi-square	32.735[a]	19	.026
Likelihood ratio	37.603	19	.007
Linear-by-linear association	25.082	1	.000
No. of valid cases	153		

Source: Author

The data presented in the table indicates that 19.0% of the participants expressed a high level of satisfaction, 27.5% reported being satisfied, 34.6% remained neutral, 14.4% conveyed dissatisfaction, and 4.6% expressed a high level of dissatisfaction with regards to the impact of enhanced training on their productivity and efficiency.

H0: There is no significant association between the gender of the respondents and adoption of training and retention of employee. Based on the data presented in the table, it can be deduced that the calculated p value stands at 0.026, which falls short of the established significance level of 0.05. With a minimum expected count of 0.44, the null hypothesis is upheld. Consequently, the analysis indicates a lack of noteworthy correlation between respondents' gender and their inclination towards adopting training initiatives and employee retention.

The Above table indicates that out of 153 respondents, co-efficient of correlation between age of the respondents and training factors influencing employee retention is -0.016. It is below 1. So, there is negative relationship between these ages of the respondents and training factors influencing employee retention.

Table 36.3 Correlation analysis relationship between age of the respondents and training factors influencing employee retention.

		Age of the respondents	Training
Age of the respondents	Pearson correlation	1	-.016
	Sig. (2-Tailed)		.847
	N	153	153
Training factors influencing employee retention	Pearson correlation	-.016	1
	Sig. (2-Tailed)	.847	
	N	153	153

Source: Author

Table 36.4 Independent *T*-Test relationship between experience of the respondents with adoption of training and retention of employee.

	Experience of the respondents	N	Mean	Std. deviation	Std. error mean
Study on training and retention of employee	1 to 2years	37	2.1158	.75581	.12425
	3 to 5years	63	2.2449	.41167	.05187

Independent samples test									
	Levene's test for equality of variances		T-Test for equality of means						
								95% Confidence interval of the difference	
	F	Sig.	T	df	Sig. (2-tailed)	Mean difference	Std. Error Difference	Lower	Upper
Study on training and retention of employee — Equal variances assumed	34.903	.000	-1.107	98	.271	-.12907	.11663	-.36051	.10238
Equal variances not assumed			-.959	48.778	.342	-.12907	.13464	-.39968	.14154

Source: Author

The mean difference of the above p value is 0.000 and the sig value is less than .050 (5%). So, there is significant relationship between independent variables such as experience of the respondents with impact on adoption of training and retention of employee.

Conclusion

The Conclusion must be clearly marked as shown. When referring to other Sections in the Letter, please use the Section heading, or describe the relevant Section as the 'following' or 'preceding' Section in relation to the current Section in the text.

Acknowledgments

This Section is optional but can be used to recognize the support from certain funds or organizations, for example: 'This work was supported by *insert organization here* (grant ABCD-1234X)'. Please try to avoid personal acknowledgments, such as individuals, and please do not include any thanks to the Editorial staff.

Manuscripts with incorrect email ID and incomplete author details would be rejected without further scope for peer review.

References

Brockman, P., French, D., and Tamm, C. (2014). REIT organizational structure, institutional ownership, and stock performance. *Journal of Real Estate Portfolio Management*, 20(1), 21–36.

Cella, C. (2009). Institutional Investors and Corporate Investment. United Sates: Indiana University, Kelley School of Business.

Chuang, H. (2020). The impacts of institutional ownership on stock returns. *Empirical Economics*, 58(2), 507–533.

Clark, G. L., and Wójcik, D. (2005). Financial valuation of the German model: the negative relationship between ownership concentration and stock market returns, 1997–2001. *Economic Geography*, 81(1), 11–29.

Dasgupta, A., Prat, A., and Verardo, M. (2011). Institutional trade persistence and long-term equity returns. *Journal of Finance*, 66(2), 635–653.

Demsetz, H., and Lehn, K. (1985). The structure of corporate ownership: causes and consequences. *Journal of Political Economy*, 93(6), 1155–1177.

Dyakov, T., and Wipplinger, E. (2020). Institutional ownership and future stock returns: an international perspective. *International Review of Finance*, 20(1), 235–245.

Gompers, P. A., and Metrick, A. (2001). Institutional investors and equity prices. *Quarterly Journal of Economics*, 116(1), 229–259.

Han, K. C., and Suk, D. Y. (1998). The effect of ownership structure on firm performance: additional evidence. *Review of Financial Economics*, 7(2), 143–155.

Kennedy, P. (1985). A Guide to Econometrics. Cambridge: MIT Press.

La Porta, R., Lopez-de-Silanes, F., and Shleifer, A. (1999). Corporate ownership around the world. *Journal of Finance*, 54(2), 471–517.

Manawaduge, A. S., Zoysa, A., and Rudkin, K. M. (2009). Performance implication of ownership structure and ownership concentration: Evidence from Sri Lankan firms. In Paper presented at the Performance Management Association Conference. Dunedin, New Zealand.

The below line is approximately the maximum length of a manuscript allowed (if it were to fill all five pages)

37 A study on emotional intelligence at work place with reference to engineering industry

Yogeswaran, M.,ᵃ Jegadeeswari, S.,ᵇ Nandhini, A.ᶜ and Swathi Newashini, S.ᵈ

Karpagam Academy of Higher Education India

Abstract

The term "emotional intelligence" gained traction due to its pivotal role. While traditional intelligence is crucial for life success, emotional intelligence is vital in fostering relationships and achieving goals within the human world built on connections. Through various measures, individuals can self-observe and comfortably understand emotions, social perceptions, and others' behavior, even in challenging scenarios. This leads to improved self-control, enhanced social decision-making, and ultimately elevates success rates. Effective success depends on heightened awareness, self-emotion regulation, and understanding others. This study explores the correlation between leadership programs and students' emotional intelligence development. Existing research emphasizes the link between emotional intelligence and academic success, yet there's a dearth of studies on its evolution among students. Qualitative data highlights students' most impactful components: mandatory workshops, teamwork, and the shared cohort experience. These elements significantly contribute to emotional intelligence development in students.

Keywords: Emotional competence, emotional intelligence, productivity, workplace

Introduction

Emotions intricately intertwine with every facet of human existence—every action, choice, and evaluation. Those with emotional intelligence grasp this reality and employ their cognitive faculties to govern their emotions, rather than allowing emotions to dictate their actions. Over the preceding two decades, the concept of emotional intelligence (EI) has risen to prominence as a pivotal gauge of an individual's acumen, competencies, and proficiencies in professional, educational, and personal realms. Cumulative research findings underscore EI's influential role in shaping job performance, motivation, decision-making, managerial efficacy, and leadership triumphs.

In daily existence, each individual communicates their thoughts and feelings. Emotions, repositories of valuable insights, shed light on relationships, conduct, and the multifaceted tapestry of human existence. Recent investigations underscore the constructive nature of emotions, contributing positively to both workplace accomplishments and personal decision-making, thereby enhancing overall performance.

Problem statement: Employees are the cornerstone of any organization, essential for its success. Without the right employees in optimal positions, operations cannot thrive. Productivity is inherently linked to content and dedicated employees. Resolving conflicts among staff members is crucial for a harmonious work environment. Addressing satisfaction within the company is key to mitigating these issues. However, cultivating satisfied and loyal employees proves challenging for industries. Research endeavors to gauge employee satisfaction levels, identify organizational needs and prioritize wants, create favorable working conditions, evaluate satisfaction with existing social security systems, and propose enhancements to these social security initiatives. Scope of the study: The research aims to enhance employees' emotional intelligence within the workplace, uncovering the factors influencing varying performance levels among individuals. By exploring emotional intelligence, the study reveals insights into organizational challenges, facilitating strategic decision-making and interventions to enhance employee performance. This effort involves identifying and understanding organizational issues, empowering the organization to strategize and implement measures that promote improved employee performance.

Objective: This study aims to analyze the factors affecting employee emotional intelligence at work while also assessing the level of awareness employees possess regarding emotional intelligence and its significance within the workplace environment. The research design is descriptive, employing a probability sampling technique across eight engineering organizations with a sample size of 120. Primary data is gathered through a precisely crafted questionnaire administered directly to consumers, enabling swift

ᵃyogeswaransriyogi@gmail.com, ᵇsjegadeeswari15@gmail.com, ᶜnandhini.aruchamy@kahedu.edu.in,
ᵈswathinivashini@gmail.com

information collection. Tools utilized include Simple Percentage Analysis and Correlation Analysis.

Literature Review

Dhani et al. (2019) conducted a research project in 2019 titled "Exploring the link between emotional intelligence and job performance: a study in the Indian context." Their study aimed to investigate the correlation between emotional intelligence and job performance among middle managers in Indian organizations. The research sample encompassed 685 managers from diverse industries such as banking, energy, healthcare, IT, and advertising. They utilized the DKEIT assessment tool to measure employee emotional intelligence and job performance, employing correlation and regression analyses to reveal the connection between the variables. The findings suggested that high emotional intelligence in employees led to stronger working relationships, fostering positive interactions and ultimately enhancing job performance.

Raid (2020) investigated the impact of emotional intelligence on organizational performance using a sample of 154 participants. They employed a 29-item questionnaire to collect data and tested their research hypothesis through multiple regression analysis. The findings showed significant and positive correlations between emotional intelligence and organizational performance. Additionally, the study highlighted a notable distinction in how emotional intelligence influences organizational performance compared to factors like age and experience.

Mayer (2021) discussed the evolving understanding of emotions, acknowledging their complex and individual nature, posing challenges in establishing a universally accepted definition or theory. Scientifically conceptualizing something deeply experiential is a formidable task. Various theories, such as Lazarus' cognition role before emotional perception, the facial feedback theory linking expressions to emotions, Sapir-Whorf's language shaping thought, and Chomsky's separate faculties of language and perception, attempt to grasp emotions' essence and human experience. The realm of theories and concepts in this domain appears boundless.

Results and Discussions

Table 37.1 indicates that 51.7% strongly agree on facing financial stress-related mental issues, while 35.0% disagree with health-related mental stress. Additionally, 47.5% strongly agree with experiencing depression-related mental issues, 39.2% agree on insecurity-related mental issues, and 35.0% strongly

Table 37.1 Health issues faced by the respondents.

Health issues	Strongly agree		Agree		Disagree		Strongly disagree	
	Res	Per%	Res	Per%	Res	Per%	Res	Per%
Financial stress	62	51.7%	33	27.5%	11	9.2%	14	11.7%
Health issues	33	27.5%	26	21.7%	42	35.0%	19	15.8%
Depression	57	47.5%	32	26.7%	21	17.5%	10	8.3%
Insecurity feeling	25	20.8%	47	39.2%	29	24.2%	19	15.8%
Relationship challenges	42	35.0%	33	27.5%	30	25.0%	15	12.5%

Source: Author

Table 37.2 Strategies adopted to overcome stress.

Strategies adopted	Respondents	Percentage%	Rank
Exercise	20	16.7	II
Deep breathing	17	14.2	III
Meditation	11	9.2	V
Talk to someone	29	24.2	I
Dancing	14	11.7	IV
Sleep	29	24.2	I
Total	120	100.0	

Source: Author

Table 37.3 EI Relational domain self-assessment.

Self-assessment	Strongly agree	Agree	Neutral	Disagree	Strongly disagree
Can show empathy and match my feelings	42	50	19	2	7
Believe that people can find common	42	50	8	17	3
People usually feel inspired	42	45	19	10	4
Can easily meet and initiate conversation	49	41	14	10	6
Discovering the emotional domain	42	50	14	10	4

Source: Author

Table 37.4 Correlation analysis - education qualification and challenges faced by the respondents.

		Correlations		
			Educational qualification	Challenges you faced
Kendall'stau_b	Educational qualification	Correlation coefficient	1.000	.909**
		Sig.(2-tailed)	.	.000
		N	120	120
	Challenges you faced	Correlation coefficient	.909**	1.000
		Sig.(2-tailed)	.000	.
		N	120	120
Spearman'srho	Educational qualification	Correlation coefficient	1.000	.959**
		Sig.(2-tailed)	.	.000
		N	120	120
	Challenges you faced	Correlation coefficient	.959**	1.000
		Sig.(2-tailed)	.000	.
		N	120	120

**.Correlation is significantatthe0.01level(2-tailed).

	Correlations		
		Educational qualification	Challenges you faced
Educational qualification	Pearson correlation	1	.949**
	Sig.(2-tailed)		.000
	N	120	120
Challenges you faced	Pearson correlation	.949**	1
	Sig.(2-tailed)	.000	
	N	120	120

Source: Author

agree on facing relationship challenges. Table 37.2 illustrates respondents' preferred coping strategies: 24.2% prioritize talking to someone and sleep, followed by 16.7% favoring exercise, 14.2% opting for deep breathing, 11.7% choosing dancing, and 9.2% selecting meditation.

Findings and Suggestions

In the findings, the majority of respondents fell within the 25-35 age range (36.7%) and were married (90.8%). Financial stress was strongly agreed upon by 51.7% of respondents, while lack of social support was ranked first by 23.3%. The majority rated their relationships with co-workers (55%), supervision by superiors (50.8%), physical working environment satisfaction (41.7%), and job emotional satisfaction (30.8%) as excellent Polychroniou (2009).

The suggestions section discusses the potential impact of a disaster on employee performance and emotional intelligence. Despite a slight improvement in emotional intelligence, the disaster's gravity, bringing employees close to death, likely impacted overall performance. Managing change competently and meeting employee needs is crucial Singh (2008). Additionally, the intriguing negative correlation between emotional intelligence and stress levels aligns with broader research, where despite large participant pools, emotional intelligence often correlates positively with individual integration.

Conclusions

Research has highlighted a strong link between employees' emotional intelligence levels, notably observing a prevalent trend of higher emotional intelligence, especially among critical care software-oriented professionals. Careful interpretation of these outcomes is crucial. The findings imply the advantages of cultivating empathy among healthcare providers, potentially enhancing employee performance and caregiving effectiveness. Further investigation is needed to identify the most effective strategies for instilling this environment when employees join the facility.

References

Dhani, P., Sherawat, A., and Sharma, T. (2019). Social and Emotional Competencies Predicting Success for Male and Female Executives, (1st edn., vol. 27). *Journal of Management Development.*

Mayer , (2021). The importance of emotional intelligence in the workplace: why it matters more than personality. ZERO RISK HR. https://www.zeroriskhr.com/post/theimportance-of-emotional-intelligencein-the-workplace-why-it-mattersmore-than-personality.

Polychroniou, P. V. (2009). Relationship between emotional intelligence and transformational leadership of supervisors. *Team Performance Management: An International Journal,* 15(7/8), 343–356. doi:10.1108/13527590911002122.

Raid, M. D. (2020). Emotional intelligence as a predictor of academic and/or professional success. *American Journal of Pharmaceutical Education,* 70(3).

Singh, K. (2008). Emotional intelligence & work place effectiveness. *Indian Journal of Industrial Relations,* 44(2), 292–302.

38 A study on employee job satisfaction and retention in manufacturing sector

Manoj, T.[a], Esakimuthu, R.[b] and Nandhini, A.[c]

Karpagam Academy of Higher Education, Coimbatore, Tamil Nadu, India

Abstract

Human resources encompass various elements in assembling worker groups within a business, including manpower, skills, employees, and related factors. This function, known as Human Resources, handles crucial assessments of a business's workforce, covering aspects like labor regulation compliance, managing employee benefits, and diverse recruitment and selection activities. Employee retention involves intentional efforts by employers to keep their workforce, viewed as a strategic approach rather than just an outcome. Prolonged retention is termed "retention." Strategies for retaining employees should attract and retain them effectively. Organizational effectiveness signifies a company's competence in achieving its objectives, reflecting its performance in fulfilling its mission. Six Sigma stands as a methodology aimed at comprehensively enhancing the efficiency of business processes.

Keywords: Employees attrition, HR practices, retention

Introduction

Organizations can retain skilled, productive staff and reduce turnover by nurturing a positive work environment that encourages engagement, shows appreciation, offers competitive compensation and perks, and advocates for work-life balance. Staff retention is critical as it enhances effectiveness, productivity, morale, customer experience, and cuts expenses. Employee retention tactics encompass rules and procedures aimed at motivating employees to stay. Examples include flexible work schedules, feedback, career development opportunities, and fostering a strong organizational culture.

In a highly competitive landscape where HR managers often poach talent, businesses face the challenge of retaining essential employees. Loyalty is no longer the sole driver for employees who now have numerous opportunities. Businesses hire and release staff for various reasons, necessitating employers to acknowledge and address both personal and professional influences. Enterprises are increasingly aware of these dynamics, implementing diverse strategies to retain their workforce. Hence, an effective retention strategy becomes a crucial tool for recovery.

Problem statement: When an employee requests a salary significantly higher than the company's financial capacity, retaining that employee becomes a challenging task. Every organization operates within a fixed wage budget that can be adjusted to a certain extent but not beyond a specific threshold for individual employees.

Objective: The research aims to explore employee retention issues and investigate the correlation between job satisfaction and employee retention. It seeks to delve into the factors influencing employees' decisions to stay within an organization and understand how job satisfaction levels contribute to their likelihood of remaining with the company.

Research Methodology

The research design adopted is descriptive in nature. Data collection involves five organizations from the manufacturing sector chosen for the study. Primary data, obtained directly from original sources without modification, is integral to addressing specific research questions and comes in qualitative and quantitative forms. Techniques like surveys, interviews, observations, and experiments aid in collecting primary data. Random sampling, a technique enabling random sample selection, was utilized. The sample size comprises 125 employees. Tools employed include Simple Percentage Analysis, Weighted Average Method, and Correlation Analysis to analyze the collected data.

Literature Review

O'Meara and Petzall (2017) emphasize the strategic alignment of an organization's future needs with the individuals pivotal to its success, advocating for the systematic identification, engagement, nurturing, and retention of exceptional personnel. This strategic

[a]manojthangavel9597@gmail.com, [b]muthucomhsr@gmail.com, [c]nandhini.aruchamy@kahedu.edu.in

approach carries implications for the community, business, and the workforce. A comprehensive strategy is deemed crucial, serving as a cornerstone in understanding how to both attract and retain highly qualified candidates.

In Sanjeev Sharma's (2016), article, "A right way to recruit an employee is to win his heart" Sharma he delves into factors contributing to the disregard of retention despite its heightened significance. Sharma likens retention to a pop-up fly ball that can be lost if not handled properly, noting its intangibility, influence on human behavior, inability to be measured, and tendency to be overlooked. He emphasizes the importance of retention and outlines ten impactful factors, including financial rewards, promotions, transfers, career advancement opportunities, engaging work, autonomy, leadership, intangible psychological rewards, goal-setting, and job satisfaction.

Neumark (2016) notes that the importance of employee retention variables evolves over time, influenced by economic shifts, workplace changes, labor market dynamics, industry competition, and employee attitudes. He stresses the need to value and incorporate employee input, highlighting that retention strategies aim to motivate staff, necessitating an understanding of employee perspectives throughout the process.

Discussions, Findings and Recommendations

The data presented in the table provides insights into the significance and correlations between various factors—such as age, salary, education, designation, experience, and gender—with the quality of work life, job satisfaction, and their connection to employee retention. The statistical analysis conducted reveals notable findings that aid in understanding these relationships within organizational settings.

Table 38.1 Issues in employee retention.

HR Policies		Yes (%)	No(%)
1	Employee-centered HR policies	88	12
2	Initiatives aimed at sustaining employee motivation	69.6	30.4
3	Satisfaction with working hours	11.2	88.8
4	Security of job	40	60
5	Resolution of grievances	72.8	27.2
Compensation benefits		Yes (%)	No(%)
1	Salaries are at par with others at the same level doing similar job	81.6	18.4
2	Adequate perks	86.4	13.6
3	Post-retirement benefits	26.4	73.6
4	Establishing a connection between performance and appropriate rewards.	93.6	6.4
5	Foreign trips	62.4	37.6
Work Pressure		Yes (%)	No(%)
1	Stress of target completion	58.4	41.6
2	Fluctuating targets	88	12
3	Unnecessary paperwork	24.8	75.2
4	Excessive competition in the IT industry	78.4	21.6
Relations with superior		Yes (%)	No(%)
1	Fulfilling the expectations of one's superiors.	71.2	28.8
2	Acknowledgment of exerted efforts from superiors.	48.8	51.2
3	Accessibility of superiors	84	16
4	Compatibility with immediate superior	77.6	22.4

Source: Author

Table 38.2 Weighted Average Method-Job satisfaction.

Job satisfaction	Strongly disagree	Disagree	Neutral	Agree	Strongly agree	Respondents	Mean score	Rank
	1	2	3	4	5	Total score		
Welfare measures	6	4	19	28	69	126		
	6	8	57	112	345	528	4.190476	1
Insurance schemes/medical benefits/fringe benefits	4	10	19	64	29	126		
	4	20	57	256	145	482	3.825397	3
Salary and compensation	2	16	35	29	44	126		
	2	32	105	116	220	475	3.769841	4
Compliant and grievance handling mechanism	2	20	27	47	30	126		
	2	40	81	188	150	461	3.65873	8
Growth and promotions	10	14	22	35	45	126		
	10	28	66	140	225	469	3.722222	6
Fair and transparent policies	4	13	21	46	42	126		
	4	26	63	184	210	487	3.865079	2
Training and development opportunities	4	17	30	35	40	126		
	4	34	90	140	200	468	3.714286	7
Supervision quality/supervisors' Skill and knowledge	7	14	23	40	42	126		
	7	28	69	160	210	474	3.761905	5

Source: Author

Table 38.3 Table showing descriptive statistics and correlation analyses for employee retention, job satisfaction, and quality of work life among 126 participants.

Variable	Mean	Std. Deviation	N	Pearson correlation with employee retention	Sig. (2-tailed)
Employee retention	1.96	0.512	126	-	-
Job satisfaction	1.98	0.521	126	0.777**	0
Quality of work life	1.96	0.512	126	0.896**	0

Source: Author

Examining the significance levels compared to the standard threshold of 0.05, it becomes evident that certain variables exhibit associations with the quality of work life. For instance, education, designation, and experience showcase significance levels below 0.05, leading to the acceptance of alternative hypotheses (H1) and the rejection of null hypotheses (H0). This indicates a discernible relationship between these variables and the quality of work life within the studied context. Conversely, factors such as age, salary, and total experience display no substantial variance concerning the quality of work life.

The significance levels exceeding 0.05 align with the acceptance of null hypotheses, indicating the absence of a statistically significant connection between these variables and the quality of work life in this specific scenario.

Furthermore, the weighted average rank analysis sheds light on the contributors to job satisfaction. It identifies welfare measures, fair policies, insurance schemes, medical benefits, and fringe benefits as the most influential factors in enhancing job satisfaction within the studied framework. These findings highlight the critical role played by these aspects in fostering a positive and satisfactory work environment for employees Das and Moharana (2017).

Additionally, the correlations between quality of work life, job satisfaction, and employee retention emerge as noteworthy. Both quality of work life and job satisfaction exhibit positive correlations with employee retention Yang (2007). Particularly striking is the robust association observed between the quality of work life and employee retention, emphasizing the significant impact of a conducive work environment on retaining employees within the organization. This underlines the importance of creating an atmosphere that promotes a high-quality work life and job satisfaction, thereby positively influencing employee retention rates Trauth (2012).

The conclusions drawn from this analysis provide valuable insights for organizational decision-makers. Understanding the factors that influence the quality of work life and job satisfaction can guide strategies aimed at enhancing these aspects, ultimately contributing to improved employee retention Moore and Kirkland (2007). Focusing on aspects such as education, designation, and experience that demonstrate significant associations with the quality of work life can aid in tailoring initiatives targeted at elevating these factors within the workplace Sharma (2005).

Moreover, acknowledging the critical role played by welfare measures, fair policies, and various benefits in driving job satisfaction underscores the importance of robust HR policies and employee-centric approaches in creating a positive work environment Kothari (2004). By prioritizing these aspects, organizations can potentially boost employee satisfaction and, consequently, retention rates.

In conclusion, the comprehensive analysis of these variables and their relationships provides valuable insights into the intricate dynamics between organizational factors, employee satisfaction, and retention. These insights serve as a guide for organizational leaders in formulating targeted strategies aimed at creating conducive work environments and bolstering employee satisfaction and retention within the organization.

Conclusions

Employee retention stands as a significant concern for many organizations due to its impact on productivity and performance. While monetary incentives play a pivotal role in maintaining employee motivation, they aren't the sole drivers. Factors such as recognition, feedback, career development, work-life balance, and organizational culture profoundly influence employee happiness and loyalty. This study delves into diverse strategies aimed at fostering workplace satisfaction and enhancing employee engagement with the company. It also investigates the priorities and preferences of employees concerning the factors that most significantly impact them. The objective of this study is to conduct a comprehensive and insightful analysis of the variables influencing employee retention, aiming to provide practical recommendations for its improvement.

References

Das, S., and Moharana, T. R. (2017). Employee empowerment and 11 organizational effectiveness: an empirical study on central public sector enterprises in India. *ITHIHAS The Journal of Indian Management*, 7(4), 40–51.

Kothari, C. R. (2004). Research Methodology: Methods and Techniques. New Age International.

Moore, D. S., and Kirkland, S. (2007). The Basic Practice of Statistics, (Vol. 2). New York: WH Freeman.

Neumark, D. (2016). Behavioural efficiency: an emerging term in management sciences. *Pakistan Economic Review*, 1(1), 69–102.

O'Meara and Petzall (2017). The principal factors that have an effect on the retention in pharmaceutical sector in India. *International Journal of Pharmaceutical Sciences Review and Research*, 2(1), 30–39.

Sharma, A. K. (2005). Text Book of Correlations and Regression. Discovery Publishing House.

Sharma, S. (2016). Role of learning management system in retention of employee in BPO industries in Chennai city. *Journal of Business and Management*, 14(2), 8–16.

Trauth, E. M. (2012). The Culture of an Information Economy: Influences and Impacts in the Republic of Ireland. Springer Science and Business Media, (pp. 1–445).

Yang, J. T. (2007). Knowledge sharing: investigating appropriate leadership roles and collaborative culture. *Tourism Management*, 28(2), 530–543. Electronic copy available at: https://ssrn.com/abstract=3939562.

39 An analysis on employee-attrition in footwear industry

Aishwarya, B., Reshmi, S.[a], Sivakrithika, N., Sujith, B.[b] and Sujitha, S.

Karpagam Academy of Higher Education, Coimbatore, Tamil Nadu, India

Abstract

Employees represent the organization's most invaluable resources, contributing both in terms of quantity and quality. As such, maintaining a stable and promising workforce has become an imperative challenge for employers over time, resulting in heightened attrition rates within organizations. This research paper endeavours to uncover the multifaceted causes of attrition, exploring its impact on both employers and employees. Furthermore, the paper delves into unconventional factors contributing to attrition, while also highlighting the potential benefits it can bring. The study also addresses the influence of leadership styles in managing attrition. Additionally, the paper offers insights into potential solutions to address this issue.

Keywords: Attrition, employee, employer, leadership, management, organization, productivity, retention

Introduction

Employee attrition, encompassing terminations, retirements, and fatalities, poses a significant challenge for businesses worldwide. The issue is particularly acute in sectors like the software industry, where retaining skilled personnel proves challenging. Companies grapple with understanding why their employees depart, prompting extensive investigations even by private HR consultants to discern dissatisfaction roots.

Upon hiring, human resources invests in training newcomers to acclimate them to the job and workplace culture, aiming to nurture their professional growth. Yet, regardless of a company's size, staff turnover remains a ubiquitous concern. Employees often seek higher salaries and improved working conditions, triggering companies to estimate and mitigate personnel churn.

However, divulging attrition data is typically avoided to safeguard the company's reputation among loyal workers and clients. Businesses, including major players like TATA and Reliance, are implementing strategies to tackle this issue. Initiatives such as flexible working hours and healthcare benefits aim to alleviate employee dissatisfaction.

Addressing employee attrition involves multifaceted approaches. Competitive pay, comprehensive benefits, and career growth opportunities demonstrate an employer's commitment, fostering employee loyalty. Creating an inclusive environment valuing diversity, transparent communication, and teamwork enhances job satisfaction, encouraging prolonged tenures. Flexible work arrangements cater to work-life balance needs, significantly impacting employee commitment.

Regular feedback, performance appraisals, and recognition of achievements bolster engagement and happiness. Involving employees in decision-making processes and wellness programmes underscores the company's dedication to their well-being. Promoting a positive work-life balance is vital, preventing burnout and reducing attrition.

Conducting comprehensive exit interviews yields valuable insights, guiding improvements and addressing underlying issues. Encouraging continuous learning through skill development programmes signals commitment to employees' growth, enhancing motivation. Acknowledging exceptional performance cultivates morale and loyalty.

Effective management and leadership significantly influence employee retention. Each company, unique in culture and challenges, requires tailored strategies. Monitoring employee satisfaction, conducting surveys, and adapting policies based on feedback prove crucial in reducing attrition while fostering a motivated workforce.

In essence, mitigating attrition demands a holistic approach encompassing fair compensation, career advancement, work-life balance, and supportive leadership, with continuous evaluation and adaptation being imperative for sustained success.

Problem Statement

The need for investigation arises from the challenge of understanding the impact of emissions alongside the rapid expansion of businesses. A critical issue faced by organisations is the costly problem of staff attrition. This necessitates a study to delve into the complex connections between employee motivation, job

[a]reshmiselvaraj03092000@gmail.com, [b]sujithasundaram1999@gmail.com

satisfaction, and retention. This research holds importance for both industry practitioners dealing with turnover and academia. Companies heavily investing in employee development and retention strategies can greatly benefit from the insights gained through this investigation.

Objectives of Study

- To investigate employee attrition in selected footwear organisation
- To pinpoint the underlying factors contributing to employee attrition within the organization

Research Methodology

- Research design: Descriptive research analyses data on current circumstances, procedures, trends, and cause-and-effect relationships for interpretation.
- Sample design: Utilised random sampling, selecting a smaller group from a larger one with equal probability.
- Sample size: Study involved three footwear companies with a total sample size of 120.
- Sources of data collection: Utilised both previously gathered and new data, involving various technologies and collection methods.

- Primary data: Gathered core information through a questionnaire.
- Tools used for analysis: Employed simple percentage analysis, Chi-square test, and correlation analysis for data interpretation.

Results and Discussion

The table indicates varying levels of satisfaction among respondents regarding personal growth opportunities: 28.3% highly satisfied, 30.0% satisfied, 21.7% neutral, 11.7% dissatisfied, and 8.3% highly dissatisfied. Overall, the majority express contentment with personal development prospects.

Table 39.2 Opportunities for personal growth and development.

Particulars	No. of respondents	Percent
Highly satisfied	34	28.3
Satisfied	36	30.0
Neither satisfied nor dissatisfied	26	21.7
Dissatisfied	14	11.7
Highly dissatisfied	10	8.3
Total	120	100.0

Source: Author

Review of Literature

Table 39.1 Studies on employee attrition: authors, methodologies, and insights.

Author name	Reference	Study	Methodology	Conclusion	Insights
Bansal	(2019)	Focuses on HR role, attrition, and organizational effectiveness	Utilised simple random sampling and percentage calculation for attrition rate determination	Tailored retention strategies are essential; no universal solution for attrition. Understanding impact on operations.	Attrition management key via HR; Factors like salary, growth prospects, policies affect attrition; Unique solutions needed.
Gayathri and Thaiyalnayaki	(2020)	Explores reasons for female attrition in IT firms	Mixed primary (questionnaires) and secondary data sources. Survey method; purposive sampling of 473 valid responses	Identifies attrition factors: work environment, career lack, culture, compensation, and supervisor support impact females.	Work environment, career growth, and supervisor support significant in female attrition. Mixed data sources and survey method used.
Arora et al.	(2021)	Focuses on software industry's HR challenges	Employed primary data collection through well-structured questionnaires. Questionnaire administered to 100 BPO workers.	High attrition rates impact software companies; attracting and retaining workforce problematic.	Software industry faces HR challenges; Attrition affects budget; Both primary and secondary data collection utilized.

Source: Author

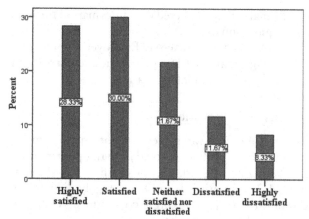

Figure 39.1 Bar chart depicting opportunities for personal growth and development
Source: Author

Table 39.3 Chi-square test – gender and factors that lead to employee attribution.

H0: There is no significant relationship between the gender of the respondents and factors that leads to employee attrition in the organization.

Pearson Chi-square	Value	df	Asymp. sig. (2-sided)
	115.671a	19	.000
Likelihood ratio	139.905	19	.000
Linear-by-linear association	82.820	1	.000
N of valid cases	120		

Source: Author

Table 39.4 Correlation analysis: relationship between the age of the respondents and effect of retention in the organization.

Correlation

		Age of the respondents	Retention
Age of the respondents	Pearson Correlation	1	.886
	Sig. (2-tailed)		.000
	N	120	120
Effect of retention in the organization	Pearson Correlation	.886	1
	Sig. (2-tailed)	.000	
	N	120	120

. Correlation is significant at the 0.01 level (2-tailed)
Source: Author

The table suggests a significant correlation between respondents' gender and factors contributing to employee attrition, with a p value of 0.000, significant at the 5% level. Accepting the alternative hypothesis indicates a meaningful association between gender and organisational attributes influencing attrition, supported by a minimum expected count of 0.30.

According to the above table, the co-efficient of correlation between the respondents' ages and the impact of retention in the organisation is.886 out of 120 respondents. It's down there. Therefore, there is a strong correlation between respondents' ages and organisational retention.

From the above table it clearly shows that the regression value of R is .964 (i.e.) there is an impact on expectation of employees to retain them in the organization. The coefficient of the relation explains that the R square value is .930; which mean 93.0% of respondents was impact on expectation of employees to retain them in the organization.

Table 39.5 Regression analysis: relationship between salary of respondents and expectation of employees to retain them in the organization.

Model	R	R Square	Adjusted R Square	Std. Error of the estimate
1	.964a	.930	.929	2.98565

a- Predictors: (Constant), gender of the respondents
Source: Author

The F statistic value was 1567.108, and the p value was smaller than the alpha value (0.05) at $p = 0.000$. By independent variables, I mean The respondents' salaries had an impact on the dependent variables concurrently. Employees are expected to stay with the organisation. The regression model's R square coefficient of determination is 0.93. The P value was lower (0.05) than alpha. This demonstrates that there is a strong correlation between respondents' salaries and their anticipation that the company will keep them on.

Table 39.6 ANOVA.

Model		Sum of squares	df		Mean square	F	Sig.
	Regression	13969.338	1		13969.338	1567.108	.000a
1	Residual	1051.862		118	8.914		
	Total	15021.200		119			

Predictors: (Constant), Salary of Respondents

Dependent variable: Expectation of Employees to Retain them in the Organization

Source: Author

Table 39.7 Coefficients.

Model	Unstandardized coefficients		Standardized coefficients	t	Sig.
	B	Std. Error	Beta		
1 (Constant)	-.410	.644		-.637	.526
Salary of the respondents	10.121	.256	.964	39.587	.000

a. Dependent variable: Expectation of employees to retain them in the organization

Source: Author

Findings

The findings reveal various sentiments among respondents regarding organisational aspects. Notably, 40.0% strongly agree on compensation and benefits, while 33.3% strongly agree on increased employee loyalty. Additionally, 40.0% agree on reduced hiring costs. Moreover, 30.0% express strong agreement regarding a highly skilled workforce. Positive company culture sees agreement from 31.7%, but 39.2% strongly disagree on maintaining morale. Job security elicits strong satisfaction from 30.0%, and 33.3% strongly find current salary offerings satisfactory. Further, 45.8% are satisfied with prevailing working conditions, and 38.3% highly satisfied with organisational morale. Engaging activities' freedom is strongly agreed upon by 40.0%, while rewards and incentives garner 38.3% agreement. Work-life balance satisfaction is at 28.3%. Relationships between respondent gender and attrition factors, age and retention impact, gender and engagement techniques, salary and retention expectations are discerned. However, no substantial gender-related correlation with attrition factors is evident.

Recommendations

To improve, the company must foster a stress-free environment, prioritize work-life balance, and promote open communication Chellammal and Magesh (2018). Cultivating strong relationships among peers and varying job tasks can prevent boredom and stress Cathrine (2019). Providing transportation facilities for punctuality and equitable compensation policies Cangelosi et al. (1998) with employee benefits are vital for enhancing motivation and overall workplace satisfaction Marufu et al. (2021).

Conclusion

The primary objective of any organization is to generate profits. However, in order to achieve optimal profitability, the organization must place a greater emphasis on its employees and implement strategies for their long-term retention. The findings of this study reveal that insufficient growth prospects and inadequate salaries are the primary drivers compelling employees to seek new job opportunities. This research emphasizes that to mitigate attrition, industries should facilitate internal employee growth by embracing innovative technologies and implementing effective training initiatives. Within the scope of this study, employee salary emerges as the most pivotal factor contributing to high attrition rates. Additionally, management must ensure that employees are fairly compensated for their contributions within the organization they are employed in.

References

Arora, S., Rawat, S., Bisht, P., and Srivastava, P. (2021). A study on the possible reasons for attrition of junior doctors in India. 5(2), 31–35 .

Bansal, S. (2019). A study on nurses' attrition factors and retention techniques. 8(1), 168–178 , ISSNo: 2249-0558.

Cangelosi, J. D., Markham, F. S., and Bounds, W. T. (1998). Factors related to nurse retention and turnover: an updated study. *Health Marketing Quarterly*, 15(3), 25.

Cathrine, T. (2019). Attrition analysis and retention strategies among staff nurses–a survey study. *Indian Journal of Community Health*, 31(2), 257–261.

Chellammal, K., and Magesh, R. (2018). A study on nurses attrition factors and retention techniques. *International Journal of Management, IT and Engineering*, 8(1), 168–178.

Gayathri, K., and Thaiyalnayaki, M. (2020). A study on driving forces leading to nurses' attrition at home healthcare services. 68(1).

Marufu, T. C., Collins, A., Vargas, L., Gillespie, L., and Almghairbi, D. (2021). Factors influencing retention among hospital nurses: systematic review. *British Journal of Nursing*, 30(5), 302–308.

40 An empirical study on third-party logistics performance in selected organisation

Mahendran, A., Sowbarni, G.[a], A. Nandhini[b] and E. Rajeswari[c]

Karpagam Academy of Higher Education, Coimbatore, Tamil Nadu, India

Abstract

Successful enterprises strategically employ logistics and supply chain management to curtail expenses, boost competitiveness, and streamline operations. In today's business milieu, logistics orchestrates the seamless movement of goods, merging physical, organizational, and informational aspects. This investigation aims to scrutinize how a firm's logistics management—encompassing transportation, warehousing, packaging, inventory, and information handling—affects efficiency and effectiveness. The reduction of costs in each logistical facet significantly impacts overall expenses, enhancing business efficacy. This study pinpoints pivotal logistics activities crucial for a company's triumph. Empirical research involving 80 companies in the Republic of Macedonia validates the overarching hypothesis, emphasizing the necessity of adept inventory, storage, warehousing, transportation, and information handling for logistics managers. The findings accentuate the urgency for optimal logistics operations management to bolster overall business efficiency and ensure heightened customer satisfaction.

Keywords: Competitive advantage, customer satisfaction, effectiveness, supply chain

Introduction

In recent times, there has been a significant surge in attention towards logistics, marking its escalating significance over the past two decades. This evolution has been closely intertwined with substantial environmental shifts. Presently, logistics services have emerged as a sought-after business strategy owing to their potential to cut costs and augment customer value. Previously confined to operational realms within purchasing and distribution departments, contemporary logistics services are undergoing a transformation, propelled by strategic alliances, technological advancements, and an intensifying competitive landscape.

Internal factors, such as the adoption of decision support systems, information system integration, heightened performance expectations, and the impact on traditional functional domains, also contribute to this shift. Globalization, technological innovations, customer-centric approaches, and outsourcing practices have become pivotal drivers sparking heightened interest in logistics, compelling organizations to seek competitive edges. Logistics, encompassing resource flow management from origin to destination, isn't merely limited to goods but extends to meeting diverse customer or business requisites. It intricately weaves together information integration, transportation, inventory, warehousing, handling, packaging, and often, security measures. While contemporary manufacturing logistics complexity can be modelled, analyzed, visualized, and optimized via factory simulation software, its landscape remains in a continual state of evolution.

Problem Statement

Amidst today's intense business competition, survival and sustained growth pose challenges. Businesses resort to diverse strategies for stability, including outsourcing operations, notably within the logistics sector. While using portions of third-party logistics (3PL) proves beneficial, this study aims to uncover the potential impact of fully embracing 3PL. Existing research lacks a focused analysis of outsourcing's specific positive effects on individual 3PL components, a gap this study aims to address, contributing to a clearer understanding of its role in logistics.

Scope of the Study

This study examines how different aspects of 3PL optimization affect customer satisfaction, gathering insights from relevant employees. It explores various third-party logistics concepts impacting customer contentment, identifies transit issues faced by 3PLs, and presents crucial analyses and conclusions. Third-party logistics providers streamline supply chains, offering expertise to save time and costs for outsourced operations.

[a]sowba13@gmail.com, [b]Nandhini.aruchamy@kahedu.edu.in, [c]rajiguna84@gmail.com

Objectives of the Study

- The study focuses on the company's third-party logistics performance
- To gauge how satisfied wholesalers are with dealing with third-party logistics

Research Methodology

- Research design: Delegates from the automobile service sector were chosen for assessment via convenient sampling method to ensure comprehensive representation.
- Sampling design: Six organizations were selected using non-probability sampling. Convenient sampling was employed for population sampling.
- Sample size: A total of 120 samples were included.
- Data sources: Primary data gathered from both primary and partner sources.
- Primary data: Collected from automotive sector experts through structured interviews.

Literature Review

Table 40.1 Insights into logistics performance and 3PL dynamics: key findings from recent studies.

Author name	Reference	Study finding	Inference/insights
Large and Hartmann	(2017)	Emphasizes customer-specific adaptation as vital for 3PL performance.	Customized logistics services are crucial for 3PL success, fostering lasting relationships and contract renewals.
Knemeyer, A.M., Murphy, P.R.		Compares users and 3PL providers on relationship marketing factors.	Trust and effective communication are pivotal in sustaining business relationships.
Bülbül et al.	(2018)	Uses employee ratings to assess company performance against competitors.	Employee-rated assessments offer insights into a company's relative performance.
Karagöz and Akgün	(2019)	Defines logistics performance as efficiency, effectiveness, and differentiation.	Logistics performance involves resource management, goal attainment, and value for customers.

Source: Author

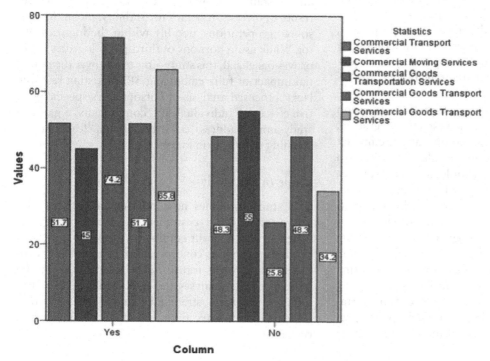

Figure 40.1 Product services of third-party logistics performance
Source: Author

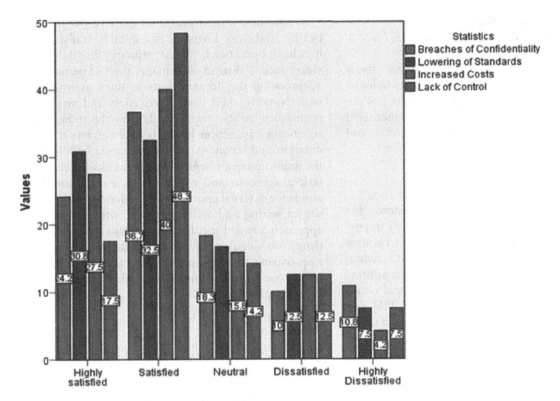

Figure 40.2 Ranking critical issues in logistics outsourcing
Source: Author

- Statistical tools: Utilized simple percentage analysis for assessment purposes.

Results and Discussion

The assessment of logistics performance and the strategic role of 3PL services play a pivotal role in contemporary business operations. This analysis delves into various factors influencing logistics performance evaluation, ranging from inventory management to transportation and technological integration. Moreover, it explores the prevalent product services employed in 3PL performance within firms, shedding light on the key preferences among respondents. Additionally, the critical issues impacting logistics outsourcing and the level of satisfaction towards these concerns provide insights into the challenges and contentment levels within the logistics landscape.

Logistics performance evaluation:
- Inventory management stands out at 31.7% consideration, followed by facilities/warehouses (24.2%), purchasing/sourcing (18.3%), transportation (14.2%), and information/communication technology (11.7%).
- Inventory management holds the highest priority (31.7%).

Third-party logistics services:
- 74.2% utilize commercial goods transportation services, 65.8% engage in packing and moving services.
- 55.0% do not use commercial moving services.
- 51.7% benefit from commercial goods transport and commercial transport services.
- Dominant service: commercial goods transportation (74.2%).

The study highlights the significance of inventory management in logistics performance evaluation and the widespread utilization of commercial goods transportation services in third-party logistics, shaping firms' operational landscapes.

Critical issues in logistics outsourcing ranking:
- Lack of control:
  - Highly satisfied: 17.5%, satisfied: 48.3%.
  - Majority satisfaction (48.3%) relates to lack of control.
- **Increased costs:**
  - Highly satisfied: 27.5%, Satisfied: 40.0%.
  - Second-highest satisfaction (40.0%) observed for increased costs.
- **Lowering of standards:**
  - Highly satisfied: 30.8%, satisfied: 32.5%.

- **Breaches of confidentiality:**
  - Highly satisfied: 24.2%, satisfied: 36.7%.

The data illustrates varying satisfaction levels among respondents concerning critical issues in logistics outsourcing. Notably, lack of control receives the highest satisfaction (48.3%), followed by increased costs (40.0%), lowering of standards (32.5%), and breaches of confidentiality (36.7%).

Findings

Findings reveal that among factors considered for logistics performance, inventory holds primary importance (31.7%), followed by facilities and warehouses (24.2%) Kenyon and Meixell (2007). Regarding third-party logistics, commercial goods transportation services (74.2%) dominate, while critical issues in outsourcing, such as lack of control (48.3%) and increased costs (40.0%), show varying satisfaction levels Kumar et al. (2006).

These results signify the significance of inventory management and transportation in logistics, emphasizing the preference for specific 3PL services Lambert and Burduroglo (2000). The data also highlights concerns regarding control and cost in outsourcing, underlining areas for improvement and focus within logistics strategies.

Conclusion

In addressing optimization strategies for third-party logistics (3PL) performance, it's imperative to acknowledge the impact of tailored initiatives. Implementing measures to enhance 3PL performance requires astute planning and execution within logistics companies. The crucial focus areas encompass refining processes for cost reduction and ensuring heightened operational efficiency. These measures contribute significantly to elevating overall performance and bolstering competitiveness in the market.

In conclusion, the integration of third-party logistics by Rightway Logistics has notably transformed logistical operations. While primary dispatch providers lack a distinct advantage, their expertise and adeptness in the domain position them as frontrunners. Notably, their cost-effectiveness and analytical proficiency bolster their standing in the industry. A significant distinction arises between external coordination and second-party coordination, highlighting the importance of integrated frameworks for effective task assignment and management. Future considerations for external coordination underscore the necessity of setting and fulfilling goals. Although various approaches exist for enhancing external coordination, there's no singular, universally recommended model, emphasizing the ongoing need for tailored strategies to navigate the complexities of this aspect within logistics management.

References

Bülbül et al. (2018). Logistics learning capability: Sustaining the competitive advantage gained through logistics leverage. *Journal of Business Logistics*, 28(2), 57–82.

Karagöz and Akgün (2019). Role of supply chain practices on customer satisfaction in the printing industry in Kenya: a case study of Morven Kester East Africa limited. *International Journal of Academic Research in Business and Social Sciences*, 4(10), 128–143.

Kenyon, G. N., and Meixell, M. J. (2007). Success factors and cost management strategies for logistics outsourcing. *Journal of Management and Marketing Research*, 7(1), 1–17.

Kumar, V., Fantazy, K. A., Kumar, U., and Boyle, T. A. (2006). Implementation and management framework for supply chain flexibility. *Journal of Enterprise Information Management*, 19(3), 303–319.

Lambert, D. M., and Burduroglo, R. (2000). Measuring and selling the value of logistics. *The International Journal of Logistics Management*, 11(1), 1–16.

Large, N., and Hartmann, R. (2017). Supply Chain Logistics Management. New York: McGraw Hill.

41 Employee engagement and its impact on organizational success

Mahintha, T., Arulprakasam, E.[a], Chitra, P.[b] and Sarojadevi, R.[c]

Karpagam Academy of Higher Education, Coimbatore, Tamil Nadu, India

Abstract

Employees constitute the fundamental cornerstone of any industry, serving as the bedrock upon which its success is built. The potency of any industry is contingent upon the fervor and dedication of its workforce. Employee engagement, a dynamic interaction between an organization and its employees, emerges as a critical determinant in attaining organizational objectives. It fosters a sense of inclusion and consequently culminates in contentment. Forward-looking enterprises envision their employees as reservoirs of zeal, eagerness, and proactive drive, aspiring for their self-improvement and unwavering commitment to delivering excellence. Essentially, companies aspire for their workforce to be wholeheartedly involved. This state of engagement is realized when individuals perceive that their contributions are valued by the organization, their efforts contribute substantively to organizational progress, and significantly, their individual aspirations for growth, rewards, and compensation are intricately interwoven with the company's trajectory.

Keywords: Employee engagement, human resources strategies, organization

Introduction

Employee engagement stands apart as a distinct entity, separate from worker satisfaction, motivation, and organizational subculture. The well-being and contentment of employees should rank as a primary concern for any thriving company, ensuring customer satisfaction and optimal outcomes. In simpler terms, contented employees contribute to delighted customers, and a multitude of contented customers translates to contented stakeholders.

The engagement of workers, whether on an emotional or intellectual level, holds paramount importance for the organization's success. The positive sentiments that employees harbor toward their company and employers significantly influence customer satisfaction in terms of service, loyalty, and engagement. Moreover, engagement has the potential to imbue each employee with the drive to excel, encouraging the acquisition of new skills and the generation of innovative ideas. Our study will delve into an exploration of literature reviews, followed by an elucidation of data collection methods, thereby elucidating the empirical approaches and outcomes of our empirical tests, alongside a comprehensive discussion and conclusion.

Problem Statement

Addressing low employee engagement in corporate HR within the packaging industry is critical. With a focus on aligning roles, this issue impacts job satisfaction, productivity, and product quality. To remain competitive, companies seek effective methods to gauge and elevate engagement, recognizing its profound impact on performance.

Objectives of the Study

- To study the contemporary strategies employed by companies for employee engagement and selection
- Quantifying the influence of training and job satisfaction on employee engagement

Research Methodology

- Research design: Descriptive research delineates observed occurrences and current phenomena.
- Sampling design: Utilized convenience sampling techniques.
- Sample size: Engaged seven engineering organizations, totaling a sample size of 120.
- Data sources: Emphasized primary data, freshly gathered through questionnaires, a prevalent method.
- Statistical tools: Employed simple percentage analysis, Chi-square test, and correlation analysis.

Results and Discussion

Employee satisfaction and engagement
The below data illustrates the satisfaction levels of employees regarding various benefits. It showcases

[a]eapcas@gmail.com, [b]chitraxing24@gmail.com, [c]rajendransaro@gmail.com

Literature Review

Table 41.1 Exploring influential factors on employee engagement and market dynamics: insights from literature.

Author	Reference	Insights	Study findings
Vijay Anand and Banu	(2019)	Employee engagement is influenced by job responsibilities, rewards, growth opportunities, teamwork, and communication. It serves as a retention tool. Remuneration and benefits have the most significant impact.	Various factors like role, environment, training, and managerial relationships are linked to employee engagement.
Mokayo and Kipyegon	(2020)	Employee engagement is connected to personal growth, performance management, remuneration, and recreational amenities. Remuneration plays a major role, while recreational facilities have the least impact.	Emphasizes the influence of remuneration on engagement, while recreational facilities have minimal effect on employee engagement.
Duke et al.	(2021)	Kenya's market for Indian textiles proposes rural electrification using decentralized technologies. Varying product quality and consumer confusion between brands exist.	Focuses on market failure in solar home system components, suggesting solutions and highlighting potential quality issues in other components and markets.

Source: Author

the varying degrees of satisfaction, with percentages indicating how employees perceive different facets of their training programs, learning transfer, managerial support, and more.

- Satisfaction level with benefits offered:
  - Highly satisfied: 25.0%
  - Satisfied: 44.2%
  - Dissatisfied: 15.8%
  - Highly dissatisfied: 15.0%
- Satisfaction with training's knowledge acquisition curriculum:
  - Highly satisfied: 30.0%
  - Satisfied: 35.8%
  - Dissatisfied: 19.2%
  - Highly dissatisfied: 15.0%
- Transfer of learning from training to work:
  - Highly satisfied: 20.8%
  - Satisfied: 57.5%
  - Dissatisfied: 13.3%
  - Highly dissatisfied: 8.3%
- Training and development aiding in learning new ideas:
  - Highly satisfied: 18.3%
  - Satisfied: 65.8%
  - Dissatisfied: 11.7%
  - Highly dissatisfied: 4.2%
- Manager's encouragement and assistance in training and education:
  - Highly satisfied: 35.8%
  - Satisfied: 49.2%
  - Dissatisfied: 10.0%
  - Highly dissatisfied: 5.0%

- Majority (65.8%) of respondents are satisfied with innovation.

Determinants to measure employee engagement
- Methods used to measure employee engagement:
  - Personnel meetings: 34.2%
  - Observation: 25.8%
  - Performance: 19.2%
  - Inspection opportunities: 20.8%

Majority (34.2%) measure engagement through personnel meeting

Statistical analyses
The Chi-square test examines the association between the age group of respondents and their departments' engagement within the organization. The analysis accepts the null hypothesis, suggesting no significant relationship between these variables.

The correlation analysis explores the relationship between respondents' monthly income and their perception of being appreciated and recognized by the company. It demonstrates a strong positive correlation ($r = 0.810$, $p < 0.01$) between these variables, indicating that as income increases, feelings of appreciation and recognition by the company also increase. Nonparametric correlation tests (Kendall's tau_b and Spearman's rho) support this significant positive relationship.

- Association between age group and department of engagement:
  - Calculated Chi-square value is lesser than the table value.

- Null hypothesis accepted: No significant relationship found.
- Correlation between monthly income and appreciation by company:
  - Pearson correlation: 0.810**
  - Significant positive correlation (0.01 level) between income and appreciation by the company.

Overall, the results suggest varying satisfaction levels regarding training, different methods to measure engagement, and a correlation between income and appreciation by the company. However, no significant relationships were found between certain factors, indicating no direct associations between age groups and departmental engagement or different ways of measuring engagement.

Findings

- A majority of 45.8% of respondents express satisfaction with opportunities for professional growth Yalabik et al. (2017).
- Among the respondents, 35.0% indicate a high level of satisfaction with training.
- Approximately 27.5% of the respondents express satisfaction with talents and expertise.
- About 31.7% of the respondents agree with the introduction of new ideas.
- Nearly 39.2% of the respondents mention that the company sometimes implements their ideas.
- Around 68.3% of the respondents consistently choose "Always." Kim-Soon and Manikayasagam (2015).
- Approximately 50.8% of the respondents note insufficient arrangements to address employee problems.
- About 35.0% of the respondents express satisfaction with positional responsibilities.
- A significant majority, comprising 61.7% of respondents, find their roles challenging.
- A substantial majority of 65.8% of respondents express satisfaction with innovation.
- About 34.2% of the respondents indicate using personnel meetings as a method to measure engagement.
- A substantial 71.7% of the respondents highly value that their ideas and suggestions are taken into consideration.

Recommendations

- To diversify its talent pool, the industry should avoid solely depending on internal promotions in employee recruitment. Relying on internal advancements might limit fresh recruits with significant potential from contributing to the company's progress.
- Improving employee compensation is crucial for the company to attract skilled external candidates who are both qualified and interested in joining the organization.
- Considering a reduction in the probationary period from a year to approximately six months could alleviate prolonged uncertainty regarding permanent employment, reducing apprehension among newly hired employees.

Conclusion

Human resource management, akin to the pivotal role of the heart in a living organism, remains foundational for organizational functionality. Regardless of sector, the competence and engagement of the workforce dictate an organization's success. Achieving desired outcomes mandates meticulous recruitment, aligning abilities and adaptable talents with designated roles. This symbiotic match ensures optimal performance, mirroring the harmony between the heart and the body's functions.

The precision in recruiting individuals capable of seamlessly integrating into their roles defines the efficiency and efficacy of an organization. It's not merely about filling positions but about orchestrating a symphony where each member contributes uniquely. Thus, management's emphasis on strategic recruitment, aligning human potential with organizational objectives, ultimately determines the organization's ability to thrive. Just as the heart regulates the body's functions, strategic HR practices regulate an organization's operational rhythm, shaping its success trajectory.

References

Anand, V. V., and Banu, C. V. (2019). A research paper on the effect of employee engagement on job satisfaction in IT sector. *Journal of Business Management and Social Sciences Research*, 3(5), 31–39.

Duke, R. D., et al. (2021). Employee engagement and its impact on organizational success - a study in manufacturing company, India. *IOSR Journal of Business and Management*, 18(4), 52–57.

Kim-Soon, N., and Manikayasagam, G. (2015). Employee engagement and job satisfaction. Retrieved January, 14, 2017.

Mokayo, S. O., and Kipyegon, M. J. (2020). Engagement and job satisfaction, 2015. Retrieved from https://www.researchgate.net.

Yalabik, Z. Y., Rayton, B. A., and Rapti, A. (2017). Facets of job satisfaction and work engagement. In Evidence-Based HRM: A Global Forum for Empirical Scholarship, (Vol. 5(3), pp. 248–265). Emerald Publishing Limited.

42 The study of efficiency and effectiveness of warehouse management in the automobile manufacturing industry

Vignesh, V., Arulprakasam, E.[a], Nandhini, A.[b] and Sarojadevi, R.[c]

Karpagam Academy of Higher Education, Coimbatore, Tamil Nadu, India

Abstract

The purpose of this article is to study how inventory management, understood as a set of planning and control decisions and procedures, is organized and driven by task complexity and market dynamics. Design/methods/approaches. The difference between production and distribution warehouses was found to be related to the relationship between grade change and PE. Furthermore, TC seems to be the main driving force behind the peculiarity of the warehouse management system (WMS). Limitations/Impacts of the Study Such a feature is the first step in defining common warehouse functionality and helps managers choose the best software for their warehouse operations. Uniqueness/value the article identifies fundamental aspects of warehouse management, makes them measurable, tests them, and assesses their impact on WMS specificity.

Keywords: Logistic information system, supply chain management, warehouse management

Introduction

Warehouse managers are the backbone of store networks, handling vital tasks like stockpiling, product planning, and inventory management (Langevin and Ripopel, 2005). This article explores how adopting Warehouse Management Systems (WMS) impacts the accumulation of auto parts inventory in Saudi Arabia. Split into four sections, it delves into the importance of automotive parts in the country, the role of the automotive industry in managing traffic operations and storage, and the significance of the WMS in this setup.

The second part details the research approach, explaining why and how data was collected. It offers insights into the evaluation process and the investigation's coordination. By examining the influence of WMS on auto parts inventory, this study aims to shed light on the automotive sector's organizational dynamics in Saudi Arabia, highlighting the critical role played by effective warehouse management systems in this industry's success.

Problem Statement

India currently leads the global car supply chain, offering extensive business opportunities worldwide. Car companies adapt diverse development models based on their requirements, aiming for surveillance and competitive edge. As the automotive landscape evolves with new vehicle offerings, the approach of delegates has shifted in the recent year. In today's heavily automated realm, the training and advancement requirements for professionals in auto companies and public roles often go overlooked. This oversight stems from the industry's belief that prolonged setups might hamper overall company capacity. Consequently, amidst this modernization, there's a pressing need to reevaluate strategies to ensure both industry growth and the development of skilled professionals.

Objectives of the Study

- To study the warehouse process well- streamlined and ensure equipment automation to make tasks less difficult for the employees
- To facilitate data for short- and long-term planning and control of management
- To keep material cost under control and low cost of production

Research Methodology

- Research design: Utilized descriptive studies for individual or group characteristics, structuring data collection and analysis.
- Sampling techniques: Employed a probability sampling method, selecting six manufacturing companies for the study.
- Sample size: Set the sample size at 150 for the study.
- Sources of data: Gathered primary data from experts in the vehicle alliance sector through a well-

[a]eapcas@gmail.com, [b]Nandhini.aruchamy@kahedu.edu.in, [c]rajendransaro@gmail.com

organized arrangement. Utilized secondary data from various sources such as research articles, internet portals, magazines, and newspapers.

- Statistical tools: Employed statistical analysis tools including simple percentage analysis, Chi-square tests, and correlation analysis.

Literature Review

Table 42.1 Insights into India's automobile industry: perspectives from various studies.

Author name	Reference	Insights	Study findings
Hameedu	(2018)	India leads in automobile production, focusing on goods categorized for duty, reduction, or exclusion under AIFTA.	India prioritizes protecting its natural rubber sector, contrasting with Thailand's lack of similar measures.
Baby	(2019)	Approximately 60,000 hectares are under automobile development; estimates a 70% increase in the next five years in liquid gold production.	Ribbed Smoked Sheets (RSS) dominate 70% of India's automobile production.
Viswanathan	(2020)	Advocates for increased women participation in automobile plantations after skill development to address labor shortages.	Emphasizes the need for women to join automobile plantation jobs after training in various production processes.

Source: Author

Results and Discussion

In examining respondent demographics and their perceptions, this study encompasses educational qualifications and work experience among participants. Insights reveal a majority of postgraduates (45.3%) and a significant proportion with 5 to 6 years' experience (37.3%). Moreover, associations between education levels and beliefs regarding warehouse management system (WMS) functionality, such as minimizing losses and optimizing space, are highlighted. Additionally, a positive correlation surfaces between respondents' income and shipment frequency. These findings underscore the interplay between education, experience, and perceptions in the context of WMS functionalities and shed light on complex correlations within the warehouse management domain. The details of the data and findings are given below.

Educational qualification of respondents
- Graduate: 11.3%
- Postgraduate: 45.3%
- Diploma: 26.7%
- Others: 16.7%
- Insights: 45.3% are postgraduates, 26.7% hold diplomas, 11.3% are graduates, and 16.7% fall under 'Others.'

Work experience of respondents
- Below 2 years: 30.7%
- 2 to 5 years: 24.0%
- 5 to 6 years: 37.3%
- Above 6 years: 8.0%

- Insights: 37.3% have 5 to 6 years' experience, 30.7% below 2 years, 24% 2 to 5 years, and 8% above 6 years.

Warehouse management system impact on loss minimization
- Significant association found between education level and belief in minimizing losses via WMS movement.

Warehouse management system's space utilization impact
- Significant association detected between educational level and belief in WMS optimizing space usage.

Correlation analysis - monthly income and shipment frequency
- Positive correlation identified between respondents' monthly income and shipment frequency received in the last year.
- Factors like identifying system problems, computerizing warehouse functions, stock distribution, and experience showed varying correlations.

The study revealed a dominance of postgraduates (45.3%) and 5 to 6 years' experienced respondents (37.3%). Significantly, education level affects perceptions on WMS functions like loss minimization and space utilization. Moreover, a positive correlation between respondents' income and shipment frequency was noted. However, varied correlations emerged between factors impacting the warehouse system, indicating nuanced relationships within these parameters.

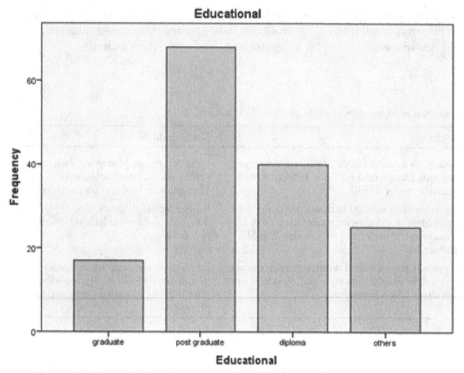

Figure 42.1 Chart depicting educational qualification of the respondents
Source: Author

Findings:
- Majority, 37.3% of respondents, hold 5 to 6 years of experience.
- Significant association found between Warehouse Management minimizing losses and educational levels (p < 0.05).
- No significant association detected between warehouse stock distribution and age (p > 0.05).
- No significant correlation observed between monitoring stock levels and age (p > 0.05).
- Gender does not significantly impact the effect of warehouse management in minimizing losses (p > 0.05).
- Similarly, gender doesn't significantly affect the role of transportation management in load balancing (p > 0.05).

Recommendations
- Historically, warehouses stored goods, now viewed as critical assets, posing cost challenges for businesses due to their toxic nature Maister (1976).
- Warehouses hold accountability for boosting organizational performance and fulfilling commitments made to advocacy groups Roodbergen and Vis (2006), Kulwiec (1985), Luo (2010).
- Turnaround time measures the duration for order processing and packaging before dispatch

to meet delivery deadlines effectively Dejax (1988).

Conclusion

In summary, the automobile industry involves a vast network of individuals spanning various functional areas and departments. The rising costs associated with developing automobile models have prompted automakers to explore solutions to this ongoing challenge. Upon review, it's evident that auto manufacturers have adopted diverse strategies, particularly in localized design, product/tooling design, manufacturing, and supplier relations. The discussion in this segment primarily focused on the intricacies of manufacturing auto parts.

This exploration highlights the industry's adaptability and its continuous quest for innovation to address cost challenges. The proactive adoption of different approaches, especially in design and manufacturing, underscores the industry's commitment to efficiency and product quality. As the automotive sector evolves, it remains committed to finding new ways to optimize production, emphasizing efficiency and excellence. This ongoing commitment ensures the industry's resilience and ability to adapt to change while driving advancements in auto manufacturing.

References

Baby, K. (2019). Commercialisation of Agriculture-Automobiles, Kurukshetra, Jan-2015, (pp. 17–20).

Dejax, P. J. (1988). A methodology for warehouse location and distribution systems planning. In Freight Transport Planning and Logistics: Proceedings of an International Seminar on Freight Transport Planning and Logistics Held in Bressanone, Italy. July 1987 (pp. 289–318). Berlin, Heidelberg: Springer Berlin Heidelberg.

Hameedu, S. (2018). Part of automobile producers societies in Kerala. *Global Journal of Current Research and Academic Review, 2*(2), 159–166.

Kulwiec, R. A. (Ed.). (1985). Materials Handling Handbook (2nd edn.). New York: Wiley.

Luo, Z. (2010). Service Science and Logistics Informatics: Innovative Perspectives. IGI Global.

Maister, D. H. (1976). Centralisation of inventories and the "Square Root Law". *International Journal of Physical Distribution and Logistics Management, 6*(3), 124–134.

Roodbergen, K. J., and Vis, I. F. A. (2006). A model for warehouse layout. *IIE Transactions, 38*(10), 799–811.

Viswanathan, P. K. (2020). More women need to enter automobile jobs. *Automobile Asia, 30*(6), 68–71.

43 Employees satisfaction on monetary benefits in IT sector

Brindha, A., Esakimuthu[a] and Sivakrithika, N.[b]

Karpagam Academy of Higher Education, Coimbatore, Tamil Nadu, India

Abstract

Job satisfaction is integral to any organization's structure, significantly impacting its success. Understanding and implementing factors that foster it are crucial. Monetary and non-monetary incentives notably influence employee satisfaction. They aid in defining employee values within the organization. However, prioritizing benefits in incentive policies can be challenging. This article examines incentives and their organizational impact. It delves into various financial and non-financial incentives, exploring their connection to immediate and lasting job satisfaction levels. Additionally, it outlines the advantages for both employees and organizations by incorporating these incentives. The study aims to comprehend the relationship between job satisfaction and incentives, determining whether monetary or non-monetary motives exert a greater influence on employee performance.

Keywords: Employees, growth, job satisfaction, monetary benefits, organization, pay, performance, recognition, relationship, training

Introduction

This research aims to mitigate the influence of compensation on both employee performance and job satisfaction within the information technology (IT) industry. However, many industries offer their employees a good compensation structure in order to improve performance and give them a sense of fulfilment at work. Many organizations are currently engaging in layoffs, retrenchments, and salary reductions. Every employee must have complete financial security at all times since the total shutdown and the onset of deductions have created a sense of uncertainty in the minds of the workforce. Most organizations' total costs are heavily influenced by wages and salaries. Pay in the form of wage or "salaries" is the main economic incentive or financial reward since it attracts people to an organization and ensures their loyalty, cooperation, and best efforts. Wages and salaries are viewed from the perspective of employees as the cost of their work or contributions to the company. Therefore, it must be enough for their basic needs, to live a better lifestyle, and to save for the future. At the same time, labor costs, which reflect the human component of manufacturing, demand ongoing monitoring, measurement, and analysis.

Problem Statement

Monetary benefits are pivotal in employment dynamics, anchoring the employer-employee relationship via wages. Employees seek diverse rewards like salaries, bonuses, and insurance, while management ensures legal compliance for financial gains and safety. These factors collectively improve output, worker satisfaction, and labor relations. This study scrutinizes Trichy's IT Sector's human resource management regarding monetary benefits, aiming to unravel the link between financial gains, employee performance, and job satisfaction.

Objectives of the Study

- Evaluate employees' perceptions regarding the monetary benefits offered in their workplace.
- Explore how employee monetary benefits influence both job satisfaction and work performance.

Scope of the Study

The study aims to examine the correlation between wages, job satisfaction, and employee performance across the corporate sector, utilizing questionnaires for data collection, emphasizing the importance of prioritizing employee well-being for enhanced efficiency and productivity while exploring the intersection of job satisfaction and performance in driving increased profits.

Research Methodology

- Research design: Utilized a descriptive study method for systematic data collection and analysis within a conceptual framework.
- Sampling design: Employed a probability sampling technique across ten selected IT organizations.

[a]muthucomhsr@gmail.com, [b]sivakrithika.nellaiappan@kahedu.edu.in

- Sampling size: Utilized a sample size of 120 participants.
- Data collection: Primarily gathered through questionnaires to analyze as primary data.

- Tools and techniques: Utilized methods including weighted average, Chi-square test, and analysis of variance.

Literature Review

Table 43.1 Research study overview: monetary incentives impacting participation, employee motivation, and renewable fuel development.

Author name	Reference	Study findings	Insights/interpretation
Abdelazeem	(2023)	Monetary incentives enhance survey participation. Research aims for a systematic review of RCTs to evaluate their impact on survey engagement.	Using monetary incentives could boost survey participation, aiding in obtaining more reliable and unbiased data.
Al-Belushi	(2022)	Investigates how monetary incentives affect Shinas College of Technology employees' motivation. It examines their significance and effectiveness, targeting the most suitable incentive type.	Understanding the impact of monetary incentives on employees' motivation helps in tailoring effective strategies to boost workforce morale and productivity at the college.
Ebrahimi	(2022)	Advocates for using winter carinata crops as a renewable jet fuel (RJF) source in the southeastern US. Monetary incentive programs (PCP, BCAP, BAP) analyzed for RJF commercialization.	Winter carinata crops could serve as a viable biomass source for RJF production. Monetary incentives like PCP, BCAP, and BAP could aid in RJF commercialization, despite associated higher costs.

Source: Author

Results and Discussion

The following section presents a comprehensive analysis of diverse methodologies and statistical tests used to evaluate employee performance, satisfaction, and the correlation with demographic factors and monetary benefits. Through the weighted average method, Chi-square tests, and ANOVA, the study explores nuances within various facets of employee engagement and satisfaction. Examining aspects such as salary, work environment, job security, age, education, work experience, and demographic segmentation, this analysis unveils critical insights into the interplay between these factors and their impact on employee performance and satisfaction within the surveyed population.

Weighted average method - employee performance
- Salary and remuneration: The mean score indicates moderate satisfaction (3.3), ranking 6th.
- Work environment: Reveals higher satisfaction (3.8), ranked 4th.
- Job security: Scores 3.7, ranking 5th.
- Reward, promotion, compensation, health and safety measures: All scored equally (4.0), ranking 3rd.
- Work-life balance: Scores relatively higher (4.1), ranking 2nd.

- Career development, policies, leadership: Score similarly (4.0), ranking 3rd.
- Open communication policy: Tops the chart with the highest satisfaction score (4.2).

Interpretation: The study highlights areas requiring attention for enhanced job satisfaction, emphasizing the importance of competitive salaries, conducive work environments, and strengthened job security measures.

Chi-square test - age and monetary benefits
- 18-25 Age group: Displays high monetary benefits.
- 26-35 Age group: Indicates comparatively lower monetary benefits.
- Statistical significance: The calculated p value (<0.05) confirms a significant correlation between age and monetary benefits.

Interpretation: Distinct differences in monetary benefits across age groups underscore the need to tailor compensation structures to different age demographics for equitable satisfaction.

Chi-square test - educational qualification and monetary benefits

- Graduates: Enjoy substantial monetary benefits.

- **Others:** Receive comparatively lower monetary advantages.

Statistical significance: The p value (<0.05) indicates a meaningful relationship between education and monetary benefits.

Interpretation: Educational qualifications significantly impact monetary benefits, suggesting a need to revise compensation strategies to ensure fairness and equality across educational backgrounds.

Chi-square test - working experience and monetary benefits

- **6-10 Years' exper'ience:** Shows elevated monetary benefits.
- **16 and above years experience:** Experience relatively lower monetary advantages.
- **Statistical significance:** The p value (<0.05) confirms a substantial correlation between work experience in the IT sector and monetary benefits.

Interpretation: Work experience significantly influences monetary benefits, highlighting the importance of rewarding experience while addressing disparities for more experienced individuals.

ANOVA - Employee performance and demographic segmentation

- **Gender, location, education, computer knowledge:** Show no significant variation in employee performance.
- **Age, marital status, organization hierarchy, scale of pay:** Display significant variations in employee performance based on demographic factors.

Interpretation: Demographic factors such as age, marital status, organizational hierarchy, and pay scales notably affect employee performance, signaling the need for targeted strategies to optimize performance based on these factors.

Findings

- **Demographics:**
  - Majority of respondents are female (58.3%), aged 26-35 (44.2%), graduates (60.8%), with less than 5 years of experience (45.8%), rural (49.2%), unmarried (57.5%), affirming computer knowledge (96.7%), and in middle-level positions (58.3%).
- **Gender and monetary benefits:**
  - Male respondents experience higher monetary benefits. No significant association between gender and monetary benefits (p

- **Age and monetary benefits:**
  - Respondents aged 18-25 enjoy greater monetary benefits than those aged 26-35. Significant correlation between age and monetary benefits (p < 0.05).
- **Education and monetary benefits:**
  - Graduates receive elevated monetary benefits. Significant association between education and monetary benefits (p < 0.05).
- **Work experience and monetary benefits:**
  - 6-10 years of experience correlates with higher monetary benefits. Significant correlation between work experience in IT sector and monetary benefits (p < 0.05).
- **Location and monetary benefits:**
  - Rural respondents receive more monetary benefits compared to semi-urban ones. Significant relationship between location and monetary benefits (p < 0.05).
- **Marital status and monetary benefits:**
  - Unmarried respondents encounter higher monetary benefits. No significant association between marital status and monetary benefits (P > 0.05).
- **Computer knowledge and monetary benefits:**
  - Respondents answering "No" about computer knowledge experience elevated monetary benefits. No significant association between computer knowledge and monetary benefits (p > 0.05).
- **Organization hierarchy and monetary benefits:**
  - Middle-level positions correlate with greater monetary benefits. Significant relationship between organization hierarchy and monetary benefits (p < 0.05).
- **Earnings and monetary benefits:**
  - Respondents earning "Upto 5000" experience enhanced monetary benefits. Significant correlation between earnings and monetary benefits (p < 0.05).
- **Employee performance:**
  - Gender, education, location, marital status, computer knowledge show no significant variation in performance (p > 0.05).
  - Age, work experience in it, organization hierarchy exhibit notable variations in performance (p < 0.05).

Recommendations

Recommendations stemming from this study encompass various strategies for organizational enhancement:

- Employers should proactively offer reasonable and equitable incentives, acknowledging employees' dedication, loyalty, and responsibilities. Fair compensation fosters loyalty and commitment Kinnear and Sutherland (2000).

- Augmenting financial benefits can significantly enhance overall job satisfaction among employees, thereby potentially improving their performance.
- Management must actively monitor and assess the impact of rewards on employee job satisfaction to ensure efficacy and relevance Milkovich and Newman (2004).
- While acknowledging the influence of salary on job satisfaction and performance, this study remains inconclusive regarding the underlying mechanisms governing this relationship, necessitating further investigation.
- The study recognizes limitations, such as the absence of perspectives from select respondents on sensitive matters, indicating the importance of considering varied viewpoints.
- Implementation of a fair remuneration policy should be complemented by embracing technological advancements, refining processes, adopting innovative techniques, and encouraging novel ideas to effectively enhance employee satisfaction and organizational performance.

Conclusion

This study contributes significantly to the landscape of human resource management, enriching it with valuable insights and practices. By affirming the correlation between financial rewards and employee job satisfaction and performance, this assessment underscores their intrinsic relevance within organizational frameworks. Notably, it sheds light on the intricate dynamics between financial incentives and job satisfaction, revealing that while job satisfaction might not invariably serve as the sole mediator between financial rewards and job performance, it remains a pivotal aspect warranting attention.

Moving forward, further research endeavors hold the potential to deepen our understanding of human resources. By delving into the complexities of employee motivation plans, future studies can become instrumental in aligning these plans with both the immediate aspirations of employees and the overarching objectives of the organization. This holistic approach will likely facilitate the establishment of more nuanced strategies that foster a symbiotic relationship between employee satisfaction, performance, and organizational goals, thereby contributing to the comprehensive development of effective human resource management practices.

References

Abdelazeem, B. (2023). Usage of monetary incentive impact the involvement in surveys? a systematic review and meta-analysis of 46 randomized controlled trials. *Research Article*, 134–138.

Al-Belushi, F. (2022). Impact of monetary incentives on employee's motivation: shinas college of technology, oman - a case study. *International Journal of Management, Innovation and Entrepreneurial Research*, 11–15.

Ebrahimi, S. (2022). Renewable jet fuel supply chain network design: application of direct monetary incentives. *Applied Energy*, 310, 118569.

Kinnear, L., and Sutherland, M. (2000). Determinants of organisational commitment amongst knowledge workers. *South African Journal of Business Management*, 31(3), 106–112.

Milkovich, G. M., and Newman, J. M. (2004). Compensation (8th edn.). Burr Ridge, IL: Irwin McGraw-Hill.

44 A study on effectiveness of the interviewing process in software industries in Coimbatore

Ishwarya, R., Divya, K. V.[a] and Nagalakshmi, N.[b]

Karpagam Academy of Higher Education, Coimbatore, Tamil Nadu, India

Abstract

This study focuses on investigating the effectiveness of interviewing processes within Coimbatore's software industries. Its primary goal is to discern the critical role these procedures play in the industry. By exploring how the right talent recruitment significantly impacts an organization's success, the research scrutinizes various recruitment strategies, selection techniques, the selection process itself, and identifies best practices aimed at optimizing talent acquisition. The analysis delves deeply into these elements to understand how they interconnect and contribute to organizational success within the context of software firms in Coimbatore. The aim is to offer valuable insights that can refine and improve the recruitment frameworks employed by these industries. Ultimately, this examination seeks to shed light on the profound impact of streamlined and effective talent acquisition processes on the overall success and sustainability of software industries in the region.

Keywords: Employee, interview process, recruitment, selection, technique

Introduction

The concept of selection and recruitment has been an age-old practice, rooted in the early stages of human assessment. Throughout history, effective leadership has always entailed choosing the right individuals for specific roles, evident even in ancient activities such as hunting. Over time, the methods of selection have evolved, yet the fundamental objective remains unchanged. With the advent of modern management, industries began systematically evaluating human capabilities, leading to the establishment of human resources departments. These departments oversee various aspects concerning employees, ranging from payroll management to addressing grievances. Within the recruitment process, companies commonly adopt two distinct approaches: internal and external sourcing. Primarily, internal recruitment, through methods like promotions or transfers, remains a prevalent choice for most organizations when filling job vacancies. This enduring practice reflects the enduring significance of selecting the most fitting individuals for specific roles, echoing the historical imperative of efficient selection methodologies.

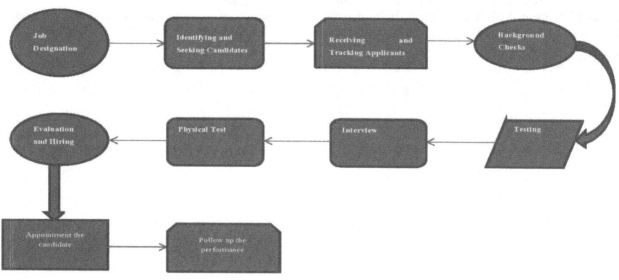

Figure 44.1 Recruitment process
Source: Author

[a]divyaponnu07@gmail.com, [b]lavanyaa2302@gmail.com

Literature Review

Table 44.1 Comparative overview of recruitment and selection perspectives in various studies.

Author name	Area of study	Study findings	Insights
Pentilla (2018)	Social media	Applicants sometimes falsify information to secure jobs. Social media aids hiring due to cost and time benefits, offering access to candidates' comprehensive profiles.	Social media's cost-effectiveness attracts candidates, yet its use demands careful scrutiny to verify information amid the hiring process.
Aswathappa (1997)	HR strategies	Robust HR strategies are vital in service industries, relying on people as a prime asset for competitive advantage. Absence of suitable HR practices imperils organizational survival.	Effective human resource management is pivotal in service sectors, where leveraging human potential defines a company's competitive edge, contrasting with industrial sectors.
Carless (2020)	Social networking	Social networks serve as job platforms but traditional hiring methods persist.	Despite the prevalence of social networking sites for job searches, conventional hiring methods remain dominant in business practices.
Ofori and Aryeetey (2022)	Recruitment and selection	Literature often treats recruitment and selection as separate processes, despite their interdependence. Insufficient candidate pools impede effective selection.	The separation of recruitment and selection in literature hampers understanding their interconnected nature, particularly when inadequate candidate pools hinder the selection process.
Valvis (2020)	Recruitment and selection	Recruitment involves seeking potential candidates, distinct from the selection process.	Distinguishing between recruitment's focus on attracting candidates and the distinct selection process is crucial for businesses to function optimally.
White (2021)	Police agencies	Global police agencies prioritize recruitment and selection. Identified issues in hiring and training officers.	Police agencies globally recognize the significance of recruitment and selection, identifying key challenges in hiring and training officers for future effectiveness.
Mohammed (2021)	Public vs private	Comparative study of hiring and selection practices in public vs private manufacturing firms in Bangladesh.	Study compares recruitment and selection processes between public and private manufacturing enterprises in Bangladesh.
Bennet (2022)	Recruitment and selection	Recruitment crafts job descriptions; selection aligns qualifications with job requirements. Person specification aids in selection.	Recruitment involves job detailing, while selection matches qualifications to job needs using person specification, ensuring suitability for roles.

Source: Author

Problem Statement

The study focuses solely on the recruitment and selection practices employed within software industries, emphasizing the necessity for ethical hiring procedures and the acquisition of employees. The aim is to complete an organizational study by delving into recruitment and selection methods, identifying optimal approaches for finding and hiring individuals. Additionally, it seeks to discern the most successful hiring and selection methods and their consequential impact on organizational outcomes.

Objectives of Study

- To study the hiring and selection procedures in the software industry.
- To evaluate the efficiency of the interviewing procedure in the software industry.

Research methodology

- Employed a descriptive research type in the selected research area of Coimbatore's Software industries, utilizing random sampling for sample selection.

- Incorporated both primary and secondary data sources in the study's analysis.
- Engaged nearly 150 respondents for data collection purposes.
- Utilized statistical tools such as the simple percentage method, Chi-square method, and correlation method in the study's analysis.

Data Analysis and Interpretation

The following section presents an insightful analysis of crucial aspects within an organizational context, encompassing the effectiveness of the interviewing process, HR department performance, employees' views on job evaluation during recruitment, and selection techniques for job roles. This examination, conducted within Coimbatore's Software industries, provides a comprehensive understanding of employees' perceptions, utilizing diverse statistical methods. Additionally, correlations between factors such as age groups and the effectiveness of interviews, as well as the relationship between experience and HR performance, are examined. These findings shed light on pivotal facets influencing organizational dynamics and employee engagement within this sector.

Effectiveness of the interviewing process

- **Excellent**: 65 (43.33%)
- **Good**: 32 (21.33%)
- **Moderate**: 27 (18%)
- **Poor**: 26 (17.33%)
- **Total**: 150 (100%)

Interpretation: Among respondents, 43.33% rated the interviewing process as excellent, while 21.33% deemed it good. Approximately 18% considered it moderate, and 17.33% found it poor.

HR department's performance

- **Highly satisfied**: 53 (35.33%)
- **Satisfied**: 51 (34%)
- **Dissatisfied**: 27 (18%)
- **Highly dissatisfied**: 19 (12.67%)
- **Total**: 150 (100%)

Interpretation: Concerning the HR department, 35.33% of employees were highly satisfied, 34% were satisfied, 18% were dissatisfied, and 12.67% were highly dissatisfied.

Employees' views on job evaluation in recruitment procedure

- **Always**: 33 (22%)
- **Satisfied**: 43 (28.67%)
- **Average**: 40 (26.67%)
- **Neutral**: 19 (12.67%)
- **Bad**: 15 (10%)
- **Total**: 150 (100%)

Interpretation: In terms of job evaluation during recruitment, 22% of employees stated evaluations occurred always, 28.67% were satisfied, 26.67% felt average, 12.67% remained neutral, and 10% deemed it bad.

Selecting technique for job

- Most employees suggested the use of aptitude tests as the primary selecting technique during interviews.

Chi-square test: age group vs effectiveness of interviewing process

- Conducted a Chi-square test between respondents' age groups and the effectiveness of the interview process.
- **Result**: The calculated value was greater than the table value, rejecting the null hypothesis. No significant relationship was found between respondents' age groups and the effectiveness of the interviewing process.

Correlation: experience vs HR department's performance

- **Pearson correlation**: 0.914** (significant at 0.01 level, positive correlation)
- **Nonparametric correlations**: Showed significant positive relationships between experience of the respondents and HR department's performance.

Interpretation: The data revealed a strong positive correlation between respondents' experience and the HR department's performance, indicating that as experience increased, satisfaction with the HR department also increased significantly.

In summary, the analysis demonstrates varying perceptions of the interviewing process, HR department's performance, and job evaluation procedures among employees. While no significant relationship was found between age groups and the effectiveness of interviews, a positive correlation was evident between employee experience and satisfaction with the HR department's performance.

Findings

- 43.3% of respondents rated the effectiveness of the interviewing process and other selection instruments as "excellent."
- 35.33% of employees expressed high satisfaction with the HR Department.
- 28.7% of respondents indicated satisfaction with job evaluation during recruitment procedures.
- 50.0% of respondents reported always using aptitude tests in their selection process.
- The study found no significant relationship between respondents' age groups and the effectiveness of the interviewing process.
- However, there were established relationships between respondents' experience and the performance of the HR department.

Recommendations

- Clearly outline the recruitment and selection procedures for a prompt response from applicants, as indicated by this study.
- Ensure the HR team responds swiftly, aligning criteria with deadlines to prevent employee loss to competitors.
- Implement innovative strategies such as networking, visiting institutions, and updating traditional recruitment methods to attract enthusiastic candidates.
- Utilize panel interviews more frequently due to their cost and time effectiveness in selecting top candidates.
- Develop specialized and cost-effective procedures for hiring and selection to benefit the company financially.
- Prioritize hiring staff capable of handling unforeseen scenarios and demonstrating adaptability to address future market challenges.
- Establish clear recruiting and selection policies communicated by senior management to provide recruiters with a clear roadmap.

Conclusion

In the ever-evolving landscape of recruitment and selection, companies persistently adapt and refine their methodologies and tools, albeit the fundamental principles enduring through time. The evaluation of human resources remains a critical and pivotal activity, ensuring the timely deployment of suitable individuals. This responsibility, integral to the company's success, presents significant challenges, where the ramifications of adept or erroneous decisions reverberate profoundly. The meticulous selection of competent personnel secures the company's future, while an ill-fated choice can precipitate dire consequences. Hence, human resource departments vigilantly allocate considerable attention to this imperative task, recognizing its profound impact on organizational prosperity.

The core recruitment and selection process, while rooted in tradition, has undergone significant transformation. Embracing the changing dynamics of industries and workforce expectations, companies strive to amalgamate innovation and efficiency into their selection frameworks. This adaptability ensures the continuous evolution of recruitment strategies, allowing companies to navigate the intricacies of talent acquisition effectively. As businesses navigate the complex terrain of personnel selection, they persistently seek refinement and enhancement to align with contemporary paradigms, safeguarding their competitive edge in the dynamic market landscape.

References

Aswathappa, K. (1997). Human Resources and Personnel Management. New Delhi: Tata McGraw-Hill Publishing Company Ltd.

Bennett (2022). Recruitment and Selection Practices of Organizations: A Case Study of HFC Bank (GH) LTD. Kwame Nkrumah University of Science and Technology.

Carless (2020). Impact of personal recruitment on organizational development: a survey of selected nigerian workplace. *International Journal of Business Administration*, 4(2), 3.3583. Retrieved from www.sciedu.ca/ijba.

Mohammed, M. (2021). Recruitment and selection. *Managing and Developing*, 12–32 .

Ofori and Aryeetey (2022). Recruitment & selection practices in manufacturing firms in Bangladesh. *The Indian Journal of Industrial Relations*, 436–448.

Penttila (2018). An investigation into recruitment and selection practices and organizational performance. *International Journal of Economics, Commerce, and Management*, 2(11), 1–11. ISSN 2348-0386.

Valvis (2020). Using Recruitment Agencies to Obtain the Best Candidates. Târgoviște, Romania: Valahia University.

White, M. D. (2021). A study of the recruitment and selection process. *SMC Global Industrial Engineering Letters*, 2(1), Retrieved from www.iiste.org.

45 A study on cash management analysis of selected cement industries

Sudhakaran, A.[a], Deva, S.[b] and Nagalakshmi, N.[c]

Karpagam Academy of Higher Education, Coimbatore, Tamil Nadu, India

Abstract

Finance stands as an indispensable cornerstone for businesses, wielding immense influence over modern management strategies. The effective management of finances reigns supreme in steering managerial decisions, with financial statements serving as pivotal tools in this arena. These statements not only aid decision-making but also wield significant influence in framing the contours within which managerial choices are made. Ensuring solvency demands a judicious amalgamation of appropriate capital sources, timely acquisition, and cost-effectiveness. The process of financial analysis, encompassing the interpretation and analysis of financial statements, serves as the compass for discerning a company's fiscal prowess and vulnerabilities. By methodically connecting the dots across balance sheets, profit and loss accounts, and other operational data, financial analysis unveils a comprehensive view of a firm's financial landscape, empowering decision-makers with actionable insights.

Keywords: Cash management, finance, performance, ratio

Introduction

In contemporary economic landscapes, small or nascent businesses face the peril of collapse amidst economic downturns, grappling with plummeting revenues and inadequate cash management. The repercussions of such downturns, exemplified by the recession of 2008–2009, are exacerbated when banks curtail short-term loans or revolving credit, conventional lifelines for firms navigating cash flow challenges. Struggling business owners resort to leveraging personal resources, including mortgaging homes, maxing out credit cards, or tapping into retirement funds, striving to salvage their enterprises. However, irrespective of economic prosperity, many small firms perennially grapple with cash flow constraints, especially during their formative years.

Entrepreneurs and managers, cognizant of these challenges, can adopt proactive measures to mitigate such issues, safeguarding their companies' ongoing sustainability. This exigency assumes critical importance in industries pivotal to global economic sustenance, such as cement production, an elemental component for construction, infrastructure, and urban development worldwide.

Challenges in Cement Industries

Ramco Cements industries: Ramco Cements, originating in 1961 under Shri P.A.C. Ramasamy Raja's guidance, has burgeoned into one of the nation's largest cement manufacturers. With 11 state-of-the-art production facilities in India, we prioritize our employees' welfare, fostering inclusive growth where organizational progress mirrors employee development. Our proactive measures in employee engagement and retention manifest in well-planned townships equipped with educational, healthcare, and recreational facilities. We relentlessly pursue excellence, aiming to redefine industry standards, garnering accolades for our contributions.

Chettinad Cement industries: A three-generation legacy thrives at Chettinad Cement since its inception in 1962 at Puliyur. The company adapts dynamically, catering to the Southern Indian market's diverse cement needs, facilitating countless residential, commercial, and engineering projects. Our versatile manufacturing unit crafts various cement types, efficiently distributed through a reliable road tanker fleet, tailoring offerings to consumer demands.

Dalmia Cement industries: Jaidayal Dalmia's pioneering vision birthed Dalmia Cement in 1939, marking India's maiden indigenous cement venture. A subsidiary of Dalmia Bharat Ltd, our company, headquartered in New Delhi and listed on major stock exchanges, exemplifies a rich legacy coupled with contemporary achievements.

India Cement industries: India emerges as the world's second-largest cement producer, harnessing extensive limestone reserves. The private sector claims 98% of India's total capacity, with the top 20 companies contributing 70% to national production. The country's burgeoning demand for cement, driven by

[a]21MBAP116@kahedu.edu.in, [b]devasezhiyan@gmail.com, [c]nagalakshmi.nagendran@kahedu.edu.in

infrastructural development, augurs a promising growth trajectory.

UltraTech Cement industries: Noteworthy investments and expansions characterize UltraTech Cement's trajectory, with a recent capital infusion of Rs. 12,886 crore (US$ 1.65 billion) to bolster capacity. Their cement products garnering Environmental Product Declaration (EPD) certificates underscore their commitment to sustainability, reflected in a substantial increase in cement production.

The cement industry, while pivotal to global development, grapples with multifaceted challenges like heightened demand, escalating costs, environmental regulations, and competition from alternative materials. To surmount these hurdles, the industry pivots towards innovation, adopting sustainable practices like renewable energy integration, waste material recycling, and the development of low-carbon cements. Additionally, the application of digitalization and automation emerges as promising avenues for bolstering output, reducing emissions, and enhancing quality and performance. As the industry navigates these challenges, collaboration, innovation, and sustainable practices remain pivotal to cementing a resilient future.

Literature Review

Table 45.1 Perspectives on cash management: insights from diverse author.

Author	Year	Study
Khan and Jain		Defining cash as the immediate currency of liquid assets, including money, checks, and bank instruments. Additionally, it encompasses "near cash" assets easily convertible into cash.
Watson and Head		Stressing cash management involves maximizing available cash, optimizing returns on idle funds, and mitigating losses due to fund transmission delays.
Zimmerer et al.		Highlighting the importance of not hoarding excess cash, as it could have been lucratively invested elsewhere. Cash hoarding restricts business growth and profitability.
Davidson et al.		Addressing cash flow issues, despite a good customer base and reputation, leading to challenges in innovation, expansion, and talent acquisition. Lack of a safety margin for unforeseen expenses is a key concern.
Westerfield		Differentiating between actual cash and cash equivalents, asserting the importance of understanding this distinction for practical cash management.
Git Philip		Connecting cash management significance to economic scenarios marked by inflation, interest rate hikes, and currency depreciation. Effective management becomes crucial for businesses' financial health during such periods.
Donaldson		Advocating multiple cash budgets to accommodate deviations from predictions, enabling better planning for unforeseen circumstances, instead of relying on a singular outcome.
Gallagher		Stating the trade-off between liquidity and profitability in cash management. Striking an ideal cash balance is critical; excessive cash impedes long-term investments, while insufficient cash affects liquidity.
Denver		Historically, cash management controlled liquidity for meeting daily obligations. Inadequate attention to liquidity control in businesses results in tying up financial assets. Recent studies reveal this negligence, especially among small enterprises.
Ekanem		Discussing various elements critical for effective cash management. Emphasizing payment habits, expediting cash inflow from clients, and optimizing payment systems, including accounts receivable.

Source: Author

Cash, as described by different authors, encompasses immediate liquid assets, including cash equivalents. Effective cash management involves optimizing available cash, understanding the trade-off between liquidity and profitability, and planning for unforeseen circumstances through diverse cash budgets.

Neglecting cash management ties up financial assets, impacting liquidity, especially among small enterprises. Crucial elements for effective management involve improving payment habits, expediting cash inflow, and optimizing payment systems across diverse business sectors.

Problem Statement

Managing surplus funds poses a dilemma for companies: idle cash generates no returns, limiting profitability; yet, future needs hinder its disposal. While bank deposits yield minimal interest, investing in marketable securities offers better returns. Businesses, including service, yarn manufacturing, and cement industries, face this quandary balancing growth and industry-specific banking requirements.

Objectives of the Study

- Assessing the influence of cash management on the financial performance of chosen cement industry entities.
- Evaluating the financial progress of selected cement industry players in India.

Hypotheses of the Study

- H0: There is no variation among liquidity ratio and accounts receivables.
- H1: There is variation among liquidity ratio and accounts receivables.

Research Methodology

The research methodology involves analyzing the cement industry's financial performance using quantitative tools like ratio and correlation analysis, primarily drawing data from annual reports spanning 2018 to 2022.

Analysis and Interpretation

The following tables discloses about ratio analysis for selected cement industries:

India Cement industries exhibit a high standard deviation. Ramco, Chettinad, Dalmia, India, UltraTech, and Orient Cement show positive skewness in their current ratio. Indian and Andhra cement display leptokurtic behavior, while others are platykurtic (Kurtosis < 3).

UltraTech Cement industries demonstrate low Standard Deviation. Ramco, UltraTech, and Orient Cement display negative skewness in their current ratio. All companies exhibit platykurtic fixed assets ratio (Kurtosis < 3).

Dalmia Cement industries display a high standard deviation. Ramco, UltraTech, Orient Cement, and others exhibit positive skewness in their current ratio. All companies portray platykurtic liquidity ratios (kurtosis < 3).

Orient Cement industries demonstrate a low standard deviation. JSW Cement, JK Lakshmi Cement, and other companies show positive skewness in their absolute liquidity ratio. JSW Cement displays leptokurtic behavior, while others exhibit platykurtic ratios (Kurtosis < 3)

Andhra Cement industries show high Standard deviation. Ramco, Shree, UltraTech, Andhra Cement, exhibit negative skewness in debtors' turnover ratio. All show platykurtic ratios (Kurtosis < 3).

Ultra Cement industries demonstrate a low standard deviation. Anthra Cement and other companies

Table 45.2 Current ratio.

Years	Ramco cement	Chettinadu cement	Dalmiya cement	India cement	UltraTech cement
2017– 2018	0.44	0.85	0.85	0.78	1
2018– 2019	0.41	0.82	0.82	0.87	0.97
2019– 2020	0.49	0.56	0.56	0.84	0.94
2020-2021	0.47	0.9	0.9	0.99	1.37
2021-2022	0.45	1.03	1.03	0.13	1.92
Total	2.26	4.16	4.16	3.61	6.2
Average ratio	0.452	0.832	0.832	0.722	1.24
Standard deviation	0.0303315	0.171959298	0.1719592	0.33966	0.41827
Co-efficient of variance	6.7105092	20.6681848	20.668184	47.0445	33.7314
Skewness	-0.225764	-0.986816404	-0.986804	-1.1894	1.45835
Kurtosis	-0.139413	2.052913997	2.0529139	4.08362	1.42708

Source: Secondary data

Table 45.3 Fixed asset ratio.

Years	Ramco cement	Chettinadu cement	Dalmiya cement	India cement	UltraTech cement
2017– 2018	0.47	0.7	4.31	1.11	0.66
2018– 2019	0.47	0.56	8.5	0.96	0.65
2019– 2020	0.54	0.57	7.97	0.98	0.73
2020-2021	0.32	0.96	4.85	0.93	1.05
2021-2022	0.25	1.41	2.62	0.98	0.92
TOTAL	2.05	4.2	28.25	4.96	4.01
Average ratio	0.41	0.84	5.65	0.992	0.802
Standard deviation	0.1202081	0.357141429	2.5060626	0.0690651	0.17598
Co-efficient of variance	29.319061	42.51683673	44.355091	6.9622163	21.9430
Skewness	-0.526767	1.303799806	0.1297222	1.7308109	0.77578
Kurtosis	-1.818919	1.036548184	-2.204647	3.5229355	-1.5568

Source: Secondary data

Table 45.4 Liquidity ratio.

Years	Ramco cement	Chettinadu cement	Dalmiya cement	India cement	UltraTech cement
2017– 2018	0.47	0.7	4.31	1.11	0.66
2018– 2019	0.47	0.56	8.5	0.96	0.65
2019– 2020	0.54	0.57	7.97	0.98	0.73
2020-2021	0.32	0.96	4.85	0.93	1.05
2021-2022	0.25	1.41	2.62	0.98	0.92
TOTAL	2.05	4.2	28.25	4.96	4.01
Average Ratio	0.41	0.84	5.65	0.992	0.802
Standard Deviation	0.1202081	0.357141429	2.5060626	0.0690651	0.17598
Co-efficient of Variance	29.319061	42.51683673	44.355091	6.9622163	21.9430
Skewness	-0.526767	1.303799806	0.1297222	1.7308109	0.77578
Kurtosis	-1.818919	1.036548184	-2.204647	3.5229355	-1.5568

Source: Secondary data

Table 45.5 Absolute liquidity ratio.

Years	Ramco cement	Chettinadu cement	Dalmiya cement	India cement	UltraTech cement
2017– 2018	1073.86	54.69	-130	307.82	-3132.46
2018– 2019	966.07	112.32	-367	886.82	-3684.08
2019– 2020	765.98	396.01	791	661.44	-3016.91
2020-2021	671.88	-54.69	-674	297.67	-2005.03
2021-2022	552.61	112.32	-859	123.55	-2733.02
Total	4030.4	396.01	396.01	396.01	396.01
Average ratio	806.08	154.63	154.63	154.63	154.63
Standard deviation	212.81894	166.5804555	644.67100	310.386	614.475
Co-efficient of variance	26.401715	107.7284198	416.91198	200.728	397.384
Skewness	0.1958466	1.265638888	1.2677251	0.63110	0.52100
Kurtosis	-1.753170	2.567678143	1.6788085	-1.3126	1.10222

Source: Secondary data

Table 45.6 Debt turnover ratio.

Years	Ramco cement	Chettinadu cement	Dalmiya cement	India cement	UltraTech cement
2017– 2018	14.92	4.8	135.55	0.82	16.61
2018– 2019	14.44	5.61	16.89	5	18.36
2019– 2020	11.19	9.12	89.4	-0.7	13.19
2020-2021	9.38	4.86	61.58	1.23	8.11
2021-2022	12.61	7.05	57.6	1.88	10.07
TOTAL	62.54	31.44	361.02	8.23	66.34
Average ratio	12.508	6.288	72.204	1.646	13.268
Standard deviation	2.2957722	1.824409494	43.858302	2.10137	4.29929
Co-efficient of variance	18.354430	29.01414589	60.742206	127.665	32.4034
Skewness	-0.401176	1.141586353	0.4233641	1.08646	-0.00304
Kurtosis	-1.406395	0.34180355	0.6515587	2.08612	-2.11156

Source: Secondary data

Table 45.7 Net profit ratio.

Years	Ramco cement	Chettinadu cement	Dalmiya Cement	India Cement	UltraTech cement
2017– 2018	16.5	10.07	12.27	6.45	26.45
2018– 2019	11.68	12.66	9.87	7.06	19.16
2019– 2020	10.56	10.69	4.38	7	15.25
2020-2021	11.04	17.26	4.43	8.29	19.67
2021-2022	8.84	24.62	7.14	9.38	24.76
TOTAL	58.62	75.3	38.09	38.18	105.29
Average ratio	11.724	15.06	7.618	7.636	21.058
Standard deviation	2.8702055	6.041328496	3.4492419	1.1844956	4.52880
Co-efficient of variance	24.481453	40.11506306	45.277526	15.511991	21.5063
Skewness	1.4636061	1.252568065	0.4633693	0.8693902	0.00927
Kurtosis	2.8953520	0.815265208	-1.753480	-0.579294	-1.4992

Source: Secondary data

Table 45.8 Gross profit ratio.

Years	Ramco cement	Chettinadu cement	Dalmiya cement	India cement	UltraTech cement
2017–2018	0.51	0.53	1.53	0.57	1.07
2018–2019	0.5	0.63	1.66	0.55	1.11
2019–2020	0.57	0.58	1.47	0.63	1.15
2020-2021	0.6	0.55	1.95	0.74	1.33
2021-2022	0.54	0.59	1.52	0.71	1.51
Total	2.72	2.88	8.13	3.2	6.17
Average ratio	0.544	0.576	1.626	0.64	1.234
Standard deviation	0.0415932	0.038470768	0.1942421	0.0836660	0.18352
Co-efficient of variance	7.6458214	6.678952799	11.946009	13.072812	14.8720
Skewness	0.3974631	0.331947369	1.6021002	0.1920903	1.01109
Kurtosis	-1.578068	-0.30953250	2.3831056	-2.55	-0.3994

Source: Secondary data

Table 45.9 Correlation.

	Current ratio	Liquidity ratio	Stock Turnover ratio	Debtor turnover ratio	Net profit ratio	Expenses ratio	Working capital ratio
Pearson correlation	1.000	.142	-.074	.026	.265	.029	-
Sig.(2-tailed)		.324	.608	.858	.063	.844	.280
N	50	50	50	50	50	50	50
Pearson correlation	.142	1.000	-.423	-.174	.049	-.102	-.071
Sig.(2-tailed)	.324		.002	.227	.734	.481	.626
N	50	50	50	50	50	50	50
Pearson correlation	-.074	-.423	1.000	.104	.212	.302	-
Sig.(2-tailed)	.608	.002		.471	.139	.033	.800
N	50	50	50	50	50	50	50
Pearson Correlation	.026	-.174	.104	1.000	.151	.024	-.098
Sig.(2-tailed)	.858	.227	.471		.295	.870	.497
N	50	50	50	50	50	50	50
Pearson correlation	.265	.049	.212	.151	1.000	-.011	-.024
Sig.(2-tailed)	.063	.734	.139	.295		.940	.870
N	50	50	50	50	50	50	50
Pearson Correlation	.029	-.102	.302	.024	-.011	1.000	-.024
Sig.(2-tailed)	.844	.481	.033	.870	.940		.869
N	50	50	50	50	50	50	50
Pearson correlation	-.156	-.071	-.037	-.098	-.024	-.024	1.000
Sig.(2-tailed)	.280	.626	.800	.497	.870	.869	
N	50	50	50	50	50	50	50

Source: Primary data

display negative skewness in gross profit ratio, while all companies exhibit platykurtic ratios (Kurtosis < 3) in Gross Profit Ratio.

JSW Cement Industries exhibit high standard deviation. Chettinadu, JSW, Orient Cement, and others display positive skewness in inventory turn over ratio. All exhibit platykurtic ratios (Kurtosis < 3).

Findings

The company's financial indicators presented dynamic shifts over the study period. Notably, the working capital turnover ratio exhibited considerable fluctuations, soaring from 3.64 to 75.56, highlighting a significant surge in turnover. Inventory turnover displayed varying efficiencies, with 2021-22 depicting improvement but contrasting with lower performance in 2018-19. The inventory conversion period fluctuated notably, ranging between 163 days (2018-19) and 51 days (2021-22), indicating variable operational efficiency.

Moreover, the debtor's turnover ratio showcased an ascending trajectory, implying improved liquidity with shorter collection periods in specific years. Conversely, the gross profit ratio declined consistently, while the net profit ratio fluctuated. Although the current asset ratio remained satisfactory despite fluctuations, the creditor turnover ratio's increase to 5.01 indicated enhanced liquidity due to a shorter average payment period in 2017-2018. Furthermore, the current assets turnover ratio portrayed an upward trend, whereas the fixed asset turnover ratio increased while the cash position ratio consistently declined

Conclusion

The recommendations highlight the paramount need for the company to curtail cash expenditures and bolster short-term investments to fortify its cash reserves. Achieving a delicate balance between profitability and liquidity hinges upon maintaining a substantial cash balance, an indispensable facet for sustained financial stability. Rigorous monitoring of the cash conversion cycle remains pivotal to ensure seamless cash flow management throughout the fiscal year. It's imperative to strive for augmented working capital through long-term sources, heralding financial liberation and reinforcing the company's fiscal management and performance.

Emphasizing the expansion of consumer sales and overall profitability, providing diverse credit options becomes crucial. Prioritizing local sales over exports stands as a strategic approach to bolster overall profitability. The conclusion underscores the necessity for enhanced cash management practices and streamlining of the cash management system. Accumulating excess cash without strategic utilization risks detrimental impacts on profitability. Strategic investment or purposeful allocation of surplus cash is vital for improved profitability and capital enrichment. Effective control and management of surplus liquidity above the ideal cash balance level promises enhanced profitability and financial robustness. While challenges persist, proactive governance and directed efforts can significantly enhance cash management practices, akin to the observed improved practices in residence halls

References

Bari, R. R. (Year). Cash Planning & Management. New Delhi: Triveni Publications, (pp. 2).

Baumol, W. J. (Year). The transactions demand for cash: an inventory theoretical approach. *Quarterly Journal of Economics*, 66(4), 545–556.

John, K. M. (Year). Cash management practices of small business owners in the cape coast metropolitan area of Ghana. *Asian Economic and Financial Review*, 2(1), 40–58.

Marfo-Yiadom, E. (Year). A survey of cash management practices of selected firms in accra-tema metropolitan area of Ghana. *The Oguaa Journal of Social Studies*, 3, 165–182.

Richards, N. D., and Laughlin, E. L. (Year). A cash conversion cycle approach to liquidity analysis. *Financial Management*, (Spring), 32–38.

Singhri, S. S., and Kaupisch, J. A. (Year). cash management in a developing economy. *Review of Management, Economic and Political Weekly*, 5(35), 95.

46 A study on employee selection process in atlas export private limited, Karur

Parthasarathy S.[a], Anish Kumar, S.[b], Shrie Bhubaneswari, N.T.[c]

Karpagam Academy of Higher Education, Coimbatore, Tamil Nadu, India

Abstract

In the domain of human resource management, the efficacy of the employee selection process is paramount for fostering a workforce characterized by reduced absenteeism and turnover issues. This undertaking involves meticulous candidate screening, not only to save time and resources but also to mitigate accidents and bolster employee morale. This discourse inquiries into the textile industry's evolution, current trends, and a concise industry profile. Specifically scrutinizing Atlas Export Pvt Ltd., its 3CI score exceeding 50, coupled with a modal factor of 1.0, highlights its comparative strength in contrast to other textile entities. The study encompasses a comprehensive analysis of the company's board of directors and capital, acknowledging their pivotal roles. Moreover, the selection process conscientiously considers external factors, aligning with societal influences to uphold fairness in candidate evaluations. Employing a disproportionate random sample of 150 respondents and utilizing SPSS tools like percentage analysis, chi-square analysis, and correlation, the research underlines the imperative need to refine recruitment strategies. The study advocates enhancements to attract top-tier candidates and foster the sustained engagement of skilled professionals in the hiring process.

Keywords: Selection process, textile, recruitment, employee productivity and motivation

Introduction

The selection procedure is a critical aspect of workforce management. This involves the identification and elimination of applicants based on their qualifications to fill specific roles within a company. Referred to as employee selection, it encompasses the strategic placement of individuals in various industry, departmental, or divisional positions, aligning their abilities and credentials with organizational needs. The effectiveness of this process hinges on precise matching, ensuring optimal performance, and reducing issues such as employee absences and turnover. The careful selection of the most qualified candidate not only enhances workforce efficiency but also contributes to time and cost savings for the business. Central to this process is candidate screening, involving rigorous testing to assess each applicant's suitability for the designated position. In essence, a well-executed selection process is vital for cultivating a high-performing and stable workforce.

Problem Statement

The problem lies in the aftermath of employee selection, where suboptimal choices lead to diverse issues, including heightened staff turnover and ongoing costs for training. This necessitates firms to implement a scientific and impartial selection process, aligning with societal fairness and governmental regulations, to ensure sustained workforce stability and compliance with legal frameworks.

Objectives

To determine how employees at Karur's Atlas Textile Exports Pvt Ltd feel about the hiring process.

- To confirm employees' perceptions of the training programs available.
- To evaluate the effect of the hiring and training processes on worker productivity.

Hypothesis of Study

- Null hypothesis: No significant relationship exists between respondents' educational qualifications and the need for an impartial, equal-opportunity selection process.
- Alternative hypothesis: A significant relationship may exist, necessitating an impartial, equal-opportunity selection process.
- Null hypothesis: No relationships exist between respondents' experience and organizations encouraging employees.
- Alternative hypothesis: Relationships exist between respondents' experience and organizations encouraging employees.

[a]21MBAP038@kahedu.edu.in, [b]anishkumars3991@gmail.com, [c]shrie.bhubaneswari@gmail.com

Research Methodology

Disparate stratified random samples were chosen for several reasons:

- Inclusion of statistics on various aspects of Karur's location.
- Facilitation of a management control system in the textile sector.

- The sample size, determined by information collection needs, comprises 150 respondents for this investigation.
- Secondary data was compiled from publications, newspapers, and project reports.
- Three SPSS tools—percentage analysis, chi-square analysis, and correlation—were utilized to conduct the research.

Literature Review

Insights into employee selection: a comparative overview of various studies in the textile industry

Table 46. 1 Analysis and interpretation.

Author name	Study	Findings (insights/interpretation)
Jones et al.	HR theories emphasize robust employee selection methods.	Hiring can be internal, external, or online; insights from textile industry history aid policy development.
Kanar and Collins	Research finds content employees, necessitating adjustments due to evolving hiring processes.	Evolving processes impact operations; HR adept at talent placement; effective employment strategy.
Allen et al.	Studies show character features and signaling impact job pursuit decisions.	Virtual worlds reveal behaviors; comprehensive recruitment needed in textile sector.
Silzer et al.	Recruitment extends to retention; talent management crucial for retaining candidates.	Effective talent management involves addressing the innate vs. gained talent debate.
Laumer et al.	Virtual worlds reduce faking; accurate information elicited.	Virtual worlds expose job-relevant behaviors accurately, reducing faking and social desirability.
Korsten 2018	Talent management challenges require executable recruitment strategies.	Implementing executable strategies crucial for overcoming talent management challenges.
C.J.,& Bell, B. S.	Negative reputation hinders employee attraction; messaging can alter perceptions.	Effective messaging can positively impact company reputation, influencing job seekers' perceptions.
Krause	Video conferencing in interviews receives higher evaluations; AI aids assessment.	Video conferencing, with AI-assisted assessments, garners higher interview evaluations.
EndahSetyowati	Selection processes lack objectivity, exhibit administrative roadblocks.	Arbitrary processes show a lack of objectivity; administrative roadblocks hinder effective selection.
Tausczik&Pennebaker	Study explores language usage in digital interviews; AI assesses broader personality.	AI-based assessments in digital interviews evaluate broader aspects of candidate personality.
Charles ObioraOmekwu	Hiring issues in Nigerian textile workers require addressing bias and nepotism.	Addressing bias and nepotism crucial for unbiased hiring; proper procedures ensure fairness.
C. Siddarth1 and Ramamurthy	Employee selection vital for fabric company growth; HR development empowers workers.	Selection crucial for growth; HR development empowers workers for increased responsibilities.
Navdeep Singh Gill	Quick, fair, and accurate selection vital for organizational success.	Success relies on a quick, fair, and accurate selection process, with criteria influencing employment rates.
Mahmood Aziz may	Research examines race and gender distinctions in internal advertising.	No significant differences found in hiring procedures based on race and gender in internal advertising.
AdjeareSoloman	"Choice through" involves management judgment; employers seek culturally aligned candidates.	Selection involves management judgment; employers compete for culturally aligned candidates for innovation.

Source: Author

Conclusion

The conclusion must be clearly marked as shown. When referring to other sections in the letter, please use the section heading, or describe the relevant section as the 'following' or 'preceding' section in relation to the current Section in the text.

References

Allen, D. B., Mahto, R. V., & Otondo, R. F. Studies show character features and signaling impact job pursuit decisions. Virtual worlds reveal behaviors; comprehensive recruitment needed in textile sector.

Brockman, P., French, D. and Tamm, C. (2014). REIT organizational structure, institutional ownership, and stock performance. J. Real Estate Portf. Manag. 20(1):21 36.

Cella, C. (2009). Institutional investors and corporate investment. United Sates: Indiana University, Kelley School of Business.

Chuang, H. (2020). The impacts of institutional ownership on stock returns. Empir. Econ. 58(2):507 533.

Clark, G. L. and Wójcik, D. (2005). Financial valuation of the German model: the negative relationship between ownership concentration and stock market returns, 1997–2001. Econ. Geogr. 81(1):11 29.

Dasgupta, A., Prat, A. and Verardo, M. (2011). Institutional trade persistence and long-term equity returns. J. Finance. 66(2):635 653.

Demsetz, H. and Lehn, K. (1985). The structure of corporate ownership: causes and consequences. J. Polit. Econ. 93(6):1155 1177.

Dyakov, T. and Wipplinger, E. (2020). Institutional ownership and future stock returns: an international perspective. Int. Rev. Finance. 20(1):235 245.

Gompers, P. A. and Metrick, A. (2001). Institutional investors and equity prices. Q. J. Econ. 116(1):229 259.

Han, K.C. and Suk, D.Y. (1998). The effect of ownership structure on firm performance: Additional evidence. Rev. Financ. Econ. 7(2):143 155.

Kenne Author Name Study Findings (Insights/Interpretation)

Jones et al. HR theories emphasize robust employee selection methods. Hiring can be internal, external, or online; insights from textile industry history aid policy development.

Kanar, A. M., Collins Research finds content employees, necessitating adjustments due to evolving hiring processes. Evolving processes impact operations; HR adept at talent placement; effective employment strategy.

Silzer et al. Recruitment extends to retention; talent management crucial for retaining candidates. Effective talent management involves addressing the innate vs. gained talent debate.

Laumer, Eckhardt, & Weitzel Virtual worlds reduce faking; accurate information elicited. Virtual worlds expose job-relevant behaviors accurately, reducing faking and social desirability.

Korsten 2018 Talent management challenges require executable recruitment strategies. Implementing executable strategies crucial for overcoming talent management challenges.

C.J.,& Bell, B. S. Negative reputation hinders employee attraction; messaging can alter perceptions. Effective messaging can positively impact company reputation, influencing job seekers' perceptions.

Krause Video conferencing in interviews receives higher evaluations; AI aids assessment. Video conferencing, with AI-assisted assessments, garners higher interview evaluations.

EndahSetyowati Selection processes lack objectivity, exhibit administrative roadblocks. Arbitrary processes show a lack of objectivity; administrative roadblocks hinder effective selection.

Tausczik&Pennebaker Study explores language usage in digital interviews; AI assesses broader personality. A I-based assessments in digital interviews evaluate broader aspects of candidate personality.

Charles ObioraOmekwu Hiring issues in Nigerian textile workers require addressing bias and nepotism. Addressing bias and nepotism crucial for unbiased hiring; proper procedures ensure fairness.

C. Siddarth1 and R. Ramamurthy Employee selection vital for fabric company growth; HR development empowers workers. Selection crucial for growth; HR development empowers workers for increased responsibilities.

Navdeep Singh Gill Quick, fair, and accurate selection vital for organizational success. Success relies on a quick, fair, and accurate selection process, with criteria influencing employment rates.

Mahmood Aziz may Research examines race and gender distinctions in internal advertising.No significant differences found in hiring procedures based on race and gender in internal advertising.

Soloman, A. "Choice through" involves management judgment; employers seek culturally aligned candidates. Selection involves management judgment; employers compete for culturally aligned candidates for innovation.dy, P. (1985). A Guide to Econometrics, MIT Press, Cambridge.

La Porta, R., Lopez-de-Silanes, F., and Shleifer, A. (1999). Corporate ownership around the world. J. Finance. 54(2):471 517.

Manawaduge, A. S., Zoysa, A., and Rudkin, K. M. (2009). Performance implication of ownership structure and ownership concentration: Evidence from Sri Lankan firms. Paper presented at the Performance Management Association Conference. Dunedin, New Zealand.

47 A study on process management in supply chain industry

Mohamed Ayman, S., Dr. R. Manju Shree, Nagalakshmi, N.[a] and Deva, S.[b]

Karpagam Academy of Higher Education, Coimbatore, Tamil Nadu, India

Abstract

This academic study delves into the assimilation of new technology within firms, specifically focusing on process management and its implications in the Indian context. Over the past two decades, the concept of integrating process management has been a prevalent theme, notably through Rogers' framework, which serves as the foundation for this thesis. The research investigates how Indian organisations adopt frameworks for incorporating new process management technology, clarifying and refining the original framework through various modifications. The project offers insights into the stages involved in integrating process management technology, drawing from existing literature and theories. Moreover, the findings and conclusions shed light on specific steps essential for introducing process management technology into supply chain management. This study thus contributes to understanding the effective implementation of technology within Indian organisations, providing a methodological framework for future research and practical applications.

Keywords: Management, process, supply, technology

Introduction

This research paper aims to explore the impact of process management on the field of logistics. To achieve this goal, an extensive review of leading academic and professional journals in logistics has been conducted. The paper will delve into the logistics structure in an upcoming section, followed by an examination of the enablers of logistics process management. Additionally, the paper will discuss the effects of e-commerce on logistics, followed by a section contemplating the future of this field.

The role of logistics has evolved significantly from being a passive, cost-absorbing function to assuming a pivotal position in business operations. By delivering superior services to clients, logistics now plays a crucial role in aiding businesses to gain a competitive advantage, as noted by Sum and Teo (1999), Bowersox and Closs (1996), and Bowersox and Daugherty (1995). In response to heightened global competition and increased customer expectations, an increasing number of companies are outsourcing their logistics operations to third-party logistics (3PL) providers (Vaidyanathan, 2005). This strategic move allows them to focus on their core strengths, adapting to the evolving business landscape.

Review of literature

Carter et al. (2015) studied that productivity enhancement strategies for casting manufacturing companies are the main topic of investigation. A better plant structure, material handling systems, and automation have been identified as areas in the casting sector where production time can be shortened. The same resulted in reduced material handling difficulty or worker weariness, it was decided. time taken to carry materials from the casting machine to the furnace and decrease in labour requirements.

Chau (2013) used simulation to increase efficiency in the food processing sector. An Arena simulation model was created to examine the impact of the process on the production line's productivity. All bottlenecks were eliminated through changes to the production line, which also improved machine utilisation by eliminating lineups. Production roughly increased, and average total time dropped. It is projected that the higher net profit will take time to pay back the new capital investment.

The case study on material handling and supply management in fertiliser production is the subject of this essay. Because the conveyors frequently break down, the author made the point that the fertiliser company's bagging line operation for bagging and conveying to final delivery to the truck is a serious concern. Granules of fertiliser that were stuck at the conveyors for packaging and bagging caused corrosion, which ultimately led to the breakdown of the conveyor roller (Bowersox and Closs, 2012).

China's growth in manufacturing productivity is examined by in a study by Banker and Kauffman (2013). It was determined that the industrial strength of a chain depends on input growth and advancements in technical development.

[a]lavanyaa2302@gmail.com, [b]devasezhiyan@gmail.com

An effort is made to examine the importance of choosing a material handling system design for the industry while taking into account issues with material flow design, such as the choice of material handling equipment, design of flow paths, facility layout, routing, etc. for connected product design in the sector (Chen et al., 2014). It has been noted that material handling costs should be minimised in terms of duration, travel distance, frequency, and overall cost. According to the survey, material handling is a crucial activity in the industrial sector. Any manufacturing company's profitability may be impacted by its choice of the best material handling equipment for a certain application. It has been determined that the material handling system significantly affects productivity.

In a machine shop that houses a range of machine tools, this study focuses on several problems frequently encountered by SMEs in parts handling systems during various processing phases (Chatterjee et al., 2012). To minimise manufacturing costs, manufacturing cycle times, ensure smooth material flow, and maintain competitiveness, low-cost material handling systems are required. Numerous chances are recognised to exist in SMEs to modernise and enhance current facilities by utilising low-cost automation solutions. It has been noted that low-cost automation technologies enable managers to reduce worker engagement in material handling for comparatively modest cost investments. In addition to enhancing safety and contributing greatly to product quality and organisational productivity, this immediately lowers the parts rejection rate.

Problem Statement

The problem statement has a significant impact on the process planning and execution since it affects the amount of time, money, and resources required. Expectations and deliverables' relationship is subsequently impacted by this. Process management is consequently a crucial managerial skill and is essential to the project's success. When the charter is agreed upon, not all of the requirements may be known. Therefore, it is the manager's duty to obtain precise needs and secure the sponsor's and stakeholders' approval. It is known as **collect requirements**. The procedure is based on the verified requirements. What is included and excluded in the project is described in the scope definition. The Work Breakdown Structure, a graphical representation of the scope, is then created using this information.

Objectives of the Study

- To know about the process management system followed in Aymu Exports and Imports

- To study the storage management system and delivery system followed are adopted in Aymu Exports and Imports.

Study Hypotheses

- With a significant value of greater than 0.05 (.166), the null hypothesis (Ho) is accepted, indicating no variation between sales turnover, remuneration, and education. The alternative hypothesis (H1) is rejected based on this outcome.

- Similarly, with a significant value higher than 0.05 (.152), the null hypothesis (Ho) is accepted, implying no variation between return on investment, supplier, and education. The alternative hypothesis (H1) is consequently rejected.

- Furthermore, a significant value exceeding 0.05 (.316) leads to accepting the null hypothesis (Ho), indicating no variation between delivery to highest value, job education, and their relationship. Consequently, the alternative hypothesis (H1) is rejected.

- Additionally, a significant value above 0.05 (.425) results in the acceptance of the null hypothesis (Ho), signifying no variation between market share system and education. Hence, the alternative hypothesis (H1) is rejected.

- Lastly, with a significant value surpassing 0.05 (.436), the null hypothesis (Ho) is accepted, indicating no variation between customer recognition and education, consequently leading to the rejection of the alternative hypothesis (H1).

Research Methodology

- Conducted a mail survey targeting logistics firms affiliated with India International Freight Forwarders Association and Ministry of Communications (MOC), totalling 1,245 providers.

- Contacted top logistics managers via phone to obtain names, addresses, and permission for questionnaire completion.

- Mailed questionnaires and study objectives cover letter to willing respondents, including a self-addressed, stamped envelope for easy return.

- Distributed 760 questionnaires to interested companies; received 104 usable completed questionnaires.

- Analysed data from the sample of 104 supply chain management service providers using statistical tools: ANOVA, rank analysis, and simple percentage analysis.

Analysis and Interpretation

This section presents a comprehensive analysis of the socio-economic profile of respondents based on gender, age, educational qualifications, income levels, years of experience, and rank analysis. Among the 104 participants surveyed, this examination reveals key demographic insights: a predominantly male population, primarily aged between 21 to 40 years, with Graduate qualifications and an income range of 10,000-15,000. Additionally, the analysis underscores the pivotal role of process management in influencing critical aspects such as customer satisfaction, sales turnover, and market share within the supply chain industry.

- **Gender:** 94.2% male, 5.8% female: Out of 104 respondents, the majority are male.
- **Age:** 38.5% (31-40), 35.6% (21-30), 24.0% (41-50): Predominantly, respondents fall within the age brackets of 31-40 and 21-30.
- **Educational qualification:** 8.7% HSC, 46.2% diploma, 45.2% graduate: The majority hold Graduate qualifications.
- **Income:** 15.4% below 5,000, 15.4% 5,000-10,000, 39.4% 10,000-15,000, 29.8% above 15,000: Most respondents earn 10,000-15,000.
- **Experience in years:** 34.6% below 5, 27.9% 5-10, 26.0% 10, 11.5% above 15: The majority have less than 5 years of experience.
- **Rank analysis:**
  - **Mean ranking:** Customer satisfaction (1), sales turnover (2), market share (2), return on investment (4), stockholder value (5), profit (6).
  - **Importance:** Process management significantly influences customer satisfaction, sales turnover, and market share within the supply chain industry.

These findings highlight a predominantly male respondent pool, primarily within the age brackets of 21-40 years, holding graduate qualifications, earning between 10,000-15,000, and having less than 5 years of experience. Moreover, process management significantly affects key aspects like customer satisfaction, sales turnover, and market share in the supply chain sector, as evidenced by the rank analysis.

ANOVA analysis

The ANOVA (analysis of variance) section presents an assessment of multiple factors influencing the supply chain management process. Through a comprehensive analysis, it scrutinises the significance of various elements including sales turnover, return on investment, delivering value to stakeholders, market share expansion, customer recognition, and more. This statistical approach aims to elucidate the potential impact of these factors on the dynamics of supply chain operations.

- **Sales turnover:** Between groups SS: 5.99, within groups SS: 115.66, Total SS: 121.65
  - **F-value:** 1.73, **Sig.:** .166
- **Return on Investment:** Between groups SS: 6.04, within groups SS: 111.80, total SS: 117.85
  - **F-value:** 1.80, **Sig.:** .152
- **Delivering value to SH:** Between groups SS: 3.23, within groups SS: 90.16, Total SS: 93.38
  - **F-value:** 1.19, **Sig.:** .316
- **Increasing Market Share:** Between groups SS: 3.33, within groups SS: 118.32, total SS: 121.65
  - **F-value:** .94, **Sig.:** .425
- **Customer Recognition:** Between groups SS: 3.31, within groups SS: 120.22, total SS: 123.53
  - **F-value:** .92, **Sig.:** .436

The ANOVA results for various factors related to the supply chain management process indicate non-significant differences in sales turnover, return on investment, delivering value to SH, increasing market share, and customer recognition. Each factor's F-value suggests no substantial variation between groups and within groups. These findings, with p-values above .05 (sales turnover: .166, return on investment: .152, delivering value to SH: .316, increasing market share: .425, customer recognition: .436), fail to reject the null hypothesis, implying no significant impact of these factors on the supply chain process. Other factors, such as competitive product, product availability, low product prices, profit potential, promotion and merchandising support, and brand popularity, also showed non-significant differences in their respective F-values and p-values, indicating no major influence on the supply chain process based on this analysis.

Findings

- **Success** in each phase of the assimilation process significantly impacts subsequent phases, although it doesn't guarantee overall success due to external influences like economic, industry, or legal changes.
- Real-world applications must integrate the study's findings into supply chain management practices.
- Observations from interviews yield recommendations aimed at enhancing the success of IT assimilation within supply chain management.

- Implementing **these recommendations can contribute to a more** successful IT assimilation process, yet external factors may still influence outcomes beyond direct control.

Recommendations

This research project set out to answer a number of questions to fulfil two objectives. What has been accomplished is a partial fulfilment of this goal. Phases of the assimilation process have been identified along with the steps within each phase. However, there are several important topics that have not been addressed by this study and which could form the basis for further research. As the findings show, current measures seem inadequate to measure process management investments. While many authors have suggested new measures, one must determine if indeed they are beneficial and useful. As well, new controls might be researched to find new ways to tighten up the control management has over its Process management investment. This study lacks true generalize ability because of the small sample size and the focus on food manufacturers. A larger study that could be shown to be representative of some population of logistics organizations would provide data that could be statistically manipulated.

Conclusion

Our findings must be evaluated in light of the study's limitations, even if it significantly contributes to the literature and has substantial managerial implications. First, because of the distinctiveness of Chinese culture and India's transitional economy, our conclusions were derived from a Chinese context and might not necessarily apply to other nations. The generalizability of our findings may be significantly impacted by cultural and economic factors. The findings of our study may not be applicable to other industrial contexts because we only looked at 3PL firms. Additionally, as the data were gathered through self-reported surveys, there may have been personal bias. To lessen the chance of self-report bias, future studies should include more impartial metrics. Last but not least, the measures—especially the first-order process management constructs—need to be improved.

References

Banker, R. D., and Kauffman, R. J. (2013). Strategic contributions of information technology: an empirical study of ATM network. In Proceedings of the Ninth International Conference on Information Systems, (pp. 141–150).

Bowersox, D. J., and Closs, D. J. (2012). Logistical Management: The Integrated Supply Chain Process. McGraw-Hill.

Carter, J. R., Pearson, J. N., and Peng, L. (2015). Logistics barriers to international operations: the case of the People's Republic of India. *Journal of Business Logistics*, 18(2), 129–145.

Chatterjee, D., Grewal, R., and Sambamurthy, V. (2012). Shaping up for e-commerce: institutional enablers of the organizational assimilation of web technologies. *MIS Quarterly*, 26(2), 65–89.

Chau, P. Y. K. (2013). Re-examining a model for evaluating information centre success using a structural equation modelling approach. *Decision Sciences*, 28(2), 309–334.

Chen, C. H., Lin, B. S., Li, L. L., and Chen, P. S. (2014). Logistics management in India: a case study of Haier. *Human Systems Management*, 23(1), 15–27.

48 Employee perception toward training and development with private banks

Indhumathi, M., Sujith, B.[a], Arul Kumar, M.[b], Reshmi, S.[c] and Sujitha, S.[d]

Karpagam Academy of Higher Education, Coimbatore, Tamil Nadu , India

Abstract

This study delves into the realm of training and development initiatives within private banks, acknowledging their pivotal role in personnel management within the banking sector. Employing a mixed-methods approach, blending quantitative survey data with qualitative insights from interviews, the research explores how employees perceive training programs in private banks and the consequent impact on their commitment to professional growth. Findings reveal that favorable perceptions align with training programs seen as relevant and conducive to job progress. A supportive organizational culture emerges as a key factor influencing employee views, emphasizing the importance of fostering continuous learning. The study uncovers challenges faced by employees, such as time constraints and discrepancies between training content and job roles, which may diminish enthusiasm for training initiatives. The insights generated by this research provide valuable guidance for private banks aiming to tailor training programs to employee needs, heighten job satisfaction, and ultimately elevate organizational performance. Contributing to the knowledge base on talent management, this study presents a nuanced analysis of employee sentiments towards training and development in the private banking industry.

Keywords: Employee perceptions, Madurai district, private banks, training and development

Introduction

In the fiercely competitive banking sector, the performance, efficiency, and customer service of private banks hinge on the expertise and knowledge of their employees. Recognizing this, training and development have become integral components of talent management strategies within private banks. This study focuses on the Madurai District, a region rich in cultural heritage and economic significance, housing several private banks. Understanding employee perspectives on training and development is paramount for these institutions to maintain industry leadership and foster a highly skilled and motivated workforce. The research employs a mixed-methods approach, combining quantitative survey data and qualitative interviews to comprehensively explore employee views on the significance, efficacy, and impact of training and development activities on individual career development and organizational performance. The study aims to provide nuanced insights that can guide private banks in aligning training initiatives with employee needs, ultimately enhancing job satisfaction, engagement, and overall organizational performance in the Madurai District's banking sector.

Review of Literature

- Tejaswi and Srinivasan (2023) acknowledged the effectiveness of Sibar Auto Parts Ltd.'s training program but suggest a need for more impactful initiatives.
- Mohanty and Arka (2019) reported 57% employee support for training policies, with disagreement on alignment with the company's strategy (59%). Ambivalence exists among 53% of employees regarding job aids during training, and 51% are indifferent about receiving preference for new assignments post-training. Only 47% express satisfaction.
- Akilandeswari and Chitra (2018) found positive and effective attitudes toward training in IT organizations.
- Rahman and Kalaskar (2018) noted increased perceived value and satisfaction among employees participating in training programs.
- Jency's study (2016) highlighted the importance of employees' attachment to training, managerial efforts, acknowledgment of contributions and alignment with organizational goals.
- John Benedict (2016) emphasized the need for suitable and efficient training evaluations that go beyond knowledge retention.
- Palaniammal et al. (2015) emphasized the enduring value of training as employees retain acquired skills, contributing to increased productivity.
- Singh and Gaur (2014) emphasized the strategic linkage of training with organizational goals, em-

[a]sujithb8@gmail.com, [b]rmarul1992@gmail.com, [c]reshmiselvaraj03092000@gmail.com, [d]sujithasundaram1999@gmail.com

phasizing motivation, attitude, and emotional intelligence.

- Murty and Fathima (2013) highlighted the positive impact of training and development in public sector organizations, shaping favorable employee attitudes in the industrial landscape.

Problem Statement

Private banks in the Madurai District face the challenge of staying competitive while ensuring ongoing employee training. The study aims to understand employee attitudes towards training and development, investigating their views on program significance and effectiveness. This insight will help private banks tailor training efforts to enhance organizational performance, boost employee engagement, and support the banking sector's growth in Madurai.

Objective of the Study

To ascertain the employee perception toward training and development

Scope of the Study

This study investigates employee perspectives on training and development in private banks within Madurai District. Focusing on various positions, including frontline employees and managers, it explores the diversity of training programs, encompassing both soft and technical skills. The research aims to understand employees' views on the significance and impact of these programs on personal and professional development. While providing recommendations for enhancing training initiatives, the study acknowledges privacy and ethical standards. Limitations include participant biases and contextual influences. Overall, the research contributes valuable insights into talent management practices in Madurai's regional banking sector, offering actionable suggestions for improving employee engagement and training programs.

Research Methodology

- **Data collection:** Primary data is essential for the study, collected through interviews for detailed and specific participant information. Interview schedules ensure consistent, standardized responses, enhancing the reliability of the data collection process.
- **Sampling and sample size:** Convenient sampling is valuable when accessing the entire population is challenging. Enables quick data collection from readily available individuals. Used in gathering data from 150 employees at private banks in Madurai.

Framework of Analysis

It employed the weighted average ranking test alongside simple percentage analysis for comprehensive evaluation of the collected data.

Significance of the Study

The study on employee perceptions of training and development at private banks in the Madurai District holds significant value, benefiting stakeholders such as banks, employees, clients, and the broader banking sector. It aids private banks in crafting effective talent management strategies by understanding employee sentiments, fostering a more skilled and engaged workforce. The findings guide resource allocation, allowing banks to optimize training investments and create clear career pathways for staff. Improved employee training enhances customer service quality, ultimately boosting customer satisfaction. The study contributes to advancing talent management knowledge in the banking sector, providing insights for other institutions to enhance their training programs. It signifies the study's potential to positively influence the functionality, character, and competitiveness of private banks in the Madurai District, fostering a supportive organizational culture and continual improvement.

Analysis and Interpretation

The analysis and interpretation of the socio-economic profile of employees in private banks operating in the Madurai District provide valuable insights into their demographics and perspectives on training and development. Examining factors such as gender distribution, age groups, marital status, years of employment, and monthly income establishes a foundational understanding of the respondent pool. Additionally, a thorough investigation into the factors influencing employee perception towards training and development, as determined through the Kaiser-Meyer-Olkin measure and Bartlett's test, uncovers the significant contributors shaping their views. This comprehensive examination lays the groundwork for informed recommendations to enhance training strategies in Madurai's private banking sector.

Gender distribution: Among the 160 respondents, 31.25% (50) are male, while 68.75% (110) are female.

Age groups: Employees up to 25 years old constitute 25.0% (40 respondents).

The age group between 25 and 35 years makes up 52.5% (84 respondents).

Employees above 35 years old account for 22.5% (36 respondents).

Marital status: Married employees represent 61.25% (98 respondents) of the sample. Unmarried employees make up 38.75% (62 respondents) of the sample.

Years of employment: Employees with less than one year of experience constitute 6.875% (11 respondents). The category of 1 to 3 years of employment makes up 47.5% (76 respondents). Employees with 3 to 5 years of experience represent 31.25% (50 respondents). Employees with more than 5 years of experience account for 14.375% (23 respondents).

Monthly income: Employees with a monthly income of up to Rs. 25,000 make up 30% (48 respondents). The income range between Rs. 25,001 and Rs. 40,000 constitutes 40% (64 respondents).Employees earning above Rs. 40,000 account for 30% (48 respondents). Employee perception factors on training and development:

KMO and Bartlett's test: The KMO measure of sampling adequacy is 0.891, indicating suitability for factor analysis.

Bartlett's test of sphericity has a significant value (p = 0.000), confirming the suitability of the data for factor analysis.

Rotated component matrix: Significant factors contributing to employee perception include high morale and performance, quality training programs, performance and productivity dependence on T&D, employees' enhancement, regular training programs, efficiency gains, fostering positive attitude, and others.

Contribution of factors: The first factor contributes 19.668%, while the cumulative contribution of seven factors is 75.803%.

In summary, the socio-economic profile reveals a predominantly female workforce, primarily aged between 25 and 35 years, and married. Regarding perception on training and development, factors like morale, program quality, and productivity dependence significantly influence employees, contributing to 75.803% of the overall perception. The study provides comprehensive insights into employee demographics and perception factors, crucial for enhancing training strategies in private banks in Madurai.

The study reveals a diverse socio-economic profile of private bank employees in Madurai. A majority of respondents are female (68.75%), aged 25-35 (52.5%), and married (61.25%). Employees with 1-3 years of experience form the largest group (47.5%). In terms of monthly income, 40% earn Rs. 25,001-40,000. Factor analysis identifies key factors influencing perceptions of training and development, such as high morale, comprehensive quality training, and the importance of training for career growth. Cumulatively, these factors contribute to 75.803% of the variance. These findings inform targeted strategies for enhancing training programs and talent management in Madurai's private banking sector.

Conclusion

In conclusion, this study underscores several key suggestions for private banks operating in the Madurai District to enhance their training and development initiatives. Firstly, banks should focus on tailoring comprehensive training programs to meet the diverse needs of employees at various career levels, ensuring that materials are current, relevant, and aligned with organizational goals. Encouraging a culture of continuous learning through regular training opportunities is essential for keeping employees abreast of industry innovations. Establishing a supportive training atmosphere, addressing unfavorable perceptions through employee feedback, and involving employees in program design and planning are crucial steps to maximize the impact of training programs. Additionally, recognizing and rewarding staff participation in learning opportunities fosters a culture of lifelong learning.

In the broader context, the findings suggest that private banks in the Madurai District can significantly enhance job performance, increase employee satisfaction, and foster a culture of ongoing learning and development by implementing these recommendations. By aligning training activities with strategic objectives and addressing specific needs, banks can improve overall organizational performance and gain a competitive advantage in the banking sector.

It is evident that training and development play a pivotal role in cultivating a knowledgeable, motivated, and adaptable workforce. The study's limitations, confined to the Madurai District, call for future research to explore the long-term impact of training on employee retention and organizational success in diverse contexts. In conclusion, private banks must recognize the importance of understanding employee perceptions to refine talent management, nurture continuous learning, and cultivate a skilled and motivated workforce vital to the banking sector's success in the Madurai District.

References

Akilandeswari, P., and Chitra, V. (2018). A study on employee's perception towards training program - with special reference to IT industries in Chennai. *International Journal of Pure and Applied Mathematics*, 118(18), 1701–1708.

Jency, S. (2016). A study on employee perception towards training and development at Indian rare earth limited (IREL). *International Journal of Applied Research*, 2(8), 705–708.

John Benedict, D. (2016). An ascertainment of training and development programme in Neyveli lignite corporation limited. *Ahead - International Journal of Recent Research Review*, 1(5), 59–63.

Mohanty, S., and Arka, M. (2019). A study on employee perception on training and development at sail. *Navajyoti, International Journal of Multi-Disciplinary Research*, 3(2), 9.

Murty, T. N., and Fathima, F. (2013). Perception and attitude of employees towards training and development in public sector unit. *Abhinav International Monthly Refereed Journal of Research in Management and Technology*, 2(3), 141–147.

Palaniammal, V. S., Kanimozhi, G., Saravanan, B., and Saranya, M. (2015). A study on training programme at sugar mills co-op ltd company. *Journal of Emerging Technologies and Innovative Research (JETIR)*, 2(8), 3241–3252.

Rahman, K. M., and Kalaskar, P. B. (2018). Perceptions of employees towards training and development: an empirical study. *International Research Journal of Human Resources and Social Sciences*, 5(03), 294–301.

Singh, N., and Gaur, A. (2014). Impact of training and development in Indian health care. *International Journal of Human Resources Management*, 3(2), 13–22.

Tejaswi, N., and Srinivasan, K. (2023). A study on employee perception towards training and development in Sibar-Autoparts private limited, Tirupati. *Journal of Emerging Technologies and Innovative Research (JETIR)*, 10(6), 671–679.

49 Factors influence employee retention in the textile industry

Lalith Kumar, M., Renukadevi, S.[a], Arul Kumar, M.[b], Velmurugan, R.[c] and Sudarvel, J.[d]

Karpagam Academy of Higher Education, Coimbatore, Tamil Nadu, India

Abstract

In this research, our focus is on discerning the determinants of employee retention within the Udumalpet textile industry, a prominent hub in India. Employee retention poses a significant challenge globally, and Udumalpet's textile sector, renowned for its labor-intensive nature, is not exempt. Investigating factors such as job satisfaction, compensation, work-life balance, career advancement opportunities, organizational culture, and leadership styles, we employ a mixed-methods approach encompassing qualitative insights from semi-structured interviews with employees and quantitative data gathered through structured surveys. The study probes into region-specific nuances impacting retention in Udumalpet's textile sector. By unveiling challenges faced by the industry, our findings provide actionable recommendations for both business professionals and policymakers. Addressing these concerns has the potential to enhance job satisfaction, elevate employee retention, and cultivate a more conducive work environment, ultimately contributing to heightened organizational success and boosted morale within the Udumalpet textile sector.

Keywords: Compensation and benefits and career development, employee retention, job satisfaction, textile industry Udumalpet

Introduction

Udumalpet, a significant textile hub in India, grapples with the universal challenge of retaining skilled workers in its crucial textile sector. This industry's labor-intensive nature necessitates the preservation of experienced personnel for effective production processes. The study aims to scrutinize diverse factors influencing employee retention, encompassing workplace conditions, organizational culture, pay structures, and opportunities for professional growth. By understanding these elements, stakeholders can formulate strategies to reduce turnover and improve the working environment. Subsequent sections will inquire into an extensive literature review on employee retention, covering key aspects like pay, benefits, work-life balance, career advancement, organizational culture, and leadership philosophies. Utilizing a mixed-methods approach, the study seeks to bridge the gap between academic insights and practical applications, contributing to industry efforts in effectively addressing the intricate challenge of employee retention within Udumalpet's textile sector.

Problem Statement

The Udumalpet textile industry grapples with a critical problem—retaining skilled workers. High turnover jeopardizes long-term viability and productivity. Issues such as monotonous tasks, inadequate pay, poor work-life balance, and unsupportive culture contribute to the challenge. This study aims to offer insights and recommendations through a mixed-methods approach to address the complex issue of employee turnover.

Objective

- To identify factors that influence employee retention in textile industry.

Research Methodology

- **Data collection:**
    - Primary data through interviews.
    - Ensures detailed and specific participant information.
    - Interview schedule for question consistency.
    - Standardized, reliable data collection process.
- **Sampling and size:**
    - Convenient sampling for quick data collection.
    - Useful when entire population access is challenging.
    - Data gathered from 200 Udumalpet workers.

Framework of Analysis

- **The collected data has been analyzed by** employing simple percentage and factor analysis.

[a]renudeepak005@gmail.com, [b]rmarul1992@gmail.com, [c]drvelsngm@gmail.com, [d]j.sudarvel@gmail.com

Literature Review

Table 49.1 Insights on employee retention: varied perspectives from academic studies.

Author name	Study	Findings (insights/interpretation)
Dahiya and Nandal (2021)	Factors influencing the textile industry	Training, job satisfaction, career development, work-life balance, communication, and rewards are positively linked to retention. Policies like better pay, flexible hours, and rewarding deserving employees enhance employee retention.
Badre (2020)	Determinants affecting employee retention	Well-structured policies, learning opportunities, development, growth, retirement benefits, and plans significantly impact employee retention.
Chandrasekara (2020)	Factors influencing Rich Light Exports Ltd	Work environment, motivation, and hygiene factors impact variables. Focus on motivation, and workplace environment crucial for employee retention.
Prabusankar (2017)	Elements influencing retention in manufacturing	Compensation, professional advancement, proximity, and relationships positively affect dedication. Fair pay, growth opportunities, and a good working atmosphere are crucial for employee commitment.
Kossivi and Kalgora (2016)	Factors influencing employee retention	Development opportunities, compensation, work-life balance, management, environment, social support, autonomy, and training majorly influence employee retention.
Patgar and Vijayakumar (2015)	Factors determining employee quit or stay	Competitive compensation, flexible work schedules, recognition, career advancement, promotions, job stability, and training impact retention. Balanced intrinsic and extrinsic motivational factors are vital for reducing staff turnover.
Shoaib et al. (2009)	Correlation between retention and various factors	A strong correlation was found between employee retention and career growth opportunities, supervisor assistance, working environment, rewards, and work-life policies.

Source: Author

Significance of the Study

The investigation into factors affecting employee retention in the Udumalpet textile sector holds immense significance for the sector and the broader economy. Recognizing and addressing turnover issues can enhance competitiveness, ensuring a stable, skilled workforce, improving product quality, and reducing operational disruptions. High turnover negatively impacts income equality, job security, and economic growth, emphasizing the need for retention-focused policies. Policymakers and HR professionals can leverage insights to create a retention-friendly environment, fostering employee happiness and loyalty. The study's broader implications extend to influencing strategic decisions, policy-making, and long-term prosperity, making it a valuable contribution to understanding and improving employee retention in the Udumalpet textile sector.

Analysis and Interpretation

In this comprehensive examination of employee retention factors within the Udumalpet textile sector, a detailed demographic overview sets the stage, revealing gender, age, qualification, income, work experience, and residential distribution among respondents. Transitioning to the core of the study, a robust factor analysis unveils critical elements influencing retention. Beyond demographic insights, this analysis informs strategic decision-making for policymakers and HR professionals, offering targeted solutions. The study's significance extends beyond Udumalpet, presenting a roadmap for future research. Now, dives into the nuanced fabric of employee retention, exploring the intricate interplay of demographics and key factors crucial for organizational stability and success.

Demographic overview

- **Gender distribution**
  - The study's respondents are predominantly female (62.0%), with males constituting 38.0% of the sample.
- **Age distribution**
  - Respondents are diversified across age groups: 35.0% up to 30 years, 30.0% between 31-40 years, 30.0% between 41-50 years, and 5.0% between 51-60 years.
- **Qualification profile**
  - Respondents' qualifications vary, with 45.0% up to high school certificate, 10.0% diploma holders, 25.0% graduates, and 20.0% possessing other qualifications.

- **Monthly income breakdown**
  - Monthly income distribution shows 15.0% earning up to Rs. 15,000, 60.0% between Rs. 15,001 and Rs. 25,000, 15.0% between Rs. 25,001 and Rs. 35,000, and 10.0% earning above Rs. 35,000.
- **Work experience profile**
  - Respondents' work experience is diverse, with 30.0% having up to 2 years, 37.0% with 2--4 years, 18.0% with 5-10 years, and 15.0% having more than 10 years of experience.
- **Area of residence**
  - The majority reside in rural areas (62.0%), followed by 18.0% in urban and 20.0% in semi-urban areas.

Employee retention factors

- **Factor analysis suitability**
  - The Kaiser-Meyer-Olkin (KMO) measure (0.741) and Bartlett's test of sphericity confirm data suitability for factor analysis, signifying its appropriateness.
- **Factors influencing retention**
  - The rotated component matrix identifies key factors contributing to employee retention.
    - Notable contributors (loading above 0.5) include team collaboration, flexible work arrangements, performance feedback, recognition, transparent policies, employee well-being, advancement opportunities, incentives, exit interviews, career growth, training programs, social responsibility, work-life balance, employee relationships, compensation, alignment with values, diversity, communication, job security, management, employee empowerment, conflict resolution, and health and safety.
- **Factor contribution**
  - Factor one contributes significantly (38.863%) to employee retention, with additional factors contributing 9.612%, 8.331%, 6.541%, 4.655%, and 4.372%, accumulating to a total of 72.373%.

Findings

- **Significance beyond demographics**
  - The demographic profile provides a foundation for understanding employee retention factors. The factor analysis probes into significant contributors, offering nuanced insights beyond demographic attributes.

- **Strategic implications**
  - Policymakers and HR professionals can leverage this comprehensive analysis to formulate targeted retention strategies based on scientific insights, addressing specific concerns raised by the workforce.
- **Future research direction**
  - This study not only contributes to the understanding of employee retention in the Udumalpet textile sector but also suggests avenues for future research using a mixed-methods approach in similar circumstances.

Conclusion

Navigating Udumalpet's dynamic textile sector demands a nuanced approach to understanding and managing employee retention. This study, employing a mixed-methods strategy, probes into factors influencing retention, from work-life balance to salary and leadership styles. The findings affirm established principles in organizational psychology, emphasizing the complexity of these variables. Demographically, the workforce presents unique disparities in gender, age, qualifications, income, experience, and geography, underlining the need for tailored retention strategies.

Recommendations, derived from both demographic insights and literature, offer a strategic blueprint. A holistic approach, accommodating diversity and crafting customized solutions, emerges as key to enhancing engagement and satisfaction. The Udumalpet textile industry can, thus, foster a positive culture, support career growth, and acknowledge diverse backgrounds, fostering organizational success and contributing to local economic growth.

Looking forward, the study advocates for longitudinal research to track evolving retention dynamics, cross-sector comparisons, and analyses of technological and organizational impacts on retention. These future avenues aim to provide actionable insights, enabling the Udumalpet textile industry to meet the evolving challenges of retaining a skilled and diverse workforce, ensuring sustained prosperity in this competitive landscape.

References

Badre, P. (2020). Analyzing the factors affecting employee retention in IT organizations At STPI Nagpur. *Our Heritage*, 68(1), Available at SSRN: https://ssrn.com/abstract=3847996.

Chandrasekara, P. G. R. B. (2020). Factors and their influence on employee retention of the apparel sector employees in anuradhapura district. *International Jour-*

nal of Scientific and Research Publications, 10(7), 543–558.

Dahiya, J., and Nandal, V. (2021). Employee retention – a matter of concern in the textile industry of haryana. *Webology*, 18(4), 2507–2514.

Kossivi, B., Xu, M., and Kalgora, B. (2016). Study on determining factors of employee retention. *Open Journal of Social Sciences*, 4, 261–268. http://dx.doi.org/10.4236/jss.2016.45029.

Patgar, S., and Vijayakumar, N. (2015). A study on the factors affecting employee retention in a textile industry.

International Journal of Recent Research in Civil and Mechanical Engineering (IJRRCME), 1(2), 1–5.

Prabusankar, R. (2017). A study on factors affecting employee retention in manufacturing enterprises in Coimbatore district. *International Journal of Management*, 8(2), 123–128.

Shoib, M., Noor, A., Tirmizi, S. R., and Bashir, S. (2009). Determinants of employee retention in telecom Sector of Pakistan. In Proceedings of the 2nd CBRC, Lahore, (pp. 14).

50 Financial performance of Subam Papers Private Limited in Tirunelveli

Muthukumar, M., Saroja Devi, R.,ᵃ Krishnaveni, V.ᵇ and Arulprakasam, E.ᶜ

Karpagam Academy of Higher Education, Coimbatore, Tamil Nadu, India

Abstract

India's paper industry, primarily serving packaging needs, witnessed a substantial growth from 20.37 million tons in 2017–2018 to 25 million tons in 2019–2020, expanding at approximately 10% annually. The study delves into Subam Papers Private Limited's financial accounts, revealing losses during the research period. To ensure future profitability, the company should consider internal and external factors. Despite losses, the company effectively utilizes its resources, maintaining a high inventory. To secure profits in the coming years, strategic attention to financial elements is crucial. This abstract highlight the Indian paper industry's growth, Subam Papers Private Limited's financial insights, and emphasizes the company's need for future profitability through prudent management and strategic decisions.

Keywords: Private Limited's financial accounts, revealing losses

Introduction

Financial performance analysis is crucial for understanding a company's strengths and weaknesses by examining the components of the balance sheet and profit and loss account. This analysis, conducted by company management or external parties like creditors and investors, delves into the relationship between financial statement sections, providing insights into the company's status. It assesses profitability, financial stability, and aids in forecasting both short- and long-term growth. The evaluation involves various analytical techniques to comprehend a firm's financial health, assisting in anticipating future earnings, debt management, and overall profitability. Financial performance, reflecting a company's operational efficacy and policy outcomes, is pivotal for gauging success in achieving financial objectives. The process is essential for comparing businesses in the same sector and assessing market dynamics. Shifting focus to India's paper industry, it emerges as a vital sector intertwined with societal progress, education, and health, playing a central role among forest-based industries. The diverse raw materials, including agricultural by-products and residues, highlight its significance, positioning it as a pivotal forest-based industry.

Review of Literature

- Mehta (2020) investigated the Indian paper industry's sustainable development, highlighting its rapid expansion and the imperative to integrate sustainability measures. The study underscores the ongoing conflict between the paper industry's growth and environmental concerns, despite recent strides in environmental sustainability.
- Sharma (2021) advocates for automating the corrugated paper industry to enhance profitability, citing the competitive edge achieved by nations like "China" and "Sri Lanka". Existing literature on the corrugated paper sector is limited, presenting a novel and valuable research opportunity to contribute substantially to the field.
- Zimmerer et al. (2022) emphasized on the delicate balance between maintaining adequate cash reserves for debt coverage and avoiding the drawbacks of excessive idle funds. The authors caution against hoarding cash for unforeseen events, arguing that investing idle funds could yield more profitable returns, enhancing overall company growth and profitability.

Problem Statement

The problem under investigation pertains to understanding the financial performance of Subam Papers Private Limited, with a focus on establishing cause-and-effect relationships, evaluating growth performance, and assessing asset utilization within Paper Mills Ltd., incorporating diverse financial indicators such as cost, sales, profit margin, financial ratios, and overall financial health to inform strategic decision-making and shape the company's future trajectory.

ᵃrajendransaro@gmail.com, ᵇkrishnaveni.rkv99@gmail.com, ᶜeapcas@gmail.com

- Within groups: 1.75784 (Df = 40, mean square = 0.043946)
- Total: 12.62274 (Df = 49)

Interpretation: The significant level (Sig.) is less than 0.05, indicating a rejection of the null hypothesis. The variation in the balance sheets is industry-related.

ANOVA in debt ratio in Subam Papers Ltd:
- Between groups: 23.80741 (D f= 9, mean square = 2.645268, F = 13.465, Sig. = 0.000)
- Within groups: 7.85793 (Df = 40, mean square = 0.196448)
- Total: 31.66534 (Df = 49)

Interpretation: The significant level (Sig.) is less than 0.05, indicating a rejection of the null hypothesis. The variation in the balance sheets is industry-related.

ANOVA in Net Profit Ratio in Subam Papers Ltd:
- Between groups: 7.18E+09 (Df = 9, mean square = 7.98E+08, F = 1.0017, Sig. = 0.322)
- Within groups: 3.19E+10 (Df=40, Mean Square=7.97E+08)
- Total: 3.91E+10 (Df=49)

Interpretation: The significant level (Sig.) is greater than 0.05, indicating acceptance of the null hypothesis. There is no significant variation among balance sheets in the industry.

ANOVA in gross profit ratio in Subam Papers Ltd:
- Between Groups: 1305.279 (Df = 9, mean square = 145.031, F = 2.2123, Sig. = 0.322)
- Within groups: 2556.682 (Df = 39, mean square = 65.55596)
- Total: 3861.961 (Df = 48)

Interpretation: The significant level (Sig.) is greater than 0.05, indicating acceptance of the null hypothesis. There is no significant variation among balance sheets in the industry.

ANOVA in receivable turnover ratio in Subam Papers Ltd:
- Between groups: 0.261527 (Df = 9, mean square = 0.029059, F = 21.031, Sig. = 0.322)
- Within groups: 0.055266 (Df = 40, mean square = 0.001382)
- Total: 0.316793 (Df = 49)

Interpretation: The significant level (Sig.) is greater than 0.05, indicating acceptance of the null hypothesis.

Objectives of the Study
- To compare the financial position of Subam paper companies in the paper industry using their financial ratios.
- To find out the efficiency of financial operation of selected companies in paper industry

Research Methodology

The researcher used descriptive study and evaluation is based on secondary data that was gathered from yearly reports, journals, and magazines. The statistics, graphs, and diagrams that are provided to describe the study's statistical data serve as the foundation for the analysis and suggestions. The time the researcher spent gathering and analyzing data for the Tirunelveli-based Subam Papers private limited company's profitability analysis. The most recent five years of data, from 2018 to 22, are used. The analyst selects ANOVA, correlation, Skewness, Kurtosis, mean, and other statistical metrics have all been used.

Data Analysis and Interpretation

In this financial analysis of Subam Papers Ltd., we employ analysis of variance (ANOVA) to scrutinize key ratios, such as current ratio, liquid ratio, debt ratio, net profit ratio, gross profit ratio, receivable turnover ratio, and payable turnover ratio. Each ratio undergoes ANOVA to assess variations among balance sheets, providing insights into the industry's financial dynamics Hingorani et al. (2005). Additionally, we explore correlations between liquidity and profitability ratios Tan (2018). Through meticulous statistical examination, this study unveils the nuanced financial landscape of Subam Papers Ltd., shedding light on crucial industry trends and relationships between key financial indicators Morarji and Devi (2015).

ANOVA in current ratio in Subam Papers Ltd:
- Between groups: 3.403168 (Df = 9, mean square = 0.37813, F = 10.995, Sig. = 0.000)
- Within groups: 1.37552 (Df = 40, mean square = 0.034388)
- Total: 4.778688 (Df = 49)

Interpretation: The significant level (Sig.) is less than 0.05, indicating a rejection of the null hypothesis. The variation in the balance sheets is industry-related.

ANOVA in liquid ratio in Subam Papers Ltd:
- Between groups: 10.8649 (Df = 9, mean square = 1.207211, F = 27.470, Sig. = 0.000)

There is no significant variation among balance sheets in the industry.

ANOVA in payable turnover ratio in Subam Papers Ltd:

- Between groups: 8184390 (Df = 9, mean square = 909376.6, F = 3.6837, Sig. = 0.322)
- Within groups: 9627725 (Df = 39, mean square = 246864.8)
- Total: 17812115 (Df = 48)

Interpretation: The significant level (Sig.) is greater than 0.05, indicating acceptance of the null hypothesis. There is no significant variation among balance sheets in the industry.

Relationship between liquidity ratio and profitability ratio - correlations:

- Current ratio vs. liquid ratio: Pearson correlation = 0.142 (Sig. = 0.324)
- Current ratio vs. debt ratio: Pearson correlation = -0.074 (Sig. = 0.608)
- Current ratio vs. gross profit ratio: Pearson correlation = 0.026 (Sig. = 0.858)
- Current ratio vs. net profit ratio: Pearson correlation = 0.265 (Sig. = 0.063)
- Current ratio vs. receivable turnover ratio: Pearson correlation = 0.029 (Sig. = 0.844)
- Current ratio vs. payable turnover ratio: Pearson correlation = -0.156 (Sig. = 0.280)
- Liquid ratio vs. debt ratio: Pearson correlation = -0.423 (Sig. = 0.002)
- Liquid ratio vs. gross profit ratio: Pearson correlation = -0.174 (Sig. = 0.227)
- Liquid ratio vs. net profit ratio: Pearson correlation = 0.049 (Sig. = 0.734)
- Liquid ratio vs. receivable turnover ratio: Pearson correlation = -0.102 (Sig. = 0.481)
- Liquid ratio vs. payable turnover ratio: Pearson correlation = -0.071 (Sig. = 0.626)

Interpretation: The correlation coefficients indicate varying degrees of association between different financial ratios. The correlation between liquid ratio and debt ratio is notably strong (Pearson correlation = -0.423).

Conclusion

In this financial analysis of Subam Papers Ltd., we employ analysis of variance (ANOVA) to scrutinize key ratios, such as current ratio, liquid ratio, debt ratio, net profit ratio, gross profit ratio, receivable turnover ratio, and payable turnover ratio. Each ratio undergoes ANOVA to assess variations among balance sheets, providing insights into the industry's financial dynamics. Additionally, we explore correlations between liquidity and profitability ratios. Through meticulous statistical examination, this study unveils the nuanced financial landscape of Subam Papers Ltd., shedding light on crucial industry trends and relationships between key financial indicators.

References

Devi, R. S., Sudarvel, J., Velmurugan, R., and Mahadevan, M. (2022). Application of altman's Z score model: the financial soundness of sun pharmaceutical industries in India. *IBMRD's Journal of Management and Research*, 11, 96–100.

Hingorani, N. L., Ramanthan, A. R., and Grewal, T. S. (2005). Management Accounting. New Delhi: Prentice Hall of India.

Morarji, A., and Devi, R. S. (2015). A study on financial status of ceramic tiles Ltd. *Pezzottaite Journals, International Journal of Applied Financial Management Perspectives*, 4(3), 1842–1849.

Tan, Y. (2018). Profitability and competition: review of literature and directions of future research. *Investment Management and Financial Innovations*, 14, 62–73.

51 Profitability analysis of the selected India cement industry

Surya, K. S.[a], Saroja Devi, R.[b], Meena Suguanthi, G.[c] and Arulprakasam, E.[d]
Karpagam Academy of Higher Education, Coimbatore, India

Abstract

In the realm of global cement production, India stands as the second-largest producer, contributing over 7% of the total installed capacity. The private sector holds a dominant position, controlling 98% of the capacity, while the public sector holds the remaining 2%. The top 20 cement companies in India collectively manufacture nearly 70% of the country's cement. Bolstered by extensive, high-quality limestone reserves, India's cement industry is poised for substantial growth. Projections indicate a 5.68% compound annual growth rate (CAGR) in cement consumption from FY16 to FY22. This study delves into a profitability ratio analysis of key cement firms during the 2018-2022 period, navigating the complexities introduced by the COVID-19 pandemic. The analysis evaluates companies' risk profiles based on strengths and weaknesses, revealing a dynamic pattern in profitability ratios within the acceptable range of 5 to 10% for net profit. Factors influencing profit fluctuations include sales variations, shifts in operational profit, and increased operating and administrative costs. The study recommends a strategic reassessment of sales and cost-management tactics to optimize return on investment and fortify future profitability amid changing market conditions.

Keywords: COVID-19 pandemic, FY16 to FY, revealing a dynamic pattern in profitability ratios

Introduction

In the financial landscape, a critical responsibility of a financial manager is to consistently evaluate a company's profitability, discerning the contributing factors to both high and low returns. This assessment involves scrutinizing changes in retained earnings, various reserves, and surplus, where an upswing in these elements signals enhanced profitability, while a reduction indicates a decline. Profits, being the primary goal of any business, necessitate a focus on retaining profitable clients through customer profitability analysis (CPA). Simply put, profitability analysis reviews a company's expenses and earnings to determine its overall profitability, considering gross profit and operating profit as crucial indicators.

Shifting gears to the cement industry, India holds a prominent position as the world's second-largest cement manufacturer, contributing over 8% to global installed capacity. Positioned for substantial growth, the industry is integral to India's infrastructure and construction expansion. However, it faces pivotal challenges and opportunities, including the environmental impact of CO_2 emissions, innovation, and global competitiveness. Key trends and issues in the cement sector encompass the COVID-19 pandemic's repercussions, the imperative to reduce carbon footprints, demand for durable and high-performance cements, exploration of new markets, industry consolidation, and regulatory considerations. While the cement industry anticipates moderate growth in the aftermath of the global pandemic, proactive strategies are essential to navigate risks such as societal unrest, trade disputes, climate change, and geopolitical conflicts, ensuring sustained development and innovation.

Problem Statement

The challenge lies in effectively investing surplus funds, as keeping idle cash offers no returns, impacting the company's profitability, and permanent disposal is impractical given potential future requirements, necessitating a strategic approach to generate returns, such as investing in marketable securities, to outperform conventional bank interest and enhance financial prospects.

Review of Literature

- Zimmerer et al. (2020) firms must balance holding sufficient cash for debt obligations with the drawbacks of unprofitable idle funds. Hoarding cash limits opportunities for profitable investments, hindering overall growth and profitability.
- Donaldson (2021) advocates for comprehensive cash budgeting to account for deviations from anticipated results. Creating budgets for best and worst-case scenarios aids better planning for unforeseen circumstances.
- Ekanem (2022) studied that profit management is a broad topic with industry-specific considerations. Efficient payment habits, including prompt

[a]21MBAP057@kahedu.edu.in, [b]rajendransaro@gmail.com, [c]meenasuganthi.govindaraj@kahedu.edu.in, [d]eapcas@gmail.com

interest-bearing payments and quick collection from clients, are crucial for exerting control and generating additional revenue. Addresses the importance of payment systems, specifically accounts receivable, in enhancing business efficiency and financial performance.

Objectives of the Study

- To examine relationship between profitability of selected companies in cement industry.
- To study the relationship between the Liquidity ratio and turnover ratio selected cement industry.

Research Methodology

- Descriptive research methodology used in this study.
- Emphasis on profit in a general and specific context.
- Secondary data sourced from websites, audited business reports, and financial platforms.
- Profitability analysis focuses on identifying financial strengths and weaknesses.
- Relationship established between balance sheet items and profit and loss account.
- Metrics include gross profit to net revenue, net operating profit to net revenue, and return ratios.
- Perspectives considered: shareholders and management.
- Primary data source: company's annual reports from 2018 to 2022.

Sample size

- Population: All types of businesses across various industries.
- Selection challenges: Difficult to choose a sample due to diverse industries; researcher's discretion.
- Basis for selection: Reflects the current industry state and business growth.
- Selected companies in the cement industry: Ultratech Cement, Shree Cements, Ambuja Cements, ACC Cements, JK Cements, Ramco Cement, JK Lashami Cement, Star Cements, Sagar Cement
- Data sources: Annual reports of selected companies.
- Timeframe: From 2018 to 2022.

Framework of analysis

- Tools used
- Ratio analysis
- Coefficient of variance
- ANOVA
- Skewness
- Kurtosis

Analysis and Interpretation

In this comprehensive financial analysis, we look into the profitability and liquidity metrics of prominent cement companies, including Ultratech, Shree Cements, Ambuja Cements, and more Hingorani et al. (2005). Focusing on key ratios like Net Profit, Gross Profit, and Operating Ratio, we explore trends, variations, and correlations across the years 2017 to 2022 Tan (2018). The examination includes ANOVA tests and correlation analyses, shedding light on significant differences and relationships that shape the financial landscape of the cement industry McDonald (2019). This meticulous exploration provides valuable insights for stakeholders seeking a nuanced understanding of the financial health of these industry leaders Borio et al. (2019).

Analysis and interpretation of profitability ratios in selected cement industry

Net profit ratio

- Formula: net profit ratio = (net profit/net sales) * 100.
  - **Companies' net profit ratios (2022-2017):**
  - Ultratech: 7.49, 6.03, 13.42, 12.36, 13.94.
  - Shree Cements: 14.07, 8.11, 13.19, 18.36, 16.61.
  - Ambuja Cements: 13.09, 13.1, 15.74, 14.89, 13.04.
  - ... *(data for all companies)*
  - **Average net profit ratio:** 10.64.
  - **Standard deviation (SD):** 3.63.
  - **Coefficient of variation:** 34.10%.

ANOVA in net profit ratio

- **Significant difference**
  - High significant difference among companies ($p < 0.001$).
  - Negative skewness observed for Ultratech, Shree Cement, ACC Cements, Ramco Cement, Star Cement, and JKLashami Cement Bolt et al. (2020).
  - All companies exhibit platykurtic distribution (Kurtosis < 3).

Gross profit ratio

- **ANOVA result**
  - No significant difference among companies ($p > 0.05$).
  - Accept **alternative** hypothesis; reject null hypothesis Guo (2021).

Operating ratio

- Formula: operating ratio = (operating expenses + cost of goods sold) / net sales Jonesa et al. (2022).

Companies' operating ratios (2022-2017):
- Ultratech: 19.74, 17.69, 21.28, 25.38, 21.58.
  - Shree Cements: 25.14, 22.63, 30.86, 31.41, 25.49.
  - Ambuja Cements: 16.65, 18.41, 23.27, 22.96, 15.3.
  - ... *(data for all companies)*
  - **Average operating ratio:** 21.13.
  - **Standard deviation (SD):** 2.83.
  - **Coefficient of variation:** 13.39%.

ANOVA in operating ratio
- **Significant difference**
  - High significant difference among companies ($p < 0.001$).
  - Negative skewness observed for JKLashami Cement Devi et al. (2022).
  - All companies exhibit platykurtic distribution (kurtosis < 3).

ANOVA in operating profit ratio
- **Significant difference**
  - High significant difference among companies ($p < 0.001$).
  - Accept alternative hypothesis; reject null hypothesis Morarji and Devi (2015).

Relationship between liquidity ratio and account receivable ratio:
- **Correlations (Pearson)**
  - Current ratio and liquid ratio: Positive correlation (0.142).
  - Stock turnover ratio and debtors turnover ratio: Negative correlation (-0.074).
  - Net profit, expenses ratio, and working capital ratio: Positive correlations.
- **Interpretation**
  - Correlation coefficients range from -1 to +1.
  - Negative correlation for stock turnover ratio; positive correlations for others.

In summary, the analysis provides insights into the profitability and liquidity of selected cement companies, revealing variations and correlations that impact their financial performance. The financial analysis of selected cement companies reveals noteworthy trends. Net Profit Ratios exhibit variability, with Ultratech and Shree Cements showcasing negative skewness. ANOVA tests confirm significant differences in net profit and gross profit ratios among the companies. Operating ratios display positive skewness in JK Lakshmi Cement, hinting at unique operational dynamics. Correlation coefficients highlight varying relationships, such as a negative correlation in stock turnover ratio. Overall, the study underscores nuanced financial dynamics, providing stakeholders with crucial insights into the profitability and liquidity nuances that distinguish these cement industry giants.

Conclusion

In light of the study's insights, several strategic suggestions emerge for enhancing the company's financial health. Firstly, the company should focus on expanding its output to boost revenue. Maintaining a secure current ratio at 2:1 is crucial, necessitating a reduction in current obligations for enhanced liquidity. Efficient reserve management is advised, preparing the business for potential losses during modernization. Cost reduction strategies, particularly in administrative expenses, are recommended. Competitive salaries must be retained to attract and retain skilled professionals, ultimately elevating productivity. The company's revenue, efficiency, and financial position can further improve through strategic management of working capital and equity investments.

Analyzing the company's profitability from 2017–2018 to 2021–2022 revealed fluctuating but satisfactory profitability ratios. While these ratios offer monetary insights, they may lack a comprehensive business portrayal. Profit fluctuations are attributed to sales variations, operational shifts, and rising operating costs. The study emphasizes the need for a proactive policy update to counter declining returns, advocating altered sales and cost-management strategies for enhanced future profitability.

References

Bolt, W., De Haan, L., Hoeberichts, M., van Oordt, M. R. C., and Swank, J. (2020). Bank profitability during recessions. *Journal of Banking and Finance,* 36(9), 2552–2564.

Borio, C., Gambacorta, L., and Hofmann, B. (2019). The influence of monetary policy on bank profitability. *International Finance,* 20(1), 48–63.

Devi, R. S., Sudarvel, J., Velmurugan, R., and Mahadevan, M. (2022). Application of altman's Z Score model: the financial soundness of sun pharmaceutical industries in India. *IBMRD's Journal of Management and Research,* 11, 96–100.

Guo, R. R. (2021). The determinants of profitability in processed food industry in Indonesia. *Journal of Business and Entrepreneurship,* 6(4).

Hingorani, N. L., Ramanthan, A. R., and Grewal, T. S. (2005). Management Accounting. New Delhi: Prentice Hall of India.

Jonesa, V., Newman, W., Lovemore, S., and Ongai, W. (2022). Literature review of the impact of Covid-19 Lockdown on the working capital management and profitability of firms. *Journal of Accounting, Finance and Auditing Studies,* 8(3), 64–85.

McDonald, J. (2019). The determinants of firm profitability in Australian Manufacturing. *The Economic Record,* 75(229), 115–126.

Morarji, A., and Devi, R. S. (2015). A study on financial status of ceramic Tiles Ltd. *Pezzottaite Journals, International Journal of Applied Financial Management Perspectives,* 4(3), 1842–1849.

Tan, Y. (2018). Profitability and competition: review of literature and directions of future research. *Investment Management and Financial Innovations,* 14, 62–73.

52 A study on cash management in ZF electronics TVS (India) Pvt limited, Madurai

Venkateshwar, Geetha Bai, B.[a] and Meena Suguanthi, G.[b]

Karpagam Academy of Higher Education, Tamil Nadu, Coimbatore

Abstract

Modern business world, cash serves multiple functions. It enables payment by cheques acts as storage for earmarked funds, and serves as a reservoir to meet emergencies. Cash is a crucial element of working capital. The primary objective of this study is to analyze cash management in ZF Electronics TVS (India) Private Limited in Madurai. The project type is analytical and descriptive research. The study utilizes secondary data, specifically the financial statements of the company from 2017-18 to 2021-22. Tools such as trend analysis, ratio analysis, cash flow statement, and comparative balance sheet are employed. The study aims to assess how the company's short-term obligations are met by liquidity ratios and its short-term solvency position. It should be noted that the findings of this study are specific to ZF Electronics TVS (India) Private Limited in Madurai and may not be generalized to a broader context.

Keywords: Reservoir, solvency, trend analysis

Introduction

The introduction highlights the multifaceted role of cash as a widely accepted medium of exchange in the market, encompassing various forms such as coins and banknotes. It signifies the value of money in facilitating transactions for goods, debt, and services. Within the context of accountancy and finance, cash is delineated as a crucial component of current assets, embodying immediate or near-instantaneous accessibility. The study delves into cash management within ZF Electronics TVS (India) Private Limited in Madurai, employing analytical and descriptive research methodologies. The focus is on scrutinizing short-term solvency positions and liquidity ratios to assess the company's adeptness in meeting current obligations. The subsequent sections elaborate on the four critical aspects of cash management: cash planning, managing cash flows, determining optimal cash levels, and optimizing surplus cash.

The principles and strategies outlined encompass the maximization of cash receipts, minimization of cash payments, and efficient utilization of cash, considering its implications on overall financial performance. The study emphasizes the significance of effective cash management for business survival, particularly for startups facing initial cash constraints. General principles by Harry Gross, such as anticipating predictable variations in cash needs, preparing for unexpected events, and maximizing cash receipts while minimizing payments, provide a comprehensive framework. The study's context is the manufacturing facility of ZF Electronics TVS (India) Private Limited in Madurai, a collaboration between TVS Group and ZF Electronics Corporation, specializing in electro-mechanical components, sensors, and precision snap-action switches.

Review of Literature

Chintha and Prasad (2021) analyzed 36 Muscat securities market-listed companies.

- Explored connections between cash management and financial performance.
- Found significant positive correlations between financial ratios (ROA, ROE, Net Profit Ratio) and cash management ratios (Cash Ratio, Operating Cash to Debt Ratio).

Faque (2022) emphasized the pivotal role of cash (liquidity) management in financial governance.

- Explored the delicate balance between bankruptcy and success.
- Advocated a hybrid strategy, incorporating adaptability to new advancements in cash management systems.

Sankar et al., (2021), focused on effective financial management.

- Emphasized the preparation of cash reserves for future emergencies.

[a]geethabhojan@gmail.com, [b]meenasuganthi.govindaraj@kahedu.edu.in

- Assessed the efficiency in managing cash, inventories, debtors, and creditors.
- Used ratio analysis on secondary data (2016-2020) from the company's website and annual reports.
- Aimed to evaluate the financial viability of the company's cash management plan.

Objectives of the Study

Primary objective: To study the cash management in ZF Electronics TVS (India) Private Limited, Madurai.

Secondary objectives: To know the sources of cash inflow and uses of cash outflow in the company. To determine how short term/current obligations of the company are met.

Sampling design

Period of Study: The time it took the researcher to gather and analyze the data on the cash management at ZF Electronics TVS (India) Private Limited in Madurai during a three-month period. The most recent five years of data, from 2017–18 to 2021–22, are used.

Sample size: The secondary data used for this study is last five years financial statements of the company from 2017-18 to 2021-22.

Sources of data collection

In this study, both primary and secondary data were utilized. Annual reports and profit and loss accounts from the company's five-year balance sheets from 2017–18 to 2021–22 serve as secondary data in this study. A technique for tracking changes and trends in a company's balance sheet over time is called a comparative balance sheet study.

Cash flow statement: A cash flow statement, also known as a statement of cash flows, is a financial statement used in financial accounting that breaks down the analysis into operating, investing, and financing activities. It illustrates how changes in balance sheet accounts and income effect cash and cash equivalents.

Data Analysis and Interpretation

In scrutinizing ZF Electronics TVS (India) Private Limited's financial health, this comprehensive analysis delves into key financial ratios, providing insights into liquidity, leverage, asset turnover, profitability, and cash flow Akinsulire (2019). Examining the company's performance over the past five years, these ratios unveil trends and fluctuations, offering a nuanced understanding of its operational and financial dynamics Pandey (2019). From liquidity challenges to

leveraging strategies, asset efficiency to profitability shifts, and effective cash management, this exploration navigates through critical financial metrics, guiding stakeholders and decision-makers in evaluating ZF Electronics TVS (India) Private Limited liquidity ratios:

Current ratio: The current ratio, indicating a firm's ability to meet short-term obligations, has fluctuated over the years. It decreased from 1.45 to 1.43 (2017-19) but increased to 1.58 in 2019-20. Subsequently, it decreased to 1.25 (2020-21) and increased again to 1.14 (2021-22). With values consistently below the ideal 2:1 ratio, the company must take steps to enhance its current ratio Alfred (2019).

Quick ratio: The quick ratio remained relatively stable, fluctuating from 0.90 to 0.96 (2017-20) before decreasing to 0.83 (2020-21) and 0.79 (2021-22). Despite aligning with the ideal 1:1 ratio, maintaining this position is advisable Prassanna Chandra (1994).

Cash ratio: The cash ratio increased from 0.02 to 0.07 (2017-19), reached 0.05 (2019-20) and 0.07 (2020-21), but decreased to 0.01 (2021-22). This ratio suggests a need for caution, as the company should strive to maintain or improve its cash position Kothari (1999).

Net working capital ratio: The net working capital ratio, depicting the ability to manage current obligations, increased to 0.22 (2019-20) but decreased to 0.12 (2020-21) and 0.07 (2021-22). Maintaining or improving this ratio is crucial for effective current obligation management Maheshwari (1993).

Leverage ratios

Debt ratio: The debt ratio remained constant at 0.50 over the five years, indicating that 50% of the company's assets were financed by debt and the remaining by owner's equity.

Asset turnover ratios

Net asset turnover: Net asset turnover decreased from 0.24 to 0.20 (2017-19) but showed an improvement at 0.34 (2021-22). This indicates fluctuations in asset efficiency.

Net current assets turnover: Net current assets turnover fluctuated, decreasing from 0.42 to 0.34 (2017-19), then improving to 0.62 (2021-22).

Profitability ratios

Net profit ratio: Net profit ratio fluctuated, decreasing from 108.28 to 101.26 (2017-19), increasing to 297.47 (2019-20), then decreasing to 133.75 (2020-21) and 26.59 (2021-22).

Return on net asset: Return on net assets fluctuated, decreasing from 0.26 to 0.20 (2017-19), increasing to 0.24 (2020-21), then decreasing to 0.09 (2021-22).

Return on equity: Return on equity decreased from 0.40 to 0.34 (2017-19), increased to 0.39 (2019-20), then decreased to 0.21 (2021-22).

Cash flow

The cash flow statement reveals efficiency, with increasing net cash flows from operations. Net cash from investing and financing activities varies annually, indicating dynamic cash flows. Inflow from operating activities ranged from 11.69 to 14.84. Net cash from investing activities ranged from 147.78 to 125.05, while financing activities showed small variations. The net increase in cash and equivalents fluctuated from 150.52 to 138.28. This suggests that ZF Electronics TVS (India) Private Limited has been effectively managing its cash, with a consistent increase in cash flows over the years. The analysis of ZF Electronics TVS (India) Private Limited's financial metrics reveals noteworthy trends. Despite a fluctuating current ratio below the ideal 2:1, the quick ratio maintains stability around the desired 1:1 mark. The cash ratio, while varying, suggests the need for prudent cash management. Net working capital ratio indicates an ability to meet current obligations. Stable debt ratios at 0.50 signify consistent financing choices. Asset turnover ratios depict a dip in efficiency, notably recovering in 2021-22. Profitability ratios fluctuate, indicating evolving net profit margins. Lastly, the cash flow statement highlights consistent positive cash flows, affirming the company's effective cash management.

Conclusion

In conclusion, the evaluation of ZF Electronics TVS (India) Private Limited's financial metrics highlights areas for enhancement in its cash management system. The proposed measures encompass the development of a robust cash flow forecasting system to anticipate needs and optimize working capital cycles. Additionally, prudent investments, collaboration with stakeholders for favorable terms, and employee training are crucial steps. By implementing these suggestions, the company can optimize cash utilization, supporting operations and investments while maintaining financial stability.

Summarily, while leverage ratios show improvement, liquidity ratios exhibit fluctuations, emphasizing the need for continuous attention to working capital. The company's profitability, asset utilization, and liquidity have witnessed fluctuations, signaling the importance of focusing on efficiency, debt management, and sustaining a steady cash flow. The positive trend in the cash flow statement indicates an efficient cash management approach, vital for ZF Electronics TVS (India) Private Limited's long-term financial stability.

References

Akinsulire, O. (2019). Financial Management, (4th edn.). Palm Avenue, Mushin: Ceemol Nigeria Publishers.

Alfred, D. (2019). Corporate Finance, (2nd edn.). Lagos: High Rise Publishers.

Kothari, C. R. (1999). Research Methodology, (2nd edn.). New Delhi: Wishwaprakash Publishers.

Maheshwari, S. N. (1993). Financial Management-Principles and Practice. New Delhi: Sultan Chand and Sons (Third Revised and Enlarged Edition).

Pandey, I. M. (2019). Financial Management, (9th edn.). New Delhi: Vikas Publishing.

Prassanna Chandra (1994). Financial Management-Theory and Practice. (3rd edn.). New Delhi: Tata McGrew Hill Publishing Company Limited.

53 Impact of organizational culture on the effectiveness of organisation with reference to agro industry

Karthik, V., Haripriya, V.[a] and Nagalakshmi[b]

Karpagam Academy of Higher Education, Coimbatore, Tamil Nadu, India

Abstract

Organisational culture plays a pivotal role in shaping the efficacy and overall triumph of enterprises, particularly in the dynamic landscape of agrobusiness. Focusing on the agricultural industry's multifaceted realm, this study employs a mixed-methods approach to scrutinise the nuanced influence of organisational culture on operational efficiency, innovation, employee contentment, and overall success within agro industry entities. Elements such as values, social norms, leadership paradigms, and communication styles are integral variables under examination. The research encompasses a diverse spectrum of agro industry organisations, ranging from familial farms to major international corporations, employing surveys, interviews, and data analysis to glean insights. By delving into the nexus between cultural factors and decision-making processes, employee engagement, and adaptive capacities to market shifts, environmental concerns, and emerging technologies, the study aims to elucidate how organisational culture shapes success in the agricultural sector. The resultant findings are poised to guide agricultural leaders and decision-makers in fostering positive cultural transformations that amplify organisational performance, sustainability, and resilience, while underscoring the imperative for a culture attuned to the distinctive challenges and opportunities of the agriculture industry. This research further augments our understanding of the pervasive impact of organisational culture across diverse industries.

Keywords: Business, culture, organisational culture, organization, performance

Introduction

The global economy's stability and food production hinge significantly on agriculture, farming, and related sectors constituting the agro industry. In the face of rapid technological advancements, heightened consumer demands, and environmental considerations, the effectiveness and adaptability of agro industry organisations gain paramount importance. Organisational culture emerges as a key determinant influencing an organisation's ability to thrive in this challenging landscape. This study delves into the intricate relationship between organisational culture and the efficacy of firms in the agricultural sector, scrutinising elements like leadership styles, communication preferences, and values. With a mixed-methods approach encompassing qualitative and quantitative methodologies, a diverse range of agro industry entities is surveyed and interviewed. The aim is to unravel the nuanced ways in which organisational culture impacts decision-making, employee satisfaction, operational efficiency, and adaptability to the dynamic agricultural landscape. By shedding light on these dynamics, this research seeks to offer valuable insights for executives and decision-makers in shaping cultures that foster creativity, productivity, and overall success in the agriculture industry. The study underscores the imperative for organisational culture to align with the distinctive challenges and opportunities of agrobusiness, contributing to the broader discourse on the significance of culture across industries and promoting the growth and resilience of organisations crucial for global food security and economic prosperity.

Problem Statement

The critical significance of human resources in organisations is underscored by the imperative role of effective organisational culture, as a lack thereof hampers success; hence, the pressing problem lies in the global demand for research addressing the nexus between organisational culture and human resources management, essential for fostering employee motivation, job satisfaction, and overall organisational development.

Objectives of the Study

- To study the organizational culture adopted in agro industries
- To analyze the work environment and work culture

Research Methodology

Research design: Research design is descriptive in nature

---

[a]haripriyavaradharaj@gmail.com, [b]lavanyaa2302@gmail.com

Sources of data collection

Primary data: The primary data collected a fresh and for the first time and happen to be original in character. In this study primary data was collected directly from respondents (employees) with the help of questionnaires.

Sampling design: Simple random sampling techniques was adopted to select the sample from the population

Sampling size: Five agro companies were chosen for the study. Sample size is 163

Tools used for analysis: In the study there were one types of tools used to analyse the collected data. They are

- Simple percentage analysis
- Chi-squared test
- Correlation analysis

Review of Literature

- Sujarwo (2019), investigates impact of organisational culture and work environment on partial employee performance.
- Explores the relationship between organizational commitment and partial employee performance.
- Study conducted at PT. Ciwangi Berlian Motor with 152 participants using saturation sample approach.
- Utilizes path analysis to reveal combined influence of organizational culture on worker performance through organizational commitment (0.172) and direct impact of organizational culture on worker performance (0.252).
- Gautam (2020), aims to find connections between workplace culture, employee satisfaction, and behavior in SMEs.
- Standardized questionnaire with 376 respondents.
- Applies Preacher and Hayes Process Macro, confirmatory factor analysis, and regression analysis.
- Emphasizes significant influence of workplace culture on job satisfaction and work habits.
- Sample size of 39 employees chosen from a population of ten.
- Tedla (2021), conducts an exploratory case study on successful strategies for cultivating a fruitful organizational culture and improving performance.
- Involves twenty senior managers from a corporate organization in Ethiopia.
- Uses semi structured face-to-face interviews with experienced applicants.

- Outcomes highlight defined corporate values and the societal benefits of self-regulatory corporate social responsibility.

Analysis and Interpretation

In this segment, the study's results and subsequent discussions unfold, shedding light on diverse facets of organisational culture's influence Lee and Yu (2004). Examining respondents' perspectives, we explore the impact of culture on loyalty, ethical behaviour, employee development, and the creation of a positive work environment. Furthermore, statistical analyses, including Chi-square and correlation tests, dissect the relationships between variables such as educational qualification, company performance, and monthly income concerning recommendations based on organisational culture Lim (1995). These findings offer nuanced insights into the intricate dynamics at play within organisations, guiding future considerations for cultivating and leveraging effective organisational cultures.

Organizational culture fosters loyalty and commitment
- 29.4% Strongly agree, 30.1% agree, 23.3% neutral, 11.0% disagree, 6.1% strongly disagree.
- The majority (59.5%) concurs that organizational culture fosters loyalty and commitment.

Culture teaches good behavior
- 24.5% Strongly agree, 35.6% agree, 17.8% neutral, 8.6% disagree, 13.5% strongly disagree.
- A significant majority (60.1%) believes that culture imparts morality and ethical behavior.

Organization culture helps to develop employees
- 36.2% Strongly agree, 25.8% agree, 8.0% neutral, 11.0% disagree, 19.0% strongly disagree.
- The majority (62.0%) strongly agrees that organizational culture aids in employee development.

Organization culture makes a good working environment
- 33.7% Strongly agree, 31.3% agree, 12.3% neutral, 8.6% disagree, 14.1% strongly disagree.
- A substantial proportion (65.0%) strongly agrees that organizational culture contributes to a positive working environment.

Chi-square test on educational qualification and culture's impact on company performance
- Null hypothesis: No significant association between educational qualification and culture's impact on company performance.

- Chi-square test values: Pearson 13.585, likelihood ratio 14.859, linear-by-linear association 2.162.
- p-values for all tests are greater than 0.05, accepting the null hypothesis.
- No significant difference found between educational qualification and the perceived impact of culture on company performance.

Correlation analysis on monthly income and recommending the company due to organizational culture

- Pearson correlation between monthly income and recommending the company: -0.050.
- Significance level (2-tailed): 0.527.
- A negative relationship exists between monthly income and recommending the company based on organizational culture.

Findings From the Study

- 30.1% of the respondents are agree towards culture of the organization creates loyal and commitment.
- 35.6% of the respondents are agree towards culture teaches good behavior and moral things.
- 36.2% of the respondents are strongly agree toward culture of the organization really helps to develop the employees.
- 34.4% of the respondents are agree towards culture leads to improve the performance of this company.
- 33.7% of the respondents are strongly agree toward culture of this organization makes a good working environment.
- 31.3% of the respondents are strongly agree toward culture helps to work without stress.
- 25.2% of the respondents are neutral toward culture creates innovative work environment.
- 31.3% of the respondents are agree toward employees would recommend the company to work
- 32.5% of the respondents are neutral toward culture controls their innovativeness and ability.
- 25.8% of the respondents are agree toward controls relationship between employees.
- 27.6% of the respondents are agree toward controls labor union activities.
- 25.2% of the respondents are neutral toward criticism in the current culture.
- 35.6% of the respondents are strongly agree toward need changes on the current culture.
- 31.3% of the respondents are strongly agree toward current culture is only well suitable.
- 28.2% of the respondents are agree culture develops a good employee and employer relationship.

- 27.0% of the respondents are strongly agree toward culture treats all employees as same.
- 34.4% of the respondents are agree toward culture creates conflicts in the relationship.
- 31.3% of the respondents are Strongly agree toward culture of the organization team sprit among the employees.
- 36.8% of the respondents are agree toward culture leads to employees rapport with other departments.
- 36.2% of the respondents are strongly agree toward culture maintains strong flow of communication among the employees.
- 33.7 of the respondents are agree toward culture motivates employees to freedom of sharing ideas to others.
- 35.0% of the respondents are strongly agree toward culture creates employees loyalty on each other.
- There is no significance difference between the educational qualification of the respondents and culture leads to improve the performance of company.

In summary, the study's findings reveal a consensus among respondents on the positive impact of organizational culture on loyalty, ethical behavior, employee development, and a conducive working environment. Additionally, the analysis suggests that there is no significant association between educational qualification and the perceived impact of culture on company performance. The negative correlation between monthly income and recommending the company based on organizational culture indicates a nuanced relationship that warrants further exploration.

Conclusion

The comprehensive investigation into the intricate relationship between organizational culture and the effectiveness of agro organizations offers valuable insights and recommendations for enhancing performance, adaptability, and sustainability in the agriculture industry. The study recommends broadening the scope of research to include external stakeholders such as farmers, suppliers, and clients, acknowledging their perspectives on organizational culture. Additionally, it suggests adopting culturally sensitive evaluation techniques and exploring regional variations in organizational culture within the agro industry.

The study underscores the significance of effective leadership styles, particularly transformational and servant leadership, in fostering innovation and sustainability within agro organizations. Building deeper partnerships with stakeholders aligns with cultures promoting sustainability and ethical practices, enhancing the organization's effectiveness. The research advocates the use of data visualization techniques to communicate findings and emphasizes the importance of aligning organizational culture with sustainability goals in the agriculture sector.

Furthermore, the study encourages the use of ethnographic research techniques to understand routine behaviors and interpersonal interactions shaping organizational culture. It recommends evaluating the impact of organizational culture on crisis response and exploring the role of knowledge sharing in innovation and problem-solving. The study concludes by highlighting the dynamic nature of the relationship between culture and productivity in the agriculture industry, calling for continued exploration and research to further unravel the transformative influence of organizational culture within this pivotal sector.

References

Gautam, P. K. (2020). Strategic human resource practices and innovation performance - the mediating role of knowledge management capacity. *Journal of Business Research*, 62, 104–114.

Lee, S. K. J., and Yu, K. (2004). Corporate culture and organizational performance. *Journal of Managerial Psychology*, 19(4), 340–359.

Lim, B. (1995). Examining the organizational culture and organizational performance link. *Leadership and Organization Development Journal*, 16(5), 16–21.

Sujarwo, E. (2019). Relationship between organizational culture and performance in Estonian schools with regard to their size and location. *Baltic Journal of Economics*, 7(1), 3–17.

Tedla, T. B. (2021). Organizational culture and job satisfaction. *The Journal of Business and Industrial Marketing*, 18(2/3), 219–236.

54 Role of material handling systems in shipping companies

Sanjay, V.[a], Dhanya, K. S.[b] and Chitra, P.[c]

Karpagam Academy of Higher Education, Coimbatore, Tamil Nadu, India

Abstract

In the quest to enhance operational efficiency, the imperative for a continuous material handling system (MHS) transcends industry size. This study delves into the pivotal role of MHS in expediting material transfer across diverse scales of enterprises. Focusing on the shop floor, the study underscores how an efficient MHS significantly impacts production cycle duration. It scrutinizes the optimal design of material handling systems, encompassing principles, types of equipment, business benefits, and global relevance. Central to the shipping sector's intricate operations, MHS stands as a linchpin for effective functionality in this dynamic industry. The paper accentuates the multifaceted role of MHS in shipping, addressing challenges and proposing solutions for supply chain optimization, safety enhancement, and environmental sustainability. Acknowledging the critical function of MHS, stakeholders and decision-makers are urged to comprehend its significance for success in a swiftly evolving global marketplace, fostering customer satisfaction, cost reduction, and a sustainable future for the shipping industry.

Keywords: Management, material handling system, operation time, production cycle

Introduction

Material handling is a pivotal aspect encompassing the movement of raw materials, processing during manufacturing, and distribution of finished products, bridging the gap between production and consumption. This process involves the protection, storage, and control of materials throughout their life cycle, employing manual, semi-automated, and automated equipment. Unlike manufacturing, which focuses on form utility, material handling creates space and time utility through waste treatment, storage, and management. The integral role of material handling systems (MHS) in the global shipping industry is paramount, providing efficiency, safety, and revenue enhancement. In an era of globalization and just-in-time supply chains, shipping companies heavily rely on MHS for streamlined operations. This research delves into the extensive scope of MHS, exploring their role in accelerating processes, reducing operational costs, and minimizing environmental impact. The study also anticipates the influence of emerging technologies on maritime material handling practices, emphasizing their contribution to efficient supply chain management, safety improvement, and environmental sustainability in the shipping industry. A comprehensive understanding of material handling systems is crucial for those navigating the complexities of contemporary shipping logistics.

Problem Statement

The prominent issue addressed in this study revolves around the challenges faced by MHS within the shipping industry, impeding their optimal functionality and efficacy; these challenges present formidable obstacles for shipping companies, impacting their competitiveness, customer satisfaction, and operational cost reduction, despite the vital role of efficient material handling in their overall success.

Scope of the Study

Effective material management plays a crucial role in project cost reduction. Premature material purchases may tie up capital with surplus stocks, incurring interest charges. Inadequate safeguards may lead to material deterioration or theft during storage. Missing paperwork for specific tasks can cause delays and additional costs. Timely material movement is essential in material handling, and measuring performance is vital for efficient management and control.

Objectives of the Study

- To study about the material management system adopted in the logistic companies
- To identify the problem faced by the employees while handling materials

[a]sanjayvasudevan028@gmail.com, [b]dhanyaks998@gmail.com, [c]chitraxing24@gmail.com

- To study the effectiveness of material handling system with respective to cost control and cost reduction, delay and delivery

Research Methodology

The preparation of the study design, often known as "research design," is the next challenge following establishing the research problem. A study design is a set of parameters for data collecting and analysis that aims to combine procedural economics and relevance to the research objective. As a result, the design contains a flowchart of the researcher's steps, from developing the hypothesis and considering its operational implications through doing the final data analysis.

Sample design: Sampling is the process of choosing a subset of a population or populations in order to draw conclusions or estimates about the population or populations. In other words, it is the procedure for learning details about the entire population by looking at just a small section of it.

Sampling techniques: The sampling technique used in this study is "convenience sampling" where the population element is sampled based on ease of access. It can be called convenience.

Sample size: Two shipping companies were chosen for the study. Sample size is 130

Methods of data collection
- Primary data
- Secondary data

Primary data: The main focus is on the original and newly collected by the researcher. In this study, primary data was collected by questionnaire. A questionnaire is a common way to collect primary data.

Tools for analysis of data
- Simple percentage analysis
- Correlation analysis

Review of Literature

Otundo et al. (2020) convened forums across counties to mitigate supplier risks linked to real estate matters, fostering discussions on specialty products, new technologies, and efficient public service delivery. Emphasizing operations in Kenya, the study aimed to assess the impact of inventory management procedures on county performance, specifically addressing supply chain access and inventory control.

Lenin et al. (2021) endeavored to address gaps in material handling within logistics facilities, recognizing its significant role in reducing project expenses. By minimizing procurement expenditures, the study aimed to curb overall project costs, particularly in construction, where improper material handling can escalate expenses. The investigation sought to identify factors influencing material availability and inventory, impacting logistics lead times and causing cost overruns.

Phu et al. (2022) explored three facets of material handling logistics: waste-increasing factors, effective solutions, and general issues at construction sites. Utilizing a materiality index (RII) and surveying project engineers, site engineers, and contractors, the study analyzed data through inferential statistics. Results indicated a noteworthy level of agreement among respondents regarding effective material handling techniques, waste-increasing factors, and material handling-related problems in construction logistics projects.

Review of Literature

In this comprehensive examination of material handling practices within diverse industries, key facets such as methods of material handling, preferred services, perceived advantages, prevalent challenges, and the evaluation of material handling systems are scrutinized. The survey, encompassing 130 respondents, unveils nuanced insights into the choices, obstacles, and contentment levels associated with material handling procedures. From the prevalence of manual handling to the challenges faced in ensuring courtesy, disclosure, and impartiality, this analysis delves into the intricacies of material management. Additionally, the evaluation of material handling systems sheds light on factors influencing satisfaction levels, providing a holistic understanding of contemporary material handling dynamics.

Methods of material handling analysis handling system
- Mechanical: 41.5%
- Manual: 46.2%
- Both: 12.3%

The analysis reveals that 46.2% of respondents prefer the manual method for material handling.

Service using material handling analysis
- Sustainable foundations: 27.7%
- Creative thinkers: 38.5%
- Client for life: 22.3%
- People build success: 11.5%

The majority (38.5%) opts for creative thinkers in material handling services.

Advantages of material handling analysis
- Good quality material: 57.7%
- Moral standard: 15.4%
- Better coordination: 11.5%
- Better performance: 15.4%

The majority (57.7%) recognizes good quality material as a primary advantage.

Challenges in handling materials
- Courtesy: 33.1%
- Disclosure: 32.3%
- Impartiality: 23.1%
- Mutual understanding: 11.5%

The primary challenge (32.3%) is identified as disclosure in handling materials.

Evaluation of MHS
Highly satisfied/satisfied/dissatisfied/highly dissatisfied
- Cost of operations: 46.9% satisfied
- Tooling storage: 38.5% highly satisfied
- Safety: 34.6% dissatisfied
- Operators' performance: 60.8% Highly Satisfied
- Tooling handling quickness: 57.7% highly satisfied
- Material handling quickness: 43.1% highly satisfied
- Setup time: 52.3% satisfied

The highest satisfaction (60.8%) is recorded in operators' performance.

Correlation analysis
- Correlation between income per month and facility of security features: 0.945
- Significant at the 0.01 level (2-tailed)
- Positive correlation relationship.

The analysis indicates a strong positive correlation (0.945) between Income per month and facility of security features in this firm.

Findings of the study
- Majority 40.0% of the respondents are using Interior work.
- Majority 59.2% of the respondents are negotiating materials from suppliers.
- Majority 89.2% of the respondents are satisfied with the interior design and electrical work in this firm.
- Majority 46.2% of the respondents are manual method adopt material handling system.
- Majority 40.0% of the respondents are highly satisfied in interior design and electrical work.

- Majority 38.5% of the respondents are using Creative thinkers.
- Majority 33.8% of the respondents are Neutral with helps to reduce the cost.
- Majority 57.7% of the respondents are Good quality material.
- Majority 44.6% of the respondents are single sources of practice.
- Majority 30.0% of the respondents are said problem finding materials delay service in your firm.
- Majority 34.6% of the respondents are guard service facility.
- Majority 52.3% of the respondents are highly satisfied in exiting method of storing the materials
- Majority 32.3% of the respondents are handling with Disclosure.
- Majority 40.0% of the respondents are highly satisfied in material maintenance in store division.

Conclusion

In conclusion, the correlation analysis reveals a significant and positive association between "Income per month" and the "facility of security features in this firm." While this correlation emphasizes the strong link between a company's monthly revenue and its security infrastructure, it is important to note that correlation does not imply causality. The findings underscore the importance of financial resources in shaping a company's ability to enhance security measures, urging businesses to consider strategic security investments aligned with their income levels.

Furthermore, the suggestions provided offer actionable recommendations based on the observed correlation. Low-income businesses are encouraged to invest in security infrastructure, allocate budget proportionately to revenue, conduct regular risk analyses, and prioritize employee education. The emphasis on adopting cutting-edge technologies, adapting security policies to financial needs, and collaborating with industry peers reflects a holistic approach to security enhancement. Regular evaluations and compliance with regulations, along with a focus on eco-friendly security options, demonstrate the ongoing commitment to security improvement.

In a dynamic and connected world, the study reinforces the role of financial resources in bolstering a company's ability to safeguard assets, personnel, and data. While the correlation highlights a positive relationship, prudent resource allocation and continuous evaluation are essential for effective security management. Businesses are encouraged to integrate these recommendations into their strategic planning and risk management activities to navigate the evolving landscape of security challenges.

References

Bowersox, D., Closs, D., Cooper, M. B., and Bowersox, J. Logistics Management reference Book by Foreign/ International Authors. McGraw Hill Education.

Lenin, P., et al. (2021). Material and Logistics Management Book by L.C. Jhamb. Everest Publishing House, India.

Myerson, P. A. Supply Chain and Logistics Management Made Easy: Methods and Applications for Planning, Operations, Integration, Control and Improvement, and Network. Paul Boge.

Otundo, J. B., et al. (2020). Logistics Management: Supply Chain Imperative. Pearson Education India.

Phu, N. L., et al. (2022). Logistics Management Reference Book by S. K. Bhattacharya. S. Chand & Company, India.

55 Job satisfaction and job involvement: conceptual framework

Vivekhini, M., Ranjith, R.[a], Nandhini, A.[b] and Sujith, B.[c]

Karpagam Academy of Higher Education, Coimbatore, Tamil Nadu, India

Abstract

This study aims to investigate the relationships between employees' job involvement, job satisfaction, job performance, and turnover intention within the context of Bangladesh. Utilizing structured questionnaires with validated scales, data were collected from 120 participants across four food processing companies. The survey covered aspects such as job involvement, job satisfaction, job performance, turnover intention, and demographic details. Through correlation analysis and ANOVA, the study seeks to unravel the intricate interconnections among these variables. The research endeavors to provide valuable insights into the nuanced factors influencing employee dynamics in the specific work environment of Bangladesh.

Keywords: Job involvement, job satisfaction, organization, relationship

Introduction

Work engagement is more than a mere system component; it involves recognizing each employee's unique attributes and active contributions to organizational objectives. The management's acknowledgment of these contributions fosters a sense of importance for each employee in the overall functioning of the organization. Looise et al., (2018) research highlights the pressing need to enhance work engagement, emphasizing the importance of involving employees in decision-making processes. Environmentally-conscious employees, in particular, exhibit heightened long-term focus and motivation. The triumphs and setbacks of an organization are deeply intertwined with its workforce's dedication to achieving set aims. Companies must proactively evaluate the strengths and weaknesses of their employees, considering their relevance to the organization's success.

Problem Statement

The challenge lies in achieving employee engagement within the food processing sector, where assessing and enhancing engagement has become a prevalent yet complex pursuit due to the intricate interplay of workplace factors impacting work, productivity, production force, and progress. The difficulty in hiring suitable personnel compounds the issue, despite existing prerequisites to incentivize participation, as revealed by research on leadership styles emphasizing employees' desire for involvement in decision-making processes across various organizations, underscoring the crucial role of engaged employees in achieving organizational goals and ensuring organizational survival.

Objectives of the Study

- To identify factors affecting job satisfaction and job commitment
- To Assess the impact of job satisfaction and work commitment on employee retention

Research methodology
Research design: The chosen research design for the studies is a descriptive design.
Sampling design: The study employed convenience sampling techniques.
Sample size: Four food processing companies were chosen for the study. Sample taken for the study is 120 respondents.

Data sources
Primary data: Primary data refers to recently gathered information that has not been previously recorded. The collection of primary data predominantly entails methods such as personal interviews and surveys.

Tools and techniques used
- Simple percentage analysis
- Chi-square test
- Correlation analysis
- ANOVA
- Independent sample t-test

[a]ranjy111@gmail.com, [b]Nandhini.aruchamy@kahedu.edu.in, [c]sujithb8@gmail.com

Review of Literature

Renwick (2018)'s study "investigating workplace interpersonal conflict" involved 36 employer-employee pairs from 10 organizational units, utilizing employment engagement measures. An additional sample of employees (n = 169) from the same subunits assessed the organizational environment through the organizational characteristics profile. CIS results reveal congruent perceptions within employee-employer pairs regarding conflict topics and sources, with technical and administrative issues being most prevalent, and differences in perception and knowledge identified as primary causes.

Kadekodi (2019) highlighting forestry's potential in addressing climate change, this sector holds ecological, economic, and social significance. Effective implementation demands substantial investment and sustainable long-term planning, necessitating a comprehensive examination of forestry alternatives. Such analysis should consider impacts on carbon stocks, necessary investments, forest resource valuation, effects on GNP and livelihoods, demand regulation, employment, and international trade to fully comprehend the multifaceted implications of forestry solutions.

Study by Brigid and Bechtold (2022) investigated into organizational culture formation and its industry impact, this exploration scrutinizes the establishment of inclusion and participation as cultural norms. The research underscores the imperative for fundamental shifts in assumptions about human nature, organizational philosophies, and business strategies within organizations to facilitate effective participation.

Analysis and Interpretation

The results and discussion section comprehensively analyses job involvement, job satisfaction, and commitment factors concerning age and gender Chu et al. (2005). Employing ANOVA, correlation analysis, independent t-tests, and Chi-square tests, the study examines the intricate relationships within these variables. The findings reveal the absence of significant variations in job involvement across diverse age groups and affirm consistent associations between different facets of job satisfaction. Additionally, the examination of gender-based differences in commitment factors underscores the uniformity in employee perceptions Cohen and Vigoda (2000). This section highlights the invaluable insights obtained from scrutinizing employee perspectives, providing pertinent implications for organizational strategies and human resource management.

Results and Discussion

ANOVA (Job involvement and age of an employee): The analysis aimed to examine the variation in job involvement based on employee age. Accepting the null hypothesis (H0) for all variables (EL Q1 to EL Q10) as p-values exceed 0.05, the study finds no significant variation. This implies that factors like liking the industry, emotional bonding with the organization, and reluctance to change industries are not substantially influenced by age.

Correlation analysis (Job satisfaction): Correlation coefficients reveal strong positive relationships between job satisfaction and its sub-questions (JS Q1 to JS Q5). A notable correlation exists between job satisfaction and JS Q2, indicating high correlation levels. Similarly, reverse relationships are highly correlated, signifying consistent associations between different aspects of job satisfaction.

Independent t-test (Performance appraisal and gender): Levene's test for equality of variances ensures the assumption of equal variances. With p-values exceeding 0.05 for all variables (JC Q1 to JC Q9), the study upholds null hypotheses, indicating no significant gender-based differences in perceptions related to commitment factors.

Chi-square test (Employee loyalty and job commitment): The Chi-square test assesses the association between employee loyalty and job commitment. With a significance level of 0.045 (< 0.05), the null hypothesis (H0) is accepted, indicating no meaningful association between employee loyalty Q2 and job commitment Q1.

In conclusion, the study reveals that job involvement, job satisfaction, and commitment factors show no substantial variations based on age or gender. The results emphasize the importance of recognizing that certain aspects of employee perception remain consistent across different demographic groups, providing valuable insights for HR strategies and organizational policies.

The study's findings indicate that age does not significantly influence job involvement. Job satisfaction exhibits strong positive correlations across its various dimensions. Gender-based differences in commitment factors show no substantial variations. The Chi-square test concludes no meaningful association between employee loyalty and job commitment. In summary, the results emphasize the stability of job involvement across age groups, consistent patterns in job satisfaction, and uniform perceptions of commitment factors irrespective of gender. These insights contribute valuable implications for organizations, suggesting the need for targeted strategies to enhance job satisfaction and recognizing the universal nature of commitment factors.

Conclusion

In conclusion, the study offers several key suggestions aimed at enhancing the work environment and overall employee experience. Recognizing the prevalent perception of heavy workloads, the organization is urged to take necessary steps to alleviate this burden, promoting a more balanced and manageable workload for employees. Additionally, there is a recommendation to improve the benefits and services offered to employees, fostering a culture of encouragement and support within the organization. Effectively planning and implementing welfare activities is highlighted as a strategy to not only enhance the internal work environment but also to positively shape the organization's public image. Furthermore, emphasizing the communication of rules and regulations, coupled with providing robust safety measures, is essential for creating a secure and compliant work environment.

In a broader context, the study underscores the significance of employee training and onboarding processes in influencing the quality of customer service. A well-conducted onboarding process reflects the organization's commitment to its employees, shaping their initial experiences and contributing to longer tenures within the industry. By addressing these suggestions, organizations can foster a positive work culture and, in turn, positively impact employee retention and satisfaction.

References

Brigid and Bechtold (2022). Work centrality and post-award work behavior of lottery winners. *The Journal of Psychology*, 138, 404–420.

Chu, C., Lee, M., Hsu, H., and Chen, I. (2005). Clarification of the antecedents of hospital nurse organizational citizenship behaviour – an example from a Taiwan regional hospital. *Journal of Nursing Research*, 13, 313–324.

Cohen, A., and Vigoda, E. (2000). Do good citizens make good organizational citizens? an empirical examination of the relationship between general citizenship and organizational citizenship behavior in Israel. *Administration and Society*, 32, 596–625.

Kadekodi, G. K. (2019). The long arm of the job: parents' work–family conflict and youths' work centrality. *Applied Psychology*, 63(1), 151–167.

Renwick, P. A. (2018). Job involvement: a brief of literature. *Management and Labour Studies*, 34(3), 397–404.

56 A study on employee health, safety and welfare measures

Sarankarthik, A. S. and Chitra, P.[a]

Karpagam Academy of Higher Education, Coimbatore, Tamil Nadu, India

Abstract

This study underscores the critical importance of maintaining a workplace free from hazardous materials, including substances like benzene, chlorine, and harmful microorganisms, along with various elements, tools, and procedures that may pose threats to health and safety. In instances where complete elimination of such hazards is impractical, the responsibility lies with the enterprise to inform individuals about potential risks, preventive measures, and safe work practices, alongside providing additional protective measures for a secure workplace. Contrary to a unilateral approach to safety, the study emphasizes a collective responsibility, asserting that workplace hazards are best addressed through effective communication and collaboration between employees and the employer. This shared responsibility involves a proactive identification of risks and the implementation of appropriate measures to ensure a safe working environment. The research design employed encompasses various analytical methods, including percentage analysis, Chi-square analysis, correlation analysis, and weighted average, to gather necessary data for addressing challenges within the operational framework of the workplace safety paradigm.

Keywords: Employees work performance and loyalty, responsibility and health safety welfare, work environment

Introduction

The introduction highlights the imperative set by the Occupational Safety Act of 1993, mandating employers to establish and uphold a work environment that prioritizes safety and minimizes risks to employees. This commitment involves ensuring freedom from hazardous substances like benzene, chlorine, and microorganisms, as well as potential risks associated with products, equipment, and processes that could cause harm. In situations where complete elimination of risks is unfeasible, employers are obligated to inform workers about potential dangers, preventive measures, and safe working practices, providing additional safeguards for a secure workplace. The introduction categorizes occupational hazards into six groups: mechanical, physical, biological, chemical, psychosocial, and ergonomic issues, thereby setting the stage for a comprehensive exploration of the diverse challenges and safety considerations within the occupational landscape.

Types of occupational hazards
Common workplace hazards are categorized in six groups:

- Mechanical hazard (confined space, equipment related injury,
- Physical hazard (noise, vibration, lighting, electricity)
- Biological hazards (bacteria, virus, tuberculosis)
- Chemical hazards (acids, base, heavy metals, fire hazards, particulates (dust/fiber material)
- Psychosocial hazards (stress, violence)
- Ergonomic issues (material handling, machine design, personal factors)

Scope of the Study

The implementation of the Anatomic Assurance Act (2007), stemming from revisions to the Factories Act (1951), expanded its jurisdiction beyond factories to encompass all workplaces where individuals are engaged in temporary or permanent work, aiming to ensure the safety and well-being of individuals at work. The problem statement revolves around the need for employers to comply with safety regulations, rules, and procedures outlined in the Act, thereby fulfilling their obligation to safeguard the safety of themselves and all individuals in the workplace through the adoption of necessary precautions and the consistent use of appropriate safety measures and control systems.

Objectives of the Study

Primary objectives: The present study finds out employee safety measures with reference to chola spinning mills private limited at erode.
Secondary objectives

- To study health safety welfare measures offer to the employees
- To access the satisfaction level of employees towards health safety welfare measures.

[a]chitraxing24@gmail.com

- To study the impact of welfare measures on employees work performance and loyalty.

Limitation of the study

- The advisers did not accommodate the able advice for study.
- It was actual difficult to aggregate the advice from the employees, because the advisers were active with their assignment schedule.
- The time of the abstraction was actual abbreviate period.
- The sample admeasurement of the abstraction was 150 respondents only.

Research Methodology

Research methodology describes the analysis procedure, which includes the overall analysis architecture and the abstracts accumulating method.

Research design: An analysis architecture is the specialization of admeasurement and action for the information bares to break problems in the all-embracing operational arrangement of framework of the project that stipulates what advice is to be calm from which sources by what procedure. There are three types of research design.

- Explorative research design
- Descriptive research design
- Experimental research design

The research design that is used by the investigator is descriptive Research design.

Statistical tools used
The commonly used statistical tools for analysis of collected data are:

1. Percentage analysis
2. Chi-square analysis
3. Correlation analysis
4. Weighted average.

Review of Literature

Table 56.1 Charting the landscape of workplace health and safety: insights from diverse studies across industries and regions.

Author name	Study	Findings
Mohan (2017)	Occupational Health and safety management in manufacturing industries	Few companies are implementing safety systems effectively. Slow, consistent efforts are necessary for developing a safety culture, involving improvements in safety standards and job promotion. Methods like behavior-based safety (BBS) significantly reduce workplace accidents.
Rumchev (2018)	Organizational factors on safety in Taiwan and Japan	Organizational factors influencing safety differ in Taiwan and Japan due to cultural distinctions. Taiwanese management tends to be "Top-Down Directive," with top management dictating safety policies. In contrast, Japanese safety management adopts a "Bottom-Up Participative" approach, involving employee participation in safety activities.
Joykutty (2019)	Issues in employee health and safety in Bangalore industries	The study highlights employee awareness of workplace health and safety measures in both private and public sector manufacturing industries in Bangalore. There is a robust commitment to the health and safety of workers in these industries.
Johannson et al. (2020)	Piece rate pay and its impact on health and safety	Recent research focuses on the impact of piece-rate pay on health and safety. The study analyzes relevant and high-quality research papers, indicating a substantial interest in musculoskeletal injury, physical exertion, pain, and occupational injury. Increased accident rates are associated with negative health and safety effects.
Ramachandran (2021)	Awareness, knowledge, and lifestyle correlates to coronary heart disease	The study investigates awareness, knowledge, and lifestyle behaviors related to coronary heart disease among laborers in Singapore. Coronary heart disease is a leading cause of death for women globally, and the study aims to understand the awareness and risk factors among laborers.
Dennis (2022)	Workplace health promotion measures and labor market outcomes	Examines the average effects of firm-provided workplace health promotion measures on labor market outcomes. Health circles/courses positively impact management and job stability across various age groups, with a notable strengthening effect on the labor force attachment of older employees (51–60).

Source: Author

Analysis and Interpretation

In exploring the intricate dynamics of employee satisfaction, this study employs a multifaceted approach, delving into the interplay of demographic factors and their influence on perceptions of health, safety, and welfare measures in the workplace. Through Chi-square, correlation, ANOVA, regression, and independent T-test analyses, we scrutinize the relationships between age, gender, education, experience, and income, unravelling the nuanced fabric of employee sentiments Wilkins (2011). As we navigate through each statistical lens, this research unveils critical findings, offering a holistic understanding of how these variables shape the landscape of employee satisfaction in organizational settings Zhu et al. (2011). Chi-square analysis: relationship between age and employee satisfaction

- **Hypotheses:** The null hypothesis (Ho) posits no significant link between respondent age and satisfaction with health safety welfare measures; the alternative hypothesis (H1) suggests a significant connection Prasad (2005).
- **Results:** The Chi-square tests reveal a Pearson Chi-square value of 116.067, with a p-value of 0.024. As the p-value is greater than 0.05, the null hypothesis is accepted. This suggests no substantial association between age and employee satisfaction, emphasizing non-significance Ramasamy (2005).

Correlation analysis: impact of gender on work performance and loyalty
- **Correlations:** Analyzing 150 respondents, the correlation coefficient between gender and the impact of welfare measures on work performance and loyalty is -0.083. With a value below 1, it indicates a negative relationship, signifying that gender isn't significantly linked to the impact of welfare measures on work performance and loyalty.

One way ANOVA test: education and employee welfare
- **ANOVA results:** The ANOVA test on educational qualifications influencing employee welfare indicates a significant impact ($F = 4.134$, $p = 0.003$). This signifies a rejection of the null hypothesis, affirming an association between educational qualifications and employee welfare.

Regression analysis: experience and satisfaction with health safety welfare measures
- **Regression model:** The regression analysis highlights that experience of the respondents contrib-

utes to a 5.1% impact on satisfaction with health safety welfare measures. The F-statistic value of 7.961, with $p = 0.000$, asserts a significant positive relationship between experience and satisfaction.

Independent T-test: income and work performance/loyalty impact
- **T-Test results:** For the impact of income on work performance and loyalty, the mean difference isn't significant ($p > 0.05$). This indicates no substantial relationship between income levels and the impact of welfare measures on work performance and loyalty.

Key findings:
- 38.7% of respondents are aged 25-30 years.
- 62.0% are male, and 70.7% are married.
- 32.7% hold a degree, and 28.7% have 0-5 years of experience.
- 56.0% earn Rs.10,000-15,000.

Employee perceptions:
- Positive views on security, retirement benefits, and institution management.
- Mixed feelings about welfare schemes' impact on productivity and effectiveness.
- Satisfaction with working conditions and facilities.

Relationships:
- No significant age-related satisfaction differences.
- Negative correlation between gender and work performance/loyalty impact.
- Educational qualifications impact employee welfare significantly.
- Positive relationship between experience and satisfaction.
- No significant income-related impact on work performance/loyalty.

This comprehensive analysis sheds light on various facets of employee satisfaction, providing nuanced insights into age, gender, education, experience, and income's role in shaping perceptions of health, safety, and welfare measures in the workplace. The study reveals that there is no significant relationship between the age of respondents and employee satisfaction with health, safety, and welfare measures. Gender shows a negative correlation with the impact of welfare measures on work performance and loyalty. Educational qualifications significantly impact employee welfare. Experience positively influences satisfaction levels with health, safety, and welfare.

However, no significant relationship is found between respondents' income and the impact of welfare measures on work performance and loyalty. These nuanced insights shed light on the complex interplay of demographic factors in shaping employee perceptions and satisfaction within organizational environments.

Conclusion

The study underscores the importance of refining health assurance and welfare measures through comprehensive discussions involving various stakeholders. It recommends advancing the existing techniques to ensure better anticipation of employee well-being. The establishment of a separate appraisal committee during the evaluation period is proposed to eliminate biases and personal prejudices, fostering fair evaluations. The evaluation system, integral to health assurance measures, plays a crucial role in retaining employees within the organization. The suggestion emphasizes the need for supervisors to cultivate positive relationships with workers, offering recognition for their efforts and providing guidance during health assurance processes.

In conclusion, health assurance and welfare measures serve as fundamental pillars for organizational success. Acknowledging employees as valuable assets, the study advocates for a focus on job appraisal techniques and development programs. While affirming the current effectiveness of the existing system, the conclusion encourages the adoption of innovative approaches to enhance the overall efficiency of health assurance and welfare measures. The alignment of organizational policies with employee behaviors fosters a strong sense of commitment, ultimately contributing to increased effectiveness in the workplace. The study concludes with a call for strategic measures to further improve the health assurance and welfare measures system.

References

Dennis, P. M. (2022). Employee health and safety practices: an exploratory and comparative study of the shipping and manufacturing industries in Ghana. 7(23), 81–95.

Johannson, Rask, and Stenberg (2020). Employees' health and safety requirements. *European Integration Studies*, (3), 76–85.

Joykutty, L. M. (2019). Demonstrating the economic value of occupational health services. *Occupational Medicine*, 52, 477–483.

Mohan, A. (2017). Occupational health and safety management in manufacturing industries. (Include additional details if available).

Prasad, L. M. (2005). Business Communication, (4th edn.).

Ramachandran, H. J. (2021). Employee safety, health, and welfare measures in the pharmaceutical industry: an empirical study. *Annals of the Romanian Society for Cell Biology*, 25(6), 682–692.

Ramasamy, T. (2005). Principles of Management. (8th Revised edn.). Himalaya Publishing House.

Rumchev (2018). Bottom-up participative where top management answer employees' (Include additional details if available).

Wilkins, J. R. (2011). Construction workers' perceptions of health and safety training programs. *Construction Management & Economics*, 29(10), 1017–1026.

Zhu, W., Singh, J., and Norton, K. (2011). Going Safely Overseas. *Industrial Management*, 53(6), 26–30.

57 Factors affecting employee absenteeism in manufacturing industries

Ruban, V., Sudarvel, J.[a], Shrie Bhubaneswari, N.T.[b], Velmurugan, R.[c] and Mathan Kumar, V.[d]

Karpagam Academy of Higher Education, Coimbatore, Tamil Nadu, India

Abstract

This study investigates factors contributing to employee absenteeism in manufacturing industries in the Coimbatore district. Recognizing absenteeism's adverse impact on productivity, the research employs a mixed-methods approach, combining quantitative analysis of absenteeism data with qualitative insights from surveys and interviews. The findings highlight diverse factors influencing absenteeism, encompassing personal issues like health and job dissatisfaction, as well as organizational factors such as working conditions and leadership styles. The results underscore the need for tailored absence management strategies, proposing region-specific measures like targeted wellness programs, addressing transportation challenges, and adapting policies to socio-economic nuances. Key interventions, including cultivating a supportive work environment, transparent communication, and fair treatment practices, are crucial for reducing absenteeism rates. This study contributes to understanding absenteeism dynamics in the Coimbatore district, enabling businesses to implement effective interventions, enhance employee satisfaction, and foster overall industrial progress in line with the region's unique characteristics.

Keywords: Coimbatore district, employee absenteeism, employee retention and workforce productivity, manufacturing industries

Introduction

The global manufacturing sector grapples with a significant challenge—employee absenteeism—and its repercussions on productivity and organizational effectiveness. In the context of Coimbatore district's thriving manufacturing industry, understanding the factors contributing to absenteeism is crucial for regional firms' growth and competitiveness. This study delves into the causes of employee absenteeism in Coimbatore's industrial sector, encompassing textiles, engineering, and automotive industries. By employing a mixed-methods approach, the research combines quantitative analysis of past absenteeism data with qualitative insights from surveys and interviews. The study explores unique absenteeism concerns arising from the district's diverse manufacturing landscape, including seasonal fluctuations, travel challenges, and local socioeconomic factors. The findings aim to inform context-sensitive strategies, enabling businesses to implement targeted interventions like improved health programs and customized HR policies, fostering a more productive and engaged workforce. In summary, this research illuminates the intricate factors influencing absenteeism in Coimbatore's industrial sectors, offering practical insights for sustainable growth and competitiveness.

Review of Literature

Table 57.1 Unravelling absenteeism: insights from diverse studies in manufacturing industries.

Author	Study	Findings
James (2020)	Stress as the primary cause of absenteeism in manufacturing industries.	Effective management of absenteeism is crucial for maintaining productivity and efficiency.
Joshi and Balu L (2019)	Factors influencing absenteeism: personal characteristics, work-related factors, job satisfaction, and training.	Focusing on these aspects can lower company absence rates, with reduced job satisfaction being a key contributor.
Waye, (2017)	Absenteeism as a common issue; satisfaction of Maslow's hierarchy of needs reduces absenteeism.	Prioritizing corporate culture, wellness initiatives, and addressing factors that lower profitability can decrease absenteeism rates.

[a]j.sudarvel@gmail.com, [b]shrie.bhubaneswari@gmail.com, [c]drvelsngm@gmail.com, [d]mathankumar010@gmail.com

Author	Study	Findings
Rahman (2016)	Absenteeism as a significant issue in the Indian textile industry; multiple factors influence absenteeism.	Working conditions, uncertainty about the future, and negative perceptions contribute to workplace absenteeism.
Kozioł (2016)	Absence primarily due to illness; suggested method involves a clear absence policy and employee training programs.	Managing sickness absenteeism requires identifying causes and implementing effective training and promotion initiatives.
Nanjundeswaraswamy (2016)	Employee dissatisfaction and interpersonal relationships as key factors in absenteeism.	Organization's culture, atmosphere, and income from other sources contribute to employee absenteeism.
Silpa (2015)	Employee attitudes toward absenteeism; factors include bad working environment, job ennui, and inadequate leadership.	Improved working conditions, higher rewards, and better benefits can help reduce absenteeism.
Senou (2015)	Employment position and supplementary revenue as crucial factors influencing teacher absenteeism.	Permanent teachers exhibit higher absenteeism, and additional income sources reduce absence.
Prabhu (2013)	Absenteeism as a gauge of employee satisfaction; dissatisfaction with wages not a major factor.	Bonuses based on performance and paid time off for holidays can reduce absenteeism.
Drakopoulos (2011)	Causes of absenteeism include accidents at work, other errands, and low job satisfaction.	Absence rates higher in UK manufacturing companies than in Greek companies, with male rates higher than female rates.
Singh et. al (2016)	Investigation into the harmful effects of absenteeism on organizational performance.	The study offers managerial tactics to reduce absenteeism and encourage attendance at work.
Beulah and Raju (2014)	Study on unscheduled employee absenteeism in the BPO sector.	Factors affecting absence and efforts to reduce it due to financial impact on the company.
Rathod and Reddy (2012)	Study on problems, causes, and corrective actions associated with absenteeism in the Titan Industry.	Recommendations to enhance the company's prospects and foster organizational growth by lowering employee absenteeism.

Source: Author

Problem Statement

The industrial businesses in Coimbatore district grapple with a widespread issue of employee absenteeism, adversely affecting productivity and overall company performance. This study addresses the pressing problem by delving into the specific causes of high absenteeism rates in the district's diverse manufacturing sector, aiming to uncover insights crucial for tailored interventions. Despite the acknowledged absenteeism challenge, prior studies lack a comprehensive exploration of the unique manufacturing context in Coimbatore. By examining human and organisational dimensions, the research seeks to understand health-related issues, job satisfaction levels, and workplace stressors. Additionally, the study considers regional elements such as transportation challenges and socioeconomic factors influencing attendance. The ultimate goal is to provide actionable insights for targeted interventions, fostering employee engagement and productivity in the district's industrial landscape.

Objective of the Study

To identify the factors that affect employee absenteeism in manufacturing industries.

Scope of the Study

This study aims to explore the factors influencing employee absenteeism in the manufacturing businesses of the Coimbatore district, focusing on both individual and organizational causes specific to the local manufacturing sector. With a primary focus on the Coimbatore district in India, the research delves into various industrial subsectors like textiles, engineering, automotive components, and machinery manufacturing. It investigates personal factors such as health concerns and job satisfaction, alongside organizational aspects like working conditions and leadership styles. The study also considers unique challenges posed by the manufacturing environment, including transportation issues, seasonal variations, and socioeconomic factors impacting absenteeism.

Research Methodology

Data collection: Primary data is essential for this study, collected through interviews for detailed information directly from participants. Using an interview schedule ensures consistency and standardized responses, enhancing the reliability of the data collection process. Sampling and sample size: Convenient sampling is valuable when accessing the entire population is challenging.

It allows quick data collection from readily available individuals, and for this study, 240 workers from Coimbatore's manufacturing industries were sampled.

Framework of analysis: Data analysis involved simple percentage calculations and factor analysis for a comprehensive understanding of the collected information.

Limitations

- Due to the district-specific focus and distinctive manufacturing ecosystem, findings may not be very generalizable outside of the Coimbatore district.
- The availability and reliability of absence data provided by involved manufacturing organisations are essential to the research.
- Personal interpretations and prejudices may colour qualitative insights, which could affect the analysis.
- Since some influences might not immediately fall under the purview of the study, it's possible that not all external factors that affect absenteeism were taken into account.

Analysis and Interpretation

This section delves into the demographic profile of 240 respondents in the Coimbatore district's manufacturing industries Brockman et al. (2014). Examining age groups, gender, marital status, educational qualifications, monthly income, and work experience provides a comprehensive understanding of the study's participants Cella (2009). Furthermore, factor analysis scrutinizes variables influencing employee absenteeism Chuang (2020). The Kaiser-Meyer-Olkin measure and Bartlett's test affirm the data's suitability for this analysis Clark and Wójcik (2005). The rotated component matrix reveals significant factors contributing to absenteeism, with cumulative percentages aiding in prioritizing interventions Dasgupta et al. (2011). Together, these analyses offer a nuanced exploration

of workforce characteristics and crucial absenteeism determinants Demsetz and Lehn (1985).

Demographic analysis of respondents

- **Age group:** The majority (57%) fall within the 25 to 35 age range, with 35% aged between 35 and 45. Those above 45 and up to 25 years each represent 4% Dyakov and Wipplinger (2020).
- **Gender:** Males dominate at 76.67%, while females constitute 23.33% of the total respondents, indicating a higher participation of males Gompers and Metrick (2001).
- **Marital status:** Married respondents make up a larger portion (68%) compared to unmarried respondents, who constitute 32%.
- **Educational qualification:** Respondents with school-level education form the largest group at 48%, followed by undergraduates at 35%. Postgraduates constitute 13%, and those with a diploma comprise 4%.
- **Monthly gross income:** The majority (75%) fall into the income range of Rs. 15001-18000. Respondents with monthly incomes of Rs.18001 to Rs.22000 make up 17%.
- **Experience in years:** The largest group (68%) has up to 5 years of experience. Those with 6-10 years constitute 24%, and respondents with 11-15 years and above 15 years each make up 4%.

Factor analysis results

- **KMO and Bartlett's test:** The KMO measure (0.867) and Bartlett's test of sphericity (Chi-square: 4104.745, Sig: 0.000) suggest the data is suitable for factor analysis Han and Suk (1998).
- **Rotated component matrix:** Significant factors contributing to employee absenteeism include lack of job resources, commuting challenges, inadequate benefits, low job satisfaction, job burnout, and more Kennedy (1985).
- **Cumulative percentage:** Six factors contribute significantly, with the first factor alone contributing 43.066%, and the cumulative percentage of the top six factors reaching 70.313%.

The demographic analysis provides valuable insights into the respondent characteristics, aiding in understanding how various factors may influence absenteeism. The factor analysis identifies key contributors, emphasizing the importance of addressing issues like job resources, commuting challenges, and inadequate benefits to mitigate absenteeism effectively. The cumulative percentage indicates that focusing on the top six factors can significantly impact employee absenteeism. This comprehensive understanding guides targeted interventions for improved employee retention and organizational performance.

The demographic analysis uncovered a predominant age group (25-35 years), a majority of male respondents, and a significant number of married individuals with school-level education. Monthly income was concentrated in the Rs.15001-Rs.18000 bracket. Regarding experience, a majority had up to 5 years. Factor analysis identified key contributors to absenteeism, including job-related stressors, inadequate benefits, and workplace culture. Cumulatively, these factors explained 70.31% of absenteeism. These findings imply the need for targeted interventions addressing specific demographic groups and workplace aspects to mitigate absenteeism and enhance overall workforce well-being.

Conclusion

Mitigating Employee Absenteeism: Key Recommendations
- To combat absenteeism, organizations should:
- Equip employees and offer skill-enhancing training.
- Introduce remote work and consider commuting incentives.
- Improve leave policies and offer holistic wellness programs.
- Conduct regular feedback sessions and involve employees in decisions.
- Establish transparent policies and encourage breaks.
- Distribute work evenly and reassess responsibilities.
- Train managers and promote a culture of openness.
- Evaluate job duties regularly and offer growth opportunities.
- Clearly define expectations and communicate openly.
- Introduce remote work options and flexible scheduling.
- Provide resources and foster a stress-friendly environment.
- Make counselling available and destigmatize mental health discussions.
- Regularly update policies and ensure clear communication.
- Uphold safety procedures and encourage open reporting.
- Promote free communication between staff and management.
- Offer routine check-ups and wellness initiatives.

- Provide sufficient rest and rotate shifts fairly.
- Introduce initiatives for employee recognition and rewards.
- Encourage cooperation, support, and set a positive example.
- Invest in leadership skills and foster open communication.
- Set achievable project timelines with employee input.
- Offer mentorship and communicate clear promotion paths.

This study identifies factors influencing absenteeism, providing insights for tailored interventions. A comprehensive strategy, incorporating these recommendations, can create a motivated and engaged workforce, benefiting both employees and the manufacturing industry. Further research opportunities include longitudinal studies, sector-specific causes, and the impact of technology on absenteeism.

References

Brockman, P., French, D., and Tamm, C. (2014). REIT organizational structure, institutional ownership, and stock performance. *Journal of Real Estate Portfolio Management*, 20(1), 21–36.

Cella, C. (2009). Institutional Investors and Corporate Investment. United States: Indiana University, Kelley School of Business.

Chuang, H. (2020). The impacts of institutional ownership on stock returns. *Empirical Economics*, 58(2), 507–533.

Clark, G. L., and Wójcik, D. (2005). Financial valuation of the German model: the negative relationship between ownership concentration and stock market returns, 1997–2001. *Economic Geography*, 81(1), 11–29.

Dasgupta, A., Prat, A., and Verardo, M. (2011). Institutional trade persistence and long-term equity returns. *Journal of Finance*, 66(2), 635–653.

Demsetz, H., and Lehn, K. (1985). The structure of corporate ownership: causes and consequences. *Journal of Political Economy*, 93(6), 1155–1177.

Dyakov, T., and Wipplinger, E. (2020). Institutional ownership and future stock returns: an international perspective. *International Review of Finance*, 20(1), 235–245.

Gompers, P. A., and Metrick, A. (2001). Institutional investors and equity prices. *The Quarterly Journal of Economics*, 116(1), 229–259.

Han, K. C., and Suk, D. Y. (1998). The effect of ownership structure on firm performance: additional evidence. *Review of Financial Economics*, 7(2), 143–155.

Kennedy, P. (1985). A Guide to Econometrics. Cambridge: MIT Press.

58 Employee perception toward welfare measures in spinning mills with reference to Namakkal district

Selsiya, N., Sudarvel, J.[a], Shrie Bhubaneswari, N. T.[b] and Velmurugan, R.[c]

Karpagam Academy of Higher Education, Coimbatore, Tamil Nadu, India

Abstract

The study explores employee perceptions of welfare measures in Namakkal district's spinning mills, recognizing the significance of well-being for enhanced productivity and job satisfaction in this labor-intensive sector. Utilizing a mixed-method approach, structured interviews and questionnaires gather both qualitative and quantitative data from employees and management representatives across multiple spinning mills. Secondary data supplements the investigation, providing insights into industry context and existing welfare practices. The research evaluates the implementation and effectiveness of welfare programs, considering healthcare benefits, safety measures, working conditions, training opportunities, and recreational facilities. Findings identify the strengths and weaknesses of current welfare initiatives, offering valuable insights for managerial improvements. The report addresses challenges in implementing comprehensive welfare standards in spinning mills and suggests proactive, employee-centered strategies to enhance staff loyalty, foster a positive workplace, and contribute to sustainable growth in the Namakkal spinning industry.

Keywords: Employee welfare measures, healthcare benefits, Namakkal, safety provisions, spinning mills, working conditions

Introduction

The introduction highlights the vital role of the spinning mill sector in providing employment to a significant portion of India's workforce, crucial to the textile industry's success. Emphasizing the pivotal link between worker health and mill sustainability, the term "employee welfare measures" encompasses a range of initiatives aimed at enhancing worker productivity, job satisfaction, and overall quality of life. Focusing on Namakkal, a key industrial hub in India with numerous spinning mills, the study investigates the impact of existing employee welfare programs on productivity, staff morale, and job satisfaction. Employing a mixed-method approach, structured interviews and surveys with employees and management representatives will gather qualitative and quantitative data, complemented by secondary data for contextualization. The research holds significance for spinning mill management, policymakers, and textile industry stakeholders, offering insights into current welfare practices and proposing recommendations for enhancement. The study aspires to guide spinning mills in creating a conducive work environment, fostering employee well-being, satisfaction, and loyalty, thereby contributing to sustained growth in Namakkal's spinning industry.

Review of Literature

In his study Sekar (2012) found that workers express minimal satisfaction with health benefits and welfare facilities beyond factory premises. Effective management is crucial for cleanliness, dust elimination, artificial humidification, and waste disposal. Employee contentment linked to demographics: education, work history, monthly income, and employment category.

Mohideen and Ishaq (2015)'s study concluded that 44% rate satisfaction with company's financial facilities as average. Negative opinions on mill's house-rent allowance; 18% report excellent festival advances.

Poongavanam et al. (2017): Welfare amenities in building regions deemed satisfactory despite a negative general sentiment.

Vijaya Ramya and Geetha (2019) found correlation between gender and challenges in obtaining leave for illness or emergencies.

Nithyavathi (2016) emphasizes health behaviors' impact on employee fulfilment; suggests improving travel options.

Antony (2017)'s study was non-financial benefits alongside cash benefits crucial for workforce satisfaction.

Sethuram and Sankari (2018) studied on availability of labor welfare measures significantly influences

[a]j.sudarvel@gmail.com, [b]shrie.bhubaneswari@gmail.com, [c]drvelsngm@gmail.com

employees' job performance. Studies show limitations: small sample sizes and insufficient exploration of the relationship between demographic factors and employee welfare measures.

Problem Statement

The spinning mill sector in Namakkal, India, grapples with the implementation of effective employee welfare measures in a labor-intensive environment, posing concerns about worker happiness and well-being. This study addresses the pressing issue of evaluating and enhancing welfare measures in Namakkal's spinning mills, which may lack comprehensive policies, potentially impacting workers' development and health. Inadequate welfare policies can lead to diminished morale, job satisfaction, increased absenteeism, and higher turnover rates. The challenge extends to ensuring health and safety in spinning mills, necessitating examination of existing safeguards. The study aims to provide insightful analysis and practical recommendations to enhance employee well-being, job satisfaction, and the overall performance and sustained growth of the spinning sector in Namakkal.

Objective of the Study

Employee perception toward welfare measures in spinning mills

Research Methodology

Data: The data required is primary in nature. Collecting primary data through interviews can be an effective method for gathering detailed and specific information directly from the participants. By using an interview schedule, you can ensure consistency in the questions asked and obtain standardized responses, making the data collection process more reliable.

Sampling and sample size: Convenient sampling can be a useful approach when it is difficult to access or reach the entire population of interest. It allows researchers to collect data quickly and easily from individuals who are readily available or accessible. Thus, by employing convenient sampling technique, data have gathered from 360 employees working at textile industry in Namakkal district.

Framework of analysis: The collected have been analyzed by employing simple percentage and weighted average ranking test.

Significance of the Study

The study on employee perception of welfare measures in Namakkal's spinning mills holds great significance for the entire spinning industry, providing valuable insights for employees, management, policymakers, and the sector as a whole. By understanding and addressing employee views on welfare measures, the study aims to enhance employee health, job satisfaction, and overall quality of life. This employee-centric approach can foster dedication, productivity, and positive morale, reducing turnover rates and associated costs. The study's findings offer actionable insights for spinning mills, aiding in the development of effective welfare policies. Policymakers can use the results to formulate industry-wide welfare guidelines, emphasizing the social responsibility of the spinning sector. The study contributes to existing knowledge on worker welfare in Namakkal's spinning mills, serving as a resource for future research. Overall, its impact lies in fostering a conducive work environment, promoting employee well-being, and supporting the sustainable growth of spinning mills in Namakkal.

Analysis and Interpretation

This analysis and interpretation delve into the intricate tapestry of employee welfare policies within Namakkal spinning mills, dissecting data segmented across various demographic factors. The study meticulously evaluates the preferences and prioritization of welfare measures among the workforce, shedding light on the critical interplay between organizational objectives and employee requirements.

The data is segmented based on demographic factors: gender, age, marital status, educational qualification, years in working service, and shift of work.

Gender: 74 respondents (61.7%) are male, and 46 respondents (38.3%) are female.

Age: Respondents are distributed across age groups as follows: 18-25 years (20.8%), 25-35 years (39.2%), 36-45 years (24.2%), and above 45 years (15.8%).

Marital status: 51.7% of respondents are married, while 48.3% are unmarried.

Educational qualification: The majority has higher secondary (30.8%) and graduate (30.8%) qualifications.

Years in working service: 40.0% have less than 4 years, 26.7% have 4-8 years, 24.2% have 8-12 years, and 9.2% have above 12 years of service.

Shift of work: 35.8% work day shifts, 43.3% work half shifts, 14.2% work day and night shifts, and 6.7% work full night shifts.

Statutory welfare measures: The following welfare measures are ranked based on respondents' preferences:

Drinking water: 4.20
Lighting: 4.10

Medi-claim insurance scheme: 4.03
Changing rooms: 3.93
Sexual harassment policy: 3.91
Latrines and urinals: 3.70
Washing places: 3.58
First aid appliances: 3.39
Maternity and adoption leave: 3.15
Facilities for sitting: 3.12
Canteen facilities: 3.02
Rest rooms: 3.00
Spittoons: 2.74

Non-statutory welfare measures:
Respondents rank the following non-statutory welfare measures:

Flexible working hours: 4.18
Work-life balance initiatives: 4.17
Transportation assistance: 3.98
Employee loans and advances: 3.85
Employee assistance programs (EAPs): 3.59
Employee wellness programs: 3.58
Work environment: 3.37
Professional development: 3.23
Employee engagement activities: 3.18
Retirement plans: 3.09
Health benefits: 3.07
Financial education: 2.65
Paid time off (PTO): 2.58
Recognition and rewards: 2.56

These rankings provide insights into the prioritization of welfare measures, with flexible working hours and work-life balance initiatives topping the non-statutory measures, while drinking water and lighting are deemed most crucial among statutory measures. In conclusion, this study underscores the paramount significance of statutory and non-statutory welfare measures in the holistic success of spinning mills and the well-being of their workforce. The weighted average ranking test provides a comprehensive hierarchy of priorities, spotlighting the nuanced preferences of employees. From flexible work schedules to recognition and rewards, the study advocates for a sincere commitment to employee wellness programs as a strategic investment fostering sustainable growth. However, the path to ideal employee welfare is an ongoing journey, demanding continual adaptation to stay attuned to evolving workforce dynamics. The study's insights offer a roadmap for spinning mills in Namakkal to embrace a holistic strategy for employee well-being, ensuring a harmonious coexistence between personnel and organizational prosperity. Looking forward, the future scope of the study suggests avenues for long-term monitoring, qualitative research, technological integration, and a global perspective to continuously enhance and adapt employee welfare initiatives in the ever-evolving landscape of the spinning mill industry.

Conclusion

In conclusion, this study navigates the intricate landscape of employee welfare policies in Namakkal spinning mills, highlighting the pivotal role played by both statutory and non-statutory measures in shaping workforce well-being and organizational success. The weighted average ranking test unveils a nuanced hierarchy, elucidating the prioritization of welfare initiatives by the workforce, ranging from flexible schedules to recognition and rewards.

The findings underscore the symbiotic relationship between organizational objectives, employee needs, and a nurturing workplace environment. The commitment to employee well-being emerges as a strategic investment, fostering morale, productivity, and organizational reputation. However, the pursuit of ideal employee welfare is ongoing, necessitating continual adaptation and innovation to align with evolving needs.

Spinning mills are urged to perceive employee welfare not merely as a legal obligation but as a pathway to excellence, ensuring a harmonious coexistence between the workforce and the business. The study's insights should guide Namakkal spinning mills towards a holistic approach to employee well-being, steering clear of a bleak and unfulfilling future.

The study's robust framework lays the foundation for future exploration, urging researchers to delve into areas such as long-term monitoring of employee perspectives, extending welfare policy comparisons, and incorporating qualitative research for a comprehensive understanding of employee experiences. Additionally, exploring the impact of technology, assessing inclusivity, and examining the efficacy of welfare metrics in dynamic work settings present promising avenues for further research. Continuous dialogue, data-driven insights, and an innovative mindset are advocated to sustain the relevance and effectiveness of welfare measures amidst the evolving landscape of the spinning mill industry.

References

Antony, J. (2017). A study on effectiveness of labour welfare measures in loss-making public-sector undertakings in Kerala. *International Journal of Innovative Research in Management Studies (IJIRMS)*, 2(7), 5–12.

Mohideen, A. S., and Ishaq, M. (2015). Labour welfare measures in L.S. mills limited, Theni, Tamilnadu. *Interna-*

tional Journal of Computing and Corporate Research, 5(3).

Nithyavathi, K. (2016). A study on safety and welfare measures provided to the employees in the textile industry in Tirupur district. *International Journal of Research in Management, Economics and Commerce,* 6(10), 51–59.

Poongavanam, S., Rengamani, D., Srinivasan, R., and Prasad, R. (2017). Employee welfare measures and industrial hygiene in civil construction company - a study. *International Journal of Civil Engineering and Technology,* 8(7), 69–77.

Sekar, M. (2012). Health and welfare measures in Tamilnadu spinning mills, India. *Indian Streams Research Journal,* 2(1).

Sethuram, S., and Sankari, S. S. (2018). Perception of employees on labour welfare measures and its impact on job performance at christy friedgram industry, Tiruchengode. *International Journal of Science and Research (IJSR),* 7(6), 1047–1050.

Vijaya Ramya, V., and Geetha (2019). Employees' perception towards safety and welfare measures in spinning mills at Rajapalayam region. *International Journal of Advance Research, Ideas and Innovations in Technology,* 5(3).

59 Employees' job satisfaction in textile industries in Coimbatore district

Deepika, S., Naveena, R.[a], Sivakrithika, N.[b], Ramyaprabha, N.[c] and Mathan Kumar, V.[d]

Karpagam Academy of Higher Education, Coimbatore, Tamil Nadu, India

Abstract

In this investigation, the examination of job satisfaction levels among employees within the textile industry in Coimbatore district offers valuable insights into organisational dynamics. The study, encompassing 360 randomly selected employees from diverse textile enterprises, underlines the pivotal role of job satisfaction in influencing employee motivation, productivity, and overall well-being. Notably, the findings reveal a commendably high level of job satisfaction among Coimbatore District's textile workforce. Key determinants of satisfaction include the work environment, compensation and benefits, and growth opportunities. Positive interpersonal relationships, recognition for contributions, and job stability also emerged as significant contributors to job happiness. However, the study identifies areas for improvement, notably in work-life balance and stress management. This research contributes to our comprehension of employee satisfaction within the unique context of Coimbatore's textile sector, offering actionable insights for management practices and human resource policies aimed at cultivating a supportive and joyful work environment conducive to heightened employee retention and productivity.

Keywords: Coimbatore, employee, job satisfaction, textile industries

Introduction

Coimbatore district in southern India boasts a rich history and a formidable presence in the textile sector, functioning as a pivotal hub for textile production and trade. The industry's growth is underpinned by factors such as the abundance of skilled labour, favourable governmental regulations, access to raw materials, and a robust network of textile-related businesses. Comprising spinning, weaving, dyeing, printing, and clothing production, the local textile industry serves both domestic and international markets, significantly contributing to the region's economic prosperity and employment landscape.

Given the textile industry's crucial role in global economic development, Coimbatore District's thriving textile sector anchors numerous local jobs. Job satisfaction emerges as a pertinent concern, directly influencing overall productivity, efficiency, and competitiveness. This research inquires into employee job satisfaction within Coimbatore's textile industries, aiming to provide insights that enable companies to cultivate a content and supportive work environment. Recognizing employees as the industry's backbone, the study focuses on the critical impact of job satisfaction on productivity, motivation, and talent retention. Ultimately, a satisfied workforce contributes to enhanced efficiency, competitiveness, and the retention of valuable institutional knowledge in the textile sector.

Review of Literature

Table 59.1 Exploring job satisfaction: insights from various studies and authors.

Author name	Study	Findings/insights
Ramapriya and Sudhamathi (2020)	Explored positive correlation between employment content, career progression, work-life balance, and job security.	Found significant relationship between job-related factors and overall job satisfaction and retention.
Ravi (2019)	Identified factors contributing to employee satisfaction and dissatisfaction in the Bangalore garment industry.	Highlighted areas for improvement in specific factors affecting employee satisfaction in the garment industry.

[a]naveenasriram@gmail.com. [b]sivakrithika.nellaiappan@kahedu.edu.in, [c]ramyameena1990@gmail.com, [d]mathankumar010@gmail.com

Author name	Study	Findings/insights
Pal (2019)	Found high job satisfaction among employees but noted deficiencies in working environment, incentives, recognition, and promotion programs.	Emphasized importance of addressing specific organizational elements to sustain high employee satisfaction and commitment.
Sreerekha et al. (2019)	Indicated overall job satisfaction among employees, with specific concerns raised about pay and recognition.	Revealed mixed sentiments on job satisfaction with specific areas of concern like pay and recognition.
Pizam (2020)	Revealed distinct characteristics of hospitality industry workers and their lower levels of job and life satisfaction.	Found hospitality industry workers expressed lower satisfaction with work and life compared to workers in other sectors.
Ozturkoglu et al. (2018)	Highlighted significance of ergonomics in determining job satisfaction for Turkish automotive workers.	Emphasized the role of ergonomics in job satisfaction for Turkish automotive workers.
Halkos et al., (2017)	Explored effects of job stress and dissatisfaction during crises on employees.	Investigated impact of job stress and dissatisfaction during crises on employees.
Buhler and Scott (2009)	Advocated for a culture prioritizing employee satisfaction.	Stressed the financial benefits of prioritizing employee satisfaction.
Stride et al., (2008)	Offered benchmarking data for organizational commitment, mental health, and job satisfaction.	Provided benchmarking data for organizational commitment, mental health, and job satisfaction.
Rowan (2008)	Provided practical advice on maximizing job happiness and navigating workplace challenges.	Offered practical advice on maximizing job happiness and overcoming workplace challenges.
Esen (2007)	Explored factors contributing to job satisfaction across industries, staff sizes, and demographics.	Studied factors contributing to job satisfaction across industries, staff sizes, and demographics.
Hochheiser (1998)	Emphasized role of positive relationships in workplace success.	Stressed importance of positive relationships for workplace success.

Source: Author

Problem Statement

The textile sector in Coimbatore district serves as a crucial driver of economic growth, generating numerous employment opportunities, yet the industry's sustained success hinges on the contentment and well-being of its workforce. Despite its significance, there exists a notable dearth of research into the specific factors shaping employee job satisfaction in this sector. This information gap poses challenges for textile firms in tailoring initiatives to address the unique needs of their workforce, potentially resulting in diminished employee engagement and retention. This research aims to address these gaps, investigating the current levels of job satisfaction among textile workers in Coimbatore district, identifying the factors influencing job satisfaction, and providing evidence-based recommendations to enhance employee well-being, thereby contributing to the overall success of the textile industry in the region.

Objective of Study

- To identify the key factors influencing job satisfaction in the textile sector.

Scope of Study

This research probes into employee work satisfaction within Coimbatore district's textile companies, specifically focusing on factors influencing job contentment. Concentrated solely on the thriving textile industry of Coimbatore district, the study aims to gather actionable insights. Participants from diverse roles and departments will be recruited, ensuring representation across experience levels and functions. The findings, while contextualized for the local textile sector, may offer broader implications for enhancing employee satisfaction and organizational effectiveness in related industries.

Research Methodology

Data
- Primary data is essential, gathered through participant interviews for precision and in-depth insights.
- Using an interview schedule ensures consistency and standardized answers, enhancing the trustworthiness of the data collection process.

Sampling and sample size
- Convenient sampling is beneficial when access to the entire population is challenging.

- Enables quick data collection from readily available individuals.
- Employed convenient sampling to gather data from 360 textile workers in Coimbatore district.

Framework of analysis
- Analyzed collected data using simple percentage and factor analysis.

Significance of Study

This research on job satisfaction in Coimbatore district's textile industry is crucial for stakeholders and the sector at large. By identifying satisfaction factors, the study aids companies in fostering positive work environments, enhancing employee well-being, and boosting overall job satisfaction. Satisfied employees are more productive and committed, leading to increased efficiency and competitiveness. The findings offer insights for policymakers, informing decisions on labor regulations and industry support while supporting sustainable growth in the textile sector. The study's impact extends beyond Coimbatore, influencing global industry practices and policies for enhanced employee satisfaction and business performance.

Analysis and Interpretation

In examining the job satisfaction of textile workers in Coimbatore district, this study investigates key demographic factors and utilizes factor analysis to identify critical elements influencing job contentment Boucher (2004). The demographic profile encompasses age, gender, marital status, educational qualification, monthly income, work experience, and shift preferences Cammann et al. (1983). Subsequently, the Kaiser-Meyer-Olkin (KMO) measure and Bartlett's test affirm the data's suitability for factor analysis Cranny et al. (1992). The rotated component matrix unveils multiple factors significantly contributing to job satisfaction Penn (2008). Recognizing the pivotal role of these factors is essential for textile industries aiming to enhance workplace conditions and employee well-being.

Demographic profile of employees
Age:

- Below 25 Years: 24.2%
- 25-35 Years: 22.5%
- 36-45 Years: 30.8%
- Above 45 Years: 22.5%

Interpretation: The age distribution shows a diverse workforce, with the majority falling between 36-45 years, indicating a mix of experience levels.

Gender:
- Male: 60.0%
- Female: 40.0%

Interpretation: The gender distribution reflects a male-dominated workforce with 60%, suggesting potential gender-related dynamics in the workplace.

Marital status:
- Married: 45.0%
- Unmarried: 55.0%

Interpretation: Nearly half of the employees are married, implying potential differences in work-life balance and priorities between married and unmarried individuals.

Educational qualification:
- School level: 21.7%
- Graduate: 41.7%
- Postgraduate: 20.8%
- Others: 15.8%

Interpretation: A significant portion holds at least a graduate degree, indicating a relatively educated workforce with diverse qualifications.

Monthly income:
- Below Rs 15,000: 33.3%
- Rs 15,000-20,000: 30.8%
- Rs 21,000-25,000: 23.3%
- Above Rs 25,000: 12.5%

Interpretation: The income distribution highlights a majority earning below Rs 20,000, signaling potential financial considerations affecting job satisfaction.

Work experience:
- Below 3 Years: 33.3%
- 3-5 Years: 46.7%
- 6-10 Years: 13.3%
- Above 10 Years: 6.7%

Interpretation: The work experience distribution suggests a blend of both experienced and relatively new employees, impacting their perspectives and expectations.

Shift of the employee:
- Day shift: 35.8%
- Half shift: 40.8%
- Day and night: 15.0%
- Full night: 8.3%

Interpretation: The varied shift distribution reveals diverse work schedules, potentially influencing factors like work-life balance and job satisfaction.

Job satisfaction of textile workers

The collected data, suitable for factor analysis, met the criteria as follows:

Factor analysis suitability:
- Kaiser-Meyer-Olkin (KMO): 0.941 (Acceptable)
- Bartlett's test of sphericity: Chi-square = 13526.829, p = 0.000 (Suitable for factor analysis)

Interpretation: The high KMO value and significant p-value from Bartlett's test confirm that the collected data is suitable for factor analysis, providing a solid foundation for interpreting job satisfaction factors.

Top 10 identified factors influencing job satisfaction out of 43:

1. Recognition and appreciation
2. Job security
3. Workload and stress levels
4. Work environment and facilities
5. Employee empowerment
6. Skill development and training
7. Career growth opportunities
8. Work-life policies
9. Communication with management
10. Job role and responsibilities

Interpretation: These ten factors are highlighted as significant contributors to job satisfaction among textile workers out of a total of 43 factors identified in the rotated component matrix. They encompass various aspects of the work environment and employee experience, emphasizing key areas crucial for enhancing overall job satisfaction. These factors collectively shape the work experience and well-being of the employees, highlighting areas crucial for enhancing job satisfaction.

Factor contribution to job satisfaction:
- Factor 1: 39.768%
- Factor 2: 12.691%
- Factor 3: 5.491%
- Factor 4: 3.331%

- Factor 5: 2.759%
- Factor 6: 2.298%
- **Total cumulative: 66.337%**

Interpretation: Factor 1 plays a dominant role in influencing job satisfaction, contributing nearly 40%, with the cumulative total of the six factors reaching 66.337%, emphasizing the importance of these factors in the overall job satisfaction of textile workers.

Findings and Inferences

The study reveals that key factors influencing job satisfaction among Coimbatore District textile workers include recognition, job security, workload, and communication. Through factor analysis, these aspects collectively contribute 66.337% towards job satisfaction. Demographically, the majority are aged 36-45, married, hold graduate degrees, earn below Rs 15,000, and have 3-5 years of work experience. Male employees dominate, with day-and-half shifts being the most common. These findings highlight critical areas for employers to focus on, offering actionable insights to enhance workplace conditions and overall job satisfaction in the local textile industry.

Conclusion

In conclusion, this research sheds light on the pivotal factors influencing job satisfaction among textile workers in Coimbatore district. Recognition, job security, workload, work environment, and career advancement emerged as crucial determinants, collectively contributing to 66.337% of the variance in job satisfaction. By implementing tailored strategies, such as recognition programs, transparent communication, and initiatives promoting work-life balance, textile companies can enhance job satisfaction, leading to improved employee retention and overall organizational performance. Satisfied employees are more engaged and committed, contributing to increased productivity and reduced turnover costs.

Moving forward, this study opens avenues for future research. Longitudinal studies can track changes in job satisfaction over time, offering insights into evolving patterns. Comparative analyses across different sectors within the textile industry can reveal industry-specific challenges and opportunities. Assessing the effectiveness of interventions and exploring the relationship between job satisfaction, employee well-being, and turnover rates can further enrich our understanding of workforce dynamics. Continuous research in these areas will empower textile firms to craft informed strategies, fostering employee well-being and organizational success.

References

Boucher, J. (2004). How to Love the Job You Hate: Job Satisfaction for the 21st Century. Beagle Bay Books.

Buhler, P., and Scott, J. (2009). The Employee Satisfaction Revolution: Understanding and Unleashing the Power of a Satisfied Workforce. Prestwick House, Inc.

Cammann, C., Fichman, M., Jenkins, Jr., D., and Klesh, J. R. (1983). Assessing the Attitudes and Perceptions of Organizational Members. John Wiley & Sons, Inc.

Cranny, C. J., Smith, P. C., Cain, P., and Stone, E. F. (1992). Job Satisfaction: How People Feel about their Jobs and How it Affects their Performance. Lexington Books.

Esen, E. (2007). Job Satisfaction. Society for Human Resource Management.

Hochheiser, R. M. (1998). It's a Job Not a Jail: How to Break Your Shackles When You Can't Afford to Quit. Simon & Schuster.

Ozturkoglu, O., Saygılı, E. E., and Ozturkoglu, Y. (2018). A manufacturing-oriented model for evaluating the satisfaction of workers – evidence from Turkey. *International Journal of Industrial Ergonomics*, 54, 73–82.

Penn, J. (2008). How to Enjoy Your Job. Lulu Publishers.

Ramapriya, M., and Sudhamathi, S. (2020). Impact of job satisfaction on employee retention in garment industry. *International Journal of Multidisciplinary Educational Research*, 9(12), 68–72.

Sreerekha, T., Saranya, R., Prabhu, V. S., and Dayalarajan, A. (2019). Job satisfaction of employees in Tirupur garment industry. *International Journal for Research Trends and Innovation*, 4(4), 1–4.

60 Employee perception towards quality of work life in the paper industry in Coimbatore

Petchimuthu, S., Ramyaprabha, N.[a], Shrie Bhubaneswari, N.T.[b], Naveena, R.[c] and Smruthymol, J.[d]

Karpagam Academy of Higher Education, Coimbatore, Tamil Nadu, India.

Abstract

This research investigates employee perceptions of the quality of work life (QWL) within Coimbatore's paper industry, acknowledging the notorious challenges posed by its demanding work environment. The study adopts a mixed-methods approach, incorporating both quantitative and qualitative data collection methods. By comprehending the factors influencing employee well-being, the research aims to contribute to the development of a resilient and enduring workforce. The findings are anticipated to be of interest to industry stakeholders, policymakers, and human resource professionals, offering valuable insights to identify and address issues affecting employee satisfaction, productivity, and retention. Furthermore, this study contributes to a deeper understanding of work-life within the Indian paper sector, serving as a foundational resource for future research endeavors in related fields. As the paper industry grapples with unique challenges, this investigation seeks to shed light on the specific nuances of QWL, facilitating informed strategies for sustainable employee management.

Keywords: Coimbatore, paper industry, quality of work life, working conditions, work-life balance

Introduction

The paper industry, a significant contributor to India's economy, plays a crucial role in Coimbatore's industrial landscape, offering employment and raw materials. Acknowledging the importance of employee well-being for industrial success, the concept of "quality of work life" (QWL) becomes pivotal. This study delves into the unique challenges faced by paper industry employees in Coimbatore, where the demanding nature of the sector may impact job satisfaction. Recognizing that a positive QWL enhances engagement, motivation, and loyalty, the research employs a mixed-methods approach to explore the factors influencing work-life satisfaction. By examining variables such as working conditions, workload, compensation, and work-life balance, the study aims to identify areas for improvement. The findings will not only benefit local stakeholders but also contribute valuable insights for scholars, policymakers, and human resource specialists nationally, aspiring to foster a more contented, motivated, and engaged workforce in Coimbatore's paper industry.

Review of Literature

Table 60.1 Insights into work life: authors, studies, and key findings.

Author Name	Study	Key Findings
Matheswaran and Latha (2019)	Enhancing employees' quality of work life	Opportunities for decision-making, comments, and suggestions, along with improved support, motivation, salaries, and benefits, enhance work life quality, leading to improved performance, commitment, and organizational image.
Sumathi and Velmurugan (2017)	Private sector employees' satisfaction	Private sector employees are content with conditions and job security but dissatisfied with health and safety policies and leave options.
Nanjundeswaraswamy and Swamy (2013)	Gender-based differences in work life satisfaction	Male employees are happier than females; demographics have no significant impact on work life quality. A substantial correlation is found between the quality of work life for teaching and non-teaching staff.

[a]ramyameena1990@gmail.com, [b]shrie.bhubaneswari@gmail.com, [c]naveenasriram@gmail.com, [d]jayalalsmruthy@gmail.com

Author Name	Study	Key Findings
Subhashini and Gopal (2013)	Factors influencing female employees' satisfaction	Female employees value the work environment and job security but are less satisfied with permissible leave. Improved work conditions contribute to higher production.
Jerome (2014)	Impact of working conditions on performance	The quality of working life affects performance, revealing the company's shortcomings in meeting basic employee needs.
Pandey and Khan (2016)	Importance of quality of work life (QWL)	QWL is crucial for attracting and retaining personnel. The study emphasized the link between QWL, worker performance, and factors influencing career growth and performance appraisal, calling for more research.
Aarthy and Nandhini (2016)	Impact of faculty members' QWL on institutions	Faculty members' QWL significantly influences institutions and students. The study found a modest level of QWL among faculty members.
Sumathi and Gunadundari (2016)	Challenges faced by highly skilled women	Skilled women often lose jobs due to reasons like parenthood. Organizations prioritizing work-life balance sustain work-life policies more effectively.
Rusu (2016)	Job and life satisfaction in organizational behavior	High job and life satisfaction positively impact motivation and task performance. The study utilized data from the European Working Condition Survey to understand Romania's employed population's interaction with various aspects of work life.
KiranBala et al. (2013)	Factors affecting employer expectations and employee needs	A systematic questionnaire explored various aspects of the working environment, compensation, welfare, stress, and relationships. Meeting employee needs enhances organizational goodwill and helps retain employees.
Sinha (2013)	Association between QWL and job satisfaction	Found a significant and positive association between QWL and job satisfaction. Public sector banks exhibited higher levels of QWL and job satisfaction compared to private sector banks.
Daud (2010)	Relationship between organizational commitment and QWL	Explored the relationship between QWL and organizational commitment among Malaysian company employees. The study used a quantitative method and records series sampling technique, revealing a positive correlation between QWL and organizational commitment.

Source: Author

Problem Statement

In the context of Coimbatore's pivotal paper sector, the pressing issue lies in the significant impact of the QWL on employee job satisfaction, well-being, and overall productivity. The demanding nature of the paper manufacturing process and work environment raises concerns among employees regarding factors influencing their QWL. This study's primary objective is to comprehensively assess the quality of work life within Coimbatore's paper sector, identifying factors that enhance or diminish employee QWL. The investigation seeks to unravel the potential repercussions of these factors on job satisfaction and general well-being, addressing a critical need for understanding and addressing challenges in this vital segment of the local economy.

Objective of the Study

- To ascertain the employee perception on quality of work life in the paper industry in Coimbatore.

Scope of Study

The study on Coimbatore's paper sector quality of work life acknowledges its limitations, focusing solely on this industry. Exclusions include related sectors like packaging or printing. The diverse workforce sample might not cover all roles due to practical constraints. Utilizing mixed methods, surveys, and interviews, the research faces limitations in interview sample size and time constraints. Cultural differences might impact data collection, and inaccuracies may affect study conclusions. Despite these challenges, the study aims to provide valuable insights for improving work conditions, job satisfaction, and overall well-being in Coimbatore's paper industry, potentially guiding research in analogous sectors.

Research Methodology

Data collection

- Primary data is essential for this study.

- Utilizing interviews ensures detailed, participant-specific information.
- An interview schedule ensures question consistency and standardized responses, enhancing data reliability.

Sampling and sample size
- Convenient sampling is valuable when accessing the entire population is challenging.
- It facilitates quick data collection from readily available individuals.
- In this study, 240 employees in Coimbatore's paper industry were sampled using the convenient sampling technique.

Framework of analysis
- Data analysis involves simple percentage and factor analysis.
- These methods aid in comprehensively evaluating the collected data.

Significance of Study

The study on the quality of work life in Coimbatore's paper sector holds crucial implications for stakeholders, offering benefits to employers, managers, and human resource specialists. It aids in understanding factors influencing workers' well-being, thereby presenting opportunities for enhancing productivity. Focusing on work-life balance, the research identifies variables affecting job satisfaction and proposes improvements for the working environment. These findings benefit businesses in retaining skilled labor, enhancing overall productivity, and influencing policy development for government agencies. Beyond industry relevance, the study contributes to the broader discourse on work-life balance, potentially influencing societal well-being. Its significance lies in improving conditions for both employees and the Coimbatore paper industry, fostering a more rewarding and sustainable work experience.

Comprehensive Analysis

In this analysis, we delve into the socio-economic profile of employees in Coimbatore's paper industry, exploring demographics, work experiences, and monthly income Gupta (2012). Additionally, we examine the appropriateness of the data for factor analysis through the Kaiser-Meyer-Olkin (KMO) measure and Bartlett's Test of Sphericity. Our focus extends to factor analysis results, identifying key contributors to employee perceptions on work life quality Kubendran et al. (2013). The cumulative impact of these factors provides valuable insights, shedding light on nuanced aspects crucial for crafting interventions to enhance work life quality in this dynamic industrial landscape.

Demographic profile
- Age distribution reveals that 39.2% of respondents are in the 30-40 years bracket, followed by 35.0% in the 40-50 years range.
- Gender representation indicates 66.67% male and 33.33% female participants.
- Educational qualifications vary, with 37.5% holding a Bachelor's degree and 23.3% possessing a Master's degree.
- Work experience spans different durations, with 37.5% having 1-4 years and 32.5% working for 5-9 years.
- Monthly income distribution indicates that 39.2% earn between 10000-15000, and 35.0% earn between 15001-20000.

Insights into Demographics: The data provides a comprehensive snapshot of participant demographics, essential for understanding how age, gender, education, work experience, and income influence perceptions of work life quality in Coimbatore's paper industry.

KMO and Bartlett's test
- The Kaiser-Meyer-Olkin (KMO) measure is 0.871, indicating suitable sampling for factor analysis.
- Bartlett's test of sphericity yields a significant result (p-value: 0.000), confirming data appropriateness for factor analysis.

Factor analysis results
- Factor analysis identifies significant contributors to employee perceptions on work life quality.
- Key factors include relationships with superiors and colleagues, training effectiveness, work stress, and compensation-related aspects.
- Cumulatively, these factors contribute to 75.408% of the variance in employee perceptions.

Factor loadings and contributions
- Factors with loadings above 0.5 include Relationship with superiors, Training effectiveness, Work stress, Job security, Job stress, Homework, Co-operation from other departments, and Motivating environment.
- Factor one contributes 23.635%, while cumulative contributions of identified factors reach 75.408%.

The study's demographic insights lay the groundwork for understanding perceptions of work life quality. The KMO and Bartlett's Test validate the appropriateness of data for factor analysis. Factor analysis identifies key factors influencing employee perceptions, contributing to a substantial cumulative variance. This nuanced understanding can guide interventions for enhancing work life quality in Coimbatore's paper industry.

Conclusion

In summarizing our study on the quality of work life in Coimbatore's paper industry, several key recommendations emerge as crucial for enhancing employee satisfaction and overall well-being. The emphasis on cultivating strong interpersonal relationships, promoting effective training initiatives, involving employees in decision-making processes, and implementing work-life policies all contribute significantly to the improvement of the work environment. Safety measures, equitable reward systems, professional development opportunities, and a diverse and inclusive workplace are additional factors that contribute to a positive work culture. By addressing these aspects, organizations in the paper sector can cultivate a more engaged and content workforce, fostering long-term prosperity.

The study highlights the importance of factors such as relationships with colleagues and superiors, training effectiveness, workload management, job security, and opportunities for professional growth. Acknowledging and addressing these elements can create a workplace that not only meets employees' expectations but also propels the industry toward sustained success. While recognizing the study's limitations, including data collection constraints, the findings set the stage for further research and industry-wide initiatives to continually improve work-life quality.

Looking ahead, future research could explore longitudinal studies to trace the evolution of work-life quality over time in the paper sector. Comparative analyses with other regions or industries could reveal industry-specific challenges and best practices. Exploring the impact of technological advancements, the relationship between organizational culture and employee well-being, and the effects of external factors on work-life quality are promising avenues for future investigations. Additionally, examining generational perspectives, sustainable work practices, and the success of specific work-life balance policies

can further enrich our understanding. These potential research directions aim to guide stakeholders in the Coimbatore paper industry and beyond toward the continuous improvement of employee well-being and overall industry sustainability.

References

Aarthy, M., and Nandhini, M. (2016). Influence of the demographic factors on quality of work life of the engineering college faculty members in Coimbatore district. *International Journal of Commerce and Management Research*, 2(10), 28–31.

Daud, N. (2010). Investigating the relationship between quality of work life and organizational commitment amongst employees in Malaysian firms. *International Journal of Business and Management*, 5(10), 75. https://doi.org/10.5539/ijbm.v5n10p75.

Gupta, C. B. (2012). Human Resource Management (Text and Case). Sultan Chand & Sons.

Jerome, S. (2013). A study on quality of work life of employees at Jeppiaar cement private ltd: Perambalur. *International Journal of Advance Research in Computer Science and Management Studies*, 1(4), 49–57. ISSN: 2321-7782 (Online).

KiranBala , B., Selvam, K. G., et al. (2013). A study on quality of work life in aditya trading solution pvt. ltd, Trichy. *International Journal of Research in Management and Technology (IJRMT)*, 3(1), 24–30. ISSN: 2249-9563.

Kubendran, V., Muthukumar, S., and Priyadharshini, M. (2013). Impact of quality of work life on the performance of the employees in IT organizations. *Indian Journal of Economics and Development*, 1(3), 82–85.

Matheswaran, V. P., and Latha, G. (2019). A study on quality of work life among employees. *International Journal of Scientific Development and Research (IJSDR)*, 4(9), 66–70.

Rusu, R. (2016). The influence of quality of work life on work performance. Nicolae Bălcescu land forces academy, Sibiu, Romania, DE GRUYTER open. *International Conference Knowledge-Based Organization*, 22(2), 960–965. https://doi.org/10.1515/kbo-2016-0084.

Subhashini, S., and Gopal, C. S. R. (2013). Quality of work life among women employees working In garment factories in Coimbatore district. *Asia Pacific Journal of Research*, 1(7), 22–29.

Sumathi, V., and Velmurugan, R. (2017). Quality of work life of employees in private companies with reference to Coimbatore. *International Journal of Multidisciplinary Research and Development*, 4, 128–131.

61 A study on work environment and work culture among the employees in select paint company

Umamaheswari, R. and Ramadevi, V.[a]

Karpagam Academy of Higher Education, Coimbatore, Tamil Nadu, India

Abstract

This research examines of the work environment and culture prevalent among employees in a specific paint company, aiming to decipher their impact on employee satisfaction, engagement, and overall organizational performance. Employing the chosen paint company as a case study allows for a nuanced exploration of work cultures within the paint industry. The research methodology adopts a mixed-methods approach, integrating surveys, interviews, and observational data. Surveys will quantify employees' perceptions of their work environment, encompassing factors such as the physical workplace, managerial support, teamwork, communication, and opportunities for professional growth. Interviews will provide qualitative insights into employees' experiences, challenges, and suggestions for improvement, while observations will assess organizational interactions and standard procedures. The study's outcomes will illuminate both positive and negative aspects of the culture and working environment at the selected paint firm, facilitating targeted improvements. Furthermore, the research contributes to an enhanced understanding of workplace dynamics within the paint industry, offering potentially transferable insights for other sectors. Ultimately, this study aspires to furnish practical recommendations for the selected paint company and analogous businesses, fostering a more supportive and efficacious workplace conducive to employee satisfaction, engagement, and overall success.

Keywords: Paint company and employees, work culture, work environment

Introduction

In the contemporary competitive business landscape, an organization's triumph is intricately tied to the quality of its work environment and the prevailing corporate culture, significantly influencing overall success and the well-being of its workforce. This study aims to scrutinize the working conditions and corporate culture within a carefully selected paint firm, a pivotal player in both consumer and industrial markets, impacting manufacturing and construction sectors. The ability of organizations in the paint industry to attract and retain talent, foster innovation, and achieve operational excellence is profoundly shaped by their work environment and culture. Challenges, such as product safety, stringent quality control, and evolving environmental regulations, pose distinctive hurdles for workers in this sector. This investigation seeks to unravel the impact of these elements on employees' experiences. Probing into the expansive concept of the "working environment," the study explores its encompassing physical components, including tools, air, noise, and light, while also acknowledging its psychological dimensions, encompassing how individuals feel and the organizational structures influencing their work. By understanding these dynamics, the study aims to provide valuable insights into cultivating a conducive and supportive workplace.

Need for the Study

Recognizing the impact of workplace environment on employee well-being is crucial, as negative perceptions can lead to chronic stress. The term "working environment" encompasses procedures, tools, and conditions affecting productivity. Internal and external factors, such as policies, culture, and working relationships, shape the office environment. This research addresses the identified issue of how the work environment and culture significantly influence employee performance, emphasizing the importance of understanding these dynamics for enhancing morale and productivity.

[a]drramadevi77@gmail.com

Review of Literature

Table 61.1 Studies on workplace dynamics: exploring the interplay of environment, job satisfaction, and employee performance.

Author name	Study	Insights
Aggarwal et al. (2023)	Workplace culture and job satisfaction	The study explores the positive association between an employee's workplace environment and job satisfaction. A supportive work atmosphere benefits both the corporation and employees, fostering increased effectiveness in job responsibilities. Research indicates a positive correlation between employee performance and job satisfaction, emphasizing the productivity boost associated with happy workers.
Marbun and Jufrizen (2022)	Workplace efficiency and employee contribution	Employees thrive in a comfortable workplace, contributing efficiently to organizational goals. Effective cooperation among coworkers and other workplace elements is crucial. A conducive work environment is essential for retaining employees as valuable assets. The study underscores the impact of the work environment on task performance and the creation of a shared work culture for external adaptation and internal integration.
Sarwar et al. (2022)	Workplace in health services	Examining workplace, employee performance, and happiness in a healthcare setting, the study at RumahSakitSwasta reveals a positive influence of job satisfaction on employee performance. The work environment also positively affects both job satisfaction and performance in the healthcare sector.

Source: Author

Objective of the Study

- To understand the demographic profile of the employees.
- To analyse the prevailing work environment in the organization
- To assess the work culture in the organization.
- To obtain suggestions the respondents to improve work environment and work culture in the organization

Limitations of the Study

- Due to the shortage of time and other constraints, the study has been limited to 120 respondents only.
- This study restricted Coimbatore only, so it may not universally applicable.
- The accuracy of the information depends upon the respondents.
- The scope of the study is limited to the Coimbatore unit only.

Research Methodology

- Describes procedures for data collection and assessment.
- Allows readers to evaluate study validity and reliability.
- Encompasses various techniques for research, including tests, experiments, questionnaires, and critical analysis.

Research design

- Descriptive research design chosen for its exploratory nature.
- Aims to discover information about who, what, when, where, and how.
- Simplest descriptive studies observe variables' size, form, distribution, or existence.

Sampling design

- Simple random sampling with personal judgment approach.
- Target population: Workers at Nexon Paints Pvt. Ltd.
- Population serves as the survey base with a sample size of 120.

Sources of data collection

- Primary data collected through personal interviews, questionnaires, etc.
- Secondary data gathered from company reports, website, textbooks, journals, newspapers, magazines, and the internet.

Tools used for analysis

1. Simple percentage analysis
2. Chi-square test
3. Correlation
4. ANOVA
5. Independent test

Findings and Analysis

This section presents a comprehensive analysis of the socio-economic profile of respondents and its implications on various workplace dynamics Deal and Kennedy (2005). Examining factors such as gender, age, family types, marital status, educational qualification, experience, and salary levels, the findings shed light on the diverse composition of the study sample Schein (2004). Statistical tools, including Chi-Square analysis, correlation analysis, One-Way ANOVA, and Independent T-Test, are employed to discern relationships between variables Guptha (2000). These insights serve as a foundation for understanding the intricate interplay between socio-economic factors and workplace aspects, guiding subsequent interpretations and recommendations for organizational enhancement Kothari (1997).

Findings
- **Gender**
  - 63.3% male and 36.7% female respondents.
  - Gender distribution may influence gender-related analyses or considerations in study outcomes Putti (1980).
- **Age**
  - Majority (40%) are up to 30 years old.
  - Considerable representation in the younger age brackets Alhabri et al. (2013).
- **Family types**
  - 60.8% from nuclear families, indicating a significant representation Chittipa (2015).
- **Marital status**
  - Balanced distribution between married (54.2%) and unmarried respondents Dimitrios (2017).
- **Educational qualification**
  - Diverse educational background with degree holders as the largest group Fakhar et al. (2018).
- **Experience**
  - Even distribution across experience levels, with a notable portion having 2-4 years of experience Fatima et al. (2019).
- **Salary levels**
  - Diverse salary distribution, with a significant portion earning between Rs.10,000 and Rs.15,000.

Chi-square analysis
- **Gender and physical work environment**
  - Null hypothesis accepted; no significant correlation found between gender and the physical work environment.

Correlation analysis
- **Age group and psychological work environment**
  - Weak negative association between age group and psychological work environment.

One-way ANOVA test
- **Educational qualification and organization work environment**
  - Significant relationship; rejecting the null hypothesis.

Independent T-test:
- **Experience and impact on work culture**
  - No meaningful connection found between respondents' experiences and their impact on work culture.

Interpretation
- **Gender and physical work environment**
  - Null hypothesis accepted; no meaningful association found.
- **Age group and psychological work environment**
  - Weak negative association between age group and psychological work environment.
- **Educational qualification and organization work environment**
  - Significant relationship found; rejecting the null hypothesis.
- **Experience and impact on work culture**
  - No significant connection found between respondents' experiences and their impact on work culture.

In conclusion, the study provides a comprehensive understanding of the socio-economic profile of the respondents and their correlation with various workplace aspects. The findings highlight diverse demographics, indicating the need for nuanced analyses in interpreting the study's outcomes. Additionally, the statistical tests employed reveal specific relationships between certain variables, guiding future investigations and organizational interventions.

Conclusion

In conclusion, the study emphasizes a series of recommendations to enhance the organisational environment. The company should focus on maintaining a conducive building with comfortable working hours, adequate lighting, and ventilation to foster productivity. Ensuring the availability of hygienic canteen facilities and necessary tools for job tasks is imperative. Stress-free work environments, work-life balance, clear role clarity, and satisfactory allowances contribute significantly to employee motivation. Safety, healthcare measures, and fostering positive relationships between superiors and subordinates are essential aspects. Regular feedback mechanisms and promotional opportunities further enhance employee engagement. Acknowledging job performance and fostering a positive leadership approach and team spirit is vital for a thriving workplace culture.

In essence, the study highlights that organisational culture profoundly influences employee performance and satisfaction. The shared norms and values within an organisation shape interaction and significantly impact productivity and happiness. Regardless of industrial or technological advancements, the study asserts the indispensability of organisational culture. The findings reveal a positive sentiment among employees in the paint industry, indicating contentment with their work environment and culture. Thus, creating a comprehensible and supportive organisational culture is pivotal for aligning individual values with corporate objectives, fostering efficiency, and ensuring employee satisfaction.

References

Alhabri, M. A., et al. (2013). Impact of organizational culture on employee performance. *International Review of Management and Business Research*, 2(1), 168–172.

Chittipa, N. (2015). A study on corporate culture and its impact on job satisfaction. *Journal of International Conference on Business, Economics and Accounting*, 1–4 .

Deal, T., and Kennedy, A. (2005). Corporate Cultures. Penguin Books. (First published by Addison Wesley, Revised Edition).

Dimitrios, B. (2017). Organizational culture and job satisfaction. *Journal of International Review of Management and Marketing*, 4(3), 132–144.

Fakhar, S., et al. (2018). Impact of organizational culture on employee job performance. *Journal of Business Studies Quarterly*, 5(2), 56–58.

Fatima, R., et al. (2019). Relationship between job satisfaction and organizational culture. *European Journal of Experimental Biology*, 2(4), 1029–1033.

Guptha, C. B. (2000). Human Resource Management.

Kothari, C. R. (1997). Research Methodology - Methods and Techniques (2nd edn.).

Putti, J. M. (1980). The Management of Securing and Maintaining the Workforce. Ram Nagar, New Delhi: S Chand & Co Ltd.

Schein, E. H. (2004). Organizational Culture and Leadership (3rd edn.). Jossey-Bass: San Francisco.

62 Impact of welfare measures on job satisfaction of employees concerning the engineering industry

Abinaya, V., Amritha, S.[a], Sumathi, G.[b], Sujith, B.[c] and Ranjith, R.[d]

Karpagam Academy of Higher Education, Coimbatore, India

Abstract

In this scholarly inquiry, the focus lies in determining the optimal approach for examining employee welfare measures, acknowledging the pivotal role that an organization's workforce plays as its most invaluable asset. Employee welfare encompasses an array of services, amenities, and benefits strategically provided by employers to enhance productivity and motivate workers. The overarching objective is to comprehend the employee, striving towards elevating the quality of life for the working class and fostering the holistic development of their personalities. The study looks into diverse facets such as housing options, healthcare provisions, and educational benefits for both children and adults. By adopting a descriptive research methodology, this paper seeks to unravel the multifaceted dimensions of employee welfare, shedding light on its profound impact on individual workers and their families. In doing so, it contributes to the broader discourse on fostering a conducive work environment that nurtures the well-being and overall development of the workforce.

Keywords: Employee, job satisfaction, welfare measures

Introduction

In the contemporary corporate landscape, the satisfaction of employees has emerged as a pivotal determinant of organizational performance, particularly in the dynamic and competitive realm. The engineering sector, renowned for its intricate projects and technical innovation, relies significantly on a qualified and motivated workforce. Recognizing this, businesses have increasingly acknowledged the significance of welfare programs in elevating staff morale and overall well-being. These measures encompass a spectrum of non-monetary incentives and services aimed at enhancing the standard of living both within and beyond the workplace.

The engineering industry, comprising diverse disciplines such as mechanical, electrical, civil, and software engineering, faces unique challenges in attracting and retaining talent. Engineers undertake demanding roles requiring creativity, problem-solving, and commitment, making the preservation of job satisfaction crucial to prevent burnout, enhance productivity, and stimulate innovation. This study seeks to explore the impact of welfare policies on job satisfaction within the engineering sector, examining the effectiveness of various programs employed by organizations and their influence on employee happiness and morale. Through this investigation, the research aims to contribute insights into the role of welfare policies in cultivating a positive workplace culture, fostering employee engagement, and promoting retention.

Employee welfare, defined as efforts for an employee's comfort and intellectual or social improvement beyond monetary compensation, involves various benefits, services, and facilities. In recognizing people as an organization's most valuable asset, the accounting profession is tasked with determining and recording the value of human assets. Unlike other assets that depreciate, human assets appreciate over time, especially when supported by investments in welfare and training programs. This study digs into the notion that the value of human assets significantly rises when factors contributing to the aging process, such as anxieties and adverse environments, are mitigated or slowed down, emphasizing the enduring importance of prioritizing employee well-being.

Statement of Problem

Exploring the broad scope of "employee welfare," which spans social security, housing, childcare, and canteen services, enhances morale and loyalty. Elevated employee well-being contributes to heightened productivity, job satisfaction, and resilience against societal challenges. This not only benefits individuals but also boosts the group's reputation and community appeal. Research on labor welfare in cotton mills sheds light on facilities and services

[a]amrithasurendran02051998@gmail.com, [b]sumathiganesh18@gmail.com, [c]sujithb8@gmail.com, [d]ranjy111@gmail.com

improving workers' health, financial status, and social standing.

Scope of the Study

This study offers valuable insights into the organizational and environmental facets of cotton mills. It aids management in addressing workplace issues, enhancing motivation, and providing career development training. Employee feedback enables informed adjustments to future welfare facilities. The report concludes with suggestions, empowering management to identify and rectify weaknesses in employee management.

Objectives of the Study

- To examine the employee perception of welfare measures.
- To measure factors influencing job satisfaction.
- To assess the impact of welfare measures and job satisfaction on employee productivity.

Research Methodology

Research design
The research design is descriptive.

Sampling design
The sampling technique used in this study is convenience sampling.

Sample size
Seven engineering organizations were chosen for the study. The sample size is 120.

Data Sources

Primary data: The researcher's original and recent data collection is their main objective. Primary data for this study was gathered by questionnaire. One common method of gathering primary data is using a questionnaire.

Statistical Tools

1. Simple percentage method
2. Chi-square test
3. Correlation analysis
4. ANOVA

Review of Literature

In his 2020 study, Srinivas (2020) evaluated the welfare amenities in Bangalore, gauging employee satisfaction. He noted that the corporation primarily provides medical care, cafeteria services, and a secure work environment, with employees expressing contentment. Additionally, in Chennai's cotton manufacturing sector, Srinivas endeavored to identify prevailing social security and labor welfare laws.

Nanda and Panda (2021) asserted that enhanced welfare practices have elevated productivity and fostered a positive work environment. Their organization offers diverse programs, including medical benefits, death benefits, insurance policies, housing, transportation options, and recreational activities, maintaining facilities and departments in optimal condition. Stringent safety procedures further emphasize the organization's commitment to employee welfare, health, and safety.

Harshani and Welmilla (2021) proposed a study investigating the impact of employee welfare facilities on cabin crew retention in Sri Lankan cotton mills. The research focused on examining the relationship between employee retention and welfare benefits among workers in Sri Lankan cotton mills, incorporating fabric, cotton, and related product industries. Two hypotheses were formulated and tested, with employee retention and welfare facilities representing the dependent and independent variables, respectively.

Results and Findings

The study delves into the correlation between socio-economic factors and welfare measures, exploring employees' opinions on lighting, ventilation, and working hours. Utilizing chi-square tests and correlation analysis, the research evaluates associations and identifies key findings. The null hypothesis is rejected, indicating a significant gap between education levels and pension and gratuity. Correlation analysis reveals a favourable association between employer-sponsored welfare measures and job satisfaction. Findings highlight varying degrees of employee satisfaction across welfare domains, from acceptable working hours to disagreements on lighting, ventilation, and facilities provided by the organisation.

Table 62.1 Proper lighting facility.

Lighting	No. of respondents	Percentage %
Strongly disagree	44	36.7
Disagree	18	15.0
Neutral	12	10.0
Agree	21	17.5
Strongly agree	25	20.8
Total	120	100.0

Source: Author

Table 62.2 Proper ventilation facilities.

Ventilation	No. of respondents	Percentage %
Strongly disagree	24	20.0
Disagree	45	37.5
Neutral	12	10.0
Agree	17	14.2
Strongly agree	22	18.3
Total	120	100.0

Source: Author

Table 62.3 Employee opinion about working hours.

Working hours	No. of respondents	Percentage %
Strongly disagree	27	22.5
Disagree	51	42.5
Neutral	15	12.5
Agree	27	22.5
Total	120	100.0

Source: Author

Note: The subsequent sections provide detailed insights into each aspect explored in the study.

Interpretation: Significant dissatisfaction with lighting; 36.7% strongly disagree, 15.0% disagree.

Interpretation: Ventilation concerns; 57.5% disagree, 28.3% agree (combined strongly and agree).

Interpretation: Work hours dissatisfaction; 65% disagree, 22.5% agree (combined strongly and agree).

Chi-square test – socio-economic factor and welfare measures

Null hypothesis:
H0 – No significant association between socio-economic factors and employer-offered welfare measures.

Chi-square test statistics
Pearson Chi-square: 26.878a
Likelihood ratio: 29.023
Linear-by-linear association: 0.174
Significance level
Asymp. Sig. (2-sided): 0.008
Rejection of null hypothesis (p-value < 0.05).
Interpretation: Indicates a significant association between socio-economic factors and welfare measures.

Note:
12 cells (60.0%) have expected counts less than 5, with a minimum expected count of 0.13.

Correlation analysis
Correlation between welfare measures and job satisfaction:
Pearson correlation: 0.510**
Significance (2-tailed): 0.000
Positive and significant correlation at the 0.01 level.

Association
Favourable association between employer-sponsored welfare programs and employees' job satisfaction.

Findings
Acceptable working hours:
Majority (45.8%) of respondents find working hours acceptable.

Drinking water
Majority (35.0%) strongly agree with the availability of drinking water.

Lighting
Majority (36.7%) strongly disagree with the organization's lighting.

Ventilation
Majority (37.5%) disagree with the ventilation provided.

Working hours
Majority (42.5%) disagree with the working hours.

Space for employees
Majority (40.0%) strongly disagree with the space provided for employees.

Washing facilities
Majority (36.7%) disagree with the washing facilities.

Shelter and restroom facilities
Majority (33.3%) are neutral about shelter and restroom facilities.

Normal temperature
Majority (43.3%) agree with the normal temperature.

Facilities provided
Majority (42.5%) disagree with facilities provided.

First aid medical facilities
Majority (27.5%) are neutral about first aid medical facilities.

Hygienic and healthy food

Majority (40.0%) are neutral about hygienic and healthy food.

Employee provident fund

Majority (30.0%) strongly disagree with the Employee Provident Fund.

Note: The percentages in the findings are based on the total number of respondents (120).

Findings, Results, and Inferences

The study's findings reveal diverse sentiments among respondents, with notable disparities in opinions on working conditions Karthi and Poongodi (2016). A significant proportion expresses dissatisfaction with lighting, ventilation, and working hours Mishra and Manju (2007). Correlation analysis establishes a positive link between employer-sponsored welfare measures and heightened job satisfaction Rathore and Tanwar (2017). Chi-square tests expose a substantial association between socio-economic factors and employer-provided benefits, particularly pension and gratuity. The rejection of the null hypothesis signifies a pronounced gap, emphasising the need for tailored welfare strategies Patro (2017). Overall, the study underscores the nuanced relationship between socio-economic factors, employee welfare, and job satisfaction, prompting a call for targeted interventions to address identified concerns.

Conclusion

In conclusion, the significance of employee welfare facilities cannot be overstated, as they profoundly impact employee happiness and, consequently, productivity. The findings highlight the pivotal role of human resources in organizational dynamics, with a keen interest in enhancing welfare facilities for the overall well-being of employees. The study reveals that the current welfare provisions, encompassing HR allowances, a well-equipped medical pantry, safety measures, and complimentary food in the canteen, are satisfactory to the staff.

However, the study also identifies avenues for improvement. Employees express contentment with the existing welfare facilities but highlight a desire for enhancements, particularly in areas such as restroom availability, preventive measures, and medical facilities. The suggestion to maintain a clean and orderly environment further emphasises the importance of creating conducive workspaces. By addressing these suggestions and continually upgrading welfare provisions, the organization can not only meet current expectations but also foster a workplace environment that minimizes absenteeism, enhances efficiency, and boosts employee morale, thereby contributing to sustained productivity and overall organizational success.

References

Harshani, M. D. R., and Welmilla, I. (2021). A study on impact of employee welfare facilities on job satisfaction. *International Journal of Advance Research and Innovative Ideas in Education*, 3(5), 822–826.

Karthi, G., and Poongodi, T. (2016). A study on employee health and safety welfare measures with special reference to RBR garments, Tirupur. *Intercontinental Journal of Human Resource Management*, 3(1), 20–26.

Mishra, S., and Manju, B. (2007). Principles for successful implementation of labour welfare activities. From police theory to functional theory.

Nanda and Panda (2021). The welfare state in historical perspective. *European Journal of Sociology/Archives europeennes de sociologie*, 2(2), 221–258.

Patro, C. S. (2017). Employee welfare measures in public and private sectors: a comparative analysis. In Public Health and Welfare: Concepts, Methodologies, Tools, and Applications (pp. 1026–1042). IGI Global.

Rathore, N., and Tanwar, M. (2017). A comprehensive literature review of effect on employees welfare in service industries. *International Journal of Management and Social Sciences Research*, 6(12), 30–32.

Srinivas (2020). A study of "labour welfare facilities" at Ahmednagar forgings limited, Pune. *International Journal of Entrepreneurship and Business Environment Perspectives*, 3(4), 1257.

63 Problems faced by employees in material handling in automobile industries

Kumar, M., Sujith, B.[a], Kumar, A.[b] and Ranjith, R.[c]
Karpagam Academy of Higher Education, Coimbatore, Tamil Nadu, India

Abstract

Material handling is a critical but challenging aspect in Kanchipuram's automobile industry, renowned for its significant role in India's automotive manufacturing sector. This study focuses on understanding the unique difficulties faced by workers engaged in material handling procedures within this industrial setting. It aims to comprehensively identify, examine, and overview challenges such as handling heavy components, ensuring safety with hazardous materials, addressing ergonomic concerns, optimizing facility layouts, managing inventory, bridging skill gaps through training, and improving communication. By illuminating these issues, the study provides insights for industry stakeholders, stressing the necessity to address challenges for enhanced operational effectiveness, employee well-being, and the region's status as an automotive hub. Emphasizing the need for targeted interventions and technological advancements, the research contributes to a deeper understanding of material handling in Kanchipuram's automobile sector, paving the way for practical solutions promoting sustainable growth and competitiveness.

Keywords: Automobile industry, material handling, problems, workplace safety

Introduction

Kanchipuram, a significant industrial hub in India, has played a pivotal role in advancing the automotive manufacturing sector, contributing significantly to economic growth and technological progress. At the heart of this industrious region lies the intricate process of material handling, crucial for the efficiency and success of vehicle production. Material handling encompasses diverse tasks, ensuring the smooth flow of parts from storage to assembly and distribution, pivotal for manufacturing precision, operational fluidity, and employee safety within the automotive industry. This study delves into the multifaceted challenges faced by material handling employees in Kanchipuram's automotive sector, extending beyond the physical demands of lifting objects. From addressing ergonomic concerns to navigating complex inventory management, mitigating safety risks related to hazardous materials, and harnessing emerging technologies, each challenge presents a facet of the intricate material handling landscape. The research aims to elucidate these complexities, offering a comprehensive understanding to enhance operational efficiency, employee well-being, and the competitive edge of Kanchipuram's automotive industries. The subsequent sections will explore these challenges in detail, proposing potential solutions aligned with industry best practices and innovative adaptations tailored to the region's unique context, ensuring sustained success in India's automotive landscape while prioritizing the welfare of the workforce.

Review of Literature

Table 63.1 Navigating material handling challenges: insights from diverse studies illuminate solutions for a smoother workflow in industries.

Author name	Study	Findings
Bala and Velumoni (2022)	Correlation between age and material handling challenges	The study reveals a negative correlation between age and the frequency of material handling problems. Younger individuals tend to face problems more frequently than older ones. However, it's important to note that correlation doesn't imply causation. An independent sample t-test examines the impact of experience on material handling improvements, aiming to find if there's a significant difference in average improvement scores between individuals with different levels of experience.

[a]sujithb8@gmail.com, [b]rmarul1992@gmail.com, [c]ranjy111@gmail.com

Author name	Study	Findings
Jagdish, (2022)	Material handling challenges in manufacturing sectors	Issues identified include a lack of proper machine handling equipment, compromising worker safety and breaks, and resulting in low productivity and efficiency. The study suggests solutions such as investing in appropriate handling tools, prioritizing safety measures, offering regular breaks, and adopting automation to improve efficiency and reduce costs. While the study focuses on human labor-intensive material handling, it notes the broader literature covered a wider range of challenges and solutions in material handling.
MHI's Annual Industry Report of 2018	Challenges faced by managers in the material handling industry (2018)	The report highlights the challenges of hiring skilled workers and meeting customer demands. Hiring difficulties indicate a potential shortage of qualified individuals impacting overall efficiency. Meeting customer demands suggests challenges in areas like supply chain complexity and fluctuating market demands. The report emphasizes the need for continuous improvement and compliance with laws and regulations. It's important to note that the information is from 2018, and consulting recent reports is recommended for an accurate understanding of current challenges.
Deshmukh and Bahale (2013)	Case study on inefficiencies in material handling in the manufacturing of ginning machines	The case study identifies inefficiencies in material handling within a ginning machine manufacturing company. It suggests adjustments to the internal material handling system to enhance material flow and overall effectiveness.
Jack (2012)	Case study on supply and material flow management in fertilizer manufacturing	The case study highlights issues with conveyor breakdowns in a fertilizer company's bagging line operation. The problem is caused by fertilizer grains getting stuck in packaging and bagging conveyors, leading to corrosion and conveyor roller failure.

Source: Author

Problem Statement

The vital automobile industries in Kanchipuram, India, crucial for regional economic growth and technological progress, confront a pressing issue. Material handling, a pivotal process influencing production efficiency, product quality, and worker safety, is marred by multifaceted challenges. From managing heavy components to ensuring safety with hazardous materials, addressing ergonomic concerns, and incorporating evolving technologies, employees grapple with obstacles that imperil operational effectiveness and well-being. This study seeks to comprehensively investigate and analyze these challenges, offering insights for strategic interventions and innovative solutions. Failure to address these hurdles may lead to diminished operational efficiency, compromised product quality, increased workplace injuries, and jeopardize the industries' competitiveness globally. The research aims to foster safe and efficient material handling practices, ensuring the sustained growth and prosperity of Kanchipuram's automotive sector.

Objective of the Study

To identify the problems faced by employees in material handling.

Scope of the Study

This study aims to delve into material handling challenges within Kanchipuram's automobile industry. Focusing on issues like handling heavy components, safety, ergonomic concerns, and facility inefficiencies, it explores how this impact efficiency, employee well-being, and industry competitiveness. Limited to Kanchipuram's automotive sector, the research involves qualitative analysis through interviews with managers and employees. It assesses the effects of challenges on production elements and proposes potential solutions, emphasizing local material handling improvement. However, the study excludes broader business aspects and may not reflect future industry changes. It seeks to inform scholars, policymakers, and industry stakeholders about material handling complexities in the regional auto manufacturing industry.

Research Methodology

- Data collection: Primary data is crucial for this research, obtained through effective interviews to gather detailed, participant-specific information. An interview schedule ensures consistency in questioning, providing standardized responses for reliable data.

- Sampling strategy: Convenient sampling proves useful when accessing the entire population is challenging. This approach allows quick data collection from readily available individuals, with 240 workers from Kanchipuram district's automobile companies.
- Analysis framework: Analysis involves employing simple percentages and the weighted average ranking method. These methods aid in systematically evaluating and interpreting the collected data for meaningful insights.

Significance of the Study

The study on material handling challenges in Kanchipuram's automobile industry is pivotal, offering insights and benefits to stakeholders. Addressing these challenges can enhance operational efficiency, streamline production, and optimize resource use. Improved material handling leads to enhanced product quality, reduced faults, and increased customer satisfaction. It also addresses safety concerns, reducing workplace injuries and boosting morale. By tackling these issues, the automotive sector gains a competitive edge, fostering economic growth, job creation, and increased income in Kanchipuram. The study contributes to existing knowledge, guiding future research and informing regulatory bodies. It advocates for advanced technologies, promoting collaboration for positive changes in material handling practices, benefiting operational efficiency, worker safety, and overall economic prosperity in Kanchipuram's automotive sector.

Analysis and Interpretation

In profiling the socio-economic characteristics of respondents and examining the prominent challenges faced by workers in material handling, a comprehensive understanding emerges Brockman et al. (2014). The majority of respondents are male, aged between 25-35 years, and possess undergraduate qualifications, offering a snapshot of the demographic involved Beamon (1998). Transitioning to the challenges, the study identifies critical issues such as time-intensive retrieval of stored goods, redundant rehandling of products, and communication gaps Beason (1999). These challenges, reflected in the weighted average rankings, illuminate areas demanding immediate attention and strategic interventions to enhance material handling practices in Kanchipuram's automobile industries Figura (1996).

Socio-economic profile

- **Gender:** 90.0% of respondents were male, and 10.0% were female Trebilcock (2002).

- **Age:** The largest age group was 25-35 years (28.3%), followed by Up to 25 years (25.0%), 35-45 years (26.7%), and Above 45 years (20.0%).
- **Qualification:** The majority had UG qualifications (42.5%), followed by School level (38.3%) and Others (19.2%).
- **Monthly income:** The highest income range was Rs. 20,000-30,000 (27.5%), with other ranges as below Rs. 20,000 (25.0%), Rs. 30,000-40,000 (23.3%), and Above Rs. 40,000 (24.2%).
- **Experience:** The largest experience group was 2-5 years (51.7%), followed by 5-10 years (20.0%), below 2 years (15.8%), and Above 10 years (12.5%).

Problems faced by workers in material handling

1. **Excessive time spent retrieving stored goods:** Ranked 1st, with a mean score of 4.18 Vallet (1999).
2. **Excessive rehandling of the same product:** Ranked 2nd, with a mean score of 4.17.
3. **Poor communication:** Ranked 3rd, with a mean score of 3.98 Welgama and Gibson (1996).
4. **Excess temporary storage:** Ranked 4th, with a mean score of 3.85.
5. **Inadequate storage:** Ranked 5th, with a mean score of 3.84.
6. **Unused vertical space:** Ranked 6th, with a mean score of 3.59.
7. **Lack of proper machine handling equipment:** Ranked 7th, with a mean score of 3.58.
8. **Excessive bending over to access or work on product:** Ranked 8th, with a mean score of 3.55.
9. **Manual loading or unloading of goods:** Ranked 9th, with a mean score of 3.37.
10. **High damage rate:** Ranked 10th, with a mean score of 3.43.
11. **Back-ups in service departments:** Ranked 11th, with a mean score of 3.18.
12. **Crowded operating conditions:** Ranked 12th, with a mean score of 3.09.
13. **Lack of scalability:** Ranked 13th, with a mean score of 3.08.
14. **Excess handling of single pieces versus unit loads:** Ranked 14th, with a mean score of 3.07.
15. **Lack of skilled labors:** Ranked 15th, with a mean score of 2.65.
16. **Obstacles in material flow:** Ranked 16th, with a mean score of 2.58.
17. **Loading and unloading same time:** Ranked 17th, with a mean score of 2.56.
18. **Excess temporary storage:** Ranked 18th, with a mean score of 2.44.

19. Inventory management: Ranked 19th, with a mean score of 2.44.

The weighted average ranking test indicates that the top three problems faced by workers in material handling are excessive time spent retrieving stored goods, excessive rehandling of the same product, and poor communication. These findings provide valuable insights for addressing challenges and improving material handling practices in the surveyed demographic. The findings reveal significant challenges in material handling for workers in Kanchipuram's automobile sector, with excess time spent on retrieving stored goods, excessive rehandling of products, and communication deficiencies ranking highest. The study identifies key areas for improvement, including the need for efficient storage solutions, streamlined communication, and reduced redundancy in handling procedures. These insights underscore the critical role of effective material handling in enhancing operational efficiency and worker well-being. Addressing these challenges can lead to a more productive and competitive automotive industry in Kanchipuram, benefiting both the workforce and the overall sector.

Conclusion

In addressing the identified challenges of material handling in Kanchipuram's automotive sector, various strategic recommendations emerge. Prioritizing efficient storage systems, streamlined material flow, enhanced communication, ergonomic designs, and investment in proper handling equipment can significantly improve operational efficiency and worker well-being. Additionally, fostering employee training, technology integration, safety protocols, damage reduction measures, and addressing staffing issues are essential steps. These strategies aim to optimize loading/unloading, facilitate continuous improvement, consider environmental sustainability, and foster collaboration with suppliers.

In conclusion, the study underscores the critical issues hindering material handling in Kanchipuram's automotive sector, impacting productivity, safety, and competitiveness. Implementing the proposed strategies is crucial for long-term success and growth, ensuring the industry's continued prominence in India's automotive landscape. The study's significance lies in guiding stakeholders towards specialized solutions, fostering collaboration, and transforming material handling challenges into strategic advantages for the region's automotive industry.

The future scope involves quantitative analysis, exploring advanced technologies, creative problem-solving approaches, comparative studies, longitudinal assessments, environmental impact studies, skill development, supply chain optimization, employee engagement, and staying updated on technological advancements. This ongoing research will further elevate the industry's operational excellence and technological leadership.

References

Beamon, B. M. (1998). Performance, reliability, and performability of material handling systems. *International Journal of Production Research*, 36(2), 377–393. DOI: 10.1080/002075498193796.

Beason, M. (1999). Here is a new material handling solution. *Textile World*, 149(2), 61–63.

Brockman, P., French, D., and Tamm, C. (2014). REIT organizational structure, institutional ownership, and stock performance. *Journal of Real Estate Portfolio Management*, 20(1), 21–36.

Deshmukh, S. S., and Bahale, A. P. (2013). Inefficiencies in material handling and alternatives for their improvement in a ginning machine manufacturing company.

Drum, D. (2009). Asset tracking: material handling benefits. *Material Handling Management*, 64(6), 36–38.

Figura, S. Z. (1996). Reducing the risk of material handling. *Occupational Hazards*, 58(8), 30–32.

Mohan Bala, B. A., and Velumoni, D. (2022). A study on challenges faced in material handling management at manufacturing industries Chennai. *International Journal of Current Research and Techniques (IJCRT)*, 10(5), ISSN: 2320-2882.

Trebilcock, B. (2002). Modern materials handling. *ABI/INFORM Global*, 57(14), 29.

Vallet, M. (1999). Better material handling improves work flow. *Fused Deposition Modelling (FDM)*, 71(14), 74.

Welgama, P. S., and Gibson, P. R. (1996). An integrated methodology for automating the determination of layout and materials handling system. *International Journal of Production Research*, 34(1), 2247–2264.

64 A study on employees' work-life balance in engineering industries with special reference to Dindigul

Mohan Kumar, G., Saritha Mol, K. K.[a], Ebenezer Paul Rajan T. Y.[b], Easwaran, P.[c] and P. Soni Pawar[d]

Karpagam Academy of Higher Education, Coimbatore, Tamil Nadu, India

Abstract

The pursuit of work-life balance, a multifaceted concept within human resource management, involves harmonizing various facets of an individual's existence. This study explores the nuanced dynamics of achieving this equilibrium, particularly within the context of Engineering Industries in Dindigul, encompassing a sample of 150 individuals through convenience sampling and a descriptive study methodology. The findings suggest that the organization, cognizant of its personnel's professional development, has successfully maintained a manageable workload by equitably distributing tasks among staff members. The workplace is conducive, prioritizing both family and job responsibilities equally. Recommendations emanating from the study advocate the expansion of work-life programs to mitigate conflicts between family and work. Moreover, the proposal to formulate and implement a comprehensive work life balance policy focuses on the organization's commitment to fostering an environment where employees can adeptly navigate their professional and personal realms. In essence, the majority of employees demonstrate adeptness in balancing these spheres, illuminating a positive correlation between organizational initiatives and the successful management of work and personal life.

Keywords: Dindigul, employees, engineering Industries, work-life balance

Introduction

In today's high-demand workplaces, particularly in industries like engineering, achieving work-life balance is crucial for employees' well-being, job satisfaction, and productivity. Focusing on the challenging engineering sector in Dindigul, this study showcases the dynamics of work-life balance, considering the industry's long hours, strict standards, and tight deadlines. Understanding the variables influencing balance becomes paramount in this context. The study aims to investigate these factors, identify areas for improvement, and provide valuable guidance for organisations and individuals in promoting work-life balance. Dindigul's expanding engineering businesses offer a unique backdrop for this research, allowing an assessment of prospects and challenges tied to work-life balance. By gathering insights through a comprehensive survey covering various workplace aspects, the study anticipates offering valuable information to enhance policies and procedures for better work-life balance. Ultimately, the research contributes to the understanding of work-life balance in Dindigul's engineering sector, aspiring to foster a more harmonious and effective workplace.

Review of Literature

Table 64.1 Insights on work-life balance: a comparative overview of key findings and inferences from multiple studies.

Author name	Study findings	Inferences
Tirta, et al. (2020)	Job happiness, healthy work-life balance, and rewards significantly boost employee retention. Keeping employees on staff reduces training and recruitment costs, requiring less effort to find new talent.	Enhancing job satisfaction through factors like happiness, work-life balance, and recognition can positively impact employee retention, leading to cost savings for training and recruitment.
Irawanto et al. (2021)	Working from home, work-life balance, and work stress negatively impact job satisfaction. Working from home can positively affect job satisfaction in Indonesia's collectivist climate.	Remote work has both negative and positive effects on job satisfaction. While it may increase stress and negatively impact work-life balance, it can also be beneficial, especially in a collectivist culture like Indonesia's.

[a]sarithasabitha@gmail.com, [b]drebenezerpaulrajan.ty@kahedu.edu.in, [c]easwar83@gmail.com, [d]sonipawar2008@gmail.com

Author name	Study findings	Inferences
Oyibo (2020)	Work-life balance is crucial for employee performance. Systemic obstacles in Nigeria, including leadership failure and socio-economic issues, hinder the implementation of work-life balance policies.	Achieving work-life balance is vital for employee performance. However, challenges in Nigeria, such as leadership failures and socio-economic issues, impede the effective implementation of policies to address work-life imbalance.
Otuya (2020)	Globalized economies and changes like work impact work-life balance. Balancing personal and professional obligations is challenging, affecting employee satisfaction.	The evolving nature of work in a globalized economy poses challenges for achieving work-life balance. Balancing personal and professional obligations is crucial for employee satisfaction and requires effective strategies from both employers and employees.

Source: Author

Need for the Study

Satisfied employees, considered valuable assets for any organization, play a pivotal role in enhancing productivity; however, factors such as challenges in balancing work and personal life, the impact of job position on this balance, and the influence of long working hours on individual efficiency presses the need for a comprehensive study to identify and address these dynamics within the workforce.

Objectives of the Study

- To study employees' work-life balance with special reference to Engineering Industries, Dindigul.
- To examine the demographic profile of the respondents.
- To determine the impact of work-life balance on employee job satisfaction and work performance.

Research Methodology

Primary data
- Conducted personal interviews and prepared questionnaires.
- Majority of questions had multiple-choice answers.
- Utilized a structured interviewing technique.
- Employed both Tamil and English during interviews.
- Considered employees' educational backgrounds in presenting the interview schedule.

Secondary data
- Derived from earlier sources, including studies and surveys.
- Also includes data from tests conducted by other parties.

- Utilized various sources such as the Internet, books, journals, and company records to gather secondary data.

Tools used for analysis
- Percentage method
- ANOVA test
- Factor analysis

Analysis

Demographic profile of respondents
Interpretation: The majority (76%) of the respondents are male.

Interpretation: The majority of respondents are over 45 years old.

Interpretation: The majority (82%) of respondents are married.

Table 64.2 Gender.

Gender	No. of respondents	Percentage
Male	114	76.0
Female	36	24.0
Total	150	100.0

Source: Author

Table 64.3 Age.

Education	No. of respondents	Percentage
Up to 25 years	20	13.3
25 - 35 years	9	6.0
36 - 45 years	59	39.3
Above 45 years	62	41.3
Total	150	100.0

Source: Author

Table 64.4 Marital status.

Particulars	No. of respondents	Percentage
Married	123	82.0
Unmarried	27	18.0
Total	150	100.0

Source: Author

Table 64.5 Shift timing segregations.

Income	No. of respondents	Percentage
7.00 am - 3.30 pm	62	41.3
9.00 am - 6.00 pm	63	42.0
3.30 pm - 12.00 am	25	16.7
Total	150	100.0

Source: Author

Interpretation: The majority work the 9.00 am - 6.00 pm shift.

Interpretation: The majority of responders are quite satisfied with their workplace.

One way ANOVA test

- Marital status and family/personal life impact on job performance
- Between groups: 0.072, within groups: 1217.868
- Significance: 0.789
- Interpretation: Accepting null hypothesis; no significant impact of marital status on family/personal life interference with job performance.

Work life balance – factor analysis
KMO and Bartlett's test

- KMO:.838
- Bartlett's Test: Chi-Square: 4603.221, df: 780, Sig:.000
- Interpretation: Data suitable for factor analysis based on KMO and Bartlett's Test.

Rotated component matrix

Factors/components contributing significantly to work life balance include

- Company culture
- Supervision and leadership
- Job autonomy
- Training and development
- Work hours
- Compensation and benefits
- Career advancement opportunities
- Health and wellness programs
- Job security and more

Table 64.6 Location of the workplace.

Particulars	No. of respondents	Percentage
Highly satisfied	43	28.7
Satisfied	23	15.3
Neutral	32	21.3
Dissatisfied	26	17.3
Highly dissatisfied	26	17.3
Total	150	100.0

Source: Author

Cumulative percentage of these factors: 73.169%.

Interpretation: These factors contribute significantly to employees' Work-Life Balance.

Summary

The demographic profile indicates a predominantly male, older, and married respondent base, with the majority working the 9.00 am - 6.00 pm shift and expressing satisfaction with their workplace. The ANOVA test suggests no significant impact of marital status on family/personal life interference with job performance. Factor analysis identifies key contributors to Work-Life Balance, with a cumulative percentage of 73.169%. The findings provide valuable insights into organizational strategies and employee well-being.

Recommendations

Organizational suggestions

- Cultivate an employee-focused culture by promoting well-being programs, diversity, and work-life balance initiatives, emphasizing corporate culture's importance.
- Stress the significance of conducive physical and social workplace environments, fostering collaborative, secure spaces to enhance employee relationships.
- Acknowledge the focus on policy, personal values, and well-being by adjusting rules to aid stress management, self-care, and work-life balance, aligning with employee needs.
- Tailor benefit plans and training courses based on factor analysis outcomes, addressing employee preferences such as technology, career development, and health.
- Improve working conditions by actively seeking employee feedback and maintaining open communication channels.
- Enhance or provide support programs for family responsibilities, acknowledging the significance of childcare and elder care assistance.

Employee suggestions:

- Assess personal principles aligning with job roles and seek organizations sharing similar values or aligning with personal beliefs.
- Prioritize self-care and stress management by dedicating time to hobbies, meditation, and activities improving well-being.
- Utilize training opportunities for career advancement to enhance skills and boost promotion prospects.
- Develop time management skills for a balanced personal and professional life.
- Maintain open communication with supervisors and colleagues to address workload concerns and improve the working environment.
- Discuss flexible work options with employers for better work-life balance.
- Utilize employer-provided programs for elder care, childcare, and health.
- Establish a network of allies within and outside the workplace for support.

Remember, achieving work-life balance is dynamic. Regular evaluation and adaptation of strategies by both organizations and individuals are crucial for effective alignment between work and life. Factor analysis findings serve as a starting point for this process.

Conclusion

In conclusion, the findings derived from the factor analysis conducted on work-life balance and working conditions within the engineering sectors of the Dindigul region provide valuable insights for both organizations and individuals. The results focus on the pivotal role of a supportive corporate culture characterized by robust supervision, effective leadership, job autonomy, training opportunities, fair compensation, and health initiatives. The cultivation and sustenance of such cultures should be a top priority for organizations seeking to enhance the well-being and job satisfaction of their workforce. By prioritizing the establishment of conducive work environments, organizations can foster a positive atmosphere that empowers employees to maintain a healthy balance between their professional and personal lives.

Furthermore, the study highlights the multifaceted influences on work-life balance, encompassing both physical and social aspects of the workplace. Access to modern equipment, pleasant working environments, transparent performance evaluations, and positive colleague connections emerge as crucial factors in promoting better employee performance. Aligning personal values, well-being practices, and compliance with organizational standards further contributes to achieving an optimal work-life balance. In light of these findings, organizations and individuals alike are encouraged to consider cultural norms, support systems for childcare and elder care, self-care initiatives, and stress management activities. In essence, the analysis provides a roadmap for stakeholders in the Dindigul engineering sectors, emphasizing the symbiotic relationship between supportive cultures, favorable workplace conditions, and individual well-being in the pursuit of an improved work-life balance.

References

Bataineh, K. A. (2019). Impact of work-life balance, happiness at work, on employee performance. *International Business Research*, 12(2), 99–112.

Darko-Asumadu, D. A., Sika-Bright, S., and Osei-Tutu, B. (2019). The influence of work-life balance on employees' commitment among bankers in Accra, Ghana. *African Journal of Social Work*, 8(1), 47–55.

Hussain, A. H. M. B., and Endut, N. (2019). Do decent working conditions contribute to work-life balance: a study of small enterprises in Bangladesh. *Global Business Management Research*, 6(1), 1–15.

Khan, O. F., and Sajidkirmani, M. (2019). Impact of work environment on work-life interface of women employees. *International Journal of Linguistics and Literature (IJLL)*, 7(4), 47–58.

Oludayo, O. A., Falola, H. O., Obianuju, H., and Demilade, F. (2019). Work-life balance initiatives as a predictor of employees' behavioral outcomes. *Academy of Strategic Management Journal*, 17(1), 1–17.

Pathak, A. (2019). Work-life balance and job satisfaction: a literature review. *International Journal of Computer Sciences and Engineering*, 7(3), 182–187.

Wong, P., Bandar, N. F. A., and Saili, J. (2019). Workplace factors and work-life balance among employees in selected services sector. *International Journal of Business and Society*, 18(1), 677–684.

65 A study on the perception of consumers with supply chain processing at Titanium pigments industry

Thiyakarajan, M., Geetha Bai[a], Ramadevi, V.[b], Easwaran, P.[c] and Soni Pawar, P.[d]

Karpagam Academy of Higher Education, Coimbatore, Tamil Nadu, India

Abstract

Within the intricate domains of industries like paints, coatings, plastics, and cosmetics, the titanium pigments market stands as a linchpin, demanding meticulous supply chain management. This academic exploration dives into consumer perceptions of supply chain processes in the titanium pigments sector, employing a mixed-methods research approach. Through in-depth interviews with supply chain specialists, industry experts, and stakeholders, coupled with a structured survey targeting consumers of titanium pigments-based products like paints, the study aims to fathom the nuances of supply chain efficiency and its impact on customer satisfaction. Addressing critical facets such as customer perceptions of supply chain responsiveness, dependability, and sustainability, along with preferences for eco-friendly production and transparent sourcing, the outcomes promise insights for refining processes, optimal resource allocation, and elevating customer contentment. Consequently, aligning supply chain practices with consumer expectations positions the titanium pigments sector for sustained growth and heightened global competitiveness.

Keywords: Consumer perception, consumer satisfaction, eco-friendly sourcing, supply chain efficiency, supply chain processing, titanium pigments, transparency

Introduction

Supply chain management (SCM) is the intricate orchestration of goods flowing from suppliers to customers with the primary goal of reducing overall costs through efficient coordination across the supply chain echelons. This involves employing analytical tools and optimization software, as detailed in academic journals and market resources. Interviews with senior management from prominent companies in Iceland and India reveal challenges in SCM implementation Lambert and Cooper (2000). Varied perceptions among departments, such as marketing, logistics, and manufacturing, lead to biased data input into SCM tools, compromising their effectiveness and fostering blame between departments.

The supply chain is a multifaceted network encompassing individuals, organizations, resources, activities, and technologies involved in producing and selling a product or service. SCM, introduced by Keith Oliver in 1982, has become a management buzzword, emphasizing integrated business processes to create value. Logistics, a vital SCM component, manages the flow of goods and information between entities, playing a pivotal role in post-procurement processes, Cooper et al. (1997). Addressing SCM challenges requires recognizing the interconnected nature of the supply chain, where decisions in one part impact the entire system. Effective SCM implementation is crucial for cost optimization and heightened customer satisfaction, urging companies to foster collaboration among departments for supply chain-wide success Table 65.1.

Review of Literature

Table 65.1 Insights into supply chain management: perspectives, challenges, and collaborative strategies from leading authors.

Author name	Problem statement	Insights
Ellram and Copper (2019)	SCM aligns perspectives into a cohesive entity, ensuring synchronization within and between firms, reducing betrayal risks through transparent information sharing.	SCM integrates perspectives, emphasizing transparency to reduce betrayal risks.

[a]geethabhojan@gmail.com, [b]drramadevi77@gmail.com, [c]easwar83@gmail.com, [d]sonipawar2008@gmail.com

Bowersox and Closs (2019)	In the modern market, integrating customers and suppliers is vital for competitiveness. SCM involves coordinating diverse participants, with essential information sharing for effective integration.	SCM necessitates integrating customers and suppliers, emphasizing information sharing's importance.
Pagh (2020)	Effective SCM requires equal stakes in risks and rewards among supply chain members, fostering cooperation for sustained industry motion.	SCM's effectiveness relies on equal stakes, cooperation, and a common objective for supply chain participants.
Drozdowski (2020)	Production cost reduction demands SCM policies, synchronized cooperation, and long-term relationships among supply chain partners. Synchronization from suppliers to distribution is crucial for SCM implementation.	SCM implementation requires synchronized cooperation, long-term relationships, and policies to reduce production costs.
Tyndall et al. (2021)	Meeting consumer expectations requires close collaboration, utilizing recent technologies. Definitions of SCM vary, and the supply chain concept predates its formal definition.	SCM requires collaboration and technology for meeting consumer expectations. Definitions vary, and the supply chain concept precedes SCM's formal definition.

Source: Author

Objectives of the Study

- To know about the customer perception towards the supply chain management system of the pigments company
- To assess the problems faced by the customer in the supply chain management process.

Research Design

This research follows a descriptive research design.

Sampling Design

The researcher has used convenience sampling to collect data.

Methodology

An extent of 120 respondents were picked using a multistage stratified purposive sampling procedure.

Data Sources

Primary data: A well-structured questionnaire has been used to collect primary data from the respondents.

Secondary data: Data is gathered from various sources such as internet campaigns, research articles, magazines, newspapers, etc.

Statistical Tools

The following statistical tools were employed in the research: Simple percentage analysis, correlation, ANOVA, and T-test.

Findings and Analysis

This analysis explores key correlations and associations within a business environment, focusing on the dynamics between years of experience, satisfaction levels, and positions within a company. Utilizing statistical tools such as Pearson correlation, ANOVA, and T-Test, the study aims to unravel intricate relationships. The findings shed light on how experience influences perceptions, the interplay between customer satisfaction and product presentation, and the impact of organizational positions on opinions about service quality.

Demographic features: The demographic profile of the respondents reveals that 81.7% are male, while 18.3% are female. In terms of age, the majority (44.2%) fall in the 41-50 years range. Regarding positions in the company, 40% of respondents work as workers, followed by foremen (30.8%) and quality controllers (18.3%). In terms of income, 40% fall in the Rs. 5,000 – Rs. 10,000 range.

Perception of supply chain process

Examining the respondents' perception of the supply chain process, 45.0% consider it primarily as a relationship with the customer, while 32.5% perceive it as an internal operation. The least emphasized aspect is collective efficacy, with only 7.5% of respondents acknowledging its importance.

Minimizing fill rate time and delivery activity

When evaluating the company's efforts to avoid delays in customer deliveries, 52.5% of respondents believe that timely delivery is achieved. Regarding delivery activities, 42.5% rate it as good, while 19.2% consider it excellent. These findings suggest a positive perception of the company's delivery efficiency.

Consumer risk policy and quality of service:

In terms of consumer risk policy, 30.0% of respondents are highly satisfied, and 31.7% are satisfied.

Regarding the quality of service, 37.5% find it average, with 22.5% considering it excellent. This indicates a mixed perception of consumer risk policies and service quality.

Factors in effective production and supply chain relationships

Respondents identify the reliability of supply as the key factor (45.0%) ineffective production and supply chain relationships, followed by trust (25.0%) and top management support (25.0%). Mutual interest is considered the least significant factor, with only 5.0% of respondents emphasizing its importance.

Logistics operation and cost

Concerning logistics operations, 57.5% of respondents view their company's operations as efficient. In terms of logistics cost compared to industry standards, 60% find it high, while 24.2% perceive it as very high. These results suggest a need for cost optimization in logistics.

Supply chain department challenges

When evaluating challenges faced by the supply chain department, 39% of respondents highlight problems during storage, followed by packaging (39.2%). Testing of packaging and evaluation of defective raw materials are considered challenges by 19.2% and 9.2% of respondents, respectively.

Product presentation to the customer

The process quality for better product presentation is perceived positively, with 37.5% rating it as excellent. An additional 35.8% find it good, indicating a generally favorable opinion regarding product presentation.

Level of usage with customer perception

In terms of level of usage with customer perception in supply chain management, 45.8% of respondents exhibit very high usage in E-commerce, while 34.1% express very high usage in inbound transportation. Outbound transportation and freight forwarding also receive significant endorsements for very high usage.

Principal objectives in developing production

The principal objectives in developing production and supply chain collaboration are generally well-received. Notably, 53.3% strongly agree that benefits to the client are a crucial objective, followed by improved customer service (51.7%). Overall supply chain cost reduction is strongly agreed upon by 43.3% of respondents.

Correlation analysis: years of experience and opinion about quality of service

The table indicates a strong positive correlation (Pearson's r = 0.874, p < 0.01) between years of experience and the opinion about the quality of service. Both Kendall's tau_b and Spearman's rho also confirm a significant correlation (p < 0.01), reinforcing the positive relationship. These findings suggest that as the years of experience increase, respondents tend to hold a more positive opinion about the quality of service.

ANOVA analysis: satisfaction level of customer on time taken for delivery and quality for better product presentation to the customer

The null hypothesis (Ho) stating no significant relationship is rejected in favor of the alternative hypothesis (H1), suggesting a significant relationship between customer satisfaction with delivery time and the quality of product presentation. The Levene test indicates unequal variances among groups (p < 0.05). The F-value of 345.211 is highly significant (p < 0.01), affirming the existence of a relationship. Multiple comparisons reveal significant mean differences across all groups, emphasizing the relationship between satisfaction level and product presentation quality.

T-Test: position of the company and opinion about quality of service

The T-Test results support the alternative hypothesis (H1) that there is a significant relationship between the position of the company and the opinion about the quality of service. The calculated t-values for both variables are highly significant (p < 0.01), indicating a positive relationship. This suggests that individuals in different positions within the company hold varying opinions about the quality of service.

Results

Years of experience and quality of service opinion
Strong positive correlations (Pearson, Kendall, and Spearman) suggest that as respondents gain more experience, their opinions about the quality of service become more favorable.

Satisfaction level and product presentation

The ANOVA results reject the null hypothesis, confirming a significant relationship between customer satisfaction with delivery time and the quality of product presentation. Variances among groups indicate the need for attention to specific areas of improvement.

Position of the company and quality of service opinion
The T-Test supports the alternative hypothesis, establishing a significant relationship between the position of the company and opinions about service quality. This implies that different roles within the company influence perceptions of service quality.

Inferences

The examination of correlations between years of experience and opinions about service quality reveals a strong positive relationship, evident through significant Pearson, Kendall's tau_b, and Spearman's rho coefficients. This implies that as experience increases, so does a positive perception of service quality. In terms of customer satisfaction and product presentation, an ANOVA analysis suggests a significant relationship Cooper and Ellram (1993). The T-Test further corroborates this, indicating a strong association between the position within a company and opinions about service quality.

Additionally, the study uncovers that respondents with higher experience levels exhibit more positive opinions about service quality. In the context of customer satisfaction and timely delivery, the findings showcase that efficient logistics operations positively impact customer satisfaction Drozdowski (1986). Furthermore, the analysis identifies a noteworthy relationship between the position of the company and opinions about service quality, indicating that individuals in certain positions may perceive service quality differently. Overall, these insights provide a nuanced understanding of the intricate dynamics influencing opinions, satisfaction levels, and organizational roles within the studied business environment.

Recommendations

Here are the recommendations from this study based on the results and analysis:

- Supply chain management success hinges on transparency; employing blockchain technology allows traceability from raw materials to final products, fostering trust.
- Establishing closer ties with suppliers is crucial for effective supply chain management.
- Utilize advanced technologies like AI and machine learning for accurate demand forecasting.
- Develop a robust risk management strategy to mitigate potential disruptions in the supply chain.
- Invest in collaborative platforms for real-time communication to address issues, manage inventory efficiently, and adapt to changes promptly.

- Regularly assess the supply chain for inefficiencies using lean management or Six Sigma strategies.
- Share information about the supply chain's complexity with consumers to build transparency.
- Ensure an efficient communication system within the supply chain.
- Well-trained and motivated staff significantly impact supply chain efficiency.
- Supply chain management is an ongoing process requiring continuous adaptation and improvement.

Supply chain management is an ongoing process that requires adaptation and continuous improvement. By implementing the above suggestions, the company can enhance supply chain's efficiency, resilience, and the overall perception consumers have about supply chain management efforts of companies.

Conclusion

In conclusion, the exploration into supply chain management practices within the examined pigment manufacturing company has unveiled a commendable landscape of effective strategies. The company not only exhibits established practices but also demonstrates a commitment to innovation in supply chain operations. Despite these strengths, critical areas, particularly concerning consumer relations and quality management, have emerged as focal points for improvement. This acknowledgment suggests a proactive approach by the company toward refining customer satisfaction and ensuring product quality.

Looking ahead, the company's forward-thinking approach involves the adoption of green supply chain measures, signaling a strategic response to evolving challenges. This prospective initiative aligns with contemporary sustainability goals, showcasing the company's commitment to responsible business practices. In essence, while celebrating existing successes in supply chain management, this study highlights the imperative for continual improvement and adaptation. By addressing identified concerns and embracing environmentally conscious strategies, the company positions itself not only for operational resilience but also for contributing positively to broader industry and societal objectives.

References

Aguezzoul, A. (2019). Use of artificial intelligence in supply chain management pactices and 3PL selection. 17(4), 272–290.

Barreto, L., Amaral, A., and Pereira, T. (2017). Industry 4.0 implications in logistics: an overview. *Procedia Manufacturing*, 13, 1245–1252.

Cooper, M. C., Lambert, D. M., and Pagh, J. D. (1997). Supply chain management: more than a new name for logistics. *The International Journal of Logistics Management*, 8(1), 1–14.

Cooper, M. C., and Ellram, L. M. (1993). Characteristics of supply chain management and the implications for purchasing and logistics strategy. *The International Journal of Logistics Management*, 4(2), 13–24.

Drozdowski, T. E. (1986). At BOC they start with the product. *Purchasing*, 62(2), 5–11.

Ellram, L. M., and Cooper, M. C. (1990). Supply chain management, partnership, and the shipper-third party relationship. *The International Journal of Logistics Management*, 1(2), 1–1.

Grover, P. (2020). Understanding artificial intelligence adoption in operations management – insights from the review of academic literature and social media discussions. *Journal of Business Logistics*, 22(2), 1–25.

Lambert, D. M., and Cooper, M. C. (2000). Issues in supply chain management. *Industrial Marketing Management*, 29(1), 65–83.

Uckelmann, D. (2008). A definition approach to smart logistics. In International Conference on Next Generation Wired/Wireless Networking, (pp. 273–284). Springer, Berlin, Heidelberg.

66 A comparative analysis on consumer awareness and willingness to use solar energy in the Ranipet district

Chandirasekar, B. and Karan, M.

Saveetha College of Liberal Arts and Sciences Saveetha Institute of Medical and Technical Sciences, Chennai, Tamil Nadu, India

Abstract

Solar energy is a sustainable resource that has impacted every aspect of human existence globally. The Indian government launched the Jawaharlal Nehru National Solar Mission (JNNSM) on January 11, 2010, aiming to promote the adoption of solar power. The energy landscape in India has undergone significant transformation due to solar power in recent years. Decentralized and distributed applications of solar energy have brought numerous benefits to millions of individuals in Indian communities, providing lighting, cooking, and other energy needs in an eco-friendly manner. Despite challenges, the populace in India is gradually transitioning from traditional energy sources to renewable solar energy. This research aimed to assess public awareness of government solar energy initiatives and individual knowledge about solar power. A closed-ended questionnaire was administered both online and offline to gather data from residents in the study area. In an online survey conducted in the Ranipet district of Tamil Nadu, 100 participants were involved. The study hypothesis was tested using the Chi-square test, revealing that while residents are aware of solar energy systems, they have not yet embraced the transition from conventional to solar power. It is imperative for the government and other entities to take appropriate measures to encourage individuals to adopt cost-effective, renewable solar energy systems.

Keywords: Awareness on solar energy, renewable energy, solar energy

Introduction of the Study

In essence, solar energy represents the process wherein sunlight is converted into electric power through the use of solar panels. Employing lenses, mirrors, and tracking systems, sunlight is harnessed, directly or indirectly, for utilization in photovoltaic (PV) and concentrated solar power (CSP) applications. The integration of automatic solar irrigation systems has facilitated the widespread deployment of solar panels on various infrastructures such as roads, traffic lights, and street lighting, reflecting the everyday use of solar energy by many individuals. The significance of green energy in reducing environmental impact has garnered considerable research attention globally (Sangroya and Nayak, 2017). Solar systems not only contribute to environmental preservation but also offer on-demand electricity for residential roofs and walls. By harnessing renewable resources, solar power generation reduces reliance on coal-based energy production. Moreover, energy storage in batteries ensures uninterrupted power supply during adverse weather conditions and winter months. Shortening the electricity supply chain by eliminating the need for electric transformers aids in enhancing system efficiency and mitigating electrical accidents, thereby presenting expanded employment opportunities for electrical engineers.

There has been an observable alteration in consumer consciousness regarding solar power and its benefits, as evidenced by research on consumer awareness of solar energy adoption (Consumer Awareness in Solar Energy: Workshop Proceedings, 1978). According to empirical evidence, attitudes, ecological awareness, subjective standards, perceived behavioural control, and perceptions of solar energy benefits all exert a favourable influence on consumers' intentions to procure solar energy. Conversely, environmental apprehensions did not significantly affect purchasing intentions for solar energy (Asif et al., 2023). The results suggest that consumers in rural regions of Pakistan are inclined and have the intention to utilise solar energy and biofuels for both domestic and commercial purposes. Moreover, these findings corroborate similar findings from Malaysia, indicating that branding, economic factors, and philanthropic motives significantly impact Pakistani consumers' willingness to adopt solar panels and biofuel. Additionally, significant attributes include ease of use, quality of retailer service, and comprehension of climate change (Yin et al., 2023). The study reveals that consumers' choices regarding the adoption of renewable energy are influenced by emotional and societal factors, alongside financial considerations (Sangroya and Nayak, 2017). The findings confirm that cost, performance, and

ªSmartgenpublications2@gmail.com

governmental initiatives strongly influence consumer purchasing decisions. However, factors such as environmentally friendly products, company and product information, environmental concerns, and social influence were deemed less significant (Kumar et al., 2019). Consumer intention to purchase is notably affected by attitude, perceived behavioural control, and energy-related concerns. Conversely, subjective norms and energy awareness were found to be less significant (Fathima et al., 2022). One reason for the pursuit of energy storage in the Indian context is an unreliable power grid. Furthermore, there exists a considerable capacity for captive power generation from sources like wind, biomass, diesel generators, and others. Achieving the objectives of the solar mission may be feasible through the integration of solar with such sources (Ravindra, 2017). The rationale behind the study is that garnering acceptance in commercial and residential sectors necessitates more than just economic incentives (Ravindra, 2017). Implementing regulations that incentivise residential users to adopt solar power and reduce greenhouse gas emissions is feasible and offers long-term benefits for the economy, society, and environment (Sommerfeld et al., 2017). The findings lend support to the idea that recipients' contentment is positively influenced by environmental perception. Additionally, perceived quality positively affects beneficiaries' satisfaction and trust in the state grid. However, social influence negatively impacts beneficiaries' satisfaction, while behaviour expectation directly bolsters satisfaction and indirectly supports trust in the state grid (Ding et al., 2021).

The absence of governmental regulations supporting EE/RE, the dearth of information dissemination and consumer awareness regarding energy and EE/RE, the elevated expenses associated with solar and other EE/RE technologies in contrast to traditional energy sources, and insufficient financial resources for EE/RE projects were identified as some of the most frequently mentioned obstacles (Margolis, 2006). "A renewable energy awareness scale" was devised to evaluate individuals' comprehension of renewable energy, acknowledging the importance of sustainable and renewable energy sources. A pilot study utilised a 50-item questionnaire known as the Renewable Energy Awareness Scale. Through factor analysis, a 39-item scale was devised, demonstrating a reliability coefficient of 0.944 (Morgil et al., 2006). The primary aim of this research was to assess consumers' level of awareness concerning solar energy, their inclination towards transitioning from conventional sources to solar energy, and their familiarity with government initiatives aimed at promoting solar energy. The initial segment of this manuscript outlines the study's

introduction and objectives. Subsequently, previous research findings are reviewed, followed by an elucidation of the research methodology employed. The concluding section deliberates on the analysis of this investigation.

Materials and Methods

The methodology and processes employed to conduct the investigation's research and evaluate its primary proposition are divulged in this segment of the document. There exist two hypotheses formulated to execute this examination, namely H1:H0: The implementation of solar power is not statistically associated with any demographic factors. H2: H0: There exists no statistical correlation between Awareness concerning solar energy systems and the adoption of solar energy. A modest sample survey of 100 individuals within the study locale was conducted due to uncertainty regarding the extent of solar energy usage. An internet-based questionnaire was employed to disseminate a sequence of predetermined surveys and collect essential primary data. Additionally, Cronbach's alpha test was executed to authenticate the precision and dependability of the survey questionnaire (Tsartsou et al., 2021), yielding an alpha coefficient value of 0.78. The null hypothesis was scrutinised via the Chi-square test, while simple percentage analysis was utilised to showcase primary data in tabular formats.

Findings and Discussion

Table 66.1 revealed demographic factors of the participants within the surveyed area, indicating that the bulk of individuals in the sample were males aged below 30 years, as per the outcomes of the investigation. Furthermore, the predominant proportion consisted of graduates and individuals without employment who partook in the survey. It comes as a surprise that merely 15% of the respondents have implemented solar power systems in their premises. Additionally, findings unveiled that the majority of participants possessed a profound understanding of the benefits associated with solar energy installations and government-sponsored initiatives aimed at promoting renewable energy sources. Most of them agreed with the assertions outlined in the questionnaire, affirming that solar power leads to reduced maintenance expenses, represents a sustainable energy source, can be integrated into various sections of a building, offers opportunities for surplus energy sale, and enhances the property value of buildings equipped with solar panels.

While there exists a heightened consciousness regarding solar energy systems within the surveyed

Table 66.1 Cross tabulation of demographic factors and solar energy installation behavior.

S. No.	Demographic factors	Category	Solar energy installed		Total
			Yes	No	
1	Gender	Male	11	60	71
		Female	5	24	29
2	Age group	Below 20	7	24	31
		21 to 30	2	25	27
		31 to 40	5	15	20
		41 to 50	1	18	19
		Above 50	1	2	3
3	Place of residence	Rural	9	49	58
		Urban	7	35	42
4	Educational level	Upto 12	3	15	18
		UG degree	8	47	55
		PG degree	4	20	24
		None	1	2	3
5	Income level p.m.	Upto 15,000	2	6	8
		15,001 to 30,000	6	9	15
		30,001 to 45,000	1	11	12
		Above 45,000	2	18	20
		None	5	40	45
6	Nature of employment	Daily wages	1	2	3
		Own business	2	6	8
		Agriculture	1	1	2
		Salaried group	5	34	39
		Students/others	7	41	48

Source: Primary data

Table 66.2 Results of the Chi-square test between the behaviour of solar energy installation and the demographic factors.

S. No.	Demographic variable	*p*- value	Significant level	Result
1	Age group	0.200	0.05	Insignificant
2	Gender	0.829	0.05	Insignificant
3	Educational qualification	0.856	0.05	Insignificant
4	Monthly income	0.067	0.05	Insignificant
5	Place of residence	0.877	0.05	Insignificant
6	Nature of employment	0.519	0.05	Insignificant

Source: Author

region, surprisingly, only approximately half of the participants indicated a willingness to transition from conventional energy sources to solar power Table 66.2. This reluctance stems from their prior financial investment in the existing system, signifying a high level of comfort and apprehension towards the supplementary expenses associated with adopting solar energy. The solar industry faces numerous challenges, encompassing grid connectivity infrastructure, regulatory shifts, capacity utilization, initial capital outlay, limited financing options, and consumer receptivity (Kar et al., 2016). The outcomes of the chi-square analysis revealed no significant correlation between demographic variables and solar energy adoption. Additionally, it was evident that individuals' attitudes and perceptions regarding the benefits of solar energy influenced their decision-making more than demographic factors. Furthermore, no statistical association was found between knowledge of solar energy systems and their installation.

Conclusion

People desire to implement and utilize solar power due to its dependable and sustainable nature. Through the dissemination of the subsidy programme via online platforms, print media, direct outreach, and television adverts, the government aims to motivate the populace, encouraging both urban and rural residents to adopt solar energy. Presently, many individuals express concerns regarding their financial stability and employment prospects. Should the populace embrace solar energy installation, it would create employment opportunities, particularly for the youth. Research indicates that while individuals possess awareness of solar energy, they remain uncertain about the associated costs and are unaware of available government subsidies. Simultaneously, knowledgeable individuals seek to provide clear guidance to novices regarding the benefits of solar energy systems and the installation process. As part of its corporate social responsibility endeavours, the company must take proactive steps to provide this service directly to residents of urban and rural areas at their doorsteps. Ultimately, people's decisions will be influenced more by their perceptions and feelings towards the benefits of solar energy systems rather than demographic variables. Given that solar energy is a natural resource, it is imperative to harness it for the preservation of nature and the environment.

Reference

Asif, M. H., Zhongfu, T., Ahmad, B., Irfan, M., Razzaq, A., and Ameer, W. (2023). Influencing factors of consumers' buying intention of solar energy: a structural equation modeling approach. *Environmental Science and Pollution Research International*, 30(11), 30017–30032.

Consumer Awareness in Solar Energy: Workshop Proceedings. 1978.

Ding, L., Shi, Y., He, C., Dai, Q., Zhang, Z., Li, J., et al. (2021). How does satisfaction of solar PV users enhance their trust in the power grid? - evidence from PPAPs in Rural China. *Energy, Sustainability and Society*, 11(1), 31.

Fathima, M. S., Batcha, H. M., and Alam, A. S. (2022). Factors affecting consumer purchase intention for buying solar energy products. *International Journal of Energy Sector Management*, 17(4), 820–839. https://doi.org/10.1108/ijesm-04-2022-0002.

Kumar, V., Hundal, B. S., and Kaur, K. (2019). Factors affecting consumer buying behaviour of solar water pumping system. *Smart and Sustainable Built Environment*, 8(4), 351–364. https://doi.org/10.1108/sasbe-10-2018-0052.

Margolis, R. M. (2006). Nontechnical barriers to solar energy use: review of recent literature. Researcher VI-Policy Analysis, Strategic Energy Analysis Center Energy Analysis Research Topic.

Morgil, I., Secken, N., Yucel, A. S., Oskay, O. O., Yavuz, S., and Ural, E. (2006). Developing a renewable energy awareness scale for pre-service chemistry teachers. *Turkish Online Journal of Distance Education*, 7(1), 63–74.

Ravindra, B. (2017). Are indian electricity consumers ready to become solar prosumers? In 2017 International Conference on Technological Advancements in Power and Energy (TAP Energy). https://doi.org/10.1109/tapenergy.2017.8397377.

Ravindra (2017). Dorotovic, Past and Present of the Synoptic Observations of the Sun at the National Astronomical Observatory of Japan. Astronomical Society of the Pacific Conference Series, vol. 504, p. 313 (2016)

Solar Energy Incentives Analysis: Psycho-Economic Factors Affecting the Decision Making of Consumers and the Technology Delivery System. 1978. https://doi.org/10.2172/5057752.

Sangroya, D., and Nayak, J. K. (2017). Factors influencing buying behaviour of green energy consumer. *Journal of Cleaner Production*, 151, 393–405. https://doi.org/10.1016/j.jclepro.2017.03.010.

Sommerfeld, J., Buys, L., and Vine, D. (2017). Residential consumers' experiences in the adoption and use of solar PV. *Energy Policy*, 105, 10–16. https://doi.org/10.1016/j.enpol.2017.02.021.

Tsartsou et al., 2021 Supply chain management: more than a new name for logistics. The International Journal of Logistics Management, 8(1), 1–14.

Yin, Y. C., Ahmed, J., Nee, A. Y. H., and Hoe, O. K. (2023). The rural consumer adoption of sustainable energy: A PLS-SEM-ANN approach of conceptual model development and cross-country validation of Pakistan and Malaysia. *Environmental Science and Pollution Research International*, 30(3), 5881–s5902.

67 A comparative analysis of employee job satisfaction and their effects on job performance in MNC company

Kishore Kumar, B. and Vimaladevi, S.

Department of Commerce, Saveetha College of Liberal Arts and Sciences, Saveetha University Chennai, Tamil Nadu, India

Abstract

The investigation is a result of the theme titled "An examination of job contentment" the exploration is conducted at Chennai. The examination is executed in the enterprise named Schwing Stetter Pvt Ltd., for a duration of one month. The principal objectives of the study are to comprehend the staff contentment of a vocation in an establishment, to verify the welfare perks provided to the staff, to understand the precision of job contentment in the operational atmosphere of an establishment, to discern the interconnection between staff and administration. The exploration encompasses both Primary and Secondary Data gathering approaches. Primary data were amassed by disseminating structured questionnaires and the gathered data were scrutinized employing statistical mechanisms like Independent Sample t-test, Chi-square test The complete tally of employees is 140. The samples as my respondent to examine staff Job contentment in an establishment. Questionnaires and personnel conversation methods are employed to collect the data from the employees. It is recognized that the staff complaints were not dealt with in the appropriate manner, and safety precautions are the principal predicaments where the staff becomes discontented so that there is a reduction in the staff contentment in the enterprise.

Keywords: Age, environment, employee, job satisfaction, management, organization

Introduction

The exploration of job contentment (Balasubramanian et al., 2012) is where employees express their sentiments concerning their organisation and work surroundings. Individual reactions are subsequently amalgamated and examined. An employee represents the ultimate sensation of an individual post executing a task. To the degree that an individual satisfies their prominent requirements and aligns with their anticipation's principles, the employee will experience contentment. The sentiment could be affirmative or adverse based (Kanar, 2006) on whether the requirements are met or not. Job contentment differs from motivation and morale. Encouragement pertains to the inclination to work. Satisfaction, conversely, denotes a favourable emotional condition (Buentello, 2021). Morale suggests a general disposition towards labour and work environment. It constitutes a collective phenomenon whereas (Sypniewska, 2014) Staff contentment may be contemplated as a facet of motivation and morale could similarly be a wellspring of satisfaction (Erez, 1994). Attitudes are predispositions that induce the individual to act in a specific manner. Employee contentment, on the other hand, is the ultimate sensation which might influence ensuing conduct. Hence, employee contentment embodies an employee's general stance towards their organisation. Job contentment is one of the pivotal factors that have captivated the focus of executives in an establishment as well as academicians. Various inquiries have been executed to discern the determinants of employee contentment and its impact on efficiency in an establishment (Raziq and Maulabakhsh, 2015). It remains a primary apprehension for executives. Balasubramanian (2012), deduced that jubilant employees in their work are more triumphant in the establishment. Where they harmonise their anticipations with actuality (Dickens, 1861). Whilst Mathew 1991, noted that contentment on commitment and commitment on contentment are interlinked in a mutually reinforcing manner. In their investigation Javad and Premarajan (2011) inferred that distributive fairness is more pivotal in job and remuneration contentment of the employees.

Problem Statement

Job contentment is the paramount aspect of performance evaluation within the establishment. The degree of contentment stands as the pivotal factor in the lifestyle of the operational milieu within any establishment. Thus, a research inquiry was undertaken to ascertain the findings (Dawal and Taha, 2006) within

[a]researchsmartgen@gmail.com

the enterprise SchwingStetterPvt. Ltd. This endeavour is a bid to accentuate the variabilities and observations concerning job gratification.

Significance of the Study

Employee contentment is a pivotal aspect that has captivated the focus of managers within the organization and scholars (Vanka et al., 2020). Numerous investigations have been undertaken to discern the determinants of Employee contentment and its impact on productivity within the organization. Although there is inconclusive proof that Employee contentment directly impacts productivity, contingent on numerous variables, it remains a paramount concern for managers.

Objectives of the Study

1. To find out the level of job satisfaction in the company Schwing Stetter Pvt. Ltd.
2. To observe various factors that influence the job satisfaction among the employees working in company Schwing Stetter Pvt. Ltd.

Scope and Limitations of the Study

The extent of the investigation encompasses the pivotal element that affects Job contentment for the workers affiliated with the corporation. The inquiry aids in pinpointing the aspects which sway and enhance job gratification within the establishment. While the examination resolves the dilemmas and components associated with Job fulfilment of the focal organisation termed SchwingStetterPvt. Ltd. The discoveries and the recommendations are pertinent solely for the designated enterprise and any extrapolations may be applied to any alternative exploration.

Research Methodology

Research design: This investigation was carried out among the personnel of SchwingStetterPvt. Ltd. This research might be regarded as an instance study of a corporation Table 67.1. Furthermore, the investigator endeavoured to determine the degree of job contentment within the selected entity.

Primary data collection: This investigation was undertaken among the employees of the organisation via a questionnaire distributed Figure 67.1. The primary information was obtained to facilitate subsequent examination.

Secondary data: Specific essential details regarding the human resources policies were extracted from the HR policy of the selected company. The information

was gathered from a pool of 140 participants, employing the convenience sampling approach. Statistical examination entailed percentage analysis, Chi-square analysis, and regression analysis techniques.

Hypothesis
H0: There is no significant relation between Qualifications and faces any problem while working in the company.
H1: There is a significant relation between Qualifications and faces any problem while working in the company.

Hypothesis: salary
H0S: There is no significant relationship between salary hike and job satisfaction.
H1S: There is a significant relationship between salary hike and job satisfaction.

Table 67.1 Observed frequency.

Qualification\face any problem	Yes	No	Total
Less than +2	1	44	45
Diploma	7	17	24
ITI	8	34	42
UG	13	5	18
Others	1	10	11

Source: Author

Table 67.2 Expected frequency.

Qualification\face any problem	Yes	No	Total
Less than +2	3	42	45
Diploma	9	15	24
ITI	10	32	42
UG	15	3	18
Others	3	8	11

Source: Author

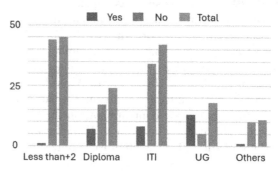

Figure 67.1 Distribution of employees and their qualifications
Source: Author

Testing of hypotheses

Analysis of Qualification and face any problem while working in the company.

Table 67.3 Observed and expected values.

O_i	E_{id}	$(O_i\text{-}E_{id})$	$(O_i\text{-}E_{id})^2$	$(O_i\text{-}E_{id})2\backslash E_{id}$
1	3	-2	4	1.333
7	9	-2	4	0.444
8	10	-2	4	0.4
13	15	-2	4	0.3
1	3	-2	4	1.333
44	42	2	4	0.095
17	15	2	4	0.3
34	32	2	4	0.125
5	3	2	4	1.333
10	8	2	4	0.5

Source: Primary data

Using Chi – square

$$Chi - square = \sum \frac{(O_i - E_{id})^2}{E} = 6.163$$

Degree of freedom = (c-1) (r-1) (2-1) (5-1) = 4, level of significant = 5%, table Value = 9.488, calculated Value = 6.163

Table 67.4 Regression analysis of the relationship between salary increment vs. overall job satisfaction.

x	y	dx	die	(dx)2	(die)2	daddy
19	33	-9	5	81	25	-45
30	40	2	12	4	144	24
21	15	-7	-13	49	169	91
48	32	20	4	400	16	80
22	20	-6	-8	36	64	48

Source: Primary data

Table 67.5 Analysis with percentage.

Variables	Age group	No. of respondents	Percentage
The age group of the respondents	Less than 20	33	23.6
	20-40	60	42.9
	40-60	39	27.9
	Above 60	8	5.7
Educational qualification	Less than +2	45	32.1
	Diploma	24	17.1
	ITI	42	30.0
	UG	18	12.9
	Others	11	7.9
Experience	Below and 1 year	44	31.4
	1-3 year	51	36.4
	3-5 year	35	25.0
	Above 5 year	10	7.1
Salary range	Less than 2000	42	30.0
	2000-3000	49	35.0
	3000-5000	29	20.7
	Above5000	20	14.3
Job nature	Temporary	22	15.7
	Permanent	118	84.3
Work environment in the organization is good	Strongly agree	23	16.4
	Agree	54	38.6
	No opinion	13	9.3
	Disagree	34	24.3
	Strongly agree	16	11.4

Source: Primary data

Accept H0: There is no significant relation between Qualifications and faces any problem while working in the company

$$Chi - square = \sum \frac{(O_i - E_{id})^2}{E_{id}} = 0.347$$

Accept H1S: There is a significant relationship between salary hike and job satisfaction.

Results and Discussions

The research findings reveal various noteworthy outcomes: Firstly, 60% of the respondent's express contentment with the work environment within the organisation. Secondly, 40% of the participants acknowledge the efficacy of the safety measures instituted by the organisation Tables 67.2, 67.3, 67.4, 67.5 and 67.6. Additionally, a majority of respondents confirm the sufficiency of machinery and tools

Table 67.6 Significant variables about salary.

Variables	Level	No. of respondents	Percentage
The salary provided by the company is fair	Strongly agree	31	22.1
	Agree	45	32.1
	No opinion	15	10.7
	Disagree	28	20.0
	Strongly disagree	21	15.0
Respondents face any problem while working in the organization	Yes	30	21.4
	No	110	78.6
Regarding the salary increment of the organization	Highly satisfied	19	13.6
	Satisfied	30	21.4
	No opinion	21	15.0
	Dissatisfied	48	34.3
	Highly dissatisfied	22	15.7
The respondent's grievance are taken care in the proper manner	Strongly agree	25	17.9
	Agree	39	27.9
	No opinion	22	15.7
	Disagree	34	24.3
	Strongly Disagree	20	14.3

Source: Author

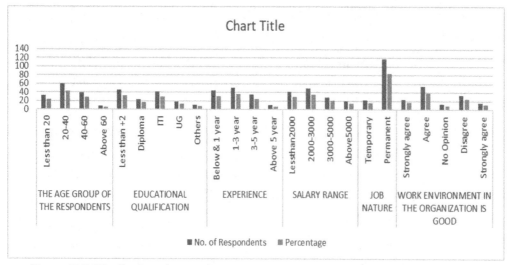

Figure 67.2 Distribution of respondents
Source: Author

provided by the organisation. Positive interpersonal relationships, both among management and staff and between colleagues, are noted to be adequately maintained. Nevertheless, concerns emerge regarding the organisation's handling of employee grievances, which appears deficient according to respondents' perceptions. Furthermore, there is an observed absence of incentives for outstanding performance recognised by management, as reported by respondents Figure 67.2. Roughly 53% of the surveyed individuals recognise the organisation's provision of satisfactory training. Moreover, most respondents affirm the organisation's provision of satisfactory vehicle maintenance and travel allowances. Furthermore, a notable portion of employees express a requirement for additional compensation for overtime work. Despite these concerns, more than 60% of employees report overall contentment with the organisation. Outcomes from the Chi-square analysis suggest that there is no notable correlation between employees' qualifications and their experience of work-related matters within the company. However, findings from the regression analysis indicate that salary increments directly influence job satisfaction, contributing to a 35% enhancement. To improve overall employee satisfaction, the organisation should concentrate on enhancing working conditions, including maintaining clean surroundings and providing adequate ventilation and lighting facilities. Additionally, efforts should be directed towards strengthening relationships between superiors and employees, as well as fostering better camaraderie among colleagues through teamwork and collaboration. Recognising employees' extra efforts, both financially and non-monetarily, is essential for motivation and morale. Regular training initiatives should be organised for all employees, and overtime compensation should be provided for those working beyond regular shifts. Furthermore, the management must address employee grievances swiftly and effectively, ideally following a standardised grievance handling procedure.

Conclusion

This examination concerning employee contentment within Lotte India enterprise limited asserts that the majority of workers are content, as demonstrated by Pawirosumarto et al. (2017). However, it is additionally observed that certain individuals desire additional amenities such as safety precautions, transportation, medical benefits, and overtime compensations, among others. The remuneration provided by the company is deemed equitable, thereby enabling employees to engage in overtime work; however, the overtime remunerations remain relatively low. It is imperative to address employee grievances adequately to enhance overall job satisfaction levels. Through the investigation, it has been determined that a significant proportion of staff members express contentment with the organisational environment and their respective roles.

References

Balasubramanian, P., Saravanan, S., and Chandar Rao, S. S. (2012). Job satisfaction among librarians in tirunelveli district, Tamil Nadu: a study. *Asian Journal of Information Science and Technology (AJIST)*, 2(1). https://search.ebscohost.com/login.aspx?direct=true&profile=ehost&scope=site&authtype=crawler&jrnl=22316108&AN=77464665&h=QRpwQE7Lyc%2F4fKEEaODosd8woVa7BgtccC3qVsKnEnSjN8KEl4VbnOH0hOmDMJDKTlWITaLO5zS%2BtWgfc2JYYQ%3D%3D&crl=c.

Buentello, A. (2021). Balance emotions and take better care of your family: create a deliberate positive emotional state: caregiver platform.

Dawal, S. Z. M., and Taha, Z. (2006). The effect of job and environmental factors on job satisfaction in automotive industries. *International Journal of Occupational Safety and Ergonomics: JOSE*, 12(3), 267–280.

Dickens, C. (1861). Great Expectations.

Erez, A. (1994). Dispositional source of job satisfaction: the role of self-deception.

Javad, S., and Premarajan, R. K. (2011). Effects of distributive and procedural justice perceptions on managerial pay and job satisfaction. *IUP Journal of Organizational Behavior*, 10(3). https://search.ebscohost.com/login.aspx?direct=true&profile=ehost&scope=site&authtype=crawler&jrnl=0972687X&AN=70220182&h=zOtDAzCVUhCPppkB1Neyga6Jtl%2F8%2BunS%2FMxM730el%2BrCAQ0cxIwe4LTcSzcpP8uwuspP9HhUc0yJEa5xKlMiew%3D%3D&crl=c.

Kanar, A. M. (2006). Positive and Negative Information Early in the Recruitment Process. Cornell University.

Pawirosumarto, S., Sarjana, P. K., and Rachmad, G. (2017). The effect of work environment, leadership style, and organizational culture towards job satisfaction and its implication towards employee performance in parador hotels and resorts, Indonesia. *Coastal Management: An International Journal of Marine Environment, Resources, Law, and Society*, 59(6), 1337–1358.

Raziq, A., and Maulabakhsh, R. (2015). Impact of working environment on job satisfaction. *Procedia Economics and Finance*, 23(January), 717–725.

Sypniewska, B. (2014). Evaluation of factors influencing job satisfaction. *Contemporary Economics*, 8(1), 57–72. https://papers.ssrn.com/abstract=2435040.

Vanka, S., Rao, M. B., Singh, S., and Pulaparthi, M. R. (2020). Sustainable Human Resource Management: Transforming Organizations, Societies and Environment. Springer Nature.

68 A comparative analysis of employee training methods and their effects on job performance

Rithish, M.[a] and Arul Mary Rexy

Department of Commerce (General), Saveetha College of Liberal Arts and Sciences Saveetha University, Chennai, India

Abstract

The objective of this investigation is to scrutinise the efficacy of the employee training and development scheme in augmenting competencies, comprehension, and job efficacy. An evaluation of the company's training and development schemes is undertaken, assessing employee contentment, comprehension, adeptness, and proficiency. Data collection was executed through a structured survey and supplementary sources such as academic literature, periodicals, and scholarly papers, subsequently analysed utilising statistical methodologies. The research methodology employed was descriptive, encompassing surveys and investigative interrogations. A sample cohort of 52 staff members was chosen via convenience sampling. The primary aim is to elevate employee effectiveness and proficiency. The outcomes were delineated via tabulations and graphical representations. Moreover, an analysis was conducted regarding the association between age, occupation, credentials, instruction, and occupational efficiency. Through the correlation test facilitated by SPSS statistical software, a substantial distinction between intrinsic and extrinsic motivation is discerned. The average and standard deviation for overall categorisation accuracy stand at 21.36 and 2.75, 17.06, and 2.83 respectively, while employment engagement is reflected by a mean and standard deviation of 45.78 and 5.34. The null hypothesis posits the absence of any correlation or linear rapport between intrinsic and extrinsic motivation. The investigation concludes that age, credentials, and training exert no significant impact on job classification or efficacy. The findings reveal no notable associations between age and occupation, credentials and instruction, and age and job efficacy. Additionally, no linear correlation is detected between intrinsic and extrinsic motivation.

Keywords: Development, employee, employment, motivation, performance, skill, skills, training

Introduction

For any commercial enterprise, the primary incentive is to pursue profit, and in today's fiercely competitive climate, businesses are placing considerable emphasis on human resources (Porter, 2011). Enhancing their profitability, once an employee is selected and positioned, they must be furnished with training facilities to continually enhance their skill levels (Cranny et al., 1992). Training has taken precedence and is frequently associated with the developmental aspect of an organisation (Brazzel and Jones, 2012). Progress is linked to the comprehensive advancement of executives; meanwhile, training is necessary to enhance the competencies required for job performance (Dwivedi, 2009). Training and development are frequently used jointly without considering whether one precedes the other (Talbot and Pora, 2018). A search on Google Scholar unveiled 16,500 articles on the topic of employee training and development, while 1453 articles were identified on the Web of Science (Talbot and Pora, 2018; Martin, 2006). The necessity for training and development is determined by the employee's performance deficiency, (Bhattacharyya, 2015) calculated

as follows: training and development needs: standard performance training and development programmes may be oriented towards individual or team performance (Penzien et al., 2020), yet the formulation and execution of training should be grounded on training needs analysis (Penzien et al., 2020). Competently trained employees are more effective and can yield more output with less input, leading to heightened productivity. Moreover, employees who are trained and possess advanced skill sets are likely to exhibit greater confidence and dedication to their work, potentially resulting in increased job satisfaction levels. Hence, investing in employee training can yield myriad benefits for the enterprise, including heightened output, enhanced productivity, and increased employee satisfaction (National Research Council, 1991; Cranny et al., 1992). There are three terms employed in the realm of learning: education, training, and development (Ackah and Agboyi, 2014). The term development encompasses a broader spectrum involving the social, mental, and physical growth of an individual. Following confusion in the usage of the terms training and development," Thus, comprehending the essence of training and development is pivotal.

[a]riteshsmartgenresearch@gmail.com

Material and Methods

The investigation was carried out at Saveetha College of Liberal Arts and Sciences and Saveetha Institute of Medical and Technical Sciences, located in Tamil Nadu, India. Ethical clearance was deemed unnecessary for this research endeavour. The primary aim of this investigation is to scrutinize the training and development initiatives, while also assessing employee satisfaction, knowledge, proficiency, and competency. Employed materials encompassed a structured survey and secondary data sources, comprising textbooks, periodicals, academic publications, and online resources. Descriptive research techniques, involving surveys and fact-finding inquiries, were employed as the research methodology. A sample size of 52 individuals was chosen via convenience sampling. Primary data collection entailed structured surveys, alongside observations, previews, and discussions with management personnel. Secondary data was garnered from textbooks, periodicals, academic reports, and online repositories. The total sample population amounted to 52, with a mean of 45.78 and a correlation significance at the 0.05 threshold level. Statistical analysis of the collected data utilised tools such as frequency distribution, percentage calculations, mean computation, and standard deviation estimation. Presentation of the study findings was achieved through tabular and graphical representations. The study zone was delineated by selecting pertinent regions of interest. In pursuing the principal aim, the training and development schemes were scrutinised for their efficacy and quality. Additionally, the investigation delved into the satisfaction levels of employees regarding these programmes, as well as their knowledge and skill proficiency.

The investigation also sought to enhance the proficiency of the workforce and elevate their effectiveness. To conduct the study, the chosen research methodology relied on a methodical and systematic quest for relevant information pertaining to a particular subject. The examination proceeded systematically, adhering to the suitable strategy and procedure tailored to the specific research dilemma. The objective was to assess the efficacy of the organisation's training and development initiatives and ascertain the contentment, understanding, proficiency, and capability of the personnel. Statistical methodologies such as mean, standard deviation, and frequency distribution were utilised to scrutinise the amassed data. An independent-samples-t-test was executed, maintaining a 95% confidence interval to establish the significance of the training and development programme's efficacy. Furthermore, the analysis explored the connection between age, occupation, qualifications, training, and work proficiency via regression analysis. Through correlation testing with SPSS statistical software, it was discerned that there exists a notable disparity between intrinsic and extrinsic motivation. The average and standard deviation for overall classification accuracy were 21.36 and 2.75, 17.06 and 2.83, respectively. The mean and standard deviation for employee engagement were 45.78 and 5.34. The null hypothesis posits no correlation or linear association between intrinsic and extrinsic motivation. By scrutinising these figures, it is plausible to draw conclusions regarding the most effective approach.

Statistical Analysis

In order to scrutinise the gathered data, analytical methods including average, deviation standard, and distribution frequency were utilised. A reliant-samples ANOVA examination was executed with a 277.95 mean square range to ascertain the importance of the programme's efficiency in training and development. Furthermore, the research probed the association amidst age, labour, eligibility, instruction, and efficacy of labour through regression scrutiny. Derived from the correlation assessment employing SPSS statistical application, it is noted that a notable disparity emerges between intrinsic and extraneous impetus.

Results and Discussions

A variety of findings derived as part of the investigation are detailed herein. Each workforce participates in the training sessions. Effective supervision of employees occurs in 90% of instances during the training and development process. Table 68.1 delineates the methodology employed in this examination, exploring the intrinsic and extrinsic motivation's link with employee engagement. A correlation test is utilised for statistical analysis to scrutinise the connection between intrinsic and extrinsic motivation and its impact on decision-making concerning training and development within the sector. The null hypothesis posits no intrinsic-extrinsic motivation association, while the alternative hypothesis suggests a relationship exists. According to the Correlation test, intrinsic motivation stands at 0.218, while extrinsic motivation registers at 0.120. Consequently, the null hypothesis can be refuted in favour of the alternative, indicating a connection between intrinsic and extrinsic motivation regarding the steel industry's selection. Table 68.2 demonstrates the correlation between employment type and intrinsic and extrinsic motivation. Statistical analysis entails a Correlation test to explore the relationship between employee engagement and intrinsic, extrinsic motivation, influencing industry selection

Table 68.1 Table showing correlation intrinsic and extrinsic motivation on training and development.

		Intrinsic motivation	Extrinsic motivation	Employee engagement
Intrinsic_motivation	Pearson correlation	1	.218	.284
	Sig (2-tailed)		.120	.041
	N	52	52	52
Extrinsic_motivation	Pearson correlation	.218	1	.598
	Sig (2-tailed)	.120		<.001
	N	52	52	52
Employee_engagement	Pearson correlation	.284	598	1
	Sig (2-tailed)	.041	<.001	
	N	52	52	52

Correlation is significant at the 0.05 level (2 tailed)
Correlation is significant at the 0.01 level (2 tailed)
Source: Author

Table 68.2 Table showing Pearson correlation for employee engagement and motivation on training methods.

		Employee_Engagement	inrinsic_motiVation	Extrinsic_motiVation
Pearson correlation	Employee_Engagement	1.000	284	.598
	Intrinsic_motivation	.284	1.000	.218
	Extrinsic_motivation	.598	.218	1.000
sig.(1-tailed)	Employee_Engagement	.021	.021	<.001
	Intrinsic_motivation	.000	.060	.060
	Extrinsic_motivatio			
N	Employee_Engagement	52	52	52
	Intrinsic_motivation	52	52	52
	Extrinsic_motivatio	52	52	52

Source: Author

Table 68.3 Table showing ANOVA and mean square on training methods.

Model	Sum of squares	df	Mean square	F	Sig
Regression	555.901	2	277.951	15.157	<.001[b]
Residual	898.559	49	18.338		
Total	1454.460	51			

a. Dependent variable Employess_Engagement
b. Predictors:(constant), Extrinsic_motivation_intrinsic_motivaton
Source: Author

– private or government. Hence, the null hypothesis can be dismissed in favour of the alternative, indicating a connection between employee engagement and intrinsic, extrinsic motivation. Table 68.3 showcases the ANOVA table and mean square for training methods, facilitating the examination of various factors affecting employer training. This approach aids in grasping each factor's importance that influences employee engagement and intrinsic-extrinsic factors. Table 68.4 depicts the outcomes of a t-test, examining the relationship between gender and intrinsic-extrinsic motivation with effective training. The null hypothesis

tested suggests no significant link between gender and intrinsic-extrinsic motivation with effective training, while the alternative hypothesis posits a significant relationship. The analysis reveals statistically significant t-values for intrinsic (5.399) and extrinsic motivation (4.889) ($p < .001$). Hence, the null hypothesis is rejected, affirming a substantial relationship between gender and intrinsic-extrinsic motivation with effective training. Moreover, the standardized coefficients (Beta) for intrinsic (.224) and extrinsic motivation (.217) indicate a moderate positive impact on employee engagement. These findings highlight the

Table 68.4 Table showing t test for gender and intrinsic, extrinsic motivation on effective training methods.

Models	Unstandardized Coefficients	Standardized coefficients	t	Sig.
	B	Beta		
1. (Constant)	20.980	.162	3.886	<.001
Intrinsic_ motivation	314	.562	1.405	.165
Extrinsic_motivation	1.060		4.889	<.001

Dependent variable Employee_Engagement
Source: Author

Table 68.5 Table showing mean score standard deviation analysis on employee engagement to intrinsic motivation and extrinsic motivation.

	Mean	Std. deviation	N
Employee_Engagement	45.7821	5.34030	52
Intrinsic _Motivation	21,3654	2.74835	52
Extrinsic_Motivation	17.0615	2.83273	52

Source: Author

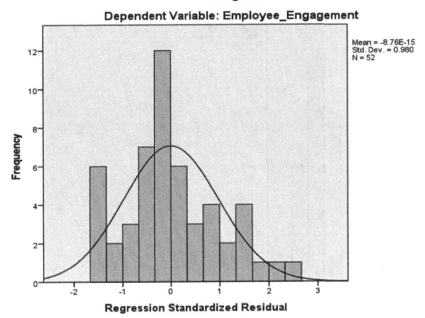

Figure 68.1 Regression standardized residual of employee engagement
Source: Author

pivotal role of gender and intrinsic-extrinsic motivation in determining effective training and employee engagement in the industry. Table 68.5 presents mean and standard deviation values for employee engagement, intrinsic motivation, and extrinsic motivation. The mean scores unveil employee engagement at 45.7821, intrinsic motivation at 21.3654, and extrinsic motivation at 17.0615. These results shed light on the levels of employee engagement and motivation, indicating a higher intrinsic motivation than extrinsic motivation. Figure 68.1 illustrates the Regression Standardized Residual of Employee Engagement, with a mean of -8.76 and standard deviation of 0.980. A mean value below 1 denotes an insignificant relationship between employee engagement and frequency. Figure 68.2 portrays Job Satisfaction Level of the Employee, with a mean of 12.19 and standard deviation of 3.908. A mean exceeding 1 signifies a significant relationship between Job Satisfaction and Frequency. Figure 68.3 showcases Organizational Commitment

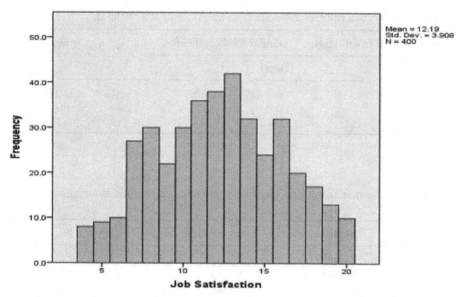

Figure 68.2 Job satisfaction level of the employee
Source: Author

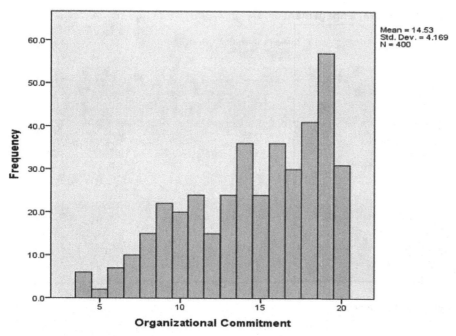

Figure 68.3 Organizational commitment of employee
Source: Author

Of Employee, with a mean of 14.53 and standard deviation of 4.169. A mean surpassing 1 indicates a substantial relationship between Organizational commitment and frequency.

Conclusion

The findings imply that these variables do not notably influence the nature of employment or work effectiveness. Age and credentials do not exert a substantial influence on the nature of employment pursued, and there exists no noteworthy correlation between credentials and instruction. In summarising this investigation, I would contend that instruction holds a greater sway on organisational advancement.

Acknowledgment

The authors would like to express their gratitude toward Saveetha College of Liberal Arts and Sciences, Saveetha Institute of Medical and Technical Sciences, MekubaPetrolubes Pvt Ltd, Ambattur Industrial Estate for providing the necessary infrastructure to carry out this work successfully.

References

Ackah, D., and Agboyi, M. R. (2014). The Effects of Training and Development on Employee Performance in the Public Sector of Ghana: A Study of the Takoradi Branch of Ghana Ports and Habours Authority (GPHA). GRIN Verlag.

Bhattacharyya, D. K. (2015). Training and Development: Theories and Applications. Sage Publications Pvt. Limited.

Brazzel, M., and Jones, B. B. (2012). The NTL Handbook of Organization Development and Change: Principles, Practices, and Perspectives. John Wiley & Sons.

Cranny, C. J., Smith, P. C., and Stone, E. F. (1992). Job Satisfaction: How People Feel about Their Jobs and How it Affects Their Performance. New York: Lexington.

Dwivedi, R. S. (2009). A Textbook of Human Resource Management. Vikas Publishing House.

Martin, V. (2006). Managing Projects in Human Resources Training and Development. Kogan Page Publishers.

National Research Council (1991). National Research Council, Division of Behavioral and Social Sciences and Education, Commission on Behavioral and Social Sciences and Education, and Committee on the Performance of Military Personnel. 1991. Performance Assessment for the Workplace: Volume I. National Academies Press.

Penzien, C. E., Tharp, J. C., Mulzer, K., Rurka, C., Abbas, C., and Chaffee, B. W. (2020). Development of a sterile compounding training and competency program at a large academic medical center. *American Journal of Health-System Pharmacy: AJHP: Official Journal of the American Society of Health-System Pharmacists*, 77(24), 2089–2100.

Porter, M. E. (2011). Competitive Advantage of Nations: Creating and Sustaining Superior Performance. Simon and Schuster.

Talbot, L., and Pora, D. (2018). Primary Care Training and Development: The Tool Kit. CRC Press.

69 A comparative analysis of the recruitment and selection process and its impact on employee satisfaction in the IT sector

Gayathri, D.[a] and Chitra, V.

Department of Commerce, Saveetha College of Liberal Arts and Sciences, Saveetha University Chennai, India

Abstract

The aim of this investigation was to examine the recruitment and selection procedure and its impact on employee contentment in the IT Industry. The research was carried out in Chennai. The scholars employed both primary and secondary data sources for the investigation. A meticulously planned questionnaire format was devised to gather primary data from the participants. A convenience sampling technique was utilised to procure the samples. The study encompassed a sample volume of 100. The researchers applied One Sample t-test and chi-square test to scrutinise the data. The findings of the examination demonstrated that there existed no correlation between the job title of the participants and their evaluation of the recruitment and selection mechanism of the firm. Additionally, there existed no discrepancy in the satisfaction level of the participants concerning the interview procedure, screening process, and announcement of outcomes. The research underscores the significance of a comprehensive and structured recruitment and selection regimen to allure and preserve talent in corporations. It furnishes a valuable reference for companies endeavouring to refine their recruitment and selection procedures.

Keywords: Human resource, interview, recruitment, screening, selection

Introduction

In today's competitive labor market, the recruitment and selection process of potential employees plays a crucial role. Human capital stands as a pivotal element within an enterprise. The triumph, expansion, and enhancement of the organization hinge on the caliber of workforce they possess. It is solely through human resources that all other assets are actively engaged and contribute to the proficient and effective operation of a business entity. The significance of Human Resource is burgeoning and gathering momentum in recent years owing to the burgeoning global commerce and a substantial demand for adept manpower. To achieve individual and organizational objectives, the unique resource termed Human Resource must be suitably positioned and acknowledged. Within an enterprise, the personnel are indispensable for the sustenance and triumph of the establishment (Kingkade, 1952). The primary function in HRM is Recruitment and Selection, meticulously tailored to augment the capabilities of an employee to align with the employer's strategic aims and objectives. Amidst the array of HR practices, Recruitment serves as the foundational function where individuals are onboarded into the organization. Recruitment embodies the process of identifying the suitable individual for a given role.

It poses a formidable challenge for organizations to execute and acquire suitable candidates. With the advancement of technology, candidate recruitment processes are increasingly conducted online. Additionally, widespread unemployment prevails. Due to meagre networks and insufficient channels, skilled and qualified candidates often elude the recruitment radar. Recruitment functions as a conduit between the employer and potential employee, enticing prospective individuals to apply for vacant positions. Selection, conversely, entails the process of sifting through applicants to discern and hire those most likely to thrive in a given role. It involves identifying the most fitting candidate for a vacant position within the organization. TCS Consultancy Services Private Ltd. operates as a non-governmental entity, specializing in Business and Management consultancy activities. Registered at the Jaipur Registrar of Companies, the company's core activities encompass offering counsel, guidance, or operational support to businesses. These activities encompass public relations, excluding paid advertisements, as well as involvement in welfare and charitable endeavors, politics, and lobbying. Additionally, the company engages in project management, planning, organization, management information, and facilitates arbitration and conciliation between management and labor.

[a]muthugayathiri@gmail.com

Examining the contentment level of the staff concerning the hiring and assortment procedure has been a subject elected by many investigators. Lately, numerous analyses have been issued in Google Scholar. Multiple exploration pieces were unearthed in google scholar over the preceding 5 years. Workforce assortment is customarily perceived as a 'dated' and 'restricted' area within HRM. Additionally, it is frequently perceived in moderately simplistic dichotomous conditions. One of the goals of our scrutiny was to elucidate the myriad stimulating advancements that have occurred in this realm in recent times. As evidenced, a multitude of these developments hold significant merit for HR practitioners functioning in establishments. However, this is merely one aspect of the equation. An equally crucial matter is to execute these advancements in establishments. One challenge is to surmount the obstinate overconfidence workforce selection decision-makers possess in their own discernment. Another associated impediment is the deficiency of awareness of these novel trends. For instance, it was noteworthy that a survey among HR professionals disclosed that two of the prime misunderstandings among these professionals concerned workforce selection, particularly the relative validity of general intellectual aptitude assessments in comparison to disposition inventories. ("Website," n.d.). Hiring and assortment possess a pivotal role in ensuring laborer effectiveness and favorable organizational outcomes. It is frequently contended that workforce selection arises not solely to replace departing employees or supplement a workforce but instead strives to institute laborers who can operate at an elevated level and exhibit dedication (French and Rumbles, 2010). The recruitment and selection process across the three sectors such as cement industry, electronic industry and sugar industry in Krishna District, Andhra Pradesh were scrutinized. The participants were content with the extant recruitment and selection process (Naveen and Raju, 2014). Amidst the internship, both the establishment and interns endeavored to impress the opposing party. 60% of the internships evolve into job proposals from the host establishments. Interns aspiring to be recruited were more inclined to employ self-promotion and ingratiation which heightened the probability of job proposals. Establishments aspiring to recruit seemed to be more amenable to interns' originality which heightened interns' application intentions (Zhao and Liden, 2011).

The investigator endeavored to bridge the research lacuna within the prevailing literature. The investigation considers elements including screening, enlistment, and assortment procedure to comprehend the contentment degree of the staff in the designated firm in Chennai Municipality. No investigation has been executed freshly to scrutinize the gratified degree of the staff concerning the enlistment and assortment procedure in TCS Consultancy Pvt. Ltd. The objective of the exploration was to scrutinize the enlistment and assortment procedure and its impact on employee contentment in the IT Domain.

Materials and Methods

The primary office of TCS Consultancy Service Pvt Ltd is situated in Chennai. Therefore, the investigation was conducted in Chennai. The study employed primary data via the feedback obtained from the participants. The primary data were scrutinized employing the t-test and chi-square examination to ascertain the outcome. The inquiry also relied on secondary data. The secondary information was amassed from journals, texts, periodicals, newspapers, and by surfing the web. A structured questionnaire format was devised to procure the primary from the participants. The surveys were disseminated among diverse divisions of the workforce at TCS Consultancy Pvt. Ltd. through a convenience sampling approach, and information was amassed from the 100 respondents. Consequently, the study's sample dimension was 100.

Result

The research demonstrates that amid the complete participants, 80% are male and every one of them falls within the age bracket of 20 years to 30 years. 90% of the participants were undergraduates and the majority are newcomers and possessing professional experience of 1-2 years. Nearly 60% of the participants were enlisted based on the origin of campus hiring (Gummadi, 2015).

It was ascertained that the corporation takes over 15 days to convey the outcome of the job application. 60% of the participants indicated that the selection procedure of the firm entails 3 stages and provided an average evaluation of the selection process of the chosen Corporation (Baker et al., 2023).

Various forms of selection assessments were carried out by the institution amongst which the bulk of the participants were chosen through individual interviews. The exploration demonstrated that the majority of the participants of the analysis are content with the selection procedure and methodology of the organization while 50% of the participants were firmly content with the screening procedure. The bulk of the participants stated that their function towards the assigned job was recognized by the corporation.

The analyst had attempted to ascertain the correlation between the two variables namely Assessment on the recruitment and selection procedure of the organization and the designation (Kingkade, 1952). From Table 69.1, based on chi-square analysis, it was discovered that 4% of Assistant Executives have ranked the recruitment and selection procedure of the firm as "Average", 20% of Support Executives have provided their rating as "Good" and 25% of the System Engineers have ranked the recruitment and selection procedure as "Very Good". Moreover, P value 0.000 was lesser than the table value of 0.05. Therefore, there was a noteworthy association between Designation and their Rating on recruitment and selection procedure in the organization.

The study also aimed to determine the satisfaction level of the participants regarding the interview process, screening process, and announcement of outcome. Table 69.2 illustrates the outcome of one sample t-test and it disclosed that the P value 0.00 was lesser than the table value of 0.05. The mean value of

Table 69.1 Association between designation and respondents' rating of the recruitment and selection process in the company.

Crosstabulation				
Designation	Rating on the recruitment and selection process of the company.			Total
	Average	good	Very good	
Support executives	3%	20%	10%	33%
Assistant executives	4%	15%	5%	24%
System engineer	3%	15%	25%	43%
Total	10%	50%	40%	100%

	Value		Asymp. Sig. (2-sided)
Pearson Chi-Square	50.000ᵃ	4	.000
Likelihood Ratio	50.040	4	.000
N of Valid Cases	100		

Source: Computed data

Table 69.2 Satisfaction level of the respondents with respect to interview process, screening process, and declaration of result.

One-sample T-Test					
	N	Mean	t	df	Sig. (2-tailed)
Interview Process	100	3.70	36.911	99	.000
Screening Process	100	3.50	29.850	99	.000
Declaration of result	100	2.80	16.629	99	.000

Source: Computed data by authors

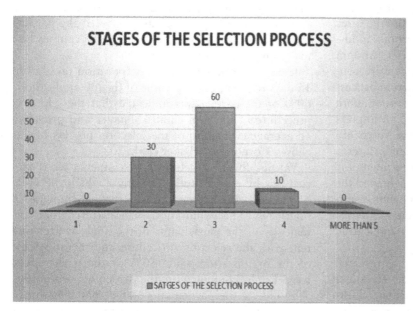

Figure 69.1 Stages of the selection process
Source: Author

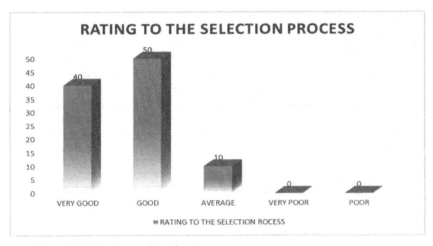

Figure 69.2 Rating to the selection process
Source: Author

the interview process and screening process were 3.70 and 3.50 respectively which surpassed the test value of 3 Figure 69.1 and 69.2. Hence, it was established that the participants were exceedingly content with the interview and screening process.

I. Designation and rating of the recruitment and selection process
II. Respondents' satisfaction level with respect to interview, screening and declaration of the result.

Discussion

The outcome revealed that the majority of the participants were content with the choice process and methodology of the organization while 50% of the respondents were deeply content with the screening procedure. The finding corresponds with the outcome of different investigations that the participants were content with the current recruitment and selection procedure (Naveen and Raju, 2014). The researchers have demonstrated that the majority of the respondents were enlisted based on the origin of campus recruitment. The finding was in contrast to the result of where the chosen organization had embraced a direct technique of hiring candidates through newspapers & periodicals. The majority of the applicant was employed by direct recruitment and also felt preliminary discussion was significant. Various forms of selection assessments were executed by the institution among which the majority of the participants were chosen through personal interaction. The outcome coincides with the finding of the other writers (Waters and Winterstein, 1991). The selection process of the organization doesn't regard advertisement as the origin of a broad spectrum. If it is taken into consideration,

the organization can enlist a vast number of skilled candidates. If the duration of communicating the outcome is lessened, capable candidates can be employed for the vacant position. In order to employ the well talented candidates, Group Debate should be the component of the selection process because during the group discussion the candidate may impart their ideas, thoughts, and the level of communication of them can also be observed. The research suggests that the organization should persist in adopting innovative recruitment and selection tactics to allure talented individuals. The organization should concentrate on nurturing its employer brand by proffering competitive salaries, staff perks, and a favorable work milieu. Additionally, the organization should invest in education and development schemes to boost the expertise of its staff (Nirmal Kumar and Thiruvekatraj, 2018).

Conclusion

Recruitment and hiring are integral aspects of human resource management, encompassing the identification and engagement of appropriate candidates for employment. The research indicates that TCS Consultancy Services Pvt. Limited in Chennai implements a thorough and organized recruitment and selection system, comprising various phases. The organization utilizes a blend of conventional and pioneering recruitment strategies to allure suitable candidates for diverse positions. Several methods, such as job boards, employee endorsements, and social networking sites, are utilized by TCS Chennai to recruit potential candidates.

The selection procedure at TCS Chennai involves a stringent assessment of candidates' credentials, expertise, and competencies. The company employs a variety of selection mechanisms, including written examinations, group interactions, and interviews, to evaluate candidates' suitability for roles. The investigation established that the selection process at TCS Chennai is impartial, equitable, and translucent. The study evidenced that employees expressed high contentment with the interview and evaluation process.

In conclusion, the research underscores the significance of a comprehensive and systematic recruitment and selection process in attracting and retaining talent within organizations. It serves as a valuable asset for organizations aspiring to enhance their recruitment and selection methodologies.

References

Baker, F. A., Blauth, L., Bloska, J., Bukowska, A. A., Flynn, L., Hsu, M. H., et al. (2023). Recruitment approaches and profiles of consenting family caregivers and people living with dementia: a recruitment study within a trial. *Contemporary Clinical Trials Communications*, 32, 101079.

French, R., and Rumbles, S. (2010). Recruitment and selection. Leading, Managing and Developing. Update of the French R&D strategy on gas-cooled reactors. Nuclear Engineering and Design, 240(10), 2401–2408. https://doi.org/10.1016/j.nucengdes.2010.02.042

Gummadi, R. K. (2015). Recruitment and Selection Practices of it Companies in Andhra Pradesh – A Study of Select Units. Zenon Academic Publishing.

Kingkade, W. B. (1952). An Evaluation of Recruitment Sources for White Collar Workers. University of Minnesota.

Naveen, S., and Raju, D. N. M. (2014). A study on recruitment selection process with reference to three industries, cement industry, electronics industry, sugar industry in Krishna DtAp, India. *OSR Journal of Business and Management*, 15(5), 60–67.

Waters, S., and Winterstein, M. (1991). The right person for the job: using occupational testing to improve recruitment and selection.

Website (n.d.). Recruitment and Selection Filip LIEVENS. Singapore Management University.

Zhao, H., and Liden, R. C. (2011). Internship: a recruitment and selection perspective. *Journal of Applied Psychology*, 96(1), 221–229.

70 A comparative study on customer preference toward various factors of decision making with reference to two wheelers

Yokesh, V.[1] and Jayanthi, L.N.[2,a]

[1]Research Scholar, Department of Commerce (General) Saveetha College of Liberal Arts and Sciences, Saveetha Institute of Medical and Technical Sciences, Saveetha University, Chennai, Tamil Nadu, India

[2]Project Guide, Department of Commerce (General) Saveetha College of Liberal Arts and Sciences, Saveetha Institute of Medical and Technical Sciences, Saveetha University, Chennai, Tamil Nadu, India

Abstract

Aim: This study reflects the preferences of Yamaha Motors' customers. Today, two-wheelers play a crucial part in our way of life. Both students and people who are employed find two wheels to be quite beneficial. Let's examine the significance of two-wheelers and their preferences. Materials and Methods: Both primary and secondary data were used to conduct the study. A questionnaire with a sample size of 104 was used to collect primary data, and websites and academic articles were used to collect secondary data. the findings and discussions. The study's conclusions show that the calculated value (3.156) is less than the table value (7.815), accepting the null hypothesis and rejecting the alternative. We can learn from this test that gender has no bearing on how well a bike works. According to the data above, 40% of respondents learned about motorcycles from their friends. Conclusion: Customers are keen to purchase two-wheelers, according to the survey's findings. Therefore, the majority of clients base their bike purchases on mileage, followed by price and maintenance requirements. Finally, I'd say that the Bike is more attractive.

Keywords: Awareness, bikes, customers, information, innovative techniques, preference, purchase, repair.

Introduction

This survey was done on the patrons of Sri Motors, a dealership for Yamaha bikes, to determine their preferences for bikes. This study aims to pinpoint the characteristics that have a significant influence on bike purchases. Due to India's rapid economic expansion, the sale of bikes has significantly increased Bijapurkar (2014). India is the world's second-largest two-wheeler producer. The majority of Indians, particularly the younger generation, favor motorcycles over automobiles. In India, about 3 lakh motorcycles are sold each month. After China, it is the second-largest motorbike manufacturer in the world. Understanding consumer behavior in the current environment using cutting-edge methods is crucial because it is no longer an easy task. A marketing manager cannot formulate the optimal sale policies and advertising strategies unless he is aware of the elements influencing consumers' purchasing habits. Understanding customer choice will offer you an idea of consumer demand since it influences what things consumers would purchase within their budget. By using this data, you can make sure you have enough product on hand to meet demand and set your product's pricing Masterson and Pickton

(2014). Marketers hardly ever provide their consumers and prospects the ability to select preferences for content and channels in an age where everyone plays video games and is accustomed to choosing characters or avatars, choosing game difficulty settings, and making a variety of other choices. The square test uses research data of the variance kind to assess the hypothesis (McMillan, 1989). The primary goal is to evaluate the noteworthy differences between two sets of provided data that are presented in tabular style. In this study, the age and preference for mileage are compared to see which age group prefers mileage more, and a test between gender and Yamaha bike awareness was done to see how many customers are aware of Yamaha bikes and how they learn about them.

According to Jain (2015) in her essay "A study of customer satisfaction of two wheelers on Yamaha," motorcycles, which are thought to be fuel-efficient, dependable, and suitable for rough roads, have contributed significantly to the two-wheeler industry's rise. According to his research, TVS-Suzuki, Hero: Honda, and Bajaj rule the two-wheeler market. According to the report, LML is facing extremely fierce competition from scooter producer and auto-maker Bajaj, which is a big competitor. However, this

[a]nirudhsmartgenresearch@gmail.com

category's dominance has been waning due to a shift in consumer preferences towards motorbikes. A significant portion of the two-wheeler industry's growth with innovative approaches has come from motorcycles, which are regarded as reliable, fuel-efficient, and suitable for a variety of environments. According to Muruganantham and Vivek (2021) in his article "A study on customer satisfaction towards after- sales service", customers who purchase two-wheelers are more concerned with the quality and performance of the bikes or scooters (Ferrell, 1990) than any other features. Instead of allowing commercials to entice them, they have started gathering data from all of the accessible sources, which they use to make the most sane and intelligent buying decision. For making the best decision, they believe that feedback from current two-wheeler users, repair, word-of-mouth recommendations from their family and friends, concepts posted on social media, and the expert opinion of two-wheeler mechanics are the most reliable, unbiased, and accurate sources of information. Bijapurkar (2009) noted in his essay "Customer perception towards major brands of two wheelers in Jaipur city and its impact on buying decision" that "customer perception" is still a research issue of great interest in an era of increasing global rivalry. Due to the fact that the average household's future disposable income will rise, future demand will outpace future supply. Studying the numerous aspects that affect customers' views and, in turn, the choices they make about purchases, becomes essential in order to live up to their expectations. To put it another way, we can say that motorcycles are a common man's mode of transportation. taking into account the fact that before purchasing a motorbike, customers have preferences in mind. The core of the entire company system should be the consumer, not the product, according to Kashani et al. (2005) in their study "A study on consumer satisfaction among Yamaha two wheeler users". As it relates to clients and their demands, customer satisfaction plays an essential and significant role. This study examines how satisfied customers are with Yamaha vehicles. Yamaha two-wheelers are renowned for their aesthetics, power, and simplicity of repair. Yamaha aims to appeal to young people. And this study has discovered the degree of customer happiness across a range of demographics, including different age groups, genders, income levels, and causes motivating them to purchase Yamaha automobiles. The majority of these users are really satisfied, which helps to keep clients. Kashani et al. (2005); National Research Council et al. (1994) stated that the marketers tamed the minds of the customers using color full television commercials with breath-taking visuals, pulsating punch

lines, repair, and celebrity endorsement in his article "Information sources for two-wheeler purchase: an analytical study with special focus on Malappuram district of Kerala." Modern consumers are extremely cunning and logical. Technological improvements have given them access to a wide range of sources from which they may quickly and easily obtain information on any product. They can no longer be duped by the graphics sorcery in television ads or by sparkling promotional items, deals, or other similar things. When an issue is identified by the buyer, the buying process begins.

The goal of this study is to give Yamaha Motors a better understanding of the brand's popularity as well as consumers' perceptions of its products and services (National Research Council et al. 1994). We can identify the markets of the other competitors thanks to the study, and we can then come up with a plan to grow those markets. The survey is being done just to learn more about our customers' preferences for Yamaha bikes. The only customers in the survey who purchased Yamahas from Sri Motors.

Materials and Methods

Research involves defining and redefining problems, formulating hypotheses or recommended solutions, gathering, organizing, and evaluating data, analyzing, and coming to conclusions. Finally, the conclusions are thoroughly tested to see if they agree with the hypotheses that were formulated. "Descriptive research" is the methodology chosen for this investigation. The quantitative or qualitative values of a variable can be referred to as data. Data cannot be understood on their own, thus the researcher must interpret the data to derive information from it.

Limitations of the Study

The study is only founded on conducted and examined surveys. A single branch of Sri Motors is the subject of the survey. Only consumers of Sri Motors are surveyed, hence the study only includes a small number of responses. Customers were constantly preoccupied with choosing a bike, making it impossible for me to speak with them and gather their information.

Scope of the Study

This study aims to give Yamaha Motors a better understanding of the brand, customers' perceptions of it, and how well they respond to its goods and services. We can identify the markets of the other competitors thanks to the study, and we can then come up with a plan to grow those markets. The survey is being done just to learn more about our customers' preferences for Yamaha bikes. The only customers in the survey who purchased Yamahas from Sri Motors.

Statistical Analysis Tools

Using Google Forms, a self-questionnaire was created for this particular study. Google Forms is a platform that enables information gathering from users via an individual survey or quiz. After that, the data is gathered and instantly connected to a spreadsheet. The survey and quiz results are entered into the spreadsheet. Utilizing cross tabulation, pie charts, bar graphs, and percentage analysis, the acquired data was examined. 19 multiple-choice questions were included in a structured questionnaire, and demographic information was also gathered.

Results

TEST - 1

To determine whether age impacts preference for mileage.

- Null hypothesis (H0): The consumers' ages and preferred mileage have no discernible link.
- Alternate hypothesis (H1): Age of customers and mileage preference are significantly correlated.

Table 70.1 Chi-square test analysis.

Observed value			
Preference towards mileage is influenced by age	Yes	No	Total
Below 20	14	3	17
20-35	56	8	64
35-50	20	1	21
Above 50	02	0	02
Grand total	92	12	104

Expected value			
Preference toward mileage is influenced by age	Yes	No	Total
Below 20	15.0	2	17
20-35	56.6	7.3	63.9
35-50	18.6	2.4	21
Above 50	1.8	0.3	2.1
Grand total	92	12	104

Calculated values				
O	E	O-E	$(O-E)^2$	$(O-E)^2/E$
14	15.0	-1.03	1.07	0.0717
56	56.6	-0.61	0.37	0.0066
20	18.6	1.42	2.02	0.1090
2	1.8	0.23	0.05	0.0301
3	2	1.03	1.07	0.5497
8	7.3	0.61	0.37	0.0512
1	2.4	-1.42	2.02	0.8357
0	0.3	-0.23	0.05	0.2307
			Grand total	1.885

Source: Author

Degree of freedom   = (R-l)*(C-l)

                        = (4-1)*(2-1)

                        = 3*1

                        = 3

Table value @5%   = 7.815

Table 70.1 The alternative hypothesis is rejected and the null hypothesis is accepted since the calculated value (1.885) is less than the table value (7.815). We can conclude from this test that age has no bearing on mileage. According to the data above, 20 to 35 respondents approved of mileage.

TEST - 2

TO determine whether gender affects Yamaha bike awareness.

- Null hypothesis (H0): The gender of the buyers and their knowledge of Yamaha bikes do not significantly correlate.

- Alternate hypothesis (H1): There is a substantial correlation between customers' awareness of Yamaha bikes and their gender.

Degree of freedom   = (R-l)*(C-l)

                        =(2-1)*(4-1)

                        = 1*3

                        = 3

Table value @5%   = 7.815

Table 70.2 The alternative hypothesis is rejected because the estimated value (3.156) is smaller than the value in the table (7.815), which accepts the null hypothesis. We can learn from this test that Yamaha bikes are not influenced by a person's gender. According to the data above, 40% of respondents learned about Yamaha bikes from their friends.

Table 70.2 Chi-square test analysis.

Observed value

Observe	Social media	Advertisement	Friends	Others	Total
Male	10	29	40	5	84
Female	4	5	8	3	20
Grand total	14	34	48	8	104

Expected values

Estimate	Social media	Advertisement	Friends	Others	Total
Male	11.3	27.4	38.9	6.4	84
Female	2.7	6.6	9.1	1.6	20
Grand total	14	34	48	8	104

Calculated values

O	E	O-E	$(O-E)^2$	$(O-E)^2/E$
10	11.3	-1.30	1.71	0.151
4	2.7	1.30	1.71	0.635
29	27.4	1.53	2.36	0.086
5	6.6	-1.53	2.36	0.361
40	38.9	1.23	1.51	0.039
8	9.1	-1.23	1.51	0.164
5	6.4	-1.46	2.13	0.330
3	1.6	1.46	2.13	1.388
			Grand total	3.156

Source: Author

Discussions

(Jain, 2015) claimed in her work "A study of customer satisfaction of two wheelers on Yamaha" that motorbikes, which are regarded as fuel-efficient, dependable, and suitable for rough roads, have contributed significantly to the rise of the two-wheeler sector. According to his research, TVS-Suzuki, Hero: Honda, and Bajaj rule the two-wheeler market. According to the report, LML is facing extremely fierce competition from scooter producer and automaker Bajaj, which is a big competitor. Analysis reveals that the estimated value (1.885) is smaller than the number in the table (7.815), accepting the null hypothesis and rejecting the alternative. We can conclude from this test that age has no bearing on mileage. According to the data above, 20 to 35 respondents approved of mileage. The alternative hypothesis is rejected and the null hypothesis is accepted since the calculated value (3.156) is smaller than the table value (7.815). We can learn from this test that Yamaha bikes are not influenced by a person's gender. According to the data above, 40% of respondents learned about Yamaha bikes from their friends.

Conclusion

Chennai is a booming metropolis, although the bulk of its residents are from the middle and upper classes. As a result, there has never been a shortage of creative two-wheelers on the market in this country. The majority of clients favored bikes over all other types of vehicles that were available here. Customers in this region must adapt to their way of life. This has encouraged the arrival of a new range of motorcycles that are readily available across the country to thrive in this market. This has increased rivalry in the bike business, but Yamaha Company has survived it by achieving the greatest market share by introducing new Yamaha Two Wheelers Bikes in the Indian business. Customers are keen to buy Yamaha two-wheelers, according to the results of the survey. Therefore, the majority of clients base their bike purchases on mileage, followed by price and maintenance requirements. In the end, I'd say that the Yamaha Two Wheelers Bike is more attractive.

References

Bijapurkar, R. (2009). We Are Like that Only: Understanding the Logic of Consumer India. Penguin Books India.

Bijapurkar, R. (2014). A Never-Before World: Tracking the Evolution of Consumer India. Penguin UK.

Ferrell, O. C. (1990). Business Ethics: Ethical Decision Making and Cases. CENGAGE Learning.

Jain, P. (2015). A study of customer satisfaction of two wheelers on Yamaha. IOSR Journal of Business and Management (IOSR-JBM), 17(8), 8–19.

Kashani, K., Jeannet, J. P., Horovitz, J., Meehan, S., Ryans, A., Turpin, D., et al. (2005). Beyond Traditional Marketing: Innovations in Marketing Practice. John Wiley Sons.

Masterson, R., and Pickton, D. (2014). Marketing: An Introduction. SAGE.

McMillan, C. J. (1989). The Japanese Industrial System.

Muruganantham, S., and Vivek, D. (2021). A study on customer satisfaction towards KTM bikes with special reference to Coimbatore city. EPRA International Journal of Multidisciplinary Research (IJMR), 7(8).

Netexplo (n.d.). Smart Cities: Shaping the Society of 2030. UNESCO Publishing.

71 A comparative study on customer satisfaction on the basis of income and age group with reference to departmental stores in Chennai

Raghul, M.[1] and Jayanthi, L. N.[2]

[1]Research Scholar, Department of Commerce (General), Saveetha College of Liberal Arts and Sciences, Saveetha Institute of Medical and Technical Sciences, Saveetha University, Chennai, Tamil Nadu, India

[2]Project Guide, Department of Commerce (General), Saveetha College of Liberal Arts and Sciences, Saveetha Institute of Medical and Technical Sciences, Saveetha University, Chennai, Tamil Nadu, India

Abstract

Aim: The study's goal is to determine consumer satisfaction with regard to Chennai's department stores. People now want creative tactics and simple access methods due to the current trend, thus in order to analyze customer satisfaction with department shops, consumers were contacted directly and information was gathered both face-to-face and through questionnaires. **Materials and Methods:** The study employed both primary and secondary data. Primary data were gathered using a questionnaire with a sample size of 100, while secondary data were gathered through websites and scholarly journals. **Results:** The study's results show that the chi-square value is 1219.46 with a 0.000 p-value. The null hypothesis is thus rejected because the p-value is greater than 0.00, and it is inferred that sample respondents' levels of satisfaction with various aspects differ from theirs. **Conclusion:** In recent years, it has been observed that department stores in the Chennai region have prospered, offering their patrons great service while utilizing ever-evolving advertising strategies. The respondents' basic characteristics, shopping preferences, and opinions on the numerous factors that contribute to service satisfaction were all included in the current study.

Keywords: Consumers, goods, innovative strategies, products, purchase, quality, reduce, satisfaction, services, shopping

Introduction

Every department store today makes an effort to persuade the consumer to buy a product in a particular department store by employing cutting-edge strategies (Oswaal Editorial Board, 2022). Departmental stores are retail establishments that sell a wide variety of goods in a single building, presenting each line of merchandise in a separate departmental stores consumer and providing the kind of product that the consumer wants. As with shopping centers and chain stores, department stores have both beneficial and negative effects on the culture around them (Winston and Sommers, 2013). However, societal changes have also had an impact on the establishments themselves. The function of departmental stores in future society, if any, will depend on how they adapt to these changes as both external technology and the social components of the retail industry continue to improve. Consumer behavior is now entirely dependent on their department stores. There are numerous actions that can be taken to resolve and lessen these issues in order to meet the challenges (Handy and Pfaff, 1975). In any case, the customer is unable to lower the risk. This demonstrates how department stores can pinpoint their issues and take the necessary actions to enhance services provided to them with the use of cutting-edge tactics (Arthur Andersen LLP, 1997). To minimize labor, the acquired data were analyzed using techniques like percentage, standard deviation, coefficient of variance, and ANOVA.

"Productivity trends in department stores 1967-86" (DIANE Publishing Company, 1994). The author has attempted to analyze the productivity patterns in department shops from 1967 to 1986 in this essay. The author claims that there are three main categories of department stores. National chains are very big companies that occasionally run more than 1000 shops. From 1.4 million in 1967 to 2.0 million in 1986, there were 45% more people working in the department store sector. In contrast to customer happiness, the author (Sasser et al., 1997) provides explicit criteria of service quality. They conclude by stating that growing competition from apparel specialty stores, off-price apparel retailers, and wholesale warehouse stores may also be limiting demand for departmental

[a]manimegalai82823828@gmail.com

stores. that giving good service has a beneficial effect on the customer's satisfaction, which should not be mistaken with service quality. Sasser et al. (1997) and Eckbo (2007) offer empirical proof that different financial performance indicators, such as revenue, revenue change, margins, return on sales, market value of equity, and current earnings, are positively correlated with customer satisfaction at the level of the customer, business unit, and company. However, they show a negative link between profitability and happiness in the retail sector, which may be because the benefits of higher satisfaction can be outweighed by the added cost in the sector.

Department stores provide a variety of merchandise in varying volumes. Department stores compete fiercely with one another (Lucy, 2021). The goal of department stores is to retain customers and foster customer loyalty. To that end, they provide a variety of services using creative marketing techniques and implement various promotional strategies to satisfy customers. Understanding customer satisfaction levels and purchasing habits is essential for any department store. (Food and Agriculture Organization of the United Nations, 2021) Department retailers may find this useful when drafting their promotional plans Figure 71.1. A study on consumer satisfaction with reference to departmental stores in Chennai is an attempt the researcher has made to gauge the level of satisfaction. This study examines the level of customer satisfaction with several service aspects provided by Chennai's department stores. The consumer has many options in this cutthroat world to choose any store to purchase high-quality goods. (FAO, 2020) It is a crucial and difficult challenge for department shops to draw customers in order to continue and grow their business in a highly competitive environment. The quality of the service is far more crucial than the technical or product quality when it comes to the many factors that help businesses establish connection with customers and maintain them as loyal customers. Therefore, the current study attempts to highlight the numerous characteristics of customer happiness, which would undoubtedly serve a purpose for the department stores to determine the quality of their service.

Material and Methods

Limitations of the study: The survey is only able to include 100 customers due to time and financial restrictions. The study's conclusions and recommendations could or might not apply to other fields. It's possible that this study won't have long-term relevance.

Scope of the study: This study examines the level of customer satisfaction with several service aspects provided by Chennai's department stores. The consumer has many options in this cutthroat world to choose any store to purchase high-quality goods. It is a crucial and difficult challenge for department shops to draw customers in order to continue and grow their business in a highly competitive environment. The quality of the service is far more crucial than the technical or product quality when it comes to the many factors that help businesses establish connection with customers and maintain them as loyal customers. In order to help department shops assess the quality of their customer service, the current study intends to highlight the numerous components of client satisfaction.

Statistical analysis and tools: By using a questionnaire to compile the data, the study's primary data was obtained from the study's participants. Part A and Part B of the questionnaire were created. Questions about the demographics of the consumers who used

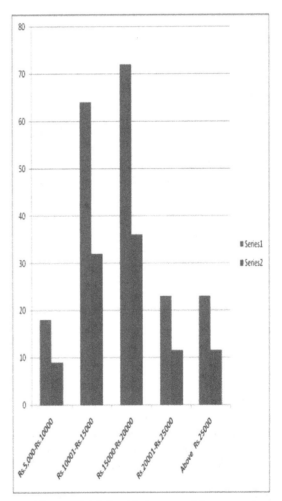

Figure 71.1 Monthly income of the respondents
Source: Author

Table 71.1 Monthly income of the respondents.

Monthly income	No of respondents	Percentage
Rs. 5,000-Rs. 10000	9	9
Rs. 10001-Rs. 15000	32	32
Rs. 15000-Rs. 20000	36	36
Rs. 20001-Rs. 25000	11	11
Above Rs. 25000	12	12
Total	100	100

Source: Author

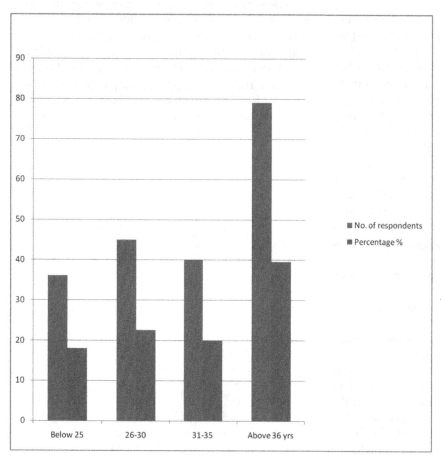

Figure 71.2 Showing the age group of the respondent
Source: Author

creative techniques were covered in the first section. Part B of the survey includes questions about consumer preferences and their level of satisfaction with department shops. On both primary and secondary data, this study is built. Structured questionnaires have been used to obtain primary data. The secondary data were gathered from websites, articles published in journals, newspapers, and publications. Tools like percentage, standard deviation, coefficient of variance, and ANOVA were used to analyze the acquired data.

Table 71.2 Showing the age group of respondents.

Age (in years)	No. of respondents	percentage
Below 25	18	18
26-30	22	22
31-35	20	20
Above 36 years	40	40
Total	100	100

Source: Author

Table 71.3 Showing have you ever availed door delivery services.

Opinion	No of respondents	Percentage
Yes	31	31
No	69	69
Total	100	100

Source: Author

Table 71.4 Chi-square test between satisfaction of various factor and level satisfaction opinion of respondents of sample respondents.

	Value	df	Asymp. Sig.
Pearson Chi-square	1219.46	72	0.000
Likelihood ratio	1184.53	72	0.000
Linear-by-linear association	.858	1	0.000
No of valid cases	100		

Source: Author

Results

In Table 71.1 out of the 100 sample respondents, it can be seen that 36% of them have monthly incomes between Rs. 15001 and Rs. 20,000, 32% between Rs. 1000 and 20,000, 11.5% between Rs. 20001 and Rs. 25,000, and 9% between Rs. 500 and 20,000. We might infer that 36% of respondents fall into the Rs. 1501–Rs. 20,000 monthly income range.

Table 71.2 reveals that out of the 100 total respondents in the sample, 39.5% are above the age of 36, 22% are between the ages of 26 and 30, 20% are between the ages of 31 and 35, and 18% are under the age of 25, according to the data. Thus, it can be said that a sizeable 40 of the sample's respondents are beyond the age of 36.

Table 71.3 demonstrates that just 31% of the 100 sample respondents have used door delivery service. 69% of the responders who are still alive had not used the door delivery service. Thus, it can be stated that 69% of survey respondents did not use the door delivery service offered by their preferred department stores.

In Table 71.4, the researcher is curious to know if there is any correlation between the level of satisfaction with certain elements and the opinions of sample respondents. To test the null hypothesis (H0), the chi-square test was chosen. The Chi-square value is 1219.46 with a p-value of 0.000, as seen in above. The null hypothesis is thus rejected because the p-value is greater than 0.00, and it is inferred that sample respondents' levels of satisfaction with various aspects differ from theirs.

Discussions

The earlier study, conducted by (DIANE Publishing Company, 1994), "has determined that growing competition from apparel specialty stores, off-price apparel retailers, and wholesale warehouse stores may also be limiting demand for departmental stores. The department stores in the Chennai region were found to be flourishing in this study, offering exceptional service to the clients by using ever-evolving advertising strategies. Sasser et al. (1997), Eckbo (2007) offer empirical proof that different financial performance indicators, such as revenue, revenue change, margins, return on sales, market value of equity, and current earnings, are positively correlated with customer satisfaction at the level of the customer, business unit, and company. The respondents' basic characteristics, shopping preferences, and opinions on the numerous factors that contribute to service satisfaction were all included in the current study. The results of the response analysis show that customers prioritized reliability, which means that they searched for the right quality products at prices below the MRP or at moderate prices as well as the availability of the entire range of products they required. They always wanted a store that would facilitate one-stop shopping, provide the necessary room and ease of movement, and represent a customer-friendly environment. The response factored into how satisfied customers felt, with timely service and helpful staff being prerequisites. Retailers should therefore pay close attention to the factors of dependability, tangibility, and responsiveness. Every retail company should regularly assess the degree of client satisfaction and make attempts to enhance creative approaches or improve the situation. The store should adapt to changes in the retail industry and take the required steps to maintain its operations and attract additional customers in this cutthroat environment. It is up to these establishments to tidy up in size and style, increase the quality and variety of their goods, and spice up their offerings as more and more trendy modern retail departmental stores sprout up in the city.

Conclusion

The study came to the conclusion that, based on the results of the response analysis, it is obvious that customers prioritized reliability, meaning that they searched first and foremost for the right quality products at prices below the MRP or at moderate prices, as well as the availability of the entire range of products they required. They always favored a store that would facilitate one-stop shopping and provide the necessary room and convenience to browse, as well as an inviting ambiance. The response factored into how satisfied customers felt, with timely service and helpful staff being prerequisites. Retailers should therefore pay close attention to the factors of dependability, tangibility, and responsiveness. Every retail business should regularly assess customer happiness.

Conflict of Interests

No conflict of interests in this manuscript

Authors Contributions

Author Raghul was involved in data collection, data analysis, and manuscript writing. Author Jayanthi was involved in conceptualization, data validation, and critical review of the manuscript.

Acknowledgments

The authors would like to express their gratitude towards Saveetha College of Liberal Arts and Sciences, SIMATS for providing the necessary infrastructure to carry out this work successfully.

References

Arthur Andersen LLP (1997). Small Store Survival: Success Strategies for Retailers. John Wiley and Sons.

DIANE Publishing Company (1994). Productivity Measures for Selected Industries and Government Services. DIANE Publishing.

Eckbo, B. E. (2007). Handbook of Corporate Finance: Empirical Corporate Finance. Elsevier.

Food and Agriculture Organization of the United Nations (2021). The Impact of Disasters and Crises on Agriculture and Food Security: 2021. Food and Agriculture Org.

Handy, C. R., and Pfaff, M. (1975). Consumer Satisfaction with Food Products and Marketing Services.

FAO (2020). The State of World Fisheries and Aquaculture 2020: Sustainability in Action. Food and Agriculture Organization of the United Nations.

Lucy, C. (2021). Stiff Competition. Fevered Publishing LLC.

Oswaal Editorial Board (2022). Oswaal CBSE Accountancy, English Core, Business Studies & Mathematics Class 11 Sample Question Papers + Question Bank (Set of 8 Books) (For 2023 Exam). Oswaal Books and Learning Private Limited.

Sasser, W. E., Schlesinger, L. A., and Heskett, J. L. (1997). Service Profit Chain. Simon and Schuster.

Winston, W., and Sommers, P. A. (2013). Consumer Satisfaction in Medical Practice. Routledge.

72 Accurate prediction of news classification using multinomial naive bayes algorithm compared with novel support vector machine

Keerthana, N. P.[a] and Christy, S.

Department of Information Technology, SIMATS, Saveetha University, Chennai, India

Abstract

The objective of this research is to achieve precise news categorization using the multinomial Naive Bayes method, contrasting it with support vector machines. Evaluating news classification involves novel support vector machine (SVM) and multinomial Naive Bayes algorithms, each with 10 iterations. Data from a Kaggle dataset, totaling 285,000 samples, underwent analysis using clinical, maintaining Gpower at 0.8 and alpha at 0.05. The study aims to assess accuracy and loss in news classification. The mean accuracy of the novel SVM is notably higher at 92.51% compared to multinomial Naive Bayes at 74.04%. An Independent sample T-Test demonstrates significance ($p < 0.05$) in accuracy and loss, indicating a notable difference between the two algorithms. This research sheds light on the strengths and weaknesses of the naive bayes algorithm and SVM in news classification. Overall, news classification using the novel SVM significantly outperforms the multinomial Naive Bayes algorithm.

Keywords: Cities, machine learning, multinomial naive bayes, news classification, novel support vector machine, text classification

Introduction

In the current categorizer system, news classification plays a crucial role. Researchers are employing an automated method to categorize news utilizing the primary algorithm support vector machine (SVM) (Ramakrishnan et al., 2020). It has been demonstrated that SVM accurately produces positive classification outcomes. The machine learning approaches of classified data are considered a feature of support vector machines (Ravikumar and Lee, 2020). Multinomial Naive Bayes is a simple technique for creating classifiers (Bajaj et al., 2016). SVMs are basically used for high-dimensional data to provide more information about city news. The value of one feature is independent of the value of every other feature, which can be used to train such classifiers (Rathi et al., 2022). The application of these algorithms is to assign feature values, represented as vectors of a finite set, and it is also useful for news readers. There are 204 articles in news classification published in IEEE Digital Explore and 115 articles in Scopus or Google Scholar Science Direct. The data was trained using machine learning techniques using SVM. This article uses machine learning to identify the illness. The approach of using machine learning and natural language processing to overcome this challenge is discussed in this study (K and Ravikumar, 2020). Multinomial Naive Bayes

classifiers are a prominent statistical technique for email filtering (Rathi et al., 2022). This application of the research discusses the strategy of employing machine learning and natural language processing to meet this difficulty. Researchers employed news classification detection in this study (Bajaj et al., 2016). Then, these probabilities can be used as inputs to the SVM algorithm, which is trained to make the final classification decision (Liu, Xu, and Liu, 2010). The combination of these two algorithms can result in improved classification accuracy compared to using either algorithm alone (Pant et al., 2018). The most cited article for training such classifiers; there isn't just one technique, but rather a family of algorithms built on the premise that, given the class variable, the value of one feature is independent of the value of every other feature (Lakshmi et al., 2022).

The drawback of the existing system is that SVM are more adept at resolving problems of this nature because they may employ regularization strategies to lessen overfitting (Sharma and Singh, 2016). As opposed to support vector machines, the multinomial Naive Bayes algorithm is used to accurately classify news articles into many categories. New York, London, and Tokyo are considered global cities with significant economic and cultural influence. The two algorithms are compared for accuracy and speed to see which performs better (Dilrukshi and De Zoysa,

---

[a]keerthanasmartgenresearch@gmail.com

Table 72.1 Support vector machine accuracy and loss for N = 10.

Iterations	Accuracy (%)	Loss (%)
1	91.05	8.95
2	93.57	6.43
3	87.75	12.25
4	96.54	3.46
5	89.73	10.27
6	94.08	5.92
7	98.65	1.35
8	85.68	14.32
9	86.61	13.39
10	97.37	2.63

Source: Author

Table 72.2 Multinomial Navie Bayes accuracy and loss for N = 10.

Iterations	Accuracy (%)	Loss (%)
1	69.06	30.94
2	72.01	27.99
3	67.09	32.91
4	74.02	25.98
5	76.08	23.92
6	66.05	33.95
7	70.03	29.97
8	65.07	34.93
9	73.03	26.97
10	64.07	35.93

Source: Author

Table 72.3 T-test group statistics with mean, std. deviation, std. error mean and confidence = 95%.

	Group	N	Mean	Std. deviation	Std. error mean
Accuracy	Support vector machine	10	92.1030	4.63643	1.46617
	Multinomial Naive Bayes algorithm	10	69.6510	4.07642	1.28908
	Support vector machine	10	7.8970	4.63643	1.46617
Loss	Multinomial Naive Bayes algorithm	10	30.3490	4.07642	1.28908

Source: Author

2013). The multinomial Naive Bayes algorithm is not affected by the sequence of words because it is based on specific words that will appear in a document (Yerekar et al., 2021)..

Materials and Methods

The study comprises two groups: Multinomial Naive Bayes algorithm and innovative support vector machine. With a sample size of 20 (Group 1 = 171, Group 2 = 171), novel support vector machines and Multinomial Naive Bayes algorithms are applied for news classification enhancement. Data collection, cleaning, and pre-processing precede organizing data for algorithm use. The dataset is sourced from Kaggle. Novel support vector machine shows 92.51% mean accuracy, while multinomial Naive Bayes records 74.04%. Both algorithms' precision is assessed using unseen test data, facilitating accuracy evaluation and potential improvements. System requirements include Intel Core I3 processor, 4GB RAM, 64-bit OS, and 1TB HDD space, with software compatibility for Windows 8, 10, 11, Google Collab Notebook, Python, and MS-Office.

Multinomial Naive Bayes algorithm (MNB)
In this investigation, the MNB classifier was subjected to five consecutive cross-validations (Zairina et al., 2017). Widely utilized in text classification tasks, MNB predicts labels based on word frequencies (Sharma and Singh, 2016). Initially, MNB constructs a vocabulary from training data, computing word likelihoods for each class (Wen and Li, 2007). Despite its efficiency with large datasets, MNB's assumption of feature independence can be sensitive to unusual words, impacting classification outcomes (Dong et al., 2016). Techniques like smoothing and feature selection are often employed to mitigate this issue. However, MNB remains a robust method, particularly suitable for text classification where the number of features is significant, as it is generally resistant to the effects of irrelevant features (Singh et al., 2019). Its pseudocode outlines its simplicity and effectiveness, making it a preferred choice for various text classification applications (Yerekar and Yerekar, 2021):

Novel support vector machine
In this study, novel SVM demonstrate the ability to classify objects based on high-dimensional feature

Table 72.4 Independent sample *T*-test is applied for the data set fixing confidence interval as 95% and support vector machine is significantly better than multinomial Naive Bayes algorithm (Independent Sample *T*- Test) significance as p = 0.045 (p < 0.05).

		Leven's test of equality of variances		T-test for equality of means					95% Confidence interval of the difference	
		F	sig.	t	df	Sig 2-tailed	Mean difference	Std error difference	Lower	upper
Accuracy	Equal variance assumed	.379	.045	11.500	18	<.001	22.45200	1.95227	18.35043	26.55357
	Equal variance did not assume			11.500	17.710	<.001	22.45200	1.95227	18.34560	26.55840
Loss	Equal variance assumed	.379	.045	-11.500	18	<.001	-22.45200	1.95227	-26.55357	-18.35043
	Equal variance does not assume			-11.500	17.710	<.001	-22.45200	1.95227	-26.55840	-18.34560

Source: Author

Table 72.5 Comparison of the SVM algorithm and MNB algorithm with their accuracy.

Classifier	Accuracy (%)	Loss (%)
SVM	92.51%	7.49%
MNB	74.04%	25.96%

Source: Author

vectors. This allows rapid categorization of articles by word count, particularly those exceeding 100,000 words. Dilrukshi et al. (2013) present insights from studies employing various preprocessing techniques to generate informative input features, notably syllable and phoneme n-grams. SVM, a supervised learning method, divides data into two groups for classification or regression tasks (Singh et al., 2019). While regression is less common, SVR, also known as novel SVR, utilizes SVM for regression analysis. Despite the emergence of more advanced algorithms, SVM remains prevalent in machine learning applications (Dilrukshi et al., 2013). The software requires a minimum system configuration of Intel Core I3 dual-core processor, 4GB RAM, 64-bit OS, 1TB HDD, and Windows 8, 10, 11, along with Python and MS-Office on a Google notebook.

Statistical analysis

The software tool version 26 of the Statistical Package for Social Sciences (SPSS) was employed for

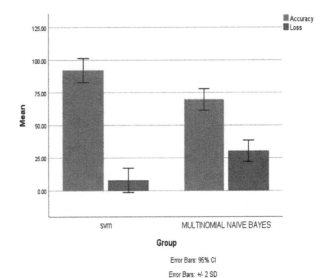

Figure 72.1 Comparison of SVM and MNB algorithm in terms of accuracy. The mean accuracy of the SVM is greater than the MNB algorithm and the standard deviation is also slightly higher than MNB algorithm. X-axis: SVM and MNB algorithm. Y-axis: Mean accuracy of detection +2 SD

Source: Author

statistical analysis. An independent sample T-test was performed to assess accuracy, along with calculations of standard deviation and standard mean errors using the SPSS tool. The significance values for both proposed and current algorithms encompass group statistical metrics. Independent variables include politics, sports, and entertainment, while dependent variables consist of accuracy and loss. This study conducts an Independent T-test as part of its research analysis.

Result

In statistical analysis, a total of 20 samples are utilized. The dataset analyzed with the MNB algorithm pertains to BBC data. Chicago, an American city, unveiled a new transportation policy in a 2015 press briefing. Employing the dataset and a category, the novel SVM algorithm categorizes news, achieving 92.51% accuracy. Table 72.1 displays MNB algorithm accuracy with N = 10 after grouping, while Table 72.2 showcases accuracy with N = 10. Mean accuracy and loss values, along with standard deviation, are tabulated in Table 72.3 using the T-test for both algorithms. The dataset is input for the multinomial Naive Bayes classifier, yielding a lower accuracy of 74.04%. Table 72.4 indicates the independent sample t-test's significance with p = 0.045, demonstrating SVM's superiority over MNB in significance. Table 72.5 contrasts accuracy and loss between SVM and MNB. A bar graph illustrates accuracy and loss for both methods.

Discussion

This study highlights the superior accuracy of the novel SVM algorithm over the Multinomial Naive Bayes algorithm. SVM achieved 92.10% accuracy, while multinomial Naive Bayes trailed at 69.65%, indicating SVM's clear superiority. SVM, renowned for its reliability, excels in text classification by categorizing documents effectively. In "News Classification Using Machine Learning Techniques," M. Sundarababu and MahajanSuthar stress the necessity of transitioning to electronic data storage to manage increasing data volumes, crucial for informed decision-making. Despite the time-consuming nature of data mining, as noted by Dilrukshi and de Zoysa, it remains essential for uncovering valuable insights. In "News classification using process of workflow with SVM," Gurmeet Kaur and Karan Bajaj address challenges in news article classification due to the rapid generation and distribution of news content, as well as limited representation of diverse perspectives and cultural backgrounds. SVMs use a hyperplane to classify data points into two classes, ensuring optimal accuracy. Additionally, the multinomial Naive Bayes algorithm complements SVM by estimating document classification likelihood within specific classes. Despite challenges like real-time classification and limited diversity in training data, SVMs remain a potent tool for text classification, offering high accuracy and versatility across various datasets and applications.

Conclusion

The Novel Support Vector algorithm performs well with a higher degree of accuracy than the Multinomial Naive Bayes Algorithm. The Support Vector Machine algorithm performs noticeably better with accuracy of 92.51% than the Multinomial Naive Bayes Algorithm accuracy of 74.04%.

Acknowledgements

The authors would like to express their gratitude towards Saveetha School of Engineering, Saveetha Institute of Medical and Technical Sciences (formerly known as Saveetha University), Best Enlist PVT Limited, Chennai for providing the necessary infrastructure to carry out this work successfully.

References

Bajaj, A., John, C., Kaur, S., and Middha, D. (2016). Cathine and alcohol involved fatality: a rare case report with a brief review of the literature. *Egyptian Journal of Forensic Sciences*, 6(4), 538–541. https://doi.org/10.1016/j.ejfs.2016.06.011.

Dilrukshi, I., and De Zoysa, K. (2013). Twitter news classification: theoretical and practical comparison of SVM against naive bayes algorithms. In 2013 International Conference on Advances in ICT for Emerging Regions (ICTer). https://doi.org/10.1109/icter.2013.6761192.

Dilrukshi, I., De Zoysa, K., and Caldera, A. (2013). Twitter news classification using SVM. In 2013 8th International Conference on Computer Science and Education. https://doi.org/10.1109/iccse.2013.6553926.

Dong, F., Guo, Y., Li, C., Xu, G., and Wei, F. (2016). ClassifyDroid: large scale android applications classification using semi-supervised multinomial naive bayes. In 2016 4th International Conference on Cloud Computing and Intelligence Systems (CCIS). https://doi.org/10.1109/ccis.2016.7790228.

Pant, G. B., Kumar, P. P., Revadekar, J. V., and Singh, N. (2018). Climate Change in the Himalayas. Cham, Switzerland: Springer International Publishing https://doi.org/10.1007/978-3-319-61654-4.

Ramakrishnan, K. M., Ramachandran, B., Ravikumar, K. G., Ravikumar, K., Putli, S., Jayaraman, V., et al. (2020). Electrical injury in pediatric patients – a case series. *Indian Journal of Burns*, 28(1), 94–97. https://doi.org/10.4103/ijb.ijb_27_19.

Rathi, R., Reddy, M. C. G., Narayana, A. L., Narayana, U. L., and Rahman, M. S. (2022). Investigation and implementation of 8D methodology in a manufacturing system. *Materials Today: Proceedings*, 50, 743–750. https://doi.org/10.1016/j.matpr.2021.05.273.

Ravikumar, A., and Lee, J. (2020). Bayesian deconvolution of rate pressure data using regularizing priors. In SPE Latin America and Caribbean Petroleum Engineering Conference. SPE. July 27, 2020. https://doi.org/10.2118/198960-ms.

Sharma, N., and Singh, M. (2016). Modifying naive bayes classifier for multinomial text classification. In 2016 International Conference on Recent Advances and Innovations in Engineering (ICRAIE), (pp. 1–7). IEEE. https://doi.org/10.1109/icraie.2016.7939519.

Singh, G., Kumar, B., Gaur, L., and Tyagi, A. (2019). Comparison between multinomial and bernoulli naïve bayes for text classification. In 2019 International Conference on Automation, Computational and Technology Management (ICACTM), (pp. 593–596). IEEE. https://doi.org/10.1109/icactm.2019.8776800.

Wen, J., and Li, Z. (2007). Semantic smoothing the multinomial naive bayes for biomedical literature classification. In 2007 IEEE International Conference on Granular Computing (GRC 2007), (pp. 648–648). IEEE. https://doi.org/10.1109/grc.2007.98.

Yerekar, A., Mungale, N., and Wazalwar, S. (2021). A multinomial technique for detecting fake news using the naive bayes classifier. In 2021 International Conference on Computational Intelligence and Computing Applications (ICICI), (pp. 1–5). IEEE. https://doi.org/10.1109/iccica52458.2021.9697244.

Yerekar, P. A., and Yerlekar, A (2021). Fake news detection using machine learning approach multinomial naive bayes classifier. *International Journal for Research in Applied Science and Engineering Technology*, 9(v). https://doi.org/10.22214/ijraset.2021.34509.

73 Analysis of consumer perception and awareness on branded and non-branded jewellery market

M. Athithyan[1] and Prameela Rani Mannava[2,a]

[1]Saveetha College of Liberal Arts and Sciences, Saveetha University Chennai, India

[2]Department of Commerce, Saveetha University Chennai, India

Abstract

This study examines consumer perceptions and awareness regarding branded and non-branded jewellery, with the goal of comprehending how individuals perceive quality, value, reputation, trustworthiness, design, and style of such items. Leveraging an analysis of prior research and primary and secondary data, a close-ended survey was administered, employing a convenient sampling approach for both online and offline data collection, with a sample size of 100. Examination through the Chi-Square test in SPSS revealed no substantial variance between educational attainment and awareness in branded and non-branded jewellery establishments. Predominantly, female respondents aged over 30, with incomes ranging from 15,000 to 30,000, were represented. The bulk of participants made selections based on recommendations from acquaintances and favoured establishments offering equitable pricing, convenient inventory management and display, a diverse selection of branded merchandise, meticulous grading and packaging, and timely availability of requisite items. Ultimately, preferences for establishments varied based on the behaviours and perspectives of participants, with contentment levels influenced by expedient service and supportive personnel.

Keywords: Branded and non-branded jewellery, customers satisfaction, gold, jewellery

Introduction

Customer contentment is a vital element that can influence consumer behaviour within the jewellery sector. In this realm, both recognized and non-branded jewellery wield potential to shape customer fulfilment. Branded jewellery typically correlates with heightened quality and status, potentially yielding greater levels of consumer gratification among those valuing such aspects. Branded jewellery might also deliver superior client assistance and post-purchase backing, thereby further amplifying customer satisfaction (Barnard, 2008).A survey undertaken to grasp the influence of celebrity endorsements in jewellery promotions on consumer conduct, notably among Lebanese women (Ahmed, 2015). Conversely, unbranded jewellery may be more attainable to a broader consumer spectrum owing to its reduced-price range. This could entice price-conscious consumers unable to afford branded jewellery. Nonetheless, non-branded jewellery might be perceived as inferior quality, potentially detracting from customer contentment. Overall, customer contentment within the jewellery sector is shaped by numerous factors encompassing product excellence, design, pricing, client care, and post-sales support. Manufacturers and retailers within the jewellery sector capable of effectively addressing these facets

are likelier to attain heightened levels of customer satisfaction and retention.Enhancing customer contentment within the jewellery sector mandates manufacturers and retailers to discern the requisites and inclinations of their target clientele. This can be realized through market exploration, customer input, and monitoring of consumer inclinations and trends. By discerning the attributes valued by their patrons and their anticipations from products and services, jewellery manufacturers and retailers can devise more efficacious marketing strategies and product assortments aligning with the preferences of their target audience. To sum up, customer satisfaction emerges as a pivotal determinant influencing consumer conduct within the jewellery sector. Both acknowledged and unbranded jewellery have potential to influence customer fulfilment, underscoring the significance for jewellery manufacturers and retailers to comprehend the determinants impacting customer satisfaction to devise more efficacious marketing strategies and product offerings.

Materials and Methods

Examined prior investigations, utilized both primary and secondary data, employed close-ended questionnaire, employed convenient sampling approach,

[a]mprameelarani9416@gmail.com

carried out surveys both online & offline, total sample size is 100, employed Chi-Square statistical test in SPSS software, summary of the investigation.

Table 73.1 shows that out of the total 100 sample respondents, 39.5% are in the age group of above 36 years, 22% are in the 26-30 age group, 20% are in the age group of 31-35, and 18% are in the age group of below 25 years. Hence, it is concluded that a considerable 40% of sample respondents are in the age group of above 36 years.

Hypothesis testing
Based on the data presented in Table 73.2, elements such as reasonable pricing, convenient stocking and presentation, diverse assortment of branded merchandise, grading and packaging standards, varying product quality, availability of essential items within the same category, and browsing ambiance are prominently valued by customers when choosing a specific jewellery store, with rankings respectively leading, following, trailing, succeeding, advancing, proceeding,

and following, and average ratings ranging from 3.10 to 4.12. Conversely, the store's location, customer service quality, home delivery options, and integrating shopping with entertainment are moderately regarded aspects for clientele. Lastly, substantial discounts and credit/debit card conveniences are of lesser importance in the decision-making process for selecting a particular jewellery outlet. In order to delineate the distinct impact of each considered aspect on the selection of a specific jewellery store by participants, the connection between the choice of jewellery store and the selection factors is examined, derived from the null hypothesis formulated to explore this correlation among the surveyed respondents.

Null hypothesis
H0 = There exists a correlation between the choice of jewellery emporium and the determinants influencing the selection process of the participants under study.

Alternate hypothesis
H1= There exists no correlation between the choice of jewellery emporium and the determinants influencing the selection process of the participants under study.

The Chi-square test has been applied. The researcher is interested in determining whether there is any association between the size of landholdings and the type of labour used for cultivating sample respondents. For this purpose, the chi-square test was selected to test the null hypothesis (H0). Table 4.26 above reveals a chi-square value of 63 with a p-value of 0.03. Therefore, since the p-value is greater than 0.05, the null hypothesis is rejected, and it is concluded that there is no

Table 73.1 Showing the age group of respondents.

Age (in years)	No. of respondents	percentage
Below 25	18	18
26-30	22	22
31-35	20	20
Above 36 years	40	40
Total	100	100

Source: Primary data collected by authors.

Table 73.2 Standard deviation analysis - factors considering the selection of jewellery shop.

Factors	Average	Standard deviation	Rank
Different quality	3.23	1.21	5
Variety ofbranded products	3.67	1.14	3
Availability of necessary goods under the same level	3.12	1.25	6
Reasonable price	4.12	1.20	1
Convenient stocking/display	3.82	1.20	2
Location of the jewellery shop	2.45	1.33	8
Shopping blend with entertainment	2.15	1.30	11
Window shopping place	3.10	1.35	7
Credit card/debit card facility	1.50	1.36	13
Huge discount	1.75	1.26	12
Customer care service	2.40	1.31	9
Home delivery	2.39	1.28	10
Grading and packing	3.35	1.26	4

Source: Author

Table 73.3 Chi-square table.

	Value	df	Asymp. Sig.
Pearson Chi-square	63	37	0.033
Likelihood ratio	623.22	108	0.032
Linear-by-linear association	15.858	1	0.029
No of valid cases	100		

Source: Author

relationship between the selection of jewellery shops and the factors influencing the selection of sample respondents (H1).

Results

It is determined that a significant 40 of participants fall within the age bracket exceeding 36 years. It could be inferred that most participants are married. It could be deduced that most participants hold a bachelor's degree. It might be inferred that a substantial proportion of respondents are homemakers. It is observed that 36% of the participants are categorized under the monthly income range of Rs.15001-Rs.20000. It is noted that 48% of the participants are categorized within the 1–3-member category. Consequently, it is acknowledged that approximately 56% of participants have been procuring goods and services from the jewellery store for under 1 year. It indicates that 56% of participants have acquired necklaces. It may be inferred that approximately 41% of the surveyed participants learned about the specific jewellery store through acquaintances who had previously visited. Thus, it is ascertained that the majority (49%) of participants were enticed by the price reductions offered by the jewellery store.

According to research by the Financial Crisis Inquiry Commission (2011), consumers demonstrate considerable understanding of the jewellery they purchase; however, there remains a lack of comprehension regarding the determinants of pricing. Thus, it falls upon store proprietors to elucidate this aspect to consumers. Survey respondents suggest a perception that branded jewellery outlets exhibit greater transparency compared to non-branded establishments. Moreover, purchasers perceive non-branded stores as providing similar pricing to branded counterparts at reduced expenses, albeit without guarantees concerning product quality.

Conclusion

From the result of the response scrutinized, based on the current investigation, it is evident that the clientele accorded precedence to the dependability facet, namely, primarily and foremostly, they sought correct quality commodities at rates beneath the MRP or reasonable rates as well as, accessibility of the entire spectrum of products required by them. They consistently favoured a shop which would facilitate one-stop shopping with indispensable space and convenience to browse, demonstrating a customer-friendly ambiance. The contentment level depended on the receptiveness wherein the service rendered was expeditious and the staff were obligated to be readily assisting. Therefore, the vendors should exhibit acute interest in the aspects of dependability, tangibility, and receptiveness. Each retail establishment should consistently assess the contentment level of the clientele and undertake endeavours to ameliorate or broaden the scenario.

References

Ahmed, R. (2015). Impact of celebrity endorsement on consumer buying behavior.

Barnard, N. (2008). Indian jewellery. Victoria and Albert Museum.

Financial Crisis Inquiry Commission (2011). The Financial Crisis Inquiry Report: The Final Report of the National Commission on the Causes of the Financial and Economic Crisis in the United States Including Dissenting Views. Cosimo, Inc.

74 Assessing customer perception towards service quality of online banking services among various demographic groups

A.K. Renuka[1,a] and B.R. Celia[2]

[1]Research Scholar, Department of Bachelor of Commerce, Saveetha college of Liberal Arts and Sciences, Saveetha Institute of Medical and Technical Sciences, Saveetha University, Chennai, India

[2]Project Guide, Department of Bachelor of Commerce, Saveetha college of Liberal Arts and Sciences, Saveetha Institute of Medical and Technical Sciences, Saveetha University, Chennai, India

Abstract

Aim: The study is an attempt to identify the underlying factors that form the customer's perception towards online banking. This study has also aimed at analyzing the level of satisfaction among customers and the ease of operation in case of online transactions as well mobile banking. **Materials and methods:** Both primary and secondary data were used to support the current investigation. Through the use of a structured questionnaire, primary data was gathered from the clients of public sector banks. In order to gauge customer satisfaction with the online banking services offered by the aforementioned public sector banks, a convenience sampling technique was used to select a sample of 200 clients. The collected data was analyzed using mean, standard deviation and one way ANOVA. **Results and discussions:** The analysis has proved that there is a significant difference between gender and their opinion on online banking transactions. It represents that there is a significant difference between the occupation of the respondents and online banking services provided by the bank. It represents that there is a significant difference among the occupation of the respondents and online banking services are easy to operate and user-friendly. **Conclusion:** The way the entire banking industry operates has been changed by online banking services. It has improved the speed and decreased the cost of bank transactions in addition to making them easier. Banks have made significant investments to build up these facilities. Mobile banking is a service provided by banks that aims to improve both the effectiveness and efficiency with which customers carry out various transactions. It also makes financial transactions more seamless. Time savings, ease of use, cost effectiveness, account information, speed, clarity of instructions, and work quality have been proven to be key drivers of online banking usage among clients. Hence Customers need to be trained on how to utilize every new technology as most of them are only familiar with the conventional banking system.

Keywords: Customer, mobile banking, online banking, services, transactions

Introduction

A bank's operations or services are referred to as banking (Horn, 2002) Online banking, usually referred to as electronic banking, is a system of electronic payments that allows clients of banks or other (Ekos Research Associates and Task Force on the Future of the Canadian Financial Services Sector, 1998) financial institutions to carry out a variety of financial transactions via the websites of those institutions. Business transactions are supported by the finance function. Daily technology advancements are changing how business transactions are conducted. Therefore, traditional finance function cannot keep up with the rate at which technology is developing (de Waal et al., 2022). E-banking is the most extensive type of this technology revolution in financial function (More and Hiray, n.d.).

E-banking is a young industry with a recent beginning, particularly in India. Internet is the finest avenue for offering customers banking services and goods due to the quick advancement of technology (Plunkett Research Ltd. 2007). Because banks want to extend their customer base, they see the Internet as being more effective than alternative distribution channels (de Waal et al., 2022). People are growing more accustomed to banking online and think that all community banks will soon be required to provide these services.

Various investigations were made on the effects of customer satisfaction with online banking services (Rashidi, 2015). This essay focuses on evaluating how customers view e-banking services. Data was gathered by a questionnaire, and ANOVA and percentages were used in a descriptive analysis. Customers were found to be utilizing E-banking

---

[a]Researchsmartgen@gmail.com

services including ATMs, home banking, and the use of credit and debit cards, to name a few (Kundra, 2020). We can infer that about 45% of people have a favorable opinion on and are satisfied with online banking. ATMs, bill payment services, and accessing bank statements are three of the most used e-banking services. A poll identified the key success criteria for the adoption of online banking. According to Shah and Braganza, different literary works claim various variables as essential to success and are typically based on subjective, perceptual data. Survey questions are based on an analysis of previous research. The information was gathered utilizing postal questionnaires from UK-based financial sector businesses that provide their services online (Sanchez-Diaz et al., 2021). Quickly responsive goods and services, organizational flexibility, the growth of services, system integration, and improved customer service top the list of elements that have been identified to be most important (Omar, 2014). A study on customer perception towards online banking services for the success of e-banking. Organizations must regard the e-banking project as a business-critical area rather than just a technological one, according to a key takeaway from this research (Ackah and Agboyi, 2014). Internal integration, which may involve channels, technology, and business processes, needs to be prioritized Ackah and Agboyi, 2014; Khosrow-Pour, 2008). In an emerging economy, this study paper discussed the (Saibaba, 2014) customer's thoughts on internet banking. Therefore, the author argues that in a developing country like India, figuring out the numerous aspects influencing consumer perception, attitude, and satisfaction with internet banking is a crucial step in developing a bank's strategy (Riscinto-Kozub, 2008). The survey was conducted on respondents selected from the northern region of India in order to obtain this information regarding Indian clients. The key findings show that customers' use of online banking services is influenced by the type of account they have, their age, and their profession. Customers attach the highest level of usefulness to the balance enquiry service among online banking services, and they rank security and trust as the most

crucial factors influencing their level of satisfaction. A study was done to support the mobile banking business model. In order to increase the number of people who can utilize mobile banking, the causes were found and investigated (Lee, 2012). He discovered that users still have numerous issues with everything from telecom providers to banks, handsets to software application assistance for using services. Discussions on how customers in the Coimbatore region perceive the services offered by IOB and ICICI banks. Both public and private sector banks' characteristics, such as those related to internet banking, ATM services, personnel availability, and attitude, have been contrasted. According to the report, ICICI Bank offers its clients superior services than Indian Overseas Bank. "A study on customer satisfaction towards net banking with special reference to general banking customers" was to learn more about the variables affecting customer satisfaction with regard to net banking services as well as services offered by the general banking sector (Fulgence, 2012).

A study on online banking services was conducted to highlight the perception of customers towards online banking. The survey was conducted to analyze the level of satisfaction among customers using online banking services. It also was done to highlight the level of awareness and usage among various age groups of customers.

Materials and Methods

To analyze the objectives of the study a structured questionnaire was used to collect the primary data. The researcher has adopted a descriptive research study since it describes the state of affairs as it exists at present. A sample of 200 was taken for this study. The probability sampling method was used in the survey. The data was analyzed using statistical tools in SPSS like frequency analysis, independent T-test analysis and One-way ANOVA

The collected data were classified, tabulated and analyzed with the statistical tools (SPSS) from the mean score analysis on the online banking services provided by the bank.

Results and Discussions

Table 74.1 Table showing mean score analysis on the online banking services provided by bank.

Particulars	Gender	N	Mean	Std. deviation
The online banking services provided by the bank.	Male	79	2.27	0.843
	Female	67	2.34	1.008

Source: Author

Table 74.2 Table showing t test for gender and online banking services provided by the bank.

T-test for equality of means

Particulars	t[a]	df[b]	Sig.[c] (2-tailed)
Online banking services provided by the bank	0.506	144	0.014* significant

Source: Author

Table 74.3 Table showing one-way analysis for occupation and online banking services provided by the bank.

	Sum of squares	df[a]	Mean square	F[b]	Sig.[c]
Between groups	5.364	3	1.788	2.163	0.005** Significant
Within groups	117.376	142	0.827		
Total	122.740	145			

Source: Author

Table 74.4 Table showing one-way analysis for occupation and online banking services are easy to operate and user-friendly.

	Sum of squares	df[a]	Mean square	F[b]	Sig.[c]
Between groups	2.795	4	0.699	0.748	0.001** Significant
Within groups	131.732	141	0.934		
Total	134.527	145			

Source: Author

Table 74.1 shows that female respondents (2.34) have the highest mean and more focus on 'online banking services' compared to the male respondents (2.27).

Table 74.2 shows the t-test for gender and online banking services provided by the bank. It depicts that there is a significant difference at 0.014 level among the customers, with respect to gender towards online banking services provided by the bank. The online banking services provided by the bank is significant at 0.014 level and hence the hypothesis is rejected.

Table 74.3 shows ANOVA for occupation and online banking services provided by the bank. It represents that there is a significant difference among the occupation of the respondents and online banking services provided by the bank. The significance is at 0.001 level and the hypothesis is rejected.

Table 74.4 shows the one way ANOVA to identify the difference between the occupation of the respondents and online banking services are easy to operate and user-friendly. The significance is at 0.001 level and the hypothesis is rejected.

Conclusion

Online banking is having a significant impact on banking relationships. The way the entire banking industry operates has been changed by online banking services. It has improved the speed and decreased the cost of bank transactions in addition to making them easier. Banks have made significant investments to build up these facilities. The capacity of a bank to convince clients to switch to online banking determines the success of online banking. Customers need to be trained on how to utilize every new technology because they are only familiar with the conventional banking system. Overall, online banking boosts operational effectiveness, lowers costs, and provides a platform for customers to get value-added services, meeting all the requirements. This survey shows that although consumers are aware of the advantages of internet banking, they are hesitant to use digital banking. Because they lack technical proficiency, they are used to branch banking and perceive online banking to be inconvenient. Security, safety, and a lack of trust are the main problems with online banking. The findings also demonstrate that retaining and attracting clients is greatly aided by dependability, convenience, speed, and user-friendliness.

Conflict of interests

No conflict of interests in this manuscript

Authors Contributions

Author Renuka was involved in data collection, data analysis, manuscript writing. Author Dr B R Celia was involved in conceptualization, data validation, and critical review of the manuscript.

Acknowledgments

The authors would like to express their gratitude towards Saveetha College of Liberal Arts and Sciences.

Saveetha Institute of Medical and Technical Sciences (Formerly known as Saveetha University) for providing the necessary infrastructure to carry out this work successfully.

Funding

We would also like to thank the following organizations for providing financial assistance to complete the study.

1. Saveetha University
2. Saveetha Institute of Medical and Technical Sciences
3. Saveetha College of Liberal Arts and Sciences

References

Ackah, D., and Agboyi, M. R. (2014). Adoption of Electronic Banking in Ghana Banking System: A Case Study of Guaranty Trust Bank (Ghana) Limited. GRIN Verlag.

de Waal, A., Bilstra, E., and Bootsman, J. (2022). Building the High-Performance Finance Function. IGI Global.

Ekos Research Associates, and Task Force on the Future of the Canadian Financial Services Sector (1998). Public opinion research relating to the financial services sector .

Fulgence, K. (2012). Factors Influencing Customer Satisfaction with Internet Banking. LAP Lambert Academic Publishing.

Horn, N. (2002). Legal Issues in Electronic Banking. Springer.

Khosrow-Pour, M. (2008). Encyclopedia of Information Science and Technology, (2nd edn.). IGI Global.

Kundra, D. (2020). A study on consumer behaviour towards e-banking services .

Lee, I. (2012). Strategy, Adoption, and Competitive Advantage of Mobile Services in the Global Economy. IGI Global.

More, V. S., and Hiray, A. (n.d.). Recent Trends In Business And Management. Archers & Elevators Publishing House.

Omar, A. (2014). Customer perception towards online banking services: empirical evidence from Pakistan .

Plunkett Research Ltd. (2007). Plunkett's E-Commerce & Internet Business Almanac 2008: E-Commerce & Internet Business Industry Market Research, Statistics, Trends & Leading Companie. Plunkett Research, Ltd.

Rashidi, E. (2015). Discussing the effects of internet banking on customer satisfaction.

Riscinto-Kozub, K. A. (2008). The Effects of Service Recovery Satisfaction on Customer Loyalty and Future Behavioral Intentions: An Exploratory Study in the Luxury Hotel Industry. Auburn University.

Saibaba, S. (2014). Factors influencing customers' intentions to use internet banking: model development and test. *International Journal of Innovative Technology and Adaptive Management (IJITAM)*, ISSN: 2347-3622.

Sanchez-Diaz, I., Vural, C. A., and Halldórsson, A. (2021). Assessing the inequalities in access to online delivery services and the way COVID-19 pandemic affects marginalization. *Transport Policy*, 109(August), 24–36.

75 Assessing satisfaction of programming content among Tamil news channel viewers

Rahul Kumar, S. and Celia, B. R.

Saveetha College of Liberal Arts and Science, Saveetha University, Chennai, India

Abstract

Tamil media outlets, known as news channels, deliver information, including news, discussions, and informative content, in the Tamil language. These channels focus on reporting local, national, and international events, aiming to offer viewers a comprehensive insight into matters affecting their daily lives. Their programming typically encompasses breaking news, political updates, weather forecasts, sports highlights, business updates, entertainment gossip, and human-interest stories. Alongside news segments, they host panel debates, discussions, and interviews with experts and prominent figures. To gauge viewer satisfaction with the content, a study was conducted among Tamil news channel audiences. A sample of 100 viewers was randomly selected, and a descriptive analysis was carried out to assess preferences, utility, and trustworthiness of these channels. Findings indicated significant disparities among viewers based on gender and age groups concerning the reliability and usefulness of the information presented. It's imperative for these channels to deliver credible, evidence-based information, avoiding sensationalism in sensitive matters. Additionally, the content should be informative and beneficial to the audience. Overall, Tamil news channels play a vital role in educating and keeping viewers informed about crucial issues and global events, fostering a sense of connection to the world.

Introduction

Tamil Nadu, situated in the southern part of India, boasts a diverse cultural legacy and historical background. The state's media landscape thrives, with numerous news outlets providing comprehensive coverage of local affairs and beyond. Initially, Doordarshan monopolised news broadcasting, but with the onset of privatization, a plethora of channels emerged, catering to both entertainment and information needs. Notable among them are Sun News, Puthiya Thalaimurai, Thanthi TV, News7 Tamil, and Polimer News Blair (2017). These television networks delve into a wide array of topics, including local, regional, and national news, sports, entertainment, and business. Complementing traditional television broadcasts, online news portals offer real-time updates on Tamil Nadu's events and developments. Digital media platforms have revolutionized news consumption, allowing people to stay abreast of current affairs even while on the move. Collectively, the Tamil Nadu media sector, with its multifaceted offerings, wields significant influence in shaping public perceptions and ensuring citizens remain well-informed about pertinent issues.

Investigation by Kempton (2022) explored television viewing preferences and behaviors within the Inuit communities of the Eastern and Central Arctic regions. The results indicated notable disparities in the consumption of various programming genres among the Inuit population (Glória et al., 2024). The fundamental premise posits that Inuit males who heavily immerse themselves in sports programming may hold a skewed perception of television's broader content (Barnett, 2011). Observations suggest that children exhibit higher television consumption rates compared to adults, displaying a preference for adult-oriented content and maintaining viewing habits into late hours. Despite transitioning from childhood to adolescence and increasing peer influence, teenagers continue to allocate significant portions of their time to television viewing (Jones et al., 2010). Their research identifies MTV programs as catalysts for transformative shifts in Asia's music landscape, with multinational rock and world music genres gaining prominence among Asian youth, overshadowing traditional styles. They also noted that approximately 48% of upper-class and 62% of middle-class Indians devote more than two hours daily to television viewing (Curtin and Shattuc, 2017). Proposals stemming from their investigation advocate for the integration of positive themes in television content, emphasizing the need to counterbalance the portrayal of crime, commercialization, and glamourization to preserve societal values.

The investigation into the satisfaction level of audiences regarding Tamil news channels aimed to uncover the diverse elements contributing to viewer

[a]Researchsmartgen@gmail.com

satisfaction with the broadcasted news content, its utility, and reliability. An analysis was undertaken to discern any notable disparities concerning gender in the perceived usefulness of news presented by these channels, to assess any significant variations in the perceived utility of news across different age groups, and to pinpoint any substantial differences among age cohorts in the perceived accuracy of news disseminated by these channels.

Materials and Methods

The investigation centers on Tamil Nadu news broadcasters. This study was carried out in Chennai with a sample size of 100 participants. The study adopts a descriptive approach. Additional information was garnered from diverse outlets such as periodicals and online platforms. Simple random sampling was employed to collect primary data. Analytical techniques encompassed t-tests, standard deviations, and one-way ANOVA for statistical assessment.

Results and Discussions

The investigation has demonstrated that female respondents (3.65) exhibit the highest mean and place greater emphasis on the 'utility of news channels' compared to the male respondents (3.64) Table 75.1.

Examination has established that there exists a notable variance at the 0.005 level among the participants, regarding gender concerning the news disseminated by news channels as being beneficial Table 75.2. The 'utility of news channels' displays significance at the 0.001 level, thus leading to the rejection of the hypothesis.

It has also emerged that a significant discrepancy exists among the age bracket of the participants and the news provided by news channels being beneficial Table 75.3. The significance is at the 0.005 level, leading to the dismissal of the hypothesis.

Analysis has similarly indicated a substantial difference among the age groups of the participants and the authenticity of the news conveyed by news channels

Table 75.1 Mean score analysis on the news which are telecasted by news channels are useful.

Particulars	Gender	N	Mean	Std. deviation
The news which are telecasted by news channels are useful	Male	39	3.64	1.013
	Female	17	3.65	0.786

Source: Author

Table 75.2 T-Test for gender and the news which are telecasted by news channels are useful.

Particulars	T - Test for equality of means		
	t^a	df^b	Sig.^{c} (2-tailed)
The news which are telecasted by news channels are useful	0.022	54	0.003* significant

Source: Author

Table 75.3 One-way analysis for age and the news which are telecasted by news channels are useful.

	Sum of squares	df^a	Mean square	F^b	Sig.^{c}
Between groups	0.202	1	0.202	0.224	0.038* significant
Within groups	48.655	54	0.901		
Total	48.857	55			

Source: Author

Table 75.4 One-way analysis for age and the news which are telecasted by news channels are true.

	Sum of squares	df^a	Mean square	F^b	Sig.^{c}
Between groups	0.202	1	0.202	0.224	0.038* significant
Within groups	48.655	54	0.901		
Total	48.857	55			

Source: Author

Table 75.4. The significance level stands at 0.005, resulting in the rejection of the hypothesis.

A commendable news channel ought to encompass a diverse array of topics spanning politics, economy, culture, education, health, sports, and entertainment. It must also deliver impartial coverage without exhibiting bias towards any particular political party or ideology. A majority of the respondents perceive that certain news broadcasts fail to provide accurate information. Therefore, television channels are urged to broadcast authentic and dependable news through their platforms. A regional news channel should concentrate on local news pertinent to the populace of Tamil Nadu. This could encompass stories revolving around local enterprises, events, and community concerns. An effective news channel should not solely relay news but also furnish comprehensive analysis and commentary on pertinent issues. This could involve interviews with experts and stakeholders, as well as panel discussions and debates.

Conclusion

Tamil news networks constitute an integral aspect of the media landscape in Tamil Nadu and other regions with a substantial Tamil-speaking populace. The privatization of television media has introduced various alternatives for spectators and facilitated the comparison of information disseminated by different channels. These networks assume a pivotal function in disseminating information and enlightening individuals regarding the most recent news, occurrences, and advancements transpiring locally, nationally, and globally. They encompass a diverse array of subjects, including politics, athletics, entertainment, commerce, and societal concerns. Utilizing an amalgamation of formats, such as live news coverage, panel discussions, and interviews, Tamil news channels deliver their content to the audience. Therefore, to summarize, the abundance of information across news networks is not the primary consideration; rather, it is the authenticity of the news that viewers seek.

References

Barnett, S. (2011). The Rise and Fall of Television Journalism: Just Wires and Lights in a Box? A&C Black.

Blair, M. K. (2017). Using digital and social media platforms for social marketing. Oxford Medicine Online . https://doi.org/10.1093/med/9780198717690.003.0012.

Curtin, M., and Shattuc, J. (2017). The American Television Industry. Bloomsbury Publishing.

Desai, M. K. (2021). Regional Language Television in India: Profiles and Perspectives. Taylor & Francis.

Glória, C. M., Dias, J. C., and Cruz, A. (2024). Pricing levered warrants under the CEV diffusion model. *Review of Derivatives Research*, 1–30 .

Grabe, M. E. (1996). Tabloid and traditional television news magazine crime stories: demography and distinction. *Journalism and Mass Communication Quarterly*, 73(4), 926–946.

Jones, K. E., Otten, J. J., Johnson, R. K., and Harvey-Berino, J. R. (2010). Removing the bedroom television set: a possible method for decreasing television viewing time in overweight and obese adults. *Behavior Modification*, 34(4), 290–298.

Kempton, M. (2022). Commercial television and primate ethology: facial expressions between granada and London Zoo. *British Journal for the History of Science* , December, 1–20.

Lu, P. J., Zhou, T., Santibanez, T. A., Jain, A., Black, C. L., Srivastav, A., et al. (2023). COVID-19 bivalent booster vaccination coverage and intent to receive booster vaccination among adolescents and adults - United States, November-December 2022. *MMWR, Morbidity and Mortality Weekly Report*, 72(7), 190–198.

Mahoney, C. (2008). Brussels versus the beltway: advocacy in the United States and the European Union. Georgetown University Press.

Vanamamalai, R. (2015). Media and minorities: media representation of dalits in Tamil Nadu. LAP Lambert Academic Publishing.

Vasanti, P. N., and Kumar, P. (2016). TV News Channels in India: Business, Content and Regulation. Academic Foundation.

76 Comparative study on removal of total dissolved solids in aquaculture wastewater by electro Fenton process with minimal national standards

Kursam Likhil Gowtham and Ganesan, R.

Department of Civil Engineering, SIMATS,Saveetha University, Chennai, India

Abstract

This investigation sought to explore reducing total dissolved solids (TDS) in aquaculture wastewater using the Innovative Electro Fenton Technique. Two sets were analyzed: one utilized the novel electro Fenton process, while the other adhered to minimal national standards. With 12 samples each, totaling 24, the study maintained an 80% pretest power, 0.05 alpha value, and 95% confidence interval. Initial TDS levels stood at 900 ppm. Post-process, the novel electro-Fenton method achieved 77.89% TDS removal, surpassing the minimal national standard's 65.00%. Statistical analysis (SPSS) yielded a significance of 0.000 (p<0.05), signifying a significant difference between the two methods. Standard deviation values were 2.898 and 0.000, while standard error values were 0.837 and 0.000, respectively. This experimental evidence indicates the superiority of the Novel Electro-Fenton approach in removing Total Dissolved Solids compared to minimal national standards.

Keywords: Aquaculture, minimal national standards, novel electro-Fenton process, pollution, total dissolved solids, water

Introduction

Aquaculture has gained significant importance in the fishing industry due to the decline of wild populations, emerging as the primary seafood source. With a 3.2% annual growth rate, it's the largest food sector globally. Reports indicate more fish consumed than produced in 2019. Organic pollutants, prevalent in household and industrial wastewater, threaten public health and ecosystems. Effective removal is crucial to prevent pollution. The novel electro Fenton method, utilizing ferrous sulfate, oxidizes aquaculture wastewater (Chung et al., 2018). Aquaculture facilities breed fish for consumption, harvesting them at peak size. Wastewater contains organic compounds leading to high total dissolved solids (TDS), a serious pollution concern (Webler et al., 2019). Electro-Fenton reduces TDS, mitigating sewage pollution and repurposing waste. Freshwater demand has increased, exacerbated by inadequate aquaculture wastewater treatment, posing food production and environmental risks (Ozturk, 2021). Aquaculture contributes to water pollution, notably through wastewater discharge containing hazardous contaminants and fertilizers (Zhang and Yang, 2011).

Numerous studies, including those on the Electro-Fenton method's application in tannery wastewater, highlight its efficacy (Kurt et al., 2007). The electro-Fenton method catalyzes hydrogen peroxide to induce oxidation, yet its use in aquaculture wastewater treatment remains underexplored. This study aims to assess the novel electro-Fenton process's capability in TDS removal from aquaculture effluent.

Materials and Methods

Tests conducted at the Saveetha School of Engineering in Chennai examined Fenton and Modified Fenton processes. Two groups were involved: a control group using Fenton and an experimental group using Modified Fenton. A sample size of 12, with an alpha of 0.05 and 80% pretest power, was determined through clinical.com pretest power calculations, resulting in 24 samples. On December 2, 2022, aquaculture effluent from Laknavaram, Telangana State, was collected and stored at 4°C. Physicochemical analysis included pH, TDS, turbidity, TS, TSS, BOD, nitrogen, and phosphorus. Effluents were tested against National Minimum Water Quality Standards.

Two methods for TDS estimation, gravimetric analysis, and conductivity, were employed. Gravimetric analysis, involving solvent evaporation and residue weighing, is the most accurate but time-consuming. Conductivity-based methods, while less accurate, are quicker and suitable for predominantly inorganic TDS. Specific conductivity directly indicates dissolved ionized solids concentration, measurable with a conductivity or TDS meter. The TDS equation correlates TDS with specific conductivity, facilitating ppm estimation.

[a]Smartgenpublications2@gmail.com

Table 76.1 Samples of testing total dissolved solids removal by using novel electro-Fenton process and compare with minimum national standards.

Sample test size	Electro Fenton process	Minimal national standards
1	76.8	65.0
2	82.6	65.0
3	80.2	65.0
4	78.7	65.0
5	75.8	65.0
6	77.3	65.0
7	78.3	65.0
8	72.5	65.0
9	74.9	65.0
10	80.2	65.0
11	76.1	65.0
12	81.3	65.0
AVG.	77.8%	65.0%

Source: Author

Table 76.2 Comparison of novel electro-Fenton process and minimal national standards. The mean is (77.89, 65.00), the standard deviation is (2.898, 0.000) and the standard error meansis (0.837, 0.000).

Group statistics

	Groups	N	Mean	Std. deviation	Std. error mean
Accuracy	Electro Fenton process	12	77.89	2.898	0.837
	MINAS	12	65.00	0.000	0.000

Source: Author

Sustainability aims to ensure future generations' needs fulfillment, particularly in rural and community areas dependent on water resources. Challenges to sustainable water treatment in impoverished regions include economic underdevelopment, technological limitations, and energy scarcity. This study evaluates advanced wastewater treatment methods for aquaculture sustainability, including Novel Electro Fenton Process, H_2O_2 catalysis, ferrous ion symbiosis, and integrated approaches.

The novel electro Fenton process, a popular electrochemical oxidation technique, is effective, affordable, and clean. This electrochemical oxidation, a recent advanced oxidation process, involves two forms: one adding external Fenton reagent and the other incorporating H_2O_2 from an external source. OH radicals, crucial in this process, result from H_2O_2 and $Fe2+$

Table 76.3 Tests: Levene's test for equality of variances and both pooled-variances and separate-variances t-tests for equality of means. A 95% confidence interval for the difference between the mean and the hypothesized test value is displayed. This represents the two-sided p-value corresponding to a t-value of 15.408 with 22 degrees of freedom. Since the p-value of the test (0.000) is less than 0.05, i.e., success in rejecting the null hypothesis. And there is no significant difference.

Independent samples test

Dependent variables	Assumptions	Levene's test for equality of variances		T-test for equality of means					95% Confidence interval of the difference	
		F	Sig	t	df	Sig (2-tailed)	Mean Difference	Std. Error Difference	Lower	Upper
Accuracy	Equal variances assumed	25.908	0.000	15.408	22	0.000	12.89167	0.83670	11.156	14.6288
	Equal variances not assumed			15.408	11.00	0.000	12.89167	0.83670	11.05010	14.73323

Source: Author

interactions. Acidic pH favors the process, with iron forming stable bonds with H_2O_2, rendering the catalyst inactive at higher pH levels.

The initial H_2O_2 concentration significantly affects novel electro-Fenton processes, with higher concentrations leading to increased contaminant removal. Optimal H_2O_2 levels enhance hydroxyl radical concentrations, improving efficiency and economic viability. For example, 84% removal of organic matter from fertilizer industry wastewater was achieved in 10

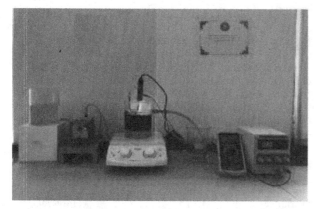

Figure 76.1 Experimental setup of the electro-Fenton-process
Source: Author

Figure 76.2 Aquaculture wastewater sample
Source: Author

minutes with a 25 mm H_2O_2 dose. Phenol and TDS deposition increase with rising H_2O_2 levels, indicating its dependency on waste type. Optimization of H_2O_2 concentration facilitates efficient phenol removal, even in stoichiometric conditions, within minutes.

Statistical Analysis

The examination in this research was conducted using IBM SPSS 22. Samples of aquaculture wastewater were taken, with 12 samples each for both the novel electro Fenton and minimum national standards. The independent variable is the sampling location, while

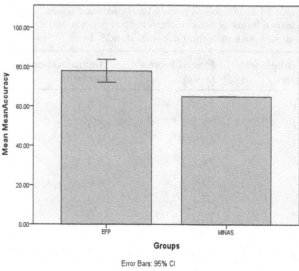

Error Bars: 95% CI

Error Bars: +/- 2 SD

Figure 76.3 A simple bar chart is graphically describing the data of group 1 and group 2. A simple bar chart can be approved by analyzing your data using an independent-samples t-test or paired-samples t-test. X-axis: comparison of the Novel Electro-Fenton Process of removal of TDS with Minimal National Standards. Y-axis: the efficiency of the removal of TDS. The Error Bar is +/- 2 SD and 95% confidence interval was taken. The average mean value of the Novel Electro-Fenton Process is 77.89% and the mean value of the Minimal National standards is 65.00%
Source: Author

pH and TDS serve as dependent variables. Attributes include total dissolved solids and minimum national standards.

Results

This study investigated aquaculture wastewater treatment using 24 samples. The novel electro-Fenton method achieved maximum TDS removal for 12 samples, meeting minimum national standards. Mean values (77.89, 65.00), standard deviation (2.898, 0.000), and standard error mean (0.837, 0.000) are detailed in Table 76.2. Levene's test for variances equality and t-tests for means equality are presented in Table 76.3, indicating success in rejecting the null hypothesis (p=0.000). No significant difference observed.

Discussions

This study utilized SPSS software version 2.6 to assess TDS elimination from aquaculture wastewater via the electro-Fenton method and compare it with minimal national standards. Comparing treatment values (77.89%) and (65.00%) showed similarity with maximum electro Fenton treatment values, likely meeting minimal national standards. Distilled water and aquaculture effluent were added. The novel electro-Fenton process exhibited a greater decrease in TDS removal percentage in aquaculture wastewater samples (Krishnanand Pavithra, 2021).

While TDS removal didn't significantly increase with increased FeSO4 dosage, there was a slight rise in turbidity (Kurt et al., 2007). Colorlessness and lack of absorbance in the visible region of treated aquaculture effluent samples suggested possible TDS removal at low $FeSO_4$ concentrations. Previous investigations have shown that aquaculture TDS removal is expedited during Fenton oxidation (Azarian et al., 2018).

This study found that the novel electro-Fenton method produced a high concentration of anions in treated wastewater and significant volumes of ferrous iron sludge. Optimization approaches can potentially reduce future high anions concentrations and significant volumes of ferrous iron sludge (Karthikeyan et al., 2012). $FeSO_4$ and interparticle gaps expedite H_2O_2 breakdown, enhancing catalytic activity and promoting rapid OH radical formation. These OH radicals increase the degradation process' effectiveness by attacking chromophoric groups. However, it was demonstrated that degradation effectiveness decreased with increased $FeSO_4$ concentration.

Conclusion

As a result of the treatment procedure, the mean TDS removal in the novel electro-Fenton process is 67.8 %, and the maximum TDS in the minimal national standards is 65.0%. According to the findings, electro-Fenton is better to treat aquaculture wastewater.

Acknowledgments

The authors would like to express their gratitude towards Saveetha School of Engineering, Saveetha Institute of Medical and Technical Science, RK Builders Pvt Ltd, for providing the necessary infrastructure and funding to carry out this work successfully.

References

Azarian, G., Miri, M., and Nematollahi, D. (2018).Combined electrocoagulation/electrooxidationprocess for the COD removal and recovery of tannery industry wastewater.*Environmental Progress and Sustainable Energy*, 37(2), 637–644. https://doi.org/10.1002/ep.12711.

Chung, M. H., Wang, C. T., Wang, J. W., Chou, W. L., and Kuo, Y. M. (2018).Application of response surface methodology on COD removal from textile wastewater by anodic chlorination and cathodicelectro-fenton process.*Desalination and Water Treatment*, 108, 144–151. https://doi.org/10.5004/dwt.2018.21953.

Ganesan, R., and Thanasekaran, K. (2011).Decolourisation of textile dyeing wastewater by modified solar photofenton oxidation. *Environmental Sciences: An International Journal of Environmental Physiology and Toxicology*, 1(6), 1168–1176.

Ganesan, R., Latha, A., and Thanasekaran, K. (2014). Treatment of textile dyeing wastewater by modified UV photo-fenton process using a new composite steel scrap/H2O2. *International Journal of Emerging Technology and Advanced Engineering*, 4, 108–113.

Karthikeyan, S., EzhilPriya, M., Boopathy, R., Velan, M., Mandal, A. B., and Sekaran, G. (2012).Heterocatalyticfenton oxidation process for the treatment of tannery effluent: kinetic and thermodynamic studies. *Environmental Science and Pollution Research International*, 19(5), 1828–1840.

Krishnan, E. P., and Pavithra, K.E.(2021). Comparative studies on colour and COD removal of reactive dyes by a novel steel scrap as a catalyst with conventional fenton process. *RevistaGestãoInovação E Tecnologias*, 11(4), 1264–1276. https://doi.org/10.47059/revistagestec.v11i4.2185.

Kurt, U., Apaydin, O., and Gonullu, M. T.(2007).Reduction of COD in wastewater from an organized tannery industrial region by electro-fentonprocess.*Journal of Hazardous Materials*, 143(1-2), 33–40.

Latha, A., Ganesan, R.,Krisnakumari, B., and Theerkadarsin, S. (2022). Comparative study of organic coagulants in water treatment.*ECS Transactions*, 107(1), 7997. https://doi.org/10.1149/10701.7997ecst.

Ozturk, D. (2021). COD removal from mixed dye wastewater using natural pyrite ore by heterogeneous fentonprocess.In Proceedings of the 7th World Congress on New Technologies. https://doi.org/10.11159/icepr21.110.

Webler, A. D., Moreira, F. C.,Dezotti, M. W. C., Mahler, C. F., Segundo, I. D. B.,Boaventura, R. A. R.,et al. (2019). Development of an integrated treatment strategy for a leather tannery landfill leachate. *Waste Management*,89(April), 114–128.

Zhang, Q., and Yang, G. (2011).The removal of COD from refinery wastewater by fentonreagent.In 2011 International Conference on Remote Sensing, Environment and Transportation Engineering. https://doi.org/10.1109/rsete.2011.5966300.

77 Comparison of customer relationship management strategies and it's impact on customer satisfaction in banking sector

Suriyavarma, G. and Vijayakumar, L.

Department of Commerce Saveetha College of Liberal Arts and Sciences, Saveetha University, Chennai, India

Abstract

This study investigates the impact of customer relationship management (CRM) strategies on customer satisfaction in the banking sector, focusing on HDFC Bank in the Cuddalore region. Empirical data collected from bank managers and customers is analyzed to identify CRM practices and assess their effectiveness. The study employs a convenience sampling method with a sample size of 100 respondents. Statistical analysis, including Chi-Square tests, is conducted to examine the relationship between age groups and managed customers according to CRM. The findings reveal no significant difference between age groups in terms of CRM effectiveness, with a calculated Chi-Square value of 11.7428, which is lower than the tabulated value of 40.99. Hence, the study accepts the Null Hypothesis. The study emphasizes the importance of CRM in fostering customer loyalty and competitive advantage in banking, suggesting opportunities for strategic enhancement.

Keywords: Customer, customer relationship management, HDFC bank, level of technology, portfolio, services, strategies

Introduction

Shaon and Rahman(2015)and also to "observe the complete business process as comprising closely linked effort to uncover, generate, and gratify customer needs." Managing and sustaining clientele is one of the primary challenges encountered by the banking sector. The requirements and anticipations of the clientele burgeon at a significantly hastened pace compared to the banks' capacity to prepare themselves to address them. As Kotlerans Fox (1995) affirms, "the finest organization globally will be ineffectual if the emphasis on 'client' is misplaced". Juslin and Hansen (2002). Entities must forge tailored propositions for clientele and guarantee relationships through enhanced customer service and the management of customer anticipations. The genesis of customer relationship management (CRM) as a strategic approach stems from several of the ensuing crucial standpoints:

The confidence of the customers is a core requirement.

- More use of new technologies with the help of CRM software to maintain important data.
- The approach must be towards relationships not only for transactions.
- More focus on customer values and time.
- Customer satisfaction is more important than self-satisfaction and profit.

- Retain existing customers who are more focused and try to increase business from them instead of targeting new customers.
- Information about current market trends. Products sold based on current economic conditions.
- Today, the market has well refined and defined CRM systems for the process of improvement.

Problem Statement

The authors have made efforts to explore the notion that CRM can be uniformly applied in the banking industry to enhance banking services. The role of CRM is markedly different from traditional forms of marketing. CRM engages not only in marketing but also in executing business as a tactic to acquire, expand, and maintain profitable customers with the goal of establishing a sustainable competitive advantage. Particularly in the banking sector, the role of CRM is exceedingly vital in guiding banks toward increased levels and magnitude of profits. Hence, there is a necessity to examine the role of CRM in the advancement and promotion of the banking sector through the lenses of practices, challenges, and the impact of CRM on the banking sector.

Need and Significance of the Study

CRM might prove beneficial in customer recognition, cross selling of goods, customer procurements

---

[a]Smartgenpublications2@gmail.com

or retention and so forth. Operational CRM, which furnishes requisite information and analytical CRM, which tracks activities and renders information more meaningful are a pair of facets of CRM. CRM units, assortment of products, client measurement and cutting-edge technology stand as some of the prerequisites for effectively executing the CRM. Over recent years, the banking sector has undergone considerable transformation, prompting the inevitability of consolidation and enhancement in banking services. Banks have acknowledged the importance of customer service not solely for business expansion but also for their very survival. They have responded so swiftly that comprehending and overseeing customer requirements becomes imperative (Panda, 2001) and robust corporate governance criteria shall wield considerable influence when assessing the potential of the contenders this time around. Hence, those aspiring companies already prioritizing CRM stand a heightened chance of securing licensure.

Literature Review andRelated Work

The examination of related literature entails methodical identifying, locating, and scrutinizing sources containing information pertaining to the research issue. These sources in the current investigation encompass books, periodicals, articles in periodicals, published studies, lexicons, unpublished theses and dissertations, as well as the internet and online platforms. A review of the literature constitutes an exploratory phase in all scientific inquiries. Categorizations of existing literatures On CRM are within Indian banks are enumerated below:

- Banking sector CRM.
- CRM application in banks
- Framework of CRM for banks in India
- Technological advancements in banks domestically and internationally.
- Indian banking sectors - hurdles and prospects

Here are five specific CRM discoveries which are focal points of each bank(Mihelis et al., 2001). Arisawa and Kambayashi,(2002)emphasized on electronic data offered to clients across various banking sectors to augment the efficiency of the system to cater to customers' needs employing banking services and aiding in CRM(Soral and Bhanawat(2009). Demands for customer service escalate manifold owing to the advent of new private banks and multinational banks-Soral and Bhanawat(2009).Sureshchandar et al. (2003) underscores that, due to advanced automation technology, foreign banks hold an edge in numerous banking domains(Almugari et al., 2020). He elucidated that IT facilitates significant CDs to raise capital

in the capital market more so than from banks. He concluded that electronic payment systems are burgeoning and garnering acceptance in the market as they facilitate cost reduction by replacing conventional methods of delivering products to customers and exploring whether technology spawn's new opportunities for banks or leads to their obsolescenceSubramanian and Gopalakrishna(2001)which commenced exerting its sway on the enterprise. It forms an integral facet of management and commands a pivotal and indispensable position in contemporary businessamenities electronically through the internet(Jindal, 2017). These amenities curtail transaction expenses andempower clients andaugment the value of banking relationships. They also deliberated services via banking, their advantages to clients, banks and drawbacks.

Objectives of the Study

To uncover the CRM strategies within HDFC bank's operations in the Cuddalore region, the study aims to evaluate the consciousness and utilization of CRM practices within the banking industry. Additionally, it seeks to delve into the satisfaction levels of HDFC customers regarding CRM initiatives and to examine how HDFC effectively manages its customers to ensure continued patronage. Furthermore, the study scrutinizes the impact of CRM implementations within HDFC. Ultimately, it proposes enhancements to HDFC bank's CRM strategies aimed at enhancing customer satisfaction and loyalty

Limitations of the Study

The investigation encompasses an exhaustive examination regarding the notion of CRM and its execution within the banking industry in Cuddaloreterritory, presented as a comparative analysis juxtaposed with HDFC banks. The scrutiny was conducted concerning assessment, expansion, and function of CRM in the advancement of the banking industry in Cuddaloreregion. Despite the research's thorough nature, it is subject to specific constraints as enumerated below. The investigation primarily hinges on data garnered from patrons of designated banks; hence, the precision of the information provided by them is dependent upon at the juncture of eliciting perceptions from the clientele. The exploration is conducted across chosen banks;thereby the discoveries may not encapsulate the entirety of the banking sector.

Scope of the Study

It is an attentive discernment for exploration of fresh facts in any sector of expertise. It necessitates numerous enlargement and exploration techniques to constitute a segment of the exploration technique. In this investigation, the examiner juxtaposed the perspectives of the clientele regarding CRM cognizance, utilization, degree of technology, and caliber of provision provided by the bank. Furthermore, the viewpoint of the bank administrators concerning the utilization and execution of customer relationship management in their operational domains was assessed.

Research Methodology

Study structure: This investigation engaged with the clientele of HSBC bank patrons, representing a case inquiry of the firm. The researcher aimed to uncover the extent of rapport with both patrons and supervisors within banking institutions. Instruments for data gathering included both primary and secondary sources. Primary Information was collected through questionnaires distributed to the clientele and supervisors, with the primary statistics facilitating subsequent scrutiny. Additionally, secondary information was derived from policy declarations pertaining to CRM. The sample comprised data from 100 participants, collected through a convenience sampling approach. The amassed data underwent analysis using statistical tools such as proportion and Chi-square, specifically applying Chi-square analysis to examine the relationship between age and managed clients in accordance with CRM practices.

Table 77.1 Responses of Participants and their Ages.

Managed age	Highly satisfied	Satisfied	dissatisfied	Highly dissatisfied	Total
Below 25	0	1	3	1	5
26– 35	16	20	20	2	58
36 – 45	8	9	9	0	26
46 – 55	2	2	3	1	8
Above 55	0	1	1	1	3
Total	26	33	36	5	100

Source: Primary Data

Table 77.2 The Chi-square values.

Chi-square value	40.999	Not significant
Yule's coefficient of association	0.547	Not significant

Source: Author

The Null hypothesis H0: *There is no significant difference between the age group and managed customers according to CRM*

The Alternative Hypothesis H1: *There is significant difference between the age group and Managed customers according to CRM*

Inference: Henceforth we acknowledge the void Hypothesis. $11.7428 < 40.99$ the determined figure is lower than the catalogued quantity. Following the preceding examination, it's deduced that there exists no notable distinction amidst age demographic and supervised clients as per CRM within HDFC Bank.

Result

As per the information gathered through questionnaires devised for both patrons and managers, one aspect that is readily apparent is that both parties possess comprehensive knowledge regarding CRM. Through adequate training, staff members demonstrate proficiency in addressing customer issues and inquiries. Given the prominence of CRM concepts, it is evident that both parties comprehend their respective roles. Despite encountering certain challenges, they remain manageable. The examination reveals that respondents express contentment with CRM's contribution to enhanced performance within the bank. The scrutiny illustrates that the entirety will perceive the bank's values in our HDFC bank. The evaluation indicates that the bank adeptly addressed your concerns, as attested by 83% of participants. Additionally, 51% of respondents expressed satisfaction with the bank's approach to problem-solving. Furthermore, 100% of respondents acknowledge the presence of a complaint box at the HDFC bank branch. Moreover, 91% of participants affirm that the bank furnishes comprehensive information on its products and services. Similarly, 91% of respondents express satisfaction with the bank's consistent communication with customers. Similarly, 91% of participants express contentment with the responsiveness of bank employees. Notably, respondents express satisfaction, believing that CRM improvements would yield better outcomes. They also emphasize the crucial role of CRM within the bank. A majority of respondents express satisfaction with the bank's adherence to CRM practices. Moreover, the majority of respondents affirm effective CRM implementation within the bank. The analysis also reveals respondent demographics; out of 100 participants, 84% are male and 16% are female, indicating a male-majority respondent pool. Additionally, 58% of respondents fall within the 26-35 age bracket, followed by 26% in the 36-45 age group, 8% in the 46-55 age range, 5% below 25 years, and 3% above

55 years, thus highlighting the predominance of respondents aged 26-35. Moreover, 43% of respondents hold postgraduate qualifications, 19% have completed HSC, 17% possess degrees, 17% fall into the 'others' category, and 4% have completed SSLC, indicating a majority of undergraduate respondents and a minority of postgraduates. Furthermore, the data indicates that 88% of respondents are married, while 12% are unmarried, underscoring a married-majority demographic within HDFC Bank. Likewise, 85% of respondents maintain accounts with HDFC Bank, while 15% do not, indicating a significant portion of respondents holding accounts with the bank.

Discussion

The examination indicates that 32% of the respondents possess a savings account, 40% of the participants hold a fixed deposit account, 15% of the individuals maintain a recurring deposit account, and 13% of the survey participants operate a current account. Thus, the majority of respondents maintain a fixed deposit account. Consequently, the investigation validates the Null hypothesis. 11.7428 < 40.99 the computed figure is lower than the designated value. From the aforementioned examination, it is deduced that there is no statistical significance between age demographics and managed clientele as per CRM in HDFC bank. In general, financial institutions are utilizing CRM as a mechanism for cultivating a customer base and augmenting sales. The misconstrued perspectives harbored by these institutions are detrimental to their overall worth, eroding the trust of their clientele. Financial institutions must undertake concerted efforts to reshape their image, should they wish to realize the potential of fostering robust relationships with their clientele. Should a bank devise novel strategies for engaging with customers that are both enticing and fulfilling, it stands to garner heightened responsiveness from its clientele.

Conclusion

This investigation offers a stride in comprehending the current customer relationship management (CRM) approaches in banking. The discoveries suggest that numerous gaps exist in the prevailing strategic CRM Strategies .This exploration serves as an illustration of the insight that can be acquired in comprehending the efficacy of front end CRM strategies in banking sector from the client viewpoint and more thorough case study scrutiny can be carried out to provide additional insights on CRM strategies in the banking realm. To fulfil the customer demand and to persist in the competition, banks necessitate dispensing the utmost quality of service. Appropriate CRM embraced by banks, will consistently aid in concentrating on augmenting the significance for client and bank.

References

Almugari, F., Bajaj, P.,Tabash, M. I., Khan, A., and Ali, M. A. (2020).An examination of consumers' adoption of internet of things (IoT) in Indian banks. *Cogent Business and Management*, 7(1), 1809071.

Arisawa, H., and Kambayashi, Y. (2002). Conceptual modeling for new information systems technologies: ER 2001 Workshops, HUMACS, DASWIS, ECOMO, and DAMA, Yokohama Japan, November 27–30, 2001. Revised Papers.Springer Science and Business Media.

Jindal, L. (2017). Customer relationship management in the banking sector.*Journal of Management Research and Analysis*, 4(3), 140–144.

Juslin, H., and Hansen, E. (2002).Strategic Marketing in the Global Forest Industries. Author's Academic Press.

Mihelis, G., Grigoroudis, E., Siskos, Y., Politis, Y., and Malandrakis, Y. (2001).Customer satisfaction measurement in the private bank sector. *European Journal of Operational Research*, 130(2), 347–360.

Panda, T. K. (2001). Creating customer lifetime value through effective CRM in financial services industry. http://dspace.iimk.ac.in/xmlui/handle/2259/552.

Shaon, S. K. I., and Rahman, H. (2015). A theoretical review of CRM effects on customer satisfaction and loyalty. *Central European Business Review; Prague*, 4(1), 23–36.

Soral, G., and Bhanawat S. S. (2009). Shareholder value creation in the Indian banking industry: an EVA analysis. *IUP Journal of Accounting Research and Audit Practices*, 8.

Subramanian, R,, and Gopalakrishna, P. (2001). The market orientation–performance relationship in the context of a developing economy: an empirical analysis. *Journal of Business Research*, 53(1), 1–13.

Sureshchandar, G. S., Rajendran, C., and Anantharaman, R. N. (2003). Customer perceptions of service quality in the banking sector of a developing economy: acritical analysis. *International Journal of Bank Marketing*, 21(5), 233–242.

78 Estimation of uberdata analysis using decision tree compared with linear regression

Kumar, V. and Kannan, N.

Department of Information Technology, Saveetha School of Engineering, SIMATS, Saveetha University, Chennai, India

Abstract

To assess Uber data precision, decision tree and linear regression (LR) were employed. The research includes two categories: Decision tree and LR Algorithm. Each category comprises 10 samples, with alpha, beta, and power values set. Their accuracies were compared across various sample sizes. Decision tree outperforms LR by 93.09%, with a significance value of .000 (p<0.005). This denotes statistical significance, indicating Decision tree's superiority in Uber data analysis and Fake News detection.

Keywords: Dataset, decision tree, linear regression, machine learning, mining,Uber data analysis

Introduction

Uber, a pioneering ride-sharing service launched in 2010, has experienced rapid growth. This study provides the first comprehensive analysis of Uber's driver-partner labor market, leveraging both survey and administrative data. The allure of Uber lies in its flexible schedule, consistent hourly earnings regardless of working hours, and freedom. Driver-partners exhibit demographic similarities to the broader workforce rather than traditional taxi drivers or chauffeurs. Many driver-partners maintain full- or part-time employment alongside their Uber commitments, underscoring the value of flexible scheduling. The desire to stabilize income fluctuations motivates many individuals to join Uber's platform (Barann et al., 2017; Cheng et al., 2011). Utilizing Uber's extensive dataset, this research examines ride data from Hyderabad and New York City, employing the k-algorithm to forecast cable demand. Efficient cable deployment is essential for reducing wait times for both passengers and drivers(Correa et al., 2017; Davis et al., 2016). The dataset facilitates an in-depth analysis of taxi demand trends, demonstrating a marked increase in Uber demand compared to traditional yellow cabs, especially during peak hours (Duan et al., 2016; Getis, 2009). Spatial and temporal models, such as spatial-temporal autoregressive (STAR) and LASSO-STAR, offer improved prediction accuracy for taxi demand. These models are vital for understanding and predicting demand fluctuations in e-hailing services (Kamarianakis and Prastacos 2003; Kamarianakis et al., 2004). The study evaluates various temporal and spatio-temporal models, including vector autoregressive (VAR), for different scenarios based on time and space lags, during both rush and non-rush hours. Results underscore the necessity of incorporating spatial components in demand forecasting models for accurate predictions. By analyzingUber's dataset, this research sheds light on the evolving landscape of e-hailing services and underscores the importance of spatial modeling in taxi demand prediction.

Materials and Methods

The investigation was conducted in the Data Analytics laboratory at the Department of Information Technology, Saveetha School of Engineering. Two groups were chosen to compare their methodologies and outcomes. Each group selected 10 sets of samples, totaling 20 samples. The sample size was set at 10, with a threshold of 0.05, G power of 80%, and a confidence interval of 95%, calculated using ClinCalc software. The study involved two sample groups: Decision tree and linear regression, with a sample size of 10 determined for each group using ClinCalc software 3.1. The classification dataset was obtained from https://www.kaggle.com/code/theod-dwaffle/uber-data-analysis, comprising 23464 rows and 12 columns containing various air quality indicators for different cities and countries. Decision Tree was utilized to forecast air quality, involving input data processing, particle detection, prediction, and accuracy enhancement (Kumar and Bishoyi, 2024; Koutsopoulos et al., 2017). The project was implemented using Python OpenCV software on a Windows 11 platform, with hardware including an Intel Core i5 processor and 16 GB of RAM. Python programming

ᵃresearchsmartgen@gmail.com

language facilitated code implementation, focusing on dataset processing and mining to enhance accuracy based on independent variables such as country, city, and air quality indicators, and dependent variables including accuracy and loss.

Data preparation

To analyze Uber data performed in the real time data sets used are semantic analysis mining. The input data set for the proposed work is sentiment analysis.

Decision tree

The most efficient and widely favored method for sorting and forecasting is the decision tree. A decision tree, resembling a flowchart, depicts tests on attributes, results, and class labels at nodes. Constructing a decision tree: segmenting the source set into subsets through attribute value tests forms a tree. This process, termed recursive partitioning, iterates on each subset. Recursion concludes when splits no longer enhance predictions or subsets hold identical target variable values. Decision tree construction suits exploratory knowledge discovery, sans parameter setup or domain expertise. Decision trees handle high-dimensional data adeptly and are often precise classifiers. Decision tree induction stands as a favored method for learning classification details. The decision tree formula is provided in the Equation. Accuracy is presented in Table 78.3 for decision trees.

$$E(A, X) = \sum_{c \in Y} p(c) \, E(c) \tag{1}$$

Where,
A → Current state.
X → Selected attribute.

Linear regression

An independent factor's value can anticipate using linear regression examination based on another factor's value. The target variable is the one sought to predict. The predictor variable is the one utilized to anticipate the other variable's value. Using one or multiple predictor variables that can most precisely anticipate the target variable's value, this method computes the coefficients of the linear equation. Linear regression minimizes the disparities between expected and actual output values by fitting a straight line or surface. Linear regression calculators employing the "least squares" approach can locate the best-fit line for a dataset of paired data. Subsequently, you establish X's value from Y's (an independent variable). The expression for the innovative linear regression is provided as in Equation (2).

$$b = s0 + s1a + \varepsilon \tag{2}$$

Where,
b = Dependent variable (target variable).
a = Independent variable (predictor variable).
s0 = intercept of the line (Gives an additional degree of freedom).
s1 = Linear regression coefficient (scale factor to each input value).
ε = random error.

Statistical analysis

The programs were executed on a Windows 11, 64-bit OS, 16 GB RAM using Google Collab software, employing Python. Statistical analysis utilized IBM SPSS version 26, examining Decision Tree and Linear

Table 78.1 Accuracy of Uber data analyzing using decision tree.

Test size	Accuracy
Test 1	98.47
Test 2	97.28
Test 3	96.85
Test 4	95.28
Test 5	94.17
Test 6	93.45
Test 7	92.15
Test 8	91.64
Test 9	91.22
Test 10	90.75

Source: Author

Table 78.2 Accuracy of Uber data analyzing using linear regression.

Test size	Accuracy
Test 1	87.64
Test 2	87.42
Test 3	87.11
Test 4	86.43
Test 5	86.27
Test 6	85.34
Test 7	84.38
Test 8	83.92
Test 9	82.14
Test 10	81.55

Source: Author

Regression. Variables include country, city, AQI values, categories, and others. T-Test assesses performance.

Results

In statistical analysis, a total of 20 samples are utilized. This data undergoes examination using both Decision Tree and linear regression techniques.

Table 78.3 Group, accuracy and loss value uses eightcolumns with eightwidth data for analyzing Uberdata.

Sl.NO	Name	Type	Width	Decimal	Columns	Measure	Role
1	Group	Numeric	8	2	8	Nominal	Input
2	Accuracy	Numeric	8	2	8	Scale	Input
3	Loss	Numeric	8	2	8	Scale	Input

Source: Author

Table 78.4 Group Statistic Analysis, Representing Decision Tree and Random Forest.

	Group	N	Mean	Std Deviation	Std. Error Mean
Accuracy	DT	10	93.960	2.19866	.69528
	LR	10	80.9150	3.14901	.99581
Loss	DT	10	6.9040	2.19866	.69528
	LR	10	19.0850	3.14901	.99581

Source: Author

Statistical analysis is conducted for these algorithms. Group and accuracy values are computed for each system. These 20 data points for each algorithm, alongside their respective losses, contribute to the statistical comparisons. Table 78.1 displays group accuracy and loss for the decision tree method, while Table 78.2 illustrates these values for linear regression. Table 78.3 encompasses group, accuracy, and loss data, utilizing 8 columns and a width of 8 for the air pollution detection system. Table 78.4 presents a statistical analysis of novel decision tree and linear regression. Additionally, Table 78.5 showcases the results of independent sample tests with a 95% confidence interval and a significance level of 0.05 (decision tree demonstrates significantly superior performance compared to Linear Regression, with p=0.000). Figure 78.1 offers a graphical comparison of mean accuracy and loss between decision tree and linear regression methods.

Discussions

The precision of a decision tree stands at 98.47%, while linear regression yields 86.57% with p = 0.363 due to abundant datasets with fewer variables, indicating decision tree's superiority over linear regression ("Urban Workers' Cardiovascular Health due to Exposure to Traffic-Originated PM2.5 and Noise Pollution in Different Microenvironments" 2023). Mean, standard deviation, and standard mean values for decision tree are 93.0690, 2.19866, and .69528, respectively. Correspondingly, for linear regression algorithms, mean, standard deviation, and standard mean values are 80.9870, 2.17456, and .68765, respectively ("Characteristics and Determinants of

Table 78.5 Independent sample tests results with confidence interval as 95% and level of significance as 0.05(random forest appears to perform significantly better than random forest with the value of p=0.179).

		Levene's Test for Equality of variance		T-Test for equality of mean						95% confidence of difference	
		F	Sig	t	df	Sig(2 - tailed)	Mean difference	Std.error difference		Lower	Upper
Accuracy	Equal variances assumed	1.958	.179	10.030	18	.000	12.18100	1.21451		9.62940	14.73260
	Equal variances not assumed	-	-	10.030	16.090	.000	12.18100	1.21451		9.60752	14.75448
Loss	Equal variances assumed	1.958	.179	-10.030	18	.000	-12.18100	1.21451		-14.73260	-9.62940
	Equal variances not assumed	-	-	-10.030	16.090	.000	-12.18100	1.21451		-14.75448	-9.60752

Source: Author

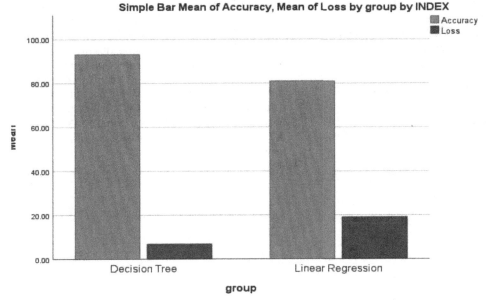

Figure 78.1 Comparison of decision tree and linear regression in terms of accuracy. The mean accuracy of decision tree is greater than linear regression and the standard deviation is also slightly higher than linear regression. x-axis: decision tree vs linear regression. Y-axis: Mean accuracy of detection + 1 SD

Source: Author

Personal Exposure to Typical Air Pollutants: A Pilot Study in Beijing and Baoding, China" 2023).Air pollution detection for review dataset utilized decision tree modulation-based categorization, achieving 98.47% accuracy. In contrast, attention-based air pollution detection attained 87.64% accuracy ("Kernel PLS with AdaBoost Ensemble Learning for Particulate Matters Forecasting in Subway Environment" 2022). Speech emotion recognition via RF yielded 98.47% accuracy, while RF using raw temporal data and datasets scored 87.64%. Our institution prioritizes evidence-based research and excels across various domains.A limitation of this model is RF's accuracy susceptibility to inconsistent data and dataset acquisition challenges ("An Analysis of the Co-Benefits of the Supply–demand for Multiple Ecosystem Services for Guiding Sustainable Urban Development" 2023). Most data is simulated, diverging from reality. Effective data preprocessing techniques and LR integration with other ML algorithms like RF may enhance accuracy in the future (Chen et al., 2022).

Conclusion

According to the experimental findings, the decision tree has demonstrated greater efficacy in forecasting Air Pollution compared to linear regression (LR). It holds potential for future fake prediction. Effective models should generate adaptable datasets, minimizing the need for extensive fine-tuning.

Acknowledgement

The authors would like to express their gratitude towards Saveetha School of Engineering, Saveetha Institute of Medical and Technical Sciences (Formerly known as Saveetha University), VeeEee Technologies Solution Pvt.Ltd.for providing the necessary infrastructure to carry out this work successfully.

References

Barann, B., Beverungen, D., and Müller, O. (2017).An open-data approach for quantifying thepotential of taxi ridesharing.*Decision Support Systems*, 99, 86–95.

Cheng, T., Wang, J., Harworth, J. Heydecker, B.G., and Chow, A.H.F. (2011).Modeling dynamic space-Time autocorrelation of urban tranportnetwork.In Geo-Computation, Session 5A: Network Complexity.

Correa, D., Xie, K., and Ozbay, K. (2017). Exploring the taxi and uberdemands in New York city: anEmpirical analysis and spatial modeling. In Transportation Research Board's 96th, Annual Meeting,Washington, D.C.

Davis, N., Raina, G., andJagannathan, K. (2016). A multi-level clustering approach for forecasting taxi travel demand. In Intelligent Transportation Systems (ITSC), 2016 IEEE 19th International Conference on (pp. 223–228).IEEE.

Duan, P., Mao G., Zhang C., and Wang S. (2016). STARI-MA-based traffic prediction with timevarying lags. In IEEE 19th International Conference on Intelligent Transportation System (ITSC),Rio, Brazil.

Getis, A. (2009). Spatial weights matrices. *Geographical Analysis*, 41(4), 404–410.

Getis, A., andAldstadt, J. (2010).Constructing the spatial weights matrix using a local statistic.In Perspectives on Spatial Data Analysis.Berlin Heidelberg: Springer, (pp. 147-163).

Kamarianakis, Y., and Prastacos, P. (2003). Forecasting traffic flow conditions in an urban network:comparison of multivariate and univariate approaches. *Transportation Research Record: Journal of the Transportation Research Board*, 1857(1), 74–84.

Kamarianakis, Y., Prastacos P., and Kotzinos, D. (2004). Bivariate traffic relations: a space-time modeling approach. In AGILE Proceedings, (pp. 465–474).

Koutsopoulos, H. N., Noursalehi, P., Zhu, Y., and Wilson, N. H. (2017). Automated data in transit: recent developments and applications. In Models and Technologies for Intelligent Transportation Systems (MT-ITS), 2017 5th IEEE International Conference on (pp. 604–609). IEEE.

Kumar, V.,andBishoyi, A. S. R. (2024).Enhancing malware detection efficiency through CNN-based image classification in a user-friendly web portal.*SPAST Reports*, 2(2).Retrieved from https://spast.org/ojspath/article/view/4949.

79 Evaluating the customer perception of service quality in online banking across different demographic segments

Renuka, A. K. and Celia, B.R.

Saveetha college of Liberal Arts and Sciences, Saveetha University Chennai, India

Abstract

The study is an attempt to identify the underlying factors that form the customer's perception toward online banking. This study has also aimed at analyzing the level of satisfaction among customers and the ease of operation in case of online transactions as well mobile banking. Both primary and secondary data were used to support the current investigation. Through the use of a structured questionnaire, primary data was gathered from the clients of public sector banks. In order to gauge customer satisfaction with the online banking services offered by the aforementioned public sector banks, a convenience sampling technique was used to select a sample of 200 clients. The collected data was analyzed using mean, standard deviation and one way ANOVA. The analysis has proved that there is a significant difference between gender and their opinion on online banking transactions. It represents that there is a significant difference among the occupation of the respondents and online banking services provided by the bank. It represents that there is a significant difference among the occupation of the respondents and online banking services are easy to operate and user-friendly. The way the entire banking industry operates has been changed by online banking services. It has improved the speed and decreased the cost of bank transactions in addition to making them easier. Banks have made significant investments to build these facilities. Mobile banking is a service provided by banks that aims to improve both the effectiveness and efficiency with which customers carry out various transactions. It also makes financial transactions more seamless. Time savings, ease of use, cost effectiveness, account information, speed, clarity of instructions, and work quality have been proven to be key drivers of online banking usage among clients. Hence customers need to be trained on how to utilize every new technology as most of them are only familiar with the conventional banking system.

Keywords: Customer, mobile banking, online banking, services, transactions

Introduction

A bank's operations or services are referred as banking (Horn, 2002). Online banking, usually referred as electronic banking, is a system of electronic payments that allows clients of banks or other financial institutions to carry out a variety of financial transactions via the websites of those institutions (Ekos Research Associates and Task Force on the Future of the Canadian Financial Services Sector, 1998). Business transactions are supported by the finance function. Daily technology advancements are changing how business transactions are conducted. Therefore, traditional finance function cannot keep up with the rate at which technology is developing (de Waal et al., 2022). E-banking is the most extensive type of this technology revolution in financial function (More and Hiray, n.d.). E-banking is a young industry with a recent beginning, particularly in India. Internet is the finest avenue for offering customers banking services and goods due to the quick advancement of technology (Plunkett Research Ltd, 2007). Because banks want to extend their customer base, they see the Internet

as being more effective than alternative distribution channels (de Waal et al., 2022). People are growing more accustomed to banking online and think that all community banks will soon be required to provide these services.

Various investigations were made on the effects of customer satisfaction with online banking services (Rashidi, 2015). This essay focuses on evaluating how customers view e-banking services. Data was gathered by a questionnaire, and ANOVA and percentages were used in a descriptive analysis. Customers were found to be utilizing E-banking services including ATMs, home banking, and the use of credit and debit cards, to name a few (Kundra, 2020). We can infer that about 45% of people have a favorable opinion on and are satisfied with online banking. ATMs, bill payment services, and accessing bank statements are three of the most used e-banking services. A poll identified the key success criteria for the adoption of online banking. According to Shah and Braganza, "different literary works claim various variables as essential to success and are typically based on subjective, perceptual data. Survey questions are based on an analysis

[a]krishsmartgenresearch@gmail.com

of previous research. The information was gathered utilizing postal questionnaires from UK-based financial sector businesses that provide their services online (Sanchez-Diaz et al., 2021). Quickly responsive goods and services, organizational flexibility, the growth of services, system integration, and improved customer service top the list of elements that have been identified to be most important (Omar, 2014). A study on customer perception toward online banking services for the success of e-banking. Organizations must regard the e-banking project as a business-critical area rather than just a technological one, according to a key takeaway from this research (Ackah and Agboyi 2014). Internal integration, which may involve channels, technology, and business processes, needs to be prioritized (Ackah and Agboyi 2014; Khosrow-Pour, 2008). In an emerging economy, this study paper discussed the customer's thoughts on internet banking (Saibaba, 2014). Therefore, the author argues that in a developing country like India, figuring out the numerous aspects influencing consumer perception, attitude, and satisfaction with internet banking is a crucial step in developing a bank's strategy (Riscinto-Kozub, 2008). The survey was conducted on respondents selected from the northern region of India in order to obtain this information regarding Indian clients. The key findings show that customers' use of online banking services is influenced by the type of account they have, their age, and their profession. Customers attach the highest level of usefulness to the balance enquiry service among online banking services, and they rank security and trust as the most crucial factors influencing their level of satisfaction. A study was done to support the mobile banking business model. In order to increase the number of people who can utilize mobile banking, the causes were found and

investigated (Lee, 2012). He discovered that users still have numerous issues with everything from telecom providers to banks, handsets to software application assistance for using services. Discussions on how customers in the Coimbatore region perceive the services offered by IOB and ICICI banks. Both public and private sector banks' characteristics, such as those related to internet banking, ATM services, personnel availability, and attitude, have been contrasted. According to the report, ICICI Bank offers its clients superior services than Indian Overseas Bank. "A Study on Customer Satisfaction towards Net Banking with Special Reference to General Banking Customers" was to learn more about the variables affecting customer satisfaction with regard to net banking services as well as services offered by the general banking sector (Fulgence, 2012).

A study on online banking services was conducted to highlight the perception of customers toward online banking. The survey was conducted to analyze the level of satisfaction among customers using online banking services. It also was done to highlight the level of awareness and usage among various age groups of customers.

Materials and Methods

To analyze the objectives of the study a structured questionnaire was used to collect the primary data. The researcher has adopted a descriptive research study since it describes the state of affairs as it exists at present. A sample of 200 was taken for this study. The probability sampling method was used in the survey. The data was analyzed using statistical tools in SPSS like frequency analysis, independent T-test analysis and one-way ANOVA

Table 79.1 Table showing mean score analysis on the online banking services provided by bank.

Particulars	Gender	N	Mean	Std. deviation
The online banking services provided by the bank.	Male	79	2.27	0.843
	Female	67	2.34	1.008

Source: Author

Table 79.2 Table showing t-test for gender and online banking services provided by the bank.

T-Test for equality of means			
Particulars	t^a	df^b	Sig.^{c}(2-tailed)
Online banking services provided by the bank	0.506	144	0.014* significant

Source: Author

Table 79.3 Table showing one-way analysis for occupation and online banking services provided by the bank.

	Sum of squares	df[a]	Mean square	F[b]	Sig.[c]
Between groups	5.364	3	1.788	2.163	0.005** Significant
Within groups	117.376	142	0.827		
Total	122.740	145			

Source: Author

Table 79.4 showing one-way analysis for occupation and online banking services are easy to operate and user-friendly.

	Sum of squares	df[a]	Mean square	F[b]	Sig.[c]
Between groups	2.795	4	0.699	0.748	0.001** Significant
Within groups	131.732	141	0.934		
Total	134.527	145			

Source: Author

Results and Discussions

The collected data were classified, tabulated and analyzed with the statistical tools (SPSS) from the mean score analysis on the online banking services provided by the bank.

Table 79.1 shows that female respondents (2.34) have the highest mean and more focus on 'Online Banking services' compared to the Male respondents (2.27).

Table 79.2 shows the t-test for gender and online banking services provided by the bank. It depicts that there is a significant difference at 0.014 levels among the customers, with respect to gender towards online banking services provided by the bank. The online banking services provided by the bank are significant at 0.014 level and hence the hypothesis is rejected.

Table 79.3 shows one-way analysis for occupation and online banking services provided by the bank. It represents that there is a significant difference among the occupation of the respondents and online banking services provided by the bank. The significance is at 0.001 level and the hypothesis is rejected.

Table 79.4 shows the one-way ANOVA to identify the difference between the occupation of the respondents and online banking services are easy to operate and user-friendly. The significance is at 0.001 level and the hypothesis is rejected.

Conclusion

Online banking is having a significant impact on banking relationships. The way the entire banking industry operates has been changed by online banking services. It has improved the speed and decreased the cost of bank transactions in addition to making them easier. Banks have made significant investments to build these facilities. The capacity of a bank to convince clients to switch to online banking determines the success of online banking. Customers need to be trained in how to utilize every new technology because they are only familiar with the conventional banking system. Overall, online banking boosts operational effectiveness, lowers costs, and provides a platform for customers to get value-added services, meeting all the requirements. This survey shows that although consumers are aware of the advantages of internet banking, they are hesitant to use digital banking. Because they lack technical proficiency, they are used to branch banking and perceive online banking to be inconvenient. Security, safety, and a lack of trust are the main problems with online banking. The findings also demonstrate that retaining and attracting clients is greatly aided by dependability, convenience, speed, and user-friendliness.

References

Ackah, D., and Agboyi, M. R. (2014). Adoption of electronic banking in Ghana banking system: a case study of guaranty trust bank (Ghana) Limited. GRIN Verlag.

de Waal, A., Bilstra, E., and Bootsman, J. (2022). Building the High-Performance Finance Function. IGI Global.

Ekos Research Associates, and Task Force on the Future of the Canadian Financial Services Sector (1998). Public opinion research relating to the financial services sector .

Fulgence, K. (2012). Factors Influencing Customer Satisfaction with Internet Banking. LAP Lambert Academic Publishing.

Horn, N. (2002). Legal Issues in Electronic Banking. Springer.

Khosrow-Pour, M. (2008). Encyclopedia of Information Science and Technology (2nd edn.), IGI Global.

Kundra, D. (2020). A Study on Consumer Behaviour Towards E-Banking Services .

Lee, I. (2012). Strategy, Adoption, and Competitive Advantage of Mobile Services in the Global Economy. IGI Global.

More, V. S., and Hiray, A. (n.d.). Recent Trends In Business and Management. Archers and Elevators Publishing House.

Omar, A. (2014). Customer perception towards online banking services: empirical evidence from Pakistan .

Plunkett Research Ltd. (2007). Plunkett's E-Commerce & Internet Business Almanac 2008: E-Commerce & Internet Business Industry Market Research, Statistics, Trends & Leading Companie. Plunkett Research, Ltd.

Rashidi, E. (2015). Discussing the effects of internet banking on customer satisfaction.

Riscinto-Kozub, K. A. (2008). the effects of service recovery satisfaction on customer loyalty and future behavioral intentions: an exploratory study in the luxury hotel industry. Auburn University.

Saibaba, S. (2014). Factors influencing customers' intentions to use internet Banking: model development and test. *International Journal of Innovative Technology & Adaptive Management (IJITAM)*, ISSN 2347-3622.

Sanchez-Diaz, I., Vural, C. A., and Halldórsson, A. (2021). Assessing the inequalities in access to online delivery services and the way COVID-19 pandemic affects marginalization. *Transport Policy*, 109, 24–36.

80 Evaluating the effect of advertising medium on consumer behavior: a comparative study of TV, online, and outdoor Ads among the different age groups

Chandirasekar, B. and Lingesh, D.[a]

Saveetha College of Liberal Arts and Sciences, Saveetha University Chennai, India

Abstract

This research conducted to measure the impact of advertising on consumer purchasing habits, to examine how people feel about advertisements and to determine the elements that influence a choice to buy the most. A pre-structured questionnaire was created for this qualitative study, and it underwent a finalization phase with the help of a pilot study including 30 participants. A survey of the residents of the Kumbakonam districts was done both online and offline. The relevant primary data were gathered from the 100 participants in a convenient sampling survey, which was carried out. The hypothesis was tested by using the ANOVA test and descriptive analysis. The responders are mostly male and in the 20 to 30 age range. Additionally, it has been discovered that creative advertising influences the minds of most individuals. The alternative hypotheses were accepted because both of the hypotheses' p values are less than 0.05. The effect of the advertising medium on customer purchasing behavior will vary depending on a number of variables, including the target market, the good or service being advertised, and the advertisement's own effectiveness. The most efficient method for influencing certain customer types may involve a combination of diverse outlets.

Keywords: Advertising, consumer behavior, demographic factors, effect of advertising

Introduction

Consumer behavior can be greatly influenced by advertising. The reason behind is that a certain product or service that a consumer may not have known about before can be made known through advertising. Additionally, businesses have the ability to enhance the perception that consumers have of their goods and services, which can affect their buying behavior. Advertising is a type of communication that aims to persuade a target audience (viewers, readers, or listeners) to buy something or do something in response to a product, piece of information, service, etc. Advertising is crucial for convincing, reminding, and educating both new and current customers to make a purchase (Manivasagan and Saravanan, 2016). A corporation can develop a strong brand identity and foster greater customer loyalty by persistently marketing a good or service. People's recommendations and opinions, including those of influencers and celebrities who support certain goods or services, can have an impact on consumers. While creating advertisements with the desired effect, marketers need to have a thorough understanding of consumer purchasing habits. The way a product is seen by people is greatly influenced by its advertising. Consumers must receive pertinent information from advertisements, which must be engaging (Edwin, 2018).

A study conducted to look at how advertising affects consumer purchasing patterns in the Nigerian context. The goal of the study was to determine whether there is a positive or negative correlation between advertising and customer purchasing habits (Edwin, 2018). The many forms of advertising, especially for those who use cosmetics, have a significant impact on consumers' purchasing choices. Repeated promotions significantly influence consumers' preferences for and purchases of cosmetics in the research area (Qadri, 2021). A study attempting to determine the impact of social media advertising on consumer purchasing behavior discovered that the availability of the product that customers are wanting to buy totally determines their online purchasing behavior (Pathak, 2019). Results from two pilot tests and four formal experiments demonstrate that virtual character spokespersons have a more favorable impact on consumers' purchase intentions than spokespersons who are real individuals, which is accomplished through the mediating role of psychological need fulfillment (Wei et al., 2023). According to a study done among teens in Gujaranwala, brand image and advertising have a considerable impact on consumer purchasing behavior and have a strong positive influence. People have a favorable mindset when they think of a brand. According to a study, teens in Gujranwala are more

[a]lin999save@gmail.com

aware of their social standing and prefer branded goods, and this awareness influences their consumer behavior in a favorable way (Malik et al., 2013).

Results of an article show that neither traditional nor online advertising has a significant direct impact on consumer purchasing decisions for branded clothing. But both have significant indirect effects because of the advertising elements and consumer attitudes that act as mediators and have a significant mediating impact (Afzal and Khan, 2015). For the current research project, numerous studies have been analyzed, and it has been discovered that none of them have examined the influence of advertising medium on customer behavior. The objectives of this study were to determine the impact of advertising on consumer purchasing behavior, to examine customer attitudes towards advertisements, and to pinpoint the variables that have the most impact on a consumer's decision to buy.

Materials and Methods

A pre-structured questionnaire was created for this qualitative study, and it underwent a finalization phase with the help of a pilot study including 30 participants.

Also, the internal consistency of the questionnaire's questions was examined using Cronbach's alpha test. A survey of the residents of the Kumbakonam districts was done both online and offline. The relevant primary data were gathered from the 100 participants in a convenient sampling survey, which was carried out. To determine whether there are any differences in the impact of advertising on demographic characteristics, two hypotheses were developed. The ANOVA test and descriptive analysis were used to evaluate the hypothesis.

Hypothesis: 01 There is no difference between gender and influence of online advertisement.
Inference: The above table represents that there is significant difference between gender and influence of online advertisement. The significance was less than 0.0001 levels, so the hypothesis (H0) was rejected and alternative hypothesis (H1) was accepted.
Hypothesis: 02 There is no difference between Hypothesis: 01 there is no difference between age and advertisement do you like.
Inference: The above table shows that there is a significant difference between age and adver-

Table 80.1 Demographic factors of the respondent.

Demographic factors	Categories	No. of respondents	Percentage
Gender	Male	82	82
	Female	18	18
Age groups	Below 20	10	10
	20-30	77	77
	30-40	13	13
	40-50	0	0
	Above 50	0	0
Income level	Below 20,000 pm	15	15
	20,000 to 30,000	33	33
	30,000 to 40,000	22	22
	40,000 to 50,000	18	18
	Above 50,000	12	12
Place of residence	Urban	68	68
	Rural	32	32
Level of education	School level	14	14
	Under graduation level	43	43
	Post graduation level	24	24
	Professional	8	8
	Illiterate	11	11

Source: Primary data

Demographic Factors

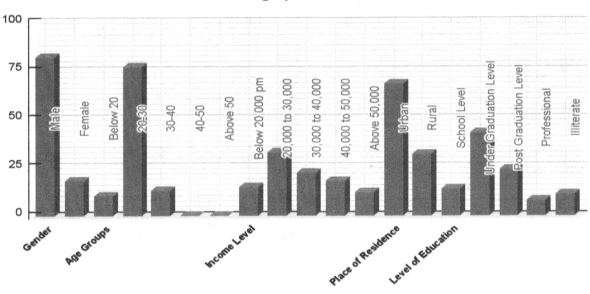

Figure 80.1 Demographic factor of the respondents
Source: Author

Table 80.2 Types of advertisements.

S. No,	Ads liked	No. of respondents	Percentages %
1	Creative	40	40
2	Informative	27	27
3	Shorts and crispy	21	21
4	Funny	12	12
	Total	100	100

Source: Primary data

Table 80.3 Source of new products.

S. No.	Source of new products	No of respondents	Percentage %
1	TV ads	23	23
2	Social media	24	24
3	Internet ads	31	31
4	Other media	22	22
	Total	100	100

Source: Primary data

Table 80.4 Advertisement of product.

S. No.	Source of new products	No. of respondents	Percentages
1	Don't remember at all	36	36
2	Remember the company but not products	36	36
3	Remember the company and product but not ad	28	28
	Total	100	100

Source: Primary data

Table 80.5 Advertising the credible.

S. No	Advertising the credible	No of respondents	Percentage %
1	Totally credible	27	27
2	Quite credible	18	18
3	Not quite	30	30
4	May be	25	25
	Total	100	100

Source: Primary data

tisement do you like. The significance was less than 0.001 levels, so the hypothesis (H0) was rejected, and alternative hypothesis (H1) was accepted.

Findings and Discussion

The results of the current study show that most respondents prefer imaginative and educational advertisements over other kinds of advertisements. Additionally, it is discovered that the main media channels where the respondents discover new items or

Table 80.6 Influence of products.

S. No.	Influences of products	No of respondents	Percentage
1	Recommendations from friends and family	24	24
2	Seeing famous people use the product	30	30
3	Personal experience	22	22
4	Others factors	24	24
	Total	100	100

Source: Primary data

Table 80.8 Buying behavior.

S. No.	Buying behavior	No of respondents	Percentage
1	Google ads	16	16
2	You tube ads	38	38
3	Face book ads	21	21
4	Instagram ads	25	25
	Total	100	100

Source: Primary data

Table 80.10 Gender and influence of online advertisement. influence of online advertisement.

	Sum of squares	df	Mean square	F	Sig.
Between groups	40.048	1	40.048	58.838	<.001
Within groups	66.702	98	.681		
Total	106.750	99			

Source: Primary data

Table 80.7 Influence of advertising.

S. No.	Influence of advertising	No of respondents	Percentage %
1	Large influence	25	25
2	Medium influence	25	25
3	Small influence	20	20
4	No influence	30	30
	Total	100	100

Source: Primary data

Table 80.9 Purchasing the product across any ads.

S. No.	Purchasing a product across any ads	No of respondents	Percentage
1	Yes	25	25
2	No	35	35
3	May be	40	40
	Total	100	100

Source: Primary data

Table 80.11 Age and advertisement do you like advertisements do you like.

	Sum of squares	df	Mean square	F	Sig.
Between groups	37.453	2	18.727	23.843	<.001
Within groups	76.187	97	.785		
Total	113.640	99			

Source: Primary data

learn about new products are social media ads and television commercials. A little over two-fifth of the respondents say they buy things after learning about them and recalling the marketing while doing so. The handiest platforms for receiving advertisements are the internet and mobile phones. TV is still a common way for people to acquire advertisements even though it is a traditional kind of media. Radio and mail-order advertisements were also discovered to have received the least degree of favor. In addition, it has been discovered that most consumers look for quality, utility, durability, and pricing in a product. These are the most crucial variables to consider when buying a new item. Most respondents agreed that they could watch effective advertisements repeatedly. This indicates that positive advertisements assist in reaching more consumers. In a study, it was discovered that advertisements and customer behavior have a substantial correlation, also discovered a considerable influence of advertising on consumer post-purchase behavior (Sharma, n.d.). Findings of a research showed that newspapers and magazines are powerful media for influencing consumers' purchasing habits behaviors (Sama, 2019).

Conclusion

The study's findings indicate that consumer behavior and attitudes are influenced by advertisements on a global scale. The results of this study demonstrated the significance of advertising in the distribution of goods. Consumer attitudes and perceptions are influenced by online advertising, it has been established. Advertising has an impact on consumer behavior and helps consumers become more aware of or subconsciously associate with a brand, which helps an organization increase sales. The material in advertisements is sufficient to draw customers' attention and raise their level of awareness. According to this study, respondents have a higher level of awareness of the impact of advertisements than was predicted. For knowledge on new items, market trends, and to compare with other products, many of them actively consume media.

Reference

Afzal, S., and Khan, J. R. (2015). Impact of online and conventional advertisement on consumer buying behaviour of branded garments. *Asian Journal of Management Sciences and Education*, 4(1), 125–135, http://www.ajmse.leena-luna.co.jp/AJMSEPDFs/Vol.4(1)/AJMSE2015(4.1-14).pdf.

Edwin, A. (2018). Conceptual review of the effects of advertising on consumer buying behaviour. SSRN .

Malik, M. E., Ghafoor, M. M., Iqbal, H. K., and Ali, Q. (2013). Impact of brand image and advertisement on consumer buying behavior. *World Applied Sciences Journal*, 23(1), 117–122. https://www.researchgate.net/profile/Qasim-Nisar/publication/308746219_Impact_of_Brand_Image_and_Advertisement_on_Consumer_Buying_Behavior/links/57ede0b008ae03fa0e829f63/Impact-of-Brand-Image-and-Advertisement-on-Consumer-Buying-Behavior.pdf.

Manivasagan, S., and Saravanan, R. (2016). Impact of advertisement on consumer behaviour for home appliances in madurai city, India. International *Journal of Innovative Research and Development*, 5(14). https://www.indianjournalofmanagement.com/index.php/ijird_delete/article/view/108577.

Pathak, S. (2019). Effects of Social Media Advertisement on Buying Behaviour. Amazon Digital Services LLC - Kdp Print Us.

Qadri, S. S. (2021). Impacts of Advertisement on Consumer's Purchasing Behavior. Cosmetic Products in Karachi. GRIN Verlag.

Sama, R. (2019). Impact of media advertisements on consumer behaviour. *Journal of Creative Communications*, 14(1), 54–68.

Sharma, S. (n.d.). Effect of advertisement on consumer behaviour . https://ijrar.org/papers/IJRAR19J2995.pdf.

Wei, H. L., Li, H., and Zhu, S. Y. (2023). Consumer preference for virtual reality advertisements with human-scene interaction: an intermediary based on psychological needs. *Cyberpsychology, Behavior and Social Networking*, 26(3), 188–197.

81 Examining the effect of brand image on consumer preference for mobile wallet: a comparison with traditional payment methods among people in Chennai district

Chandirasekar, B. and Sanjay S. M.

Saveetha College of Liberal Arts and Sciences, Saveetha University Chennai, India

Abstract

The growth of financial technology has made it possible for buyers and sellers to complete transactions using a mobile wallet payment gateway. Mobile wallets have also grown in popularity among smartphone users. The purpose of this study is to understand customer preferences for using mobile wallets for transactional purposes and to pinpoint the elements that influence those preferences. To ensure that the content of the pre-structured questionnaire was appropriate, a pilot research with 30 participants was carried out. A practical sampling strategy was utilized to acquire a sample from 100 respondents because the community of mobile wallet users is relatively large. The demographic characteristics were categorized using descriptive statistics, and the hypothesis was tested using the ANOVA test. The majority of respondents, it has been discovered, prefer to use mobile wallets because they are handy and time-saving. to determine whether there are any differences in mobile wallet usage across various employment and age categories. The findings of the ANOVA test, which was used, indicate that the P-value is less than 0.05 for both demographic factors. The findings of this study demonstrate that mobile wallets have become a crucial aspect of everyone's lives, and that usage varies depending on age and employment status.

Keywords: Consumer preference, fin-technology, mobile wallets, payment gateway

Introduction

Mobile wallets are digital systems that let users store, manage, and use their money without carrying cash or credit cards on their person. They have grown in popularity over the past few years as a result of their practicality, use, and improved security measures. The rise of e-commerce, the proliferation of smartphones, and the growing demand for easy, safe, and easily accessible payment methods have all contributed to the expansion of mobile wallets (Handa et al., 2011). By removing the need for customers to carry several credit cards in their wallets, these mobile payment systems, also known as mobile wallets, make it easier for customers to shop (Kafsh, 2015). The Indian government has placed a strong emphasis on digital payment systems as part of the Digital India project. The government launched a number of new digital payment methods through the National Payments Corporation of India in order to improve the system's uptake and settlement (NPCI). It serves as the umbrella organization for all Indian retail payment systems (Joshi, 2017). One of the major digital payment methods that showed an increase in adoption at COVID-19 is mobile wallets. People are now turning to online payment methods as a safer alternative to utilizing cash to pay for shopping, food deliveries, electricity bills, and many other things as a result of the pandemic (Kapoor et al., 2022; Benni, 2021).

Numerous studies have been conducted on mobile wallet payment gateways. Due to time restrictions, only a few articles were reviewed for the current study; their key conclusions are listed below. The study "adoption of digital wallet by consumers" discovered that users utilize mobile wallets due to its convenience, one touch technique, and time-saving technology. This research also explored the risks, difficulties, and factors that affected consumer acceptance of digital wallets (Rathore, 2018). The purposive sample method was used to gather a total of 327 responses. The findings showed that relative advantage, good infrastructure, security concerns, and touch-free transactions all had a favorable, significant impact on the desire to embrace m-wallets (Kapoor et al., 2022). In India, 243 individuals participated in a survey. Convenience, safety, complexity, trialability, compatibility, service quality, privacy, information availability, and ease of use were among the things

ᵃResearchsmartgen@gmail.com

that were noted (Sharma, 2019). A primary poll was performed across the country, and 744 people in total took part. There were 17 different hypotheses created, and PLS-SEM was used to estimate and test each one. The findings demonstrate that a number of elements, including perceived usefulness (PU), perceived ease of use (PEOU), trust, security, enabling conditions, and lifestyle suitability, significantly influence customer attitudes and intentions towards using mobile wallets (Chawla and Joshi, 2019). A study that looked at the impact of digital wallets on consumer purchases. It focused on a number of aspects that influence customer use of digital wallets, including security, credibility, usability, and promotional offers. They found that the convenience of having all of your information in one place and the fact that some consumers prefer using a digital wallet as their primary payment method (Soegoto and Sumantri, 2020). The findings of the study conducted by Jin et al. (2020) suggested that perceived utility, perceived usability, social influence, and brand image have a significant relationship on consumers' behavior to accept mobile wallets, as well as the consumers' behavior has a significant relationship on consumers' intention to accept mobile wallets. In a study to explore consumer acceptance of mobile

wallets, it was discovered that the most significant influence on people's intentions to use mobile wallets is trust (Bhimasta, 2017). There was no research found on customer preference for mobile wallet payment gateway among the numerous studies analyzed, so it is interesting to learn why consumers choose to use mobile wallets over other available options. The purpose of this study is to understand customer preferences for using mobile wallets for transactional purposes and to pinpoint the elements that influence those preferences.

Materials and Methods

The primary data was gathered using a set of pre-structured questionnaires. The first component of the questionnaire comprises demographic information, and the second section's 10 questions gauge consumers' preferences for mobile wallets. To validate the questionnaire, a pilot research with 30 participants was carried out. Data from the respondents were gathered using an online survey method. Since it is uncertain how many people use mobile wallets, a practical sample technique was used to conduct the study, which included 100 respondents in the Chennai

Table 81.1 Demographic profile of the respondents.

S. No.	Demographic factors	Categories	Frequency	Percentage
1	Gender	Male	54	54
		Female	46	46
2	Age group	Below 20	21	21
		20-30	51	51
		30-40	15	15
		40-50	11	11
		Above 50	2	2
3	Employment status	Business	19	19
		Profession	24	24
		Salaried	7	7
		Daily wages	10	10
		student	40	40
4	Level of education	Up to school level	26	26
		Undergraduate	31	31
		Post graduate	23	23
		Professional course	5	5
		None	15	15

Source: Primary data

Table 81.2 Respondents opinion about performance of mobile wallets.

S. No.	Rating	Frequency	Percentage
1	Excellent	32	32 .0
2	Very Good	29	29 .0
3	Good	22	22 .0
4	Fair	12	12 .0
5	Poor	5	5 .0
	Total	100	100

Source: Primary data

Table 81.3 ANOVA test result for age group and use of mobile wallets.

	Sum of squares	df	Mean square	F	Sig
Between groups	0.602	3	0.201	8.352	<.001
Within groups	2.308	96	0.024		
Total	2.91	99			

Source: SPSS output   P 0.01<0.05

Table 81.4 ANOVA test result for employment category and use of wallets.

	Sum of squares	df	Mean square	F	Sig
Between groups	167.349	3	55.783	112.977	<.001
Within groups	47.401	96	0.494		
Total	214.75	99			

Source: SPSS output   P0.01<0.05

district. Two null hypotheses, namely that there is no difference in the employment category in terms of use of mobile wallets and that there is no difference in the age group with respect to use mobile wallets, were developed in order to carry out the investigation. For this study's assumptions, a one-way ANOVA test was carried out in SPSS.

Findings and Discussions

The demographic characteristics of the respondents are presented in Table 81.1, which showed that most of the respondents are male and that respondents between the ages of 20 and 30 participated more frequently in the study. Google Pay, Phone Pe, and Paytm are the three mobile wallets that respondents in the research area use most frequently. Few respondents are willing to conduct their transactions via a banking company's mobile app. Additionally, it has been discovered that more student groups than other employment groups are using mobile wallets effectively. It demonstrates that the nature of employment is not a factor influencing the use of mobile wallets. Additionally, the vast majority of respondents were happy with the level of service and security offered by the mobile wallet companies, and it was discovered

that its most appealing feature is its always-available nature. A number of variables were found, including those related to comfort, security, complexity, trialability, compatibility, service quality, privacy, and the accessibility of information (Sharma, 2019).

More than half of the respondents expressed a high degree of satisfaction with how well mobile wallets performed, according to Table 81.2, which summarized the opinions of the respondents regarding their performance. Surprisingly, the majority of respondents reported having difficulties using mobile wallets when making payments, but they did not give this concern much thought because the advantages they get from using them outweigh any drawbacks. Table 81.3 of this study disclosed the result of the first hypothesis, according to which the alternative hypothesis is accepted because the ANOVA test result for hypothesis 1 is p 0.01 < 0.05. This indicates that there is a significant difference in mobile wallet use across the various age groups. The null hypothesis was rejected since Table 81.4 demonstrated that the P-value was less than 0.05 (p 0.01 < 0.05). It has been demonstrated that usage of mobile wallets varies significantly depending on the nature of the employment.

Conclusion

This survey sought to determine how Chennai customers felt about using mobile wallets for cashless transactions. Additionally, the survey aimed to comprehend customers' preferences for using mobile wallets, their degree of satisfaction with these online payment methods, and any difficulties they might encounter. Mobile wallets are anticipated to become more important in daily life as technology develops and people become more dependent on a digital lifestyle. This study assesses the user popularity of Google Pay, the most widely used mobile wallet. The survey also identifies the purchase of cinema tickets as one of the mobile wallets' most popular applications. The study is significant because it offers insightful information about Chennai consumers' use of mobile wallets and preferences, information that can be used to enhance the aesthetics and usability of these electronic payment systems. The findings of this study can also assist companies and payment providers in better understanding consumer wants so that they can develop customized goods and services. Overall, this study clarifies the expanding significance of mobile wallets in today's digital world and offers insightful data to consumers, organizations, and payment service providers.

References

Benni, N. (2021). Digital Finance and Inclusion in the time of COVID19: Lessons, Experiences and Proposals. Food and Agriculture Org.

Bhimasta, R. A. (2017). Determinant factors of consumer adoption towards intention to use mobile wallet: a case study Indonesian young generation. S2, UAJY . [Link](http://ejournal.uajy.ac.id/id/eprint/11283).

Chawla, D., and Joshi, H. (2019). Consumer attitude and intention to adopt mobile wallet in India – an empirical study. *International Journal of Bank Marketing*, 37(7), 1590–1618.

Handa, R., Maheshwari, K., and Saraf, M. (2011). Google Wallet a Glimpse into the Future of Mobile Payments. GRIN Verlag.

Jin, C. C., Seong, L. C., and Khin, A. A. (2020). Consumers' behavioural intention to accept of the mobile wallet in Malaysia. *Journal of Southwest Jiaotong University*, 55(1). [DOI](https://doi.org/10.35741/issn.02582724.55.1.3).

Joshi, M. (2017). Digital payment system: a feat forward of India. *Research Dimension*, ISSN: 2249-3867.

Kafsh, S. Z. (2015). Developing Consumer Adoption Model on Mobile Wallet in Canada. Universitéd'Ottawa / University of Ottawa.

Kapoor, A., Sindwani, R., Goel, M., and Shankar, A. (2022). Mobile wallet adoption intention amid COVID19 pandemic outbreak: a novel conceptual framework. *Computers and Industrial Engineering*, 172(October), 108646.

Rathore, H. S. (2018). Adoption of digital wallet by consumers .

Sharma, G. (2019). Mobile wallet adoption in India: an analysis. SSRN .

Soegoto, E. S., and Sumantri, M. B. R. (2020). The influence of digital wallet. *IOP Conference Series: Materials Science and Engineering*, 879(1), 012122.

82 Examining the effect of customer service on consumer preference for online vs offline electronic goods shopping

Chandirasekar, B. and Lokesh, E.

Department of Commerce (A&F), Saveetha College of Liberal Arts and Sciences Saveetha University, Chennai India

Abstract

One of India's rapidly expanding sectors, retail significantly contributes to the nation's GDP growth. For a considerable segment of the Indian populace, the conventional practice has been to procure electronic goods through offline channels. Nevertheless, over the last decade, the online retail market for electronics has experienced substantial growth, emerging as a fiercely competitive arena vis-à-vis offline counterparts and gradually supplanting it as the primary mode of electronic purchases. This investigation aimed to discern consumers' inclinations towards online versus offline shopping, comprehend the determinants influencing consumer buying choices, and grasp consumer perspectives regarding online and offline shopping. Due to the unknown population sizes of online and offline purchasers, a pragmatic sampling technique and a limited sample survey involving 100 respondents were employed. The data underwent scrutiny via descriptive statistics and the chi-square test. The study's findings reveal that the demographic characteristics of respondents, encompassing gender, age bracket, educational attainment, monthly income level, place of residence, and employment type, held no sway over their preference for purchasing mode. As per the study, individuals in the Kanchipuram district exhibit a preference for traditional methods of acquiring electronic merchandise, albeit they are also embracing online platforms for procuring a select few electronic items.

Keywords: Consumer preferences, electronic shopping, factors influencing, offline shopping, online shopping

Introduction

Consumer inclination is a concept employed in economics to delineate the choices individuals undertake to enhance their level of satisfaction (Consumer Preference, 1955). While consumers exert some influence over the commodities they procure, they aren't always capable of selecting precisely what they desire. A pivotal facet of the economic realm is consumer inclination. It constitutes one of the foremost factors impacting supply, demand, and pricing. Societal pressures to conform to specific customs or ideologies, alongside cultural principles, exert an influence on consumers. The trend toward online shopping is steadily escalating, yet a majority still favour in-person transactions, as they can physically interact with and trust the merchandise. Given the diverse nature of shopping preferences, accurately pinpointing such inclinations poses a formidable challenge (Miller, 1977; Sawant, n.d.). Individuals increasingly resort to online shopping due to their technological savvy and appreciation for internet-based transactions. Consequently, it is imperative to conduct investigations into how individuals engage with and perceive online purchasing (Emerald Group Publishing Limited, 2015).

As a consequence of technological advancement, contemporary consumers possess an understanding of the market condition, the attributes of products and services, their cost, quality, and all other elements influencing their buying choices (Consumer Preference, 1955; Miller, 1977). Moreover, consumers possess a thorough comprehension of the rivalry among manufacturers in the marketplace, rendering it remarkably straightforward to contrast, assess, and opt for a particular product based on preference. Furthermore, they now have the capability to make purchases from the comfort of their homes due to the extensive proliferation of e-commerce platforms.

Wasiq et al. (2022) investigated the factors affecting the adoption and utilization of M-commerce services amidst the pandemic and found that buying inclinations were impacted by individual, economic, feasibility, and safety considerations. An examination was conducted to gain deeper insights into the determinants affecting the online shopping patterns of consumers in America and Germany. These elements are categorised into three divisions: individuality, purchase context, and product-associated characteristics (Kühn, 2010). In this circumstance, every conventional or brick-and-mortar retailer must strategize their business approaches by assessing consumer inclination toward the purchasing mode. The purpose of this investigation was to ascertain consumers' preferences between online and offline shopping, to comprehend the determinants influencing consumer buying choices, and to understand consumer perceptions of both online and offline shopping channels.

[a]natashasmartgenresearch@gmail.com

Table 82.1 Cross tabulation on demographic factors vs opinion on safety mode of purchase.

S. No.	Demographic factors	Categories	Opinion about safety mode of purchase of electronic goods			Total
			Online	Offline	Both	
1	Gender	Male	16	23	23	62
		Female	10	10	13	33
		Others	3	2	0	5
2	Age	Up to 20	7	8	15	30
		21 to 30	11	15	5	31
		31 to 40	9	6	9	24
		41 to 50	2	4	3	9
		Above 50	0	2	4	6
3	Education qualification	Up to H.Sc.	4	4	2	10
		Under graduation	19	20	19	58
		Post-graduation	1	7	6	14
		None	5	4	9	18
4	Monthly income	Up to 15,000	2	2	1	5
		15,001 to 30,000	3	7	3	13
		30,001 to 45,000	9	11	6	26
		45,001 to 60,000	3	4	9	16
		Above 60,000	12	11	17	40
5	Place and residential	Rural	15	20	15	50
		Urban	14	15	21	50
6	Nature and employment	Daily wages	4	4	1	9
		Businessman	5	4	9	18
		Agricultural activities	4	8	4	16
		Salaried groups	5	6	4	15
		Students group	11	13	18	42

Source: Primary data

Table 82.2 Chi-square test between the respondent's demographic factors and opinion about the safety mode of purchase.

S. No.	Demographic variable	P-value	Significant level	Result
1	Gender	0.387	0.05	Insignificant
2	Age group	0.112	0.05	Insignificant
3	Educational qualification	0.333	0.05	Insignificant
4	Monthly income	0.382	0.05	Insignificant
5	Place of residence	0.417	0.05	Insignificant
6	Nature of employment	0.491	0.05	Insignificant

Source: SPSS result

Materials and Methods

As the study's populace remains undisclosed, a convenient sampling method was employed to amass insights from the inhabitants of Kanchipuram district. Moreover, 100 respondents from the surveyed area, reflecting diverse demographic profiles, actively participated in the questionnaire. Essential primary data was collected through a predetermined questionnaire, while an online survey strategy was deployed,

Table 82.3 Cross tabulation for mode of purchase and physical inspection of goods.

		Mode of purchase of electronic goods			Total
		Online	Offline	Both	
Opinion about physical inspection of good	Very important	9	8	19	36
	Important	6	11	7	24
	Indifferent	7	7	4	18
	Not important	3	3	1	7
	Not at all important	4	6	5	15
Total		29	35	36	100

Source: Primary data

Table 82.4 Chi-square test result for physical inspection and mode of purchase.

	Value	df	Asymptotic significance (2-sided)
Pearson Chi-square	9.244[a]	8	.322
Likelihood ratio	9.398	8	.310
Linear-by-linear association	2.182	1	.140
N of valid cases	100		

a. 4 cells (26.7%) have expected to count less than 5. The minimum expected count is 2.03.

Source: SPSS result

disseminated via Gmail, WhatsApp, and various social networking platforms. Secondary data was sourced from authoritative websites, literature, periodicals, and published articles. Additionally, two hypotheses were formulated, and the Chi-square test was utilised alongside SPSS software to scrutinise the primary hypothesis of the study. The Chi-square test served to evaluate the adequacy of fit or the significance of correlation between two variables (Kothari, 2004).

Findings and Discussion

The Table 82.1 illustrates the demographic makeup of the participants, indicating that the majority of respondents fell below 30 years old and identified as female. Moreover, it was revealed that a substantial portion comprised individuals holding degrees. Among those surveyed from rural locales, a prevalent interest in online shopping was evident, underscoring its ubiquity in society. Furthermore, a significant consensus among respondents favoured the perceived security of offline purchases. The majority expressed their ability to afford electronic products both online and offline, with minimal discernible discrepancies in pricing, warranty and guarantee, as well as the availability of diverse goods and services. These

demographic attributes are detailed in Table 82.1, with the chi-square test employed to ascertain their potential impact on consumer buying preferences. The outcomes of the test, as depicted in Table 82.2, revealed that factors beyond demographics influenced consumers' purchasing behaviours. Additionally, a shift was noted in respondents' attitudes towards the value of physically inspecting products when opting for offline purchases, with greater emphasis now placed on the added value associated with such transactions.

Conclusions

This investigation unveiled the behaviour and disposition of individuals regarding the method of acquisition of electronic commodities amidst online and offline platforms. This inquiry aided in comprehending the mentality and inclination of consumers positioned in Kanchipuram district. This exploration indicates that inhabitants of Kanchipuram district possess restricted acquaintance concerning attributes and functionalities offered by virtual emporiums. It illustrates that consumers within Kanchipuram district exhibit a predilection for both online and offline channels when procuring electronic merchandise. Patrons do not exhibit a robust inclination towards any specific procurement avenue, albeit they harbour a slight inclination towards the offline medium, possibly due to their constrained knowledge or adherence to traditional customs. Residents of Kanchipuram district harbour minimal trust in the security extended by online merchants for their acquired items, perhaps owing to delivery impediments or product conditions. This study brought to light that individuals in Kanchipuram district remain apathetic towards both procurement modes, opting for convenience at the moment, yet disregarding or possessing scant awareness of the diverse features and benefits accessible through online retailers. Based on the findings, it can be deduced that denizens of Kanchipuram district exhibit a preference for conventional methods when purchasing electronic goods, although they are gradually embracing the online platform for select electronic acquisitions.

Reference

Andruetto, C., Bin, E., Susilo, Y., and Pernestål, A. (2023). Transition from physical to online shopping alternatives due to the COVID-19 pandemic - a case study of Italy and Sweden. *Transportation Research Part A: Policy and Practice*, 171(May), 103644.

Consumer Preference (1955).

Emerald Group Publishing Limited (2015). A Focus on Consumer Behaviours and Experiences in an Online Shopping Environment. Emerald Group Publishing.

Gaurav, K., and Jhansi, V. (2017). Factors Influencing Customers' Perception Towards Online Shopping. GRIN Verlag.

Guruswamy, M. (2014). Online Shopping Habits And Consumer Behavior: A Study on Consumer Behavior and E-tailing. GRIN Verlag.

Hodges, L., Lowery, C. M., Patel, P., McInnis, J., and Zhang, Q. (2023). A systematic review of marketing practices used in online grocery shopping: implications for WIC online ordering. *Nutrients*, 15(2), 446, https://doi.org/10.3390/nu15020446.

Kothari, C. R. (2004). Research methodology: methods and techniques. *New Age International*.

Kühn, S. (2010). A Comparison of Online Shopping Behavior of American and German Consumers. GRIN Verlag.

Miller, M. A. (1977). The consumer and his awareness of his rights in the market place. PhD diss., Ball State University.

Sawant, S. S. (n.d.). Customer Satisfaction in Online Shopping. Archers and Elevators Publishing House.

Wasiq, M., Johri, A., and Singh, P. (2022). Factors affecting adoption and use of m-commerce Services among the customers in Saudi Arabia. *Heliyon*, 8(12), e12532.

83 Exploring online buying behavior of consumers post pandemic - a comparative analysis among demographic groups

Vigneshwaran, D. and Celia, B. R.

Saveetha College of Liberal Arts and Science, Saveetha University, Chennai, India

Abstract

This investigation explores the digital purchasing patterns of customers in Chennai following the pandemic. The global health crisis has expedited the transition towards electronic commerce and web-based shopping, necessitating a comprehensive understanding of the variables impacting digital purchasing behavior. Employing a structured questionnaire, the study surveyed 200 consumers to assess the pandemic's repercussions on their purchasing conduct. Utilizing SPSS tools, collected data underwent descriptive analysis, with One-way ANOVA employed to validate the study's hypotheses. Results indicate that convenience, safety, and the availability of discounts and promotions are primary motivators for digital purchasing behavior. Nevertheless, concerns regarding product authenticity and delivery delays persist as significant challenges for consumers. Additionally, the research unveils a rising trend of consumers utilizing social media platforms for online shopping. These findings hold implications for businesses, policymakers, and marketers seeking to bolster their online presence and enhance the digital purchasing experience. Consequently, it can be inferred that the outbreak of the pandemic has precipitated substantial changes in online purchasing behavior. Individuals have come to appreciate the convenience and time-saving aspects of home-based shopping, alongside its perceived safety due to enhanced privacy and reduced exposure to crowds.

Keywords: Behavior, consumers, e-commerce, online, pandemic, purchase, shopping

Introduction

The COVID-19 outbreak has triggered a notable transformation in consumer purchasing patterns, with a majority transitioning towards digital platforms for their transactions. Consequently, e-commerce has experienced an unparalleled surge in demand, necessitating businesses to adjust to this emerging landscape. The objective of this investigation is to examine the online purchasing conduct of consumers in Chennai, India, following the pandemic. Situated in the southern region of India, Chennai serves as a pivotal commercial center with a populace exceeding 7 million. The conventional brick-and-mortar retail framework has been disrupted by the pandemic, compelling numerous enterprises in Chennai to pivot towards e-commerce to sustain operations. This shift has resulted in a rapid expansion of online retail, as consumers increasingly rely on digital platforms to procure diverse goods and services. Through this study, our goal is to comprehend the determinants influencing consumer behavior in Chennai amidst the pandemic, encompassing factors such as health apprehensions, price sensitivity, and product accessibility. Furthermore, we intend to explore the role of technology in facilitating online shopping, encompassing the utilization of mobile devices and virtual trial features. Additionally, we will scrutinize the influence of social media on consumer behavior, alongside their perspectives on sustainability and ecological consciousness. In essence, this inquiry aims to furnish insights into the evolving purchasing patterns of Chennai consumers post-pandemic and its ramifications for local businesses.

Customer contentment stands as one of the fundamental elements in internet acquisition. Not solely the website but additionally the data customer-centric facilities and so forth entice more individuals to digital retail platforms. The exploration indicates that it's necessary to establish (Mohamed, 2003) customer rapport to foster continual acquisition. The group makeup of digital shopping patrons and their stance towards digital shopping platforms additionally centers on the cognizance level of the patrons during their digital purchases. The analyst scrutinized the demeanor of the patrons when acquiring diverse items from various platforms, and their gratification degree is also a point of concern in the inquiry. The study concerning outlook and understanding of patrons toward digital shopping fixates on elements that induce repetitive purchases and conversely the elements that instill hesitancy in patrons toward digital acquisition (Gaurav and Jhansi, 2017). The transaction assurance, product cost, product

ᵃvishalsmartgenresearch@gmail.com

standard, accessibility, promotions and advertisement, delivery time, quality comparison, convenience, and company prestige are the (Hariramani, n.d.) principal variables in digital shopping. To delve deeper into the digital shopping conduct of consumers and vendors amid the duration of the COVID-19 pandemic. The exploration strove to unearth enhanced strategies for digital vendors to offer improved choices to consumers and to undertake an examination of various trends prevalent in the market concerning digital shopping. Amid escalating extent of digital shopping and the conduct of patrons, particularly students (Kengthon, 2011). The investigation centered on the elements that predominantly impact the resolutions concerning digital shopping and the factors influencing it (Gao, 2016). The exploration posits that the overhauling of digital shopping platforms to surpass the prevailing position isn't distant.

The investigation also centered on students' inclinations toward various online purchasing platforms (Brandt, 2013). This inquiry was carried out to comprehend the digital purchasing conduct of consumers following the global health crisis. Examination was undertaken to gauge the extent of consumer familiarity with the available online shopping applications and ascertain the most favored and frequently utilized platforms. Additionally, the research strived to pinpoint the impact of the COVID-19 pandemic on consumer online purchasing behavior. The conjecture was formulated to ascertain the correlation between marital status and expenditure on digital shopping, to discern potential disparities among age demographics concerning application usage, and to scrutinize whether variances existed in employment status and the chosen payment methods for online transactions.

Materials and Methods

The research focuses on consumer behavior on online shopping. For the study, 200 people from Chennai district were chosen as a sample and polled using a questionnaire. The research is descriptive in nature. Secondary data is obtained from a variety of trustworthy sources like books, newspapers, journals, and websites. Convenient sampling technique is used to acquire primary data. The data collected through questionnaire was analyzed using the statistical tool, one way ANOVA.

Results and Discussions

Table 83.1 illustrates a noteworthy variance between marital status and expenditure on internet-based retail transactions. The statistical significance surpasses the 0.001 threshold (0.843), resulting in the absence of discernible impact. Table 83.2

Table 83.1 Table showing one-way analysis for marital status and amount spends on online shopping.

ANOVA
One-way analysis for marital status and amount spends on online shopping

	Sum of squares	df	Mean square	F	Sig.
Between groups	.030	1	.030	.039	.843
Within groups	59.358	78	.761		
Total	59.388	79			

Source: Author

Table 83.2 Table showing one-way analysis for gender and apps used for online shopping.

ANOVA
One-way analysis for gender and apps used for online shopping to buy electronic products

	Sum of squares	df	Mean Square	F	Sig.
Between groups	123.521	1	123.521	235.182	<.001
Within groups	40.967	78	.525		
Total	164.488	79			

Source: Author

Table 83.3 Table showing one-way analysis for employment status and mode of payment.

ANOVA
One-way analysis for employment status and mode of payment

	Sum of squares	df	Mean square	F	Sig.
Between groups	6.669	2	3.335	6.915	.002
Within groups	37.131	77	.482		
Total	43.800	79			

Source: Author

demonstrates a significant distinction in gender concerning the selection of applications for purchasing electronic items online. The statistical significance falls below the 0.001 level, prompting the rejection of the null hypothesis (H0) and acceptance of the alternative hypothesis (H1). Table 83.3 indicates a significant differentiation regarding employment status and preferred payment methods in online shopping. The statistical significance exceeds the 0.001 threshold (0.002), indicating negligible influence. It is imperative for online shopping service providers to exercise caution in handling customers' personal information, fostering a sense of security among them. Predominantly, individuals with higher levels of education capitalize on the online shopping opportunity. Simplifying the online purchasing process could attract a wider demographic of customers across various age groups. A primary issue encountered by customers pertains to the delivery of purchased goods. Therefore, it is advisable for retailers to ensure the accessibility of deliveries in rural areas, thereby enhancing convenience for customers.

Conclusion

Ultimately, the COVID-19 pandemic has had a considerable effect on consumers' online purchasing patterns. Customers have increasingly turned to electronic commerce platforms for their day-to-day requirements, and they have cultivated fresh routines, including utilizing portable gadgets for internet transactions. Trustworthiness and safety have emerged as pivotal considerations for consumers, who exhibit greater prudence regarding their personal data and financial particulars. Convenience and promptness in delivery have assumed paramount importance for consumers, given their emphasis on safeguarding their well-being. Consequently, brands and merchants must adjust to these shifts by furnishing a seamless online shopping encounter that caters to the evolving demands of consumers.

References

Brandt, E. (2013). The Relationship between Innovativeness and Shopping Website Feature Preferences Across Product Classes. Cleveland State University. Department of Psychology, and Ohio LINK Electronic Theses and Dissertations Center.

Gao, J. (2016). Understanding online purchase decision making: the effects of unconscious thought, information quality, and information quantity .

Gaurav, K., and Jhansi, V. (2017). Factors Influencing Customers' Perception Towards Online Shopping. GRIN Verlag.

Gupta, P. (2020). E-Commerce in India: Economic and Legal Perspectives. SAGE Publishing India.

Hariramani, S. G. (n.d.). A Study on Consumers Perception about Online Shopping in India. Archers and Elevators Publishing House.

Kengthon, W. (2011). Consumer Buying Behaviour. GRIN Verlag.

Liu, Z., Zhao, J., Yu, Z., Zhou, Z., Wang, L., and Chen, Y. (2022). How has the COVID-19 pandemic changed urban consumers' ways of buying agricultural products? evidence from Shanghai, China. *Healthcare (Basel, Switzerland)*, **10(11)**, 2264. **https://doi.org/**10.3390/healthcare10112264.

Mohamed, H. P. (2003). Customer Relationship Management: A Step. Vikas Publishing House.

Pathak, S. (2019). Effects of Social Media Advertisement on Buying Behaviour. Woven Words Publishers.

Rahman, S. (2014). Introduction to E-Commerce Technology in Business. GRIN Verlag.

Rowles, D. (2013). Mobile Marketing: How Mobile Technology is Revolutionizing Marketing, Communications and Advertising. Kogan Page Publishers.

Sawant, S. S. (n.d.). Customer Satisfaction in Online Shopping. Archers and Elevators Publishing House.

84 Green marketing: a study on buyer insolences towards eco-friendly products

Dilli G. and Rexy, A M.

Department of Commerce (General), Saveetha College of Liberal Arts and Sciences Saveetha University, Chennai, India

Abstract

The research aims to explore buyer preferences and attitudes toward eco-friendly products, focusing on consumer behavior and perceptions of green marketing. Utilizing descriptive methods, convenient sampling involved 196 participants. SPSS analyzed hypotheses, producing multivariate tables, with data analyzed using the percentage method, t-tests, and One-way ANOVA. As environmental awareness rises, consumers increasingly favor eco-friendly products, reacting positively to brands less harmful to the environment. The study assessed consumer awareness, environmental consciousness, and purchase intentions. Of 196 respondents, 65 (33%) were male, and 131 (67%) females. Those above 40 exhibited greater eco-friendly product awareness (19%), with males showing higher awareness (17%) but females exhibiting more environmental consciousness (21%) and purchase intentions (18%). Moderate positive correlations were observed between eco-friendly product awareness and environmental consciousness, and environmental consciousness and purchase intention, with a low positive correlation between eco-friendly product awareness and purchase intentions. India's green marketing field is nascent, requiring further research. Despite rising interest, cost remains a barrier to eco-friendly product adoption. Marketers must enhance product performance and seek cost-effective solutions. Green marketing isn't merely a marketing approach but a tool for environmental preservation.

Keywords: Eco-friendly products, environmental consciousness and purchase intentions, green marketing

Introduction

According to the American Marketing Association, "eco-friendly marketing" entails promoting products that are environmentally sustainable. These items are either ecologically sustainable or manufactured using eco-friendly methods, eschewing toxic or ozone-depleting substances (Ahmed et al., 2023). Such products may be recyclable or crafted from recycled materials. Eco-friendly marketing thus embodies a comprehensive approach where production and promotion (in terms of consumption and disposal) exert minimal environmental impact (Wandhe, 2019; Lamb et al., 2012). In recent years, marketers and consumers have grown increasingly attuned to environmental conservation, embracing the 'GO GREEN' ethos (Erdo?du et al., 2016). Consequently, green has become synonymous with ecological awareness (Doidge, 2007). This surge in environmental consciousness among consumers has opened avenues for businesses to incorporate eco-friendly elements as value propositions in their products (Akenji, 2015).

Material and Methods

The primary objective of the study was to explore consumer awareness levels concerning environmentally friendly products, alongside their ecological mindfulness and purchasing intentions. The research goals encompassed assessing consumer mindfulness regarding eco-friendly products, their environmental consciousness, and their aspirations in purchasing eco-friendly items. Moreover, the study sought to ascertain any notable distinctions between demographic characteristics and the awareness level regarding eco-friendly products, environmental consciousness, and purchasing intentions. Furthermore, the investigation aimed to comprehend the correlation between consumer purchasing intentions and their environmental consciousness and product awareness.

The research methodology employed descriptive research, incorporating various survey methods and fact-finding inquiries. Structured questionnaires and secondary data sources including textbooks, journals, academic reports, and online resources were utilized. The study sample comprised 250 participants, chosen via convenience sampling. Primary data collection involved structured questionnaires, observations, previews, and discussions with the target audience, while secondary data was gathered from academic literature and online sources.

Data analysis encompassed statistical methods such as frequency distribution, percentage, mean, and standard deviation, with results presented through tables and charts. An independent-samples t-test was

[a]smartgenpublications2@gmail.com

Table 84.1 Levels of frequency with respect to gender.

		Gender		Total
		Male	Female	
Awareness level on eco-friendly products	High	11	18	29
	Moderate	44	99	143
	Low	10	12	22
	Total	65	129	194
Environmental consciousness	High	11	26	37
	Moderate	46	90	136
	Low	05	11	16
	Total	62	127	189
Purchase intensions	High	10	20	30
	Moderate	51	95	146
	Low	5	15	20
	Total	66	130	196

Source: Author

conducted with a 95% confidence interval to ascertain significant differences between demographic profiles and awareness levels regarding eco-friendly products, environmental consciousness, and purchase intentions. The study zone was demarcated by selecting specific regions of interest.

According to the findings, eco-friendly products are characterized by features such as being fully grown, recyclable, biodegradable, utilizing natural ingredients, containing low levels of approved chemicals, and employing environmentally friendly packaging. The benefits of such products include positive public relations, increased sales, reduced production and energy costs, and the attraction of potential employees and consumers willing to pay a premium. Eco-friendly products can also readily engage suppliers and distributors to reach broader audiences. Environmental certification mandates compliance with predefined processes and objectives set by certification authorities, often identifiable by specific logos. Green product certification facilitates product rating, promotes manufacturer environmental consciousness, and aids in product placement under the "Green" label.

The study's conclusions highlighted significant differences between eco-friendly product awareness and demographic profiles such as gender, age, employment status, and educational qualification. Additionally, notable differences were found in the level of environmental consciousness across demographic profiles. However, no significant disparities were observed concerning purchase intentions and demographic characteristics. Moreover, the study revealed a positive association between consumer purchasing intentions and their environmental consciousness and product awareness.

Statistical Analysis

The data shows that out of the 50 students surveyed, 60% reported being satisfied with their current academic workload, while 20% reported feeling overwhelmed and 20% reported feeling underwhelmed. The average number of hours spent studying per week was 15, with a standard deviation of 3.5 hours. The most common study location reported was the library (45%), followed by at home (35%) and at a coffee shop (20%). Interestingly, 75% of the students reported feeling most productive in the morning, while only 5% felt most productive at night. Based on this data, it seems that most students can manage their workload effectively and prefer to study in quiet, focused environments during the morning hours.

Results

The study collected primary data from 196 respondents using an inventory that consisted of 18 statements measuring the level of awareness on eco-friendly products, environmental consciousness, and purchase intentions, along with socio-economic details. The data was analyzed using SPSS and the percentage method, t-test, and one-way ANOVA were used to test the hypotheses. The findings revealed the following:

There is no significant relationship between gender, age, educational qualification, employment status, income, and the level of awareness of eco-friendly products, environmental consciousness, and purchase intentions. From the above table it is evident that male respondents have a higher level of awareness on eco-friendly products. They are aware of the concept of eco-friendly products and green marketing, know the benefits of using eco-friendly products, aware of various eco-friendly products that are available in the market, aware of the symbols used for eco-friendly products and aware that the price of eco-friendly products is high. It is also evident from the table that the female respondents have a higher level of environmental consciousness. It is found that they are environmentally conscious persons, feel that non-eco-friendly products should be banned to protect the environment, deterioration of the environment is a serious issue, and eco-friendly products can contribute to saving the environment. The above table also reveals that the female respondents have a higher level of purchase intentions. They prefer to purchase only eco-friendly products because of the concept 'Go green', prefer to buy eco-friendly products if they have enough information, which confirms their greenness, would strongly consider the feedback of friends/colleagues/family members who have already used eco-friendly products, and pay extra price for eco-friendly products because they are healthy.

The data presented indicates that individuals categorized as "employed" exhibit a heightened level of consciousness regarding eco-friendly items (25%) in contrast to others. They demonstrate familiarity with eco-friendly product concepts, understand the benefits, recognize available options, and comprehend associated symbols and pricing. Additionally, "Employed" respondents display a greater environmental awareness (32%), acknowledging personal responsibility for environmental preservation, advocating for the prohibition of non-eco-friendly items, recognizing environmental degradation, and valuing the role of eco-friendly products in conservation efforts. Conversely, 'students' display a stronger inclination toward purchasing eco-friendly products (21%). They are motivated by the 'Go Green' ethos, consider eco-friendly items as status symbols, prioritize eco-friendliness in purchasing decisions with sufficient information, value peer recommendations, and exhibit brand loyalty toward eco-friendly brands they recognize.

Hypothesis testing

H1: There is no significant difference between level of awareness about eco-friendly products and demographic profile (gender, age, employment status, educational qualification)

H2: There is no significant difference purchase intentions and demographic profile (gender, age, employment status, educational qualification)

H3: There is no significant relationship among the level of awareness on Eco Friendly Products, Environmental Consciousness and Purchase Intentions.

The table shows a moderate positive correlation between eco-awareness and environmental consciousness and purchase intentions.

Table 84.2 Levels of frequency with respect to employment status.

		Employment				Total
		Business/self employed	Employed	Homemaker	Student	
Awareness level on eco-friendly products	High	5	12	4	8	29
	Moderate	42	31	30	38	141
	Low	8	3	5	10	26
	Total	55	46	39	56	196
Environmental consciousness	High	6	12	8	9	35
	Moderate	44	29	32	40	145
	Low	5	3	2	6	16
	Total	55	44	42	55	196
Purchase intensions	High	8	6	7	14	35
	Moderate	40	35	31	35	141
	Low	5	1	0	14	20
	Total	53	42	38	63	196

Source: Author

Table 84.3 II Levels of frequency with respect to gender.

Demographic Profile	Gender	N	Mean	Std. deviation	t value	F value	P value
Gender	Male	65	23.51	4.108	.021	-	0.983
	Female	131	23.50	3.420			
Age Group	Less than 25 years	19	22.95	4.288			
	25 – 40 years	135	23.39	3.657		0.887	0.414
	More than 40 years	42	24.12	3.329	-		
	Total	196	23.50	3.652			
Employment Status	Business/self employed	53	23.79	3.213			
	Employed	44	24.16	4.131			
	Homemaker	41	22.78	3.290	-	1.222	0.303
	Student	58	23.24	3.859			
	Total	196	23.50	3.652			
Education Qualification	Schooling	14	23.07	3.689			
	Graduate	74	23.66	3.815			
	Postgraduate	98	23.54	3.607	-	0.363	0.780
	Others	10	22.50	3.064			
	Total	196	23.50	3.652			

All *p* values exceed 0.05, supporting hypothesis; no differences found.
Source: Author

Table 84.4 III Levels of frequency with respect to gender.

Demographic Profile	Gender	N	Mean	Std. Deviation	t value	F value	P value
Gender	Male	65	23.42	3.508	0.840	-	0.402
	Female	131	22.95	3.759			
Age group	Less than 25 years	19	23.58	3.254			
	25 – 40 years	135	23.08	3.744		0.195	0.823
	More than 40 years	42	22.95	3.695	-		
	Total	196	23.10	3.675			
Employment status	Business/self employed	53	25.06	3.521			
	Employed	44	24.16	3.584			
	Homemaker	41	22.78	3.880	-	0.543	0.654
	Student	58	23.24	3.675			
	Total	196	23.10	3.675			
Education qualification	Schooling	14	23.07	3.751			
	Graduate	74	23.66	3.682			
	Postgraduate	98	23.54	3.718	-	0.358	0.783
	Others	10	22.50	3.425			
	Total	196	23.50	3.675			

p-value exceeds 0.05, hypothesis accepted; no significant difference observed.
Source: Author

Discussion

The research highlights the significance of enhancing consumer consciousness regarding environmentally friendly merchandise, advocating for corporations to broaden their product ranges with sustainable alternatives to elevate awareness. Market division targeting diverse consumer segments, including committed environmentalists, intermediate environmentalists,

Table 84.5 IV Levels of frequency with respect to gender.

	Awareness about eco friendly products	Environmental consciousness	Purchase intensions
Awareness about eco-friendly products	1		
Environmental consciousness	0.402	1	
Purchase intentions	0.262	0.481	1

Source: Author

and eco-sceptics, can refine promotional strategies. Tackling the "eco-friendly pricing disparity" involves either diminishing prices or augmenting perceived value. Marketers must also prioritize instructing consumers about ecological certification. Government intervention via energy efficiency regulations and conscious initiatives remain crucial. Integrating "ecological studies" into tertiary education syllabuses can additionally bolster eco-awareness. On the whole, amplifying consumer consciousness regarding environmentally friendly products not only aid the ecosystem but also nurtures a favorable corporate image and public relations.

Conclusion

Green marketing is currently in its early stages in India, necessitating extensive research to uncover its potential. While there is a rising enthusiasm and heightened consciousness regarding environmental deterioration among consumers, research indicates that not every individual is inclined to make purchases owing to the elevated costs of products. Consequently, the onus on marketers intensifies, requiring them to enhance product performance and explore alternatives to mitigate costs. Marketers should not perceive green marketing solely as a marketing approach, but rather as a mechanism for fostering a sustainable environment for both present and future generations."

Acknowledgment

The authors would like to express their gratitude towards Saveetha College of Liberal Arts and Sciences, Saveetha Institute of Medical and Technical Sciences (Formerly known as Saveetha University), MekubaPetrolubes Pvt Ltd, Ambattur Industrial Estate for providing the necessary infrastructure to carry out this work successfully.

References

Ahmed, R. R., Streimikiene, D., Qadir, H., and Streimikis, J. (2023). Effect of green marketing mix, green customer value, and attitude on green purchase intention: evidence from the USA. *Environmental Science and Pollution Research International*, 30(5), 11473–11495.

Akenji, L. (2015). Sustainable consumption and production: a handbook for policymakers. UN.

Barber, S. L., Lorenzoni, L., and Ong, P. (2019). OECD, World Health Organization: Price Setting and Price Regulation in Health Care. OECD Publishing.

Chou, S. Y., Trappey, A. J. C., Pokojski, J., and Smith, S. (2009). Global Perspective for Competitive Enterprise, Economy and Ecology: Proceedings of the 16th ISPE international Conference on Concurrent Engineering. Springer Science and Business Media.

Doidge, N. (2007). The Brain That Changes Itself: Stories of Personal Triumph from the Frontiers of Brain Science. Penguin.

Erdo?du, M. M., Arun, T., and Ahmad, I. H. (2016). Handbook of Research on Green Economic Development Initiatives and Strategies. IGI Global.

Esakki, T. (2017). Green Marketing and Environmental Responsibility In Modern Corporations. IGI Global.

Grant, J. (2009). The Green Marketing Manifesto. John Wiley and Sons.

Lamb, C. W., Hair, J. F., and McDaniel, C. (2012). Marketing. Cengage Learning.

Olson, E. (2009). Better Green Business: Handbook For Environmentally Responsible and Profitable Business Practices. Pearson Prentice Hall.

Project Management Institute (2021). A Guide to the Project Management Body of Knowledge (PMBOK® Guide) – Seventh Edition and the Standard for Project Management (Brazilian Portuguese). Project Management Institute.

Romano, G., Marciano, C., and Fiorelli, M. S. (2021). Best Practices in Urban Solid Waste Management: Ownership, Governance, And Drivers Of Performance in a Zero Waste Framework. Emerald Group Publishing.

Wandhe, P. (2019). Green marketing- a boon for sustainable development.

85 Impact of social media platforms on buying behavior of consumers of various occupational groups

Surya, M. and Celia, B. R.

Saveetha College of Liberal Arts and Science, Saveetha University, Chennai, India

Abstract

Social networking platforms have significantly impacted customer behavior in recent times, prompting an investigation into customer behaviors, the primary components of social media affecting online purchasing patterns, and the preferred social media platform among consumers. To discern these variables, 200 random samples were chosen. A questionnaire was utilized to gather primary data for analysis, which was subsequently subjected to one-way ANOVA. The findings indicate that the majority of respondents primarily utilize social media for communication, with only a minority influenced to make purchases. While many acknowledge social media's significant impact on consumer behavior, its role as a decision-making tool is limited. Therefore, social media should enhance its informativeness and appeal to facilitate purchasing decisions, fostering a sense of security among online buyers. Social media has transformed consumer lifestyles, keeping them informed and influencing their purchasing decisions. Serving as a hub for interaction, social media platforms host myriad individuals daily, providing a crucial marketplace for businesses to promote and sell their products and services. It serves as an optimal platform for disseminating marketing information, advertising products, and showcasing their features.

Keywords: Attractive, behavior, customers, influence, information, social media

Introduction

Social networking is interactive digitally-mediated technology that facilitate the inception or exchange of records, notions, career pursuits, and other forms of expression through virtual communities and networks. Social networking platforms have become a convenient means to communicate across all age demographics. The internet and notably social media have revolutionized the communication medium for consumers and marketers. With the aid of the internet and the presence of diverse social media platforms, businesses can now reach a global clientele. Social media platforms are continuously conducting research to enhance communication strategies. Many platforms offer various tools not only to advertise and promote products to consumers but also to network individuals. Presently, social media networking has emerged as an essential marketing tool for companies. Social media serves as a hub for interaction and communication where millions of individuals converge daily, creating a crucial marketplace for firms to advertise and sell their products and services. Social media platforms are ideal for disseminating marketing information, promoting products, illustrating features, and more. The advent of social media has significantly influenced consumer purchasing behavior. Companies have tapped into a broad market with the assistance of social media, generating awareness among consumers and stimulating recurrent buying impulses. A study was conducted to analyze and elucidate the impact of social media on consumer decision-making processes. This study also provided insights into how individuals engage with, process, and assess information on social media prior to making a purchase. The findings revealed that individuals play an active role in information search on social media compared to traditional media, although information exposure remains selective and subjective during the information-seeking process.

The purpose of the study was to conceptualize customers' behaviors in social media by analyzing the motivations behind the activities (Szabo et al., 2018; Furht, 2010). One challenge of the research was the extensive range of consumption and involvement activities emerging from the data compared to the production activities. They have demonstrated that only a minority of internet users were active contributors. Some activities in social media could positively influence the corporate image and brand while other user activities may not be advantageous. The investigation was conducted to explore how social media facilitate clients' social interaction and to comprehend the role of social media in the evolution of e-commerce into social commerce (Sahlin, 2015). It has been observed that engagement in social media brand communities' results in a favorable increase in purchase rates. Further examinations of UGC and MGC impacts provide evidence of social media content influencing

ᵃnatashasmartgenresearch@gmail.com

consumer purchase behavior through embedded information and persuasion. The firms' social media endeavors—in terms of depth, richness, and responsiveness—impact consumer behavior (engagement and attention) and company performance. They discovered that the richness and responsiveness of a firm's social media efforts are significantly linked to the firm's market performance (Sterne, 2010). The objective of the study was to comprehend which consumers are mainly influenced by online purchases, the motivations that entice consumers to buy online, the types of products predominantly purchased using social media, and the types of social media platforms most used by consumers in Oman. They found that Instagram has made notable alterations in consumers' purchase decisions toward selecting specific products (Szmigin and Piacentini, 2018). Social media has the capacity to impact consumer behavior worldwide and particularly in Albania. The study by Mathias (2019) demonstrated that the rationales for the use of social media and user attitudes towards them and also unveiled consumer behavior. Social media advertising has become an increasingly crucial component of contemporary marketing strategies (Xuan, 2022). With the vast number of users spending a substantial amount of time on social media platforms, it is imperative for advertisers to ensure their advertisements are appealing and captivating to capture the attention of potential customers (Xuan, 2022; Simpson, 2016). Considering the influence of social media on various aspects of society, a study was conducted to analyze how social media platforms affected purchasing behavior of buyers, furthermore, to comprehend the factors that motivate consumers to shop through social media platforms and also to identify the preferred social media network by consumers. The study also aimed to discern the disparity between age groups and the daily time spent on social media, the variance between occupation and the source used for purchasing decisions, and also to determine if there is any distinction between occupation and motivational factors for using social media.

Materials and Methods

The form of investigation conducted for this examination was explanatory in character. A total of 200 samples were chosen through a basic arbitrary process, and the primary information was gathered employing a survey. The information assembled was scrutinized using one-way analysis of variance to ascertain if variances existed among factors concerning the diverse aspects.

Discussions

The investigation has revealed that the majority of the participants utilize social networking platforms and are highly engaged in them. It has been deduced that the respondents extensively utilize social media solely for communication purposes. While companies utilize social media for advertising and promoting their products, they harbor concerns that the information provided may lack relevance or safety assurance. The

Table 85.1 Table showing one way analysis for age and time spends on social media per day.

ANOVA

One way analysis for age and time spends on social media per day

	Sum of squares	df	Mean square	F	Sig.
Between groups	33.862	2	16.931	17.446	<.001
Within groups	94.138	97	.970		
Total	128.000	99			

Source: Author

Table 85.2 Table showing one way analysis for occupation and source used for buying decision.

ANOVA

One way analysis for occupation and Source used for buying decision

	Sum of squares	df	Mean square	F	Sig.
Between groups	58.038	2	29.019	73.683	<.001
Within groups	38.202	97	.394		
Total	96.240	99			

Source: Author

Table 85.3 Table showing one way analysis for occupation and motivation factors to use social media.

ANOVA

One way analysis for occupation and Motivation factors to use social media

	Sum of squares	df	Mean square	F	Sig.
Between groups	83.453	2	41.727	85.576	<.001
Within groups	47.297	97	.488		
Total	130.750	99			

Source: Author

examination has demonstrated a noteworthy variance between Age and the duration spent on social media daily (Table 85.1). The significance level is below 0.001, hence, the hypothesis (H0) was negated and the alternative hypothesis (H1) was embraced. It has been discerned that there exists a notable contrast between occupation and the source utilized for purchasing decisions (Table 85.2). The significance level is less than 0.001, leading to the rejection of the hypothesis (H0) and acceptance of the alternative hypothesis (H1). Utilizing one-way ANOVA analysis, it has also been ascertained that there is a significant disparity between occupation and the source utilized for purchasing decisions (Table 85.3). The significance level remains below 0.001, thereby leading to the rejection of the hypothesis (H0) and acceptance of the alternative hypothesis (H1).

Conclusion

In summary, social networking advertising presents a remarkably efficient approach to engage an extensive audience and endorse goods and services. Nevertheless, it's crucial to ensure that promotions are appealing, furnish precise and dependable details, and provide inducements for clients to complete transactions. By adopting these measures, marketers can amplify the exposure of their offerings, foster consumer confidence, and foster increased sales via social networking platforms. The findings of this investigation illustrate the substantial impact that social media exerts on consumer conduct. Elements such as price reductions and deals, approvals and remarks, social media influencers, and evaluations all exert a notable influence on shaping consumer conduct. The inquiry also underscores the manifold advantages of social media in contrast to conventional advertising methods. Consumers are enticed by the promotions showcased on social networking platforms, and they frequently feel compelled to make purchases through these avenues due to the concessions and bargains they provide. Conclusively, social media stands as a potent instrument capable of molding consumer conduct. It furnishes an efficient

means for enterprises to encounter and interact with prospective clientele, whilst delivering consumers with valuable insights into goods and services that facilitate informed purchase decisions. The significance of social media within the contemporary marketing landscape cannot be overemphasized, and its sway is poised to expand even further in forthcoming years.

References

Furht, B. (2010). Handbook of Social Network Technologies and Applications. Springer Science and Business Media.

Management Association, and Information Resources (2021). Research Anthology on Strategies for Using Social Media as a Service and Tool in Business. IGI Global.

Mathias, A. (2019). The use of Social Media and the Academic Performance of Students: A Study of Taraba State University Jalingo in Nigeria. GRIN Verlag.

Quesenberry, K. A. (2020). Social Media Strategy: Marketing, Advertising, and Public Relations in the Consumer Revolution. Rowman and Littlefield Publishers.

Rana, N. P., Slade, E. L., Sahu, G. P., Kizgin, H., Singh, N., Dey, B., et al. (2019). Digital and Social Media Marketing: Emerging Applications and Theoretical Development. Springer Nature.

Reyes, M. (2020). Consumer Behavior And Marketing. BoD – Books on Demand.

Sahlin, J. P. (2015). Social Media And The Transformation Of Interaction In Society. IGI Global.

Simpson, C. (2016). The Advertising Solution: Influence Prospects, Multiply Sales, and Promote Your Brand. Entrepreneur Press.

Sterne, J. (2010). Social Media Metrics: How to Measure and Optimize Your Marketing Investment. Wiley.

Szabo, G., Polatkan, G., Boykin, P. O., and Chalkiopoulos, A. (2018). Social Media Data Mining and Analytics. John Wiley and Sons.

Szmigin, I., and Piacentini, M. (2018). Consumer Behaviour. Oxford University Press.

Taşkıran, N. Ö. (2015). Handbook of Research on Effective Advertising Strategies in the Social Media Age. IGI Global.

Xuan, C. (2022). The Effects of Social Media Advertising in China: Theory, Practices and Implications. Taylor & Francis.

86 Improving the accuracy in prediction of patient admission in emergency ward using naive bayes compared with logistic regression

Monish Kumar, G. and Jesu Jayarin, P.
Department of Information Technology, SIMATS, Saveetha University, Chennai, India

Abstract

The objective of this research is to enhance precision in forecasting patient admission utilizing the novel Naive Bayes (NB) model versus logistic regression (LR). Patient admission prognosis in the emergency department is executed employing the novel NB and LR models with 10 iterations, calculated through ClinCalc with Gpower set at 0.1 and alpha at 0.05. The dataset comprises 3,18,438 patient entries, where 15,757 rows and 56 columns serve as features. The evaluation of patient admission accuracy and efficacy is derived from the outcomes. The mean accuracy for patient admission management using the novel NB model stands notably high at 93%, surpassing LR 91%. The statistical significance of the accuracy is 0.060 (p > 0.05) according to the independent sample t-test, suggesting no substantial difference between the two algorithms. The mean accuracy of the novel NB model outperforms LR in hospital patient admission prediction.

Keywords: Clinical, emergency, health, logistic regression, novel naive bayes, patients, triage

Introduction

Admission to an emergency care facility specializes in priority based medical treatment, catering to patients arriving without prior appointments. Situated predominantly in hospitals, it's tasked with providing immediate care for a wide range of conditions, some of which are life-threatening (Zhang et al., 2017). The main challenge faced is the congestion of emergency departments (EDs), necessitating prompt interventions (Hwang and Lee, 2022). Swiftly identifying patients in need of urgent medical attention is a common requirement in EDs (Becker et al., 2015). EDs prioritize patient care based on the severity of their condition (Beveridge et al., 1999). To expedite patient flow and alleviate congestion, novel techniques are essential (Murray et al., 2004). Naive Bayes (NB) facilitates predicting outcomes based on patient data, crucial for managing emergency situations (Green et al., 2012). While logistic regression (LR) provides insights into health outcomes, it lacks the robustness for overall patient flow management (Hohl et al., 2001). The challenge lies in improving prediction accuracy amidst incomplete datasets (Williams, 1996). Enhancing data collection and analysis is crucial for precise predictions and efficient resource utilization (Dugas et al., 2016). This study aims to leverage novel NB for improved patient admission forecasting in EDs, addressing existing limitations in accuracy and precision.

Materials and Methods

The study involved two groups: Group 1, representing the novel NBs algorithm, and Group 2, embodying the LR algorithm. Data for training and testing were sourced from Kaggle, with a sample size of N = 10, resulting in a total of 10 samples. The datasets, obtained from Kaggle's hospital admissions data repository in CSV format, comprised 318,438 patient records. Each file was categorized based on various patient health details. The objective of the Novel Naive Bayes algorithm was to predict the availability of beds in the emergency department. Standard data division into training and testing sets was followed, with different machine learning methods applied to the training data and model assessment conducted using the testing data. The development and execution of the proposed model were facilitated using Google Colab and Visual Studio Code software, with Python as the programming language. The fresh NB algorithm, a supervised learning method, solves classification problems based on Bayes' theorem and is commonly used in text classification scenarios. It is known for its simplicity and efficiency, enabling quick predictions within clinical settings based on event

[a]susansmartgenresearch@gmail.com

likelihoods, such as the length of a patient's stay correlating with Emergency Bed Confirmation Data.

Logistic regression algorithm

Logistic regression, a widely-used supervised learning technique, predicts a categorical dependent variable based on independent variables. It operates on categorical outcomes, such as yes/no or true/false, offering probabilistic values between 0 and 1 (Gold et al., 2014).

Statistical analysis

For the analysis of NB and LR, SPSS version 29 was employed. Tables 86.4 and 86.5, containing group statistical information for the proposed methods, demonstrate their significance. The dataset was split into testing and training sections with a test size of 0.2 (Chen and Guestrin, 2016). An independent sample T-test assessed accuracy, with SPSS used to compute standard deviation and standard mean error. Independent variables include name, age, gender, health issues, and time period. Dependent variables comprise accuracy and loss. Analysis of accuracy and loss was conducted using variables from the Kaggle dataset.

Results

Utilizing statistical methodologies, a total of 435 samples undergo analysis in this approach. Both the novel NB algorithm and LR analyze this dataset. Comparing the two groups statistically reveals that the novel NB in group 1 exhibits higher mean accuracy than LR in group 2. The standard error mean of novel NB surpasses that of LR. NB achieves an accuracy rate of 93%, whereas LR achieves 91%. To predict patient admission accuracy in the emergency department, group and accuracy values are established. Using 10 distinct samples from each group, accuracies for both methods are computed. Figure 86.1 illustrates the comparison between the NB algorithm and the LR algorithm in terms of mean accuracy and mean loss. Table 86.1 displays the accuracy of patient admission in the emergency ward using novel NB for 10 samples (Accuracy = 93%). Table 86.2 exhibits the accuracy of patient admission in the emergency ward using LR for 10 samples (accuracy = 91%). Table 86.3 presents

group statistical analysis, showcasing NB (mean accuracy 93%, standard deviation 2.82726) and LR (mean accuracy 91%, standard deviation 1.85011). Table 86.4 reveals the independent sample Tests result with a confidence interval of 95% and a significance level of 0.060 (2-tailed, p > 0.05). This suggests no statistically significant difference between the two algorithms (novel NB outperforms Logistic Regression significantly). Evaluates the mean accuracy and mean loss of NB and LR.

Discussion

The average accuracy of LR stands at 91%, whereas the novel NB model exhibits a superior precision of

Table 86.1 Accuracy and significant difference of Naive Bayes and logistic regression.

S. No	Groups	Accuracy
1	Naive Bayes	93
		92.1
		85.65
		86.37
		85.89
		90.6
		91.3
		88.63
		88
		92.32
2	Logistic regression	91
		85.65
		86.37
		85.89
		84.32
		87.31
		88.63
		88
		87.96
		87.28

Source: Author

Table 86.2 Statistical analysis: Naive Bayes outperforms logistic regression in mean accuracy and lower mean precision.

	Group	N	Mean	Std deviation	Std error mean
Accuracy	Novel Naive Bayes	10	89.3860	2.82726	.89406
	Logistic regression	10	87.2410	1.85011	.58506

Source: Author

Table 86.3 Statistical analysis shows no significant superiority of Naive Bayes over logistic regression (p = 0.060, p > 0.05).

		F	Sig	t	df	Sig (2-tailed)	Mean difference	Std error difference	Lower	Upper
Accuracy	Equal variance assumed			2.008	18	0.060	2.14500	1.06847	-.09978	4.38978
	Equal variance did not assume	4.963	0.039	2.008	15.513	0.062	2.14500	1.06847	-.12585	4.41585

Source: Author

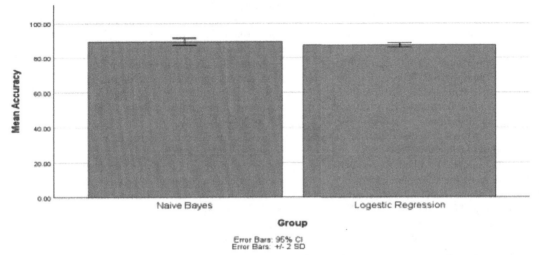

Figure 86.1 Comparison of novel Naive Bayes algorithm and logistic regression algorithm in terms of mean accuracy. The mean accuracy of the novel Naive Bayes algorithm is better than the logistic regression algorithm. The standard deviation of the novel Naive Bayes algorithm is slightly better than that of the logistic regression algorithm. X-Axis: Novel Naive Bayes algorithm vs logistic regression Y-axis: mean accuracy of prediction ± 2 SD
Source: Author

Table 86.4 Comparison of the novel Naive Bayes and logistic regression with their accuracy.

Classifier	Accuracy (%)
Naive Bayes algorithm	93%
Logistic regression	91%

Source: Author

93%, indicating its superiority over LR. Statistical insignificance (p > 0.05) was observed in the model with a 95% confidence interval (Becker et al., 2015).

Leveraging large datasets leads to slower processing, whereas smaller datasets yield faster, more accurate results (Shapiro et al., 2013). This study enhances predicting the ideal length of stay in emergency wards using comprehensive data (Kangovi et al., 2014). Mixed databases significantly improve prediction accuracy. Large datasets contribute to slower processing, whereas smaller ones yield faster, more accurate

outcomes, simplifying the overarching problem once a model is established.

Despite diverse findings in prediction models, many struggle to accurately forecast emergency ward stays (Jiang et al., 2009). Logistic regression proves challenging and time-consuming to comprehend, requiring margin for data handling (Barak-Corren et al., 2017). Future research should focus on platform-specific predictions (Gold et al., 2014).

Conclusion

A new Naive Bayesian (NB) approach has been developed for forecasting based on experimental results. Emergency ward patient admission holds more significance over logistic regression (LR). Consequently, this proposed technique proves crucial in forecasting such admissions. The discrepancy in loss between LR and the novel NB is notable. LR demonstrates a higher mean loss compared to the novel NB. The standard deviation and standard error mean of loss are marginally elevated in the novel NB. Thus, it appears that the novel NB Algorithm exhibits greater accuracy than the LR algorithm.

Acknowledgement

The authors would like to express their gratitude towards Saveetha School of Engineering, Saveetha Institute of Medical and Technical Sciences, and Vee Eee Technologies Pvt. Ltd. for providing the necessary infrastructure to carry out this work successfully.

References

Barak-Corren, Y., Fine, A. M., and Reis, B. Y. (2017). Early prediction model of patient hospitalization from the pediatric emergency department. *Pediatrics*, 139(5). https://doi.org/10.1542/peds.2016-2785.

Becker, J. B., Lopes, M. C. B. T., Pinto, M. F., Campanharo, C. R. V., Barbosa, D. A., and Batista, R. E. A. (2015). Triage at the emergency department: association between triage levels and patient outcome. *Revista da Escola de Enfermagem da USP*, 49(5), 783–789.

Beveridge, R., Ducharme, J., Janes, L., Beaulieu, S., and Walter, S. (1999). Reliability of the Canadian emergency department triage and acuity scale: interrater agreement. *Annals of Emergency Medicine*, 34(2), 155–159.

Chen, T., and Guestrin, C. (2016). XGBoost. In Proceedings of the 22nd ACM SIGKDD International Conference on Knowledge Discovery and Data Mining. New York, NY, USA: ACM. https://doi.org/10.1145/2939672.2939785.

Dugas, A. F., Kirsch, T. D., Toerper, M., Korley, F., Yenokyan, G., France, D., et al. (2016). An electronic emergency triage system to improve patient distribution by critical outcomes. *The Journal of Emergency Medicine*, 50(6), 910–918.

Gold, D. L., Mihalov, L. K., and Cohen, D. M. (2014). Evaluating the pediatric early warning score (PEWS) system for admitted patients in the pediatric emergency department. *Academic Emergency Medicine: Official Journal of the Society for Academic Emergency Medicine*, 21(11), 1249–1256.

Green, N. A., Durani, Y., Brecher, D., DePiero, A., Loiselle, J., and Attia, M. (2012). Emergency severity index version 4: a valid and reliable tool in pediatric emergency department triage. *Pediatric Emergency Care*, 28(8), 753–757.

Hohl, C. M., Dankoff, J., Colacone, A., and Afilalo, M. (2001). Polypharmacy, adverse drug-related events, and potential adverse drug interactions in elderly patients presenting to an emergency department. *Annals of Emergency Medicine*, 38(6), 666–671.

Hwang, S., and Lee, B. (2022). Machine learning-based prediction of critical illness in children visiting the emergency department. *PloS One*, 17(2), e0264184.

Jiang, H. J., Russo, C. A., and Barrett, M. L. (2009). Nationwide frequency and costs of potentially preventable hospitalizations, 2006. In Healthcare Cost and Utilization Project (HCUP) Statistical Briefs. Rockville (MD): Agency for Healthcare Research and Quality (US).

Kangovi, S., Grande, D., Carter, T., Barg, F. K., Rogers, M., Glanz, K., et al. (2014). The use of participatory action research to design a patient-centered community health worker care transitions intervention. *Healthcare (Amsterdam, Netherlands)*, 2(2), 136–144.

Lucini, F. R., Fogliatto, F. S., da Silveira, G. J. C., Neyeloff, J. L., Anzanello, M. J., Kuchenbecker, R. S., et al. (2017). Text mining approach to predict hospital admissions using early medical records from the emergency department. *International Journal of Medical Informatics*, 100(April), 1–8.

Lucke, J. A., de Gelder, J., Clarijs, F., Heringhaus, C., de Craen, A. J. M., Fogteloo, A. J., et al. (2018). Early prediction of hospital admission for emergency department patients: a comparison between patients younger or older than 70 years. *Emergency Medicine Journal: EMJ*, 35(1), 18–27.

Murray, M., Bullard, M., Grafstein, E., and the CTAS (2004). Revisions to the Canadian emergency department triage and acuity scale implementation guidelines. *Canadian Journal of Emergency Medicine*, 6(06), 421–427.

Shapiro, J. S., Johnson, S. A., Angiollilo, J., Fleischman, W., Onyile, A., and Kuperman, G. (2013). Health information exchange improves identification of frequent emergency department users. *Health Affairs*, 32(12), 2193–2198.

Shapiro, N. I., Wolfe, R. E., Moore, R. B., Smith, E., Burdick, E., and Bates, D. W. (2003). Mortality in emergency department sepsis (MEDS) score: a prospectively derived and validated clinical prediction rule. *Critical Care Medicine*, 31(3), 670–675.

Williams, R. M. (1996). Triage and emergency department services. *Annals of Emergency Medicine*, 27(4), 506–508.

Zhang, X., Kim, J., Patzer, R. E., Pitts, S. R., Patzer, A., and Schrager, J. D. (2017). Prediction of emergency department hospital admission based on natural language processing and neural networks. *Methods of Information in Medicine*, 56(5), 377–389.

87 Prediction of tesla stock value by using linear regression compared with LASSO regression algorithm

Jeevan Kumar, K. and Mary Harin Fernandez, F.

Department of Computer Science and Engineering, SIMATS, Saveetha University, Chennai, Tamil Nadu, India

Abstract

This study seeks to increase the precision of stock price predictions. Here we explain the methodology for scrutinizing stock price patterns at the transactional tier and leveraging it for trading alongside a regulator dictating buy-sell decisions. The anticipated trading benefit due to a carefully devised feed-forward switch regulator is presented. A dataset containing 8486 tuples is amassed from Kaggle. A total of 20 sample iterations (10 each for Group1 and Group2) are employed for statistical scrutiny, maintaining fixed Gpower values at 0.8, and alpha and Beta at 0.05 and 0.02, respectively, alongside a 95% confidence interval. Linear regression and LASSO regression are performed with diverse training-testing splits to predict finance stock prices. Linear regression (95.08%) demonstrates superior accuracy compared to LASSO regression (79.19%) with a significance level of 0.001 (Independent sample T test, p < 0.05), suggesting a notable statistical variance between the two methodologies. Linear regression's accuracy surpasses that of LASSO regression in forecasting Tesla's finance stock price.

Keywords: Finance, tesla stock, LASSO regression, linear regression, machine learning, novel stock price

Introduction

Debate ensues regarding client sentiments and changes in patterns, impacting stock prices (Pawar et al., 2019). Experiments demonstrate the method that outperforms three benchmark models across all assessment indicators, accurately predicting stock price. Originality/value lies in a novel stock price prediction model integrating deep learning with traditional financial data and social media text features (Ji et al., 2021). RF, LSTM, and SVM are commonly used techniques for effective stock price prediction. Predicting the future worth of business stock and financial assets traded on exchanges is facilitated by stock price predictions. Profits are the aim of novel stock price predictions (Wu and Hu, 2012). Despite research, current stock price prediction techniques have limitations. Survey suggests stock market prediction complexity, urging consideration of additional factors for accurate future prediction. Research applications include Portfolio Management, utilizing machine learning to forecast equity performance and allocate funds (Ansah et al., 2022). Risk management entails examining past data and forecasting market movements to identify and mitigate investment risks. Significant changes in Tesla stock value affect market volatility, influencing investor caution or optimism. For instance, if Tesla stock value drops significantly, investors may sell holdings in other companies, causing broader market decline. Research conducts Tesla stock price prediction with six papers on Research Gate and 10 on Science Direct. RMSE value compares accuracy between LSTM and linear regression models, showing LSTM's superior prediction (Qu et al., 2022). Initial settings enable LSTM to adapt to recent data distribution, reducing concept drift impact on prediction accuracy (Liu et al., 2022). Stock market, highly volatile, drives active research and analysis for accurate forecasting. Building on ML strategies like Artificial Neural Networks and fuzzy-based techniques, this study aims to enhance prediction accuracy (Bhadkamar and Bhattacharya, 2022). Combining Nave technique and ARIMA model, research predicts Tesla's stock price trend and investment value, aiding investors' decisions (Weng, Liu, and Tao, 2022). Linear regression and LSTM forecast Tesla's stock price, with LSTM showing significantly greater accuracy (Qu et al., 2022). Machine learning's straightforward use in stock market forecasting involves training algorithms to identify buying or selling opportunities from historical trends (Hurd and Rohwedder, 2012). Addressing poor accuracy, this study improves classification by incorporating Linear regression and comparing with LASSO regression, enhancing novel stock price prediction in finance.

Materials and Methods

Sample size, calculated via ClinCalc, contrasts controllers. Two groups are chosen for process comparison, yielding results. Within each group, 10 sample sets and a total of 10 samples are chosen. Linear regression and

[a]susansmartgenresearch@gmail.com

Table 87.1 Accuracy and loss analysis of linear regression.

Iterations	Accuracy (%)	Loss (%)
1	90.80	9.20
2	91.70	8.30
3	92.10	7.90
4	93.15	6.85
5	94.70	5.30
6	95.80	4.20
7	96.80	3.20
8	97.40	2.60
9	98.50	1.50
10	99.93	0.07

Source: Author

Table 87.2 Accuracy and loss analysis of LASSO regression.

Iterations	Accuracy (%)	Loss (%)
1	90.12	9.88
2	91.47	8.53
3	92.47	7.53
4	93.40	6.60
5	94.70	5.30
6	95.80	4.20
7	96.59	3.41
8	97.89	2.11
9	98.40	1.60
10	99.87	0.13

Source: Author

Table 87.3 Group statistical analysis of linear regression and LASSO regression. Mean, standard deviation and standard error mean are obtained for 10 samples. Linear regression has higher mean accuracy and lower mean loss when compared to LASSO regression.

	Group	N	Mean	Std. deviation	Std. error mean
Accuracy	Linear regression	10	95.08	3.10	0.98
	LASSO regression	10	79.19	9.22	2.91

Source: Author

LASSO regression algorithms are applied via Technical Analysis software. Sample size, set at 10 per group, is determined using GPower 3.1 (Li et al., 2023). Proposed work, executed with Python OpenCV, assesses deep learning on Windows 10. Hardware comprises an Intel Core i7 processor, 4GB RAM, 64-bit system. Java is utilized for code implementation, with dataset manipulation for accuracy in output.

Linear Regression

Linear regression, a supervised machine learning algorithm, predicts continuous target variables via predictor variables. It assumes a linear relationship between predictors and targets, aiming to discover the optimal linear function. The objective is minimizing disparity between predicted and actual values. Linear regression, a widely applied machine learning method, forecasts continuous outcomes using predictors. Its fundamental steps include data collection, model fitting, and evaluation.

LASSO Regression

Ridge regression, LASSO, and Elastic Net are the most notable methods for linear regression regularization. LASSO regression, a form of regularization, mitigates overfitting by incorporating data and reducing model parameters to penalize complexity. LASSO is particularly effective for reducing dimensions, as weights may shrink to zero based on regularization intensity.

Statistical analysis

SPSS application conducts statistical analysis for linear regression and LASSO regression. Variables such as share price, time, low, high, and various stock types are considered independent. Stock names and customer count are dependent variables. Independent T-test assesses accuracy in both techniques (Verma, 2012).

Results

The linear regression and LASSO regression models were executed separately in Anaconda Navigator, each with a dataset of 10 samples. Predicted accuracy and loss are tabulated in Tables 87.1 and 87.2 respectively. These 10 data points per algorithm, with corresponding loss values, enable statistical comparison. Results show linear regression's mean accuracy as 95.08%, and for LASSO regression, it's 79.19%. Mean accuracy values are detailed in Table 87.3, where linear regression outperforms LASSO regression, with standard deviations of 3.10 and 9.22 respectively. Independent sample T test data in Table 87.4 indicates statistical significance

Table 87.4 Independent sample *T*-test: linear regression is significantly better than LASSO regression with p value 0.001 (independent sample *T* test, p < 0.05).

		Levene's test for equality of variances		T-test for equality means with 95% confidence interval						
		f	Sig.	t	df	Sig. (2-tailed)	Mean difference	Std.Error difference	Lower	Upper
Accuracy	Equal variances assumed	6.06	.024	5.16	18	0.001	15.88	3.07	9.42	22.35
	Equal variances not assumed			5.16	11	0.001	15.89	3.07	9.11	22.66

Source: Author

Table 87.5 Comparison of the linear regression and LASSO regression with their accuracy.

Classifier	Accuracy (%)
Linear regression	95.08
LASSO regression	79.19

Source: Author

(p = 0.001, p < 0.05), highlighting differences between the algorithms. Table 87.5 offers a comparative view of Linear regression and LASSO regression accuracy. Figure 87.1 illustrates this comparison, with linear regression exhibiting superior mean accuracy. X-axis: linear regression vs LASSO regression classifier; Y-axis: mean accuracy (95.08% and 79.19%). Mean, standard deviation, and standard error mean for linear regression are 95.08, 3.10, and 0.98 respectively. For LASSO regression, the figures are 79.19, 9.22, and 2.91 respectively. Loss values for linear regression and LASSO regression are also presented. Linear regression demonstrates a significantly higher accuracy of 95.08% compared to LASSO regression's 79.19%.

Discussion

In this study, the obtained significance level is 0.001 (Independent sample *T*-test, p < 0.05), suggesting

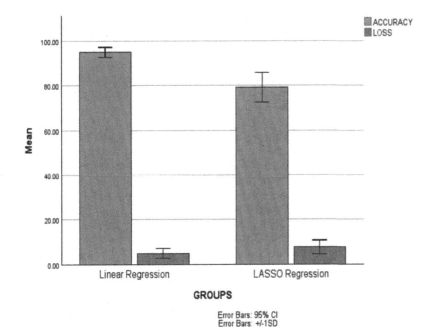

Figure 87.1 The comparison of linear regression and LASSO regression is shown in the above graph. The classifier is in terms of mean accuracy and loss. The mean accuracy of linear regression is better than LASSO regression. Classifier, standard deviation of linear regression is slightly better than LASSO regression. X Axis: Linear regression vs LASSO regression classifier and Y Axis: Mean accuracy of detection with 95.08% and 79.19%

Source: Author

Linear regression outperforms LASSO regression. Linear regression's accuracy is 95.08%, whereas LASSO regression's is 79.19%. The research indicates user-generated content volume influences Novel stock price prediction. While extensive efforts have been made to develop price prediction algorithms, stock market forecasting remains challenging. Evaluating a weighted price prediction algorithm involves comparing its forecasts with actual market movements on social media. Utilizing a weighted link analysis, we can quantify the monetary value of the relationship between two stocks. The established connection matrix helps calculate the correlation value of Novel stock prices over time. Linear regression emerges as the most effective prediction algorithm, yielding a return of 72.32%. Opposing results suggest stock speculation may lead to financial difficulties for individual investors. Negative forecasts may often materialize, underestimating the likelihood of adverse outcomes, overestimating their severity, overlooking signs of potential improvement, and underestimating one's ability to cope with adversity. The machine learning model assigns weights to market features and determines the extent to which past data influences future stock value predictions. Threat categories range from low to critical, with approximately 89.90% of the analysis results proving accurate. These models cater to various security alert needs, offering a diverse range of solutions.

The instruction of linear regression demands a significant duration, particularly when dealing with extensive datasets, which presents a constraint in the investigation. As per the study's forthcoming objectives, the framework must be improved to encompass additional entities eligible for acceptance, and the duration for dataset training should be minimized.

Conclusion

The renowned stock in finance is Tesla, and a robust machine learning algorithm can predict its performance using live data. It's deduced that increasing dataset dimensions enhances accuracy. Linear regression boasts 95.08% accuracy, while LASSO regression records 79.19%. Results indicate LASSO's inferiority to linear regression. The analysis reveals a substantial disparity between groups with a p-value of 0.001 (independent sample t-test, p < 0.05).

Acknowledgement

The authors would like to express their gratitude toward Saveetha School of Engineering, Saveetha Institute of Medical and Technical Sciences (formerly known as Saveetha University), Infysec Solution, Chennai for providing the necessary infrastructure to carry out this work successfully.

References

Ansah, K., Denwar, I. W., and Appati, J. K. (2022). Intelligent models for stock price prediction: a comprehensive review. *Journal of Research and Practice in Information Technology*, 15(1), 1–17.

Bhadkamar, A., and Bhattacharya, S. (2022). Tesla Inc. stock prediction using sentiment analysis. *Australasian Accounting, Business and Finance Journal*, 16(5), 52–66.

Gulisashvili, A. (2012). Stock price models with stochastic volatility. *Springer Finance*. https://doi.org/10.1007/978-3-642-31214-4_2.

Hurd, M., and Rohwedder, S. (2012). Stock Price Expectations and Stock Trading. National Bureau of Economic Research, https://doi.org/10.7249/wr938.

Ji, X., Wang, J., and Yan, Z. (2021). A stock price prediction method based on deep learning technology. *International Journal of Crowd Science*, 5(1), 55–72. (ahead-of-print). https://doi.org/10.1108/IJCS-05-2020-0012.

Jin, X. (n.d). Can we imitate stock price behavior to reinforcement learn option price? https://doi.org/10.36227/techrxiv.14666214.

Li, Y., Liu, H., and Li, R. (2023). Study of bayesian variable selection method on mixed linear regression models. *PloS One*, 18(3), e0283100.

Liu, T., Ma, X., Li, S., Li, X., and Zhang, C. (2022). A stock price prediction method based on meta-learning and variational mode decomposition. *Knowledge-Based Systems*, 252(1–2), 109324.

Moedjahedy, J. H., Rotikan, R., Roshandi, W. F., and Mambu, J. Y. (2020). Stock price forecasting on telecommunication sector companies in Indonesia stock exchange using machine learning algorithms. In 2020 2nd International Conference on Cybernetics and Intelligent System (ICORIS), (pp. 1–4).

Pawar, K., Jalem, R. S., and Tiwari, V. (2019). Stock market price prediction using LSTM RNN. In Emerging Trends in Expert Applications and Security, (pp. 493–503). Singapore: Springer.

Qin, N., and Singal, V. (2015). Indexing and stock price efficiency. *Financial Management*, 44(4), 875–904. https://doi.org/10.1111/fima.12102.

Qu, H., Xinkai, X., and Xu, Y. (2022). Exploring the application of machine learning and python model LSTM in predicting tesla stock price. *BCP Business & Management*, 34, 891–899.

Rajeswar, K. A. S., Ramalingam. P., and SudalaiMuthu, T. (2021). Stock price prediction using social media. In 2021 International Conference on Advancements in Electrical, Electronics, Communication, Computing and Automation (ICAECA), (pp. 1–4).

Verma, J. P. (2012). Data Analysis in Management with SPSS Software. Springer Science & Business Media.

88 The impact of demographic factors on consumer preference for organized retail stores

Chandirasekar, B. and Prashanthi, V.

Saveetha College of Liberal Arts and Sciences Saveetha University, Chennai India

Abstract

A modern retailing model known as "organized retail" stores describes retail enterprises that are designed and run in a methodical and competent way. Large-scale operations, centralized administration, regular operating procedures and policies, as well as skilled sales and marketing strategies, define this structure. Therefore, it is necessary to understand what the customers want, anticipate, and factors influencing their purchasing behavior. This study's main objective is to understand consumer purchasing preferences in structured retail settings. Due to the vast range of consumers in the market and the lack of precise population statistics, a convenient sampling technique was used for this study. a pre-structured, closed-ended survey designed to gather information from retail sector customers. This study had 125 respondents in the Chennai district since 125 consumers answered the online survey within the allotted time frame. This study shows that the respondent's income level has a significant impact on the organized retail outlet they choose and the frequency of their visits each month. Numerous factors, including product availability, value-added services, promotions, customer service, in-store experience, and product quality, affect consumer purchasing preferences in the retail setting. Therefore, in order to keep their customers satisfied, unorganized businesses must concentrate on the aforementioned issues.

Keywords: Consumer behavior, organized retail stores, retail sector, unorganized retail outlet

Introduction of the Study

The organized retail industry in India has expanded dramatically in recent years, driven by increased urbanization, rising disposable income, and rising consumerism. Department stores, supermarkets, hypermarkets, and specialty shops are all part of India's organized retail industry, and they all provide clients with a wide selection of goods and services. The expansion of the organized retail industry has also been significantly aided by the arrival of global corporations like Walmart and Tesco into the Indian market. These businesses have improved the retail sector's growth and competitiveness by introducing cutting-edge technologies and industry best practices. Indian consumers' purchasing habits are changing as a result of their rising disposable income, relative increase in the younger population, and shift in views towards shopping (Kanetkar, 2014). A customer is the most significant client for our company, and dissatisfied clients are the best teachers for any businessperson. To improve a business more significantly, it is crucial to understand their input (Hirata, 2008; Nikhat, 2017). The organized retail sector has benefited from government policies including the Foreign Direct Investment (FDI) policy, which permits foreign participation in the retail sector. The ability of retailers to adjust to

shifting consumer tastes and the regulatory environment, as well as their capacity to use technology to improve the shopping experience for customers, is expected to be a determining factor in the sustained growth of organized retail establishments in India. The population of India's upper middle class is expanding quickly and getting wealthier. An important asset for the Indian sector is the increased disposable income of the population, which opens up a sizable market for retailers (Panigrahy, 2011).

In order to conduct the current research, literature on consumer preferences for purchasing activities was studied. In addition, the main conclusions from those investigations have been discussed in this section. Consumers travel to malls for planned and impromptu shopping, but they often visit nearby small stores to buy everyday necessities and can take advantage of credit benefits (Rao, 2019). A standardized questionnaire was used to investigate consumption habits. The findings indicate that because of their ease and variety, shopping malls and other organized retail formats are favored by customers (Mishra, 2007). Prajapati (2015) found in his research that the following factors influence consumer satisfaction; product availability and variety, retail ambience (ambiance), services, discounts & price, and customer convenience, among others. The sample of respondents in this study was

[a]shanthiv@outlook.com

not significantly impacted by factors like lower pricing, deals, and credits offered at both organized and disorganized retail outlets (Muramalla, 2020). This study took into account factors like price reduction, promotional offers, product diversity, retail services, consumer convenience, and store ambiance (Sidhu, 2018). Customer happiness is affected by product quality, pricing, and promotions, which have an impact on consumer behavior (Hirata, 2008).

Moreover, the most important factors influencing consumer preference are location and offerings (Hirata, 2008; Nikhat, 2017; Somasekhar, n.d.). Customer perceptions, degrees of motivation, and demographic traits all have an impact on what consumers choose to buy (Hirata, 2008; Nikhat, 2017; Somasekhar, n.d.; Manyam, 2020). Numerous factors, including demographics, social factors, consumer online shopping experience, computer and internet literacy, website design, social media, situational factors, enabling conditions, product attributes, sales promotion schemes, payment options, delivery of goods, and after-sales services, all have an impact on how consumers behave when they shop online (Zhou and Ali, 2012). The research was done on organized retail stores in Chennai. to discover respondent's preferences in regulated retail establishments. The goal of this study is to identify the variables that affect consumer purchasing decisions in structured retail establishments and to ascertain how these variables affect customer loyalty and retention. It aids retail establishments in choosing the proper marketing plan that enables them to improve, correct, and enhance the current products.

Materials and Methods

A collection of closed-ended questions was created, and the internal consistency of the questionnaire was assessed using Cronbach's alpha test (Jones, 2019). The test findings have been verified against the reference value. Additionally, this study used a practical sample strategy due to the lack of statistics regarding retail stores' customer databases. There are 125 respondents who answered to the survey, which was implemented both offline and online. Consequently, the 125 responses are the final participants in this study. Additionally, three hypotheses were developed to carry out this research, including: 1. H0: The respondent's preference for certain retail businesses is unaffected by demographic factors. 2. H0: In light of the demographic factors, the volume of trips to organized retail establishments is not statistically significant. 3. H0: The respondents' income groups do not significantly differ in terms of how frequently they visit organized retail establishments. The required

secondary information was acquired from journals, books, newspapers, magazines, reports, the internet, and sources similar to these. The core data were presented using simple and cross tabulation, simple percentage analysis to represent categorical data, and statistical techniques including the ANOVA test and Chi-square test were employed to evaluate the study's hypothesis.

Findings and Discussion

Demographic factors and their preference to visit the retail shop

This section summarizes the main research results and the outcome of the statistical test that was carried out to verify the hypothesis. Everyone's decision-making is heavily influenced by demographic considerations. This study uses four demographic variables to analyze how those variables affect customer preferences. The demographic information and respondents' preference for organized retail stores in the Chennai district are shown in Table 88.1.

The survey indicated that the majority of the male gender and the age range of 26 to 35 are mostly involved in the purchasing activities in organized retail establishments. Students are the largest category found in the survey, and they actively participate in shopping at organized retail stores. The poll reveals that individuals, regardless of income level, choose organized retail establishments to meet their needs. The income groups belonging to below Rs. 20,000 and belonging to above Rs. 40,000 both constitute the majority of the sample.

The Chi-square test is used to determine whether the respondent's demographic characteristics, such as gender, age, monthly income, and employment, have an impact on their choice for organized retail outlets or not.

Hypothesis: 1. H0: was created to examine this possibility. It is clear from the results shown in the Table 88.2 that the P-values for the gender, age, and occupational groups are all higher than 0.05 (gender group 0.314, age group 0.067, and for occupations 0.054) and that these factors do not significantly affect a respondent's preference for an organized retail store. Furthermore, the p-value (0.008) for respondents' income level and preference for organized retail shops is lower than 0.05, indicating that the respondents' monthly income has an effect on their preference for retail shops.

Demographic factors of the respondents and their frequency of visit

The Table 88.3 implied that more than half of the respondents were men and that one-third of them

Table 88.1 The respondent's preference for structured retail shops and demographic considerations.

Demographic factors		Reason for purchase from organized retail stores						Total in %
		Low price	Better quality	Variety of products	Multi brands products	Better services	Nearest shop	
Gender	Male	15	5	15	17	6	10	68
	Female	15	8	6	10	5	13	57
Age group	Up to 25	9	5	6	6	2	8	36
	26 to 35	9	6	10	13	1	4	43
	36 to 45	4	0	2	4	6	7	23
	Above 45	8	2	3	4	2	4	23
Occupation	Student	7	4	6	8	2	7	34
	Self Employed	2	7	4	4	4	3	24
	Professionals	6	1	6	9	0	4	26
	House wife	6	1	1	2	2	6	18
	Salaried group	9	0	4	4	3	3	23
Monthly income	Below 20,000	13	6	9	6	1	9	44
	20,001 to 40,000	1	4	2	7	3	4	21
	40,001 to 60,000	4	1	1	3	6	3	18
	Above 60,000	12	2	9	11	1	7	42

Source: Primary data

Table 88.2 Chi-square result for impact of demographic factors on preferences to choose retail shop.

S. No.	Demographic variable	p- value	Significant level	Result
1	Gender	0.314	0.05	Insignificant
2	Age group	0.067	0.05	Insignificant
3	Monthly income	0.008	0.05	significant
4	Occupation	0.054	0.05	Insignificant

Source: SPSS result

Table 88.3 Frequency of visiting organized retail stores and demographic factors.

S. No.	Demographic factors	Category	Frequency of visiting organized retail stores					Total in %
			Daily	Once in a week	Once in 15 days	Once in a month	Rarely	
1	Gender	Male	13	16	22	7	10	54
		Female	11	18	14	6	8	46
2	Age group	Up to 25	11	10	7	4	4	29
		26 to 35	4	11	18	5	5	34
		36 to 45	3	8	5	2	5	18
		Above 45	6	5	6	2	4	18
3	Occupation	Student	10	11	5	3	5	27
		Self Employed	2	9	7	3	3	19
		Professionals	2	4	13	1	6	21

S. No.	Demographic factors	Category	Frequency of visiting organized retail stores					Total in %
			Daily	Once in a week	Once in 15 days	Once in a month	Rarely	
4	Monthly income	House wife	5	4	4	2	3	14
		Salaried group	5	6	7	4	1	18
		Below 20,000	16	11	8	4	5	35
		20,001 to 40,000	0	10	2	4	5	17
		40,001 to 60,000	2	6	5	1	4	14
		Above 60,000	6	7	21	4	4	34

Source: Primary data

Table 88.4 Chi-square test result between the frequency of visit and with the demographic factors.

S. No.	Demographic variable	p- value	Significant level	Result
1	Gender	0.843	0.05	Insignificant
2	Age group	0.428	0.05	Insignificant
3	Monthly income	0.01	0.05	significant
4	Occupation	0.186	0.05	Insignificant

Source: SPSS result

Table 88.5 Respondent's income level and frequency of visits in organized retail stores cross tabulation.

		Frequency of visits in organized retail stores					Total
		Daily	Once in a week	Once in 15 days	Once in a month	Rarely	
Monthly income	Below 20,000	16	11	8	4	5	44
	20,001 to 40,000	0	10	2	4	5	21
	40,001 to 60,000	2	6	5	1	4	18
	Above 60,000	6	7	21	4	4	42
Total		24	34	36	13	18	125

Source: Primary data

Table 88.6 ANOVA test result between income level and frequency of visit in organized retail stores.

ANOVA

Income level vs frequency of your visits in organized retail stores

	Sum of squares	df	Mean square	F	p-value	Significant level
Between groups	12.386	3	4.129	2.576	.057	0.05
Within groups	193.902	121	1.602			
Total	206.288	124				

Source: SPSS result

were in the 26–35 age range. Unexpectedly, more student organizations than any other group participated in the poll. Most of the respondents fall into one of two income categories: those making under Rs. 20,000 and those making over Rs. 60,000.

Hypothesis: 2. H0: The number of visits to organized retail stores is not statistically significant with the demographic characteristics. According to Table 88.4 the gender, age group, and occupation demographic parameters are not statistically associated with the frequency of visits to organized retail stores, hence the null hypothesis is accepted for the three demographic components. Also, it is discovered that there is a connection between respondents' visit frequency and income level of the respondents.

Respondent's monthly income and their frequency of visit

The following cross-tabulation shows that most of the respondents prefer to go to organized retail establishments twice in a month. Further investigation showed that individuals making more than Rs. 60,000 per month visit once every 15 days. The following hypothesis was developed and put to the test using the ANOVA test to see if there are any differences in the visiting behavior between the various income categories.

Hypothesis: 3. H_0: There is no significant difference among the different income groups in visiting the organized retail stores.

The results of the ANOVA test are shown in Table 88.6, where the p-value for testing hypothesis 3 is more than 0.05. Thus, the null hypothesis is accepted. This shows that there are no differences in the respondents' income levels when it comes to the frequency of visits to established retail locations. It indicates that people from every economic bracket are eager to visit the arranged retail establishments in the research region.

Conclusion

The study's findings suggest that a variety of factors influence consumer shopping preferences in formal retail establishments. They include product availability, value-added services, promotions, customer service, in-store experience, and product quality. Customers' purchasing patterns alter for the better when things are more affordable and readily available, and for the

worse when the quality of the products is substandard. Pricing and product availability have a favorable impact on client purchase behavior (Muramalla, 2020). Consumers should also take into account the usage of technology, as well as the personalization and customization of the buying experience. It is discovered that the respondents' income has an effect on their preferences for organized retail outlets as well as the frequency with which they frequent the shops. At the same time, no differences in income groups were discovered, indicating that all income groups in the study area visited organized retail establishments on an equal basis.

Reference

Hirata, T. T. (2008). Customer Satisfaction Planning: Ensuring Product Quality And Safety Within Your MRP/ERP Systems. CRC Press.

Kanetkar, M. (2014). An Analytical Study of Organized and Unorganized Retailing in India. LAP Lambert Academic Publishing.

Manyam, K. (2020). A study on influence of retail location attributes: does organised retail outperform unorganized retail in Karnataka, with reference to Bangalore, India.

Mishra, M. S. (2007). The consumption pattern of Indian consumers: choice between traditional and organized retail.

Muramalla, V. S. S. (2020). Retail store perceptions and buying behavior of consumers.

Nikhat, R. (2017). A Pragmatic Approach of Consumer Behaviour Towards Organized Retail Outlets – A Study of Select Cities. Zenon Academic Publishing.

Panigrahy, R. L. (2011). Problems and Prospects of Retail Marketing. Discovery Publishing House Pvt Limited.

Prajapati, S. (2015). A study of factors affecting consumer preference and satisfaction for shopping from the organized retail stores over unorganized retail stores in selected cities of Gujarat region.

Rao, V. (2019). Buying behaviour in India - the new face of retail market.

Sidhu, D. S. (2018). Shopping orientations based typology of indian consumers.

Somasekhar, G. (n.d.). Emerging Trends of Retailing in Rayalaseema Region of Andhra Pradesh. Archers & Elevators Publishing House.

Zhou, Y., and Ali, F. (2012). Factors Affecting Consumer Behaviour in Online Shopping: A Study of Students Purchasing Clothing In UK Online Market. LAP Lambert Academic Publishing.

89 The relationship between marital status and occupational stress management in the workplace: a special reference to private educational institutions

Manibharathi, A. N. and Sasikumar, T.

Department of Commerce, Saveetha College of Liberal Arts and Sciences, Saveetha University, Chennai, India

Abstract

Teaching is and remains one of the most vital professions globally and constitutes one of the most challenging and taxing occupations, especially now. In this contemporary era, particularly within India, educational institutions increasingly prioritize quantitative metrics such as marks and rankings over educational quality. While student stress receives ample attention, the occupational stress experienced by educators often goes unacknowledged, to say the least. This aforementioned occupational stress and pressure manifest prominently among teachers in privately-run establishments. This investigation underscores the importance of stress management awareness and delves into the primary causes of occupational stress among instructors in private schools situated within the Krishnagiri district of Tamil Nadu. Employing a descriptive design, the study gathered data through a questionnaire administered to 56 respondents across approximately 10 private educational institutions.

Keywords: Awareness of stress management, factors involved, major causes of occupational stress, occupational stress, private school teachers

Introduction

Teaching, stemming from its inherent essence, presents a highly demanding occupation and undeniably a pivotal one as well. This pertains to every facet of our civilized realm and particularly so in swiftly developing nations like India, boasting the largest youth populace globally. This not merely contributes to the significance of education within our nation but further exacerbates the existing pressures on educators, notably those in private establishments, which consistently attract a substantial influx of students annually. Beyond the ingrained, enduring attributes escalating the stakes, the contemporary educational era overly emphasizes the quantitative aspect over educational quality. Consequently, educators are incessantly tasked with pursuing predefined objectives, particularly within private educational institutions. Moreover, the advent of the pandemic ushering digital platforms into the educational domain has significantly augmented the workload and working hours of educators, ultimately amplifying their occupational stress. This profound escalation in occupational stress adversely impacts the mental well-being of educators, thereby not only affecting their professional endeavors but also intertwining with the future prospects of students, their personal lives, and the nation's future, given the paramount importance of education within the country. This study scrutinizes and assesses the degree of occupational stress among educators in private schools, as well as their awareness of and access to tools and strategies for managing and mitigating stress. The aim is to furnish them with the requisite knowledge to enhance their mental health, overall well-being, and the standard of education nationwide.

Methodology

The investigation concentrates on educators within independent institutions. For this examination, (Aggarwal, 2000) instructors from independent educational establishments within Krishnagiri locality were selected as a representation and surveyed utilizing a questionnaire. The study is grounded in observation (Buys, 2018). Auxiliary information is procured from an assortment of dependable origins like volumes, newspapers, periodicals, and websites. The uncomplicated haphazard sampling technique is employed to gather prime information. The answers to the surveys that were handed back to the examiners were ascertained to be suitably completed, by the initial suppositions of the study. National Research Council, Division of Behavioral and Social Sciences and Education, Board on Behavioral, Cognitive, and Sensory Sciences, and Committee on Developments in the Science of Learning with additional material from the Committee on Learning Research and Educational Practice, (2000) The statistics assembled from the

[a]smartgenpublications2@gmail.com

questionnaires were tabulated and subsequently inserted into the SPSS 23.0 rendition software.

Sampling Technique

A straightforward random sampling technique was utilized within the 'Probability sampling method' framework to designate the sample. A descriptive research design is embraced to conduct the research inquiry. Analytical tools such as t test and One-way ANOVA are applied in scrutinizing the data amassed to derive findings.

Objectives of the Investigation

To explore the degree of awareness regarding stress management among educators in private educational institutions. To identify the primary factors contributing to job-related stress among educators. To devise viable and optimal strategies to manage the professional pressure faced by educators in their roles.

Hypotheses

The following hypotheses were assumed in the study:

- **Hypothesis I:** There is no significant difference between gender and level of mental health affected by occupational stress
- **Hypothesis II:** There is no significant difference between age and awareness of stress management techniques
- **Hypothesis III:** There is no significant difference between marital status and occupational stress negatively influence personal life

Literature Review

According to Elwork (1997), in their study titled Stress management among school teachers of Palakkad district, it was suggested that the extent of job satisfaction within the educational setting could aid in diminishing the stress levels experienced by school educators. The presence of technologies and the accessibility of these technologies to educators, both in school environments and at their residences, could substantially contribute to alleviating stress associated with teaching, as technology serves as a natural stress-relieving agent that provides entertainment and positively transforms lives. The references (MRP/12th Plan/14-15/KLCA021 Dated: 10th December 2014, 1603-MRP/14-15/KLCA021/UGC-SWRO, Dated: 4th February 2015) were cited in support. According to Somerfield and McCrae (2000), determinants that significantly impact individuals' coping mechanisms for stress include factors such as their level of educational attainment and marital status. (Faure, 1972) In a study by (Frögéli et al., 2022), various facets of the professional lives of college instructors were examined, with a specific focus on discerning disparities in the perceptions of male and female, as well as junior and senior, faculty members regarding their respective responses. The findings indicated that junior faculty members reported significantly higher levels of stress across various stress dimensions compared to their senior counterparts. However, female instructors experienced greater stress related to role overload and inter-role distance compared to males (National Research Council, 2015). Research conducted by Edgell et al. (2015) concerning occupational stress among secondary school educators in the Madurai district of Tamil Nadu revealed that teachers in aided schools experience greater stress levels compared to those in government-run institutions. Furthermore, it was noted that educators experiencing elevated stress levels exhibit lower levels of job satisfaction and are more likely to consider leaving the profession, potentially never returning to teaching. Worth et al. (2015) discovered that primary school teachers experience high levels of stress, particularly those in private institutions compared to their counterparts in government schools (OECD, 2001). The study conducted by (Sachdeva and Kaur, 2014) titled "Study of occupational stress of secondary school teachers" emphasized the importance of fostering a supportive and collaborative environment within schools, providing stress and time management training, as well as recreational facilities to faculty members to mitigate occupational stress. The involvement of teachers in decision-making processes was also encouraged, alongside the provision of a conducive working environment, job security, manageable workloads, training in handling disruptive behavior, and access to various facilities (Leicht et al., 2018). Additionally, department heads should promptly report insufficient staffing and equipment shortages to school authorities (OECD and Specialists Schools and Academies Trust, 2008).

A statistical analysis was done for all the data collected for the research through tools like t-test and one-way ANOVA with the" help of SPSS 23.0 version of the software.

Results

A variety of outcomes acquired and observed from the investigation are condensed and outlined here. Concerning the 'Degree of psychological well-being is influenced by work-related pressure', (Table 89.1). Female participants (2.53) exhibit the greatest average and elevated degree of psychological well-being is impacted by work-related pressure compared to

Table 89.1 Mean score analysis on level of mental health is affected by occupational stress.

Particulars	Gender	N	Mean	Std. deviation
Level of mental health affected by occupational stress	Male	39	2.31	0.832
	Female	17	2.53	0.874

Source: Author

Table 89.2 T test for gender and level of mental health is affected by occupational stress.

Particulars	T - Test for equality of means		
	t[a]	df[b]	Sig.[c] (2-tailed)
Level of mental health affected by occupational stress	0.903	54	0.000* Significant

Source: Author

Table 89.3 One-way analysis for age and awareness of any stress management techniques.

Particulars	Sum of squares	df[a]	Mean square	F[b]	Sig.[c]
Between groups	0.673	3	0.224	0.937	0.030*
Within groups	12.452	52	0.239		
Total	13.125	55			Significant

Source: Author

Table 89.4 One-way analysis for marital status and occupational stress negatively influence personal life.

Particulars	Sum of squares	df[a]	Mean square	F[b]	Sig.[c]
Between groups	3.132	3	1.044	0.820	0.009**
Within groups	66.225	52	1.274		
Total	69.375	55			Significant

Source: Author

the male participants (2.31). The Table 89.2 illustrates that there exists a noteworthy disparity at 0.001 threshold amidst the participants, regarding gender toward degree of psychological well-being is impacted by work-related pressure. 'Degree of psychological well-being is influenced by work-related pressure' is noteworthy at 0.001 level. There exists a significant disparity amidst the age of the participants and Familiarity with any stress management strategies. The significance is at 0.005 threshold as depicted in the Table 89.3. Table 89.4 signifies that there is a substantial variance amidst the marital status of the participants and work-related pressure detrimentally affects personal life. The significance is at 0.001 threshold.

Discussion

The assertion that educators functioning within (Haque, 2022) independent educational institutions encounter considerable occupational strain owing to myriad factors such as student misbehavior, heightened workload, extended work durations, job instability, inequitable and delayed remuneration, and so forth is conspicuously apparent from the findings extrapolated from the examination of the data. It also substantiates that an insufficient number of instructors possess awareness regarding strategies to manage the strain prevalent within their profession.

Additionally, it is discerned that numerous subjective elements influence (Committee on Physical Activity and Physical Education in the School Environment, Food and Nutrition Board, and Institute of Medicine, 2013) the landscape of teachers' occupational stress, including gender, age, marital status, and similar aspects, thereby complicating the provision of a universally applicable viewpoint and recommendations on the subject matter.

Based on the outcomes of the analysis, the recommendations posited by the study entail the following:

educational institutions must uphold their commitments to providing optimal working conditions, hours, and workload for educators; fostering a transparent rapport between instructors and students (Winkelmes et al., 2019); educators should actively seek avenues for self-improvement through training and other modalities; schools ought to furnish them with requisite resources and mechanisms to alleviate and manage the occupational stress accrued in the course of their duties. Moreover, it is advisable for older educators to receive education and training on stress management methodologies and tools, while female educators should be assigned a workload commensurate with achieving a work-life balance.

Furthermore, the fixation on quantitative grades and marks prevalent in our society must be relinquished for the greater good, and educational institutions must create an improved environment for educators to discharge their duties, characterized by (Edgell et al., 2015) a salubrious work atmosphere, equitable treatment, and job security, thereby not only fostering the enhancement of educators' mental well-being and performance but also elevating the educational quality and standards of the nation holistically, securing a prosperous future for the country.

Conclusion

The investigation determined that there is insufficient recognition regarding occupational strain and techniques for managing stress among educators within independent educational institutions situated in the locale of Krishnagiri. Considering that the inquiry encompasses all principal private educational institutions sited within the vicinity, the deduction can be regarded as unanimous for the entirety of the region. Additionally, it is recommended that educational institutions within the area address this concern and furnish instructors with essential resources for handling their professional stressors.

References

Aggarwal, Y. (2000). How Many Pupils Complete Primary Education in Five Years?: Evidence from Selected DPEP Districts of Tamil Nadu. National Institute of Educational Planning and Administration.

Auer, M. E., Hortsch, H., Michler, O., and Köhler, T. (2022). Mobility for Smart Cities and Regional Development - Challenges for Higher Education: Proceedings of the 24th International Conference on Interactive Collaborative Learning (ICL2021), Volume 2. Springer International Publishing Springer, Cham.

Buys, A. M. (2018). The multi-faceted roles of learning support teachers in private schools .

Committee on Physical Activity and Physical Education in the School Environment, Food and Nutrition Board, and Institute of Medicine (2013). Educating the student body: taking physical activity and physical education to school .

Ding, G. B., Sang, Q., Han, H. J., Wang, X. M., and Wu, Y. F. (2023). Assessment of stroke knowledge and awareness among primary healthcare providers: a cross-sectional survey from the kezhou quality improvement in acute stroke care project. *Frontiers in Public Health*, 11, 1136170.

Dollard, M., Winefield, H. R., and Winefield, A. H. (Eds.). (2003). Occupational Stress in the Service Professions. CRC Press.

Dunham, J. (2002). Stress in Teaching. Routledge.

Edgell, S., Gottfried, H., and Granter, E. (2015). The SAGE handbook of the sociology of work and employment .

Elwork, A. (1997). Stress Management for Lawyers: How to Increase Personal & Professional Satisfaction in the Law. Vorkell Group

Faure, E. (1972). Learning to be: The World of Education Today and Tomorrow. UNESCO.

Frögéli, E., Annell, S., Rudman, A., Inzunza, M., and Gustavsson, P. (2022). The importance of effective organizational socialization for preventing stress, strain, and early career burnout: an intensive longitudinal study of new professionals. *International Journal of Environmental Research and Public Health*, 19(12), 7356.

Great Britain Health and Safety Executive (2007). Managing the Causes of Work-Related Stress: A Step-by-Step Approach using the Management Standards. Hse Books.

Haque, A. U. (2022). Handbook of Research on the Complexities and Strategies of Occupational Stress. IGI Global.

Hartney, E. (2008). Stress Management for Teachers. Bloomsbury Publishing.

Leicht, A., Heiss, J., and Byun, W. J. (2018). Issues and Trends in Education for Sustainable Development (Vol. 5). UNESCO Publishing.

Mills, S. H. (1990). Stress management for teachers.

National Research Council, Division of Behavioral and Social Sciences and Education, Board on Behavioral, Cognitive, and Sensory Sciences, and Committee on Developments in the Science of Learning with additional material from the Committee on Learning Research and Educational Practice (2000). How People Learn: Brain, Mind, Experience, and School: Expanded Edition. (Vol. 1). National Academies Press.

National Research Council (2015). Institute of medicine, board on children, youth, and families, and committee on the science of children birth to age 8: deepening and broadening the foundation for success.. transforming the workforce for children birth through age 8: a unifying foundation .

OECD (2001). New school management approaches .

OECD, and Specialists Schools and Academies Trust. (2008). Improving school leadership, volume 2 case studies on system leadership: case studies on system leadership .

Sachdeva, R., and Kaur, K. (2014). A Study of Occupational Stress of Secondary School Teachers. GRIN Verlag.

Sharma, K. A., Cooper, C. L., and Pestonjee, D. M. (2021). Organizational Stress Around the World: Research and Practice. Routledge.

Winkelmes, M. A., Boye, A., and Tapp, S. (2019). Transparent design in higher education teaching and leadership: a guide to implementing the transparency framework institution-wide to improve learning and retention .

Worth, J., Bamford, S., and Durbin, B. (2015). Should I Stay or Should I Go?: NFER Analysis of Teachers Joining and Leaving the Profession: Report. Slough: National Foundation for Educational Research.

90 Enhancing the precision of predicting patient admission in the emergency ward through naive bayes compared to logistic regression

Monish Kumar G and Jesu Jayarin P

Department of Information Technology, SIMATS, Saveetha University, Chennai, India

Abstract

The objective of this research is to enhance precision in forecasting patient admission utilizing the novel Naive Bayes (NB) model versus logistic regression (LR). Patient admission prognosis in the emergency department is executed employing the novel NB and LR models with 10 iterations, calculated through ClinCalc with Gpower set at 0.1 and alpha at 0.05. The dataset comprises 3,18,438 patient entries, where 15,757 rows and 56 columns serve as features. The evaluation of patient admission accuracy and efficacy is derived from the outcomes. The mean accuracy for patient admission management using the novel NB model stands notably high at 93%, surpassing LR's 91%. The statistical significance of the accuracy is 0.060 (p > 0.05) according to the independent sample t-test, suggesting no substantial difference between the two algorithms. The mean accuracy of the novel NB model outperforms LR in hospital patient admission prediction.

Keywords: Clinical, emergency, health, logistic regression, novel naive bayes, patients, triage

Introduction

Admission to an emergency care facility specializes in priority based medical treatment, catering to patients arriving without prior appointments. Situated predominantly in hospitals, it's tasked with providing immediate care for a wide range of conditions, some of which are life-threatening (Zhang et al., 2017). The main challenge faced is the congestion of emergency departments (EDs), necessitating prompt interventions (Hwang and Lee, 2022). Swiftly identifying patients in need of urgent medical attention is a common requirement in EDs (Becker et al., 2015). EDs prioritize patient care based on the severity of their condition (Beveridge et al., 1999). To expedite patient flow and alleviate congestion, novel techniques are essential (Murray et al., 2004). Naive Bayes (NB) facilitates predicting outcomes based on patient data, crucial for managing emergency situations (Green et al., 2012). While logistic regression (LR) provides insights into health outcomes, it lacks the robustness for overall patient flow management (Hohl et al., 2001). The challenge lies in improving prediction accuracy amidst incomplete datasets (Williams, 1996). Enhancing data collection and analysis is crucial for precise predictions and efficient resource utilization (Dugas et al., 2016). This study aims to leverage novel NB for improved patient admission forecasting in EDs, addressing existing limitations in accuracy and precision.

Materials and Methods

The study involved two groups: Group 1, representing the novel NB algorithm, and Group 2, embodying the LR algorithm. Data for training and testing were sourced from Kaggle, with a sample size of N = 10, resulting in a total of 10 samples. The datasets, obtained from Kaggle's hospital admissions data repository in CSV format, comprised 318,438 patient records. Each file was categorized based on various patient health details. The objective of the novel NB algorithm was to predict the availability of beds in the emergency department. Standard data division into training and testing sets was followed, with different machine learning methods applied to the training data and model assessment conducted using the testing data. The development and execution of the proposed model were facilitated using Google Colab and Visual Studio Code software, with Python as the programming language. The fresh NB algorithm, a supervised learning method, solves classification problems based on Bayes' theorem and is commonly used in text classification scenarios. It is known for its simplicity and efficiency, enabling quick predictions within clinical settings based on event likelihoods, such as the length

[a]natashasmartgenresearch@gmail.com

of a patient's stay correlating with emergency bed confirmation data.

Logistic Regression Algorithm

Logistic regression, a widely-used supervised learning technique, predicts a categorical dependent variable based on independent variables. It operates on categorical outcomes, such as yes/no or true/false, offering probabilistic values between 0 and 1 (Gold et al., 2014).

Statistical Analysis

For the analysis of NB and LR, SPSS version 29 was employed. Tables 90.4, containing group statistical information for the proposed methods, demonstrate their significance. The dataset was split into testing and training sections with a test size of 0.2 (Chen and Guestrin, 2016). An independent sample T-test assessed accuracy, with SPSS used to compute standard deviation and standard mean error. Independent variables include name, age, gender, health issues, and time period. Dependent variables comprise accuracy and loss. Analysis of accuracy and loss was conducted using variables from the Kaggle dataset.

Results

Utilizing statistical methodologies, a total of 435 samples undergo analysis in this approach. Both the novel NB algorithm and LR analyze this dataset. Comparing the two groups statistically reveals that the novel NB in group 1 exhibits higher mean accuracy than LR in group 2. The standard error mean of NB surpasses that of LR. NB achieves an accuracy rate of 93%, whereas logistic regression achieves 91%. To predict patient admission accuracy in the emergency department, group and accuracy values are established. Using 10 distinct samples from each group, accuracies for both methods are computed. Figure 90.1 illustrates the comparison between the NB algorithm and the LR algorithm in terms of mean accuracy and mean loss. Table 90.1 displays the accuracy of patient admission in the Emergency ward using novel NB for 10 samples (Accuracy = 93%). Table 90.2 exhibits the accuracy of patient admission in the emergency ward using LR for 10 samples (Accuracy = 91%). Table 90.3 presents group statistical analysis, showcasing NB (mean accuracy 93%, standard deviation 2.82726) and LR (mean accuracy 91%, standard deviation 1.85011). Table 90.4 reveals the independent sample tests result with a confidence interval of 95% and a significance level of 0.060 (two-tailed, p > 0.05). This suggests no statistically significant difference between the two

Table 90.1 Accuracy and significant difference of naive bayes and logistic regression.

S. No	Groups	Accuracy
1	Naive Bayes	93
		92.1
		85.65
		86.37
		85.89
		90.6
		91.3
		88.63
		88
		92.32
2	Logistic regression	91
		85.65
		86.37
		85.89
		84.32
		87.31
		88.63
		88
		87.96
		87.28

Source: Author

algorithms (novel NB outperforms LR significantly). Table 90.5 evaluates the mean accuracy and mean loss of NB and LR.

Discussion

The average accuracy LR stands at 91%, whereas the novel NB model exhibits a superior precision of 93%, indicating its superiority over LR. Statistical insignificance (p > 0.05) was observed in the model with a 95% confidence interval (Becker et al., 2015).

Leveraging large datasets leads to slower processing, whereas smaller datasets yield faster, more accurate results (Shapiro et al., 2013). This study enhances predicting the ideal length of stay in emergency wards using comprehensive data (Kangovi et al., 2014). Mixed databases significantly improve prediction accuracy. Large datasets contribute to slower processing, whereas smaller ones yield faster, more accurate outcomes, simplifying the overarching problem once a model is established.

Despite diverse findings in prediction models, many struggle to accurately forecast emergency ward stays (Jiang et al., 2009). LR proves challenging and

Table 90.2 Statistical analysis: Naive Bayes outperforms logistic regression in mean accuracy and lower mean precision.

ACCURACY	Group	N	Mean	Std deviation	Std error mean
	Novel Naive Bayes	10	89.3860	2.82726	.89406
	Logistic regression	10	87.2410	1.85011	.58506

Source: Author

Table 90.3 Statistical analysis shows no significant superiority of naive bayes over logistic regression (p = 0.060, p > 0.05).

		F	Sig	t	Df	Sig (2-tailed)	Mean difference	Std error difference	Lower	Upper	
Accuracy	Equal variance assumed	4.963	0.039	2.008	18	0.060	2.14500	1.06847	-.09978	4.38978	
	Equal variance did not assume			2.008	15.513	0.062	2.14500	1.06847	-.12585	4.41585	

Source: Author

Table 90.4 Comparison of the novel Naive Bayes and logistic regression with their accuracy.

Classifier	Accuracy (%)
Naive Bayes algorithm	93%
Logistic regression	91%

Source: Author

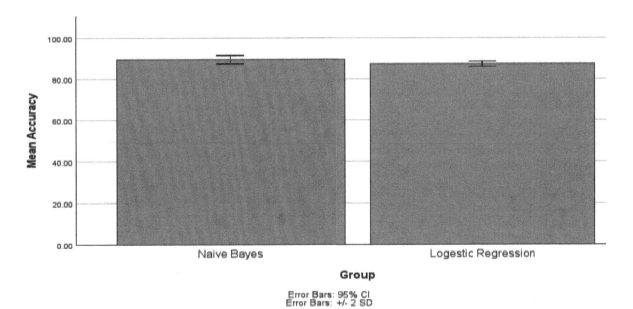

Figure 90.1 Assessing mean accuracy between Novel Naive Bayes and logistic regression algorithms reveals superiority in the former's accuracy and standard deviation, Naive Bayes Algorithm vs. Logistic Regression Y-Axis: Mean accuracy of prediction ± 2 SD

Source: Author

time-consuming to comprehend, requiring margin for data handling (Barak-Corren et al., 2017). Future research should focus on platform-specific predictions (Gold et al., 2014).

Conclusion

A new Naive Bayesian (NB) approach has been developed for forecasting based on experimental results. Emergency ward patient admission holds more significance over logistic regression (LR). Consequently, this proposed technique proves crucial in forecasting such admissions. The discrepancy in loss between LR and the novel NB is notable. LR demonstrates a higher mean loss compared to the novel NB. The standard deviation and standard error mean of loss are marginally elevated in the novel NB. Thus, it appears that the novel NB algorithm exhibits greater accuracy than the LR algorithm.

References

Barak-Corren, Y., Fine, A. M., and Reis, B. Y. (2017). Early prediction model of patient hospitalization from the pediatric emergency department. *Pediatrics*, 139(5). https://doi.org/10.1542/peds.2016-2785.

Becker, J. B., Lopes, M. C. B. T., Pinto, M. F., Campanharo, C. R. V., Barbosa, D. A., and Batista, R. E. A. (2015). Triage at the emergency department: association between triage levels and patient outcome. *Revista da Escola de Enfermagem da USP*, 49(5), 783–789.

Beveridge, R., Ducharme, J., Janes, L., Beaulieu, S., and Walter, S. (1999). Reliability of the Canadian emergency department triage and acuity scale: interrater agreement. *Annals of Emergency Medicine*, 34(2), 155–159.

Chen, T., and Guestrin, C. (2016). XGBoost. In Proceedings of the 22nd ACM SIGKDD International Conference on Knowledge Discovery and Data Mining. New York, NY, USA. ACM. https://doi.org/10.1145/2939672.2939785.

Dugas, A. F., Kirsch, T. D., Toerper, M., Korley, F., Yenokyan, G., France, D., et al. (2016). An electronic emergency triage system to improve patient distribution by critical outcomes. *The Journal of Emergency Medicine*, 50(6), 910–918.

Gold, D. L., Mihalov, L. K., and Cohen, D. M. (2014). Evaluating the pediatric early warning score (PEWS) system for admitted patients in the pediatric emergency department. *Academic Emergency Medicine: Official Journal of the Society for Academic Emergency Medicine*, 21(11), 1249–1256.

Green, N. A., Durani, Y., Brecher, D., DePiero, A., Loiselle, J., and Attia, M. (2012). Emergency severity index version 4: a valid and reliable tool in pediatric emergency department triage. *Pediatric Emergency Care*, 28(8), 753–757.

Hohl, C. M., Dankoff, J., Colacone, A., and Afilalo. M. (2001). Polypharmacy, adverse drug-related events, and potential adverse drug interactions in elderly patients presenting to an emergency department. *Annals of Emergency Medicine*, 38(6), 666–671.

Hwang, S., and Lee, B. (2022). Machine learning-based prediction of critical Illness in children visiting the emergency department. *PloS One*, 17(2), e0264184.

Jiang, H. J., Russo, C. A., and Barrett, M. L. (2009). Nationwide frequency and costs of potentially preventable hospitalizations, (2006). In Healthcare Cost and Utilization Project (HCUP) Statistical Briefs. Rockville (MD): Agency for Healthcare Research and Quality (US).

Kangovi, S., Grande, D., Carter, T., Barg, F. K., Rogers, M., Glanz, K., et al. (2014). The use of participatory action research to design a patient-centered community health worker care transitions intervention. *Healthcare (Amsterdam, Netherlands)*, 2(2), 136–144.

Lucini, F. R., Fogliatto, F. S., da Silveira, G. J. C., Neyeloff, J. L., Anzanello, M. J., Kuchenbecker, R. S., et al. (2017). Text mining approach to predict hospital admissions using early medical records from the emergency department. *International Journal of Medical Informatics*, 100, 1–8.

Lucke, J. A., de Gelder, J., Clarijs, F., Heringhaus, C., de Craen, A. J. M., Fogteloo, A. J., et al. (2018). Early prediction of hospital admission for emergency department patients: a comparison between patients younger or older than 70 Years. *Emergency Medicine Journal: EMJ*, 35(1), 18–27.

Murray, M., Bullard, M., Grafstein, E., and the CTAS. (2004). Revisions to the Canadian emergency department triage and acuity scale implementation guidelines. *Canadian Journal of Emergency Medicine*, 6(06), 421–427.

Shapiro, J. S., Johnson, S. A., Angiollilo, J., Fleischman, W., Onyile, A., and Kuperman, G. (2013). Health information exchange improves identification of frequent emergency department users. *Health Affairs*, 32(12), 2193–2198.

Shapiro, N. I., Wolfe, R. E., Moore, R. B., Smith, E., Burdick, E., and Bates, D. W. (2003). Mortality in emergency department sepsis (MEDS) score: a prospectively derived and validated clinical prediction rule. *Critical Care Medicine*, 31(3), 670–675.

Williams, R. M. (1996). Triage and emergency department services. *Annals of Emergency Medicine*, 27(4), 506–508.

Zhang, X., Kim, J., Patzer, R. E., Pitts, S. R., Patzer, A., and Schrager, J. D. (2017). Prediction of emergency department hospital admission based on natural language processing and neural networks. *Methods of Information in Medicine*, 56(5), 377–389.

91 The double-edged sword of AI-integrated education: an investigation into personalized and inclusive learning in higher education

Analisa Hamdan[1,2,a]

[1]Lecturer, Asia Pacific University of Technology and Innovation, Kuala Lumpur, Malaysia

[2]PhD Student, Sultan Idris Education University, Perak, Malaysia

Abstract

The integration of Generative AI tools in higher education offers promising avenues for enhancing personalized and inclusive learning but also presents significant challenges. This study investigates these complexities, focusing on personalized learning, inclusivity, faculty preparedness, and ethical considerations. Employing a mixed-methods research design, the study surveyed and interviewed students and faculty members from multiple higher education institutions. Using stratified random sampling, 300 students and 100 faculty members were selected. The study found that 85% of students reported enhanced engagement and academic performance due to AI's personalized learning capabilities. However, some students preferred traditional methods of teaching. In terms of inclusivity, 75% of students felt that AI tools were accessible and culturally diverse, although concerns about algorithmic biases were raised. Faculty preparedness emerged as a significant factor, with 60% of faculty members feeling inadequately prepared to effectively use AI tools, citing technical and ethical challenges. Ethical considerations were a major concern, with 70% of participants worried about data privacy and security, and 50% raising issues related to algorithmic bias. These findings align with existing literature, emphasizing the need for a balanced approach to AI integration, faculty training programs, and ethical guidelines. The study offers valuable insights for future research and practical implementations in higher education. It also underscores the urgency for educational institutions to address these challenges to fully harness the benefits of AI in academic settings.

Keywords: Ethical considerations, faculty preparedness, generative AI, higher education, personalized learning

Introduction

The introduction of Generative AI tools into higher education is a transformative development that holds immense promise for reshaping the educational landscape. These advanced technologies offer the potential to create more personalized learning experiences, tailoring educational content to meet individual student needs (Wang et al., 2019). In addition, Generative AI tools can also contribute to more inclusive learning environments by adapting to diverse learning styles and cultural backgrounds (Williams et al., 2017).

However, there are complexities and difficulties involved in integrating AI technologies into educational settings. One of the most pressing issues is the ethical considerations that come with AI deployment, such as data privacy and algorithmic bias (Smith and Smith, 2020; O'Neil, 2016). These ethical concerns are often not adequately addressed, leaving a gap in the existing body of research. Another critical area that requires attention is the pedagogical implications of AI integration. While AI tools can enhance learning,

there is a need for empirical studies that investigate how these tools align with educational theories and practices (Clark and Mayer, 2016; Reeves and Lin, 2020).

Furthermore, the preparedness of faculty members to effectively integrate and utilize these advanced AI tools remains a significant concern (Brown and Green, 2018; Adiguzel et al., 2023). Faculty development programs often lag in providing the necessary training and resources for educators to feel comfortable and competent in using such technologies (Ertmer et al., 2012).

The integration of AI in education can be seen as a double-edged sword. On one hand, it offers unprecedented opportunities for personalized and inclusive education; on the other, it raises serious questions about data ethics, educational quality, and social equity (Roberts et al., 2021). The swift advancement of AI frequently surpasses the development rate of ethical guidelines and educational frameworks. This mismatch leads to a scenario resembling the "wild west," where numerous possibilities unfold, but not all are prudent or ethically sound (Ivanov, 2023).

[a]analisa@apu.edu.my, [b]p20182002321@siswa.upsi.edu.my

While Generative AI tools offer exciting possibilities for enhancing personalized and inclusive learning, there are several challenges and gaps in the current research that need to be addressed. These include ethical considerations, pedagogical alignment, and faculty preparedness, all of which necessitate a comprehensive, multi-faceted study to fully understand the impact of Generative AI tools in higher education. Thus, the primary aim of this study is to investigate the effectiveness of Generative AI tools in facilitating inclusive and personalized learning experiences in higher education (Williams et al., 2017). The study also seeks to identify the challenges and limitations faced by faculty and students in integrating these tools into the educational process (Davis and Davis, 2019).

Research Objectives

1. To assess the effectiveness of Generative AI tools in enhancing personalized learning experiences for students in higher education.
2. To evaluate the level of inclusivity provided by Generative AI tools in educational settings.
3. To understand the preparedness and challenges faced by faculty members in integrating Generative AI tools into their teaching methods.
4. To analyse the ethical considerations associated with the use of Generative AI tools in higher education.
5. To provide recommendations for educators, policymakers, and AI developers for the successful integration of AI into higher education based on the study's findings.

Literature Review

Artificial intelligence (AI) is ushering in a transformative era in higher education. Classrooms around the world are experiencing enhanced personalized learning and a renewed emphasis on inclusivity, largely driven by AI advancements. However, with this innovation come challenges and considerations. The effectiveness of these tools, the preparedness of educators, and the ethical implications are all areas of active discussion and research. This review explores these critical topics, drawing insights from a rich body of literature, to provide a comprehensive understanding of the current landscape of AI in education.

Effectiveness of generative AI tools in personalized learning

The effectiveness of Generative AI tools in enhancing personalized learning experiences has been a subject of considerable research, and the literature on this topic is both rich and evolving. Early studies by Clark et al. (2016) and Johnson et al. (2016) laid the groundwork by emphasizing the adaptability of AI-driven platforms to individual learning styles. They found that these platforms could significantly improve student engagement and academic performance by offering real-time feedback and personalized assessments. These findings are consistent with the work of Davis and Davis (2019), who caution that the effectiveness of these tools can be influenced by various factors such as the quality of the AI algorithms and the level of faculty preparedness.

Recent contributions to this body of literature have expanded the understanding in notable ways. For instance, Zhang et al. (2023) proposes key pedagogical principles for integrating AI chatbots in classrooms. They focus on goal setting, feedback, and personalization as essential elements for promoting self-regulated learning in higher education. This study adds a layer of complexity by suggesting that the design principles behind AI tools can significantly impact their effectiveness in personalized learning.

Another recent study by Chan and Hu (2023) inquired into students' perceptions of generative AI technologies. While students are generally willing to engage with these tools, they also have concerns about accuracy, privacy, and ethical issues.

This study holds particular significance as it underscores the idea that the success of AI tools doesn't solely depend on technological prowess. It also heavily relies on how users perceive and trust these advanced tools.

Thus, the literature suggests that while Generative AI tools have significant potential to enhance personalized learning experiences, their effectiveness is contingent on multiple factors. These include the quality of the AI algorithms, faculty preparedness, pedagogical design principles, and student perceptions. As such, a multi-faceted approach is necessary for the successful integration and effectiveness of these advanced tools in higher education settings.

Level of inclusivity provided by generative AI tools
The effectiveness and inclusivity of Generative AI tools in educational settings have been subjects of considerable research. On the one hand, studies have shown that AI-driven platforms can adapt to individual learning styles, thereby improving student engagement and academic performance. Clark et al. (2016) and Johnson et al. (2016) have laid the groundwork by emphasizing the adaptability of these platforms to individual learning needs. They argue that AI tools can offer real-time feedback and personalized assessments, which are crucial for effective learning.

However, the literature also cautions that the effectiveness of these tools can be influenced by various factors. Davis and Davis (2019) note that the quality of the AI algorithms and the level of faculty preparedness can significantly impact the effectiveness of these tools. Recent contributions by Zhang et al. (2023) and Chan and Hu (2023) have further nuanced the understanding by focusing on pedagogical principles and student perceptions, respectively.

On the other hand, inclusivity in educational settings facilitated by AI tools has also garnered attention. Roberts and Simpson (2020) emphasized that AI tools could be designed to be accessible to students with disabilities and offer content that is culturally and linguistically diverse. Wang et al. (2019) further noted that AI tools could provide equal opportunities for all students to participate in the learning process. However, Smith and Smith (2020) raised concerns about algorithmic biases that could inadvertently lead to exclusionary practices.

Hence, the literature indicates that although Generative AI tools hold substantial promise for improving personalized learning experiences and fostering inclusivity, their success and inclusiveness depend on various factors. These include the quality of the AI algorithms, faculty preparedness, pedagogical design principles, and student perceptions. As such, a multi-faceted approach is necessary for the successful integration and effectiveness of these advanced tools in higher education settings.

Faculty preparedness and challenges
The role of faculty in the successful integration of AI tools is another critical variable. Green et al. (2017) found that faculty preparedness significantly impacts the effectiveness of AI tools in education. They argued that faculty training and development programs are essential for the successful implementation of AI tools. Brown and Green (2018) also noted that faculty members often face challenges such as technical issues and ethical considerations, which could limit the effectiveness of AI tools.

Recent advancements in this field have further refined the comprehension of faculty readiness. For example, Ramiz Zekaj (2023) discusses the potential advantages and disadvantages of AI in educational settings, emphasizing the need for further research and the development of best practices for AI integration. This study suggests that while AI tools like ChatGPT can significantly improve instruction, faculty preparedness in understanding these tools is crucial (Zekaj, 2023).

Jekatyerina Dunajeva (2022) focuses on the challenges faced by faculty in transitioning to online education during the COVID-19 pandemic. The study highlights the flaws in technological abilities and digital preparedness within universities, indicating a gap that needs to be filled for effective AI integration (Dunajeva, 2022).

Another study by Mohammed Amin Almaiah et al. (2022) examines the factors affecting technology adoption in higher education and finds that technological preparedness is vital in determining perceived ease of use. This study underscores the importance of faculty being well-versed in the technology they are expected to use (Almaiah et al., 2022).

Finally, Mohammed Alqahtani et al. (2022) investigates the factors that influence students' attitudes toward e-learning technologies. The study suggests that faculty preparedness can significantly impact students' satisfaction and academic performance, thereby affecting the overall effectiveness of AI tools in education (Alqahtani et al., 2022).

Thus, the literature indicates that faculty preparedness is a multi-faceted issue that significantly impacts the successful integration and effectiveness of AI tools in higher education. It is influenced by various factors including technological abilities, ethical considerations, and the need for ongoing training and development programs.

Ethical considerations in AI-integrated education
Ethical considerations in the use of AI tools in education have been a focal point in several studies. Smith and Smith (2020) emphasized the importance of data privacy and security, as well as the need to address issues related to algorithmic bias and fairness. Williams et al. (2017) also pointed out that ethical considerations are not just limited to data privacy but also include the quality and inclusivity of educational content.

Recent contributions to this field have broadened the scope of ethical considerations. Rodríguez Chávez et al. (2023) conducted a systematic review that highlighted the ethical considerations surrounding academic integrity when integrating AI into educational settings. Their work adds a new dimension by focusing on academic honesty, an often overlooked but equally important ethical consideration (Rodríguez Chávez et al., 2023).

Schutte et al. (2023) explored the reporting of ethical review decisions and ethical considerations in health professions education research. Although their study is specific to health professions, the ethical considerations they discuss, such as data privacy and algorithmic fairness, are universally relevant to AI-integrated education (Schutte et al., 2023).

Furthermore, Koretzky et al. (2023) designed a case-based undergraduate medical education workshop to introduce students to important neuroethics concepts. While the study is specific to medical education, it underscores the need for ethical training and awareness among students, a concern that extends to AI-integrated education (Koretzky et al., 2023).

Thus, the literature highlights that ethical considerations in AI-integrated education are multifaceted and intricate, covering concerns related to data privacy, algorithmic fairness, academic integrity, and ethical training.These considerations are critical for the responsible and effective use of AI tools in educational settings.

Methodology

This study employs a mixed-methods approach to provide a comprehensive understanding of the effectiveness and challenges of integrating Generative AI tools in higher education. The mixed-methods design allows for the triangulation of data, thereby enhancing the validity and reliability of the study's findings (Creswell and Clark, 2017).

The target population for this study comprises students and faculty members from higher education institutions. The study employed a stratified random sampling technique to ensure a diverse and representative sample of both students and faculty members from multiple higher education institutions (Lohr, 2019). In stratified random sampling, the population is divided into different subgroups or 'strata' based on specific characteristics, and then random samples are taken from each stratum. For this study, the strata were defined based on factors such as academic disciplines, years of teaching experience for faculty, and academic levels (e.g., undergraduate, postgraduate) for students. This approach was chosen to capture a wide range of perspectives and experiences related to the use of Generative AI tools in higher education.

A total of 400 participants were selected for the study, comprising 300 students and 100 faculty members from higher education institutions. The sample size was determined based on the need for statistical power and the feasibility of managing the data collection process within the study's timeframe and resources. After defining the strata, random sampling was conducted within each stratum to select the participants. For students, the strata included different academic disciplines and levels, while for faculty, the strata were based on academic disciplines and years of teaching experience. This ensured that the sample was not only random but also representative of the larger population, thereby increasing the validity and generalizability of the study's findings.

Data collection methods
The study employs a multi-pronged approach to data collection to ensure a comprehensive understanding of the research questions.

Surveys
1. **General Effectiveness and Inclusivity Survey:** Online surveys are administered to both students and faculty members. These surveys aim to assess the effectiveness of Generative AI tools in facilitating personalized learning and inclusivity within higher education settings. The survey instrument incorporates both Likert-scale questions and open-ended questions, allowing for the collection of both quantitative and qualitative data. This method of survey design is guided by the recommendations of Dillman et al. (2014).

2. **Faculty Preparedness for AI Integration Survey (FPAIS):** To specifically assess faculty preparedness, the FPAIS is administered. This survey focuses on technical skills, training and support, ethical considerations, perceived challenges, and resource availability. It aims to provide a comprehensive view of faculty readiness and the challenges they face in effectively using AI tools in educational settings. The FPAIS was developed in accordance with best practices for educational survey design, as outlined by Creswell and Creswell (2018).

Semi-structured interviews
Semi-structured interviews are conducted to gain more nuanced insights into the experiences and challenges associated with the use of Generative AI tools. These interviews target faculty members and a selected group of students, providing an opportunity for in-depth exploration of individual perspectives. The interview protocol is informed by the work of DiCicco-Bloom and Crabtree (2006), which offers a structured yet flexible approach to qualitative interviewing.

Validation of survey and interview questions
Before administering the survey and interview questions, they were subjected to an expert review. A panel of five experts in the fields of AI in education, educational research methods, and higher education pedagogy was convened. These experts evaluated the questions for clarity, relevance, and comprehensiveness (Creswell and Creswell, 2018). Their feedback was instrumental in refining the questions to ensure they accurately captured the constructs of interest.

A pilot test was conducted with a small sample of 20 participants (15 students and 5 faculty members) who fit the study's demographic but were not part of the main study. This pilot helped identify any ambiguities, misinterpretations, or potential biases in the questions (Dillman et al., 2014). Based on the feedback received, minor adjustments were made to enhance the clarity and flow of the questions.

After the pilot test, the reliability of the survey questions was assessed using Cronbach's alpha, a commonly used statistic for measuring internal consistency (Tavakol and Dennick, 2011). A value of 0.85 was obtained, indicating a high level of reliability and suggesting that the questions were consistently interpreted by the participants.

Post the pilot phase, the survey and interview questions underwent iterative refinement. This process ensured that the questions not only aligned with the study's objectives but also resonated with the target audience's experiences and perceptions (Creswell & Creswell, 2018).

To further validate the findings, data triangulation was employed (Carter et al., 2014). The quantitative data from the survey was cross-referenced with the qualitative data from the interviews. This approach provided a holistic understanding and added depth to the findings, ensuring that the results were not solely dependent on one method.

After the interviews were transcribed, participants were given the opportunity to review their responses. This process, known as member checking, ensured that the transcriptions accurately represented participants' views and allowed them to clarify or expand on their answers if needed (Birt et al., 2016). Throughout the data collection process, continuous monitoring was implemented (Creswell and Creswell, 2018). Any anomalies, unexpected responses, or patterns were flagged for review. This ongoing scrutiny ensured the data's integrity and the instruments' continued relevance.

Thus, the rigorous validation process undertaken for the survey and interview questions underscores the reliability and validity of the instruments used in this study. The multi-faceted approach, combining expert review, pilot testing, reliability assessment, and triangulation, ensures that the findings are both robust and grounded in the authentic experiences of the participants.

Data Analysis Tools
For the analysis of quantitative data, this study employs the Statistical Package for the Social Sciences (SPSS) as the primary tool. The data collected from the surveys undergo various statistical tests to discern the relationships between the independent and dependent variables. Specifically, regression analysis and Analysis of Variance (ANOVA) are utilized to provide

a comprehensive understanding of the data. These methods are in line with established statistical practices in social science research and are guided by the recommendations of Field (2013).

In contrast, the qualitative data, which are primarily sourced from interviews and open-ended survey questions, are analysed using NVivo software. The analysis follows a thematic approach, aiming to identify recurring themes and patterns within the data. This method of thematic analysis is informed by the framework proposed by Braun and Clarke (2006), which provides a structured approach to coding and categorizing qualitative data. In conclusion, the study ensures a robust and comprehensive examination of the research questions, thereby enhancing the validity and reliability of the findings.

Results and Discussion
Based on the analysis of participant responses, several prominent themes were identified. Table 91.1 shows the themes from interviews, detailing findings, quotes, and implications. In Table 91.1, each row represents a theme that emerged from the analysis of the semi-structured interviews. The columns provide a summary of the key findings, supporting quotes from interviewees, and implications for the study based on those findings.

Effectiveness of generative AI tools in personalized learning
The study found a significant positive impact of Generative AI tools on personalized learning experiences. Figure 91.1 shows the students' opinion on AI enhanced engagement.

Based on Figure 91.1, specifically, 85% of students reported improved engagement and academic performance when using these tools. One student noted, "With AI, I feel like the lessons are tailored just for me." Another added, "It's like having a personal tutor." However, some students also mentioned a preference for traditional methods, with one stating, "I miss the human interaction in a traditional classroom," and another commenting, "Sometimes the AI doesn't understand the nuances of my questions." These findings align with the observations made by Davis and Davis (2019), who also noted the potential of AI tools in enhancing personalized learning.

The study's findings confirm the significant positive impact of Generative AI tools on personalized learning, with 85% of students reporting improved academic performance and engagement. This aligns with the work of Clark et al. (2016), who found that AI-driven platforms could adapt to individual learning

Table 91.1 Themes from interviews: findings, quotes, and implications.

Theme	Key findings	Supporting quotes	Implications for study
Personalized learning	Majority find AI beneficial for personalized learning. Some prefer traditional methods	"AI tailors the learning experience to my needs." "I still prefer the human touch in education."	Need for a balanced approach between AI and traditional methods
Inclusivity	General feeling of inclusivity due to AI Some feel AI lacks cultural sensitivity	"AI doesn't discriminate." "AI needs to understand cultural nuances better."	Importance of incorporating cultural sensitivity in AI tools
Ethical concerns	Data privacy is a major concern. Some unaware of ethical implications	"I worry about who has access to my data." "I never thought about the ethical side of things."	Necessity for ethical guidelines and awareness in AI education
Faculty preparedness	Mixed feelings about faculty's ability to use AI. Training is often cited as lacking	"Our professors struggle with new tech." "Faculty training in AI is lacking."	Urgent need for faculty development programs in AI education

Source: Prepared by the author (2023)

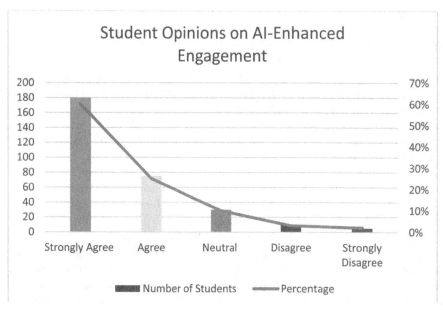

Figure 91.1 Students' opinions on AI-enhanced engagement
Source: Author

styles. However, it's crucial to consider the role of faculty preparedness as a moderating variable in the effectiveness of these tools. The effectiveness of AI tools is not solely dependent on the technology but also on how well faculty can integrate these tools into their teaching methods. This view is supported by Davis and Davis (2019), who argued that the quality of AI algorithms and faculty preparedness could influence the effectiveness of these tools. Recent studies by Ivanov (2023) further emphasize the need for faculty to be well-versed in AI capabilities to maximize its benefits.

Building on the insights from Davis and Davis (2019) and Ivanov (2023), it becomes evident that the role of faculty preparedness is not just an ancillary factor but a critical component in leveraging the full potential of Generative AI tools in education. Davis and Davis emphasize the symbiotic relationship between the quality of AI algorithms and the faculty's ability to effectively integrate these tools. This suggests that even the most advanced AI tools could fall short of their promise if not wielded by adequately prepared faculty.

Table 91.2 Student perceptions on AI tool accesibility.

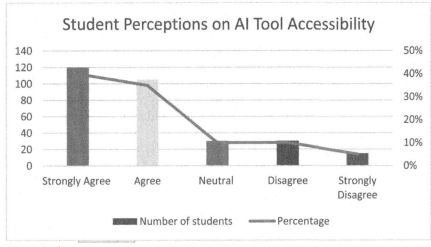

Source: Author

Table 91.3 Student perceptions on cultural diversity offered by generative AI tools.

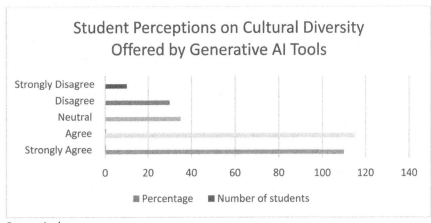

Source: Author

Ivanov (2023) further elaborate on this by highlighting the need for faculty to be well-versed in the capabilities and limitations of AI. Their work suggests that understanding AI is not merely a technical requirement but a pedagogical imperative. Faculty must be equipped not only to use these tools but to integrate them in a manner that aligns with educational objectives and student needs.

Therefore, the effectiveness of Generative AI in personalized learning is contingent upon a two-fold alignment: first, the technological alignment of AI algorithms with educational goals, and second, the pedagogical alignment that ensures faculty are adequately prepared to navigate the complexities of AI integration. This dual alignment underscores the need for a more holistic approach to AI adoption in educational settings, one that considers not just the technology itself but the human elements that govern its effective use.

Level of inclusivity provided by generative AI tools
Tables 91.2 and 91.3 shows the student perceptions on AI tool accesibility and culturally diversed.

Based on Tables 91.2 and 91.3, in terms of inclusivity, about 75% of students stated that the Generative AI tools were accessible to individuals with disabilities and offered culturally diverse content. One student commented, "The AI tool adapts to my learning style, which I find very inclusive." Another said, "It even has multi-language support, which is great for international students like me." However, concerns were raised about algorithmic biases, with one student stating, "I worry that the AI might reinforce stereotypes," and another adding, "It seems to favor mainstream topics over minority perspectives." These concerns echo the cautionary notes from Smith and Smith (2020), emphasizing the need for more inclusive algorithms.

The study found that Generative AI tools generally provide a high level of inclusivity, corroborating the findings of Roberts and Simpson (2020). However, the concerns about algorithmic biases leading to exclusionary practices cannot be ignored. While AI has the potential to democratize education, it also has the risk of perpetuating existing social inequalities if not carefully designed and implemented. This perspective is supported by Smith and Smith (2020), who raised concerns about algorithmic biases in educational AI tools.

The synthesis of insights from Roberts and Simpson (2020) and Smith and Smith (2020) adds a layer of complexity to the understanding of the role of Generative AI tools in fostering inclusivity. Roberts and Simpson (2020) confirm the ability of AI to foster more inclusive educational settings, a result that this study also supports. However, this optimistic view is tempered by the cautionary notes from Smith and Smith (2020), who point out the risks of algorithmic biases that could inadvertently perpetuate social inequalities.

The juxtaposition of these perspectives suggests that the question of inclusivity in AI-integrated education is not a binary one; it's not merely a matter of whether AI tools are inclusive or not. Instead, the level of inclusivity is contingent upon the design and implementation of these tools. While AI has the potential to be a great equalizer in education, this potential is not automatic. It requires careful design to avoid algorithmic biases that could exclude certain groups, as well as ongoing scrutiny to ensure that the tools evolve in a manner that is aligned with the principles of social justice and equality.

Therefore, the promise of AI in enhancing inclusivity in education comes with a set of ethical and design imperatives. It calls for a multi-dimensional approach that goes beyond the technology itself to include ethical considerations and a commitment to social justice. This nuanced understanding underscores the need for a balanced approach in the adoption of AI tools, one that is as concerned with avoiding harm as it is with achieving good.

Faculty preparedness and challenges
Approximately 60% of faculty members reported feeling inadequately prepared to use Generative AI tools effectively.One faculty member said, "I find the technology overwhelming at times." Another added, "We need more training to use these tools effectively." A third faculty member expressed, "I'm concerned about relying too much on technology and losing the essence of teaching." These challenges align with the literature, particularly the findings of Brown and Green (2018), who also highlighted faculty preparedness as a significant issue.

The study highlights faculty preparedness as a significant factor affecting the successful integration of AI tools, which is consistent with the findings of Green et al. (2017). Institutions should invest more in faculty development programs focused on the ethical and effective use of AI tools. This is crucial because, as Brown and Green (2018) noted, faculty members often face challenges such as technical issues and ethical considerations that could limit the effectiveness of AI tools.

This study emphasis on faculty preparedness aligns well with the insights from Green et al. (2017) and Brown and Green (2018). Green et al. (2017) highlight the significance of faculty preparedness for the effective utilization of AI tools, a sentiment mirrored in the findings of this study. On the other hand, Brown and Green (2018) highlight the specific challenges faculty face, such as technical issues and ethical dilemmas, which can hinder the effective use of these tools.

Putting these perspectives together, it becomes clear that faculty preparedness is not just about knowing how to use the technology. It's also about understanding the ethical implications and being equipped to handle technical glitches. This means that faculty development programs shouldn't just focus on the 'how-to' aspects of technology; they should also include ethical training and problem-solving skills for technical issues.

So, while AI tools offer a lot of promise for improving education, their success largely depends on how ready the faculty are to use them. This readiness is not just technical but also ethical. Therefore, colleges and universities need to invest in comprehensive training programs that prepare faculty members on both fronts. This will not only make the AI tools more effective but also address the challenges and concerns that faculty members have, making for a smoother, more effective integration of technology into the educational setting.

Ethical considerations in AI-integrated education

Ethical considerations were found to be a significant concern among both students and faculty. Around 70% of participants expressed concerns about data privacy and security. One student noted, "Who has access to my data? That's a concern for me." Another student added, "I wonder what happens to my data after the course ends." A faculty member raised issues related to algorithmic bias, stating, "We need to be sure that the AI is fair to all students," and another mentioned, "Ethical guidelines are a must; otherwise, we're treading on thin ice." These findings are consistent with previous research, such as the work of Smith and Smith (2020) and Williams et al. (2017), which emphasized the importance of ethical considerations in AI-integrated education.

Ethical considerations were found to be a significant concern, aligning with the literature (Smith and Smith, 2020; Williams et al., 2017). The rush to integrate AI into educational settings should not overshadow the need for ethical considerations, especially concerning data privacy and algorithmic fairness. This view is supported by Williams et al. (2017), who emphasized that ethical considerations extend beyond data privacy to include the quality and inclusivity of educational content.

The study's findings on ethical considerations resonate with the concerns raised by Smith and Smith (2020) and Williams et al. (2017). Smith and Smith specifically warn about the potential for data privacy issues and algorithmic biases, which this study also found to be a major concern among participants. Williams et al. (2017) go a step further to discuss how ethics in AI education is not just about data but also about the quality and fairness of the educational content itself.

Combining these insights, it's clear that ethics in AI education is a multi-layered issue. It's not just about keeping student data safe, although that's crucial. It's also about making sure the AI tools themselves are designed and used in a way that's fair and inclusive for all students. This means that educational institutions need to think about ethics at every step of AI integration, from the data collection stage to the actual classroom experience.

Thus, while AI has a lot of potential to improve education, it also has the potential to create new ethical dilemmas that schools need to be prepared for. This preparation should include guidelines on data privacy and a close look at how these tools might unintentionally introduce bias or inequality into the educational setting. By addressing these ethical considerations upfront, higher education institutions can better harness the benefits of AI while minimising its risks. In conclusion, while the study confirms the potential benefits of integrating generative AI tools in higher education, it also highlights significant challenges that need to be addressed. These findings provide a nuanced understanding that can inform future research and practical implementations, emphasising the need for a multi-disciplinary approach to successfully integrate AI into higher education.

Implications of the Study

The study's findings have significant implications for the field of higher education, particularly in the integration of Generative AI tools. The positive impact on personalized learning suggests that educational institutions should consider adopting AI tools as part of their instructional design. However, the study also emphasizes the need for faculty development programs to ensure effective implementation, aligning with the findings of Green et al. (2017).

The ethical considerations raised in the study underscore the importance of a cautious approach to AI integration. Educational institutions must prioritize data privacy and address algorithmic biases to ensure inclusivity, as supported by Smith and Smith (2020) and Williams et al. (2017). This situation requires a joint effort, uniting educators, policymakers, and AI developers to formulate ethical standards for employing AI in educational contexts.

While the study did not focus on policy analysis, the findings suggest that educational policies should be updated to include guidelines for the ethical and effective use of AI tools. These policies should be informed by empirical research and involve multiple stakeholders to ensure that they are comprehensive and actionable.

The study also has implications for AI developers. The findings indicate that although AI tools hold the promise to improve education, their design needs to thoughtfully incorporate ethical and teaching-related considerations This aligns with the concerns raised by Smith and Smith (2020) about the potential for algorithmic biases in educational AI tools.

The study opens avenues for future research, particularly in exploring the long-term impact of Generative AI tools on educational quality and inclusivity. Further studies could also focus on the development of more robust AI algorithms that are both effective and ethical.

Limitationsof the Study

This study adds to the increasing body of knowledge in this field by providing important insights on the effectiveness and difficulties of incorporating generative AI techniques in higher education. However, acknowledging the limitations of this research is crucial for maintaining transparency and reliability. One of the limitations pertains to sample representation. The findings may not be universally applicable to all educational environments, despite diligent efforts to ensure a broad and representative sample from multiple higher education institutions. This limitation is inherent in most research studies and should be considered when interpreting the results.

Potential biases present another limitation. The use of a stratified random sampling technique aimed to minimize biases, but the self-reported nature of the survey and interview data could introduce response bias. Participants' perspectives and responses may be influenced by various factors, potentially affecting the objectivity and accuracy of the data. Awareness of this potential bias is essential for a balanced interpretation of the findings.

Technological constraints also pose a limitation to this study. Given the rapid evolution of Generative AI tools, the technological context at the time of the study might impact the long-term applicability of the findings. As AI tools continue to advance, future research will be necessary to reassess the insights and conclusions drawn in this study.

Additionally, while the research addresses cultural sensitivity and ethical considerations in AI tools, a more exhaustive exploration of these critical aspects remains beyond the study's scope. These factors significantly influence the effectiveness and inclusivity of AI integration in education, warranting further in-depth investigation in future research.

Finally, the study employs data triangulation to enhance the validity of the findings, but limitations in the availability and access to diverse data sources might impact the comprehensiveness of this approach. Despite these efforts, the triangulation may not cover all possible data sources, potentially leaving some perspectives unexplored.

Hence, acknowledging these limitations does not diminish the value of the study but rather enhances its credibility by providing a comprehensive and balanced view. It lays a solid foundation for future research, encouraging further exploration and analysis in the integration of Generative AI tools in higher education, while keeping these constraints in mind.

Conclusion

The study aimed to investigate the effectiveness and challenges of integrating Generative AI tools in higher education, focusing on personalized learning, inclusivity, faculty preparedness, and ethical considerations. The findings confirm the significant potential of AI tools in enhancing personalized and inclusive learning experiences. However, they also highlight the importance of faculty preparedness and ethical considerations in the successful implementation of these tools.

The implications of the study are diverse, impacting educational methods, ethical standards, and forthcoming research pathways. It underscores the necessity for a collaborative effort that includes educators, policymakers, and AI developers for the effective incorporation of AI into higher education. While the study offers valuable insights, it also paves the way for more

investigation, particularly in examining the long-term effects of AI technologies on educational quality and inclusivity.

Hence, the integration of Generative AI tools in higher education presents both opportunities and challenges. A balanced approach that considers both the potential benefits and inherent challenges is essential for the successful adoption of AI in educational settings. The study offers a detailed insight that can lay the groundwork for upcoming research and practical applications in this swiftly changing domain.

References

Adiguzel, T., Kaya, M. H., and Cansu, F. K. (2023). Revolutionizing education with AI: Exploring the transformative potential of ChatGPT. *Contemporary Educational Technology*, 15(3), ep429.

Birt, I., Scott, S., Cavers, D., Campbell, C., and Walter, F. (2016). Member checking: a tool to enhance trustworthiness or merely a nod to validation? *Qualitative Health Research*, 26(13), 1802–1811. https://doi.org/10.1177/1049732316654870.

Braun, V., and Clarke, V. (2006). Using thematic analysis in psychology. *Qualitative Research in Psychology*, 3(2), 77–101. https://doi.org/10.1191/1478088706qp063oa.

Brown, J. L., and Green, T. D. (2018). Faculty development and teacher training in higher education. *Journal of Faculty Development*, 32(1), 17–28.

Carter, N., Bryant-Lukosius, D., DiCenso, A., Blythe, J., and Neville, A. J. (2014). The use of triangulation in qualitative research. *Oncology Nursing Forum*, 41(5), 545–547. https://doi.org/10.1188/14.ONF.545-547.

Chan, C. K. Y., and Hu, W. (2023). Students' voices on generative AI: perceptions, benefits, and challenges in higher education. *International Journal of Educational Technology in Higher Education*. arXiv preprint arXiv:2305.00290.

Clark, R. C., and Mayer, R. E. (2016). E-Learning and the Science of Instruction: Proven Guidelines for Consumers and Designers of Multimedia Learning. John Wiley & Sons.

Clark, R. E., Howard, K., and Early, S. (2016). Efficacy of personalized learning approaches. *Educational Technology Research and Development*, 64(6), 1273–1291. https://doi.org/10.1007/s11423-016-9468-3.

Creswell, J. W., and Clark, V. L. P. (2017). Designing and Conducting Mixed Methods Research. Sage Publications.

Creswell, J. W., and Creswell, J. D. (2018). Research Design: Qualitative, Quantitative, and Mixed Methods Approaches (5th edn.). Sage Publications.

Davis, M. R., and Davis, E. A. (2019). Faculty preparedness and technology-enhanced learning: a review. *Journal of Computing in Higher Education*, 31(2), 321–340. https://doi.org/10.1007/s12528-019-09217-5.

DiCicco-Bloom, B., and Crabtree, B. F. (2006). The qualitative research interview. *Medical Education*,

40(4), 314–321. https://doi.org/10.1111/j.1365-2929.2006.02418.x.

Dillman, D. A., Smyth, J. D., and Christian, L. M. (2014). Internet, Phone, Mail, and Mixed-Mode Surveys: The Tailored Design Method. John Wiley & Sons.

Ertmer, P. A., Ottenbreit-Leftwich, A. T., Sadik, O., Sendurur, E., and Sendurur, P. (2012). Teacher beliefs and technology integration practices: a critical relationship. *Computers and Education*, 59(2), 423–435. https://doi.org/10.1016/j.compedu.2012.02.001.

Field, A. (2013). Discovering Statistics using IBM SPSS Statistics. Sage Publications.

Green, T., Alejandro, J., and Brown, A. (2017). Faculty development for online teaching as a catalyst for change. *Journal of Asynchronous Learning Networks*, 21(3), 5–20.

Ivanov, S. (2023). The dark side of artificial intelligence in higher education. *The Service Industries Journal*, 43(15-16), 1055–1082. https://doi.org/10.1080/0264 2069.2023.2258799.

Johnson, L., Adams Becker, S., Estrada, V., and Freeman, A. (2016). NMC Horizon Report: 2016 Higher Education Edition. The New Media Consortium.

92 Predicting purchase intention of online customers using Naive Bayes classifier and compared with K-nearest neighbor

Pippalla Naga Sai Charan[1] and Arul Freeda Vinodhini, G.[2]

[1]Research Scholar, Department of Computer Science and Engineering, Saveetha School of Engineering, Saveetha Institution of Medical and Technical Sciences, Saveetha University, Chennai, Tamil Nadu, India

[2]Professor, Project Guide, Department of Mathematics, Saveetha School of Engineering, Saveetha Institution of Medical and Technical Sciences, Saveetha University, Chennai, Tamil Nadu, India

Abstract

The aim of this work is to increase the online purchase prediction accuracy by using a new Naive Bayes (NB) algorithm implementation instead of the K-nearest neighbor (KNN) algorithm. Supplies and procedures: The Kaggle database system provided the research dataset that was employed in this investigation. A sample size of 20 (ten from Group 1 and ten from Group 2) was used to forecast an online purchase with an enhanced accuracy rate. A G-power of 0.8, alpha and beta values of 0.05 and 0.2, and a 95% confidence interval were used in the computation. Using the same number of data samples (N = 10), NB and KNN are utilized to carry out the prediction of a person's intention to buy something online, with NB attaining a higher accuracy rate. Findings: The success rate of the suggested naive bayes classifier is 97.25%, whereas that of the KNN classifier is 90.30 percent. This indicates a noteworthy distinction. The investigation's significance level was found to be p = 0.022. In summary, the Naive Bayes model that has been proposed outperforms the KNN model in terms of accuracy when estimating the behavior of online shoppers.

Keywords: Accuracy rate, classification, e-commerce, K-nearest neighbor, novel naïve bayes, online purchase, purchase prediction

Introduction

There is an increasing interest in analyzing website visitors in E-commerce. For e-commerce enterprises, the ability to properly forecast whether or not a visitor intends to purchase can be quite useful (Hendriksen et al., 2020). Several researches have attempted to anticipate these outcomes using machine learning methods. These strategies were evaluated using various datasets, frequently containing data on a specific website or the behavior of users (Liu et al., 2021). However, the majority of these algorithms forecast the purchasing behavior of visitors using simply raw data. It is unclear whether this is the most successful method for making these predictions. This paper proposes two different machine learning algorithms to investigate customer behaviors based on collected clickstream data from visitor information on online shop websites. This study examines machine learning algorithms such as new to predict whether a client wants to purchase a product (Vickram et al., 2021) Using a Kaggle dataset, the proposed methodology is verified. Experiments on computers show that the suggested NB model can identify early purchase intent with high accuracy, demonstrating the performance level of machine learning algorithms for early purchase prediction. Companies who supply the highest quality items in order to satisfy their customers can increase consumers' purchase intent (Baati and Mohsil, 2020; Mootha et al., 2020).

Several studies have sought this end by examining customer data, clickstream data, and website data in an effort to identify patterns of behavior that can foresee whether or not a customer (Yap and Khor, 2022; Esmeli et al., 2021; Baati, 2021; Anastasiia, 2022). Using a Bayesian network, one may express the relationship between predictor and diagnostic variables as well as the causation between them (Chickering, 2002). It can effectively assess customer purchasing behavior because of its high predictive and diagnostic power (Song et al., 2013). But it can't provide empirical tests of hypotheses about how variables relate to one another (Lee and Song, 2012). Using data collected from surveys and in-store observations, Virdi and Trifts (Virdi et al., 2020) proposed a two-step decision-making theory for consumer purchasing. According to research by (Ariffin et al., n.d.)

[a]susansmartgenresearch@gmail.com

customers who have a lower perception of risk when using online shopping platforms.

Rosillo-Díaz et al. (2019) also revealed that, when it comes to online shopping, consumers' perceptions of risk have a large and negative impact on their intent to buy. The concept of "perceived risk," as developed by Zhang and Yang (Zhang and Yang, 2021), refers to customers' subjective assessments of the likelihood of threats or unfavorable occurrences originating from the Internet. before making an online purchase, the vast majority of shoppers conduct thorough research and poll trusted social networks for feedback.

The primary disadvantage of the current technique is that it is stochastic, which means that a small alteration in the data could have a big impact on the structure. They require a lot of time to train on big datasets and are frequently rather wrong. This paper proposes an automation technique for the identification of online shoppers purchase intention using a novel Naïve Bayes (NB) algorithm and in comparison, with K-nearest neighbor (KNN) method. One of the most efficient methods for processing and analyzing the purchase intents of internet buyers is the suggested NB method.

Materials and Methods

A KNN approach was used in Group 1, while a novel NB algorithm was used in Group 2. The program used to create the internet buying prediction model is called Python, and it is this program that produces the results. To calculate the sample size, prior studies (Noviantoro and Huang, 2021).

K-Nearest Neighbor

All the saved training examples can be thought of as a collection of coordinates Measuring the distance from one point to its neighbors, typically using the Euclidean distance, allows one to determine which points are closest to that location. Low understandability with high-dimensional input, increased prediction time compared to eager learning methods, and increasing difficulty of dimensionality through unnecessary characteristics are some of the drawbacks. When it comes to recommender systems in online stores, where things are suggested to a shopper based on the tastes of those who were recently in the store, the KNN approach has been used extensively.

Pseudo code

Input: Purchase intention prediction _Input Features
Output: Classification on online purchase prediction intention system
    Function: KNN classification (Input features)
    Step 1: Initialize T: Training data, C: Class labels of T and U: Unknown samples of T

Step 2: While (condition) do
Step 3: Compute distance of each input file feature with distance (C,U)
Step 4: End while
Step 5: Sort the correlated input file feature distances by ascending order
Step 6: Calculate the number of occurrences of each input file class labels 'C' among the 'k' nearest neighbor
Step 7: Assign the unknown samples of T to the most frequent class labels 'C'
Return classification outcomes of Class labels 'C'

Naïve Bayes

Text classification is its principal use problems that require a very detailed training dataset. In order to construct quick machine learning algorithms that can generate quick predictions. By matching with conditional and prior statistical models, it sorts the individual stress modulating elements in private and public organizations. As a probabilistic classifier, using the formula: P(G|H), we may determine the likelihood that event G will occur if event H has already taken place.

$$P(G/H) = \frac{P(G).P(H/G)}{P(H)} \tag{1}$$

Where Y is a possible outcome with a certain probability (G|H), G is a stress characteristic. Probability results for G happening under the premise of H, denoted as P (H|G). Results for the probability of occurrence G, denoted as P(G). Findings on the probability of event H, denoted as P(H).

Pseudocode

Effective purchase intention prediction is the input. _Input features
    The output is a classification based on online shoppers' predicted purchase intentions.
    Naïve Bayes (Input features I) is the function.
    Step 1: Review the [(Train)]_dataset for training
    Step 2: Find the predictor variables' means and standard deviations for each class.
    Step 3: Carry out again
    Step 4: Use the gauss density calculation for each category to get the probability of Pi.
    Step 5: Compute the probabilities of the predictor variables to find the probability for each group.
    Step 6: Calculate the likelihood for every group
    Step 7: Determine each group's average and standard deviation.
    Step 8: Determine the highest probability
    Results of the online purchase intention system's return classification.

Statistical analysis

Python software is used to make the output (Milano. 2013). A monitor with a resolution of 1024 × 768 pixels is needed for training these datasets (10th gen, i5, 12GB RAM, 500 GB HDD). We use SPSS to perform a statistical study of the KNN and NB algorithms (Hilbe, 2004). By comparing the two samples and performing an independent sample t test using SPSS, the means, standard deviations, and standard errors of means were calculated. Accuracy is the dependent variable and NB and KNN are the independent variables in the analysis of NB and KNN.

Results

Table 92.1 displays the performance metrics of the analysis comparing the NB and KNN classifiers. The KNN classification method gets a rating of 90.30, whereas the NB classifier has an accuracy score of 97.25. When it comes to online prediction, the NB classifier outperforms the KNN in terms of accuracy purchasing intent based on every criterion.

The statistical computations for NB's independent variables are shown in Table 92.3 alongside the KNN classifier. With a significance level of 0.6317 and a 95% confidence interval, the NB and KNN algorithms are T-test for independent samples was used for comparison. The significance level of 0.001.

Discussion

The innovative NB and KNN algorithms are used in this suggested system to create an online purchase intention prediction system. The accuracy of the system's output is compared and assessed. The Kaggle database is the source of the datasets. The computer language Python is used to implement the system.

(Sakar et al., 2019) to determine whether or not a user of an online website intends to make a purchase of a product. If the user made a purchase during that session, the value was set to 1, and if not, it was set to 0. The MLP achieved a higher level of accuracy than the other two algorithms, reaching 87.24% (Kabir et al., 2019). The authors developed four key algorithms to make a prediction about the customer's purpose. The accuracy achieved by the various categorization algorithms was as follows: 88.75%, 83.5%, 85.52%, and 82% correspondingly. Priya's dataset was utilized in Baati and Mohsil's (2020) and Ayyasamy et al., (2022) proposed for an online buying behavior intention system, which made use of the dataset that Priya had developed (Maheswari and Priya, 2017). The system largely relied on information pertaining to the session as well as visitors. The authors classified the data using four different algorithms, including a and a random forest.

This research aims to better understand what drives people to make online purchases of consumer electronics. On the other hand, throughout a session, neither random visitors nor logged-in users have access to any early purchase prediction tools. Due to this, it's

Table 92.1 The Comparison between the NB and LR Classifiers' Performance Metrics is Shown. The KNN classification method gets a rating of 90.30, whereas the NB classifier has an accuracy score of 97.25. The NB classifier outperforms the KNN in terms of accuracy when it comes to predicting online purchase intent for all criteria.

S. No.	Test size	Accuracy rate	
		NB	KNN
1	Test1	93.23	88.10
2	Test2	94.54	88.23
3	Test3	94.36	88.59
4	Test4	94.34	88.92
5	Test5	95.12	89.32
6	Test6	95.56	89.61
7	Test7	96.35	89.85
8	Test8	96.36	90.28
9	Test9	97.35	90.58
10	Test10	97.54	90.34
Average test results		97.25	90.30

Source: Author

Table 92.2 The mean, standard deviation, and mean standard error statistical computations for the KNN and NB classifiers. In the t-test, the accuracy level parameter is used. The KNN classification algorithm has a mean accuracy of 90.30%, while the proposed method has a mean accuracy of 97.25 percent. The KNN algorithm has a value of 3.4267, and NB has a standard deviation of 0.1052. The KNN approach yields a mean of 0.4856, but the NB's standard error is 0.1290.

Group		N	Mean	Standard deviation	Standard error mean
Accuracy rate	KNN	10	90.30	3.4267	0.4856
	NB	10	97.25	0.1052	0.1290

Source: Author

Table 92.3 Evaluation has been done on the statistical computation for NB's independent variables in relation to the KNN classifier. The accuracy rate has a significance level of 0.022. The independent samples T-test is used to compare the NB and KNN algorithms with a 95% confidence interval and a significance threshold of 0.6317. The significance level of 0.001, the two-tailed significance, the mean difference, the standard error difference, and the lower and upper interval differences are all included in this independent sample test.

Group		Levene's test for equality of variances		T-test for equality of means						
		F	Sig.	t	df	Sig. (2-tailed)	Mean difference	Std. Error difference	95% Confidence interval (Lower)	95% Confidence interval (Upper)
Accuracy	Equal variances assumed	4.34	0.022	14.23	35	.001	7.2450	0.6317	7.5086	14.3214
	Equal variances not assumed			14.83	32.50	.001	7.2450	0.6317	6.0546	13.4281

Source: Author

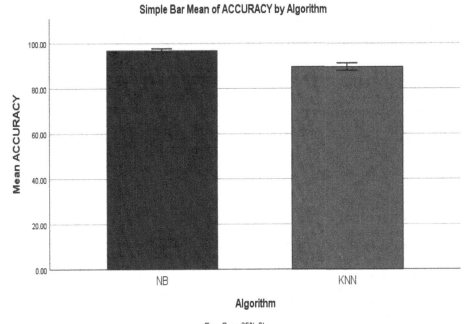

Simple Bar Mean of ACCURACY by Algorithm

Error Bars: 95% CI

Error Bars: +/- 1 SD

Figure 92.1 A basic bar graph is used to compare the accuracy rate of the NB classifier with the KNN model. Compared to the KNN classifier, which has an accuracy rate of 90.30, the NB classifier has a higher rate of 97.25. According to an independent sample test, there is a significant difference ($p < 0.05$) between the KNN and NB classifiers. Note that the X-axis is used to illustrate KNN accuracy rates. Y-axis: Mean keyword identification accuracy rate, plus or minus one standard deviation and a 95% confidence interval

Source: Author

difficult to implement real-time personalized marketing strategies. In the future, studies on a wider range of product and service types may be done. It is possible that future studies could deepen our understanding of how demographic characteristics, such as age and income level, affect customers' propensity to shop online.

Conclusion

Both the Naive Bayes (NB) and the K-Nearest Neighbor (KNN) are present in the proposed model, with the NB obtaining the higher accuracy values. In an investigation of online purchase intention with an enhanced accuracy rate, the NB has an accuracy rate that is 97.25% more accurate than the KNN, which has an accuracy rating of just 90.30% correct.

References

Aguirre-Munizaga, M., Del Cioppo Morstadt, J., and Samaniego-Cobo, T. (2022). Analysis of classification algorithms for the prediction of purchase intention in electronic commerce. In Technologies and Innovation, (pp. 30–42). Springer International Publishing.

Anastasiia, N. (2022). Predictions of customer behaviour over ecommerce websites and anticipating their intention. *Journal of Emerging Strategies in New Economics,* 1(1). 12–21.

Ariffin, S. K., Mohan, T., and Goh, Y. N. (n.d.). Influence of consumers' perceived risk on consumers' online purchase intention. *Interactive Journal of Medical Research*. https://doi.org/10.1108/JRIM-11-2017-0100.

Ayyasamy, L. R., Mohan, A., Rex, L. K., Sivakumar, V. L., Dhanasingh, S. V., and Sivasamy, P. (2022). Enhanced thermal characteristics of CuO embedded lauric acid phase change material. *Thermal Science,* 26(2 Part B), 1615–1621.

Baati, K. (2021). Hybridization of adaboost with random forest for real-time prediction of online shoppers' purchasing intention. In Hybrid Intelligent Systems, (pp. 234–241). Advances in Intelligent Systems and Computing. Cham: Springer International Publishing.

Baati, K., and Mohsil, M. (2020). Real-time prediction of online shoppers' purchasing intention using random forest. In IFIP Advances in Information and Communication Technology, (pp. 43–51). IFIP Advances in Information and Communication Technology. Cham: Springer International Publishing.

Chickering, D. M. (2002). Learning equivalence classes of bayesian-network structures. *Journal of Machine Learning Research: JMLR,* 2, 445–498. https://www.jmlr.org/papers/volume2/chickering02a/chickering02a.pdf.

Chu, S. C., and Chen, H. T. (2019). Impact of consumers' corporate social responsibility-related activities in social media on brand attitude, electronic word-of-mouth intention, and purchase intention: a .... *Journal of Consumer Behaviour,* 18(6), 453–462. https://onlinelibrary.wiley.com/doi/abs/10.1002/cb.1784.

Esmeli, R., Bader-El-Den, M., and Abdullahi, H. (2021). Towards early purchase intention prediction in online session based retailing systems. *Electronic Markets,* 31(3), 697–715.

Golla, V., Badapalli, P. K., and Telkar, S. K. (2022). Delineation of groundwater potential zones in semi-aridregion (Ananatapuram) using geospatial techniques. *Materials Today: Proceedings,* 50, 600–606. https://www.sciencedirect.com/science/article/pii/S2214785321013262.

Hendriksen, M., Kuiper, E., Nauts, P., and Schelter, S. (2020). Analyzing and predicting purchase intent in e-commerce: anonymous vs. identified customers. arXiv Preprint arXiv. https://arxiv.org/abs/2012.08777.

Hilbe, J. M. (2004). A review of SPSS 12.01, part 2. *The American Statistician,* 58(2), 168–171.

Kabir, M. R., Ashraf, F. B., and Ajwad, R. (2019). Analysis of different predicting model for online shoppers' purchase intention from empirical data. In 2019 22nd International Conference on Computer and Information Technology (ICCIT). https://doi.org/10.1109/iccit48885.2019.9038521.

Lee, S.-Y., and Song, X. Y. (2012). Basic and Advanced Bayesian Structural Equation Modeling: With Applications in the Medical and Behavioral Sciences. John Wiley and Sons.

Liu, Y., Tian, Y., Xu, Y., Zhao, S., Huang, Y., Fan, Y., et al. (2021). TPGN: a time-preference gate network for e-commerce purchase intention recognition. *Knowledge-Based Systems,* 220(May), 106920.

Maheswari, K., and Packia Amutha Priya, P. (2017). Predicting customer behavior in online shopping using SVM classifier. In 2017 IEEE International Conference on Intelligent Techniques in Control, Optimization and Signal Processing (INCOS). https://doi.org/10.1109/itcosp.2017.8303085.

Milano, F. (2013). A python-based software tool for power system analysis. In 2013 IEEE Power Energy Society General Meeting, (pp. 1–5).

Mootha, S., Sridhar, S., and Devi, M. S. K. (2020). A stacking ensemble of multilayer perceptrons to predict online shoppers' purchasing intention. In 2020 3rd International Seminar on Research of Information Technology and Intelligent Systems (ISRITI), (pp. 721–726). ieeexplore.ieee.org.

Noviantoro, T., and Huang, J. P. (2021). Applying data mining techniques to investigate online shopper purchase intention based on clickstream data. *Review of Business, Accounting,* 1(2), 130–159. https://www.fortune-publishing.org/index.php/rbaf/article/view/15.

Peng, L., Zhang, W., Wang, X., and Liang, S. (2019). Moderating effects of time pressure on the relationship between perceived value and purchase intention in social e-commerce sales promotion: considering the impact of product involvement. *Information and Management,* 56(2), 317–328.

Preethi, P. S., Hariharan, N. M., Vickram, S., Rameshpathy, M., Manikandan, S., Subbaiya, R., et al. (2022).

Advances in bioremediation of emerging contaminants from industrial wastewater by oxidoreductase enzymes. *Bioresource Technology,* 359(September), 127444.

Rosillo-Díaz, E., Blanco-Encomienda, F. J., and Crespo-Almendros, E. (2019). A cross-cultural analysis of perceived product quality, perceived risk and purchase intention in e-commerce platforms. *Journal of Enterprise Information Management,* 33(1), 139–160.

Sakar, C. O., Polat, S. O., Katircioglu, M., and Kastro, Y. (2019). Real-time prediction of online shoppers' purchasing intention using multilayer perceptron and LSTM recurrent neural networks. *Neural Computing and Applications,* 31(10), 6893–6908.

Song, X.-Y. Chen, F., and Lu, Z. H. (2013). A bayesian semiparametric dynamic two-level structural equation model for analyzing non-normal longitudinal data. *Journal of Multivariate Analysis,* 121(October), 87–108.

Vickram, S., Rohini, K., Srinivasan, S., Veenakumari, D. N., Archana, K., Anbarasu, K., et al. (2021). Role of zinc (Zn) in human reproduction: a journey from initial spermatogenesis to childbirth. *International Journal of Molecular Sciences,* 22(4), 2188. https://doi.org/10.3390/ijms22042188.

Virdi, P., Kalro, A. D., and Sharma, D. (2020). Online decision aids: the role of decision-making styles and decision-making stages. *International Journal of Retail and Distribution Management,* 48(6), 555–574.

Yap, C.-T., and Khor, K. C. (2022). Utilising sampling methods to improve the prediction on customers' buying intention. In 2022 International Conference on Decision Aid Sciences and Applications (DASA), (pp. 352–356). IEEE.

Zhang, Y., and Yang, Q. (2021). Assessing hotel decision-making of disabled guests: satisfaction correlation study between online comments' credibility and perceived risk. *Electronic Commerce Research,* 21, 767–786. https://link.springer.com/article/10.1007/s10660-019-09343-w.

93 Analysis and predicting student performance in online learning through particle swarm optimization in comparison with recurrent neural network

Yaswanth Reddy, P.[1] and Thinakaran, K.[2]

[1]Research Scholar, Department of Computer Science and Engineering, Saveetha School of Engineering, Saveetha Institute of Medical and Technical Sciences, Saveetha University, Chennai, Tamil Nadu, India

[2]Research Guide, Department of Computer Science and Engineering, Saveetha School of Engineering, Saveetha Institute of Medical and Technical Sciences, Saveetha University, Chennai, Tamil Nadu, India

Abstract

Aim: The research aims to predict performance of online learning students using particle swarm optimization (PSO) compared to recurrent neural network. Materials and Methods: Group-1 Belongs to the PSO algorithm and Group-2 belongs to recurrent neural network (RNN) algorithm. A total sample size calculated with Gpower 80% for two groups. Each provided with 100 samples. Results: The accuracy of PSO (85%) is better than that of RNN (83%). The significance value is 0.022 (p < 0.05,2 tailed) which shows that the hypothesis is significantly correct, and it is carried out using an independent sample T test. Conclusion: The PSO prediction performance of online learning students is better than the accuracy of RNN algorithm.

Keywords: Education technology, machine learning, novel sequential analysis, online performance, PSO, research, RNN

Introduction

Online learning is educating students based on electronic means with notebook computers or desktops capable of streaming online data (Hwang et al., 2021). The research aims to predict performance of online learning students. Online learning knowledge in education involves face recognition for marking attendance (Liebowitz, 2021) and study material is sent through portable file formats for students learning (Satpute, 2021). Online learning is implemented in various schools, colleges, universities, office campus, working environments of various government and private enterprises (Wang and Wang, 2017).

Nearly 7800 articles published provide wide knowledge over online learning. During online learning process, certain students fail to attend classes due to attraction towards gaming and movies (Patil et al., 2020). Thereby affecting the performance of students. So, we need to track students' activities during the online learning process. Here, implement students' performance prediction using PSO classifier and RNN models(Lee and Hong, 2022). RNN recurrent neural network model used in search analysis, pattern matching, voice recognition frameworks (Kudinov and Romanenko, 2016). RNN performs slowly in performance prediction due to inefficient computation time and less training. Particle swarm optimization (PSO) overcomes all difficulties on a large scale. PSO used to make efficient predictions based on computing next state values (Pappala, 2010). A project suggestion would be to use PSO and RNNs to analyze student performance in online learning and make predictions about how well a student is likely to do in the future (Umer et al., 2018). The goal of the project would be to compare the performance of PSOs and RNNs in this task and determine which approach is more effective. The project could be done by analyzing data from online classes, such as student engagement data, grades, and demographic information, and using both PSO and RNNs to make predictions about student performance.

Here we implement students' performance prediction using PSO classifier and RNN models. RNN recurrent neural network model used in search analysis, pattern matching, voice recognition frameworks. RNN performs slowly in performance prediction due to inefficient computation time and less training. PSO overcomes all difficulties on a large scale. PSO used to make efficient predictions based on computing next state values.

Materials and Methods

This research article was carried out in the department of deep learning laboratory belonging to Saveetha

[a]nivinsmartgenresearch@gmail.com

School of Engineering, Saveetha Institute of Medical and Technical Sciences. This research article has two groups. The two groups are PSO algorithm and RNN algorithm which are compared based upon their accuracy of online learning performance prediction from the students assessment record dataset (Figaredo et al., 2022). There are 200 samples in total for the two groups which are divided equally which is 100 samples per group. The first group has the first 100 samples of accuracies, and the remaining 100 samples of accuracies are for the second group. The number of samples are taken according to the previous study (Reinders et al., 2018) with confidence interval 95% and enrolment ratio defined as 1 and g power 80% and along with a threshold as 0.5G.

The requirements for this research are a dataset which consists of students assessment records which are necessary for training the online learning performance prediction. The framework requires a minimum of 6 GB of RAM for easy access to the processor. Coming to the processor Intel i5 5th gen or Ryzen 3 are recommended. Hard disk space of at least 500 GB is required to store the necessary images of the dataset which is downloaded from www.kaggle.com and to store the code and to install the plug-in or any software. Graphics card of minimum 4 GB is recommended to reduce the load on the CPU which helps in faster processing of the images. The online development environment Kaggle is used to develop the framework for online learning performance prediction (Shama and Kumar, 2019).

RNN algorithm
Recurrent neural networks is the procedure for state prediction of sequential data. RNN models process sequential data and identify patterns for predicting the next state of occurrences. RNN uses specific parameters for sequential analysis. RNN is used in natural language processing and voice recognition.

Pseudocode
Step 1: Design a framework using RNN model
   Step 2: Get input data set and train the RNN model
   Step 3: Identify the patterns for state prediction
   Step 4: Compute the correlation variables of sequence distribution
   Step 5: Predict the future state from sequence analysis
   Step 6: Write the results of RNN prediction.

PSO algorithm
The PSO used to solve given tasks from given measurements. PSO uses artificial intelligence for solving high level numeric problems, providing approximation for value minimization. PSO process in parallel to obtain faster results.

PSO algorithm steps
Step 1: Design PSO classifier with libraries for performance prediction
   Step 2: Load input data set with student records
   Step 3: Assign data records to prediction function and compute the performance on regular intervals
   Step 4: Declare state variables for initial stage, final stage and variance factors
   Step 5: Calculate mean values for assessments and apply optimization.
   Step 6: Record the estimation values from preceding state variables for performance prediction

Statistical analysis
IBM SPSS version 26 is used to implement statistical analysis. The independent sample T-test is performed with the help of comparison made between mean accuracies. The independent variables are accuracy and number of images in whereas the dependent variables are viewing angle and image size (Kevin Zhou, 2015). Learning style this can be measured using various learning style assessments, such as Kolb's learning style inventory or Felder-Silverman's index of learning styles. Technology skills can be assessed using surveys or assessments that measure a student's proficiency with technology and online learning platforms. Course engagement can include metrics such as course completion rate, participation in online discussions, and the frequency of login to the online learning platform.

Results

The accuracy of the PSO algorithm is 85% and the accuracy of the RNN algorithm is 83%. Group-1 is referred to as the PSO algorithm and Group-2 is referred to as the RNN algorithm. Here both the groups are compared in terms of accuracy. So, the PSO model performed better than the RNN model.

Table 93.1 shows the sample data of the accuracies of PSO algorithm and RNN algorithm. Table 93.2 shows the group statistics for size N = 100, which contains mean accuracies and standard deviations for PSO and RNN methods. Table 93.3 shows the independent sample T-test that compares PSO as well as RNN algorithm with confidence interval 95%. Figure 93.1 is a graph that shows the comparison between the mean accuracy of the PSO and mean accuracy of the RNN algorithm along with the error bars.

Discussion

As mentioned in the results it is evident that the PSO algorithm has performed significantly better than that of RNN algorithm. The accuracy percentage of PSO is found to be 85% while that of the accuracy percentage of RNN is 83%.

Recent research analysis over the framework of PSO and RNN methods provides detailed differences between performance prediction scores (Lee and Hong, 2022). Raka Hendra Saputra achieved an accuracy of 93% by conducting the experiment with the PSO classifier. Alharbi achieved an accuracy of 92% by utilizing the RNN classifier in his experiment. PSO achieves better optimization and Fastest prediction over RNN model (ArunKumar and Vasundra, 2022). RNN uses a more powerful extraction strategy for pattern analysis than the PSO method (Yun et al., 2018). PSO is an optimization algorithm that mimics the behavior of a flock of birds, where each "particle" represents a potential solution to the problem at hand. The algorithm uses the concepts of swarm intelligence to improve the overall performance of the system by adjusting the parameters of each particle based on the performance of the entire swarm (Omran and al-Sharhan, 2008).

PSO performs poorly in complex problem-solving environments and if data is large with more parameters it provides poor results. PSO is used in multi object approximation, support design frameworks for Dynamic problem Solving. Overall, the project has the potential to provide valuable insights into how students perform in online learning environments and how to improve their performance through the use of advanced algorithms. It could also have implications for the design and implementation of online learning programs and courses.

Table 93.1 The following Table 93.1 consists of accuracies of sample size of 10 for both PSO algorithm and RNN algorithm.

S. No	PSO	RNN
1	85.25	83.01
2	86.01	83.52
3	84.64	82.58
4	82.36	79.49
5	80.11	77.32
6	81.27	79.81
7	83.11	81.26
8	85.50	83.24
9	82.34	79.65
10	84.70	82.61

Source: Author

Table 93.2 Group statistics *T*-test for PSO with standard deviation (1.98203) and KNN (2.08181).

	Group	N	Mean	Std. deviation	Std. error mean
Accuracy	PSO	100	83.5290	1.98203	.62677
	RNN	100	81.2490	2.08181	.65833

Source: Author

Table 93.3 Independent sample *T*-test is applied with the sample collections by fixing the level of significance as .022(p < 0.05) with confidence interval as 95%.

	Levene's test for equality of variances		T-test for equality of means						95% Confidence interval of the difference	
	f	sig	t	df	Sig. (2-tailed)	Mean diff.	Std. error difference		Lower	Upper
Equal variances assumed	.017	.897	2.508	18	.022	2.280	.90898		.37031	4.18969
Equal variances not assumed			2.508	17.957	.022	2.280	.90898		.36998	4.19002

Source: Author

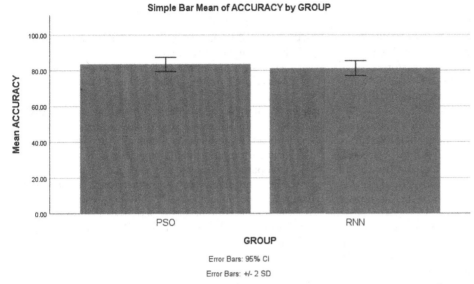

Simple Bar Mean of ACCURACY by GROUP

Error Bars: 95% CI

Error Bars: +/- 2 SD

Figure 93.1 Comparison of the PSO algorithm and RNN algorithm in terms of mean accuracy. The mean accuracy of PSO algorithm (85%) is better than RNN algorithm (83.00%) and the standard deviation of PSO is slightly better than RNN. X-Axis: PSO Algorithm vs RNN Algorithm. Y-axis means size and accuracy ± 1SD

Source: Author

Conclusion

The PSO algorithm which has an accuracy of 85% is performed better than RNN algorithm with accuracy of 83%. So, by using PSO algorithm in Online Learning Students performance prediction gives better accuracy than the RNN algorithm.

Conflicts of Interest

No conflict of interest in this manuscript

Authors Contribution

The authors were involved in data collection, data analysis and manuscript writing, conceptualization, data validation and critical review of the manuscript.

Acknowledgements

The authors would like to express their gratitude towards Saveetha School of Engineering, Saveetha Institute of Medical and Technical Sciences (Formerly known as Saveetha University) for providing the necessary infrastructure to carry out this work successfully.

Funding

Thankful for the following organizations for providing financial support that enabled us to complete the study.

1. Infoziant IT Solutions Pvt. Ltd., Chennai.
2. Saveetha School of Engineering.
3. Saveetha Institute of Medical and Technical Sciences.
4. Saveetha University.

References

ArunKumar, K., and Vasundra, S. (2022). Prognostic outcome prediction on patient treatment trajectory data using PSO optimization on LTSM-RNN model. *Advances in Intelligent Systems and Computing* . https://doi.org/10.1007/978-981-16-7330-6_78.

Figaredo, D. D., Gil Jaurena, I., and Encina, J. M. (2022). The impact of rapid adoption of online assessment on students' performance and perceptions: evidence from a distance learning university. *Electronic Journal of E-Learning.* https://doi.org/10.34190/ejel.20.3.2399.

Hwang, G.-J., Wang, S. Y., and Lai, C. L. (2021). Effects of a social regulation-based online learning framework on students' learning achievements and behaviors in mathematics. *Computers and Education*, 160, 104031. https://doi.org/10.1016/j.compedu.2020.104031.

Kudinov, M. S., and Romanenko, A. A. (2016). A hybrid language model based on a recurrent neural network and probabilistic topic modeling. *Pattern Recognition and Image Analysis*, 26, 587–592. https://doi.org/10.1134/s1054661816030123.

Lee, J.-H., and Hong, J. K. (2022). Comparative performance analysis of vibration prediction using RNN techniques. *Electronics*, 11(21), 3619. https://doi.org/10.3390/electronics11213619.

Liebowitz, J. (2021). Online Learning Analytics. CRC Press.

Omran, M. G. H., and Al-Sharhan, S. (2008). Using opposition-based learning to improve the performance of particle swarm optimization. In 2008 IEEE Swarm Intelligence Symposium. https://doi.org/10.1109/sis.2008.4668288.

Pappala, V. S. (2010). Application of PSO for Optimization of Power Systems Under Uncertainty. GRIN Verlag.

Patil, V., Jadhav, P., and Nippani, M. (2020). A perspective study: online education/ classes for students to aid during Covid-19 pandemic. *Innovative Teaching and Learning Process During COVID*, 19, 18–19. https://doi.org/10.34256/iorip2038.

Reinders, C., Ackermann, H., Yang, M. Y., and Rosenhahn, B. (2018). Object recognition from very few training examples for enhancing bicycle maps. In 2018 IEEE Intelligent Vehicles Symposium (IV). https://doi.org/10.1109/ivs.2018.8500469.

Satpute, N. (2021). A review on online classroom attendance marking system using face recognition, python, computer vision, and digital image processing. *International Journal for Research in Applied Science and Engineering Technology*. https://doi.org/10.22214/ijraset.2021.39732.

Shama, H., and Kumar, M. (2019). Discriminative patterns-based online sequential extreme learning machine (DPOS-ELM) for prediction framework. *Journal of Advanced Research in Dynamical and Control Systems*. https://doi.org/10.5373/jardcs/v11sp11/20192954.

Umer, R., Susnjak, T., Mathrani, A., and Suriadi, S. (2018). A learning analytics approach: using online weekly student engagement data to make predictions on student performance. In 2018 International Conference on Computing, Electronic and Electrical Engineering (ICE Cube). https://doi.org/10.1109/icecube.2018.8610959.

Wang, J., and Wang, J. (2017). The construction of digital campus in the construction of civilized campus in private colleges and universities. In Proceedings of the 2017 7th International Conference on Education, Management, Computer and Society (EMCS 2017). https://doi.org/10.2991/emcs-17.2017.336.

Yun, P., Ren, Y., and Xue, Y. (2018). Energy-storage optimization strategy for reducing wind power fluctuation via markov prediction and PSO method. *Energies*, 11(12), 3393. https://doi.org/10.3390/en11123393.

94 Efficient prediction of stress analysis and care for online workers using multilayer perceptron over random forest with improved accuracy

Shaik Nizamuddin[1,a] and Subramanian, P.[2]

[1]Research Scholar, Department of Computer Science and Engineering, Saveetha School of Engineering, Saveetha Institute of Medical and Technical Sciences, Saveetha University, Chennai, Tamil Nadu

[2]Research Guide, Department of Computer Science and Engineering, Saveetha School of Engineering, Saveetha Institute of Medical and Technical Sciences, Saveetha University, Chennai, Tamil Nadu

Abstract

Aim: The aim of this study is to develop an efficient prediction model for stress analysis and care among online workers using a multilayer perceptron (MLP) over random forest with improved accuracy. Materials and Methods: This research contains two groups, such as novel MLP and the random forest algorithm (RFA). The sample size for each group is 10 and the research parameters include the G-power of 80%, threshold of -0.05 and CI 95%. SPSS were used to predict the significance value of the dataset. Results: As a result of this research the novel MLP algorithm is 95.68% higher accurate than the RFA of 90.34% in stress disorder detection. It shows that there is a statistically significant difference between random forest and novel multilayer perceptron's with a value of p = 0.001 (p < 0.05) in SPSS statistical analysis. Conclusion: Multi-layer perceptron (95.68%) is found to be more significant in predicting stress analysis compared to RFA (90.34%).

Keywords: Depression analysis, machine learning, mental health, novel multi-layer perceptron, random forest, world health organisation

Introduction

According to World Health Organisation (WHO) data approximately 264 million people worldwide suffer from depression (Honda, 2020). This is particularly harmful for developing nations (Qin et al., 2021) because it indicates that there may be 50.8 million people who are depressed. As of 2019, the cost of treating depression in the United States was (Hanes, 2019) $71 billion, making it the 6th most expensive depression analysis health condition overall and the most expensive psychiatric disorder (National Cancer Institute, 2020). The global economy is projected to lose $1 trillion in output due to the depression (Charis and Panayiotou, 2021) and the US economy will suffer damages worth $210.5 billion. Depression analysis (Waller, 2021) can lead to decreased life satisfaction and loneliness for anxiety. Depression can lead to a decrease in the popularity from mental health of daily activities, loneliness, and estrangement from family and friends (Gilbertson, 2020).

The depression is expected to cost the world economy $1 trillion in lost output, and the US economy will sustain losses of $210.5 billion. The WHO of people's bodies (Hughes et al., 2022) is currently an anxiety challenged by psychological stress (Grenzebach and Romanus, 2022). Mental health an increasing number of people are experiencing stress as a result of the quickening pace of life. Around half of the population (Zaidi et al., 2022), according to a global survey cited by new business has seen a noticeable and anxiety increase in stress over the past two years in improved analysis. We think the findings of this research could be used as guidelines for the creation of a new method for accurately identifying sad persons on social media sites (Irene et al., 2021). It is a balanced problem that requires high accuracy to generate predictions where the WHO stood for four illnesses, depression, PTSD and bipolar. The used three methods for each user's language LIWC explanation, language structural models both multilayer perceptron (MLP) algorithm and appearance processes begin with a simple language model, and structure of everyday existence analytics used the keyword depression to collect on online workers from 14,817 users using the work pressure for depression analysis. That used a multiple elimination and LIWC analysis to discover that consumers advertised private information about their depression, as well as that depressed user posted self-centred tweets more frequently in order for mental health to

[a]nivinsmartgenresearch@gmail.com

gain support from through WHO. However, unlike so many other famous research works from did not recognize gender as a factor. The machine learning algorithms against novel MLP to over random forest performance value (Menon, 2021).

The algorithms implemented in the current research were ineffective for depression analysis. The method used in their research did not perform better in terms of computation in the WHO. The research gap is that the insertion may fail while adding larger amounts of data, necessitating rehashing, as in random forest tables in mental health. The main aim of this research is to improve the efficiency of predicting for random forest in stress analysis using the multi-layer perceptron with signature algorithm.

Materials and Methods

This research was carried out in the artificial intelligence and machine learning laboratory at the Department of Computer Science and Engineering, Saveetha School of Engineering, Chennai. This research uses two groups. (group 1) the random forest algorithm (RFA) (Youngberg, 2021) has 10 sample sizes and (group 2) has 10 sample sizes for the novel MLP algorithms (Reyes et al., 2023). Each sample size was predicted using the G power Tools with version 3.1.10 and resulting in 20 sample sizes with 80%, a threshold of 0.05% and a confidence interval of 95%. The Kaggle repository was used to obtain a (https://www.kaggle.com/datasets/laavanya/stress-level-detection) dataset including a collection of stocks (Youngberg, 2021).

The data was obtained from the free source websites IEEE-dataport.org and Google Schloar. The dataset which has 20 columns and 200 rows, was used to estimate software effort with the novel MLP and random forest classifiers. This research endeavour is evaluated for display using the Computer Vision programme from a Jupyter notebook. The system combinations employed an Intel Core i5 CPU with 8GB of RAM. The software configuration of the machine is 64-bit Windows OS, 64-bit CPU, and 512 SSD.

Novel multilayer perceptron classifiers

A class of feed-forward artificial neural network is called a novel multi-layer perceptron. The name MLP is vague it can refer to any feed-forward ANN or more accurately to networks made up of several layers of activation functions with thresholds of activation see terminology. When novel multi-layer perceptron's' have just one hidden layer are sometimes referred to as mental health neural network models. A minimum of three levels of nodes makes up an MLP to the input layer, the hidden layer, and the output layer. Each node with the exception of the novel perceptron is a neuron that employs a nonlinear activation function. Backpropagation of novel perceptron is a supervised learning method used by MLP during training. MLP differs from a linear perceptron due to its numerous layers and non-linear activation by the WHO.

Pseudocode for novel multilayer perceptron algorithm
Input: The options vector for every user.
   Step 1: Initially select the number of trees to be generated e. g., K.
   Step 2: At step k (1 < k < K).
   Step 3: A vector is generated representing samples (data selected for creating tree).
   Step 4: Construct tree – h(x).
   Step 5: Using any decision tree algorithm.
   Step 6: Each tree casts 1 vote for the most popular class at X.
   Step 7: The class at X is predicted by selecting the class with maximum votes.
Output: The user ID identification results.

Random forest classifiers

Random forest algorithms, also known as random decision forests, are ensemble learning techniques for classification, regression, and other tasks. The work involves creating a large number of decision trees during the training phase, and then being able to produce the class that represents the mean of the classes (for classification) or the mean/average prediction (for regression). Decision trees have a tendency to overfit their training set, and random decision forests are accurate for this improved analysis. Although random forests typically outperform decision trees, are less accurate than gradient boosted trees from the WHO. Their effectiveness meanwhile can be impacted by data features for random forests. A common method of depression analysis for many applications of machine learning is the use of decision trees. Gain knowledge from trees and their performance in perceptron.

Pseudocode for random forest algorithm
INPUT:
The random forest rectifiers.
   Step 1: Random forest chosen train file using random forest.
   Step 2: From the train file, random vectors are selected using any criteria tree.
   Step 3: Classifier tree building algorithm
   Step 4: A random forest is created using a large number of trees.
   Step 5: Each variable is classified after passing through the random forest for example 10.
   Step 6: Will be classified as 1, -10 as 1, and -1 as -1.
   Step 7: So that each Tree casts one vote.

Step 8: Every change in the independent variable will produce a forest of results.

Step 9: The class at X is predicted by choosing the class with the most votes.

arbitrary column.

Step 10: Title column

1 3 2- 1- 3- 4- 8

< 0

= < 3- 1

OUTPUT: Random forest (RF) = 1

Statistical analysis

The statistical analysis, IBM SPSS 26 is employed while Jupyter/Google Colab can be used to put the methods into practice. In IBM SPSS 22.0.1, it has been compared how the modified novel MLP and random forest algorithms perform (Youngberg, 2021). The independent variables are Id, A1 score, A2 score, A3 score, A4 score, A5 score, A6 score, A7 score, A8 score, A9 score, A10 score, age, gender, nationality, jaundice, autism, country of res, used app before, result, age desc, and relation. An impartial sample T-test was used to calculate the means, median, statistical significance, and standard mean error.

Results

The accuracy of the novel multi-layer perceptron algorithm is 95.68% and the accuracy of the RFA is 90.34%. The independent sample t-test significance is 0.001. There exists a statistical significance difference between two algorithms. Group 1 is referred to the RFA and group 2 is referred to the novel multi-layer perceptron algorithm. Here both the groups are compared in terms of accuracy. So, the RFA is better than the MLP algorithm for improved analysis.

Table 94.1 Comparison between MLP and RFA algorithm with N = 10 samples of the dataset with the highest performance of 92.20% and 97.78% in the sample (when N = 1) using the dataset size = 200 and the 70% of training & 30% of testing data.

S. No	MLP	RFA
1	97.78	92.20
2	97.67	92.10
3	96.88	91.50
4	96.78	91.20
5	95.90	90.55
6	95.89	90.30
7	94.67	89.50
8	94.55	89.25
9	93.50	88.50
10	93.20	88.30
Accuracy	**95.68**	**90.34**

Source: Author

Table 94.2 Group Statistics was done for Logged data from simulation for 10 Iterations between MLP (95.68%) algorithm and RF (90.34%). The accuracy of the RF algorithm is high compared to the MLP algorithm.

	Group	N	Mean	Std. deviation	Standard error mean
Accuracy	MLP	10	95.6820	1.64359	.51975
	RFA	10	90.3400	1.41927	.44881

Source: Author

Table 94.3 Independent sample test was done for logged data from simulation for 10 iterations to fix the confidence interval to 95%. It shows that there is a statistically significant difference between random forest and novel MLP with a value of p = 0.001 (p < 0.05) in SPSS statistical analysis. The results produced statistical significance p < 0.001.

		Levene's test for equality of variance		T-test for equality of means					95% Confidence interval of the difference	
		F	sig	t	df	Significance (2-Tailed)	Mean difference	Std. error difference	lower	Upper
Accuracy	Equal variances assumed	.324	0.577	7.779	18	<.001	5.34200	.68671	3.89928	6.78472
	Equal variance not assumed			7.779	17.626	<.001	5.34200	.68671	3.89708	6.78692

Source: Author

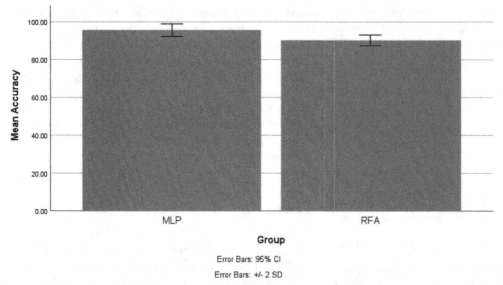

Figure 94.1 Comparison between MLP (95.68%) and RF (90.34%) in terms of mean accuracy. The mean accuracy of MLP is better than RF and standard deviation of MLP slightly better than RF. Xaxis RFA Vs MLP y axis mean accuracy 95%. The average detection accuracy is within +/-2SD

Source: Author

Table 94.1 shows random forest and novel MLP. Table 94.2 shows the group statistics for size N = 10 which contain mean accuracies and standard deviations standard error method for random forest and novel MLP algorithms. Table 94.3 shows the independent sample T-test that compares RFA as well as novel multi-layer perceptron with confidence interval 95% from random forests. It shows that there is a statistically significant difference between random forest and novel MLP with a value of p = 0.001 (p < 0.05) in SPSS statistical analysis. Figure 94.1 is a graph that shows the comparison between the mean accuracy of the random forest and mean accuracy of the novel MLP algorithms along with the error bars. Table 94.1 shows result comparison of proposed x algorithm and y algorithm in this proposed along achieved the accuracy of 80% to the existing one technique. The total no. of sample taken analysis is 10.

Discussion

model using class labels to minimise resource complexities. The future work of upcoming studies will be on improving the earlier and more precise diagnosis of stress and depressive disorders. It is my hope that this research will add to this rich legacy.

Conclusion

The multilayer perceptron (MLP) and random forest algorithm (RFA) implementation methods were statistically analysed for the detection of depression and stress RFA. The RFA has an accuracy rating of 90.34% whereas the MLP seems to have an accuracy value of 95.68%. The novel MLP classifiers appear to be more efficient at detecting depression and stress than the RFA. In this article the MLP consistently outperformed the RFA at detecting fake currency, with an accuracy of about 95.68% relative to 90.34%. MLP typically produces a result with a standard deviation that is more predictable propagations to the given significantly (p < 0.05) as observed in Table 94.3 of results corresponding to machine learning; the features are not comparable results indicating MLP of the accuracy This classifies consumer journal articles by widely mentioned topics to use the vocabularies from DBpedia, Freebase, and YAGO2s.

The comparison of RFA (90.34%) for the (Jain et al., 2022) depression detection has an accuracy of (95.68%) for MLP. The proposed technique of reported RF is used to identify Intellectual disabilities and has an accuracy rate of 95%. The accuracy of the RFA concept is higher at 90.34%. According to their research, RF is a parameter used in both traditional and modern methods to measure the detection of (Larkin and Chantler, 2020) stress and depression disorder, and it offers the highest accuracy 90.34%), and the ranges between when compared to other machine learning techniques. The use of RF for mental retardation disorder detection for improved analysis (Barone et al., 2022) will raise serious issues because research suggests RF by using machine learning and deep learning techniques on depression analysis novel MLP.

The limitations of this research is RFA and applied to the stress analysis data set as input. All of the parameters for the provided feature variable cannot be taken into consideration by this model during training. In the upcoming project, Asperger disorder will be identified using a classification

Declarations

Conflicts of Interest
No conflicts of Interest in this manuscript.

Authors Contribution

SN contributed to data collecting, data analysis, idea development, and article writing. Author PS, was involved in data validation and paper critical assessment.

Acknowledgements

The authors would like to express their gratitude towards Saveetha School of Engineering, Saveetha Institute of Medical and Technical Sciences (Formerly known as Saveetha University) for providing the necessary infrastructure to carry out this work successfully.

Funding

Thanks to the following organisations for providing financial support that enabled us to complete the research.

1.   Cyclotron Technologies, Chennai.
2.   Saveetha School of Engineering.
3.   Saveetha Institute of Medical and Technical Sciences.
4.   Saveetha University, Chennai.

References

Barone, R., Cirnigliaro, L., Saccuzzo, L., Valdese, S., Pettinato, F., Prato, A., et al. (2022). PARK2 microdeletion in a multiplex family with autism spectrum disorder. *International Journal of Developmental Neuroscience: The Official Journal of the International Society for Developmental Neuroscience.* https://doi.org/10.1002/jdn.10246.

Charis, C., and Panayiotou, G. (2021). Depression conceptualization and Treatment: Dialogues from Psychodynamic and Cognitive Behavioral Perspectives. Springer Nature.

Gilbertson, T. (2020). Reconnecting with your Estranged Adult Child: Practical Tips and Tools to Heal your Relationship. New World Library.

Grenzebach, J., and Romanus, E. (2022). Quantifying the effect of noise on cognitive processes: a review of psychophysiological correlates of workload. *Noise and Health*, 24(115), 199–214.

Hanes, C. (2019). The great depression in the United States. Handbook of Cliometrics. https://doi.org/10.1007/978-3-030-00181-0_40.

Honda, M. (2020). Reverse Depression Naturally: Alternative Treatments for Mood Disorders, Anxiety and Stress. Hatherleigh Press.

Hughes, A. M., Sanderson, E., Morris, T., Ayorech, Z., Tesli, M., Ask, H., et al. (2022). Body mass index and childhood symptoms of depression, anxiety, and attention-deficit hyperactivity disorder: a within-family mendelian randomization study. *eLife*, 11, e74320. https://doi.org/10.7554/eLife.74320.

Irene, D. S., Surya, V., Kavitha, D., Shankar, R., and Thangaraj, S. J. J. (2021). An intellectual methodology for secure health record mining and risk forecasting using clustering and graph-based classification. *Journal of Circuits Systems and Computers*, 30(08), 2150135.

Jain, S., Pandey, K., Jain, P., and Seng, K. P. (2022). Artificial Intelligence, Machine Learning, and Mental Health in Pandemics: A Computational Approach. Academic Press.

Larkin, K. T., and Chantler, P. D. (2020). Stress, depression, and cardiovascular disease. In Cardiovascular Implications of Stress and Depression. (pp. 1–12). Academic Press. https://doi.org/10.1016/b978-0-12-815015-3.00001-5.

Menon, J. (2021). PNS88 classifying high medical expenditure patients using logistic regression and random forest methods. *Value in Health*, 24, S188–S189. https://doi.org/10.1016/j.jval.2021.04.942.

National Cancer Institute (2020). Pediatric psychiatric disorder. *Definitions*. https://doi.org/10.32388/bwnz0y.

Qin, Q., Shen, J., Reece, K. S., and Mulholland, M. R. (2021). Developing a 3D mechanistic model for examining factors contributing to harmful blooms of margalefidinium polykrikoides in a temperate estuary. *Harmful Algae*, 105, 102055. https://doi.org/10.1016/j.hal.2021.102055.

Reyes, J., Komarow, L., Chen, L., Ge, L., Hanson, B. M., Cober, E., et al. (2023). Global epidemiology and clinical outcomes of carbapenem-resistant pseudomonas aeruginosa and associated carbapenemases (POP): a prospective cohort study. *The Lancet. Microbe*, 4(3), e159–e170. https://doi.org/10.1016/S2666-5247(22)00329-9.

Waller, R. C. (2021). Depression, Anxiety, and other Things we Don't Want to Talk About. Thomas Nelson.

Youngberg, C. (2021). Machine Learning for Beginners Book: Decision Trees and Random Forests Work: Classification Machine Learning Algorithms. Independently Published.

Zaidi, S. F., Saeed, S. A., Khan, M. A., Khan, A., Hazazi, Y., Otayn, M., et al. (2022). Public knowledge, attitudes, and practices towards herbal medicines; a cross-sectional study in western Saudi Arabia. *BMC Complementary Medicine and Therapies*, 22(1), 326.

95 Maximizing the accuracy of fraudulent behavioral activities in online payment using ResNet-50 over GoogleNet classifier for improved accuracy

Veera Mahesh, S.[1] and Mary Valantina, G.[2]

[1]Research Scholar, Department of Computer Science and Engineering, Saveetha School of Engineering, Chennai, India

[2]Research Guide, Corresponding Author, Department of Computer Science and Engineering, Saveetha University, Chennai, India

Abstract

Aim: The purpose of this study is to predict online fraudulent activities using two different classifiers namely ResNet-50 and GoogleNet. Materials and Methods: The collection of data and training of the model must be done. The number of groups chosen for this study are two and the machine learning (ML) algorithms used for this approach are Novel ResNet–50 and GoogleNet. Each group contains 10 samples, and it totals 20 samples. For SPSS calculation, a G power value of 0.95 is used. The significance value is 0.001 ($p < 0.05$). Result: The training and testing of fraudulent behavior detection in online payment methods using ResNet-50 and GoogleNet has to be done. A greater proportion of 98.76% accuracy is attained by ResNet-50 which is larger than 96.76% accuracy attained by GoogleNet classifier. Conclusion: The essentiality of recommendation of online payment fraud detection is defined in the study and a strong face recognition-based fraud detection is proposed. The performance analysis of the suggested system is reviewed and compared. From the results, the effectiveness of the proposed technique is visualized, and the ResNet-50 classifier is more accurate.

Keywords: Credit card, fraud detection, GoogleNet, machine learning, novel ResNet-50, online payment, work

Introduction

The Reserve Bank of India regulates National Electronic Funds Transmission (NEFT) or, an electronic means of online money transfer (Pendharkar and Narasimham, 1980). There are no additional transaction fees for money transfers done through NEFT (Understanding Online Payment Options, 2010). And this is the second method of performing money transfer via banks. But this method is time consuming in nature (Montague, 2010). The recommendation of machine learning techniques by researchers to work classification and prediction within a limited time period is more effective in recent times (Appalasamy et al., 2012). The applications of ML are food quality prediction, bitcoin price prediction, patient health monitoring system, deposit account, credit card, burst-out, and first-party (Sajter, 2022).

From 2007 to 2022, a total of 1820 articles were reviewed and it contains 640 from IEEE Xplore, 300 from Researchgate, 450 from Google scholar and 430 from Elsevier.

Puh and Brkic (2019) proposed credit card fraud detection using random forest (RF), logistic regression (LR), support vector mechanism (SVM) to bring a revolution in fraudulent actions identification. Srivastava et al. (2008) used the total amount transferred as attributes and HMM is presented within this identification. Naik (2018) used various ML approaches such as KNN, RF, LR, AdaBoost, to identify undesirable activities on credit card transactions. Ghobadi and Rohani, (2016) performed classification of fraudulent activities from the selected dataset and this study recommended LR, KNN, neural network respectively. Kalaiselvi et al. (2018) used a dataset which counts 30,000 legal transactions and performed analysis on it.

The drawback of novel ResNets is that as networks go deeper, error detection becomes more difficult. Furthermore, if the network is too thin, learning may not be very effective. Although ResNets produced deeper networks, Inception produced larger networks. And the drawback for GoogleNet classifier is that adding additional parameters also increases your model's propensity for overfitting. All bottleneck approaches are thus employed to prevent a parameter explosion on the inception layers. As can be seen above, it represents a significant departure from the sequential designs where previously seen ML is a promising technique to identify fraudsters with greater accuracy rate. The conventional

---

[a]krishsmartgenresearch@gmail.com

approaches utilized lower sized dataset to identify and test the users. This study used the maximum volume of the dataset and aim is to work on prediction processes within it at higher accuracy.

Materials and Methods

This project was done at the Information Security Laboratory, (Saveetha Institute of Medical and Technical Sciences), Saveetha School of Engineering. The Novel RestNet-50 and GoogleNet classifiers were used in this investigation, as well as 20 samples.

Anyone can download and share the Google dataset search for free online without being constrained by the law or their ability to utilize money. Clinccalc.com is used to calculate the sample size, where the alpha value is taken as 0.05, power is taken as 0.8 and beta is taken as 0.2 (Ghobadi and Rohani, 2016). Most ML frameworks can be used with these frequently updated datasets. The fact that free datasets cannot be altered is their main drawback.

ResNet-50
The CNN classifier with 50 layers is named ResNet-50 (Liu et al., 2021). Also having characteristics of jump connection and residual learning structure. It consisted of a sequence of convolutional blocks with average pooling (Khan et al., 2021). There are five convolutional layers present within it. For classification Softmax layer is used. It uses skip connection to connect with the previous layer. This skip connection having neural network to maximize accuracy. It presents two mappings.

Pseudocode
Input: Training dataset
   Output: Accuracy
   Step 1: Begin
   Step 2: Take the dataset
   Step 3: For neighbors x in image do
   Step 4: For neighbors y in image do
   Step 5: Normalize the training data
   Step 6: Define sequential model
   Step 7: Add models of layers using 'model. add(*Layer_type*)'
   Step 8: Load dataset.
   Step 9: Perform pre-processing
   Step 10: The collection of features from input has to be done.
   Step 11: From selected, classification is performed.
   Step 12: For ten samples, the accuracy value is calculated.
   Return accuracy
   End

GoogleNet
This classifier comprises 22 layers and it totals nine inception modules. It is entirely different from AlexNet and ZF-Net. The designing of it depends on inception architecture which adds an inception block on CNN also having multiscale transformations utilizing split, change and combine ideas (Kim and Cha, 2016). The inception layer is different among several other deep learning architectures which contains a predefined convolutional layer for each layer.

Pseudocode
Input: Training dataset
   Output: Accuracy
   Step 1: Begin
   Step 2: Take the dataset
   Step 3: For neighbors x in image do
   Step 4: For neighbors y in image do
   Step 5: Normalize the training data
   Step 6: Define sequential model
   Step 7: Add models of layers using 'model. add(*Layer_type*)'
   Step 8: Import and read the dataset.
   Step 9: Noise removal and several other techniques to reduce unwanted content from the dataset takes place.
   Step 10: Classification of the dataset into classes
   Step 11: Choosing of hyperplane
   Step 12: Performs classification.
   Return accuracy
   End

A system with Windows OS and hard disk capacity of 50 GB is used. Ram of 8GB and Language used id Python, either implemented in Jupyter (Anaconda) or Google Colab. The processor used is intel i5. Independent variables for face detection in images/videos. Dependent variables are improved accuracy values.

Statistical analysis
The statistical study of the suggested model was carried out using SPSS (IBM 2021) and the Python Google collab tool to evaluate the algorithm's efficiency (Gee, 2014). The independent variables are fraud detection (input parameters). The dependent variables are the accuracy variables (output parameters).

Results

Identification of fraudsters activities from selected dataset using ResNet-50 and GoogleNet is studied and prediction is performed in an effective manner; the recommended study provides better performance than GoogleNet classifier.

Table 95.1 represents the accuracy comparison of the conventional and proposed methods.

Table 95.2 defines the mean and standard deviation of the group and accuracy of the ResNet-50 and GoogleNet algorithms were 95.4540%, 2.44310, 93.4840% and 2.02444, respectively. In comparison to the GoogleNet approach, the ResNet-50 had a lower standard error of 0.77257.

Table 95.3 involves the independent sample test that revealed a substantial variation in accuracy among the suggested two stages and the standard single stage. Since $p < 0.05$, there is a substantial variation between the two methods.

Figure 95.1 shows the accuracy and mean accuracy calculation of the findings, the prediction of fraudulent activities in online transaction using ResNet-50 and GoogleNet algorithms were reviewed. Conventional method and the proposed over selected input. The proposed method attained a mean accuracy of 95.4540%, which is greater than the conventional method of 93.4840%. The significance value is 0.004 ($p < 0.05$).

Table 95.1 The ResNet-50 attained accuracy of 98.76% compared to GoogleNet having 96.76%.

Execution	ResNet-50	GoogleNet
1	92.26	90.26
2	92.60	91
3	93.13	92.13
4	93.95	92.95
5	95.11	93.01
6	95.84	93.84
7	96.42	94.42
8	98	95
9	98.47	95.47
10	98.76	96.76

Source: Author

Discussion

The proposed algorithm obtained accuracy of 98.76% which is larger than accuracy attained by GoogleNet having 96.76%. The statistically significant difference between ResNet-50 and GoogleNet is p = 0.004 (p < 0.05).

Table 95.2 The mean and standard deviation of the group and accuracy of the existing and proposed methods were 95.4540%, 2.44310, 93.4840% and 2.02444, respectively.

	Group statistics				
	Group name	N	Mean	Standard deviation	Standard Error Mean
Efficiency	Proposed	10	95.4540	2.44310	0.77257
	Existing	10	93.4840	2.02444	0.64018

Source: Author

Table 95.3 The independent sample test revealed a substantial variation in accuracy among the suggested two stages and the standard single stage.

		Independent sample test								
				T-test for equality of means						
Levene's test for equality of variance				t	df	Sig. (2-tailed)	Mean difference	Std. error difference	95% confidence interval of the difference	
		F	Sig.						Lower	Upper
Efficiency	Equal variance assumed	.731	.404	1.963	18	0.001	1.9700	1.00335	-.13795	4.07795
	Equal variance not assumed			1.963	17.399	0.001	1.9700	1.00335	-.14318	4.08318

Source: Author

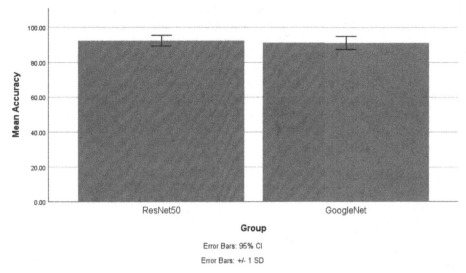

Figure 95.1 Mean accuracy comparison of ResNet-50 and GoogleNet classifier on fraudulent behavior detection. X-axis represents ResNet-50 and GoogleNet classifier; Y-axis represents mean accuracy ± 1SD

Source: Author

Itoo et al. (2021) proposed KNN classifier in comparison with several other classifiers such as NB, LR. Similar findings that recommended the classifier obtained accuracy of 72%. (Sharma et al., 2021) performed credit card fraud detection using artificial neural network (ANN) and improved the F1 score of 0.91. Preeti and Ashima (2019) did a survey of fraudulent detection using seven classifier algorithms. Among that, the dissimilarity findings of the ANN achieved a greater prediction accuracy of 99%. Faraji, (2022) proposed varieties of ML approaches such as logistic regression, decision tree, random forest, KNN and XGboost classifier. The accuracy attained are 81%, 99%, 99%, 86% and 99%. Researcher applied supervised classifier algorithm over Kaggle dataset and attained 96% accuracy.

The drawback of novel ResNet-50 is that while it can train on a sizable dataset, the accuracy may not be maximized, and the result will most likely depend on the quality of the data. More storage is required for the training procedure. The accuracy of the suggested technique will be improved by adding more classifiers over novel ResNet-50 in the future, which will encourage additional research on it.

Conclusion

The essentiality of recommendation of online payment fraud detection is defined in the study and a strong face recognition-based fraud detection is proposed. The performance analysis of the suggested system is reviewed and compared. From the results, the effectiveness of the proposed technique is visualized, and the ResNet-50 classifier is more accurate. Based on the capacity and volume of the data, we created a variety of machine learning models and evaluated their performances against diverse datasets. We may understand the model performance in real-time by comparing the models to a different dataset with a sizable volume.

Conflict of Interests

No conflict of interest in these manuscripts.

Authors Contributions

The authors were involved in data collection, data analysis, manuscript writing, conceptualization, data validation, and critical review of the manuscript.

Acknowledgments

The authors would like to express their gratitude towards Saveetha School of Engineering, Saveetha Institute of Medical and Technical Sciences (Formerly known as Saveetha University) for providing the necessary infrastructure to carry out this work successfully.

Funding

We thank the following organizations for providing financial support that enabled us to complete the study.

1. TechGrader, Chennai.
2. Saveetha University

3. Saveetha Institute of Medical and Technical Sciences
4. Saveetha School of Engineering

References

Aman (2021). Credit card fraud detection using machine learning and data science. *International Journal for Research in Applied Science and Engineering Technology* . https://doi.org/10.22214/ijraset.2021.37200.

Appalasamy, P., Mustapha, A., Rizal, N. D., Johari, F., and Mansor, A. F. (2012). Classification-based data mining approach for quality control in wine production. *Journal of Applied Sciences*, 598–601. https://doi.org/10.3923/jas.2012.598.601.

Faraji, Z. (2022). A review of machine learning applications for credit card fraud detection with a case study. *SEISENSE Journal of Management*, 5(1), 49–59. https://doi.org/10.33215/sjom.v5i1.770.

Gee, S. (2014). Fraud and Fraud Detection, + Website: A Data Analytics Approach. John Wiley & Sons.

Ghobadi, F., and Rohani, M. (2016). Cost sensitive modeling of credit card fraud using neural network strategy. In 2016 2nd International Conference of Signal Processing and Intelligent Systems (ICSPIS). https://doi.org/10.1109/icspis.2016.7869880.

Itoo, F., Meenakshi, and Singh, S. (2021). Comparison and analysis of logistic regression, naïve bayes and KNN machine learning algorithms for credit card fraud detection. *International Journal of Information Technology*, 13(4), 1503–1511. https://doi.org/10.1007/s41870-020-00430-y.

Kalaiselvi, N., Rajalakshmi, S., Padmavathi, J., and Karthiga, J. B. (2018). Credit card fraud detection using learning to rank approach. In 2018 Internat2018 International Conference on Computation of Power, Energy, Information and Communication (ICCPEIC) ional Conference on Computation of Power, Energy, Information and Communication (ICCPEIC). https://doi.org/10.1109/iccpeic.2018.8525171.

Khan, M. A., Gairola, S., Jha, B., and Praveen, P. (2021). Smart Computing: Proceedings of the 1st International Conference on Smart Machine Intelligence and Real-Time Computing (SmartCom 2020), 26-27 June 2020, Pauri, Garhwal, Uttarakhand, India. CRC Press.

Kim, Y.-G., and Cha, E. Y. (2016). Streamlined GoogLeNet algorithm based on cnn for korean character recognition. *Journal of the Korea Institute of Information and Communication Engineering*, 20(9), 1657–1665. https://doi.org/10.6109/jkiice.2016.20.9.1657.

Liu, J., Du, W., Zhou, C., and Qin, Z. (2021). Rock image intelligent classification and recognition based on Resnet-50 model. *Journal of Physics: Conference Series*, 2076(1), 012011. https://doi.org/10.1088/1742-6596/2076/1/012011.

Montague, D. (2010). Essentials of online payment security and fraud prevention. https://doi.org/10.1002/9781118386750.

Naik, H. (2018). Credit card fraud detection for online banking transactions. *International Journal for Research in Applied Science and Engineering Technology*, 6(4), 4573–4577. https://doi.org/10.22214/ijraset.2018.4749.

Pendharkar, V. G., and Narasimham, M. (1980). Recent evolution of monetary policy in India**extracted by permission of the governor of the reserve bank of India from reserve bank of India Bulletin (Apr. 1966). Money and Monetary Policy in Less Developed Countries . https://doi.org/10.1016/b978-0-08-024041-1.50019-3.

Preeti, S., and Ashima (2019). Analysis of various credit card fraud detection techniques. *International Journal of Computer Sciences and Engineering*. https://doi.org/10.26438/ijcse/v7i6.12121216.

Puh, M., and Brkic, L. (2019). Detecting credit card fraud using selected machine learning algorithms. In 2019 42nd International Convention on Information and Communication Technology, Electronics and Microelectronics (MIPRO). https://doi.org/10.23919/mipro.2019.8757212.

Sajter, D. (2022). Overseas transaction fees: sending money via Bitcoin vs. banks. *Zagreb International Review of Economics and Business*, 25, 65–83. https://doi.org/10.2478/zireb-2022-0025.

Sharma, P., Banerjee, S., Tiwari, D., and Patni, J. C. (2021). Machine learning model for credit card fraud detection- a comparative analysis. *The International Arab Journal of Information Technology*, 18(6), 789–796. https://doi.org/10.34028/iajit/18/6/6.

Srivastava, A., Kundu, A., Sural, S., and Majumdar, A. K. (2008). Credit card fraud detection using hidden markov model. *IEEE Transactions on Dependable and Secure Computing* . https://doi.org/10.1109/tdsc.2007.70228.

Understanding Online Payment Options. (2010). Essentials of Online Payment Security and Fraud Prevention. https://doi.org/10.1002/9781118386750.ch1.

96 Classification of target customers for online advertising using Wide Resnet CNN and comparing its accuracy over ELM-CNN algorithm

Vamsi Krishna Polina[1] and Malathi, K.[2]

[1]Research Scholar, Department of Computer Science and Engineering, Saveetha School of Engineering, Saveetha Institute of Medical and Technical Sciences, Saveetha University, Chennai, Tamil Nadu, India

[2]Project Guide, Corresponding Author, Department of Computer Science and Engineering, Saveetha School of Engineering, Saveetha Institute of Medical and Technical Sciences Saveetha University, Chennai, Tamil Nadu, India

Abstract

Aim: The proposed study aims at the novel image classification of target customers for online advertising using Wide Resnet CNN and comparing its accuracy over extreme learning machine convolutional neural networks (ELM-CNN) algorithm. **Materials and Methods:** The age and gender are discovered by using ELM-CNN with sample size of 10 and Wide Resnet with sample size 10. Based on the identified age and gender distinct advertising will be displayed. **Results:** A prediction accuracy of 93.8% was achieved using Wide Resnet method while 82.6% was achieved with ELM-CNN method. The significance value obtained in statistical analysis is 0.02 ($p < 0.05$). **Conclusion:** It shows that the identification of age and gender is considerably better in Wide Resnet than ELM-CNN.

Keywords: ELM-CNN, machine learning, neural networks, novel image classification, online advertising, Wide Resnet

Introduction

The representation-based age and gender recognition plays a very important role in the interaction activities of individuals is increasing daily on social media, which makes the inclusion of gender and age identification in intelligent applications like security, online advertising biometric registration, commercial networks and video surveillance. Advertising practices and techniques based on age and gender are researched extensively today to boost the effectiveness of advertisement across numerous social media platforms. Deep learning techniques will produce a competitive advantage for online advertisements over traditional practices through larger precision in displaying digital ads to specific people. Deep learning techniques improve the accuracy of targeted advertising by predicting the most important ads for users based on age and gender.

In the last 5 years, there are around 445 research articles published in science direct on age and gender identification. Abirami et al. (2020) estimate age and gender from a single face real-time image using convolutional neural network (CNN). This study made a try to classify human age and gender both at the coarser and finer level. A feed forward propagation neural network is used in coarser level whereas 3-sigma control limit final classification is done in finer level classification of age groups includes children, middle-aged adults, and old-aged adults. To overcome the overfitting problem, a pretrained CNN as a facial feature extractor is employed in this work. Caffe is one of the most popular libraries for deep learning. Liu et al. (2017) study used CNN for facial novel image classification. Convolutional neural network is one of the artificial neural networks. (Tsimperidis, Yucel, and Katos, 2021) were some of the early researchers who used a neural network which was trained on a small set of near- frontal facial picture dataset to classify gender. After that (Rosso, 2017) supplied a point of view-invariant look version of local scale-invariant functions to categorize age and gender. Recently age and gender novel image classification has collected enormous attention, providing direct and fastest means for getting implicit and demanding social data. (Fu et al. (2010) created an in depth investigation of age classification and we are able to learn additional data about recent situation from Ref. Classifying age from the human facial pictures was introduced by Shah et al., 2017; Deena et al., 2022; Thanigaivel et al., 2022; Shah et al., 2017. All of these above strategies have been effectively verified in records restricted to Age classification, which are not suitable for unrestricted images in sensitive packets. Our proposed

[a]malathieng@gmail.com

approach does not automatically classify age and gender from facial images, but also successfully handles unlimited facial imaging tasks

Materials and Methods

The study setting of the proposed work was done in the data analytics lab of Saveetha School of Engineering, Saveetha Institute of Medical and Technical Sciences. The two groups corresponding to two algorithms for the proposed system are extreme learning machine convolutional neural networks (ELM-CNN) and Wide Resnet. A sample size of 10 per group, a total of 20 sample sizes were carried out for our study with Gpower with 95% confidence and 80% test power (Beaujean, 2014).

Extreme learning machine convolutional neural networks

The ELM-CNN was proposed by Huang et al. ELM-CNN can be implemented as a stack of blocks with a specified operation (convolution, pooling, and nonlinearity). Each ELM-CNN block has an input feature map. This is the output feature map from the previous layer (in the first layer, the input feature map is the input training data set), and an output feature map (with the exception of the last layer that generates the class grades). First, the input weights and hidden layer bias are randomized, and then the training data sets are combined from SLFN with to determine the output weights (Yu, 2017).

In the training phase, for the given ELM CNN architecture, we randomly initialized all the filters. The data is then propagated through the network by directly calculating the output of each block. If the block is a CONV layer, the training is done first and then the output can be estimated after learning the convolution kernels (Pantraki et al., 2017). The convolution operation is transformed into a matrix multiplication. Therefore, each local window is unrolled into a vector, and then all local windows are grouped in a single matrix. We also unroll each filter to a vector (Ahmed and Viriri, 2020).We repeat the previous operations on all the filters and input feature maps, then connect the vectorized version of all local windows, all filters in the first dimension and the second dimensions in sequence order. The system architecture for ELM CNN was shown in Figure 96.1

Pseudocode
Input: x-> Dataset 'X' values

  T ->, target values,

  L -> number of hidden nodes.

Output: ELM parameters.

  Generate randomly the input weights and the bias Wand b.

  Compute the hidden matrix H = G(XW+ b).

  Compute the output weights β = H*T.

  Return the ELM parameters W, b, and β.

Wide Resnet

Wide Resnet was introduced by (Zagoruyko and Komodakis 2016). It consists of residual units or blocks with bypass connections, also called identity connections. The output of the previous layer is added to the output of the next layer in the remaining block.

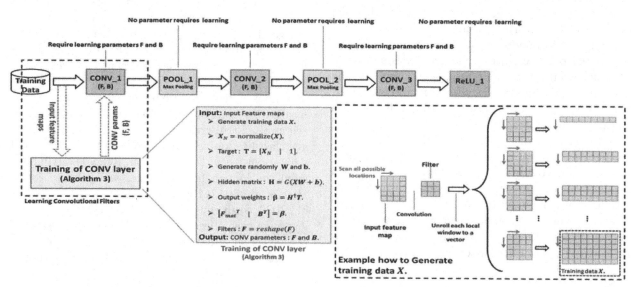

Figure 96.1 System architecture for ELM CNN algorithm
Source: Author

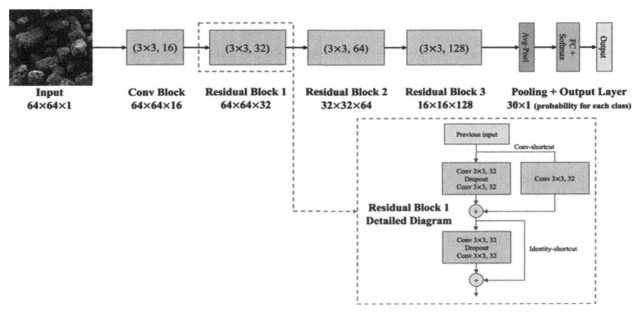

Figure 96.2 System architecture for Wide Resnet algorithm
Source: Author

Table 96.1 The results of the predicted output of the age and gender with accuracy using ELM CNN.

S.NO	Input Image	Predicted output		
		Age	Gender	Accuracy (%)
1	Im1	22	Male	83
2	Im2	21	Male	82
3	Im3	25	Male	84
4	Im4	65	Male	85
5	Im5	21	Male	80
6	If1	20	Female	83
7	If2	21	Female	82
8	If3	25	Female	82
9	If4	46	Female	84
10	If5	23	Female	81

Source: Author

Table 96.2 The experimental results of the predicted output of the age and gender with accuracy using Wide Resnet.

S. No	Input image	Predicted output		
		Age	Gender	Accuracy (%)
1	Im1	19	Male	92
2	Im2	20	Male	94
3	Im3	19	Male	93
4	Im4	61	Male	92
5	Im5	17	Male	94
6	If1	9	Female	96
7	If2	18	Female	91
8	If3	19	Female	93
9	If4	38	Female	96
10	If5	21	Female	97

Source: Author

The jump or jump can be 1, 2 or even 3. When adding, the dimensions of x can differ from F (x) due to the convolution process, which leads to a decrease in its dimensions. The remaining block has a 3 × 3 convolution layer followed by a stack normalization layer and a ReLU activation function. This, in turn, is continued by a 3 × 3 convolution layer and a stack normalization layer. The hop connection basically skips these two layers and adds directly before the ReLU transformation function, so the residual blocks are repeated to form a residual network. The system architecture for Wide Resnet was shown in Figure 96.2.

Pseudocode
  Input: All images are rescaled and given as input
  Output: Accuracy, precision and recall.
  Wide Resnet layer parameters are generated.

Steps:
1. Divide into m mini-batches.
2. Randomly choose a mini-batch, I_t.
3. Using i get partition I_t 1.
4. Average the weights.

Table 96.3 Analysis of ELM CNN and Wide Resnet algorithms. Mean accuracy value, standard deviation and standard error mean for ELM CNN and Wide Resnet are obtained for 10 iterations. It is observed that Wide Resnet acquired better accuracy than the ELM CNN algorithm.

	Group	N	Mean	Std. deviation	Std. error mean
Accuracy	ELM CNN	10	82.6000	1.50555	0.47610
Accuracy	Wide Resnet	10	93.8000	1.98886	0.62893

Source: Author

Statistical Analysis

The statistical comparison of the age and gender identification using two sample groups was done through SPSS version 28.0. Analysis was done for mean, standard deviation, independent T-test. Table 96.3 represents the statistical results mean and standard deviation of accuracies obtained from the ELM-CNN and Wide Resnet.

Results

The analysis was performed using ELM CNN and Wide Resnet. Each group is executed with 10 different number of image datasets to obtain 10 different outputs which display the age and gender of the given person, and the suggested advertisement based on age and gender. The sample group images are used in IBM SPSS tool to calculate the independent sample T-Test which gives the significance value which is used to evaluate ELM CNN and Wide Resnet. For comparing both models, 10 different input image datasets are used and the received accuracy values are recorded. Wide Resnet showed better results and has been categorized as a better algorithm than extreme learning machine convolutional neural networks in the prediction of age and gender. Table 96.1 and 96.2 shows the comparison of output results for ELM-CNN and Wide Resnet.

Discussion

Wide Resnet appears to produce the most compatible results with minimal standard deviation. ELM CNN appears to produce the most variable results with its standard deviation. There is a statistically significant difference ELM CNN and Wide Resnet algorithms. (p < 0.05 independent sample T test). It is clearly evident that Wide Resnet is a better algorithm for age and gender identification with 93.8% accuracy than ELM CNN with 83% accuracy.

There are many investigations done over the most recent five years that have results in line with the discoveries in our study. (Hatipoglu and Kose. 2017). In this task transfer of learning techniques with fine-tuning of the ConvNet into the new training set of persons of interest is impossible because the images are unlabeled; that is, the configuration is completely unsupervised. Hence, the traditional face clustering methods focus on finding effective face representation or appropriate dissimilarity measure between faces (Hsu et al., 2021) propose the random occlusion, a facts augmentation method on facial photos the usage of simple image processing strategies for age and gender recognition (Qawaqneh et al., 2017; Singh et al.. 2021; Sivakumar, Radha Krishnappa, and Nallanathel, 2021; Vidhya Lakshmi et al., 2020; Singh et al., 2021). In this work Wide Resnet gives better results than the ELM-CNN. Many authors published that Wide Resnet gives better results than ELM-CNN. But in some cases like low resolution images, blurred images may give low accuracy.

Limitations are, the study is particularly focused on a set of range of ages, so the age is identified in between those ranges after the detection. Once in a while the age or gender prediction can be incorrect so that the counseled advertisement is irrelevant to a person, this could show up due to numerous factors like low resolution of the photo, blurred photograph and the lightning situations. The Future work of this study can be working on enhancing the resolution and quality of images captured there by increasing the accuracy of the age and gender prediction.

Conclusion

In this research, based on the comparison accuracies of Wide Resnet and extreme learning machine convolutional neural networks (ELM CNN), it is clearly evident that Wide Resnet is a better algorithm for age and gender identification with 93.8% accuracy than ELM CNN with 83% accuracy.

References

Abirami, B., Subashini, T. S., and Mahavaishnavi, V. (2020). Gender and age prediction from real time facial images using CNN. *Materials Today: Proceedings*, 33, 4708–4712. https://doi.org/10.1016/j.matpr.2020.08.350.

Ahmed, M., and Viriri, S. (2020). Facial age estimation using transfer learning and bayesian optimization based on gender information. *Sampling Theory in Signal and Image Processing. An International Journal*, 11. https://doi.org/10.5121/SIPIJ.2020.11604.

Beaujean, A. (2014). Sample size determination for regression models using Monte Carlo methods in R. 19(12). http://dx.doi.org/.

Deena, S. R., Vickram, A. S., and Manikandan, S. (2022). Enhanced biogas production from food waste and activated sludge using advanced techniques–a review. *Bioresources*. https://www.sciencedirect.com/science/article/pii/S0960852422005636.

Fu, Y., Guo, G., and Huang, T. S. (2010). Age synthesis and estimation via faces: a survey. *IEEE Transactions on Software Engineering*, 32(11), 1955–1976.

Hatipoglu, B., and Kose, C. (2017). A gender recognition system from facial images using SURF based BoW method. In 2017 International Conference on Computer Science and Engineering (UBMK). https://doi.org/10.1109/ubmk.2017.8093405.

Hsu, C.-Y., Lin, L. E., and Lin, C. H. (2021). Age and gender recognition with random occluded data augmentation on facial images. *Multimedia Tools and Applications*, 80(8), 11631–11653. https://doi.org/10.1007/s11042-020-10141-y.

Liu, X., Li, J., Hu, C., and Pan, L. S. (2017). Deep convolutional neural networks-based age and gender classification with facial images. In 2017 First International Conference on Electronics Instrumentation & Information Systems (EIIS). https://doi.org/10.1109/eiis.2017.8298719.

Pantraki, E., Kotropoulos, C., and Lanitis, A. (2017). Age interval and gender prediction using PARAFAC2 and SVMs based on visual and aural features. *IET Biometrics*, 6(4), 290–298. https://doi.org/10.1049/iet-bmt.2016.0122.

Qawaqneh, Z., Mallouh, A. A., and Barkana, B. D. (2017). DNN-based models for speaker age and gender classification. In 10th International Conference on Bio-Inspired Systems and Signal Processing, (pp. 106–11).

Rosso, P. (2017). Author profiling at PAN: from age and gender identification to language variety identification (invited Talk). In Proceedings of the Fourth Workshop on NLP for Similar Languages, Varieties and Dialects (VarDial). https://doi.org/10.18653/v1/W17-1205.

Shah, S. Y., Ismail, M., Khan, S., and Ahmad, N. (2017). Age classification using facial image features in DCT domain. *Sindh University Research Journal-SURJ (Science Series)*, 49(3), 535–539.

Singh, A., Rai, N., Sharma, P., Nagrath, P., and Jain, R. (2021). Age, gender prediction and emotion recognition using convolutional neural network. In Proceedings of the International Conference on Innovative Computing & Communication (ICICC). https://doi.org/10.2139/ssrn.3833759.

Identification of customer group for online targeted advertising using novel learning representation of fully connected CNN in terms of accuracy compared over ELM-CNN algorithm

Vamsi Krishna Polina[1] and Malathi, K.[2]

[1]Department of Computer Science and Engineering, Saveetha School of Engineering, Saveetha Institute of Medical and Technical Sciences, Saveetha University, Chennai, Tamil Nadu, India

[2]Research Scholar, Project Guide, Department of Computer Science and Engineering, Saveetha School of Engineering, Saveetha Institute of Medical and Technical Sciences, Saveetha University, Chennai, Tamil Nadu, India

Abstract

Aim: The aim is to identify a customer group for novel online targeted advertising using learning representation of fully connected convolutional neural networks (CNN) in terms of novel accuracy compared over extreme learning machine convolutional neural networks (ELM-CNN). **Materials and Methods:** The age and gender are discovered by using ELM-CNN with sample size of 10 and fully connected CNN with sample size 10. Based on the identified age and gender distinct advertising will be displayed. In this work we get 95% confidence interval and pretest power of 80%. **Results:** A prediction novel accuracy of 93.6% was achieved using fully connected CNN method while 82.6% was achieved with ELM-CNN method. The significance value obtained in statistical analysis is 0.04 ($p < 0.05$). **Conclusion:** It shows that the identification of age and gender is considerably better in fully connected CNN than ELM-CNN.

Keywords: Accuracy, age and gender, extreme learning machine convolutional neural networks, fully connected CNN, machine learning, neural networks, novel online advertising, targeted customers

Introduction

Automated gender and age classification are a major task in computer vision. Age and gender classification plays an important role in real world applications such as visual surveillance, forensic science, targeted advertising etc. Human gender classification has also been linked to the advent of social media and networks with a variety of automated systems. One such application is online advertisements. Advertising techniques and strategies focused mainly on age and gender have been researched comprehensively to improve the effectiveness of commercials on various social media platforms (Hsu et al., 2021). These advancements also mitigate marketing with significantly boosting advertisements based on individuals (Liu and Liu, 2017).

Social media and big data are the terms that quickly come into sight for the massive photos and advertisements. In the last five years, ScienceDirect has published around 63 study articles on age and gender identity. Many of these studies use neural networks to classify images. (Chao et al. (2013) used local binary patterns for texture-based classification tasks. Support vector machines were used to estimate weight vectors and project images to obtain a rank score (Srivastava et al., 2017). Significant improvements have been proposed at convolutional neural networks (CNN), owing in large part to the reorganization of processing devices and the advent of recent blocks. Li et al. (2021) has compared the performance of deep learning networks against the conventional handcrafted methods and reported a prediction error of 24.23% using a temporal convolution network. Predicted age and gender from a face real-time photo using CNN (Azarmehr et al., 2015). This takes a look and tries to classify human age and gender each on the coarser and finer stage. To triumph over the overfitting problem, Caffenet, a pretrained CNN as a facial function extractor, becomes employed. Caffe is one of the most famous libraries for deep studying (convolutional neural networks in particular). Deena et al., 2022; Thanigaivel et al., 2022; Duan et al., 2018 take a look at used CNN for facial photo type. Support vector machine technique is targeted for face recognition problems (Kumar et al., 2017). The input statistics is selected from the FERET database of male and females labeled with the digits 1 and 2 respectively. Then suitable kernel characteristic is chosen manually,

[a]khilsmartgenresearch@gmail.com

and exceptional outcomes are received whilst the use of RBF kernel characteristic. Adjustable parameter values of the RBF kernel are decided on experimentally (Hatipoglu and Kose, 2017).

The appearance of the face differs due to a number of factors including variations in light, the effects of facial appearance on individual bone structure. While there are potential practical uses like computer-aided customer relationship management, there has been relatively little work in the age of automation and gender recognition due to its many challenges. The aim of this work is to predict the age and gender of facial images using the convolutional neural networks of the extreme machine learning machine and a new fully connected CNN.

Materials and Methods

The study setting of the proposed work was done in the data analytics lab of Saveetha School of Engineering, Saveetha Institute of Medical and Technical Sciences. The two groups corresponding to two algorithms for the proposed system are extreme learning machine convolutional neural networks (ELM-CNN) and fully connected CNN. A sample size of 10 per each group, totally 20 sample sizes have been carried out for our study using Gpower with 95% confidence and 80% pretest power (Beaujean, 2014).

For this project I used an IMDB-WIKI dataset collected from (IMDB-WIKI - 500k+ face images with age and gender labels). In this dataset there are a large number of human faces with gender, name and age information. For our pretrained models use a default width and height on all four sides of images (the default settings). The required samples for this analysis are done using G power calculation (p = 0.075). The data is divided into two parts: 90% for training and 10% for validation. Training and testing for age and gender classifications are carried out using the standard 5-time cross-validation process(Tursunov et al., 2021) Age and gender recognition is carried out using ELM-CNN compared with fully Connected CNN both with sample size of 20.

Extreme learning machine convolutional neural networks

The ELM-CNN was developed by Huang et al. ELM-CNN can be implemented as a stack of blocks with a specific operation (convolution, grouping, and nonlinearity). Each ELM-CNN block has an input feature map. This is the output feature map from the previous layer (in the first layer, the input feature map is the input training dataset) and an output feature map (with the exception of the last layer that generates the

class grades). First, the input weights and hidden layer bias are randomized, and then the training data sets are combined from SLFN to determine the output weights.

In the training phase, for the given ELM-CNN architecture, we randomly initialized all the filters. Next, the data is propagated through the network by directly computing the output of every block. If the block is a CONV layer, first, the training is performed, and then the output can be estimated after learning the convolutional kernels. The convolution operation is converted into a matrix multiplication. Therefore, each local window is unrolled into a vector, and then all local windows are grouped in a single convolutional kernel. The convolution operation is converted into a matrix multiplication. Therefore, each local window is unrolled into a vector, and then all local windows are grouped in a single convolutional kernel. The convolution operation is converted into a matrix multiplication. Therefore, each local window is unrolled into a vector, and then all local windows are grouped in a single convolutional kernel. The convolution operation is converted into a matrix multiplication. Therefore, each local window is unrolled into a vector, and then all local windows are grouped in a single matrix. We also unroll each filter to a vector. Reshaping the fillers and local windows to vectors needs to be done in the same direction to keep the same results of the multiplication operation. We repeat the previous operations on all the filters and input feature maps, then connect the vectorized version of all local windows, all filters in the first dimension and the second dimensions in sequence order. The system architecture for ELM CNN was shown in Figure 97.1

Pseudocode
Input: Dataset X, target T, and the number of hidden nodes L.
Output: ELM parameters.

Generate randomly the input weights and the bias W and b.

Compute the hidden matrix $H = G(XW + b)$.

Compute the output weights $\beta = H*T$.

Return the ELM parameters W, b, and β.

Fully connected CNN
Neurons in a fully connected layer have complete connections to all the activities of the previous layer, as seen in normal neural networks. Therefore, its activation can be calculated with a matrix multiplication followed by a biased offset. The main advantage of fully connected networks is that they are "structural agnostic", i.e. do not need to make any special assumptions about the input. worse performance than special

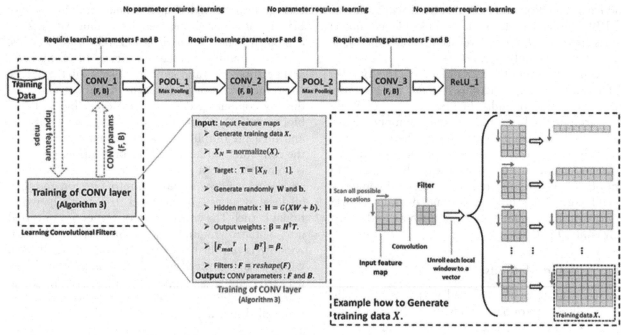

Figure 97.1 System architecture for ELM CNN algorithm
Source: Author

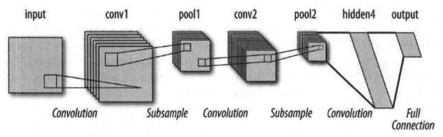

Figure 97.2 System architecture for Fully Connected CNN algorithm
Source: Author

purpose networks that fit the structure of the problem space. The fully connected CNN architectures explicitly assume that the inputs are images, which allows some properties to be encoded in the model architecture (Budiman, 2019). The CNN is simply a string of layers and each layer of the CNN converts one active volume into another through a distinguishable function. The system architecture for a fully connected CNN has been shown in Figure 97.2.

Pseudocode

Input: All images are rescaled and given as input
  Output: Accuracy, precision and recall.
  Fully connected CNN layer parameters are generated.

Steps:
1. Input volume
2. Convolution layer stride
3. Max pool layer stride 2
4. Flatten layer
5. Fully connected layer ReLU activation
6. Soft-max activation

Statistical analysis

The statistical comparison of the age and gender identification using two sample groups was done through SPSS version 28.0. Analysis was done for mean, standard deviation, independent T-test. Table 97.3 represents the statistical results mean and standard deviation of accuracies obtained from the ELM-CNN and Fully connected CNN.

Results

The analysis was performed using ELM-CNN and fully connected CNN and their results are shown in Figure 97.3a and b. Each group is executed with 10

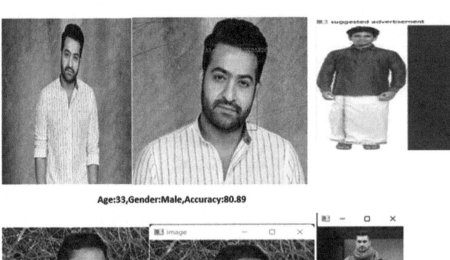

Age:33,Gender:Male,Accuracy:80.89

Age:22,Gender:Male,Accuracy:83.20

Age:10,Gender:Female,Accuracy:80.0

Figure 97.3 Output screenshots of age and gender prediction by the given input images with accuracy using ELM CNN algorithm

Source: Author

different number of image datasets to obtain 10 different outputs which display the age and gender of the given person and the suggested advertisement based on age and gender. The sample group images are used in IBM SPSS tool to calculate the independent sample T-Test which gives the significance value which is used to evaluate ELM-CNN and fully connected CNN. For comparing both models, 10 different input image datasets are used, and the received accuracy values are recorded. Fully connected CNN showed better results and has been categorized as a better algorithm than extreme learning machine convolutional neural networks in the prediction of age and gender. Tables 97.1 and 97.2 shows the comparison of output results for ELM-CNN and fully connected CNN.

Discussion

Fully connected CNN appears to produce the most compatible results with minimal standard deviation. ELM-CNN appears to produce the most variable results with its standard deviation. There is a statistically significant difference between ELM-CNN and fully connected CNN algorithms ($p < 0.05$ independent sample T-test). It is clearly evident that Wide Resnet is a better algorithm for age and gender identification with 93.6% accuracy than ELM-CNN with 83% accuracy.

Multiple studies conducted in the last 5 years have shown results that are consistent with the conclusions of our study. Discusses grouping images into

Table 97.1 The Results of the Predicted Output of the Age and Gender with Accuracy using ELM CNN.

S.NO	Input Image	Predicted Output		
		Age	Gender	Accuracy(%)
1	Im1	22	MALE	83
2	Im2	21	MALE	82
3	Im3	25	MALE	84
4	Im4	65	MALE	85
5	Im5	21	MALE	80
6	If1	20	FEMALE	83
7	If2	21	FEMALE	82
8	If3	25	FEMALE	82
9	If4	46	FEMALE	84
10	If5	23	FEMALE	81

Source: Author

Table 97.2 The Experimental Results of the Predicted Output of the Age and Gender with Accuracy Using Fully Connected CNN.

S.NO	Input Image	Predicted Output		
		Age	Gender	Accuracy(%)
1	Im1	19	MALE	92
2	Im2	28	MALE	91
3	Im3	20	MALE	93
4	Im4	61	MALE	92
5	Im5	19	MALE	93
6	If1	8	FEMALE	91
7	If2	20	FEMALE	94
8	If3	17	FEMALE	95
9	If4	40	FEMALE	98
10	If5	21	FEMALE	97

Source: Author

Table 97.3 Analysis of ELM CNN and Wide Resnet Algorithms. Mean Accuracy value, standard Deviation and Standard Error Mean for ELM CNN and Wide resnet are obtained for 10 iterations.It is observed that Wide resnet acquired better accuracy than the ELM CNN algorithm.

	Group	N	Mean	Std.Deviation	Std.Error Mean
Accuracy	ELM CNN	10	82.6000	1.50555	0.47610
Accuracy	Fully Connected CNN	10	93.6000	2.41293	0.76303

Source: Author

Table 97.4 Independent Sample Test for Significance and Standard Error Determination. *P* value is less than 0.05 considered to be statistically significant and 95% confidence intervals were calculated.(p=0.02).

		Levene's test for equality of variances		T- test for equality of means						
		F	Sig	t	df	sig.(2-tailed)	Mean difference	Std.Err or difference	95% candidates interval of the difference	
									Lower	upper
Accuracy	Equal variances assumed	2.166	.158	-12.231	18	.013	-11.00000	0.89938	-12.88953	-9.11047
	Equal variances not assumed			-12.231	15.085	0.13	-11.00000	0.89938	-12.91604	-9.08396

Source: Author

individual identities contained in data fed with a large number of face images. In this task, fine-tuned learning techniques could not be transferred from ConvNet to the new trainer of interests training set because the images were not labeled; that is, completely unattended installation. The author reported 93.79% accuracy in determining age and gender using their proposed Mobile Net model (Nguyen et al., 2013). The authors proposed the Additive Angular Margin Loss (ArcFace) facial recognition feature to obtain highly distinguishing features and reported an accuracy of 92.56%. Hsu et al., 2021; Sivakumar et al.,

2021; Lakshmi et al., 2020 proposed randomization, a method of data enhancement on face images using simple image processing techniques for age and gender recognition. Haider et al. (2019), in this work fully connected CNN gives better results than the ELM-CNN. Many authors published that fully connected CNN gives better results than ELM-CNN. The negatives such as in some cases like low resolution images, blurred images it may give low accuracy. Large training needed for fully connected CNN to get better accuracy.

The limitation is, the study specifically focused on a subset of age groups, so age was determined between these groups after detection. people, it can appear due to many factors such as low image resolution, blurred photography and lightning situations. Future work on this study may involve improving the resolution and quality of captured images by increasing the accuracy of age and gender prediction.

Conclusion

In this research, based on the comparison accuracies of fully connected CNN extreme learning machine convolutional neural networks (ELM-CNN), it is clearly evident that Wide Resnet is a better algorithm for age and gender identification with 93.6% accuracy than ELM-CNN with 83% accuracy.

Conflict of interest

No conflict of interest in this manuscript.

Authors contribution

Author PVK was involved in data collection, data analysis, manuscript writing, Author CS was involved in conceptualization, data validation, and critical review of manuscript.

Acknowledgements

The Authors would like to impress their graduates towards Saveetha School of Engineering, Saveetha Institute of Medical and Technical Sciences (formerly known as Saveetha University) for providing the necessary infrastructure to carry out this work successfully.

Funding

We thank the following organizations for providing the financial support that enabled us to complete the study.

1. Finura Bioteks
2. Saveetha University
3. Saveetha Institute of Medical and Technical Sciences
4. Saveetha School of Engineering

References

Azarmehr, R., Laganière, R., Lee, W. S., Xu, C., and Laroche, D. (2015). Real-time embedded age and gender classification in unconstrained video. In Proceedings of the IEEE Conference on Computer Vision and Pattern Recognition Workshops, (pp. 57–65). http://ieeexplore.ieee.org/stamp/stamp.jsp?tp=&arnumber=7301367.

Beaujean, A. (2014). Sample size determination for regression models using Monte Carlo methods in R. 19. http://dx.doi.org/.

Budiman, F. (2019). SVM-RBF parameters testing optimization using cross validation and grid search to improve multiclass classification. *Scientific Visualization*, 11(1), 80–90. https://doi.org/10.26583/sv.11.1.07.

Chao, W.-L., Liu, J. Z., Ding, J. J., and Wu, P. H. (2013). Facial expression recognition using expression-specific local binary patterns and layer denoising mechanism. In 2013 9th International Conference on Information, Communications & Signal Processing. https://doi.org/10.1109/icics.2013.6782964.

Deena, S. R., Vickram, A. S., and Manikandan, S. (2022). Enhanced biogas production from food waste and activated sludge using advanced techniques–a review. *Bioresources* . https://www.sciencedirect.com/science/article/pii/S0960852422005636.

Duan, M., Li, K., Yang, C., and Li, K. (2018). A hybrid deep learning CNN-ELM for age and gender classification. *Neurocomputing*, 275, 448–461 https://doi.org/10.1016/j.neucom.2017.08.062.

Haider, K. Z., Malik, K. R., Khalid, S., Nawaz, T., and Jabbar, S. (2019). Deepgender: real-time gender classification using deep learning for smartphones. *Journal of Real-Time Image Processing* 16(11), 15–29. https://doi.org/10.1007/s11554-017-0714-3.

Hatipoglu, B., and Kose, C. (2017). A gender recognition system from facial images using SURF based BoW method. In 2017 International Conference on Computer Science and Engineering (UBMK), (pp. 989–993). IEEE. http://ieeexplore.ieee.org/stamp/stamp.jsp?tp=&arnumber=8093405.

Hsu, C.-Y., Lin, L. E., and Lin, C. H. (2021). Age and gender recognition with random occluded data augmentation on facial images. *Multimedia Tools and Applications*, 80(8), 11631–11653. https://doi.org/10.1007/s11042-020-10141-y.

Kumar, S., Singh, S., and Kumar, J. (2017). A study on face recognition techniques with age and gender classification. In 2017 International Conference on Computing, Communication and Automation (ICCCA), (pp. 1001–1006). IEEE. http://ieeexplore.ieee.org/stamp/stamp.jsp?tp=&arnumber=8229960.

Lakshmi, S. V., Ramalakshmi, M., Rakshith, R. K., Christobel, M. J., Kumar, P. P., Priyadharshini, B., et al. (2020). An integration of geospatial technology and standard precipitation index (SPI) for drought vulnerability assessment for a part of Namakkal district, South India. *Materials Today: Proceedings*, 33(January), 1206–1211.

Li, Y., Chen, R., Sensale-Rodriguez, B., Gao, W., and Yu, C. (2021). Real-time multi-task diffractive deep neural networks via hardware-software co-design. *Scientific Reports*, 11(1), 1–9.

Liu, C., and Liu, J. (2017). The role of metonymy in advertisements. In Proceedings of the 2017 International Conference on Humanities Science, Management and Education Technology (HSMET 2017). https://doi.org/10.2991/hsmet-17.2017.205.

Nguyen, P., Tran, D., Huang, X., and Ma, W. (2013). Age and gender classification using EEG paralinguistic features. In International IEEE/EMBS Conference on Neural Engineering, November, (pp. 1295–1298).

Sivakumar, V. L., Krishnappa, R. R., and Nallanathel, M. (2021). Drought vulnerability assessment and mapping using multi-criteria decision making (MCDM) and application of analytic hierarchy process (AHP) for namakkal district, Tamilnadu, India. *Materials Today: Proceedings*, 43(January), 1592–1599.

Srivastava, A., Mahmood, A., and Srivastava, R. (2017). A comparative analysis of SVM random forest methods for protein function prediction. In 2017 International Conference on Current Trends in Computer, Electrical, Electronics and Communication (CTCEEC), September, (pp. 1008–1010).

Thanigaivel, S., Vickram, S., Dey, N., Gulothungan, G., Subbaiya, R., and Govarthanan, M., et al. (2022). The urge of algal biomass-based fuels for environmental sustainability against a steady tide of biofuel conflict analysis: is third-generation algal biorefinery a boon? *Fuel*, 317(June), 123494.

Tursunov, A., Mustaqeem, Choeh, J. Y., and Kwon, S. (2021). Age and gender recognition using a convolutional neural network with a specially designed multi-attention module through speech spectrograms. *Sensors*, 21(17), 5892.

98 Lack of accuracy in envisioning the spread of COVID-19 over online social networks based on geographical location identification using novel naive bayes algorithm comparing support vector machine algorithm

Arani Girish[1] and Shri Vindhya, A.[2]

[1]Research Scholar, Department of Computer Science and Engineering, Saveetha School of Engineering, Saveetha Institute of Medical and Technical Sciences, Saveetha University, Chennai, India

[2]Project Guide, Corresponding Author, Department of Computer Science and Engineering, Saveetha School of Engineering, Saveetha Institute of Medical and Technical Sciences, Saveetha University, Chennai, India

Abstract

Aim: The goal of this research work is to intensify the efficiency percentage of geographical location identification to alleviate impact of covid using machine learning classifiers by comparing novel Naive Bayes (NB) algorithm and support vector machine (SVM) algorithm. Materials and Methods: NB algorithm with sample size = 10, G-power (value = 0.8) and SVM algorithm with sample size = 10 were predicted many times to evaluate the efficiency percentage. NB is evaluated by using its weights and configurations. Results and Discussion: NB algorithm has better efficiency (55%) when compared to SVM algorithm efficiency (36%). The results achieved with significance value p = 0.889 (p > 0.05) shows that two groups are statistically insignificant. Conclusion: NB algorithm performed significantly better than the SVM algorithm.

Keywords: COVID-19, COVID hotspot, efficiency, geographical location identification, novel naive bayes algorithm, support vector machine algorithm

Introduction

The aim of this research is to anticipate pandemic spread of COVID-19 using geographical location identification using novel Naive Bayes (NB) algorithm and to compare proposed algorithm with support vector machine (SVM) algorithm. In this case the experiment aims to improve the rate of efficiency in detecting social distancing violations between locations (Murphy, 2020). With the recent wave and rapid transmission of the coronavirus pandemic (Lange, 2022), the spread of covid is merely increasing. The proposed method was formerly used to become aware of the hotspots of covid inflamed areas. Geographical location identification model proposed in this research to identify the covid hotspots by using Novel random forest algorithm (Jayant, 2020). Related research concludes that the naive bayes algorithm has better efficiency and faster detection time. The applications of this research method facilitate in identifying the covid hotspots with geographical location (Smith, 1981).

The second part of the study focuses on tracking individual movement patterns during the COVID-19 pandemic using geolocation. Around 126 papers were published in IEEE Xplore and 182 publications were in google scholar on identifying hotspots on detecting physical distancing. These records were utilized to investigate the causes and consequences of COVID-19 (Wanner, 2020). A methodology for spread of COVID-19 using geographical location identification using hotspots with social distancing during the coronavirus pandemic(Simonov et al., 2020). On a national or worldwide scale, measuring the spatial structure of social networks is frequently challenging. We solve this problem in this research by calculating social connections between locales using collected data from social networks. Close research discusses the challenges within hotspot identifying the covid hotspot areas(Matheri et al., 2022). Another research illustrates how these connection measurements may be used to forecast the geographic spread of contagious illnesses.(Mahapatra, 2021). In every other method the writer proposed a technique that overcomes detection disasters and efficiently detects the covid hotspots while surprising alternate passes off in geographical location (Higgs et al., 2022; Deena et al., 2022; Thanigaivel et al., 2022; Higgs et al., 2022). The drawback of the existing geographical location identification is less efficiency in detecting

[a]keerthanasmartgenresearch@gmail.com

objects in hotspots especially when they are in motion and detecting less frames per second. The main aim of our proposed system is to improve efficiency in detecting social geographical location identifications for identifying COVID-19 using the novel NB algorithm.

Materials and Methods

This research work was performed at Cyber Forensic Laboratory, Saveetha School of Engineering, SIMATS (Saveetha Institute of Medical and Technical Sciences). The proposed work contains two groups. Group 1 is taken as NB and Group 2 as SVM (Padmanaban, n.d.). The NB algorithm and SVM algorithm were evaluated a different number of times with a sample size of 10 with confidence interval of 95%, and with pretest power of 80% and maximum accepted error is fixed as 0.05 (Gupta et al., 2019; Sivakumar et al., 2021; Lakshmi et al., 2020).

After dataset collection, the null values and unimportant content in the datasets were removed by preprocessing and data cleaning steps. After cleaning and preprocessing the data, an ideal input for the detection model is produced, which are processed into the detection model using OpenCV library and efficiency of both novel NB algorithm and SVM algorithm is calculated. The learning process of NB and SVM algorithms are given

Naive Bayes algorithm

The NB algorithm is a supervised learning algorithm that is built on the Bayesian theorem and mainly used for solving classification problems. It is primarily used in text classification, which includes a high-dimensional training data set (Ghosh and Senthilrajan, n.d.). The NB algorithm contains many decision trees. Table 98.5 shows the pseudocode for NB algorithm from dataset processing to output generation.

Support vector machine algorithm

Support vector machine algorithm is a supervised machine learning algorithm and mainly used for solving classification and regression challenges (Kumar, 2019). In the SVM algorithm, each data item is represented as a point in n-dimensional space where n is the number of characteristics of the data item. It is used to obtain exposure odds ratio in the presence of multiple explanatory variables. The process is very common to multiple linear regression, except that the response is binomial. The result is the effect of each variable on the exposure odds ratio of the observed event of interest. Table 98.6 predicts the SVM algorithm.

The detection model gives the following procedure. Table 98.1 gives the source of covid affected hotspots. The hotspots are processed using the open csv library and each frame is detected at once. It is displayed as a graph that may indicate the number of tweets at a certain place in the frame, which is then translated into a top-down perspective. The top-down view may be used to estimate the position of each hotspot. It is possible to measure and scale the distance between each hotspot. Any distance less than the permitted distance between any two places as a warning, according to the predefined minimum distance. Python programming language was used to implement this work.

The following are minimum hardware requirements to implement this model processor: intel i5, RAM 8GB, 500 GB HDD storage.

Software specifications are concerned with the resources that must be installed in the target system in order to get an application to work. The minimal software specifications for this model to work are windows operating system version 7/8/10, Python programming language version 3 or above, Google collab.

Table 98.1 Dataset name- name, extension and source.

S. No	Dataset name	Dataset extension	Dataset source
1	Covid19_tweets	CSV	Kaggle.com
2	world cities	CSV	Kaggle.com

Source: Author

Table 98.2 Efficiency of Naive Bayes algorithm and support vector machine algorithm. The Naive Bayes algorithm is 19% more efficient than the random forest algorithm.

Iteration no.	Naive Bayes (%)	SVM (%)
1	60	41
2	58	40
3	57	39
4	56	38
5	55	37
6	54	36
7	53	35
8	52	34
9	51	33
10	50	32

Source: Author

Table 98.3 Group statistics of Naive Bayes algorithm and support vector machine algorithm with the mean value of 54.60% and 36.50%.

Group	N	Mean (%)	Std. deviation	Std. error mean
NB	10	54.60	3.204	1.013
SVM	10	36.50	3.028	0.957

Source: Author

Table 98.4 Independent sample *T*-test is performed for the two groups for significance and standard error determination. The significance value p = 0.889 (p > 0.05) shows that two groups are statistically insignificant.

	Equal variance	Levene's test for equality of variance		T-test for equality of means						95% Confidence interval of the difference	
		F	Sig	t	df	Sig (2-tailed)	Mean difference	Std. error difference		Lower	Upper
Accuracy	Assumed	0.20	.889	12.984	18	.001	18.100	1.394		15.171	21.029
	Not assumed			12.984	17.943	.001	18.100	1.394		15.171	21.029

Source: Author

Table 98.5 Pseudocode for Naive Bayes algorithm.

1. Start the program
2. Load the data (train set, test set).
3. Remove unwanted variables from the dataset
4. Visualization of data set
5. Import Naive Bayes model from sklearn.linear_model
6. Fit train set and test set to Naive Bayes model.
7. Do K-fold cross validation on our train set
8. Predict the geographical location identification of train set
9. Measure the accuracy of the model on test set
10. Compile model
11. End the program

Source: Author

Table 98.6 Pseudocode for support vector machine algorithm.

1. Start the program
2. Load the data (train set, test set).
3. Remove unwanted variables from the dataset
4. Visualization of data set
5. Import SVM model from sklearn.linear_model
6. Fit train set and test set to SVM model.
7. Do K-fold cross validation on our train set
8. Predict the geographical location identification of train set
9. Measure the accuracy of the model on test set
10. Compile model
11. End the program

Source: Author

Statistical analysis

IBM SPSS is used for statistical analysis. The independent variable is user id and the dependent variable is tweet location and country (McCormick and Salcedo, 2017). The independent T-Test analysis is performed.

Results

Table 98.1 shows the dataset for several users and their locations. Table 98.2 represents the simulated efficiency of novel NB and SVM algorithms. Table 98.3 represents group statistics of NB and SVM algorithm with the mean value of 54.60% and 36.50%

respectively. Table 98.4 represents the independent T-test analysis of both the groups with significance value p = 0.889 (p > 0.05) states that both groups are statistically insignificant. Figure 98.1 shows architecture for geographical location identification using novel NB algorithm, from dataset processing to output of each frame.

Figure 98.2 shows the bar graph analysis based on efficiencies of two algorithms. The mean efficiencies of novel NB and SVM are 55% and 36% respectively. From the results obtained it is inferred that the novel NB algorithm is more efficient than the SVM algorithm.

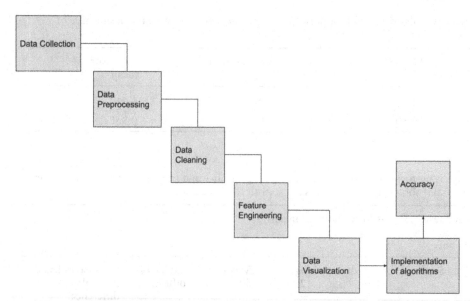

Figure 98.1 Architecture for geographical location identification using novel Naive Bayes algorithm, from dataset collection to accuracy calculation

Source: Author

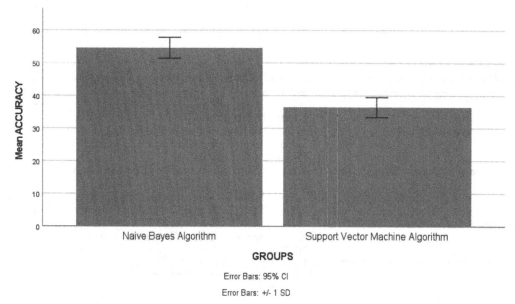

Figure 98.2 Bar graph analysis of novel Naive Bayes algorithm and support vector machine algorithm. Graphical representation shows the mean efficiency of 55% and 36% for the proposed algorithm NB algorithm and SVM respectively. X-axis: NB vs SVM, Y-axis: Mean precision ± 1 SD

Source: Author

Discussion

In this research work, NB and SVM algorithm were evaluated for predicting the efficiency of geographical location identification in covid hotspots using twitter. After validating the two models using the same datasets it was observed that the NB algorithm has better performance than the SVM algorithm. The novel NB detection model for finding COVID-19 hotspots and geographical location identification between hotspots was developed, which makes use of OpenCV library to process the identifying the location. The proposed model detects the objects and their distances using NB, and displays a user's tweets by location detected. The datasets from different ranges of location helped in improving the efficiency percentage.

The research resulted in less development of efficiency in detecting geographical location identification between covid hotspots (Xu et al., 2022). A similar work in identification of covid hotspots and areas distance calculation using NB algorithm (Ghosh and Senthilrajan, n.d.). The results achieved after all iterations on each dataset showed a constant 55% efficiency. The model proposed resulted in achieving more than 19% increase of efficiency compared to the existing model (Sang, 2022). The similar research carried out is about covid hotspots identification which is best for future researchers who are interested in covid hotspots detection (Kuznetsov and Sadovskaya, 2021). There aren't any such contrary findings with regards to existing item detection for geolocation identification of covid hotspots.

The proposed system of this paper is to get the information about the geographical location identification on predicting the hotspots of COVID-19 pandemic. Although our proposed system is faster than SVM algorithm in detecting covid hotspot areas, it is generally extracting only limited features from the hotspots and it is limited to testing only hotspots data (Syetiawan et al., 2022). Further, this research work can be improved by identifying the impact of covid on people living in geographical locations.

Conclusion

In this research work, prediction of efficiency percentage for geographic location identification using Naive Bayes algorithm appears to have enhanced efficiency (55%) when compared to support vector machine algorithm (36%). Location identification has been successfully employed for geographical location identification for tweet counts by users. The results reveal the maximum number of true positives compared to true negatives from all the observations.

Conflict of Interest

The author declares no conflict of interest.

Authors Contribution

The authors were involved in data collection, data analysis, and manuscript writing, in conceptualization, data validation, and critical review of manuscript.

Acknowledgement

The authors would like to express their gratitude towards Saveetha School of Engineering, Saveetha Institute of Medical And Technical Sciences (Formerly known as Saveetha University) for providing the necessary infrastructure to carry out this work successfully.

Funding

We thank the following organizations for providing financial support that enabled us to complete the research.

1. Indigitech, Chennai, Tamil Nadu.
2. Saveetha University.
3. Saveetha Institute of Medical And Technical Sciences.
4. Saveetha School of Engineering.

References

Deena, S. R., Vickram, A. S., and Manikandan, S. (2022). Enhanced biogas production from food waste and activated sludge using advanced techniques–a review. *BioResources* . https://www.sciencedirect.com/science/article/pii/S0960852422005636.

Ghosh, A., and Senthilrajan, A. (n.d.), Implementing naive bayes algorithm for detecting spam emails on datasets. https://doi.org/10.20944/preprints202005.0241.v1.

Gupta, S., Kapil, R., Kanahasabai, G., Joshi, S. S., and Joshi, A. S. (2019). SD-measure: a social distancing detector. https://ieeexplore.ieee.org/document/9242628.

Higgs, G., Langford, M., and Llewellyn, M. (2022). Towards an understanding of inequalities in accessing residential and nursing home provision: the role of geographical approaches. *Health and Social Care in the Community*, 30(6), 2218–2229. https://doi.org/10.1111/hsc.13770.

Jayant, A. (2020). Data science and machine learning series: bayes theorem and the naive bayes classifier .

Kumar, D. (2019). Machine learning series: the support vector machine (SVM) in Python .

Kuznetsov, A., and Sadovskaya, V. (2021). Spatial variation and hotspot detection of COVID-19 cases in Kazakhstan, 2020. *Spatial and Spatio-Temporal Epidemiology*, 39(November), 100430.

Lakshmi, S. V., Ramalakshmi, M., Rakshith, R. K., Christobel, M. J., Kumar, P. P., Priyadharshini, B., et al. (2020). An integration of geospatial technology and standard precipitation index (SPI) for drought vulnerability assessment for a part of Namakkal district, South India. *Materials Today: Proceedings*, 33(January), 1206–1211.

Lange, P. W. (2022). Response to characteristics of nursing homes associated with COVID-19 outbreaks and mortality among residents in Victoria, Australia. *Australasian Journal on Ageing*, 41(2), 345. https://doi.org/10.1111/ajag.13047.

Mahapatra, A. (2021). COVID-19: Separating Fact from Fiction. Penguin Random House India Private Limited.

Matheri, A. N., Belaid, M., Njenga, C. K., and Ngila, J. C. (2022). Water and wastewater digital surveillance for monitoring and early detection of the COVID-19 hotspot: industry 4.0. *International Journal of Environmental Science and Technology: IJEST*, 1–18 .

McCormick, K., and Salcedo, J. (2017). SPSS Statistics for Data Analysis and Visualization. John Wiley & Sons.

Murphy, P. (2020). COVID-19: Proportionality, Public Policy and Social Distancing. Springer Nature.

Padmanaban, H. (n.d.). Comparative analysis of naive bayes and tree augmented naive bayes models. https://doi.org/10.31979/etd.n7jg-e3uh.

Sang Minh, N. (2022). Impact of the COVID-19 pandemic on bank efficiency in Vietnam. *Banks and Bank Systems*, 17(1), 13–23. https://doi.org/10.21511/bbs.17(1).2022.02.

Simonov, A., Sacher, S. K., Dubé, J. P. H., and Biswas, S. (2020). The persuasive effect of fox news: non-compliance with social distancing during the Covid-19 pandemic .

Sivakumar, V. L., Krishnappa, R. R., and Nallanathel, M. (2021). Drought vulnerability assessment and mapping using multi-criteria decision making (MCDM) and application of analytic hierarchy process (AHP)

for Namakkal District, Tamilnadu, India. *Materials Today: Proceedings*, 43(January), 1592–1599.

Smith, D. M. (1981). Industrial Location: An Economic Geographical Analysis. John Wiley and Sons.

Syetiawan, A., Harimurti, M., and Prihanto, Y. (2022). A spatiotemporal analysis of COVID-19 transmission in Jakarta, Indonesia for pandemic decision support. *Geospatial Health*, 17(s1). https://doi.org/10.4081/gh.2022.1042.

Thanigaivel, S., Vickram, S., Dey, N., Gulothungan, G., Subbaiya, R., Govarthanan, M., et al. (2022). The urge of algal biomass-based fuels for environmental sustainability against a steady tide of biofuel conflict analysis: is third-generation algal biorefinery a boon? *Fuel*, 317(June), 123494.

Wanner , R. M. (2020). COVID-19 stadium ideas for social distancing: six feet from everybody, OK?

Xu, Z., Zhang, H., and Huang, Z. (2022). A continuous markov-chain model for the simulation of COVID-19 epidemic dynamics. *Biology*, 11(2). https://doi.org/10.3390/biology11020190.

99 Stress of employees toward private sector banks with reference to Palakkad district

Vishal, K.[1] and Usha, M.[2]

[1]Research Scholar, Department of Management, Karpagam Academy of Higher, Education, Coimbatore, Tamil Nadu, India

[2]Associate Professor, Department of Management, Karpagam Academy of Higher, Education, Coimbatore, Tamil Nadu, India

Abstract

In recent years, the banking industry, particularly in India, has been subjected to a number of important developments. The Palakkad district's private sector banks function within the greater context of economic changes, technology improvements, shifting consumer expectations, and regulatory reforms. Inside the framework of this discussion, we examine the levels of stress that are experienced by personnel working inside major financial organizations. The study's objectives involve identifying significant demographic factors and their impact on job stress and formulating evidence-based strategies for organizations to enhance employee well-being. The methodology involves a comprehensive analysis of a dataset, encompassing demographic variables such as gender, age, family type, area of residence, educational qualification, and occupation, in conjunction with job stress metrics. Statistical techniques, including ANOVA and chi-square tests, are employed to reveal significant relationships. Key findings emerge, emphasizing the significance of gender, family type, age, and area of residence in influencing job stress. Gender disparities are evident in pay stress, emphasizing the need for gender-inclusive practices. Family type significantly impacts both pay and promotion stress, underlining the importance of family-friendly policies. The study concludes by advocating for data-driven strategies, diversity and inclusion initiatives, and commitment to continuous improvement within organizations. These insights provide actionable guidance for organizations striving to cultivate a positive, inclusive work environment that meets the diverse needs of employees, ultimately fostering higher job stress and productivity.

Keywords: Private sector banks and workplace, stress of employees

Introduction

Efficient management of employee stress is crucial for the success of an organisation. Enhanced employee satisfaction heightens the probability of them being motivated, efficient, and committed to their employment. In the context of private sector banks in Palakkad district, it is essential to assess and understand the level of stress among employees, as this can have a significant impact on the overall performance of these financial institutions. To evaluate employee stress in private sector banks, we have designed a comprehensive questionnaire consisting of various statements related to different aspects of the work environment. An organization's capacity to effectively handle employee stress is crucial for achieving success. Enhanced employee satisfaction heightens the probability of their motivation, efficiency, and commitment toward their task. The value of this research rests in the fact that it provides an understanding of the varied issues that bank personnel in the Palakkad area encounter within the wider context of the dynamics of the banking

industry. The management of employee stress is not only essential for the health and happiness of people but also for the efficiency of organizations, levels of production, and the quality of service provided to customers. For the purpose of conducting a study on the levels of stress experienced by workers in private sector banks in the Palakkad area, it is necessary to investigate empirical data, get qualitative insights, and maybe conduct surveys or interviews with the workers themselves. These kinds of research projects have the ability to give a complete knowledge of the nature, causes, and possible solutions to the stress that is experienced in these financial institutions. This study eventually aims to shed light on the challenges faced by the workforce in the banking sector and to propose viable strategies for enhancing employee well-being and organizational performance by delving into the stress endured by employees in private sector banks within the Palakkad district. This is accomplished by looking into the stress encountered by employees in private sector banks within the Palakkad district. Thus, the study is to analyse the stress of employees

[a]amritasmartgenresearch@gmail.com

towards employees working in private sector banks with reference to Palakkad district.

Statement of Problem

In the demographic area of Palakkad district, employees working in private sector banks encounter several challenges that affect their job stress and overall well-being. The following problem statement encapsulates the key issues faced by these employees: "Employees in private sector banks in Palakkad district" face significant challenges related to job stress, stemming from issues such as inadequate compensation, limited promotion opportunities, suboptimal supervision, distress with fringe benefits, insufficient contingent rewards, cumbersome operating procedures, strained coworker relationships, varying degrees of fulfillment in the nature of work, and communication gaps within the organization. These challenges collectively contribute to decrease employee morale, reduce motivation, and potential disengagement, ultimately impacting the banks' ability to deliver quality services and maintain a positive work environment. This problem statement highlights the multifaceted nature of the issues faced by employees in private sector banks in Palakkad district and emphasizes the need for strategic interventions and improvements to address these challenges effectively.

Objectives of the Study

- To study the demographic variables of the employees working in private sector banks.
- To analyse the stress of the respondents towards pay, promotion opportunities, supervision, fringe benefits, contingent rewards, operating procedures, coworkers, nature of work, and communication.
- To find the impact of demographic varaibles on level of stress of the respondents towards various dimensions taken for the study.

Scope of the Study

- The research focuses primarily on the demographic region of Palakkad district in Kerala, India, taking into account the distinctive socio-cultural and economic elements that might potentially impact employee stress inside private sector banks in this locality.
- The primary emphasis of this study is to be on personnel who are employed in private sector banks located in the Palakkad area.
- This research aims to conduct a complete investigation into the nine factors of employee happi-

ness, including compensation, promotion chances, supervision, fringe benefits, contingent incentives, operational procedures, teammates, nature of job, and communication.

Research Methodology

Descriptive research: The present study used a descriptive research approach.

    Primary data collection: Questionnaire using survey method.

    Secondary data: Articles, journals and websites.

    Sampling method: Convenience sampling is the method used for selecting respondents. This approach entails the selection of participants based on their availability and voluntary participation.

    Sample size: The objective of this research is to collect data from a sample of 325 individuals employed in private sector banks located in the Palakkad area.

    Data analysis tools: Percentage analysis, descriptive statistics, Kruskall Wallis test and one-way ANOVA

Limitations of the Study

- The presented data may not be fully representative of the total population, which might introduce bias into the obtained results.
- The survey methodology is dependent on data that is self-reported, which introduces the possibility of response bias.
- The study's narrow scope on Palakkad district and the use of convenience sampling may restrict the extent to which the results can be applied to other geographical areas or the whole of the private sector banking industry in India.

Data Analysis and Interpretation

The majority of respondents are male, accounting for 58.1% of the total respondents, while females make up 41.9% of the total. This suggests that there are more male respondents in the survey. The largest age group among the respondents is those between 31 and 40 years old, representing 40.5% of the total respondents. This indicates that a significant portion of the respondents falls in this age range. On the other hand, respondents above 50 years old are the smallest group at 3.5%. Urban residents make up the majority of the respondents, constituting 39.9% of the total. Semi-urban and rural areas have 28% and 32.1% of the respondents, respectively. This suggests that a higher percentage of respondents come from urban areas.

    Respondents with a postgraduate education level are the majority, comprising 34.4% of the total respondents. Undergraduates and professionals also

Table 99.1 Demographic Variables.

Demographic variables	Particulars	Frequency	Percent
Gender	Male	218	58.1
	Female	157	41.9
	Total	375	100
Age	Up to 30 years	54	14.4
	31 – 40 years	152	40.5
	41 – 50 years	156	41.6
	Above 50 years	13	3.5
	Total	375	100
Area	Rural	120.5	32.1
	Semi-urban	105	28
	Urban	149.5	39.9
	Total	375	100
Educational qualification	Higher secondary	57.5	15.3
	Undergraduate	107	28.5
	Postgraduate	129	34.4
	Professional	68.5	18.3
	Others	13	3.5
	Total	375	100

Source: Author

Table 99.2 Stress of respondents pay.

Particulars	N		SDA	DA	N	A	SA	Mean	SD
(PA1)	325	FRQ	108	5	109	106	48	2.95	1.398
		%	28.7	1.3	28.9	28.3	12.8		
(PA2)	325	FRQ	176	20	16	104	60	2.60	1.639
		%	46.9	5.3	4.3	27.6	15.9		
(PA3)	325	FRQ	69	20	41	118	128	3.58	1.462
		%	18.4	5.2	10.8	31.5	34.1		
(PA4)	325	FRQ	54	14	38	115	155	3.81	1.382
		%	14.3	3.6	10.1	30.7	41.3		

Source: Author

represent substantial portions at 28.5% and 18.3%, respectively. This indicates that a significant proportion of respondents have higher educational qualifications. Conversely, those with "higher secondary" and other qualifications make up smaller percentages at 15.3% and 3.5%, respectively.

Stress Toward Dimensions of the Study

The combined percentage of those who agree (28.3%) and strongly agree (12.8%) is notable. The mean score of 2.60 suggests that, on average, respondents tend to disagree with the statement that raises are too few and far between. The majority of respondents fall into the "strongly disagree" category (46.9%), indicating that they do not feel that raises are infrequent. However, there is a notable percentage of respondents who either agree (27.6%) or strongly agree (15.9%) with this statement. The mean score of 3.58 suggests that, on average, respondents tend to agree with the statement that they feel unappreciated by the organization when considering their pay. In summary, the data

Table 99.3 Stress of respondents toward promotion.

Particulars	N		SDA	DA	N	A	SA	Mean	SD
(PR1)	350	FRQ	44	29	98	136	69	3.42	1.212
		%	11.7	7.6	26.1	36.1	18.4		
(PR2)	350	FRQ	35	51	35	155	101	3.63	1.265
		%	9.3	13.5	9.2	41.2	26.8		
(PR3)	350	FRQ	16	40	78	139	104	3.73	1.099
		%	4.1	10.5	20.7	37.1	27.6		
(PR4)	350	FRQ	50	73	63	86	103	3.32	1.399
		%	13.3	19.5	16.8	22.9	27.5		

Source: Author

Table 99.4 Stress of respondents towards supervision.

Particulars	N		SDA	DA	N	A	SA	Mean	SD
(SV1)	350	FRQ	17	24	120	135	80	3.63	1.028
		%	4.5	6.3	31.9	36	21.3		
(SV2)	350	FRQ	80	137	43	84	32	2.60	1.272
		%	21.3	36.5	11.5	22.3	8.4		
(SV3)	350	FRQ	26	39	56	130	125	3.77	1.211
		%	6.9	10.3	14.8	34.7	33.3		
(SV4)	350	FRQ	62	61	36	86	131	3.43	1.501
		%	16.4	16.3	9.6	22.9	34.8		

Source: Author

Table 99.5 Stress of Respondents toward supervision.

Particulars	N		SDA	DA	N	A	SA	Mean	SD
(SV1)	350	FRQ	17	24	120	135	80	3.63	1.028
		%	4.5	6.3	31.9	36	21.3		
(SV2)	350	FRQ	80	137	43	84	32	2.60	1.272
		%	21.3	36.5	11.5	22.3	8.4		
(SV3)	350	FRQ	26	39	56	130	125	3.77	1.211
		%	6.9	10.3	14.8	34.7	33.3		
(SV4)	350	FRQ	62	61	36	86	131	3.43	1.501
		%	16.4	16.3	9.6	22.9	34.8		

Source: Author

indicates that while respondents are relatively neutral about whether they are being paid fairly for their work, they tend to disagree with the perception that raises are infrequent. However, a significant portion of respondents feels unappreciated regarding their pay, and the majority is satisfied with their chances for salary increases.

The mean score of 3.32 suggests that, on average, respondents tend to be somewhat neutral in their stress with their chances for promotion. The data

indicates that respondents generally perceive that those who perform well have a fair chance of being promoted and that career advancement opportunities are comparable to other places. However, there is some variation in respondents' perceptions of promotion opportunities, with a significant portion feeling neutral or dissatisfied with their chances for promotion.

The mean score of 3.43 suggests that, on average, respondents tend to have a positive opinion of their

Table 99.6 Stress toward communication.

Particulars	N		SDA	DA	N	A	SA	Mean	SD
Co1	350	FRQ	53	89	5	171	58	3.24	1.347
		%	14.1	23.6	1.3	45.6	15.3		
Co2	350	FRQ	42	107	6	127	94	3.33	1.400
		%	11.1	28.4	1.6	33.9	25.1		
Co3	350	FRQ	36	96	35	137	72	3.30	1.295
		%	9.5	25.6	9.2	36.5	19.2		
Co4	350	FRQ	67	83	10	97	119	3.31	1.538
		%	17.9	22.1	2.5	25.9	31.6		

Source: Author

Table 99.7 Comparison between demo graphic profile (gender, type of family) and their acceptance towards job stress based on pay.

Demographic variables	Particulars	N	Mean rank	Chi-square	Asymp. sig.
Gender	Male	436	389.74	4.571	0.033
	Female	314	355.72		
	Total	750			
Type of family	Joint	329	344.10	12.501	0.000
	Nuclear	421	400.03		
	Total	750			

Source: Author

Table 99.8 Comparison between demo graphic profile (gender, type of family) and their job stress based on promotion.

Demographic variables	Particulars	N	Mean rank	Chi-square	Asymp. sig.
Gender	Male	436	386.26	2.609	0.106
	Female	314	360.56		
	Total	750			
Type of family	Joint	329	346.69	10.529	0.001
	Nuclear	421	398.01		
	Total	750			

Source: Author

supervisors. The data suggest that, on average, respondents have a positive perception of their supervisors' competence, fairness, interest in subordinates' feelings, and likability. Most respondents perceive their supervisors in a favorable light.

The mean score of 3.43 suggests that, on average, respondents tend to have a positive opinion of their supervisors. The data indicate that, on average, respondents have a positive perception of their supervisors' competence, fairness, interest in subordinates' feelings, and likability. Most respondents perceive

their supervisors in a favorable light, with a notable percentage strongly agreeing with positive statements about their supervisors.

The effective management of employee stress is crucial for the success of an organisation. Enhanced employee satisfaction heightens the probability of them being motivated, efficient, and committed to their work. The combined percentage of those who agree (25.9%) and strongly agree (31.6%) is significant, indicating a perception of inadequate communication regarding work assignments. In summary,

Table 99.9 Comparison between demo graphic profile (age, area, educational qualification, occupation, no of children, no. of earning members, no. of on earning members, monthly income, total family expense) and their job stress based on supervision.

Demographic variables	Particulars	N	Mean	SD	F	Sig
Age	Up to 30 years	108	3.14	0.755	11.254	.000
	31 – 40 Years	304	3.47	0.573		
	41 – 50 years	312	3.35	0.536		
	Above 50 years	26	3.04	0.780		
	Total	750	3.36	0.608		
Area	Rural	241	3.34	0.634	4.399	.013
	Semi-urban	210	3.28	0.537		
	Urban	299	3.43	0.626		
	Total	750	3.36	0.608		
Educational qualification	Higher secondary	115	3.33	0.597	1.801	.127
	Undergraduate	214	3.38	0.688		
	Postgraduate	258	3.30	0.546		
	Professional	137	3.46	0.604		
	Others	26	3.38	0.506		
	Total	750	3.36	0.608		
Occupation	Private sector employee	129	3.43	0.605	.895	.466
	Government sector employee	175	3.33	0.530		
	Business	269	3.34	0.573		
	Farmer	81	3.33	0.707		
	Others	96	3.41	0.737		
	Total	750	3.36	0.608		

Source: Author

the data indicates that, on average, respondents tend to have mixed perceptions of communication within the organization. While they generally view communications as good, there are concerns about the clarity of organizational goals, a lack of awareness about organizational activities, and incomplete explanations of work assignments. There may be opportunities to improve communication to address these concerns.

Ho1: There is no relationship between demo graphic profile (gender, type of family) and their Job stress based on pay

A relationship exists between the type of family (0.000) and job stress related to pay. Specifically, respondents from joint families have a lower mean rank (344.10) compared to respondents from nuclear families (400.03), suggesting that, on average, respondents from nuclear families have higher job stress related to pay than those from joint families.

H02: There is no relationship between demo graphic profile (gender, type of family) and their Job stress based on promotion

A relationship exists between the type of family (0.001) and job stress related to promotion. Specifically, respondents from nuclear families have a higher mean rank (398.01) compared to respondents from joint families (346.69), suggesting that, on average, respondents from nuclear families have higher job stress related to promotion than those from joint families.

H03: There is a significant difference between (age, area, educational qualification, occupation, no of children, no. of earning members, no. of on earning members, monthly income, total family expense) and their Job stress based on supervision

- Age and area of residence have a significant impact on job stress related to supervision.
- Educational qualifications and occupation do not have a significant impact on job stress related to supervision.
- For the variables where significant differences were observed, post-hoc tests can be conducted to further explore and identify specific groups that

exhibit significant variations in job stress related to supervision.

Findings

Stress toward pay

A significant percentage of respondents agreed (28.3%) or strongly agreed (12.8%) that raises were infrequent.

However, the majority disagreed with the perception of infrequent raises, and the mean score suggested overall disagreement.

A notable portion of respondents (43.5%) felt unappreciated regarding their pay.

Stress toward promotion

Respondents were somewhat neutral (mean score: 3.32) about their chances for promotion.

There was variation in perceptions, with a significant portion feeling neutral or dissatisfied with their chances for promotion.

Stress toward supervision

On average, respondents had a positive opinion of their supervisors (mean score: 3.43).

Respondents generally perceived their supervisors as competent, fair, interested in subordinates' feelings, and likable.

Stress toward communication

Respondents had mixed perceptions of communication within the organization.

While they generally viewed communications as good, there were concerns about the clarity of organizational goals, lack of awareness about organizational activities, and incomplete explanations of work assignments.

Comparison of demographic profiles with job stress

There was a significant relationship between the type of family and job stress related to pay and promotion.

Respondents from nuclear families experienced higher job stress related to pay and promotion compared to those from joint families.

Age and area of residence significantly impacted job stress related to supervision.

Educational qualifications and occupation did not show significant impacts on job stress related to supervision.

Suggestions

- The study suggests a need for organizations to address concerns related to pay, promotion, and communication.

- Strategies to improve the perception of appreciation for work and clarity in communication may enhance overall job satisfaction.
- Organizations should consider tailoring strategies based on demographic factors, such as family type, age, and area of residence, to effectively manage job stress.
- Given the significant difference in pay stress between genders, organizations should consider conducting pay equity audits to ensure that compensation is fair and equal for all employees regardless of gender.
- Organizations should also focus on creating an inclusive workplace culture to address any gender-related disparities in job stress.
- Recognizing the impact of family type on job stress, organizations can implement family-friendly policies and benefits to support employees from joint families, such as flexible work hours and childcare support.
- For employees from nuclear families, organizations can focus on career development and growth opportunities.

Conclusion

In summary, the analysis of job stress and its association with demographic factors reveals important insights for organizations aiming to enhance employee well-being and productivity. Gender disparities are evident in pay stress, highlighting the need for pay equity audits and gender-inclusive workplace practices. Family type significantly impacts both pay and promotion stress, emphasizing the importance of family-friendly policies. Age and area of residence influence supervision stress, suggesting the need for tailored training and communication strategies. While educational qualification and occupation do not exhibit major effects in this dataset, continuous monitoring is essential. Organizations should adopt data-driven strategies, promote diversity and inclusion, and maintain a commitment to continuous improvement to cultivate a workplace where employees from diverse backgrounds feel valued and satisfied.

References

Dobre, O. I. (2013). Employee motivation and organizational performance. *Review of Applied Socio-Economic Research*, 5(1), 53.

Ganguly, A. K., and Chattopadhyay, S. (2020). The employees perception on technology adoption in banks: an empirical study on two major private banks. *American Journal of Business and Management Research*, 1(3), 1–12.

Gupta, V., Kulkarni, S., and Khatri, N. (2018). Leadership and management of private sector undertakings in an emerging economy. Indian Institute of Management Ahmedabad India Research and Privateations WP, (2018-01), 04.

Helina, S. T., and Rathiha, D. R. (2018). Transformation in banks through e-banking services–employee's perception. *International Journal of Management Studies*, 69 –76.

Kulkarni, A. A., and Metre, D. S. G. (2020). A comparative study of customer stress of urban co-operative bank with special reference to Pune, Mumbai and Nagpur regions. *International Journal of Management*, 11(9).

Kumar, A., and Kumar, R. (2017). Factor influencing job stress of employees: a study on BEML: India. *ZENITH International Journal of Business Economics and Management Research*, 7(12), 130–139.

Manjunatha, M. K., and Renukamurthy, T. P. (2017). Stress among banking employee-a literature review. *International Journal of Research -GRANTHAALAYAH*, 5, 207–213.

Mohanadasan, T. (2022). Customer relationship management skill: a sector-wise analysis of the variation among the bank managers in Kerala. *Journal of Positive School Psychology*, 9406 –9417.

Ok, U., and Prakash, A. (2019). A comparative study on CRM of traditional scheduled bank and new private sector bank in Kerala. *IJRAR-International Journal of Research and Analytical Reviews (IJRAR)*, 6(2), 615–623.

Sadanandan, R. (2001). Government health services in Kerala: who benefits? *Economic and Political Weekly*, 3071 –3077.

Srivastava, G., and Mittal, A. (2013). Customer's expectation from service quality of private and private sector bank: a comparitive study. *International Journal on Customer Relations*, 1(1), 38.

Subeesh, M. M. (2015). Quality of work life among the employees of mass media industry in Kerala (Doctoral dissertation, Dept. of Commerce and Management Studies, University of Calicut, 2015.).

Suginraj, M. (2016). A study on stress management of security guards with special reference to Trivandrum district. *International Journal of Research -GRANTHAALAYAH*, 4(5SE), 12–17.

Sukthankar, S. V., Chonkar, V., Rath, R. C., and Jain, V. K. (2020). An appraisal of goa urban cooperative bank: an empirical study. *Splint International Journal of Professionals*, 7(4), 94–100.

100 Predicting purchase intention of online customers using Naive Bayes classifier and compared with decision tree

Pippalla Naga Sai Charan[1] and Manikandan, N.[2]

[1]Research Scholar, Department of Computer Science and Engineering, Saveetha School of Engineering, Saveetha Institution of Medical and Technical Sciences, Saveetha University, Chennai, India

[2]Project Guide, Department of Computer Science and Engineering, Saveetha School of Engineering, Saveetha Institution of Medical and Technical Sciences, Saveetha University, Chennai, India

Abstract

Aim: This study compare the performance of the Naive Bayes (NB) algorithm to that of the decision tree (D-Tree) method, with the goal of determining whether the former is more effective at predicting future online purchases. This will be accomplished by comparing the two algorithms side-by-side. Materials and Methods: The data set that was utilized for this analysis was obtained from the Kaggle network. The sample size for the online purchase prediction with a higher rate of accuracy was 20 (Group 1 = 10 and Group 2 = 10), and calculations were performed using G-power 0.8, alpha and beta values of 0.05 and 0.2, and a 95% confidence interval. NB with N = 10 samples and D-Tree with N = 10 samples are used to predict the online purchase intent with an enhanced accuracy rate. Results: The proposed naive bayes achieves a 97.25% success rate compared to the decision tree classifier's 91.80% success rate. This represents a significant difference. The significance level of the investigation was determined to be p = 0.034. Conclusion: The suggested NB model obtains a greater rate of accuracy than the D-Tree model when it comes to the estimation of the behavior of making purchases online.

Keywords: Accuracy rate, classification, decision tree, e-commerce, novel Naïve Bayes, online purchase, purchase prediction

Introduction

Online shopping's popularity has grown alongside the amount of people who have access to the internet, drawing more and more focus to the importance of advertising on the web (Merugu and Mohan, 2020; Wadhawan and Arya, 2020). For various preferences of user behavior prediction study has become a hot direction in light of the influx of information and the widespread and non-targeted exploitation of Internet advertising (Rausch et al., 2022). In this research, we attempt to develop a model that can predict a user's buying intentions and divide them into two groups, those who plan to shop and those who don't. The application of machine learning techniques to address the issue of user interest analysis is a rapidly developing area of study in the study of e-commerce. This research develops a novel Naïve Bayes (NB) method to predict the customer purchase intention in the e-commerce products and compare the results with decision tree (D-Tree) algorithm (Moon et al., 2021; Dey et al. 2020). Based on the experimental findings, the proposed NB approach improves recognition accuracy and throughput. NB classification is frequently used in clinical diagnosis, text analysis, e-mail filtering, and information retrieval because to its high efficiency and strong classification accuracy (Golpour et al., 2020).

There have been a vast number of studies over the past five years aimed at analyzing customer interest in making a purchase of a particular online product (Wibowo and Oesman, 2020; Aldossari et al., 2020; Shafin et al., 2020; Bashir et al., 2021). A total of 67 exam papers were made available through IEEE Explore, while 97 were located using a Google Scholar search. According to Solomon (Solomon and Panda, 2004), "search behavior" is defined as the process of looking for information online in order to make a decision, such as an online purchase. Based on a probabilistic model, the naive Bayes technique was developed by Zuev and Moore (2005). All of the classification attributes must be uncorrelated and normally distributed for this method to work. The linearly separable ideas can all be described by the Bias classifier, as demonstrated by Sun et al., (2009). To predict purchasing intent from user activity on an e-commerce website, Vieira (Vieira, 2015) contrasted conventional machine learning methods and proposed a classifier. Zhang et al. proposed a methodology for predicting consumers' purchase intent based on their mobile search habits (Zhang et al., 2016). By employing a regression analysis, Franjkovi (Franjković, 2017) investigated the connection between the price-image dimensions and consumer desire to make a purchase. She came to the

[a]manimegalai82823828@gmail.com

conclusion that the price-image dimension Quality for money had the greatest impact on consumers' propensity to make a purchase, followed by Price level and Price perceptibility. To foretell purchases made by users during in-progress sessions in an online shop, Suchacka and Stemplewski (Suchacka and Stemplewski, 2017) developed a neural network model. The Hidden Markov Model, a stochastic instrument typically employed in data extraction, is being utilized to forecast consumers' propensity to make purchases on the internet in another study (Varol and Marquez, 2020). Web server logs are gathered, cleansed, and analyzed by the team. Based on findings, Lee et al., (2022) presented a method that combines NB and D-Tree to comprehend the categorization of intention problems.

The main problem with the current approach is that it is vulnerable to instability due to its reliance on the sample proportion in the given dataset. There are some situations in which it performs badly and recognition accuracy is low. In order to address this shortcoming, this work proposes a unique NB algorithm for determining the intent to buy among online shoppers. The decision tree algorithm is used to evaluate the outcomes. The dataset has been used from the Kaggle repository. Based on the experimental results, it is clear that the suggested NB technique outperforms the use of conventional decision tree classifiers in terms of both recognition accuracy and processing speed. When applied to the task of automatically forecasting online shoppers' intent to buy, this new method points in the right direction.

Materials and Methods

The investigation was carried out in the Computer Science and Engineering Department's Software Laboratory at Saveetha University. In this particular research study, the dataset was obtained from the Kaggle repository. The database is structured so that 75% of it is dedicated to training, and 25% is for testing. There are two sets taken, and each set has ten data samples; the total number of samples taken into consideration is twenty. Group 1 was a D-Tree algorithm and Group 2 was a novel NB algorithm. Python is the software that is used for the online buying prediction model, and it is this software that generates the output. The sample size was determined by using previous research from (Xu et al., 2020) at clinicalc.com. The threshold for the calculation was set at 0.05, the G power was set at 80%, and the confidence interval was set at 95%.

Decision tree
D-Trees are a type of decision - making tool that employs a tree-like graph or representation of decisions and the potential repercussions, such as the outcomes of random events, the costs and benefits of resources, and the value of the decisions themselves. That's one way to show off an algorithm you've written. Not only are D-Trees a popular machine learning technique, but they are also widely used in the field of operations research, particularly in the field of decision analysis, to determine which course of action is most likely to result in the desired outcome. Each node inside a decision tree represents a "test" on an attribute (such as whether a coin is headed up or down), each branch reflects the result of that test, and each leaf node indicates a class name. The branches from the tree's center outward symbolize different ways of organizing information. Predicted values of different options are calculated using a decision tree and the highly associated influence diagram in decision analysis.

Pseudo code
Input: Purchase intention prediction_Input features

Assign training and testing dataset for purchase intention prediction system

Output: Classification on purchase intention prediction of online customers

Function: D-Tree (Input features I)

Step 1: if tree is of the form Leaf (purchase intention_detect) then

Step 2: return detect

Step 3: else if tree is of the form Node (Input features I, left, right) then

Step 4: if Input features I = no in test point then

Step 5: return Decision_Tree_Test (left, test point)

Step 6: else

Step 7: return Decision_Tree_Test (right, test point)

Step 8: end if

Step 9: end if

Return classification outcomes for the purchase intention prediction system.

Naïve Bayes
The basic concept of NB classification is fairly simple, in some fields it is the easiest and most productive classification technique. Calculate the likelihood of occurrence in each category in this category for the items to be categorized that have been given in the data set, and then identify the item to be classified as having the highest probability. If the data collected are independent of one another and according to the same allocation of random variable series, the intensity of the occurrence can be used before probability of the occurrence, according to the large number theorem. Similarly, the frequency of incidence of each sample can be used to determine the probability value of the

sample data in the data set under the constraint of a NB model, that is, the ratios between each feature of the sample are independent of one another. It simply necessitates less training and testing data. Each characteristic is classified independently. The value assumption of the NB classifier is that variables within each group are independent of each other. The classifiers perform effectively even when the isolate criterion is violated. Bayes's theorem provides a straightforward formula for determining conditional probability using mathematics. Using the formula P(G|H), one may determine the likelihood that event A will occur if event B has already taken place.

$$P(G/H) = \frac{P(G).P(H/G)}{P(H)} \qquad (1)$$

Posterior probability is defined as P(G|H). Likelihood, denoted by P(H|G), is the probability that event H will occur given that event G has indeed taken place. The probability of event H occurring in a given class G is denoted by the notation P(G). The chance of any event happening, denoted by P(H), is referred to as a predictor probability value.

Pseudocode

Input is efficient prediction of purchase intention _ Input Features

Output is Classification on Purchase intention prediction of online customers

Objective: Naive Bayes (Input features I)
Step 1: Examine the Training dataset
Step 2: Find the mean and standard deviation of each class's predictor variables.
Step 3: Repeat
Step 4: Estimate the probability of p i for each class using the Gauss density equation.
Step 5: Continue until the probabilities of all predictor variables (p 1, p 2,..., p n) are computed.
Step 6: Provide the training and testing parameters to the train test split() method.
Step 7: Assign test size and random state as parameters for data splitting using Naive Bayes training.
Step 8: Compute the probability for each class
Step 9: Calculate the Mean and Standard deviation for each class.
Step 10: Maximize your likelihood
Step 11: Return classification results of the online purchase intent system.

Statistical analysis

The output is created with Python software (Kaifosh et al., 2014). Training these datasets requires a display with a resolution of 1024×768 pixels (10th gen, i5, 12GB RAM, 500 GB HDD). In order to do a statistical analysis of the NB and KNN algorithms, we employ SPSS (Frey, 2017). Means, standard deviations, and standard errors of means were computed by using SPSS to run an independent sample t test and then compare the two samples. When analyzing NB

Table 100.1 The performance measurements of the comparison between the NB and D-Tree classifiers are presented in Table 100.1. The NB classifier has an accuracy rate of 97.25, whereas the D-tree classification algorithm has a rating of 91.80. With a greater rate of accuracy, the NB classifier surpasses the D-Tree in predicting online purchase intent across all criteria.

S. No.	Test size	Accuracy rate	
		NB	D-Tree
1	Test1	93.23	89.10
2	Test2	94.54	89.23
3	Test3	94.36	89.59
4	Test4	94.34	89.92
5	Test5	95.12	90.32
6	Test6	95.56	90.61
7	Test7	96.35	90.85
8	Test8	96.36	91.28
9	Test9	97.35	91.58
10	Test10	97.54	91.74
Average test results		**97.25**	**91.80**

Source: Author

Table 100.2 The statistical calculations for the NB and D-Tree classifiers, including mean, standard deviation, and mean standard error. The accuracy level parameter is utilized in the t-test. The Proposed method has a mean accuracy of 97.25 percent, whereas the D-Tree classification algorithm has a mean accuracy of 91.80 percent. NB has a standard deviation of 0.1351, and the D-Tree algorithm has a value of 2.6467. The mean of NB's standard error is 0.1864, while the D-Tree method is 1.8256.

Group		N	Mean	Standard deviation	Standard error mean
Accuracy rate	D-Tree	10	91.80	2.6467	1.8256
	NB	10	97.25	0.1351	0.1864

Source: Author

Table 100.3 The statistical calculation for independent variables of NB in comparison with the D-Tree classifier has been calculated. The significance level for the rate of accuracy is 0.034. Using a 95% confidence interval and a significance threshold of 0.7532, the NB and D-Tree algorithms are compared using the independent samples T-test. This test of independent samples includes significance as 0.001, significance (two-tailed), mean difference, standard error difference, and lower and upper interval difference.

Group		Levene's test for equality of variances		T-test for equality of means						
		F	Sig.	t	df	Sig. (2-tailed)	Mean Difference	Std. Error Difference	95% Confidence Interval (Lower)	95% Confidence Interval (Upper)
Accuracy	Equal variances assumed	6.78	0.034	14.65	37	.001	9.9950	0.7532	8.3256	15.1244
	Equal variances not assumed			14.70	33.56	.001	9.9950	0.7532	7.0752	12.2891

Source: Author

and KNN, accuracy is the dependent variable and NB and KNN are the independent variables.

Results

Figure 100.1 compares the NB classifier's accuracy to that of the D-TREE classifier. The NB prediction model has a greater accuracy rate of 97.25 than the D-Tree classification model, which has a rate of 91.80. The NB classifier differs considerably from the D-Tree classifier (test of independent samples, p 0.05). The NB and D-Tree precision rates are shown along the X-axis. Y-axis: Mean keyword identification accuracy, 1 SD, with a 95%confidence interval.

The performance measurements of the comparison between the NB and D-Tree classifiers are presented in Table 100.1. The NB classifier has an accuracy rate of 97.25, whereas the D-Tree classification algorithm has a rating of 91.80. With a greater rate of accuracy, the NB classifier surpasses the D-Tree in predicting online purchase intent across all criteria.

Table 100.2 illustrates the statistical calculations for the NB and D-Tree classifiers, including mean, standard deviation, and mean standard error. The accuracy level parameter is utilized in the t-test. The proposed method has a mean accuracy of 97.25%, whereas the D-Tree classification algorithm has a mean accuracy of 91.80 percent. NB has a standard deviation of 0.1351, and the D-Tree algorithm has a value of 2.6467. The mean of NB's standard error is 0.1864, while the D-Tree method is 1.8256.

Table 100.3 displays the statistical calculations for independent variables of NB in comparison with the D-Tree classifier. The significance level for the rate of accuracy is 0.034. Using a 95% confidence interval and a significance threshold of 0.7532, the NB and D-Tree algorithms are compared using the independent samples T-test. This test of independent samples includes significance as 0.001, significance (two-tailed), mean difference, standard error difference, and lower and upper interval difference.

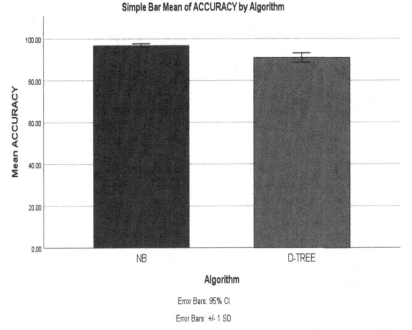

Figure 100.1 Comparing the accuracy of the NB classifier to that of the D-Tree algorithm has been evaluated. The NB prediction model has a greater accuracy rate of 97.25 than the D-Tree classification model, which has a rate of 91.80. The NB classifier differs considerably from the D-Tree classifier (test of independent samples, p 0.05). The NB and D-Tree precision rates are shown along the X-axis. Y-axis: Mean keyword identification accuracy, 1 SD, with a 95% confidence interval

Source: Author

Discussion

This study used two supervised machine learning algorithms are used to evaluate the online purchase intentions of the customers. The suggested method is successful and efficient, according to tests done on synthetic and actual data sets. Our experimental results demonstrate the viability of our suggested NB methodology in terms of both effectiveness and accuracy when compared to D-Tree prediction methods. The experimental results show that NB has a higher accuracy rate than D-Tree in predicting purchase rate, with an accuracy rate of 97.25%, while the accuracy rate of D-Tree was 91.80%.

Some similar studies are Crone and Soopramanien (Crone and Soopramanien, 2005) tested the efficacy of logistic regression and neural networks in predicting customers' actions when buying online. Classification accuracy for neural networks was 57%, whereas logistic regression was 54.4%. Students' online purchase intentions were studied by Islam et al., (2011). Multiple regression analysis led them to the conclusion that consumers' perceptions of an online store's practicality, user friendliness, compatibility, and safety all play a significant role in shaping their preferences. Using RFID data and a Bayesian network. Zuo and Yada (2014) demonstrated a

quantitative data analysis process of purchasing behavior selection overstay time. It was determined that compared to other common prediction models, the Bayesian network is the most accurate. To anticipate customers' online purchasing behavior, Shi and Ghedira (Shi and Ghedira, 2016) suggested a prediction model. Linear discriminant analysis, support vector machines, decision trees C5.0, and NB were the four techniques employed for classification. The accuracy of the NB classification (C5.0 algorithm) was 90%.

The proposed method has a low rate of accuracy while processing samples of low quality, which is a limitation. The suggested approach is based solely on website data and training data generated by algorithms. This will likely be more effective in the future as ecommerce and customer-focused businesses and demands increase. Increases in customer-generated results can be expected as the adoption of cloud computing and e-commerce becomes more widespread. The process can be automated even further, with the result shown in a desktop program. More enhancements can be made so that the work can be used in an AI setting. Future technologies that rely on customer input or results, including sales team and logistics management, can benefit from this method as well.

Conclusion

This research proposed a supervised machine learning-based technique for the prediction of online purchase intention in e-commerce product. Both the NB and D-Tree may be seen in the suggested model, with the NB achieving better accuracy. When comparing NB to D-Tree, which has an accuracy rate of 91.80% for analysis of online purchase intent, NB is 97.25% more accurate.

Conflicts of Interest

No conflict of interest in this manuscript

Authors Contributions

The authors were involved in data collection, data analysis & manuscript writing, in conceptualization, data validation, and critical review of manuscripts.

Acknowledgment

The authors would like to express their gratitude toward Saveetha School of Engineering, Saveetha Institute of Medical and Technical Sciences (Formerly known as Saveetha University) for successfully carrying out this work.

Funding: We thank the following organizations for providing financial support that enabled us to complete the study.

1. Company name.
2. Saveetha University
3. Saveetha Institute of Medical and Technical Sciences
4. Saveetha School of Engineering

References

Aldossari, B. S., Alqahtani, F. M., Alshahrani, N. S., Al-hammam, M. M., Alzamanan, R. M., Aslam, N., et al. (2020). A comparative study of decision tree and naive bayes machine learning model for crime category prediction in Chicago. In Proceedings of 2020 the 6th International Conference on Computing and Data Engineering, (pp. 34–38). ICCDE 2020. New York, NY, USA: Association for Computing Machinery.

Bashir, A. K., Khan, S., Prabadevi, B., Deepa, N., Alnumay, W. S., Gadekallu, T. R., et al. (2021). Comparative analysis of machine learning algorithms for prediction of smart grid stability. *International Transactions on Electrical Energy Systems*, 31(9), e12706. https://doi.org/10.1002/2050-7038.12706.

Crone, S. F., and Soopramanien, D. (2005). Predicting customer online shopping adoption-an evaluation of data mining and market modelling approaches. In DMIN, (pp. 215–221).

Dey, S., Wasif, S., Tonmoy, D. S., Sultana, S., Sarkar, J., and Dey, M. (2020). A comparative study of support vector machine and naive bayes classifier for sentiment analysis on amazon product reviews. In 2020 International Conference on Contemporary Computing and Applications (IC3A), (pp. 217–220). ieeexplore.ieee.org.

Franjković, J. (2017). Prices and price image of retailer. Thesis of the postgraduate specialist study. Osijek: Faculty of Economics in ….

Frey, F. (2017). SPSS (Software). The International Encyclopedia of Communication Research Methods , November, 1–2.

Golpour, P., Ghayour-Mobarhan, M., Saki, A., Esmaily, H., Taghipour, A., Tajfard, M., et al. (2020). Comparison of support vector machine, naïve bayes and logistic regression for assessing the necessity for coronary angiography. *International Journal of Environmental Research and Public Health*, 17(18), 6449. https://doi.org/10.3390/ijerph17186449.

Islam, M. A., Yulihasri, E., and Daud, K. A. K. (2011). Factors that influence customers' buying intention on shopping online. *International Journal of Marketing Studies*, 3(1), 128.

Kaifosh, P., Zaremba, J. D., Danielson, N. B., and Losonczy, A. (2014). SIMA: Python software for analysis of dynamic fluorescence imaging data. *Frontiers in Neuroinformatics*, 8(September), 80.

Lee, C. S., Cheang, P. Y. S., and Moslehpour, M. (2022). Predictive analytics in business analytics: decision tree. *Advances in Decision Sciences, Taichung*, 26(1), 1–29.

Merugu, D. P., and Mohan, D. V. K. (2020). Customer satisfaction towards online shopping with reference to Jalandhar city. *International Journal of Management (IJM)*, 11(2), 36–47. https://papers.ssrn.com/abstract=3552410.

Moon, N. N., Talha, I. M., and Salehin, I. (2021). An advanced intelligence system in customer online shopping behavior and satisfaction analysis. *Current Research in Behavioral Sciences*, 2(November), 100051.

Rausch, T. M., Derra, N. D., and Wolf, L. (2022). Predicting online shopping cart abandonment with machine learning approaches. *International Journal of Market Research*, 64(1), 89–112.

Shafin, M. A., Hasan, M. M., Alam, M. R., Mithu, M. A., Nur, A. U., and Faruk, M. O. (2020). Product review sentiment analysis by using NLP and machine learning in Bangla language. In 2020 23rd International Conference on Computer and Information Technology (ICCIT), (pp. 1–5). ieeexplore.ieee.org.

Shi, F., and Ghedira, C. (2016). Intention-based online consumer classification for recommendation and personalization. In 2016 Fourth IEEE Workshop on Hot Topics in Web Systems and Technologies (HotWeb), (pp. 36–41).

Solomon, M. R., and Panda, T. K. (2004). Consumer Behavior, Buying, Having, and Being. Pearson Education India.

Suchacka, G., and Stemplewski, S. (2017). Application of neural network to predict purchases in online store. In Information Systems Architecture and Technology: Proceedings of 37th International Conference on Information Systems Architecture and Technology – ISAT 2016 – Part IV, (pp. 221–231). Springer International Publishing.

Sun, Q., Dong, N., Chen, Z., and Yuan, Z. (2009). A modified neural network based predictive control for nonlinear systems. *International Journal of Modelling, Identification and Control*, 8(2),91–97. https://doi.org/10.1504/ijmic.2009.029020.

Varol, S., and Marquez, A. (2020). An empirical study on assessing brand loyalty in automobile industry using hidden markov model. *Academy of Marketing Studies Journal; London*, 24(1), 1–13.

Vieira, A. (2015). Predicting online user behaviour using deep learning algorithms. *arXiv [cs.LG]*. arXiv. http://arxiv.org/abs/1511.06247.

Wadhawan, N., and Arya, R. K. (2020). Understanding e-commerce: a study with reference to competitive economy. *Journal of Toxicology and Environmental Health. Part B, Critical Reviews*, 7(8), 805–809.

Wibowo, A. H., and Oesman, T. I. (2020). The comparative analysis on the accuracy of K-NN, naive bayes, and decision tree algorithms in predicting crimes and criminal actions in Sleman regency. *Journal of Physics. Conference Series*, 1450(1), 012076.

Xu, Y., Chen, Z., Peng, M. Y. P., and Anser, M. K. (2020). Enhancing consumer online purchase intention through gamification in China: perspective of cognitive evaluation theory. *Frontiers in Psychology*, 11(November), 581200.

Zhang, M., Chen, G., and Wei, Q. (2016). Discovering consumers' purchase intentions based on mobile search behaviors. In Advances in Intelligent Systems and Computing, (pp. 15–28). Advances in Intelligent Systems and Computing. Cham: Springer International Publishing.

Zuev, D., and Moore, A. W. (2005). Traffic classification using a statistical approach. In Passive and Active Network Measurement, (pp. 321–324). Springer Berlin Heidelberg.

Zuo, Y., and Yada, K. (2014). Using bayesian network for purchase behavior prediction from RFID data. In 2014 IEEE International Conference on Systems, Man, and Cybernetics (SMC), (pp. 2262–2267).

101 Predicting purchase intention of online customers using Naive Bayes classifier and compared with random forest

Pippalla Naga Sai Charan[1] and G. Arul Freeda Vinodhini[2]

[1]Research Scholar, Department of Computer Science and Engineering, Saveetha School of Engineering, Saveetha Institution of Medical and Technical Sciences, Saveetha University, Chennai, India

[2]Professor, Department of Mathematics, Saveetha School of Engineering, Saveetha Institution of Medical and Technical Sciences, Saveetha University, Chennai, India

Abstract

Aim: The purpose of this study is to determine whether the Naive Bayes (NB) algorithm is more efficient and accurately predicting online purchases than the random forest (RF) technique. This will be performed via side-by-side comparison of the two algorithms. Materials and methods: The data set that was utilized for this analysis was obtained from the Kaggle network. The sample size for the online purchase prediction with a higher rate of accuracy was 20 (Group 1 = 10 and Group 2 = 10), and calculations were performed using G-power 0.8, alpha and beta values of 0.05 and 0.2, and a 95% confidence interval. NB with n = 10 samples and RF with n = 10 samples are used to predict the online purchase intent with an enhanced accuracy rate. Results: The proposed naive bayes achieves a 97.25% success rate compared to the RF classifier's 91.80% success rate. This represents a significant difference. The significance level of the investigation was determined to be $p = 0.034$. Conclusion: When it comes to the prediction of the behavior of purchasing items online, the NB model that has been suggested achieves a superior rate of accuracy than the RF approach that has been suggested.

Keywords: Accuracy rate, classification, e-commerce, novel naïve bayes, online purchase, purchase intention, random forest

Introduction

Digital marketing is considered the preferred strategy when compared to traditional marketing. Researchers and academicians can utilize it for social media marketing and to forecast the purchase intent of customers (Dastane, 2020; Batu et al., 2020). With the rapid growth of the internet, E-commerce has experienced significant expansion. E-commerce is a resounding success due to the convenience of viewing and purchasing things online, as well as having them delivered to your home. E-commerce also serves virtually every industry, from electronics to fashion to food. The number of visitors to E-commerce websites is increasing rapidly, while the number of transactions has remained stable (Et al. 2021; Nabieva, 2021; Vickram et al., 2021; Et al. 2021; Nabieva, 2021). A novel Naïve bayes (NB) method has been proposed for determining whether a user intends to purchase a product. The proposed system is tested, and its efficiency is measured, against the random forest (RF) technique (Rajesh Kumar et al., 2021; Zare et al., 2020). The outcomes showed that by utilizing the NB algorithm, the performance of the approach could be enhanced, and a more accurate prediction effect could be attained when attempting to forecast consumers' purchase intent on e-commerce platforms. There is significant practical value for the

effective functioning of e-commerce platforms since this work may be used as a reference for enhancing the accuracy of predicting consumers' purchasing intention on e-commerce platforms. The NB classification approach is frequently used in medical diagnosis, text analysis, e-mail filtering, and information retrieval because of its high efficiency and strong classification accuracy (Vergura et al., 2020).

There are a number of approaches that have been suggested for researching online shoppers' intent to buy (Cheong et al., 2020; Lăzăroiu et al., 2020; Naseri et al., 2021; Rahman et al., 2020). A total of 133 exam papers were made available through IEEE Explore, while 183 were located using a Google Scholar search. An SVM classifier-based framework was proposed by K. Maheswari and P. A. A. Priya (Maheswari and Priya, 2017). Our methodology is built on a model of user sessions to predict future consumer behavior. The past purchases of users during a session are used to anticipate their behavior going forward. According to research by Ngwe et al. (Ngwe et al., 2022), if you help shoppers find what they're looking for, you can boost your odds of making a sale. Consumers' cross-channel search and purchase patterns are interconnected (Zhai et al., 2020). Based on the users' (shoppers') in-store physical mobility developed a methodology for real-time purchase pattern prediction (Kim et al., 2020; Sai

[a]riteshsmartgenresearch@gmail.com

Preethi et al., 2022; Kim et al., 2020). Cameras and object recognition algorithms were utilized to identify shopping behavior. However, it is difficult and expensive to put these mechanisms into action. On the other hand, models that forecast whether or not a customer will make a purchase online are reliable, simple to implement, and easy to incorporate (Mokryn et al., 2019). In (Li et al., 2015), they looked at the efficacy of many machine learning (ML) models in predicting users' purchases. The meta-model approach have presented takes into account choices made regarding evaluation tools (Hernández et al., 2021). They generated c4.5 variations by cross-validating the candidates 10 times. They used a Bayesian statistical analysis to rank the evaluation metrics gathered from various sources. For better accuracy while dealing with an uneven number of classes and noisy features (Shih and Ting, 2019) implemented a genetic model called KNN for improving feature weights and class weights via the distance function. The model greatly enhanced the classification outcome. Combining DT, NN, and logistic regression into a single ML model improved its performance, as demonstrated by Suh et al. (Suh et al., 2004) who used association rules (AR) to generate model attributes.

The main drawbacks of the conventional approach are its difficulty, class imbalanced data, and low accuracy rate. To address this restriction, this research introduces a novel NB algorithm for predicting online purchase intention and compares it to the decision tree (DT) technique. An experimental result demonstrates that the new NB method outperforms the conventional RF method. Moreover, analyses of efficiency and complexity were a part of the examination. The evaluation demonstrated that the proposed approach outperformed the state-of-the-art alternatives.

Materials and Methods

The investigation was carried out in the Computer Science and Engineering Department's Software Laboratory at Saveetha University. In this particular research study, the dataset was obtained from the Kaggle repository. The database is structured so that 75% of it is dedicated to training, and 25% is for testing. There are two sets taken, and each set has ten data samples; the total number of samples taken into consideration is twenty. Group 1 was a D-tree algorithm and Group 2 was a novel a RF algorithm. Python is the software that is used for the online buying prediction model, and it is this software that generates the output. The sample size was determined by using previous research from (Khan et al., 2021) at clinicalc.com. The threshold for the calculation was set at 0.05,

the G power was set at 80%, and the confidence interval was set at 95%.

Random forest

RF is a supervised learning model that falls under the genre of supervised learning. RF is helpful for machine learning classification and regression problems. The "learning from data" notion is the foundation of ensemble learning. The main concept of the random forest method is to generate a huge variety of decision trees. RF is a classification algorithm comprised of many decision trees on distinct subsets of the given dataset, with the means used to reduce error. Instead, of relying on a single decision tree, the random forest algorithm combines the predictions of numerous interconnected decision trees to forecast the eventual outcome. A higher sample size is preferable to reduce the likelihood of overfitting. The RF functions similarly to the decision tree, with the difference that only a random subset of characteristics is available following each split. RF generates forecasts for each DT by combining a huge number of trees. The development process can be characterized as follows: Choose random nodes from the training set, then create decision trees from the input (second step), determining the number of decision trees, and repeating steps 1 and 2 until a decision tree is constructed for all input data (third step). RF estimates the ultimate outcome based on the majority of votes using each decision tree. Even if the end results are consistent, they cannot predict every case.

Pseudo code

Step 1: Input is analysis of human emotion via speech recognition_Input Features

Step 2: Output is classification on purchase intention prediction of online customers

Step 3: Function: Random Forest (Input features Var = 1…n)

Step 4: for each (condition) do

Step 5: Arbitrarily select 'r' features from the Input features Var = 1…n

Step 6: Choose the Training and Testing dataset for Input features Var = 1…n

Step 7: Compute the root vertex to construct tree using the finest divide point among 'r' features

Step 8: Partition the vertex into sibling vertex utilizing finest divide point

Step 9: Reiterate 1 to 5 steps until all numbers of vertices are clutched.

Step 10: Reiterate 4 to 6 to construct a random forest tree for creation of Trees T.

Step 11: End for each

Step 12: Return classification results

Naïve Bayes

NB is a simple algorithm for supervised machine learning. The Bayesian probability principle is the basis for the NB classifier. The categorization approach predicts future prospects based on past experience using statistical and probability calculations. NB is a straightforward method for modeling techniques that represent class occurrences, expressed as vectors of functional meaning including class labels. The advantage of Nave Bayes is that it just requires a limited number of training data to determine classification parameters. Nave Bayes is a classifier with a strong bias and low variance, and it can develop a good classifier even with a little data set. This approach presupposes that an object's characteristics are independent. This method's classification technique has the advantage of using only minimal training data to estimate the required parameter. It is easy to use and highly efficient. The primary characteristic of this classifier is a naive assumption (a strong assumption) of independence for any event or condition. Although the assumption is not particularly valid (it is "aïve"), experience indicates that NB's categorization also works effectively. The condition of independence greatly simplifies the probability model construction equations in NB.

$$P(G/H) = \frac{P(G).P(H/G)}{P(H)} \qquad (1)$$

Posterior probability is defined as P(G|H). Likelihood, denoted by P(H|G), is the probability that event H will occur given that event G has indeed taken place. The probability of event H occurring in a given class G is denoted by the notation P(G). The chance of any event happening, denoted by P(H), is referred to as a predictor probability value. Many real-world applications of Bayes parameter estimation employ a maximum probability strategy; in other words, the naive bayes approach makes it possible without embracing Bayesian probability or Bayesian techniques.

Pseudocode

Input is efficient prediction of purchase intention _ Input Features

Output is Classification on Purchase intention prediction of online customers

Objective: Naive Bayes (Input features I)

Step 1: Analyze the Training dataset
Step 2: Compute the mean and standard deviation of the predictor variables for each class.
Step 3: Repeat

Step 4: Using the Gauss density equation, estimate the probability of Pi for each class.
Step 5: Proceed until the probabilities of all predictor variables (p1, p2,..., Pn) have been obtained..
Step 6: Generates the training and testing parameters to the train test split() function.
Step 7: Assign test size and random state as variables for data splitting using NB training.
Step 8: Calculate the probabilities for each class.
Step 9: Calculate the mean and standard deviation for each class.
Step 10: Maximize your likelihood
Step 11: End for each Return Classification outcomes

Statistical analysis

The output is created with Python software (Shmueli et al., 2019). Training these datasets requires a display with a resolution of 1024×768 pixels (10th gen, i5, 12GB RAM, 500 GB HDD). In order to do a statistical analysis of the NB and KNN algorithms, we employ SPSS (Hilbe, 2004). Means, standard deviations, and standard errors of means were computed by using SPSS to run an independent sample t test and then compare the two samples. When analyzing NB and KNN, accuracy is the dependent variable and NB and KNN are the independent variables.

Results

Figure 101.1 compares the NB classifier's accuracy to that of the RF classifier. The NB prediction model has a greater accuracy rate of 97.25 than the RF classification model, which has a rate of 88.90. The NB classifier differs considerably from the RF classifier (test of independent samples, p 0.05). The NB and RF precision rates are shown along the X-axis. Y-axis: Mean keyword identification accuracy, 1 SD, with a 95% confidence interval.

The performance measurements of the comparison between the NB and RF classifiers are presented in Table 101.1. The NB classifier has an accuracy rate of 97.25, whereas the RF classification algorithm has a rating of 88.90. With a greater rate of accuracy, the NB classifier surpasses the RF in predicting online purchase intent across all criteria.

Table 101.2 illustrates the statistical calculations for the NB and RF classifiers, including mean, standard deviation, and mean standard error. The accuracy level parameter is utilized in the t-test. The Proposed method has a mean accuracy of 97.25%, whereas the RF classification algorithm has a mean accuracy of 88.90%. NB has a standard deviation of 0.1424, and the RF algorithm has a value of 3.6147. The mean of NB's standard error is 0.1789, while the RF method is 1.6789.

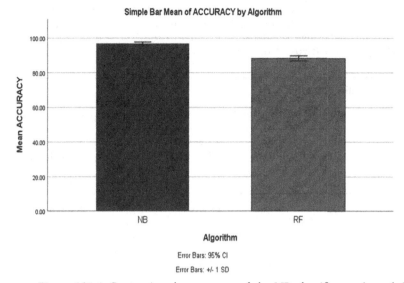

Figure 101.1 Comparing the accuracy of the NB classifier to that of the RF algorithm has been evaluated. The NB prediction model has a greater accuracy rate of 97.25 than the RF classification model, which has a rate of 88.90. The NB classifier differs considerably from the RF classifier (test of independent samples, p 0.05). The NB and RF precision rates are shown along the X-axis. Y-axis: Mean keyword identification accuracy, 1 SD, with a 95% confidence interval
Source: Author

Table 101.1 The performance measurements of the comparison between the NB and RF classifiers are presented in Table 101.1. The NB classifier has an accuracy rate of 97.25, whereas the RF classification algorithm has a rating of 88.90. With a greater rate of accuracy, the NB classifier surpasses the RF in predicting online purchase intent across all criteria.

S. No.	Test size	Accuracy rate	
		NB	RF
1	Test1	93.23	86.10
2	Test2	94.54	86.23
3	Test3	94.36	86.59
4	Test4	94.34	86.92
5	Test5	95.12	87.32
6	Test6	95.56	87.61
7	Test7	96.35	88.85
8	Test8	96.36	88.28
9	Test9	97.35	8.58
10	Test10	97.54	88.74
Average test results		97.25	88.90

Source: Author

Table 101.2 The statistical calculations for the NB and RF classifiers, including mean, standard deviation, and mean standard error. The accuracy level parameter is utilized in the t-test. The Proposed method has a mean accuracy of 97.25 percent, whereas the RF classification algorithm has a mean accuracy of 88.90 percent. NB has a standard deviation of 0.1424, and the RF algorithm has a value of 3.6147. The mean of NB's standard error is 0.1789, while the RF method is 1.6789.

Group		N	Mean	Standard deviation	Standard error mean
	RF	10	88.90	3.6147	1.6789
Accuracy rate	NB	10	97.25	0.1424	0.1789

Source: Author

Table 101.3 The statistical calculation for independent variables of NB in comparison with the RF classifier has been calculated. The significance level for the rate of accuracy is 0.037. Using a 95% confidence interval and a significance threshold of 0.8533, the NB and RF algorithms are compared using the independent samples T-test. This test of independent samples includes significance as 0.001, significance (two-tailed), mean difference, standard error difference, and lower and upper interval difference.

Group		Levene's test for equality of variances		T-test for equality of means						
		F	Sig.	T	df	Sig. (2-tailed)	Mean difference	Std. error difference	95% Confidence interval (lower)	95% Confidence interval (upper)
Accuracy	Equal variances assumed	2.45	0.037	13.45	35	.001	6.5650	0.8533	9.5524	13.1144
	Equal variances not assumed			15.72	31.51	.001	6.5650	0.8533	7.0567	11.9341

Source: Author

Table 101.3 displays the statistical calculations for independent variables of NB in comparison with the RF classifier. The significance level for the rate of accuracy is 0.037. Using a 95% confidence interval and a significance threshold of 0.8533, the NB and RF algorithms are compared using the independent samples T-test. This test of independent samples includes significance as 0.001, significance (two-tailed), mean difference, standard error difference, and lower and upper interval difference.

Discussion

This study proposed an automated system for predicting online purchase intentions of the customers based on two distinct machine learning algorithms, including a NB and RF. According to the results of experiments conducted on both synthetic and actual data sets, the proposed strategy is both successful and efficient. When compared to RF prediction approaches, the results of our experiments show that our proposed NB methodology is superior in terms of both its efficiency and its accuracy. This conclusion was reached as a direct consequence of the findings of our experiments. Based on the outcomes of the experiment, NB has a better accuracy rate than RF when it comes to predicting purchase rate. NB's accuracy rate was found to be 97.25%, while the accuracy rate of RF was found to be 88.90%.

Several publications and articles explore the topic of purchase prediction. Some similar studies (Lo et al., 2016) suggested purchase prediction models for verified Pinterest members in order to study both long-term and short-term patterns of behavior. The authors conducted a series of experiments testing prediction models using extracted features at several points in time prior to the purchase action, and they discovered that consumers' propensity to buy increased over time. Prediction models with features based on the entire timeline up until just before purchase action performed better in experiments, it was found. The authors of (XingFen et al., 2018; Golla et al., 2022; XingFen et al., 2018) offered a method to foresee customers' goods purchases. The authors studied the raw data from a single e-commerce website collected over the course of three months in 2016. Their research could lead to major breakthroughs in promoting e-commerce platforms and locating potential customers. Also interested in analyzing the purchase conversion rate, (Sakar et al., 2019) looked into how customers navigated a single E-commerce site. The factors that influence a consumer to repurchase a product were studied by (Kumar et al., 2019; Ayyasamy et al., 2022; Kumar et al., 2019). The authors used machine learning techniques and found that the Naive bayes classification model accurately predicted repurchase intent with a 96.58% success rate.

The training data was insufficient for the proposed NB approach, which requires huge volumes of data to correctly discover patterns in the data and make accurate predictions. Using more data would have certainly led to more accurate predictions, but training times were excessively long as a result. The future study could focus on optimizing the usage of the available data rather than tweaking and investigating the possibilities of different algorithms. Researchers need to do more work to differentiate between sequential and static datasets in order to better serve their clients.

Conclusion

This study compares two categorization algorithms that use e-commerce website session data to determine which one performs best. The primary goal of the job is to estimate how likely it is that site visitors will make a purchase. The proposed model Naive Bayes (NB) has got high accuracy values from the existing experiments. When comparing the two methods for analyzing a consumer's propensity to make a purchase online, NB's accuracy rate is 97.25%, while RF's is 88.90%.

Declaration

Conflicts of Interest

No conflict of interest in this manuscript

Authors Contributions

The author's name was involved in data collection, data analysis & manuscript writing. The author guide name was involved in conceptualization, data validation, and critical review of manuscripts.

Acknowledgment

The authors would like to express their gratitude towards Saveetha School of Engineering, Saveetha Institute of Medical and Technical Sciences (Formerly known as Saveetha University) for successfully carrying out this work.

Funding: We thank the following organizations for providing financial support that enabled us to complete the study.

1. Company name.
2. Saveetha University
3. Saveetha Institute of Medical and Technical Sciences
4. Saveetha School of Engineering

References

Ayyasamy, L. R., Mohan, A., Rex L. K., Sivakumar V. L., Dhanasingh, S. V., and Sivasamy, P. (2022). Enhanced thermal characteristics of CuO embedded lauric acid phase change material. *Thermal Science*, 26(2 Part B), 1615–1621.

Batu, R. L., Situngkir, T. L., and Krisnawati, I. (2020). Pengaruh digital marketing terhadap online purchase decision pada platform belanja online shopee. *Ekonomi and Bisnis*, 18(2), 144–152. http://sisdam.univpancasila.ac.id/uploads/berkas/penelitian/Jurnal_Nasional_08112021181426.pdf#page=65.

Cheong, J. W., Muthaly, S., Kuppusamy, M., and Han, C. (2020). The study of online reviews and its relationship to online purchase intention for electronic products among the millennials in Malaysia. *Asia Pacific Journal of Marketing and Logistics*, 32(7), 1519–1538.

Dastane, D. O. (2020). Impact of digital marketing on online purchase intention: mediation effect of customer relationship management. *Journal of Asian Business Strategy*, 10, 142–158. https://papers.ssrn.com/abstract=3605954.

Erlangga , H. (2021). Effect of digital marketing and social media on purchase intention of SMEs food products. *Turkish Journal of Computer and Mathematics Education (TURCOMAT)*, 12(3), 3672–3678.

Golla, V., Badapalli, P. K., and Telkar, S. K. (2022). Delineation of groundwater potential zones in semi-aridregion (Ananatapuram) using geospatial techniques. *Materials Today: Proceedings*, 50, 600–606. https://www.sciencedirect.com/science/article/pii/S2214785321013262.

Hernández, V. A. S., Monroy, R., Medina-Pérez, M. A., Loyola-González, O., and Herrera, F. (2021). A practical tutorial for decision tree induction: evaluation measures for candidate splits and opportunities. *ACM Computing Surveys*, 54(1), 1–38.

Hilbe, J. M. (2004). A review of SPSS 12.01, Part 2. *The American Statistician*, 58(2), 168–171.

Khan, M, R., Iqbal, M., and Lodhi, A. J. (2021). Influencer marketing on instagram: effects of promotional posts on purchasing behavior of consumers. pu.edu.pk. 2021. *Journal of Political Studies*, 28, 119–132, http://pu.edu.pk/images/journal/pols/pdf-files/10-v28_1_2021.pdf.

Kim, D. H., Lee, S., Jeon, J., and Song, B. C. (2020). Real-time purchase behavior recognition system based on deep learning-based object detection and tracking for an unmanned product cabinet. *Expert Systems with Applications*. 143, 113063. https://doi.org/10.1016/j.eswa.2019.113063.

Kumar, A., Kabra, G., Mussada, E. K., Dash, M. K., and Rana, P. S. (2019). Combined artificial bee colony algorithm and machine learning techniques for prediction of online consumer repurchase intention. *Neural Computing and Applications*, 31(2), 877–890.

Lăzăroiu, G., Neguriţă, O., Grecu, I., Grecu, G., and Mitran, P. C. (2020). Consumers' decision-making process on social commerce platforms: online trust, perceived risk, and purchase intentions. *Frontiers in Psychology*, 11(May), 890.

Li, Q., Gu, M., Zhou, K., and Sun, X. (2015). Multi-classes feature engineering with sliding window for purchase prediction in mobile commerce. In 2015 IEEE International Conference on Data Mining Workshop (ICDMW), (pp. 1048–1054).

Maheswari, K., and Packia Amutha Priya, P. (2017). Predicting customer behavior in online shopping using SVM classifier. In 2017 IEEE International Conference on

Intelligent Techniques in Control, Optimization and Signal Processing (INCOS). https://doi.org/10.1109/itcosp.2017.8303085.

Mokryn, O., Bogina, V., and Kuflik, T. (2019). Will this session end with a purchase? inferring current purchase intent of anonymous visitors. *Electronic Commerce Research and Applications*, 34(March), 100836.

Nabieva, N. M. (2021). Digital marketing: current trends in development. *Theoretical and Applied Science*. https://elibrary.ru/item.asp?id=44813129.

Naser i, R. N. N., et al. (2021). An overview of online purchase intention of halal cosmetic product: a perspective from Malaysia. *Turkish Journal of Computer and Mathematics Education (TURCOMAT)*, 12(10), 7674–7681.

Ngwe, D., Els, M., Schwam, D., and Gupta, S. (2022). Cross-merchant spillovers in coalition loyalty programs. Available at SSRN 4094153. https://doi.org/10.2139/ssrn.4094153.

Rahman, A., Yazdani, D. M. N., Bakar, A., Hamid, A., and Al Mamun, A. (2020). Brand image, eWOM, trust and online purchase intention of digital products among Malaysian consumers . xajzkjdx.cn. 2020. http://www.xajzkjdx.cn/gallery/462-mar2020.pdf.

Rajesh Kumar, E., Aravind, A., Jotheeswar Raghava, E., and Abhinay, K. (2021). Decision making among online product in e-commerce websites. In Inventive Computation and Information Technologies, (pp. 529–536). Singapore: Springer.

Sai Preethi, P., Hariharan, N. M., Vickram, S., Rameshpathy, M., Manikandan, S., Subbaiya, R., et al. (2022). Advances in bioremediation of emerging contaminants from industrial wastewater by oxidoreductase enzymes. *Bioresource Technology*, 359(September), 127444.

Sakar, C. O., Polat, S. O., Katircioglu, M., and Kastro, Y. (2019). Real-time prediction of online shoppers' purchasing intention using multilayer perceptron and LSTM recurrent neural networks. *Neural Computing and Applications*, 31(10), 6893–6908.

Shih, Y.-H., and Ting, C. K. (2019). Evolutionary optimization on k-nearest neighbors classifier for imbalanced datasets. In In 2019 IEEE Congress on Evolutionary Computation (CEC), (pp. 3348–3355).

Shmueli, G., Bruce, P. C., Gedeck, P., and Patel, N. R. (2019). Data Mining for Business Analytics: Concepts, Techniques and Applications in Python. John Wiley & Sons.

Suh, E., Lim, S., Hwang, H., and Kim, S. (2004). A prediction model for the purchase probability of anonymous customers to support real time web marketing: a case study. *Expert Systems with Applications*, 27(2), 245–255.

Vergura, D. T., Zerbini, C., and Luceri, B. (2020). Consumers' attitude and purchase intention towards organic personal care products. an application of the S-O-R model. *Sinergie Italian Journal of Management*, 38(1), 121–137.

Vickram, S., Rohini, K., Srinivasan, S., Veenakumari, D. N., Archana, K., Anbarasu, K., et al. (2021). Role of zinc (Zn) in human reproduction: a journey from initial spermatogenesis to childbirth. *International Journal of Molecular Sciences*, 22(4), 2188. https://doi.org/10.3390/ijms22042188.

XingFen, W., Xiangbin, Y., and Yangchun, M. (2018). Research on user consumption behavior prediction based on improved XGboost algorithm. In 2018 IEEE International Conference on Big Data (Big Data), (pp. 4169–4175).

Zare, M., Shakeri, H., and Mahmoudi, R. (2020). Ecommerce: an efficient digital markcting data mining framework to predict customer performance. *Journal of the International Academy for Case Studies Preview Publication details PUBLICATION DETAILS×Scholarly Journal Journal of the International Academy for Case StudiesJordan Whitney Enterprises, Inc Citation/Abstract Coverage*, 10(1), 1–8.

Zhai, X., Shi, P., Xu, L., Wang, Y., and Chen, X. (2020). Prediction model of user purchase behavior based on machine learning. In 2020 IEEE International Conference on Mechatronics and Automation (ICMA), (pp. 1483–87). ieeexplore.ieee.org.

102 Enhancing covidpatient emotion predictiononline: novel logistic regression vs. naive bayes

Harshitha, G. and Vindhya, A.[a]

Saveetha University, Chennai, Tamil Nadu, India

Abstract

This research aims to predict the emotions of COVID-19 patients on social media by comparing the effectiveness of a novel logistic regression (LR) algorithm with the traditional Naive Bayes (NB) algorithm. Employing LR and NB with sample sizes of 10 each, accuracy was assessed multiple times, yielding a 95% confidence interval and a G-power value of 0.8. The LR algorithm exhibited superior accuracy (61%) compared to NB (46%). Statistical analysis with p=0.506 (p>0.05) indicated no significant difference between the two groups. Consequently, it was concluded that the LR algorithm outperforms NB in accurately recognizing the emotions of COVID-19 patients on social media. This finding underscores the potential of advanced algorithms in enhancing the understanding of patient sentiments during public health crises like the COVID-19 pandemic.

Keywords: COVID-19, COVIDSenti dataset, emotions, naive bayes algorithm, novel logistic regression algorithm, social media

Introduction

The primary objective of this research is to assess the accuracy of recognising the emotions of COVID-19 patients through social media by comparing the novel logistic regression (LR) algorithm with the Naive Bayes (NB) algorithm. Social scientists and psychologists have shown a growing interest in understanding human psychology and mental health due to the extensive information available on social media platforms (Qurashi, 2022). Platforms like Twitter have been utilised for data collection in psychological and behavioural science research, predicting personality types (Rahman et al., 2022), and analysing internet trends. There is also a curiosity about how individuals express their emotions during significant events such as natural disasters, political upheavals, and terrorism incidents (Nivetha and Inbarani, 2022). Constructing a social computer capable of understanding human communication requires a thorough understanding of various factors (Aslan et al., 2022). During the COVID-19 pandemic, social media, particularly Twitter, served as a crucial platform for people to express a wide range of emotions amidst rising cases and stricter lockdown measures (Imbalzano et al., 2021). Social media also facilitated the application of natural language processing and machine learning techniques to analyse data. However, a study employing deep learning to analyse sentiment in World Health Organisation tweets found shortcomings in providing public guidance (Kentour and Lu, 2021). The applications of the novel LR algorithm include enhancing business understanding and identifying factors influencing profitability, while NB finds applications in spam filtering, document classification, and sentiment prediction.

Sentiment analysis was utilised to investigate the impact of a statewide lockdown in India due to the COVID-19 epidemic, revealing that the majority of Indians agreed with the government's decision on the initial nationwide lockdown in the fight against COVID-19 (Kandasamy et al., 2021). Over 100 articles in IEEE Xplore are related to the emotions of COVID-19 patients, illustrating how individuals were affected emotionally during the pandemic (Pathuri et al., 2021). However, it's noted that despite the increase in COVID-19 cases, no research has employed language models for sentiment analysis (Pathuri et al., 2021). Our model explores the various emotions expressed over time concerning the rise in cases, economic impact, and varying levels of lockdowns, which significantly affected the population's psychology (Cabezas et al., 2021). Given the uncertainties surrounding the epidemic, our research serves as a tool to quantify and validate emotional and psychological issues (Ahmed, Aurpa, and Anwar, 2021). Despite NB's drawback of lesser accuracy in detecting emotions in frames, our proposed system aims to enhance accuracy in detecting emotions of COVID-19 patients using novel LR algorithms and NB algorithms. The results and discussion section elaborates on the findings, while the concluding part discusses the implications of the research and its future trajectory (Shofiya and Abidi, 2021).

[a]vindhisaveetha@gmail.com

Table 102.1 Dataset name, dataset emotions, dataset source.

S.No	Dataset name	Dataset emotions	Dataset source
0	3204	sad.	Agree the poor in India are treated badly their poor's seek a living in Singapore and are treated like citizens they are given free medical treatment given food daily sim cards to call home to tell their family that they are fine if COVID-19 case treated foc in hospitals
1	1431	joy	if only i could have spent the with this cutie vcsakshi_s i n g h coast crossing republik
2	4624	fear	joebiden's coronavirus web address lands on a donation page for his campaign he is profiting from fear demopos
3	4646	anger	maybe if i bolt my front door shut coronavirus will stay out
4	2530	sad	The coronavirus disappearing in Italy shows this to "intellectuals" who say lockdowns do not work …

Source: Author

Materials and Methods

This research, conducted at Saveetha School of Engineering's Cyber Forensic Laboratory in Chennai, employed machine learning algorithms to train the affective tweets dataset. Pre-processing, using a lexicon of 70,000 English words, aimed to enhance data quality. The study evaluates classifier effectiveness on the COVIDSenti dataset and aims to enhance performance by extracting significant attributes from tweets. The proposed technique improved accuracy and efficiency on COVID-19-related Twitter posts, addressing issues such as overfitting, noise, and dataset size. The study includes classification algorithms, with separate training and testing sections for the COVIDSenti dataset, ensuring robust analysis.

Logistic regression

Logistic regression is a predictive analytic approach used in machine learning for classification problems, determining the likelihood of a target variable. It follows a probability-based notion, as depicted in Figure 102.1 (Kumar, 2022). The emotion recognition model's procedure is outlined accordingly.

Naive bayes

Naive Bayes is a probabilistic machine learning technique widely employed in classification tasks such as spam filtering and sentiment prediction. It operates independently on features, influenced by Rev's works (Zhang, Li, and Lu, 2017). Figure 102.2 illustrates the complete model procedure, with the emotion recognition model following a similar process. Table 102.1 presents tweet data reflecting people's emotions, showcasing the impact of Python programming language in this study.

Hardware and software requirements

Minimal hardware requirements for CPU implementation include an Intel i5 processor and 256 GB storage. Software specifications necessitate IOS, Python 3 programming language, or Google Colab for operation.

Statistical analysis

IBM SPSS is employed for statistical analysis, with text emoticons as dependent variables and sentiments as independent variables. T-Test analysis is conducted independently to analyse data accurately, with 10 iterations for proposed and current algorithms for accuracy assessment (Omer et al., 2022).

Results

This study evaluates DL, hybrid-based, and transformer-based models on four COVIDSenti datasets. Utilizing the proposed method, sentiment categorization performance was assessed. Table 102.1 displays the dataset profile. Simulated accuracy analysis of novel LR and NB is shown in Table 102.2. Group statistical analysis (Table 102.3) indicates mean accuracies of 61.15% and 46.11%, with p=0.506 (insignificant). Mean accuracies (Figure 102.4) for novel LR and NB are 61.1% and 46.1%. Results suggest novel LR's superiority.

Conclusion

The conclusion must be clearly marked as shown. When referring to other Sections in the Letter, please use the Section heading, or describe the relevant Section as the 'following' or 'preceding' Section in relation to the current Section in the text.

References

Brockman, P., French, D., and Tamm, C. (2014).REIT organizational structure, institutional ownership, and stock performance.*Journal of Real Estate Portfolio Management*, 20(1), 21–36.

Cella, C. (2009).Institutional Investors and Corporate Investment.United Sates: Indiana University, Kelley School of Business.

Chuang, H. (2020). The impacts of institutional ownership on stock returns.*Empirical Economics*, 58(2), 507–533.

Clark, G. L., and Wójcik, D. (2005). Financial valuation of the German model: the negative relationship between ownership concentration and stock market returns, 1997–2001. *Economic Geography*, 81(1), 11–29.

Dasgupta, A., Prat, A., and Verardo, M. (2011). Institutional trade persistence and long-term equity returns. *Journal of Finance*, 66(2), 635–653.

Demsetz, H., and Lehn, K. (1985). The structure of corporate ownership: causes and consequences. *Journal of Political Economy*, 93(6), 1155–1177.

Dyakov, T., and Wipplinger, E. (2020). Institutional ownership and future stock returns: an international perspective. *International Review of Finance*, 20(1), 235–245.

Gompers, P. A., and Metrick, A. (2001).Institutional investors and equity prices.*Quarterly Journal of Economics*, 116(1), 229–259.

Han, K.C., and Suk, D.Y. (1998). The effect of ownership structure on firm performance: additional evidence. *Review of Financial Economics*, 7(2), 143–155.

Kennedy, P. (1985). A Guide to Econometrics. Cambridge:MIT Press.

La Porta, R., Lopez-de-Silanes, F., and Shleifer, A. (1999). Corporate ownership around the world.*Journal of Finance*, 54(2), 471–517.

Manawaduge, A. S., Zoysa, A., and Rudkin, K. M. (2009). Performance implication of ownership structure and ownership concentration: Evidence from Sri Lankan firms. In Paper Presented at the Performance Management Association Conference. Dunedin, New Zealand.

103 Earn while you learn - a study among arts and science college students in Coimbatore

Sarath Kumar, G. and Gayathiri, M.[a]

Karpagam Academy of Higher Education, Coimbatore, Tamil Nadu, India

Abstract

The "earn while you learn" strategy, pivotal for college students, blends practical skill development with financial relief. In Coimbatore, Tamil Nadu, India, arts and science college students are the focal point of an investigation into the determinants guiding their preference for this approach. Utilizing factor analysis and a mix of quantitative and qualitative methods, a comprehensive questionnaire captured details encompassing demographics, education, employment status, job types, hours worked, and financial impacts. Findings highlighted influential factors, with component loadings of 0.5 or higher, advocating for the "earn while you learn" approach. Notably, these encompassed networking, interpersonal skills, skill acquisition, time management, and robust leadership capabilities. These pivotal insights offer valuable guidance for educational institutions, policymakers, and career advisors to craft tailored strategies and support systems. Such initiatives strive to harmonize work and study for arts and science college students, fostering an optimal balance beneficial for their holistic development.

Keywords: Academic performance and career prospects, balancing work and learning, earn while you learn, part-time employment, work-study programs

Introduction

The concept of "earning while learning" has gained substantial momentum as students aim to alleviate the financial strain of education while gaining practical work exposure. This approach intertwines work and education, enabling individuals to earn an income while pursuing academic pursuits. Part-time jobs, internships, apprenticeships, and cooperative education programmes facilitate this balance, allowing simultaneous skill acquisition and financial support.

Conventional education often burdens students with financial stress and loans. "Earn-while-you-learn" initiatives present a remedy, offering income opportunities that mitigate educational costs, reduce loan reliance, and enhance financial stability. Moreover, these programs furnish invaluable real-world experiences, cultivating practical skills, industry knowledge, and professional networks.

While immensely beneficial, such programmes pose challenges. Balancing work and learning necessitates effective time management and aligning opportunities with educational goals. In this study, the researcher delves into the "earning while learning" concept, focusing on arts and science college students. Exploring various models, benefits, challenges, and impacts of these programs, this research aims to provide actionable strategies for students to optimise their work-study balance. The findings aim to enrich existing literature on student employment, offering insights that enhance the educational journey and future prospects of Coimbatore's arts and science college students.

Review of Literature

Table 103.1 Insights into student financial behaviours and academic performance.

Author name	Study	Findings
Jeevitha and Priya (2019)	Explored Coimbatore students' spending and saving habits. Most saved less than spent, differing in spending areas. Preferred saving through bank accounts.	Majority saved less than spent, varied in spending. Predominantly saved via bank accounts.

[a]muthugayathiri@gmail.com

Author name	Study	Findings
Wang and Chen (2017)	Examined factors influencing spending/saving habits of students reliant on parental pocket money. Gender disparities in spending revealed. High spending on fast food, movies, transport; leftovers saved for the future.	Investigated spending/saving habits of students using parental pocket money, uncovering gender-based spending differences. High spending on fast food, movies, transport; remainder saved for the future.
Ha et al. (2016)	Explored part-time work among university students. Age, course, major affected job uptake. Limited impact on academics except physically demanding roles.	Explored student part-time work, noting age, course, major influencing job uptake. Minimal academic impact except for physically demanding roles.
Ajide (2015)	Investigated Lagos youths' spending patterns. Significant gender-based differences in spending, reliant on family pocket money. Noted positive correlation between pocket money and spending.	Explored Lagos youths' spending patterns, highlighting gender-based differences using family pocket money. Identified positive pocket money-spending correlation.
Tessema et al. (2014)	Studied paid employment's impact on student satisfaction/GPA. Non-employed students had higher GPA/satisfaction. GPA declined with over 11 hours' work, affecting graduation.	Explored employment's impact on student satisfaction/GPA. Non-employed had higher GPA/satisfaction. GPA declined with over 11 hours' work, impacting graduation.
Staff et al. (2010)	Investigated first-year students' employment and academic achievement. Over 20 hours' work negatively affected grades; ≤ 20 hours' on-campus work had positive impact.	Explored first-year students' employment and academic achievement. Over 20 hours' work hurt grades; ≤ 20 hours' on-campus work positively impacted.

Source: Author

Research Gap

Despite ample global research on "earn while you learn" among college students, there exists a dearth of specific investigations concentrating on arts and science students in Coimbatore, with most studies conducted in varied geographical settings or diverse disciplines, leaving uncharted territory in exploring the cultural and socioeconomic determinants influencing part-time work practices among these students. Additionally, there remains a notable gap in comprehending the ramifications of part-time employment on academic performance, career aspirations, and the holistic well-being of students within this distinct context.

Problem Statement

The lack of comprehensive investigation into the practice of "Earn while you learn" among arts and science college students in Coimbatore necessitates a study addressing the prevalence, motivations, types of employment, work-study balance challenges, and the perceived impact on academic performance to gain insights crucial for understanding the phenomenon and its implications for student experiences and career prospects in this specific context.

The objective of the study is to ascertain preference for prefer part time job while studying

Scope of the Study

The study's scope on "earn while you learn" involves exploring part-time employment or internships in higher education, encompassing program analysis, job identification, student and employer views, academic performance, institutional support, and economic impact. The study's depth relies on research goals, resources, and the target population's specifics.

Research Methodology

1. Research approach: Using mixed methods—quantitative and qualitative—to explore part-time work's experiences, motivations, challenges, and impacts among arts and science students in Coimbatore.

2. Sampling strategy: Employing stratified and random sampling methods to gather a diverse, representative sample from arts and science colleges, encompassing various disciplines, ages, and genders.

3. Data collection: Utilizing a questionnaire for quantitative data from 160 students, covering demographics, education, employment status, job types, hours, motivations, and impacts. Secondary data sourced from journals, newspapers, government sites.

Table 103.2 Socio-economic profile.

Particulars	Numbers (n = 160)	Percentage
Age (years)		
Upto 19	12	7.5
20 – 22	132	82.5
Above 23	16	10.0
Gender		
Male	144	90.0
Female	16	10.0
Education stream		
Arts	80	50.0
Science	74	46.3
Management	6	3.7
Educational qualification		
UG	84	52.5
PG	76	47.5
Year of study		
First year	28	17.5
Second year	36	22.5
Final year	96	60.0
Type of family		
Joint	14	8.7
Nuclear	146	91.3
Number of earning members		
1	2	1.3
2	92	57.5
3	48	30.0
4	14	8.7
5& above	4	2.5
Monthly income (Rs.)		
Up to 5000	44	27.5
5001-7500	80	50.0
Above 7500	36	22.5
Family Income (Rs.)		
Up to 20000	20	12.4
20001-40000	130	81.3
Above 40000	10	6.3
Family expenditure		
Upto5000	20	12.5
5001-13000	112	70.0
Above 13000	28	17.5
Basis of income		
Daily	34	21.3
Weekly	28	17.4
Monthly	98	61.3

Source: Author

Table 103.3 KMO and Bartlett's test.

Kaiser-Meyer-Olkin measure of sampling adequacy.		.760
Bartlett's test of sphericity	Approx. Chi-square	874.201
	Df	91
	Sig.	.000

Source: Author

4. Analysis tools: Employing factor analysis to uncover significant factors influencing the preference for 'Earn while you learn' among arts and science students in Coimbatore.

Significance of the Study

This study on "earn while you learn" among arts and science students in Coimbatore is crucial. It uncovers motivations for part-time work, aiding in developing strategies to ease financial burdens. By examining job types and impacts on academics, it highlights work-study integration. This research adds to the limited knowledge in this specific context, guiding future studies and policies. Its significance lies in informing institutions and policymakers to address financial concerns, promote work-study balance, and enhance students' educational experiences and career prospects in Coimbatore.

Limitations of the Study

Limitations of this study on "earn while you learn" among Coimbatore's arts and science students include potential constraints in generalizing findings to the wider student population. Time constraints might impact thorough data collection and analysis. External factors like economic fluctuations and job market changes could affect part-time work experiences, but these complexities fall beyond the study's scope, potentially impacting comprehensive understanding.

Findings of the Study

Simple percentage analysis: The following table states about socio-economic profile of the study.

Most students are aged between 20-22, predominantly male, studying arts at the undergraduate level, mostly in their final year. They mostly belong to nuclear families, with two earners, earning Rs. 5001-7500 monthly, with family incomes between Rs. 20001-40000 and expenditures Rs. 5001-13000 per month. They predominantly earn on a monthly basis.

Factor analysis: Preference for preferring the part time job

Table 103.4 Rotated component matrix[a].

Factors	Component			
	1	2	3	4
To build professional network	.891			
To develop interpersonal skills	.860			
To gain skills and experience	.821			
To manage time wisely	.753			
To build strong management skills	.752			
To gain work experience	.626			
To increase friendship network				
To gain confident				
To stand on my own		.777		
To stand independent		.686		
Learn to manage money		.631		
Family financial condition			.869	
To meet education expenses			.715	
To meet pocket expenses				.838
Eigen values	4.542454	1.826125	1.553582	1.060554
Percentage of variance	32.4461	13.04375	11.09702	7.575388
Cumulative percentage of variance	32.4461	45.48985	56.58687	64.16226

Source: Author

The KMO and Bartlett's test validate the data for factor analysis. KMO (>0.70) confirms variable suitability. Bartlett's test (874.201) with a significant p-value (Sig. .000) indicates strong variable correlation, supporting factor analysis. This method unveils influential reasons for student part-time job preferences in higher education.

Factor analysis will uncover key influences on students' part-time job preferences, like financial needs or skill development. Interpreting results meticulously—factor loadings, eigenvalues, and scree plots—reveals factors and their significance in explaining data variance. Accurate reporting of results, including extracted factors and statistical measures, fortifies research quality, offering insightful reasons behind students' part-time job choices in higher education.

The factor analysis revealed four significant factors driving the perception of "Earn while you learn" among arts and science students in Coimbatore. Factors include Professional Development and Time Management, Financial Independence and Management, Financial Considerations (family and education expenses), and Pocket Expenses. Each factor encompasses specific variables highlighting the importance of professional growth, financial independence, family circumstances, and meeting pocket expenses in influencing students' attitudes towards part-time work for educational purposes.

The investigation discerns four pivotal factors shaping the inclination toward "earn while you learn" among arts and science students in Coimbatore. Factor 1 accentuates professional growth and time management, while factor 2 underscores financial independence and expense regulation. Factor 3 scrutinizes family financial dynamics and education expenditures, whereas factor 4 addresses personal expense coverage. These insights serve as a compass for institutions and policymakers, aiding in tailoring bespoke support mechanisms. Such tailored interventions cater to the nuanced needs of Coimbatore's student populace, nurturing their holistic development and fostering success across academic and vocational domains within the educational sphere.

Recommendations

Based on the topic of "earn while you learn" among arts and science college students in Coimbatore, here are some suggestions that could be considered:

- Tailored career guidance programs by Coimbatore's educational institutions.

- Forge partnerships with local entities for student internships.
- Workshops on financial literacy: budgeting, saving, and planning.
- Initiate mentorship by arts and science professionals.
- Strengthen in-house academic support services.
- Collaborate with local employers for flexible work arrangements.
- Continuous assessment of part-time employment's impact on students.

These initiatives aim to assist arts and science students in Coimbatore to balance work and study effectively, enhancing employability, financial stability, and educational experience.

Conclusion

Understanding the significance of "earn while you learn" among Coimbatore's arts and science students underscores its multifaceted impact on financial stability and skill development. Despite study limitations, the insights offer promise for enhancing the city's educational framework. Part-time work provides financial backing and practical skills but demands adept time management and academic equilibrium, warranting deeper understanding of its prevalence, challenges, and impacts.

Educational institutions can empower students through tailored career guidance, internships, and financial literacy workshops. Collaborations with employers, research-driven initiatives, and flexible schedules are pivotal in nurturing a seamless transition from academia to the professional realm. Moreover, delving into further research avenues – spanning longitudinal studies, mental health assessments, and

intersectional analyses – holds the potential to enrich policies and comprehensive support frameworks for Coimbatore's students navigating part-time employment. These initiatives foster a conducive environment for informed policy-making and holistic student development.

References

Ajide, F. M. (2015). The spending pattern among youth in Lagos, Nigeria. IOSR Journal of Business and Management, 17(4), 66–73.

Cefai, C., and Camilleri, L. (2011). The dietary habits of Maltese university students. *Malta Medical Journal*, 23(2).

Ha, C. N., Thao, N. T., and Son, T. D. (2016). Student part-time employment: case study at ton duc thang university in Vietnam. In Proceedings of ICERI 2016 Conference, 9th International Conference of Education, Research and Innovation at Seville, Spain, 14th to 16th November, (pp. 3193–3201).

Jeevitha, P., and Priya, R. K. (2019). A study on saving and spending habits of college students with reference to Coimbatore city. *International Journal of Research and Analytical Reviews*, 6(1), 463z–466z.

Staff, J., Schulenberg, J. E., and Bachman, J. G. (2010). Adolescent work intensity, school performance, and academic engagement. *Sociology of Education*, 83(3), 183–200.

Tessema, M. T., Ready, K. J., and Astani, M. (2014). Does part-time job affect college students' satisfaction and academic performance (GPA)? The case of a Mid-Sized public university. *International Journal of Business Administration*, 5(2), 1–10.

Wang, Y.-C., and Chen, C.-J. (2017). College students part-time jobs: factors and challenges for future careers. In 2017 6th IIAI International Congress on Advanced Applied Informatics (IIAI-AAI) (pp. 1–4). IEEE. 10.1109/IIAI-AAI.2017.18.

104 A study on preference and problems of online lottery

Nandha Kumar, K., Jothi, K.[a] and Velmurugan, R.[b]

Karpagam Academy of Higher Education, Coimbatore, Tamil Nadu, India

Abstract

Online lotteries have become increasingly popular, offering easy access and convenience to players. However, this rise in popularity brings significant challenges that need to be addressed. This study aims to explore the key issues faced by online lottery players and the broader implications of these problems. From the risk of addiction to inadequate regulatory frameworks, the study delves into how these factors can negatively impact individuals and the community. The goal is to highlight the importance of responsible gambling practices and the need for effective measures to safeguard players in the online gambling environment. By understanding these challenges, we can work towards creating a safer and more responsible gambling landscape.

Keywords: Gambling, online lottery, problems

Introduction

Online lottery, facilitated through digital means such as websites and mobile apps, offers players the convenience of participating in a range of lottery games, including popular ones like Powerball and EuroMillions, from the comfort of their own homes. This accessibility, while appealing, comes with significant drawbacks that should not be overlooked. The foremost among these is the risk of addiction, which can lead to serious financial troubles and disrupt both personal and professional lives. Furthermore, the odds of winning in these lotteries are generally quite low, meaning most participants will end up losing their money. The sector's regulatory grey areas in some jurisdictions also raise concerns about potential fraud, unscrupulous operators, and privacy breaches.

Excessive engagement in online lotteries can have detrimental social impacts. It often leads to strained family relationships, conflicts, and social withdrawal, as gambling takes precedence over personal commitments. This form of gambling is particularly enticing to vulnerable individuals, such as those with a predisposition to gambling addiction or those in financial distress, who may be lured by the prospect of significant winnings. Given these risks, it's crucial for players to select reputable and licensed platforms that prioritize data security and have clear privacy policies, ensuring a safer and more responsible gambling experience.

Review of Literature

Burns et al. (1990) noted that younger individuals, often with lower income levels, are more inclined to play lotteries, possibly due to advertising, optimism, or financial aspirations. Scholes (2012) highlighted the increased risk of substance use and mental health issues among online gamblers, including teenagers. Saranya Devi and Jayasheela (2017) found that teenagers are particularly vulnerable to the adverse effects of online gambling due to immaturity and accessibility. Foote (2018) determined that factors like age, gender, and pre-gambling emotions influence the severity of gambling problems. Bernadeta et al. (2019) and Morgan et al. (2022) both identified gambling issues among UK university students, influenced by year of study and gender. Kumar (2021) discussed the lower odds of winning in online lotteries compared to traditional ones and warned about the prevalence of online lottery scams, emphasizing the need for caution and verification of lottery platforms.

Research Gap

From the above literature review, it is ascertained that youngsters more particularly affected by online lottery and many of the online lottery players lose their hard-earned money. Only few studies have been carried out to identify the reason for preferring online lottery and problems associated with it. Further, no such studies have been carried out in Coimbatore district. Thus, in order to fill this research gap, the present study has been carried out.

Problem Statement

Despite the convenience and variety offered by online lottery platforms, including access to various games and enhanced security, they present significant

[a]jothikrishnasamydr@gmail.com, [b]drvelsngm@gmail.com

challenges such as addiction, financial risks, regulatory compliance issues, data security concerns, and the impersonal nature of digital interactions, which this study aims to investigate.

Objectives of the Study

- To ascertain reason for preferring online lottery
- To identify the problems on playing with online lottery

Scope of the Study

The present study focuses on the Coimbatore district of Tamil Nadu and aims to investigate the socio-economic profile of online lottery players, understand the reasons for their preference for online lottery, and examine the problems associated with playing online lottery alone.

Research Methodology

- **Data Collection Method**: A well-structured questionnaire will be used to collect primary data on the socio-economic backgrounds, reasons for preference, and problems faced by online lottery players in Coimbatore district, Tamil Nadu.
- **Sampling method and size**: Snowball sampling, which involves initial participants referring others, will be employed to gather data from 90 respondents in Coimbatore district, Tamil Nadu, due to the hard-to-reach nature of the target population.
- **Data analysis technique**: The data will be analyzed using simple percentage methods and the weighted average rank test to understand the preferences and challenges faced by online lottery players.

Significance of the Study

This study is crucial for understanding the complexities of online lottery, focusing on consumer protection, responsible gambling, and policy development, while addressing issues like addiction, economic impacts, and the need for international collaboration to create safer gambling environments and inform policymaking.

Limitations of the Study

The study's findings may not fully represent the broader population due to potential sampling bias. Snowball sampling might lead to a non-random sample, as initial participants often refer to similar individuals. Additionally, responses could be skewed by factors like social desirability or recall bias, making

generalization to the entire population or other contexts cautious.

Findings

Socio economic profile
The following Table 104.1 discloses about socio-economic profile of the study.

Table 104.1 Socio economic profile.

Particulars	Numbers (n = 90)	Percentage
Age		
Up to 25	51	56.7
26 – 35	33	36.7
Above 35	6	6.7
Gender		
Male	87	96.7
Female	3	3.3
Marital status		
Married	87	96.7
Unmarried	3	3.3
Educational qualification		
SSLC	3	3.3
H. Sc.,	12	13.3
Under graduate	30	33.3
Postgraduate	27	30.0
Professional	18	20.0
Occupation		
Business	42	46.7
Employee	33	36.7
Agriculture	6	6.7
Student	9	10.0
Monthly income (Rs.)		
Up to 10000	9	10.0
10000 – 20000	75	83.3
Above 20000	6	6.7
Family expenditure (Rs.)		
Up to 7500	9	10.0
7501 – 15000	75	83.3
Above 15000	6	6.7
Type of family		
Joint	57	63.3
Nuclear	33	36.7
Status in family		
Head	36	40.0
Member	54	60.0

Source: Author

The majority of online rummy players are male, predominantly aged around 25, indicating a stronger inclination towards the game among younger men. Interestingly, most players are married and have undergraduate qualifications. Businessmen and employees form the bulk of this group, with monthly incomes generally between Rs. 10,000 to Rs. 20,000. Their family expenditures typically range from Rs. 7,500 to Rs. 15,000, suggesting moderate financial backgrounds. Notably, many players come from joint families, pointing to online rummy's role as a leisure activity within family contexts.

Online rummy playing behavior

The following Table 104.2 portrays the online rummy playing behavior of sample respondents in Coimbatore district.

The majority of respondents discovered online rummy through friends, highlighting the importance of personal referrals in its popularity. Regular engagement is evident as they play weekly, dedicating around three hours per session, making it a consistent leisure activity. Financially, they typically invest Rs. 101 to Rs. 150 per game, indicating a moderate spending level. Interestingly, some report earning profits, reflecting the potential for financial gains in online rummy.

Preference toward online rummy

To understand the main reasons which induce respondents to prefer online rummy, a weighted average rank test is employed. The following Table 104.3 discusses the reason for preferring online rummy by the sample respondents.

The weighted average rank test reveals that respondents prefer online rummy primarily for its unlimited game variety, showing a high value for diverse gaming options. The ease of playing on various devices

Table 104.2 Online lottery playing behavior.

Particulars	Numbers (n = 90)	Percentage
Source of awareness		
Advertisement	39	43.3
Friends	51	56.7
Frequency of playing online rummy		
Daily	30	33.3
Weekly	54	60.0
Monthly	6	6.7
Duration of playing online rummy (hours)		
One	6	6.7
Two	21	23.3
Three	48	53.3
Above three	15	16.7
Investment in online rummy (Rs.)		
Up to 100	33	36.7
101- 500	54	60.0
Above 500	3	3.3
Monthly income from online rummy (Rs.)		
Up to 1000	51	56.7
2000	33	36.7
Above 2000	6	6.7

Source: Author

Table 104.3 Preference toward online rummy.

Preference	SA	A	NO	DA	SDA	Total	Mean Score	Mean rank	Rank
Easy to play on all devices	27	42	15	3	3	90	357	3.97	2
	135	168	45	6	3				
Unlimited variety of games	42	33	9	6	0	90	381	4.23	1
	210	132	27	12	0				
Premium rewards and benefits	9	42	30	9	0	90	321	3.57	5
	45	168	90	18	0				
Fraud and collusion protection	21	9	45	12	3	90	303	3.37	6
	105	36	135	24	3				
Comfort and convenience	12	42	30	3	3	90	327	3.63	4
	60	168	90	6	3				
The newbie benefits	27	42	6	15	0	90	351	3.90	3
	135	168	18	30	0				

Source: Author

like smartphones and computers is another key factor, indicating the importance of convenience and accessibility. Additionally, benefits for new players, such as sign-up bonuses and tutorials, are well-appreciated. Comfort and flexibility of playing from home or any preferred location at convenient times are significant attractions. Moreover, the opportunity to earn premium rewards and benefits, enhancing the overall gaming experience, is also a priority for players.

Recommendations

To combat online lottery issues, the Tamil Nadu Government has enacted a ban under the 1997 Regulation Act and introduced strict legal actions against offenders. Awareness campaigns educate the public on the risks and illegality of online lottery, promoting responsible gambling. The government collaborates with law enforcement, operates consumer complaint mechanisms, and actively blocks illegal lottery websites, encouraging public reporting of such activities.

Key suggestions include establishing a comprehensive regulatory framework, implementing age verification, promoting responsible gaming, and strengthening consumer protection. Public awareness and financial management among players are emphasized. Collaborative efforts between stakeholders and continuous research and monitoring are vital. Players are advised to budget responsibly, play with caution, and stay alert to scams, treating online lottery as entertainment, not income.

Conclusion

The study highlights several critical issues faced by online lottery players, such as loneliness, financial losses, addiction, overspending, and time mismanagement. These findings underscore the urgency of implementing measures to mitigate these problems and encourage responsible gaming practices in the online lottery sector. Proposals include establishing a regulatory framework, enforcing age verification, adopting responsible gaming measures, and enhancing consumer protection. Additionally, educational and awareness initiatives are essential to inform players about responsible gambling and the risks of excessive lottery participation.

Future research in this area is vital to deepen our understanding of the challenges in online gambling. Investigating the prevalence and impact of online lottery addiction, assessing the effectiveness of regulatory frameworks and consumer protection, and studying the financial implications and social consequences of online lottery participation are key areas. Research could also explore the vulnerability of specific populations like youth and low-income individuals and evaluate the effectiveness of responsible gambling measures. Comparative studies across different jurisdictions would provide further insights, helping to identify best practices and inform policy recommendations.

References

Bernadeta, et al. (2019). The prevalence of e-gambling and of problem e-gambling in Poland. *International Journal of Environment Research and Public Health*, 17, 1–15.

Burns, A. C., Gillett, P. L., Rubinstein, M., and Gentry, J. W. (1990). An exploratory study of lottery playing, gambling addiction and links to compulsive consumption. In Goldberg, M. E., Gorn, G., and Pollay, R. W. (Eds.), Advances in Consumer Research (Vol. 17, pp. 298–305). Association for Consumer Research.

Devi, S., and Jayasheela, G. (2017). A study on problems faced by teenagers due to internet gambling. *International Journal of Innovative Science and Research Technology*, 2(11), 212–213.

Foote, B. (2018). Predictors of gambling-related problems in adult internet gamblers (Doctoral dissertation, Walden University).

Kumar, R. (2021). Indian Online Lottery: Advantages and Disadvantages. Augusta Free Press. https://augustafreepress.com/news/indian-online-lottery-advantages-and-disadvantages/.

Morgan, et al. (2022). Gambling problems among students attending university in the United Kingdom: Associations with gender, financial hardship and year of study. *Journal of Gambling*, 1–21 .

Scholes, A. (2012). Relationships between online gambling, substance use and mental health: a review. Retrieved from https://acuresearchbank.acu.edu.au/.

105 A study talent management among college teaching staff in Coimbatore district

Rakulram, S. and Rathnapriya, B.[a]

Karpagam Academy of Higher Education, Coimbatore, Tamil Nadu, India

Abstract

This study examines the talent management practices among college teaching staff in Coimbatore District, with a focus on job satisfaction as a key factor in effective talent management. Talent management is an essential in education field, as it directly impacts the attraction, development, and retention of skilled faculty. The research explores the key components of talent management, including recruiting qualified candidates, fostering professional development, offering competitive compensation, enhancing employee engagement, and ensuring work-life balance. It also identifies the key factors influencing talent management, such as institutional culture, leadership support, resource availability, and effective communication. This study provides the valuable insights for college administrators and stakeholders to develop strategies that attract, nurture, and retain talented staff. Ultimately, this research aims to enhance educational quality, foster academic.

Keywords: College teaching staff, employee engagement, professional development, recruitment, retention, talent management

Introduction

In the dynamic realm of educational institutions, the pivotal role of talent management in fostering success and growth cannot be overstated. Specifically, within the sphere of college teaching staff, talent management denotes the strategic orchestration employed by institutions to allure, nurture, inspire, and retain accomplished faculty members. The adept handling of faculty talent emerges as a linchpin in augmenting the overall quality of education and fostering an enriched academic milieu within colleges. Nestled in the verdant landscapes of Tamil Nadu, India, Coimbatore district stands as a beacon of educational excellence, housing a myriad of colleges offering a diverse array of courses and programs. These institutions, cognizant of the profound impact of competent teaching staff on educational delivery, ardently strive to attract and retain such talents. Therefore, a profound comprehension and judicious implementation of talent management strategies in this district can wield a transformative influence on the academic outcomes and standing of these colleges, thereby contributing significantly to their mission of delivering exceptional education to students.

Review of Literature

Table 105.1 Insights into diverse talent management studies: authors, focus areas, and key discoveries.

Author name	Study	Findings
Sathyanarayana et al. (2022)	Talent management and employee retention in Indian IT	Identified job engagement, working environment quality, and open communication as crucial factors in talent management.
Das (2022)	Conceptual analysis of talent management	Findings emphasise the importance of talent management.
Sen et al. (2023)	Talent management's impact on organizational Performance	Strategies aligning with company strategy significantly impact business revenues.
Yildiz and Esmer (2023)	Systematic review of talent management strategies	Identified seven fundamental talent management functions.

[a]priyamidhun2014@gmail.com

Author name	Study	Findings
Lokhande (2023)	Talent management's role in organizational performance	Stressed HR's critical role, effective hiring, and strategic actions in talent management.
Shafique (2023)	Impact of talent management on employees' work outcomes	Concluded that talent management positively influences productivity and quitting intentions.

Source: Author

Table 105.2 Socio economic profile of the respondents.

Particulars		Numbers (n = 170)	Percentage
Gender	Male	64	37.6
	Female	106	62.4
Age	21 – 35	127	74.7
	Above 35	43	25.3
Qualification	Postgraduate	68	40.0
	M. Phil.	24	14.1
	Ph. D	78	45.9
Professional qualification	Trained	114	67.1
	Untrained	56	32.9
Experience	Up to 5 years	112	65.9
	6 - 10 years	36	21.2
	11 - 15 years	10	5.9
	Above 15 years	12	7.1
Marital status	Married	74	43.5
	Unmarried	96	56.5
Type of college	Government	16	9.4
	Aided	60	35.3
	Private	94	55.3
Nature of college	Boys	8	4.7
	Girls	8	4.7
	Co – education	154	90.6
Location of college	Urban	110	64.7
	Rural	60	35.3

Source: Author

Problem Statement

In the educational landscape of Coimbatore District, an investigation into talent management practices among college teaching staff is imperative to comprehend the intricacies of the talent management process and its impact on job satisfaction. The study aims to delve into the methods employed for talent acquisition, development, motivation, and retention within the teaching staff, taking into account potential challenges such as intense competition from other institutions, limited resources for recruitment and retention, and the availability of qualified educators. The primary goal is to evaluate the relationship between talent management practices and the performance and job satisfaction of college teaching staff. By unraveling how these strategies influence crucial outcomes, the study seeks to provide recommendations aimed at enhancing faculty performance and job satisfaction, addressing the nuanced challenges inherent in talent management within the educational context of Coimbatore District.

Objective of the study
The study seeks to achieve two primary objectives: firstly, to uncover the intricacies of the talent

Table 105.3 Assessment of job satisfaction among college faculties.

S.NO	Job Satisfaction	HS 5	S 4	N 3	DS 2	HDS 1	Total	Mean score	Rank
1	My job is quite interesting.	67	79	20	4	0	170	4.229	1
		335	316	60	8	0	719		
2	My job gives sense of accomplishment.	44	84	31	11	0	170	3.947	10
		220	336	93	22	0	671		
3	I am respected with my job.	67	71	28	4	0	170	4.182	4
		335	284	84	8	0	711		
4	I feel uncomfortable with my job.	35	75	48	8	4	170	3.759	23
		175	300	144	16	4	639		
5	My job is challenging enough to achieve the goals of organization.	51	99	20	0	0	170	4.182	4
		255	396	60	0	0	711		
6	My job is creative.	52	102	16	0	0	170	4.212	2
		260	408	48	0	0	716		
7	My job develops my abilities.	60	86	24	0	0	170	4.212	2
		300	344	72	0	0	716		
8	My income is adequate for normal expenses.	35	91	44	0	0	170	3.947	10
		175	364	132	0	0	671		
9	My pay is fare.	20	99	47	4	0	170	3.794	21
		100	396	141	8	0	645		
10	My income provides luxuries.	20	76	44	23	7	170	3.465	28
		100	304	132	46	7	589		
11	My Job is insecure.	40	72	35	15	8	170	3.712	26
		200	288	105	30	8	631		
12	My pay is less than I deserve.	28	82	48	12	0	170	3.741	24
		140	328	144	24	0	636		
13	I am well paid.	52	68	31	15	4	170	3.876	19
		260	272	93	30	4	659		
14	I am under paid.	32	75	44	11	8	170	3.659	27
		160	300	132	22	8	622		

Source: Author

management process, encompassing acquisition, development, motivation, and retention strategies; and secondly, to assess the level of job satisfaction. Through these dual lenses, the research aims to provide concise insights into the interplay between talent management practices and subjective job contentment.

Research methodology
1. Data collection: Collected data via an Interview schedule focusing on the profile, talent management, and job satisfaction of college teaching staff.

2. Source of data: Primary data gathered through a structured questionnaire distributed in both hard and soft copies.
3. Sampling design: Employed convenience sampling, collecting data from 170 respondents in Coimbatore city.
4. Area of study: The study focuses on Coimbatore district.
5. Framework of analysis: utilized simple percentage analysis and weighted average rank for data analysis.

Significance of the study

This study proves invaluable for both college management and teaching staff by providing insights into the talent management process for college teaching faculties. It serves as a practical guide, offering tangible assistance in navigating and optimizing talent management strategies within the academic context. The findings of this research contribute to enhancing the understanding and implementation of effective talent management practices, fostering an environment conducive to the professional growth and satisfaction of teaching staff while simultaneously aiding the managerial decision-making process within the college.

Limitations of the study

This study confines its scope to respondents in Coimbatore city, thus cautioning that the outcomes may not be universally applicable to other geographical locations. The research exclusively focuses on the teaching profession, highlighting the specificity of its findings to this particular occupational domain. This limitation underscores the need for careful consideration when extrapolating and generalizing the study's results to broader contexts, emphasizing the localized nature of the investigation within the specified demographic and professional boundaries of Coimbatore city and the teaching profession.

Findings of the study

Simple percentage analysis: Socioeconomic profile of respondents revealed in the following Table.

The socio-economic profile reveals a predominant female representation among teachers, aged between 21 and 35, with a majority holding Ph.D. qualifications and being professionally trained. Most teachers have less than 5 years of experience, are unmarried, and work in private co-education colleges located in urban areas.

Applying the weighted average rank method to assess job satisfaction among college faculties:

Utilizing the weighted average rank method to identify key reasons influencing the choice of the teaching profession, as disclosed in the study results.

According to the results of the Weighted Average Rank test, the majority of individuals express satisfaction with their teaching profession, citing factors such as the intrinsic interest in teaching, the creative nature of the job, and the development of personal abilities. Positive sentiments are also associated with aspects like supportive and stimulating colleagues, respectful treatment, and a challenging work environment aligned with organizational goals. On the flip side, some concerns are raised, including perceptions of gossipy or lazy colleagues, issues with management supervision, and feelings of being underpaid or insecure in the job. The diverse array of responses highlights the multifaceted nature of job satisfaction among college faculties.

Recommendations

Recommendations for enhancing faculty development, talent management, job satisfaction, and working conditions, tailored to different demographics and institutional settings in the academic landscape.

*   Attend faculty development for growth, conduct orientation programs.
*   Postgraduate teachers improve talent management through higher qualifications and international publications.
*   Urban teachers enhance talent management using institutional facilities and engaging in co-consultancy.
*   MPhil-qualified teachers improve satisfaction with leave for Ph.D. pursuits; unmarried teachers limit admin work.
*   Aided college teachers improve job satisfaction with better working environments and support for higher studies.
*   Male faculty receive higher incentives for qualifications; rural faculty improve satisfaction through infrastructure and living standards.

Conclusion

Faculty members aiming to enhance talent management are recommended to engage in a comprehensive set of strategies, including attending development programs, conducting orientations, pursuing higher qualifications like a Doctorate or NET exam, publishing in international conferences, utilizing institutional facilities, offering consultancy services, and providing supportive measures like leaves and free consultants.

Tailored interventions for specific demographics, such as improving the working environment for unmarried and aided college teachers, offering competitive salaries and incentives, and enhancing infrastructure in rural colleges, collectively contribute to fostering increased job satisfaction and elevating overall competency levels among teachers.

References

Das, P. K. (2022). An introduction to the study of talent management. *World Journal of Education and Humanities*, 4(2), ISSN 2687-6760 (Print), ISSN 2687-6779 (Online).

Lokhande, J. (2023). Talent management and its impact on organization performance: a conceptual framework. *Journal of Emerging Technologies and Innovative Research*, 10(2), e823–e825.

Sathyanarayana. S., Pushpa, B. V., and Gargesa, S. (2022). Talent management practices and its impact on intention to stay in the organization. *Asian Journal of Economics, Business and Accounting*, 22(24), 86–104.

Sen, J., Harianto, A., and Satrianny, I. P. (2023). Talent management in human resource management to improve organizational performance. *Indonesian Journal of Contemporary Multidisciplinary Research (MODERN)*, 2(2), 95–108.

Shafique, M. (2023). Impact of talent management on employees' work outcomes. *International Research for Advanced Research*, 4(1), 405–414.

Yildiz, R. O., and Esmer, S. (2023). Talent management strategies and functions: a systematic review. *Industrial and Commercial Training*, 55(1), 93–111.

106 Problems faced by fisherman in Nagapattinam

Vishva and Gayathiri, M.[a]

Karpagam Academy of Higher Education, Coimbatore, Tamil Nadu, India

Abstract

This study delves into the challenges faced by the fishing community in Nagapattinam, a coastal district in Tamil Nadu, India, where dependence on marine resources is pivotal for livelihoods. It identifies and analyses various issues impacting the economic, social, and environmental well-being of these fishermen. Key challenges include erratic weather patterns, overfishing, poor infrastructure, limited financial resources, and insufficient government support. The research highlights that a significant number of fishermen struggle with financial constraints and face difficulties in fishing throughout the year and across different sea regions. To mitigate these issues, the study proposes several solutions: enhancing weather forecasting systems, encouraging sustainable fishing practices, investing in infrastructure development, easing access to credit and insurance, and implementing robust government support programs. These recommendations aim to improve the overall well-being and resilience of the fishing community in Nagapattinam.

Keywords: Challenges, climate change, government support, insurance, overfishing, problems, weather patterns

Introduction

Nagapattinam, a coastal district in Tamil Nadu, India, is known for its thriving marine resources and fishing community. Fishing, a generational livelihood, faces numerous challenges that affect the fishermen's lives, economic stability, and well-being. This introduction explores these challenges, providing insight into the complex factors impacting the fishermen's lives.

Climate change and erratic weather patterns, including increased cyclonic activities and unpredictable monsoons, pose significant risks to the fishermen. These conditions not only threaten their safety but also cause damage to their fishing equipment, leading to financial losses. Overfishing is another major concern, as intensified fishing activities and unsustainable practices have led to depleted fish stocks, reducing catch sizes and threatening long-term sustainability.

The region's inadequate infrastructure exacerbates these problems. Limited access to credit and insurance options makes it difficult for fishermen to invest in modern equipment, repair vessels, or handle the aftermath of accidents and natural disasters. Additionally, the lack of comprehensive government support in terms of policies, regulations, and initiatives for sustainable fishing and social welfare leaves the fishing community vulnerable.

Addressing these issues requires a thorough understanding of the specific problems and their root causes. The study aims to develop targeted interventions and sustainable solutions, delving deeper into these challenges and proposing potential solutions to enhance the resilience and prosperity of Nagapattinam's fishermen.

Review of Literature

Muringai et al. (2020) highlighted the diverse pressures faced by small-scale fishing communities in Lake Kariba, Zimbabwe, including environmental, social, political, and economic challenges impacting fish production. Kinseng et al. (2019) identified issues faced by fishermen in Banyuwangi, Indonesia, such as unpredictable weather and decreased catches. Jahan et al. (2018) focused on the fish biodiversity and socio-economic status of fishermen in Belia Bael, noting a variety of fish species and the demographic characteristics of the fishing community. Jarin (2018) studied fishermen in Dagupan City, finding most to be young adult males with primary education. Kotni (2017) examined the marine fisheries value chain in Andhra Pradesh, India, identifying challenges in infrastructure, export, and various other sectors. Salim et al. (2017) observed that improved education and healthcare positively impact fishermen's lifestyles.

Despite existing research, there remains a significant gap in comprehensively understanding the multifaceted problems faced by fishermen in Nagapattinam, necessitating an interdisciplinary approach to fully address these issues and involve fishing communities, policymakers, and researchers.

[a]muthugayathiri@gmail.com

Problem statement

The fishing community in Nagapattinam, Tamil Nadu, is confronting multifaceted challenges, including the adverse effects of climate change, overfishing, unsustainable practices, insufficient infrastructure, and a lack of government support, all of which severely impact their livelihoods and overall well-being, necessitating targeted solutions and interventions.

The objective of the study is to identify the problems faced by fishermen.

Scope of the study

This study delves into the challenges faced by the fishing community in Nagapattinam, a coastal district in Tamil Nadu, India, aiming to identify and analyze their specific problems. It addresses issues like climate change, overfishing, insufficient infrastructure, financial constraints, and the lack of government support, using qualitative methods like interviews and focus groups. The study's goal is to offer recommendations for sustainable fishing practices, infrastructure improvements, financial support, and government interventions, primarily focused on Nagapattinam but potentially applicable to other similar coastal communities. However, it is tailored to the unique situation in Nagapattinam and may not cover all challenges faced by fishermen elsewhere.

Research methodology

- **Research design**: Employing a mixed-methods design combining qualitative and quantitative approaches for a thorough understanding of the challenges faced by fishermen in Nagapattinam.
- **Data collection**: Gathering primary data from 180 fishermen using interview schedules with close-ended questions, supplemented by secondary data from various sources, and analyzing statistically for patterns and trends.
- **Sampling method**: Utilizing purposive sampling to ensure a diverse representation of fishermen across different age groups, experience levels, and practices for a well-rounded perspective.
- **Analysis Framework**: Applying inferential statistics, including simple percentage analysis and weighted average analysis, to identify significant factors contributing to the fishermen's challenges.

Significance of the Study

This study on Nagapattinam's fishermen is vital for understanding their unique challenges and guiding sustainable fisheries management, policy development, and the improvement of livelihoods, by providing insights into the dynamics affecting their well-being, informing adaptive strategies and interventions, and serving as a valuable resource for global knowledge exchange in fisheries management and coastal community resilience.

Limitations of the Study

In studying the problems faced by fishermen in Nagapattinam, it's important to consider limitations like potential biases (selection, response, interviewer) and the representativeness of a possibly small sample size, which might not fully encapsulate the diverse experiences and perspectives of all fishermen in the region. The study may be subject to various biases, including selection bias, response bias, and interviewer bias.

Findings of the Study

Simple percentage analysis

The following table discloses the socio economic profile of the respondents.

Table 106.1 Socio Economic Profile of the Respondents.

Particulars	Numbers (n = 180)	Percentage
Age		
18 – 25	10	5.6
26 – 30	49	27.2
31 – 35	77	42.8
Above 35	44	24.4
Gender		
Male	156	86.7
Female	24	13.3
Educational qualification		
Illiterate	37	20.6
SSLC	61	33.9
HSC	82	45.6
Status in family		
Head	81	45.0
Member	99	55.0
Type of family		
Joint	54	30.0
Nuclear	126	70.0
Monthly income (Rs.)		
Up to 19000	23	12.8
19001-25000	126	70.0
Above 25000	31	17.2

Particulars	Numbers (n = 180)	Percentage
Family income (Rs.)		
Up to 12000	1	0.6
12001-30000	174	96.7
Above 30000	5	2.7
Family expenditure		
Upto 20000	153	85.0
Above 20000	27	15.0
Number of earning members		
1	17	9.4
2	115	63.9
3 and above	48	26.7
Area of residence		
Urban	80	44.4
Semi Urban	100	55.6

Source: Author

Most fishermen in the study are males aged 31-35, with a High School certificate, living in nuclear families in semi-urban areas. Their personal monthly income ranges from Rs. 19,001 to 25,000, while family income is typically Rs. 12,001 to 30,000. They generally spend up to Rs. 20,000 and have two earning members per family.

Weighted average analysis

To identify the prominent reasons that induce a person to have general problems in fishing. A weighted average and rank test has been employed. The following table discloses the results of the study.

The weighted average rank test reveals that the primary problems faced by the majority of fishermen include a lack of finance, difficulty in capturing fish throughout the sea and year, high petrol and diesel expenses, and troubles with officials from other countries.

Table 106.2 General problems towards fisherman.

Problems	1	2	3	4	5	Sum	Mean	Rank
Overfishing	2	8	36	88	46	180	3.93	6
	2	16	108	352	230	708		
High petrol diesel expenses	0	6	32	58	84	180	4.22	4
	0	12	96	232	420	760		
No regular income	0	38	54	68	20	180	3.39	9
	0	76	162	272	100	610		
Damage of boat	8	34	92	18	28	180	3.13	11
	8	68	276	72	140	564		
Trouble from other country's officials	2	8	20	88	62	180	4.11	5
	2	16	60	352	310	740		
Unable to capture fish all over the year	0	0	28	68	84	180	4.31	3
	0	0	84	272	420	776		
Poor monsoon	8	62	58	76	16	220	3.14	10
	8	124	174	304	80	690		
Perishable nature of product	2	28	40	68	42	180	3.67	8
	2	56	120	272	210	660		
Unable to spend time with family	6	10	54	70	40	180	3.71	7
	6	20	162	280	200	668		
Lack of finance	0	2	20	58	100	180	4.42	1
	0	4	60	232	500	796		
Unable to capture fish all over the sea	0	8	20	46	106	180	4.39	2
	0	16	60	184	530	790		

Source: Author

Conclusion

In conclusion, the fishermen of Nagapattinam face a myriad of challenges that significantly impact their livelihoods and overall well-being. These challenges include adverse effects of climate change, overfishing, inadequate infrastructure, limited financial support, and insufficient government backing. To mitigate these issues, a range of strategies needs to be implemented. These include enhancing weather forecasting, enforcing sustainable fishing regulations, improving access to essential resources, facilitating credit availability, and encouraging collaborative efforts between various stakeholders. Additionally, diversifying income sources and offering vocational training can bolster the resilience of fishermen against the uncertainties of fishing seasons.

However, it's important to recognize that these conclusions are based on hypothetical scenarios and require empirical research specific to Nagapattinam for validation. Engaging comprehensively with the local community, government, NGOs, and researchers will ensure the relevance and effectiveness of any proposed solutions. By tackling these problems effectively, not only can the livelihoods of Nagapattinam's fishermen be improved, but also the health of the marine ecosystem and the sustainability of the fishing industry can be safeguarded.

Future research should aim to deepen our understanding of the socio-economic impacts on Nagapattinam's fishing community, explore the role of women in the industry, assess the environmental impacts of fishing practices, and investigate alternative livelihood options. Such research will be crucial in developing targeted, context-specific interventions, contributing to sustainable fisheries management and the overall well-being of the fishing community in Nagapattinam.

References

Brahmane , V. T., Solanki, V. M., Patel, M. R., and Baraiya, K. G. (2016). Socio-economic status and scope for improvement of Navi bandar fishing village of Saurashtra. *Advances in Life Sciences*, 5(10), 4039–4042.

Jahan, M. I., Alam, M. S., Karim, M. S., Sultana, N., Mamun, M., and Rafiquzzaman, S. (2018). Assessment of fish diversity and socio-economic condition of fishermen in Bangladesh. *Asian Journal of Medical and Biological Research*, 4(1), 69. doi:10.3329/ajmbr.v4i1.36824.

Jarin, S. A. (2018). Socio-economic status and environmental problems affecting the fishermen along the river tributaries of Dagupan city. *Asia Pacific Journal of Multidisciplinary Research*, 6(1), 82–87.

Kinseng, R. A., Mahmud, A., Hamdani, A., and Hidayati, H. N. (2019). Challenges to the sustainability of small-scale fishers livelihood in Banyuwangi regency, East Java, Indonesia. *IOP Conference Series: Earth and Environmental Science*, 352, 1–13.

Kotni (2017). Management and socio-economic conditions of fishermen in Andhra Pradesh. *Journal of Fisheries*, 1(1), 30-36.

Muringai, R. T., Naidoo, D., and Mafongoya, P. (2020). The challenges experienced by small-scale fishing communities of lake Kariba, Zimbabwe. *The Journal for Transdisciplinary Research in Southern Africa*, 16(1), 1–16.

Salim, S. S., Narayanakumar, R., Sathiadhas, R., Antony, B., and Manjusha, U. (2017). Assessment of socio-economic status of fishers across different sectors in Tamil Nadu. *Fishery Technology*, 54(4), 291–293.

107 A study on problems faced by small-scale industries in Coimbatore district

Chandru, G.[a] and Lakshmi Priya, N.[b]

Karpagam Academy of Higher Education, Coimbatore, Tamil Nadu, India

Abstract

This study delves into the challenges faced by small-scale industries in Coimbatore, crucial for the country's growth. Highlighting obstacles such as insufficient capacity utilization, ineffective management, and financial constraints, the research emphasizes the need for addressing these issues to facilitate unimpeded production and enhance marketability. The findings contribute valuable insights to the ongoing discourse on creating a conducive environment for small-scale industries, aiming to optimize their role in the broader economic landscape.

Keywords: Challenges, financial assistance, small-scale industries

Introduction

The significance of small-scale industries in the economic fabric of Coimbatore district, renowned for its industrial prowess, cannot be overstated. These enterprises are pivotal contributors to local employment, production, and entrepreneurial opportunities, yet they grapple with a host of challenges that impede their growth. This multifaceted array of issues, encompassing market dynamics, financial constraints, infrastructure limitations, and regulatory hurdles, underscores the need for a nuanced analysis. Employing factor analysis as a robust methodology, this study aims to identify and categorize these challenges, offering valuable insights for targeted interventions. Recognizing the integral role of small-scale industries in fostering a conducive business environment and promoting sustainable economic development, this research seeks to inform strategies and policies that can empower these enterprises to overcome obstacles, enhance competitiveness, and fully realize their potential as drivers of regional prosperity.

Review of Literature

Table 107.1 Synopsis of key findings in studies on business development challenges and solutions in various sectors.

Author	Study	Findings
Rajamani et al. (2022)	Financial access for new entrepreneurs	Emphasizes financial access importance; highlights adverse effects of financial barriers and advantages of business characteristics.
Singh and Kaur (2021)	SMEs in India	Advocates government focus on banking sector development and education to encourage SME businesses.
Leo Francis and Haris (2021)	Challenges in "make-to-order" and "make-to-stock" organizations	Identifies five criteria determining challenges in manufacturing organizations, including design, manufacturing, technology, raw material collection, and marketing.
Kumar and Mookiah (2020)	Industrial businesses and financial aid	Respondents seek government financial aid due to environmental changes affecting industrial businesses.
Gawali1 and Gadekar (2017)	MSMEs failure causes	Attributes MSMEs failure to poor financial management and managerial inefficiency, advocates improved financial skills for survival and growth.
Kateshiya (2017)	Contemporary production techniques	Analyzes the need for modern production techniques, infrastructure, and government support in production units.

[a]chandru040500@gmail.com, [b]lakshmipriya.navaneethakrishnan@kahedu.edu.in

Author	Study	Findings
Ramcharran (2016)	Effectiveness of bank loans in Indian SME sector	Investigates SME sector operation, measures bank loan effectiveness, and rates in Indian SMEs.
Khuriyati and Kumalasari (2015)	End of pipe treatment technique	Reveals the ineffectiveness of the end-of-pipe treatment technique due to high cost.
Mukherjee (2018)	Challenges in Indian economy	Identifies challenges in the Indian economy, including high borrowing costs, raw material availability, insufficient infrastructure, and a shortage of skilled labor.
Onukwuli et al.(2014)	Barriers in business	Identifies barriers such as difficulty in assessing credit, insufficient competence and administrative skills, information technology gaps, and challenges in R&D investment.

Source: Author

Problem Statement

Small-scale industries in India grapple with a myriad of challenges, hindering their development and growth. Issues encompass insufficient capacity utilization, ineffective management, financial constraints, raw material shortages, marketing and export hurdles, working capital deficiencies, technological lag, labor problems, cash flow issues, and power shortages. Despite their historical contributions to economic growth, these enterprises face unique obstacles that curtail their potential, exacerbated by increased competition from large-scale businesses. Government initiatives, initially beneficial, have lost efficacy as the economy evolved, leaving many small-scale industries struggling to survive. Their distinct organizational structure places them at a disadvantage, necessitating a comprehensive understanding and strategic interventions to address their multifaceted issues.

Objective of the study
The primary objective of this study is to systematically identify and understand the challenges faced by small-scale industries in Coimbatore district, shedding light on issues such as insufficient capacity utilization, ineffective management, and financial constraints.

Research methodology
1. Data collection: Collection of primary data achieved through the administration of questionnaires for study purposes.
2. Sampling technique: Utilization of a simple convenience sampling method, involving 180 small-scale industries in Coimbatore district.
3. Analysis tools: Employed simple percentage calculations and Factor Analysis for analyzing the collected data.

Significance of the study
This study holds significant relevance for entrepreneurs and laborers in small-scale industries, particularly those grappling with the challenges prevalent in the Indian business landscape. Small-scale industries, once benefiting from reserved production items, now contend with fierce competition due to economic liberalization and globalization. The study underscores the need for swift government intervention, advocating the formulation of welfare schemes tailored to address the unique challenges faced by these enterprises. By proactively tackling these issues, the government can empower small-scale industries to unlock their full potential, fostering not only their growth but also their substantial contribution to overall economic development.

Limitations of the study
This survey specifically targeted selected areas within the Coimbatore region, emphasizing a focused approach to data collection. Geographical specificity ensures a detailed and contextual understanding of the factors at play within the identified areas. By homing in on these particular locations, the survey aims to provide nuanced insights that are reflective of the unique dynamics and challenges present in the selected Coimbatore areas, contributing to a more targeted and regionally relevant analysis.

Findings of the study
Percentage analysis of small-scale industry operators:

Insights from respondent data

In the study, 180 small-scale industries were surveyed, revealing that 51.7% operated for four to six years. The majority of industries employ up to four workers (58.3%), with experienced personnel (63.9%) having 6 to 10 years of experience. Sole proprietors constitute 85% of businesses, while 91.7%

Table 107.2 Profile of the respondents.

Year of establish	Frequency	Percent
Up to 3 years	18	10.0
4 - 6 years	93	51.7
7 -10 years	63	35.0
Above 10 years	6	3.3
Total	180	100.0
N. of workers emp	Frequency	Percent
Up to 4 members	105	58.3
5 - 7 Members	57	31.7
8 - 10 Members	18	10.0
Total	180	100.0
Experience	Frequency	Percent
Up to 5 years	18	10.0
6 - 10 years	115	63.9
More than 10 years	47	26.1
Total	180	100.0
Type of firm	Frequency	Percent
Sole trader	153	85.0
Partnership	21	11.7
Private company	6	3.3
Total	180	100.0
Procurement of RM	Frequency	Percent
Local market	165	91.7
National	12	6.7
International	3	1.7
Total	180	100.0
Finished product	Frequency	Percent
Local market	156	86.7
National	21	11.7
International	3	1.7
Total	180	100.0
Location	Frequency	Percent
Urban	93	51.7
Semi-urban	72	40.0
Rural	15	8.3
Total	180	100.0
Nature of organization	Frequency	Percent
Manufacturer	126	70.0
Service	54	30.0
Total	180	100.0
Gender	Frequency	Percent
Male	180	100.0
Age	Frequency	Percent
Up to 30 years	26	14.4

Year of establish	Frequency	Percent
31 - 40 years	22	12.2
41 - 50 years	78	43.3
Above 50 years	54	30.0
Total	180	100.0
Annual income	Frequency	Percent
Less than 1 lakh	3	1.7
1 - 2 lakh	12	6.7
2 - 3 lakh	84	46.7
Above 3 lakh	81	45.0
Total	180	100.0
Generation of entrepreneur	Frequency	Percent
1st Generation	165	91.7
2nd Generation	15	8.3
Total	180	100.0
Type of unit	Frequency	Percent
Capital intensive	99	55.0
Labor intensive	81	45.0
Total	180	100.0

Source: Author

Table 107.3 KMO and Bartlett's test.

KMO and Bartlett's test		
Kaiser-Meyer-Olkin Measure of sampling adequacy.		.769
Bartlett's test of sphericity	Approx. Chi-square	2207.152
	df	276
	Sig.	.000

Source: Author

source raw materials locally. Additionally, 86.7% sell finished goods in local markets, with 51.7% of industries located in cities. Manufacturers represent 70% of the businesses, all owned by men. In terms of age, 43.3% fall in the 41–50 range, and 46.7% earn an annual salary of nearly 3 lakhs, while 91.7% of owners are first-generation entrepreneurs.

Factor analysis of challenges in Coimbatore district preliminary evaluation

Preliminary validation: assessing data suitability for factor analysis using KMO and Bartlett's test.

In this study, factor analysis is utilized to discern key factors affecting challenges in Coimbatore District's small-scale industries. Preceding the analysis, the KMO measure and Bartlett's Test of Sphericity confirm data suitability. The KMO measure, surpassing the 0.70 threshold, affirms dataset adequacy. Bartlett's Test of Sphericity, with a significant p-value and a substantial test statistic, indicates the correlation matrix's suitability. These tests collectively assure the data's appropriateness for factor analysis, permitting a comprehensive exploration of the factors influencing challenges faced by small-scale industries in Coimbatore District. The outcomes demonstrate that the collected data is well-suited for factor analysis, offering a foundation for identifying influential factors affecting these industries.

Rotated components matrix analysis:
Utilizing a rotated components matrix and criteria assessment: Eigen values and component loadings analysis. This approach involves evaluating Eigen Values greater than unity and component loadings of 0.5 and above to discern meaningful factors.

Table 107.4 Rotated component matrixa.

Rotated component matrix

	Component							
	Factor 1	Factor 2	Factor 3	Factor 4	Factor 5	Factor 6	Factor 7	Factor 8
Facing open competition with large-scale industries	0.91							
The financial institutions are not sufficient	0.901							
Rental problems of business establishment	0.763							
It is difficult to get loans from authorized financial institutions		0.853						
The credit worthiness of SSI'S is weak		0.754						
Private money lenders demand high rate of interest		0.721						
Discretion of authorities of financial institutions also creates financial problem		0.552						
Buyer – seller meet is arranged by SIDCO			0.841					
Ancillary SSI units are forced to sell their products in a local market			0.736					
The productions of SSI must travel long distance for marketing			0.622					
Lack of technology				0.717				
SSI are not considered as skill development centers				0.71				
Difficulty in making frequent purchase of raw materials					0.801			
Frequent purchase of raw material affects the quality of production					0.768			
Competition in marketing the productions					0.517			
Within the limited hours of power supply, it is difficult to complete the production						0.87		
There is no special staff to deal with government agencies regarding raw material supply							0.801	

Rotated component matrix

	Component							
	Factor 1	Factor 2	Factor 3	Factor 4	Factor 5	Factor 6	Factor 7	Factor 8
Poor quality raw materials affects the image of the products produced							0.746	
Storage cost of raw material								0.82
Eigenvalues	4.497	2.928	2.275	1.989	1.723	1.48	1.326	1.181
% of Variance	18.739	12.201	9.478	8.287	7.178	6.169	5.525	4.92
Cumulative %	18.739	30.941	40.418	48.705	55.882	62.051	67.576	72.496

Source: Author

- Factor 1: Challenges in open competition, financial institutions, and business establishment rental issues.
- Factor 2: Loan challenges, weak credit, high-interest rates, and financial authority discretion problems.
- Factor 3: Marketing hurdles, forced selling, and travel challenges for SSI productions.
- Factor 4: Technology deficiency and SSIS not recognized as skill development centers.
- Factor 5: Raw material purchase difficulties, quality impact, and production marketing competition.
- Factor 6: Production challenges within limited power supply hours.
- Factor 7: Insufficient staff for government agencies, raw material quality affecting product image.
- Factor 8: High storage costs for raw materials.
- These identified factors encapsulate diverse facets of the challenges confronting small-scale industries in Coimbatore, offering crucial insights for targeted interventions and performance enhancement.

Recommendations

- Foster partnerships between small and large industries for resource leverage and market access.
- Improve financial support with specialized institutions and enhance financial literacy for small-scale industries.
- Address rental issues through industrial zones, incentives, and shared manufacturing spaces.
- Enhance creditworthiness and financial skills through training for small-scale industries.
- Connect small-scale industries with buyers through trade fairs and online platforms for marketing.
- Promote technology adoption and skill development for a modern workforce.

- Collaborate on power supply improvements and explore renewable energy options.
- Improve raw material access and quality through direct linkages and bulk purchases.
- Strengthen coordination with government agencies for regulatory support.
- Promote networking among small-scale industries for shared knowledge and joint marketing efforts.
- A comprehensive strategy for addressing identified factors and problems in Coimbatore district's small-scale industries.

Conclusion

In conclusion, industries serve as a cornerstone of national economic growth, creating jobs and improving living standards. However, small businesses encounter challenges, primarily stemming from limited access to capital, hindering investments in marketing, inventory, and equipment. Furthermore, inadequate infrastructure and logistical support pose difficulties for small businesses dependent on shipping and transportation, impacting their competitiveness.

References

Gawali, R. B., and Gadekar, A. (2017). Financial management practices in micro, small and medium enterprises. *International Journal of Research in Finance and Marketing*, 7(6), 45–59.

Kateshiya, S. (2017). Problems of Small Scale Industry in Jamnagar City in the Context of Brass Part Units. Abhinav Publication, (vol. 6(8)), UGC APPROVED Online ISSN-2277-1166.

Khuriyati, N., and Kumalasari, D. (2015). Cleaner production strategy for improving environmental performance of small-scale cracker industry. *Agriculture and Agricultural Science Procedia*, 3, 102–107.

Kumar, S., and Mookiah, S. (2020). Contemporary scenario of small-scale industries in Tirunelveli district. *Journal* of *Xi'an University of Architecture and Technology*, 12, 1155.

Leo Francis, K., and Haris, N. (2021). Analysis of challenges faced by small and medium enterprises in Kerala: a comparison study on make-to-stock and make-to-order industries. *International Research Journal of Engineering and Technology (IRJET)*, 8(8).

Mukherjee, S. (2018). Challenges to Indian micro small scale and medium enterprises in the era of globalization. *Journal of Global Entrepreneurship Research*, 8, 1–19.

Onukwuli, A. G., Akam, U. G., and Onwuka, E. M. (2014). Challenges of small-scale industries in sustainable development in Nigeria.

Rajamani, K., Jan, N. A., Subramani, A. K., and Raj, A. N. (2022). Access to finance: challenges faced by micro, small, and medium enterprises in India. *Inzinerine Ekonomika-Engineering Economics*, 33(1), 73–85.

Ramcharran, H. (2016). Bank Lending to Small Business in India: Analyzing Productivity and Efficiency. QREF, June-16, Elsevier.

Singh, P., and Kaur, C. (2021). Factors determining financial constraint of SMEs: a study of unorganized manufacturing enterprise in India. *Journal of Small Business and Entrepreneurship*, 33(3), 269–287.

108 Consumer satisfaction toward chain of restaurant with special reference to Coimbatore city

Prakash, J.[a] and Sudarvel, J.[b]

Karpagam Academy of Higher Education, Coimbatore, Tamil Nadu, India

Abstract

This study scrutinizes the determinants of consumer satisfaction within a restaurant chain in Coimbatore city, against a backdrop of burgeoning industry competition. Aiming to delineate the key factors that influence customer contentment and loyalty, this research employs a mixed-methods approach. Initial qualitative inquiries, through in-depth interviews, will shed light on customer experiences and perceptions concerning service quality, food, ambience, pricing, and other pivotal satisfaction influences. This will be complemented by a quantitative survey, capturing broader satisfaction levels and demographic nuances. Analytical rigor will be maintained through content analysis of interviews and statistical methods for survey data. The outcomes promise to enrich academic discourse on consumer behavior in the restaurant sector, offering empirical insights for future scholarly inquiries. Concurrently, the findings will arm industry practitioners with strategic knowledge to augment customer satisfaction, foster loyalty, and secure competitive leverage, thereby catalyzing sustainable business growth.

Keywords: Coimbatore city, consumer satisfaction, food quality, restaurant industry, service quality

Introduction

In Coimbatore, a city in Tamil Nadu celebrated for its culinary richness, this study examines consumer satisfaction in its rising restaurant chains. It recognizes that satisfaction is crucial for the success and reputation of these establishments, influencing customer loyalty and repeat patronage. The research investigates various determinants of satisfaction, including food quality, service, cleanliness, menu variety, timeliness, and value. It aims to understand consumer experiences and expectations, providing insights for restaurant owners to refine their offerings and for consumers to make informed dining choices. The ultimate goal is to enhance Coimbatore's dining culture, ensuring enjoyable and rewarding experiences for both diners and restaurant owners.

Problem Statement

This study investigates the factors influencing consumer satisfaction with the growing chain restaurants in Coimbatore, amidst a diverse and competitive culinary landscape.

Review of Literature

Study	Key findings
Arefin and Hossain (2022)	Restaurants need to enhance product and service attributes like food quality, menu diversity, freshness, and consistency for customer satisfaction.
Zibarzani et al. (2022)	Used machine learning to analyze trip advisor reviews, focusing on how restaurant quality factors affect customer satisfaction.
Bishwas et al., (2021)	Found a strong positive correlation between customer satisfaction and factors like restaurant decor, cleanliness, service, management benefits, and food variety.
Rajput and Gahfoor (2020)	Identified a positive link between customers' intention to revisit fast food restaurants and factors like satisfaction, food quality, service quality, and environment.
Kanchanamala (2019)	Concluded that demographic factors like age, gender, marital status, income, and residence do not significantly influence satisfaction towards restaurant services.
Moreira Junior et al. (2019)	Noted a generally positive satisfaction index for various restaurant aspects but found internal decoration was less favorably evaluated.

[a]jayap9292@gmail.com, [b]j.sudarvel@gmail.com

Study	Key findings
Karjaluoto et al. (2015)	Highlighted that customer satisfaction and loyalty are influenced by service quality, reliability, and cost during initial service interactions.
Wansink and Sigirci (2014)	Revealed that higher spending on food correlates with greater customer satisfaction, suggesting a perceived link between price and food quality.
Andaleeb and Conway (2006)	Identified employee responsiveness as the most influential factor on customer satisfaction, followed by price and food quality, while physical design had less impact.

Source: Author

Table 108.1 Analysis of the data.

Age	Frequency	Percentage	Age	Frequency	Percentage
Below 30 years	60	20.4	Professional	22	7.5
30 – 40 years	164	55.8	Home maker	32	10.9
Above 40 years	70	23.8	Student	92	31.3
Total	294	100	Total	294	100
Gender	Frequency	Percentage	Area of residence	Frequency	Percentage
Male	180	61.2	Urban	152	51.7
Female	114	38.8	Semi- urban	58	19.7
Total	294	100	Rural	84	28.6
Marital status	Frequency	Percentage	Total	294	100
Married	140	47.6	Type of family	Frequency	Percentage
Unmarried	154	52.4	Joint family	54	18.4
Total	294	100	Nuclear family	240	81.6
Education qualification	Frequency	Percentage	Total	294	100
Up to SSLC	10	3.4	Monthly income	Frequency	Percentage
HSC	58	19.7	Up to 20000	48	16.3
UG Degree	112	38.1	20001 – 40000	232	78.9
PG Degree	68	23.1	Above 40000	14	4.8
Professional	42	14.3	Total	294	100
Others	4	1.4	Preferable food	Frequency	Percentage
Total	294	100	Veg	54	18.4
Profession	Frequency	Percentage	Non- veg	78	26.5
Agriculturist	18	6.1	Both	162	55.1
Business	22	7.5	Total	294	100
Employee	108	36.7			

Source: Author

Research Gap

Existing literature lacks focus on chain restaurants' impact on consumer satisfaction in Coimbatore, with most studies being general or on independent restaurants.

Objective of the study

To assess consumer satisfaction with restaurant chains in Coimbatore, understanding key satisfaction factors.

Scope of the study

This study focuses on consumer satisfaction within Coimbatore's restaurant chains, considering factors like food quality, service, menu variety, and pricing. It aims to identify areas for improvement and explore demographic impacts on satisfaction.

Research methodology

A mixed-method approach, combining quantitative surveys and qualitative interviews/focus groups, will

Table 108.2 Consumer satisfaction scores.

Satisfaction	SA	A	N	DA	SDA	Score	Mean Score	Rank
	5	4	3	2	1			
Varieties available	90	82	90	24	8			
	450	328	270	48	8	1104	3.7551	1
Interior decoration	50	96	106	36	6			
	250	384	318	72	6	1030	3.5034	9
Parking facility	68	64	88	62	12			
	340	256	264	124	12	996	3.38776	16
Drive inn facility	58	74	104	52	6			
	290	296	312	104	6	1008	3.42857	13
Neatness and cleanliness	56	84	98	50	6			
	280	336	294	100	6	1016	3.45578	11
Amenities	76	72	94	48	4			
	380	288	282	96	4	1050	3.57143	4
Price	48	90	94	54	8			
	240	360	282	108	8	998	3.39456	15
Taste	80	72	98	36	8			
	400	288	294	72	8	1062	3.61224	3
Quality of food	82	74	98	32	8			
	410	296	294	64	8	1072	3.64626	2
Quantity of food	56	100	90	44	4			
	280	400	270	88	4	1042	3.54422	6
Appearance of the staff	64	82	84	54	10			
	320	328	252	108	10	1018	3.46259	13
Safety and security	62	82	78	56	16			
	310	328	234	112	16	1000	3.40136	14
Server behavior	71	66	84	68	5			
	355	264	252	136	5	1012	3.44218	12
Time taken to serve food	60	72	58	88	16			
	300	288	174	176	16	954	3.2449	17
Freshness of food	78	56	54	42	64			
	390	224	162	84	64	924	3.14286	18
Crowd maintenance	52	82	134	22	4			
	260	328	402	44	4	1038	3.53061	7
Private dining	64	88	96	40	6			
	320	352	288	80	6	1046	3.55782	5
Consistent service	68	70	108	40	8			
	340	280	324	80	8	1032	3.5102	8

Source: Author

be used to study consumer satisfaction in Coimbatore's chain restaurants.

Data Collection

Data will be collected through structured questionnaires and in-depth interviews or focus groups, exploring consumer satisfaction levels and experiences.

Framework of analysis

Simple percentage and Weighted Average methods will be used to analyse the collected data.

Limitations

The study's findings might be specific to Coimbatore and not generalizable. Consumer satisfaction being subjective, the study acknowledges limitations in self-reported data.

Significance of the study

The study is significant for understanding consumer satisfaction in Coimbatore's chain restaurants, aiding in business improvement, customer retention, and contributing to academic and industry knowledge. It aims to provide insights into future strategies, aligning restaurant operations with customer expectations for success.

Analysis and Interpretation

This analysis suggests restaurants should cater to a predominant demographic of 30-40-year-old, mostly male, unmarried professionals, predominantly educated to undergraduate level and residing in urban areas. Menus and marketing should thus align with these characteristics, offering trendy, health-conscious options, social dining experiences, and promotions for young professionals. Additionally, family-friendly environments and diverse menus catering to both vegetarian and non-vegetarian preferences are essential, considering the nuclear family structure and varied dietary inclinations of this demographic. By considering these demographic factors, restaurants can tailor their offerings and experiences to meet the preferences and expectations of the majority of consumers, thereby enhancing consumer satisfaction and driving customer loyalty.

Consumer satisfaction toward chains of restaurants
Weighted average results reveal that customer satisfaction in Coimbatore's restaurant chains hinges on several factors. Menu diversity ranks highest, with consumers valuing a broad range of culinary options. Food quality, encompassing freshness, taste, and hygienic preparation, is crucial. Taste itself is a

significant determinant, with well-seasoned and delicious meals enhancing satisfaction. Amenities, including comfort and cleanliness, play a vital role. Options for private dining and events are appreciated for their exclusivity. Portion size, offering value for money, and efficient crowd management during peak times are also key contributors to customer satisfaction. These insights guide restaurant managers in Coimbatore to improve dining experiences and foster customer loyalty.

Conclusion

In the competitive realm of restaurant chains, consumer satisfaction is paramount. Achieving this hinge on a multifaceted strategy that addresses various aspects of the dining experience. Key to this is consistency; ensuring uniform quality across all locations builds customer trust and reliability, essential for a positive reputation.

Excellent customer service is another critical element. Training staff to be friendly, attentive, and responsive enhances the dining atmosphere and shows a commitment to customer care. A diverse menu catering to different dietary preferences, including options for customization, addresses the diverse needs of customers, elevating their overall experience.

The physical environment of the restaurant also significantly impacts customer satisfaction. A focus on cleanliness, an appealing ambiance, and efficient management of waiting times respect the customer's time and contribute to a positive dining experience. Furthermore, offering value for money through reasonable pricing and customer loyalty programs incentivizes repeat visits.

References

Brockman, P., French, D., and Tamm, C. (2014). REIT organizational structure, institutional ownership, and stock performance. *Journal of Real Estate Portfolio Management*, 20(1), 21–36.

Cella, C. (2009). Institutional Investors and Corporate Investment. Indiana University, Kelley School of Business.

Chuang, H. (2020). The impacts of institutional ownership on stock returns. *Empirical Economics*, 58(2), 507–533.

Clark, G. L., and Wójcik, D. (2005). Financial valuation of the German model: the negative relationship between ownership concentration and stock market returns, 1997–2001. *Economic Geography*, 81(1), 11–29.

Dasgupta, A., Prat, A., and Verardo, M. (2011). Institutional trade persistence and long-term equity returns. *Journal of Finance*, 66(2), 635–653.

Demsetz, H., and Lehn, K. (1985). The structure of corporate ownership: causes and consequences. *Journal of Political Economy*, 93(6), 1155–1177.

Dyakov, T., and Wipplinger, E. (2020). Institutional ownership and future stock returns: an international perspective. *International Review of Finance*, 20(1), 235–245.

Gompers, P. A., and Metrick, A. (2001). Institutional investors and equity prices. *Quarterly Journal of Economics*, 116(1), 229–259.

Han, K. C., and Suk, D. Y. (1998). The effect of ownership structure on firm performance: additional evidence. *Review of Financial Economics*, 7(2), 143–155.

Kennedy, P. (1985). A Guide to Econometrics. MIT Press, Cambridge.

109 A study on materials management system

Allwin, Y. and Usha, M.

Karpagam Academy of Higher Education, Coimbatore, Tamil Nadu, India

Abstract

Achieving quality in materials management is a deliberate and strategic effort, driven by innovative and intelligent initiatives. The evaluation process encompasses meeting delivery deadlines, stock development, cargo completion, financial procedures, and inventory accuracy. Leaders play a crucial role in overseeing stock bases and ensuring control over fresh deliveries. In large organisations, a dedicated purchasing division manages supplies, adjusting stock bases based on purchased costs. The complexities of goods handling in air transportation involve meticulous processes and adherence to regulations. A dedicated goods handling division acquires production materials before handing over responsibilities to plant material managers. This module delves into the multifaceted responsibilities of forwarders, covering booking strategies, payload detection, customer complaint resolution, compliance with air cargo rules (e.g., the Montreal Convention), and comprehensive security frameworks.

Keywords: Efficiency, inventory, procurement

Introduction

In the intricate landscape of materials management, the establishment of networks, circuits, and stock associations plays a pivotal role, shaping the parameters for network execution. Companies strategically formulate comprehensive material requirements, sourced under various restrictions, with the Materials Manager at the helm of decision-making. This involves determining distribution quantities for each stacking zone, devising material stimulation plans, selecting stock levels for raw materials, work-in-progress, and finished goods, and disseminating information across the extensive production association. Roles like Materials manager, inventory control manager, and material planner are integral to this domain. The primary challenge faced by materials managers is ensuring a reliable material supply for production, hindered by factors such as premium payload, frequent stock changes, and production demands.

Overcoming issues like jumbled bills of materials and shipping errors, material managers have navigated the evolution of materials management in the commercial sector. This exploration delves into the stages of materials management, covering sorting, procurement/purchasing, materials handling, transportation, and receiving.

Essentiality of Investigation

Material handling heads at Spectra Plast bear the weight of orchestrating and controlling vital components, encompassing material prices, reserves, and consumption. Given that materials constitute a substantial portion of production costs, minimizing these expenses is crucial for enhanced profitability. Optimal material availability is indispensable for uninterrupted production, as any shortage in materials can lead to project delays and production halts, impacting the overall operational capacity.

Review of Literature

Table 109.1 Overview of studies on material management in various contexts.

Author name	Study	Findings
Eckert et al. (2020)	Inventory management impact on customer satisfaction	Identified shipping issues and assessed overall customer happiness.
SantuKar et al. (2020)	Material management challenges in the steel industry	Incorrect material supply significantly affects goods' schedule and cost performances.
Narimah Kasim (2021)	Challenges in tracking goods on construction sites	Inappropriate handling and storage hindered tracking, impacting project costs.
Bekr et al. (2022)	Role of material management in maximizing resources	Emphasized planning, regulating material flow, and maximizing resources for enhanced customer service.

Source: Author

[a]ushakarthic6969@gmail.com

Objective of the Study

The investigation aims to identify challenges in material handling within Spectra Plast India Pvt Ltd in Coimbatore, examining the adopted method/system and understanding organizational challenges. The study seeks feedback on how materials management responds to suggestions.

Scope of the Study

The examination in Coimbatore delves into the administration and load treatment of Spectra Plast products. It explores employee assessments regarding secure material handling, scrutinizing adherence to safety standards. The research encompasses an analysis of strategic actions and working conditions, aiming to understand the employee perspective. Additionally, the study aims to acquire inventory levels for future reference in effective management.

Research Methodology

Solving a research problem involves employing research techniques, which serve as a systematic and scientific source for studying how research is conducted. Methodology encompasses the processes researchers use to describe, understand, and predict occurrences, with methods hindering or facilitating data production, gathering, and interpretation. These methods, serving as the means for collecting necessary data to evaluate explanations, are integral to the research process.

1. Research design: Configuration for inquiry, guiding gathering and analysis of material, instructive and perceptive in character.
2. Sources of data
   (a) Primary data: Crucial information obtained through buyer surveys, using open-ended and closed-ended questions.
   (b) Secondary data: Supplementary information gathered from published sources for the current article.
3. Test questions: Frequently used method, surveying participants with various question formats for flexibility in responses.
4. Interrogation methods examining: Selection of a portion for conclusion about the total, using "accommodation inspecting" in this examination.
5. Accommodation sampling: Units selected based on the ease of access to the test.
6. Test size: Consistent with information's disposition, 130 respondents used for crucial information in this inquiry.
7. Statistical tools: Simple percentage analysis, Chi-square analysis, correlation, and ANNOVA employed for analysis.

Unravelling Insights: Data Analysis and Interpretation in Academic Research

As illustrated in the table, 49.2% of respondents express satisfaction with the existing material storage method, while 33.1% are highly satisfied. Conversely, 3.1% are dissatisfied, and 3.8% very dissatisfied. The majority, 49.2%, convey contentment with the current storage technique.

As per the table, 46.9% are content with operational costs, 38.5% highly satisfied with tool storage, 34.6% dissatisfied with safety. After improvements, 60.8% highly satisfied with operators' performance in the material handling system evaluation.

Comparing Results with Hypotheses

Chi-Square analysis
[Annexture the tables]

The presented tables encapsulate a thorough investigation into the interplay between age and opinions concerning quality control measures in polymer production. This analysis hinges on testing null and alternative hypotheses, aiming to discern any significant correlation. The case processing summary (Table 109.4) outlines that 130 cases were valid, contributing to a comprehensive examination of age-opinion dynamics.

The subsequent Chi-square tests (Table 109.5) delve into statistical values, including Pearson Chi-square, likelihood ratio, and linear-by-linear association. Impressively, all values indicate a complete rejection of the null hypothesis, emphasising a substantial correlation between age and opinions regarding polymer quality control measures.

Table 109.2 Content with the current material storage approach: an academic evaluation.

S No	Exiting method of storing the materials	No. of respondents	Percentage (%)
1	Highly satisfied	43	33.1
2	Satisfied	64	49.2
3	Neutral	14	10.8
4	Dissatisfied	4	3.1
5	Highly dissatisfied	5	3.8
Total		130	100

Sources: Primary data

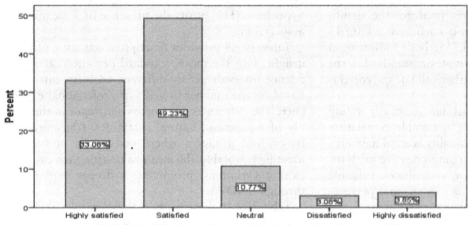

Figure 109.1 Contentment with current material storage practices: an academic assessment
Source: Author

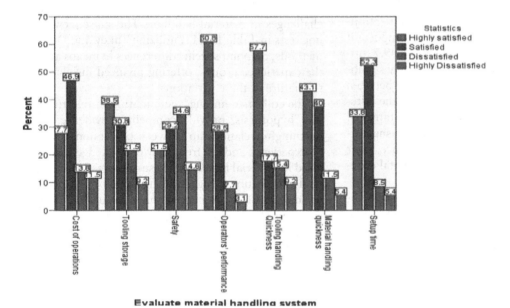

Figure 109.2 Assessing Material Handling System Post-Implemented Changes: Academic Evaluation
Source: Author

Table 109.3 Assessing material handling system post-establishment changes: academic inquiry.

Changes/satisfaction level	Highly satisfied	Satisfied	Dissatisfied	Highly dissatisfied
Cost of operations	27.70%	46.90%	13.80%	11.50%
Tooling storage	38.50%	30.80%	21.50%	9.20%
Safety	21.50%	29.20%	34.60%	14.60%
Operators' performance	60.80%	28.50%	7.70%	3.10%
Tooling handling	Quickness	57.70%	17.70%	15.40%
Material handling quickness	43.10%	40.00%	11.50%	5.40%
Setup time	33.80%	52.30%	8.50%	5.40%

Sources: Primary data

Further insights are derived from symmetric measures (Table 109.6), employing Kendall's tau-b and tau-c. Notably, these measures reinforce the significant correlation, with a tau-b coefficient of 0.841 and a tau-c coefficient of 0.755, both indicating a robust association. The asymptotic standard error and approximate T values further validate the correlation's strength.

In conclusion, the findings unequivocally refute the null hypothesis, affirming a notable correlation between age and opinions on quality control measures in polymer production. This comprehensive analysis, supported by statistical rigor, contributes valuable insights into the nuanced dynamics shaping perspectives within the polymer manufacturing domain.

Analysis of Correlation

[Annexture of the tables]

The correlation analysis, detailed in Tables 109.7 and 109.8, thoroughly explores the intricate relationship between Years of Experience and the Important Criteria considered by the company. Table 109.7, utilizing Pearson correlation, establishes a highly significant positive correlation ($r = 0.869, p < 0.01$) between the duration of professional experience and the criteria deemed important by the company. This statistical significance underscores a robust connection, suggesting that as professionals gain more experience, their perspectives align more closely with the pivotal criteria prioritized by the organization.

In Table 109.8, Kendall's tau_b correlation coefficient further confirms the positive correlation ($\tau\_b = 0.866, p < 0.01$) between experience in years and the importance attributed to specific criteria. The consistency in results across distinct correlation measures enhances the reliability of the findings. In essence, these results robustly affirm a positive and statistically significant correlation between years of professional experience and the significance attached to specific criteria by the company. This implies a progressive alignment of perspectives with organizational priorities as professionals accrue more experience, offering invaluable insights for strategic decision-making and human resource management.

ANOVA Analysis

[Annexture of the tables]

The ANOVA analysis, detailed in Tables 109.9, 109.10, and 109.11, investigates the potential correlation between professionals' years of experience and the frequency of challenges encountered in material handling. The null hypothesis (H0) proposes that there is no substantial relationship between these variables, whereas the alternative hypothesis (H1) posits the presence of a meaningful association.

Table 109.9 provides descriptive statistics, offering insights into the mean, standard deviation, and confidence intervals across different problem categories based on the number of years of professional experience. The categories encompass shortages in the supply of equipment, natural calamities, transportation issues, and instances where no specific problem is identified. Notably, the mean values for each category exhibit variations, prompting a deeper exploration through ANOVA.

Table 109.10 presents the ANOVA results, revealing a statistically significant disparity in means across distinct levels of professional experience ($p < 0.05$). The robust F-statistic of 632.326 underscores substantial variations between the groups, suggesting that professionals with varying experience levels face distinct challenges in material handling. The subsequent post hoc tests in Table 109.11, utilizing Tukey and Duncan methods, pinpoint specific differences in means among the experience groups, offering nuanced insights into the nature of these variations.

The collective findings, culminating in rejecting the null hypothesis, provide compelling evidence for a meaningful relationship between professionals' years of experience and the frequency of challenges encountered in material handling. These outcomes carry practical implications, suggesting that tailored strategies for material management should consider the diverse experiences of professionals within an organization. Addressing challenges in material handling may necessitate targeted approaches that align with the varying expertise levels of the workforce.

Means Plot

The computed F-value of 632.326, accompanied by a p-value of 0.000 (less than 0.05), indicates a significant association between professionals' years of experience and challenges faced in material handling. Therefore, the alternative hypothesis (H1) is accepted, underscoring the practical relevance of this correlation.

Descriptive Statistics

The respondent profile reveals diversity, with 30% being men, and a significant 43.1% falling between ages 31 and 40. Predominantly, 53.8% hold the role of quality controller, while 78.5% refrain from accepting material handling equipment or supplier-supplied

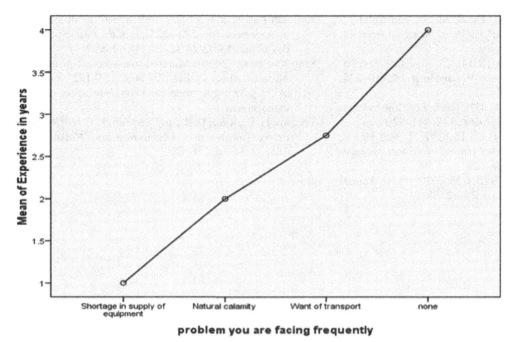

Figure 109.3 Problems re facing analysis with years
Source: Author

items. A substantial 89.2% prioritize product examinations before storage or display. Business practices indicate 71.5% selling scrap items to other firms and 33.8% expressing neutrality towards materials handling. These findings offer a brief yet insightful snapshot of the varied demographics and practices prevalent among respondents in their approach to material handling in business operations.

Recommendations

- Industries are pivotal in monitoring global dynamics and public concerns, applied in diverse products.
- Polymer Science and Engineering explores research, maintenance, and the vast potential of materials.
- The focus is on sliding cases, presenting current states and revealing the science behind them.
- Leading experts offer insights, recommendations, and evaluative guidelines for material management and organization.
- Vignettes illustrate typical applications, providing a glimpse into practical scenarios.
- The examination encompasses plastics, fibres, composites, and other materials, integral in films and coatings.
- Clear-cut preparation methods and synthesis lead to unparalleled support in various industries.

Conclusion

Industries constitute a distinct field of study, delving into the transformation of polymers or elastomers into marketable products. This involves the preparation of latex, processing of manufactured or common polymers, and various handling stages before reaching the final product. The key techniques for managing raw polymers include vulcanization, calendaring, and rumination. Notably, polymers have found widespread applications in diverse products, with the growing prevalence of logistics equipment attributed to the significant rise in automobile usage. This interdisciplinary exploration sheds light on the crucial role of polymers in contemporary manufacturing processes, underscoring their adaptability and integral role in various industries.

References

Begum, R. A., Siwar, C., Pereira, J. J., and Jaafar, A. H. (2022). *Resources, Conservation and Recycling*, 48, 86–98, (pp. 13–21).

Bekr, G. A., Cox, R. F., Issa, R. R., and Ahrens, D. (2018). *Journal of Construction Engineering and Management*, 129, 142–151 . P.F., 22–30.

Eckert, et al. (2020). Asvanthappa BT, Nursing Administration, (1st edn.), New Delhi: Jaypee Brothers, (pp. 13–20).

Ekanayake, L. L., and Ofori, G. (2004). *Building and Environment*, 39, 851–861 .

Hassan, S. H., Ahzahar, N., Fauzi, M. A., and Eman, J. (2021). *Procedia - Social and Behavioural Sciences*, 42, 175 –181.

Hughes, R., and Thorpe, D. (2014). *Construction Innovation: Information, Process, Management*, 14, 210–228, (pp. 12–18).

Jarkas, A. M., and Bitar, C. G. (??). *Journal of Construction Engineering and Management*, 138, 811–820 .

Kaming, P. F., Olomolaiye, P. O., Holt, G. D., and Harris, F. C. (2022). *International Journal of Project Management*, 15, 21–30 (pp. 56–62).

Makulsawatudom, A., and Emsley, M. (2001). 17th Annual ARCOM Conference, (pp. 281–290).

Narimah Kasim, et al. (2021). Indian institute of materials management, (pp. 221 –225). http://www.iimm.org/index.php/2016-02-24-12-20-24/crimm.

SantuKar, et al. (2020). Material management in nursing. *Material Management (Online)*, 165–172. Available at http://www.nursingplanet.com./education/material management.

Thomas, H. R., Riley, D. R., and Sanvido, V. E. (2019). *Journal of Construction Engineering and Management*, 125, 39–46 (pp. 56–63).

110 A study on employee Absenteeism with reference to textile industries

Kumar, B. K. and Usha, M.[a]

Karpagam Academy of Higher Education, Coimbatore, Tamil Nadu, India

Abstract

The term "textiles" encompasses yarns, threads, and wools processed through spinning, weaving, tufting, knotting, and other methods to create fabric. Mass production and modern industrial technology have drastically evolved this ancient craft, rendering traditional weaves unrecognizable to an ancient Roman weaver. Natural fibers have long been integral to the industry, with a richer history dating back to 500AD, progressing through inventions and technological advancements. Key advantages include a robust raw material production, a diverse labor force, cost-effective labor, strong export potential, and minimal import reliance. This sector, deeply rooted and traditional, experiences high domestic and international demand. Its export basket spans cotton yarn, synthetic fabrics, wool and silk textiles, various clothing, and other manufactured goods, catering to a wide market.

Keywords: Evolution of textiles, export potential, fabric production, historical development, industrial technology, labor force, natural fibers, raw materials, Textiles, traditional sector

Introduction

Absenteeism, a regular pattern of skipping tasks or commitments, was historically perceived solely as a management issue framed in economic terms. It was linked to poor individual performance and viewed as breaching the implied employee-employer contract. However, recent research delves deeper, interpreting absenteeism as a signal of social, medical, or psychological adjustment to work. For smooth operation, both in the production process and the entire organization, employee presence during designated hours is crucial. Yet, the occurrence of absenteeism in Indian industry significantly disrupts work, escalates labor costs, diminishes productivity, and fosters indiscipline.

Defined explicitly as unapproved absences from work, absenteeism involves situations where workers, despite available employment, choose not to report without informing the employer adequately. This behavior impacts productivity and discipline. It's important to note that absenteeism excludes approved leaves, holidays, vacations, or other authorized time-offs per collective bargaining agreements.

Combatting Workplace Absenteeism

The following steps can help you minimize or regulate absence:
- Choosing personnel by carefully evaluating their goals, value systems, sense of duty, and sensitivity.
- Using a humanistic strategy to address the personal issues of employees.
- Identifying and addressing employee complaints in a proactive manner.
- Providing clean working environments.
- Offering welfare programs and extra benefits while balancing the needs of the workers and the organization's resources.

Validity of the study

Bojaraj Textile Ltd witnesses a surge in staff absenteeism due to illness, personal matters, and workplace conditions. Left unaddressed, this trend jeopardizes the company's excellence. Despite unpaid leaves, absenteeism incurs substantial costs, disrupting workflows, impeding timely deliveries, and intensifying expenses, notably with sick leave allowances. To curb these challenges, cost-effective measures must be implemented. Management, faced with multiple contributing factors, necessitates prompt action to tackle excessive absence rates in affected units.

Objectives of the study

- To Identify reason for Absenteeism
- To determine factor, influence in job Satisfaction
- To identify employee performance on quality of work life

Scope of the study

Employee absenteeism, stemming from personal and family obligations, affects every business, impacting industry output, expansion, and sales. Addressing this, motivating workers through specialized training

[a]ushakarthic6969@gmail.com

and leave benefits can mitigate absenteeism and lower turnover rates, aiding the company. Research focuses on resolving this issue to optimize productivity and employee commitment.

Literature Review

Table 110.1 Studies on employee absenteeism author insights and findings.

Author name	Study	Findings
Beulah et al., (2019)	Analyses unplanned textile sector absenteeism's factors, performance assessment, and strategies to reduce it. High turnover costs impact company finances due to frequent replacements.	Examines unplanned absenteeism factors in the textile sector, proposes strategies for reduction, highlighting high turnover's financial toll through frequent replacements.
Susan Michie (2021)	Reviews literature on factors contributing to employee psychological illness and absenteeism: long work hours, stress, organizational deficiencies, limited involvement in decision-making, and unclear job roles.	Examines factors causing employee psychological illness and absenteeism: long work hours, stress, organizational issues, limited decision-making involvement, and unclear job roles.
Steven G. Aldana (2022)	Studies how high absenteeism relates to health risks and employee reluctance in health programs. Advises employers to consider health initiatives' impact on absenteeism and overall employee expenses.	Explores the correlation between high absenteeism, health risks, and employee resistance to health programs. Suggests employers weigh health initiatives' impact on absenteeism and overall employee costs.

Source: Author

Research Methodology

- Research design: Employed a descriptive research design for data collection, measurement, and analysis.
- Sample design: Utilized company's HR data, selecting 120 responders via convenience sampling.
- Data collection: Conducted a descriptive study focusing on respondent traits and demographics.
- Primary data: Gathered via questionnaires, processed into graphs, tables, and conclusions.
- Secondary data: Ratio analysis to compare multiple data series for meaningful comparisons.
- Tools used: Employed Chi-square test, correlation, ANOVA, and simple percentage method.

Analysis and Interpretation

The analysis and interpretation encompass findings from surveys conducted among respondents within the organization. Table breakdowns reveal gender distribution and perceptions compared to other local entities. Additionally, an independent samples test explores various workplace factors and their potential gender-related implications. Despite the meticulous examination, the study failed to refute the null hypothesis across the tested variables, suggesting no significant gender-specific differences in factors impacting work satisfaction. These insights provide a comprehensive understanding of how perceptions and gender dynamics intersect within the workplace environment.

The examination of data through Chi-square tests, ANOVA, and correlation analysis unveils crucial insights into the relationship between demographic factors, workplace conditions, and employee satisfaction. Chi-square tests reveal no age-related association with work satisfaction factors, while ANOVA demonstrates consistency across various job-related aspects. Additionally, correlation analysis illuminates strong positive correlations between timely payments, fair compensation, and overall job satisfaction. These analyses provide comprehensive perspectives on employee perceptions, shedding light on the intricate interplay between demographic attributes and workplace contentment.

1. **Gender of the respondents**
- Male respondents: 66.2%
- Female respondents: 33.8%

2. **Comparison to other organizations in the locality**
- Strongly agree: 41.5%
- Agree: 29.2%
- Undecided: 29.2%

3. **Independent samples test**
   Variables examined:
- Feeling safety at the workplace
- Culture and values of the company
- Rules, regulations, and job-related policies
- Lighting, ventilation, drinking water facilities
- Availability of material/tools/equipment for the job

- Fairness in management behavior
- Management recognition of employee job
- Organization commitment to professional development

Test findings
- Study failed to reject the null hypothesis (H0) due to a significant value > 0.05 (p = 0.100).
- No gender-specific difference in factors impacting work satisfaction (H0 retained).
- Study results lacked sufficient evidence to refute the null hypothesis (H0).
- No gender-related difference in factors affecting work satisfaction (H0 retained).
- Similar results found for all variables tested, supporting the null hypothesis (H0).

The investigation could not reject the null hypothesis (H0) due to significant values exceeding 0.05 (p = 0.100). All findings led to the retention of the null hypothesis (H0) for gender-related differences in work satisfaction factors.

4. Chi-square tests
Test results:
- No correlation found between age and factors affecting work satisfaction (p = 0.000).
- Alternative hypothesis (H1) accepted, rejecting null hypothesis (H0) for age-related work satisfaction.
- Consistent findings across tests indicating no association between age and work satisfaction factors.
- Null hypothesis (H0) accepted due to insignificant p-values, implying no relationship between age and work satisfaction factors.

5. ANOVA
ANOVA test results:
- No variation observed among variables concerning emergency payment, salary comparisons, overtime wages, and material benefits.
- Null hypothesis (H0) retained as p-values (>0.05) indicated no significant difference in assessed aspects.

6. Correlation
Correlation findings
- Strong correlation observed between timely wage payments and fair compensation for work (correlation coefficient = 1.000).
- Positive associations noted between adequate wages, covering basic needs, and ability-based earnings.
- High correlation (0.907) between fair compensation and earnings commensurate with abilities.

- Moderate positive correlation found between various aspects of wage satisfaction, indicating consistent positive relationships.
- Overall, significant positive associations between timely payments, fair wages, and satisfactory job-related payments were highlighted.

Findings
- Male respondents constitute the majority of the sample (55%).
- The majority of responders, comprising 79.2%, are married.
- Approximately 58.3% of responders fall within the age range of 30 to 40 years.
- Graduates make up approximately 35% of the respondents.
- Future prospects serve as a motivating factor for the majority of responders (23.3%).
- About 27.5% of respondents believe that the workplace environment impacts their work.
- 31.7% of respondents perceive that wage policy influences their work.
- 35% of respondents agree that other sources of income impact their work.
- 35% of respondents believe that employee absenteeism and the leadership style of immediate superiors are interrelated.
- Approximately 39.2% of respondents consider employee illness and absence as problems.
- 29.2% of respondents believe that job stability influences absenteeism.
- 5% of respondents stated that an employee's relationship motivated them to work in the manufacturing industry.
- 53.3% of respondents are utilizing their sick days.
- 35% of respondents expressed satisfaction with an employee's departure.

Recommendations
- To diminish absenteeism, the company could enhance leave benefits.
- Offering elevated compensation and benefits based on the financial health of the company can reduce absenteeism.
- Providing employees and their families with generous financial assistance and leave during illness.
- The company should reduce employees' workload while prioritizing their health and ensuring adequate relaxation.
- To devise methods for reducing absenteeism, maintain accurate absence records and conduct an analysis of the causes of absence.

- The majority of workers are unaware of any authorized Earn, Casual, or Medical leaves. Hence, it's vital to educate the workforce about leave policies.
- Upgrade the bus's internal facilities to ensure that absenteeism will soon be reduced.

Conclusion

In any organizational framework, the workforce stands as its paramount asset, dictating the rhythm of operational efficiency. The pivotal nature of employee presence within the stipulated work hours is fundamental, underscoring the smooth functioning of production processes and the broader organizational ecosystem. The pervasive challenge of absenteeism confronts numerous enterprises today, bearing consequential costs that pose substantial hurdles for effective management. For Bojaraj Textile, boasting a lean workforce, any dips in attendance precipitate marked productivity losses, significantly impacting on the company's bottom line.

The study reveals a modest absenteeism rate within the organization, attributing the phenomenon to personal, work-related, and general concerns. Addressing these multifaceted reasons becomes imperative, with recommendations emerging as beacons of hope for curbing absenteeism's adverse effects. Implementation of these strategic recommendations holds promise in substantially mitigating the absenteeism predicament. By embracing these tailored approaches, there exists the potential to transform the landscape, fostering an environment conducive to enhanced attendance and heightened productivity within Bojaraj Textile and akin organizations.

References

Akila, R., and Indumathi, M. K. (2019). Employee absenteeism and its impact. *International Journal of Research in Commerce, Economics and Management*, 103(7), 703–723.

Beulah, G., and Venkatrama Raju, D. (2019). A study on factors influencing employee absenteeism in spinning industry. *International Journal of Business and Administration Research Review*, 2(5), 98, April-June 2014, E-ISSN - 2347-856X, ISSN - 2348-0653.

Chowdhury, S. (2022). A study of absenteeism in a manufacturing company. In MIT-SOM PGRC KJIMRP National Research Conference (Special Issue).

Galdana, S. G. (2022). Optimal workforce configuration incorporating absenteeism and daily workload variability. *Socio-Economic Planning Sciences*, 27(2), 91–96, June 1993.

Iverson, D., Olekalns, M., and Erwin, P. J. (Year). Affectivity, organizational stressors, and absenteeism: a causal model of burnout and its consequences. *Journal of Vocational Behavior*, 52(1), 1–23.

Iverson, R. D. (2022). Affectivity, organizational stressors, and absenteeism: a causal model of burnout and its consequences. *Journal of Vocational Behavior*, 52(1), 1–23.

Patel, A., and Thakkar, S. (2019). A Study on Causes of absenteeism among employees in retail shops. *ISBR Management Journal*, 1(1).

Poongavanam, S. (2020). Employee absenteeism – a case study of leather firm in Vellore. *International Journal of Research in Social Sciences*, 7(10).

Rahman, T. H. (2021). A study on causes of absenteeism among employees in retail shops. *ISBR Management Journal*, 1(1).

Singh, T., et al. (2020). An investigation into the impact of absenteeism on the organizational performance of a private security company in Durban, Kwazulu-Natal.

111 A study on employee perception toward performance appraisal

Sherin M.F. and Usha, M.[a]

Karpagam Academy of Higher Education, Coimbatore, Tamil Nadu, India

Abstract

In the contemporary landscape, the internet has become the primary avenue for individuals seeking information about businesses, rendering traditional directories obsolete. In 2017, a staggering 97% of people turned to online sources to discover local businesses, as reported by Adaptive Marketing. This underscores the imperative for businesses to establish a digital presence, primarily through a website, in order to connect with their target audience and foster business growth. Irrespective of the industry, this discourse explores the compelling reasons behind the necessity for businesses to embrace a website in 2020. The article underscores the significance of continual individual and procedural development, focusing on addressing weaknesses to enhance organizational performance. Emphasizing the pivotal role of performance evaluation in organizational life, the narrative highlights its multifaceted nature, encompassing aspects such as assessing work performance, setting goals, and administering rewards. It elucidates how a well-executed performance evaluation system can positively impact employee satisfaction, fostering a conducive environment for increased productivity and organizational success.

Keywords: Business growth, online presence, organizational success, performance evaluation, website development

Introduction

In the dynamic realm of workforce management, assessing employee performance is pivotal for organizational success and individual growth. Performance evaluation, employing methods from monetary incentives to strategic placements, delves into past contributions and future potential. Distinguishing employment from performance evaluations is crucial; the former gauges competence in job duties, while the latter appraises overall capacity.

Periodic evaluations, structured and aligned with schedules, ensure a comprehensive analysis of individual and collective performance. An astute evaluation process considers perspectives of both staff and evaluator, informing decisions, enhancing productivity, and achieving organizational objectives. Evaluations impact strategic decision-making, influencing promotions, pay raises, and long-term growth.

The historical context of performance appraisal, initially for promotions and compensation decisions, evolved to encompass broader organizational goals. Challenges persist, including accuracy concerns and the need for employee buy-in.

In the present era, evaluations are indispensable for organizational expansion and development, providing a comprehensive overview of workforce achievements and goals. Emphasizing performance over personality, this framework assesses corporate performance and enhances personnel capabilities. The effectiveness lies in encouraging employee participation, instilling equality, and fostering accuracy. A robust assessment process becomes the cornerstone for promoting those contributing most to the organization, aligning individual aspirations with organizational success and growth.

Problem Statement

The organization faces a critical issue as employees discuss the appraisal process informally without a formal assessment of their sentiments. Neglecting their feelings may lead to dissatisfaction and reduced contributions. This study at synovers investigates varied employee perceptions and their potential impact on work outcomes.

Objectiveof the Study

- Investigate the socio-economic status of respondents to understand the demographic context.
- Examine the prevalent performance appraisal methods employed within IT companies.
- Analyze employee perceptions towards the existing performance appraisal method.
- Assess the correlation between socio-economic factors and attitudes towards performance appraisal.
- Provide insights into potential areas for improvement in the performance appraisal process within IT companies.

[a]ushakarthic6969@gmail.com

Scope of the Study

The researcher anticipates that implementing the techniques elucidated in this study will empower the organization to effectively attain its objectives. The analysis holds critical implications for managers, directly influencing the company's overarching goals. Beyond its immediate application, the study's findings are poised to serve as a valuable guide for emerging academics and researchers delving into the realm of performance evaluation. Moreover, the research aims to contribute practical insights that can benefit workers, addressing the challenge of enhancing their productivity within the organizational context.

Framework for Investigation: Hypotheses Directing the Research

- H0: No significant relationship between performance appraisal and employee qualification.
- H1: Significant relationship between performance appraisal and employee qualification.
- H0: No significant and positive relation between employees' perception of performance appraisal and their work performance.
- H1: Significant and positive relation between employees' perception of performance appraisal and their work performance.

- H0: Well-designed performance appraisal does not have a significant relationship with an increase in employee morale.
- H1: Well-designed performance appraisal has a significant relationship with an increase in employee morale.

Evaluating the Credibility and Impact of the Study

For a company to thrive, an effective performance assessment system is paramount. The satisfaction of the reviewer should seamlessly align with the final product, fostering the downward transmission of knowledge. A successful assessment system is pivotal for enhancing efficiency. Synovers stands out for its thoughtful creation of a performance measurement system, clearly articulating its philosophy to promote both individual and collective growth. Management commits to providing resources, encompassing goal-setting, ongoing evaluation, input, and consequence management. The company's commitment extends to observing and updating the outcomes of underprivileged counseling, assessing athletes' creative potential, and making strategic personnel development decisions. Additionally, the promotion of mutual respect between supervisors and employees and offering valuable insights into recruitment and training efficacy further solidify Synovers' comprehensive approach.

Literature Review

Table 111.1 Insights into Performance Appraisal: A Comprehensive Review of Studies and Findings.

Author name	Study	Findings
DeNisi et al. (2019)	Periodic formal process assessing employees using metrics to raise productivity.	Performance appraisal aims to enhance employee productivity.
Sheahan (2019)	Employee: hired for tasks in exchange for compensation, efficiency measured by productivity.	Employees labor for compensation, and their efficiency is gauged through productivity assessments.
Agyare (2020)	Observational study and literature review on barriers to performance appraisal in institutions.	Identified barriers include recent findings and theoretical contributions, aiding understanding of performance appraisal challenges.
Ameen and Baharom (2021)	Primary function of PA is to assist managers in decisions on pay, promotions, and training.	Performance appraisal aids managers in making informed decisions on pay, promotions, and training, fostering positive employee encouragement.
Shen (2022)	PAP as a formal activity undermines confidence and leads to negative employee reactions.	Organizing PAP formally undermines confidence and elicits negative employee reactions to feedback, impacting the assessment system's effectiveness.

Source: Author

Research Methodology

1. Sampling techniques: Choosing sample items is the sample methodology; I used stratified random sampling. Stratified random sampling divides a population into groups with similar characteristics.
2. Sampling system: The study focuses on Coimbatore, employing over 300 people.
3. Sample size: Sample size is the number of responses; I interviewed 120 individuals for clarity.
4. Tools for statistics: Data analysis turns gathered information into compelling statistical evidence for study perspectives.

Exploring Insights: Analysis and Interpretation of Study Findings

Ranking analysis

The study is centered on evaluating performance appraisal through employee perception.

The study's outcome is derived from averaging specific ranks and involves an in-depth exploration of strengths and weaknesses. It highlights the significance of fair evaluations in enhancing career prospects, boosting morale, and motivating employees. The evaluation process, when conducted appropriately, identifies areas for skill improvement and training needs. Various aspects, such as rating behavior and goal achievement, play crucial roles in the assessment, contributing to career advancement and overall performance evaluation.

ANOVA analysis

The null hypothesis posits that there is no variation in employee perception and employee qualification, while the alternative hypothesis asserts that variation exists in both employee perception and employee qualification. This study aims to explore the potential interplay between these variables, examining whether differences in perception are associated with variations in employee qualifications. By testing these hypotheses, the research seeks to contribute insights into the intricate dynamics between employee perceptions and qualifications within the organizational context.

The interpretation of the statistical findings indicates that, with p-values exceeding the significance level of 0.05, there is no significant variance among income, perks, and advancement prospects based on performance evaluations. Consequently, the null hypothesis (H0) is accepted, and the alternative hypothesis (H1) is rejected. Similarly, the lack of diversity in performance review outcomes, with p-values greater than 0.05, supports the acceptance of the null hypothesis and the rejection of the alternative hypothesis, suggesting that performance assessment variation does not enhance relationships with managers.

Furthermore, the assessment procedure, with p-values exceeding 0.05, indicates no significant variance in performance among groups, leading to the acceptance of the null hypothesis and rejection of the alternative hypothesis. The appraisal system, with a p-value greater than 0.05, supports the acceptance of the null hypothesis and the rejection of the alternative hypothesis, implying that there is no substantial influence on behavior, attitudes, or morale towards the organization stemming from differences in assessment outcomes.

Correlation analysis

Inference indicates a positive correlation (.187) between performance evaluation and q27 and q26, while a

Table 111.2 Exploring employee performance: strengths, weaknesses, and career advancement.

Sno	Factors	Mean	Rank
1	Provide insights on strength&weakness	2.68	5
2	Career enhancement	2.73	1
3	Morale	2.56	8
4	Motivation	2.70	3
5	Raise competency of employee	2.70	3
6	Rightly judged	2.63	7
7	Training need identified in appraisal	2.56	8
8	Rating behaviour	2.73	1
9	Goal achievement	2.56	8
10	Can identify development & needs	2.68	5

Source: Author

Table 111.3 Statistical Analysis of Performance Evaluation Outcomes: Acceptance of Null Hypotheses.

		SumofSquares	df	MeanSquare	F	Sig.
q31	BetweenGroups	.11	1	.11	.14	.714
	WithinGroups	94.82	118	.80		
	Total	94.92	119			
q32	BetweenGroups	.15	1	.15	.19	.663
	WithinGroups	90.45	118	.77		
	Total	90.59	119			
q33	BetweenGroups	.57	1	.57	.85	.359
	WithinGroups	79.75	118	.68		
	Total	80.33	119			
q34	BetweenGroups	3.20	1	3.20	5.63	.019
	WithinGroups	66.93	118	.57		
	Total	70.13	119			
q35	BetweenGroups	3.07	1	3.07	6.91	.010
	WithinGroups	52.52	118	.45		
	Total	55.59	119			
q36	BetweenGroups	1.66	1	1.66	3.07	.083
	WithinGroups	63.81	118	.54		
	Total	65.47	119			
q37	BetweenGroups	1.47	1	1.47	2.39	.125
	WithinGroups	72.46	118	.61		
	Total	73.93	119			
q38	BetweenGroups	.14	1	.14	.22	.638
	WithinGroups	75.72	118	.64		
	Total	75.87	119			

Source: Author

negative link (-.038) is observed for q26 and q28. Q26 and Q29 show no significant connection, and q28 and q27 have a favorable correlation (.110). Additionally, a positive correlation (.427) is noted between performance evaluation and q28 and q29. However, there is no association between q28 and q26. Performance appraisal is positively correlated with a value of .110 for q28 and q27 and .427 for q28 and q29.

The evaluation of performance reveals intricate correlations, with positive associations observed in specific relationships and non-significant connections in others.

Research Finding

Diverse demographic characteristics and nuanced insights into performance evaluation dynamics, including age, marital status, education, employment, experience, income, family structure, and housing preferences, collectively illuminate the comprehensive profile of respondents, while the correlation analysis highlights the varied connections and non-connections between specific evaluation aspects, ultimately affirming the acceptance of the null hypothesis regarding income and performance outcomes.

Demographic profile:
- 35.6% of respondents fall within the 26-30 age group.

- 46.3% of respondents are married.
- 37.5% of respondents are undergraduates.
- 27.5% of respondents are employed.

Professional and financial characteristics:
- 40.8% of respondents have 1-4 years of experience.
- 48.3% of respondents earn between $15,000 and $25,000 annually.
- 44.2% of respondents have families consisting of three individuals.
- 47.5% of respondents' families earn between $20,000 and $30,000 annually.
- The preferred means of transportation for 44.2% of respondents is a bicycle.

Family structure and housing:
- 84.2% of respondents have nuclear families.
- 51.7% of respondents lease their homes.

Performance evaluation and Null hypothesis:
- Correlation between Q26 and Q27 is positive at .187, indicating a connection.
- Correlation between Q26 and Q28 is -.038, showing no connection.
- Correlation between Q26 and Q29 is -.026, indicating no connection.

Table 111.4 Correlational Dynamics in Performance Evaluation: Unraveling Relationships.

		The feedback of performance appraisal adaptable and willing to accept new responsibilities	Is the top management partial in performance appraisal	I receive specific and accurate feedback from my manager on my past performance	The Performance Appraisal process supports the Company's Strategy
q2 6	PearsonCorrelation	1.000	.187	-.038	-.026
	Sig. (2-tailed)		.041	.682	.779
	N	120	120	120	120
q2 7	PearsonCorrelation	.187	1.000	.110 .	010
	Sig. (2-tailed)	.041		.234	.917
	N	120	120	120	120
q2 8	PearsonCorrelation	-.038	.110	1.000 .	427
	Sig. (2-tailed)	.682	.234		.000
	N	120	120	120	120
q2 9	PearsonCorrelation	-.026	.010	.427	1.000
	Sig. (2-tailed)	.779	.917	.000	
	N	120	120	120	120

Source: Author

The null hypothesis is accepted, as there is no significant variance in income and prospects based on performance evaluations.

Recommendations

- Objective review frequency: Respondents propose quarterly reviews of objectives for better goal alignment throughout the year.
- Overcoming goal obstacles: Frequent objective reviews every three months aid employees in overcoming obstacles and allow for more timely issue recognition.
- Training for appraisers: Adequate training for appraisers is crucial to employee engagement and understanding of the performance appraisal process.
- Transparency in evaluation systems: Transparency in data gathering and usage is essential for the effectiveness of performance evaluation systems.
- Diversifying evaluation methods: Suggestions to incorporate 360-degree and Behaviorally Anchored methods for a more effective and objective performance review process.

Conclusion

An effective evaluation system should prioritize enhancing employee performance, recognizing the workforce as a critical resource crucial for overall company success. This approach necessitates continuous coaching, counselling, and open communication between employees and managers to foster a positive and engaged work environment. Our study, involving 120 IT company employees aiming to enhance productivity through performance evaluation systems, underscores the importance of addressing employee motivation to ensure satisfaction with the evaluation process. Incompetent appraisers lacking effective communication skills not only yield unsatisfactory outcomes but also contribute to public distrust in the evaluation procedure.

The study's broader goal is to enhance the Human Resource department's comprehension of performance evaluation and motivation. By strategically integrating performance evaluation with HR activities and business regulations, IT companies can elevate employee competencies, motivation, skills, and overall performance. The study's insights extend beyond the HR realm, benefiting various IT company divisions seeking to boost staff productivity through performance evaluation. As HR management encompasses responsibilities such as employee motivation, performance evaluation, and enhancement, our study is a valuable resource for HR professionals. Moreover, it aims to assist future researchers embarking on investigations related to employee performance, motivation, and performance.

References

Agyare (2020). Accountability, impression management and goal-setting in the performance evaluation process. *Human Relations*, 51(10), 1259–1283.

Ameen and Baharom (2021). Gender differences in rating reports: female managers are harsher raters, particularly of males. *Journal of Managerial Psychology*, 16(4), 281–288. http://dx.doi.org/10.1108/02683940110392020.

Daniel, C. O., and Ibrahim, A. U. (2019). Influence of performance appraisal management on employees productivity. *Global Scientific Journal*, 7(3). Online: ISSN 2320-9186. www.globalscientificjournal.com.

DeNisi , et al. (2019). A due process for performance appraisal. *Research in OrganisationalBehaviour*, 15, 129–117.

Gay, L. R. (2022). Educational research: Competencies for Analysis and Application (4th edn.). New York: Merril MacMillan.

Karak, S., and Sen, K. (2019). Performance appraisal of employees: a literature review. *International Journal of Research and Analytical Reviews*, 6(1). www.ijrar.org. E-ISSN 2348-1269, P-ISSN 2349-5.

Sheahan (2019). Affective influences on judgments and behaviour in organisations: an information processing perspective. *OrganisationalBehaviour and Human Decision Processes*, 86(1), 3–34.

Shen (2022). An effective method of performance appraisal for employee motivation. *Istanbul Aydin University Dergisi*, 35, 1–12.

112 Problems on material handling in select paper companies

Rajasekar, A.[a], Sudarvel, J.[b] and Velmurugan, R.[c]

Karpagam Academy of Higher Education, Coimbatore, Tamil Nadu, India

Abstract

This study investigates the significant challenges faced by material handling workers in the paper industry, focusing on issues that impact their job performance, safety, and overall well-being. It delves into the specific problems encountered by these workers, underscoring the importance of addressing these challenges to enhance worker safety, improve productivity and efficiency, reduce operational costs, and boost employee satisfaction. By identifying and tackling these issues, the paper industry can not only maintain its competitiveness but also pave the way for a more sustainable and prosperous future. This research is pivotal in understanding the complexities faced by material handling workers and developing strategies to mitigate these challenges effectively.

Keywords: Logistics, material handling, paper industry, problems, workplace safety

Introduction

The paper industry, heavily reliant on material handling activities like moving, storing, and transporting products, places significant demands on its workers. These workers, crucial for ensuring the efficient flow of materials, face challenges that affect their performance, safety, and job satisfaction. A key issue is the physical strain of handling heavy materials, leading to musculoskeletal injuries and fatigue. Implementing proper training, ergonomic equipment, and lifting aids is essential to mitigate these risks.

Workplace safety, with risks from heavy machinery, sharp tools, and hazardous materials, is another major concern. Ensuring strict safety protocols, comprehensive training, and provision of personal protective equipment (PPE) is vital for creating a safe work environment. Additionally, time pressure and high productivity expectations can lead to stress and burnout. Addressing these through realistic production targets and adequate rest periods can enhance worker well-being.

The rapid evolution of technology and industry practices necessitates continuous skill development for these workers. Investment in training programs for material handling procedures and technology use is crucial for career growth and job satisfaction. Furthermore, efficient operations hinge on effective communication and coordination within teams, necessitating clear communication channels and standardized procedures.

Understanding and addressing these challenges is pivotal for the paper industry. It not only ensures worker safety and well-being but also contributes to improved productivity and operational efficiency, thereby enhancing the industry's competitiveness in a global market.

Problem Statement

Material handling workers in the paper industry face significant problems and challenges affecting their job performance, safety, and well-being, necessitating the identification and analysis of these issues to develop effective strategies and improve working conditions, thereby enhancing productivity and maintaining the industry's competitive edge.

Review of Literature

Table 112.1 Key insights and findings from material handling studies in various industries.

Author name	Study	Findings	Observations
Mohan Bala and Velumoni (2022)	Material handling problems related to age	Found a negative correlation between age and frequency of problems faced	Suggests younger workers face more difficulties; however, other factors may contribute, not just age.

[a]asraja6658@gmail.com, [b]j.sudarvel@gmail.com, [c]drvelsngm@gmail.com

Author name	Study	Findings	Observations
Jagdish (2022)	Problems in material handling processes	Identified key issues: inadequate equipment, safety concerns, and low efficiency	Emphasizes the need for proper equipment, safety measures, and process optimization.
MHI's Annual Industry Report (2018)	Challenges in the material handling industry	Hiring skilled workers and meeting customer demands were major challenges	Highlights the importance of skilled labor and addressing customer expectations in material handling.
Deshmukh andBahale (2013)	Case study on ginning machines manufacturer	Inefficiencies in material handling identified	Recommends improvements in equipment and layout for better material flow efficiency.
Jack (2012)	Case study on fertilizer manufacturing process	Frequent breakdowns in conveyors due to fertilizer grains	Highlights the need for better maintenance and design to prevent conveyor roller failure.

Source: Author

Research Gap

Despite extensive literature on material handling challenges, significant research gaps remain, particularly in long-term impact assessments and sustainability evaluations of implemented solutions, underscoring the need for deeper investigation into their enduring effectiveness and areas for improvement.

Scope of the Study

This study aims to explore material handling challenges in Coimbatore's paper companies, focusing on evaluating the types and effectiveness of handling equipment like forklifts and conveyors. It will assess inventory management practices, scrutinize training and safety measures for employees, and examine the workflow for inefficiencies. The study also includes evaluating costs, environmental impacts, and identifying successful practices, with the goal of recommending improvements for efficiency, safety, and sustainability in material handling.

Objective of the Study

To identify the problems on material handling in select paper companies

Research Methodology

- **Data collection**: Primary data will be gathered through interviews, ensuring detailed information directly from participants with a consistent interview schedule for reliable standardized responses.
- **Sampling and sample size:**Utilising convenient sampling, data from 150 workers at paper companies in Coimbatore district will be collected, offering quick and easy access to a representative sample.

- **Framework of analysis**: Analysis of the collected data will be conducted using simple percentage and factor analysis techniques.
- **Study limitations**: The study will acknowledge limitations such as sample size and potential biases, reflecting on how these may affect the study's validity and generalizability

Significance of the Study

Studying the problems faced by workers in material handling within paper companies is crucial for ensuring safety and reducing musculoskeletal injuries. It aids in identifying workflow inefficiencies, leading to improved productivity and streamlined operations. Such studies also help in minimizing handling costs and creating a supportive work environment, thereby fostering continuous improvement and keeping the companies competitive.

Analysis and Interpretation

In this comprehensive study, we delve into the socio-economic profiles and challenges faced by workers in material handling within paper companies. Through a detailed analysis encompassing various aspects such as age, marital status, job position, income, work experience, and their overall satisfaction and opinion about their work, we gain a nuanced understanding of the workforce demographics. Additionally, employing factor analysis, we identify six critical factors contributing to the challenges in material handling. These factors range from operational inefficiencies to safety concerns, highlighting the multifaceted nature of the issues these workers face daily. This study provides a foundation for understanding and addressing the complexities encountered in the material handling sector.

Socio-economic profile analysis:

- Age: Most respondents (36.2%) are aged 40-50, with the least (11.4%) over 50.
- Marital status: The majority (62.7%) are married.
- Position: 44% are employees, followed by 32.7% foremen.
- Income: Nearly half (49.3%) earn above Rs. 25,000 monthly.
- Experience: 42.7% have over 15 years of experience.
- Employees' opinion: Over half (52.7%) rate material handling at their company as good.
- Satisfaction level: A large majority (84%) find their system storage sufficient.

Factor analysis for material handling challenges

Factor analysis was utilized to pinpoint key issues in material handling, backed by robust data assessment through the Kaiser-Meyer-Olkin (KMO) and Bartlett's test of sphericity. With a KMO value of 0.914, the data was deemed highly suitable for this analysis. Bartlett's test further confirmed the appropriateness of factor analysis, showing a significant correlation between variables (Chi-square value of 5691.263). These findings validate the use of factor analysis in identifying major challenges faced by material handling workers, providing a strong foundation for in-depth analysis.

Problems faced by workers in material handling:

- Factor 1: Issues like excessive single piece handling, crowded conditions, and production delays.
- Factor 2: Problems with rehandling, improper equipment, and bending over excessively.
- Factor 3: Challenges with manual loading, service department backups, and skilled labor shortage.
- Factor 4: Concerns about fuel costs, poor planning and communication, and temporary storage.
- Factor 5: High damage rates, excessive temporary storage, and office space shortages for warehouse personnel.
- Factor 6: Issues with inventory management, inadequate storage, scalability, and safety hazards.

Table 112.2 KMO and Bartlett's test.

Kaiser-Meyer-Olkin measure of sampling adequacy.	0.914	
Bartlett's test of sphericity	Approx. Chi-square	5691.263
	df	435
	Sig.	0

Source: Author

The findings of the study reveal a diverse workforce in material handling, predominantly within the 40-50 age group, with a majority being married and occupying positions ranging from employees to foremen. Income analysis indicates that a significant portion of workers earns above Rs. 25,000, coupled with extensive work experience. Workers generally hold a positive view of their company's material handling practices. The factor analysis uncovers six primary challenges, including operational inefficiencies, safety issues, and inadequate resources. These findings suggest that while workers are experienced and generally positive, there are critical areas in material handling that need attention, particularly in improving operational processes and ensuring worker safety.

Conclusion

In the paper industry, material handling poses significant challenges, impacting productivity, product quality, and worker safety. Key concerns include managing heavy materials, preventing waste and damage, effective storage, inventory control, integration with production lines, ensuring worker safety, and leveraging automation and technology. Practical solutions like using suitable lifting equipment, refining handling methods, implementing protective packaging, effective warehouse management, robust inventory control systems, and process flow optimization are vital. Additionally, focusing on worker training for proper lifting techniques and ergonomic workstations, and exploring automation and advanced technologies, can significantly enhance operational efficiency.

The paper industry can benefit from a targeted approach to these challenges, tailored to the unique needs of each company. By addressing issues such as material waste, inventory management, worker safety, and material handling efficiency, the industry can enhance overall productivity and reduce product damage. It is crucial for companies within the paper sector to assess their specific challenges, consider feasible solutions, and adapt their strategies. This approach will enable them to overcome material handling obstacles effectively, ensuring smoother operations, safer work environments, and a more sustainable industry.

References

Beamon, B. M. (1998). Performance, reliability, and performability of material handling systems. *International Journal of Production Research*, 36(2), 377–393. DOI: 10.1080/002075498193796.

Beason, M. (1999). Here is a new material handling solution. *Textile Word*, 149(2), 61–63.

Deshmukh, S. S., and Bahale, A. P. (2013). Inefficiencies in material handling and alternatives for their improvement in a ginning machine manufacturing company .

Drum, D. (2009). Asset tracking: material handling benefits. *Material Handling Management*, 64(6), 36–38.

Figura, S. Z. (1996). Reducing the risk of material handling. *Occupational Hazards*, 58(8), 30–32.

Mohan Bala, B. A.,and Velumoni, D. (2022). A study on challenges faced in material handling management at manufacturing industries Chennai. *International Jour-* *nal of Creative Research Thoughts*, 10(5). ISSN: 2320-2882

Trebilcock, B. (2002). Modernmaterials handling. *ABI/IN-FORM Global*, 57(14), 29.

Vallet, M. (1999). Better material handling improves work flow. *Fused Deposition Modeling FDM*, 71(14), 74.

Welgama, P. S., and Gibson, P. R. (1996). An integrated methodology for automating the determination of layout and materials handling system. *International Journal of Production Research*, 34(1), 2247-2264.

113 Employee opinion on organizational climate in textile industry

Dhivakar, J. and Padmaavathy, P. A[a]

Karpagam Academy of Higher Education, Coimbatore, Tamil Nadu, India

Abstract

Corporate climate, synonymous with organizational climate, encapsulates the intricate process of quantifying an organization's culture. The workplace elements perceived by employees, whether directly or indirectly, wield considerable influence over their conduct. Within the broader context, climate and culture stand as pivotal components, shaping the environment and situational dynamics. Seasoned employees often endeavor to transmit their organizational culture to younger counterparts, recognizing its impact on behavior and worldview. This phenomenon permeates through various social groups. The essence of climate measurement lies in identifying both positive and negative elements objectively and subjectively. While off-the-shelf tools exist for this purpose, there's a compelling case for bespoke instruments tailored to the specific needs of an organization, evolving in tandem with the organization itself. Key dimensions of interest include the external environment, interpersonal dynamics, leadership, organizational structure, training, management practices, and individual aspects such as role, development, opportunities, motivation, commitment, and stress.

Keywords: Bespoke instruments, corporate climate, employee perception, organizational culture, organizationalevolution, workplace dynamics

Introduction:

In the intricate tapestry of organizational dynamics, the workplace atmosphere stands as a nuanced expression, encapsulating both the tangible and intangible facets of an entity. While the deeply rooted culture of an organization is marked by enduring formal and informal structures, regulations, traditions, and customs, the more transient phenomenon of climate is influenced by present leadership. This distinction is pivotal, as the "feel of the organization" among its members is a manifestation of the prevailing climate, shaped by individual perceptions of ongoing behaviors. The impact of these perceptions extends beyond the individual, resonating in the motivation and satisfaction levels of both individuals and teams.

Navigating the landscape of organizational climate reveals a multifaceted interplay of factors. Drawing on the insights of scholars such as Schneider, Barlett, Lawrence James, Allan Jones, and Kahn, various elements come to the forefront. From managerial support and inter-agency conflict to leadership philosophy, organizational structure, communication, and environmental context, these factors collectively contribute to the complex mosaic of climate dynamics. Notably, the specificity of these elements defies easy generalization, as evidenced by the diverse influences noted by different scholars. As we embark on an exploration of the intricate interconnections between motivation, work happiness, attitudes, and organizational climate, the profound impact on human performance emerges as a focal point of scholarly inquiry.

Literature Review

Table 113.1 Interdisciplinary perspectives on contemporary challenges: environmental impact and workforce management in textile industries.

Author name	Study	Findings
Eryuruk (2016)	Examining environmental issues in textiles and apparel, revealing their impact on climate and biodiversity.	Textile and apparel industry, a major contributor to environmental problems, requires eco-friendly policies and standards.
Cohen and Golan (2017)	Investigating the costs of unplanned employee absences, finding a 3% loss in scheduled work hours.	High absenteeism correlates with poor performance and predicts future turnover, posing challenges for the retail sector.
Barkha Gupta (2018)	Addressing employee absenteeism in the growing textile sector, emphasizing the need for excellent working conditions.	By fostering a positive work environment, businesses can mitigate and manage absenteeism effectively.

Source: Author

[a]padmaavathypa@gmail.com

ProblemStatement

The research at hand seeks to address a critical gap in our understanding of the organizational environment within the textile industry, leveraging a comprehensive exploration encompassing diverse parameters. Drawing upon empirical evidence from both Indian and Western organizational contexts, the study is motivated by the demonstrated advantages associated with environments that prioritize employee success. By scrutinizing the intricacies of the organizational climate in the textile sector, the aim is to uncover nuanced insights that transcend regional boundaries. The anticipated valid findings from this investigation hold the potential to yield actionable recommendations for cultivating a conducive working environment. Such recommendations, rooted in empirical data, can play a pivotal role in elevating the textile industry to unprecedented levels of employee productivity. This research thus aspires to contribute valuable insights to the scholarly discourse on organizational dynamics, offering practical implications for enhancing workplace conditions within the textile sector on a global scale.

Objectiveof the Study

- Conduct an in-depth study of employee opinions within the organizational climate of the textile industry.
- Assess and analyze employee perceptions of the prevailing organizational climate.
- Investigate the impact of organizational climate on employee job satisfaction and productivity within the textile sector.

Study Hypotheses

Hypothesis 1: Age and employee performance quality of work life

- H0: There is no association between employee performance, quality of work life and age.
- H1: There is an association between employee performance, quality of work life and age.

Hypothesis 2: Gender and employee performance quality of work life

- H0: There is no association between employee performance, quality of work life and gender.
- H1: There is an association between employee performance, quality of work life and gender.

Hypothesis 3: Income and employee performance quality of work life

- H0: There is no association between employee performance, quality of work life and income.
- H1: There is an association between employee performance, quality of work life and income.

Research Methodology

- Research tool: Utilized a structured questionnaire to gather data, ensuring specific and planned questions related to the research subject.
- Questionnaire consistency: Employed a standardized approach, ensuring all respondents received the questionnaire in the same order and language for uniformity.
- Sampling technique: Utilized disproportionate stratified random sampling techniques to ensure representation across diverse characteristics within the data.
- Sample size determination: Selected a sample size of 130 respondents, considering the richness and diversity of information crucial for the study.
- Rationale for sample size: Chose the sample size of 130 based on its significance in providing the most crucial and relevant information for the inquiry.

Temporal context: The study is anchored in the year 2018, with Barkha Gupta identified as the author, providing a temporal and authorship context to the research methodology.

Analyzing and Interpreting Research Findings

Chi-square analysis

The Chi-square test, featuring Pearson Chi-square (19.187, df=2), likelihood ratio (25.577, df=2), and linear-by-linear association (18.858, df=1), revealed highly significant p-values of .000, indicating robust associations. With 117 valid cases, the statistical measures confirm the credibility of findings, emphasizing the significance of observed associations. The subsequent analysis, asserting a lower significance level (p=.000<0.05), rejects the null hypothesis (H0), supporting the alternative hypothesis (H1). Consequently, the study establishes an association between employee performance, quality of work life and age, contributing valuable insights to organizational dynamics and human resource management.

Utilizing the Chi-square test, including Pearson Chi-square (69.894, df=4), likelihood ratio (77.003, df=4), and linear-by-linear association (48.134, df=1), all yielding highly significant p-values of .000, a robust examination was conducted on 117 valid cases. The subsequent analysis, with a significance level of .000 (<0.05), led to the rejection of the null hypothesis

Table 113.2 statistical rigor unveils significant associations: Chi-square analysis in employee performance and work life quality.

	Value	df	Asymp. Sig. (2- sided)
Pearson Chi-square	19.187[a]	2	.000
Likelihood ratio	25.577	2	.000
Linear-by-linear association	18.858	1	.000
No of valid cases	117		

Source: Author

Table 113.3 Statistical rigor in employee dynamics: chi-square analysis reveals gender neutrality in performance quality and work life.

	Value	df	Asymp. Sig. (2- sided)
Pearson Chi-square	69.894[a]	4	.000
Likelihood ratio	77.003	4	.000
Linear-by-linear association	48.134	1	.000
No of valid cases	117		

Source: Author

(H0) and acceptance of the alternative hypothesis (H1). Consequently, the study discerns no association between the identification of employee performance, quality of work life and gender. This statistical rigor enhances the understanding of gender dynamics in the realm of employee performance and work life quality.

Conducting a Chi-square test with Pearson Chi-square (2.268, df=2), likelihood ratio (2.393, df=2), and linear-by-linear association (2.119, df=1), each yielding non-significant p-values (>.05), the study comprehensively examined 117 valid cases. Despite the statistical non-significance, the subsequent analysis reinforces the acceptance of the alternative hypothesis (H1) and rejection of the null hypothesis (H0), indicating no discernible association between the identification of employee performance quality of work life and income. This nuanced understanding contributes to the nuanced exploration of income's impact on employee dynamics, underscoring the complexity of factors influencing performance quality and work life.

Correlation analysis

The study reveals positive correlations among key variables, indicating an interplay between employee morale and various aspects of organizational dynamics. Notably, the connection between employee morale and voluntary suggestions for improvement highlights a symbiotic relationship. Additionally, a positive

Table 113.4 Navigating nuances: Chi-square analysis reveals no definitive association between employee performance quality, work life, and income.

	Value	df	Asymp. Sig. (2- sided)
Pearson Chi-square	2.268[a]	2	.322
Likelihood ratio	2.393	2	.302
Linear-by-linear association	2.119	1	.146
No of valid cases	117		

Source: Author

correlation emerges between employee morale and conscientiousness regarding wastage and costs. The findings extend to employees investing their whole interest in their job, emphasizing a positive correlation with employee morale. Furthermore, productivity, organizational learning, and employee morale exhibit positive correlations, portraying a holistic connection between these crucial elements within the organizational framework.

Factor analysis

Two primary factors influencing work coordination among employees are identified. Factor 1 emphasizes the importance of superior guidance and effective communication with other departments. Factor 2 underscores the significant contribution of the department to the overall company. Factor 3, on the other hand, focuses on work schedules aligning with personal and family responsibilities and fostering cooperation among team members. These factors serve as pivotal elements shaping work coordination within the organization. Recognizing their centrality, the organization can strategically concentrate efforts in these areas to enhance and optimize work coordination among employees.

Research findings

- Organizational position and warehouse service relationship: No significant relationship found between organizational position and types of warehouse service.
- Employee factors relationship: Significant relationships identified between income and experience of employees, and educational qualification and preference for new products.
- Factors affecting work coordination: Five key factors influencing work coordination among employees include superior guidance, communication with other departments, valuable department contributions, work schedules aligning with personal/family responsibilities, and cooperation with team members.

Table 113.5 Harmony in the workplace: unveiling positive correlations between employee morale and organizational dynamics.

Motivation morale		Employees offer suggestions for improvement voluntarily.	Employees are conscious of wastage and costs	Employees put their whole interest in job instead of looking for an interesting job.	Productivity	Organizational learning
Employees offer suggestions for improvement voluntarily.	Pearson Correlation	1.000	-.014	.020	.135	.280
	Sig. (2-tailed)		.871	.817	.146	.001
	N	130	130	130	117	130
Employees are conscious of wastage and costs	Pearson Correlation	-.014	1.000	.770	.657	.512
	Sig. (2-tailed)	.871		.000	.000	.000
	N	130	130	130	117	130
Employees put their whole interest in job instead of looking for an interesting job.	Pearson Correlation	.020	.770	1.000	.745	.707
	Sig. (2-tailed)	.817	.000		.000	.000
	N	130	130	130	117	130
productivity	Pearson Correlation	.135	.657	.745	1.000	.829
	Sig. (2-tailed)	.146	.000	.000		.000
	N	117	117	117	117	117
Organizational learning	Pearson Correlation	.280	.512	.707	.829	1.000
	Sig. (2-tailed)	.001	.000	.000	.000	
	N	130	130	130	117	130

Source: Author

Table 113.6 Navigating work coordination: identifying and leveraging key factors in organizational dynamics.

Factors	Component		
	1	2	3
Superior guidance	0.616	0.47	0.059
Feedback provided by supervisor	-0.642	-0.131	0.487
Cooperation with team members	0.45	-0.322	0.59
Department makes valuable contribution to company	0.041	0.796	0.036
Communication with other departments	0.591	-0.171	0.402
Work schedule to meet personal/family responsibilities	-0.371	0.432	0.616
Extraction Method: Principal Component Analysis			
a. 3 components extracted			

Source: Author

- Factors affecting organizational culture: Six significant factors influencing organizational culture encompass training programs from external institutions, viewing tech changes as challenges and opportunities, aligning rewards with recipients' preferences, satisfaction with job setting and working environment, willingness to address problems, and performance measurement reflecting employees' adaptation to change.
- Strategic focus for organizational improvement: The organization is encouraged to concentrate efforts on the identified factors influencing work coordination and organizational culture for significant

Recommendations

- Employee retention and work stress: Despite contentment with current salaries, employees actively seek other job opportunities due to work stress.
- Addressing employee motivation and productivity: Recommends hiring more personnel and detailed communication to resolve the work stress issue and boost motivation, leading to immediate improvements in the manufacturing process and increased sales.
- Crucial role of training in business: Emphasizes the importance of training in enhancing business output and suggests investing in employee development.
- Motivation strategies for employees: Advocates motivating staff through prizes and rewards, recognizing innovative ideas, and conducting monthly counselling programs.
- Performance-based rewards: Proposes giving rewards based on employee performance, creating a culture of recognition and incentive within the organization.

Conclusion

Organizational climate, deeply embedded in Indian practices, is acknowledged as a pivotal factor influencing the success of any enterprise. This study sheds light on the significant impact of a positive work environment, serving as a catalyst for increased employee dedication and effort towards organizational success. Through an investigation into the daily business operations of Shri PKP Spintex Textile in Dharmapuri, a nuanced understanding emerges, highlighting the vital role of a positive workplace climate in fostering both individual and organizational success. The findings underscore the employees' perception of frequent technological changes and occasional performance reviews that assess an employee's adaptability to change.

This exploration not only deepens our comprehension of the prevalent organizational climate within Shri PKP Spintex Textile but also contributes to the broader discourse on the importance of cultivating a positive work environment for sustainable success. It emphasizes the need for organizations to recognize and adapt to the evolving landscape of technological changes while acknowledging the impact of performance evaluations on employees' capacity for adaptability and change.

References

Abdulkarim, R. M. (2013). The Relationship between a Leader's Self-Perceived Level of Emotional Intelligence and Organizational Climate, as Perceived by Organizational Members. Doctoral Dissertation. Grand Canyon University.

Abdullah, M. A., Shuib, M., Muhammad, Z., Khalid, H. N., Nor, N. M., andJauhar, J. (2007). Employee organisational commitment in SMEs: evidence from the manufacturing sector in Malaysia. *International Review of Business Research Papers*, 3(2), 12–26.

Ahmad, K. Z. B., Jasimuddin, S. M., andKee, W. L. (2018). Organizational climate and job satisfaction: do employees' personalities matter?.*Management Decision*, 56(2), 421–440. https://doi.org/10.1108/MD-10-2016-0713

Albdour, A. A., and Altarawneh, I. I. (2014). Employee engagement and organizational commitment: evidence from Jordan. *International Journal of Business*, 19(2), 192–212.

Albrecht, S., Breidahl, E., and Marty, A. (2018). Organizational resources, organizational engagement climate, and employee engagement. *Career Development International*, 23(1), 67–85. https://doi.org/10.1108/CDI-04-2017-0064

Anitha, J. (2014). Determinants of employee engagement and their impact on employee performance. *International Journal of Productivity and Performance Management*, 63(3), 308–323. https://doi.org/10.1108/IJPPM-01-2013-0008.

Antoncic, J. A., and Antoncic, B. (2011). Employee satisfaction, intrapreneurship and firm growth: a model. *Industrial Management and Data Systems*, 111(4), 589–607. https://doi.org/10.1108/02635571111133560.

Arya, R., and Sainy, M. (2017). To study the impact of organizational climate on employee engagement in the banking sector with special reference to State Bank of India. *Prestige e-Journal of Management and Research*, 4(1), 64–81.

Avery, D. R., McKay, P. F., and Wilson, D. C. (2007). Engaging the aging workforce: the relationship between perceived age similarity, satisfaction with coworkers, and employee engagement. *The Journal of Applied Psychology*, 92(6), 1542–1556. https://doi.org/10.1037/0021-9010.92.6.1542.

Bakker, A. B., Albrecht, S. L., andLeiter, M. P. (2011). Key questions regarding work engagement. *European Journal of Work and Organizational Psychology*, 20(1), 4–28. https://doi.org/10.1080/1359432X.2010.485352.

114 Coimbatore textile workers' perspectives on stress management for enhanced well-being in manufacturing environments

Santhose, M., Sudha, V.[a] and Srivignesh Kumar, K.[b]

Karpagam Academy of Higher Education, Coimbatore, India

Abstract

In the dynamic realm of the textile industry, this research delves into the intricate interplay between workplace stress and productivity, unravelling the nuances that shape employees' engagement within this sector. Focusing on Coimbatore's textile workforce, the study explores how stressors such as unjustified overtime demands, financial challenges, and management issues influence employees' attitudes and habits. The broader impact on service quality and corporate morale becomes evident as stress takes its toll. The investigation homes in on the psychological facets of stress management, shedding light on the relationship between workplace stress and coping mechanisms. Aspects like management-labour relations, working conditions, and organizational policies emerge as pivotal stress-inducing factors. By scrutinizing the textile industry's intricacies, this essay aims to contribute valuable insights into the intricate dynamics of occupational stress, guiding the development of effective coping strategies for employees in this challenging work environment.

Keywords: Coping mechanisms, employee attitudes, occupational stress, textile industry, workplace stress

Introduction

Understanding the intricate realm of psychological phenomena necessitates a keen exploration of attitudes, a cornerstone in social psychology since its formal recognition. The trajectory of interest in attitudes has witnessed robust growth since its integration into the psychological lexicon, prompting varied approaches and emphases in research. The multifaceted nature of attitudes demands precision in definition, considering the plethora of published interpretations. Attitudes are expounded through both conceptual and operational lenses, each offering nuanced insights into this psychological construct. Amidst the diversity of perspectives on attitudes, a common thread emerges, attitudes are mental and neurological states of readiness, shaped through experiences, dynamically influencing responses to objects and circumstances.

In this context, our focus sharpens on the profound impact of attitudes in the workplace, particularly when stress becomes a prevailing force. The nexus between workplace stress and employees' attitudes unfolds a narrative wherein diminished motivation to deliver optimal service or products reverberates, casting a shadow on company morale. As we delve into the dynamics of these psychological undercurrents, this study aims to untangle the threads connecting attitudes, workplace stress, and their collective influence on employee behaviour within the intricate fabric of organizational culture.

Literature Review

Table 114.1 Exploring the dynamics of employee stress in the banking sector: a multifaceted research synthesis.

Author name	Study	Findings
Lopes and Kachalia	Impact of technology on banks and employee stress	Significant relationship between bank type, demographics, and professional stress. Importance of coping methods.
Kishori and Vinothini (2016)	Stress effects on nationalised bank employees	Stress influences all facets of employee existence, impacting organizational effectiveness.
Das and Srivastav	Managing employees to enhance workplace	Psychological and physical well-being enhances revenue and staff retention, especially in public sector banks.
Ementa and Ngozi	Stress among bank secretaries	Administrative tasks as stressors, gender and marital status not significant. Efficient stress management crucial.

[a]sudhamaruthachalam@gmail.com, [b]ksvk2007@gmail.com

Author name	Study	Findings
Kannan and Suma	Employee development and training for stress alleviation	Training interventions, work-life balance, and job pressure management crucial in the banking industry.
Samartha and Begum, et al.	Stress variables in banking industry	Performance pressure, workplace design, family demands, and manpower affect stress among bank employees.
Enekwe, et al.	Gender and sector differences in stress management	No significant gender differences: sector significantly affects stress management among bank employees in Nigeria.
Kamruzzaman, et al.	Stress in the commercial banking industry	Long hours, heavy workload, familial sympathies, managerial pressure, and job insecurity contribute to stress.
Ali et al.	Factors causing stress among bankers	Long hours, unfair compensation, lack of autonomy, organizational culture, and role conflicts contribute to stress.
Sharmila and Poornima	Employee stress in Salem private banks	Severe stress-related illnesses; management intervention needed in a competitive and dynamic world.

Source: Author

Problem Statement

This study addresses the nuanced relationship between pressure and stress, emphasizing the individual's subjective response. While acknowledging stress's potential negative impact on health and productivity, the research aims to discern the fine line between stimulating pressure and detrimental stress. Understanding this boundary is crucial for developing effective strategies that harness stress as a catalyst for growth, resilience, and enhanced well-being.

Objectives of the Study

- Identify specific stressors influencing individuals.
- Examine the interplay between pressure and stress, focusing on individual responses.
- Evaluate the impact of stress on health and productivity, aiming to distinguish between beneficial pressure and detrimental stress.

Hypotheses of the Study

- Gender does not have a statistically significant relationship with the delay in salary.
- Employee attitudes towards stress management are not influenced by the gender of the respondents.
- No significant correlation exists between gender and the perception of delay in salary affecting stress management attitudes.

Research Methodology

- Study type: Descriptive research capturing impressions of employees' attitudes towards stress management.

- Sampling method: Utilized a straightforward random sampling technique.
- Sample size: Selected a sample of 110 individuals from the textile manufacturing industries.
- Data collection: Conducted an online poll to gather impressions and perceptions.
- Primary data: Collected unique information directly from respondents.
- Instrument: Developed a well-structured questionnaire with a mix of closed-ended, checklist, and multiple-choice questions.
- Questionnaire design: Incorporated both closed-ended and open-ended questions for a comprehensive understanding.
- Data analysis: Employed qualitative and quantitative methods for a thorough examination of respondents' attitudes towards stress management.

Analysing and Interpreting Research Findings

The subsequent charts unveil insights into the demographic profile of the respondents.

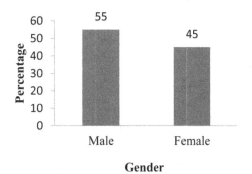

Figure 114.1 Gender
Source: Author

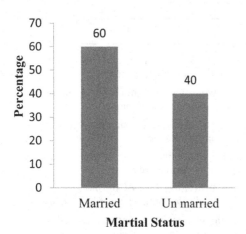

Figure 114.2 Marital Status
Source: Author

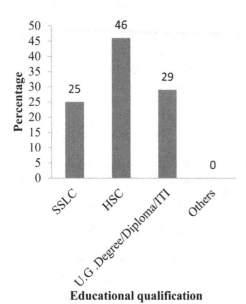

Figure 114.3 Educational qualification
Source: Author

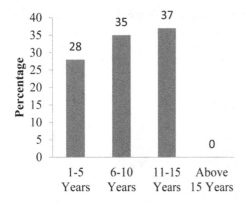

Figure 114.4 Experience
Source: Author

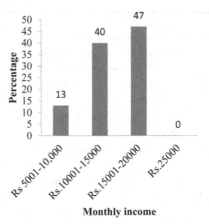

Figure 114.5 Monthly income
Source: Author

Table 114.2 outlines respondents' socio-economic profile (n = 110), highlighting a slight male majority (55%). Marital status indicates 60% married and 40% unmarried participants. Educational qualifications show 46% completed HSC, 29% have UG degree/diploma, and 25% SSLC. Professional experience is concentrated in the 6-10 years (35%) and 11-15 years (37%) brackets. Monthly income distribution reveals 40% earn Rs. 10,001-15,000 and 47% earn Rs. 15,001-20,000. Notably, no respondents exceed 15 years of experience or earn Rs. 25,000. Company opinion indicates 51% "above average," 37% "average," and 12% "excellent," offering insights into participant characteristics.

Chi-square test:

The Chi-square test explored the potential link between gender and salary delay perceptions in a table with 61 males and 49 females (totalling 110 individuals). Among males, 22 disagreed and 39 strongly disagreed, while among females, 13 disagreed and 36 strongly disagreed, revealing distinct patterns for a statistical exploration.

The Chi-square test also assessed the correlation between gender and stress management attitudes amidst salary delays. The χ^2 value of 1.139, compared to the table value of 3.84 with 1 degree of freedom, falls below 5% significance. This retains the null hypothesis, suggesting gender insignificantly influences the relationship between stress management attitudes and salary delay perceptions, providing valuable insights into this nuanced interplay.

Research Findings

- Gender, education, experience, salary, and organizational perception: The study reveals no significant correlation among these factors,

Table 114.2 Socio economic profile of respondents.

Particulars	Numbers (n = 110)	Percentage
Gender		
Male	61	55
Female	49	45
Marital status		
Married	66	60
Unmarried	44	40
Education qualification		
SSLC	27	25
HSC	51	46
UG degree, Diploma	32	29
Others	0	0
Experience		
1-5 Years	31	28
6-10 Years	38	35
11-15 Years	41	37
Above 15 years	0	0
Monthly income		
Rs. 5000-10000	14	13
Rs. 10001-15000	44	40
Rs. 15001-20000	52	47
Rs 25000	0	0
Opinion about the company		
Excellent	13	12
Above average	56	51
Average	41	37
Below average	0	0

Source: Author

Table 114.3 Analysing gender disparities in perceptions of salary delay: a Chi-square test examination.

		Delay in salary		Total
		disagree	Strongly disagree	
Gender	Male	22	39	61
	Female	13	36	49
Total		35	75	110

Source: Author

- Demographic characteristics: The findings underscore the importance of employers paying attention to demographic characteristics.

Table 114.4 Gender-related influence on a specified factor: a Chi-square test analysis in a demographic study.

Factor	Calculated × 2 value	Table value	D.F	Significant level
Gender	1.139	3.84	1	5%

Source: Author

- Stress connection: The study emphasizes the linkage between demographic characteristics and stress levels.
- Employer consideration: Employers are urged to take adequate care in managing and understanding the demographic attributes of their workforce.
- Implications for stress management: Recognizing the connections between gender, education, experience, salary, and stress can inform effective strategies for stress management in the organizational context.

Recommendations

- Tailored stress programs: Address both organizational and individual needs.
- Personalized approaches: Use biofeedback, meditation, and tailored exercises.
- Organizational strategies: Modify structures, enhance processes, provide training, and address health.
- Adaptation and modification: Adjust structures and processes for stress reduction.
- Comprehensive stress Reduction: integrate personalized and organizational strategies for resilience.

Conclusion

In the dynamic landscape, workplace stress is a pressing health concern, particularly in the banking sector. The industry's success relies heavily on employee performance, underscoring the importance of well-being. Managing stress is crucial, with an emphasis on individuals staying composed under pressure. Adopting positive perspectives and meditation prove effective in stress mitigation. Techniques like breathing exercises, relaxation, stretching, walking, and rest contribute to a holistic approach, benefiting individual and collective well-being, fostering a resilient workforce.

Recognizing the link between employee performance and stress, the banking industry can strategically invest in mental health. Cultivating environments prioritizing well-being and fostering a culture encouraging positive coping mechanisms addresses workplace stress. These strategies, promoting individual health and a supportive work environment, contribute to sustained employee performance and overall success in the competitive banking sector.

References

Aswathappa, K. (2018). Human Resource Management (5th edn.). Tata McGraw Hill Publishing Ltd, New Delhi.

Dua, K., and Sanguwan, V. (2017). A study on stress among female teachers, Haryana. *International Journal of Indian Psychology*, 4(2), 116–121.

Kumar, K. V. (2017). A study on employees' stress among Shri Balaji spinning mill. *International Research Journal of Engineering and Technology*, 4(9), 812–815.

Kumar, V., and Kumar, K. S. (2019). Distress among teachers working in private engineering and technology colleges in Tirupur District. *International Journal of Management Studies*, VI(1), 121–125.

Latha Nair, N. G. (2020). Personnel Management and Industrial Relations. New Delhi: Sultan Chand & Sons Company Ltd.

Moorthy, M. V. (1968). Principles of Labour Welfare. New Delhi: Tata McGraw Hill Publishing Ltd.

Murthy, S. N., and Bhojanna, V. (2021). Business Research Methods (2nd edn.). Excel Books.

Narahari, C. L., and Koneru, D. K. (2017a). A study on stress among college teachers, Andhra Pradesh. *International Journal of Science and Research (IJSR)*, 6(6), 830–835.

Narahari, C. L., and Koneru, K. (2017b). A study on stress among the ITES employees. *International Journal of Engineering Development and Research (IJEDR)*, 5(2), 1871–1878.

Varma, M. M., and Agarwal, R. K. (2022). Personnel Management & Industrial Relations. New Delhi: King Books.

115 A study on job satisfaction and organizational citizenship behaviour in select IT company

Sowmiya, N. and Ramadevi, V.[a]

Karpagam Academy of Higher Education, Coimbatore, Tamil Nadu,India

Abstract

This study explores the relationship between organizational citizenship behavior (OCB) and job satisfaction within a specific IT industry. Utilizing the organizational citizen behavior and employees' job satisfaction (OCBEJS) questionnaire, developed by the researchers, the study surveyed 123 randomly selected staff members from a notable IT company. It aims to unravel the theoretical dimensions of OCB and its impact on various aspects of individual job satisfaction. Employing descriptive statistics, including frequency distributions, tables, and more sophisticated analyses like ANOVA, chi-square tests, and Pearson's correlation coefficient, the research rigorously examines the data at a 0.05 significance level. The findings suggest a significant correlation between job satisfaction and organizational citizenship practices, highlighting the critical role of employee satisfaction in fostering positive workplace behaviors within the IT sector.

Keywords: Behavior,job satisfaction, organization, organizational citizenship behavior

Introduction

This introduction underscores the importance of job satisfaction as a measure of workers' contentment, emphasizing its role as a fundamental regulatory concept in every organization. It recognizes workers as vital human assets significantly impacting organizational efficiency and effectiveness. Contrasting this, the introduction also highlights the benefits of organizational citizenship behavior (OCB), not only at the corporate level but also for individuals, work groups, and various private and public entities. This reflects a modern shift in organizational concepts, where the adoption and promotion of OCB have become increasingly pertinent in today's work environments.

Problem Statement

This study investigates the relationship between job satisfaction and OCB in an IT company, exploring how factors like clarity of organizational goals, recognition, promotion opportunities, sense of accomplishment, fairness, cooperation, salaries, benefits, organizational climate, willingness to help, obedience to rules, and attendance at non-mandatory meetings influence OCB. With job satisfaction as the independent variable and OCB as the dependent variable, it aims to establish whether job satisfaction significantly impacts OCB and institutional performance.

Objectives of the Study

- To determine the factors influencing job satisfaction.
- To measure the employees organizational citizenship behavior in the unit.
- To measure the impact of job satisfaction on employees' organizational citizenship behavior.

Limitation of the Study

- The study focuses on the select IT company in the select city.
- The company provided limited time to access information.
- The study was conducted within a limited time period.
- Employees were unresponsive and busy, making it difficult to collect data.

[a]drramadevi77@gmail.com

Review of Literature

Table 115.1 Impact of organizational behavior on employee performance and satisfaction: a comparative study across sectors.

Author name	Year	Study	Findings
Shrestha andBhattarai	2022	Relationship between job satisfaction and OCB in education	Positive correlation between job satisfaction and OCB, enhancing teachers' performance and student achievement.
Dorta-Afonso et al.	2023	Impact of high-performance work systems on job satisfaction in hospitality	Identified burnout as a mediating factor linking high-performance work systems to employee outcomes in tourism and hospitality.
Albloush et al.	2020	Influence of OCB on job performance in Greater Amman Municipality	OCB positively impacts job performance, with perceived training opportunities partially mediating this relationship.

Source: Author

Research Methodology

- **Research design**: Utilized a descriptive design focusing on efficiently combining data collection and analysis with the study's relevance and purpose.
- **Descriptive studies**: Aim to describe characteristics of individuals or groups, focusing on specific predictions and narrating various aspects.
- **Sample design**: Involves studying a portion of the population to infer about the whole; random sampling was used in this study.
- **Sample size**: Based on employee opinions and expectations; 123 respondents were sampled for this study.
- **Simple random sampling**: Ensures each participant has an equal chance of selection, representing the broader population objectively.
- **Data collection methods**
- **Primary data**: Gathered through questionnaires distributed to employees in a select IT company.
- **Secondary data**: Sourced from pre-existing materials like web sites, publications, annual reports, and internet resources.
- **Analysis tools**:Applied ANOVA and factor analysis along with correlation techniques for data analysis.

Analysis and Interpretation

This study explores the intricate relationship between job satisfaction and OCB using a comprehensive five-factor model derived from 18 variables. The factors – Altruism, Courtesy, Sportsmanship, Conscientiousness, and Civic Virtue – encompass a range of behaviors from task performance to interpersonal relations, pivotal in shaping OCB within an organization. Correlation analysis reveals a strong interconnection between these factors, particularly altruism and courtesy. Further analysis through ANOVA and factor analysis demonstrates the varying impact of demographic factors like age, gender, education, and work experience on organizational commitment. This detailed examination provides crucial insights into the dynamics of job satisfaction and its significant influence on employee OCB.

Factor extraction for job satisfaction and OCB

A five-factor model was developed from 18 variables, focusing on OCB in job satisfaction.

- Factor 1: "Altruism" includes tasks, attitudes, company reputation, committee involvement, work preparation, organizational updates, and rule obedience.This factor is composed of seven items, ranging in loadings from 0.693 to 0.854. It includes behaviors like consistently performing assigned tasks (loading 0.888), maintaining a positive attitude (0.888), contributing to the company's reputation (0.707), being active in committees (0.673), completing pending work (0.673), staying updated with organizational changes (0.558), and obeying rules (0.548).
- Factor 2: "Courtesy covers initiation for organizational improvement, decision-making, task accomplishment, and compliance with company policies.Comprising four items, this factor's loadings range from 0.541 to 0.825.It encompasses initiating organizational betterment (0.825), readiness for positive change (0.798), completing challenging tasks (0.555), and following policies (0.541).
- Factor 3: "Sportsmanship" involves newcomer assistance, co-worker support, and organizing office celebrations.This factor includes three items, with

loadings from 0.568 to 0. 829.It involves helping newcomers (0.829), lending a hand to co-workers (0.662), and organizing office events (0.568).

- Factor 4: "Conscientiousness" includes volunteering for meetings and being mindful of others' jobs.Represented by two items, their loadings are 0.608 and 0.805.This includes volunteering for meetings or committees (0.805) and being mindful of others' work (0.608).
- Factor 5: "Civic virtue" relates to timely work completion and building internal relationships. Consisting of two items, with loadings of 0.641 and 0.839.It covers completing work on time (0.839) and making efforts for good internal relationships (0.641).

Correlation analysis

Key findings from correlation analysis:

- Volunteering for meetings or committees showed significant positive correlations with several behaviors, indicating its strong association with positive organizational actions.
- Organizing office celebrations positively correlated with other citizenship behaviors, highlighting its impact on workplace dynamics.
- Helping newcomers demonstrated a strong positive relationship with co-worker assistance, indicating a culture of support and orientation.
- Employees ready to make decisions for positive changes showed high correlations with other proactive behaviors, reflecting a commitment to organizational improvement.
- Efforts to build good relationships within the organization had notable correlations with other aspects of OCB, emphasizing the value of interpersonal relations at work.
- Mindful behavior affecting others' jobs showed significant positive correlations, underlining its importance in the work environment.
- Performance of assigned tasks had strong positive correlations with various elements of OCB, suggesting its integral role in overall job performance.
- Interpretation:The correlation values (ranging from 0.259 to 0.446) indicate a positive relationship between aspects like altruism and courtesy within the organizational context. This suggests that actions promoting altruism also enhance courteous behavior, contributing to a positive organizational culture.

ANOVA results
- Gender: No significant variance with organizational commitment.
- Age: Significant differences found, impacting organizational commitment.
- Education: No significant impact on organizational commitment.
- Work experience: Variances exist, affecting organizational commitment.
- Location: No significant correlation with organizational commitment.
- Salary: No significant variance with organizational commitment.

Total variance of 76.905% explained by all four factors in the model. Variance explained by individual factors varies before and after rotation, showing the significance of each component in influencing job satisfaction and employee OCB. These analyses provide comprehensive insights into the factors influencing job satisfaction and their impact on organizational citizenship behavior, revealing key areas for enhancing employee performance and satisfaction in organizational settings.

Factor analysis

Total variance of 76.905% explained by all four factors in the model.

Variance explained by individual factors varies before and after rotation, showing the significance of each component in influencing job satisfaction and employee OCB.

These analyses provide comprehensive insights into the factors influencing job satisfaction and their impact on organizational citizenship behavior, revealing key areas for enhancing employee performance and satisfaction in organizational settings.

Conclusion

The study's findings suggest a direct relationship between job satisfaction and organizational citizenship behavior (OCB), indicating that employees' discretionary behaviors can be positively influenced by enhancing various aspects of job satisfaction. Factors such as fair treatment, adequate salaries, benefits, allowances, supportive organizational climate, opportunities for career growth, and equitable promotion policies are pivotal in motivating staff. When employees feel valued and fairly compensated, they are more likely to engage proactively in activities that exceed their formal duties, thus contributing significantly towards achieving organizational goals.

In conclusion, the favorable link between job satisfaction and OCB underscores the importance of nurturing employee contentment within an organization. Job satisfaction not only boosts morale but also

Table 115.2 Eigen values factors underlying job satisfaction on employee's organizational citizenship behavior.

Component	Initial Eigenvalues	Extraction Sums of Squared Loadings		Rotation Sums of Squared Loadings					
	Total	% of Variance	Cumulative %	Total	% of Variance	Cumulative %	Total	% of Variance	Cumulative %
1	7.678	42.656	42.656	7.678	42.656	42.656	4.158	23.1	23.1
2	2.037	11.317	53.973	2.037	11.317	53.973	3.511	19.507	42.607
3	1.664	9.245	63.218	1.664	9.245	63.218	2.654	14.744	57.351
4	1.325	7.362	70.58	1.325	7.362	70.58	1.962	10.899	68.25
5	1.138	6.325	76.905	1.138	6.325	76.905	1.558	8.655	76.905
6	0.788	4.375	81.28						
7	0.743	4.126	85.406						
8	0.625	3.472	88.878						
9	0.459	2.551	91.429						
10	0.312	1.735	93.164						
11	0.299	1.663	94.826						
12	0.275	1.529	96.355						
13	0.218	1.214	97.569						
14	0.164	0.913	98.482						
15	0.156	0.869	99.351						
16	0.117	0.649	100						
17	2.17E-16	1.21E-15	100						
18	6.28E-17	3.49E-16	100						

Source: Author

encourages employees to exhibit discretionary behaviors that are beneficial to the organization. These findings highlight that OCBs are not just desirable traits but essential components for enhancing organizational performance and efficiency. As such, institutions should focus on strategies that enhance job satisfaction to leverage the potential benefits of OCB, thus fostering an environment where employees are motivated to contribute beyond their required roles for the overall betterment of the organization.

References

Albloush, A., Taha, S., Nassoura, A., Vij, A., Bohra, O. P., Masouad, N., et al. (2020). Impact of organizational citizenship behavior on job performance in Jordan: The mediating role of perceived training opportunities. *International Journal of Psychosocial Rehabilitation*, 24(5), 5584-5600. https://doi.org/10.37200/IJPR/V24I5/PR2020264.

Dorta-Afonso, D., Romero-Domínguez, L., and Benítez-Núñez, C. (2023). It's worth it! high performance work systems for employee job satisfaction: the meditational role of burnout. *Science Direct*, 108(10), 103364. https://doi.org/10.1016/j.ijhm.2022.103364.

Shrestha, M., and Bhattarai, P. C. (2022). Contribution of job satisfaction to organizational citizenship behavior: a survey of Nepal school teachers. *Journal of School Administration Research and Development*, 7(1), 36–49. Retrieved from https://files.eric.ed.gov/fulltext/EJ1343750.pdf.

116 A study on work-life balance among police personnel in Coimbatore city

Karthick , S. and Lakshmi Priya, N.[a]

Karpagam Academy of Higher Education, Coimbatore, Tamil Nadu, India

Abstract

This article delves into the significant challenge of achieving a healthy work-life balance for police officers, a critical aspect of their job satisfaction and overall well-being. Given the unpredictable nature of policing, coupled with long and irregular shifts, and the constant readiness for emergencies, police officers uniquely struggle to balance their professional responsibilities with personal and family needs. The article not only explores the root causes of these work-life balance issues within the police force but also proposes viable solutions. Emphasizing the importance of work-life balance for officer well-being, retention, organizational performance, and community relations, it underscores the necessity for police departments to support their officers in this endeavour. The article offers practical recommendations for police agencies to foster a more balanced work environment, ultimately contributing to the health and effectiveness of the police force.

Keywords: Police department,work-life balance

Introduction

In the demanding field of law enforcement, achieving a healthy work-life balance is crucial yet challenging. Police officers, committed to ensuring public safety, often face unforeseen difficulties and high-stress situations, which can adversely affect their personal life and well-being. Recognizing the importance of this balance, police departments globally are increasingly prioritizing their personnel's well-being. This article examines the concept of work-life balance within the police force, exploring the unique challenges officers face due to the unpredictable nature of their job, irregular shifts, and the need to be constantly available. It delves into the various factors impacting officers' ability to balance their professional and personal lives and discusses strategies and programs designed to assist them in achieving a more harmonious work-life balance.

Review of Literature

Table 116.1 Studies on work-life balance and stress factors in law enforcement personnel.

Author name	Reference	Study
Anju and Punia	2022	Work overload, role ambiguity, and excessive working hours contribute to work-life balance issues in police.
Yadav et al.	2022	Lack of guaranteed time off and consistent working hours among police despite peer and superior support.
Elango and Michael Fonceca	2021	Women police officials' job demands impede family time; work-life balance linked more to time management than salary.
Manojand Shivalingappa	2021	Challenges in balancing personal and professional lives for traffic police officers; suggests improved salaries and workplace conditions.
Banurekha et al.	2020	Studied organizational features, work hours, and family management affecting women in law enforcement.
Poonam Kaushal and Jai Singh Parmar	2019	Younger police officers struggle more with work-life balance due to various factors like extended working hours.
Naganandhini and Malliga	2019	Recommended implementing a shift system for police personnel.
Shanmughavadivu andSethuramSubbiah	2018	Moderate work-life balance and occupational stress in married women police.

[a]lakshmipriya.navaneethakrishnan@kahedu.edu.in

Author name	Reference	Study
Yawalkarand Sonawane	2016	Suggested a work-life balance model for police, including wellness and counselling programs.
Kazmi and Singh	2015	Correlation between job satisfaction, work-life balance, and stress in police.
Kaur and Jain	2014	Impact of autocratic behaviour of superiors on police subordinates' stress levels.

Source: Author

Problem Statement

The challenging work-life balance in police departments, marked by demanding, irregular shifts and high stress, significantly impacts officers' personal well-being, potentially leading to stress, burnout, strained relationships, lower job satisfaction, and increased attrition, thereby affecting the department's overall effectiveness.

Objective of the Study

To identify the work-life balance among police personnel in Coimbatore city

Research Methodology

Data: Primary data required for the study has been collected through questionnaire.

Sampling:Data was collected by employing a convenience sampling method from 160 respondents in Coimbatore city.

Tools employed

The collected data have been analyzed by Simple percentage and Factor Analysis.

Significance of the Study

The significance of this study stems from its potential to enhance police officers' well-being, boost organizational effectiveness, bolster public safety, and inform policy and practice improvements, thereby fostering a healthier and more sustainable work environment within police departments.

Scope of the Study

The study encompasses an analysis of police departments' existing policies and initiatives, such as shift scheduling, flexible work arrangements, time-off policies, wellness programs, and organizational culture, to assess their effectiveness in promoting a healthier work-life balance for police officers and identify potential areas for improvement.

Table 116.2 Assessment of data suitability: Kaiser-Meyer-Olkin and Bartlett's test results.

Kaiser-Meyer-Olkin measure of sampling adequacy.	0.798	
Bartlett's test of sphericity	Approx. Chi-square	2771.984
	df	630
	Sig.	0

Source: Author

Findings and Interpretation

In this section, we delve into the comprehensive results of a factor analysis conducted on a dataset collected from respondents within the police department in Coimbatore district. The analysis reveals fifteen distinct factors that shed light on various facets of work-life balance, ranging from job satisfaction and family responsibilities to challenges related to work-related conflicts and social engagements. These factors offer valuable insights into the intricate dynamics that influence the work-life equilibrium of police officers in the region. By understanding these factors, we aim to inform strategies and policies tailored to enhance the well-being and work-life balance of these dedicated professionals.

Key findings of the study:

- Age group: 35% aged 31-40.
- Education: 41.3% have HSC qualification.
- Marital status: 58.8% are married.
- Monthly income: 32.5% earned Rs. 35,001 - 45,000.
- Family Expenditure: 46.3% spent Rs. 25,001 - 35,000.
- Multiple earners: 56.3% have more than one family earner.
- Family type: 90% are in nuclear families.
- Relatives in police: 63.7% have no police relatives.
- Residential area: 37.5% live in rural areas.
- Designation: 33.8% are Police constables.

- Experience: 42.5% have experience in their role.
- Recruitment: 67.5% were directly recruited.
- Work zone: 38.8% work in the west zone.
- Facility satisfaction: 100% are satisfied with facilities.
- Working hours: 48.8% work over 12 hours. These findings inform demographics, income, family structure, recruitment, and work-life balance satisfaction, offering insights for tailored policies in the Coimbatore police department.

KMO and Bartlett's test

The KMO value and Bartlett's test of sphericity both indicate that the collected data is suitable for factor analysis. Specifically, the KMO value is greater than 0.70, which suggests that the data is highly suitable for factor analysis. Additionally, the large value of Bartlett's test of sphericity (2771.984, df: 630, sig. .000) further supports the appropriateness of factor analysis and indicates that the sample size is adequate for conducting the analysis. These results confirm that you can proceed with factor analysis to identify the prominent factors that determine the work-life balance of employees in the police department using the collected data. Factor analysis will help uncover underlying dimensions or factors that contribute to work-life balance in this specific context.

Factor analysis summary:Fifteen factors are identified by locating Eigen values greater than unity. Factors which have a component loading of 0.5 and above are said to be significant.

- Factor 1- Job satisfaction and clarityvariables: Pleasure in job, lack of job clarity, preference for teamwork.
- Factor 2- Work-related challengevariables: Difficulty attending parent-teacher meetings, workload distribution, extra hours dedication.
- Factor 3- Stress and household dutiesvariables: Struggle with household responsibilities, stress under tight deadlines.
- Factor 4- Meeting expectations and communicationvariables:Meeting colleagues' expectations, lack of communication during family emergencies.
- Factor 5- Family time and exam supportvariables: Helping children with exams, lack of time for family and friends.
- Factor 6- Work-life flexibility and pressurevariables: Flexibility in work schedule, work-related pressure in group tasks.
- Factor 7- Family well-being and caregivingvariables: Meeting family's basic needs, inability to care for sick family members.

- Factor 8- Social engagement challengesvariable: Struggle to attend and enjoy parties.
- Factor 9- Community involvement and multitaskingvariables: Participation in community activities, multitasking challenges.
- Factor 10- Expense and travel issuesvariables: Expense reimbursement challenges, discomfort with travel duration.
- Factor 11- Leave requests during emergenciesvariable: Ease of requesting leave during social emergencies.
- Factor 12- Social contributions and hostingvariables: Contributions to the underprivileged, hosting gatherings.
- Factor 13- Department privileges and financial obligationsvariables: Enjoying department privileges, managing financial obligations.
- Factor 14- Job preferencesvariable: Preference for working alone over with colleagues.
- Factor 15- Meeting supervisor expectations variable: Difficulty in meeting supervisor and senior expectations.

These factors provide insights into the complex dimensions affecting work-life balance among the respondents in the police department, helping inform strategies for improvement.

The study's findings reveal a multifaceted picture of work-life balance among police department respondents in Coimbatore district. Key results include a predominant age group of 31-40 years, with HSC as the most common educational qualification, and a significant portion married with monthly incomes ranging from Rs. 35,001 to 45,000. Family dynamics highlight a prevalence of nuclear families, while direct recruitment and extended working hours are common. Factor analysis identifies 15 distinct factors, shedding light on various aspects of work-life balance, such as job satisfaction, stress, and social engagement. These insights inform potential strategies to enhance the well-being of police officers, facilitating improved work-life equilibrium.

Conclusion

In conclusion, prioritizing work-life balance for employees in the Coimbatore district police department is paramount for their well-being and job satisfaction. The findings from our study, facilitated by factor analysis, have provided valuable insights into the multifaceted nature of work-life equilibrium. These insights, in turn, have led to a range of meaningful suggestions for enhancing work-life balance within the department.

Our recommendations encompass various aspects of job design, organizational policies, and support mechanisms, all aimed at fostering a harmonious blend of personal and professional life for police officers. These measures include promoting clarity in job objectives, encouraging teamwork, addressing meeting conflicts, equitable workload distribution, family support initiatives, time management training, employee assistance programs, recognition of work-life balance efforts, community engagement opportunities, administrative streamlining, professional development, enhanced supervisor support, and the encouragement of regular breaks and vacations.

By implementing these suggestions, the Coimbatore district police department can create an environment that not only supports its officers' well-being but also boosts overall job satisfaction and productivity. Prioritizing work-life balance is not just a moral imperative; it is an investment in the department's efficiency and effectiveness. Ultimately, by embracing these measures, the police department can set a positive example and lead the way in promoting work-life equilibrium in the demanding field of law enforcement.

References

Anju, M., and Punia, B. K. (2022). Organisationalpredictors of work-life conflicts amongst police personnel in Indian state. *Journal of Positive School Psychology*, 6, 1979–1998.

Banurekha, R., Saranya, K., Sachin, S. S., and Praveen, M. A. (2020). Work-life balance of police in India. *International Journal of Research in Engineering and Management*,4246–253.

Elango, L., and Michael Fonceca, C. (2021). Data on work-life balance experienced by women police officials of Tirupattur District, Tamil Nadu, India. *International Journal of Aquatic Science*, 12(02), 667–673. ISSN: 2008-8019.

Kaur, R.,and Jain, P. (2014). Work and family life balance among police personnel: acase study of Punjab Police .

Kazmi, A. B., and Singh, A. P. (2015). Work-life balance, stress, and coping strategies as determinants of job satisfaction among police personnel. *Indian Journal of Health and Wellbeing*, 6(12), 1244, ISSN-p-2229-5356, e-2321-3698.

Manoj, H. R.,andShivalingappa, B. P. (2021). Work-life balance among police personnel with special reference to traffic police personnel. *Journal of Emerging Technologies andInnovative Research*, 8(11).

Naganandhini, J., and Malliga, A. L., (2019). Social and family factors influencing the work-life balance of employees in Tamilnadu police service with special reference to Dindigul district. *International Journal of Southern Economic Light (JSEL)*, 7, 2019–2020, Print ISSN: 2277-5692.

Shanmughavadivu, N., and Sethuramasubbiah, A. (2018). Occupational stress and work-life balance among married women police. *International Journal of Research in Social Sciences*, 8(1), 746–761, ISSN: 2249-2496, Impact Factor: 7.081.

Yadav, R., Khanna, A., and Chenab (2022). Quality of work life, emotional and physical well-being of police personnel in India. *International Journal of Police Science and Management*, 24(1), 89–99.

Yawalkar, V. V., and Sonawane, M. A. (2016). A study of work-life balance; challenges before jalgaonpolice department. ISSN (ONLINE): 2250-0758, ISSN (PRINT): 2394-6962. *International Journal of Engineering and Management Research*, 6(1),82–84.

117 Job satisfaction of Neyveli Lignite corporation limited workers

Kamalesh, S.[a], Dhivyadharshini, M.[b] and Saranya, T.[c]

Karpagam Academy of Higher Education, Coimbatore, Tamil Nadu, India

Abstract

Job satisfaction profoundly impacts employee well-being and organizational success. This abstract outline a study focusing on job satisfaction among Neyveli Limited employees, a prominent Indian public sector entity. The research explores factors influencing job satisfaction and their implications for job performance and organizational outcomes. Using standardized scales and open-ended interviews, the study assessed pay, work-life balance, career growth, supervision, and workplace environment. Preliminary findings indicate moderate to high job satisfaction levels among Neyveli Limited workers. Notably, competitive compensation, career opportunities, supportive supervision, and a positive work environment significantly contribute to their satisfaction. This summary offers a concise insight into the study on Neyveli Limited employees' job satisfaction. The comprehensive research report provides detailed survey analysis, interview insights, and recommendations to enhance overall job satisfaction within the organization.

Keywords: Job satisfaction, NeyveliLignite Corporation Limited, public sector.

Introduction

Job satisfaction significantly impacts employees' overall well-being and performance within an organization, representing their subjective assessment of fulfillment and contentment at work. Understanding employees' job satisfaction is pivotal for creating a positive work atmosphere, boosting morale, and increasing productivity. This study focuses on scrutinizing the job satisfaction among Neyveli Limited employees, a key player in India's power generation and mining sectors, employing a diverse workforce across various departments.

Factors influencing job satisfaction encompass compensation, job security, career growth, work-life balance, autonomy, work environment, and relationships. This research combines quantitative and qualitative methods, employing surveys to gauge various dimensions like pay, security, promotions, and qualitative interviews to delve deeper into employees' experiences.

Ultimately, this study aims to furnish insights for Neyveli Limited's management, pinpointing areas of satisfaction and potential improvements. It contributes to the job satisfaction discourse, especially in public sector organizations, offering recommendations to elevate employee satisfaction and foster a more motivated workforce, thus enhancing organizational effectiveness. Table117.1 summarizes the literature review.

Table 117.1 Literature review.

Authors	Study findings
Velmurugan and Menon (2021)	Found that the working environment, recognition from management, promotion policies, career development opportunities, and the adoption of technology significantly impact employees' job satisfaction.
Somasekharan and Velmurugan (2018)	Discovered that job satisfaction and quality of work life in private sector banks are influenced by factors like age, gender, educational qualification, working conditions, and career growth opportunities. They highlighted differences in expectations between age groups and the importance of addressing these generational disparities. Also, emphasized the role of gender biases and the need for an inclusive work environment.
Pandey and Khare (2016)	Explored the relationship between job satisfaction, organizational commitment, and employee loyalty in manufacturing and service industries. They found that higher job satisfaction and organizational commitment positively influence employee loyalty. Identified factors affecting loyalty, such as leadership quality, career development, work-life balance, and job security.

[a]kamaleshshanthi@gmail.com, [b]saikutti1997@gmail.com, [c]saranyaveerakkumar93@gmail.com

Authors	Study findings
Singh and Jain (2016)	Stressed the importance of employee job satisfaction in maintaining productivity, addressing workforce needs, and creating a work environment conducive to exceptional performance and work-life balance.
Velmurugan(2016)	Identified salary, working time, professional growth opportunities, and work autonomy as significant factors influencing teacher job satisfaction. Higher salaries, reasonable workloads, professional development, and decision-making autonomy positively impacted job satisfaction among teachers. Mentioned the impact of relationships, recognition, resources, student engagement, and school environment on satisfaction.
Prabhaharan et.al (2014)	Concluded that HRM practices significantly impact job satisfaction, job involvement, work ethics, and pay practices. Highlighted the positive relationship between HRM practices and employee motivation, as well as the negative impact of poor practices on turnover.
BakoticandBabic (2013)	Emphasized the importance of improving working conditions to enhance job satisfaction, particularly for workers facing challenging environments.
Damodaran (2011)	Identified employment status as a significant determinant of employee job satisfaction, noting variations due to economic and organizational benefits.

Source: Author

Problem Statement

The problem focuses on evaluating current job satisfaction levels among Neyveli Limited employees, crucial for identifying improvement areas. It involves examining facets like compensation, career growth, work-life balance, supervisor support, and company culture. Addressing challenges such as inadequate compensation, limited career growth, or unsupportive culture allows targeted interventions for enhanced satisfaction, fostering a positive work environment and organizational outcomes.

Study Objective and Scope

The goals are to gauge workspace awareness, assess work life quality, and pinpoint factors impacting job satisfaction levels.

This study investigates the factors influencing job satisfaction among NLC employees, considering both internal and external aspects. Internally, employee reorganization plays a role, while external factors encompass economic benefits and personal characteristics. Moreover, organizational care for employee welfare, such as leave policies and medical allowances, can reduce inequality, affecting both productivity and job satisfaction.

Research Methodology

The sampling design involved gathering data through convenience sampling from 160 respondents in Cuddalore district. The analysis framework encompassed methods such as simple percentage, T-Test, weighted average, and factor analysis. simple percentage analysis categorized respondents by their demographic and socio-economic profiles, while the independent sample 'T' Test compared means between independent groups. Weighted average rank was employed to enhance data accuracy by multiplying each data point value by an assigned weight and summing them. Factor analysis aimed to discern significant factors affecting the impact of Chinese product requirements on employability. The study's significance lies in shedding light on the neglect of employee welfare in industries despite their contribution to economic growth. It emphasizes organizations' responsibility for employee well-being and underscores the value of job satisfaction in enriching the workforce, providing insights to achieve higher job satisfaction.

Findings

The data indicates demographic and professional details of 160 respondents. In terms of age, individuals between 25 to 35 years constitute 28.8%, followed by 36 to 40 years (22.5%), 41 to 45 years (30.0%), and above 50 years (18.8%). Gender distribution shows 100.0% male respondents and no female representation. Marital status indicates that 82.5% are married, while 17.5% are unmarried. Regarding education qualifications, SSLC holders constitute 35.0%, followed by ITI (32.5%), diploma (26.3%), and Degree holders (6.3%). Experience distribution reveals 36.3% with 6 to 10 years, 38.1% with 11 to 15 years, and 25.6% with above 20 years of experience. Salary-wise, 6.3% earn below 15000, 23.8% between 20000-30000, 46.3% between 40000-50000, and 23.8% above 60000. Finally, 82.5% work up to 8 hours, while 17.5% work beyond 8 hours.

The gathered data for Neyveli Limited workers' job satisfaction appears ideal for factor analysis. Initial tests - Kaiser-Meyer-Olkin (KMO) and Bartlett's test

Table 117.2 KMO And Bartlett's test.

KMO and Bartlett's test		
Kaiser-Meyer-Olkin measure of sampling adequacy.		.79
Bartlett's test of sphericity	Approx. Chi-square	985.54
	df	105
	Sig.	0.0

Source: Author

of sphericity - were conducted. KMO, measuring sample adequacy, exceeded 0.70, signaling suitability for factor analysis. Bartlett's test, with a statistic of 877.366 and p < 0.05, confirmed the data's appropriateness. These results affirm that the data is fit for factor analysis, enabling the identification of key factors affecting job satisfaction among Neyveli Limited workers.

Rotated Component Matrix

The correlations between survey items and identified components. The matrix features five components, each associated with specific survey statements. For instance, component 1 reflects opinions related to compensation fairness, job interest, and potential testing. Component 2 encompasses sentiments regarding the impact of supervision on job performance and the realization of career ambitions. Component 3 involves perceptions about refreshing physical work situations, pollution-free environments, and pleasant work morale due to the surroundings. Component 4 pertains to supervision aligning personal and organizational goals, efficient rewards, and supportive superiors. Lastly, Component 5 includes aspects of supervision quality and well-maintained workplaces. These components aid in understanding the diverse factors influencing job satisfaction among the respondents.

The factor analysis conducted on data from Neyveli Limited workers reveals critical aspects influencing job satisfaction. This analysis identified five key factors based on variables with significant component loadings. These factors shed light on various dimensions impacting employees' contentment and fulfillment in their roles.

Factor 1 underscores the significance of fair compensation and the positive influence of supervision on job performance. This suggests that equitable pay and effective supervision play pivotal roles in fostering job satisfaction among the workforces.

Factor 2 highlights the importance of a refreshing work environment and the job's intrinsic interest. Factors such as physical work situations and a pollution-free environment contribute significantly to employees' comfort and satisfaction. An engaging and pleasant work environment enhances morale and positively impacts job satisfaction levels.

Factor 3 focuses on the direction provided by supervision and the acknowledgment of efficiency through rewards. This indicates that employees value guidance from their supervisors and feel motivated when their efforts are recognized and rewarded.

Factors 4 and 5 emphasize the challenging nature of the job that tests employees' potential and the quality of supervision received. These factors reflect the significance of career realization and the importance of supportive, attentive, and caring superiors.

The recommendations provided aim to address these key factors, considering the diverse workforce and their unique needs and aspirations. Encouraging diversity and inclusivity within the organization can be instrumental in promoting equal opportunities for all employees, irrespective of age, gender, or educational background. Creating policies and practices that foster diversity, and an inclusive work culture can significantly enhance job satisfaction.

Offering training and development programs can empower employees to progress in their careers and increase job satisfaction. It's essential to extend opportunities for further education and skill development beyond basic qualifications like SSLC or ITI, especially considering the workforce's educational profile.

Improving work-life balance emerges as another critical aspect, especially for employees with 11-15 years of experience. This can involve initiatives such as flexible working hours, wellness programs, and support for personal commitments, contributing to enhanced job satisfaction.

Regularly reviewing and ensuring competitive compensation and benefits packages aligned with industry standards is crucial. Benchmarking salaries against industry norms can attract and retain top talent, further enhancing job satisfaction levels.

Creating clear career paths and growth opportunities within Neyveli Limited is vital for employee motivation and retention. Promotions, skill development, and professional advancement avenues can significantly contribute to job satisfaction.

Fostering open communication and engagement can strengthen the sense of belonging among employees. Regular team-building activities, recognition programs, and inclusive decision-making processes can positively impact job satisfaction.

It's important to note that these recommendations should be customized according to Neyveli Limited's specific goals and work environment. Additionally, addressing grievances, empowering employee work styles, encouraging further education, retraining, and promoting family welfare can further enrich the work culture and job satisfaction at Neyveli Limited. These efforts collectively contribute to building a motivated, engaged, and satisfied workforce essential for the organization's success.

Future Studies

Engage in a comprehensive longitudinal study tracking changes in job satisfaction among Neyveli Limited workers to unveil trends and factors behind fluctuations. Conduct qualitative research via in-depth interviews or focus groups, unraveling nuanced aspects beyond quantitative measures. Explore organizational climate's impact, including leadership, communication, teamwork, and values on job satisfaction. Investigate external influences like industry trends, economics, and regulations on satisfaction levels and their interplay with internal factors. Evaluate Neyveli Limited's implemented initiatives, assessing their efficacy in enhancing job satisfaction and associated outcomes. By delving into these domains, further research can offer actionable insights, fostering improved job satisfaction and organizational success among Neyveli Limited workers.

Conclusion

The researchers aimed to assess employee job satisfaction in NLC Ltd., a public sector enterprise, painting a positive picture of satisfaction and job security from personal interviews. The atmosphere promotes skill enhancement, fostering a serene environment with close communication and effective grievance handling. Job satisfaction is vital, reflecting individual expectations and fulfillment. Employees take pride in serving NLC, with satisfaction playing a pivotal role in the organization's success.

The analysis of job satisfaction among Neyveli Limited workers employed factor analysis, confirming sample adequacy through KMO and Bartlett's Test. It identified five key factors influencing job satisfaction, accompanied by demographic insights, including age, gender, marital status, education, experience, salary range, job nature, and working hours.

General suggestions emerged, advocating diversity, professional growth, better work-life balance, competitive compensation, career advancement, and enhanced employee engagement. These recommendations are based on available data and require further in-depth exploration aligned with Neyveli Limited's specific context and objectives for more tailored conclusions.

References

Carmeli, A. (2005). Exploring determinants of job involvement: an empirical test among senior executives. *International Journal of Manpower*, 26, 457–472.

D'souza, A. (2011). A study on employee satisfaction with special reference to a.p.s.r.t.c. sangareddy bus depot. *Journal of Research in Commerce and Management*, 3(1), 61–69.

Hyz, A. (2010). Job satisfaction and employee performance of break banking staff; an empirical investigation. *Acta Universities Lodziensis*. 86–95 .

Martin, A., and Roodt, G. (2005). Perception of organizational commitment, job Satisfaction and turnover intentions in a post merger South African territory institution. *SA Journal of Industrial Psychology*, 34(1), 23–31.

Sahinidis, A. G., and Bouris, J. (2008). Employee perceived training effectiveness relationship to employee attitudes. *Journal of European Industrial Training*, 32(1), 63–76.

Shanmugam, A., and Velsamy, R. S. S.(2015). A study on the job satisfaction, job involvement and work ethics of the engineers of the neyveli lignite corporation limited. *Asia Pacific Journal of Research*, 1(11),163–170.

118 A study on ill effects on playing online video games in Karaikal

Mahendiran, R. and Soni Pawar, P.[a]

Karpagam Academy of Higher Education, Coimbatore, Tamil Nadu, India

Abstract

This study delves into the negative impacts of online video gaming on individuals in Karaikal, examining its physical, psychological, and social consequences. With the increasing popularity of online gaming, the research, through a survey of Karaikal's gaming community, investigates various aspects such as gaming duration, physical health, psychological well-being, academic performance, and social interactions. The analysis reveals that excessive gaming is linked to physical issues like sedentary lifestyles, poor posture, and obesity risks. Psychologically, it is associated with increased stress, anxiety, and depression. Academically, excessive gaming correlates with lower grades and diminished focus. Socially, it contributes to isolation and poor communication skills. These findings underscore the need for awareness of online gaming's potential harms and recommend promoting balanced gaming habits, physical activities, and real-world social engagement.

Keywords: Ill effects, playing online video games, Karaikal

Introduction

This study delves into the negative impacts of online video gaming on individuals in Karaikal, examining its physical, psychological, and social consequences. With the increasing popularity of online gaming, the research, through a survey of Karaikal's gaming community, investigates various aspects such as gaming duration, physical health, psychological well-being, academic performance, and social interactions. The analysis reveals that excessive gaming is linked to physical issues like sedentary lifestyles, poor posture, and obesity risks. Psychologically, it is associated with increased stress, anxiety, and depression. Academically, excessive gaming correlates with lower grades and diminished focus. Socially, it contributes to isolation and poor communication skills. These findings underscore the need for awareness of online gaming's potential harms and recommend promoting balanced gaming habits, physical activities, and real-world social engagement.

Review of literature

Table 118.1 Impacts of online gaming on academic performance and social behavior: a comparative study.

Author name	Reference	Study
Li, et al	2023	Found that online gaming fulfills personal growth, social needs, and enhances academic performance.
Rajathi and Ravisankar	2022	Revealed negative impacts of online gaming on educational performance, leading to poor grades and physical distress.
Pajarillo-Aquin	2019	Discovered high academic performance in respondents despite engagement in online gaming.
Aswathy et al.	2019	Reported a high addiction rate to adventure games like PUBG among males in Ernakulam, causing health issues and reduced social interactions.
Valdez et al.	2020	Demonstrated that online gaming alleviates stress, enhances teamwork, and improves academic understanding, but cautioned against addiction.
Aviso et al.	2021	Observed the rise of online gaming in the Philippines due to COVID-19, highlighting both mental health risks and cognitive benefits.
Garcia et al.	2018	Players acknowledged online gaming's negative impact on academic performance.
Dumrique and Castillo	2017	Found positive effects of online gaming on social behavior and academic performance, with respondents maintaining good grades.

Source: Author

[a]sonipawar2008@gmail.com

Problem Statement

This study aims to investigate the adverse effects of playing online video games on individuals in Karaikal, focusing on the impact on their physical health, psychological well-being, academic performance, and social interactions, with the goal of developing strategies to promote responsible gaming and improve overall well-being.

Objective of the Study

To identify the Ill effects on playing online video games

Scope of the Study

This study aims to explore the negative impacts of online video gaming among Karaikal residents, examining physical health, psychological state, academic performance, and social interactions. Involving a diverse range of gamers, it employs a survey method to gather data on their gaming habits and related well-being aspects. While focused on online gaming's ill effects and based on self-reported data, this research will offer crucial insights for promoting responsible gaming and enhancing individual well-being in Karaikal.

Research Methodology

The study's necessary data was gathered through a questionnaire. Questions focus on the profile of the impact of online video game usage, preferences, and issues.

Data collection: Primary data was collected using a structured questionnaire, distributed in both hard and soft copy formats, focusing on the impact and issues related to online video game usage.

- **Source of data:** The questionnaire was designed to gather detailed information about online video gaming habits, preferences, and associated problems among the respondents.
- **Sampling design:** Utilized convenience sampling to collect data from 150 school students in Karaikal city, chosen for their accessibility and practicality within the study's context.
- **Sampling limitations:** Acknowledges the limitations of convenience sampling, including potential non-representativeness and limited generalizability of findings to the broader population of school students in Karaikal.
- **Area of study:** Focused on Karaikal city, specifically 17 out of 32 towns, including Edatheru, Keezhaiyur (South), and Kottucherry, among others, to gather diverse responses.

- **Framework of analysis:** Employed Simple Percentage Analysis and Factor Analysis to interpret the collected data and draw conclusions about the effects of online gaming.

Significance of the Study

This study on the ill effects of online gaming in Karaikal is significant as it raises awareness about the negative consequences of excessive gaming, such as sedentary behavior, poor posture, and obesity risks. It also explores psychological impacts like increased stress and anxiety, highlighting the need for mental health support. Additionally, the study examines the detrimental effects on academic performance and social interactions, prompting the development of educational strategies and social skill enhancement. Ultimately, it aims to guide policy and interventions for healthier gaming habits in Karaikal.

Limitations of the Study

This study on online gaming's ill effects in Karaikal faces limitations, including potential sampling bias impacting generalizability, and relies on self-reported data prone to recall or social desirability bias. Focusing solely on online gaming, it may not fully reflect the range of gaming impacts or capture long-term effects, necessitating caution in interpreting causality.

Significance of the Study

This study on online gaming's ill effects is crucial, highlighting its growing prevalence and potential risks to public health, particularly for vulnerable groups like children and adolescents. It explores the psychological impact, including addiction and mental health issues, and its influence on educational outcomes and social relationships. The findings guide policies, interventions, and strategies for responsible gaming, supporting mental health professionals, educators, and families in managing and mitigating these effects.

Analysis and Interpretation

The study conducted in Karaikal city delves into the multifaceted ill effects of playing online video games among its youth. Focused on a demographic primarily between 10-20 years, predominantly higher secondary students in urban settings, this research investigates the intricate dynamics of gaming's impact on various aspects of life. Utilizing factor analysis, the study explores how excessive gaming intertwines with mental and physical health, educational performance, and social behavior. This introduction sets the stage for a nuanced exploration of the complexities surrounding online gaming habits, highlighting their prevalent nature and the diverse challenges they pose to young individuals in Karaikal. The study on the ill effects of playing online video games in Karaikal city reveals several insights:

- **Demographics**: The predominant age group engaged in online gaming is 10-15 years, with a significant number of higher secondary students and most living in urban areas. Families with four members are common among gamers.
- **Gaming preferences**: Adventure games are favored, and most gamers use their parents' gadgets, typically playing for about an hour.
- **Factor analysis**: The data is suitable for factor analysis, indicated by the KMO measure (.742) and Bartlett's test (Chi-square 449.197, Sig. .000).
- **Ill effects - factor 1**: Interpersonal conflict, poor emotional regulation, and lack of motivation are key issues, with loadings of .761, .652, and .546 respectively.
- **Ill Effects - factor 2**: Health concerns such as obesity, exhaustion, and suicidal thoughts are significant, with component loadings of .891, .685, and .588.
- **Ill Effects - factor 3**: Financial losses in games, cross-platform issues, and addiction have loadings of .705, .695, and .662.
- **Ill Effects - factor 4**: Behavioral issues like short temper and prolonged gadget use are noted, with loadings of .806 and .751.
- **Ill effects - factor 5**: Mental disturbance and educational impact are critical, with loadings of .841 and .812.

These factors and their loadings indicate the strength of their association with the negative impacts of online gaming. This comprehensive analysis provides a deep understanding of the various dimensions of how online gaming affects individuals in Karaikal.

The study in Karaikal revealed significant insights into the consequences of online gaming among young individuals. Most participants, primarily adolescents, showed a strong preference for adventure games, with usage mostly on family gadgets. Notably, one-hour gaming sessions were most common. Factor analysis identified five key areas of concern: interpersonal conflict, health issues like obesity and exhaustion, addictive behaviors including monetary loss, temperamental changes due to prolonged device use, and negative impacts on mental health and education. These findings underscore the multifaceted influence of online gaming on young individuals, highlighting the need for balanced gaming habits to mitigate adverse effects on health, behavior, and academic performance.

Conclusion

The study on the ill effects of playing online video games in Karaikal offers critical suggestions for mitigating these adverse impacts. Key among these is regulating gaming time to prevent overindulgence and ensuring regular breaks during sessions to avoid mental and physical fatigue. It's essential to balance virtual gaming with real-life interactions, fostering healthy relationships and emotional well-being. Implementing emotional regulation strategies and maintaining physical health through exercise, balanced diet, and sufficient sleep can counteract sedentary gaming habits. Additionally, mindful financial management in gaming, especially regarding in-game purchases, can prevent monetary losses and associated stress.

In conclusion, the study underscores the multifaceted negative effects of online gaming, highlighting issues like interpersonal conflicts, emotional and motivational challenges, health problems, financial losses, addiction, and educational impacts. Addressing these requires a holistic approach, combining time management, emotional and physical health maintenance, and financial prudence. These measures, alongside professional support for severe cases, can foster a healthier gaming culture. Future research should delve deeper into psychological, cognitive, social, and physiological aspects, exploring age-specific impacts, different gaming genres, and cultural influences. Understanding these factors will pave the way for effective interventions, promoting balanced gaming habits and overall well-being.

References

Aswathy, V., Devika, E., and Girish, S. (2019). A study on impact of online gaming and its addiction among youth with special reference to Kerala. *International Journal of Management, IT and Engineering, 9*(6).

Aviso, A., Bachelor, Maderazo, M., Katleene, A., Castro, C. J., Quiroga, C. J., Espineda, J., and Vincent, V. (2021). Impact on the behavior of students due to online technology gaming and its effect on their academic performance .

Garcia, K., Jarable, N., and Paragas, J. (2018). Negative effects of online games on academic performance. *Southeast Asian Journal of Science and Technology, 3*(1). Available at: https://www.sajst.org/sajst/article/download PDF.

Li, F., Zhang, D., Wu, S., Zhou, R., Dong, C., and Zhang, J. (2023). Positive effects of online games on the growth of college students: a qualitative study from China. *Frontiers in Psychology*, 14, 1008211. https://doi.org/10.3389/fpsyg.2023.1008211.

Pajarillo-Aquin, I. (2019). The effect of online games on the academic performance of the students in the college of teacher education. *International Journal of Advanced Research in Management and Social Sciences,* 8(3), 74–86.

Rajathi, V. M. A., and Ravisankar, S. (2022). A study on the impact of online games to the academic performance of the students in Tamilnadu (Dharmapuri District).

International Journal of Research Publication and Reviews, 3(6), 4526–4532.

Valdez, F., Baylen, R., Bustamante, A., Cabiles, G., Vallente, A. M., and Ablen, A. (2020). Effects of online gaming on academic performance of GAS students at Bestlink college of the Philippines. *Ascendens Asia Singapore – Bestlink College of the Philippines Journal of Multidisciplinary Research,* 2(1).

119 Employee retention with reference to IT sector in Coimbatore

M. Pavithra[a] and G. Sumathi[b]

Karpagam Academy of Higher Education, India

Abstract

Employee retention poses a critical challenge for organizations, notably within the swiftly expanding information technology (IT) sector. This study endeavors to scrutinize the determinants impacting employee retention within IT firms situated in Coimbatore, a key city in India's IT domain. It delves into various factors influencing retention, encompassing organizational culture, salary structures, career growth opportunities, and work-life equilibrium. By drawing insights from this research, the study aims to furnish recommendations for enhancing staff retention strategies tailored to Coimbatore's IT firms. These recommendations will primarily focus on fortifying work-life harmony, augmenting professional advancement avenues, refining compensation and benefits, and fostering a nurturing organizational ethos.

Keywords: Career development, Coimbatore, compensation, employee retention, IT sector, job satisfaction, organizational culture, work-life balance

Introduction

The information technology (IT) industry has seen remarkable growth in Coimbatore, Tamil Nadu, emerging as a crucial sector for economic advancement. However, retaining skilled personnel has become a challenge due to fierce competition. High turnover rates disrupt growth and productivity, prompting Coimbatore-based IT firms to seek methods to enhance employee happiness, engagement, and loyalty. This study focuses on understanding factors influencing employee retention in the city's IT industry. It aims to identify variables impacting workers' decisions to stay or leave their jobs, enabling tailored strategies for retention. The study delves into organizational culture, professional growth opportunities, compensation, and work-life balance as critical retention factors specific to Coimbatore's IT sector. By examining these aspects, the research aims to address unique challenges faced by local organizations. Findings will offer actionable insights to enhance personnel retention strategies for Coimbatore IT firms and contribute valuable knowledge to HR experts and researchers. Ultimately, the study's objective is to equip organizations with effective strategies to bolster retention, foster loyalty, and maintain a competitive edge in Coimbatore's IT market.

Literature Review

Author	Study focus	Method	Key findings
Comfort Osaro (2017)	Talent management and employee retention in textile companies	Survey research, utilizing previous findings	Significant relationship between talent strategies and staff retention
Muppuri. Nagabhaskar (2017)	Motivating factors influencing employee retention	Analysis of motivating factors	Identified factors: monetary incentives, job characteristics, career progression, recognition, management, work-life balance
Bidisha Lahkar Das, Dr. Mukulesh Baruah (2018)	Review of employee retention research	Literature review, identification of influencing factors	Emphasized factors: pay practices, leadership, career development, flexible work schedules, working environments
Bliss (2019)	Impact of employee departure on organizations	Analysis of productivity loss and knowledge transfer	Loss of output, social capital, and clients; knowledge transfer to competitors

[a]mpavithra.9272@gmail.com, [b]sumathiganesh18@gmail.com

Author	Study focus	Method	Key findings
Hendricks (2019)	Retention challenges in organizations	Examination of retaining highly qualified personnel	Struggles in retaining in-demand skilled workers
Jane (2019)	Use of trainers as retention tools	Assessment of training programs' impact	Importance of strategic training for recruitment and retention
St. Thomas, Minneapolis, MN (2020)	Motivational elements and organizational behavior	Exploration of motivational theories	Application of theories to explain staff retention
Ramlall (2020)	Forecasting the cost of employee turnover	Estimation of turnover cost	Estimated turnover cost equaling 150% of employee yearly wage
Bender (2020)	Competence transfer and retention	Focus on global knowledge transfer	Significance of global assignments in knowledge dissemination
Abassi and Hollman (2021)	Impact of dysfunctional turnover	Examination of dysfunctional turnover	Hindrance to innovation, services, productivity
Dawkin, Reich (2021)	Research on customer retention rates	Analysis of client relationship duration	Extended client relationship linked to higher retention percentages

Source: Author

Problem Statement

Employee retention poses a significant challenge in Coimbatore's IT industry due to the high demand for skilled workers and the numerous career prospects available to them. Elevated turnover rates negatively impact an organization's growth, stability, and productivity. Hence, it becomes imperative to identify the causes behind employee churn and devise actionable strategies to retain talented IT professionals. Understanding the factors influencing employee retention, such as competitive compensation and benefits, and cultivating a robust organizational culture to address these elements, is crucial. The study seeks to address the following research question:

What are the primary factors affecting employee retention in Coimbatore's IT sector?

By addressing these research inquiries, the study endeavors to shed light on the unique challenges faced by IT organizations in Coimbatore concerning employee retention. The resultant conclusions aim to assist organizations in formulating strategies that enhance employee satisfaction, engagement, and loyalty, thereby reducing turnover rates and enhancing organizational performance.

Objective: To identify the factors influencing employee retention in the IT Industry. Table 119.1. Socio economic profile of respondents examining the unique difficulties faced by organizations in this area are the problems that this study seeks to solve. Organizations may undertake focused efforts to improve work-life balance, give professional development opportunities, provide

Research Methodology

This study is based on descriptive research design and involved in administering questionnaires as a tool for research work. Data has been collected from the employees of the IT industries. For the present study simple random sampling method was used. A total of 120 IT respondents have been selected as sample. The questionnaire used in this study. To analyze the data, the simple percentage method and Factor analysis method has been used.

Significance of the Study

The study's implications for various stakeholders in Coimbatore's IT sector, including businesses, employees, HR professionals, and researchers, are substantial. Its significance lies in the provision of valuable insights to IT firms, enabling them to enhance their employee retention programs by pinpointing factors influencing staff turnover. This allows for tailored initiatives addressing job satisfaction, career growth, work-life balance, compensation, and company culture, ultimately fostering a stable and proficient workforce, reducing turnover rates, and retaining top talent. For IT industry workers in Coimbatore, the study's conclusions shed light on elements influencing their job satisfaction and decisions to stay with their employers. It empowers them to make informed career choices, considering factors crucial for job retention. Moreover, it could pave the way for improved career development schemes, a better work-life balance, and a more inclusive organizational environment, enhancing overall working conditions. Human resource professionals are pivotal in ensuring employee retention. The study's findings offer actionable insights for HR experts, aiding in tailoring retention strategies to Coimbatore's IT industry's unique requirements. These conclusions can guide HR practices, policies, and initiatives geared toward bolstering retention rates through the promotion of positive organizational cultures, improved work-life balance, and heightened job satisfaction. Contributing to existing knowledge, the study delves into the intricacies of employee retention within Coimbatore's IT industry. It enriches understanding of factors impacting retention and highlights challenges specific to this sector. These findings serve as a platform for further research, exploring additional contextual factors influencing employee retention. Ultimately, the study's significance lies in its potential to boost job satisfaction, elevate retention rates, and foster a conducive work environment within Coimbatore's IT sector.

Data Analysis and Interpretation

The survey results highlight a predominant presence of females, constituting 75.0% of the respondents. A substantial 35% belong to the age group below 25 years. Marital status reflects a majority of approximately 56.67% being married individuals. Educationally, a significant 66.6% hold qualifications at the Under graduate level. Additionally, the survey reveals that 40.8% of respondents reported a monthly income below 15000 units.In our sample of 120 participants, 75.0% were female, and 25.0% were male.

Regarding age distribution, 35.0% were up to 25 years old, 29.2% were between 25 and 31 years old, 20.0% were between 31-50 years, and 15.8% were above 50 years. Marital status reflected 56.67% being married, and 43.33% were unmarried. Educationally, 66.67% held undergraduate degrees, 25% were postgraduates, and 8.33% possessed professional qualifications. Lastly, in terms of monthly income, 40.8% earned below Rs. 15,000, 30.0% earned between Rs. 15,001 and Rs. 25,000, 16.7% earned between Rs. 25,001 and Rs. 35,000, 8.3% earned between Rs. 35,001 and Rs. 45,000, and 4.2% earned above Rs. 45,000.

Factor Analysis

To identify the prominent factors that influence the employee retention in IT industry, factor analysis is employed. Kaiser-Meyer-Olkin (KMO) and Bartlett's test of sphericity has been used as pre-analysis testing for suitability of the entire sample for factor analysis.

Table 119.1 KMO and Bartlett's test.

Kaiser-Meyer-Olkin measure of sampling adequacy.		.898
Bartlett's test of sphericity	Approx. Chi-square	4958.456
	df	741
	Sig.	.000

Source: Author

Rotated component matrix[a]							
	Component						
	1	2	3	4	5	6	7
Opportunities for innovation	.819						
Employee surveys and feedback	.814						
Diversity and inclusion efforts	.769						
Effective communication channels	.580						
Workload management	.560						
Employee empowerment and autonomy	.555						
Employee wellness initiatives	.516						
Career development opportunities	.512						
Communication and transparency	.512						
Transparent career progression paths		.812					
Strong leadership development programs		.795					
Workforce diversity and inclusion		.728					
Employee well-being initiatives		.702					
Employee feedback and suggestions mechanisms		.661					

Rotated component matrix[a]

	Component						
	1	2	3	4	5	6	7
Collaborative and supportive team culture		.633					
Employee benefits and perks		.594					
Performance-based incentives		.523					
Conflict resolution and supportive environment			.687				
Performance feedback and evaluation			.640				
Employee engagement			.607				
Work-life balance			.591				
Recruitment and on boarding process			.569				
Competitive compensation and benefits				.706			
Employee retention metrics and analytics				.671			
Meaningful employee involvement in decision making				.650			
Recognition and rewards				.554			
Employee workload and resource management				.550			
Work environment and facilities					.640		
Flexible work arrangements					.629		
Challenging and meaningful work					.598		
Employee recognition programs						.727	
Team dynamics						.633	
Employee satisfaction surveys							.581
Continuous learning and skill development opportunities							.553

Source: Author

The result of KMO and Bartlett's Test is found greater than 0.70. Hence the collected data is fit for employing factor analysis. Further the large value of Bartlett's test of sphericity (4958.456, Df:898, Sig. .000) indicated the appropriateness of factor analysis i.e., the sample was adequate

Recommendations and Conclusions

Employee retention is pivotal in Coimbatore's IT sector, impacting key stakeholders. This study holds significance for IT firms, staff, HR, and researchers, revealing crucial retention elements for tailored strategies. It advocates an innovative, collaborative environment fostering employee ownership. Open communication, shaped by frequent surveys, enhances job satisfaction. Combating bias and promoting inclusivity through training is vital. Transparent communication channels inform staff of organizational decisions, while workload management aids work-life balance. Encouraging autonomy and career growth boosts employee satisfaction. Wellness programs and competitive benefits elevate well-being. Recognizing achievements and teamwork bolsters collaboration. Continuous learning

ensures industry relevance. Adapting these insights can revolutionize Coimbatore's IT landscape, retaining top talent, and ensuring organizational success. Tailoring these suggestions to fit workforce preferences is key for implementation. This study highlights critical factors, emphasizing innovation, inclusivity, and effective communication for robust retention strategies, imperative for sustained organizational growth and competitiveness.

References

Advantage in Bahrain post. *International Journal of Core Engineering and Management*, 4, 1–17 .

Abbasid and Holman (2018). Staff retention and empowerment: functions of leadership. *Clinical Laboratory Management Review*, 16(6), 391–398.

Campbell and Baldwin (2017). Employee Retention: Your Keyto Bottom Line Success. Vantage Point 2005.

Elangovan (2018). Buildinga high-retention culturein healthcare. *Clinical Laboratory Management Review*, 18(5), 259–266.

Gomez-Mejia, B., and Cardy (2019). Strategies for staff retention advance/lab admin. 13(2), 14.

Gupta, N. (2020). Retention of employee community health workers in Dhaka urban slums: a prospective cohort study. *Human Resources for Health*, 12(1), 1–11. Doi:10.1186/1478-4491-12-29.

Neumark, D. (2016). Organizational retention strategies and employee performance of zenith bank in Nigeria. *African Journal of Economic and Management Studies*, 1(1).

O'Meara and Petzall (2017). Retention management for the twenty-first century. *Harvard Business Review,* 86, 1–8.

Paskett, E. D. (2020). Human resource management. 9, 11, P.No.234-256.

Shao, Y. (2021). A review into talent management, talent retention and its scope for learning organizations. *International Journal of Knowledge Management and Practices*, 2(1), 1–11.

Sharma, S. (2016). A Study of Employee Retention Issues in the Textiles Industry. (6th edn.), American Psychological Association, (pp. 1–58).

Zheng and Lamond (2019). Strategic Management Theory. New York: Houghton Mifflin; 2004.

120 Financial inclusion of *Pradhan Mantri Jan Dhan Yojana* scheme in Dharapuram

Narmadha, R., Mathan Kumar, V.[a] and Naveena, R.[b]

Karpagam Academy of Higher Education, Coimbatore, Tamil Nadu, India

Abstract

The *Pradhan Mantri Jan Dhan Yojana* (PMJDY) scheme is an initiative launched by the Indian government with the aim of promoting financial inclusion among the marginalized sections of society. An overview of the PMJDY plan and its effects on achieving financial inclusion in India are given in this abstract. Its primary goals include ensuring that all people have access to banking services, fostering financial literacy, and ensuring everyone has access to credit, insurance, and pension plans. People are urged to create bank accounts under the plan that have no minimum balance restrictions. Account users get access to basic banking services such deposit accounts, remittances, overdraft options, and debit cards. Additionally, the program has a focus on offering accessible financial services, such as microinsurance and pension plans. The PMJDY scheme has been instrumental in advancing financial inclusion in India by providing access to banking services, promoting financial literacy, and facilitating the delivery of government benefits. While progress has been made, sustained efforts are necessary to ensure that individuals actively utilize the accounts and leverage the benefits offered by the scheme to improve their overall financial well-being.

Keywords: Financial inclusion, NITI Aayog, SDG, welfare schemes

Introduction

The *Pradhan Mantri Jan Dhan Yojana* (PMJDY) is a flagship financial inclusion program launched by the Government of India. It was launched on August 28, 2014, with the intention of giving the unbanked people access to complete financial services and fostering financial literacy across the nation. Every family in India is expected to have access to a basic banking account thanks to the PMJDY initiative. It focuses on assisting underserved groups in society, such as low-income people, women, and rural communities that have historically been shut out of the official financial system. The government wants to empower these people economically and build a more inclusive financial environment, so it gives them access to banking services. The provision of a zero-balance savings account, a RuPay debit card, and access to a variety of financial services are among the key components of the PMJDY plan. The accounts formed under this program include simple services including depositing and withdrawing money, sending money overseas, and accessing insurance and pension plans. Account holders can obtain credit through the program's overdraft capabilities, which allows them to meet their financial demands. The PMJDY scheme encourages the use of technology to enable easy banking services. To improve account holders' financial accessibility and convenience, it promotes the use of electronic payment systems, online banking, and mobile banking. The program also emphasizes fostering financial knowledge among account holders, empowering them to decide wisely about financial planning, investing, and saving. Since its start, the PMJDY plan has reached important milestones. A significant portion of the population has now entered the official financial system thanks to the opening of millions of bank accounts under the plan. Additionally, it has made it easier for the government to deposit subsidies, pensions, and other welfare payments directly into beneficiaries' bank accounts, improving the efficiency and transparency of social welfare program delivery. Overall, the PMJDY has become a key project in India's quest for financial inclusion. The program aims to improve the financial well-being of millions of economically disadvantaged citizens and contribute to the overall socio-economic development of the country by providing financial services to the unbanked population, giving people access to credit and insurance, and promoting financial literacy.

Literature Review

The PMJDY has garnered significant attention from researchers and scholars exploring the impact of the scheme on financial inclusion in India. The following review of literature provides an overview of key studies and findings related to the PMJDY.

[a]mathankumar010@gmail.com, [b]naveenasriram@gmail.com

1. Chandrasekaran and Niranjan (2016)study examines various government initiatives for financial inclusion in India, including the PMJDY. It highlights the scheme's success in expanding access to banking services and increasing the number of bank accounts. However, it also identifies challenges such as low utilization of accounts, inadequate financial literacy, and the need for better customer service.

2. Research article by Mishra (2017)evaluates the PMJDY as a catalyst for financial inclusion in India. It discusses the scheme's objectives, implementation, and impact on various sections of society. The study concludes that the PMJDY has contributed significantly to increasing financial inclusion, particularly among marginalized populations, but emphasizes the importance of addressing challenges related to account usage and financial literacy.

3. Study by Seth and Mahajan (2018)assesses the impact of the PMJDY on financial inclusion in India through an empirical analysis. It examines factors such as the number of accounts opened, deposits, and utilization patterns. The research highlights the scheme's success in bringing the unbanked population into the formal financial system but emphasizes the need for increased account usage and improved financial literacy.

4. Basu and Das (2019)study evaluates the effectiveness of the PMJDY in achieving financial inclusion objectives. It analyzes factors such as the number of accounts opened, account activity, and customer satisfaction. The research concludes that the scheme has significantly enhanced financial inclusion, particularly among marginalized sections, but recommends measures to improve account usage and promote financial literacy.

5. Sharma (2020)research article examines the impact of the PMJDY on financial inclusion and inclusive growth in India. It explores the scheme's achievements, challenges, and future prospects. The study concludes that the PMJDY has played a vital role in expanding financial inclusion and emphasizes the need for sustained efforts in improving account usage, financial literacy, and infrastructure.

Overall, the reviewed literature demonstrates that the PMJDYhas made significant strides in promoting financial inclusion in India. However, it also highlights the challenges related to account utilization, financial literacy, and service quality that need to be addressed to maximize the scheme's impact and ensure the sustained empowerment of marginalized populations.

Problem Statement

The Government of India has launched a large program for financial inclusion called the PMJDY. Although the program has significantly increased access to financial services, there are still a number of obstacles that must be overcome for it to be implemented successfully and succeed in the long run.

The limited use of accounts formed under the PMJDY program is one of the major issues. Many account users fail to actively use their accounts for deposits, transactions, and other banking activity, particularly in rural areas and low-income sectors. The intended advantages of financial inclusion are hampered by this lack of account activity, and the objective of empowering people economically is undermined.

The requirement for increased financial knowledge and awareness among PMJDY account users is another difficulty. Many people, especially those from socially marginalized groups, do not have the requisite knowledge and comprehension of financial ideas, goods, and services. This may result in underuse of the available banking resources and limit account users' capacity to make wise financial decisions.

It is a huge task to guarantee that PMJDY account holders across the nation receive high-quality banking services. Some places, especially those that are distant and rural, could have poor infrastructure and few banking options. Long wait times, limited access to ATMs, and poor customer service may discourage account users from regularly utilizing their accounts and reduce the scheme's overall efficacy.

While the PMJDY program seeks to increase financial inclusion across all facets of society, it is important to make sure that vulnerable populations including women, elderly people, and people with disabilities are also included. Addressing the particular difficulties these groups have in obtaining and using financial services under the plan deserves special consideration.

There is a higher danger of fraud and security breaches as a result of the proliferation of digital banking services and the usage of technology in the PMJDY program. Account holders could have trouble comprehending and implementing safe banking practices, which leaves them open to financial fraud and identity theft. To preserve confidence and protect the interests of PMJDY account holders, it is essential to implement strong security measures and to raise awareness of cybersecurity issues. The PMJDYmust be implemented well if it is to be successful in the long run. To maximize the advantages of financial inclusion for everybody, efforts should be made to encourage active account usage, develop financial literacy, raise service standards, ensure the inclusion of vulnerable groups, and bolster security measures.

Study Objectives

1. To measure intensity of utilization of PMJDY scheme.
2. To assess problem on utilization on PMJDY scheme.

Methodology

Data required for the study has been collected through an interview schedule. Questions pertain to profile of PMJDY scheme users on awareness, utilization, problems and satisfaction towards PMJDY Scheme.

Source of Data

The primary data are collected through a well framed and structured questionnaire.

Sampling Design

Data collected by employing convenience sampling method from 200 respondents in Dharapuramtaluk.

Frame Wok of Analysis

- Simple percentage
- Factor analysis
- Weighted average rank

Analysis and Interpretation

The following table narrates about socio-economic profile of the study.

1. Age distribution among the surveyed individuals indicates a dominant presence of respondents above the age of 41, comprising 76% of the total. In contrast, the younger age groups, particularly those aged 21-30, constitute a significantly smaller proportion, representing only 0.5% of the sample.
2. The gender distribution reveals a relatively balanced representation, with males constituting 52% and females representing 48% of the surveyed population, totaling 200 respondents.
3. Regarding educational qualifications, the majority of respondents possess Secondary School Leavingcertificate (SSLC), accounting for 58% of the sample. Illiterate individuals make up 25%, while Higher Secondary certificateHSC) holders represent 17% of the respondents.
4. Occupation-wise, the data demonstrates a significant majority engaged in agriculture, comprising 73.5% of the surveyed population. Other forms of employment, including self-employment, for-mal employment, and daily wage work, represent smaller proportions of 7.5%, 5.5%, and 15.5%, respectively.
5. A notable majority of respondents reside in rural areas, constituting 80% of the total population. In contrast, individuals residing in semi-urban areas represent a smaller yet considerable proportion, accounting for 20% of the sample.
6. Family type analysis reveals a dominance of nuclear families among the respondents, representing 66% of the surveyed population. Joint families, while significant, comprise a comparatively smaller proportion, constituting 34% of the sample.
7. Monthly income distribution showcases that a majority of individuals earn incomes between 25,001 and 50,000 units, accounting for 73.5% of the surveyed population. Those earning up to 25,000 units represent 10.5%, while earners above 50,000 units constitute 17% of the sample.
8. Monthly expenditure data indicates that a significant majority, 93%, spend between 12,001 and 50,000 units, reflecting a balanced expenditure pattern. A smaller proportion spends up to 12,000 units (5.5%), while only 2% report expenditures above 50,000 units.
9. Sources of information about the PMJDY Scheme vary, with the highest information source being relatives, accounting for 42.5% of the sample. Friends and newspaper sources represent 16% and 15%, respectively, while TV advertisements and other sources contribute smaller yet notable proportions of 3.5% and 24%, respectively, among the respondents.

The above Table 120.1 illustrate that majority respondents are mostly used ATM required of the PMJDY scheme and it followed by fund transfer, financial literacy program, overdraft facility, cheque collection, smart card, demand draft and passbook.

Weighted average rank test

To identify the level of utilization on PMJDY Scheme weighted average rank test is employed.

Factor Analysis

To identify the prominent factors that influence a level of problem in PMJDY Scheme, factor analysis is employed. Kaiser-Meyer-Olkin (KMO) and Bartlett's test of sphericity has been used as pre-analysis testing for suitability of the entire sample for factor analysis.

Table 120.1 Table showing level of utilization on PMJDY scheme.

Utilization	High	Moderate	Low	Total	Mean score	Rank
	3	2	1			
Cheque collection	65	111	24	200	2.2	5
	195	222	24	441		
Demand draft	63	87	50	200	2.1	7
	189	174	50	413		
Fund transfer	103	82	15	200	2.4	2
	309	164	15	488		
Overdraft facility	79	105	16	200	2.3	4
	237	210	16	463		
Financial literacy program	104	83	13	200	2.4	2
	312	166	13	491		
ATM	123	60	17	200	2.5	1
	369	120	17	506		
Passbook	50	76	74	200	1.8	8
	150	152	74	376		
Smart card	107	18	75	200	2.2	5
	321	36	75	432		

Source: Primary data

Level of problem on PMJDY scheme
KMO and Bartlett's test

Kaiser-Meyer-Olkin measure of sampling adequacy.		.661
Bartlett's test of sphericity	Approx. Chi-square	432.543
	df	15
	Sig.	.000

The result of KMO and Bartlett's test is found greater than 0.70. Hence the collected data is fit for employing factor analysis. Further the large value of Bartlett's test of sphericity (432.543, Df:15, Sig. .000) indicated the appropriateness of factor analysis i.e., the sample was adequate.

Rotated component matrix[a]

Rotated component matrix[a]	Component	
	1	2
Delay in availing loan	.863	
Len thing procedure on opening an account	.858	
Delay in opening account	.800	
Lengthy documentation procedure	.777	
Technological issue		.870
Connectivity challenges (ATM network)		.867
Eigen values	2.748	1.522
Percentage of variance	45.797	25.371
Cumulative percentage	45.797	71.168

Two factors are identified by locating Eigen Values greater than unity. Factors which have a component loading of 0.5 and above are said to be significant. From the rotated components matrix, delay in availing loan, lengthening procedure on opening an account, delay in opening account, lengthy documentation procedure has a component loading of 0.5 and above. Hence, these four variables form first factor. In the second factor, technological issues and connectivity challenges (ATM network) are found to be significant.

Conclusions

The study's recommendations aim to bolster the Pradhan Mantri Jan Dhan Yojana (PMJDY) scheme, ensuring enhanced financial inclusion and empowerment, especially among India's marginalized communities. These suggestions advocate for active utilization of PMJDY accounts, promoting financial education, and improving customer service for account holders. Encouraging digital literacy, particularly in rural areas, is crucial for safe and accessible financial service access. Collaborations with self-help and microfinance organizations will assist in reaching underserved communities and tailoring financial products to meet their specific needs.

Addressing the financial inclusion challenges faced by women, seniors, and people with disabilities requires targeted programs and specialized financial services. Strengthening financial infrastructure, both physical and digital, in underserved regions is essential to ensure reliable access to financial services. Collaboration between public and private entities can expedite financial inclusion measures and improve service delivery.

Continuous evaluation and adaptation of PMJDY implementation strategies are crucial to meet evolving demands and ensure program efficacy. The scheme has notably increased awareness and participation among villagers, enabling access to financial services like ATM usage, cash transfers, and check collection, enhancing economic conditions in rural areas. The majority of the populace is content with the interest rates offered on deposits and loans, indicating satisfaction with the scheme's provisions.

In conclusion, the PMJDY scheme has significantly impacted rural India, facilitating financial accessibility, aid distribution, and banking services. Implementing these recommendations could fortify the scheme's impact, contributing to broader economic growth and empowerment for India's marginalized communities.

References

Basu, S., and Das, P. (2019). Financial inclusion in India: an evaluation of the Pradhan Mantri Jan Dhan Yojana. *Journal of Contemporary Issues in Business and Government*, 25(2), 34–42.

Chandrasekaran, S., and Niranjan, S. (2016). Financial inclusion in India: a review of government initiatives and challenges. *International Journal of Management Research and Reviews*, 6(4), 405–416.

Mishra, B. P. (2017). Pradhan Mantri Jan Dhan Yojana (PMJDY): a catalyst for financial inclusion in India. *International Journal of Social Science and Economic Research*, 2(1), 270–277.

Seth, N., and Mahajan, R. (2018). Financial inclusion through Pradhan Mantri Jan Dhan Yojana in India: an empirical study. *International Journal of Engineering and Management Research*, 8(3), 228–232.

Sharma, N. (2020). Pradhan Mantri Jan Dhan Yojana: an inclusive revolution in Indian banking sector. *Journal of Commerce and Accounting Research*, 9(1), 61–66.

121 Problems faced by coconut cultivators in Coimbatore

Santhosh, K.[a] and Mathan Kumar, V.[b]

Karpagam Academy of Higher Education, Coimbatore, Tamil Nadu, India

Abstract

Coconut cultivation constitutes a vital facet of Coimbatore's agricultural landscape, playing a pivotal role in the state of Tamil Nadu, India. However, the practitioners of this industry grapple with multifaceted challenges, intricately impacting their productivity and economic viability. This abstract elucidates prominent issues confronting coconut cultivators in Coimbatore, notably the menace posed by pests and diseases. The pervasive presence of coconut mites, rhinoceros beetles, and the red palm weevil poses a substantial risk, causing extensive harm and jeopardizing the vitality of coconut palms. Concurrently, ailments such as bud rot, root wilt, and leaf blight compound the adversities faced by cultivators. The spectre of fluctuating weather patterns and climate change looms large, with erratic rainfall, prolonged droughts, and heightened cyclonic activity adversely affecting water availability for coconut palms. Elevated temperatures and evolving climatic conditions further exacerbate challenges by fostering the proliferation of pests and diseases. Compounding these issues is the limited adoption of modern agricultural practices and technology, perpetuating the reliance on traditional, less efficient methods. The dearth of awareness and training in contemporary techniques, encompassing intercropping, integrated pest management, and improved irrigation systems, curtails the potential productivity and economic gains of coconut farming in Coimbatore.

Keywords: Coconut, cultivators, farmers, problems and Coimbatore

Introduction

Coconut cultivation constitutes a pivotal facet of Coimbatore's agricultural landscape in Tamil Nadu, India. However, the local coconut cultivators grapple with multifarious challenges that impinge upon their productivity and overall financial viability. This synopsis seeks to elucidate the primary predicaments confronting coconut cultivators in Coimbatore. Paramount among these challenges are pest and disease infestations, with the coconut mite, rhinoceros beetle, and red palm weevil posing substantial threats. Their incursions result in considerable harm to coconut palms, engendering diminished yields and potential tree fatalities. Furthermore, ailments like bud rot, root wilt, and leaf blight compound the tribulations faced by cultivators. The region's susceptibility to fluctuating weather patterns and climate change exacerbates the conundrum. Unpredictable rainfall, prolonged droughts, and heightened cyclone frequency compromise water availability, inducing water stress and diminished productivity in coconut palms. Moreover, escalating temperatures and evolving climatic dynamics foster pest and disease proliferation, compounding extant challenges. The adoption of archaic agricultural practices further impedes progress, as many farmers persist in utilising traditional methods, such as manual pollination and inefficient irrigation. Insufficient awareness and training in contemporary techniques, encompassing intercropping, integrated pest management, and enhanced irrigation systems, further curtail coconut farming's productivity and economic viability in Coimbatore.

Problem Statement

The pivotal role of coconut farming in Tamil Nadu's economy, where 60% of producers depend on it as a primary income source, underscores a critical problem statement: the socio-cultural importance of coconuts clashes with the economic challenges faced by farmers, whose financial situations hinge on the marketability and pricing dynamics of coconut products, thereby necessitating a balanced approach to sustain both societal and economic aspects.

Objectives of the Study

To identify the production problems of coconut cultivators.

Methodology: Data required for the study has been collected through interview schedule. Questions pertain to profile of coconut cultivators, cultivation pattern, marketing practices, problems on production and marketing practices of coconut cultivators.

Data: Data required for the study is primary in nature. Thus, primary data is collected by making use of interview schedule. Questions pertaining to Profile of coconut cultivators, cultivation pattern, marketing practices, problems on production of coconut cultivators.

[a]santhoshmsd79763@gmail.com, [b]mathankumar010@gmail.com

Sample: By adopting convenient sampling method 242 responses are collected through interview schedule.

Study area: Data collected from Pollachitaluk of Coimbatore district.

Framework of analysis: The collected data has been analyzed by making use of statistical tool like weighted average method.

Review of Literature

Table 121.1 Exploring agricultural dynamics: a synopsis of diverse studies on coconut farming and Agro marketing.

Author name	Reference	Study
Shafiai andMoi (2017)	Examining the potential of Islamic agricultural financing to assist farmers in land development, utilizing interviews and a questionnaire to analyze literature and identify financial challenges during the cultivation cycle.	This study explores how Islamic agricultural financing can support farmers in land development, revealing financial difficulties faced by surveyed farmers during the second cultivation cycle despite banking opportunities.
Ashik (2018)	Investigating the socio-economic conditions of Kerala's coir sector, utilizing percentage analysis and Chi-square tests on data from 123 respondents to identify issues like labor shortage, lack of government support, and low pay rates.	This research aims to understand the socio-economic aspects of Kerala's coir sector, highlighting major challenges such as labor shortage, governmental neglect of traditional practices, and issues related to low wages and worker health through statistical analyses.
Shanthini andRamane (2018)	Analyzing 15 years of secondary data (2000-01 to 2015-16) to study coconut growth trends across states, emphasizing the impact of yield on overall coconut output, with Kerala being an exception in terms of favorable growth rates.	This study examines 15 years of secondary data to assess coconut growth trends, noting significant yield impacts on overall output across states, except in Kerala, where growth rates remain consistently favorable.
Chellasamy, et al.	Investigating coconut sales in the Hassan district, categorizing farmers into marginal, small, and big groups, and presenting a taxonomy of marketing channels, with Channel IV proving effective in the marketing of coconut products.	This research explores coconut sales in the Hassan district, categorizing farmers by size and proposing marketing channels, finding Channel IV to be effective for coconut product marketing.
Palanivelu and Muthukrishnan	Evaluating variables influencing coconut farmers' satisfaction, analyzing marketing strategies, and suggesting improvements based on findings, with a sample of 240 farmers indicating a shift toward alternative agricultural products.	The study assesses factors affecting coconut farmers' satisfaction, examines marketing strategies, and suggests improvements based on a sample of 240 farmers, revealing a shift toward alternative agricultural products in Coimbatore.
Elangovan, Mohanraj	Advocating for the use of e-commerce in agro marketing, providing online platforms for farmers to sell perishable goods, expand beyond local markets, and access a broader customer base, while offering features to enhance farm management and labor opportunities.	This research promotes e-commerce in agro marketing, facilitating online sales for farmers, expanding market reach, and providing tools for farm management and labor engagement, ultimately contributing to the strategic success of agro marketing.

Source: Author

Findings

In this comprehensive exploration of coconut cultivators, we delve into the demographic fabric and production challenges shaping the landscape of coconut farming. Examining key parameters such as residence, age, gender, education, income, expenditure, family size, and family type provides a nuanced understanding of the cultivators' socio-economic backdrop. Additionally, an insightful analysis of perceived challenges in coconut production unveils priorities and areas of concern. This holistic overview aims to illuminate the intricate dynamics that influence coconut cultivation, offering a foundation for informed interventions and strategic planning to bolster the resilience and prosperity of coconut farming communities.

Demographic profile of coconut cultivators:
- **Area of residence:**
  - Rural: 162 (66.9%)

- Semi urban: 80 (33.1%)
- Total: 242 (100.0%)
- **Age of coconut cultivators**
  - Up to 32 years: 39 (16.1%)
  - Between 32-55 years: 166 (68.6%)
  - Above 55 years: 37 (15.3%)
  - Total: 242 (100.0%)
- **Gender of the cultivator**
  - Male: 165 (68.2%)
  - Female: 77 (31.8%)
  - Total: 242 (100.0%)
- **Educational qualification**
  - Illiterate: 15 (6.2%)
  - SSLC: 181 (74.8%)
  - HSC: 19 (7.9%)
  - Under-graduation: 19 (7.9%)
  - Post-graduation: 8 (3.3%)
  - Total: 242 (100.0%)
- **Monthly income**
  - Below 31000: 10 (4.1%)
  - Between 31000-68550: 218 (90.1%)
  - Above 68550: 14 (5.8%)
  - Total: 242 (100.0%)
- **Monthly expenditure**
  - Below 11000: 20 (8.3%)
  - Between 11000-27250: 198 (81.8%)
  - Above 27250: 24 (9.9%)
  - Total: 242 (100.0%)
- **Size of the family**
  - Up to 2 Members: 79 (32.6%)
  - 3 to 5 Members: 116 (47.9%)
  - Above 5 Members: 47 (19.4%)
  - Total: 242 (100.0%)
- **Type of the family**
  - Joint family: 166 (68.6%)
  - Nuclear family: 76 (31.4%)
  - Total: 242 (100.0%)

Perceived problems on production of coconut cultivators

- **Weighted average rank:**
  - Nutritional deficiency (mean score: 4.140)
  - Attack of pests and diseases (mean score: 3.880)
  - Increase price of fertilizers (mean score: 1.049)
  - Seasonal low yield (mean score: 1.036)
  - Water scarcity during summer seasons (mean score: 1.015)
  - Unfavorablesoil and climatic conditions (mean score: 1.013)
  - Defective pollination and fertilization (mean score: 1.011)

- Formation of abscission layer (mean score: 0.931)

Insights:
- **Demographic overview:**
  - The majority of coconut cultivators reside in rural areas (66.9%).
  - The age group between 32-55 years constitutes the largest segment of cultivators (68.6%).
  - Male cultivators dominate the demographic profile (68.2%).
  - SSLC is the predominant educational qualification (74.8%).
  - Most cultivators fall within the monthly income range of Rs. 31000-68550 (90.1%).
  - Monthly family expenditure is mainly between Rs. 11000-27250 (81.8%).
  - Families with 3 to 5 members are the most common (47.9%).
  - Joint families prevail among coconut cultivators (68.6%).
- **Production challenges:**
  - The weighted average rank indicates that the most significant problem faced by coconut cultivators is nutritional deficiency, followed by the attack of pests and diseases.
  - Other challenges include the increase in the price of fertilizers, seasonal low yield, water scarcity during summer seasons, unfavorable soil and climatic conditions, defective pollination and fertilization, and the formation of the abscission layer.

In summary, this comprehensive analysis of coconut cultivators' demographics and perceived production challenges provides valuable insights for policymakers, agricultural experts, and stakeholders aiming to enhance the well-being and productivity of coconut farming communities. Understanding the nuances of their socio-economic context is essential for implementing targeted interventions and sustainable agricultural practices.

Findings from the study reveal a predominant presence of rural, middle-aged male cultivators with SSLC education and a monthly income between Rs. 31000-68550. The majority reside in joint families with 3 to 5 members, facing challenges like nutritional deficiency and pest attacks. The weighted average rank positions nutritional deficiency as the foremost concern. These insights illuminate the socio-economic landscape of coconut cultivators, guiding interventions for sustainable agriculture. Policymakers can leverage these results to address key challenges and enhance the overall well-being of coconut farming communities by tailoring strategies that align with their demographic profile and production constraints.

Conclusion

In conclusion, our systematic study of coconut cultivation in Coimbatore underscores the pressing challenges faced by cultivators, with nutritional deficiency topping the weighted average rank analysis. Demographic insights reveal a predominant profile: rural residents, aged 32-55, predominantly male, SSLC-educated, earning Rs. 31,000-68,550 monthly, with 3-5 member families in joint setups. These findings illuminate the nuanced socio-economic fabric of coconut cultivators. To address challenges and enhance livelihoods, our suggestions advocate for training, financial support, market linkages, value addition, infrastructure investment, research reinforcement, women's empowerment, cooperative collaboration, policy advocacy, and climate-smart farming. Implementation of these recommendations promises to fortify coconut cultivation, boost growers' prosperity, and ensure high-quality produce for the market. Collaborative efforts from stakeholders are imperative to usher in positive change, strengthen coconut farming, and uplift the socio-economic landscape of cultivators.

References

Ashik, A. (2018). Socio-economic conditions of coir workers in Kerala. *International Journal of Pure and Applied Mathematics*, 118(20), 4389–4397.

Fausayana, I., Abdullah, W. G., andDawid, L. O. (2018).Risk analysis of coconut product marketing.*International Journal Of Research-Granthaalayah*, 6, 138–148.

Shafiai, M. H. M., andMoi, M. R. (2017). Financial problems among farmers in Malaysia: Islamic agricultural finance as a possible solution . 11(4), 1–16.

Shanthini, G., and Ramane, R. V. (2018). An analysis of growth trends of coconut crop in India. *International Journal of Research in Management, Economics and Commerce*, 08(3), 78–85.

122 Problems on material handling, storage, and packaging in selected logistic companies in Coimbatore

Krishna Kumar M.[a], Sudarvel, J.[b] and Velmurugan, R.[c]

Karpagam Academy of Higher Education, Coimbatore, India

Abstract

This study delves into the challenges inherent in material handling, storage, and packaging operations within selected logistic companies situated in Coimbatore. The primary objective is to meticulously identify and analyze specific issues encountered by these companies, aiming to propose viable solutions and enhancements. By focusing on these challenges, the overarching goal is to elevate worker performance, safety standards, and operational efficiency within the warehousing domain of these logistic entities. The research uncovers prominent issues, including physical strain from manual lifting, inefficient workflow designs, inadequate safety measures, and the underutilization of available technologies. The insights derived from this study provide valuable information for logistic organizations, not only in Coimbatore but also in broader contexts, offering guidance on how to discern and address the primary difficulties faced by personnel engaged in material handling, storage, and packaging. The implementation of the proposed solutions holds the potential to cultivate a safer warehouse environment, augment operational efficacy, and bolster worker contentment, contributing to the overall progress and success of the logistics sector.

Keywords: Material handling, packaging, storage, warehousing, workers and problems

Introduction

Material handling, storage, and packaging are essential elements of warehouse operations in the logistics sector. The efficient management of these processes guarantees the free flow of commodities and is essential for satisfying client requests. However, there are several difficulties that store, and package materials frequently deal with, which have an effect on their well-being and productivity. In Tamil Nadu, India's bustling city of Coimbatore is home to a sizable number of logistic firms that operate warehouses. To handle resources, store them properly, and package them for shipment, these businesses primarily rely on the skills and efforts of their employees. For areas of development and steps to be put in place to increase their performance and general job satisfaction, it is essential to comprehend the difficulties these companies confront in material handling, storage, and packing. This research intends to investigate and analyze the unique issues faced by employees working in material handling, storage, and packaging within certain Coimbatore logistic enterprises. The research tries to examine these issues in order to determine their root causes and suggest feasible remedies to address them. With this study, the warehouse industry's production will be increased overall, worker effectiveness will be increased, and safety will be promoted.

Logistics firms in Coimbatore might profit greatly by solving the difficulties that employees have when handling, storing, and packing materials. These include greater customer satisfaction, decreased risk of accidents and injuries, higher operational efficiency, and increased market competitiveness. The remainder of this study will examine the difficulties faced by personnel engaged in material handling, storage, and packaging within the chosen logistic organizations. Researchers, managers, and practitioners in the logistics sector would benefit greatly from the results, which will help them develop practical solutions to these problems and enhance the material handling, storage, and packing procedures in warehouse operations.

[a]mkrishna122000@gmail.com, [b]j.sudarvel@gmail.com, [c]drvelsngm@gmail.com

Review of Literature

Table 122.1 Exploring challenges in material handling and logistics: a comparative overview of key studies.

Author name	Reference	Study
Venkatesan et al. (2023)	Common problems include inadequate packaging, lack of labor and handling equipment, misplacing and stealing supplies, lack of planning, site space, high population, insufficient supervision, delay in permissions, and ignorance of handling.	The study by Venkatesan et al., identifies challenges in material handling and transportation, encompassing issues such as inadequate packaging, labor and equipment shortages, theft, planning lapses, space constraints, population density, supervision deficiencies, delayed permissions, and handling ignorance.
Mohan and Velumoni (2022)	There's a negative correlation between age and material handling difficulties; younger individuals are more prone to issues. The study employs an independent sample t-test to assess the impact of experience on material handling improvements.	Bala andVelumoni's research discover a negative association between age and material handling issues, indicating that younger individuals are more likely to face difficulties. The study employs an independent sample t-test to examine the impact of experience on material handling improvements.
Jagdish (2022)	Problems include lack of machine handling equipment, safety negligence, low productivity, and efficiency in manual processes. The study suggests solutions like investing in proper tools, prioritizing safety, adopting automation, and enhancing training.	Raghunandan Jagdish's study highlights issues like insufficient machine handling tools, safety oversights, and low productivity in manual material handling. Solutions proposed include investing in equipment, prioritizing safety measures, adopting automation, and improving training to enhance efficiency.
iThink logistics (2019)	Major issues faced by Indian logistics companies: Lack of skilled personnel, slow technology adoption, warehousing and taxation discrepancies, and shortage of drivers and delivery staff.	iThink logistics outlines significant challenges for logistics companies in India, encompassing a lack of skilled personnel, slow technology adoption, warehousing and taxation discrepancies, and a shortage of drivers and delivery staff.
Bagyalakshmi and Thangaraj (2018)	Logistic companies face problems such as poor infrastructure, temperature control storage issues, heavy competition, and dispatch time delays.	Bagyalakshmi and Thangaraj's study reveals major challenges for logistic companies, including poor infrastructure, temperature control storage issues, intense competition, and delays in dispatch times.
MHI's Annual Industry Report of 2018	Challenges managers faced in 2018: Difficulty in hiring qualified staff and meeting consumer requests. This may indicate a shortage of skilled individuals in the industry affecting overall operations.	MHI's Annual Industry Report of 2018 highlights challenges faced by managers, including difficulties in hiring qualified staff and meeting consumer demands, potentially suggesting a shortage of skilled individuals impacting overall operational efficiency.

Source: Author

Problem Statement

The study addresses the challenges encountered in material handling, storage, and packaging within selected logistic companies in Coimbatore, aiming to identify specific impediments to worker effectiveness, safety, and overall productivity, with the ultimate goal of formulating strategies and solutions to enhance worker performance and contribute to increased productivity and operational efficiency in the logistics sector.

Scope of the Study

The study aims to identify and assess challenges faced by employees in Coimbatore-based logistics companies engaged in material handling, storage, and packaging operations. By selecting a diverse sample of businesses, considering various industries and sizes, and gathering detailed employee information, the study seeks to explore issues such as ergonomic difficulties, safety risks, inadequate training, and communication inefficiencies Beamon (1998). Using interviews, questionnaires, and observations, the study will analyze the impact of these problems on employee performance, satisfaction, and well-being. Both quantitative and qualitative data will be utilized to measure the scope and severity of the identified issues, delving into root causes such as organizational rules, managerial techniques, work environment, technology usage, and employee engagement Beason (1999). The study's scope may be adjusted based on available resources, time constraints, and research goals.

Objective of the Study

To identify the problems with material handling, storage, and packaging in selected logistic companies.

Research Methodology

- Primary data collection via interviews is crucial for detailed and specific information.
- An interview schedule ensures consistency and standardized responses, enhancing the reliability of data collection.
- **Sampling and sample size:**Convenient sampling is valuable when accessing the entire population is challenging. It allows quick data collection from readily available individuals, and 166 workers at logistic companies in Coimbatore were sampled using this approach.
- **Framework of analysis:** Analysis involved simple percentage and factor analysis.
- **Significance of the study:**Addressing material handling issues enhances logistical operations' productivity and efficiency.Streamlining operations, providing training, and ensuring proper tools can increase worker productivity, leading to improved operational results, lower expenses, and heightened customer satisfaction.
- **Employee health and safety:**Prioritizing health and safety provides a market advantage, fostering a reputation for being employee-friendly.Recognizing and resolving worker-related issues attracts and retains qualified personnel, supporting overall competitiveness in the logistics sector.
- **Policy implications:**Study conclusions inform industry policies and compliance efforts, guiding politicians, industry groups, and regulatory authorities. Insights help create effective policies, standards, and laws to protect workers' safety and wellbeing.
- **Contributions to knowledge:**The research adds to existing knowledge in logistics, particularly in packing, storage, and material handling. Focusing on Coimbatore-specific issues generates fresh ideas, best practices, and suggestions applicable locally and in similar contexts, contributing to the logistics sector's knowledge base.

Analysis and Interpretation

In this comprehensive study, an exploration into the challenges encountered by logistic companies in Coimbatore unfolds, delving into demographic profiles, safety perceptions, material handling intricacies, and packaging complexities Figura (1996). The research employs a multifaceted approach, utilizing factor analysis and weighted average tests to discern key influencers and prioritize prevalent issues Drum (2009). As we navigate through the nuanced layers of logistic operations, this study aims to not only unravel challenges but also illuminate strategic recommendations, offering a holistic understanding crucial for enhancing productivity, worker satisfaction, and operational efficiency in the logistics landscape.

Demographic profile:
- Majority respondents fall in the 36-45 age range (33.7%).
- Predominantly male respondents (80.7%).
- Educational qualification is primarily up to higher secondary (57.8%).
- Most respondents earn a monthly income between 12,000 and 20,000 (39.8%).

Safety and Satisfaction:
- Safety in material handling reported as good by most respondents (32.5%).
- High satisfaction with equipment used for material handling (33.7%).

Material handling problems:
Frequent problems faced:

- Labor cost (30.12%)
- Unsafe conditions (18.67%)
- Shortage of place (20.48%)
- Shortage of trained manpower (30.72%).

Factor analysis:
- Kaiser-Meyer-Olkin measure of sampling adequacy: 0.795.
- Bartlett's test of sphericity: Chi-square = 4379.234, df = 325, Sig = 0.000.
- Factors influencing storage issues identified through factor analysis.

Weighted average test on packaging problems:
Major problems identified:

- Shortage of trained manpower
- Inconsistent packing quality
- Lack of packing automation
- Increase in the cost of packing
- Inefficient packing layout or design.

Conclusion:
- Demographic insights highlight the age, gender, education, and income distribution of respondents.

- Safety and satisfaction levels provide a glimpse into the overall well-being of workers.
- Material handling problems, as identified, emphasize key challenges faced in logistic companies.
- Factor analysis sheds light on significant factors influencing storage problems, contributing to a nuanced understanding.
- Weighted average test on packaging problems prioritizes issues, enabling focused intervention strategies.

Implications and recommendations:
- Addressing the shortage of trained manpower is crucial in mitigating material handling challenges.
- Enhancing safety measures and equipment satisfaction can improve overall working conditions.
- Strategic solutions are needed for consistent packing quality and automation adoption.
- Policy implications involve tailoring interventions based on demographic insights and problem prioritization.

Significance of the Study:
- The study's significance lies in its comprehensive approach to understanding logistic challenges.
- Demographic and problem-specific insights offer valuable inputs for targeted interventions.
- Recommendations based on factor analysis and weighted average tests provide actionable steps for logistic companies.
- The study contributes to the broader understanding of logistic challenges and offers practical solutions.

In conclusion, the study illuminates the multifaceted nature of challenges faced by logistic companies in Coimbatore, emphasizing the importance of addressing demographic variations, material handling issues, and packaging concerns. The nuanced insights provided through statistical analyses offer a foundation for informed decision-making and strategic planning in the logistics sector. The study reveals significant insights into the demographic composition, safety perceptions, and operational challenges faced by logistic workers in Coimbatore. Findings indicate a predominant age group of 36-45, a male-dominated workforce, and prevalent education levels up to higher secondary. Material handling safety is generally perceived as good, and workers express high satisfaction with equipment. Logistic companies primarily grapple with a shortage of trained manpower, inconsistent packing quality, and limited automation. The factor analysis identifies key variables driving storage issues, emphasizing the multifaceted nature of challenges. Recommendations include addressing manpower

shortages and enhancing automation to elevate operational efficiency and worker well-being.Conclusion

In conclusion, the logistics companies in Coimbatore grapple with multifaceted challenges in material handling, storage, and packaging. Issues such as a shortage of educated labor, variable packing quality, and the lack of packing automation contribute to inefficiencies in material handling processes Deshmukh and Bahale (2013). Storage-related challenges encompass poor lighting, outdated equipment, and inadequate pest control, impacting overall facility management Trebilcock (2002). Meanwhile, packaging-related hurdles, including the lack of skilled labor and ineffective layout designs, affect the efficacy, efficiency, and affordability of packaging procedures Vallet (1999). Addressing these challenges is crucial for optimizing operations. Strategies such as employee training, the implementation of standard operating procedures, exploration of automation technologies, and optimization of packaging designs can enhance overall logistics processes. Improved lighting, infrastructure, and communication among various departments further contribute to streamlined material handling, storage, and packaging. Investing in these areas enables logistics firms to boost customer satisfaction, reduce costs, and ensure effective and efficient logistics operations.

References

Bagyalakshmi, K., and Thangaraj, B. (2018). A study on problems faced by logistics companies in cargo handling with reference to Coimbatore city. *Global Journal for Research Analysis,* 7(8).

Beamon, B. M. (1998). Performance, reliability, and performability of material handling systems. *International Journal of Production Research,* 36(2), 377–393. DOI: 10.1080/002075498193796.

Beason, M. (1999). Here is a new material handling solution. *Textile World,* 149(2), 61–63.

Deshmukh, S. S., and Bahale, A. P. (2013). Inefficiencies in material handling and alternatives for their improvement in a ginning machine manufacturing company .

Drum, D. (2009). Asset tracking: material handling benefits. *Material Handling Management,* 64(6), 36–38.

Figura, S. Z. (1996). Reducing the risk of material handling. *Occupational Hazards,* 58(8), 30–32.

Mohan, B. B. A., and Velumoni, D. (2022). A study on challenges faced in material handling management at manufacturing industries Chennai. *International Journal of Creative Research Thoughts,* 10(5), ISSN: 2320–2882.

Trebilcock, B. (2002). Modern materials handling. *ABI/INFORM Global,* 57(14), 29.

Vallet, M. (1999). Better material handling improves workflow. *Fused Deposition Modeling,* 71(14), 74.

Venkatesan, V. D.,Dhadve, P. P., and Panchal, H. (2023). Material handling storage and packaging challenges in sandozprivate limited. *International Research Journal of Modernization in Engineering Technology and Science,* 05(02).

123 Profitability analysis: a study of selected pharma companies in India

Kishore, R.[a] and M. Nandhini[b]

Department of Management, Karpagam Academy of Higher Education, India

Abstract

The primary aim of this study was to assess the pharmaceutical industry's profitability, acknowledging that a company's operational and financial strategies significantly influence its overall profit. Financial gains stem from the disparity between actual and credited returns on investment, while operating profit derives from the difference between income and total operational expenses. India stands as a prominent global steel manufacturer, boasting competitiveness due to abundant reserves and accessible, inexpensive labor. Within companies, the financial sector holds a pivotal role, being deemed their lifeblood across various pursuits. Management prioritizes evaluating all operational facets, recognizing profitability as the ultimate result of the cumulative decisions and policies shaping a business's trajectory.

Keywords: Current asset, current liability, financial statement, liquidity, profit, solvency

Introduction

Profitability analysis in cost accounting delves into an organization's production profitability, often categorized by products, clients, locations, channels, or transactions. Assessing a company's efficacy relies heavily on its profitability, often evaluated using ratios that link net profit from the profit and loss statement to sales, assets, or equity levels. Higher ratios signify better business profitability, although these ratios lack predefined benchmarks for evaluation. A thorough examination of these ratios uncovers the factors influencing profitability. Analysts employ correlation analysis to trace financial ratios over time, presenting the company's operations as an accurate input-output model for assessment. Factors such as economies of scale, scope, mechanization, and brand investment often drive profitability.

This analysis remains a crucial aspect of financial modeling and is essential for those pursuing financial modeling certification. Every company prioritizes profitability, and profitability ratios serve as fundamental tools for both management and investors. These metrics determine the company's bottom line for managers and the return on equity for investors. Profitability measures guide management decisions and are vital for demonstrating success to equity investors, especially those external stakeholders who've invested in the company. At the end of each quarter or year, profitability ratios, as elucidated below, showcase a company's asset utilization and overall performance efficiency.

Problem Statement

In today's economy, achieving substantial profits in business proves challenging, often becoming a secondary goal. Without profits, a business struggles to function, especially in the global market. To attain even marginal profits, a company must expand its operations, driving higher sales and consequently, increased profits. Beyond revenue, factors like goodwill, reputation, and trustworthiness significantly contribute to a firm's overall wealth and value. Analyzing profitability is crucial for a business's seamless functioning, necessitating a balance between financial and operational efficiency.

Scope of Study

The research delves into the role of profitability analysis within the pharmaceutical industry. Profitability ratios serve as key indicators, showcasing a company's efficiency and success. Various profitability ratios, serving as decision-making tools, offer insights into a company's financial health. Companies conduct profitability analysis to optimize their business potential and assess fluctuations in profit or loss over a five-year period.

Objectives of Study

Analyzing a chosen pharmaceutical firm's profitability passion involves exploring its financial status and understanding how financial elements affect its passionate performance in the market. Understanding these factors is crucial.

[a]kishoregtx7@gmail.com, [b]nandhini1817@gmail.com

Research Methodology

The analysis focused on the annual financial statement of the organization, utilizing ratio analysis from balance sheets, income statements, cash flow statements, and shareholder equity statements of selected pharmaceutical companies. The study aimed at predicting financial efficiency through an analytical research design. Covering the period from 2017-2018 to 2021-2022, data collection involved primary sources, including discussions with financial executives, and secondary sources, obtained from the companies' annual reports. Ten pharmaceutical companies were selected for this analysis, including Sun Pharma, Torrent Pharma, Zydus Life, Ajanta Pharma, Alembic Pharma, Natco Pharma, Eris Life, Marksams Pharma, Bliss GVS Pharma, and Aunh Pharma. The tools used included ratio analysis and correlation analysis to assess and interpret the financial data.

Results and Discussion

Table 123.1 depicts that Eris Life, and Bliss GVS Pharma have negative skewness, whereas other firms have positive skewness. Leptokurtic observed on Torrent Pharma and AnuhPharma because Kurtic value larger than 3 and platykurtic observed on other firms because Kurtic value less than 3.

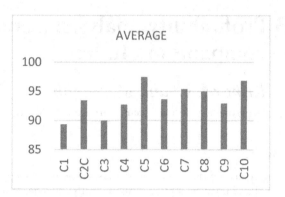

Figure 123.1 Gross profit – average
Source: Author

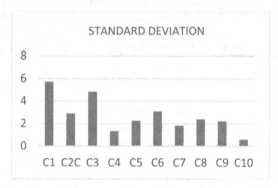

Figure 123.2 Gross profit – standard deviation
Source: Author

Table 123.1 Literature review.

Authors	Research focus
Duy and Flaaten (2015)	Explores government subsidies for offshore fishing vessels in Vietnam, finding that subsidy programs improved vessel profitability, particularly quasi-lump sum fuel cost support.
Ash et al. (2015)	Examines the financial health of paper firms in northern Australia, attributing their decline to rising production costs and falling paper prices. Investigates technology interventions (e.g., genetic gain in cattle) to bolster profitability in the paper industry.
Padula et al. (2015)	Compares the profitability and inventive performance of technology-specialist SMEs to vertically integrated SMEs, positing that technology specialists, specializing upstream in creating ideas, outperform due to deeper inventive experience and flexible structures.
Ukaegbu (2014)	Investigates the relationship between working capital efficiency and business profitability across different industrialization levels, discovering a negative link between profitability and cash conversion cycles, indicating reduced profitability with longer cycles.
Maryska and Doucek (2015)	Emphasizes the need for precise economic information at various levels within a company and discusses the relevance of activity-based costing (ABC) in understanding detailed cost structures of products or services for enhanced financial perception and accounting.
Day and Venkataramanan (2006)	Studies the impact of considering fixed manufacturing costs in product pricing and composition decisions, exploring how shared resources in manufacturing affect profitability decisions in similar product lines through conjoint and cost data analysis.

Source: Author

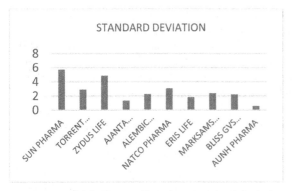

Figure 123.3 Net profit ratio – standard deviation
Source: Author

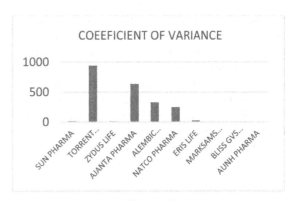

Figure 123.4 Coefficient of variance
Source: Author

Figure 123.5 Average correlation analysis
Source: Author

Table 123.2 illustrates that Sun Pharma, Torrent Pharma, NatcoPharma, and MarksamsPharma exhibit negative skewness, while other firms display positive skewness. Ajanta Pharma demonstrates leptokurtic behavior, indicated by a Kurtosis value exceeding 3,

while other firms appear platykurtic as their Kurtosis values fall below 3. The profit ratio and operating profit ratio exhibit a positive correlation. Specifically, the correlation value between gross profit ratio and operating ratio stands at (-)0.012, denoting a negative correlation between these metrics. Conversely, the correlation value between net profit ratio and gross profit ratio is notably high at 0.988, indicating a strong positive correlation between them. Similarly, the correlation between net profit ratio and operating profit ratio registers at 0.122, showcasing a positive correlation between these factors. Moreover, the correlation value between net profit ratio and operating ratio is (-)0.012, illustrating a negative correlation between these parameters. Conversely, the correlation value between operating profit ratio and gross profit ratio is 0.132, indicating a positive correlation. Likewise, the correlation between operating profit ratio and net profit ratio stands at 0.122, suggesting a positive relationship between these metrics. Additionally, the

Table 123.2 Gross profit ratio.

Year 2017-2022	C1	C2C	C3	C4	C5	C6	C7	C8	C9	C10
17 -18	86.58	90.4	92.86	92.85	99.62	97.34	92.83	94.68	94.33	97.18
18 -19	84.52	90.43	87.11	92.35	96.39	91.60	94.84	95.21	90.06	97.16
19 - 20	84.78	94.07	82.92	91.02	94.19	90.53	96.98	98.84	91.08	97.28
20 - 21	97.04	96.40	94.50	94.75	97.50	92.16	97.30	93.82	95.04	96.56
21 - 22	93.80	95.96	92.65	92.58	99.43	96.53	94.90	92.43	94.2	95.88
Total	446.72	467.28	450.04	463.55	487.13	468.16	476.85	474.98	464.71	484.06
Average ratio	89.344	93.456	90.008	92.71	97.426	93.632	95.37	94.996	92.942	96.812
Standard deviation	5.72	2.90	4.85	1.34	2.26	3.08	1.82	2.39	2.22	0.59
Coefficient of variance	32.71	8.42	23.48	1.8	5.10	9.52	3.32	5.72	4.92	0.35
Skewness	0.70	-0.24	-0.91	0.63	-0.53	0.48	-0.36	1.16	-0.63	-1.26
Kurtosis	-2.23	-3.01	-0.94	1.88	-0.77	-2.84	-0.92	2.06	-2.50	0.47

Source: Author

correlation value between operating profit ratio and operating ratio is 0.514, signifying a positive correlation between these aspects. Finally, the correlation value between operating ratio and gross profit ratio is (-)0.012, indicating a negative correlation, while the correlation between operating ratio and net profit ratio also shows a negative relationship at (−)0.012. Conversely, the correlation between operating ratio and operating profit ratio is noted as 0.514, indicating a positive correlation between these parameters.

Findings and Suggestions

Negative skewness was observed in Eris Life, MarksamsPharma, Bliss GVS Pharma, and AunhPharma, while other companies exhibited positive skewness in their Current Ratio. MarksamsPharma showed leptokurtosis, with a kurtosis value greater than 3, while other companies' Current Ratio demonstrated platykurtic distribution, with kurtosis values less than 3. Similarly, negative skewness was noticed in Sun Pharma, Alembic Pharma, Eris Life, and AunhPharma, with other companies displaying positive skewness in their Liquid Ratio. All companies exhibited platykurtic distribution in their Liquid Ratio, with kurtosis values less than 3. AunhPharma exhibited negative skewness in their Cash Ratio, while other companies showed positive skewness. AunhPharma also displayed leptokurtosis, with a kurtosis value greater than 3, while other companies' Cash Ratio demonstrated platykurtic distribution, with kurtosis values less than 3. Negative skewness was observed in Torrent Pharma, Zydus Life, Ajanta Pharma, Alembic Pharma, Eris Life, and Bliss GVS Pharma, while other companies showed positive skewness in their Gross Profit Ratio. Torrent Pharma and AunhPharma exhibited leptokurtosis, with kurtosis values greater than 3, while other companies' Gross Profit Ratio displayed platykurtic distribution, with kurtosis values less than 3.

The pattern continued with negative skewness noticed in Torrent Pharma, Zydus Life, Alembic Pharma, Eris Life, Bliss GVS Pharma, and AunhPharma, while other companies exhibited positive skewness in their net profit ratio. Torrent Pharma displayed leptokurtosis, with a kurtosis value greater than 3, while other companies' net profit ratio demonstrated platykurtic distribution, with kurtosis values less than 3. Moreover, negative skewness was observed in Sun Pharma, Torrent Pharma, NatcoPharma, and MarksamsPharma, while other companies showed positive skewness in their operating profit ratio. Ajanta Pharma exhibited leptokurtosis, with a kurtosis value greater than 3, while other companies' operating profit ratio displayed platykurtic distribution, with kurtosis values less than 3. Similarly, negative skewness was noticed in Sun Pharma, Torrent Pharma, Zydus Life, NatcoPharma, MarksamsPharma, and AunhPharma, while other companies displayed positive skewness in their operating ratio. All companies exhibited platykurtic distribution in their operating ratio, with Kurtosis values less than 3. In addition, negative skewness was observed in Sun Pharma, Zydus Life, and Bliss GVS Pharma, while other companies showed positive skewness in their inventory turnover ratio. All companies exhibited platykurtic distribution in

Table 123.3 Correlation analysis.

		GPR	NPR	OPR	OP
GPR	Pearson correlation	1	.988**	.132	-.012
	Sig. (2-tailed)		.000	.361	.932
	N	50	50	50	50
NPR	Pearson correlation	.988**	1	.122	-.012
	Sig. (2-tailed)	.000		.397	.935
	N	50	50	50	50
OPR	Pearson correlation	.132	.122	1	.514**
	Sig. (2-tailed)	.361	.397		.000
	N	50	50	50	50
OP	Pearson correlation	-.012	-.012	.514**	1
	Sig. (2-tailed)	.932	.935	.000	
	N	50	50	50	50

**. Correlation is significant at the 0.01 level (2-tailed).

GPR = Gross profit ratio, NPR = Net profit ratio, OPR = Operating profit ratio, OP = Operating profit

Source: Author

their inventory turnover ratio, with Kurtosis values less than 3.

Negative skewness was noticed in Eris Life, MarksamsPharma, Bliss GVS Pharma, and AunhPharma, while other companies exhibited positive skewness in their total assets turnover ratio. All companies displayed platykurtic distribution in their total assets turnover ratio, with Kurtosis values less than 3. Moreover, negative skewness was observed in Torrent Pharma, Alembic Pharma, Eris Life, and MarksamsPharma, while other companies showed positive skewness in their fixed assets turnover ratio. Torrent Pharma and AunhPharma exhibited leptokurtosis, with Kurtosis values greater than 3, while other companies' fixed assets turnover ratio demonstrated platykurtic distribution, with Kurtosis values less than 3. Finally, Debtors turnover ratio showcased positive skewness across all companies, with Sun Pharma exhibiting leptokurtosis, having a Kurtosis value greater than 3, while other companies displayed platykurtic distribution, with kurtosis values less than 3. In the creditors turnover ratio, negative skewness was noticed in Eris Life, MarksamsPharma, Bliss GVS Pharma, and AunhPharma, while other companies showed positive skewness. Sun Pharma exhibited leptokurtosis, with a Kurtosis value greater than 3, while other companies' creditors turnover ratio demonstrated platykurtic distribution, with kurtosis values less than 3. Lastly, negative skewness was observed in MarksamsPharma and AunhPharma, while other companies displayed positive skewness in their investment turnover ratio. Sun Pharma, Torrent Pharma, Zydus Life, Ajanta Pharma, Alembic Pharma, NatcoPharma, and Bliss GVS Pharma exhibited leptokurtosis, with kurtosis values greater than 3, while other companies' investment turnover ratio demonstrated platykurtic distribution, with Kurtosis values less than 3.

Correlation Analysis

The correlation between gross profit ratio and net profit ratio is a highly positive 0.988, indicating a strong relationship between them. Similarly, gross profit ratio and operating profit ratio exhibit a positive correlation, albeit weaker at 0.132. However, the correlation between gross profit ratio and operating ratio is slightly negative at (-)0.012, showing an inverse relationship. Likewise, net profit ratio and gross profit ratio maintain a highly positive correlation of 0.988, mirroring their close association. Net profit ratio also shows a positive correlation with operating profit ratio at 0.122. Conversely, the correlation between the net profit ratio and operating ratio remains negative at (-)0.012. Operating profit ratio demonstrates a positive correlation of 0.132 with gross profit ratio and a slightly stronger positive correlation of 0.514 with operating ratio. It also positively correlates with the net profit ratio at 0.122. Operating ratio and gross profit ratio exhibit a negative correlation of (-)0.012, indicating an inverse relationship. Similarly, the operating ratio shows a negative correlation of (-) 0.012 with net profit ratio. However, the operating ratio and operating profit ratio maintain a strong positive correlation of 0.514.

Conclusion

Transforming excess current assets, notably cash and bank balances, into viable investments can substantially bolster a company's earnings potential. This strategy not only optimizes the utilization of surplus resources but also ensures a more dynamic financial portfolio, enabling the generation of additional revenue streams. Simultaneously, maintaining equilibrium between current assets and liabilities is pivotal for the corporation's financial resilience. Such balance mitigates liquidity risks and fortifies the organization's ability to meet short-term obligations, reinforcing its overall financial stability.Diversifying perks across various plans is imperative for the organization to cater to a wide spectrum of preferences among its stakeholders. By offering a variety of benefits, the company can effectively engage and retain employees while also enhancing its appeal to potential recruits. Moreover, expanding current operations or innovating new products holds immense potential for revenue growth. Active efforts to escalate production capacities are indispensable in maximizing profit margins and sustaining an upward trajectory for the business. An enhanced reserves policy is recommended to fortify the company's financial preparedness. Elevating the reserve levels allows for meticulous planning, encompassing potential losses, modernization initiatives, and future business expansions. Interestingly, the company maintained lower reserves compared to previous periods, signifying the need to instigate measures aimed at curbing administrative expenses for greater financial prudence.In conclusion, the industry encountered formidable challenges this year, impacting various firms, including ours. While profitability analysis remains a cornerstone of financial management, several factors have encumbered our company's profitability. This research emphasizes the criticality of robust financial management practices for ensuring efficient business operations. Delving into profitability and financial statement analysis, this study elucidates comprehensive analytical approaches that can significantly augment both profitability and liquidity. Such insights gleaned from these studies serve as a foundation for future financial planning and sustained evaluation of the company's profitability trends over time.

References

Ash, A., Hunt, L., McDonald, C., Scanlan, J., Bell, L., Cowley, R., et al. (2015). Boosting the productivity and profitability of northern Australian beef enterprises: exploring innovation options using simulation modelling and systems analysis. *Agricultural Systems*, 139, 50–65.

Day, J. M., and Venkataramanan, M. A. (2006). Profitability in product line pricing and composition with manufacturing commonalities. *European Journal of Operational Research*, 175(3), 1782–1797.

Duy, N. N., and Flaaten, O. (2015). Government support and profitability effects–vietnamese offshore fisheries. *Marine Policy*, 61, 77–86.

Maryska, M., and Doucek, P. (2015). Reference model of cost allocation and profitability for efficient management of corporate ICT. *Procedia Economics and Finance*, 23, 1009–1016.

Padula, G., Novelli, E., and Conti, R. (2015). SMEs inventive performance and profitability in the markets for technology. *Technovation*, 41, 38–50.

Ukaegbu, B. (2014). The significance of working capital management in determining firm profitability: Evidence from developing economies in Africa. *Research in International Business and Finance*, 31, 1–16.

124 The effect of workforce diversity on job satisfaction of lecturers in Malaysia

S. Sudharshan[a], D. Vishnu Vardhan[b] and R. Gayathiri Chitra[c]

Karpagam Academy of Higher Education, Coimbatore, India

Abstract

Job satisfaction is a crucial factor to consider when assessing a workforce because it is connected both directly and indirectly to organizational efficiency and effectiveness. Nowadays, diversified workforce is the key factor of success in any business. Therefore, the primary goal of this study is to determine how workforce diversity affects lecturers' job satisfaction utilizing simple percentage analysis, independent sample t-test, correlation, analysis of variance (ANOVA), and regression. Gender, age, education, and experience all refer to this varied cultural background. In Malaysia, 200 respondents from public and private college lectures participated in this study. To get the necessary primary data, a structured questionnaire was used. The outcome of the study revealed that, of the other variables being examined, only the amount of education had a significant impact on the employee's job satisfaction. This study also provides academicians in Malaysia with helpful recommendations.

Keywords: Age diversity, diversity, educational diversity, gender diversity, job satisfaction, workforce

Introduction

Diversity in the workforce refers to the disparities among employees regarding age, gender, ethnicity, culture, and education levels. For the past decade, Malaysia has been experiencing a significant increase in workforce diversity due to globalization and other related factors. The diverse workforce has changed the landscape of the workplace, creating both advantages and disadvantages. One of the significant effects of workforce diversity in the Malaysian context is on lecture satisfaction. This study's goal is to determine how lecturer satisfaction in Malaysia is affected by workforce diversity, including its positive and negative effects. Workforce diversity refers to the range of individual variances inside a company. Diversity has many different aspects, including differences in race, ethnicity, gender, age, religion, ability, and sexual orientation, education, and skills. Workforce diversity can have many benefits for organizations, such as enhancing creativity, innovation, problem-solving, decision-making, and customer satisfaction.

Gender diversity is a term that refers to the recognition and respect of multiple genders and gender identities within a society or organization. Gender diversity can have positive impacts on various aspects of social and economic development, such as education, health, human rights, and innovation. Age diversity is a crucial component of any organization since it allows for the workplace to be enriched by a variety of perspectives, experiences, and abilities. Age diversity can also enhance creativity, innovation, and problem-solving abilities, as well as foster a culture of mutual learning and respect. Education diversity is a term that refers to the variety of perspectives, backgrounds, experiences, and identities that students and educators bring to the learning environment. Education diversity can enhance the quality of education by fostering critical thinking, creativity, collaboration, and cultural awareness

Experience Diversity

Experience diversity is a term that refers to the variety of backgrounds, perspectives, and skills that people bring to a workplace or a team. Experience diversity can enhance creativity, innovation, and problem-solving by allowing different viewpoints and approaches to emerge.

Job Satisfaction

The degree of happiness and involvement that employees have with their jobs, employers, and working environments is measured by their job satisfaction. Job satisfaction can affect various aspects of organizational performance, such as productivity, retention, customer service, innovation, and profitability. Therefore, it is important for managers and leaders to monitor and improve employee's job satisfaction levels regularly.

[a]sakthisudharshan420@gmail.com, [b]vishnuvardhanvvn@gmail.com, [c]gayathrirathnamr@gmail.com

Literature Review

Authors	Study focus
Joseph and Selvaraj (2015)	Analyzing the impact of workforce diversity on employee performance within Singaporean organizations, with a specific focus on diversity in age, gender, and ethnicity. The study suggests favorable outcomes if managed effectively, while mismanagement of diversity may lead to unfavorable results.
Gallego-Alvarez et al. (2010)	Investigating the influence of gender diversity on the performance of Spanish firms registered on the Madrid Stock Exchange from 2004 to 2006. Utilizing the CNMV database for corporate governance information, the research implies that higher gender diversity in companies doesn't necessarily correlate with improved performance based on market and accounting criteria, suggesting a limited impact of gender diversity on business performance.
Kunze et al. (2011)	Examining the evolution of perceived age discrimination within organizations and its impact on overall efficiency. The study delves into the effects of age diversity on perceptions of age discrimination at organizational levels and the consequential effects on firm performance via the mediation of employees' affective engagement. Highlighting the link between perceived age discrimination and the success of age diversity, the findings underscore the implications for managing diverse workforces effectively.
Aksoy (1998)	Investigating the connection between training and employment by analyzing educational markers used in hiring processes such as diplomas, grades, courses, and experience. Emphasizing the significance of aligning education with workplace value, the study suggests policy and perspective changes for educators and employers to better facilitate students' transition from education to employment.
Mcdaniel and Schmidt (1988)	Utilizing data from 16,058 individuals to explore the relationship between work experience and job performance across various occupational groupings. Analyzing data from the private sector and focusing on factors like experience duration and job complexity, the study identifies these as moderators affecting the association between work experience and job performance, suggesting a stronger correlation in populations and jobs with lower experience levels and cognitive demands, thereby supporting the casual model of job performance.
Annierah M., et al.	Investigating the correlation between teachers' personal characteristics (age, length of service, education level) and job happiness in the Cotabato Region of the Philippines. The study, conducted in 200 elementary public schools and 12 primary schools in Cotabato City, found significant connections between certain personal attributes (age, educational level, employment duration) and job satisfaction. The majority of teacher respondents were married women with master's degrees and an average teaching experience of 11 to 15 years, rating their job efficiency as very satisfactory.

Source: Author

Problem Statement

The leadership lacks the necessary expertise to successfully manage workforce diversity. Many of them were unaware of the elements that go into successful diversity management. Additionally, the impact of a diverse workforce on job satisfaction has received less attention in earlier studies. Enhancing job performance and organizational performance is always a result of job satisfaction. Therefore, the purpose of this study is to ascertain how workforce diversity affects lecturers' job satisfaction in Malaysia.

Research Objectives

1. To analyze the lectures demographic profile in Malaysia.
2. To check the relationship between workforce diversity and job satisfaction.

Hypotheses of the Study

H0: There is no significant relationship between workforce diversity and job satisfaction.

Research Methodology

The research methodology is a systematic and critical investigation into phenomenon. The researcher has interpreted the data through descriptive methods to systematically formulate the process that explores and describes the participant's responses. In this study Snowball sampling method was adopted. The sample size for the survey conducted was 200 respondents. Two different sorts of data are employed. Both main and secondary data describe them. To determine the relationship between workforce diversity and job satisfaction, this study used statistical techniques such basic percentage analysis and correlation.

Analysis and Interpretation

The employees demographic profile provides meaningful insight to the research topic. Hence, employee's demographic profile such as gender, age, marital status, educational qualification, ethnicity, designation, monthly income and experience are the information collected from the employees. Simple percentage analysis is used to categorize the employees belong to which group.

Objective 1: To analyze the lectures demographic profile in Malaysia.

Table 124.1 explains the distribution of sample employees based on their gender. It is classified into male and female. Out of 200 sample lectures, 76 belong to male category which is 38% and 124 belongs to female category which is 62%.

From the information it is inferred that majority of the female employees have participated in this survey.

Table 124.2 shows the distribution of sample lectures based on their Age. Age is classified into four groups namely below 20-29 years old, 30-39 years old, 40-49 years old and 50 years old and above. Out of 200 sample lectures 30 belongs to 20-29 years age group category which is 15.00 percent, 86 belongs to 30 to 39 years age group category which is 43%, 74 belongs to 40 to 49 years age group category which is 37% and 10 lectures belongs to 50 years and above age group which is 5%.

From the information it is inferred that most of the participants belong to 30 to 39 years age group.

Table 124.3 indicates the distribution of sample lectures based on their marital status. It is classified into unmarried and married. Out of 200 lectures, 152 belong to married category which is 76% and 48 lectures belongs to unmarried category which is 24%.

From the information it is noted that majority of the Married employees have participated in this survey.

Table 124.4 predicts the distribution of lectures based on their ethnicity. It is classified into Malay, Chinese and Indian. Out of 200 lectures, 116 belongs to Malay which is 58.00 percent, 48 belongs to Chinese which is 24.00 percent and 36 belongs to Indian which is 18.00 percent.

From the information it is observed that the majority of the Malay lectures have participated in this survey.

Table 124.5 predicts the distribution of lectures based on their educational qualification. It is classified into postgraduate, doctorate and post doctorate. Out of 200 lectures, 38 belong to post graduate which is 19%, 152 belongs to Ph.D which is 76% and 10 belongs to postdoc which is 5%.

Table 124.1 Distribution of employees based on their gender.

Gender	Frequency	Percent
Male	76	38.00
Female	124	62.00
Total	200	100

Source: Primary data computed

Table 124.2 Distribution of employees based on their age.

Age	Frequency	Percent
20-29 years old	30	15.00
30-39 years old	86	43.00
40-49 years old	74	37.00
50 years old and above	10	5.00
Total	200	100

Source: Primary data computed

Table 124.3 Distribution of employees based on their marital status.

Marital status	Frequency	Percent
Unmarried	48	24.00
Married	152	76.00
Total	200	100

Source: Primary data computed

Table 124.4 Distribution of employees based on their ethnicity.

Educational qualification	Frequency	Percent
Malay	116	58.00
Chinese	48	24.00
Indian	36	18.00
Total	200	100

Source: Primary data computed

Table 124.5 Distribution of employees based on their educational qualification.

Educational qualification	Frequency	Percent
Postgraduate	38	19.00
Doctorate	152	76.00
Post doctorate	10	5.00
Total	200	100

Source: Primary data computed

From the information it is observed that the majority of the Ph.D lectures have participated in this survey.

Table 124.6 shows the distribution of sample employees based on their experience. It is classified into up to 5 years, 5 to 10 years, 11 to 15 years and above 15 years. Out of 200 sample employees, 80 employees have the 11 to 15 years' experience (40%), 50 employees have above 15 years' experience which is 25%, 46 employees have the 5 to 10 years' experience which is 23%, 24 employees have the upto 5 years of experience which is 12%.

From the above information it is found that majority of the employees have the 11 to 15 years of experience.

Table 124.7 predicts the distribution of sample employees based on their tenure with the current organization. It is classified into less than 5 years, 5-10 years, 11-15 years and more than 15 years. Out of 200 sample, 98 belongs to 5-10 years which is 49%, 46 belong to less than 5 years category which is 23%, 40 employees belong to 11-15 years category which is 20% and 16 belongs to more than 15 years category which is 8%.

From the information it is observed that majority of the 5-10 years respondents have participated in this survey.

Table 124.8 predicts the distribution of sample employees based on their designation. Designation is classified into lecturer, senior lecturer, associate professor and professor. Out of 200 sample employees, 74 employees belong to associate professor which is 37%, 52 employees belong to senior lecturer category which is 26%, 50 employees belongs to professor category which is 25% and 24 employees belongs to lecturer category which is 12%.

From the information it is observed that majority of the Associate Professor have participated in this survey.

Objective 2: To examine the relationship between workforce diversity and job satisfaction.

Relationship between workforce diversity and job satisfaction

In this analysis gender diversity, age diversity, educational background diversity, and work experience diversity are the workforce diversity factors that have been considered as the independent variables. Job satisfaction has been taken as the dependent variable. Further, correlation analysis has been carried out. The result is presented below.

H_o: *Workforce diversity has not related with job satisfaction.*

The Pearson correlogram test (Table 124.9) validates the hypothesis: workforce diversity significantly relates to job satisfaction (p = 0.001 at 1% significance level). Calculated correlation values (r = 0.136

Table 124.6 Distribution of employees based on their years of experience.

Experience	Frequency	Percent
Up to 5 years	24	12
5 to 10 years	46	23
11 to 15 years	80	40
Above 15 years	50	25
Total	200	100.0

Source: Primary data computed

Table 124.9 Relationship between workforce diversity and recruitment.

Workforce diversity	Job satisfaction	
	r-value	p-value
Gender diversity	0.323	0.001
Age diversity	0.296	0.001
Educational background diversity	0.156	0.001
Work experience diversity	0.136	0.004

Source: Primary data computed

Table 124.7 Distribution of employees based on their tenure with current organization.

Designation	Frequency	Percent
Less than 5 years	46	23.00
5-10 years	98	49.00
11-15 years	40	20.00
More than 15 years	16	8.00
Total	200	100

Source: Primary data computed

Table 124.8 Distribution of employees based on their designation.

Designation	Frequency	Percent
Lecturer	24	12
Senior lecturer	52	26
Associate professor	74	37
Professor	50	25
Total	200	100

Source: Primary data computed

to 0.323) indicate the strength of this relationship. Gender diversity displays the strongest correlation ($r = 0.323$), followed by age ($r = 0.296$), education ($r = 0.156$), and work experience diversity ($r = 0.136$). This confirms a substantial, positive link between workforce diversity and job satisfaction, with gender diversity exerting the most significant influence. Nonetheless, educational background and work experience exhibit comparatively weaker ties with job satisfaction.

Conclusions

The study on Malaysia's education sector reveals robust diversity in various facets except education-related diversity. Emphasizing job relevance, encouraging individuals with additional qualifications can augment diversity. To enhance educational diversity, offering value-added and technical courses online and offline would uplift the sector. Recognizing experienced individuals' achievements is vital to boost satisfaction, facilitating physical exchanges with other universities or countries. In this contemporary era, workforce diversity significantly boosts job satisfaction, particularly through gender diversity. However, educational background and work experience diversity show weaker associations with satisfaction. Educating employees on embracing diversity fosters a more productive work environment, encouraging skill development and self-confidence through non-resistance to diversity.

References

Aksoy, H. H. (1998). Relationship between education and employment: how do employers use educational indicators in hiring? (Results from a participatory observation). In Presented in World Council for Curriculum & Instruction Region VI, North American Chapter Interdisciplinary Education Conference Theme: Educational Networking: Making Connections for the 21st Century, (pp. 1–33).

Darwin Joseph, R. (2014). Age diversity and its impact on employee performance in Singapore. *The International Journal of Research and Development in Technology and Management Science-Kailash*, 21(5), 79–98.

Darwin Joseph, R. and Selvaraj, P. C. (2015). The effects of workforce diversity on employee performance in Singapore organizations. *International Journal of Business Administration*, 6(2), 17–29.

Gallego-Alvarez, I., and Garcia-Sanchez, I. M., and Rodriguez-Dominguez, L. (2010). The Influence of gender diversity on corporate performance. *Revista de Contabilidad-Spanish Accounting Review*, 13(1), 53–88.

Kaur, N., and Arora, P. (2020). Acknowledging gender diversity and inclusion as key to organizational growth: a review and trends. *Journal of critical Reviews*, 7(6), 125–131, ISSN: 2394-5125.

Kunze, F., Boehm, S. A., and Bruch, H. (2011). Age diversity, age discrimination climate and performance consequences- a cross organizational study. *Journal of Organizational Behavior*, 32(2), 264–290.

Mcdaniel, M. A., and Schmidt, F. L. (1988). Job Experience correlates of job performance. *Journal of Applied Psychology*, 73(2), 327–330.

Okafor, C. N., Obi-Anike, H. O., and Adeyemi, O. S. (2020). Does ethno-religion diversity influence firms performance? evidence from federal health institutions in Nigeria. *International Journal of Advanced Science and Technology*, 29(2), 3365–3383.

Sloka, B., et al. (2015). Employers' needs and expectations for qualified employees (Case study on the opinions in one of the regions in Latvia). *Economics and Business*, 27(1), 69–75. doi.10.1515/eb-2015-0011.

Usop, A. M., Kadtong, M. L., and Usop, D. A. S. O. (2013). The significant relationship between work experience and job satisfaction in Philippines. *International Journal of Human Resource Management and Research (IJHRMR)*, 3(2), 9–16. ISSN: 2249-6874.

Wang, M., and Fang, Y. (2020). Age diversity in the workplace: facilitating opportunities with organizational practices. "The Gerontological society of America". *Public policy and Aging Report*, 30(3), 119–123.

Wieczorek-Szymanska, A. (2020). Gender diversity in academic sector – case study. faculty of economics, finance and management, institute of management, university of Szczecin, 70-453 Szczecin, Poland; anna.wieczorek-szymanska@usz.edu.pl, 1–20, https:// doi:10.3390/ admsci10030041.

125 Socially responsible public procurement: the implementation in Malaysia's public organizations

Nur Faiza Ishak[1,a] and Vinesh Thiruchelvam[2,b]

[1]Ph.D in Management, Asia Pacific University of Technology and Innovation, Malaysia

[2]Chief Innovation and Enterprise Officer, Asia Pacific University of Technology and Innovation, Malaysia

Abstract

The emerging needs of social inclusion represent a potential sustainable opportunity to meet the UN SDG's Goals, specifically Target 12.7. While ensuring that public money is being spent in such a way to achieve long-term benefit, sustainable public procurement is another effort to spur economic growth by minimising the environmental harm and benefitting society through social impact. The motivation to this study is to understand the current practices of sustainable procurement, specifically in social criteria within Malaysia's public organisation. By utilising dataset published in the ePerolehan database between 2019 – 2021 from the awarded procurement notices, this study qualitatively used text mining content analysis technique for consistency purposes. This study contributes to significant findings where social criteria inclusion can be clustered under four different categories; namely employees sourcing requirements, working conditions, work benefit and cultures.

Introduction

Nowadays, public procurement is no longer limited to obtaining the lowest price possible but involves a more comprehensive requirement to achieve the best value for money. According to Organisation for Economic Co-operation and Development (OECD) (2019), public procurement accounts for a significant amount of spending, where approximately 12% of GDP and 29% of government expenditure in OECD member countries. This proves that the governments have huge spending power and spend public money to secure inputs and resources to achieve their objectives. By doing so, the governments will create a significant impact on key stakeholders and broader society. In OECD countries, there is a growing trend of using public procurements as a policy instrument to achieve some policy objectives (OECD, 2019). Traditionally, as public procurement is deemed to achieve a specific target, they are now being used strategically to add more benefits to the surrounding environment (Nijboer et al., 2017). Furthermore, Grandia and Meehan (2017) established that public procurement could focus on societal needs and achieve certain societal goals such as reducing unemployment, encouraging innovation and supporting small local businesses. Besides, public procurement power may be an important driver towards influencing sustainable policy by leveraging markets through significant public purchases (Andhov and Mitkidis, 2017). To achieve greater sustainability,

governments need to adapt their purchasing activities in the market continuously. Not only that, being the single biggest spender in the country, purchasing through public procurement will promote sustainability solutions and further spur more demand (Knutsson and Thomasson, 2014).

As for Malaysia's context, SDGs targets and indicators are closely associated with the 12th Malaysia Plan (12 MP) from 2021 – 2025. Malaysia is committed to pursuing green growth and adopting sustainable consumption and production concepts (EPU, 2021c). In the earlier issue of the 11th Malaysia Plan (11 MP) and based on the year 2016 – 2017 performance, even though the government undertook sufficient measures to achieve a sustainable economy, challenges remain to accomplish the target, mainly due to insufficient coordination, low awareness and unsustainable development across the country (Ministry of Economic Affairs, 2018). Hence, sustainable initiatives through the public procurement process is a decision-making process in which the decisions of procurers serve sustainable development goals, helping create shared value and delivering commercial value creation. Besides, organisations can obtain supplies and services that benefit the environment, society, and the economy by incorporating sustainability into the public procurement processes.

Despite various initiatives taken during the review term, plenty of action must be addressed, especially in sustainable public procurement (SPP). Purposely,

[a]nfaizaishak@gmail.com, [b]dr.vinesh@staffemail.apu.edu.my

the more sustainable the goods and services that the government purchases, the greater the impact on the market, society and the environment. Moreover, sustainable procurement strategies have proved to be able to transform the market, save money, improve financial viability, increase the competitiveness of eco-industries, protect natural resources, and stimulate job creation, all of which contribute to sustainable development (Islam et al., 2017).

Recent work from the literature observed that the majority of the researchers focused on the environmental dimension of sustainability. For example, Neto and Gama Caldas (2018) conducted a review of green criteria being used in food products and catering services. Similarly, (Braulio-Gonzalo and Bovea, 2020b) analysed the green criteria being actively proposed and compared them to the existing sustainability tools within the office building sectors. Nevertheless, another study context in the overall dimension of sustainability was by Braulio-Gonzalo and Bovea (2020a) where they critically reviews all three dimensional of sustainability criteria implementation in the furniture sector.

With these current trends focusing on the green criteria, this study addresses the social criteria being incorporated specifically within Malaysia's public organisation sector. Mainly, the motivation of this study is to understand the current practices of social criteria for public procurement of public organisations. At the same time, this study aims to identify the commonly used social criteria in public procurement.

Literature Review

Unlike the environmental dimension, very little attention is paid to the social dimension (Benchekroun et al., 2019). Semple (2017) described socially responsible public procurement as an effort to contribute social benefits or human rights aspects that can result in greater equality and work-life balance improvements. Generally, the inclusion of social criteria can be as simple as "respecting human rights", "providing a safe working condition", "fair wages" or avoiding child labour (Benchekroun et al., 2019; Grandia and Kruyen, 2020; Hyacinth et al., 2017; Montalbán-Domingo et al., 2019). Most importantly, the inclusivity will also be able to support fair and ethical trade, and at the same time avoid the exploitation of human resources or unethically sourced materials (Stoffel et al., 2019).

Social Dimension

Social compliance seems much more accessible than environmental criteria since various provisions and legal acts related to social responsibility have been outlined and recognised globally. For example, in the context of Australia and New Zealand, they proved that almost 74% of the participating organisations actively incorporated social criteria in their procurement process (Barraket et al., 2021). However, a lower percentage was observed by Fuentes-Bargues et al. (2021) with only 18.6% of Valencia's tenders including social criteria. A comprehensive consideration of social criteria indicated the organisation's effort to ensure the well-being of their employees and provide assurance in terms of work stability and safety. On the other hand, in the context of public procurement, the incorporation of social criteria by procuring organisations mainly ensures that the winning tenderers will put up their effort to provide necessary employee benefits and further contribute to the communities. By embedding social criteria, procuring public organisations have control of whatever the tenderers are offering products or services.

Furthermore, integrating social criteria can enhance compliance with the related social and labor law such as the employment act, corporate social responsibility, supporting SMEs, offering job opportunities and establishing cultural rights. Improving public services like clean transport enhances air quality and reduces the use of toxic chemicals in cleaning products creating a healthier working environment, both of which will enhance the quality of life (European Commission, 2020). Including the social dimension in the public procurement process can further establish the right to freedom of association and collective bargaining, prohibit forced and child labor, and eliminate discrimination in the workplace and occupation (UNEP, 2011). Besides, public procurement can promote social capital by improving the living style through new job openings, resulting in greater social equity.

The exploration of the social dimension in the public procurement process can be seen through a few recent studies. Even though a study by Wontner et al. (2020) discovered that suppliers refused to incorporate socio-economic criteria since their end customers would have to bear the cost, but that can be considered a minority case. For example, Fuentes-Bargues et al. (2021) highlighted the importance of providing health and safety requirements in Spain's construction public procurement. Besides, capacity building to mainly prepare the employee with decent knowledge and expertise is also included as one of the social criteria in public procurement. (Bernal et al., 2019; Masudin et al., 2020). On the other hand, Fourie and Malan (2021) explored that South Africa's public railway organisation embedded social inclusion in terms of employee skill development, new job creation and preservation as well as gender equality in the railway industry. A compilation of commonly used social criteria from previous research is shown in Table 196.1.

Public Social Procurement Program

Compared to the environmental dimension in GPP that has been exercised for quite some time, the social context is literally new with limited policies available globally. As one of the pioneers, the European Commission intends to facilitate the uptake of socially responsible criteria in public procurement (SRPP) and to promote their use across the EU (European Commission, 2021b). According to European Commission (2021b), SRPP is grounded in the 2014 EU harmonised public procurement rules based on the Treaty principles and social aspects. Public authorities can engage in socially responsible public procurement by buying ethical products and services and using public tenders to create job opportunities, decent work, social and professional inclusion, and better conditions for disabled and disadvantaged people. On the other hand, SRPP in Australia focuses on the Indigenous Procurement Policy (2020), Equal Opportunity for

Table 125.1 Social criteria from literature.

Theme	Criteria	Literature
Employees sourcing requirements	• Ban forced/child labor • Gender equality • Employing a person with disabilities • Fair employment and human rights concerns • Integration of disabled and disadvantaged people • Promotion of equality between women and men at work • Human rights protection • Social justice and human rights	Braulio-Gonzalo and Bovea (2020); Cravero (2017); Osei-Kyei et al. (2019); Rahman and Islam (2017); Sarter et al. (2014)
Culture	• Community development • Establish the right to form trade unions • Fair & ethical trade • Freedom of association and no discrimination • Encouraging the use of official languages in each region • Consideration of ethical and fair-trade principles	Akenroye (2013); Braulio-Gonzalo and Bovea (2020); Chiarini et al. (2017); Cravero (2017); Rahman and Islam (2017); Schebesta (2018)
Working conditions	• No discrimination • Minimum wages • Promotion of acceptable working conditions (minimum wages) • Promotion of acceptable working conditions (working time standards) • Compliance with social requirements such as child labour, forced labor • Promote job stability • Compliance with legislation and collective agreements	Adjei-Bamfo and Maloreh-Nyamekye (2019); Braulio-Gonzalo and Bovea (2020); Cravero (2017); Rahman and Islam (2017); Sarter et al. (2014); Simon and Benjamin (2023)
Safety requirement	• Health and safety employees • Promotion of health and safety standards • Health and safety during work execution • Promote occupational health and safety issues • Health and safety requirements	Cravero (2017); Fuentes-Bargues et al. (2021); Masudin et al. (2020); Montalbán-Domingo et al. (2019); Simon and Benjamin (2023)
Work benefit	• Employees' welfare (compensation scheme) • Support disadvantaged or disabled groups • Access to people with disability (facilitate people with disabilities)	Adjei-Bamfo andNaloreh-Nyamekye (2019); Akenroye (2013)
Capacity building	• Training for catering staff • Staff training • Training and skill support • Training participation • Provide capacity building and training • To improve staff skills • Provide training tools • Training and upskilling • Provide jobs and training • Skills development	Akenroye, (2013); Bernal et al., (2019); Braulio-Gonzalo and Bovea, (2020); Loosemore and Reid, (2019); Masudin et al., (2020); Montalbán-Domingo et al., (2019); Neto and Gama Caldas, (2018); Sarter et al., (2014); Smith et al., (2016)

Source: Author

Women in the Workplace Policy and the Victorian Social Procurement Framework (2017) (Barraket et al., 2021; Troje, 2021). Similarly, the Canadian government has recently considered the community employment benefit policy to improve employment opportunities for under-represented groups in major infrastructure projects (Social Enterprise Ecosystem Project, 2015).

Despite the main policy on GGP, Malaysia has also initiated a public social procurement program or known as impact driven public social procurement programme (PPISK) in the year 2021 which aims to leverage the purchasing power in positive social outcomes for the country. The program offers priority to organisations and enterprises that can propose products or services that are readily available that comply with social criteria. As a start, PPISK onboarded 11 products and services that can offer social benefits such as fair opportunities, empowering local skills, improving the likelihoods of women, building safe and sustainable livelihoods to the community, offering job employment for people with disabilities or supporting aboriginal villagers (MaGIC, 2021a).

The effort in PPISK was established through three initiatives; 1) priority is given to registered enterprises/organisations that pledge to offer social inclusions, 2) no restriction of participation in any tender values, and 3) waived criteria for e*Perolehan* (e-Procurement) (MaGIC, 2021b). As a result, the Malaysian government has pledged a total of RM20 million in social procurement options that can be utilised. Besides, the effort of PPISK is expected to offer fair opportunities for businesses to grow in terms of social-impact solutions and at the same time to increase more awareness regarding the importance of sustainable growth and equitable society. Through this strategic policy too, the industry player participating in the public tendering process will have to match the social benchmarks set by the developed countries with stringent requirements to comply with.

Methodology

Utilising existing textual data sources is useful as it facilitates a good understanding of past and present policies, service systems and programs (Mackieson et al., 2019). Furthermore, government documents are considered a trustworthy data source authentically official with high-quality content (Mackieson et al., 2019). In this study, the main data sources for the analysis were interview transcripts. Upon completing this study, the researcher collected and analysed publicly available data from Malaysia's e*Perolehan* public procurement database (https://www.eperolehan.gov.

my/home) for three (3) years from 2019 – 2021 from each eleven organisations of different sectors.

e*Perolehan* system was first initiated in the year 1999 to restructure Malaysia's public procurement process and at the same time, to enhance transparency (Kassim and Hussin, 2013). Malaysia's public organisations fully utilised the e*Perolehan* system in 2018 as an independent procurement process that includes all procurement interactions and payment transactions based on the approved procuring value (Ministry of Finance, 2018). A holistic approach across an e-procurement system is proven to be one of the best global practices to ensure a good governance that leads to great accountability (Guerry et al., 2018).

The e*Perolehan* database allows public access transparently to all sorts of procurement at various statuses such as published, closed, awarded or cancelled by all ministries in Malaysia, regardless of the procurement types (direct negotiation, quotation or tender). Generally, based on Malaysia's public procurement procedures, procurement notices can be advertised for a minimum of 3 days or as long as 60 days, depending on the potential participation of tenderers (Ministry of Finance, 2020c). Typically, the more complicated the project is, the longer time will be given to obtain as many participations as possible. A procurement notice is restricted not only within the ministerial level but by any organisation with its own annual allocated budget. Since thousands of procurement notices are available on the website, it is wise to restrict the keyword of searching to specific criteria.

Hence, this dataset was used to determine their actual level of implementation through the procurement notices. However, only "awarded" procurement notices were accessed through the e*Perolehan* website from 2019 until 2021, based on the ministry participating in the interview session. Figure 125.1 shows the main page of the accessible e*Perolehan* website:

Document Analysis

Qualitative data analysis does not only involve interview transcripts or focus group discussions but also encompasses any document analysis. Typically, conducting document analysis on additional data is another act of achieving triangulation of findings across different datasets (Grandia and Kruyen, 2020; Kobayashi et al., 2018). Document analysis is one of the methods to give meaning to text documents and practical resources to a large amount of reliable data (Bathmanathan et al., 2018). Furthermore, document analysis allows researchers to obtain new findings that primary data might not be able to provide (Morgan, 2022). Similar to primary data analysis, conducting

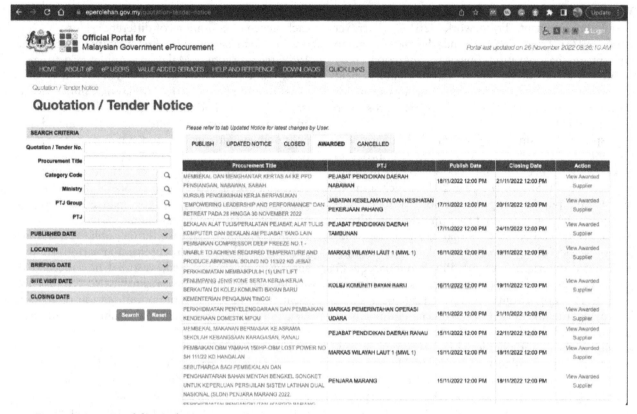

Figure 125.1 ePerolehan website
Source: Author

document analysis involves a repetitive process through a thorough examination of the whole document to review both printed and electronic materials (Koyuncu and Kılıç, 2019).

This study will be able to report the actual practices of SPP within Malaysia's public organisation by conducting document analysis on documents from all procurement notices. To process more than 27,000 procurement notices efficiently, it is not practical to manually run the conventional open coding process. Hence, this study adapted three-step computer-aided text-mining techniques by Grandia and Kruyen (2020) and Kobayashi et al. (2018), allowing pattern identification of over 27,000 documents. According to Yu et al. (2011), text mining is known as extracting related information by identifying patterns from all the documents collected. To do so, a compilation of all sustainable criteria from literature is assembled according to similar dimensions and being made into an extensive codebook to be referred to. A hybrid approach that begins with deductive coding based on a literature review was followed by an inductive approach focusing more on localised sustainable criteria to achieve comprehensive results. The overall text-mining process is using Atlas.ti version 22 software. Figure 125.2

shows the overall process flow for the text-mining process adapted in this study.

After the data collection process is complete, clustering codes are gathered based on previous studies with keywords in either sustainable procurement (Ghadge et al., 2019; Peralta Álvarez et al., 2017; Rahman and Islam, 2017; Smith et al., 2016), green procurement (Sicignano et al., 2019; Soto et al., 2020; C. Yu et al., 2020), social procurement (Akenroye, 2013; Montalbán-Domingo et al., 2021) or economic performance in procurement (Treviño-Lozano, 2021). These multidimensional criteria of sustainability served as a steppingstone before being refined into a proper subcluster and cluster accordingly. For example, nationalities, local workers, aboriginals/*Orang Asli*, age and gender criteria are grouped together under one cluster under the employees sourcing requirements. At the same time, working hours/minimum wages/insurance criteria are grouped together under the second cluster of working conditions. Besides, the synonyms, alternative spellings and translation into the Malay language were also included in the codebook under each cluster group. Including dual language and synonyms is crucial since procurement notices come in various templates and languages. For instance, "insurance" are

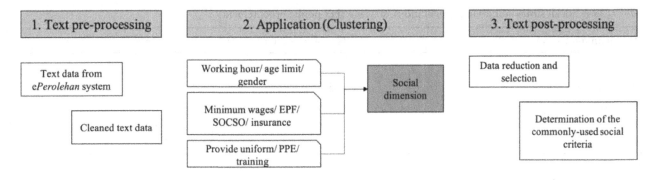

Adapted from Kobayashi et al. (2018)
Grandia & Kruyen (2020)

Figure 125.2 Text mining process
Source: Author

also defined as "*insuran*" and "*insurans*" to obtain a holistic coverage of the specific code to be discovered by the software.

Even though performing a computer-aided text mining using reliable software in qualitative analysis is relatively new, but it has been proven successful by Grandia and Kruyen (2020) and Van Lill and Marnewick (2016). Mainly because it allows data processing of a large set of documents with text identification options at minimum human intervention. The list of codes in the sub-clustered criteria was added to the Atlas.ti software in the go-list module to enhance the search criteria. Conducting computer-aided software to mine all the pre-listed code is one of the best methods for processing a large amount of data that involves cumbersome text volume. Besides, it saves time and resources with exceptional results and at the same time, improves the reliability and rigour of this study.

Data Analysis

The analysis of procurement notices provides evidence of sustainable criteria embedded in Malaysia's public procurement. Through these documents too, it is possible to assess how far the organisations have practised sustainability in their procurement notices. These documents were obtained from the *ePerolehan* system which is transparently available online at http://www.eperolehan.gov.my. The administrative data set was collected for three (3) years of 2019, 2020 and 2021, covering only the "awarded" procurement tender. This study observed a total of 27,765 procurement notices from eleven (11) organisations. Based on the documents analysis, there are situations where each procurement notice includes multiple sustainability criteria such as environmental, social or

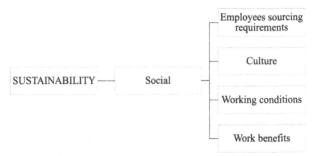

Figure 125.3 Social dimensions sub-criteria inclusions
Source: Author

economic. However, as this study focuses on the social criteria, the overall inclusivity of social dimensions in Malaysia's public procurement is concluded in Figure 125.3 below.

Furthermore, this study discovered that the overall implementation of SPP in Malaysia's public procurement is at 21.99% or 6,105 out of 27,765 procurement notices extracted from the *ePerolehan* system. This study also discovered that at least one criterion from the codebook was identified in a procurement notice that embedded sustainable criteria. For a start, the score indicates that there are still more than 80% of the procurement notices that do not include any criteria at all. In this case, social criteria have been incorporated in at least 1,816 procurement notices which represent 6.54% of overall notices. The overall inclusion of social criteria with another dimension is shown in Table 125.2 below.

From the analysis of the procurement notices, this study managed to ascertain which criteria were most frequently incorporated in the procurement notices. Even though environmental criteria are known as the familiar ones based on the GGP guidelines, the findings showed that Malaysia's public organisation

Table 125.2 Social sustainability implementations in Malaysia's public procurement.

SPP main dimension	No. of procurement notices	Overall %
Social	1,816	6.54%
Environment + social	165	0.59%
Social + economic	130	0.47%
Environment + social + economic	6	0.02%
Overall	2,117	7.62%

Source: Author

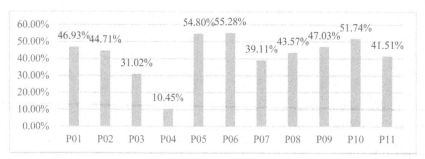

Figure 125.4 Comparison of SPP practices in 11 organisations for all dimensions
Source: Author

has been incorporating social criteria more widely than environmental ones. These frequent occurrences proved that Malaysia's public organisations had considered social dimensions in their procurement notices way ahead of the GGP guidelines focused on.

Furthermore, from the overall analysis of procurement notices, this study discovered that SPP practices within Malaysia's public procurement had been incorporated well enough in most of the organisations with more than 20% implementation as stated by Economic Planning Unit (2021b). A complete comparison between each organisation is shown in Figure 125.4. P06 has the highest percentage of implementation (55.28%) compared to other organisations whilst P04 has the least implementation of SPP with only 10.45%. Nevertheless, the organisation's performance for each dimension is explained in the next section.

Social Dimension

Unlike the environmental dimension, social inclusion is much more comprehensive and subjective. It involves anything related to society, rights, freedom, fairness, safety or well-being. Incorporating social value in public tenders will spur social responsibility and address major societal challenges that subsequently promote sustainable growth. Figure 125.5 compiles some of the most commonly used social criteria based on the document analysis.

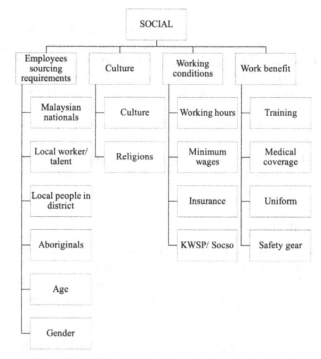

Figure 125.5 Social criteria and sub-criteria inclusions found in the *ePerolehan* system
Source: Author

Based on the interview sessions, most of the participants were unfamiliar with social inclusions in public procurement, let alone the criteria involved. This might possibly be due to the are no specific clauses

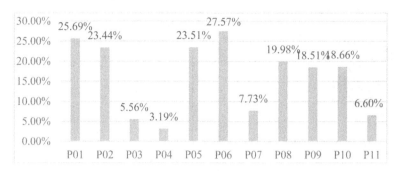

Figure 125.6 The incorporation of social criteria within Malaysia's public procurement
Source: Author

mentioned about social criteria in GGP 3.0 guidelines. However, some of the criteria are readily available through legislation and other policies such as the Employment Act 1955 and Food Act 1983. Hence, a further analysis through procurement notices yielded different results. Almost all organisations have already embedded social dimension criteria in their procurement notices without realising it. Further analysis of the procurement notices document showed that at least 2,117 (7.62%) out of 27,765 have at least one social criterion in their procurement notices for the past three years. It is impressive to discover that more than half of the participating organisations have embedded social criteria in more than 10% of their procurement notices. The overall percentage of social criteria incorporation by each organisation for three years is shown in Figure 125.6.

Why is it important for public procurement to focus on the social dimension? It is obvious that public tender involves providing services or products to the community such as supplying furniture to schools or hospitals, procuring pharmaceuticals products for public health facilities, keeping public areas well-maintained and clean, or supplying materials for identity cards, passports or driver's license to the public. Hence, to avoid employees' low morale and lack of motivation, which might lead to public users' complaints, public organisations have taken their own initiatives. Inclusivity of social dimension criteria comes from the organizations' initiatives towards their responsibility to the winning suppliers or service providers. Most of the fundamental inclusion is nothing new to the corporate world such as providing a decent working environment, basic training, minimum wages and complying with maximum working hours.

To begin with, this study differentiates the findings according to their social category through document reading and investigations. For example, the open coding of "Tenderer must appoint local staff" and "The contract workers must hold a Malaysian citizenship" is clustered together under the same category

of "employees sourcing requirements". Additionally, open coding of "not allowed to work in a double shift", "maximum working hours are 12" or "winning supplier must abide by the minimum wages order by the government" and "provide EPF & SOCSO" falls under "working conditions".

Out of all sixteen (16) social criteria discovered, the majority of the organisations focused on "working hours", "*warganegara*/Malaysians", "age" and followed by the newly emerged criteria "halal requirement". Figure 125.7 shows the compilation of social criteria frequency for all organisations.

Typically, Malaysia's public organisations focus on employees' age restrictions that the winning supplier/contractor has to adhere to. According to Tools for Information (2017), full-time employment may start at the age of 15 but certain protective regulations cover young workers aged 15 to 18. Most of the age-limit criteria stated in the procurement notices are the restriction of working age at 18 years and even some restriction to 21 years, especially for a security services contract. Besides, there are also requirements stating that if any pensioners are to be employed to fulfil the contract, they must undergo strict health and medical check-up regularly and will only be allowed to work for up to 65 years. It is crucial to ensure their employees' well-being meet the tender requirements and provide the best service to avoid any complications in the future. The following procurement notices show the organisation's commitment to the age restriction.

Product/ service group: Cleaning services "*The employees' age must not be less than 18 years old and more than 58 years old. If the employee is older than 58, they must obtain an official medical report.*" [P01].

Product/service group: Transportation service "*Medically fit and free from substance abuse. Age between 30 to 55 years old*" [P04].

Product/ service group: Security services "*Security officers must be over 18 years old and not more than 50 years old. Any security officers that are more than*

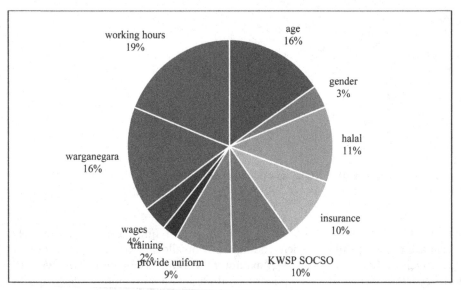

Figure 125.7 Social criteria frequency within Malaysia's public procurement
Source: Author

40 years old are subject to health approval from Public Health Officer every year." [P09].

Apart from age restriction, all organisations emphasised on the required working time for the winning contract employees. To avoid any mishandling while performing their duty, organisations also stated that no double shift is allowed where it involves not more than 12 working hours per day. This requirement is especially for security services and cleaning services to ensure the best performance from their employees to fulfil their duty.

Following that, Malaysia's Government has imposed a minimum wage order for 2020 of RM1,200 (Federal Government Gazette, 2020). It is crucial for procuring organisations to specifically mention the minimum wage order in procurement notices to protect employees' rights. Enabling such criteria will also reduce the possibility of non-compliance with the winning contract's job scope. Complying with minimum wage regulations is nothing new in the global world. The minimum wage policy is crucial to help low-income families to manage their economic sources. In this context, wages are not the only criteria but also the company's responsibility to contribute towards the Employee's Provident Fund (EPF) and Social Organisation Contribution (SOCSO). Some extracts from procurement notices related to the minimum wage criteria are compiled as follows:

Product/ service group: Security services "*To ensure that all salary payments and benefits for security guards are made according to the minimum wages orders by the government*" [P04].

Product/ service group: Agriculture farming services "*To provide a sufficient budget to pay salary, allowances, KWSP and PERKESO for two general workers*" [P07].

Product/ service group: Catering services "*Mandatory: Company must ensure to adhere to the current minimum wages order by the government*" [P01].

Furthermore, there have also been several situations where procuring organisations practise gender equality especially in security and cleaning services. Emphasizing on gender equality is nothing new. Gutberlet (2021) explained that a more experienced gender according to their work practices will be able to avoid any alienation of the work process.

In the document analysis, it was apparent that procuring organisations mentioned their preference for having a separate job description for cleaning services employees where men are required to conduct tougher tasks such as polishing carpets using chemicals and heavy machines or cleaning outside windows using a crane. Besides, there is also a preference for security services contracts where only men are allowed to work during the night shift at risky government premises. The following are a few keywords related to gender preferences in tender notices:

Product/ service group: Security services "*Must be free from any criminal records and we give priority to men.*" [P07].

Product/service group: Cleaning services "*General workers must be among women only*" [P10].

Product/service group: Transport services "*Driver must be a man within 18 to 50 years old, possess* valid driver's license and with full insurance coverage" [P04].

A new emerging criterion observed during the document analysis phase related to choices on religious food requirements such as Halal labelled products, Halal catering services and Muslim cooked food (*makanan bermasak Islam*). Furthermore, the halal requirement is one of the most important elements of the daily life of Muslims which does not necessarily apply to food items but also covers preparation and food packaging, cosmetics, pharmaceuticals, supplements and water filters (Mohamed et al., 2020; Raja Rina et al., 2013; Wan Azlan et al., 2016; Wibisono et al., 2018). Naturally, halal requirements do not only relate to environmental concerns, but also uphold diversity, empowerment, transparency, fair wages, fair trade, and consumer responsibility (Pg Hj Idris et al., 2022). R. Abdullah et al. (2018) through their study confirmed that the adoption of sustainable practices in the halal industry is still absent.

Referring to Malaysia's public infrastructure provider such as public school, higher education institution, public health facilities (clinics/hospitals) or government officers, the government are serving a multi-cultural community. Besides, it is a due fact that Malaysia is a majority Muslim country with a demographic of 61.3% of the population Muslim (Ibrahim et al., 2016). Hence, due to high demand, the halal market is widely recognised worldwide, ensuring the quality and security of the products. For this reason, the researcher decided that it is relevant to include this new finding predominantly in a Muslim country where the Islamic religion influences purchasing decisions in public organisations. A few criteria clauses extracted from procurement notices are next to support these statements.

Product/service group: Water filter "*The product must obtain Halal certification from JAKIM with a reference number. Please upload the proof of certification too*" [P03].

Product/service group: Catering services "*To provide halal breakfast and lunch for 50 pax and 15 days of class*" [P07].

Product/service group: Medical food "*To provide folic acid and iron in an airtight bottle with clear label medicine name, ingredients and expiry date. Must obtain Halal from JAKIM*".

Furthermore, the participating tenderers should also consider providing sufficient training and safety gear for their employees as part of their work benefits. In terms of training, this study discovered that organisations emphasized on training required to be provided by the winning tenderers, especially in the service group. The following examples were extracted from procurement notices.

Product/service group: Catering services "*Participating tenderers are required to send their employees to food handling courses to ensure that they have sufficient knowledge to perform their duty well.*" [P04].

Product/service group: Security services "*Security Guards must be exposed and well trained in the first aid emergency and related administrative issue when there is no officer around*" [P08].

Product/service group: Cleaning services "*to provide training for employees that involved in cleaning works*" [P10].

The same goes for providing suitable working attire such as personal protective equipment, safety boots as well as working uniforms to protect the employee's safety.

Product/service group: Catering services "*Subcontractor that is being appointed for delivery purposes must be equipped with personal protective equipment (PPE) along with hair net/ hair cover, face mask, apron and safety boots*" [P04].

Product/service group: Cleaning services "*Employees Working Attire: Employers must provide complete uniform with name tag and suitable Personal Protective Equipment*" [P06].

Product/ service group: Farming workers "*Workers must wear PPE during pesticides poisoning work*" [P07].

Discussion

As for the thematic analysis from procurement notice extraction, the findings surprisingly revealed that Malaysia's public organisations had incorporated more than 7% of the total procurement in social criteria. Compared to other countries, the Valencian public organisation only achieved 11.7% (Fuentes-Bargues et al., 2021) while New Zealand and Australia achieved 15% (Barraket et al., 2021). This finding is quite interesting since no authoritative guidelines are being released on social procurement yet. This study focuses on three (3) years of implementation (2019 – 2021) and according to GGP Guidelines 3.0 (EPU, 2020), social procurement will only begin in the year 2021 onwards. Nevertheless, most of the social criteria identified in the procurement notices include the basic employment requirement and employees' welfare. Besides, the substantial accomplishment of social criteria is also based on the current legislation available in Malaysia such as Employment Act 1955 (Employment Act 1955, 2012) and child labour (Tools for Information, 2017) or minimum wages (Federal Government Gazette, 2020). Apart from obeying the lawful act, incorporating social criteria in public tenders guarantees that suppliers and contractors will not neglect their responsibilities towards their employees. Mainly because public tenders usually involve providing facilities and services to the public and carry the government identity as the front liners who offers the services. For instance, the employees who work as security guards under security services appointed through public tenders must be protected through proper working benefits and working conditions so that they can perform their duty well in protecting public areas. Hence, it is safe to say that the legislative act is the key enabler to ensure that all organisations take it into consideration.

This study also accords with another unexpected finding where another social requirement for participating tenderers is to employ local talent and local citizens (Malaysian citizens) in most of the services. This effort is to actively address more job opportunities on a contractual basis to lower the unemployment rate. Malaysia's public organisations are also keen to engage local citizens to help eradicate social problems. According to the literature, similar findings by Osei-Kyei et al. (2019) found that job creation for local residents is another essential requirement for achieving social responsibility measures. Creating jobs for unemployed citizens through institutional pressure has also been implemented in Australia (Denny-Smith et al., 2020). At the same time, providing necessary training for a particular job scope is another essential social criterion to boost local talent. It is encouraging to know that public procurers are concerned about knowledge dissemination by enhancing the skills and expertise of the employees.

Moreover, another interesting new finding from this study is the contemplation of public organisations to consider religious and cultural requirements, which is the halal requirement for food products or catering services. The population of Muslims has grown to 18% and causing an increase in demand in the halal market (Azmi et al., 2018). Even though the halal requirement is a new criterion identified in this study, but it is not surprising at all since Malaysia is a Muslim country with a strong Halal certification body to endorse such businesses. Catering services for public health facilities or public schools and training centres must at least provide halal-certified food products as most Malaysians are Muslims. This new emerging criterion is very important for any Muslim country to ensure their rights as Muslims are protected well enough. Besides, providing non-certified halal products can furnish undesirable impressions in the community, especially in suburban areas (Wan Azlan et al., 2016).

Despite the number of implementations being relatively low, this study chooses to disagree with Jiménez et al. (2019) where the environmental dimension is more challenging to implement due to the lack of legislation to be obliged. Being a technologist country which fully utilises being a user and not an inventor, the sustainability industry in Malaysia relies on the existing product which causes the higher price and limited product availability when there's no demand. Nonetheless, after carefully deliberating all three dimensions of sustainability, this study makes a significant contribution in terms of the existing criteria used in the procurement process. Even though plenty of other criteria have been acknowledged through literature, these findings depicting local context especially in Malaysia are essential and can be used as future guidelines. A lot of consideration needs to be considered since most public organisations depend highly on product availability within their budget allocation. Furthermore, these findings may shed some light on relevant routes to be taken to increase SPP implementation in Malaysia further.

Conclusion

The overall findings provide strong support to contribute to literature. Particularly, this study extends from a single dimension (environment) to a multi-dimension of sustainability triple bottom line (environment, social and economy). By doing so, this study interpreted the current understanding and practices of public procurers regarding sustainability criteria and the common product groups involved. The empirical findings in this study provide a new discovery of social criteria being incorporated in procurement notices such as work conditions, work benefit and cultural. Besides, the social dimension is also deemed to have a higher percentage due to the strong legislation available regarding employment and social benefits.

The findings of this study are crucial especially in the context of Malaysia since social responsibility consideration is still an infant in the research world. The overall findings provide strong support to contribute to literature. By addressing the most common social criteria being incorporated will improve better inclusivity toward the employee and community. While Malaysia is still a work in progress in SPP, this study has provided evidence that Malaysia's public organisations have consistently incorporated social criteria whenever possible.

However, there were certain limitations in conducting this study. Although this study managed to shed some light, there is another limitation which is only focused on Malaysia's public organisation context. Despite the valuable findings, one single platform study makes this study is not possible to be generalised. Besides, this study employs a qualitative analysis that aims for an in-depth understanding of social criteria implementation in Malaysia. Hence, this study proposes that the study scope for future research is extended to private organisations as well as suppliers' scope of context. It is useful to shift the focus from public to private sectors with similar research settings to explore their actual state of understanding and implementation. Remarkably, the private sector is starting to act concerning sustainability interests, especially in procurement. There might be other criteria that they experience other than the ones reported in this study. Moreover, since this study is limited to documentation extraction from the e*Perolehan* system, future research could focus on a specific case study according to sector or product group for a clearer picture.

References

Employment Act 1955, Business Law Review (2012). https://doi.org/10.54648/bula1982153.

Federal Government Gazette (2020). Minimum Wages Order 2020. Federal Government Gazette, (pp. 1–11). https://www.aana.com/advocacy/federal-government-affairs.

Fourie, D., and Malan, C. (2021). Can public procurement requirements for railway transport promote economic and social sustainability in south africa? *Sustainability*, 13(21), 11923. https://doi.org/10.3390/su132111923.

Fuentes-Bargues, J. L., Bastante-Ceca, M. J., Ferrer-Gisbert, P. S., and González-Cruz, M. C. (2021). Analysis of the situation of social public procurement of works at the Valencian region (Spain). *Sustainability*, 13(1), 1–23. https://doi.org/10.3390/su13010175.

Ghadge, A., Kidd, E., Bhattacharjee, A., and Tiwari, M. K. (2019). Sustainable procurement performance of large enterprises across supply chain tiers and geographic regions. *International Journal of Production Research*, 57(3), 764–778. https://doi.org/10.1080/00207543.2018.1482431.

Grandia, J., and Kruyen, P. (2020). Assessing the implementation of sustainable public procurement using quantitative text-analysis tools: a large-scale analysis of Belgian public procurement notices. *Journal of Purchasing and Supply Management*, 26(4). https://doi.org/10.1016/j.pursup.2020.100627.

Grandia, J., and Meehan, J. (2017). Public procurement as a policy tool: using procurement to reach desired outcomes in society. *International Journal of Public Sector Management*, 30(4), 302–309. https://doi.org/10.1108/IJPSM-03-2017-0066.

Guerry, L., Martins, A., Sachdeva, P., and Mayoral, A. (2018). Public Procurement: 12 Ways Governments Can Unlock Better Value. Oliver Wyman.

Gutberlet, J. (2021). Grassroots waste picker organizations addressing the UN sustainable development goals. *World Development*, 138, 105195. https://doi.org/10.1016/j.worlddev.2020.105195.

Hyacinth, D. D., Babura, A. M., and Animashaun, A. O. (2017). Sustainable public procurement practice: panacea to good governance in Nigeria. *International Journal of Scientific Research in Social Sciences and Management Studies*, 2(1), 114–131.

Ibrahim, I. I., Johari, N. R., Nor, M. N. M., Ahmad, Z., Wahab, S. A. A. B., and Hamid N. H. (2016). Antecedence that affect advertising from an Islamic perspective in Malaysia as a muslim country. *International Academic Research Journal of Social Science*, 2(1), 55–60.

Islam, M. M., Turki, A., Murad, M. W., and Karim, A. (2017). Do sustainable procurement practices improve organizational performance? *Sustainability*, 9(12), 1–17. https://doi.org/10.3390/su9122281.

Jiménez, J. M., López, M. H., and Escobar, S. E. F. (2019). Sustainable public procurement: From law to practice. *Sustainability*, 11(22), 6388. https://doi.org/10.3390/su11226388.

Kassim, E. S., and Hussin, H. (2013). A success model for the Malaysian government e-procurement system: the buyer perspective. *International Journal of Electronic Government Research*, 9(1), 1–18. https://doi.org/10.4018/jegr.2013010101.

Knutsson, H., and Thomasson, A. (2014). Innovation in the public procurement process: a study of the creation of innovation-friendly public procurement. *Public Management Review*, 16(2), 242–255. https://doi.org/10.1080/14719037.2013.806574.

Kobayashi, V. B., Mol, S. T., Berkers, H. A., Kismihók, G., and den Hartog, D. N. (2018). Text mining in organizational research. *Organizational Research Methods*, 21(3), 733–765. https://doi.org/10.1177/1094428117722619.

Koyuncu, İ., and Kılıç, A. F. (2019). The use of exploratory and confirmatory factor analyses: a document analysis. *Education and Science*, 44(198), 361–388. https://doi.org/10.15390/EB.2019.7665.

Loosemore, M., and Reid, S. (2019). The social procurement practices of tier-one construction contractors in Australia. *Construction Management and Economics*, 37(4), 183–200. https://doi.org/10.1080/01446193.2018.1505048.

Mackieson, P., Shlonsky, A., and Connolly, M. (2019). Increasing rigor and reducing bias in qualitative research: a document analysis of parliamentary debates using applied thematic analysis. *Qualitative Social Work*, 18(6), 965–980. https://doi.org/10.1177/1473325018786996.

Van Lill, D., and Marnewick, C. (2016). Comparative analysis of Atlas.ti and Leximancer text-mining software in the field of benefits management. In 33rd Pan-Pacific Business Conference, https://doi.org/10.5930/issn.1-931649-27-6.

126 User satisfaction toward e-bikes

M. Hari Ganesh[a] and V. Haripriya[b]

Karpagam Academy of Higher Education, Coimbatore, India

Abstract

This study examines user satisfaction with e-bikes and identifies significant factors that influence satisfaction levels. The analysis involved conducting Simple percentage and factor analysis to determine the key factors that contribute to user satisfaction. In recent years, e-bikes have become more well-liked as an eco-friendly and practical form of mobility. Understanding consumer happiness with e-bikes is important for manufacturers, politicians, and anybody contemplating using this technology. This study seeks to give a thorough summary of e-bike customer satisfaction aspects. The study combines prior research, market research, and user feedback to pinpoint the crucial factors affecting user happiness. User satisfaction is significantly influenced by elements including improved riding experience, accessibility, commuting convenience, health and fitness advantages, cost savings, fun and pleasure, and sustainability awareness.

Keywords: E-bikes, electronic industry, environment pollution, two-wheelers

Introduction

In recent years, electric bicycles (e-bikes) have surged in popularity as an eco-friendly and efficient mode of transport, blending pedal power with electric motor assistance for a comfortable ride. Understanding user satisfaction with e-bikes is pivotal for policymakers, urban planners, and manufacturers seeking to optimize regulations, infrastructure, and product design. This study comprehensively assesses various factors influencing user experiences and preferences, elucidating the reasons behind e-bikes' appeal. Factors like enhanced riding experiences, accessibility, health benefits, cost-effectiveness, and sustainability awareness significantly drive user happiness, aiding potential buyers in decision-making. Recognizing these elements enables stakeholders to craft effective strategies for e-bike adoption, fostering sustainable mobility. Additionally, this research identifies avenues for further study and information gaps, offering a comprehensive resource for manufacturers, policymakers, and enthusiasts keen on e-bikes' role in sustainable transportation.

Review of Literature

Table 126.1 Literature reviews.

Authors	Key findings
Deekshu (2018)	Majority of consumers content with e-bike mileage, convinced of advantages, and willing to recommend to friends.
Bhalla (2018)	Analysis indicates electric vehicle acceptance requires increased infrastructure and environmental awareness through government and producer investments.
Javed and Khurram (2022)	Recommendations include enhancing user knowledge, giving specialists dealership opportunities, strengthening distribution networks, and lowering e-bike prices to boost sales.
Charles (2021)	Customer perceptions of e-cars influenced by oil/petrol costs; perception and petrol prices impact electric vehicle purchases.
Flores and Jansson (2021)	Users view micro automobiles as creative and fairly eco-friendly, while non-users don't share the same perspective.
Jain and Handy (2023)	Commuters' e-bike awareness increased but consideration decreased between 2019-2021. Notable rise in awareness among staff, students, and those feeling secure riding to campus.
IJSREM Journal (2022)	Majority of e-bike advertising online; minimal presence in print/TV media. Customers significantly influenced by advertisements in purchase decisions.

[a]anjurcas111@gmail.com, [b]haripriyavaradharaj@gmail.com

Authors	Key findings
Wadate et al. (2019)	Key attributes: e-bikes do not use fossil fuels, aiding in foreign exchange savings, pollution reduction, and noise-free operation.
Kumar and Padmanaban (2019)	Addressing global pollution through CO_2 emission reduction; adoption of EVs considered crucial due to transport sector's significant CO_2 emissions.

Source: Author

Research GAP

The expanding use of electric bikes has led manufacturers to create diverse models catering to varied population needs, shaping e-bikes as an integral part of transport and recreational systems. However, research on Indian e-bike users and specifically in Coimbatore remains limited, prompting this study to bridge the gap. The primary concern is understanding user satisfaction factors and their impact, a vital yet understudied aspect in the burgeoning e-bike landscape. Addressing the lack of comprehensive analysis, this research seeks to identify influential elements like safety features, pricing, eco-friendliness, and government incentives on user satisfaction. The study aims to offer insights benefiting e-bike businesses, guiding product development, marketing strategies, and customer service enhancements. Ultimately, it endeavors to elevate user happiness, align consumer expectations, and promote widespread adoption of e-bikes as an eco-friendly and efficient mode of transportation. The study's objective centers on gauging customer brand awareness and satisfaction levels concerning e-bikes.

This study delves into e-bike user satisfaction and key influencing factors, analyzing available data to identify these determinants. It covers aspects like pricing, after-sales service, eco-friendliness, and more to gauge their impact on consumer happiness. Factor analysis is essential to isolate crucial elements. Quantitative data analysis forms the core, likely requiring statistical methods and tools. It focuses solely on examined components, excluding other potential influencers not investigated. Limited to a specific timeframe or market niche, the findings are context-specific but pertinent. Not involving primary data collection or field research, the study's conclusions rely on existing information. While providing a foundational understanding, further research may validate or expand upon these identified variables in diverse contexts or demographics.

Research Methodology

This study employs primary and secondary data collection methods. Primary data, obtained Table 126.2

Table 126.2 Primary and secondary data collection methods with Percentages.

Particulars	Numbers (n = 150)	Percentage
Age		
18-25 years	30	20.0
26-35 years	98	65.3
Above 35 years	22	14.7
Gender		
Male	129	86.0
Female	21	14.0
Educational qualification		
School level	15	10.0
Under graduation	94	62.7
Postgraduation	41	27.3
Occupation		
Student	12	8.0
Private employee	114	76.0
Government employee	19	12.7
Professional	5	3.3
Type of family		
Joint	143	95.3
Nuclear	7	4.7
Locality		
Rural	1	0.7
Semi-urban	34	22.7
Urban	115	76.7
Monthly income (Rs.)		
Up to 10,000	16	10.7
10,000 to 20,000	101	67.3
20,001 to 30,000	28	18.7
Above 30,000	5	3.3
Family monthly income (Rs.)		
Up to 30,000	70	46.7
30,000–50,000	66	44.0
50,001 – 70,000	14	9.3
Above 70,000	Nil	Nil

Particulars	Numbers (n = 150)	Percentage
Are you the only earning person		
Yes	20	13.3
No	130	86.7
Satisfied as a user of e-bike		
Fully satisfied	145	96.7
Satisfied	4	2.7
Not satisfied	1	0.7
Suggest other people to buy e-bike		
Yes	141	94.0
No	9	6.0
Buy an e-bike again		
Yes	52	34.7
No	98	65.3

Source: Author

Table 126.3 KMO and Bartlett's test.

Kaiser-Meyer-Olkin measure of sampling adequacy.		.855
Bartlett's test of sphericity	Approx. Chi-square	1533.073
	df	171
	Sig.	.000

Source: Author

Table 126.4 Rotated component matrix[a].

	Component			
	1	2	3	4
Safety features	.791			
Price of the bike	.742			
After-sales service	.727			
Eco friendly	.627			
Registration fee exemption	.560			
Maximum load	.511			
Road tax exemption		.708		
Brand of the bike		.702		
Running cost		.692		
Comfort		.678		
maintenance cost		.501		
Government subsidy			.760	
Motor power			.703	
Low noise			.695	
Scrapping incentives			.530	
Riding range (Mileage)				.805
Battery life				.706
Charging time				.585
Total	7.680	1.862	1.438	1.189
% of Variance	40.421	9.800	7.569	6.259
Cumulative %	40.421	50.222	57.791	64.050

Source: Author

socio-economic profile and user satisfaction of e-bikes through a questionnaire distributed to e-bike users in Coimbatore District, offers firsthand insights. The questionnaire was designed for ease of understanding to encourage open responses. Secondary data, gathered from books, journals, and websites, complements the primary data. A total of 150 responses were analyzed using percentage and factor analysis after employing convenient sampling.

Significance of the Study

The study's outcomes offer valuable insights to governments, employers, students, and potential e-bike buyers. These insights aid manufacturers in designing more appealing e-bikes, shaping the demand-supply balance, and enhancing e-bike user experiences. The findings have potential implications for policy development, transportation strategies, and boosting e-bike sales, fostering a deeper understanding of user preferences and satisfaction.

Findings

The following table narrates socio-economic profile and user satisfaction of e-bikes.

The prevalent demographic among e-bike users comprises males aged 26 to 35, predominantly with undergraduate education, working in private sectors, residing in urban areas. Their monthly income ranges from Rs. 10,000 to 30,000, with two or more earners in the family. Despite satisfaction using e-bikes and willingness to recommend, they exhibit reluctance toward repurchase. Factor analysis aims to uncover influential elements shaping user preferences, validated by Kaiser-Meyer-Olkin and Bartlett's test of sphericity to ensure sample suitability.

The result of KMO and Bartlett's test is found greater than 0.70. Hence the collected data is fit for employing factor analysis. Further the large value of Bartlett's test of sphericity (4958.456, Df:855, Sig. .000) indicated the appropriateness of factor analysis i.e., the sample was adequate.

Locating Eigen values larger than unity reveals four elements. Significant factors are those that have a component loading of at least 0.5. From the rotated components matrix, it can be seen that safety features, price of the bike, after-sales service, ecofriendly, registration fee exemption and maximum load have a component loading of 0.5 and above. Hence, these four variables form first factor. In the second factor, road tax exemption, brand of the bike, running cost, comfort and maintenance cost are found to be significant. In the third factor, government subsidy, motor power, low noise and scrapping incentives are found to be significant. In the last factor, riding range (mileage), battery life and charging time are found to be significant.

Conclusions

The study recommends several strategies to enhance user satisfaction with e-bikes. These suggestions include highlighting safety features, competitive pricing, and eco-friendliness, emphasizing brand reputation, promoting cost savings, and providing information on government incentives. Factors like riding range, battery life, and charging time should be addressed to meet customer preferences. The study's findings underscore the importance of these elements in improving user happiness and suggest how businesses can tailor their offerings accordingly. It's crucial to customize these recommendations to suit specific markets and capitalize on the unique advantages of e-bike products. Furthermore, future research in the e-bike industry could explore social and environmental aspects, infrastructure availability, cost-effectiveness, and satisfaction comparisons between e-bikes and traditional bicycles, among other areas.

References

Bose, B. (2021). Marketing Management. Hilmalaya Publishing House.

Cappelle, J., et al. (2002). Characterisation of Electric Bicycles Performances. *Blood.*

Cappelle, J., et al. (2003). Electrically assisted cycling around the world. In Proceedings of the 20th International Battery, Hybrid and Fuel Cell Electric Vehicle Symposium.

Chatterjee, B. K. (2004). Marketing Management. Jaico Publishing House.

Cherry, C., and Cervero, R. (2007). Use characteristics and mode choice behavior of electric bike users in China. *Transport Policy.*

Cuntiffw, E.. and Still (2009). Basic Marketing. Prentice Hall of India.

Fyhri, A., and Fearnley, N. (2015). Effects of e-bikes on bicycle use and mode share. Transportation Research Part D: Transport and Environment, 36, 45–52.

Harrell, G. D. (2001). Consumer Behavior. Harcourt Brace Jovanouich, Publishers.

Jamerson, F., and Benjamin, E. (2009). Electric bike worldwide reports.

Jayashanker (2007). Marketing. Maugham Publishers.

Mathur, V. (2007). Consumer Behavior. Cyber Tech Publications.

Memoria, C. B., Joshi, R. L. (2000). Principles and practice of marketing in India, Published by Kitab Mahal, 28, Natiji Subhash Marg, New Delhi-110002.

Pilipkotler (2007). Marketing Management. Prentice Hall of India.

Pillai and Bahavathi (2007). Modern Marketing. S. Chand

Rose, G. (2002). E-bikes and urban transportation: emerging issues and unresolved questions transportation.

Saxena, R. (2005). Marketing Management. New Delhi: Tata Mcgraw-Hill Publishing Company Limited.

Sharma, D. D. (2001). Marketing Research. Sulthan Chand and Sons,

Sherlekars, A. (2004). Marketing Management. Himalaya Publishing.

Sontakki, C. N. (2009). Marketing Management. Kalayani Publishers.

127 Public perception toward smart city project in Coimbatore city

Akshaya, N.ᵃ, K. Jothiᵇ, J. Sudarvelᶜ and R. Velmuruganᵈ

Karpagam Academy of Higher Education, Coimbatore, India

Abstract

The study delves into public perception of Coimbatore's smart city project, utilizing a mixed-methods approach. Results suggest overall positive sentiment, acknowledging benefits like improved infrastructure and connectivity. Factors impacting perception include awareness, personal experiences, trust in governance, and inclusivity perceptions. The research identifies areas for enhancing public perception. Acknowledging public sentiment's importance, the study emphasizes its role in the project's long-term success and sustainability.

Keywords: Citizen engagement, Coimbatore, public perception, smart city project, sustainability, urban development

Introduction

Coimbatore's smart city initiative aims to use technology for urban improvement. This study explores public perception of the project, essential for its success. It will employ surveys and interviews to understand residents' attitudes and expectations. As smart cities focus on innovation and community benefit, the study aims to capture diverse views, considering various demographics and opinions. Examining how Coimbatore's residents perceive the smart city project will provide crucial insights for policymakers and urban planners. This research aims to contribute to India's smart city development conversation by gathering comprehensive data on public sentiment.

Review of Literature

Author(s) and Year	Summary
Trindade et al. (2017)	Analyzes the relationship between environmental sustainability and smart cities through a qualitative assessment of literature from Scopus, Science Direct, and Emerald Insight. Valuable for researchers seeking background information.
Kandpal et al. (2017)	Investigates issues and funding difficulties in building or upgrading Indian cities under the Smart cities mission. Suggests options like debt finance and FDI for financing.
Mishra (2017)	Advises tactics for governments, particularly in India, to implement for successful smart city projects, focusing on suitable finances, expertise development, and favorable regulations.
Praharaj et al. (2017)	Explores the connection between social-economic standards, city involvement, digital infrastructure in Indian cities, advocating for demand-driven policies, city sizes in citizen engagement, and awareness.
Silva et al. (2017)	Reviews the use of IoT in smart cities to address urbanization and population issues, offering insights into smart cities' characteristics, composition, design, and practical applications.
Macke et al. (2018)	Discusses smart city complexities, emphasizing an integrated approach considering objective and subjective quality of life for residents, and the need for research focusing on consumer preference and life quality.
Aggarwal and Solomon (2019)	Investigates government funding sources and institutional frameworks for smart cities, focusing on the Smart Cities Mission's financial viability and public-private partnerships.
Hameed (2019)	Emphasizes telecommunications' role in smart city infrastructure and its transition to sustainable and ecologically friendly cities, highlighting sustainability's alignment with smart city goals.

ᵃakshayaakshaya890@gmail.com, ᵇjothikrishnasamydr@gmail.com, ᶜj.sudarvel@gmail.com, ᵈdrvelsngm@gmail.com

Author(s) and Year	Summary
Camero and Alba (2019)	Explores the evolving concept of smart cities in research and city planning, highlighting the absence of a universally accepted definition and its fragmented development across multiple domains.
Praharaj and Han (2019)	Examines Indian perceptions of smart cities and their conceptual elements, stressing the importance of integrating sustainability and community concerns beyond digital technology in defining smart cities.
Rana et al. (2019)	Identifies governance, economics, technology, social, environmental, and legal barriers as impediments to smart city development in India, emphasizing governance as the most significant barrier.
Hasija et al. (2020)	Categorizes global smart city initiatives into themes of data, end-user benefit, and economic feasibility, acknowledging the infancy of academic literature and suggesting contributions from manufacturing and service operations management researchers.
Georgiadis et al. (2021)	Examines the influence of ICT applications on residents' lives and their role in municipal collaboration, highlighting ICT's importance in building sustainable smart cities.
Coelho et al. (2021)	Discusses smart contracts' use for governance in modern society, addressing the potential of blockchain-assisted tools to increase citizen involvement in decision-making, primarily through decentralized systems and voting procedures.

Source: Author

Problem Statement and Scope of the Study

Coimbatore's smart city project's success relies on public backing, making understanding public perception crucial. This study aims to explore residents' awareness, satisfaction, and concerns to guide policymakers and planners. Positive perception drives cooperation, while negativity can stall progress. The investigation will deeply analyze perceived benefits, challenges, and community expectations, aiding in engagement strategies, gap identification in knowledge dissemination, and tailored approaches for diverse demographics. Assessing public involvement in decision-making and communication channels' roles will inform better strategies. Comparative analysis with other cities globally and in India will offer unique insights. Recommendations will focus on improving communication, addressing concerns, and enhancing community participation. Ultimately, this research seeks a comprehensive understanding of residents' perceptions to optimize the smart city project and ensure successful implementation.

Data Source

The study collected data from 277 respondents in Coimbatore using convenience sampling and a structured questionnaire, analyzing data through percentages and factor analysis. Understanding public perception toward Coimbatore's smart city project is crucial for community engagement and decision-making. Positive perceptions drive collaboration and success, while negative views hinder progress.

These insights guide policymakers, aligning decisions with community needs, and enhancing well-being. Understanding public sentiment aids in identifying challenges, opportunities, and support for sustainability. It enables ongoing evaluation, ensuring project responsiveness to evolving needs, and continual enhancement for Coimbatore's smart city project's success.

Analysis and Interpretation

Socio economic profile
The following table discusses age, gender, education qualification, occupation, type of family, status in family, monthly income, family income, family expenditure, number of non- earning member and number of earning member.

The summarized findings indicate that the majority of respondents are aged between 17 and 42, predominantly male, undergraduates, employed, belong to nuclear families, and have monthly incomes ranging from Rs. 5001 to Rs. 30000. Most have family incomes between Rs. 16001 and Rs. 78000, family expenditures below Rs. 35000, with 2 to 4 non-earning and earning members in their families. The study utilizes factor analysis to explore factors influencing public perception of Coimbatore's smart city project. The Kaiser-Meyer-Olkin (KMO) test, assessing data adequacy, yielded a value above 0.70, indicating suitability for factor analysis. Bartlett's test of sphericity resulted in a p-value of .000, confirming significant differences in the correlation matrix, supporting the validity of conducting factor analysis on the data. The

Table 127.1 Analysis - I.

Age (Years)	Number (n =277)	Percentage
Up to 17	13	4.7
17 to 42	214	77.3
Above 42	50	18.0
Gender		
Male	152	54.9
Female	125	45.1
Education qualification		
Illiterate	15	5.4
SSLC	40	14.4
HSC	10	3.6
Undergraduate	132	47.7
Postgraduate	55	19.9
Professionals	25	9.0
Occupation		
Agriculture	6	2.2
Business	50	18.1
Employed	116	41.8
Self employed	19	6.9
Student	62	22.4
Home maker	22	7.9
Retired	2	.7
Type of family		
Joint	79	28.5

Age (Years)	Number (n =277)	Percentage
Nuclear	198	71.5
Status in family		
Head	67	24.2
Member	210	75.8
Monthly income		
Up to 5000	50	18.1
5001 to 30000	192	69.3
Above 30000	35	12.6
Family income		
Up to 16000	23	8.3
16001 to 78000	217	78.3
Above 78000	37	13.4
Family expenditure		
Up to 35000	247	89.2
Above 35000	30	10.8
Number of non-earning members		
Up to 2 members	25	9.0
2 to 4 members	191	69.0
Above 4 members	61	22.0
Number of earning members		
Up to 2 members	38	13.7
2 to 4 members	216	78.0
Above 4 members	23	8.3

Source: Author

Table 127.2 KMO and Bartlett's test.

Kaiser-Meyer-Olkin measure of sampling adequacy.		.869
Bartlett's test of sphericity	Approx. Chi-square	1674.230
	Df	91
	Sig.	.000

Source: Author

factor analysis aims to reveal the core drivers shaping public perception toward the smart city project. Identifying these underlying factors will offer insights into what influences the overall perception among Coimbatore's residents.

The study's factor analysis identified three influential factors driving public perception of Coimbatore's smart city project. Factor one, accounting for 42.688%, stresses improved amenities, connectivity, transportation, and safety. Factor two (9.286%) highlights healthcare and basic utilities' significance. Factor three (7.804%) emphasizes cleanliness, traffic management, and quality of life. Addressing these factors could bolster public support, benefiting the project's success.

Recommendations and conclusions

The study offers targeted strategies for improving public perception within distinct demographics. Adolescents could benefit from free Wi-Fi with enhanced safety features for accessing smart city services and education. Homemakers' perception could improve with better infrastructure like sewage, sanitation, water, and lighting. Lowering taxes on essential services and ensuring accessible healthcare can aid those with modest incomes. Enhancing 24-hour transportation could address concerns about living standards for the public. Collaborating with corporations can expedite project implementation and boost

Table 127.3 Rotated component matrix and component.

Rotated component matrix[a]

	Component		
	1	2	3
Better recreation facility	.810		
Quality of lifestyle is improved	.719		
Improved in IT connectivity	.693		
Better transportation facility is provided	.666		
Finding enough funds and sources for implementation of smart city is challenging	.619		
Smart lighting solution reduces energy consumption	.569		
Safety place of living	.524		
Better health care system		.814	
Adequate electricity supply is provided		.779	
Adequate water supply is offered		.760	
Importance is given to cleanliness and waste management			.800
Reduced traffic congestion			.719
Standard of living is improved			.504
Eigen values	5.976	1.300	1.093
Percentage of variance	42.688	9.286	7.804
Cumulative percentage of variance	42.688	51.975	59.779

Source: Author

positive perceptions. It emphasizes the need for specific data on Coimbatore's smart city perception, advocating for surveys, consultations, and media analysis for clarity. Future research should track changing perceptions over time and compare with global initiatives to identify beneficial strategies for Coimbatore's project.

Reference

Aggarwal, T., and Solomon, P. (2019). Quantitative analysis of the development of smart cities in India. *Smart and Sustainable Built Environment*.

Camero, A., and Alba, E. (2019) Sart city and information technology. 93, 84–99.

Coelho, V. N., et al. (2021). Smart account for decentralized governance on smart cities. 4(2), 881–893.

Georgiadis, A., et al. (2021). Citizens perception of smart cities 11 march 2021. 11(6), 2517.

Hameed, A. A. (2019). Smart city planning and sustainable develop. 518 (2).

Hasija, S., Shen, Z. J. M., Teo, C. P. (2020). Smart city operations: modeling challenges and opportunities. *Manufacturing and Service Operations Management*, 22(1), 203–213.

Kandpal, V., Kaur, H., and Tyagi, V. (2017). Smart city projects in India: Issues and challenges . Available at SSRN 2926260.

Macke, J., et al. (2018). Smart city and quality of life citizen perception in a Brazilian case study. 182 , 717–726.

Mishra, R. (2017). Smart city: a path of growth of India. *Journal of Public Policy and Environmental Management*, 1(3), 20–22.

Praharaj, S., and Han, H. (2019). Cutting through the clutter of smart city definitions: a reading into the smart city perceptions in India. *City, Culture and Society*, 18, 100289.

Praharaj, S., Han, J. H., and Hawken, S. (2017). Innovative civic engagement and digital urban infrastructure: lessons from 100 smart cities mission in India. *Procedia Engineering*, 180, 1423–1432.

Rana, N. P., Luthra, S., Mangla, S. K., Islam, R., Roderick, S., and Dwivedi, Y. K. (2019). Barriers to the development of smart cities in Indian context. *Information Systems Frontiers*, 21(3), 503–525.

Silva, B. N., et al. (2017). Sustainable cities and socity. 38, 697–713.

Trindade, E. P., et al. (2017). Sustainable development of smart cities-3, Article number-11, Augest 4, 2017 .

Zhao, F., et al. (2021). Smart city research a holistic and state of the art literature review. 119 , 103406.

128 The impact of employee engagement on business performance

Esakki Pandi, K.ᵃ and Ebenezer Paul Rajan, T.Y.ᵇ
Karpagam Academy of Higher Education, Coimbatore, India

Abstract

Organizational success is critically dependent on employee engagement affecting various aspects such as work culture, staff turnover, productivity, customer relationships, and profitability. The intent of this study is to evaluate and track the impact of employee engagement operational performance. The study determines the relationship between these characteristics and engagement by looking at the demographic profile of the employees and their opinions on personal, organizational, work-related, and economic issues as well as employee attrition. Data is gathered using surveys and interviews as part of the research design, which also uses a convenient sample technique. The data are analyzed and hypotheses are tested using statistical techniques like percentage analysis, chi-square testing, correlation, and ANOVA.

Keywords: Business performance, economic factors, employee attrition, employee engagement, job-related factors, organizational factors, questionnaire, statistical analysis, survey

Introduction

The enthusiasm, passion, or devotion people have towards their jobs and employers is known as employee engagement. Organizations work hard to completely engage and win over brilliant people in today's competitive climate, in addition to trying to retain them. Engaged staff members offer significant competitive advantages, such as increased output and decreased attrition rates. Organizations may develop strategies and deal with commitment and engagement difficulties by having a clear understanding of the challenges affecting employee engagement, which will help them remain competitive in the market.

Review of Literature

Authors	Focus of study	Main findings
Iswara and Riana (2019)	Impact of employee freedom on performance	Granting employees freedom and responsibility positively influences performance without waiting for superior orders.
Altehrebah and Yusr (2019)	Elements influencing employee engagement	Hypotheses including employee communication, reward/recognition, and staff development significantly relate to employee engagement.
Othman and Rapi (2019)	Variables impacting employee engagement in construction	Organizational culture strongly influences employee engagement in the construction sector.
Feng	Business investments in products due to employee engagement	Business investment in new products, advertising through online consumer dialogues, and social media to counter competitors' product advancements due to evolving employee engagement.
Allen and Meyer	Quantitative indicator of employee engagement	Employee engagement is defined as an emotional connection to work. Engagement impacts motivation for work.
Yakut, and Kara	Mediating roles of employee engagement and organizational support	Strategic human resource management alignment leads to increased productivity and reduced job satisfaction and turnover intention.
Afram et al.	Structural and psychological employee engagement	Employee engagement elements correlate with organizational performance, but engagement itself is not a significant mediator.
Ajitha	Factors driving insurance worker enthusiasm	Employee engagement policies, analyzing employee opinions, and organizational factors significantly impact employee motivation.

ᵃpandi231323@gmail.com, ᵇdrebenezerpaulrajan.ty@kahedu.edu.in

Authors	Focus of study	Main findings
Nagpal	Aspects of employee engagement in the manufacturing sector	Participation-related aspects like goals, role clarity, and communication influence manufacturing business outcomes.
Kumar and Sondhi	Employee engagement's effect on job satisfaction	Employee engagement contributes significantly to job satisfaction.
Sahoo et al. (2022)	Workplace commitment through employee engagement	Individual commitment positively influences organizational outcomes, performance, and high-quality services.
Sunny and Yajurvedi	Managerial approach to employee engagement and organizational benefits	Employee engagement's importance in achieving competitive advantages through sound managerial strategies and efficient operation.
Ganjawala1and Joshi	Relationship between customer satisfaction and employee engagement	Employee engagement significantly affects customer satisfaction in various dimensions.
Ngwane	Factors affecting government employee engagement in Gauteng	Gender, age, position, and service have significant relationships with engagement in government employees.
Tanuwijaya et al.	Influence of leadership on work engagement	Authentic leadership drives work engagement, enhancing favorable work outcomes for employees.

Source: Author

Objectives of the Study

The study aims to assess employee engagement concerning demographic factors. Additionally, it seeks to analyze the influencing elements and their effect on engagement, such as self-awareness and wellbeing. Lastly, the research intends to quantify how engagement impacts productivity through innovative work approaches and employee satisfaction.

Hypothesis of the Study

Experience and engagement with management decision making.

H0: There is no significance relationship between experience at this concern and engagement with management decision making.

H1: There is a significance relationship between experience at this concern and engagement with management decision making.

Relationship between educational qualification and opportunities at or to earn and grow

H0: There is no significant relationship between education qualification and opportunities at work to learn and grow.

H1: There is a significant relationship between education qualification and opportunities at work to learn and grow.

Research Methodology

A multistage stratified purposive sampling method was used to choose a sample of 113 workers from the service industry. Primary data was collected through structured questionnaires and interviews. Secondary data were also utilized from various sources such as research articles, internet campaigns, magazines, and newspapers. The data were analyzed and the hypotheses were tested using statistical techniques such as percentage analysis, chi-square testing, correlation, and ANOVA.

Analysis and Interpretation

Chi-square analysis

H0: There is no significance relationship between experience at this concern and engagement with management decision making.

H1: There is a significant relationship between experience at this concern and engagement with management decision making.

ANOVA

Relationship between educational qualification and opportunities at or to earn and grow

H0: There is no significant relationship between education qualification and opportunities at work to learn and grow.

Table 128.1 Experience and engagement with management decision making.

Chi-Square tests			
	Value	df	Asymp. Sig. (2-sided)
Pearson Chi-square	12.526[a]	16	.707
Likelihood ratio	13.059	16	.668
Linear-by-linear association	1.271	1	.260
N of valid cases	113		

a. 17 cells (68.0%) -expected count less than 5. minimum expected count is .25.

Chi-Square test			
	Value	df	Asymp. Sig. (2-sided)
Pearson Chi-square	22.622[a]	16	.124
Likelihood ratio	22.341	16	.133
Linear-by-linear association	7.013	1	.008
N of valid cases	113		

a. 17 cells (68.0%) expected count less than 5. The minimum expected count is .19.

Chi-Square tests			
	Value	df	Asymp. Sig. (2-sided)
Pearson Chi-square	29.612[a]	16	.020
Likelihood ratio	28.311	16	.029
Linear-by-linear association	6.508	1	.011
N of valid cases	113		

a. 17 cells (68.0%) have expected count less than 5. The minimum expected count is .11.

Chi-square tests			
	Value	df	Asymp. Sig. (2-sided)
Pearson Chi-square	23.818[a]	16	.094
Likelihood ratio	20.225	16	.210
Linear-by-linear association	4.925	1	.026
N of valid cases	113		

a. 17 cells (68.0%) have expected count less than 5. The minimum expected count is .11.
Source: Author

H1: There is a significant relationship between education qualification and opportunities at work to learn and grow.

From the analysis above, we can conclude that the determined F-value of 1.884 is a positive number. So

H1 agree. Due to the p value of 0.000 being larger than or equal to 0.05. Qualification in terms of schooling and chances to develop professionally at work are significantly correlated. At a 5% level, the findings are noteworthy.

Table 128.2 Remuneration and job satisfaction.

Correlations

		The setting of goals has greatly improved my overall performance within the organization	Reward management system increases my performance level	Skills and competences enhanced through training process	Performance of employees increases under good leadership	Individual productivity and performance elevates with effective teamwork
The setting of goals has greatly improved my overall performance within the organization	Pearson correlation	1	.410**	.285**	.375**	.206*
	Sig. (2-tailed)		.000	.002	.000	.029
	N	113	113	113	113	113
Reward management system increases my performance level	Pearson correlation	.410**	1	.302**	.287**	.247**
	Sig. (2-tailed)	.000		.001	.002	.008
	N	113	113	113	113	113
Skills and competences enhanced through training process	Pearson correlation	.285**	.302**	1	.311**	.167
	Sig. (2-tailed)	.002	.001		.001	.078
	N	113	113	113	113	113
Performance of employees increases under good leadership	Pearson correlation	.375**	.287**	.311**	1	.176
	Sig. (2-tailed)	.000	.002	.001		.063
	N	113	113	113	113	113
Individual productivity and performance elevates with effective teamwork	Pearson correlation	.206*	.247**	.167	.176	1
	Sig. (2-tailed)	.029	.008	.078	.063	
	N	113	113	113	113	113

**. Correlation is significant at the 0.01 level (2-tailed).

*. Correlation is significant at the 0.05 level (2-tailed).

Source: Author

Table 128.3 ANOVA.

		Sum of squares	df	Mean square	F	Sig.
Moral and productivity of employees is highly influenced by the effectiveness of organizational performance	Between groups	4.284	3	1.428	1.389	.250
	Within groups	112.035	109	1.028		
	Total	116.319	112			
Employee motivation is positively related to employee performance	Between groups	6.533	3	2.178	1.884	.137
	Within groups	126.015	109	1.156		
	Total	132.549	112			
Good performance is effectively addressed throughout the organization	Between groups	3.708	3	1.236	1.182	.320
	Within groups	114.009	109	1.046		
	Total	117.717	112			
The organization has high performance standards	Between groups	4.823	3	1.608	1.509	.216
	Within groups	116.080	109	1.065		
	Total	120.903	112			

		Sum of squares	df	Mean square	F	Sig.
Job performance is measured to ensure that all the employees are achieving their results	Between groups	1.443	3	.481	.513	.674
	Within groups	102.114	109	.937		
	Total	103.558	112			

Source: Author

Conclusions

The analysis found no notable link between organizational tenure and engagement in management decisions. However, positive associations were evident between goal setting and performance, reward systems and productivity, training for skill enhancement, effective leadership, teamwork, and individual productivity. The ANOVA highlighted a significant relationship between educational qualifications and learning opportunities.

Recommendations include fostering an engaging culture with open communication, setting clear expectations for employees, nurturing strong leadership, implementing comprehensive recognition and reward systems, supporting skill development, promoting work-life balance, and actively seeking employee feedback. Implementing these strategies can create an environment that prioritizes engagement, positively impacting organizational success.

In conclusion, this study underscores the pivotal role of employee engagement in organizational effectiveness. Recognizing and addressing factors like goal-setting, training, leadership, and teamwork can foster a productive and engaging workplace. By valuing engagement and implementing strategies to enhance it, businesses can boost performance, productivity, and overall success.

References

Altehrebah, S. S. A. S., and Yusr, M. M. (2019). Factors influencing employee engagement: a study of Sana'a University. *International Journal*, 2(9), 23–31.

Bekirogullari, Z. (2018). Employees engagement and empowerment in attaining personal and organisational goals. *The European Journal of Social and Behavioural Sciences*, 26(3), 290–298.

Gusti Ngurah Agung Rama Iswara, I., and Gede Riana, I. (2019). The role of job satisfaction mediate the effect of engagement on employee performance. *International Journal of Management and Commerce Innovations*, 7(2), 910–919.

Hamed, S. S. (2019). Antecedents and consequences of employees engagement. *Management Review*, 5(1), 64–71.

Khaliq, A., Kayani, U. S., and Mir, G. M. (2020). Relationship of employee training, employee engagement, teamwork with job satisfaction. *Journal of Arts and Social Sciences*, 7(2), 185–192.

Kothari, C. R. (2004). Research Methodology – Methods and Techniques, (2ndedn.). New Delhi: New Age International (P) Ltd.

Kulkarni, P., and Mutkekar, R. (2020). Role of strategic management for employee engagement and skill development for start-ups. *Vilakshan - XIMB Journal of Management*, 17(2), 79–95.

Lwin, Z. M. (2019). Factors affecting employee engagement. *International Journal of Multidisciplinary in Management and Tourism*, 1(2), 278–283.

Mohanan, M., Sequeira, A. H., and Kumar, M. S. (2012). Employee engagement and motivation. *KHOJ-Journal of Indian Management Research and Practices*,

Osborne, S., and Hammoud, M. S. (2018). Effective employee engagement in the workplace. *International Journal of Applied Management and Technology*, 16(1), 50–67.

Othman, R. B., and Rapi, R. B. M. (2019). Factors affecting employee engagement: a study among employees in the Malaysian construction industry. *International Journal of Academic Research in Business and Social Sciences*, 9(7), 784–797.

Papalexandris, N., and Galanaki, E. (2008). Leadership's impact on employee engagement differences among entrepreneurs and professional CEOs. *Leadership and Organization Development Journal*.

Rana, S., and Singh, V. (2018). Employee engagement and job satisfaction: an empirical study in IT industry. *IOSR Journal of Humanities and Social Science (IOSR-JHSS)*, 21(10), 23–29.

Sahoo, C. K., Behera, N., and Tripathy, S. K. (2022). Employeeengagement and individual commitment: an analysis from integrative review of research. *Employment Relations Record*, 10(1), 40–47.

Sengupta, N., and Sengupta, M. (2018). Status of employee engagement: an empirical study. *Journal of Management (JOM)*, 5(3), 15–23.

Sharma, M., and Bhati, M. (2018). The role of organizational factors of engagement and motivation in enhancing employees' commitment in Indian automotive industry. *Universal Journal of Industrial and Business Management*, 5(3), 29–37.

Simon, N., and Amarakoon, U. A. (2019). Impact of occupational stress on employee engagement. In 12th International Conference on Business Management (ICBM) 2019.

Suyal, S., and Negi, M. (2018). Employee engagement and its relationship with job satisfaction: a study of some selected service organization in Dehradun. *Journal of Emerging Technologies and Innovative Research (JE-TIR)*, 6(4), 93–100.

Tiwari, P., and Nagarkoti, K. (2018). Employee engagement and its effect on employee's performance. *International Journal Of Creative Research Thoughts (IJCRT)*, 6(2), 2028–2032.

Vashisht, A. (2018). Influence of employee engagement on job satisfaction: a study of consultancy firms in Guru-gram. *Apeejay ournal of Management and Technology*, 13(1), 37–46.

Venkatesh, D. A. N. (2015). Employee engagement through leadership. *American International Journal of Research in Humanities, Arts and Social Sciences*, 9(4), 333–336.

129 Unveiling the factors influencing employee attrition

Logesh, R.ª and Ebenezer Paul Rajan, T. Y[b]

Karpagam Academy of Higher Education, Coimbatore, India

Abstract

Employee attrition, or employee turnover, is a significant concern for organizations across industries. High levels of attrition can have detrimental effects on productivity, morale, and financial performance. Employees attrition, often known as staff turnover, is a problem that organisations in many different industries continue to encounter. It speaks about the frequency with which workers depart from an organisation and must be replaced. High attrition rates can lead to higher hiring expenses, decreased institutional knowledge, diminished employee morale, and even issues with productivity. This abstract presents a brief overview of employee attrition, its causes, consequences, and strategies for managing and reducing attrition.

Keywords: Compensation and benefits, employee attrition, employee engagement, employee satisfaction, job design, leadership, organizational culture, retention, talent management, turnover

Introduction

Attrition among the workforce is one of the major issues that HR managers in today's must deal with. In the construction industry, employee turnover drives up costs associated with employee training as well as productivity and the desired degree of "knowledge maturity" of the company and its workforce. The company that can maintain a long-term relationship with its employees will endure in the market, while others will eventually disappear. The stabilisation of business operations and the abundance of skilled and experienced labour that may provide a long-term solution to the high attrition the sector faces constitute the construction industry's ultimate solution. More passionate employees at all levels will aid this sector's stabilisation, expansion, and contribution to economic progress. The call centre segment in the construction industry, in particular, has a high attrition rate due to a lack of enrichment opportunities for professional advancement. The cost-effectiveness and quality of the labour force are two key factors in the expansion of the construction sector. There are countless reasons why employees may decide to leave their company, but each cause will differ depending on the type of firm.

Objectives of the Study

Understand employee perspectives on personal, organisational, job-related, and economic factors impacting attrition at Sowmya Constructions Pvt Ltd.

Evaluate employee opinions on personal, organisational, job-related, and economic factors considering age, gender, marital status, monthly income, and experience.

Investigate the relationship between personal, organisational, job-related, and economic factors and employee attrition.

Identify the influence of personal, organisational, job-related, and economic factors on employee attrition rates.

Literature Review

Table 129.1 Insights into employee attrition: diverse perspectives and strategies for retention.

Author Name	Study	Findings/insights/interpretation
AMARAM (2021)	Emphasised the need for strategic hiring and employee integration to combat attrition.	Hiring the right applicants and integrating them effectively into the organization is crucial in curbing attrition. Overwhelmed employees tend to withdraw, impacting their productivity and causing discontent. Balancing care for employees with productivity expectations is essential to prevent high turnover.
Park (2021)	Highlighted the importance of employee ownership and autonomy in enhancing performance.	Granting employees ownership of their work and allowing autonomy fosters responsibility and motivation. Providing opportunities for increased responsibilities as employees progress in their roles contributes to a sense of accountability towards outcomes.

[a]rslogeshlogu@gmail.com, [b]drebenezerpaulrajan.ty@kahedu.edu.in

Author Name	Study	Findings/insights/interpretation
Booyens (2021)	Stressed the significance of effective supervision in ensuring resource utilization and goal achievement.	Effective supervision involves assessing organisational efficiency, rectifying mistakes, maintaining standards, and achieving objectives through appropriate resource usage.
Nel, et al. (2020)	Identified the existence of psychological contracts in addition to employment agreements.	Psychological contracts, alongside employment contracts, outline mutual expectations between employees and organizations when entering a working relationship.
Habeck, Kroger and Tram (2020)	Explored how offering benefits reduces attrition rates and impacts employee retention.	Providing benefits decreases the likelihood of employee departure and increases the likelihood of them staying.
Booyens (2020)	Defined job orientation's goal in easing employee transition and shaping work expectations.	Job orientation aims to familiarize employees with their roles, reducing anxiety, fostering positive attitudes, and establishing realistic work expectations.
Mouton (2019)	Linked excessive workload to stress-related illnesses and its impact on turnover intention.	Overloading employees with excessive work leads to stress-related health issues, associating workload with inadequate compensation and motivating turnover.
Ichniowski (2019)	Identified social connections at work as crucial stress-relieving factors and their impact on turnover.	Positive social ties between employees relieve stress, while unhealthy relations lead to turnover and absenteeism.
Kevin et al. (2019)	Proposed various criteria predicting turnover, advocating for employee-centric management strategies.	Long-term employee retention requires strategies like job redesign, autonomy, significance, identity, open book management, empowerment, and strategic recruitment.
Hamermesh (2019)	Stressed the importance of understanding turnover complexity and aligning individuals with suitable roles.	Comprehending the intricacies of turnover and aligning individuals with fitting roles aids in maintaining productivity and loyalty.
Khera and Gulati (2018)	Explored HRIS's role in HR planning within IT companies.	HRIS can efficiently manage employee information, determine vacancies, and evaluate qualifications for positions.
Kossivi et al. (2016)	Highlighted factors influencing employee retention.	Employee retention relies on various factors such as development opportunities, pay, work-life balance, leadership, culture, social support, autonomy, training, and development.
Goswami, and Jha (2016)	Advocated addressing attrition causes and nurturing employee assets.	Ignoring attrition reasons neglects the value of employees as vital resources. Recognizing their aspirations, creativity, and offering advancement opportunities, respect, and a collaborative atmosphere creates an organization that excels in domestic and international markets.

Source: Author

Research Methodology

The data analysis and interpretation section delves into comprehending employees' perspectives on stress factors across personal, organizational, job-related, economic, and employee attrition domains. Through detailed examination using descriptive statistics, ANOVA, t-tests, correlations, and regression analyses, this section aims to illuminate the nuanced variations in employee perceptions. It explores the impact of gender and marital status on these perceptions, unveiling crucial insights into the diverse factors influencing employee stress levels. By scrutinizing these facets, this study seeks to unravel critical patterns and associations, providing a comprehensive understanding of stress-related dynamics in the workplace.

- Research methodology: A systematic approach guides the research process, detailing strategies for scientific proposals.
- Sampling: Convenient sampling selects 130 employees from the population for data collection.
- Data collection: Primary data sourced via questionnaires, observations, interviews, and feedback from managers and employees.
- Secondary data: Utilization of previously gathered information subjected to statistical analysis from various sources.
- Data sources: HR records, manuals, policies, library resources, media, and the internet aid in gathering secondary data.
- Analysis techniques: Statistical methods like regression analysis employed to evaluate and test hypotheses.

Data Analysis and Interpretation

Employee perception towards stress factors
- *Personal factors*
  - Mean values range from 2.3000 to 2.5000.
  - Standard deviation ranges from 1.02121 to 1.12882.
  - Employees perceive issues balancing work-life responsibilities and emotional challenges.
- *Organizational factors*
  - Mean values range from 2.1077 to 2.4923.
  - Standard deviation ranges from 0.90001 to 1.14287.
  - Concerns about changing management strategies and inadequate organizational support for self-improvement.
- *Job related factors*
  - Mean values range from 2.2243 to 2.4462.
  - Standard deviation ranges from 0.98092 to 1.05148.
  - Employees experience work pressure, lack of flexibility, and cooperation issues.
- *Economic factors*
  - Mean values range from 2.1308 to 2.5385.
  - Standard deviation ranges from 0.95529 to 1.11639.
  - Mixed perceptions on salary satisfaction, job benefits, and standard of living improvements.
- *Employee attrition*
  - Mean values range from 2.3692 to 2.6231.
  - Standard deviation ranges from 1.00580 to 1.05114.

- Concerns about unpleasant work environments, lack of recognition, and work overload.

Impact of gender and marital status
- *Gender*
  - Significant variations in stress perceptions based on gender.
  - Male employees perceive higher stress levels across multiple factors compared to female employees.
- *Marital status*
  - Significant differences in stress perceptions between married and unmarried employees.
  - Stress factors vary significantly based on marital status.

Influence of stress factors
- Personal and employee attrition factors significantly impact stress levels.
- Regression analysis suggests these factors contribute significantly to increased employee stress levels.

Hypothesis testing results
- Null hypotheses rejected for various stress factors, implying significant variations in perceptions.
- Associations between satisfaction indices and work-related factors established.

Findings
- Employee attrition and personal factors notably impact employee stress levels.
- Strong correlation exists between satisfaction and welfare indices.
- Substantial association found between designation and income level.
- Significant link detected between HRM challenges and an open work environment.
- Independent sample t-test revealed for specific data constructs.
- Levene's test confirms significance in constructs like 'liking about the company' and 'satisfaction with the job'.
- Employee attrition as an HR challenge shows significance with an HRM strategy in place.
- Null hypothesis rejected, confirming a significant association between certain constructs.

The study's findings present a comprehensive exploration of stress factors impacting employees across diverse domains. Highlighting the pivotal impact of Employee Attrition and personal factors on stress levels, the research delves into correlations between satisfaction indices, income levels, and HRM challenges. By employing various statistical tests like t-tests, Levene's test, and independent sample t-tests, this investigation uncovers significant associations between constructs such as job satisfaction, company preferences, and HR strategies combatting Employee Attrition. These findings shed light on the nuanced interplay of stress elements within the workplace, offering valuable insights for organisations aiming to understand and manage employee stress more effectively.

Recommendations

- Graduates require comprehensive pre-job training to align with job demands effectively.
- Businesses can utilize innovative technologies to offer career growth opportunities, reducing attrition rates.
- Regular meetings and exit interviews help understand staff expectations, with periodic assessments and training for development.
- Immediate implementation of effective recommendations is crucial for company progress.
- Enhancing employee salaries is essential for company welfare.
- Maintaining manageable workloads contributes to employee satisfaction and productivity.
- Enhance career prospects within the company to retain talent effectively.
- Establishing proper work schedules fosters a conducive work environment.
- Regular training updates with contemporary techniques benefit employee growth.
- Acknowledging and rewarding valuable contributions bolster employee morale.
- Nurturing strong interpersonal relationships among colleagues fosters a healthy work culture.

Conclusion

The study highlights the potential of innovative technologies in construction businesses, offering a pathway for reducing attrition rates by fostering internal career advancement. It underscores the pivotal role of employee satisfaction in devising a robust staff retention strategy. Often overlooked is the profound impact of employee contentment not just on internal operations but also on client relations and overall business profitability. Adaptability emerges as a key trait for HR managers in the construction industry, crucial in nurturing, motivating, and retaining talent effectively.

Effective communication of policies to workers proves vital in the management of construction projects, shaping the work environment and employee perceptions. The study underscores the success of the training programs at Sowmya Construction Pvt Ltd, positioning it as a significant contributor to employee welfare and development. The comprehensive attrition analysis uncovers multifaceted insights beneficial for the workforce, shedding light on areas for potential enhancement and employee-centric strategies.

References

Booth, S., and Hamer, K. (2017). Labour turnover in the retail industry: predicting the role of individual, organisational and environmental factors. *International Journal of Retail and Distribution Management*, 35(4), 289–307.

Budhwar, S. P., Varma, A., Malhotra, N., and Mukherjee, A. (2019). Insights into the Indian call centre industry: can internal marketing help tackle high employee turnover? *Journal of Services Marketing*, 23(5), 351–366.

Burns, A. C., and Bush, R. F. (2020). Marketing Research, (6th edn.). New York: Pearson Education, Inc.

Gardner, D. G. (2019). Employee focus of attention and reaction to organisational change. *The Journal of Applied Behavioural Science*, 23(3), 11–288.

Gustafson, C. M. (2021). Staff turnover: retention. *International Journal of Contemporary Hospitality Management*, 14(3), 106–110.

130 A study on import procedure toward Sailink logistics Pvt Ltd, Chennai

A. *Karthikeyan*[a], *Nithya, J.*[b] and *R. Gayathiri Chitra*[c]

Karpagam Academy of Higher Education, Coimbatore, India

Abstract

The economy's backbone often resides in logistics, and Sailink Private Limited's import processes and logistics activities serve as focal points in this study. Importation, a crucial facet of commerce, involves the acquisition of goods from overseas for various purposes—be it for individual, corporate, or governmental utilization in production or direct resale. This research delves into the correlation between educational background and import criteria, employing a convenience sampling approach. Statistical tools such as ANOVA and simple percentage analysis were utilized in the study. Notably, the findings reveal a positive correlation between several factors, underlining the significance of educational qualifications in shaping import-related decision-making processes. This study sheds light on the interconnectedness of academic background and the criteria governing imports, contributing to a more comprehensive understanding of this intricate facet of the economy.

Keywords: Educational qualification, export, goods, import, requirements

Introduction

In today's fast-paced landscape, distinguishing oneself from competitors is vital for business success, and this often hinges on effective export-import strategies. A substantial segment of our economy thrives on logistics, where the quality of imports and exports plays a pivotal role in establishing trustworthiness with clients. While prioritizing quality production is paramount, understanding logistics - the process of efficiently moving goods from origin to destination - becomes equally crucial to meet consumer demands. Logistics encompasses diverse specializations including shipping, material handling, packaging, and warehousing. Exploring these facets can be facilitated through online import/export courses, aiding in the selection of optimal strategies. This field involves the intricate management and integration of various components to streamline operations and cut costs for businesses. Ultimately, the core responsibility of logistics lies in delivering the right product to the right consumer, at the right time, location, quantity, condition, and cost.

Literature Review

Table 130.1 Insights into economic dynamics: relationships between trade, investment, and growth - a comparative review.

Author	Study	Findings
Bakari et al. (2019)	Investigated Brazil's economy from 1970 to 2017, exploring the interrelationship between domestic investment, exports, imports, and economic growth using the VECM approach.	Short-term impacts revealed mutual influence among domestic investment, exports, imports, and economic growth. However, long-term effects indicated a detrimental relationship between imports and economic growth. Notably, certain factors had no discernible impact on each other.
Devkota (2019)	Explored long-term correlations in India's exports, imports, and economic growth, identifying unidirectional causal links between exports and imports, and GDP and imports.	Found equilibrium long-run connections between India's exports, imports, and economic growth, observing causality from exports to imports and GDP to imports.
El Alaoui (2015)	Analysed Moroccan yearly time series data from 1980 to 2013, examining the nexus between exports, imports, and economic growth.	Identified bidirectional causality between economic growth and imports, one-way causality from exports to imports, and no causal relationship between exports and economic growth based on Granger causality results.

[a]keyankarthi5931@gmail.com, [b]nithyajnithya@gmail.com, [c]gayathrirathnamr@gmail.com

Author	Study	Findings
Ogunmokun (2016)	Discussed environmental and social implications linked with metal mining, citing cobalt as an example with significant non-economic costs due to its association with unfavourable regions like the Congo.	Highlighted the generic nature of most metals traded on exchanges, suggesting a less urgent need for a comprehensive approach since refined products are essentially similar, regardless of the producer.
Taghavi et al. (2012)	Examined Iranian economic growth with a VAR approach, focusing on imports, exports, and related variables.	Found a positive correlation between exports and economic growth, in contrast to a negative correlation between imports and economic growth in the Iranian context.

Source: Author

Problem Statement

The Regulation of Imports and Exports Act addresses the challenge of effectively managing the movement of hazardous waste, ensuring proper handling, while also balancing the significance of imports and exports in fostering the economic growth of nations with varying resources and expertise.

Objectives of the Study

- Analyze the demographic profile of employees at Sailink Logistics Pvt Ltd.
- Examine the import procedures adopted by Sailink Logistics Pvt Ltd.
- Assess employees' perspectives regarding the correlation between essential import requisites and educational qualifications.

Hypotheses of the Study

H0: There is no significant relationship between education qualification and basic requirements to import goods

   Research methodology

- Employing research methodology systematically addresses research problems.
- Descriptive research design was utilized for this study.
- Utilization of convenience sampling involving Sailink Pvt Ltd staff.
- Total population: 402 employees; questionnaire distributed to 150, 132 responded.
- 120 usable responses selected; 12 incomplete responses excluded from the sample.
- Statistical tools such as simple percentage analysis and ANOVA employed.
- Aim: Investigate the link between educational attainment and import requisites' minimum standards.

Analysis and Interpretations

The section delves into a comprehensive analysis of Sailink Pvt Ltd employees' demographic profile and their understanding of import procedures. By scrutinizing gender distribution, age demographics, and educational qualifications, a nuanced understanding of employee backgrounds is established. The subsequent exploration focuses on the correlation between education levels and the comprehension of import requisites. Through robust statistical analyses, such as ANOVA and multiple comparison tests, this study aims to unveil the relationship between education and import standards among employees, shedding light on potential influences shaping their understanding of import procedures within the company.

Demographic profile analysis
The demographic breakdown of respondents provides crucial insights into the study's focus:

- **Gender distribution:**
  - Male respondents: 96.7%
  - Female respondents: 3.3%
- **Age groups:**
  - 31–40 years: 40.0%
  - 21–30 years: 29.2%
  - Above 40 years: 20.0%
  - Below 20 years: 10.8%
- **Educational qualifications:**
  - Higher secondary: 39.2%
  - Illiterate: 28.3%
  - Undergraduate: 19.2%
  - Postgraduate: 13.3%

Overwhelmingly male respondents (96.7%) indicate a gender imbalance within the surveyed employee pool, potentially impacting diversity. The largest age bracket (40.0%) falling between 31–40 years suggests a dominant middle-aged workforce in Sailink Pvt Ltd. Higher secondary education (39.2%) emerges as the

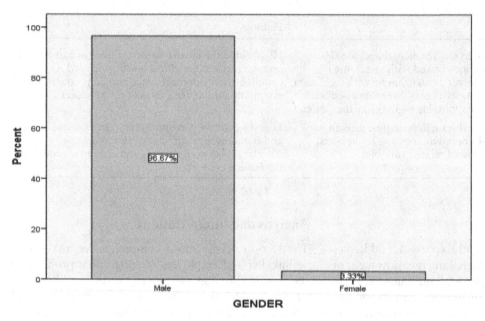

Figure 130.1 Chart – Gender of the respondents
Source: Author

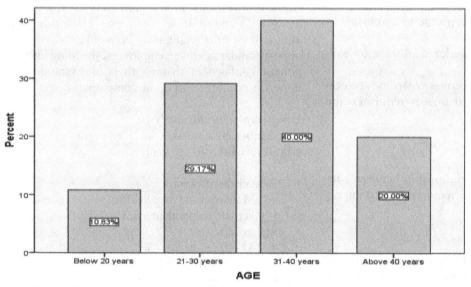

Figure 130.2 Age group of the respondents
Source: Author

primary educational background, possibly influencing employees' understanding of import procedures. The skewed gender ratio, predominant middle-aged workforce, and emphasis on higher secondary education might influence perspectives on import procedures and their understanding among employees.

Hypothesis testing - relationship between education and import requirements
Objective 2 aims to examine the correlation between education levels and import prerequisites.

ANOVA analysis:
- F-value: 606.754 indicates a substantial relationship between education and import standards.
- P-value: Less than 0.05 signifies a strong association between education levels and import requisites.

Interpretation: The significant F-value and P-value (<0.05) confirm a robust link between employees' education levels and their comprehension of import requirements. Acceptance of alternate hypothesis

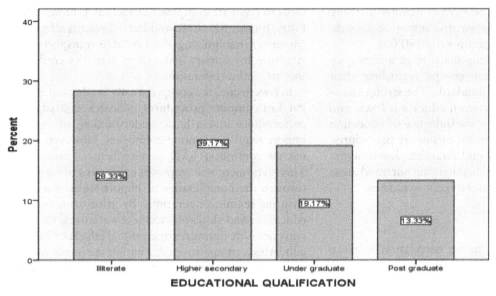

Figure 130.3 Educational qualification of the respondents
Source: Author

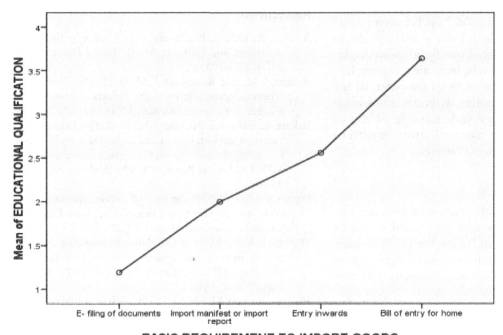

Figure 130.4 Homogenous educational qualification (mean)
Source: Author

(H1): Strong association between education levels and import standards. Education significantly correlates with import requisites.

Multiple comparison analysis: The multiple comparison analysis reveals substantial disparities in mean scores among different educational backgrounds. These variations denote diverse levels of comprehension concerning import prerequisites among employees with distinct educational qualifications. Such disparities highlight the potential need for targeted training or educational interventions to bridge knowledge gaps effectively within the workforce.

Homogeneity and post hoc tests:
• Homogeneity of variances tested positive.

The computed F-value (606.754) signifies a strong correlation between education and import standards, corroborated by a significant p-value (<0.05).

Positive results in homogeneity tests affirm consistency among education groups regarding their understanding of import standards. The strong statistical association found between education levels and import requisites highlight the influence of education on employees' comprehension of import procedures. The data suggests varied understanding levels across educational qualifications, highlighting potential areas for targeted training or development initiatives.

Findings

The findings illustrate a strong correlation between employees' education levels and their grasp of import requisites within Sailink Pvt Ltd. Analyzing demographic profiles highlighted a male-dominated, predominantly middle-aged workforce with higher secondary education as the primary qualification. Statistical analyses, including ANOVA, affirm a significant relationship (F-value: 606.754) between education and import standards (p value < 0.05). Multiple comparison tests underscored significant mean disparities across educational levels, indicating varying levels of comprehension. This suggests the potential for tailored educational initiatives to bridge knowledge gaps, enhancing employees' understanding of import procedures and fostering more effective compliance within the company's import practices.

Conclusion

The study reveals a tangible connection between age, educational qualifications, and the pivotal requisites for importing goods within Sailink Pvt Ltd. The intricacies of managing an import/export business pose inherent complexities and risks, distinctly different from domestic or international market operations. Navigating this terrain requires meticulous planning and a forward-thinking approach to fortify the company's growth trajectory. It's imperative to establish a robust foundation, laying emphasis on initiatives that strengthen employees' technical acumen, foster a deep understanding of basic management principles, and instill comprehension of both government regulations and import processes.

Building upon the existing operational framework, the company's growth strategy should involve a multifaceted approach. Bolstering employees' proficiency in fundamental management practices and the intricacies of import regulations becomes crucial. This proactive stance is essential to equip them with the necessary tools to navigate complexities such as E-filing, Bill of Entry, Import Manifest, and Entry Inwards effectively. Moreover, maximizing the available transport infrastructure for import and export activities could further streamline operations.

In conclusion, the comprehensive analysis of Sailink Pvt Ltd's import procedures indicates a satisfactory performance and a basic understanding of essential import requisites among employees. However, focusing on continuous skill development is paramount. This investment will empower employees to maneuver through the complexities of import logistics adeptly, ensuring seamless operations. By prioritizing ongoing education and skill enhancement initiatives, the company not only optimizes operational efficiency but also cultivates a competitive edge within the import/export landscape. This strategic approach sets the stage for sustained growth, consolidating the company's position in the market and augmenting its potential for long-term success.

References

Alvarez, R. (2020). Explaining export success: firm characteristics and spillover effects. *World Development*, 35(3), 377–393.

Andraz, J. M., and Rodrigues, P. M. M. (2014). What causes economic growth in Portugal: exports or inward FDI? *Journal of Economic Studies*, 37(3), 605–622.

Bakari, S., Fakraoui, N., and Tiba, S. (2019). Domestic investment, export, import and economic growth in Brazil: an application of vector error correction model. MPRA (Munich Personal RePEc Archive, Paper No. 95528).

Devkota, M. L. (2019). Impact of export and import on economic growth: time series evidence from India. *Dynamic Econometric Models*, 19, 29–40.

El Alaoui, A. (2015). Causality and cointegration between export, import and economic growth: Evidence from Morocco. MPRA (Munich Personal RePEc Archive, Paper No. 65431).

Hashim, K., and Masih, M. (2014). What causes economic growth in Malaysia: Exports or imports? MPRA (Munich Personal RePEc Archive, Paper No. 62366).

Lee, M., and Son, B. (2015). Korean strategies for export markets. *Long Range Planning*, 26(6), 99–106.

Ogunmokun (2016). [The effect of export financing resources and supply-chain skills]. (Unpublished raw data).

Taghavi, M., Goudarzi, M., Masoudi, E., and Gashti, H. P. (2012). Study on the impact of export and import on economic growth in Iran. *Journal of Basic and Applied Scientific Research*, 2(12), 12787–12794.

Uddin, G., Khan, S., and Alam, M. (2010). An empirical study on export, import and economic growth in Bhutan. *Indian Development Review*, 8(1), 95–104.

131 A stress management study among employees directed at Pepy technologies at Coimbatore

Sugitha[a], G. Priyadharshini[b] and P.H. Hemamalini[c]

Karpagam Academy of Higher Education, Coimbatore, India

Abstract

The current landscape of India's information technology (IT) industry is marked by unprecedented competitiveness, exacerbated by the influx of technological advancements and the entry of international firms into the market. This surge in projects has intensified competition, resulting in heightened stress levels and consequent health issues among IT professionals. Consequently, a vast majority of employees are actively seeking relief from this mounting pressure. Recognizing the urgency of the situation, this study aims to delve into the specific challenges faced by the IT sector, particularly concerning stress management. Workplace stress has profound implications on the physical and emotional well-being of employees, prompting the need for targeted interventions. This research not only identifies the detrimental effects of stress but also proposes strategies and initiatives aimed at aiding individuals in coping with these pressures, thereby contributing to a healthier and more resilient workforce within the IT industry.

Keywords: Employee well-being, health issues, Indian IT industry, stress management, workplace stress

Introduction

Employee stress management encompasses a wide spectrum of approaches, encompassing training, guidance, and educational interventions elucidating the impact of stress on individuals or groups. It serves as a pivotal discipline nurturing the development of coping mechanisms and resilience against stressors. Stress management techniques and psychotherapies form a crucial armamentarium in controlling stress levels, particularly chronic stress, thereby enhancing day-to-day functionality. These strategies not only mitigate stress but also aid in bolstering mental and emotional well-being.

Understanding stressors' diverse effects on individuals, both physically and psychologically, underscores the significance of tailored stress management techniques. The signs and symptoms of stress vary based on individual circumstances, demanding a nuanced approach to address them effectively. By equipping individuals with an array of stress-relieving tools and strategies, stress management studies aim to fortify individuals against the detrimental impacts of stress, fostering healthier and more resilient work environments.

Validity of the Study

- Understanding workplace stress and its impact on employees constitutes the primary objective of this project.

- Investigating the correlations between stress-inducing factors and their influence on job-related stress among employees in the workplace.
- Identifying effective strategies aimed at reducing stress levels, fostering an environment conducive to skill development among the staff.

Problem Statement

Rising stress levels significantly impact modern society, especially within the workforce, affecting employee health and performance. This issue leads to illness, high turnover, and increased absenteeism, necessitating urgent attention and comprehensive strategies within organizations to mitigate its detrimental effects.

Objectives of the Study

- Determine the underlying causes of stress.
- Identify the metrics or indicators of stress.
- Determine effective strategies and steps to mitigate and overcome stress.

[a]Sugithashanmugarajan663@gmail.com, [b]priyaacc.in@gmail.com, [c]hemamalini2007ster@gmail.com

Literature Review

Table 131.1 Insights into occupational stress: perspectives from diverse studies (2019-2021).

Year	Authors	Summary
2019	Tatheer	Pakistani bankers report high work stress due to organizational politics and bureaucracy, affecting work and health.
2019	Georgiou and Michailidis	Focus on work stress influenced by education, leisure, habits. Alcohol consumption is highlighted as a primary stress factor.
2019	Sinha and Subramanian	Different organizational levels experience varied role stress influenced by resources, job factors, and role expectations.
2020	Pratibha	Stress harms private bank employees' quality of life, suggesting stress management programs to improve the work environment.
2020	Karthik	Stress affects work performance positively or negatively; moderate stress levels lead to better performance. Aim is stress reduction, not elimination.
2020	Swaminathan and Rajkumar	Study examines stress across age groups, professions, work hours, and identifies role overload, self-distance, stagnation as stress factors.
2021	Satija and Khan W.	Occupational stress management crucial to prevent negative employee attitudes due to job stress and emotional intelligence.
2021	Shani and Pizam	Hotel employees in Central Florida suffer work-related depression; study links depression to occupational stress.

Source: Author

Research Methodology

- Geographical diversity: Focus extends beyond a single region, acknowledging stress as a ubiquitous factor experienced by individuals across varied settings.
- Scope: Main emphasis lies in analyzing employee stress across multiple departments of Pepy Technologies Ltd.
- Timeframe: A three-month duration was allocated for the comprehensive study.
- Data collection: Primary data sourced through a questionnaire, while secondary data obtained from company records and relevant periodicals.
- Research design: Descriptive approach used to comprehend current environment and consumer behavior in the study.
- Hypothesis: H1 postulated a significant correlation between respondents' salaries and attitudes towards overtime compensation.
- Population and sample: All clients of Pepy Technologies Ltd. in Coimbatore constituted the survey's population. A sample of 120 employees randomly selected for opinions and expectations.
- Sampling unit: Pepy Technologies Ltd. in Coimbatore served as the study's sampling unit.
- Statistical tools: Utilized correlation and ANOVA analyses for data evaluation in the study.

Analysis and Interpretation

The analysis undertaken delves into two key aspects—correlation between educational qualifications and job performance, and the relationship between respondents' ages and stress coping mechanisms. The correlation study presents compelling evidence of a strong positive link between higher educational qualifications and efficient job performance. Additionally, the ANOVA investigation explores the nuanced relationship between respondents' ages and various stress coping methods, revealing significant correlations. This comprehensive exploration sheds light on crucial associations within the dataset, illuminating the interplay between educational attainment, job efficiency, age demographics, and stress management approaches among the respondents.

Correlation analysis: educational qualification and efficient job performance
- **Pearson correlation (parametric)**
  - Educational qualification and efficient job performance:
    - Strong positive correlation ($r = 0.935^{**}$).
    - Significant at $p < 0.01$ level (2-tailed).
- **Nonparametric correlations**
  - **Kendall's tau_b:**
    - Correlation between educational qualification and efficient job performance:

- Strong positive correlation ($\tau = 0.839**$).
  - Significant at $p < 0.01$ level (2-tailed).
- **Spearman's rho:**
  - Correlation between educational qualification and efficient job performance:
    - Strong positive correlation ($\rho = 0.874**$).
    - Significant at $p < 0.01$ level (2-tailed).
- **Interpretation:** Positive correlation found between educational qualifications and the assurance of efficient job performance.

ANOVA analysis: respondents' ages and coping with stress

- **Null hypothesis (Ho):** No significant correlation between respondents' ages and stress coping methods.
- **Alternative hypothesis (H1):** Significant correlation exists between respondents' ages and stress coping methods.
- **ANOVA results:**
  - F-value: 436.948, $p < 0.05$ (significant).
  - Indicates acceptance of H1: Respondents' ages and stress coping methods are significantly correlated.
- **Post hoc analysis:**
  - Multiple comparison tests showed significant mean differences between various stress coping methods across age groups.
  - Age significantly correlates with preferred stress coping methods among respondents.

This concise interpretation highlights a strong positive correlation between educational qualifications and efficient job performance. Furthermore, it confirms a significant relationship between respondents' ages and their chosen stress coping mechanisms, supporting the alternative hypothesis.

Findings

- Age range: 30.0% of respondents fall within the age bracket of 25 to 35 years.
- Marital status: A majority (55.0%) of respondents are married.
- Family members: 61.7% have up to four family members.
- Education: 38.3% possess a high school diploma.
- Annual income: 45.0% earn less than Rs. 15,000 per annum.
- Job experience: 41.7% have up to five years of work experience.
- Satisfaction with services: 34.2% agree with the services provided.
- Overtime compensation: 40.8% advocate for overtime compensation.
- Perception of work-related stress: 39.2% strongly believe work-related stress is an issue.
- Perception of job load: 30.8% agree with their job load.
- Working conditions: 24.2% agree with the prevailing working conditions.

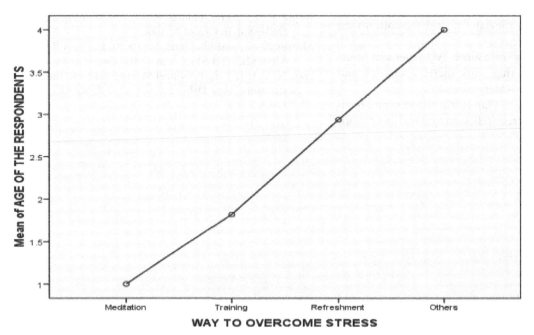

Figure 131.1 Means for groups in homogeneous subsets – age of the respondents
Source: Author

- Adherence to rules: 33.3% strongly agree with rules and regulations.
- Job security: 36.7% feel their jobs are secure.
- Importance of job efficiency: 55.0% strongly consider job efficiency as crucial.
- Family support: 40.8% receive family support.
- Coping mechanism: 40.8% seek refreshment to combat stress.
- Work pressure: 43.3% perceive excessive pressure to complete tasks.
- Neutral responses: 30.8% offered neutral views.
- Beliefs regarding job efficiency: 55.0% strongly believe in the importance of job efficiency.

Recommendations

- **Image projection and therapy:** Management should project a positive image and offer therapy to reduce stress and boost workplace confidence.
- **Balanced goal setting:** Encourage sensible goal-setting for studies and personal life to avoid undue pressure on employees.
- **Workload management:** Avoid overburdening staff with trivial tasks and allocate reasonable workloads to maintain employee well-being.
- **Employee-centric support:** Offer employee-centric benefits like personal and school loans to address their financial needs.
- **Target completion:** Rather than pressuring employees to meet targets, provide extra time and support for slower performers.
- **Promotion of understanding:** Establish meditation and yoga programs to enhance mutual understanding and alleviate mental tension among staff.
- **Unity and safety measures:** Management must take actions fostering unity, increase salaries, and provide necessary safety measures.
- **Celebratory culture:** Plan cultural events and festivals to create a stress-relieving and inclusive work atmosphere.

- **Counselling services:** Consider counselling as a means to mitigate stress levels effectively.

Conclusion

The findings strongly advocate for a proactive stance by employers towards mitigating both short-term and long-term stressors among personnel. This imperative isn't solely about fostering employee well-being; it directly impacts the business's profitability and reputation. Acknowledging and addressing stress levels can significantly bolster the overall operational efficiency and organizational culture. Hence, it's pivotal for employers and top-level officials to heed these recommendations, initiating measures that resonate with their workforce's well-being.

Moreover, the inclusivity of stress-relieving measures, such as counselling accessible to all employees irrespective of their hierarchical position within the organization, underlines the importance of a holistic approach. This fosters a supportive environment and underscores the employer's commitment to prioritizing employees' physical and mental health. Embracing these recommendations isn't just an ethical consideration but a strategic move towards creating a conducive and sustainable work environment that ultimately benefits both employees and the business at large.

References

Aswathappa, K. (2008). Human Resource Management, (5th edn.). New Delhi: Tata McGraw Hill Publishing Ltd.

Gupta, C. B. (2001). Human Resource Management. New Delhi: Sultan Chand & Sons.

Murthy, S. N., and Bhojanna, V. (2008). Business Research Methods, (2nd edn.). New Delhi: Excel Books.

Nair, N. G. L. (2001). Personnel Management and Industrial Relations. New Delhi: Sultan Chand & Sons Company Ltd.

132 A financial performance study of selected listed companies with particular relation to India's Cement industries

Devika[a], G. Rajeswari[b] and P.H. Hemamalini[c]

Karpagam Academy of Higher Education, Coimbatore, India

Abstract

The essence of financial performance lies in appraising a security's value through fundamental factors impacting a company's current operations and future potential on a broader scale. This assessment extends beyond individual companies, encompassing the industry level. The focus here is on gauging the profitability of the cement sector reliably and leveraging this analysis to forecast the annual growth rate of a company. Utilizing five years' worth of secondary data, the study scrutinizes the workforce composition, shedding light on management strategies employed by these firms in navigating their circumstances. It draws overarching conclusions discernible among these companies. The comprehensive evaluation of the cement industry's performance includes assets, liabilities, revenues, expenses, and net operational outcomes over a specific timeframe. Scrutinizing these components is crucial to enhance the usefulness of financial information. Once interpreted accurately, these findings can be disseminated among intended users for informed decision-making.

Keywords: Cement sector, financial performance, industry-level analysis, operational outcomes, profitability assessment

Introduction

Finance encapsulates the creation, management, and scrutiny of financial investments, delineating how and why individuals, corporations, or governments acquire and allocate funds. This domain is broadly categorized into corporate, personal, and public finance, each illuminating distinct fiscal facets. Essential to this realm are financial performance reports, serving as formal portrayals of an entity's financial activities and status. These reports, crafted by corporate management, provide a snapshot of current financial positions. Typically comprising a balance sheet, income statement, owner's equity statement, and cash flow analysis, these reports offer a comprehensive overview. Regular auditing of financial performance is customary among corporations, governments, and entities, ensuring precision for investment, financing, and tax considerations. Within the field of finance, the study of investments investigates how assets and liabilities evolve amidst varying risk and uncertainty. Ultimately, finance is construed as the adept management of monetary resources, underpinning the science governing money.

Objectives of the Study

- To evaluate the financial growth of specific cement industries through trend analysis.
- To conduct a comparative and analytical examination of the financial statements belonging to selected cement industry companies.

Literature Review

Table 132.1 Exploring financial insights in the cement industry: a review of research findings.

Author name	Study	Findings/insights/interpretation
Mohanakumar and George (2020)	Explored the impact of economic reforms on the cement sector, particularly automated manufacturing, focusing on cement trucks and buses.	Economic reforms have prompted a significant influx of new market entrants, emphasizing the need for optimal product mix and radial cement selection for substantial investments.
Deepa and Babu (2018)	Examined liquidity ratios' role in assessing a company's ability to cover current obligations, impacting stability, financial health, and debt repayment.	Liquidity ratios hold pivotal importance for market analysts, creditors, and potential investors, with absolute liquidity ratio reflecting cash availability for immediate obligations.

[a]devikad803@gmail.com, [b]rajiganeshamoorthi1@gmail.com, [c]hemamalini2007ster@gmail.com

Author name	Study	Findings/insights/interpretation
Acharekar et al. (2019)	Investigated various input requirements for the cement industry and analyzed liquidity through ratio assessment, studying the significance of different working capital sources.	This study delved into the diverse input needs of the cement sector and scrutinized the importance of different working capital sources in determining liquidity.
Suresh (2019)	Explored how economic, industrial factors, and fundamental company characteristics influence investment decisions.	Fundamental and industrial aspects significantly influence investment decisions, as revealed by this research.
Tulsian (2020)	Emphasized that a company's net income alone does not suffice in assessing its effectiveness and success, highlighting the need for correlation with various financial indicators.	Statistical methods including ratio analysis, mean, standard deviation, and correlation unveiled strong interconnections between profitability, short-term capital, and long-term capital for cement industry businesses.

Source: Author

Research Methodology

- Study design: Employing an analytical approach aligns with the study's aim of performance analysis estimation.
- Secondary data sources: Company annual reports and official records serve as primary secondary data sources.
- Study objectives: Determine liquidity, solvency, profitability, and turnover ratios, conduct comparative analysis, and offer organizational improvement recommendations.
  - Tools and techniques utilized: Analysis of variance and correlation analysis

Data Analysis and Interpretation

Current ratio

Table 132.2 Analysis of variance for current ratio showing significant variance among chosen cement industry companies' ratios.

Analysis of variance (ANOVA)	CR	SOS	df	Mean square	F	Sig.
Between groups	11.199	6	1.866	19.782	0	0.000
Within groups	2.642	28	0.094			
Total	13.84	34				

Result Sig. value: 0.000

The alternative hypothesis (H1) is accepted over the null hypothesis (H0), signifying significant variance in the cement industry's current ratio.

Gross profit ratio

Table 132.3 Analysis of variance for gross profit ratio demonstrating no significant differences in the ratios among selected cement industry enterprises.

Analysis of variance (ANOVA)	GPR	SOS	df	Mean square	F	Sig.
Between groups	348.373	6	58.062	3.263	0.015	0.000
Within Groups	498.219	28	17.794			
Total	846.592	34				

Result: Sig. value: 0.015

The null hypothesis (H0) is accepted, indicating no significant difference in the gross profit ratio among chosen cement industry companies.

Net profit ratio

Table 132.4 Analysis of variance for net profit ratio displaying noteworthy differences among selected cement industry companies' ratios.

Analysis of variance (ANOVA)	NPR	SOS	df	Mean square	F	Sig.
Between groups	605.161	6	100.86	9.656	0	0.000
Within groups	292.471	28	10.445			
Total	897.632	34				

Result Sig. value: 0.000

The alternative hypothesis (H1) is supported, revealing substantial variance in the cement industry's net profit ratio.

Operating profit ratio

Table 132.5 Analysis of variance for operating profit ratio revealing substantial differences among chosen cement industry enterprises' ratios.

Analysis of variance (ANOVA)	OPR	SOS	df	Mean square	F	Sig.
Between groups	725.281	6	120.88	6.803	0	0.000
Within groups	497.509	28	17.768			
Total	1222.79	34				

Result Sig. value: 0.000

The alternative hypothesis (H1) is supported, indicating significant variation in the cement industry's operating profit ratio.

Long term debt equity ratio

Table 132.6 Analysis of variance for long term debt equity ratio indicating significant differences among chosen cement industry entities' ratios.

Analysis of variance (ANOVA)	LDR	SOS	df	Mean square	F	Sig.
Between groups	0.89	6	0.148	11.873	0	0.000
Within groups	0.35	28	0.012			
Total	1.24	34				

Result Sig. value: 0.000

The alternative hypothesis (H1) is accepted, signifying significant differences in the long-term debt equity ratio among selected cement industry companies.

Inventory turnover ratio

Table 132.7 Analysis of variance for inventory turnover ratio indicating substantial differences in ratios among the selected cement industry enterprises.

Analysis of variance (ANOVA)	ITR	SOS	df	Mean square	F	Sig.
Between groups	570.76	6	95.127	20.394	0	
Within groups	130.606	28	4.665			
Total	701.367	34				

Result Sig. value: 0.000

The alternative hypothesis (H1) is supported, signifying substantial variation in the inventory turnover ratio among chosen cement industry companies.

Fixed asset turnover ratio

Table 132.8 Analysis of variance for fixed asset turnover ratio showcasing noteworthy differences among selected cement industry enterprises' ratios.

Analysis of variance (ANOVA)	FTR	SOS	df	Mean square	F	Sig.
Between groups	30.239	6	5.04	39.152	0	
Within groups	3.604	28	0.129			
Total	33.843	34				

Result Sig. value: 0.000

The alternative hypothesis (H1) is accepted, demonstrating significant differences in the fixed asset turnover ratio among chosen cement industry companies.

Results

The analysis revealed several correlations among key financial ratios. A negative correlation (-0.239) was observed between the operating profit ratio (OPR) and asset turnover ratio (ATR). Similarly, the ATR exhibited a negative correlation (-0.108) with the net profit ratio (NPR). Conversely, a positive correlation was identified between the ATR and inventory turnover ratio (ITR) with a correlation coefficient of 0.005. Moreover, a negative correlation was observed between the NPR and both the ATR and OPR, both registering (-)0.108 and (-)0.784 respectively. Furthermore, the NPR demonstrated a negative correlation (-0.258) with the ITR. Conversely, the ITR showcased a positive correlation with both the ATR and OPR.

Findings

- Chosen cement companies' present ratios show no significant differences.
- Significant differences exist in gross profit ratios among selected cement companies.

- Net profit ratios among chosen cement companies lack significant differences.
- No significant differences in operating profit and long-term debt equity ratios among chosen cement companies.
- Inventory turnover ratios among chosen cement companies show no statistically significant differences.
- Fixed asset turnover ratio among chosen cement companies exhibits no significant differences.
- Negative correlation between OPR and ATR (-0.239). Negative correlations exist between ATR and NPR (-0.108), ATR and ITR (0.005). OPR and NPR have negative correlations with ATR. Positive correlation observed between ATR and ITR.
- OPR and ATR have a negative correlation (-0.239). OPR and NPR show a positive correlation (0.784). ITR and OPR display a negative correlation (-0.085). Negative correlations are evident among ATR, ITR, and OPR. Positive correlation observed between ATR and ITR.
- Negative correlations found between ATR and NPR (-0.108), OPR and NPR (-0.784), ITR and NPR (-0.258). Negative correlations among ITR, OPR, and NPR.
- Positive correlation observed between ATR and ITR (0.005). Negative correlation between OPR and ITR (-0.085). Negative correlation found between ITR and NPR (-0.258). Negative correlations of OPR and NPR with ITR. Positive correlation between ATR and ITR.

Recommendations

- Enhance Liquidity Utilization: Optimize the use of existing liquidity resources for productive ventures.
- Utilize Credit Facilities: Leverage offered credit facilities to benefit the company's operations.
- Improve Debt Capital Efficiency: Enhance the effective utilization of debt capital to augment the company's resources.
- Maximize Resource Efficiency: Focus on maximizing overall efficiency and returns on invested

capital by utilizing existing resources more effectively.
- Diversify Funding Sources: Expand funding sources, particularly for research and development, to boost future revenue generation.

Conclusion

The research conducted on financial performance through ratio analysis in the cement industry, based on a comprehensive analysis spanning five years, offers insightful observations. While the current and liquid ratios depict the present financial stability, insights into the long-term financial position are discerned through proprietary and debt equity ratios. The effectiveness of performance in this sector is further gauged by activity and profitability ratios. Through this analysis, it's evident that the company exhibits a commendable financial robustness, underscored by its performance metrics evaluated over the past five years.

This study emphasises the multifaceted nature of financial assessment in the cement industry, highlighting the significance of varied ratios in portraying different aspects of financial health. The comprehensive evaluation using diverse ratios unveils the company's financial strength, affirming its solidity and resilience within the industry. The insights gleaned from this research not only validate the current stability but also provide valuable cues for strategic financial decisions aimed at sustaining and enhancing the company's position in the dynamic market landscape.

References

Acharekar, P., et al. (2019). A study of working capital management of cement industries in India. *International Referred Journal of Engineering and Science*, 2(8), 12–17.

Mohanakumar, S., and Tharian George, K. (2020). Impact of economic reforms on the cement industry. *Economic and Political Weekly*, 36(12), 1044–1050.

Tulsian, M. (2020). Profitability analysis: comparative study. *IOSR Journal of Economics and Finance*, 3(2).

133 A study of employees' mental health by the motivation in car dealership industry

Kalaivani, K. and Venkatachalam[a]

Karpagam Academy of Higher Education, Coimbatore, India

Abstract

Every organization is designed or built with long-term engagement with customers and employees. Happy customers and satisfied employees are the biggest assets of any organization. Whatever the industry is, a motivated worker will always make a big difference in achieving the organization goals and his personal goals. Motivation Programs can be done through various levels like rewards, bonuses, incentives, etc. But without mental health motivating employees becomes a tall mountain to climb.

Keywords: Employee, mental health, organization, workplace

Introduction

The automotive industry's projected creation of 5 crore jobs by 2030 underlines the vital link between motivation, rewards, and employee well-being. As India's automobile sector expands, attention to motivation and mental health is paramount, given its significant GDP contribution and global standing. Maruti Suzuki is the largest manufacturer, catering to a youthful demographic's increasing vehicle ownership aspirations. A survey at SRT TATA, Coimbatore, highlights the positive correlation between employee support and heightened motivation. Incorporating mental health initiatives into motivation programs, overseen by the employee welfare department, is crucial. Strategies include fostering a safe work environment, promoting mental well-being, encouraging healthy competition, providing accessible support, validating contributions, and maintaining effective communication. However, factors like unmonitored workload, personal issues, conflicts, and poor management communication can negatively impact mental health. Prioritizing employee well-being enhances productivity and organizational success, as engaged employees are better positioned to contribute effectively.

Objectives

- To identify the risk factors that affect mental health of employees.
- To find the factors that resolve psychological health issues of employees.
- To know the best support system for a Positive work environment in the organization.

Problem Statement

This study aims to identify challenges stemming from employees' inadequate mental health within organizations. With over half of global workers experiencing such issues, the resultant inefficiencies hamper productivity and necessitate comprehensive understanding and intervention strategies.

Review of Literature

Table 133.1 Insights into employee mental health studies.

Author name	Study	Findings (insights or interpretation)
Butterworth et al. (2006)	Explores employee psychological wellness, highlighting the role of transactional leadership and training in motivation. Rewards promote commitment and enhance emotional and mental well-being at work.	Transactional leadership, training, and rewards foster employee commitment, improving emotional and mental well-being in the workplace.
Björklund et al. (2013)	Identifies rising mental health challenges in the workplace, particularly in healthcare. Company atmosphere significantly impacts employee psychological well-being, influenced by factors such as relationships, leadership, and communication.	The healthcare sector faces escalating mental health issues, with company atmosphere crucially impacting employee well-being, influenced by various workplace dynamics.

[a]venkatachalam.s@kahedu.edu.in

Author name	Study	Findings (insights or interpretation)
Bronkhorst et al. (2015)	Explores the efficacy of MI health coaching in addressing various mental health issues. Implementation in medical centers results in significant improvement over three months, indicating effectiveness in occupational settings.	MI health coaching proves effective in improving mental health within medical centers, demonstrating its utility for addressing a range of mental health concerns in the workplace.
Dagenais-Desmarais et al. (2018)	Investigates the relationship between different workplace stimuli and psychological fitness. Structural equation modeling reveals a direct link, highlighting the importance of addressing internal factors over time.	Workplace stimuli directly impact psychological fitness, necessitating attention to internal factors for sustained well-being over time.
Nadeak et al. (2019)	Examines the impact of changes on mental well-being through a survey of 77 employees. Results show both positive and negative changes in work motivation over 18 months, underscoring the importance of fostering positive energy for successful career development.	Changes in the workplace exert both positive and negative effects on work motivation, emphasizing the need for organizational support to mitigate negative changes and promote career success.

Source: Author

Research Methodology

- Utilized existing research data to establish a comprehensive findings repository sourced from 100 organization employees.
- Employed statistical methodologies including percentage analysis and one-way ANOVA to discern significant mean variations across factors.
- Hypothesized the absence of a correlation between departmental divisions (sales and service) and detrimental factors affecting employee mental well-being.

Data Analysis

- Employees predominantly fall within the 25-30 age bracket, suggesting a youthful workforce conducive to updated technology adaptation.
- Male employees notably outnumber females, aligning with industry trends, although women are more prevalent in administrative roles.
- Sales departments dominate over service sectors, indicating the industry's focus on revenue generation.
- Factors detrimentally impacting employee mental health include excessive workload, management conflicts, and low salaries.
- Resolutions to psychological health issues prioritize positive work environments and flexible working hours.
- Preferred support systems for mental health encompass psychological training and flexible scheduling.
- One-way ANOVA analysis indicates a significant relationship between departmental divisions and mental health factors.

- Key findings highlight the importance of youth in the workforce, gender disparities, and the influence of departmental dynamics on mental health.
- Suggestions emphasize mental health training implementation and the role of employee welfare departments in fostering positive work environments through activities like yoga and team-building exercises.

Conclusion

In light of these findings, fostering a positive working environment and fostering equality among employees emerges as a pivotal strategy. The indicators of good mental health, as recommended by employees, hold promise for the long-term success of organizations. The correlation between decreased motivation levels and heightened stress and depression emphasizes the significance of cultivating supportive managerial relationships. Employees working under positive and supportive managers demonstrate enhanced productivity and effectiveness, emphasizing the profound impact of workplace atmosphere on performance. Ultimately, the nexus between a positive work environment and robust mental health yields higher productivity levels, thus facilitating the achievement of both organizational and individual goals. It becomes evident that prioritizing employee well-being is not only ethically imperative but also strategically advantageous for organizational success.

References

Bjorklund, C., Jensen, I., and Lohela-Karlsson, M. (2013). Is a change in work motivation related to a change in mental well-being? *Journal of Vocational Behavior*, 83(3), 571–580.

Bronkhorst, B., Tummers, L., Steijn, B., and Vijverberg, D. (2015). Organizational climate and employee mental health outcomes. *Health Care Management Review*, 40(3), 254–271. DOI: Lippincott Williams & Wilkins.

Butterworth, S., Linden, A., McClay, W., and Leo, M. C. (2006). Effect of motivational interviewing-based health coaching on employees' physical and mental health status. *Journal of Occupational Health Psychology*, 11(4), 358–365.

Dagenais-Desmarais, V., Leclerc, J.-S., and Londei-Shortall, J. (2018). The relationship between employee motivation and psychological health at work: a chicken-and-egg situation? *Work and Stress*, 32(2), 147–167. DOI: 10.1080/02678373.2017.1317880.

Nadeak, B., Sasmoko, S., Iriani, U. E., Naibaho, L., Sormin, E., and Juwita, C. P. (2019). Building employees' mental health: the correlation between transactional leadership and training program with employees' work motivation at XWJ factory. *Indian Journal of Public Health Research and Development*, 10(6), 1373–1379. ISSN 0976-5506.

134 An impact of employee motivation on organizational performance: a special reference with car dealership industries

Kalaivani, K.[a] and Venkatachalam, S.

Karpagam Academy of Higher Education, Coimbatore, India

Abstract

In contemporary business strategy, prioritizing employee motivation is paramount. Irrespective of a company's product appeal, marketing prowess, or financial resources, low staff morale poses a significant hurdle to profitability. Today's organizations recognize that employee satisfaction correlates with productivity. Engaged employees, emotionally and intellectually invested in their company's goals and values, are the linchpin of success. Motivated employees don't just fulfil their basic job duties; they exceed expectations, driving the business forward with their initiative and dedication. Consequently, fostering a culture of motivation is not merely a luxury but a strategic imperative for companies aiming to thrive in the competitive marketplace.

Keywords: Competitive marketplace, employee motivation, engagement, productivity, profitability

Introduction

The automotive industry, particularly in India, is poised for significant growth, with projections indicating it will become a global leader by 2030. India's large youth population favors the adoption of autonomous vehicles, suggesting a promising future for the sector. Forecasts predict the creation of five crore jobs in the automotive field by 2030, reflecting its substantial economic impact. Moreover, with over 14,000 automobile companies and Maruti Suzuki leading the pack, the industry's influence is undeniable. The presence of 4,897 car dealers across 523 cities underscores the extensive reach of the automotive market, supported by the Federation of Automobile Dealers Association of India (FADA). Recognizing the importance of a motivated workforce, various strategies emerge to enhance employee engagement and satisfaction within the motorcar sector. Methods such as establishing trust, setting targets, fostering a positive environment, and offering rewards aim to boost productivity and nurture a sense of loyalty among employees, ultimately benefiting both the organization and its customers. Factors influencing employee motivation, including recognition, opportunities for development, financial incentives, work-life balance, and non-monetary perks, further underscore the need for proactive management strategies to drive success in the automotive industry.

Objectives

- To identify the demographic profile of employees.
- To know the factors that influence the effectiveness of employee motivation.
- To know the impact of employee motivation on organizational performance

Problem Statement

The study aims to address the problem of productivity setbacks stemming from employee demotivation within car dealership companies. Identifying the most effective motivation techniques is crucial to mitigate delays in work completion and enhance overall productivity.

Literature Review

Table 134.1 Studies on employee motivation and productivity in organizational settings.

Author name	Reference	Study
Bhavani and Sharavan	(2015)	This study emphasizes the importance of engaging employees in decision-making processes to enhance organizational success and productivity through building trust and involvement.

[a]clicktokv@gmail.com

Author name	Reference	Study
Bawa	(2017)	The impact of motivation on productivity is analyzed, drawing on Maslow's hierarchy of needs theory. Strategies for motivating employees are discussed, considering individual needs and theories.
Nilsson	(2017)	This study explores how aligning employee and organizational goals lead to increased production and achievement. Various motivational strategies are examined based on economic, social, and psychological factors.
Seeht Saad	(2018)	Effective motivation techniques for organizations are investigated, focusing on how joyful employees contribute to increased productivity through challenging tasks and clear communication.
Jain et al.	(2019)	Employee motivation is identified as a critical aspect for organizational success, particularly in the era of globalization. The study underscores the significance of motivation in achieving targets.

Source: Author

Research Methodology

- Research procedure entails a methodical plan to address a research problem, providing the foundational structure for the study.
- Descriptive research, involving 70 respondents, employs simple random sampling to ensure each subset member has an equal chance of selection.
- The study utilizes simple percentage analysis and the weighted average method for data analysis.

Results and Findings

This dataset explores the significance of employee motivation in organizational contexts, analyzing factors like age, marital status, income, and work experience. These insights inform strategies to boost productivity and satisfaction within the workforce.

Employees age:
- The majority fall within 31-40 age bracket (42.85%).
- 35.71% are aged 21-30, while 21.43% are above 40.

Marital status:
- 67.14% of respondents are married, 32.86% unmarried.

Income level:
- 32.86% earn Rs. 15000-20000.
- 20% earn Rs. 20000-25000.
- 24.27% earn Rs. 25000-30000.
- 22.87% earn above Rs. 30000.

Work experience:
- 32.86% have 0-3 years.
- 30% have 3-6 years.
- 21.43% have 6-9 years.
- 15.71% have above 9 years.

Factors influencing employee motivation:
- Wages and salaries rank highest (1st).

- Followed by reward and recognition (2nd), personal growth (3rd), working environment (4th), and interpersonal relationship (5th).

Impact of employee motivation:
- 38.6% believe motivation enhances work performance.
- Others attribute it to attitude (20%), job satisfaction (22.8%), and goal setting (18.6%).

Feel the stimulation of work:
- 20% find smart work stimulating.
- 27.2% value knowledge exploration.
- 17% are motivated by meeting weekly targets.
- 35.8% are stimulated by developing new skills.

Findings:
- The majority are aged 30-40, married, earning Rs. 15000-20000, with 0-3 years of experience.
- Wages and salaries are the top motivator.
- Employees value work-life balance and personal development.

Suggestions:
- Increase salaries for those with 0-3 years' experience.
- Implement retention strategies for employees with over 10 years' experience.
- Enhance focus on work-life balance for better motivation.

Conclusion

In conclusion, it's evident that motivated employees are the cornerstone of organizational success. Their enthusiasm not only drives individual performance but also inspires their colleagues to excel, fostering a culture of continuous improvement within the workplace. It's imperative for organizations to prioritize employee motivation as it directly impacts engagement levels, strengthening the bond between employers and employees. By investing in motivational strategies, such as recognition programs, career development opportunities, and a supportive work environment, companies can cultivate a workforce that is committed, productive, and aligned with the organization's goals. Ultimately, nurturing employee motivation isn't just beneficial for individuals; it's a strategic imperative for the long-term prosperity and sustainability of the organization as a whole.

References

Bawa, M. A. (2017). Employee motivation and productivity: a review of literature and implications for management practice. *International Journal of Economics, Commerce and Management*, 5(12), 662–673.

Bhavani, S. A., and Sharavan, A. (2015). A study effectiveness of employee engagement in automobile industry. *International Journal of Economics and Management Sciences*, 4, 295. https://doi.org/10.4172/21626359.1000295.

Jain, A., Gupta, B., and Bindal, M. (2019). A study of employee motivation in organization. *International Journal of Engineering and Management Research*, 9(6), 65–68.

Nilsson, K. (2017). The influence of work environmental and motivation factors on seniors' attitudes to an extended working life or to retire: a cross-sectional study with employees 55-74 years of age. *Open Journal of Social Sciences*, 5(07), 30.

Seeht Saad, D. D. M. Z. (2018). The impact of employee motivation on work performance. *International Journal of Scientific and Research Publications*, 8(3), 295–308.

Somasekharan, T. M., and Velmurugan, R. (2019). Factors influencing the job satisfaction of bank employees in Kerala: evidence from five major private sector banks in Ernakulam district. *Journal of Advanced Research in Dynamical and Control Systems*, 11(1), 634–638.

Sumathi, V., and Velmurugan, R. (2018). Job satisfaction of female faculty in arts and science colleges in Coimbatore district. *International Journal of Engineering and Technology*, 7(3.6), 129–133.

Suryakumar, M., Velmurugan, R., and Sudarvel, J. (2019). HRM practices and its influence on employee performance towards job satisfaction in selected IT companies. *International Journal of Scientific and Technology Research*, 8(12), 3052–3054.

Velmurugan, R., and Uma, A. (2022). Job satisfaction of select school teachers in Coimbatore district. *International Journal of Early Childhood Special Education*, 14(4), 65–72.

Velmurugan, R., Sumathy, M., and Sridhar, K. M. (2020). Job transition among school teachers in Coimbatore city. *International Journal of Disaster Recovery and Business Continuity*, 11(1), 722–727.

135 Benchmarking digital privacy: Malaysian e-commerce transparency and control

Priya Sukirthanandan[1,a] and Mudiarasan Kuppusamy[2,b]

[1]Faculty of Business, University of Cyberjaya, Malaysia

[2]School of Graduate Studies, Unirazak, Malaysia

Abstract

The research examines data privacy practices among e-commerce platforms in Malaysia, highlighting leaders like Lazada, Shopee, and Lelong, which prioritize transparency and user control. Conversely, platforms like Ezbuy and Qoo10 lag behind in data privacy measures. Transparency and control are crucial for building trust in digital commerce. The study underscores the importance of clear privacy policies and user options for managing personal data. Results suggest that businesses with higher transparency tend to excel in management areas, emphasizing the need for consumer awareness and informed decision-making. This analysis aids both businesses and consumers in understanding data privacy standards, fostering better practices and choices in Malaysia's online marketplace.

Keywords: Benchmarking, data privacy, e-commerce, privacy policies, transparency, user control

Introduction

Customers willingly share personal information online, despite privacy concerns, benefiting businesses. Understanding motivations and consequences of data disclosure is crucial for e-commerce success. Privacy rules, especially regarding transparency and control, significantly impact user interfaces and innovative platforms. The internet's rapid evolution and global accessibility further emphasize the need for vigilant data protection. As cyberattacks and data breaches rise, customers' fears grow, fueled by ongoing disputes over cookies and wallet strategies. Recent incidents, like those involving Shopify, Facebook, Alibaba, and eBay, underscore the significant impact of data privacy issues on e-commerce performance, posing financial and reputational risks.

In the era of information and technology, frequent cyberattacks and data breaches are prevalent, heightening concerns about data privacy. Over the past decades, the global e-commerce sector has faced numerous privacy challenges, amplifying operational, financial, and reputational risks. The scale of data privacy issues in today's data-driven world impacts millions or even billions of users simultaneously. Notable incidents, such as those involving Shopify, Facebook, Alibaba, and eBay, highlight the far-reaching consequences of data privacy concerns. As the internet becomes increasingly pervasive, addressing these challenges becomes paramount to maintaining trust and safeguarding the e-commerce sector's performance and integrity.

Literature Review

Table 135.1 Benchmarking data privacy practices in Malaysian e-commerce.

Author name	Study
Shevchuk (2021)	Privacy concerns on the rise in Malaysia's e-commerce sector due to multiple data vulnerabilities.
Surfshark (2022)	Malaysia ranks 11th globally in data breaches during Q2 2022, with around 665,200 Malaysians compromised.
Murugiah (2022); Chee-Beng (2022)	Report on Malaysia's 3,699 personal data breaches since 2017, based on the findings of the Personal Data Protection Department (PDPD) Director.
Abas and Zulkifli (2022)	Limited studies in Malaysia, especially in the e-commerce industry; most research focuses on the role of privacy in small and medium enterprises.

Source: Author

[a]priya@cyberjaya.edu.my, [b]arasan@unirazak.edu.my

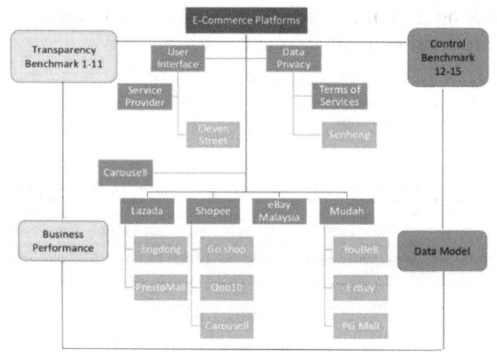

Figure 135.1 Schematic diagram for benchmarking of e-commerce platform
Source: Author

Research Methodology

Schematic analysis:
- Indicates the filling of key indicators by e-commerce platforms.
- Benchmarking from 1-11 focuses on data privacy transparency.
- Control benchmark from 12-15 indicates the level of control.
- Yellow color signifies effective transparency in companies.

Data privacy and control benchmarks:
- Yellow color represents effective transparency in benchmarks 1-11.
- Grey color signifies significant control in benchmarks 12-15.
- Companies have notable control in data privacy and control areas.

Information security testing:
- Testing process for information security is clear.
- Management of comparisons clearly defines what is being measured.
- Individuals and businesses collaborating show a high level of full disclosure.

High level of full disclosure:
- Represents business entities with a significant degree of control.
- Focuses on collection of information security and governance domains.

- Emphasizes transparency in the collaboration of information control.

This methodology aims to provide a clear understanding of how e-commerce platforms handle data privacy, control benchmarks, information security testing, and the level of disclosure in collaboration between individuals and businesses.

Result and Analysis

The success of e-commerce platforms depends on their contribution to data control and privacy. Companies like Go Shop, eBay Malaysia, Eleven Street, and Senheng prioritize data protection, earning high internal benchmarking rankings. Their strategies focus on safeguarding customer information, reflecting a commitment to privacy. Internal data protection not only serves as a foundation for third-party collaborations but also enhances overall business performance. The careful handling of data contributes to the genuine outcome and facilitates external business improvement.

The graph displays the distribution of points (1-400) for e-platforms concerning data modelling, performance, privacy, and security. The blue line signifies the range, reflecting customer satisfaction levels across platforms like Ezbuy, Qoo10, PG Mall, YouBeli, and Jingdong. Meanwhile, the red line, with a ratio of

Word	Internal Benchmarking	Performance Benchmarking	Practice Benchmarking	Length	Count	Label
Lazada	6	4	1	4	371	Transparency
Shopee	7	5	2	11	254	Control
Lelong	8	6	8	7	221	Transparency
Mudah	4	7	11	3	154	Transparency
PrestoMall	5	8	12	8	132	Transparency
Carousell	1	1	13	8	123	Control
Ezbuy	2	2	14	6	118	Transparency
Qoo10	3	3	15	8	113	Transparency
PG Mall	9	9	9	5	105	Control
YouBeli	10	13	10	3	104	Transparency
Jingdong	11	14	3	3	101	Control
Go Shop	12	15	4	7	98	Transparency
eBay Malaysia	15	10	5	3	91	Transparency
Eleven Street	14	11	6	6	81	Control
Senheng	13	12	7	7	70	Transparency

Figure 135.2 Benchmarking matrix from NVivo software
Source: Author

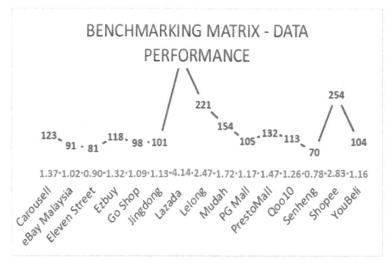

Figure 135.3 Benchmarking matrix
Source: Author

1-3 points, represents performance benchmarking for e-commerce platforms such as Lazada, Shopee, Lelong, Mudah, PrestoMall, and Carousell. These indicators gauge the success levels of online stores, emphasizing the importance of technology, quality, and worker engagement in shaping e-commerce practices.

In essence, the chart illustrates the advantages of using e-platforms for record-keeping, data modelling, and data protection. The varying share values indicate different success levels in comparisons among retailers. The feedback loop from clients serves as a crucial benchmark for businesses, determining success or potential warning signs. The comparative analysis of high-quality data from diverse e-commerce platforms highlights the significance of technology and quality standards, linking them to employee information and overall standards of excellence in the e-commerce landscape.

The data privacy benchmarking for e-commerce platforms in Malaysia reveals opportunities for improvement across the board. Most platforms have room to enhance transparency and control scores,

Table 135.2 Data privacy benchmarking for E-commerce platforms in Malaysia.

E-Commerce platform	Transparency	Control	Total
Lazada	9	5	14
Shopee	9	5	14
Lelong	6	5	11
Mudah	6	4	10
PrestoMall	6	5	11
Carousell	6	3	9
Ezbuy	6	3	9
Qoo10	6	3	9
PG Mall	7	4	11
YouBeli	6	3	9
Jingdong	6	4	10
Go Shop	6	3	10
eBay Malaysia	6	3	9
11 Street	6	5	11
Iprice	6	5	11

Source: Author

emphasizing the need to better inform users about data practices and provide more choices over personal data. Elevating transparency and control can bolster customer trust, loyalty, and satisfaction, benefiting platform reputation, competitiveness, and profitability.

Lazada and Shopee stand out as top performers with a total score of 14, showcasing exemplary transparency and control. Their high transparency score of 9, indicating clear data privacy policies, and a solid control score of 5, granting users substantial data management options, position them as leaders. Meanwhile, others lag behind, with varying levels of transparency and control, urging a collective effort to fortify data privacy practices and elevate customer confidence in the long run.

Conclusion

In the realm of e-commerce data privacy benchmarking in Malaysia, Lazada, Shopee, and Lelong emerge as top performers, boasting scores of 14, 14, and 11, respectively. These platforms excel in providing transparent and comprehensive privacy policies, offering users control over their data through various tools and options. Conversely, Ezbuy, Qoo10, and Go shop lag behind with lower scores, indicative of weaker data privacy practices and less user control. Despite optimized performance, some platforms lack clarity in terms of

data procedures and limit users' control over their information.

The process of data privacy benchmarking involves assessing and comparing the privacy practices of different e-commerce organizations. Transparency and control are pivotal principles, ensuring customers are informed about data collection, usage, and protection. However, the evaluation reveals a disparity in information security measures among online shopping platforms, highlighting the need for standardized practices and improved transparency.

The quality of products and services also plays a crucial role in participants' responses to e-commerce platforms, influencing their performance. Benchmarking and evaluation practices aid in comparing business efficiency and data security against industry standards. The results indicate Lazada's leading position, emphasizing the importance of transparency and control in enhancing e-commerce business performance. This information is vital for both companies and consumers, guiding informed choices based on individual privacy preferences. Overall, there exists a significant correlation between transparency, accountability, and effective business management in the e-commerce landscape.

References

Bowman, L., Kwok, K. O., Redd, R., Yi, Y., Ward, H., Wei, W. I., et al. (2021). Comparing public perceptions and preventive behaviours during the early phase of the COVID-19 pandemic in Hong Kong and the United Kingdom: cross-sectional survey study. *Journal of Medical Internet Research*, 23(3), e23231.

Chee-Beng, T. (2022). The Baba of Melaka: Culture and identity of a Chinese Peranakan Community in Malaysia. Strategic Information and Research Development Centre.

Dunn, M. (2020). Making gigs work: digital platforms, job quality and worker motivations. *New Technology, Work and Employment*, 35(2), 232–249.

Hill, M., and Swinhoe, D. (2021). The 15 biggest data breaches of the 21st century. Retrieved from URL.

Kaur, D., Uslu, S., Rittichier, K. J., and Durresi, A. (2022). Trustworthy artificial intelligence: a review. *ACM Computing Surveys (CSUR)*, 55(2), 1–38.

Lăzăroiu, G., Kovacova, M., Kliestikova, J., Kubala, P., Valaskova, K., and Dengov, V. V. (2018). Data governance and automated individual decision-making in the digital privacy general data protection regulation. *Administratie si Management Public*, (31), 132–142.

Mohammed, Z. A., and Tejay, G. P. (2017). Examining privacy concerns and ecommerce adoption in developing countries: the impact of culture in shaping individuals' perceptions toward technology. *Computers and Security*, 67, 254–265.

Murugiah, S. (2022). Malaysia ranked 103 on global gender gap index 2022 . Retrieved September 2, 2022.

Sandle, T. (2022). Avoiding errors with the batch release process: best practice CGMPs .

Shevchuk, V. (2021). Innovative optimization directions of investigative (detective) activity in modern conditions. *Theory and Practice of Forensic Science and Criminalistics*, 24(2), 8–25.

136 Exploring strategies to expand the Xiaohongshu app's presence in Singapore and Malaysia: an examination of the expansion of Chinese social media abroad

Yin Ying[1], Mudiarasan Kuppusamy[2,a] and Benjamin Chan Yin Fah[2,b]

[1]Faculty of Business, University of Cyberjaya, Malaysia

[2]School of Graduate Studies, Unirazak, Malaysia

Abstract

This article discusses China's unique social media landscape, which is shaped by the country's culture, politics, and regulatory environment. Chinese social media platforms, such as WeChat, Weibo, and Xiaohongshu are highly integrated and innovative, with virtual red envelopes and mini programs driving user engagement. However, expanding these platforms overseas presents challenges, such as cultural differences, regulatory environment, and competition. The article focuses on the case of Xiaohongshu (RED). It proposes strategies to improve customer loyalty and functionality in the context of e-commerce, using the Unified Theory of Acceptance and Use of Technology 2 (UTAUT2) as the theoretical framework. The article highlights the importance of understanding the cultural norms and preferences of the target audience, complying with local laws and regulations, and finding ways to differentiate Chinese social media platforms from established players in the market.

Keywords: Chinese social media landscape, cultural differences, customer loyalty, regulatory environment, WeChat, Weibo, Xiaohongshu (RED)

Introduction

Xiaohongshu, also known as Little Red Book or RED, is a popular social e-commerce platform that originated in China. Launched in 2013, Xiaohongshu has quickly become a go-to app for Chinese consumers interested in fashion, beauty, lifestyle, and travel. The platform combines social media and e-commerce, allowing users to share their experiences, discover new products, and make purchases within the app. With its high-quality user-generated content, strong community aspect, and gamification features, Xiaohongshu has attracted millions of users and has become a valuable marketing tool for businesses looking to reach Chinese consumers. As this application got popular in a comparatively short time, it is good to review it from the perspective of user behavior and engagement on this application.

There are some challenging key factors that need to be considered when expanding social media (Chinese social media platforms) or applications such as Xiaohongshu overseas. Some of the crucial challenges could be cultural differences, environment, and competition.

Malaysia and Singapore are both considered to be developed countries, with high internet and smartphone penetration rates. This makes them attractive markets for Xiaohongshu, as they have a growing middle class that is increasingly interested in e-commerce and online shopping.

Furthermore, both Malaysia and Singapore have a strong cultural connection to China, which could make Xiaohongshu's expansion into these markets easier. There is already a sizable Chinese community in both countries, and many Malaysians and Singaporeans are familiar with Chinese culture and language. This could make it easier for Xiaohongshu to market its platform to these audiences and establish a foothold in the market.

Marketing Xiaohongshu in Southeast Asia: challenges and opportunities

Marketing a Chinese social media platform like Xiaohongshu in overseas markets, particularly in Southeast Asia, presents a unique set of challenges and opportunities. The region's cultural, linguistic, and regulatory diversity requires marketers to carefully consider the factors impacting customer loyalty and engagement in cross-cultural marketing (Pemarathna, 2019b). Understanding these factors can provide valuable insights into how to create tailored marketing strategies that address the specific needs and preferences of users in countries such as Malaysia and Singapore. In order to successfully market Xiaohongshu in Southeast Asia, it is essential to explore the challenges and opportunities arising from

[a]arasan@unirazak.edu.my, [b]benjamin_chan@unirazak.edu.my

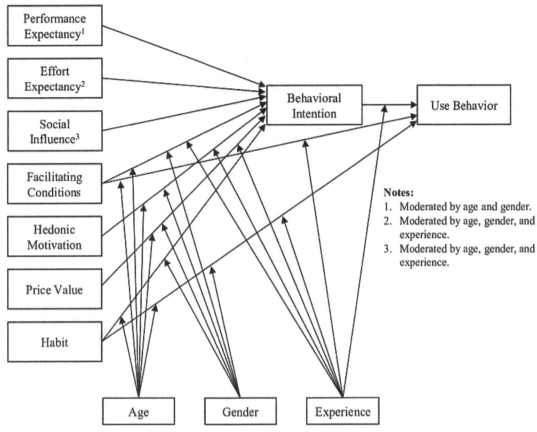

Figure 136.1 The conceptual framework of UTAUT2 model
Source: Author

the region's cultural, linguistic, and regulatory landscape (Van-Tien Dao et al., 2014). By identifying and addressing potential barriers to adoption and usage, Xiaohongshu developers can devise strategies to overcome these obstacles and establish a strong presence in these countries.

Xiaohingshu presence in Malaysia and Singapore
Xiaohongshu (RED) has swiftly emerged as a leading lifestyle app in China, Malaysia and Singapore. Founded in 2013 by Miranda Qu and Charlwin Mao, the Chinese platform initially allowed users to exchange shopping experiences and recommendations for international products. Today, Xiaohongshu has transformed into a comprehensive lifestyle app, captivating users with a wide range of topics including fashion, beauty, travel, and food. The platform's success in Malaysia and Singapore is largely due to its unique features, cultural compatibility, the significant impact of Key Opinion Leaders (KOLs) who influence purchasing decisions, and the convenience of cross-border e-commerce. As Xiaohongshu continues to evolve, it is poised to maintain its strong presence in these markets, offering local consumers

a trusted source of lifestyle inspiration and shopping opportunities (Lian et al., 2021; Tian et al., 2021). For Xiaohongshu to succeed in Malaysia and Singapore, it must address factors like language, localized content, and regulations, fostering customer loyalty and functionality based on UTAUT2 model.

Methodology

Research design
The research design stands as the backbone of any academic study, laying the blueprint for the structured and systematic execution of the research process. It encapsulates the formal procedures and protocols to be followed, serving not only as a roadmap guiding the trajectory of the research but also as a justification for the selection of certain methodologies and approaches over others(De-Madaria et al., 2021). The design of the research is therefore central to achieving the pre-determined objectives and goals, providing a path to the answers the study seeks to uncover. In the case of this particular study, the chosen research design adopts a quantitative approach, focusing on the collection and interpretation of numerical data

and statistics(Asenahabi, 2019). The choice of this approach is reflective of the study's primary aim: an investigation into the factors contributing to the successful employability of graduates from technology institutions in China.

The application of quantitative research design is suitable for this study as it allows for a more precise measurement and analysis of the defined variables. This methodology offers the opportunity to collect data from a large sample size, enhancing the statistical power and generalizability of the findings. Moreover, it facilitates the examination of relationships and patterns between variables, making it possible to ascertain the most significant factors contributing to graduate employability in Chinese technology institutions.

Furthermore, the quantitative approach lends itself to a robust, objective evaluation of the success factors, reducing the scope for subjectivity or bias that might potentially cloud the research outcomes. The standardized data collection and analysis methods typically associated with quantitative research ensure high reliability and consistency in the study's findings. Therefore, the decision to use a quantitative research design in this study is primarily based on its ability to yield results that are reliable, objective, and generalizable (Creswell, 2009). This methodological choice is premised on the inherent strength of quantitative research, which allows for precise measurement and analysis of numeric data. In the context of this study, this involves examining the factors that contribute to the employability of graduates from technology institutions in China. These factors are quantifiable and lend themselves to statistical analysis, which makes a quantitative approach suitable.

Furthermore, this quantitative approach is expected to enable a large-scale assessment of the situation. With a sufficiently large sample size, findings could be generalizable to a broader population, thereby ensuring the wider applicability of the research conclusions. This generalizability is crucial in the study's objective to provide valuable insights and recommendations that may influence, and shape future policies and strategies aimed at enhancing graduate outcomes in the technology sector.

The intended outcomes of this study serve an instrumental role in shaping the strategic direction for the expansion of the Xiaohongshu app in Malaysia and Singapore. By understanding the dynamics of graduate employability within China's technology sector, this study can help inform strategies for developing Chinese social media overseas. The assumption underlying this part of the study is that graduates who possess certain success factors would be more likely to contribute to the successful expansion and adaptation of Chinese social media apps like Xiaohongshu in foreign markets. By employing a quantitative research design, the study intends to map out these success factors and establish how they translate into real-world success in overseas markets. This approach enables the measurement and comparison of key variables across different settings, providing a more comprehensive understanding of how to successfully expand Chinese social media overseas. This broader understanding can then be used to refine the strategic decisions regarding the expansion of the Xiaohongshu app into the Malaysian and Singaporean markets.

Study setting and unit of analysis

The setting of this study is the burgeoning digital landscape of Southeast Asia, with a concentrated focus on the markets of Malaysia and Singapore. The choice of these countries as our arena of investigation is motivated by their high degree of internet penetration, burgeoning e-commerce markets, and cultural proximity to China which makes them attractive for Chinese app expansion. Furthermore, these countries have a substantial Chinese diaspora, suggesting that there may already be a familiar cultural milieu conducive to the adoption of a Chinese social media platform like Xiaohongshu.

The unit of analysis for our research is twofold. On one hand, we analyze the firm level, investigating Xiaohongshu's current strategies, functionalities, and market positioning. We seek to understand the operational decisions that Xiaohongshu has made and how these decisions have affected its ability to appeal to users outside of its home market. This involves a deep dive into the app's functionalities, its unique selling propositions, and its approach to foreign markets to date. This firm-level analysis will provide insights into the potential capabilities and weaknesses of Xiaohongshu as it seeks to expand.

On the other hand, we conduct a user level analysis, exploring the adoption behaviors, preferences, and perceptions of potential users in Malaysia and Singapore. Through this, we aim to uncover the factors influencing the acceptance and usage of Xiaohongshu in these markets. We will utilize the Unified Theory of Acceptance and Use of Technology 2 (UTAUT2) model as the theoretical underpinning for this analysis, as it integrates key aspects of user behavior including performance expectancy, effort expectancy, social influence, facilitating conditions, hedonic motivation, price value, and habit into the analysis. This dual-layered unit of analysis will facilitate a comprehensive understanding of both the supply (Xiaohongshu) and demand (users in Malaysia and Singapore) sides of the equation. In this way, the study will not only propose strategies for Xiaohongshu to improve its functionalities and market position but will also provide insights into how these strategies can be effectively aligned with user expectations and preferences in the target markets.

Target population

The target population and the method of surveying are both crucial components of a successful research design. In the context of this study, the target population has been specifically defined as users of the Xiaohongshu application who have substantive experience in using the platform. More specifically, this population is further narrowed down to include only those users who reside in the two key Southeast Asian markets under examination, Malaysia and Singapore. By focusing on this subset of users, the research seeks to gain insights that are contextually relevant and deeply rooted in the cultural and market dynamics of these two countries.

The method of data collection selected for this study is surveying. Surveys, being a widely-used tool in quantitative research, offer several advantages, such as the ability to reach a large number of participants and to collect a substantial amount of data in a relatively short time frame. In this study, the surveys would be designed to solicit detailed responses about the users' experiences and perceptions of the Xiaohongshu application, capturing the factors that influence their usage patterns, preferences, and satisfaction levels.

The rationale for selecting this particular population and method of data collection stems from the research objectives. By focusing on experienced users residing in Malaysia and Singapore, the study can gather rich, location-specific insights into the factors that may influence Xiaohongshu's successful expansion into these markets. The survey method, on the other hand, allows for a comprehensive collection of data that can be statistically analyzed to identify patterns, trends, and correlations, all of which are invaluable in informing the strategic direction of Xiaohongshu's expansion efforts. Overall, this targeted population and survey method form an integral part of the research design, shaping the data collection process and ultimately influencing the validity and relevance of the study's findings. By focusing on experienced Xiaohongshu users in Malaysia and Singapore and employing a systematic survey method, this study aims to produce findings that are both reliable and contextually informed, providing a robust foundation for understanding and facilitating Xiaohongshu's expansion into these key Southeast Asian markets.

Data collection methods

An online survey will be designed and disseminated among current Xiaohongshu application users in Malaysia, and Singapore. The survey will contain a series of close-ended questions aimed at understanding user behaviour, satisfaction levels, and perceptions of the application's features. For robustness, the sample size will be statistically representative of the user base. The respondents will be selected using a random sampling technique to eliminate bias and ensure the generalizability of the findings. Besides, the app's usage data will also be collected, subject to user consent and data privacy norms, to analyze patterns, preferences, and engagement levels. This data will be augmented by insights from secondary sources like app analytics, user reviews, and market reports to substantiate the survey findings. The collected data will be analyzed using advanced statistical techniques to identify correlations, trends, and patterns that could inform effective strategies for expanding the Xiaohongshu app in Malaysia and Singapore.

Survey instrument design

The design of the survey instrument for this research proposal draws heavily on the precedent set by prior studies, utilizing an approach of adopting and adapting questions from these investigations to ensure a comprehensive and robust questionnaire. Core studies that significantly influence this instrument include those conducted by Finney et al (2016) and Salignac et al (2019), as well as a questionnaire crafted by the Bureau of Consumer Financial Protection for their financial well-being survey. The survey instrument consists of two sections: Section 1 is dedicated to Demographic information. This section is critical as it seeks to capture essential information about the respondents, including their age, gender, occupation, education level, and other relevant details. This data will help to contextualize the responses, allowing for a deeper analysis of how different demographic factors may influence the variables of interest in the study.

The other section, Section 2, features a variety of questions designed to probe the independent and dependent constructs of the study. These questions will be methodically structured and rely on a five-point Likert scale, enabling respondents to express their agreement or disagreement with each statement. Importantly, the questions have been adopted and adapted from previous research studies, ensuring their validity and reliability in measuring the constructs intended. The precise nature of these questions will be displayed in the forthcoming table.

Data Analysis Technique

The data analysis technique for the study "Exploring Strategies for Expanding the Xiaohongshu App in Malaysia and Singapore: A Study on Developing Chinese Social Media Overseas" will be a comprehensive, multi-step process grounded in quantitative methods. Once the data from the surveys and app usage is collected, it will undergo a rigorous cleaning process to remove any inconsistencies or errors, ensuring the reliability and validity of the results.

This dataset will then be subjected to descriptive statistical analysis to identify central tendencies, dispersion measures, and patterns, thereby providing an overall understanding of user behavior, perceptions, and satisfaction levels across the different markets. Comparative analysis will be employed to discern any significant differences in app usage and user opinions between Malaysia, and Singapore for a more granular view. Further, inferential statistical methods, such as chi-square tests for independence and ANOVA, will be utilized to examine any significant associations or differences among various demographic groups and their app usage behavior or preferences. These methods will allow for a deeper understanding of how different groups interact with the Xiaohongshu app, informing segmentation and targeted marketing strategies.

To glean insights from the app usage data, a time series analysis will be conducted to uncover trends and patterns over time, while regression analysis will be applied to determine the impact of specific app features on user engagement and satisfaction. Machine Learning algorithms, like clustering, might be used to categorize users based on their engagement patterns, aiding user profiling. Lastly, sentiment analysis techniques will be applied to user reviews and comments to understand the users' emotions toward the app's features. Once quantified through sentiment scores, this text data will complement the survey and app usage data to provide a comprehensive perspective on user attitudes. All the findings will be visualized using data visualization tools, such as bar charts, pie charts, heat maps, and trend lines, to facilitate intuitive understanding and communication of results. This rigorous and detailed quantitative analysis will provide robust, actionable insights that can inform effective strategies for Xiaohongshu's expansion in Malaysia and Singapore.

Results

The survey in this study is divided into two parts. The first part focuses on the fundamental utilization of Xiaohongshu by consumers, encompassing aspects such as whether they use Xiaohongshu, the frequency of shopping on the platform, and their usage patterns. This section also explores the search behavior for individual product prices and the primary categories users search for on Xiaohongshu.

The second part constitutes the core of the questionnaire. It comprises a total of 16 questions designed to assess the perceived risks associated with Xiaohongshu, including perceived product efficacy risk, perceived service risk, and the level of trust compared to other platforms (such as Facebook, Instagram, Lazada, and peer-to-peer purchasing). Additionally, it covers respondents' experiences with negative reporting and their cross-platform purchasing behavior.

In October 2022, this research was undertaken, and the authors using google survey, an online questionnaire service, with a smaller sample size. A total of 376 test questionnaires were distributed online. The preliminary test results indicated that five questionnaires were deemed invalid, leaving 371 valid responses. Following the analysis using PLS SEM, both reliability and validity tests fell within the desired range.

Prior to participating in the study, participants received information outlining the study's objectives. After providing informed consent, they were permitted to proceed. The study adhered to guidelines set by the institutional ethical committee. Given that the primary focus of this research is on Xiaohongshu users, the initial question on the Google Survey served as a screening question. In other words, respondents who were Xiaohongshu users continued with the questionnaire, while those who were not Xiaohongshu users were directed to stop answering the questions directly.

The authors distributed the questionnaire simultaneously through WeChat, China's leading social network, and Whatapp, another leading social network, and personal computers (PCs). Both snowball and convenient sampling approaches were employed to ensure a diverse sample, and respondents completed the survey online. A 2-yuan reward was offered to encourage respondents to complete the survey. To mitigate sampling bias resulting from non-random sampling, the authors conducted these operations in the background of the questionnaire system.

The authors took several measures to enhance data quality:

a. Implemented a speed test to filter out gratuitous or casual responses.
b. Required respondents to match all answer options to complete the questionnaire and receive the reward.
c. Included a reminder section; if response time exceeded 25 minutes, the system would automatically close, marking the survey as invalid.

d. Inserted the same question in the middle of the survey; discrepancies in responses were flagged as indicative of an invalid questionnaire.

A total number of 376 questionnaires were gathered. Following the screening and elimination of returned questionnaires, 366 valid responses remained, resulting in an effective rate of 97.34%. The data from these 366 questionnaires were further scrutinized based on the question: "Do you use the Xiaohongshu application?" Seventy respondents indicated that they had never used Xiaohongshu. Consequently, the authors established a sample size of 296 for this study.

Discussion

In Figure 136.2, there are two indicator items with loading < 0.70 are removed. performance of Xiaohongshu item 2, with loading 0.355 and living-std3 with loading 0.359. After these modifications,

the PLS-SEM model has 17 indicating items. Digital, Social network, E-commerce, Communication are four factors of higher performance for us. 85.7% (R2 = 0.857) of performance is caused by the four factors. The positive path coefficient (beta) indicates that increasing in four factors will cause performance increased.

E-commerce has become an essential part of modern retail, and its growth is expected to continue in the future. Some predictors of the future direction of e-commerce include: There are eight predictors; mobile commerce, personalization, voice commerce, augmented reality, same-day delivery, social commerce, sustainability, cross-border e-commerce.

Communication is an essential part of human interaction and has been significantly impacted by advances in technology. Some predictors of the future direction of communication include: there are seven predictors; the rise of remote work, artificial intelligence and machine learning, virtual and

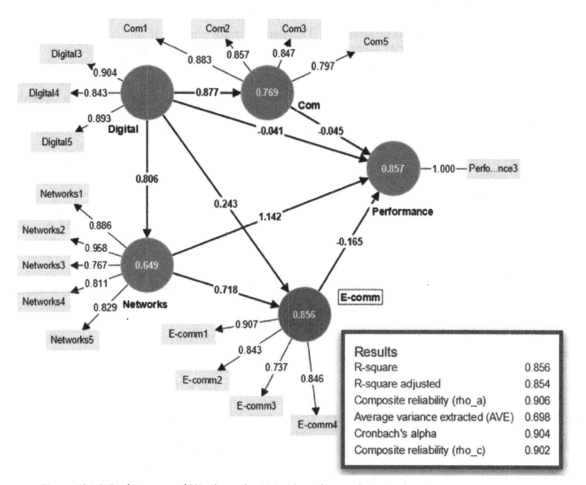

Figure 136.2 Performance of Xiaohongshu PLSc algorithm analysis result
Source: Author

augmented reality, personalization, the Internet of Things, increased privacy and security, multilingual communication.

Social network has significant value for its users. Firstly, it serves as a platform for individuals to share their authentic and personal experiences, recommendations, and insights. Users can discover new products, travel destinations, fashion trends, beauty tips, and much more through real-life stories and reviews shared by fellow users. This wealth of information helps users make informed decisions and enrich their lifestyle choices. Secondly, it fosters a sense of community and connection among like-minded individuals. Users can engage in conversations, exchange ideas, and build relationships based on shared interests and passions. Moreover, RED provides a space for businesses and brands to connect with their target audience, enabling them to showcase their products and services in an engaging and interactive manner. Overall, RED adds value to users' lives by facilitating knowledge sharing, community building, and access to a wide range of lifestyle-related content.

Digital holds significant value for its users. Firstly, it provides a convenient and accessible platform for users to explore a vast array of content and products. Users can browse through various categories such as fashion, beauty, travel, food, and more, all at their fingertips. This digital accessibility allows for effortless discovery and inspiration.

Secondly, RED offers personalized experience through its algorithm-driven recommendations. The platform analyzes users' preferences, browsing history, and engagement patterns to deliver tailored content and product suggestions. This personalization enhances the user's experience, making it more relevant and engaging.

Additionally, the digital nature of RED enables users to connect and interact with a diverse community of like-minded individuals from around the world. Users can follow, comment, and engage with content creators and fellow users, fostering connections and facilitating knowledge exchange.

Furthermore, the digital platform of RED serves as a marketplace where users can directly purchase products showcased on the platform. This seamless integration of content and commerce creates a convenient and efficient shopping experience for users.

Xiaohongshu has been growing rapidly over the past decade, here are some examples of the four factors:

1. User behavior:
   The way people interact with technology and use digital platforms will also influence the direction of the digital landscape. For example, the increas-

ing use of mobile devices for accessing the internet has led to the rise of mobile-first design.

2. Regulatory environment:
   Governments and regulatory bodies will continue to play a role in shaping the digital landscape. For example, regulations around data privacy and cybersecurity will impact the development of digital platforms and technologies.

3. Economic factors:
   Economic factors such as market demand and consumer spending will also play a role in shaping the digital landscape. For example, the rise of e-commerce has been driven by the increasing preference for online shopping.

4. Global events:
   Major global events such as pandemics, natural disasters, and political upheavals can also have a significant impact on the digital landscape. For example, the COVID-19 pandemic led to a rapid shift toward remote work and digital communication.

Conclusion

The popularity of the social media app, Little Red Book, can be attributed to several factors, as analyzed through the application of PLS-SEM. Firstly, the digital factor of Xiaohongshu user-friendly interface and intuitive design contribute to its appeal, ensuring a seamless and enjoyable user experience. Secondly, the social network factor of Xiaohongshu emphasis on user-generated content and authentic recommendations creates a trustworthy and reliable environment, fostering user engagement and loyalty. Thirdly, the communication factor of Xiaohongshu personalized recommendations, driven by advanced algorithms, cater to individual interests and preferences, enhancing user satisfaction, the ecommerce factor of Xiaohongshu. Additionally, the app's strong community aspect, facilitating connections among like-minded individuals and promoting social interactions, contributes to its popularity. Moreover, the integration of content and commerce within the app enables users to conveniently discover and purchase products, further enhancing their value. In conclusion, the success and popularity of RED can be attributed to its user-friendly design, authentic content, personalized recommendations, strong community engagement, and seamless integration of content and commerce.

Xiaohongshu is particularly popular for its focus on beauty, fashion, travel, and food content. Users can share their experiences and recommendations related to these topics, as well as discover new products and trends. The app also features e-commerce functionality that allows users to purchase products directly from the app.

Xiaohongshu has become an important platform for both consumers and businesses in China's digital landscape, with many brands and influencers using the app to promote their products and reach potential customers. The app's unique combination of social networking and e-commerce has made it a valuable platform for businesses looking to tap into China's growing consumer market.

References

Abdulahi, A., et al. (2014). A study on the negative effects of social networking sites such as Facebook among Asia Pacific university scholars in Malaysia. *International Journal of Business and Social Science*, 5(10). www.ijbssnet.com.

Acheampong, P. et al. (2017). Determinants of behavioral intentions of 'Generation-Y' adoption and use of computer-mediated communication tools in Ghana. *British Journal of Interdisciplinary Research*, 8, 1. http://onlinejournal.org.uk/index.php/BJIR/index.

Agyei, J., et al. (2020). Influence of trust on customer engagement: empirical evidence from the insurance industry in Ghana. *SAGE Open*, 10(1).

Ahmed, A. M., et al. (2014). Event-based mobile social networks: services, technologies, and applications. *IEEE Access*, 2, 500–513.

Ain, N. U., Kaur, K., and Waheed, M. (2016a). The influence of learning value on learning management system use: an extension of UTAUT2. *Information Development*, 32(5), 1306–1321.

Akram, W., and Kumar, R. (2017). A study on positive and negative effects of social media on society. *International Journal of Computer Sciences and Engineering*, 5(10), 351–354. http://www.ijcseonline.org/full_paper_view.php?paper_id=1527.

Almegbel, H., and Aloud, M. (2021). Factors influencing the adoption of mhealth services in Saudi Arabia: a patient-centered study. *IJCSNS International Journal of Computer Science and Network Security*, 21(4), 313–324. https://doi.org/10.22937/IJCSNS.2021.21.4.39.

Al'Uqdah, S. N., Jenkins, K., and Ajaa, N. (2019). Empowering communities through social media. *Counselling Psychology Quarterly*, 32(2), 137–149.

Alwahaishi, S., and Snasel, V. (2013). Factors influencing the consumers'adoption of mobile internet a fuzzy approach for the topological data analysis view project security of mobile devices and communication, financed by technology agency of the Czech Republic view project factors influencing the consumers' adoption of mobile internet. https://www.researchgate.net/publication/257922017.

Amedie, J. (2015). Scholar commons the impact of social media on society pop culture intersections the impact of social media on society. http://scholarcommons.

scu.edu/engl_176http://scholarcommons.scu.edu/engl_176/2.

Asenahabi, B. M. (2019). Basics of research design: a guide to selecting appropriate research design. *International Journal of Contemporary Applied Researches*, 6(5), 76–89. www.ijcar.net.

Bail, C. A., et al. (2018). Exposure to opposing views on social media can increase political polarization. *Proceedings of the National Academy of Sciences of the United States of America*, 115(37), 9216–9221.

Belanger, F., Hiller, J. S., and Smith, W. J. (??). Trustworthiness in electronic commerce: the role of privacy, security, and site attributes. www.elsevier.com/locate/jsis.

Borghouts, J., et al. (2021a). Barriers to and facilitators of user engagement with digital mental health interventions: systematic review. *Journal of Medical Internet Research*, 23(3).

Boschetti, F., Hughes, M., Jones, C., and Lozano-Montes, H. (2018). On decision makers' perceptions of what an ecological computer model Is, What It Does, and its impact on limiting model acceptance. Sustainability, 10(8).

Boyd, D. M., and Ellison, N. B. (2007). Social network sites: definition, history, and scholarship. *Journal of Computer-Mediated Communication*, 13(1), 210–30.

Busalim, A. H., Ghabban, F., and AbRazakCheHussin. (2021). Customer engagement behaviour on social commerce platforms: an empirical study. *Technology in Society*, 64.

Carr, C. T., and Hayes, R. A. (2015). Social media: defining, developing, and divining. *Atlantic Journal of Communication*, 23(1), 46–65.

Choi, J., Lee, H. J., Sajjad, F., and Lee, H. (2014). The influence of national culture on the attitude towards mobile recommender systems. *Technological Forecasting and Social Change*, 86, 65–79.

Chu, S. C., Chen, H. T., and Gan, C. (2020). Consumers' engagement with corporate social responsibility (CSR) communication in social media: evidence from china and the United States. *Journal of Business Research*, 110, 260–71.

Creswell, J. W. (2009). Research Design : Qualitative, Quantitative, and Mixed Methods Approaches. SAGE.

De-Madaria, E., et al. (2021). Design and validation of a patient-reported outcome measure scale in acute pancreatitis: the pan-promise study. *Gut*, 70(1), 139–147.

Dong, T., Liang, C., and He, X. (2017). Social media and internet public events. *Telematics and Informatics*, 34(3), 726–39.

Escobar-Rodríguez, T., Carvajal-Trujillo, E., and Monge-Lozano, P. (2014). Australasian journal of educational technology factors that influence the perceived advantages and relevance of facebook as a learning tool: an extension of the UTAUT. http://newsroom.fb.com/Key-.

Aljohani, N. F. N. (2022). Towards an effective M-Health application: exploring factors affecting the adoption and acceptance of M-Health applications in Saudi Arabia Certificate of Original Authorship.

Fedorko, I., Bacik, R., and Gavurova, B. (2021). Effort expectancy and social influence factors as main determinants of performance expectancy using electronic banking. *Banks and Bank Systems*, 16(2), 27–37.

Fulk, J., Schmitz, J., and Steinfield, C. W. (1990). A social influence model of technology use understanding online creative collaboration over multidimensional networks view project Boundary Spanning over Enterprise Social Media View Project. https://www.researchgate.net/publication/238734420.

Gharaibeh, M. K., Arshad, M. R. M., and Gharaibh, N. K. (2018). Using the UTAUT2 model to determine factors affecting adoption of mobile banking services: a qualitative approach. *International Journal of Interactive Mobile Technologies*, 12(4), 123–34.

Greve, G. (2014). The moderating effect of customer engagement on the brand image – brand loyalty relationship. *Procedia - Social and Behavioral Sciences*, 148, 203–10.

Grizane, T., and Jurgelane, I. (2016). Social media impact on business evaluation. *In Procedia Computer Science*, Elsevier B.V., 190–96.

He, X., and Pedraza-Jiménez, R. (2015). Chinese social media strategies: Communication key features from a business perspective. *Profesional de la Informacion*, 24(2), 200–209.

International Information Management Corporation, and Institute of Electrical and Electronics Engineers. Mauritius Subsection. 2014 IST-Africa Conference & Exhibition : 06-09 May 2014, Mauritius.

Jeffres, Leo, and Kimberly A Neuendorf. In a Mobile Era, Do Visual Media Cultivate a Singular View of the Public Sphere? https://www.researchgate.net/publication/314207895.

Ji, Mindy F., and Wendy Wood. 2007. "Purchase and Consumption Habits: Not Necessarily What You Intend." Journal of Consumer Psychology 17(4): 261–76.

Johnson, Hayley. 2017. "#NoDAPL: Social Media, Empowerment, and Civic Participation at Standing Rock." Library Trends 66(2): 155–75.

Kaplan, Andreas M. 2015. "Social Media, the Digital Revolution, and the Business of Media." JMM International Journal on Media Management 17(4): 197–99.

Kaun, Anne, and Julie Uldam. 2018. "Digital Activism: After the Hype." New Media and Society 20(6): 2099–2106.

Khechine, Hager, Benoit Raymond, and Marc Augier. 2020. "The Adoption of a Social Learning System: Intrinsic Value in the UTAUT Model." British Journal of Educational Technology 51(6): 2306–25.

Kim, Jiyeon, and Sandra Forsythe. 2007. "Hedonic Usage of Product Virtualization Technologies in Online Apparel Shopping." International Journal of Retail and Distribution Management 35(6): 502–14.

Kim, MyungJa, Namho Chung, and Choong Ki Lee. 2011. "The Effect of Perceived Trust on Electronic Commerce: Shopping Online for Tourism Products and Services in South Korea." Tourism Management 32(2): 256–65.

Lally, Phillippa, and Benjamin Gardner. 2013. "Promoting Habit Formation." Health Psychology Review 7(SUPPL1).

Lee, Claire Seungeun. 2021. "Online Fraud Victimization in China: A Case Study of BaiduTieba." Victims and Offenders 16(3): 343–62.

Leidner, Dorothy E., Ester Gonzalez, and Hope Koch. 2018. "An Affordance Perspective of Enterprise Social Media and Organizational Socialization." Journal of Strategic Information Systems 27(2): 117–38.

Li, Xiaoqing, Xiaogang He, and Yifeng Zhang. 2020. "The Impact of Social Media on the Business Performance of Small Firms in China." Information Technology for Development 26(2): 346–68.

Lian, K., Chen, Z., and Zhang, H. (2021). From the Perspective of Feminism: Market Positioning of Xiaohongshu. In 5th International Seminar on Education, Management and Social Sciences (ISEMSS 2021). Atlantis Press.

Lin, Jiabao, ZhimeiLuo, Xusen Cheng, and Lei Li. 2019. "Understanding the Interplay of Social Commerce Affordances and Swift Guanxi: An Empirical Study." Information and Management 56(2): 213–24.

Loureiro, Sandra M.C., Luisa Cavallero, and Francisco Javier Miranda. 2018. "Fashion Brands on Retail Websites: Customer Performance Expectancy and e-Word-of-Mouth." Journal of Retailing and Consumer Services 41: 131–41.

Merhi, Mohamed, Kate Hone, and Ali Tarhini. 2019. "A Cross-Cultural Study of the Intention to Use Mobile Banking between Lebanese and British Consumers: Extending UTAUT2 with Security, Privacy and Trust." Technology in Society 59.

Möller, Judith, Robbert Nicolai van de Velde, Lisa Merten, and Cornelius Puschmann. 2020. "Explaining Online News Engagement Based on Browsing Behavior: Creatures of Habit?" Social Science Computer Review 38(5): 616–32.

Montag, Christian, Benjamin Becker, and Chunmei Gan. 2018. "The Multipurpose Application WeChat: A Review on Recent Research." Frontiers in Psychology 9(DEC).

Moore, Gary C., and IzakBenbasat. 1991. "Development of an Instrument to Measure the Perceptions of Adopting an Information Technology Innovation." Information Systems Research 2(3): 192–222.

Nikolopoulou, Kleopatra, VasilisGialamas, and KonstantinosLavidas. 2021. "Habit, Hedonic Motivation, Performance Expectancy and Technological Pedagogical Knowledge Affect Teachers' Intention to Use Mobile Internet." Computers and Education Open 2: 100041.

Oh, Sujin, Xinran Y. Lehto, and Jungkun Park. 2009. "Travelers' Intent to Use Mobile Technologies as a Function of Effort and Performance Expectancy." Journal of Hospitality and Leisure Marketing 18(8): 765–81.

Okazaki, Shintaro. 2009. "Social Influence Model and Electronic Word of Mouth: PC versus Mobile Internet." International Journal of Advertising 28(3): 439–72.

Osatuyi, Babajide. 2015. "Personality Traits and Information Privacy Concern on Social Media Platforms."

Journal of Computer Information Systems 55(4): 11–19.

Parveen, Farzana, Noor IsmawatiJaafar, and AininSulaiman. 2015. "Role of Social Media on Information Accessibility." In Pacific Asia Conference on Information Systems, PACIS 2015 - Proceedings, Pacific Asia Conference on Information Systems.

Pemarathna, Rmmd. 2019a. Impact of Xiaohongshu on Its User Based and Society: A Review.

Pemarathna, Rmmd. 2019c. Impact of Xiaohongshu on Its User Based and Society: A Review. https://www.researchgate.net/publication/333974009.

Podhovnik, Mag Mag Phil Edith. "Language in International Business. Diminishing the Cross-Cultural Divide with Cultural Scripts." https://www.researchgate.net/publication/267323352.

Qomariah, Nurul. 2021. "The Role of Promotion and Service Quality in Increasing Consumer Satisfaction and Loyalty in Pawnshops." Journal of Economics, Finance And Management Studies 04(10). http://ijefm.co.in/v4i10/17.php.

Raman, Arumugam, and Yahya Don. 2013a. "Preservice Teachers' Acceptance of Learning Management Software: An Application of the UTAUT2 Model." International Education Studies 6(7): 157–64.

Razak, FahmiZaidi Bin Abdul, Azlina Abu Bakar, and Wan Salihin Wong Abdullah. 2017. "How Perceived Effort Expectancy and Social Influence Affects the Continuance of Intention to Use E-Government. A Study of a Malaysian Government Service." Electronic Government 13(1): 69–80.

Richards, Deborah, Patrina H.Y. Caldwell, and Henry Go. 2015. "Impact of Social Media on the Health of Children and Young People." Journal of Paediatrics and Child Health 51(12): 1152–57.

Schober, Michael F. et al. 2016. "Social Media Analyses for Social Measurement." Public Opinion Quarterly 80(1): 180–211.

Sewandono, Raden Edi, ArmanuThoyib, DjumilahHadiwidjojo, and AinurRofiq. 2022. "Performance Expectancy of E-Learning on Higher Institutions of Education under Uncertain Conditions: Indonesia Context." Education and Information Technologies.

Sheikh, Zaryab et al. 2017. "Acceptance of Social Commerce Framework in Saudi Arabia." Telematics and Informatics 34(8): 1693–1708.

Sobré-Denton, Miriam. 2016. "Virtual Intercultural Bridgework: Social Media, Virtual Cosmopolitanism, and Activist Community-Building." New Media and Society 18(8): 1715–31.

"Social Media Revolution."

"Social Media RP Full Intro."

Sousa, Sonia, David Lamas, and Paulo Dias. A Model for Human-Computer Trust Contributions Towards Leveraging User Engagement.

Sudari, SuciAyu, Arun Kumar Tarofder, Ali Khatibi, and JacqulineTham. 2019. "Measuring the Critical Effect of Marketing Mix on Customer Loyalty through Customer Satisfaction in Food and Beverage Products." Management Science Letters 9(9): 1385–96.

Sweet, Kayla S., Jennifer K. LeBlanc, Laura M. Stough, and Noelle W. Sweany. 2020. "Community Building and Knowledge Sharing by Individuals with Disabilities Using Social Media." Journal of Computer Assisted Learning 36(1): 1–11.

Tamilmani, Kuttimani, Nripendra P. Rana, and Yogesh K. Dwivedi. 2017. "A Systematic Review of Citations of UTAUT2 Article and Its Usage Trends." In Lecture Notes in Computer Science (Including Subseries Lecture Notes in Artificial Intelligence and Lecture Notes in Bioinformatics), Springer Verlag, 38–49.

Tamilmani, Kuttimani, Nripendra P. Rana, and Yogesh K. Dwivedi. 2021. "Consumer Acceptance and Use of Information Technology: A Meta-Analytic Evaluation of UTAUT2." Information Systems Frontiers 23(4): 987–1005.

"The Next Wave" Emerging Digital Life in South and Southeast Asia.

Tian Guang. 2012. "Key Issues in Cross-Cultural Business Communication: Anthropological Approaches to International Business." AFRICAN JOURNAL OF BUSINESS MANAGEMENT 6(22).

Tian, W., Xiao, Y., and Xu, L. (2021). What XiaoHongShu users care about: an analysis of online review comments. In 2021 International Conference on Public Relations and Social Sciences (ICPRSS 2021) (pp. 386–391). Atlantis Press, https://www.kuchuan.com.

Toole, Jameson L., Carlos Herrera-Yaqüe, Christian M. Schneider, and Marta C. González. 2015. "Coupling Human Mobility and Social Ties." Journal of the Royal Society Interface 12(105).

Turetken, Oktay, Jan Ondracek, and WijnandIJsselsteijn. 2019. "Influential Characteristics of Enterprise Information System User Interfaces." Journal of Computer Information Systems 59(3): 243–55.

"Understanding Social Media in China."

Valente, Thomas W. SOCIAL NETWORKS EISEWER Social Networks IX I IYYh) 60-89 Social Network Thresholds in the Diffusion of Innovations*.

Van-Tien Dao, W., Nhat Hanh Le, A., Ming-Sung Cheng, J., and Chao Chen, D. (2014). Social media advertising value. *International Journal of Advertising*, 33(2), 271–294.

Wallis, Cara. 2011. 5 International Journal of Communication New Media Practices in China: Youth Patterns, Processes, and Politics. http://ijoc.org.

Wang, Junsong, and YanhuiJia. 2021. "Social Media's Influence on Air Quality Improvement: Evidence from China." Journal of Cleaner Production 298.

Wang, Shiliang, Michael J Paul, and Mark Dredze. Exploring Health Topics in Chinese Social Media: An Analysis of SinaWeibo. http://wubi.sogou.com/dict/cell.php?id=272.

Wang, Yan. 2016. "Brand Crisis Communication through Social Media: A Dialogue between Brand Competitors on SinaWeibo." Corporate Communications 21(1): 56–72.

Weber, Matthew S., Janet Fulk, and Peter Monge. 2016. "The Emergence and Evolution of Social Networking Sites as an Organizational Form." Management Communication Quarterly 30(3): 305–32.

Weger, Harry, and Mark Aakhus. 2003. "Arguing in Internet Chat Rooms: Argumentative Adaptations to Chat Room Design and Some Consequences for Public Deliberation at a Distance." Argumentation and Advocacy 40(1): 23–38.

Xu, Li, Xiaohui Yan, and Zhengwu Zhang. 2019. "Research on the Causes of the 'TikTok' App Becoming Popular and the Existing Problems." Journal of Advanced Management Science: 59–63.

Xu, Qiong, and Richard Mocarski. 2014. "A Cross-Cultural Comparison of Domestic American and International Chinese Students' Social Media Usage." 4(4): 374–88. http://jistudents.org.

Yang, Shuiqing, Bin Wang, and Yaobin Lu. 2016. "Exploring the Dual Outcomes of Mobile Social Networking Service Enjoyment: The Roles of Social Self-Efficacy and Habit." Computers in Human Behavior 64: 486–96.

Yuan, Shupei, Wenjuan Ma, ShaheenKanthawala, and Wei Peng. 2015. "Keep Using My Health Apps: Discover Users' Perception of Health and Fitness Apps with the UTAUT2 Model." Telemedicine and e-Health 21(9): 735–41.

Zendle, David, and Henrietta Bowden-Jones. 2019. "Is Excessive Use of Social Media an Addiction?" The BMJ 365.

Zeng, Jing, Crystal Abidin, and Mike S Schäfer. 2021. Research Perspectives on TikTok and Its Legacy Apps: Introduction. http://ijoc.org.

Zhang, Xin, Liang Ma, Bo Xu, and Feng Xu. 2019. "How Social Media Usage Affects Employees' Job Satisfaction and Turnover Intention: An Empirical Study in China." Information and Management 56(6).

Zhang, Xingting, Dong Wen, Jun Liang, and Jianbo Lei. 2017. "How the Public Uses Social Media Wechat to Obtain Health Information in China: A Survey Study." BMC Medical Informatics and Decision Making 17.

Zunzunegui, María-Victoria, Beatriz E Alvarado, Teodoro Del Ser, and Angel Otero. 2003. Social Networks, Social Integration, and Social Engagement Determine Cognitive Decline in Community-Dwelling Spanish Older Adults. http://psychsocgerontology.oxford-journals.org/.

137 Digital pathways to Riyadh: investigating social media's role in tourist engagement within the Saudi capital

Naji Khaled Abdo Qaid and Maniyarasi Gowindasamy[a]

Faculty of Business, University of Cyberjaya, Malaysia

Abstract

This study delves into the digital pathways shaping tourist engagement in Riyadh, Saudi Arabia, with a focus on social media interactions. Employing a mixed methodology, quantitative data was meticulously analyzed. The experimental approach involved primary data collection through online surveys (nine questionnaires) and face-to-face interviews (six questionnaires) with 500 diverse respondents in Riyadh, spanning students, professionals, teachers, and more. Demographic details and social media activities, such as likes, shares, and reviews, were scrutinized. The study highlights the positive impact of social media on tourists' behavior and decision-making, supported by the reliability analysis using "Cronbach's alpha" for data gathered from both survey types.

Keywords: Riyadh, Saudi capital, sustainable tourism, sustainable tourism development, tourism development, tourism industry

Introduction

In today's rapidly evolving technological landscape, communication technologies, particularly social media platforms like Facebook, Twitter, and Instagram, have become integral to daily life. This shift has transformed the way people exchange information, share images, and engage on social media, making it easier and faster. Social media's increasing significance is evident in its impact on various aspects, from staying updated on news to reshaping organizational marketing strategies, replacing traditional channels like television and radio (Klingmann, 2023; Alsheikh et al., 2022).

The focus of this study is on the role of digital pathways, specifically social media platforms, in enhancing tourist engagement in Riyadh. The research indicates that the use of social media has positively influenced tourist attraction in the Saudi capital, with tourists benefiting from real-time updates, political news, scientific data, and social interactions. Additionally, the study examines demographic backgrounds of visitors from January to June 2023, shedding light on activities that positively impact tourists' behavior and decision-making processes in selecting destinations (Taibah, Al-Hilali, and Huzaim, 2023 ; Al-Mohmmad and Butler, 2021; Dudley, 2013). The reliability of the data collected from 500 respondents is affirmed through Cronbach's alpha analysis, further reinforcing the study's credibility.

Literature Review

Table 137.1 Exploring diverse methodologies in tourism research: a survey of recent studies.

Author name	Study
Al-Gasawneh and Al-Adamat (2020)	Surveyed various papers with diverse methodologies and results, focusing on tourist behavior and decision-making processes for destination selection.
Buluk (2015)	Utilized quantitative research methods to support findings in their paper.
Alghamdi and Plunkett (2021)	Employed a mixed methodology, including interviews conducted periodically over the years.
Acharjee and Ahmed (2023)	Applied regression analysis approach to explain their concept in a detailed manner.

Source: Author

[a]maniyarasi@cyberjaya.edu.my

Research Methodology

This research explores the effects of social media on tourist behavior in Riyadh, Saudi Arabia. By employing both descriptive and experimental methods, it aims to understand how platforms like Instagram, Facebook, Youtube, and Twitter influence tourist engagement and decision-making. The study also extends its focus to assessing the impact of social media on individuals working in the local tourism sector. Through a combination of primary and secondary data collection, this research aims to shed light on the intricate dynamics shaping the tourism landscape in Riyadh.

Sampling technique:
- Involves a sample of 500 respondents for statistical analysis.
- Combines primary and secondary data sources.

Data collection methods:

Questionnaires:
- Utilizes open-ended questionnaires for data gathering.
- Circulated among 500 respondents, covering a wide range of information.
- Employed Likert scale approach for responses.

Sampling period:
- Research conducted with respondents who visited Riyadh between January 2023 to June 2023.

Primary data collection:
- Online questionnaires sent to tourist agencies, students, business stakeholders, and travelers.
- Incorporates a Likert scale for responses (agree, strongly agree, disagree, strongly disagree, neutral).

Face-to-face interviews:
- Conducted with students, university professors, lecturers, residents, tourist guides, etc.
- Utilizes a variable-based question survey method with a rating scale from 1 to 5 (severe disagreement to strong agreement).

Result and Analysis

The study involved gathering data from 500 respondents through both primary and secondary methods. The primary approach utilized nine questionnaires, with respondents indicating their agreement levels on a Likert scale. Additionally, secondary data collection involved six questionnaires where respondents rated items on a scale of 1 to 5. This comprehensive data collection process encompassed demographic information and social media activities influencing tourist behavior and decision-making. The analysis, validated through Cronbach's alpha, ensured the reliability and authenticity of the findings. Ultimately, the research concludes that social media significantly impacts tourist engagement in Riyadh, fulfilling the study's primary objective.

By employing both primary and secondary data collection techniques, the study amassed diverse insights into tourist behavior in Riyadh. Through nine questionnaires utilizing the Likert scale and six surveys

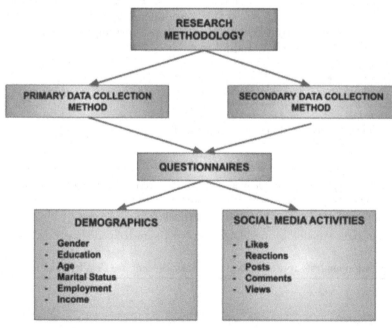

Figure 137.1 Representing research methodologies
Source: Author

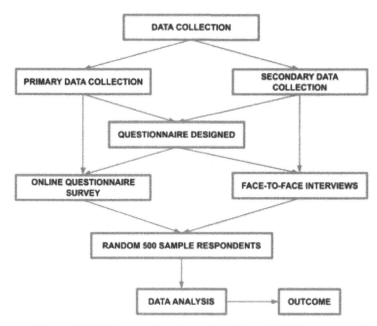

Figure 137.2 Representing data collection methodology on sample respondents with data analysis and outcome
Source: Author

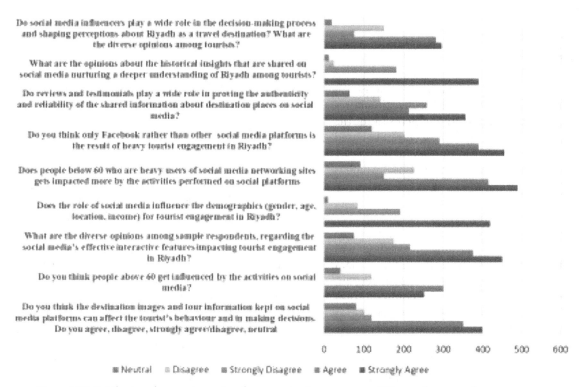

Figure 137.3 Likert scale questionnaires for quantitative survey on 500 sample respondents
Source: Author

employing a rating scale of 1 to 5, the research captured a broad spectrum of demographic data and social media activities shaping tourist decisions. The application of Cronbach's Alpha further authenticated the reliability of the data analysis. The study's culmination indicates a substantive role of social media in enhancing tourist engagement within the Saudi capital, Riyadh, thus achieving its principal research aim.

In addition to this, a secondary data collection approach was also used in this paper, which was

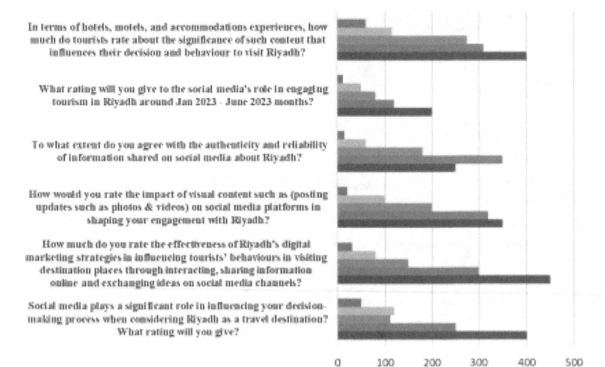

Figure 137.4 Variables-based questionnaires for quantitative survey on 500 sample respondents
Source: Author

conducted by face-to-face interviews (Al-Gasawneh and Al-Adamat, 2020). A total of six questionnaires were created for the sample respondents and the responses gathered were based on a variable-based survey in which the sample had to respond between 1 (very good response) to 5 (very bad response) which is shown in Figure 137.4.

Reliability analyses and implications
For analyzing the authenticity and reliability of the information Cronbach's alpha analysis method was implemented to deduce how much the gathered data is reliable and authorized given by the sample respondents. "Cronbach's alpha" is the most common form of reliability coefficient. This analysis is a method for assessing the consistency by comparison the quantity of shared variance, or covariance with the quantity of overall variance among the complete data gathered (Al-Gasawneh and Al-Adamat, 2020). Implementing Cronbach's alpha analysis can sometimes provide incorrect analysis of the gathered data due to the variance chosen. If the analysis of the collected responses is done incorrectly, this method will prove to be inefficient in determining how much data is authenticated and reliable in the study. It is a time-consuming method, because if "Cronbach's alpha" coefficient is over 0.7 then it implies good reliability. However, it

can vary depending on the number of questionnaires that have been used in the study.

Advantages of social media's role in tourist engagement
While social media has some implications, it also has major benefits that play a significant role in engaging more tourists in Riyadh with wide demographic backgrounds from around the globe. The primary and secondary methods that were implemented in the study helped researchers in gathering a good amount of data. Implementing the Likert scale and variable-based survey methodologies has aided the researchers in collecting not only better quantity but also quality of data. Sample respondents appreciated not only the quality of the questionnaires distributed to them which was from January 2023 - June 2023 but also the survey methodologies used which were Likert scale and variable-based.

Conclusion

This study has achieved the outcome of the tourist engagement in Riyadh through social media which was the main objective of this paper. This study has shown to be true that social media applications positively affect tourists' behavior and their decision-making processes about the intention of choosing the visiting destinations. Researchers can work on exploring particularly those social media features that typically affect the tourist's behavior and their decision-making process in choosing the visiting destination in Riyadh. In addition, they can also add more questionnaires to the Likert scale, and variable-based surveys to prove the in-depth demographics of the tourists traveling to Riyadh. In addition to this, future researchers can investigate the wide scope of the travelers such as gathering a sample of a greater number of respondents instead of only 500 that have been taken in this paper. Moreover, they can also work on collecting the data searched by the travelers before and after visiting Riyadh.

References

Al-Gasawneh, J. A., and Al-Adamat, A. M. (2020). The Relationship between perceived destination image, social media interaction and travel intentions relating to Neom city. *Academy of Strategic Management Journal*, 19(2), 1–12.

Alghamdi, A. (2023). A hybrid method for customer segmentation in Saudi Arabia restaurants using clustering, neural networks and optimization learning techniques. *Arabian Journal for Science and Engineering*, 48(2), 2021–2039. https://doi.org/10.1007/s13369-022-07091-y.

Alghamdi, A. A., and Plunkett, M. (2021). The perceived impact of social networking sites and apps on the social capital of Saudi postgraduate students: a case study. *Future Internet*, 13(1), 20. https://doi.org/10.3390/fi13010020.

Al-Mohmmad, S., and Butler, G. (2021). Tourism SME stakeholder perspectives on the inaugural 'Saudi seasons': an exploratory study of emerging opportunities and challenges. *Tourism and Hospitality Management*, 27(3), 669–687. https://doi.org/10.20867/thm.27.3.11.

Alsheikh, D. H., Abd Aziz, N., and Alsheikh, L. H. (2022). Influencing of e-word-of-mouth mediation in relationships between social influence, price value and habit and intention to visit in Saudi Arabia. *Humanities and Social Sciences Letters*, 10(2), 186–197. https://doi.org/10.18488/73.v10i2.3010.

Baber, R., and Baber, P. (2023). Influence of social media marketing efforts, e-reputation and destination image on intention to visit among tourists: application of S-O-R model. *Journal of Hospitality and Tourism Insights*, 6(5), 2298–2316. https://doi.org/10.1108/JHTI-06-2022-0270.

Buluk, B. (2015). The effects of social media on before and after visiting a destination: a research in Gallipoli Peninsula. *Journal of International Social Research* . https://doi.org/10.17719/jisr.20154115096.

Dudley, D. (2013). Riyadh Looks beyond Religious Tourism. MEED: Middle East Economic Digest.

Klingmann, A. (2023). Rescripting Riyadh: how the capital of Saudi Arabia employs urban megaprojects as catalysts to enhance the quality of life within the city's neighborhoods. *Journal of Place Management and Development*, 16(1), 45–72. https://doi.org/10.1108/JPMD-06-2021-0062.

Martiasari, L. D., and Hendratmi, A. (2022). Menilai halal awareness dan lifestyle terhadap keputusan menginap di hotel syariah. *Jurnal Ekonomi Syariah Teori Dan Terapan*, 9(4).

138 Harmonizing leadership and agility: a new paradigm for digital talent management

Alper Kaplan and Maniyarasi Gowindasamy[a]

Faculty of Business, University of Cyberjaya, Malaysia

Abstract

In navigating the digital age, successful talent management hinges on the inseparable qualities of leadership and agility. This study underscores the transformative impact of agile leadership in attracting, developing, and retaining digital talent, becoming a strategic norm for fostering innovation. Looking forward, the future of digital talent management entails continuous technological advancements, evolving leadership paradigms, and organizational revolution. To stay competitive, organizations must prioritize proactive upskilling and reskilling initiatives amid the rise of AI and automation. Leadership, too, will pivot toward individual's adept at turning digital challenges into opportunities, while addressing diversity, inclusion, and ethical considerations. The evolution of technology poses political challenges, underscoring the need for institutions guiding followers towards an ethos aligned with the changing demands of the digital era.

Keywords: Agile leadership, digital talent management, ethical considerations, innovation, upskilling and reskilling

Introduction

In today's digital era, the intertwined dynamics of stimulated metabolism, leadership development, and recruitment form a critical partnership for organizational success. The ability to go beyond mere responsiveness and embrace agility and innovation has become essential for companies navigating the fast-paced digital landscape. This agility, at the intersection of leadership and talent management, is pivotal for organizations to adapt swiftly, seize opportunities, and minimize unpredictability. Leaders, evolving from equilibrium sustainers to revolutionary mentors, play a crucial role in shaping an organizational culture that thrives in the digital terrain, fostering adaptability and innovation.

The core of this transformative journey lies in digital talent management, where innovative recruitment and training-oriented HR strategies are imperative to attract, develop, and retain the right employees. In this context, the paper delves into the intricate links between organizational agility, leadership development, and digital talent management. It recognizes the symbiotic relationship between these factors, emphasizing their combined impact on an organization's performance in contemporary society. Utilizing a comprehensive methodology that involves a critical review of literature, analysis of conference records, and extraction of data from industry reports, the study aims to provide a nuanced understanding of the complex dynamics governing leadership, agility, and digital talent management. The synthesis of insights from diverse sources establishes a robust foundation for exploring how these elements interact and shape the organizational landscape (Begeç and Akyuz, 2023).

Literature Review

Table 138.1 Insights into talent management and leadership agility.

Author	Study
Siddique et al. (2023)	Organizational agility and digital talent intersect, fostering innovation and performance. Enhances commitment, retention, and continuous learning for digital professionals.
Begeç and Akyuz (2023)	Leadership shifts to flexible structures, emphasizing orchestration, collaboration, and innovation. Drives success through cross-functional teamwork in the digital era.
Choudhury et al. (2021)	Collaborative and transformational leadership are crucial for managing change and promoting innovation. Strategic use of technology and data literacy support informed decision-making.
Asfahani (2021)	Leadership development focusing on strategic thinking cultivates agility, enhancing adaptability and innovation. Leaders drive proactive responses for organizational agility.

[a]maniyarasi@cyberjaya.edu.my

Author	Study
Gilmore (2023)	Outsourcing improves talent management, balancing global skills with local needs. Challenges include mapping global resources, retaining talent, and continuous upskilling in a dynamic digital landscape.
Syamsuri et al. (2022)	Digital talent management faces challenges in balancing global skills with local needs. Organizations need strategies for talent acquisition, involvement, and retention in the dynamic digital landscape.

Source: Author

Study objective

- Foster agile leadership culture for attracting, developing, and retaining digital talent effectively.
- Implement proactive upskilling initiatives to adapt to evolving technological landscapes in talent management.
- Evolve leadership paradigms towards addressing inclusion, diversity, and ethics in digital challenges and opportunities.

Analysis

In navigating the challenges of survival, organizations often resort to extreme tactics for resilience. Yet, the crux lies in prioritizing leadership development and fostering digital talent agility. A symbiotic relationship emerges, where the culture of leadership agility significantly impacts an organization's prowess in attracting, nurturing, and retaining digital talent. Vital to cultivating a robust organizational culture are leadership development programs, steering towards the core of an agile culture crucial for effective digital talent management. Successful entities like Google and Amazon attribute their triumphs to agile leadership development, fostering an environment that embraces change, encourages innovation, and guides teams through dynamic landscapes, ultimately yielding top-tier digital talent sourcing and a competitive edge in volatile markets. Agile leaders, akin to digital magnets, allure prospective employees seeking innovative environments, shaping the employer's brand as a hub for digital professionals immersed in cutting-edge innovations (Alqarni et al., 2023).

Through agility-centric leadership development programs, organizations not only empower leaders with critical skills but also instill attitudes conducive to fostering a noble team. The transformative effects are evident in an organization's ability to adapt to change, experiment with novel ideas, and champion innovation. Such programs contribute to crafting an employer's brand, portraying the organization as a haven for digital professionals eager to engage with exciting, avant-garde initiatives. The resulting employer attractiveness is particularly pronounced in the realm of competitive digital positions, where candidates are drawn to firms explicitly showcasing their innovative fluidity. This emphasis on agility not only shapes leaders but also propels organizations towards a distinct identity – one that resonates as a dynamic and cutting-edge space for digital experts (Alqarni et al., 2023).

Findings, implications and future trends

In today's digital landscape, successful talent management hinges on two key pillars: leadership and agility. These elements are intrinsically linked and vital for navigating the challenges of the digital age. The ability to integrate leadership with agility is crucial for organizational survival amidst rapid technological advancements. Agile leadership, in particular, has proven revolutionary in attracting, nurturing, and retaining digital talent, positioning organizations for effective competition in the market. The synergy between leadership and agility is not just advantageous but has become a strategic imperative, shaping institutional norms and fostering innovative creativity in digital talent management.

Looking ahead, the future of digital talent management is marked by ongoing technological evolution, evolving leadership paradigms, and transformative organizational structures. As we move forward, companies must embrace change and innovation as core principles to maintain competitiveness in the dynamic digital environment. Emerging technologies like AI and automation, coupled with evolving integration approaches, necessitate a diverse skill set aligned with the demands of the digital workforce. To address these shifts, forward-thinking talent management practices must prioritize proactive upskilling and reskilling initiatives to equip employees with the necessary competencies.

Furthermore, leadership paradigms are poised to undergo significant transformations, emphasizing the importance of leaders who can effectively navigate digital challenges while promoting inclusivity, diversity, and ethical considerations. As technology continues to evolve, it brings forth political challenges that require proper institutional frameworks and ethical guidelines for stakeholders to adhere to. Therefore, organizations must cultivate a culture that embraces change and fosters ethical practices to effectively address the evolving nature and demands of emerging technologies.

In summary, the future of digital talent management requires a holistic approach that integrates leadership, agility, and technological literacy. By embracing change, fostering innovation, and prioritizing ethical considerations, organizations can effectively navigate the complexities of the digital landscape and position themselves for sustained success in the digital age.

Conclusion

In conclusion, the dynamic nature of today's digital landscape demands a holistic approach to talent management, where leadership and agility stand as the cornerstones of success. As organizations navigate the challenges posed by rapid technological advancements, the symbiotic relationship between leadership development and digital talent agility emerges as a strategic imperative. Drawing inspiration from successful entities like Google and Amazon, fostering an agile culture not only attracts top-tier digital talent but also shapes an organization's identity as a dynamic hub for innovation. Looking ahead, the future of digital talent management requires a commitment to ongoing technological evolution, transformative leadership paradigms, and ethical considerations. Embracing change, fostering innovation, and prioritizing inclusivity and diversity are essential elements for organizations aiming to thrive in the ever-evolving digital age. By adopting this holistic approach, companies can position themselves for sustained success and resilience in the competitive and dynamic digital landscape.

References

Ahmad, J., Sanusi, A., Hamid, H., Laduppa, H., and Nilwana, A. (2021). Agility leadership and its effect on motivation and discipline: a review of learning supervision during Covid-19. *AIP Conference Proceedings*, 2438(1). https://doi.org/10.1063/5.0071615.

Ahmed Mohamed Bashandy, E., Shaaban Mohammed, T., Ali Ahmed, F., and Thabet, M. (2022). Exploring the relation between toxic leadership, nurses passion for work and organizational agility. *Egyptian Journal of Health Care*, 13(4), 1892–1906. https://ejhc.journals.ekb.eg/article_337022.html.

Alqarni, K., Agina, M. F., Khairy, H. A., Al-Romeedy, B. S., Farrag, D. A., and Abdallah, R. M. (2023). The effect of electronic human resource management systems on sustainable competitive advantages: the roles of sustainable innovation and organizational agility. *Sustainability*, 15(23), 16382. https://doi.org/10.3390/su152316382.

Asfahani, A. (2021). The impact of modern strategic human resources management models on promoting organizational agility. *Academy of Strategic Management Journal*, 20(2), 1–11.

Begeç, S., and Akyuz, G. A. (2023). Requirements of collaborative and transformational leadership in digital ecosystems: techno-orchestrating leaders in a VUCA world. *Revista de Administração de Empresas*, 63, e2022-0155.

Choudhury, A., Behl, A., Sheorey, P. A., and Pal, A. (2021). Digital supply chain to unlock new agility: a TISM approach. *Benchmarking: An International Journal*, 28(6), 2075–2109.

Gilmore, D. (2023). Harmonizing outsourcing to keep clinical trials on track. *Applied Clinical Trials*, 32(11), 12–14.

Siddqiue, M. U., Arshad, A., Ghaffar, A., and Fazal-Ur-Rehman, M. (2023). Examining the impact of servant leadership on employee agility and organizational performance: an empirical study in the software industry. *Journal of Business and Management Research*, 2(2), 1004–1021.

Syamsuri, A., Dalimunthe, R. F., Gultom, P., and Siahaan, E. (2022). New paradigm: HR professional transformation in manufacturing company. Retrieved from https://dupakdosen.usu.ac.id/handle/123456789/7195.

Turner, P. (2022). Complementarity in Organizations: Strategy, Leadership, Management, Talent and Engagement in the Fourth Industrial Revolution. Springer Nature.

139 People, processes, and technology in cybersecurity: Malaysian insights

Leoparken Pillay and Maniyarasi Gowindasamy[a]

Faculty of Business, University of Cyberjaya, Malaysia

Abstract

This paper presents a comprehensive literature review exploring the intersection of people, process, and technology in Cybersecurity Governance, with a specific focus on the Malaysian context. The study emphasizes the importance of Cybersecurity governance in addressing these challenges and offers practical implications for policymakers, industry professionals, and academics. It also explores interactions among People, Process, and Technology in the Malaysian context, highlighting the adoption of human-centric design in Cybersecurity systems and the alignment of local processes with technological capabilities. The findings contribute to the existing body of knowledge in Cybersecurity Governance, emphasizing the need for a more focused understanding of the interplay between people, process, and technology in Malaysia. The future trends in Cybersecurity governance in Malaysia are anticipated to involve a continued emphasis on integrating people, process, and technology for a robust defense against evolving cyber threats.

Keywords: Cyber threats, cybercrime trends, cybersecurity, digital infrastructure, governance, human-centric design, ITS frameworks, people, process, risk management, security controls, technology, technology adoption, top-level management

Introduction

The introduction of this paper aims to provide a comprehensive literature review exploring the intersection of people, process, and technology in Cybersecurity Governance, with a specific focus on the context of Malaysia. The purpose is to analyze and synthesize existing research, theories, and literature in this domain to enhance our understanding of the interplay between these three key elements within the Cybersecurity Governance framework. The goal is to establish a foundation for the subsequent exploration by providing a thorough understanding of the current state of knowledge in this area.

This study is to clearly articulate the identified gap or problem within the realm of Cybersecurity Governance, specifically focusing on the interrelation of people, process, and technology. This problem statement will highlight the need for a more focused understanding of how these elements interact within the unique context of Malaysia. The paper highlights the potential contributions of the study to the existing body of knowledge in Cybersecurity Governance, particularly within the Malaysian context. The significance may be framed in terms of practical implications for policymakers, industry professionals, or academics. The concept of Cybersecurity governance is explored, acknowledging the existence of various frameworks for cybersecurity management that primarily focus on defining and constructing security controls. However,

the study emphasizes the lack of practical guidance for boards in defining their Cybersecurity Governance. Cybersecurity Governance, as explained, involves offering a strategic perspective on how an organization manages its security. This encompasses elements like articulating risk appetite, constructing accountability frameworks, and outlining decision-making responsibilities. Effective governance ensures that cybersecurity activities align with the organization's strategic goals. The discourse notes that while many boards recognize the need for specific attention to cybersecurity risks, they often struggle to formulate a comprehensive approach that genuinely manages risk, as opposed to implementing generic control frameworks. In recent years, the spread of cyber threats has underscored the necessity for robust Cybersecurity Governance frameworks. This is particularly relevant in a country like Malaysia, where rapid technological advancements coexist with an evolving threat landscape.

Background

Malaysia has witnessed substantial growth in its digital infrastructure, accompanied by an escalating number of cyber incidents. According to Singh et al. (2021), the surge in technological advancements, coupled with the propagation of inadequately secured infrastructures and platforms in the realms of big data and the Internet of Things (IoT), has substantially elevated the vulnerability to cybercrime attacks. The

[a]maniyarasi@cyberjaya.edu.my

unprecedented global impact of the COVID-19 pandemic has further exacerbated the scenario, fostering an environment in which cybercriminals exploit vulnerabilities to breach cognitive barriers and extract sensitive information. Besides the researcher embarks on an exploration of cybercrime threats within the context of Malaysia, spanning the period from 2008 to 2020, elucidating the trends and repercussions associated with this growing threat. Exploring into the realm of cyber-criminology, the study investigates the factors contributing to the surge in technological growth. The research findings underscore that the consequences of cyber-attacks extend far beyond financial losses and damage to reputations; they now encompass a systemic failure on a global scale.

Significance

People, process, and technology play a distinct yet interconnected role in Cybersecurity Governance. People are often the first line of defense, with their awareness and behavior crucial in mitigating cyber threats. Processes provide the framework for implementing security measures, while technology offers the tools to enforce them. In the Malaysian context, with its unique socio-cultural landscape and technological advancements, it is paramount to tailor Cybersecurity strategies that resonate with the local environment. The government and businesses alike have recognized the imperative to fortify their cybersecurity defenses. Cybersecurity governance, defined as the set of policies, processes, and technologies implemented to protect digital assets, becomes a cornerstone in this endeavor. Understanding how people, processes, and technology intersect in this context is pivotal for effective governance.

Researcher Maleh et al. (2021) addresses the growing threat of cybercrime and the imperative for organizations to reassess their cybersecurity principles in the digital era. The author emphasizes the critical role of Cybersecurity Governance in effective defense and risk management. Without proper governance, vulnerabilities persist, leading to compromised assets. In response to the evolving cyber threat landscape, the paper proposes a capability maturity framework for assessing and enhancing Cybersecurity Governance in organizations. According to another case study done under Information Security Governance in Malaysia researcher Talib et al. (2023) investigates the critical role of top-level management in ensuring effective information security governance within the Malaysian government sector. It is supported that today's interconnected environment, characterized by increasing cyber threats and reliance on online transactions, the commitment

and involvement of top management are deemed essential. The findings highlight significant issues, including top management constraints, resource limitations, employee resistance to information security practices, and organizational culture. These challenges collectively jeopardize the confidentiality, integrity, and availability of valuable information assets. Another researcher Teoh et al. (2018), explores into the challenges encountered in the implementation of Cybersecurity measures at the organizational level, focusing on a case study of the government sector in Malaysia.

The challenges identified are categorized into three pillars: People, Process, and Technology. Under the People pillar, the researcher finds the challenges include the lack of skills among employees, a collective lack of responsibility for cybersecurity, and the inherent vulnerability of human error. Lack of skills is addressed through the importance of ongoing training and certifications to keep human resources updated on the latest cybersecurity trends. Moving on to the process pillar, researcher finds challenges revolve around the absence of detailed implementation plans, the misplacement of human resources with cybersecurity skills, and the inadequate allocation of budget. Lack of implementation plans is linked to the need for clear timelines, guidelines, and strategies to ensure effective execution. Besides, under the Technology pillar fast-paced evolution poses difficulties for organizations to keep up with Cybersecurity measures, necessitating dependence on vendor updates and training initiatives. Participants emphasize the need for constant updating of knowledge and skills to counteract the evolving landscape of cyber threats. As organizations strive to secure their digital assets, the interplay between people, processes, and technology becomes a focal point. The objective of this literature review is to examine the intricate relationship among these components within the specific context of Malaysia.

Interactions: People, Process, and Technology

Human-centric design in Malaysian cybersecurity systems:

Recognizing the unique socio-cultural factors in Malaysia, there is a growing emphasis on human-centric design in cybersecurity systems. Interfaces and training programs are tailored to resonate with the local population, fostering a sense of ownership and responsibility in cybersecurity practices. Extending the understanding of human factors in cybersecurity, researcher Rohan et al. (2021) academic work investigates into the critical realm of cybersecurity, emphasizing the significance of human factors in protecting information systems, data, and digital assets from cyber threats. The study draws upon a comprehensive analysis of 24 articles presented at a prominent conference on human factors in cybersecurity over the past six years. The study identifies 17 human factors, with human awareness, privacy perception, trust perception, behavior, and capability emerging as the top five contributors. The work underscores the need to augment technological safeguards with a deeper understanding of human-nature-related cybersecurity concerns. Additionally, it provides new insights and recommendations to enhance the overall cybersecurity framework.

Alignment of local processes with technological capabilities

The synergy between processes and technology is evident in the Malaysian cybersecurity landscape. Processes must be agile to adapt to evolving threats, and technology must align with these dynamic processes. According to a study conducted by Shariffuddin and Mohamed (2020), it critically examines the interaction between Information Technology Security (ITS) and Information Technology Governance (ITG) to address both strategic and operational issues. The researcher observes that failure to address the issues adequately could result in severe financial consequences, posing a risk to the business and threatening the organization's sustainability in the short and long term. Previous studies have demonstrated that the absence of technical controls, weak governance, and inadequate oversight at the enterprise stakeholders' level can lead to catastrophic events. Hence, the synergy between ITS and ITG is imperative to enhance the overall security posture of an enterprise. The paper conducts an in-depth examination of these common ITS frameworks, highlighting their shortcomings and emphasizing the necessity for an improved framework. Additionally, the paper scrutinizes frameworks governing ITG, weighing their advantages and disadvantages. These themes are then integrated into ITG practice blocks aligned with structure, process, and relational mechanisms spanning people, process, and technology domains. While the integration of people, process, and technology presents opportunities for a robust cybersecurity posture, challenges persist. Balancing technological innovation with the need for a skilled workforce, addressing cultural factors influencing human behavior, and ensuring regulatory compliance without restraining agility are ongoing challenges in the Malaysian context.

Summary and Future Projection

In conclusion, the study identifies a critical gap in existing Cybersecurity Governance literature, emphasizing the need for a focused understanding of how these elements interact in the unique Malaysian context. The significance of addressing people, process, and technology in Malaysia is underscored by the country's substantial digital growth, increasing cyber incidents, and the evolving threat landscape. The paper explores into the challenges and the interactions among these components are explored, highlighting the importance of human-centric design in cybersecurity systems and the alignment of local processes with technological capabilities. The findings of the literature review contribute to the existing body of knowledge in Cybersecurity Governance and offer practical implications for policymakers, industry professionals, and academics. Moving forward, the paper suggests the necessity for a more comprehensive approach in defining Cybersecurity Governance for boards, particularly in the Malaysian context, and emphasizes the ongoing challenges of balancing technological innovation, workforce development, cultural factors, and regulatory compliance. The future trends in Cybersecurity Governance in Malaysia are likely to involve a continued emphasis on the integration of people, process, and technology for a robust and adaptive defense against evolving cyber threats.

References

Maleh, Y., Sahid, A., and Belaissaoui, M. (2021). A maturity framework for cybersecurity governance in organizations. *EDPACS*, 63(6), 1–22.

Mohd Noor, M. (2022). Addressing cyber security vulnerabilities and initiatives in Malaysia maritime industry. *Journal of Maritime Research*, XIX(III), 89–95, Retrieved from.

Rohan, R., Funilkul, S., Pal, D., and Chutimaskul, W. (2021). Understanding of human factors in cybersecurity: a systematic literature review. In 2021 International Conference on Computational Performance Evaluation (ComPE), Shillong, India (pp. 1–8). IEEE.

Shariffuddin, N., and Mohamed, A. (2020). IT security and IT governance alignment: a review. In Proceedings of the 3rd International Conference on Networking, Information Systems and Security (NISS '20) (pp. 1–8).

Singh, M. M., Frank, R., and Wan Zainon, W. M. N. (2021). Cyber-criminology defense in pervasive environment: a study of cybercrimes in Malaysia. *Bulletin of Electrical Engineering and Informatics*, 10(3), 1658–1668.

Talib, S., Abdul Munir, R., Abdul Molok, N. N., and Ahmad, M. R. (2023). Information security governance issues in Malaysian government sector. *Journal of Information Systems and Digital Technologies*, 5(2), 1–18.

Teoh, C. S., Mahmood, A. K., and Dzazali, S. (2018). Cyber security challenges in organisations: a case study in Malaysia. ResearchGate.

140 Analysis of financial health of a government company in Kerala

Rejimon, A. V.[a] and Usha

Karpagam Academy of Higher Education, Coimbatore, India

Abstract

This research investigates the intricate interplay between company performance, financial distress, and the likelihood of bankruptcy while inquiring into the liquidity position's influence on financial stability. It scrutinizes the firm's profitability and the solidity of its cash reserves. Factors such as high fixed costs, illiquid assets, managerial inefficiency, and bureaucratic hurdles exacerbate the risk of financial distress, particularly during economic downturns, diminishing returns on investment. Employing models like the Zmijewski and Springate Models, underpinned by financial ratios, this study reveals an initial susceptibility to bankruptcy, albeit later resilience. It identifies subpar liquidity and solvency levels, advocating for bolstering working capital through long-term funds for optimal fixed asset utilization. By enhancing our theoretical comprehension and furnishing actionable recommendations, this research highlights the imperative of mitigating insolvency, bankruptcy, and financial distress, thereby safeguarding firms' financial well-being.

Keywords: Bankruptcy, financial distress, financial models, financial ratios, insolvency, liquidity

Introduction

In today's business milieu, facing financial challenges is commonplace, particularly post the 2008 global financial crisis. Acknowledging the escalating importance of financial distress, the European Commission in 2014 introduced new criteria to detect early signs of financial hardship in corporations. The impact of financial troubles transcends a company's operations, affecting stakeholders and the broader economy, urging proactive measures for prediction and mitigation. This study diverges from traditional industry-centric analyses, focusing on individual companies to address the root causes of financial distress and foster their transformation into financially robust entities. Utilizing Univariate and Multiple Discriminant financial models, we aim to diagnose and remedy financial issues effectively. The use of early warning system models is crucial for accurate assessment of a company's financial health, given the transient nature of business strength. Motivated by numerous corporate collapses in the Indian Public sector, our study scrutinizes a public sector company using robust financial analysis models to inform governmental interventions aimed at revitalizing distressed firms. By providing actionable insights into the financial dimensions contributing to distress, this study empowers stakeholders to preempt and recover from financial adversity, fortifying business resilience and the broader economy.

Objectives

- Primary objective: Analyze the financial distress of a government company.
- Secondary objectives:
  - Indicate the liquidity position of the firm.
  - Ascertain the profitability of the firm.
  - Determine the probability of bankruptcy of the firm.
  - Evaluate the soundness of the cash position of the firm.

Literature Review

Table 140.1 Insights into financial distress and predictive models.

Author	Study	Findings (insights or interpretation)
Altman (1993)	Defines financial distress terms	Altman provides a comprehensive definition of financial distress terms like bankruptcy, failure, insolvency, and default, aiming to overcome discrepancies in their usage.

[a]Reji01@yahoo.com

Author	Study	Findings (insights or interpretation)
Platt and Platt (2002)	Definition and impact of financial distress	The platts define financial distress as a stage preceding bankruptcy or liquidation, emphasizing its severity and need for resolution.
Foster (1986)	Identifying financial distress	Foster defines financial distress as severe liquidity issues necessitating operational or structural reevaluation, underlining its critical nature.
Lütz and Kranke (2013)	Causes and consequences of financial fragility	Financial fragility arises from various factors such as debt repayment difficulties, leading to negative outcomes like bankruptcy initiation.
Asutay and Othman (2020)	Profitability's role in financial distress	High profitability reduces the likelihood of financial distress, but excessive profitability may limit a company's performance.
Amendola et al (2015)	Financial strain in government enterprises	Financial strain in government enterprises can lead to severe consequences, including company destruction, highlighting the significance of addressing financial issues.
Konstantaras and Siriopoulos (2011)	Determinants of financial status	Financial status is influenced by factors like profitability, liquidity, and trading on equity, with lower profitability and liquidity increasing the risk of financial distress.
Du Jardin (2015)	Importance of liquidity in bankruptcy theory	Liquidity is crucial in bankruptcy theory, as it reflects a company's ability to meet short-term obligations, influencing its resilience in financial distress scenarios.
John (1993)	Coping mechanisms in financial distress	Coping mechanisms for financial distress include selling assets, renegotiating credit terms, or risking collapse, highlighting management's dilemma in mitigating financial crises.
Beaver (1966), Altman (1968), Gissel et al. (2007)	Evolution of financial distress models	Financial distress models have evolved from basic accounting ratios to sophisticated methodologies, resulting in more accurate predictions of financial distress.
Ohlson (1980)	Ohlson's financial distress model	Ohlson's model utilizes multidimensional logic analysis and financial ratios to predict financial distress accurately, enhancing bankruptcy prediction.
Zmijewsky (1984)	Zmijewsky's financial distress model	Zmijewsky's model employs profit analysis to predict financial distress, demonstrating a high accuracy rate in identifying troubled companies.

Source: Author

Research Methodology

- This study examines the likelihood of financial distress in a government company in Kerala using the Zmijewski and Ohlson O-Score Models.
- Forecasting financial downturns is crucial for businesses, investors, and stock market regulators to anticipate adverse impacts.
- Data from the government manufacturer, discussions with officials, and official records were utilized for analysis.
- Secondary data sources included corporate websites, company journals, and annual reports spanning from 2013–14 to 2018–19.
- Multivariate financial distress models, such as the Zmijewski and Ohlson O-Score Models, were employed to evaluate financial health.
- These models assess the company's financial structure, liquidity, solvency, and profitability for comprehensive analysis.

Data analysis and findings

The analysis probes into the financial distress of a government company in Kerala, employing the Zmijewski and Springate models. Results highlight persistent distress over the years, driven by inadequate working capital, poor retained earnings, and underutilized assets. Findings inform strategic recommendations for enhancing financial health and mitigating distress.

Zmijewski model: Zmijewski's financial distress model calculates a score using a formula involving working capital, retained earnings, EBIT, and market value of equity. A company is considered insolvent if its Z score is below 0.5 and solvent if above.

$$Z = 6.56 \, X1 + 3.26 \, X2 + 6.72z3 + 1.05X4 \quad (1)$$

Springate model: The Springate Model calculates a distress score using variables like working capital, retained earnings, EBIT, market value of equity, sales efficiency, equity to fixed assets, and working capital efficiency.

$$Z = 0.1\,X\,1 + 0.6\,X\,2 + 0.03\,X\,3 + 0.05\,X\,4 + 0.12\,X\,5 + 0.23\,X\,6 + 0.17X7 \qquad (2)$$

Zmijewski's financial distress model assesses a company's solvency using ratios: X1 (working capital/total assets), X2 (retained earnings/total assets), X3 (EBIT/total assets), X4 (market value of equity/book value of total liabilities). A score below 0.5 indicates insolvency. Springate's model includes additional ratios: X5 (sales/total assets), X6 (equity/fixed assets), X7 (working capital/sales). A score below 0.862 signifies bankruptcy. Both models use ratios to evaluate financial health, with specific thresholds for solvency or bankruptcy.

Empirical results

In Table 140.1, Zmijiewski's financial distress model reveals that the company faced challenges in its overall working capital, marked by an inadequate situation due to a significant disparity between current assets and liabilities. The retained profits variable suffered due to sustained losses, while the EBIT variable performed well, and the X4 variable showed notable improvements in equity-to-external liability ratio. Despite improvement in the final three years, the company's financial health remained subpar, indicating ongoing economic challenges.

Table 140.2 displays the outcome of the Springate financial model analysis. The company's working capital situation was below ideal, driven by a

substantial gap in the growth of current assets and liabilities. Retained profits suffered from sustained losses, while EBIT showed a positive trend. The X4 variable demonstrated significant improvements in the equity-to-external liabilities ratio. However, negative results in sales efficiency and working capital efficiency, along with all indicators signaling financial distress, collectively contributed to the company being classified as financially distressed from 2014 to 2023.

Findings and Recommendations

Findings

- The firm's current working capital situation is insufficient, primarily attributed to an inadequate ratio of current assets to current liabilities.
- Retained earnings were considered inadequate due to insufficient profits generated during the assessment period.
- The EBIT variable did not grow significantly, resulting from a decline in sales revenue and unmanageable operating expenses.
- Market value of equity showed growth throughout the study period; however, inadequate profitability made it unsatisfactory.
- The Zmijewski model categorized the firm as distressed for the initial six years, but recent improvements indicate a positive shift.
- Sales efficiency suffered due to a shortage of working capital and underutilization of investments in fixed and non-fixed assets.
- To address these issues, a thorough evaluation of working capital management and investment utilization is recommended, focusing on maximizing

Table 140.2 Zmijewski Model Analysis.

Year	X1 -Working capital variable	X2 - Retained earnings variable	X3 - Earnings before interest and taxes (EBIT) Variable	X4 - market value of equity to book value of total liabilities variable	Zmijewski Model: The Z score	Firm's financial health
2023	0.4066751	0.376024408	1.063873	3.3477907	5.194363493	Healthy
2022	-0.0692152	-0.3502406	0.942786	2.2030756	2.726406012	Healthy
2021	-0.7687543	-0.79586009	1.191883	2.0839388	1.711207821	Healthy
2020	0.4953326	-1.42124705	3.253396	0.7112686	3.038750237	Healthy
2019	0.3375132	-2.94830181	1.281082	0.6587788	-0.67092775	Distressed
2018	-0.2962954	-4.10562729	0.706393	1.0025287	-2.69300123	Distressed
2017	0.0455712	-4.49067797	0.179958	0.9176748	-3.347474	Distressed
2016	0.5874045	-3.90832338	-0.823988	0.4921701	-3.65273655	Distressed
2015	-3.2001207	-3.00567291	-0.83896	0.7674633	-6.27728993	Distressed
2014	-1.4280571	-1.91199913	-0.26112	0.6013471	-2.99982936	Distressed

Source: Author

Table 140.3 Springate score analysis table.

Year	X1 - Working Capital variable	X2 - Retained earnings variable	X3 - Earnings before interest and taxes (EBIT) Variable	X4 - market value of equity to book value of total liabilities ratio	X5= Sales efficiency ratio	X6-Equity to Fixed assets	X7 = working capital efficiency	Springate Score	Firm's Financial Health
2023	0.061993151	0.11534491	0.158314487	3.188372059	1.14055878	1.38711644	0.054353	0.7047182	Distressed
2022	-0.010551098	-0.10743577	0.140295572	2.098167213	1.03863181	0.4992618	-0.01016	0.2813397	Distressed
2021	-0.11718815	-0.24412886	0.177363601	1.984703597	0.96777853	-0.5135595	-0.12109	-0.076211	Distressed
2020	0.075508025	-0.43596535	0.48413631	0.677398703	1.06022422	-1.6591453	0.071219	-0.447904	Distressed
2019	0.051450178	-0.90438706	0.190637219	0.627408356	0.84002062	-4.6515732	0.061249	-1.459045	Distressed
2018	-0.045166974	-1.25939487	0.105117969	0.954789198	1.0609366	-5.2309998	-0.04257	-1.792316	Distressed
2017	0.006946837	-1.37750858	0.026779449	0.873976026	1.19074138	-4.704274	0.005834	-1.719411	Distressed
2016	0.089543365	-1.1988722	-0.122617223	0.468733433	1.06404536	-4.4888028	0.084154	-1.581044	Distressed
2015	-0.487823272	-0.92198555	-0.124845185	0.730917412	1.21325216	-2.7934588	-0.40208	-1.134432	Distressed
2014	-0.217691629	-0.5865028	-0.038857185	0.572711565	1.17394077	-1.5230251	-0.18544	-0.587148	Distressed

Source: Author

asset efficiency and ensuring sufficient working capital for operational needs.

- Working capital efficiency underperformed during the assessment period, primarily due to insufficient working capital and poor management of current assets and liabilities.
- The Springate financial model classified the firm as unhealthy or distressed, mainly due to imbalances in working capital, EBIT, sales efficiency, and working capital efficiency variables.

Recommendations

- Address the working capital problem by conducting a comprehensive study of current assets and liabilities, identifying imbalances, and making calculated changes for overall improvement.
- Conduct a strategic evaluation of cost control, profit retention, and revenue creation plans to address the retained earnings issue, emphasizing areas for increased earnings.
- Tackle the EBIT problem through a thorough examination of sales income and operational costs, aiming to find economical solutions, streamline processes, and explore revenue-increasing opportunities.
- Improve the sales generation variable by conducting a thorough evaluation of working capital management and investment use, with a focus on maximizing asset efficiency and ensuring sufficient working capital for operational requirements.
- Address equity variables by examining elements influencing profitability, including pricing tactics, revenue streams, and cost structures, to identify opportunities for enhancement and strategic modifications.
- Enhance overall working capital efficiency through effective management techniques for current assets and liabilities, coupled with a strategic evaluation of working capital needs.
- Resolve issues by conducting a thorough analysis of each variable's impact and implementing strategic modifications in sales efficiency, working capital efficiency, and effective working capital and EBIT management.

Conclusion

In summary, our analysis employing the Zmijewski, Z-Score, and Springate models unveils critical financial facets. The company's weak working capital, inadequate retained earnings, and faltering EBIT underscore immediate concerns. Despite stock market gains, profitability remains elusive, dissuading potential investors.

Addressing these challenges necessitates strategic interventions. A thorough review of asset-liability balance is crucial to rectify working capital deficiencies. Simultaneously, targeted efforts in cost management, profit retention, and revenue augmentation are vital for bolstering retained earnings. Furthermore, a comprehensive evaluation of sales revenue and operational costs is necessary to streamline processes and explore revenue-generating avenues. These strategic steps are instrumental in guiding the company towards improved financial resilience, fortified working capital, sustained retained earnings growth, and enduring profitability. Implementation of these measures will fortify the company's financial position, ensuring long-term stability.

References

Alifiah, M. N. (2014). Prediction of financial distress companies in the trading and services sector in Malaysia using macroeconomic variables. *Procedia - Social and Behavioral Sciences*, 129, 90–98. [Online]. Available at: https://doi.org/10.1016/j.sbspro.2014.03.652.

Altman, E. (1993). Corporate Financial Distress and Bankruptcy, (3rd edn.). New York: Jogh Wiley & Sons.

Altman, E. I. (1968). Financial ratios, discriminant analysis and the prediction of corporate bankruptcy. *Journal of Finance*, 23(4), 589. [Online]. Available at: https://doi.org/10.2307/2978933.

Arnold (2007). Corporate Financial Management, (2nd edn.). Pearson Education Limited.

Asutay, M. and Othman, J. (2020). Alternative measures for predicting financial distress in the case of Malaysian Islamic banks: assessing the impact of global financial crisis. *Journal of Islamic Accounting and Business Research*, 11(9), 1827–1845. [Online]. Available at: https://doi.org/10.1108/jiabr-12-2019-0223.

Beaver, W. H. (1966). Financial ratios as predictors of failure. *Journal of Accounting Research*, 4, 71. [Online]. Available at: https://doi.org/10.2307/2490171.

Du Jardin, P. (2015). Bankruptcy prediction using terminal failure processes. *European Journal of Operational Research*, 242(1), 286–303. [Online]. Available at: https://doi.org/10.1016/j.ejor.2014.09.059.

Foster (1986). Financial Statement Analysis, (2nd edn.). Englewood Cliffs: Prentice-Hall.

Plumley, D., Serbera, J.-P., and Wilson, R. J. (2020). Too big to fail? accounting for predictions of financial distress in English professional football clubs. *Journal of Applied Accounting Research*, 22(1), 93–113. [Online]. Available at: https://doi.org/10.1108/jaar-05-2020-0095.

Zmijewski, M. E. (1984). Methodological issues related to the estimation of financial distress prediction models. *Journal of Accounting Research*, 24, 59–82.

141 How humanised are our workplaces: a dipstick study of Indian industry

C. Suriyaprakash and B. Arul Senthil[a]

Jansons School of Business, Coimbatore, India

Abstract

The primary objective of the research is to study the human factors and humanising factors as practiced in a cross-section of Indian industries and to identify the impact of gender, age, employment levels, and years of experience on these factors. A survey questionnaire was administered to 235 employees across industries in India. The study was conducted through Google Forms. The researchers employed T-Test and one-way ANOVA to test all variables using descriptive statistics for better understanding. The results show that human factors and humanising factors are perceived to be high in Indian industries and there is no significant difference in perception of the same with gender, age, employment levels, and years of experience.

Keywords: Age, employment levels, gender, human factors, humanising factors

Introduction

Throughout history, work has been seamlessly integrated into daily life, from hunting and gathering to the agrarian era. However, the industrial revolution disrupted this harmony, prioritising efficiency and profit over holistic living. The workplace transformed into a mechanised environment, alienating workers from their true selves.

In contemporary times, human resource management grapples with the complexity of defining the "human" element. Capitalism and professionalism have deepened the schism between personal and professional identities, prompting individuals to adopt masks of detached professionalism. This disconnects sacrifices authenticity for productivity, neglecting individual well-being.

Revitalising the workplace necessitates a shift toward re-humanisation, prioritising the holistic needs and aspirations of individuals over profit-driven motives. It requires recognising the intrinsic humanity of workers and fostering environments where authenticity is valued and nurtured. This approach not only enhances employee satisfaction and well-being but also fosters a more productive and sustainable workplace culture.

Literature Review

Table 141.1 Authors, studies, and insights on rehumanizing workplaces.

Author(s)	Study	Findings/interpretation
Abbas and Awan (2017)	Employees play a critical role in an organization's success, especially in sectors like oil and gas. Emotional commitment stems from a desire to belong and aligns with the company's moral standards, fostering a sense of identity and engagement in organizational activities.	Employee emotional commitment, rooted in a desire to belong and aligned with the company's moral standards, fosters identity and engagement.
Linda and Fitria (2016)	Affective commitment among employees, driven by emotional ties to the organization, results in allegiance, willingness to make sacrifices, and reduced turnover intentions.	Emotional ties to the organization lead to allegiance, sacrifices, and reduced turnover intentions.
Meyer and Allen (1997)	Emotional commitment enhances employee allegiance and diminishes turnover intentions, showcasing the importance of emotional connections in the workplace.	Emotional commitment strengthens allegiance and reduces turnover intentions, highlighting the significance of emotional connections.

[a]aruljansons@gmail.com

Author(s)	Study	Findings/interpretation
Arnold and Bowie (2003); Bowie (1998); Kennedy et al., (2016); Margolis (2001); Phillips and Margolis (1999); Pirson et al. (2016); Sayer (2007)	Previous studies emphasise humanness as fundamental for individuals and organizations, primarily defining them.	Previous research underscores humanness as crucial for individuals and organizations.
Haarjärvi and Laari-Salmela (2022)	This study explores the demonstration of humanity in an R&D organization known for high employee satisfaction, uncovering hidden ethical implications in organizational actions.	The study reveals hidden ethical implications in organizational actions through the demonstration of humanity in an R&D organization.

Source: Author

The review explores human and humanizing factors vital for rehumanizing workplaces, focusing on fostering environments valuing and motivating individuals. Human and humanizing factors are crucial for valuing and motivating individuals, thus rehumanizing workplaces.

The review provides insights into factors contributing to rehumanizing workplaces, balancing individual needs and organizational strategies.A nuanced understanding of factors contributing to rehumanizing workplaces is offered, balancing individual needs and organizational strategies.The paper advocates for rehumanizing workplaces to protect well-being, mental health, and social capital, with implications for broader environmental sustainability. Rehumanizing workplaces is crucial for safeguarding well-being, mental health, and social capital, extending to broader environmental sustainability.

The paper presents hypotheses exploring potential differences in perceptions of human and humanizing factors among employees based on demographic and employment characteristics.

Hypotheses aim to investigate variations in employee perceptions of human and humanizing factors based on demographic and employment characteristics.

Hypotheses

The researchers framed the following hypotheses based on the differentiation of employee's profile.

- H1: There is no significant difference between male and female on human factors and humanising factors.
- H2: There is no significant difference among age groups on human factors and humanising factors.
- H3: There is no significant difference between different levels of employment on human factors and humanising factors.
- H4: There is no significant difference between work experience and no work experience on human factors and humanising factors.

Research Methodology

- Survey questionnaire distributed to 235 Indian employees across various industries.
- Utilized Google Forms for data collection.
- Instrument comprised 20 Likert-type scale questions.
- Questions assessed perception of human factors and humanising factors.
- **Scale ranged from strongly disagree to strongly agree.**

Results and Discussions

This data analysis examines the weighted averages of human and humanizing factors within an organization, exploring their distribution across gender, age, level of employment, and years of work experience. The study aims to identify any significant variations and their implications for fostering a more humane workplace culture.

Gender comparison
T-Test results for human factors: No significant difference between female ($\mu = 21.229$, $\sigma = 7.249$) and male ($\mu = 21.381$, $\sigma = 6.749$) employees (F = 0.480, Sig. = 0.489).

T-Test results for humanizing factors: No significant difference between female ($\mu = 15.760$, $\sigma = 4.992$) and male ($\mu = 16.496$, $\sigma = 5.392$) employees (F = 0.477, Sig. = 0.490).

Age comparison
One-way ANOVA results for human factors: No significant difference among age groups (<30, 31–40, 41–50, >50) (F = 0.086, Sig. = 0.968).

One-way ANOVA results for humanizing factors: No significant difference among age groups (<30, 31–40, 41-50, >50) (F = 0.524, Sig. = 0.666).

Level of employment comparison
One-way ANOVA results for human factors: No significant difference among top leadership, middle

Table 141.2 Weighted average of human factors and humanizing factors.

Human factors

	Items	Strongly agree	Agree	Neutral	Disagree	Strongly disagree	Weighted average
1	Employees are recognised and treated as human first, resource second.	20	40.9	18.3	17.3	3.8	3.56
2	People are put first above everything else while making business decisions.	11.1	31.1	20.9	31.9	5.1	3.11
3	A trusting environment is created with the belief that people want to do a good job.	29.4	43.8	17.9	8.1	0.9	3.93
4	A safe and secure workplace is provided from physical, emotional, and mental threats.	30.2	37.9	15.7	12.3	3.8	3.78
5	Employees are treated as unique, individual human beings, with unique, individual wants and needs, who need unique, individual support.	18.3	36.6	20.4	20	4.7	3.43
6	Work and workplace is suited to the employees and not the other way around.	10.6	39.1	25.5	22.1	2.6	3.32
7	The workplace embraces diversity, ensures equity, and effects inclusion.	19.6	42.6	25.5	10.2	2.1	3.67
8	Employees are cared for, encouraged, and appreciated.	23	42.1	23.8	10.6	0.4	3.76
9	It is believed that organisation thrives only when people thrive.	37.9	42.6	11.5	6.8	1.3	4.09

Humanizing factors

	Items	Strongly agree	Agree	Neutral	Disagree	Strongly disagree	Weighted average
1	Shared outcomes and expectations are communicated.	21.3	48.5	20	9.4	0.9	3.80
2	Behaviours, team norms, and values that matter are clearly defined.	20	49.4	18.7	10.2	1.7	3.75
3	Agile goals are established to define individual outcomes and measures of productivity.	15.7	49.4	24.3	8.1	2.6	3.67
4	Transparency is built into goals within and across teams.	14.5	46.8	19.6	15.7	3.4	3.53
5	Leaders' check-in (show concern and care) and not check-up (follow up on work alone).	19.1	35.7	25.5	17.4	2.1	3.51
6	Progress is measured against goals and clearly defined performance criteria	17.9	52.3	17.4	10.6	1.7	3.73
7	Contributions are recognised and rewarded toward agreed upon outcomes.	23.4	43.4	21.7	10.2	1.3	3.77

Source: Author

management, and entry-level positions (F = 1.650, Sig. = 0.194).

One-way ANOVA results for humanizing factors: No significant difference among top leadership, middle management, and entry-level positions (F = 2.010, Sig. = 0.136).

Years of work experience comparison
One-way ANOVA results for human factors: No significant difference among different experience levels (< 5, 5–10, 10–20, >20 years) (F = 0.085, Sig. = 0.968).

One-way ANOVA results for humanizing factors: No significant difference among different experience levels (< 5, 5–10, 10–20, >20 years) (F = 1.200, Sig. = 0.310).

Summary of findings and implications
Gender does not significantly influence human and humanizing factors, suggesting a gender-neutral approach to improving workplace conditions.

Age and level of employment also do not significantly This analysis reveals that gender, age, level of employment, and years of work experience do not

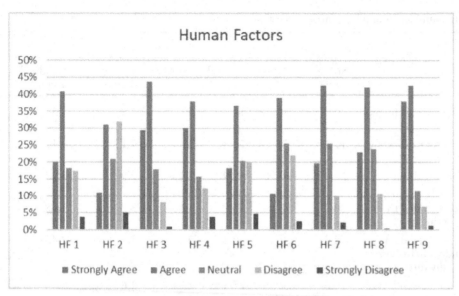

Figure 141.1 Percentage of each item in human factors
Source: Author

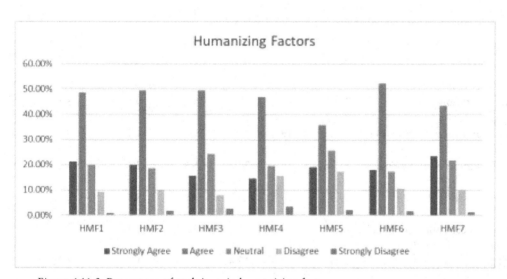

Figure 141.2 Percentage of each item in humanizing factor
Source: Author

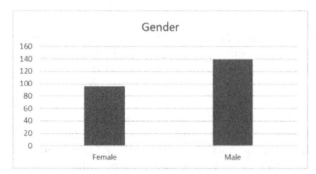

Figure 141.3 Human factors and humanizing factors on gender
Source: Author

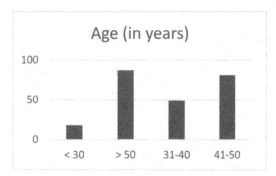

Figure 141.4 Human factors and humanizing factors on age
Source: Author

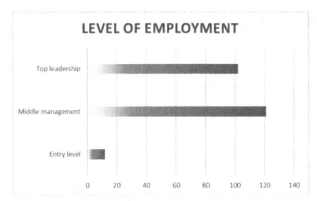

Figure 141.5 Human factors and humanising factors on level of employment
Source: Author

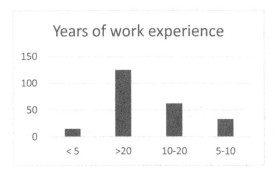

Figure 141.6 Human factors and humanizing factors on years of work experience
Source: Author

significantly impact the perception of human and humanizing factors within the workplace. These findings underscore the importance of adopting inclusive strategies to promote a compassionate and equitable organizational culture.

Conclusion

The comprehensive research conducted across various demographic factors such as gender, age, employment levels, and years of experience elucidates that these variables do not yield notable disparities in workplace attitudes or behaviours. Consequently, a broad approach holds promise for greater efficacy compared to targeted interventions aimed at enhancing specific facets of the work environment. The findings suggest a lack of significant differentiation in observed characteristics among gender, age cohorts, job hierarchies, and tenure, underscoring the notion that distinct behavioural or attitudinal delineations in the workplace are not evident. Thus, the implementation of tailored strategies tailored to individual gender, age demographics, or occupational strata may not be imperative for cultivating a contented and inclusive workplace milieu. Instead, prioritizing diversity and adopting a universal strategy emerges as pivotal for enhancing workplace dynamics and fostering a culture of inclusivity and satisfaction.

References

Abbas, Q., and Awan, S. H. (2017). Impact of organizational politics on employee performance in public sector organizations. *Pakistan Administrative Review*, 1(1), 19–31.

Arnold, D., and Bowie, N. (2003). Sweatshops and respect for persons. *Business Ethics Quarterly*, 13(2), 221–242.

Bowie, N. E. (1998). A kantian theory of capitalism. *Business Ethics Quarterly*, 8(S1), 37–60.

Haarjärvi, T., and Laari-Salmela, S. (2022). Site-seeing humanness in organizations. *Business Ethics Quarterly*, 1–37.

Kennedy, J., Kim, T., and Strudler, A. (2016). Hierarchies and dignity: a confucian communitarian approach. *Business Ethics Quarterly*, 26(4), 479–502.

Linda, M. R., and Fitria, Y. (2016). The influence of perceived organizational support on work-life balance with transformational leadership as the moderating variable.

Margolis, J. (2001). Responsibility in organizational context. *Business Ethics Quarterly*, 11(3), 431–454.

Meyer, J. P., and Allen, N. J. (1997). Commitment in the Workplace: Theory, Research, and Application. Sage Publications.

Phillips, R. A., and Margolis, J. D. (1999). Towards an ethics of organization. *Business Ethics Quarterly*, 9(4), 619–638.

Pirson, M., Goodpaster, K., and Dierksmeier, C. (2016). Guest editors' introduction: Human dignity and business. *Business Ethics Quarterly*, 26(4), 465–478.

142 Impact of COVID-19 on shifting consumer behavior patterns

Frough Eid Mohammad[1] and Mudiarasan Kuppusamy[2,a]

[1]Faculty of Business, University of Cyberjaya, Malaysia

[2]School of Graduate Studies, Unirazak, Malaysia

Abstract

This research explores the impact of COVID-19 on consumer purchasing behavior in Malaysia, highlighting the role of attitudes and product types over mere awareness of the pandemic. Utilizing the Theory of Planned Behavior (TPB), the study reveals that positive attitudes towards the pandemic and the relevance of product types significantly shape consumer intentions and behaviors, while awareness alone does not lead to behavioral change. The findings emphasize the importance of targeted strategies by policymakers and marketers to influence consumer behavior effectively during health crises. design the first page of this paper in a standard way.

Keywords: Consumer purchasing behavior, COVID-19 impact, strategic marketing, theory of planned behavior

Introduction

The evolution of human civilization has seen a series of crises, from pandemics to wars, causing severe economic challenges. The recent COVID-19 pandemic, which emerged in late 2019 in Wuhan, China, has had a profound impact globally. With its effects on the lower respiratory tract, the virus led to a slowdown in the economy and triggered changes in shopping trends. Governments worldwide implemented measures like tax reductions and financial support to mitigate the impact on people's lives. However, despite these efforts, COVID-19 significantly altered consumer purchasing behavior, with changes likely to be long-lasting. Factors like technology, religion, and crises also influence shopping habits. The outbreak affected various sectors, particularly electronics, housing, and clothing, with the most significant impact observed in food and hygiene product purchases. People shifted from in-person to online shopping, changing their food priorities and preferences. The pandemic also redirected focus towards healthcare and personal hygiene products, disrupting international orders. In Malaysia, the epidemic led to economic setbacks, triggering a surge in online shopping as 73% of Malaysians became more optimistic about it in light of the pandemic.

Problem Statement

The COVID-19 pandemic has profoundly impacted global economies and daily lives, prompting shifts in consumer behavior worldwide. This study explores how the crisis has influenced purchasing habits in Malaysia, delving into changes such as a preference for online shopping, stockpiling, and altered product priorities. Despite extensive research on the global scale, there"s a gap in understanding these effects specifically in the Malaysian context, prompting this investigation into the evolving landscape of consumer buying behavior in the wake of COVID-19.

Objectives

- To examine the impact of consumer awareness of COVID-19 on changes in purchasing behavior during the pandemic.
- To analyze how attitudes towards the pandemic influenced consumer purchasing behavior throughout the COVID-19 crisis.
- To investigate the influence of product type on the evolution of consumer purchasing behavior during the COVID-19 pandemic

[a]arasan@unirazak.edu.my

Literature Review

Table 142.1 Consumer behavior dynamics: exploring influences of needs, technology, religion, and crises.

Author	Study
Hopper (2020)	Identifies needs encompassing basic physical and social aspects.
Hale et al. (2019)	Discusses Maslow's hierarchy, from physiological to self-realization.
Goswami and Chouhan (2021b)	Highlights technology's impact on consumers, shaping business and marketing.
Arenas-Gaitán et al. (2019)	Describes technology's influence on consumerism and buying behavior.
Eroğlu (2014)	Notes the surge in internet usage, driving changes in consumer behavior.
Sarofim and Cabano (2018)	Explores religion's role in shaping consumer behavior through decrees and taboos.
Agarwala et al. (2019)	Emphasizes religion's direct influence on shopping behavior and societal aspects.
D'Haene et al. (2019)	Connects religion to food and clothing purchasing habits.
Laguna et al. (2020)	Shows a shift in consumer priorities towards fundamental needs during the COVID-19 crisis.

Source: Primary data

Hypothesis

- H1: Consumer awareness of COVID-19 was positively related to the evolution of consumer behavior during the COVID-19 pandemic.
- H2: Pandemic attitudes are positively related to the evolution of consumer behavior during the COVID-19 pandemic.
- H3: Product Type is related to the evolution of consumer behavior during the COVID-19 pandemic.
- H4: During the COVID-19 pandemic, changes in shopping priorities are positively associated with consumer behavior.
- H5: Consumer behavior is positively related to the change in shopping methods during the COVID-19 pandemic

Analysis and Interpretation

The COVID-19 pandemic has significantly shaken up our daily lives, prompting a deep dive into understanding its impact on consumer behavior. Mazza et al. (2020) stress the importance of grasping how anxiety and uncertainty have played a role. The TPB, a versatile framework (Alexa et al., 2021; Alaimo et al., 2020), shines a light on these changes, especially in the realm of purchasing habits. TPB's three pillars - attitudes, subjective norms, and perceived behavioral control - become key players in a crisis, driving noteworthy shifts in how people buy and make decisions (Ajzen, 2020; Obschonka et al., 2015).

The demographic snapshot indicates a majority female population (62%) with most individuals aged 25–54 (50%). Education levels are high, with 40% holding a Bachelor's degree and 25% having

Table 142.2 Demographics.

Demographic variable	Category	%
Gender	Male	38.00%
	Female	62.00%
Age groups	15 - 24	20.00%
	25 - 54	50.00%
	55 - 64	25.00%
	65 and above	5.00%
Education levels	High school qualification	10.00%
	Certificate/diploma	25.00%
	Bachelor's degree	40.00%
	Post-graduate qualification	25.00%
Employment status	Not employed	15.00%
	Self-employed	35.00%
	Private (company employee)	30.00%
	Government employee	15.00%
	Retired	5.00%
Income levels	Less than RM4850 per month	60.00%
	RM4850 - RM10959 per month	30.00%
	RM10960 and above per month	10.00%

Source: Primary data

post-graduate qualifications. Self-employment is significant at 35%, and the majority earn below RM4850 per month (60%).

Table 142.3 Factor loading, and construct reliability and validity.

Constructs	A	å	CR	(AVE)
AOC1	0.847	0.854	0.898	0.641
AOC2	0.883			
AOC3	0.825			
AOC4	0.823			
AOC5	0.594			
ATP1	0.791	0.848	0.893	0.627
ATP2	0.65			
ATP3	0.849			
ATP4	0.841			
ATP5	0.81			
PT1	0.816	0.846	0.89	0.619
PT2	0.757			
PT3	0.783			
PT4	0.82			
PT5	0.757			
BI1	0.843	0.87	0.911	0.719
BI2	0.857			
BI3	0.852			
BI4	0.84			
CB1	0.781	0.781	0.873	0.697
CB2	0.889			
CB3	0.832			

Source: Primary data

Table 142.4 Path coefficient and hypothesis testing.

Hypothesis	Path coefficient	Standard deviation	T statistics
AOC -> BI	0.015	0.1	0.152
ATP -> BI	0.238	0.12	1.986
BI -> CB	0.685	0.06	11.426
PT -> BI	0.627	0.1	6.281

Source: Primary data

Our study on COVID-19 awareness, attitudes, product preferences, behavioral intention, and customer behavior found strong support for our measurement model. All constructs, including awareness, attitudes towards the pandemic, product types, behavioral intention, and customer behavior, demonstrated high reliability and validity. Factor loadings, Cronbach's alpha, composite reliability, and average variance extracted all surpassed recommended thresholds, ensuring the robustness of our scales. These findings provide a solid foundation for analyzing the structural relationships in our research on the impact of COVID-19 on behaviors.

The study found that knowing about the virus didn't really impact how people intended to behave (p > .05). However, having a positive attitude toward the pandemic did influence behavioral intentions significantly (p < .05). Behavioral intentions strongly predicted actual customer behavior (p < .001), and the type of product also had a significant impact on intentions (p < .001). In essence, attitudes and the kind of product are key factors in shaping how consumers change their behavior during the pandemic.

Future Scope

The findings of this study offer valuable insights for shaping consumer behavior post-COVID-19. Acknowledging that people's attitudes towards the pandemic greatly influence their actions, it's crucial for policymakers and marketers to create strategies that not only share information but also positively impact perceptions. For businesses, recognizing the impact of product types on consumer intentions emphasizes the need to tailor product development and marketing to match the changing needs during health crises. Applying these insights can lead to more effective communication and product strategies, encouraging adaptive consumer behaviors in line with current health guidelines.

Conclusion

The study applied the Theory of Planned Behavior to assess changes in Malaysian consumer behavior due to COVID-19, with a demographic focus on a primarily female and educated cohort. The measurement model confirmed high reliability and validity for constructs related to COVID-19 awareness, attitudes, product preferences, behavioral intention, and customer behavior, paving the way for precise hypothesis testing.

Key findings from the structural model analysis include the non-significant impact of COVID-19 awareness on behavioral intentions, suggesting that mere awareness does not lead to behavioral change. In contrast, a positive attitude toward the pandemic significantly influenced behavioral intentions, underscoring the role of individual perceptions in shaping proactive behaviors. Additionally, intentions were found to be powerful predictors of actual customer behavior, and the type of product significantly impacted consumer intentions. These insights indicate that attitudes and product types are crucial in driving consumer behavior during a crisis, highlighting the importance of targeted communication and product strategies to effectively influence consumer actions in the face of health crises.

References

Agarwala, R., Mishra, P., and Singh, R. (2019). Religiosity and consumer behaviour: a summarizing review. *Journal of Management, Spirituality and Religion*, 16(1), 32–54. https://doi.org/10.1080/14766086.2018.1495098.

Alexa, L., Apetrei, A., and Sapena, J. (2021). The COVID-19 lockdown effect on the intention to purchase sustainable brands. *Sustainability (Switzerland)*, 13(6). https://doi.org/10.3390/su13063241.

Arenas-Gaitán, J., Sanz-Altamira, B., and Ramírez-Correa, P. E. (2019). Complexity of understanding consumer behavior from the marketing perspective. In Complexity (Vol. 2019). Hindawi Limited. https://doi.org/10.1155/2019/2837938.

Ben Hassen, T., El Bilali, H., Allahyari, M. S., and Charbel, L. (2021). Food shopping, preparation and consumption practices in times of COVID-19: case of Lebanon. *Journal of Agribusiness in Developing and Emerging Economies*. https://doi.org/10.1108/JADEE-01-2021-0022.

D'Haene, E., Desiere, S., D'Haese, M., Verbeke, W., and Schoors, K. (2019). Religion, food choices, and demand seasonality: evidence from the Ethiopian milk market. *Foods*, 8(5), 167. https://doi.org/10.3390/foods8050167.

Di Crosta, A., Ceccato, I., Marchetti, D., La Malva, P., Maiella, R., Cannito, L., et al. (2021). Psychological factors and consumer behaviour during the COVID-19 pandemic. *PLoS One*, 16(8), e0256095. https://doi.org/10.1371/journal.pone.0256095.

Edeh, F. O., Aryani, D. N., Subramaniam, T. A., Kee, D. M. H., Samarth, T., Nair, R. K., et al. (2021). Impact of COVID-19 Pandemic on consumer behavior towards the intention to use e-wallet in Malaysia. *International Journal of Accounting and Finance in Asia Pacific*, 4(3), 42–59. https://doi.org/10.32535/ijafap.v4i3.1205.

Eger, L., Komárková, L., Egerová, D., and Mičík, M. (2021). The effect of COVID-19 on consumer shopping behavior: generational cohort perspective. *Journal of Retailing and Consumer Services*, 61, 102542. https://doi.org/10.1016/j.jretconser.2021.102542.

Eroğlu, E. (2014). The changing shopping culture: internet consumer behavior. *Review of Business Information Systems*, 18(1). http://dunya.com.

Fathollah, S., Aghdaie, A., Piraman, A., and Fathi, S. (2011). An analysis of factors affecting the consumer's attitude of trust and their impact on internet purchasing behavior. *International Journal of Business and Social Science*, 2(23), 147–158.

143 Consumer preferences on electric vehicles and its prospective in Indian scenario

Kandavel, R. and Padmavathy, N.[a]

Jeppiaar University, Chennai, Tamilnadu, India

Abstract

This study enquires into the intricacies of consumer preferences, particularly regarding the expanding market for electric vehicles (EVs). By scrutinizing the elements driving consumer choice in favor of EVs, it aims to shed light on both theoretical frameworks and empirical evidence. Employing a quantitative approach through surveys, data from 265 respondents in Chennai, Coimbatore, and Tiruchirappalli, Tamilnadu, India, is analyzed. The study uncovers the factors underpinning consumer preferences for EVs, alongside exploring various usability features. Through a descriptive research design and convenience sampling method, it identifies key insights pivotal for companies in their marketing strategies, aiding them in the selection, targeting, and positioning of EVs. This research serves not only to enrich academic discourse on consumer behavior but also to offer practical guidance to industry stakeholders navigating the evolving landscape of sustainable transportation.

Keywords: Consumer preferences, electric vehicles, and influential factors

Introduction

Electric vehicles (EVs) offer a promising solution to combat the environmental challenges posed by traditional fuel-based automobiles. With their reliance on electric engines instead of internal combustion motors, EVs aim to tackle issues such as pollution, global warming, and the depletion of natural resources. While the concept of EVs has been around for some time, recent years have witnessed a surge in interest, driven by growing concerns over carbon emissions and environmental impact. In India, significant steps towards promoting EV adoption were initiated in 2010, aligning with global efforts to reduce pollution and carbon footprint. The introduction of initiatives like the faster adoption and manufacturing of hybrid and EV highlights the commitment to creating a sustainable transportation ecosystem. However, despite the momentum towards EV adoption, there remains a dearth of research on consumer preferences in this sector. This study seeks to address this gap by investigating the factors influencing consumer choices regarding EVs. By examining existing literature and empirical studies, it aims to provide insights that can inform policymaking and enhance the effectiveness of initiatives aimed at promoting EV adoption.

Importance of Study

Understanding consumer preferences for electric contribute crucial for a company's success and contributes to the economy indirectly. It's imperative to identify the factors influencing these preferences, particularly given the limited research in this area compared to traditional EV attributes like driving range and performance.

Scope of Study

A comprehensive examination of consumer preferences enables companies to construct precise value propositions. These propositions, encompassing promises of delivered value and consumer belief in experiencing such value, are applicable across various organizational facets, including consumer accounts, products, or services. The development of a value proposition hinges upon a meticulous review and analysis of the benefits, costs, and overall value proposition, aligning with the organization's objectives towards both current and prospective consumers.

[a]padmajeppiar@yahoo.com

Literature Review

Table 143.1 Factors influencing electric vehicle adoption.

Author name	Study	Findings/insights/interpretation
Driving range	Driving range is crucial for EV adoption, with longer ranges positively influencing consumer decisions. Psychological factors, policy attributes, and social influences also shape EV preference.	Driving range significantly impacts EV adoption, alongside psychological, policy, and social factors.
Environmental	Psychological motives, including environmental concerns, influence EV preference. Cultural differences affect the symbolic value of EVs, impacting consumer perceptions. Policy measures and social influences further shape EV adoption rates.	Psychological motives, cultural differences, policy measures, and social influences impact EV preference and adoption.
Performance	Performance factors and emissions considerations influence EV preference. Gender differences and policy attributes also shape consumer perceptions. Social influences play a significant role in EV adoption decisions.	Performance, emissions, gender differences, and policy measures affect EV preference. Social influences also significantly impact EV adoption.
Policy attributes	Policy incentives, such as tax reductions, significantly influence EV adoption rates. Social influences also play a role in shaping consumer preferences. However, the effectiveness of policy measures varies across different incentives.	Policy incentives, social influences, and the effectiveness of policy measures impact EV adoption rates.
Social influence	Social factors, such as peer behavior and norms, significantly impact EV adoption. Public reviews and market share among social networks influence consumer preferences. However, the extent of social influence may vary depending on cultural contexts and individual perceptions.	Social factors significantly influence EV adoption, with public reviews and market share playing a role. However, the impact of social factors varies across cultures and individual perceptions.
Warranty	Warranty positively influences EV adoption rates by addressing consumer concerns about battery life. However, the significance of warranty effects varies across studies, highlighting the importance of consumer experience in EV adoption.	Warranty positively impacts EV adoption by addressing battery life concerns. However, its significance varies, emphasizing the role of consumer experience.

Source: Primary data

Objectives

The research objectives have taken an overall overview and attempt to indicate the comprehensive notion of consumer preference for electric vehicles. Largely study has focused on the following objectives:

- To identify the factors affecting consumer preference for electric vehicles.
- To analyze factors and their relationship with electric vehicles.
- To assess the influence of factors of EVs on electric vehicles.

Hypothesis of Study

H1: Driving range, environmental friendliness, performance, policy attributes, social influences and warranty have significant relationships with electric vehicles.

H2: Electric vehicle factors namely driving range, environmental friendliness, performance, policy attributes, social influences and warranty have significantly influenced electric vehicles.

Research Methodology

- Research design: Descriptive and quantitative methods were employed, using a structured questionnaire for data collection and analysis.
- Primary data: Collected from EV consumers in Chennai, Coimbatore, and Tiruchirappalli, India, through a Likert scale questionnaire.
- Secondary data: Derived from websites, magazines, and articles to support primary findings.
- Sampling design: Convenience sampling utilized due to the exhaustive nature of studying all consumers. 300 questionnaires distributed, yielding 265 usable responses.

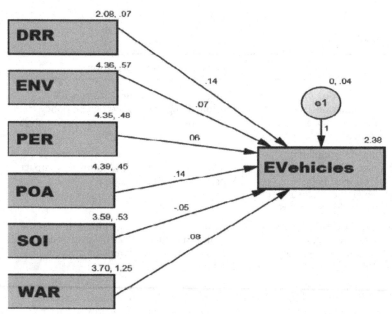

Figure 143.1 Multiple regression path analysis of factors and electric vehicles
H: *Several factors significantly influence electric vehicles, including driving range, environmental friendliness, performance, policy attributes, social influences, and warranty*
Source: Author

- Pre-testing: Questionnaire pilot study conducted with 100 respondents to ensure validity and refine wording.
- Reliability: Internal consistency assessed using Cronbach's alpha, resulting in an overall reliability score of .812.

Analysis and Interpretation

This analysis probes into consumer preferences and factors influencing EV adoption in India. It explores rankings of key factors, correlation with EVs, model fit, regression weights, and offers practical suggestions to accelerate the transition toward EVs in the Indian automotive market.

Consumer preference on electric vehicles

Consumer preference on electric vehicles is most powerful promotion strategic in current Indian scenario. The study highlights key determinants of consumer preference. Respondents prioritized environmental friendliness and driving range, while policy attributes and warranty were comparatively less preferred.

- Environmental friendliness (mean: 3.76) ranked highest, followed by driving range (mean: 3.47), and performance (mean: 3.20).
- Social influences (mean: 3.05) and policy attributes (mean: 2.93) were also considered, while warranty (mean: 2.75) ranked lowest.

Relationship between factors and electric vehicles

H: Driving range, environmental friendliness, performance, policy attributes, social influences and warranty are having significant relationship with electric vehicles.

- Pearson correlation test revealed significant relationships between driving range, environmental friendliness, performance, policy attributes, social influences, and warranty with electric vehicles.
- Social influences showed the highest correlation (r = 0.812), followed by policy attributes (r = 0.801), and performance (r = 0.797).

Model fit summary

- The model demonstrated a good level of prediction (R = 0.663), with factors such as driving range, environmental friendliness, performance, policy attributes, social influences, and warranty explaining 44% of the variance in electric vehicles.

Regression weights of factors

- Multiple regression analysis showed significant relationships between all factors and EVs, with driving range, environmental friendliness, policy attributes, and warranty displaying the highest weights.

Suggestions

- Establishing visible charging infrastructure, optimizing parking spaces for charging stations, offering subsidies for commercial purchases, and mandating electric vehicle purchase for proposed new smart cities.

- Encouraging firms, schools, and colleges to use electric vehicles, implementing electric buses, offering cash back incentives for battery returns, and adopting vehicle-to-grid technology are also suggested.

The study aims to accelerate the transition from conventional ICE vehicles to electric vehicles in India, underscoring the importance of consumer-related research in this context.

Conclusion

The study's findings suggest that the initial introduction of electric vehicles (EVs) into the mainstream market may not be perceived as significant advancements. However, this interpretation likely oversimplifies a complex issue, as previous research indicates varying attitudes among adopters towards embracing technology. This study aligns with recent research on EV uptake, indicating multiple early adopter segments, each with distinct characteristics and preferences. While individual creativity may not singularly influence EV acceptance, it emphasizes the importance of considering psychological constructs such as creativity alongside other factors. Integrating inherent creativity with other mental constructs could aid in identifying adopter categories with specific inclinations towards EV adoption. This insight is crucial for manufacturers and policymakers to target marketing and implementation efforts towards adopters more likely to embrace EV technology, serving as conduits for knowledge dissemination, catalysts for change, and influencers within their communities.

References

Ajzen, I. (1991). The theory of planned behavior. *Organizational Behavior and Human Decision Processes*, 50(2), 179–211.

Anable, J., Kinnear, N., Hutchins, R., Delmonte, E., and Skippon, S. (2016). Consumer segmentation and demographic patterns. Report for Energy Technologies Institute Plug-in Vehicles Infrastructure Project (April 2011). Transport Research Laboratory Published Project Report PPR769.

Araghi, Y., Kroesen, M., Molin, E., and van Wee, B. (2014). Do social norms regarding carbon offsetting affect individual preferences towards this policy? results from a stated choice experiment. *Transportation Research Part D: Transport and Environment*, 26, 42–46.

Axsen, J., and Kurani, K. S. (2011). Interpersonal influence in the early plug-in hybrid market: observing social interactions with an exploratory multi-method approach. *Transportation Research Part D: Transport and Environment*, 16(2), 150–159.

Axsen, J., Kurani, K. S., McCarthy, R., and Yang, C. (2011). Plug-in hybrid vehicle GHG impacts in California: integrating consumer-informed recharge profiles with an electricity-dispatch model. *Energy Policy*, 39(3), 1617–1629.

Axsen, J., Orlebar, C., and Skippon, S. (2013). Social influence and consumer preference formation for pro-environmental technology: the case of a U.K. workplace electric-vehicle study. *Ecological Economics*, 95, 96–107.

Bamberg, S., and Möser, G. (2007). Twenty years after hines, hungerford, and tomera: a new meta-analysis of psycho-social determinants of pro-environmental behaviour. *Journal of Environmental Psychology*, 27(1), 14–25.

Bockarjova, M., Knockaert, J., Rietveld, P., and Steg, L. (2014). Dynamic consumer heterogeneity in electric vehicle adoption. Transportation Research Board Annual Meeting 2014 Paper.

Dimitropoulos, A., Rietveld, P., and Van Ommeren, J. N. (2013). Consumer valuation of changes in driving range: a meta-analysis. *Transportation Research Part A: Policy and Practice*, 55, 27–45.

Dittmar, H. (1992). The Social Psychology of Material Possessions: To have is to be. New York, NY: St Martin's Press.

144 Factors influencing job satisfaction of migrant workers in Coimbatore district

R. Velmurugan[1,a], M. Kalimuthu[2], S. Karthik[3], Maksud A. Madraswale[4], K. Srivignesh Kumar[1] and M. Prakash[5]

[1]Karpagam Academy of Higher Education, Coimbatore, Tamil Nadu, India

[2]Dr.N.G.P. Arts and Science College, Coimbatore, Tamil Nadu, India

[3]Kalasalingam Academy of Research and Education, Krishnankoil, Srivilliputhur, Tamil Nadu, India

[4]Associate professor, School of Management, Presidency university, Bengaluru, India

[5]CHRIST (Deemed to be University), Bengaluru, Karnataka, India

Abstract

Recent years have seen a rise in the phenomenon of migration for employment, which has resulted in a more diversified and dynamic global workforce. Migrant workers contribute to a variety of businesses and sectors, which is essential to the economic growth of host nations. Their job satisfaction, though, continues to be a major source of worry. This summary gives a general overview of the variables affecting migrant workers' job satisfaction, highlighting significant aspects like pay, working conditions, social support, and cultural assimilation. This study intends to shed light on the complex interactions between these variables and their effects on migrant workers' overall well-being and job satisfaction through an examination of the literature already in existence and empirical data. The results of this study can help policymakers, employers, and other stakeholders implement initiatives that improve migrant employees' job satisfaction, creating more effective, peaceful, and inclusive work environments.

Keywords: Cultural integration, employment conditions, job satisfaction, migrant workers

Introduction

The contemporary era is characterized by unprecedented global interconnectedness, prompting significant migration in pursuit of economic opportunities. This trend has led to a diverse cohort of migrant workers whose welfare is intricately linked to various factors, from economic disparities to technological advancements. Central to their well-being is the nature of their employment arrangements, particularly in terms of remuneration. Pay not only facilitates basic needs but also determines access to essential services like healthcare and education, shaping overall financial security. Adequate training programs further enhance workers' integration and job performance, underlining the importance of fair compensation. Regularity in salary payments ensures financial stability, enabling workers to plan for short-term needs and long-term aspirations. Additionally, work schedules impact the balance between personal and professional life, affecting job satisfaction. The work environment, encompassing physical comfort, social interactions, and welfare policies, significantly influences migrant workers' overall experience and societal contributions. Recognizing and addressing the multifaceted needs of migrant workers is not only ethically imperative but also strategically beneficial for fostering inclusive and prosperous communities.

Literature Review

Table 144.1 Factors influencing job satisfaction among migrant workers: a synthesis of findings.

Author name	Study	Findings (Insights)
Nasurdin and Kim-Soon (2013)	Wage disparities between migrant and native workers influence job satisfaction.	Migrant workers may experience dissatisfaction due to discrepancies in wages compared to native workers.
Pereira and Elfering (2014)	Cultural integration and a sense of belonging play significant roles in shaping job satisfaction.	A sense of belonging and cultural integration positively impacts job satisfaction among migrant workers.

[a]drvelsngm@gmail.com

Author name	Study	Findings (Insights)
De Jong et al. (2015)	Equitable wages and benefits are essential for fostering job satisfaction.	Fair remuneration and benefits contribute to higher levels of job satisfaction among migrant workers.
Jiang et al. (2015)	Positive supervisor support and effective leadership styles contribute to higher job satisfaction.	Supportive leadership and positive supervisor interactions enhance job satisfaction among migrant workers.
Durmaz and Terzi (2016)	Positive relationships with co-workers contribute to a supportive work environment and higher job satisfaction.	Strong interpersonal relationships at work foster a supportive environment and increase job satisfaction.
Kumar et al. (2016)	Recognition and appreciation from supervisors and colleagues positively influence job satisfaction.	Acknowledgment and appreciation from peers and superiors enhance job satisfaction among migrant workers.
Lee et al. (2016)	Poor working conditions can lead to dissatisfaction among migrant workers.	Unsatisfactory working conditions negatively impact job satisfaction among migrant workers.
Ding et al. (2017)	Experiences of unfair treatment can lead to dissatisfaction and negatively affect psychological well-being.	Unfair treatment can result in lower job satisfaction and adverse effects on psychological health.
Qureshi et al. (2017)	Job engagement and a sense of involvement contribute to higher levels of job satisfaction among migrant workers.	Active engagement and involvement in job roles are associated with increased job satisfaction among migrant workers.
Wardak et al. (2017)	Language barriers hinder social interactions and contribute to lower job satisfaction among migrant workers.	Language barriers impede social interactions and lead to decreased job satisfaction among migrant workers.
Bashir and Ramay (2018)	Empowered migrant workers tend to experience higher levels of job satisfaction.	Empowerment and decision-making authority positively correlate with increased job satisfaction among migrant workers.
Chen et al. (2018)	Perceived job meaningfulness influences job satisfaction among migrant workers.	A sense of job meaning and societal contribution positively affect job satisfaction among migrant workers.
Fozdar and Torezani (2018)	Poor health and well-being can lead to dissatisfaction and reduced job performance.	Deteriorating health and well-being contribute to decreased job satisfaction and performance among migrant workers.
Hassan et al. (2018)	Ensuring workplace safety and fairness promotes higher job satisfaction among migrant workers.	Workplace safety, fairness, and suitable accommodations enhance job satisfaction among migrant workers.
Hossain et al. (2018)	Engaging job designs lead to higher job satisfaction among migrant workers.	Varied and engaging job tasks positively correlate with increased job satisfaction among migrant workers.
Li et al. (2018)	Decision-making authority and skill application contribute to higher job satisfaction among migrant workers.	Autonomy and skill utilization are associated with increased job satisfaction among migrant workers.
Soltani et al. (2018)	Job security is linked to higher levels of job satisfaction among migrant workers.	Perceived job security is positively associated with increased job satisfaction among migrant workers.
Khaleel et al. (2019)	Limited autonomy and skill utilization in jobs contribute to dissatisfaction among migrant workers.	Jobs with restricted autonomy and limited skill utilization are associated with decreased job satisfaction among migrant workers.
Kim and Yun (2019)	Successful cultural adaptation correlates with higher levels of job satisfaction.	Adaptation to host culture is positively linked with increased job satisfaction among migrant workers.
Ma et al. (2019)	Perceptions of fairness, equity, and justice within the workplace significantly affect job satisfaction.	Fairness and equity perceptions within the workplace strongly influence job satisfaction among migrant workers.
Al-Khawaldeh et al. (2020)	Social support networks and integration within the host country enhance job satisfaction among migrant workers.	Support networks and integration in the host country positively impact job satisfaction among migrant workers.

Author name	Study	Findings (Insights)
Islam et al. (2020)	Opportunities for skill development and training positively correlate with job satisfaction among migrant workers.	Skill development opportunities enhance job satisfaction among migrant workers.
Nguyen and Nguyen (2020)	Perceived fairness fosters job satisfaction among migrant workers.	Fair treatment is associated with increased job satisfaction among migrant workers.
Rashid et al. (2020)	Balancing work and personal/family life contributes to higher job satisfaction among migrant workers.	Achieving work-life balance is associated with increased job satisfaction among migrant workers.
Chien et al. (2021)	Family and social support networks impact the well-being and job satisfaction of migrant workers.	Support from family and social networks positively influences the well-being and job satisfaction of migrant workers.
Hassan et al. (2021)	Workplace conflict and stress negatively affect job satisfaction among migrant workers.	Workplace conflict and stress are linked to decreased job satisfaction among migrant workers.
Li et al. (2021)	Organizational support and employee well-being policies contribute to job satisfaction among migrant workers.	Organizational support and employee-centric policies enhance job satisfaction among migrant workers.
Salma et al. (2021)	Prospects for growth within the organization positively influence job satisfaction among migrant workers.	Opportunities for growth within the organization lead to increased job satisfaction among migrant workers.
Yurtseven et al. (2021)	Perceived opportunities for growth and advancement within jobs are associated with higher job satisfaction.	Opportunities for growth and advancement within jobs correlate with increased job satisfaction among migrant workers.

Source: Author

Research Gap

Prior research has identified several key themes and elements that affect migrant workers' job satisfaction, including wage inequalities, cultural integration, interpersonal relationships, supervisor support, working conditions, recognition, empowerment, meaningful work, fairness, social support networks, skill development, work-life balance, workplace conflict, and growth opportunities. It appears that many of the studies cited use quantitative techniques. In-depth interviews and focus groups used in qualitative research can give participants deeper insights into the viewpoints and lived experiences of migrant workers about job satisfaction.

Problem statement

The study addresses the complex dynamics of job satisfaction among migrant workers in Coimbatore district, aiming to identify challenges and propose solutions. Through empirical investigation, it seeks to foster understanding and catalyze positive change toward a more inclusive and harmonious community.

Objectives

• To identify the socio-economic profile of migrant workers

• To ascertain factors influencing migrant workers' job satisfaction

Scope of study

The Coimbatore district of Tamil Nadu has been the exclusive focus of the current study. Additionally, elements affecting migrant employees' job satisfaction alone and their socioeconomic profile are included in the interview schedule

Research methodology

• Data: Primary data collected through interviews is essential for this study's investigation.
• Sampling: Information was gathered from 600 migrant workers in Coimbatore district using convenience sampling.
• Analysis framework: Data underwent analysis using simple percentages and factor analysis techniques.

Limitations of the study

• Methodology: Information was obtained through an interview schedule, acknowledging potential biases in primary data that may constrain the study.

- Limitations: Biases in primary data also constrain this investigation; hence, results must be extended with utmost caution.

Significance of study

The study on variables affecting migrant workers' job satisfaction has wide-reaching implications. Migrant workers can negotiate better conditions and make informed decisions, while employers benefit from increased productivity and retention. Policymakers can create fair labor laws, NGOs can advocate for worker rights, and researchers can deepen understanding. Ultimately, the study impacts various stakeholders, fostering a more just and equitable work environment.

Findings

The analysis probes into the socio-economic profile and factors influencing job satisfaction among migrant workers in Coimbatore district, offering insightful recommendations for enhancing their workplace experiences.

Socio-economic profile of migrant workers

- **Age:** The majority fall between 21 and 30 years old, primarily contributing to various industries.
- **Gender:** Predominantly male, making significant contributions to the labor force.
- **Education:** A substantial portion is SSLC graduates, showcasing diverse knowledge and skills.
- **Marital status:** Many are unmarried, despite being devoted family members, indicating dedication to work.
- **Monthly income:** A considerable percentage earn above Rs. 15,000 monthly, reflecting significant family contributions.
- **Family expenditure:** Typically allocate Rs. 6,001–8,000 monthly for family expenses, prioritizing stability.
- **Earning members:** Mostly have two earners and one non-earning or dependent relative, ensuring financial stability.
- **Occupation:** Many works as Masons, contributing significantly to construction and infrastructure projects.
- **Languages known:** Primarily communicate in Hindi, reflecting the multilingual nature of the workforce.
- **Working hours:** Majority work longer than 12-hour shifts, demonstrating dedication and commitment.

Factors influencing job satisfaction

- **Factor analysis suitability:** Kaiser-Meyer-Olkin (KMO) measure and Bartlett's test of sphericity confirm data suitability for analysis.
- **Influential factors:** Identified factors include periodicity of salary payment, leisure time offered at the workplace, superiors' support, and workplace facilities.
- **Significant components:** Workplace welfare programs, co-workers' support, and cleanliness are also significant factors.
- **Cumulative influence:** These factors collectively contribute to 78.027% of job satisfaction among migrant workers.

Recommendations for enhancing job satisfaction

1. **Periodicity of salary payment:** Ensure regular and transparent payment schedules.
2. **Leisure time offered at workplace:** Establish dedicated rest areas and support regular breaks.
3. **Superiors support:** Foster open communication and provide mentorship.
4. **Facilities offered at workplace:** Maintain clean and comfortable facilities.
5. **Welfare measures:** Introduce health and wellness programs.
6. **Co-workers support:** Encourage a collaborative workplace culture.
7. **Neighbors support:** Foster community interaction.
8. **Work timing:** Implement flexible schedules where possible.
9. **Training program:** Schedule frequent and tailored training sessions.
10. **Cleanliness at accommodated place:** Maintain sanitary living conditions.
11. **Salary:** Ensure fair and consistent pay scales.
12. **Hygiene at workplace:** Establish stringent hygiene standards.

Employers and organizations can enhance job satisfaction and overall wellbeing by prioritizing these recommendations and regularly seeking feedback from migrant workers

In conclusion, the socio-economic profile and factors influencing job satisfaction among migrant workers in Coimbatore district highlights the importance of tailored interventions to enhance their well-being and workplace experiences.

Conclusion

In conclusion, the study sheds light on several critical factors shaping the job satisfaction of migrant workers in the Coimbatore district. The regularity of income payments and availability of leisure time significantly impact job happiness. Moreover, supportive management, workplace amenities, welfare measures, and social support networks play pivotal roles. Clean and hygienic living conditions, fair pay, and participation in training programs also influence overall satisfaction. This comprehensive understanding underlines the complexity of factors contributing to migrant workers' job satisfaction.

Moving forward, further research in this field holds immense potential. Longitudinal studies can track how job satisfaction evolves over time, while cross-cultural comparisons can reveal universal versus context-specific factors. Sector-specific investigations and qualitative methodologies, such as focus groups and interviews, offer deeper insights into migrant workers' experiences. Additionally, exploring the impact of technology, health, diversity, and intervention programs can enrich our understanding and inform targeted strategies for improving migrant workers' well-being and working conditions. Through continued research and collaborative efforts, scholars, policymakers, and stakeholders can pave the way for a more equitable and supportive environment for migrant workers.

References

Al-Khawaldeh, A., Othman, M., and Al-Dmour, H. (2020). The impact of migrant workers on job satisfaction. *International Journal of Applied Management and Technology*, 19(2), 73–88.

Bashir, S., and Ramay, M. I. (2018). Impact of employee empowerment on job satisfaction: an empirical analysis of Pakistani banking sector. *The Pakistan Development Review*, 57(4), 681–698.

Chen, G., Chen, X. P., and Meindl, J. R. (2018). How can leaders achieve high employee performance?: the impact of cultural intelligence, positive psychology, and authentic leadership. *Organizational Dynamics*, 47(3), 147–156.

De Jong, G. F., Madamba, A. B., and Kaplan, D. H. (2015). The economic integration of immigrants in 18 European countries. *International Migration Review*, 49(3), 731–766.

Ding, Y., Chang, C. W., and Li, Y. (2017). Chinese immigrants' perceived discrimination and subjective well-being: the moderating role of enculturation. *International Journal of Intercultural Relations*, 57, 55–64.

Durmaz, Y., and Terzi, H. (2016). The impact of interpersonal relationships on job satisfaction among migrant workers: A social exchange perspective. *Procedia-Social and Behavioral Sciences*, 235, 131–138.

Fozdar, F., and Torezani, S. (2018). The well-being and job satisfaction of temporary migrant workers in Australia: a research note. *Australian Journal of Social Issues*, 53(4), 344–358.

Hassan, A., Chang, D. C., and Salim, R. M. (2018). Work environment factors and job performance of foreign workers in Malaysia. *International Journal of Academic Research in Business and Social Sciences*, 8(10), 279–295.

Hassan, A., Chang, D. C., Salim, R. M., and Riaz, F. (2021). Workplace conflict, stress, and job satisfaction: a study of foreign workers in Malaysia. *Journal of Workplace Behavioral Health*, 36(3), 194–213.

Hossain, M. M., Rahman, M. M., and Khan, M. F. H. (2018). Job satisfaction and job performance of migrant workers in Malaysia: the moderating role of job engagement. *Journal of Global Mobility: The Home of Expatriate Management Research*, 6(1), 28–46.

145 Adoption of AI marketing by small and medium enterprises in Malaysia: examining the success factors

Wang Chuan-Fu[1] and Mudiarasan Kuppusamy[2,a]

[1]Faculty of Business, University of Cyberjaya, Malaysia

[2]School of Graduate Studies, Unirazak, Malaysia

Abstract

In exploring artificial intelligence (AI)-driven marketing for small and medium enterprises (SMEs) in Malaysia, the study delves into crucial success factors such as CSF adoption, effective communication, individual skills, SMEs privacy, and technological infrastructure. Employing a partial least squares structural equation modeling (PLS-SEM) model and a quantitative research methodology with a sample of 380 stakeholders, including small business managers and enterprise owners, the survey uncovers significant potential and relationships among these critical factors. The evolving landscape of small businesses and marketing trends highlights the importance of equal attention to each CSF for successful AI adoption in Malaysia. The findings suggest a promising avenue for SMEs in leveraging AI for marketing, emphasizing the need for continued research into these critical success factors to further advance AI adoption in the Malaysian business landscape.

Keywords: AI infrastructure, AI SMEs marketing, communication, CSF adoption, skills

Introduction

Small and medium enterprises (SMEs) are increasingly tapping into the power of artificial intelligence (AI) tools like chatbots and customer service automation. Building a strong connection and personalized AI marketing is becoming essential for SMEs' success (Žigienė et al., 2019 ; Giusti et al., 2019; Dora et al., 2022). The adoption of AI in SMEs plays a crucial role in economic extension and market development (Tan and Lee, 2022; Zainon et al., 2022; Muthusamy and Chew, 2020). Critical success factors highlight the importance of incentives and business technology adoption schemas (Sumra et al., 2022). However, the sustainability of SMEs is at stake, with 57% to 72% facing failure due to limited AI applications, impacting markets like Malaysia, where SMEs contribute significantly to GDP, national exports, and employment (El-Chaarani et al., 2023; Barclay et al., 2022; Amiri et al., 2023; Khan et al., 2022; Alam, 2022). Aiming for long-term success, only 76% of start-ups remain operational beyond two years (Andembubtob et al., 2023).

Literature Review

Table 145.1 Navigating AI success in SMEs: insights from critical studies and strategies.

Author name	Study
Jadhav et al., 2021	Critical success factors for SME adoption in Malaysia - 97.4% SMEs, with focus on services and manufacturing.
Wong et al., 2022	AI-driven marketing success factors, emphasizing programmatic media buys (Alam and Kuppusamy, 2023).
Ghobakhloo and Iranmanesh, 2021	Effective communication with SMEs for AI success, selecting appropriate messaging strategies.
Owusu et al., 2020	Construction SMEs at 87.3%, highlighting the importance of AI adoption for sustained small businesses.
Sumra and Alam, 2021	Non-alignment of critical success factors in SMEs adoption through AI marketing tools.
Jiwasiddi and Mondong, 2018	AI-driven components mitigating issues in sales and marketing's external financing.

[a]arasan@unirazak.edu.my

Author name	Study
Baabdullah et al., 2021	Use of sensors for self-improvement in SMEs, addressing operational logic challenges in marketing.
Ristyawan, 2020	Corporate strategy for marketing in widely accepted SMEs businesses - assembling effective strategies.

Source: Author

Resource-based theory

The SMEs adoption of AI with the critical success factors implies the use of resource-based theory that indicates the use of resources for the competitive advantage. Barney in 1991 research on firm resources and competitive advantage provides the heterogeneity and use of resources in a valuable manner to gain the attention and potential outcomes (Baharuden et al., 2019). The theory highlights the importance of strategic marketing while focusing on numerous resources that include the efficient application of technological infrastructure and advancement. The critical success factors where marketing becomes the central phenomenon through technological advancement support the evaluation of the AI potential for SMEs adoption (Peyravi et al., 2020; de Vries et al., 2018).

Conceptual framework

The critical success factors are centralized tools for the development of conceptual framework where the use of technological infrastructure and development (Khayer et al., 2020; Peyravi et al., 2020; de Vries et al., 2018). Through business-related communication, marketing is connected to the individual skills, SMEs' privacy, and adoption. The challenge for risk management for SMEs is the accurate tracking and AI processing of the less expensive sensors towards the successful adoption of SMEs. In the conceptual framework for better SMEs business adoption, these critical success factors are given a specific role.

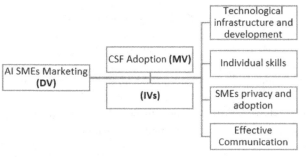

Figure 145.1 Conceptual framework
Source: Hariharan, 2019; Priyadarshinee et al., 2017; Tjebane et al., 2022

Dependent variable (DV): AI SMEs marketing.
Mediating variable (MV): CSF adoption
Independent variables (IVs): Technological infrastructure and development, individual skills, SMEs privacy and adoption, effective communication.

The marketing of SMEs business and small operations through the AI based advance technology is paramount for the critical success factors. These factors are adopted to engage the SMEs in Malaysia for the favorable and positive outcome of the SMEs marketing. The factors are inter-linked and acting in the framework as independent variables. These included the technological infrastructure and development which is the major issues for the AI adoption in SMEs of Malaysia (Priyadarshinee et al., 2017).

Hypothesis

- H1: The CSF adoption is significantly co-related with AI SMEs marketing
- H2: The technological infrastructure is significantly co-related with CSF adoption
- H3: The individual skills are significantly co-related with CSF adoption
- H4: The privacy and adoption are significantly co-related with CSF adoption
- H5: The effective communication is significantly co-related with CSF adoption

Methodology

This study focuses on utilizing quantitative research methodology to explore the adoption of AI marketing among SMEs in Malaysia, aiming to enhance their operational sustainability (Oliva et al., 2022). It underscores the importance of quantitative research in understanding critical success factors pivotal for the effective adoption of AI marketing (Bernardi et al., 2022), relying on numerical data for robust statistical analysis and interpretation.

Data collection:
- Collection of data for quantitative research through survey questionnaires.
- Approach participants in a meaningful way to gather information (Amrita et al., 2018; Basri, 2020).

- Use of a scoring system (1 = Strongly disagree, 2 = Disagree, 3 = Neutral, 4 = agree, 5 = Strongly agree).

Data Analysis:

- Analysis of data for AI-driven marketing tools and validation of critical success factors.
- Processing raw material to derive meaningful insights (Žigienė et al., 2019).

Data modeling approach (PLS-SEM):

- Utilization of partial least squares structural equation modeling (PLS-SEM) for SMEs-based AI marketing behavior.
- Testing theories for confirmation of results (Chatterjee et al., 2022).

Variables considered:

- Estimation of complex models for variables including infrastructure and development, individual skills and SMEs, SMEs privacy and adoption, effective communication, and AI processing, sensor devices (Kumar et al., 2019).

By employing quantitative research methodologies, this study aims to contribute to the understanding of critical success factors in AI marketing adoption among SMEs in Malaysia. The utilization of PLS-SEM provides a robust framework for testing theories and confirming results, allowing for a comprehensive analysis of various variables influencing AI adoption.

Results and analysis

In the context of SMEs in Malaysia, the research emphasizes the pivotal role of AI-driven marketing for business success. With a focus on businesses with varying years of experience, the study reveals that SMEs aged 6-15 years contribute significantly (47.89%), showcasing the value of AI adoption. The research spans two decades, involving 119 participants (31.31%), highlighting the enduring impact of AI on SMEs. Investment-wise, businesses with 0-5 million (47.36%) lead, underlining the influence of

capital on AI adoption. The R-square values further affirm the relevance of AI in SMEs marketing.

The marketing strategies for SMEs, driven by critical success factors, emphasize the workforce's size. Businesses with 36-65 staff (34.73%) play a substantial role, reflecting the significance of employee strength in SMEs. The study underscores the positive correlation between critical success factors and AI-driven marketing, with 48.15% response rate. Notably, high-status SMEs (52.89%) exhibit a strong inclination towards AI-based marketing. Technical businesses dominate responses (73.42%), showcasing a preference for skill-based approaches, while non-technical businesses contribute 26.57% to the research, emphasizing diversity in SME specifications.

In a study employing PLS-SEM, participants aged 9-29 constituted 38.68%, with reliable responses from 30-40 (32.36%), 41-50 (23.42%), and 51 onwards (6.57%). Males (65.52%) dominated, correlating with AI in SMEs. Expenditure of 1000 –5000 MYR had 43.94% participation. Effective communication (0.649) and individual skills (0.140) significantly influenced CSF adoption, reinforcing AI SMEs marketing (0.422). Regression revealed positive relationships, with technological infrastructure being a strong CSF (r-square 0.421). Cronbach alpha showed high

Table 145.2 Exploring factors contributing to performance.

	R-square	R-square adjusted
AI SMEs marketing	0.422	0.42
CSF adoption	0.317	0.312
SMEs privacy and adoption	0.374	0.373
Effective communication	0.422	0.42
Individual skills	0.314	0.311
Technological infrastructure	0.421	0.371

Source: Author

Table 145.3 Assessing the reliability and validity of constructs in AI and SMEs.

	Cronbach's alpha	Composite reliability (rho_a)	Composite reliability (rho_c)	Average variance extracted (AVE)
AI SMEs marketing	0.827	0.873	0.869	0.797
CSF adoption	0.793	0.797	0.852	0.891
Effective communication	0.888	0.89	0.913	0.799
Individual skills	0.738	0.717	0.868	0.771
SMEs privacy and adoption	0.771	0.796	0.83	0.786
Technological infrastructure	0.676	0.737	0.821	0.865

Source: Author

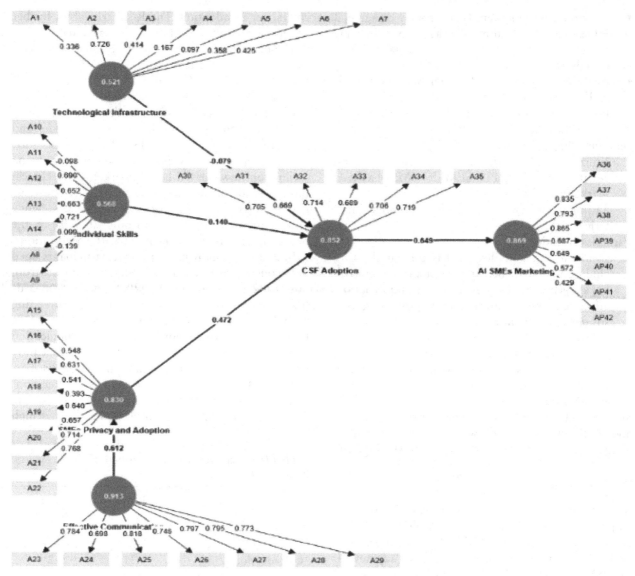

Figure 145.2 Critical success factors for SMEs in Malaysia
Source: Author

internal consistency: AI SMEs marketing (0.827), CSF adoption (0.793), effective communication (0.888), individual skills (0.738), and SMEs privacy and adoption (0.771). Critical success factors had acceptable composite reliability (0.873) and average variance (0.797), validating the study's reliability for AI adoption in Malaysian SMEs.

Effective communication plays a pivotal role in composite reliability, registering a value of 0.890 with an average variance of 0.799. This directly impacts communication within SMEs, crucial for business success in Malaysia. Individual skills contribute significantly, with a CR value of 0.717 and an average variance of 0.771. SMEs' privacy and adoption of AI show a CR value of 0.796, reflecting the importance of privacy in AI-based operations. The technological

infrastructure, with a CR value of 0.737 and average variance of 0.865, underscores the compliance required for AI-based development in small businesses, leveraging available technological capabilities.

The developed model for this research on the use of AI in SMEs in Malaysia reveals that technological infrastructure, individual skills, privacy, and effective communication are independent variables influencing CSF adoption, which in turn mediates AI SME marketing. The absence of negative relations between these constructs, demonstrated by 0 values, strengthens the model. Evaluation of AI potential for SMEs through CSF adoption is effectively illustrated, showing significant and reliable values for model fit in the context of Oman. Critical success factors play a vital role in fostering AI adoption among SMEs in Malaysia, highlighting their importance in driving AI-driven markets through SMEs marketing tools.

Conclusion

The practical contribution of this research has persuaded the owners and managers of small businesses to believe that they have essential components such as technological infrastructure and growth, personal skills, and communication. The significant effects of computational intelligence (AI) on the SMEs company environment compelled the management and smaller staff, including the employees of various production and marketing components, to restructure their skills and training for technological advances learning. The court and the taxing authorities are easing their oversight of skills and the regulation of SMEs, which is reducing cost trial and error. Allocating products and brands is the cost experiment for all of the stakeholders in order to better comprehend consumers.

References

Alam, M. (2022). Understanding and improving digital tourism events in Pakistan. In Technology Application in Tourism Fairs, Festivals and Events in Asia (pp. 233–247). Singapore: Springer Singapore.

Alam, M., and Bahrein, K. (2021). Image branding factors & facilitating model of tourism destinations management during Covid-19 in Pakistan. *Journal of Tianjin University Science and Technology*, 54(10), 428–444. DOI: 10.17605/OSF.IO/956PY.

Alam, M., and Kuppusamy, M. (2023). Integrated management for image branding; a prospective outlook from Abbottabad as a tourism destination valley of Pakistan. In BESRA Germany, International Conference on Recent Developments in Social Science and Digital Economy / Washington DC.

Alam, M., Kuppusamy, M., and Kunasekaran, P. (2023). The role of destination management in mediating the determinants of Cyberjaya tourism image branding. *Cogent Business and Management*, 10(3), 2259579.

Amiri, A. M., Kushwaha, B. P., and Singh, R. (2023). Visualisation of global research trends and future research directions of digital marketing in small and medium enterprises using bibliometric analysis. *Journal of Small Business and Enterprise Development*, 30(3), 621–641.

Sumra, K. B., Ahmad, M. S., and Alam, M. (2020). Informal economy, social inequalities and street vendors in Pakistan: governance, politics and tourism in pandemic.

Sumra, K. B., Alam, M., and Aftab, R. (2022a). Artificial intelligence for strengthening administrative and support services in public sector amid COVID-19: challenges and opportunities in Pakistan. In Advances in Data Science and Intelligent Data Communication Technologies for COVID-19: Innovative Solutions Against COVID-19 (pp. 153–172).

Sumra, K. B., Alam, M., and Iftikhar, H. (2022b). Cities poor management in social protection and Covid-19: transgender inequalities and opportunity bias.

Sumra, K. B., Alam, M., Noor, K. B. M., Hali, S. M., and Iftikhar, H. (2022c). Factors affecting artificial intelligence and management of institutional response to the event of coronavirus in Pakistan. *Pertanika Journal of Social Sciences & Humanities*, 30(4).

Sumra, K. B., and Alam, M. M. (2021). Promoting religious tourism management for creating a soft image of Pakistan. In Global Development of Religious Tourism (pp. 149–174). IGI Global.

146 Adoption of building information modeling for management of construction project success

Yin Rui[1] and Mudiarasan Kuppusamy[2,a]

[1]Faculty of Business, University of Cyberjaya, Malaysia

[2]School of Graduate Studies, Unirazak, Malaysia

Abstract

In Malaysia, the widespread adoption of building information modelling (BIM) in construction faces several challenges, such as financial constraints, limited understanding of BIM, weak implementation, and inadequate governmental support. A quantitative research approach, employing a survey with 382 respondents and utilizing SPSS software, revealed that integrating BIM significantly enhances precast construction efficiency. The study emphasized the positive impact of BIM tools like clash detection and 3D/4D/5D modelling in precast projects, demonstrating their effectiveness in ensuring timely project completion. The findings highlight the need for future research to explore BIM's broader applications beyond Malaysia for improved construction outcomes and sustainable practices.

Keywords: 3D/4D/5D BIM, BIM, current installation, precast construction

Introduction

The implementation of Building Information Modelling (BIM) in precast projects, as highlighted by Plebankiewicz et al. (2015), offers a transformative approach to traditional methods. Maghiar et al. (2015) emphasize that modeling excellence enhances manufacturing efficiency and the effective utilization of resources in construction. Unlike conventional methods, precast construction prioritizes detail design and prefabrication, leading to improved efficiency (Smith, 2014). Specific planning and execution tailored to the unique nature of precast projects are crucial (Tserng et al., 2014; Wu and Issa, 2015; Tushar et al., 2022).

BIM clash detection, as outlined by Sumra et al. (2022) and Alam (2022), becomes instrumental in establishing a rational sequence for prefab component installation through 3D modeling. This not only fosters communication between owners and designers but also addresses conflicts and uncertainties in precast fabrication execution (Ismail, 2022). However, challenges persist, with Duan and Liu (2023) noting a growing gap between manufacturing and construction due to the persistence of conventional approaches. Despite these issues, the real case of using BIM in precast construction, as advocated by Qin (2021) and Ali (2021), demonstrates its superiority over traditional methods, mitigating the disconnect between architectural drawings and the final product (Philip and Kannan, 2021; Jiankang et al., 2022).

Literature Review

Table 146.1 Advancements in precast construction: a collaborative and sustainable approach.

Author name	Study
Fung, 2022	Prefabricated concrete installation's ability to withstand significant pressure
Sumra et al., 2020	Prefabricated construction technology involving casting concrete in a controlled environment
Heinbach et al., 2023	Precast construction supporting building structures, particularly parking structures
Ullah et al., 2019	Resistance of precast construction to dents, chips, and related damage
Ben Mahmoud et al., 2022	Improved quality and safety in construction projects through real-time collaboration
Banerjee and Nayaka, 2022	Collaborative aspects of construction projects facilitated by real-time coordination
Kahre et al., 2022	Enhanced quality and safety in construction through improved collaboration

Source: Author

[a]arasan@unirazak.edu.my

The theory refers to the better understanding and implication of five key steps for the implementation of BIM technology in a technical manner (Juan-Valdés et al., 2018). The implementation of BIM as well as application actions in prefabricated structures involve BIM understanding, argumentation, choices, execution, and approval (Alam and Bahrein, 2021; Newell and Goggins, 2019). The environment of BIM as per the conventional precast of BIM relates to the BIM implementation as it is required for the precast construction models in Malaysia (Shirowzhan, 2020; Karampour, 2021).

The proposed conceptual framework is to integrate the key variables of this research on adopting BIM as a successful method of construction project. The design illustrates the current state of implementation of BIM, as well as the resulting and predicting of the different strategies used under the BIM framework (Ren and Zhang, 2021). The current installation in the precast construction is assessed using the multi-dimensional strategy and modelling of 3D/4D/5D as the progressive elements of construction (He et al., 2021; Basta et al., 2020). The construction of building specification is connected with the agreements for the various phases of construction project completion (Gbadamosi et al., 2019).

Hypothesis
- H1: There is a positive association between improved precast construction efficiency and the adoption of BIM.
- H2: There is a positive association between improved precast construction efficiency and current installation in precast construction.

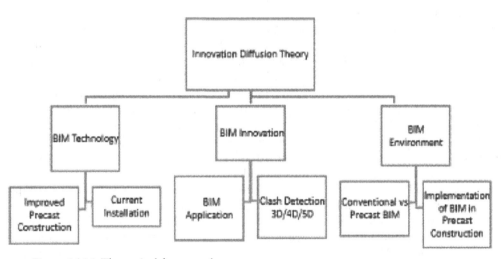

Figure 146.1 Theoretical framework
Source: Wang et al., 2022; Shirowzhan, 2020; Karampour, 2021

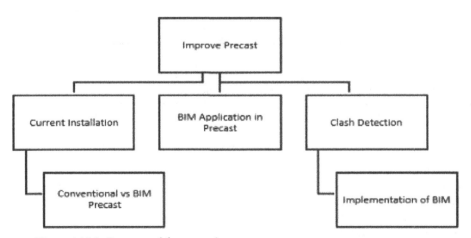

Figure 146.2 Conceptual framework
Source: He et al., 2021; Basta et al., 2020; Gbadamosi et al., 2019

- H3: There is a positive association between improved precast construction efficiency and BIM application in precast construction.
- H4: There is a positive association between improved precast construction efficiency and clash detection with 3D/4D/5D BIM.
- H5: There is a positive association between improved precast construction efficiency and conventional vs BIM precast construction.

Research methodology

This research investigates how precast construction projects can benefit from BIM adoption. Traditional methods face data challenges. The study aims to understand project completion and BIM integration using quantitative analysis. Insights will inform systematic interventions for improved construction practices.

Data collection:
- Survey questionnaires are employed, targeting participants involved in precast building projects, including engineers, QS supporting staff, consultants, designers, and workers (Alam et al., 2023; Hussein et al., 2021; Li, 2021).

Participant selection:
- Quantitative selection of participants is undertaken for the establishment of BIM modeling in precast construction (Wu et al., 2021; Hussein et al., 2021; Mohammed et al., 2022; Ding et al., 2019; Chaokromthong & Sintao, 2021).
- Simple random sampling is utilized to determine the sample size from a population of 75,000, following Krejcie and Morgan's recommendations, resulting in a sample size of 382 respondents (Ismail, 2021; Mutale, 2021; Tamang, 2021).

Data analysis:
- SPSS is chosen as the tool for data analysis, specifically to address queries regarding clash detection within 3D/4D/5D BIM models and to compare conventional vs BIM usage in precast construction (Fang et al., 2023; Alyatama and Al-Sabah, 2023; Darwish et al., 2020).
- The application of SPSS is essential for analyzing variables related to BIM adoption, contributing to the development of a comprehensive framework (Chao et al., 2021; Guo et al., 2021).

Result and analysis

In examining the participant demographics, the data highlights a predominant age group of 26-40, comprising 64 individuals, constituting 16.8% of the study. The 41–60 age bracket exhibits a substantial 311 participants, contributing 81.4%. Gender-wise, 248 males (64.9%) and 134 females (35.1%)

engaged in the research. Educational backgrounds vary, with 27 participants (7.1%) holding basic education, 93 (24.3%) intermediate, and 262 (68.6%) possessing postgraduate degrees. Experience-wise, 27 individuals (7.1%) have 5 years, 93 (24.3%) have 10 years, and 262 (68.6%) boast 20 years in precast construction.

The study's robustness is affirmed by a high Cronbach's alpha value of .947, reflecting the reliability of the 46 research items. This underscores the significance of BIM methodologies in construction, particularly in precast construction, as evidenced by their applicability in the current installation processes within manufactured buildings.

The efficiency of improved precast construction is reflected in frequency statistics, connected to current installations. Out of 382 valid responses, 75 respondents reported a mean value of 1.00, highlighting effectiveness.

The correlation study explores the relationships between various variables, such as IPC, CIP, BIM, CD, CB, and IB. The values in the table indicate the strength and direction of these connections. Positive values signify a positive relationship, while negative values indicate an inverse association. For instance, IPC and CIP exhibit a strong positive correlation of 1.000. These correlation coefficients help researchers understand the degree of coordination between different variables, providing valuable insights into their interdependence

The decision tree analysis reveals relationships between independent variables. Non-technical visuals show 53% agreement for improved pre-cast construction based on 206 responses, with a significant p-value (0.000) and chi-square (382). Current precast

Table 146.2 Reliability statistics.

Cronbach's alpha	N of items
0.947	46

Source: Author

Table 146.3 Frequency statistics.

		IPC	CIP	BIM	CD	CB	IB
N	Valid	382	382	382	382	382	382
	Missing	0	0	0	0	0	0
Minimum		1	1	1	1	1	1
Percentiles	25	2	2	2	2	2	2
	50	4	4	4	4	4	4
	75	4	4	4	4	4	4

Source: Author

Table 146.4 Correlation.

	IPC	CIP	BIM	CD	CB	IB
IPC	1	1.000**	1.000**	1.000**	1.000**	1.000**
	0.371	0.371	0.268	0.202	0.449	0.211
	382	382	382	382	382	382
CIP	1.000**	1	1.000**	1.000**	1.000**	1.000**
	0.268	0.218	0.202	0.449	0.211	0.333
	382	382	382	382	382	382
BIM	1.000**	1.000**	1	1.000**	1.000**	1.000**
	0.202	0.218	0.202	0.449	0.211	0.289
	382	382	382	382	382	382
CD	1.000**	1.000**	1.000**	1	1.000**	1.000**
	0.449	0.318	0.202	0.449	0.211	0.289
	382	382	382	382	382	382
CB	1.000**	1.000**	1.000**	1.000**	1	1.000**
	0.211	0.202	0.449	0.211	0.289	0.348
	382	382	382	382	382	382
IB	1.000**	1.000**	1.000**	1.000**	1.000**	1
	0.449	0.211	0.289	0.348	278	0.383
	382	382	382	382	382	382

Source: Author

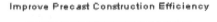

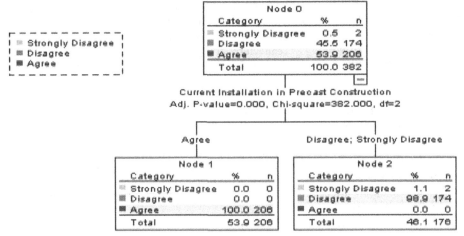

Figure 146.3 Tree analysis

Source: Author

installation has a 53.9% agreement vs 46.1% (176 responses).

In principle component analysis, a value of 1.000 at both initial and extraction levels ensures communalities reflect variable skills. It fosters transition from conventional to BIM construction methods.

The dataset summary indicates a perfect model fit, with R and R-square values both at 1.000, showcasing the accuracy in predicting targeted field values. This suggests minimal disruption in results, aligning with the BIM method for construction. The Durbin Watson values (0-4) signify a robust model, indicating no autocorrelation in the research sample. Overall, the findings underscore the efficiency of precast construction, showcasing technological strides in constructing reinforced buildings, promoting

Table 146.5 Principal component analysis; communalities.

	Initial	Extraction
Improve precast construction efficiency (IPC)	1	1
Current installation in precast construction (CIP)	1	1
BIM application in precast construction (BIM)	1	1
Clash detection with 3D/4D/5D BIM (CD)	1	1
Conventional vs BIM precast construction method (CB)	1	1
Implementation of BIM precast Construction project (IB)	1	1
Extraction method: principal component analysis.		

Source: Author

eco-friendly practices, and ensuring timely project completion.

Conclusion

In the arena of precast construction research, a key focus lies in analyzing data provided by respondents engaged in multiple data connections. These respondents highlight the efficacy of precast construction, particularly through the adoption of building information modelling (BIM). BIM plays a crucial role in ensuring successful project completion by incorporating clash detection tools in 3D/4D/5D, enhancing overall construction activities and project management.

The application of BIM in precast construction goes beyond just clash detection, encompassing effective management of 3D/4D/5D. This integration facilitates conflict resolution and ensures safer construction sites, underscoring the pivotal role of BIM in precast activities. The utilization of BIM in prefabricated buildings not only involves clash detection but also emphasizes effective leadership, where the virtual model created through BIM planning and execution becomes a vital tool for assessing modifications before initiating physical work.

References

Abdelghany, A. H. (2021). The potential of adopting blockchain technology with BIM implementations in the construction industry ecosystem–a review paper.

Alam, M. (2022). Understanding and improving digital tourism events in Pakistan. In Kuppusamy, M. (Ed.), Technology Application in Tourism Fairs, Festivals and Events in Asia, (pp. 233–247). Singapore: Springer Singapore.

Alam, M., and Bahrein, K. (2021). Image branding factors and facilitating model of tourism destinations management during Covid-19 in Pakistan. *Journal of Tianjin University Science and Technology*, 54(10), 428–444. DOI: 10.17605/OSF.IO/956PY.

Alam, M., and Kuppusamy, M. (2023). Integrated management for image branding: a prospective outlook from Abbottabad as a tourism destination valley of Pakistan. In BESRA Germany, International Conference on Recent Developments in Social Science and Digital Economy / Washington DC.

Alam, M., Kuppusamy, M., and Kunasekaran, P. (2023). The role of destination management in mediating the determinants of Cyberjaya tourism image branding. *Cogent Business & Management*, 10(3), 2259579.

Ali, A. (2021). Precast concrete fabrication process improvement through BIM-based paperless system implementation.

Alyatama, S., and Al-Sabah, R. (2023). Construction planning and scheduling of a precast house extension using a multi-objective genetic algorithm and 4D building information modeling. *QScience Connect*, 2023(2), 1.

Banerjee, A., and Nayaka, R. R. (2022). A comprehensive overview of BIM-integrated cyber-physical system architectures and practices in the architecture, engineering, and construction industry. *Construction Innovation*, 22(4), 727–748.

Basta, A., Serror, M. H., and Marzouk, M. (2020). A BIM-based framework for quantitative assessment of steel structure deconstructability. *Automation in Construction*, 111, 103064.

Ben Mahmoud, B., Lehoux, N., Blanchet, P., and Cloutier, C. (2022). Barriers, strategies, and best practices for BIM adoption in Quebec prefabrication small and medium-sized enterprises (SMEs). *Buildings*, 12(4), 390.

147 Success factors for e-paper display adoption by Malaysian industries

Meng Ching-Lin[1] and Mudiarasan Kuppusamy[2,a]

[1]Faculty of Business, University of Cyberjaya, Malaysia
[2]School of Graduate Studies, Unirazak, Malaysia

Abstract

This research, employing quantitative methodology, explores the application of conceptual designs in e-paper technology for logistics, manufacturing, and education. Utilizing the PLS-SEM model and data from 381 respondents, the study highlights the significant impact of e-paper display adoption on user behavior and change factors. It emphasizes technical attributes, energy efficiency, and ecological considerations, connecting them to performance expectancy and successful technology adoption. The findings endorse the broader application of e-paper in Malaysia, stressing the need for technological infrastructure across various industries for stable and sustainable business practices.

Keywords: E-paper display technology, Malaysian industries, satisfaction and gratification, social factors

Introduction

The adoption of e-paper display technology in Malaysian industries is influenced by unique features like bi-stability, flexibility, and excellent readability in diverse lighting conditions (Lee et al., 2010). Comparisons with other display technologies, such as LCD, LED, and OLED, highlight e-paper's strengths and limitations. The environmental advantages, like energy efficiency and waste reduction, contribute to its appeal (Amasawa et al., 2018). Understanding the factors impacting e-paper implementation in industries is currently lacking, presenting an opportunity to explore user behavior and perceptions (Hamilton et al., 2021). Bridging this gap could enhance the broader application of e-paper technology, considering technical aspects, energy efficiency, and ecological implications (Johnstone et al., 2020).

The complexity of e-paper's performance expectancy, offering energy-saving benefits but falling short in areas like refresh rates and color displays, is a critical consideration (Ali Rabbani et al., 2023; Chigrinov and Kudreyko, 2021). The role of facilitating conditions, encompassing infrastructure and technical support, is crucial in realizing the technology's potential in practical implementation (Walrave et al., 2021; Lowitzsch et al., 2020; Malik, 2020; Abdullah, 2020). A comprehensive exploration of these facets, coupled with a comparative analysis against alternative display technologies, can provide valuable insights for a more informed and widespread adoption of e-paper display technology.

Literature Review

Table 147.1 Economic and environmental perspectives on e-paper technology adoption.

Author name	Study
Al-Mamary, 2022	E-paper success factors, focusing on economic aspects and efficient resource use.
Montanarella and Kovalenko, 2022	Modern systems often require significant upfront investments.
Litvina et al., 2019	Discussing financial factors beyond acquisition costs for technological upgrades.
Cao et al., 2020; Dong et al., 2021	Examining additional expenses associated with tech upgrades, potentially deterring organizations with tight budgets.
Drabicki et al., 2023	Describing the economics of implementing new technology, emphasizing e-paper's efficient resource use.
Liu et al., 2021	Highlighting advantages of e-paper displays in material usage and energy consumption during production.
Dezaki and Bodaghi, 2023	Pointing out that traditional displays are less eco-friendly despite using e-paper.

Source: Author

[a]arasan@unirazak.edu.my

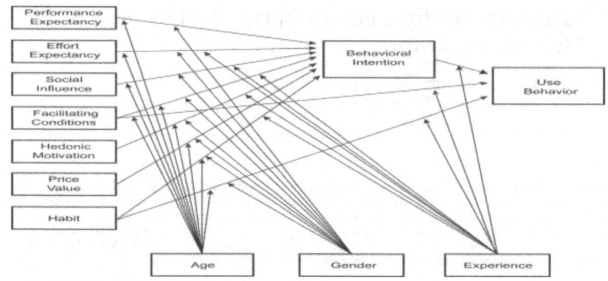

Figure 147.1 Conceptual framework
Source: Author

Research methodology

This study adopts a positivist research philosophy, focusing on obtaining knowledge through observable phenomena and empirical evidence. Aligned with the quantitative nature of the research, rooted in positivism, it employs an online questionnaire based on the UTAUT2 model to investigate factors influencing the adoption of E-paper display technologies in Malaysian industries. The study emphasizes objective knowledge through systematic, quantitative methods, utilizing structural equation modelling for data analysis, aiming to test predetermined hypotheses and draw conclusive findings regarding key constructs like behavioral intention and performance expectancy.

Data collection strategy:

* Quantitative research is fundamentally based on numerical data and statistical techniques, allowing for the analysis of large amounts of data, theory testing, and drawing statistically significant conclusions (Wei Asper et al., 2022).

* To explore factors contributing to the adoption of E-paper display technologies within Malaysian industries, the study employs a highly structured, quantitative data collection strategy.

* The primary data collection method is an online questionnaire, designed to yield high-quality data from individuals actively engaged in relevant industrial sectors and meeting inclusion criteria.

Questionnaire structure and segmentation:

* The questionnaire is segmented into multiple sections, each focusing on a different construct of the UTAUT2 model, such as behavioral intention, use behavior, hedonic motivation, social influence,

performance expectancy, and facilitating conditions (Hafter, 2023; Oke and Fernandes, 2020).

* Each section utilizes Likert-scale items and multiple-choice questions to capture respondents' perspectives and experiences (Lowitzsch et al., 2020).

Data analysis with structural equation modelling:

* Structural equation modelling (SEM) is employed with the AMOS software package to assess causal relationships among the study's constructs: performance expectancy, hedonic motivation, social influence, and facilitating conditions toward behavioral intention and use behavior (Kaufman, 2022).

* Before running the SEM analysis, a series of data quality tests, including Cronbach's Alpha for reliability and exploratory factor analysis for validity, are executed. Multi-collinearity and normality checks are undertaken to ensure the data's suitability for SEM.

Result and analysis

The analysis considers age groups to assess the impact of e-paper displays across industries. It notes significant participation from individuals aged 0-14, 15-34, and 51-65 or older, indicating diverse involvement. Gender ratios show 59% male and 41% female engagement. Education levels vary, with 19% at short-cycle tertiary education, 27% bachelor's degree holders, and 37% master's degree participants, reflecting a spectrum of knowledge.

Statistical measures like mean, median, and standard deviation elucidate the data distribution and variance within success factors related to e-paper adoption. Skewness and kurtosis values indicate asymmetry and

Table 147.2 Frequency analysis.

	Mean	Median	Obv min	Obv max	Std Dev	N Obv
E-Paper display adoption	0	0.21	4.356	1.732	1	381
Facilitating conditions	0	0.227	3.334	1.9	1	381
Hedonic motivation	0	0.226	2.994	1.665	1	381
Performance expectancy	0	0.031	2.814	2.221	1	381
Social influence	0	0.089	3.416	1.851	1	381

Source: Author

Table 147.3 Correlation analysis.

	E-Paper display adoption	Facilitating conditions	Hedonic motivation	Performance expectancy	Social influence
E-paper display adoption	1				
Facilitating conditions		1			
Hedonic motivation			1		
Performance expectancy				1	
Social influence					1

Source: Author

Table 147.4 R & R-square values.

	R-square	R-square adjusted
E-paper display adoption	0.27	0.268
Facilitating conditions	0.525	0.522
Hedonic motivation	0.344	0.391
Performance expectancy	0.533	0.565
Social influence	0.311	0.352

Source: Author

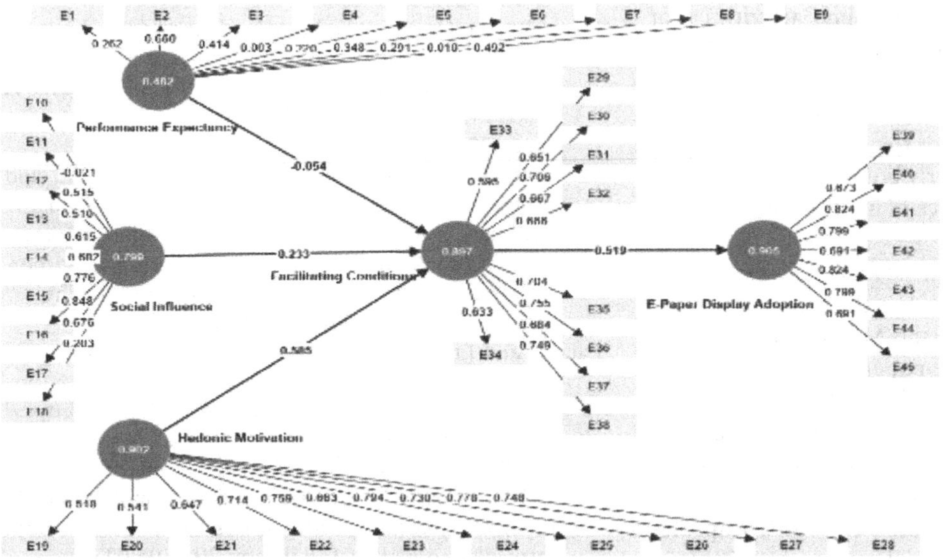

Figure 147.2 PLS-SEM model
Source: Author

variability, informing about the dataset's distribution characteristics. Construct validity assessments suggest robust measures, with values over 50% for e-paper adoption, facilitating conditions, hedonic motivation, performance expectancy, and social influence, underscoring the evaluation's reliability.

Regression analysis demonstrates the explanatory power of the model in predicting e-paper adoption success factors. R-square values highlight the fitness of the partial least squares structural equation modelling (PLS-SEM) model, showing correlations between adoption and facilitating conditions, as well as hedonic motivation. The model incorporates perceived behavioral control and UTAUT framework, emphasizing user-friendly interfaces and performance expectations as catalysts for adoption.

The technical aspects of e-paper, including its composition and comparison with LCD displays, underscore its versatility and performance expectancy. The development of e-ink technology and the use of plastic for layer containment reflect advancements driving e-paper's evolution. Social influence emerges as a significant factor, shaping perceptions and adoption patterns. Overall, e-paper's potential lies in its adaptability, efficiency, and alignment with user expectations, paving the way for broader integration across various sectors.

Conclusion

The degree to which a person believes in a particular system is what helps to raise performance expectations. Performance expectations refer to how technology is used and how easily consumers may use tools and devices to influence their behavior. Individual beliefs play a pivotal role in enabling activities that are associated with the noteworthy prognosis of prolonged and intensive technology utilization. Trust and efforts or the satisfaction indicate the positive association of the success factors for the performance expectancy. Offering of the quarterly bonus are a motivation for the rewarded performance in multiple industries of Malaysia.

The research contribution is to be examined and assessed the success factors for the e-paper display adoption while focusing on the Malaysian industries. It is centered around the e-paper impacts those are based on the criteria of traditional displays with the required time to operate for the e-paper managerial operations. Requirement of constant power for the operations of e-paper which is powered by the small battery or the use of solar panel. Tiny microcapsules are filled with the charge particles that are contributing for the easy and effective service delivery towards the e-paper display adoption. The digital signs and the public information display contribute for the change management which is extensively using the e-paper for the tracking of official records and transactions.

References

Alam, M. (2022). Understanding and improving digital tourism events in Pakistan. In Technology Application in Tourism Fairs, Festivals and Events in Asia (pp. 233–247). Singapore: Springer Singapore.

Alam, M., and Bahrein, K. (2021). Image branding factors and facilitating model of tourism destinations management during Covid-19 in Pakistan. *Journal of Tianjin University Science and Technology*, 54(10), 428–444. DOI: 10.17605/OSF.IO/956PY.

Alam, M., and Kuppusamy, M. (2023). Integrated management for image branding; a prospective outlook from abbottabad as a tourism destination valley of Pakistan. In BESRA Germany, International Conference on Recent Developments in Social Science and Digital Economy / Washington DC.

Alam, M., Kuppusamy, M., and Kunasekaran, P. (2023). The role of destination management in mediating the determinants of Cyberjaya tourism image branding. *Cogent Business and Management*, 10(3), 2259579.

Al-Mamary, Y. H. S. (2022). Understanding the use of learning management systems by undergraduate university students using the UTAUT model: credible evidence from Saudi Arabia. *International Journal of Information Management Data Insights*, 2(2), 100092. https://doi.org/10.1016/j.jjimei.2022.100092.

Cao, J. X., Qin, Z., Zeng, Z., Hu, W. J., Song, L. Y., Hu, D. L., et al. (2020). A convolutional neural network for ghost image recognition and waveform design of electrophoretic displays. *IEEE Transactions on Consumer Electronics*, 66(4), 356–365. https://doi.org/10.1109/TCE.2020.3032682.

Dong, B., Shi, Q., Yang, Y., Wen, F., Zhang, Z., and Lee, C. (2021). Technology evolution from self-powered sensors to AIoT enabled smart homes. *Nano Energy*, 79, 105414. Elsevier Ltd. https://doi.org/10.1016/j.nanoen.2020.105414.

Drabicki, A., Cats, O., Kucharski, R., Fonzone, A., and Szarata, A. (2023). Should I stay or should I board? willingness to wait with real-time crowding information in urban public transport. *Research in Transportation Business and Management*, 47, 100963. https://doi.org/10.1016/j.rtbm.2023.100963.

Du, K., and Li, J. (2019). Towards a green world: How do green technology innovations affect total-factor carbon productivity. *Energy Policy*, 131, 240–250. https://doi.org/10.1016/j.enpol.2019.04.033.

Duarte, P., and Pinho, J. C. (2019). A mixed methods UTAUT2-based approach to assess mobile health adoption. *Journal of Business Research*, 102, 140–150. https://doi.org/10.1016/j.jbusres.2019.05.022.

148 The impact of digital transformation on quality management in the banking sector of Malaysia

Huang Chih Hung[1] and Mudiarasan Kuppusamy[2,a]

[1]Faculty of Business, University of Cyberjaya, Malaysia

[2]School of Graduate Studies, Unirazak, Malaysia

Abstract

The digital transformation has significantly improved the quality management of the banking sector, enhancing customer satisfaction. Utilizing tools such as viable banking solutions, mobile banking technology, QR-code scanning, and E-payments ensures effective and secure transactions. Conducting 09 interviews revealed consistent responses, with qualitative data analysis using NVivo software 12. The study indicates a noteworthy impact, suggesting that digital transformation enhances quality management practices in the Malaysian banking sector. The research recommends prioritizing the quality management of mobile banking technology to address challenges in e-payments and online transaction traffic. Future research should focus on supporting secure payment processes to uphold the economic and social welfare of banking clients.

Keywords: Banking, digital, quality management, technology, transformation

Introduction

The digital transformation in the banking sector involves upgrading processes and introducing new operational methods through electronic devices, revolutionizing money exchange and enhancing customer experiences. This evolution emphasizes trust, faith, and the provision of accurate information in banking transactions, ultimately aiming for increased profitability. The sector embraces open-source quality control and advanced technology, aligning with best practices for sustainable services. Quality management, facilitated by skilled staff, institutionalizes practices within organizations, fostering efficiency and reliability.

The transition from traditional banking to electronic realms brings about better monetary outcomes, exemplified by the 1997 directive from Bank Negara Malaysia to merge local banks for quality improvement. The digital era is pivotal for commercial banking, with a focus on successful money services and the transformative impact of technologies on banking operations. Accelerated digital banking features interconnect with quality management, necessitating a close examination of the research question: the management of impacts on the quality of the banking sector due to digital transformation.

Literature Review

Table 148.1 A comprehensive exploration of digital transformation and customer-centric leadership.

Author name	Study
Ramamoorthy et al. (2018)	E-services and payment privacy transformation in the Malaysian banking sector
Chang et al. (2020)	E-services and payment privacy impact on the banking sector in Malaysia
Islam et al. (2020)	Influence of QR-code technology on banking transformations in Malaysia
Mosteanu and Faccia (2020)	QR-code implications for the evolution of the banking sector in Malaysia
Ghadge et al. (2020)	Technological changes and managerial processes in the Malaysian banking sector
Ni (2020)	Quality management in online and digital services based on existing and renovated concepts
Albuhisi and Abdallah (2018)	Connection between digital transformation and effective outcomes in banking
Kitsios et al. (2021)	Digital transformation's influence on banking services and applications in Malaysia
Abad-Segura et al. (2020)	Review of Vial's (2019) categorical and personalized repayment strategy

[a]arasan@unirazak.edu.my

Author name	Study
Salloum et al. (2019)	Digital transformation's contribution to the improved banking sector based on digital leadership
Llopis-Albert et al. (2021)	Banking leadership's focus on customer experience and excellence in digital banking

Source: Author

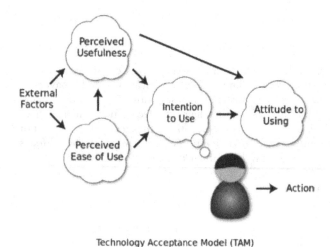

Figure 148.1 Technology acceptance model
Source: Khatoon et al., 2020

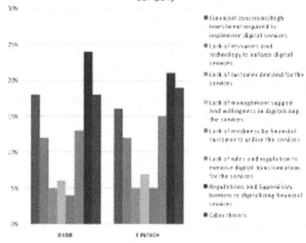

Figure 148.2 Conceptual framework
Source: Gangi et al., 2018; Disemadi, 2019

Figure 148.3 Comparison of Challenges: Faced by Transactions
Source: Author

Research methodology

Sampling:
- Purposive sampling, a non-probability technique, selected based on specific participant characteristics (Pakurár et al., 2019; Sumra et al., 2020; Brock and Von Wangenheim, 2019).

Questionnaire development:
- Development of a questionnaire as the research instrument.
- Ensured proper procedure in formulating each statement of the interview guide (Heavin and Power, 2018; Zouari and Abdelhedi, 2021).

Qualitative data analysis:
- Transcription used in analyzing qualitative data.
- Recorded interview audios processed through analysis and transcription (Alolayyan et al., 2018).
- NVivo Software version 12 employed for qualitative research analysis of digital transformation and its impacts (Wessel et al., 2021).
- Design support from NVivo Software 12 for pragmatic research and thematic analysis to organize research findings (Alam and Bahrein, 2021).

Result and analysis

The key areas of the data analysis use the demographic information of the participants and the findings from the collected data (Abbas, 2020). The participant characteristics are chosen based on the consideration of the viable banking solutions, leverage of power and intention to use, mobile banking technology, QR-code scanning and E-payments for security and payment privacy (Rabbani et al., 2021). The age connection between the 31 Years to 52 Years among the participants is according to the position and contribution to the research on digital transformation in the banking sector Figure 148.3.

The 60% male and 40% female contribution to the research on digital transformation for the banking sector is attributable as it reflects original and

Table 148.2 Features of the research participants.

Position	Specialization	Age	Gender	Exp	Education
Chief executive officer	Operations and digital banking	52 years	Male	25 Years	Post-graduate
President	Digital development and banking	54 years	Male	17 Years	Graduate
Vice-president	Digital sales in banking	47 years	Male	15 Years	Post-graduate
Manager	Banking business intelligence	40 years	Female	12 Years	Post-graduate
Controller	Banking customer intelligence	39 years	Male	10 Years	Graduate
Deputy manager	Banking Digital Procurement	33 years	Male	11 Years	Post-Graduate
Branch manager	Digitalization	31 years	Female	12 years	Graduate
Banking associate	Digital dealings	33 years	Female	09 Years	Graduate
Credit analyst	Digital credit facilitator	37 years	Male	13 years	Post-graduate

Source: Author's development

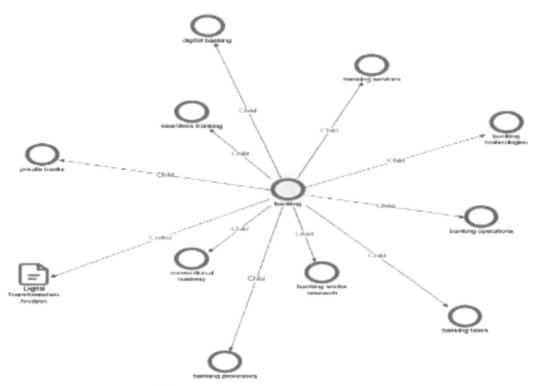

Figure 148.4 Digital Transformation of Banking Codes
Source: NVivo Software 12

experienced outcome. The experience of 17 years followed by 15 years are acceptable for the relatively higher positions of officers in the banking sector. These reflect the 12 years of experience followed by 10 years for vice-president, manager, and controller to reform the manual transfer of services into the digital services. The contribution of the deputy and branch manager leads toward the 11 and 12 years and 09 and 13 years of experience which costs for the quality management in banking.

The digital transformation has an impact on the verification of the deliverable quality standards of technology use in the financial sector. The assurance for the quality control are the leading areas of impacts on the products, services, and culture of banking. Quality management impacts from the available codes indicate the defect-free banking products which enable the seamless experience and outstanding transactions.

These codes and child connection with each of the concepts constructed as per the output from

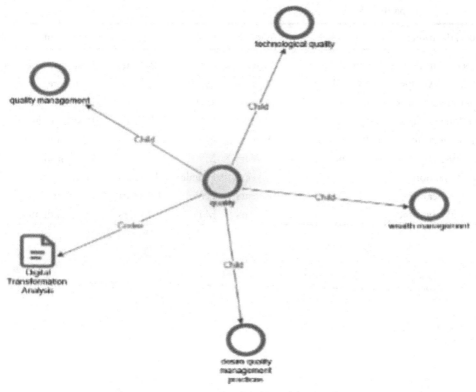

Figure 148.5 Quality management and technological use analysis
Source: NVivo Software 12

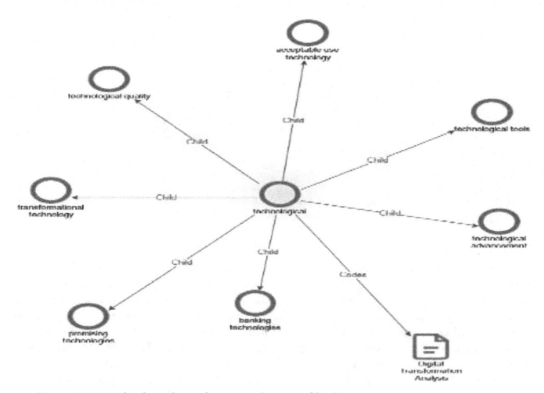

Figure 148.6 Technological transformation elements of banking sector
Source: NVivo Software 12

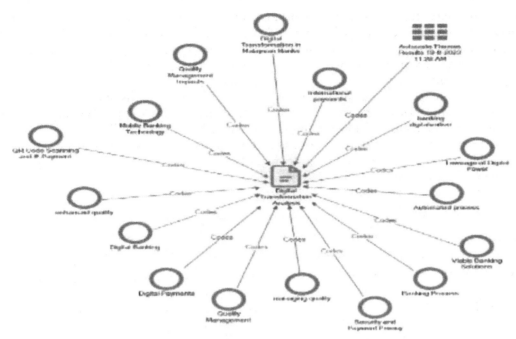

Figure 148.7 Quality management of digital transformation in banking sector
Source: NVivo Software 12

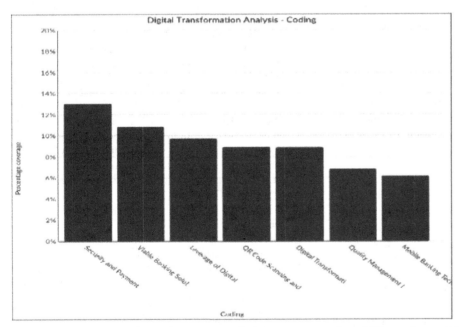

Figure 148.8 Digital transformation analysis in percentage from NVivo software 12
Source: NVivo Software 12

participant observation provides the managing of financial needs through advance digital means. The codes' illustrations of the development of technology for banking show how financial services have been able to take advantage of these developments for the benefit of its clients.

The instructions show how the financial system, company procedures, and changing business models are facilitating the process of recovery. Real-time data, which enables intelligent choices, has a similar ratio, and versatility aids in investing changes about job-related and the customer excursion. Banking businesses are guided by the digital transformation where electronic payments are unique credential of service those are adopted by the banks.

The digitalization of banking and the indication of reduced transaction expenses are made possible by it. For payments internationally, where banking digitalization is supporting the entire quality control process, automated handling of workable banking solutions is helpful. As international payments to control the digital transformation, viable banking solutions are connected to the effective administration of banking. The viable banking solutions connects with the quality management of banking in Malaysia as it is using the international payments for the regulation of the digital transformation. Banking digitalization and the process of quality management is efficient as illustrated from the respondent of this research in a practical way.

The banks are using multiple strategies to overcome the flaws in the process of transformation for mobile banking technology which has higher impacts on the quality management. This is to use digital transformation for the scanning of QR code where the analysis of coding engaged with improve customer efficiency. Banking services with the digital transformation reflects the innovative practices for the financial services. Most of the respondents agree that innovative steps are essential for meeting customer outlook. The digital wallets with the evolving role of advancement in artificial intelligence is supporting the data analytics for the quality management. Increasing efficiency is the enabling of banking to improve the speed and processing of manual labor into the accuracy of services.

Conclusion

The impacts of the digital transformation on the quality management of banking sector provides for the interlinking connection between the leverage of digital power, Key banking transformation, QR-code services and E-payment, security and payment privacy and viable banking solutions. The data-driven decision making of banking managers and CEOs is based on the risks of digitalization. It is to ensure the quality management factors with the collaboration of Fintech and open banking.

The research implications for the assistance and support of the financial working are influenced by the banking leverage of digital power, key banking transformation, QR-code services and E-payment, security and payment privacy and viable banking solutions. The startups' efforts to reinvent secure and anonymous payment are being thwarted by rivals from monetary solutions. Smart cards, also called chip cards, that are activated through a mobile device are used to facilitate online payment platforms, creating a digital purse. The scope of the digital business strategy is the scale and speed of banking value creation for digital banking. The shifts in customer expectations are the practical implications for the CEOs, managers, controllers, senior management of the banks. The use of technology for improved quality leadership is what is driving the technology use in banking.

References

Abad-Segura, E., González-Zamar, M. D., Infante-Moro, J. C., and Ruipérez García, G. (2020). Sustainable management of digital transformation in higher education: global research trends. *Sustainability*, 12(5), 2107.

Abbas, J. (2020). Impact of total quality management on corporate green performance through the mediating role of corporate social responsibility. *Journal of Cleaner Production*, 242, 118458.

Al Ahbabi, A. R., and Nobanee, H. (2019). Conceptual building of sustainable financial management and sustainable financial growth. Available at SSRN 3472313.

Alam, M. (2022). Understanding and improving digital tourism events in Pakistan. In Technology Application in Tourism Fairs, Festivals and Events in Asia (pp. 233–247). Singapore: Springer Singapore.

Alam, M., and Bahrein, K. (2021). Image branding factors and facilitating model of tourism destinations management during Covid-19 in Pakistan. *Journal of Tianjin University Science and Technology*, 54(10), 428–444. DOI: 10.17605/OSF.IO/956PY.

Alam, M., and Kuppusamy, M. (2023). Integrated management for image branding; a prospective outlook from Abbottabad as a tourism destination valley of Pakistan. In BESRA Germany, International Conference on Recent Developments in Social Science and Digital Economy / Washington DC.

Alam, M., Kuppusamy, M., and Kunasekaran, P. (2023). The role of destination management in mediating the determinants of Cyberjaya tourism image branding. *Cogent Business and Management*, 10(3), 2259579.

Albuhisi, A. M., and Abdallah, A. B. (2018). The impact of soft TQM on financial performance: the mediating roles of non-financial balanced scorecard perspectives. *International Journal of Quality and Reliability Management*, 35(7), 1360–1379.

Alhababsah, S., and Yekini, S. (2021). Audit committee and audit quality: an empirical analysis considering industry expertise, legal expertise, and gender diversity. *Journal of International Accounting, Auditing and Taxation*, 42, 100377.

Allan, G. (2020). Qualitative research. In Handbook for Research Students in the Social Sciences (pp. 177–189). Routledge.

149 The influence of destination marketing factors on destination image and intention to revisit

Han Zhenning[1] and Mudiarasan Kuppusamy[2,a]
[1]Faculty of Business, University of Cyberjaya, Malaysia
[2]School of Graduate Studies, Unirazak, Malaysia

Abstract

In this study, we delve into the crucial factors influencing tourists' intentions to revisit Malaysia, focusing on destination marketing aspects such as communication effectiveness and accessibility. By examining these factors through a quantitative research approach involving 381 participants from the tourism sector and relevant stakeholders, we uncover significant insights. Leveraging SPSS software, we conduct various tests to analyze the data against our research objectives. Our findings underscore the pivotal role of communication, attraction, destination information access, and overall accessibility in shaping tourists' intentions to return and enhancing Malaysia's destination image. We advocate for strategic destination management, emphasizing the need for targeted marketing efforts and harnessing technology to attract repeat visitors. Furthermore, we propose further investigation into each factor's individual impact to refine destination marketing strategies and bolster Malaysia's position as a premier tourism destination. This research contributes valuable insights for effective destination management and underlines the importance of continuous improvement in marketing strategies to sustain Malaysia's appeal to travelers.

Keywords: Accessibility, communication, destination marketing, image, revisit intention

Introduction

Tourist destinations thrive on repeat visits, relying on the amenities and activities managed by destination authorities. Marketing plays a pivotal role in influencing tourists' choices, aiming to create enticing experiences and raise awareness of specific locations. Effective communication strategies are crucial for destination marketing, fostering positive perceptions and enhancing reputation. Such efforts not only boost tourism but also stimulate local economies, fostering sustainable growth. Attractions, entertainment options, and diverse experiences are key components of destination marketing, enticing travelers to explore new places. Promotional activities, including conventional sales tactics and advertising, further promote destinations, aligning with organizational objectives and communication strategies. In the case of Malaysia, factors such as communication effectiveness, attractiveness, information accessibility, and overall convenience drive tourists' intentions to revisit, highlighting the core values of destination marketing in fostering enduring appeal and positive perceptions.

Literature Review

Table 149.1 Overview of destination marketing studies and insights.

Author name	Study	Findings/insights/interpretation
Han et al., 2019	The role of advertising in shaping destination image and attracting repeat visitors.	Utilizing advertising effectively contributes to a destination's appeal, encouraging tourists to consider revisiting.
Soliman, 2021	Collaborative approaches to destination marketing, with a focus on Malaysia.	Cooperative efforts enhance awareness of specific destinations, such as Malaysia, among potential travelers.
Youssef et al., 2019	Historical perspective on destination marketing, citing the case of Detroit in 1895.	Detroit's early marketing efforts laid the foundation for modern destination promotion strategies.
Chen et al., 2020	Historical context of destination marketing, referencing the Convention and Businessmen League in 1896.	The establishment of organizations like the Convention and Businessmen League marked the formalization of destination marketing practices.

[a]arasan@unirazak.edu.my

Author name	Study	Findings/insights/interpretation
Beritelli and Laesser, 2018; Ruiz-Real et al., 2020; Ivars-Baidal et al., 2021	Destination marketing strategies for sustainable tourism development.	Targeted marketing initiatives contribute to sustainable tourism practices and product development.
Joyner et al., 2018	Successful destination marketing campaigns, including Sin City's "Stays here" campaign.	Effective marketing campaigns, like Sin City's "Stays here," demonstrate the impact of strategic destination marketing.
Bausch and Unseld, 2018	Brand management and long-term marketing objectives in destination branding.	Destination branding involves long-term strategies aimed at establishing and managing brand identity.
Hahm and Severt, 2018; Okumus and Cetin, 2018	Brand management strategies for tourism destinations.	Strategic brand management contributes to the successful marketing and branding of tourism destinations.
Alcántara-Pilar et al., 2018	Considerations in destination marketing, including interaction, visual appeal, and accessibility.	Destination marketing involves various factors, such as interaction, visual appeal, and accessibility, to shape destination image.
Gardiner and Scott, 2018	Historical limitations in the conceptualization of tourist destination image.	Theoretical and conceptual limitations have influenced the understanding of tourist destination image since the 1970s and 1980s.
Lin et al., 2020	Perception and mindset in destination marketing.	Tourists' perceptions and mindsets play a crucial role in destination marketing, influencing their travel decisions and experiences.
Vinyals-Mirabent, 2019; Alam and Kuppusamy, 2023; Grundner and Neuhofer, 2021; del Barrio-Garcia and Prados-Peña, 2019	Factors influencing destination image, including communication, attractiveness, and accessibility.	Various factors, such as communication effectiveness and attractiveness, shape tourists' perceptions of destinations and influence their revisit intentions.
Al-Ansi and Han, 2019	The role of destination attractiveness in encouraging repeat visits.	Attractive destinations have a higher likelihood of enticing tourists to revisit, contributing to sustained tourism growth.
Losada and Mota, 2019; Zhang et al., 2018; Kovačević et al., 2018	The importance of destination image and tourist satisfaction in destination marketing.	Tourists' perceptions of a destination and their satisfaction play crucial roles in destination marketing effectiveness.
David-Negre et al., 2018	The significance of travel guides in promoting destination-specific experiences.	Travel guides play a vital role in promoting destination-specific experiences and mitigating travel-related challenges for tourists.

Source: Author

Conceptual Framework

The allure of tourists with revisit intentions hinges on the captivating image of destinations, shaping potential travelers' perceptions (Dedeoğlu et al., 2019). Destination marketing's framework, emphasizing image promotion, influences tourists' revisit intentions significantly (Jiménez-Barreto et al., 2020; Mahdzar and Gani, 2018). The correlation between destination marketing factors and destination image is pivotal for effective tourism service delivery, encompassing communication, attractiveness, information access, and accessibility.

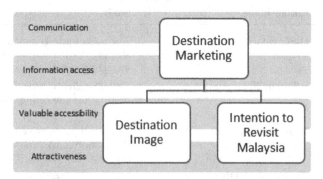

Figure 149.1 Conceptual framework
Source: Jiménez-Barreto et al., 2020; Dedeoğlu et al., 2019

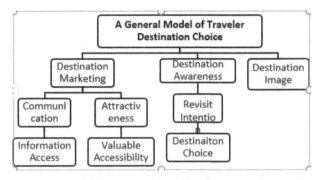

Figure 149.2 A general model of traveler destination choice

Source: Hassan and Hemdi, 2018; Saad et al., 2022

Table 149.1 Case processing summary.

	N	Percent
Included	381	100.0%
Excluded	0	0.0%
Total	381	100.0%

Source: Made by Author

Table 149.2 Reliability statistics.

Cronbach's alpha	N of items
0.94	31

Source: Author

A general model of traveler destination choice

Theoretical frameworks explore destination marketing's role in shaping tourist perceptions and revisit intentions in Malaysia (Kanwel et al., 2019). Key factors include communication, attractiveness, information access, and accessibility (Zins and Abbas Adamu, 2023; Rahman et al., 2022). Models like the General Model of Traveler Destination Choice highlight these factors' influence on visitors' decisions to return (Alam et al., 2023; Jahandide et al., 2020).

Research Methodology

- Quantitative research methodology enhances Malaysia's destination image and tourist revisit intentions (Yağmur and Aksu, 2020; Cheng et al., 2020; Mohammad et al., 2022).
- Descriptive research identifies factors impacting marketing and tourist intentions (Al-Dweik, 2020).
- Deductive approach explores destination marketing's role in shaping Malaysia's tourism image (Yağmur and Aksu, 2020; Jahandide et al., 2022; Liang and Xue, 2021).
- Positive research paradigm integrates destination marketing factors (Cheng et al., 2020).
- Quantitative methodology facilitates detailed analysis of marketing factors' impact on tourism (Mohammad et al., 2022; Schofield et al., 2022; Liang and Xue, 2021; Hassan and Hemdi, 2018).
- Survey sample of 381 participants drawn from a population of 50,000 (Zins and Abbas Adamu, 2023).
- Questionnaire employs Likert scale for comprehensive data collection (Jahandide et al., 2022; Cheng et al., 2020; Liang and Xue, 2021).
- SPSS software aids in statistical analysis for enhancing destination image and tourist intentions (Manyangara et al., 2023; Yağmur and Aksu, 2020)

Results and Discussions

This data analysis explores the multifaceted dynamics of destination marketing and its impact on tourists' revisit intentions and perceptions of Malaysia. Examining participant demographics, reliability, descriptive statistics, and correlation analysis offers insights into the effectiveness of marketing strategies in shaping destination image and visitor intentions.

- Factors influencing repeat visits encompass destination marketing, destination image, and facilitating factors.
- Participant demographics: 11.7% aged 18-25, 17.3% aged 26-34, 31% aged 35-45, and 205 male participants (54%), 175 female participants (46%).
- Destination marketing experience ranges from 0-17 years, with varying proportions across different experience brackets.
- Sample size: 381 participants included for effective data analysis.
- Reliability statistics: Cronbach's Alpha = .940, indicating excellent reliability Table 149.2).
- Descriptive statistics: Mean values for various factors range from 1.8793 to 3.2782, with standard deviation representing variability (Table 149.3).
- Frequency statistics present mean, median, mode, standard deviation, and skewness for different factors (Table 149.4).
- Correlation analysis reveals positive relationships among destination image, revisit intention, communication, and information access.
- Model summary indicates high model fit with R Square = 1.000, suggesting accuracy in predicting destination marketing outcomes.
- Study underlines

Table 149.3 Descriptive statistics.

	N	Minimum	Maximum	Mean	Std. deviation	Skewness		Kurtosis	
	statistic	statistic	statistic	statistic	statistic	Statistic	Std. error	statistic	Std. error
Destination marketing	381	1.00	4.00	3.2782	1.05195	-.889	.125	-.920	.249
Destination image	381	1.00	4.00	3.2782	1.05195	-.889	.125	-.920	.249
Destination revisit Intention	381	1.00	4.00	3.2782	1.05195	-.889	.125	-.920	.249
Communication	381	1.00	4.00	3.2782	1.05195	-.889	.125	-.920	.249
Information access	381	1.00	4.00	3.2782	1.05195	-.889	.125	-.920	.249
Valuable accessibility	381	1.00	4.00	3.0814	1.01369	-.225	.125	-1.874	.249
Attractiveness	381	1.00	4.00	1.8793	.55830	1.149	.125	5.398	.249
Valid N (listwise)	381								

Source: Author

Table 149.4 Frequency statistics.

	Destination marketing	Destination image	Destination revisit intention	Communication	Information access	Valuable accessibility	Attractiveness
N Valid	381	381	381	381	381	381	381
Missing	0	0	0	0	0	0	0
Mean	3.2782	3.2782	3.2782	3.2782	3.2782	3.0814	1.8793
Median	4.0000	4.0000	4.0000	4.0000	4.0000	4.0000	2.0000
Mode	4.00	4.00	4.00	4.00	4.00	4.00	2.00
Std. Deviation	1.05195	1.05195	1.05195	1.05195	1.05195	1.01369	.55830
Skewness	-.889	-.889	-.889	-.889	-.889	-.225	1.149
Std. error of Skewness	.196	.196	.196	.196	.196	.196	.196

Source: Author

Table 149.5 Model Summaryc.

Model	R	R Square	Adjusted R Square	Std. Error of the Estimate	Change statistics						Durbin-Watson
					R Square Change	F Change	df1	df2	Sig. F Change		
1	1.000	1.000	1.000	.00000	1.000	.321	3	377	.000		.339

a. Predictors: (constant), attractiveness, information access, valuable accessibility

b. Not computed because there is no residual variance.

c. Dependent variable: destination marketing

Source: Author

- the effective use of destination marketing factors, particularly destination image, in influencing revisit intentions.

- Importance of communication, information, accessibility, and attractiveness in shaping destination perceptions and intentions.

- Emphasis on enhancing subconscious and conscious mediation of destination attention through effective marketing strategies.
- Availability of amenities in vacation resorts serves as a key factor in attracting tourists and promoting destination appeal.

Conclusion

The research on the destination marketing factors for destination image and intention to revisit Malaysia are to analyze and examine the factors of destination image, revisit intention, communication, information access, valuable accessibility, and attractiveness. The image of the destination is inter-related with the revisit intention of tourist that provides for the access to comprehensive and timely information. Managers and the destination marketing representatives unfold the role of tourism destination visibility by practically presenting promotional tools of easy and accessible accommodation, shared communication among traveling agents and organization of special events for valuable accessibility. The real-life experiences are demonstrated by the platforms of the social media those are including Facebook, TikTok and Instagram. The factors of the communication, information access, valuable accessibility and attractiveness of a destination are encouraging features for the improve destination image to revisit Malaysia.

References

Afshardoost, M., and Eshaghi, M. S. (2020). Destination image and tourist behavioural intentions: a meta-analysis. *Tourism Management*, 81, 104154.

Alam, M. (2022). Understanding and improving digital tourism events in Pakistan. In Technology Applica-tion in Tourism Fairs, Festivals and Events in Asia (pp. 233–247). Singapore: Springer Singapore.

Alam, M., and Bahrein, K. (2021). Image branding factors and facilitating model of tourism destinations management during Covid-19 in Pakistan. *Journal of Tianjin University Science and Technology*, 54(10), 428–444. DOI: 10.17605/OSF.IO/956PY.

Alam, M., and Kuppusamy, M. (2023). Integrated management for image branding; a prospective outlook from abbottabad as a tourism destination valley of Pakistan. In Presented at BESRA Germany, International Conference on Recent Developments in Social Science and Digital Economy / Washington DC.

Alam, M., Kuppusamy, M., and Kunasekaran, P. (2023). The role of destination management in mediating the determinants of Cyberjaya tourism image branding. *Cogent Business and Management*, 10(3), 2259579.

Al-Ansi, A., and Han, H. (2019). Role of halal-friendly destination performances, value, satisfaction, and trust in generating destination image and loyalty. *Journal of Destination Marketing and Management*, 13, 51–60.

Alcántara-Pilar, J. M., Blanco-Encomienda, F. J., Armenski, T., and Del Barrio-García, S. (2018). The antecedent role of online satisfaction, perceived risk online, and perceived website usability on the affect towards travel destinations. *Journal of Destination Marketing and Management*, 9, 20–35.

Al-Dweik, M. R. (2020). Influence of event image and destination image on visitor satisfaction and intentions to revisit. *African Journal of Hospitality, Tourism and Leisure*, 9(4), 418–433.

Bausch, T., and Unseld, C. (2018). Winter tourism in Germany is much more than skiing! consumer motives and implications to Alpine destination marketing. *Journal of Vacation Marketing*, 24(3), 203–217.

Ben Youssef, K., Leicht, T., and Marongiu, L. (2019). Storytelling in the context of destination marketing: an analysis of conceptualisations and impact measurement. *Journal of Strategic Marketing*, 27(8), 696–713.

150 A robust stock market price prediction model utilizing the random forest algorithm

Ravi Thirumalaisamy[1], R. Velmurugan[2], Mahmoud Abouraia[1] and J. Sudarvel[2,a]

[1]Modern College of Business and Science, Sultanate of Oman

[2]KarpagamAcademy of Higher Education, Coimbatore, India

Abstract

This study explores the intricate world of stock market trading, emphasizing the challenge of analyzing the inherent nonlinear properties of stock market data. Focused on enhancing forecast accuracy, the paper introduces a hybrid machine learning model for stock price prediction. This model integrates the Whale Optimization Algorithm (WOA), a swarm intelligence algorithm, and the random forest (RF) machine learning model. Using Bombay Stock Exchange (BSE) data, the study involves dataset pre-processing, feature extraction through technical indicators, WOA-based feature selection, and RF model training/ testing. Evaluation metrics include MBE, RMSE, and MAPE, with comparisons against models like ABC-NB, ACO-SVM, and PSO-DT for validation.

Keywords: Machine learning, MAPE, MBE, RF, RMSE, stock prediction, WOA

Introduction

The stock market's equity serves as a long-term predictor of GDP per capita, influencing a nation's economic output. Economics divides into microeconomics (individuals, enterprises) and macroeconomics (national decisions affecting the entire economy). Due to the economy market's inherent non-linearity, thorough assessments are crucial for reliable trading. Two main analysis types exist: technical and fundamental. Fundamental analysis evaluates a company using both quantitative and qualitative indicators, requiring specialized knowledge. In contrast, technical analysis relies on intrinsic patterns like volume and price to deduce oscillations and key points. The buying and selling of financial products are centralized in a stock market or equity market (Thakkar and Chaudhari, 2021).

The share price, also known as the "stock price," is the price of shares in an equity market, where stocks of various publicly listed firms are traded. The company's stock price is a reliable indicator of its financial performance. Investors commonly rely on three main strategies for predicting the stock market: fundamental analysis, technical analysis (charting), and technology methods (ML) (Nti et al., 2020).

Literature Review

Table 150.1 ML and deep learning for risk reduction in trend prediction.

Author name	Study
Wu, D. (2021)	Proposed a hybrid model using ELM and wavelet transform for stock trend prediction, demonstrating enhanced accuracy on a dataset of 400 stocks.
Alotaibi, (2021)	Developed a stock market prediction model with feature extraction, selection, and Red Deer Adopted Wolf Algorithm for accurate predictions.
Nabipour, (2020)	Constructed an ML and deep learning model for trend prediction, highlighting the superiority of deep learning on both continuous and binary data.
Vijh, (2020)	Predicted closing prices for five businesses using an ANN and RF-based model with enhanced variables from financial datasets.
Wang, (2019)	Integrated news effects into a hybrid time-series predictive neural network model for stock price prediction, showing improved accuracy compared to baseline methods.

Source: Author

[a]drvelsngm@gmail.com, [b]j.sudarvel@gmail.com

Technical analysis

Technical analysis aims to predict stock market behavior by analyzing historical price charts and technical indicators. After pre-processing historical stock prices, relevant indicators are computed and input into predictive models Alotaibi (2021). Many stock market prediction methods utilize technical analysis techniques to forecast future stock value patterns. However, quantitative data alone may not capture the full complexity of businesses' financial situations. Unstructured data from social networks and news sites can complement quantitative information, enhancing prediction systems, especially in the context of current social media trends. The simple moving average (SMA) is a commonly used technical indicator, often alongside EMA, MACD, and RSI in analyses (Nti et al., 2020).

The accessibility of extensive data insights has prompted numerous researchers to employ machine learning (ML) techniques in the stock market Nabipour et al. (2020). Some research papers have demonstrated promising outcomes from these efforts (Argade et al., 2022).

Two approaches exist for forecasting stock market behavior: predicting a stock's future price or projecting its future price direction (trend forecasting) (Gupta et al., 2019). ML has shown potential in predicting the stock market by testing and training models with social media data, historical datasets, or financial trends. ML aims to construct effective and efficient models for accurate forecasts. Various supervised ML approaches have improved stock market predictions, with the RF algorithm being widely used due to its superior results (Lawal et al., 2020). This study proposes combining the WOA with RF for stock price forecasting, leveraging soft computing and ML models in stock market analysis (Wu et al., 2021).

Research methodology

This study developed a stock price prediction model comprising four phases: data preprocessing, feature extraction, optimal feature selection, and prediction. Figure 150.1 illustrates the workflow. Technical features were derived using indicators like RSI, SMA, EMA, MACD, and OBV. Feature dimensionality, a common challenge, affecting prediction accuracy, was addressed using the WOA algorithm for optimal feature selection Vijh et al. (2020). Chosen features underwent regression analysis, and the final predictions were obtained from the RF model.

The stock price data, being a time series, underwent initial normalization. Feature extraction utilized stock technical indicators. WOA was employed for feature

selection, and the RF algorithm predicted the stock price.

Data preprocessing

The data underwent standardization to the interval [0, 1] using the following equation in preparation for the prediction model.

$$y_i = \frac{x_i - x_{min}}{x_{max} - x_{min}} (h_i - l_i) \tag{1}$$

In this case, y_i is the input or output's normalized values, x_i is the actual output or input values, x_{min} is the minimum actual output or input values, and x_{max} is the maximum actual output or input values. Additionally, h_i is the normalizing interval's upper bound (which is 1 in this scenario), and l_i is the normalizing interval's lower bound (0 in this scenario), which distinguished the useful signal from the unwanted noise in an effective manner [11].

Here, (y_i) represents the normalized input or output values, (x_i) denotes the actual input or output values, x_{min} is the minimum actual input or output value, and x_{max} is the maximum actual input or output value. h_i is the upper bound of the normalizing interval (1 in this case), and (l_i) is the lower bound (0 in this case), effectively distinguishing useful signals from unwanted noise [11].

Feature extraction

Figure 150.1 Proposed Model Workflow
Source: Author

Feature extraction in this study involved applying technical indicators to normalized data. The proposed model employed this approach, and the subsequent discussion will delve into the technical indicators.

The RSI indicator assesses whether a stock is over-bought or oversold.

The simple moving average (SMA) is obtained by summing up the latest closing values of a stock and dividing the total by the number of periods in the calculation average.

The EMA is similar to the SMA, except that the calculation of the EMA for a specific day relies on the EMA calculations for all preceding days.

The MACD, a momentum indicator, predicts stock market movements by comparing short and long-term trends. It calculates the difference between a 26-day exponential moving average and a 12-day EMA to derive the MACD.

The OBV indicator serves as both a lagging and momentum indicator, utilizing volume flow to predict stock price swings. A rising OBV indicates potential future stock price increases, while a falling OBV suggests potential declines (Wang et al., 2019).

WOA

In solving complex optimization problems within time constraints and intricate restrictions, meta-heuristic methodologies mimic biological and physiological processes. The Whale Optimization Algorithm (WOA), a bio-inspired meta-heuristic, simulates the social behavior of humpback whales, specifically the foraging method known as the bubble net. This method involves encircling, searching, and attacking prey. The algorithm initializes with random positions for whale populations and sets parameters for exploitation and exploration. Fitness evaluation is performed using various benchmark functions, with the whale exhibiting the highest fitness considered the best search agent. Adjusting the control parameter (A) influences the search agent's location. Iterations continue with adaptive movement until the whale settles in the position representing the optimal solution. Parameter 'p' is modified during iterations, and the best search operator from the latest iteration is considered the optimal solution.

Random forest

The RF method is versatile, applicable to both classification and regression problems. It utilizes a decision tree approach, randomly selecting features as dividers for multiple decision trees forming an ensemble. Each tree makes a prediction and votes for the class, with the majority determining the category. For regression, the average prediction is used. RF's key components

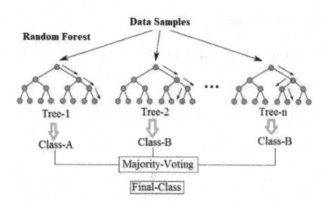

Figure 150.2 Architecture of RF
Source: Author

are random sampling of training data during tree construction and random feature selection when splitting nodes. In the process, a bootstrap sample, with the same size as the original dataset, is generated by randomly selecting entries, allowing duplicates (Argade et al., 2022).

In the next step, a random subset of input features is chosen before node separation. This involves building a decision tree using the bootstrap dataset while limiting the selection to a random subset of variables at each step.

Applying the same approach, a specified number (N) of bootstrap samples and decision trees are generated.

Currently, the data is sequentially processed, starting with the first tree and progressing through each subsequent tree.

Data pass through each branch of the RF tree, and the option with the most votes is considered. Consequently, the result is influenced by a substantial vote.

Results and discussion

To assess the proposed model's effectiveness, performance analysis was conducted on the Bombay Stock Exchange's stock dataset spanning February 3, 2017, to January 31, 2023. The predicted closing prices underwent evaluation using root mean square error (RMSE), mean bias error (MBE), and mean absolute percentage error (MAPE) to identify minimized overall prediction errors Figure 150.2. The predicted results were then compared with other ML models for validation.

Performance evaluation

Performance analysis involves three parameters: MBE, MAPE, and RMSE, computed using the following equations.

$$MAPE = \frac{1}{n}\sum_{i=1}^{n}\frac{(O_i - P_i)}{O_i} \qquad (2)$$

Table 150.2 Performance comparison on BSE dataset.

Models	RMSE	MAPE	MBE
ABC-NB	0.5842	0.934	-0.0355
ACO-SVM	0.5561	0.8493	-0.0332
PSO-DT	0.4908	0.8569	-0.0293
WOA-RF	0.411	0.7705	-0.0149

Source: Author

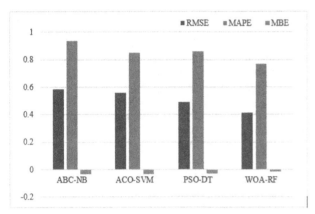

Figure 150.3 Performance comparison on BSE dataset
Source: Author

$$RMSE = \sqrt{\frac{\sum_{i=1}^{n}(O_i - P_i)^2}{n}} \qquad (3)$$

$$MBE = \frac{1}{n}\sum_{i=1}^{n}(O_i - P_i) \qquad (4)$$

Here, Q_i indicates the actual closing price, P_i indicates the predicted closing price and n indicates the data size.

Table 150.2 presents a comparative analysis of error performance among models using the BSE stock dataset. The evaluated error values for the WOA-RF model are displayed, along with a performance comparison against other models like Artificial Bee Colony-Naïve Bayes (ABC-NB), Ant Colony Optimization-Support Vector Machine (ACO-SVM), and Particles Swarm Optimization-Decision Tree (PSO-DT). The WOA-RF model demonstrated the lowest error rates across all parameters, including RMSE, MAPE, and MBE. Compared to other models, WOA-RF achieved values of 0.4110 RMSE, 0.7705 MAPE, and -0.0149 MBE. Notably, all models in this experiment yielded negative MBE values, indicating underestimation of data. In conclusion, the proposed WOA-RF model outperformed other models in this comparison.

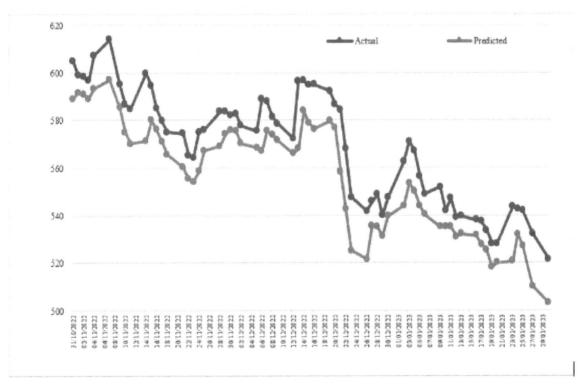

Figure 150.4 WOA-RF model
Source: Author

Figure 150.3 illustrates the performance comparison of the proposed model with other models based on RMSE, MBE, and MAPE. The evaluation covers a 65-day period from the test dataset. Figure 150.4 depicts the comparison between actual and predicted values by the WOA-RF model. The results indicate that the proposed WOA-RF model efficiently predicts the closing stock prices in this study.

Conclusion

This research proposes an effective stock price forecasting model, employing a hybrid approach combining the Whale Optimization Algorithm (WOA), swarm intelligence algorithm and the RF machine learning technique. The WOA-RF model's evaluation utilized BSE stock data from February 3, 2017, to January 31, 2023. The dataset underwent preprocessing, including normalization and application of stock technical indicators for feature extraction. The WOA algorithm facilitated feature selection from the extracted dataset features. Subsequently, the data was divided for training and testing the RF model for prediction analysis. Evaluation metrics such as RMSE, MBE, and MAPE were employed to analyze error performance. Comparative assessments were made with other models (ABC-NB, ACO-SVM, and PSO-DT) for validation. Future improvements could involve incorporating deep learning models and optimizing with advanced techniques.

References

Alotaibi, S. S. (2021). Ensemble technique with optimal feature selection for Saudi stock market prediction: a novel hybrid red deer-grey algorithm. *IEEE Access*, 9, 64929–64944.

Argade, S., Chothe, P., Gawande, A., Joshi, S., and Birajdar, A. (2022). Machine learning in stock market prediction: a review. Retrieved from SSRN: http://dx.doi.org/10.2139/ssrn.4128716.

Gupta, A., Bhatia, P., Dave, K., and Jain, P. (2019). Stock market prediction using data mining techniques. In 2nd International Conference on Advances in Science and Technology (ICAST) (pp. 1–5).

Lawal, Z. K., Yassin, H., and Zakari, R. Y. (2020). Stock market prediction using supervised machine learning techniques: an overview. In IEEE Asia-Pacific Conference on Computer Science and Data Engineering (CSDE) (pp. 1–6).

Nabipour, M., Nayyeri, P., Jabani, H. S., and Mosavi, A. (2020). Predicting stock market trends using machine learning and deep learning algorithms via continuous and binary data; a comparative analysis. *IEEE Access*, 8, 150199–150212.

Nti, I. K., Adekoya, A. F., and Weyori, B. A. (2020). A systematic review of fundamental and technical analysis of stock market predictions. *Artificial Intelligence Review*, 53, 3007–3057.

Thakkar, A., and Chaudhari, K. (2021). A comprehensive survey on portfolio optimization, stock price and trend prediction using particle swarm optimization. *Archives of Computational Methods in Engineering*, 28, 2133–2164.

Vijh, M., Chandola, D., Tikkiwal, V. A., and Kumar, A. (2020). Stock closing price prediction using machine learning techniques. *Procedia Computer Science*, 167, 599–606.

Wang, Y., Liu, H., Guo, Q., Xie, S., and Zhang, X. (2019). Stock volatility prediction by hybrid neural network. *IEEE Access*, 7, 154524–154534.

Wu, D., Wang, X., and Wu, S. (2021). A hybrid method based on extreme learning machine and wavelet transform denoising for stock prediction. *Entropy*, 23(440), 1–30.

151 A mathematical prediction model for equity markets centered on key players in the Indian stock market

Ravi Thirumalaisamy[1,a], Mahmoud Abouraia[2,b], Mohanambal Palanisamy[3,c], R. Velmurugan[4,d] and J. Sudarvel[5,e]

[1]Assistant Professor, Department of Accounting, Finance and Economics, Faculty of Business and Economics, Modern College of Business and Science, Sultanate of Oman

[2]Professor, Department of Accounting, Finance and Economics, Faculty of Business and Economics, Modern College of Business and Science, Sultanate of Oman

[3]Senior Lecturer in Mathematics, Modern College of Business and Science, Sultanate of Oman

[4]Associate Professor of Commerce, Karpagam Academy of Higher Education, Coimbatore, India

[5]Assistant Professor of Management, Karpagam Academy of Higher Education, Coimbatore, India

Abstract

This research addresses equity market prediction, crucial due to associated risks. Leveraging computationally intelligent technologies, deep learning (DL) stands out for automated feature learning, multilayer features learning, enhanced efficiency, powerful generalization, and new data detection. The study proposes a hybrid model, combining stacked denoising autoencoder (SDAE) DL technique with linear regression (LR) to forecast closing prices of top Indian stocks (Reliance Industries, TCS, HDFC Bank). Preprocessing involves handling missing values and standardization. SDAE selects features, followed by LR for prediction. Evaluation metrics include RMSE, MAPE, and correlation coefficient R for accuracy assessment.

Keywords: Deep learning, Indian stock market, LR, SDAE, statistical analysis

Introduction

The stock market, a public platform for trading equity securities, raises capital for diverse purposes like research, development, product launches, market entry, financial growth, and acquisitions (Islam et al., 2018). A share signifies ownership in a firm, impacting a nation's economy and social structure (Islam et al., 2018). Globally, economic growth hinges on financial operations' outcomes, with stocks offering high-risk, high-return potential (Le et al., 2020). Accurate predictions are vital before investing. Forecasting stock prices via time series poses challenges for investors and analysts (Le et al., 2020). Successful predictions could yield substantial profits.

The equity market is a crucial element in a nation's economic and social structure. Forecasting it poses challenges for analysts, investors, and finance scholars due to the complex, nonparametric, noisy, volatile, non-linear, chaotic, and dynamic nature of time series stock prices (Strader et al., 2020).

Stock and asset prices significantly impact economic activities and serve as indicators of the social and emotional condition, historically reflecting a country's economic status. A growing stock market suggests economic improvement, presenting investment opportunities for both foreign and domestic investors in India, a rapidly developing country. The two primary stock exchanges in India are the following:

- National Stock Exchange (NSE)
- Bombay Stock Exchange (BSE)

Established in 1875, the BSE is India's oldest stock exchange, while the NSE started trading in 1994. These exchanges list major Indian corporations. The BSE has around 5000 listed companies, surpassing the NSE's 2000. Despite having fewer listed companies, the NSE holds a significant share in trading, contributing over seventy percent of the market shares. The market's overall performance is gauged through the index, a leading predictor of stock market behavior. The two primary indicators or indexes that are tracked by the Indian stock market are:

- Sensex
- Nifty

Additional indices, like the IT, bank, and automobile indices, depict specific industry performances;

[a]ravi@mcbs.edu.om, [b]Mahmoud.Abouraia@mcbs.edu.om, [c]mohanambal@mcbs.edu.om, [d]drvelsngm@gmail.com, [e]j.sudarvel@gmail.com

however, the most crucial ones are the Sensex and Nifty. The Sensex, comprising 30 equities, reflects overall market sentiment on the BSE. Movement in the Sensex indicates the majority of stock values moving either up or down. Nifty, an indicator for NSE-listed companies, comprises 50 stocks (Kumar et al., 2021).

Previously, investors relied on personal expertise to identify market patterns, but this approach is impractical in today's vast and rapidly executed markets. Basic statistical analysis of financial data may provide insights, yet investment organizations increasingly turn to artificial intelligence (AI) systems, including machine learning (ML) and deep learning (DL) models, to analyze large real-time equity and economic data sets. These systems assist human decision-making in investments, with their features and performance now studied to identify those with superior predictive capabilities compared to other methods (Dopi et al., 2021).

Successful stock market investment demands a nuanced grasp of complexities and the interpretation of vast information. Recently, DL techniques have gained attention for their potential to enhance market forecasting compared to traditional methods. This study aims to construct a DL-based model for stock market behavior prediction, employing computational strategies rooted in soft computing and DL models to address market analysis and prediction challenges. The research utilizes an SDAE method for noise-resistant network pretraining and employs the LR method in the top layer for making stock price predictions.

Literature Review

Due to the notable depreciation of the Indian currency, precise predictions in the equity market are crucial to protect investors' interests. A study (Idrees et al., 2019) introduced an initial exploration of time series forecasting and analysis for India's economy, employing an ARIMA model to forecast the volatility of the Indian equity market. The model utilized publicly accessible time series data, and a comparative analysis between predicted and actual time series indicated an average variation of approximately five percent for Sensex and Nifty. The study suggests that the ARIMA method, known for its efficacy in handling time series data, has constructive potential for addressing real-world issues.

In Cao and Wang's (2020) study, principal component analysis (PCA) was employed to evaluate the key financial data indices for selected businesses, creating a comprehensive evaluation index for an accurate prediction model. Subsequently, both financial and transaction indicators were simultaneously utilized as input variables in stock price prediction research. Three different Back Propagation Neural Network (BPNN) algorithms were implemented. The combination of PCA and BPNN was applied for stock price prediction, and a blend of traditional stock selection analysis methods was used to develop a diverse quantitative investment stock selection approach. Comparative results favored the Bayesian regularization approach in BPNN, showcasing superior prediction accuracy.

Unexpected events can significantly impact financial markets, potentially leading to calamitous consequences. For investors, accurately quantifying the key factors influencing the aftermath of such events and efficiently assessing market reactions is crucial, especially in the context of event-driven investing strategies on a global scale. In Li et al. (2021), a CNN-based classification model was developed on a news dataset with binary labels to detect unexpected occurrences. The CNN-binary classifier determined whether the news was related to unexpected incidents, and a decision tree was proposed for specific unexpected events to reduce false positives. The identification and extraction models achieved accuracy levels of 91.3% and 93.7%, respectively.

A successful forecast provides numerous benefits, influencing financial traders' decisions on buying or selling instruments. When considering investments and stock transactions, investors often prioritize the stock price index. In Nikou et al. (2019), the study aimed to predict the closing prices of iShares MSCI UK at the end of the trading day, assessing the accuracy of ML models in stock market forecasting. Four ML algorithms—artificial neural network, SVR, RF, and LSTM—were implemented for prediction. The investigation revealed that the recurrent neural networks, specifically those incorporating LSTM blocks, outperformed other models in forecasting closing prices.

Predicting stock index prices is a common practice in academic and economic circles, but the presence of unknown noise makes it challenging. In Gao et al. (2020), four ML techniques, including MLP, CNN, Long Short-Term Memory, and an attention-based neural network, were applied to estimate index prices. The goal was to predict the next day's index price using historical data, daily trade data, macroeconomic variables, and technical indicators as input variables. The attention-based model demonstrated superior overall performance compared to the other models. In financial time series analysis, numerous indications can influence the general movement of stock prices.

Methodology

This paper proposes a DL-based stock prediction model, named SDAE-LR, to estimate the stock market's closing price. DL models are frequently used in prediction applications, leading to the development of the SDAE-LR hybrid model. The model's process flow is depicted in Figure 151.1. The stock dataset considers the top three businesses in India based on market capitalization—HDFC Bank, Reliance Industries, and Tata Consultancy Services. Market capitalization is determined by the current share price and total outstanding stocks, and historical stock data for these companies was compiled accordingly.

A. Data preprocessing

This research analyzes historical stock data for Reliance Industries, TCS, and HDFC Bank from January 1, 2020, to February 1, 2023. The dataset, in CSV format, includes columns labeled Open, Low, High, Adj Close, Close, and Volume. The data preprocessing involves inspection, standardization, and the application of technical indicators for feature extraction (Gao et al., 2020). The main emphasis is on ensuring data accuracy and completeness by eliminating any missing or inaccurate data.

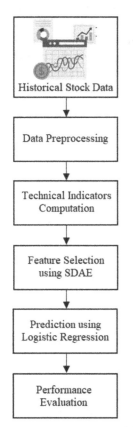

Figure 151.1 Workflow of the proposed model
Source: Author

B. Feature extraction

Feature extraction involved applying technical indicators—exponential moving average (EMA), average true range (ATR), relative strength index (RSI), and rate of change (ROC)—to standardized data.

EMAs have a shorter lag time compared to SMAs because they are more responsive to market price changes. The calculation period for the moving average influences the importance assigned to the most recent price. A higher weight is given to the most recent price when calculating the EMA with more recent price information.

$$EMA_{pdv} = \left[pdv * \left(\frac{S}{1+Days}\right)\right] + EMA_{ydv} * \left(1 - \left(\frac{S}{1+Days}\right)\right) \tag{1}$$

In equation (1), pdv represents the current day's value, ydv denotes the previous day's value, and S is the smoothing element.

ATR gauges the range sensitivity for a given day, attempting to consider the specific difference from the preceding day's close.

$$ATR = Avg\left(True_{range}, time\right) \tag{2}$$

$$True_{range} = \max(hp - lp), \left(hp - P_{past}\right), \left(P_{past} - lp\right) \tag{3}$$

Here, *hp* represents the highest price, *lp* denotes the lowest price, and P_{past} is the latest price.

RSI is computed by comparing the smoothed average absolute value of the loss over a period to the smoothed time-period average gains.

$$RSI = 100 - \left(\frac{100}{1+RS}\right) \tag{4}$$

ROC is determined by comparing current prices to prices noted a set number of days ago, calculating the percentage change in price values. It is often viewed as an indicator of overall momentum.

$$ROC = \left(\left(C_{price}/Price\right) - 1.0\right) * 100 \tag{5}$$

Equation (5) uses the variable C_{price} to represent the current stock price.

C. SDAE

The SDAE can be adapted for stock index forecasting. Its deep neural network architecture learns a condensed features representation from historical input data on volume and price for all index stocks. In the presented methodology, volume data and minute prices for each stock may initially have a predetermined corruption level, as illustrated by equation (6).

$$\hat{Z} = f(Z) \quad (6)$$

Subsequently, the corrupted sample $\hat{Z}$ is transformed into a high-dimensional intermediate output with over-completed hidden layers. The output size gradually decreases from one layer to the next until it reaches the central layers, serving as an effective nonlinear feature selection applied to the initial inputs.

For the transformation and reconstruction, weights (W_l), biases (b_l), and b_l' are employed for each layer l, as defined in equations (7) and (8). The layer's dimension is then reset by reversing the transformation using the same weights and bias settings. The Euclidean loss, derived by comparing the reconstructed data $\tilde{Z}$ to the initial input data Z, measures the difference between the two. To enhance generalization accuracy, the loss function incorporates sparsity constraints and L2 regularization. Equation (9) presents the loss function along with the learning rate λ. The loss is back-propagated into the network, and stochastic gradient descent updates the parameters.

$$h_l = g\left(W_l \hat{Z} + b_l\right) \quad (7)$$

$$\tilde{Z} = g(W_l h_l + b_l') \quad (8)$$

$$Loss = \sum\left(\tilde{Z} - Z\right)^2 + \lambda(\|W\|^2 + \|W\|^2) \quad (9)$$

After training, an LR layer was added atop to categorize the newly learned representations into two classes: decrease or increase. This pertains to predicting the movement direction of stock indices in the subsequent period. Once each layer was pre-trained, the rightmost layer was removed, and the LR layer was applied for fine-tuning every layer. Both the encoder and decoder share the same weight. This training method for an SDAE is the most efficient, converting tainted inputs into condensed feature representations in Layer four. The LR classification determines whether stock indices will increase in the next period (Li et al., 2017).

D. Logistic regression

Regression analysis is a statistical procedure used for modeling and estimating connections between variables, focusing on the relationship between a dependent variable and one or more independent variables. This concept encompasses various modeling and evaluation techniques. LR has become crucial in machine learning, primarily for classifying new data based on past data. Logistic regression and linear regression diverge in the selection of a parametric model and assumptions. Despite this distinction, logistic regression follows overarching concepts similar to linear regression, drawing motivation from the techniques used in linear regression analysis.

Let Y be the response variable, taking values of either 0 or 1. The predicted response π(x) is solely determined by the probability that the response variable assumes the value 1.

The mathematical expression for the logistic response function is presented in equation (10).

$$E(Y/x) = \pi(x) = \exp(\beta_0 + \beta_1 x) / \{1 + \exp(\beta_0 + \beta_1 x)\} \quad (9)$$

$$\eta = \beta_0 + \beta_1 x = \ln[\pi(x)/\{1 - \pi(x)\}] \quad (10)$$

Equation (11) represents the logit transform of the variable x.

The model acts as a link function between the linear expression and the probability, where the odds are given by $\pi(x)/\{1 - \pi(x)\}$, expressed as a ratio. Maximum likelihood is employed to estimate β_0 and β_1, denoted by $\widehat{\beta_0}$ and $\widehat{\beta_1}$.

Once coefficients are estimated, relevant hypotheses are tested to determine the accuracy of the model and whether the included independent variables have a significant relationship with the outcome variable. The odds ratio is given by equation (11).

$$\frac{O_{xi+1}}{O_{xi}} = \theta^{\beta_1} \quad (11)$$

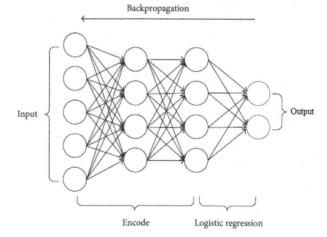

Figure 151.2 Architecture of SDAE-LR
Source: Author

The odds ratio represents the expected increase in probabilities of achieving objectives with a one-unit change in the predicted variable (Ananthakumar and Sarkar, 2017). It's crucial to note that the LR classifier is a component of the network, and the prediction outcomes are indicated by the LR layer, which is also the overall network result.

Results and Discussion

This section describes the performance of the SDAE-LR model in both experimental and evaluation aspects. The experiment was conducted separately on each of the three datasets, comparing the results with established validation methods. The data was divided into two sections: the training set, used for model training and parameter updating, and the testing set, used for data forecasting. In all approaches, ninety percent of the data were used for model training, and ten percent were employed to assess model performance.

A. Performance evaluation
In this section, accuracy metrics are employed to evaluate and compare the proposed model's performance with other models. Three traditional indicators—root-mean square errors (RMSE), mean absolute percentage errors (MAPE), and correlation coefficients (R)—are chosen as metrics for the predictive performance of the model. The equations for these indicators are presented below:

$$MAPE = \frac{1}{n}\sum_{i=1}^{n}\left|\frac{(a_i - p_i)}{a_i}\right| \tag{12}$$

$$RMSE = \sqrt{\frac{1}{n}\sum_{i=1}^{n}(a_i - p_i)} \tag{13}$$

$$R = \frac{\sum_{i=1}^{n}(a_i - b_i)(p_i - c_i)}{\sqrt{\sum_{i=1}^{n}(a_i - b_i)^2 (p_i - c_i)^2}} \tag{14}$$

The original series that must be forecast is denoted by a_i in the aforementioned equations, and the original series mean was denoted by b_i. The anticipated series was denoted by p_i and can be derived from the model output. The mean of the predicted series was denoted by c_i. n is the size of the dataset.

In the equations mentioned earlier, the original series to be forecast is represented by a_i, and its mean is denoted by b_i. The anticipated series, derived from the model output, is denoted by p_i, and its mean is represented by c_i. The dataset size is denoted by n.

Table 151.1 compares the error performance of models using the Reliance Industries stock dataset.

Table 151.1 Performance evaluation comparison on reliance dataset.

Models	RMSE	MAPE	R
BPNN	15.6836	0.8502	0.8909
PCA-NB	12.0675	0.7588	0.9250
AE-SVM	10.4338	0.6826	0.9404
SDAE-LR	9.4660	0.5574	0.9584

Source: Author

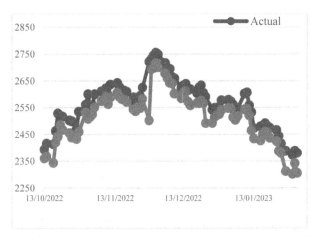

Figure 151.3 Comparison of actual values vs predicted values on reliance dataset
Source: Author

Table 151.2 Performance evaluation comparison on TCS dataset.

Models	RMSE	MAPE	R
BPNN	16.0706	0.9165	0.8738
PCA-NB	13.8261	0.7959	0.9012
AE-SVM	11.8996	0.7230	0.9259
SDAE-LR	10.0081	0.6827	0.9417

Source: Author

The evaluated error values of the SDAE-LR model are presented alongside other models such as BPNN, auto encoder-support vector machine (AE-SVM), and principal component analysis-Naïve bayes (PCA-NB). The SDAE-LR model demonstrated the lowest error rates in all parameters, including RMSE and MAPE, and a higher correlation coefficient value. Compared to other methods, the SDAE-LR model achieved 9.4660 RMSE, 0.5574 MAPE, and 0.9584 correlation coefficient. Figure 151.3 illustrates the comparison of actual values vs. predicted values for the Reliance dataset.

Table 151.2 presents a performance comparison of models using the TCS stock dataset. The SDAE-LR model exhibited the lowest error rates in all parameters,

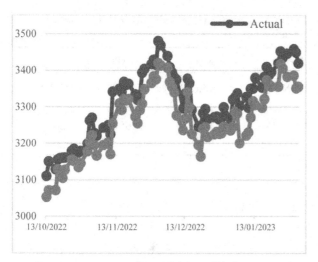

Figure 151.4 Comparison of Actual Values vs Predicted Values on TCS Dataset
Source: Author

Table 151.3 Performance Evaluation Comparison on HDFC Dataset.

Models	RMSE	MAPE	R
BPNN	13.3935	0.9058	0.9082
PCA-NB	10.1269	0.8589	0.9297
AE-SVM	9.6554	0.7011	0.9538
SDAE-LR	8.9845	0.6424	0.9640

Source: Author

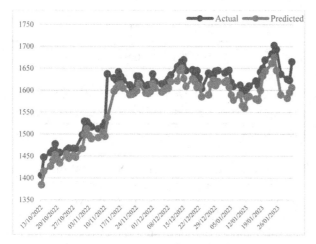

Figure 151.5 Comparison of actual values vs predicted values on HDFC dataset
Source: Author

including RMSE and MAPE, and a higher correlation coefficient value. Compared to other methods, the SDAE-LR model achieved 10.0081 RMSE, 0.6827 MAPE, and 0.9417 correlation coefficient. Figure

151.4 illustrates the comparison of actual values vs. predicted values for the TCS dataset.

Table 151.3 compares the performance of models using the HDFC stock dataset. The SDAE-LR model achieved 8.9845 RMSE, 0.6424 MAPE, and 0.9640 correlation coefficient, outperforming other methods. Figure 151.5 illustrates the comparison of actual values vs. predicted values for the HDFC dataset. The obtained results indicate that the proposed SDAE-LR model demonstrates efficient performance in predicting the closing price of the stock data in this study.

Conclusion

This study proposes a hybrid stock price prediction model utilizing both deep learning (DL) and statistical techniques to forecast the top 3 Indian stock market data. The hybrid model combines a DL method, stacked denoising autoencoder (SDAE), with a linear technique, logistic regression (LR), for predicting stock closing prices. The SDAE-LR model is evaluated using data from three Indian stocks—Reliance Industries, TCS, and HDFC—spanning from October 10, 2022, to February 1, 2023. The dataset is preprocessed to address missing values and standardization. Stock technical indicators are then applied to extract features, followed by the application of the SDAE architecture for feature selection. The data is divided into training and testing sets for LR classifier prediction. Model evaluation employs RMSE, MAPE, and correlation coefficient (R) to analyze error performances and assess accuracy. The obtained results are compared with other models (BPNN, PCA-NB, and AE-SVM) for validation. Future implementations could extend the proposed model to international stock datasets for a global stock market analysis.

References

Ananthakumar, U., and Sarkar, R. (2017). Application of logistic regression in assessing stock performances. In 2017 IEEE 15th Intl Conf on Dependable, Autonomic and Secure Computing, 15th Intl Conf on Pervasive Intelligence and Computing, 3rd Intl Conf on Big Data Intelligence and Computing and Cyber Science and Technology Congress (DASC/PiCom/DataCom/CyberSciTech), (pp. 1242–1247).

Cao, J., and Wang, J. (2020). Exploration of stock index change prediction model based on the combination of principal component analysis and artificial neural network. *Soft Computing*, 24, 7851–7860.

Dopi, G. Y., Hartanto, R., and Fauziati, S. (2021). Systematic literature review: stock price prediction using machine learning and deep learning. In International Conference on Management, Business, and Technology (ICOMBEST 2021) (pp. 52–61).

Gao, P., Zhang, R., and Yang, X. (2020). The application of stock index price prediction with neural network. *Mathematical and Computer Applications*, 25(53), 1–16.

Idrees, S. M., Alam, M. A., and Agarwal, P. (2019). A prediction approach for stock market volatility based on time series data. *IEEE Access*, 7, 17287–17298.

Islam, M. R., Al-Shaikhli, I. F. T., and Abdulkadir, A. (2018). A scientific review of soft-computing techniques and methods for stock market prediction. *International Journal of Engineering and Technology*, 7(2.5), 27–31.

Kumar, G., Jain, S., and Singh, U. P. (2021). Stock market forecasting using computational intelligence: a survey. *Archives of Computational Methods in Engineering*, 28, 1069–1101.

Le, D. Y. N., Maag, A., and Senthilananthan, S. (2020). Analysing stock market trend prediction using machine and deep learning models: a comprehensive review. In 5th International Conference on Innovative Technologies in Intelligent Systems and Industrial Applications (CITISIA) (pp. 1–10).

Li, J., Liu, G., Yeung, H. W. F., Yin, J., Chung, Y. Y., and Chen, X. (2017). A novel stacked denoising autoencoder with swarm intelligence optimization for stock index prediction. In 2017 International Joint Conference on Neural Networks (IJCNN), (pp 1956–1961).

Li, Z., Lyu, S., Zhang, H., and Jiang, T. (2021). One step ahead: a framework for detecting unexpected incidents and predicting the stock markets. *IEEE Access*, 9, 30292–30305.

Nikou, M., Mansourfar, G., and Bagherzadeh, J. (2019). Stock price prediction using DEEP learning algorithm and its comparison with machine learning algorithms. *Intelligent Systems in Accounting, Finance, and Management*, 1–11 .

Strader, T. J., Rozycki, J. J., Root, T. H., and Huang, Y. H. (2020). Machine learning stock market prediction studies: review and research directions. *Journal of Information Technology and Information Management*, 28(4), 63–83.

152 A system for predicting stock market price fluctuations

J. Sudarvel[1,a], R. Velmurugan[1], Ravi Thirumalaisamy[2] and Mahmoud Abouraia[2]

[1]Karpagam Academy of Higher Education, Coimbatore, Tamil Nadu, India

[2]Modern College of Business and Science, Sultanate of Oman

Abstract

This study addresses the challenging task of stock price prediction by proposing a system that employs neural networks and clustering techniques. The integrated K-means-deep belief network (DBN) model incorporates K-means clustering for feature selection and DBN for predicting stock closing prices. The model is evaluated using historical datasets from Amazon and Tesla. The preprocessing involves standardizing raw data through normalization, followed by the application of six technical indicators for feature extraction. K-means is utilized for feature selection, and the data is then split for DBN network training. Model evaluation employs MSE, MAE, and RMSE to analyze error performance and predict accuracy.

Keywords: DBN, k-means clustering, neural network, stock price forecasting, technical indicators

Introduction

Financial markets wield substantial influence over societal and economic realms, with assets linked to these markets holding significant value and fragility. The stock market serves as a platform for the exchange of various financial instruments, where traded equities represent ownership stakes, offering potential for elevated returns alongside inherent risks. Market volatility, characterized by erratic fluctuations, complicates the analysis of market dynamics. Fundamental analysis employs both quantitative and qualitative assessments, while technical analysis utilizes stock attributes and correlations to glean predictive insights. Such analyses play a pivotal role in investigating market liquidity, underscoring the necessity for dependable computational methodologies. A stock market functions as a public arena for companies to list and trade their stocks at predetermined prices, enabling them to secure financial resources. Investors engage in buying and selling these stocks, potentially earning dividends based on the company's profits. Shareholders may also trade stocks to capitalize on price differentials, with the global stock market witnessing substantial financial transactions, cementing its status as a pivotal financial arena.

Related Work

Predicting stock prices is challenging due to volatility, with standard data mining struggling to extract key information. A model using an encoder-decoder framework predicts movements and durations, extracting features with piecewise linear regression and CNN. A Deep Q-Network with CNN forecasts global markets, yielding profits across nations. Another model uses technical indicators and a nature-inspired algorithm with Elman neural network, optimized with grey wolf optimization, for one-day forecasts. A hierarchical attention capsule network considers news and social media, enhancing prediction accuracy. Lastly, an improved Levenberg-Marquardt algorithm for ANN outperforms ANFIS in predicting stock closing prices.

Proposed Model

This paper introduces a stock prediction model utilizing a deep neural network structure incorporating deep belief networks Thakkar and Chaudhari (2021). The model aims to comprehend influential features in the stock market. Figure 152.1 illustrates the entire process of the proposed model, encompassing each phase. Historical stock data from Amazon Inc. and Tesla Inc. was chosen for input data.

Data Processing

The model selected historical stock data from Amazon and Tesla for analysis Vui et al. (2013). The dataset covers the period from February 8, 2022, to February 7, 2023, and is formatted in CSV for accessibility. The file columns are labeled "Open," "Low," "High," "Adj Close," "Close," and "Volume."

Normalization ensures uniform significance of all data values. The Z-normalization equation (1) uses x as the actual value, μ as the mean, and σ as the

[a]j.sudarvel@gmail.com

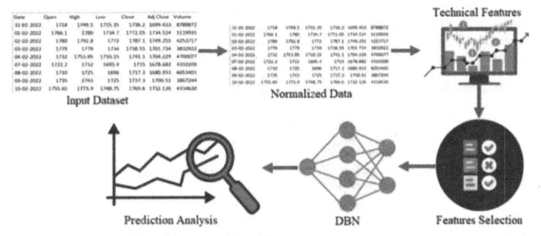

Input Dataset   **Normalized Data**   **Technical Features**

Prediction Analysis   **DBN**   **Features Selection**

Figure 152.1 Procedure of the proposed model
Source: Author

standard deviation Pauli et al. (2020). The impact of the stock data value's median on normalization is crucial. If the derived value equals the mean, it normalizes to zero; otherwise, it doesn't Soni (2011). A lower derived value yields a negative result, while a higher one yields a positive result. The normalized scores are based on the stock data value's standard deviation, which can be positive or negative. In cases of large standard deviations, indicating wide value disparities, the normalized value approaches 0.

$$z = \frac{x - \mu}{\sigma} \qquad (1)$$

Normalization began by substituting the initial stock value into the equation (1).

Technical feature extraction
Predicting stock price trends is challenging with univariate financial time series data due to its limited market information Liu et al. (2020). Essential aspects like closing, opening, low and high prices, and volume were selected and transformed into technical indicators. Technical analysis indicators are rules and patterns influencing the market.

Derived indicators include moving average (MA), relative strength index (RSI), bias, Williams %R, volume volatility, and closing price volatility. MA smoothens short-term swings, computed as the average of consecutive values Billah et al. (2016). RSI assesses overbought and oversold levels by comparing losses to returns. Bias compares the closing price to the MA, indicating discrepancies. Williams %R gauges momentum by relating the current price to past peak and lowest values. Volume volatility measures volume changes over time, while closing price volatility assesses variations in closing prices.

K-means clustering
The k-means clustering algorithm, widely recognized for grouping data, will be employed in this investigation Chen et al. (2019). However, it faces a significant issue of generating empty clusters and providing sub-optimal solutions due to random initial center selections Lee et al. (2019). Social media textual information will be grouped using the K-means clustering algorithm, correlated to the base mode of ontology, and subjected to a similarity estimation based on the Chi-square scheme. This measure aims to eliminate non-informative terms likely to be incorrect when applied to the dataset.

K-means clustering forms clusters using the nearest centroids, equivalent to the group's mean value. The method is widely used due to its ease of application to various data types but is sensitive to the initial cluster center placements. The steps of the K-means method are as follows:

1. Initialization starts by randomly selecting k data points as the centers of k clusters.
2. A search for the nearest neighbor is conducted, associating each data point with the cluster center closest to it.

The equation below identifies the data vector closest to a centroid:

$$d\left(z_p, a_j\right) = \sqrt{\sum_{k=1}^{d}\left(Z_{pk} - a_{jk}\right)^2} \qquad (2)$$

Here, d represents the dimensions of the data point vectors, z_p is the centroid of cluster P, and a_j is the vector belonging to the data point.

3. Updating the mean involves calculating the mean of the input vectors assigned to each cluster to find the new center.
4. The stopping criteria involve repeating steps 2 and 3 until there is no further variation in the computed means (Desokey et al., 2017).

Deep belief network

The restricted Boltzmann machine (RBM) is a key component of the generative model deep belief network (DBN). DBN training is sequential and layer-by-layer, using the data vector to determine the hidden layer at each level, which becomes the data vector for the next level. RBM's efficient training makes it suitable for inclusion in DBN Zhao et al. (2015). The hidden units in each layer of RBM learn higher-level features than the initial data. DBN can be viewed as well-trained neural networks with initialized weights. Dimensionality reduction is possible with a DBN structure without using class labels or backpropagation (BPNN). For classification with classes and labels, DBN is suitable. The presented backward propagation DBN model is based on the network structure in Figure 152.2, initializing weights using the greedy layer-wise contrastive divergence criteria.

The multilayer RBM now incorporates a final layer representing the desired output variables. This layer feeds the outcome of the RBM networks into the BPNN as input. A supervised BPNN performs error backpropagations and top-down fine-tuning of the architecture. The data then serves as inputs to a BPNN, addressing issues like falling into a local minimum and slow convergence time after optimizing the multilayer RBM.

The DBN method lays the groundwork for a stock price anticipation model. The subsequent explanation outlines the primary steps of the algorithm.

DBN algorithm

a. Select appropriate testing and training sets.
b. Describe the features of the two-dimensional model and represent the data collection using a matrix.
c. Initiate DBN parameter initialization, including the number of iterations, learning rate, hidden layer units, etc.
d. Input the training sets into DBN, adjust parameters, and assess prediction results using the testing sets.

Experiment analysis

This section presents the performance analysis of the proposed k-means-DBN model, focusing on both experimental and evaluation data. The experiment was conducted on datasets such as Amazon and Tesla, with separate training and testing sets extracted. The training sets were used for model training, and the test sets for predictions. Performance evaluations utilized various measurements, including mean square errors (MSE), mean absolute errors (MAE), root mean square errors (RMSE), and R-square (R^2), based on predetermined validation criteria.

A. Performance metrics

This section applies accuracy metrics to analyze and compare the proposed model's performance with other models. It specifically evaluates the accuracy of the data, utilizing three parameters: MSE, MAE, and RMSE as measures for predictive performance.

$$MSE = \frac{1}{n}\sum_{i=1}^{n}(p_i - r_i) \tag{3}$$

$$MAE = \frac{1}{n}\sum_{i=1}^{n}|p_i - r_i| \tag{4}$$

$$RMSE = \sqrt{\frac{1}{n}\sum_{i=1}^{n}(p_i - r_i)^2} \tag{5}$$

The original series mean is represented by r_i, while the anticipated series is denoted by p_i, derived from the model output. n signifies the dataset size.

Table 152.1: Compares error performance among models using the S&P500 stock dataset, including ICA-RF, ANN, SVM, and DNN. K-means-DBN achieved the lowest error rates in MSE, MAE, and

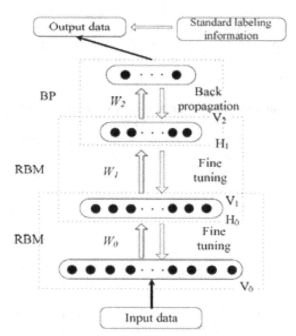

Figure 152.2 Architecture of DBN
Source: Author

Table 152.1 Performance evaluation comparison on Amazon dataset.

Models	MAE	MSE	RMSE
ANN	0.2276	0.1320	0.3633
SVM	0.2052	0.1167	0.3416
DNN	0.1885	0.1078	0.3283
k-means-DBN	0.1510	0.0845	0.2906

Source: Author

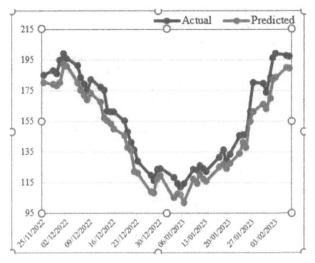

Figure 152.4 Comparison of actual vs predicted prices on tesla dataset

Source: Author

Figure 152.3 Comparison of actual vs predicted prices on amazon dataset

Source: Author

Table 152.2 Performance evaluation comparison on Tesla Dataset.

Models	MAE	MSE	RMSE
ANN	0.2638	0.1743	0.4174
SVM	0.2595	0.1525	0.3905
DNN	0.2370	0.1306	0.3613
k-Means-DBN	0.2201	0.1158	0.3402

Source: Author

RMSE parameters, demonstrating superior performance with 0.1510 MAE, 0.0845 MSE, and 0.2906 RMSE. Figure 152.3 depicts actual vs. predicted values using K-means-DBN on the Amazon dataset.

Table 152.2 presents the error performance comparison of models using the Tesla stock dataset. The K-means-DBN model achieved the lowest error rates in all parameters: MAE, MSE, and RMSE. Compared with other methods, the K-means-DBN model showed 0.2201 MAE, 0.1158 MSE, and 0.3402 RMSE. Figure 152.4 illustrates the comparison of actual vs. predicted performance using the K-means-DBN model

on the Tesla dataset. The proposed K-means-DBN demonstrated superior performances in all evaluated parameters when experimenting with both Amazon and Tesla datasets. The comparison of actual stock prices vs. predicted prices was more effective than other models, affirming the efficiency of the proposed K-means-DBN model for stock price prediction.

Conclusion

This work proposes a stock price forecasting model integrating clustering and neural network techniques. The framework forecasts closing prices using k-means clustering for feature selection and a deep belief network (DBN) for predictions. The K-means-DBN model is assessed with Amazon and Tesla stock datasets from February 8, 2022, to February 7, 2023. The dataset undergoes preprocessing, standardizing raw data with normalization. Six technical indicators are applied for feature extraction, followed by k-means clustering for feature selection. The data is then split for training and testing the DBN classifier. Model evaluation employs MSE, MAE, and RMSE to assess prediction accuracy, comparing performance with other models (ANN, SVM, DNN) for validation. Future work may involve optimizing the DBN to further enhance prediction performance.

References

Billah, M., Waheed, S., and Hanifa, A. (2016). Stock market prediction using an improved training algorithm of neural network. In 2nd International Conference on Electrical, Computer and Telecommunication Engineering (ICECTE) (pp. 1–4).

Chandar, S. K. (2021). Grey wolf optimization-elman neural network model for stock price prediction. *Soft Computing*, 25, 649–658.

Chen, Y., Lin, W., and Wang, J. Z. (2019). A dual-attention-based stock price trend prediction model with dual features. *IEEE Access*, 7, 148047–148058.

de Pauli, S. T. Z., Kleina, M., and Bonat, W. H. (2020). Comparing artificial neural network architectures for Brazilian stock market prediction. *Annals of Data Science*, 7, 613–628.

Desokey, E. N., Badr, A., and Hegazy, A. F. (2017). Enhancing stock prediction clustering using K-means with genetic algorithm. In 13th International Computer Engineering Conference (ICENCO) (pp. 256–261).

Firdaus, M., Pratiwi, S. E., Kowanda, D., and Kowanda, A. (2018). Literature review on artificial neural networks techniques application for stock market prediction and as decision support tools. In Third International Conference on Informatics and Computing (pp. 1–4).

Lee, J., Kim, R., Koh, Y., and Kang, J. (2019). Global stock market prediction based on stock chart images using deep q-network. *IEEE Access*, 7, 167260–167277.

Liu, J., Lin, H., Yang, L., Xu, B., and Wen, D. (2020). Multi-element hierarchical attention capsule network for stock prediction. *IEEE Access*, 8, 143114–143123.

Soni, S. (2011). Applications of ANNs in stock market prediction: a survey. *International Journal of Computer Science Engineering and Technology*, 2(3), 71–83.

Thakkar, A., and Chaudhari, K. (2021). A comprehensive survey on deep neural networks for stock market: the need, challenges, and future directions. *Expert Systems with Applications*, 177, 1–17.

Vui, C. S., Soon, G. K., On, C. K., Rayner, A., and Anthony, P. (2013). A review of stock market prediction with artificial neural network (ANN). In IEEE International Conference on Control System, Computing and Engineering (pp. 477–482).

Zhao, Z., Guo, J., Ding, E., Zhu, Z., and Zhao, D. (2015). Terminal replacement prediction based on deep belief networks. In International Conference on Network and Information Systems for Computers (pp. 255–258).

153 A fusion approach for forecasting stock market trends through probabilistic modeling

R. Velmurugan[1,a], J. Sudarvel[1], Ravi Thirumalaisamy[2], Mahmoud Abouraia[2] and R. Bhuvaneswari[3]

[1]Karpagam Academy of Higher Education, Coimbatore, Tamil Nadu, India
[2]Modern College of Business and Science, Sultanate of Oman
[3]Dr. Mahalingam College of Engineering and Technology, Pollachi, Tamil Nadu, India

Abstract

This study focuses on developing a hybrid model using machine learning and feature selection techniques to predict stock closing prices. The autoencoder (AE) technique is employed for feature selection, and the Naïve Bayes (NB) technique is used for price prediction. The AE-NB model is evaluated on historical stock datasets (Apple Inc. and Google) from February 8, 2022, to February 8, 2023. Pre-processing involves wavelet transform to eliminate noise. Five technical indicators are applied, followed by AE for feature selection and NB for prediction. Evaluation metrics include MAE, RMSE, and correlation coefficient R^2 to assess the model's accuracy.

Keywords: Autoencoder, feature selection, machine learning, naïve bayes, stock price forecasting

Introduction

The stock market, renowned for its allure as a dynamic investment arena, captivates both academic researchers and financial experts with its potential for predicting price movements. Traditionally, the efficient market hypothesis contends that stock prices reflect all available market information. However, advancements in computational intelligence challenge this notion, prompting an exploration of a shifting landscape. Investors, driven by the pursuit of profit, engage in the stock market, where shares represent ownership claims in companies. Accurate market forecasting is pivotal for informed decision-making, risk mitigation, and identifying profitable stocks. Amidst the complexities, accurate prediction models, drawing from diverse data sources and leveraging machine learning, have gained traction. This study proposes a machine learning-based stock prediction model, integrating an Autoencoder for feature selection and a Naïve Bayes (NB) model for predictions. Such methodologies highlight the evolving nature of stock market analysis, aiming to equip investors with robust tools for strategic decision-making amidst market uncertainties.

Related Works

Stock price prediction, a vital aspect of financial analysis, often faces challenges with nonstationary time series data. A novel approach proposed by Ji et al. (2021) integrates text attributes from social media, surpassing conventional statistical and econometric models. Employing Doc2Vec and SAE techniques, the method reduces the dimensionality of text vectors and addresses imbalances inherent in financial data. Additionally, Haar wavelet transform, and LSTM models are employed to denoise stock prices and forecast future values by amalgamating textual features and financial data. This innovative methodology exhibits superior performance in handling nonstationary stock data and harnessing text information from social media platforms.

Deep learning methods are increasingly sought after by researchers and investors for stock trend prediction due to their potential for enhanced accuracy and financial gains. A comprehensive framework incorporating financial news and sentiment analysis is introduced, featuring unique elements such as two-streams gated recurrent unit networks and Stock2Vec sentiment analysis word embeddings (Minh et al., 2018). Furthermore, Ouyang et al. (2020) proposes a three-stage architecture for identifying and predicting patterns in stock indexes, employing advanced techniques like multivariate LSTM-FCNs and Temporal Patterns Attention. Lastly, Huang et al. (2022) and Huang et al. (2018) present innovative approaches leveraging multilevel graph attention networks and modified Bayesian-LSTM models respectively, demonstrating significant advancements in stock market prediction accuracy.

[a]drvelsngm@gmail.com

Research Methodology

- Study presents a machine learning stock price prediction model.
- The model integrates wavelet transform, autoencoder, and NB.
- Utilizes historical stock data for Google, and Apple.
- Figure 153.1 depicts workflow, highlighting forecasting ability based on financial features.

Data Processing

The analysis inquiries into historical stock data of Google and Apple indices from February 8, 2022, to February 8, 2023, presented in CSV format with columns like "Open," "Low," "High," "Adj Close," "Close," and "Volume." Stock market fluctuations often introduce random noise, causing volatility and overfitting issues. Strong randomization can mitigate this, preserving data trends. Function transformation aids in noise reduction, smoothing variations without altering the trend. Wavelet transform, particularly Haar, is favored for its ability to manage nonstationary data while retaining essential features, vital for financial forecasting. This method decomposes information based on frequency and time, with acceptable computational time complexity (O(n)). The concept involves modifying data to separate valuable information and noise. Significant information is linked to higher coefficients, while noise is to lower ones. The model autonomously determines coefficient thresholds, retaining valuable data and discarding noise, contributing to enhanced stock price predictions.

Technical Feature Extraction

The feature extraction process involved applying technical indicators to the preprocessed data in the proposed model. An example of such an indicator is the simple moving average (SMA), calculated by summing up the most recent closing values of a stock and dividing by the total number of periods considered.

Another technical indicator employed was the Moving Averages Convergence/Divergence (MACD). This indicator predicts market moves by comparing short and long-term trends. To calculate MACD, the differences between a 26-day exponential moving average (EMA) and a 12-day EMA are computed.

The relative strength index (RSI) serves as a technical indicator to identify potential overbought or oversold conditions in a stock. The EMA is akin to the SMA, differing in that prior-day calculations influence the EMA for any given day. The on-balance volume (OBV) indicator, acting as both a lagging and momentum indicator, utilizes volume flow to predict stock price swings. A rising OBV may suggest future price increases, while a declining OBV may indicate potential price decreases.

Feature Selection using Autoencoder

The autoencoder (AE) is a non-recurrent, feedforward neural network, resembling a standard multi-layer artificial neural network. It operates through unsupervised learning to glean reduced informative representations of the data. Consisting of input, output, and hidden layers, the output layer has the same number of nodes as the input layer (illustrated in Figure 153.2 with $\widehat{x_1}, \widehat{x_2}, \ldots, \widehat{x_6}$ and $x_1, x_2, \ldots, x_6$). The AE learns weight vectors by treating the output layer vector as if it were the input layer vector.

A deep autoencoder is an autoencoder with multiple hidden layers. In this neural network, the primary task is to replicate its input, with the condition that one hidden layer has a reduced dimension, limiting the network's output. This constraint allows for a comprehensive representation of complex input distributions. During deep autoencoder training, backpropagation is employed to replicate the input vector

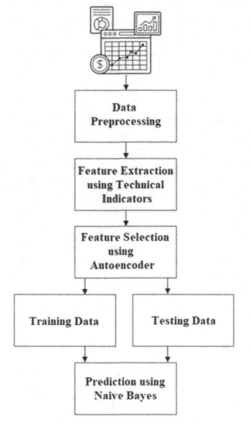

Figure 153.1 Workflow of the Proposed Model
Source: Author

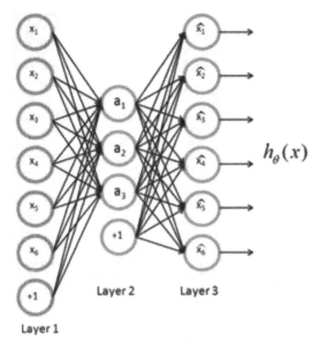

Figure 153.2 Architecture of AE
Source: Author

data. AE is employed to extract features from derived technical features, enhancing the accuracy, search space, and classification process of the NB approach.

Results and discussion

In this section, we present the performance analysis of the AE-NB model, focusing on both experimental and evaluation data. The experiment was conducted on each dataset, extracting training and testing sets. The training set was used to train the model, and predictions were based on the test set. Performance evaluations involved various metrics, including mean absolute error (MAE), root mean square error (RMSE), and R-square (R^2), aligning with predetermined validation criteria.

Performance evaluation

In this section, we evaluated error performance and compared it with other models. Specifically, the focus was on assessing data accuracy using three parameters: RMSE, MAE, and R^2 as metrics for predictive performance.

$$MAE = \frac{1}{n}\sum_{i=1}^{n}|p_i - r_i| \qquad (2)$$

$$RMSE = \sqrt{\frac{1}{n}\sum_{i=1}^{n}(p_i - r_i)^2} \qquad (3)$$

$$R^2 = 1 - \frac{(\sum_{i=1}^{n}(p_i - r_i)^2)/n}{\sum_{i=1}^{n}(a_i - r_i)^2/n} \qquad (4)$$

The original series that must be forecast is denoted by a_i in the aforementioned equations, and the original seriesmean was denoted by r_i. The anticipated series was denoted by p_i and can be derived from the model output.n is the size of the dataset.

The original series to be forecast is denoted by a_i in the given equations, and the mean of the original series is denoted by r_i. The anticipated series is represented by p_j, which is derived from the model output. n is the size of the dataset.

The error performance comparison of the models examined using the Google stock dataset is presented in Table 153.1. The AE-NB model's evaluated error values, along with a performance comparison with other models like k-Nearest neighbor (k-NN), artificial neural network (ANN), and support vector machine (SVM), are displayed in the table. The AE-NB model achieved the lowest error rates in parameters such as MAE and RMSE, accompanied by a higher correlation coefficient value. Specifically, the AE-NB model demonstrated a 0.2155 MAE, 0.3108 RMSE,

on the output layer. Numeric segments in the data are minimized using the hidden layer's output to facilitate easier identification of the input vector. The mathematical formulation involves defining the encoder and decoder functions.

Naïve bayes

The NB classifier, a probabilistic machine learning model, is employed for classification purposes using the supervised NB algorithm. This algorithm, based on Bayes' theorem, addresses classification issues and operates within the supervised algorithm framework. The NB classifier is known for its simplicity and effectiveness, playing a vital role in quickly generating accurate predictions. It establishes separate and independent relationships between characteristics through conditional probability, determining the likelihood of an event occurring.

$$P(A|B) = \frac{P(B|A)P(A)}{P(B)} \qquad (1)$$

The prior probability, denoted as P(A), the posterior probability, denoted as P(A|B), the marginal probability, denoted as P(B), and the likelihood probability, denoted as P(B|A).

This work introduces an integrated concept of NB and AE. Utilizing the probability distribution property, NB determines the potential class for stock price prediction based on existing characteristics in the stock

Table 153.1 Performance evaluation comparison on Google dataset.

Models	MAE	RMSE	R^2
k-NN	0.2682	0.3725	0.8968
ANN	0.2495	0.3541	0.9237
SVM	0.2313	0.3365	0.9489
AE-NB	0.2155	0.3108	0.9635

Source: Author

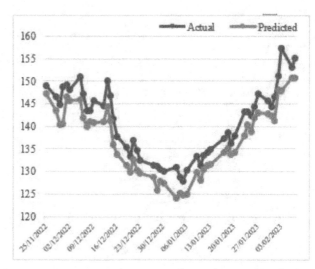

Figure 153.4 Comparison of actual vs predicted price on Apple dataset
Source: Author

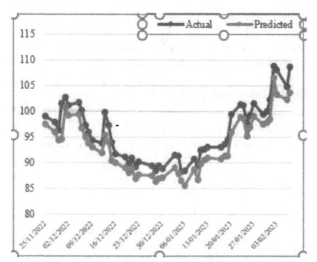

Figure 153.3 Comparison of actual vs predicted price on Google dataset
Source: Author

Table 153.2 Evaluation performance comparison on Apple dataset.

Models	MAE	RMSE	R^2
k-NN	0.2812	0.3748	0.9185
ANN	0.2645	0.3677	0.9312
SVM	0.2586	0.3521	0.9520
AE-NB	0.2305	0.3369	0.9724

Source: Author

and a correlation coefficient of 0.9635. Figure 153.3 illustrates the comparison between actual and predicted prices using the AE-NB model on the Google stock dataset.

The error performance comparison of models using the Apple stock dataset is depicted in Table 153.2. The AE-NB model demonstrated the lowest error rates in both parameters, namely MAE and RMSE, along with a higher correlation coefficient value. Specifically, the AE-NB model achieved 0.2305 MAE, 0.3369 RMSE, and a correlation coefficient of 0.9724, outperforming other methods. Figure 153.4 visualizes

the comparison between actual and predicted prices using the AE-NB model on the Apple stock dataset. The achieved results indicate superior performance of the proposed AE-NB model in all evaluated parameters for both Google and Apple datasets. The model's low error rates suggest effective stock prediction capabilities

Conclusion

This study proposes a hybrid stock price prediction model employing dimension reduction and a probabilistic classifier. The AE-NB model, integrating autoencoder (AE) for feature selection and Naïve Bayes (NB) for predicting closing prices, was assessed on Google and Apple datasets (February 8, 2022, to February 8, 2023). Preprocessing involved wavelet transform for noise elimination. Five technical indicators extracted features post-preprocessing, and AE selected relevant features. Data were then split for NB training and testing. Evaluation metrics (MAE, RMSE, R2) gauged model accuracy, outperforming k-NN, ANN, and SVM. Future applications may extend to predicting gold or oil prices.

References

Bustos, O., and Quimbaya, A. P. (2020). Stock market movement forecast: a systematic review. *Expert Systems with Applications*, 156(113464), 1–15.

Huang, B., Ding, Q., Sun, G., and Li, H. (2018). Stock prediction based on bayesian-LSTM. In ICMLC 2018: Proceedings of the 2018 10th International Conference on Machine Learning and Computing, (pp. 128–133).

Huang, K., Li, X., Liu, F., Yang, X., and Yu, W. (2022). ML-GAT: a multilevel graph attention model for stock prediction. *IEEE Access,* 10, 86408–86422.

Ibidapo, I., Adebiyi, A., and Okesola, O. (2017). Soft computing techniques for stock market prediction: a literature survey. *Covenant Journal of Informatics and Communication Technology,* 5(2), 1–28.

Ji, X., Wang, J., and Yan, Z. (2021). A stock price prediction method based on deep learning technology. *International Journal of Crowd Science,* 5(1), 55–72.

Minh, D. L., Sadeghi-Niaraki, A., Huy, H. D., Min, K., and Moon, H. (2018). Deep learning approach for short-term stock trends prediction based on two-stream gated recurrent unit network. *IEEE Access,* 6, 55392–55404.

Ouyang, H., Wei, X., and Wu, Q. (2020). Discovery and prediction of stock index pattern via three-stage architecture of TICC, TPA-LSTM and multivariate LSTM-FCNs. *IEEE Access,* 8, 123683–123700.

Patel, A., Patel, D., and Yadav, S. (2021). Prediction of stock market using artificial intelligence. In Proceedings of the 4th International Conference on Advances in Science and Technology (ICAST2021), (pp. 1–6).

Sharma, Y. K., and Kaur, R. (2019). Stock market prediction analysis: areview. *International Journal of Scientific Research and Engineering Development,* 2(6), 621–627.

Shi, C., and Zhuang, X. (2019). A study concerning soft computing approaches for stock price forecasting. *Axioms,* 8(116), 1–21.

154 Utilizing a hybrid CNN-ELM model for business analytics in stock price prediction

Ravi Thirumalaisamy[1], R. Velmurugan[2,a], J. Sudarvel[2], R. Bhuvaneswari[2] and Mahmoud Abouraia[1]

[1]Modern College of Business and Science, Sultanate of Oman

[2]KarpagamAcademy of Higher Education, Coimbatore, India

Abstract

In academic and financial research, predicting stock prices is a challenging task due to market volatility. This study introduces a deep learning (DL) model utilizing stock technical indicators (STIs) to analyze historical stock data. Seven STIs are applied to datasets from Reliance Industries and Tata Consultancy Services (TCS) sourced from Yahoo Finance. The proposed model combines a convolutional neural network (CNN) for feature extraction and an extreme learning machine (ELM) for prediction. Evaluation metrics including MSE, MAE, RMSE, and R2 demonstrate superior performance of the CNN-ELM model compared to alternative models (ANN, SVM, ELM) in stock prediction.

Keywords: Business analytics, CNN-ELM, hybrid model, stock price prediction

Introduction

The stock market, known for its complexity and unpredictability, generates vast amounts of structured and unstructured data globally, posing challenges in evaluation due to the increasing "volume," "velocity," "variety," and "veracity" of data (Nti et al., 2020). Fundamental and technical analyses are commonly used methodologies for processing stock market "Big Data." Fundamental analysis focuses on economic developments, sentiments, financial statements, and political conditions, while technical analysis involves statistical analysis of past stock price movements, using indicators like moving averages (Shah et al., 2019).

Advancements in stock market prediction have gained attention due to the challenging nature of analyzing stock movements amidst market noise. The complexity of stock pricing leads to changing elements, such as quarterly earnings announcements and market news. Market capitalization serves as the basis for calculating stock market indices, presenting a constant challenge in providing accurate predictions due to the industry's dynamic nature (Gandhmal and Kumar, 2019). Investors show interest in the stock market, driven by enhanced applications that promise profitable predictions. Successful predictions rely on obtaining advance information, with prediction methods playing a crucial role in monitoring and guiding the market (Gandhmal and Kumar, 2019).

The stock market, covering various industrial stocks in the financial industry, handles a wealth of information. Adjustments based on business status, purchases, and sales impact the market position, influenced by elements like future income estimates, news publications, and management changes. Precise predictions assist stockholders in making informed decisions (Kumar et al., 2022).

Literature Review

Table 154.1 Deep learning for stock market trends: a comprehensive review.

Author (Year)	Study
Hegazy et al. (2013)	Proposed a model with PSO and LS-SVM for daily stock prediction, addressing overfitting.
Albahli et al. (2022)	Used autoencoder and 1D DenseNet for closing stock prediction, reducing correlation among STIs.
Pang et al. (2020)	Introduced "stock vector" in LSTM model with embedded layer, showing superior performance.

[a]drvelsngm@gmail.com

Author (Year)	Study
Nabipour et al. (2020)	Addressed regression for stock groups, LSTM outperformed in forecasting Tehran stock exchange prices.
Ghani et al. (2019)	Applied various ML methods, forecasted stock trends one month ahead using Apple and Amazon data. Developed time series methods.

Source: Author

Stock Market Data Types

Stock market data falls into seven categories, essential for predictive analysis.

i. Market data
ii. Text data
iii. Macroeconomics data.
iv. Knowledge graph data
v. Image data
vi. Fundamental data
vii. Analytics data (Jiang, 2021).

Powerful software has enhanced the appeal of the stock market to investors, facilitating accurate predictions Table 154.1. Trading and investing in stock data directly influence predicting market trends. Prediction methods monitor, predict, and regulate the market, aiding in decision-making. The stock market manages diverse industrial stock information, contributing to prediction systems that bring new and existing investors together Table 154.2. The proposed research advocates a hybrid model merging CNN for feature extraction and ELM for stock price prediction.

Proposed Model

The proposed model involved three main steps: (i) Initial data acquisition from Yahoo Finance for Reliance Industries and Tata Consultancy Services, the top two companies in India by market capitalization. Stock technical indicators (STIs) were then computed using the collected stock data Table 154.3. (ii) The evaluated STIs served as inputs for a convolutional neural network (CNN), utilized for dimensionality reduction Table 154.4. The CNN model processed both the STIs with reduced correlation and datasets from Yahoo Finance to calculate deep features. (iii) The computed features were subsequently fed into an extreme learning machine (ELM) model for the final step, predicting stock prices.

Data Preprocessing

Python and TensorFlow were employed for implementing the proposed stock price prediction model. The dataset underwent zero-mean normalization and

Table 154.2 Utilized stock technical indicators.

STIs	Formula
Commodity channel index (CCI)	$CCI = \dfrac{Typical price - MA}{0.015 \times Mean deviation}$
Exponential moving average (EMA)	$EMA_t = C_t\left(\dfrac{2}{T+1}\right) + EMA_{t-1}\left(1 - \dfrac{2}{T+1}\right)$
Moving average (MA) of n days	$MA = \dfrac{1}{n}\sum_{i=1}^{n} C_i$
Stochastic oscillator (%K)	$\%K = \left[\dfrac{C_t - L_p}{H_p - L_p}\right] \times 100$
William (%R)	$\%R = \left[\dfrac{H_p - C_t}{H_p - L_p}\right] \times 100$
Moving average convergence Divergence (MACD)	$MACD = [(12day - EMA) - (26day - EMA)]$
Relative Strength Index (RSI)	$RSI = 100 - \left[\left(\dfrac{100}{1 + \left(\frac{AG}{AL}\right)}\right)\right]$

Source: Author

was then divided into training (January 3, 2022, to November 12, 2022) and test datasets (November 13, 2022, to January 12, 2023).

In Table 154.2, L_p and H_p denote the lowest and highest price rates in the previous p days, respectively, while C_t represents the present day's considered price. AL and AG stand for average loss and average gain, and L, H, and C represent "low," "high," and "close" pricing, respectively.

Convolutional Neural Network

This study introduces a CNN-based feature extractor for stock prediction, utilizing feed-forward neural networks with local receptive fields for extracting features

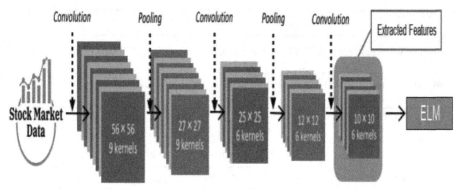

Figure 154.1 Proposed CNN architecture
Source: Author

from two-dimensional datasets. The feasibility of applying CNNs to stock price prediction is highlighted. The CNN model employs specialized layers, including pooling and convolution layers, iteratively applied, with a brief outline of the model architecture provided.

Convolution layer: Let $I = [I_{m,n}|m = \{1, ..., M\}, n = \{1, ..., N\}]$ be the input data in 2D. In addition, the kernel $I = [K_{p,q}|p = \{1, ..., P\}, q = \{1, ..., Q\}]$ is a 2D array of parameters that can be acquired by training. The equation defines the "convolution" operation, which involves evaluating dot products between components of the kernel and input.

$$u_{m,n} = \Sigma_p \Sigma_q I_{m-p,n-q} K_{p,q} + b_{m,n} \qquad (1)$$

In this context, $b_{m,n}$ denotes bias. Thus, the result $u_{m,n}$ gets transformed into the convolution layer's output $Z_{m,n}$.

$$Z_{m,n} = \phi(u_{m,n}) \qquad (2)$$

An activation function denoted as $\phi(.)$ is employed in this context. Among various types, this approach utilizes a common choice known as the rectified linear unit (ReLU), defined as in equation (3) for the activation function.

$$\phi(x) = \max(0, x) \qquad (3)$$

The input, represented by "x," leads to an output set Z(m,n), known as a feature map, with a reduced size compared to the input. This reduction results from the kernel size being smaller than the input size. In this layer, the process intuitively identifies 2D patterns on the input comparable to the kernels and transforms them into smaller-sized patterns. The convolution layer's output undergoes nonlinear down-sampling through the pooling layer to achieve the desired effect. Pooling layers are tasked with condensing and

generalizing the feature map obtained from the convolution layer Figure. 154.1. In the following equation, for example, max pooling selects the largest value within the sub region denoted by S(p,q).

$$S_{p,q} = \max_{(m,n)\in H_{p,q}} Z_{m,n} \qquad (4)$$

In this scenario, H_(p,q) designates a specific input region centered at coordinates (m,n). It's crucial to note that the pooling layer summarizes feature maps, ensuring stability against slight position variations Figure. 154.3. The key advantage of CNN lies in the ability of convolutional and down sampling layers to serve as learnable feature extractors. This allows inputting neural networks without intricate preprocessing, ensuring that valuable features are learned during training.

Extreme Learning Machine

Benefits of applying the ELM algorithm include:

1. Reduced computational overhead compared to many other machine learning techniques.
2. Faster learning rate compared to most feedforward neural network techniques.
3. Superior generalization performance compared to many other models.
4. Few nodes in the hidden layer, and they do not require tuning.

Figure 154.2 depicts the fundamental architecture of ELM, and the algorithm is outlined as follows:

ELM represents a single-layer artificial neural network, assuming L random hidden neurons and N distinct learning samples (x, y), denoted as L and N, respectively. Moreover, $x \in R^{d*N}$, $y \in R^N$ $a_i \in R^{1*d}$, $b_i \in R$, where a_i and b_i are matrices and vectors produced randomly. The output function can be expressed as shown in the following equation.

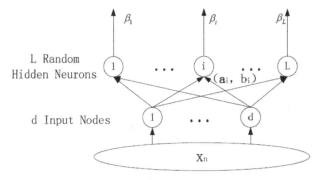

Figure 154.2 ELM architecture
Source: Author

$$fL(x_n) = \sum_{i=1}^{L} \beta_i G(a_i, b_i, x_n) = y_n \qquad (5)$$

In this instance, β symbolizes the weight vector connecting hidden neurons randomly to the outputs. The activation function G, linking the ith hidden neuron randomly with each input node, can be any infinitely differentiable function, such as the Sigmoid function depicted below.

$$G(a, b, x) = \frac{1}{1 + exp(-(a \cdot x + b))} \qquad (6)$$

The formula for equation (5) can also be expressed in the form of matrices, as shown below.

$$H \cdot \beta = Y \qquad (7)$$

where,

$$H = \begin{bmatrix} G(a_1, b_1, x_1) & \cdots & G(a_L, b_L, x_1) \\ \vdots & \ddots & \vdots \\ G(a_1, b_1, x_N) & \cdots & G(a_L, b_L, x_N) \end{bmatrix} \qquad (8)$$

$$\beta = [\beta_1 \beta_2 \dots \beta_L]^T \quad Y = [y_1 y_2 \dots y_N]^T \qquad (9)$$

Thus, the equation (5)'s least-square solution was:

$$\beta = H^\dagger Y = H^T (H H^T) Y \qquad (10)$$

In this context, the matrix H denotes the hidden layer output. Within this matrix, the ith element (h_i) signifies the output vector of the hidden layer for the input x_i. The training data output is represented as a vector Y. The only parameter to be determined through training is the value of β. The number of unique training samples serves as an upper limit for the required count of hidden nodes; in other words, the count of hidden nodes should be less than the count of training data samples.

Table 154.3 Description of historical stock Data.

Columns	Data descriptions
Date	Represents the days in the month, i.e., 03/01/2022
Low	The stock's minimum price traded during a day.
Open	The stock's opening price.
High	The stock's maximum price traded during a day.
Close	The stock's closing price.
Volume	The stock's total shares traded.
Adj. Close	The stock's adjusted closing prices, considering corporate action, like rights offerings, dividends, and stock splits.

Source: Author

Date	Open	High	Low	Close	Adj Close	Volume
03-01-2022	2365	2407.95	2363.55	2403.85	2396.635	2502073
04-01-2022	2415.9	2461	2404	2458.1	2450.722	5006225
05-01-2022	2462	2477	2432.95	2469.6	2462.187	5373618
06-01-2022	2451.2	2454	2409	2416.5	2409.246	6667483
07-01-2022	2430.95	2458.05	2411.55	2436	2428.688	6051239
10-01-2022	2452	2457	2416.05	2438	2430.682	4267365
11-01-2022	2436	2474.95	2435	2455.55	2448.179	7478681
12-01-2022	2471.3	2524.95	2465	2521.1	2513.532	6830402
13-01-2022	2521.25	2541	2508.4	2535.3	2527.69	5471871
14-01-2022	2535	2567.3	2525.85	2539	2531.379	9197773

Figure 154.3 Screenshot of the collected dataset in CSV format
Source: Author

Dataset Description

This study utilized publicly accessible historical financial stock market data, obtainable from the Yahoo Finance website. The data spans from January 3, 2022, to January 12, 2023, focusing on Reliance Industries and TCS. The collected historical stock data is structured into seven columns: Date, open, high, low, close, adj close, and volume. refer to Table 154.3 for a detailed description of these attributes.

Performance Metrics

The proposed CNN-ELM model's prediction outputs were assessed using mean absolute error (MAE), root mean square error (RMSE), mean square error (MSE), and coefficients of determination (R2). Lower values of MSE, RMSE, and MAE suggest that the model's predictions closely match the actual values. A higher R^2 value, approaching 1, indicates better predictive performance.

$$MSE = \frac{1}{N} \sum_{i=1}^{N} (\hat{y}_i - y_i) \qquad (11)$$

Table 154.4 MSE evaluation comparison.

Models	Reliance	TCS
ANN	0.121	0.1532
SVM	0.1176	0.1358
ELM	0.1052	0.1383
Proposed	0.0864	0.1106

Source: Author

$$MAE = \frac{1}{N}\sum_{i=1}^{N}|(\hat{y}_i - y_i)| \tag{12}$$

$$RMSE = \sqrt{\frac{1}{N}\sum_{i=1}^{N}(\hat{y}_i - y_i)} \tag{13}$$

$$R^2 = \frac{\sum_{i=1}^{N}(\hat{y}_i - \bar{y}_i)^2}{\sum_{i=1}^{N}(y_i - \bar{y})^2} \tag{14}$$

The number of samples is denoted by N, the value predicted by the model is denoted by $\hat{y}_i$, the actual value is denoted by y_i, and the mean value of y_i is denoted by $\bar{y}_i$.

The model achieved the lowest MSE for both tested datasets. Specifically, for Reliance Industries stock data, the research model achieved 0.0864, outperforming other models by 1.9% to 3.46%. For TCS stock data, the research model achieved a MSE of 0.1106, surpassing other models by 2.5% to 4.2%.

MAE is computed by taking the absolute difference between the predicted and observed values. The MAE comparison of the research model, which achieved the lowest MAE for both datasets. For the Reliance dataset, the model achieved a 0.2046 MAE, outperforming other models by 3.2% to 6.1%. Similarly, for TCS stock data, the research model achieved a 0.2418 MAE, surpassing other models by 2.1% to 4.5%.

RMSE is a common measure for assessing the accuracy of a prediction model compared to actual values. The RMSE comparison of the research model, which attained the lowest RMSE for both datasets. For the Reliance dataset, the model achieved a 0.2939 RMSE, outperforming other models by 3% to 5.3%. Likewise, for TCS stock data, the research model achieved a 0.3325 RMSE, surpassing other models by 3.6% to 5.8%.

The coefficient of determination, indicating the proportion by which error variance is less than the dependent variable variance. The research model achieved the highest R2 values for both datasets, reaching 0.9435 for the Reliance dataset (2.6% to 5.4% improvement) and 0.8879 for TCS stock data (2.65% to 7.7% improvement) compared to other models.

In performance analysis, the CNN-ELM model consistently outperformed other models like ANN, SVM, and ELM in stock price prediction. The CNN-ELM model exhibited superior performance across all evaluated parameters in predicting stock prices.

Conclusion

This study developed a stock price prediction model using the convolutional neural network (CNN) deep learning (DL) technique, employing seven stock technical indicators (STIs) derived from historical data of companies like Reliance Industries and TCS. The CNN extracts features based on computed STIs, and the ELM model is then trained for stock price prediction. Performance analysis, utilizing parameters such as MSE, MAE, RMSE, and R2, compared the CNN-ELM model with ANN, SVM, and ELM. The CNN-ELM model exhibited superior performance in stock prediction. Future enhancements may involve integrating the proposed model with event-based sentiment analysis for enhanced stock price prediction.

References

Albahli, S., Nazir, T., Mehmood, A., Irtaza, A., Alkhalifah, A., and Albattah, W. (2022). AEI-DNET: a novel DenseNet model with an autoencoder for the stock market predictions using stock technical indicators. *Electronics*, 11(611), 1–26.

Gandhmal, D. P., and Kumar, K. (2019). Systematic analysis and review of stock market prediction techniques. *Computers Science Review*, 34(100190), 1–13.

Ghani, M. U., Awais, M., and Muzammul, M. (2019). Stock market prediction using machine learning (ML) algorithms. *Advances in Distributed Computing and Artificial Intelligence Journal*, 8(4), 97–116.

Hegazy, O., Soliman, O. S., and Salam, M. A. (2013). A machine learning model for stock market prediction. *International Journal of Computer Science and Telecommunications*, 4(12), 17–23.

Jiang, W. (2021). Applications of deep learning in stock market prediction: recent progress. *Expert Systems with Applications*, 184(115537), 1–22.

Kumar, D., Sarangi, P. K., and Verma, R. (2022). A systematic review of stock market prediction using machine learning and statistical techniques. *Materials Today: Proceedings*, 49(8), 3187–3191.

Nabipour, M., Nayyeri, P., Jabani, H., Mosavi, A., Salwana, E., and Shahab, S. (2020). Deep learning for stock market prediction. *Entropy*, 22(840), 1–23.

Nti, I. K., Adekoya, A. F., and Weyori, B. A. (2020). A comprehensive evaluation of ensemble learning for stock-market prediction. *Journal of Big Data*, 7(20), 1–40.

Pang, X., Zhou, Y., Wang, P., Lin, W., and Chang, V. (2020). An innovative neural network approach for stock market prediction. *Journal of Supercomputing*, 76, 2098–2118.

Shah, D., Isah, H., and Zulkernine, F. (2019). Stock market analysis: areview and taxonomy of prediction techniques. *International Journal of Financial Studies*, 7(26), 1–22.

155 Analysis of performance management in Malaysian health and beauty private sector: qualitative case study

Tong Soo Mee[1], Mudiarasan Kuppusamy[2,a] and Balakrishnan Parasuraman[3,b]

[1]Faculty of Business, University of Cyberjaya, Malaysia

[2]School of Graduate Studies, Unirazak, Malaysia

[3]Faculty of Entrepreneurship and Business, Malaysia

Abstract

This paper examines the relationship between people, processes, and performance management systems in the Malaysian health and beauty industry. It highlights the importance of the retail industry in addressing issues and provides insights for policymakers, business professionals, and academics. The study emphasizes the need for a deeper understanding of the retail industry's interactions and potential threats.

Keywords: COVID-19 impact, health and beauty sector, industrial relations, organizational performance, performance management

Introduction

Performance management systems are pivotal for evaluating employee performance, ensuring well-being, and managing stress in today's evolving workplace. Within the Health and Beauty industry, these systems play a crucial role in enhancing worker performance and organizational outcomes. They address challenges such as the retail environment, evolving customer demands, and heightened responsibilities amidst workforce reductions and reduced hours. Reward management systems aim at fostering employee commitment, motivation, and development, drawing from theories like Maslow's Hierarchy of Needs (1954) to understand motivation dynamics. Despite their importance, there's ambiguity surrounding what constitutes an effective performance management system.

Instances like those at General Electric and Capital One, where such systems led to increased industrial disputes, highlight this ambiguity. Additionally, the ongoing COVID-19 pandemic has exacerbated issues such as harsh working conditions and burnout, resulting in significant job losses and legal battles. Amidst these challenges, performance management systems remain vital for setting goals, monitoring progress, and motivating employees, thereby enhancing organizational productivity. This paper enquires into the specifics of performance management within the Malaysian Health and Beauty sector, aiming to provide practical insights for policymakers, industry professionals, and academics amidst an environment of increasing industrial disputes and evolving human relations challenges.

Literature Review

Table 155.1 Overview of organizational dynamics and challenges.

Author(s)	Study	Findings/insights/interpretation
Sami (2021)	Importance of human resource efficiency and proficiency	Organizational success hinges on effective human resource management, which fosters employee motivation and performance.
Indiyati et al. (2021)	Impact of worker motivation on organizational performance	Employee motivation influences organizational outcomes such as empowerment and recognition, thereby reflecting on overall performance.
Gupta et al. (2023)	Challenges faced by workers due to labour cuts and reduced hours	Workers must maintain good customer relations despite increased responsibility stemming from reduced work hours and labor cuts.

[a]arasan@unirazak.edu.my, [b]balakrishnan@umk.edu.my

Author(s)	Study	Findings/insights/interpretation
Adamu et al. (2023)	Impact of extreme work conditions on employee performance during COVID-19	Intense work demands during the pandemic led to burnout and poor performance among workers, resulting in unfair dismissals and legal disputes in industrial relations courts.
Malaysian Lawyer (2021)	Legal implications of COVID-19 dismissals	The COVID-19 pandemic exacerbated issues of unfair dismissal and poor working conditions, leading to legal disputes and increased cases in industrial relations courts.
Bartik et al. (2020)	Survival strategies of companies during economic crisis	Smaller businesses resorted to cost-cutting measures, borrowing, or bankruptcy during economic downturns, while larger firms with reserves and government support fared better.

Source: Author

Research Methodology

Discusses data collection, interview techniques, validity, reliability, question categories, and ethical considerations.

Qualitative approach
- Utilizes a qualitative method to comprehend respondents' perspectives, emotions, and behavior.
- Employs a single case study design with semi-structured techniques: unstructured interviews, documentary reviews, direct observation, and primary data from the author.

Ethical considerations and analysis tool
- Emphasizes ethical considerations, employs QDA Miner 6 software for qualitative analysis.

Study scope
- Explores the impact of performance management in the health and beauty sector using Maslow's Theory and Robert Yin's qualitative case study.
- Involves thirty (30) health and beauty respondents in face-to-face interviews.

Research questions
- RQ1: Perception of performance management in health and beauty private sector.
- RQ2: Importance of performance management in improving industrial harmony.
- RQ3: Role of performance appraisal tool in enhancing performance.
- RQ4: Factors influencing performance of managers and non-managerial employees.

Case study characteristics
- Utilizes qualitative case study method focusing on single item, small sample size for data analysis.
- Challenges in data collection require linguistic proficiency and direct interaction.
- Evaluates advantages and disadvantages of case studies for research efficacy.

Data collection methods
- Includes direct observation, face-to-face interviews, focus groups, and qualitative methodologies like coded theme analysis.

Participant consent and privacy:
- Obtains authorization from University of Cyberjaya, explains objectives and purpose to participants.
- Records participant consent and ensures privacy protection.
- Stores data securely and uses the internet for interviews in a friendly environment.

Data security measures:
- Secures recorded audio in password-protected computer files accessible only to approved researchers.

Analysis and Findings

This analysis probes into the intricacies of performance management within the health and beauty sector in Malaysia. By examining challenges, success factors, and future directions, it aims to enhance organizational performance and continuity in this critical industry.

- The data collection process is ongoing, aiming for 30 respondents.
- Interviews conducted with 24 respondents, including nine managers and fifteen non-managers from an established company.
- Utilization of coded thematic analysis in the case study, highlighting challenges, success factors, context, and implications for performance improvement in health and beauty sector organizations.

- Identification of three contextual factors from respondent feedback, with preliminary suggestions for improvement.
- Exploration of performance management implementation in health and beauty public organizations, providing insights into experiences and indicating future research directions.

The findings highlight the significance of addressing sensitive elements within the health and beauty sector to enhance performance within the Malaysian healthcare landscape. By acknowledging and nurturing these factors, healthcare leaders stand to enhance productivity, ensure business continuity, and positively influence the sector's overall success.

The study's focus on the health and beauty sector within specific organizations highlights nuances and intricacies unique to this context. While the findings provide valuable insights for improving performance management practices within these sectors, it's essential to recognize that the study's conclusions may not be universally applicable to all organizations across Malaysia.

Efforts to refine and enhance performance management practices within the health and beauty sector are crucial for fostering organizational success and meeting the evolving needs of the healthcare landscape. Recognizing the specific challenges and success factors inherent in this sector can guide leaders in implementing targeted strategies to drive performance improvement and ensure sustained success.

The study's findings shed light on the importance of addressing sensitive elements within the health and beauty sector to enhance performance and drive success in the Malaysian healthcare industry. While the study's insights offer valuable guidance for sector-specific organizations, it's essential to approach performance management strategies with an understanding of the unique contextual factors at play. By recognizing and nurturing these factors, healthcare leaders can pave the way for increased productivity, improved business continuity, and long-term success within the sector.

Conclusion

In conclusion, this study underlines the critical need for a nuanced understanding of performance management systems in Malaysia's retail sector, amidst growing industrial incidents and a rapidly evolving business landscape. By recognizing the gap in current literature and addressing the challenges inherent in implementing these systems, organizations can better navigate the complexities of the health and beauty industry.

Moreover, the study advocates for a human-centric approach to design, aligning local processes with emerging technological capabilities to foster resilience against economic and pandemic threats. Looking ahead, the integration of people, processes, and new business technologies will be paramount for sustained growth and success in the sector. Performance management emerges as a vital tool in this regard, offering a dynamic alternative to traditional appraisal systems by facilitating goal setting, motivation, transparency, staff development, and leadership enhancement. Ultimately, this research aims to equip organizations within the health and beauty sector with actionable strategies to enhance performance management and operational efficiency in an ever-evolving landscape.

References

Adamu, A. A., Raza, S. H., and Mohamad, B. (2023). The interactive effect of mindfulness and internal listening on internal crisis management and its outcomes: the moderating role of emotional exhaustion. *Corporate Communications: An International Journal*, 28(1), 6–29.

Bartik, A. W., Bertrand, M., Cullen, Z. B., Glaeser, E. L., Luca, M., and Stanton, C. T. (2020). How are Small Businesses Adjusting to COVID-19? Early Evidence from a Survey (No. w26989). National Bureau of Economic Research.

Bartol, K. M. (2023). Pay for performance. In Handbook of Principles of Organizational Behavior: Indispensable Knowledge for Evidence-Based Management (pp. 137).

Gupta, S., Montenovo, L., Nguyen, T., Lozano-Rojas, F., Schmutte, I., Simon, K., et al. (2023). Effects of social distancing policy on labor market outcomes. *Contemporary Economic Policy*, 41(1), 166–193.

Indiyati, D., Ghina, A., and Romadhona, A. F. (2021). Human resource competencies, organizational culture, and employee performance. *International Journal of Science and Society*, 3(1), 1–10.

Malaysian Lawyer (2021). Case update: industrial court finds retrenchment due to effects of Covid-19/MCO 16 Aug 2021 was unfair (Award No.1052 of 2021). Retrieved from https://themalaysianlawyer.com.

Sami, H. M. (2021). Optimizing organizational overall performance, the use of quantitative choice of HR in carrier quarter enterprise of Bangladesh. *Canadian Journal of Business and Information Studies*, 3(3), 49–59.

The New Straits Times (2021). 30 percent of shops have closed: 300,000 workers lost jobs. Retrieved from www.nst.com.my.

Yin, R. K. (2003). Case Study Research: Design and Methods. Thousand Oaks, CA: Sage.

Young, L. C., and Wilkinson, I. R. (1989). The role of trust and cooperation in marketing channels: a preliminary study. *European Journal of Marketing*, 23(2), 109–122.

156 Assessing the influence of the COVID-19 pandemic on the employability skills among graduating students

Sonia Valas, X.[1,a], Beulah Suresh[2,b], L. Harathy[3,c], Cyril Fernandez[d] and Arivuselvee, V. J.[e]

[1]Ph.D Scholar, Auxilium College (Autonomous), Vellore and Assistant Manager, Christian Medical College, Vellore, India

[2]Head and Asst. Professor, Department of Business Administration Auxilium College (Autonomous), Vellore, India

[3]Ph.D Scholar, Auxilium College (Autonomous), Vellore, India

Abstract

Employability skills, also known as work readiness skills, encompass the vital set of abilities and standards required to enable a recent graduate to enter and thrive in a professional work environment. Employers and industry experts seek candidates who possess these essential employability skills. The emergence of the COVID-19 pandemic introduced a challenging new paradigm for students, as they had to adapt to the new norm of attending online classes to complete their prescribed coursework. This research undertakes to assess the influence of COVID-19 on the employability skills of college students. The evaluation is conducted using a self-assessment questionnaire and a proficiency test aimed at gauging their capabilities. The study involved 176 students enrolled in a reputable institution in Vellore City, Tamil Nadu, who were to be graduate in October 2022. Students were provided with self-assessments across nine primary dimensions, including collaborative work, team cooperation, social interaction, adaptability in diverse groups, communication proficiency, critical thinking and self-awareness, data analysis and problem-solving, self-management and entrepreneurship, and professionalism. In addition to this, they undertook a test to evaluate their numerical, verbal, and data analysis abilities, as well as their ability to make situational judgments. To address the "illusion of confidence," a cognitive bias wherein individuals tend to overestimate their abilities, the students were divided into two groups. One group initially completed a questionnaire designed to gauge their perception of employability skills and the impact of COVID-19 on these skills, followed by self-assessment and the proficiency test. For the second group, the proficiency test was administered first, followed by the questionnaire and self-assessment of their employability skills. The study's findings indicate that students perceive a decline in their employability skills due to the shift from traditional classroom instruction to online learning brought about by COVID-19. The research identified six critical employability skills.

Keywords: COVID-19, employability skills, graduating students

Introduction

Substantial research has been conducted the world over to identify the skills that employers expect from incoming fresh college-leaving recruits. Several skills like team playing, communication, and basic numeracy skills (and many more) have been identified by researchers who have surveyed employers' HR personnel. While the HR managers expect specific skill sets from the employees, (depending on the nature of the industry) a question arises as to whether the graduating students are aware of the expectations of prospective employers. The fundamental questions that arise are (a) How do students perceive the expectations of the industry? (b) Does the perception of a student intersect with the expectations of his/her prospective employer? (c) How do the students perceive their capability on the employable skill sought by the industry? The answers to these questions give an avenue to know in what ways the students can be given inputs so that they are aware of the expectations of the industry and equip themselves to meet the industry's expectations.

Once students perceive the requirements of the industry, they can evaluate their actual skills so that they are aware of the gap between their assessment and reality. The assessed gap between the self-rating and their actual performance on evaluation of specific skills through evaluation methods will help them to adapt to interventional training so that the gap is narrowed, and they are better equipped to face the rigors of evaluating employers. The educational institutions could use these identified gaps for developing

[a]soniavalas@cmcvellore.ac.in, [b]beulah@auxiliumcollege.edu.in, [c]harathy.reddy@gmail.com, [d]cyrilabcd@gmail.com, [e]arivuselvee.jayaraman@gmail.com

customized skill development curricula and extracurricular activities for the benefit of the students and help in addressing the demand of the market proactively. This would create a win-win situation for the students, educational institutions, and recruiting organizations.

The COVID-19 pandemic has churned the normal lifestyle across the world in the last two years. Colleges and schools were forced to adopt an online mode of delivering the course curriculum. This study aimed to investigate how this move that was thrust on the student population by the pandemic has changed their perceptions of evaluation of the market requirements of employability skills and in what ways they feel that they are affected by the online mode. Though the college is back in the classroom mode now, by investigating the reactions of the students in the final year of graduate studies on the impact of COVID-19 on employability skills, Institutions can plan to equip the students to meet the expectations of the industry.

For this purpose, a self-assessment survey and test are conducted among the students for the identification of key employable skills and their thoughts on COVID-19 induced handicaps, if any. The results of the survey and the tests help to design training programs for graduating students across the country to meet the needs of the recruiters in the industry.

Employability skills – summary from literature review
In earlier years, educational credentials and technical knowledge were used to envisage success in the workplace. However, recent research on modern-day employers emphasizes certain soft skill sets named 'employability skills' or 'work readiness skills 'that determine a recruit's job performance. Although researchers agree that these employability skills have a competitive edge, there are still arguments on the accepted specific list of skillsets since 'there is an extensive list impacting efficiency at workplace' (O'Brien et al., 2020).

Employability skills are 'basic required skills possessed by graduates equipping them to be acceptable at workplace' (Jackson, 2013).

Literature also highlights that certain important skills of social and cognitive skills are essential for employment. However, there is a 'visible gap between the workforce and the employers laying heavy pressure on the education institution for inculcating skill-based curriculum relevant for the industry' (Ratneswary, 2019).

Keeping the changing nature of the industry, the research emphasizes that the graduates being ready for work with expected skillsets indicates their ability to perform and enhance their career development (Caballero and Walker, 2010).

US employers were surveyed on hiring young graduates and found that nearly '80% attention is given for soft skills such as interest to learn new skills, decision making, teamwork, communication skills and Ability to handle data. Only 50% importance are given to knowledge or academics.' Paradoxically 'though the employers are looking for these skills, only less than two-thirds possess these skills' (Doe, 2015).

Although there are various employability skill assessment scales available, many focus on measuring the knowledge level rather than measuring the possibility of obtaining a job after graduation. Hence, there isa lot of scope for further studies to construct and validate employability measurement scales for the benefit of employers and students (Rodgers, 2012).

Organizations seeking technically skilled engineers seek not only their technical domain but also demand highly professional candidates who would add value to their organization and contribute to their productivity. Hence, there is a paradigm shift from technical-oriented engineering jobs to service-centered engineering jobs which includes both technical and soft skills. It is 'essential to provide quality investment on human capital through careful design of job-oriented course curriculum and skill-based learning process for future graduates' (Aruna, 2016).

Certain research findings state that in tertiary education, curriculum differs according to their specialization. In assessing graduating student's perspective of their work readiness, it was seen that the 'healthcare specialty seems to score higher in preparing graduates ready for work compared to business specialization' (Roberta, 2020).

From the literature, it is reckoned that employers expect certain sets of skills over and above technical skills and there is a huge gap between the expectation of the employers and the outcomes of the graduating students. It is essential to capture the required skillset expected by employers and inculcate the same in the learning process to equip the young graduates entering the industry.

Study objective
It is evident from the literature that young graduates are expected to possess certain work readiness skills which will fetch them an edge over others and success in the workplace. However, many students and the curriculum does not fulfil the expectation. There is scope for further study in this area for skills development.

This study helps to address the following questions:

a. Are students aware of specific employability skills expected of them?

b. Do students perceive that COVID-19 and consequent disruption of classes have impacted specific employability skills?

c. Are there differences between students of different academic streams in their perception of their employability skills?

d. Do students have an inherent bias in rating themselves on their employability skills?

Materials and Methods

Study area and duration

This study was carried out among final-year Undergraduate students. Five different streams of specialization were identified for the study from a reputed college in Vellore town, Tamil Nadu. This study was carried out during the final semester of the passing out graduates in July 2022. A total of 176 students participated in the study. The college selected is an all-women's college. This is a limitation of the study as the male population is excluded. However, at the gateway of selection, employers can be gender-neutral in their need for the 'soft' skills. Hence, the study findings shall find universal application.

Study instrument

Based on the study of the existing literature, a questionnaire was developed to identify employability skills and the impact of the COVID-19 lockdown in acquiring the required employability skills. To eliminate the bias of students inflating their response, which could be out of overconfidence, the questionnaire contained two parts – the first on their perception of employability skills and the second on their self-assessment on the level of employability skills they possess.

The first part of the questionnaire consists of demographic variables and the second part consists of seven statements under nine major skillsets totaling 63 statements to obtain the perception of the graduating students on a 5-point Likert scale,

SA: Strongly agree
A: Agree
NAND: Neither agree nor disagree
DA: Disagree, and
SDA: Strongly disagree

The responses are assigned values ranging from 1 to 5 based on the framing of the question.

There were 13 statements on a reverse scale. The third component of the questionnaire had self-rating questions on their level of employability skills on a scale of 1-10.

A question paper was prepared to assess the students on their numerical, verbal and data analysis ability including a situational judgment test.

The selected sample was divided into two halves.

A. For one-half, the test was administered first and then they were made to fill out the questionnaire.

B. The other half were asked first to fill out the questionnaire and then take the test.

The questionnaire was distributed to ten students to assess its appropriateness towards the objectives of the research (pilot study). Based on the feedback received from these students, relevant modifications were made to the questionnaire and finalized. The respondents of the pilot study were excluded from the main study.

Item development and scale construction

The questionnaire consists of potential employability traits selected from a basket of traits based on literature. They are:

1. Collaborative working
2. Team playing
3. Social interaction
4. Working in a diverse group
5. Communication
6. Self-awareness and critical thinking
7. Data analysis and problem-solving
8. Self-management and enterprise
9. Professionalism, responsibility and accountability.

Statistical Analysis

Test of illusion of confidence

We hypothesized that students tend to overestimate their employability skills.

> H_{01}: *There is no difference in the self-assessment (scores) of students who took the test before self-assessment and the students who took the test later.*

Chabris and Simons (2011) refer to this as an 'illusion of confidence.' They write that this illusion 'causes us to overestimate our own qualities.' To test the hypothesis, we divided the students into two groups. One group filled out the questionnaire that we devised to elicit their perception of their employability skills first and then took the test. Other group took the test first and then filled out the self-assessment tool. Both groups rated themselves on nine specific employability skills (Table 156.1). The tests assessed their verbal, numerical and analytical abilities. The students were also given a situational judgement test to solve.

The test of hypothesis shows that the null hypothesis is to be rejected. This means that there is a difference in the self-assessment made by the students who took the test first and the ones who took the test later. The students who have taken the test after the self-assessment have overestimated their employability skills compared to the students who did the self-assessment after taking the test. The set of students who took the test and did the self-assessment have attenuated their assessment.

We computed Cohen's 'd' factor. This comes as 0.1608. We interpret this as approximately 52% of

the students in the group which self-assessed after taking the test is below the average of the group which took the test before self-assessment. This is an indication that just over half the students who assessed themselves after taking the test have moderated their assessment compared to the students who did the self-assessment before taking the test. We attribute this diminution to the effect of the test we have administered them.

Differences in the test performance

To rule out the possibility of differences in the performance of tests between these two sets of students, we formulated the hypothesis:

> H_{02}: There is no difference in the performance of the students in the test administered.

The test result shows that there is no difference in the test performance of the students who took the test first and the set who took the test later. This test reinforces our first hypothesis that students have toned down their self-assessment based on their perceived performance in the tests given.

Study of the perception of employability skills

To find the perception of the students about the impact of COVID on their perceived employability skills we gave the students a set of 24 questions and asked them to answer the questions on a five-point scale. We give the outcome in Table 156.2.

We have hypothesized that the students perceive that there is no impact on their employability skills

Table 156.1 Self-rating dimensions considered in the study.

Sl. No.	Self-ratings dimensions
1	Collaborative working
2	Team playing
3	Social interaction
4	Working in diverse group
5	Communication skills
6	Critical thinking and self-awareness
7	Analyzing data and solving problems
8	Managing self and entrepreneurship
9	Professionalism

Source: Author

Table 156.2 Questions on impact of COVID-19, shift of classes to online mode, on employability skills.

Question	Questions	Mean	SD	Count SA & A	Count SDA and DA	% Count SA and A	% Count SDA and DA
1	COVID-19 has resulted in change from classroom to online learning and this has affected forming groups and physical meetings of groups, in our batch.	4.0909	0.9638	141	15	90.38%	9.62%
2	Lack of physical group meeting has affected my skills of working with my friend and batchmates.	4.1080	1.0280	142	16	89.87%	10.13%
3	Online learning has resulted in poor formation of teams in our batch.	3.6477	1.0479	105	26	80.15%	19.85%
4	I feel that my ability to be an effective team member is affected due to online classes.	3.6364	1.0816	105	24	81.40%	18.60%
5	My social interaction has been constrained due to online classes.	3.8068	1.1986	122	31	79.74%	20.26%

Question	Questions	Mean	SD	Count SA & A	Count SDA and DA	% Count SA and A	% Count SDA and DA
6	I believe that my reduced social interaction may create adjustment problems for me when I go for a job.	3.6136	1.0683	106	28	79.10%	20.90%
7	Online classes have denied me the opportunity to mix and interact with students coming from different walks-of-life.	3.8295	1.0767	119	22	84.40%	15.60%
8	Interacting with diverse groups in college will help in successful integration in work life – I feel that the COVID-19 induced classroom mode will affect such integration when I go for a job.	3.9148	0.9731	126	16	88.73%	11.27%
9	Online tests are better than writing tests with pen and paper.	3.3125	1.3603	79	52	60.31%	39.69%
10	Online classes due to COVID-19 has not affected my writing skills or speaking skills.	3.2784	1.2452	80	46	63.49%	36.51%
11	Attending college physically would have helped me in increasing my public speaking skills.	4.2898	0.9746	151	11	93.21%	6.79%
12	Lack of access to library (due to COVID-19) has affected my reading more than the prescribed textbooks.	3.6989	1.0393	111	23	82.84%	17.16%
13	My personal practices would have changed if there were offline classes	3.9318	0.9171	129	12	91.49%	8.51%
14	Because of not attending physical classes, I am not aware of the present labor market conditions.	3.6023	1.0202	101	28	78.29%	21.71%
15	Online classes are helpful in developing the habit of life-long learning.	3.4773	1.1806	95	36	72.52%	27.48%
16	I have learnt more of using computer and apps for studying, joining meetings. This would not have been possible in physical classroom sessions.	3.8750	0.9358	131	16	89.12%	10.88%
17	Online classes are more helpful in increasing my capacity to analyze and solve examination questions.	3.3920	1.1211	86	41	67.72%	32.28%
18	Lack of classrooms sessions has resulted in my loosing basic numerical skills.	3.2955	1.0919	81	38	68.07%	31.93%
19	I could have increased my skill of collecting and collating information through physical classes due to more face-to -face interaction with my batchmates.	3.8920	0.9884	121	13	90.30%	9.70%
20	By studying from home, I have used my spare time to earn some money by taking up work from home jobs or starting a small business.	3.5625	1.1936	105	35	75.00%	25.00%
21	Studying from home has increased my self-confidence.	3.5739	1.1540	100	32	75.76%	24.24%
22	Online classes have helped me to be self-disciplined – achieving academic goals by self-initiated actions.	3.4602	1.0736	94	34	73.44%	26.56%

Question	Questions	Mean	SD	Count SA & A	Count SDA and DA	% Count SA and A	% Count SDA and DA
23	COVID-19 induced online classes has prevented developing behaviors and attitudes to comply with the college as an organization and its culture.	3.7486	0.9677	104	16	86.67%	13.33%
24	I feel a lack of understanding broader community value systems in the absence of physical classes.	3.7784	1.0264	108	18	85.71%	14.29%

Legend: SDA: Strongly disagree, DA: disagree, SA: Strongly agree, A: Agree
Source: Author

Table 156.3 Test of hypothesis H03.

Test statistic
The test statistic 'T' equals 12.9195, which is not in the 95% region of acceptance: [-2.0687, 2.0687].
The 95% confidence interval of COVID 19 impact is: [3.5885, 3.8129].

P Value
The p-value equals 4.994e-12, (P(x≤12.9195) = 1). It means that the chance of type I error (rejecting a correct H0) is small: 4.994e-12 (5e-10%).
Since the p-value < α, H_{03} is rejected.

The COVID-19 impact population's average is not equal to the expected average (3).
In other words, the difference between the average of COVID-19 impact and the expected average is big enough to be statistically significant.

Effect size
The observed effect size d is large, 2.64. This indicates that the magnitude of the difference between the average of the differences and the expected average of the differences is large.

Source: Author

due to the prolonged closure of the college, because of which the instruction mode shifted from physical classroom to online mode.

> *H3: Students perceive that there is no impact on their employability skills due to the shift from classroom learning to online mode.*

The statistics of the response to the perception of employability skills are given in Table 156.2. The result of the hypothesis testing is in Table 156.3.

Since the null hypothesis is rejected, we accept the alternate hypothesis and conclude that the students perceive that their employability skills have been affected due to the COVID-19 induced change in the mode of instruction – from classroom to the online mode.

Factor analysis of perception of employability skill
The questionnaire included questions related to the impact of COVID-19. These questions were weeded out and the rest 41 questions were subjected to factor analysis. The extraction was through the principal component analysis method. In the first iteration, thirteen factors emerged. The thirteen factors cumulatively explained 63.924% of the variance. The emergent Scree plot was studied and the questions falling into each factor. The researcher saw that further reduction of factors was possible as some of the thirteen could be subsumed into other factors. The analysis was run for nine factors and the results were studied. The factors developed were studied and it was again found that some of the factors can be grouped into a single factor. Based on the analysis of the questions, the factor analysis was run again. The rotation method used was Varimax with Kaiser normalization and the rotation converged in six iterations. The result of the factor analysis is given in Table 156.4.

The six factors of employability that emanate from the factor analysis are: (1) Ability to work with diverse groups, (2) Communication skills, (3) Entrepreneurial skills, (4) Planning and Problem-Solving skills, (5) Team work and (6) Self-drive.

The minimum factor loading noticed is 0.514 and the maximum is 0.840.

The factors and the extraction sum of squared loadings and the rotation sum of squared loadings are given in Table 156.7.

All the six factors have an eigenvalue of above 1. 'Working with diverse groups' contributes the maximum variance of 24.432%, followed by 'communication' which contributes 10.386%. 'Entrepreneurial skills' contributes to 9.020% of the variance, while 'planning and problem-solving skills' explains another 8.232%. 'Teamwork' contributes 6.583% of the variance and factor 'self-drive' 6.187%. The total cumulative variance explained by the six factors is 64.841% (Table 156.7). In reducing the factors from thirteen

Table 156.4 Factors and factor loadings.

Factor no.	Employability factor	Q. No.	Items	Factor loading
1	Working with diverse groups	4.1	Interact with students coming from different cultural backgrounds.	0.812
		3.1	Important to listen to the viewpoint of others.	0.730
		4.2	Interacting with students coming from different religious backgrounds.	0.703
2	Communicating with others	5.4	Increased writing skills.	0.777
		2.5	Shared learning.	0.673
		4.3	Work productively with their teachers.	0.585
		3.4	People have complex emotions and I need to accept such a situation and respond calmly.	0.528
3	Entrepreneurial skills	8.2	By studying from home, I have used my spare time to earn some money by taking up work from home jobs or starting a small business.	0.870
		8.3	Studying from home has increased my self-confidence.	0.840
		9.4	Honesty and Integrity are highly valued traits by employers.	0.514
4	Planning and problem solving	1.3	Increase problem- solving skills.	0.826
		1.4	Improve planning skills.	0.751
5	Teamwork	1.6	Forming groups and physical meetings of groups.	0.846
		1.7	Skills of working with friends and batchmates.	0.826
6	Self-drive	9.1	Solely responsible for success and failure.	0.825
		9.2	Prioritize and schedule (my studies.)	0.771

Source: Author

Table 156.5 Factors, percentage variance and cumulative variance.

Factor No.	Factor name	Extraction sums of squared loadings			Rotation sums of squared loadings		
		Total	% of Variance	Cumulative %	Total	% of Variance	Cumulative %
1	Working with diverse groups	4.153	24.432	24.432	2.227	13.101	13.101
2	Communicating with others	1.766	10.386	34.819	2.127	12.513	25.613
3	Entrepreneurial skills	1.533	9.020	43.839	2.016	11.857	37.470
4	Planning and problem-solving skills	1.399	8.232	52.071	1.590	9.355	46.824
5	Teamwork	1.119	6.583	58.654	1.586	9.329	56.154
6	Self-drive	1.052	6.187	64.841	1.477	8.687	64.841

Source: Author

to six the cumulative variance has improved from approximately 64-65%.

Item analysis
The item adjusted to total correlation is the correlation between the scores of one omitted item and the total score of all other items. The details are given in Table 156.8. The correlation ranges from 0.17 to 0.53. Range 0.20 to 0.39 shows that there is 'good' discrimination and a value greater than 0.40 is 'very good.' Reading of the results shows that only one element (Q. 1.7) has a value of 0.17 and all others are greater than 0.254. This means moderately fair discrimination between the items. The overall

Table 156.6 Factors and Factor Loadings.

Factor No.	Employability Factor	Q. No.	Items	Factor loading
1	Working with diverse groups.	4.1	Interact with students coming from different cultural backgrounds.	0.812
		3.1	Important to listen to the viewpoint of others.	0.730
		4.2	Interacting with students coming from different religious backgrounds.	0.703
2	Communicating with others.	5.4	Increased writing skills.	0.777
		2.5	Shared learning.	0.673
		4.3	Work productively with their teachers.	0.585
		3.4	People have complex emotions and I need to accept such a situation and respond calmly.	0.528
3	Entrepreneurial skills.	8.2	By studying from home, I have used my spare time to earn some money by taking up work from home jobs or starting a small business.	0.870
		8.3	Studying from home has increased my self-confidence.	0.840
		9.4	Honesty and Integrity are highly valued traits by employers.	0.514
4	Planning and Problem solving.	1.3	Increase problem- solving skills.	0.826
		1.4	Improve planning skills.	0.751
5	Teamwork.	1.6	Forming groups and physical meetings of groups.	0.846
		1.7	Skills of working with friends and batchmates.	0.826
6	Self-drive.	9.1	Solely responsible for success and failure.	0.825
		9.2	Prioritize and schedule (my studies.)	0.771

Source: Author

Table 156.7 Factors, Percentage Variance and Cumulative Variance.

Factor No.	Factor Name	Extraction Sums of Squared Loadings			Rotation Sums of Squared Loadings		
		Total	% Of Variance	Cumulative %	Total	% Of Variance	Cumulative %
1	Working with diverse groups	4.153	24.432	24.432	2.227	13.101	13.101
2	Communicating with others	1.766	10.386	34.819	2.127	12.513	25.613
3	Entrepreneurial skills	1.533	9.020	43.839	2.016	11.857	37.470
4	Planning and problem-solving skills	1.399	8.232	52.071	1.590	9.355	46.824
5	Teamwork	1.119	6.583	58.654	1.586	9.329	56.154
6	Self-drive	1.052	6.187	64.841	1.477	8.687	64.841

Source: Author

alpha value is 0.777, which shows that the internal consistency is 'high.' The Cronbach alpha values and the squared multiple correlations along with the item-adjusted correlations. The Cronbach alpha calculated for each factor is given in Table 156.9. The authors retain Question 1.7 for this study. Probably rewording the question would elicit a better result.

Description of Factors

The factors that emerged out of the study are elaborated here.

Working with diverse groups

Working with diverse groups is the ability to respect and tolerate different points of view, values, and philosophies of life and deal constructively with people who differ from oneself.

Working with diverse groups consists of cognitive ability, affective ability, and behavioral ability. Cognitive ability includes the ability to understand the cultural difference among others and their practices as well. Affective ability includes a positive outlook towards cultural differences among others and their practices. Behavioral ability is acting in an acceptable social manner while interacting with culturally different people.

In an analysis carried out globally among 2400 companies conducted by Credit Suisse, it is found that adding one female member to the Board could generate higher net growth for the company while comparing to not having added one. Literature proves that working in a diverse group enhances work productivity. Companies focus on enriching their employee teams with different diverse groups so that it contributes to the company's intellectual strengths. The employers are looking for candidates who could have the 'adaptability skills of working in a diverse group and contribute to the team's effort.' (David and Heidi 2016)

Communication

Communication means the ability to express oneself properly in both verbal and non-verbal ways. Poor communication skills of the educated youth are a matter of serious concern, as they minimize employment opportunities.

"One of the top five skills that most employers expect is oral communication" (Bharathi, 2011). One of the 'employable skills that employers in retail industry are looking for is communication (Rajkumar, 2011). It is found that 'among others, communication skills have significant impact on the employability of engineering graduates' (Varwandkar, 2013). 'One of the major factors that affect employability skills is communication' (Nidhi and Ranjanibala, 2014). Research done by Clokie and Fourie (2016) shows that 'consistent with worldwide trends, local employers value communication competencies highly when recruiting new graduates.'

Entrepreneurial skills

UNESCO defines entrepreneurial skills as 'two kinds of competency: that of creating value and that of enabling contingency. The ability to create good customer relationships, competency to master the technology and competency to develop products or services, as well as production and logistical competences, belong to value creative competences. The competency to direct and steer business operations, the competency to develop personnel and the competency to master knowledge are all competencies which enable contingency.'

An entrepreneurial mindset will "help organizations innovate and succeed" Crayford et al. (2012). Entrepreneur skill is 'one of the elements which employer always looks for in graduates. Both descriptive analysis and interviews place an importance on the ability to work with minimal supervision and managing resources as well as taking business opportunity' (Rasul, 2013). Entrepreneurship skills build competencies in learners and increase their capabilities for putting knowledge into action and developing enterprises. Thus, a student with entrepreneurial skills has better employability skill and an advantage to the workforce, the community and the country's economy" (Mittal and Raghuvaran, 2021). "Entrepreneurial initiative was the only employability skill that plays a mediating role in the relationship between psychological capital and the employability perceived by students". Therefore, interventions designed to increase the perceived employability of undergraduate students should include components that focus on developing their psychological capital and entrepreneurial initiative' (Ayala et al., 2021). "Employability and entrepreneurial skills are crucial for sustainable industrial development in the digital era" (Singh et al., 2022).

Planning and problem-solving skills

Planning is the ability of a person to marshal the available resources to achieve a specific goal. Planning is a thinking skill. It is about thinking about ways and avenues to accomplish a task before attempting to work on it. Planning is a skill that helps individuals in strategizing for solutions to a problem at hand. Problem-solving skills are the ability to identify problems, analyze solutions, and select and implement optimal solution(s). The American Society for Quality (ASQ) (??) defines problem-solving as 'the act of defining a problem; determining the cause of the problem; identifying, prioritizing, and selecting alternatives for a solution; and implementing a solution.'

One of the skills 'listed for global competitiveness is problem-solving.' Dharma (2015) and Subramanian (2017) finds that 'problem-solving ability and communication can improve the employability of students.' Some of the top employability skills were planning, organizing, controlling and evaluation skills, and problem-solving aptitude (Teresa, 2022). Singh's (2022) study reveals that students perceive employability skills, such as project management skills as vital for their career outcomes. Soft skills, such as problem-solving are also perceived as required skills. Based on qualitative findings, Aynaz et al., (2002) find that two of the most important organizational skills that create employment in the higher education centers in Iran are problem-solving, and planning. The National Foundation Skills Framework 2022-2032 released by Australia's Department of Education, Skills and Employment (2022) lists planning and organizing, and problem-solving as some of the employability skills.

Teamwork

Teamwork is the ability to become a part of an organized group or team and work effectively. It is the skill that enables a person to work well with others in every situation and empathize with the others in the group.

The second top skill identified from an analysis of 1000 job advertisements is "teamwork" (Roger Bennett, 2002). The Confederation of British Industry's (2007), lists "teamwork' as one of the employability skills in their report. Gruzdev et al. (2018) find that among the skills sought by businesses indicated that one of the most desired soft skills is "interpersonal and teamwork skills". From a review of the literature, Fajaryati et al. (2020) noted that one of the skills that most employers seek in candidates is "team working." Study of teamwork done by Ivanova (2022) and others in the UAE shows a direct and significant correlation between the independent variable of teamwork and the dependent variable of Emirati students' personal readiness for employment.

Self-drive

Self-drive connotes the capacity to begin and succeed at a task without being forced into it by others. A self-driven individual is one who is motivated to accomplish something without any tangible reward.

In the context of the hospitality industry, Kevan (2020) states 'self-drive' is an 'important factor considered by recruiters.' 'For becoming a portfolio musician awareness of what you want, who you are and what you want to become; it is your drive that is required apart from other qualities like resilience' etc. 'The shift of work from regular, institutionalized work to more flexible, dynamic and project-based work requires self-drive,' etc (Orning, 2019). Higden in her study "Employability: The missing voice: how student and graduate views could be used to develop future higher education policy and inform curricula" found that third-year undergraduate students believe that they must be able to "access ongoing self-drive and

other such programs for enhancing employability." Those who are "non-motivated and lacking in both aptitude and self-drive (*emphasis ours*) or the resource capability within them it too less, should be classified as unemployable" (Kaushik et al., 2015).

Findings

The study shows the propensity of students to overrate their skills, in the absence of a testing mechanism that can reveal to them how skilled they are. The questionnaire gathered six factors that students perceive as employability skills. It is also seen that students perceive that COVID-19 has affected their employability skills due to the induced change in the mode of instruction from classroom teaching to online mode.

Conclusion

From this study, it is concluded that COVID-19 has impacted employability skills due to changes in the instruction mode at colleges. Colleges need to inculcate the employability skills expected by the industry in the course curriculum through Objective based curriculum or through extra-curricular activities to ensure that the graduates are ready to fit for the competitive jobs in the industry. There is scope for further enlarging the study to investigate and validate more specific skill sets expected from various industries.

References

American Society for Quality (ASQ) (??). What is Problem Solving? Retrieved from https://asq.org/quality-resources/problem-solving.

Bakay, M. E. (2022). 21st century skills for higher education students in EU countries: perception of academicians and HR managers. *International Education Studies*, 15(2), 14–24.

Bharathi, A. V. (2011).Communication skills–core of employability skills: issues and concerns. *Higher Learning Research Communications*, 6(4). Google Scholar

Caballero, C., and Walker, A. (2010). Work readiness in graduate recruitment and selection: a review of current assessment methods. *Journal of Teaching and Learning for Graduate Employability*, 1, 13–25.

Calvo, J. C. A., and García, G. M. (2021). The influence of psychological capital on graduates' perception of employability: the mediating role of employability skills. *Higher Education Research and Development*, 40(2), 293–308.

Clokie, T. L., and Fourie, E. (2016). Graduate employability and communication competence: Are undergraduates taught relevant skills? *Business and Professional Communication Quarterly*, 79(4), 442–463.

Confederation of British Industry (2007). Time well spent: embedding employability in workexperience. Retrieved from http://www.educationandemployers.org/wp-content/uploads/2014/06/timewell-spent-cbi.pdf.

Crayford, J., Fearon, C., McLaughlin, H., and van Vuuren, W. (2012). Affirming entrepreneurial education: learning, employability and personal development. *Industrial and Commercial Training*, 44(4), 187–193.

Department of Education, Skills and Employment, Australia (2022). National Foundation Skills Framework 2022 to 2032.

Dharma, D. (2015). Management education and employability skills: business' looking for more than a quality major in graduates: can academe get with-it? Yes. *Sri Lankan Journal of Human Resource Management*, 5(1), 1–75.

Doe, R. (2015). Work readiness among graduate students. Louisiana State University Doctoral Dissertations, 1008.

Fajaryati, N., Wiranto, Budiyono, and Akhyar, M. (2020). The employability skills needed to face the demands of work in the future: systematic literature reviews. *Open Engineering*, 10(1), 595–603.

Fenech, R., Baguant, P., and Abdelwahed, I. (2020). Work readiness across various specializations, higher colleges of technology, United Arab Emirates. *Academic Journal of Interdisciplinary Studies*, 9(4), E-ISSN, 2281-4612, ISSN 2281-3993.

Gruzdev, M. V., Kuznetsova, I. V., Tarkhanova, I. Y., and Kazakova, E. I. (2018). University graduates' soft skills: the employers' opinion. *European Journal of Contemporary Education*, 7(4), 690–698. https://files.eric.ed.gov/fulltext/EJ1200952.pdf [Web of Science ®], [Google Scholar].

Kumari, N. A., Rao, D. N., Reddy, M. S., and Kiranmai, C. (2014). The way forward for excellence in engineering institutions through education process reengineering. *International Journal of Soft Computing and Engineering (IJSCE)*, 6(2), 38–42, ISSN: 2231-2307.

Robinson, J. P. (2000). The workplace – a fact sheet – what are employability skills? *Alabama Cooperative Extension System*, I(3).

Rock, D., and Grant, H. (2016). Why diverse teams are smarter, harvard business review. *Diversity Latest Magazine*.

Roject, (2020) California State Polytechnic University, Pomona.

Ziadlou, A., Azari, K. N., and Negin, J. (2022). Identifying and analyzing the components of strategic intelligence with emphasis on the role of job-creating skills in higher education centers. *Journal of Development and Evolution Management*, 1401(49).

157 Strategic approaches to bias and variance in algorithmic profiling

C. Roshan Machayya[a]

R.V. University, Bengaluru, India

Abstract

Personalization and optimization are the keys in managing people across various fields like work, surveillance, and medicine. However, the reliance on emergent algorithms raises concerns about intense profiling potential. Unlike human memory, algorithms remember and process data differently, inheriting biases from their programming influences. While we often attribute intelligence to algorithms, the inherent biases compromise the benefit of doubt we give them. This paper explores how bias and variance in algorithmic processes impact management, work, surveillance, and medicine. Through case studies, it highlights the dangerous outcomes of data-driven profiling optimization, underscoring the need for a legal framework to address algorithmic processing in sensitive areas.

Keywords: AI, algorithm, bias, management, profiling, variance

Introduction

Prejudice and bias are detrimental to the equivocal opportunity for people's fair participation in society, work, and all things that govern everyday existence. We rely on software, algorithms, and artificial intelligence (AI) that has been shown time and again to incorporate serious bias in its functionality across areas (Gianfrancesco, 2018; Heilweil, 2020 ; Real-Life Examples of Discriminating Artificial Intelligence (n.d.) Esposito, 2022). Biases and prejudice are found in algorithmic programming because consciously or not, the biases of programmers make their way into AI based and algorithmic driven tools (Esposito, 2022). This issue is aggravated by the fact that algorithms make use of all available information from big data sources without picking data points and discarding irrelevant information (Esposito, 2022).

Algorithms, AI, and machines learn from a process called deep learning among many others forms of learning. This is a process that refers to training deep neural networks where the idea of depth does not reference sophistication but depth in layers of the network being trained (Mitchell, 2020). In the process of learning and teaching algorithms, AI and more specifically heavy data reliant neural networks such as Convolutional Neural Networks or ConvNets, the process of learning is conducted via a supervised learning process given that they also require a huge amount of human effort. (Mitchess, 2020). This is a process of producing intelligence in response to creating a system of communication between actual humans and machine intelligence where machine intelligence can be understood as an analysis referencing a complex of highly specialized computational systems (Zuboff, 2019). Elena Esposito remarks that machines do not have to be intelligent since they can produce information not previously considered by humans and appear interesting and as competent communication partners not because they have become intelligent, but because they no longer must try to (Esposito, 2022). Within an ecosystem of machine intelligence, AI, and algorithm interaction with human experiences, we find that our search for solutions to management problems in the areas of work, medicine, and surveillance are potentially more problematic than quantified with resolutions. While we are confronted with a future of vast unknowns in terms of technological capabilities as well as legislative measures that safeguard our interests and humanity in different aspects of everyday living, to grant the complete benefit of doubt to machine intelligence is problematic. This paper explores the disconnect between affected human experiences and the perception of a human likeness that we have consented to run our managerial affairs. To perceive a sense of human likeness in the communication between humans and machine intelligence does take us closer to the point where machines pass the Turing test. Realistically, we still do not have adequate reason to grant the notion of intelligence to machines irrespective of their pattern-based outcome capabilities because we are still far from actual intelligence (Karpathy, 2012).

[a]roshanm@rvu.edu.in

Research Methodology

This paper explores the real-world impact of algorithms, focusing on work management, medicine, and surveillance in the United States and India. Examining AI's influence on prejudice, bias, and its intersection with law, it aims to understand the consequences, considering the unique perspectives of these two countries.

Geographical focus:
- Consideration of case studies from the United States of America and India.
- Justification for choosing the United States due to its global leadership in AI development.
- Selection of India as the country of origin for the paper.

Global AI landscape:
- Brief reference to a 2023 report on the leading countries in AI development.
- Recognition of the United States as the current global leader in AI.

Case studies:
- In-depth exploration of specific cases from the United States and India.
- Highlighting the relevance of these case studies in understanding the diverse impacts of algorithms.

AI's impact on different sectors:
- Discussion on how AI influences work management, medicine, and surveillance.
- Recognition of the multifaceted consequences of AI applications in real-world scenarios.

Intersection with prejudice, bias, and law:
- Examination of AI's impact on prejudice and bias.
- Exploration of the intersection between AI, law, and human experiences.
- Consideration of legal and ethical implications arising from algorithmic decisions.

Significance of the Indian context:
- Acknowledgment of India as the country of origin for the paper.
- Insight into how the Indian context contributes to the overall understanding of AI's impact.

Bias, Variance, and Prejudice

With the biases and prejudices of actual algorithm architects making their way into algorithm designs, one must contend with what constitutes truth and validity in the real world as against the world that is produced by the data that machine intelligence gathers and creates. The essence of the problem lies in the understanding of intelligence - something remarkably subjective. Arguably, the validity of intelligence cannot lie in the idea of a machine or AI carrying out tasks that rely on pattern-based outcomes only. The worry with intelligence is the production of a world that is driven by the lack of data relevance from scouring the world of big data where 90% of all big data was produced in the last two years alone (Matz, n.d.). Ergo, the production of a post truth world driven by big data and propagated through machine learning systems coupled with social networks that shape everyday life and govern social relations (Shepard, 2022). Interestingly, 80-90 percent of generated data consisting of images, documents, audio, video, social media posts etc. is unstructured data (Davis, 2019). This will have a massive impact on everyday human experiences in different aspects of life and work that rely on effective management.

Technological advancements in AI, algorithm design, and machine intelligence are cornerstones of innovations in management in areas of work, medicine, and surveillance; it is critical to note that in the world outside of these machines, humans are essentially dealing with humans. Essentially our life experiences factor in very limited experiences that negate a lot of information and stimuli from the outside world. In essence, reality is reduced by perception, and perception is reduced by language because perception is an interface between reality and an individual delivering a version of reality adequate for individual decisions and actions adequate for individual agency (Enfield, 2022). In the midst of the limited and simplified perception of reality that has carried civilization forward all this time, the language to deal with a notion of reality and potentially managerial prejudice that comes with AI presents a danger. In the process of productivity personalization and outcome optimization, we must consider the agency of an individual in the process of creation in work and their relation to their work. At the same time, to let AI, algorithms and machine intelligence do so might result in less than favorable outcomes.

If we consider predictability in work and management optimization and favorable productivity, we must consider human experiences that are influenced by social conditions. The problem with predictive algorithms is that they are not only technical but require social and communicative conditioning of their use (Esposito, 2022).

As much as bias and prejudice is rooted in the process and outcome of memory and experiences, they do not fully limit the possibility of various outcomes for the future. On the other hand, biases within algorithms and AI curtail the future without adequate intervention. Esposito remarks that the problem is related to the management of the relationship between the past and the future, a task of memory but an outfitted system (in the guise of machine intelligence and algorithms) memorizes the past and uses this to predict the future (Esposito, 2022).

Legal Engagement: Risks and Vulnerabilities

At the moment, we lack a very serious engagement with a legal language that takes into account the vulnerabilities that AI and emergent technology exposes us to. In recent times in India, the biggest and arguably the first serious discussion on technology and law was with the Aadhaar case or the 'right to privacy judgement' (Justice [Retd.] K.S. Puttaswamy v. Union of India) where the Supreme Court of India was asked to consider the widespread use of technology and its relationship between the State, individual, corporations and society (Bhatia, 2019, 331). The reliance that we express on algorithms, machine intelligence and AI driven tools in the areas of management, work, medicine, and surveillance exposes us to massive vulnerabilities. Insofar as one finds pride in data driven optimization to guide virtually all our processes potentially, the existence of data is always one that comes with risks.

Within the first quarter of 2023 there were over 6 million data records exposed through data breaches and since the first quarter of 2020, the highest instances of data breaches were recorded amounting to breaches of 125 million data sets by the fourth quarter of 2020 (Petrosyan, 2023). The combination of social data combined with public databases, cookies, beacons and location history can lead to serious consequences (Goodman, 2015). This imposes a contingency since improper management of raw data across cyberspaces may lead to detrimental outcomes with legislation. This is because a lot of national jurisdictions lack a specific legal language to deal with this contingency. For the ones that do, for example, in the United States of America, social networks are considered as public spaces where users have no expectation of privacy in the data their service providers collect on them (Goodman, 2015). This implies that one's data is not private but constitutes a part of business records of any institution in possession of said data (Goodman, 2015). People as data principalities are potentially the biggest victims in the event of data and machine intelligence contingencies.

In essence, any surveillance agency can access any user's data irrespective of the existence of a legal language that prevents or regulates this issue. Within the United States of America as of 2015, the state spent US$ 574 per taxpayer or 6.5 cents an hour to track each and every American citizen (Goodman, 2015). In the 'right to privacy judgement' (Justice [Retd.] K.S. Puttaswamy vs Union of India) also known as the Aadhaar judgement, a nine-judge bench of the Supreme court of India laid out the judgement that the constitution of India did guarantee privacy as fundamental right (Bhatia, 2023). This verdict did not decide the extent and circumstances by which the state can surveil its citizens among others, despite providing a constitutional framework within which similar cases can be decided by courts in the future (Bhatia, 2023). Recently, India passed the Digital Personal Data Protection Bill, 2023. This policy outlines how technology companies process user data, gives the users the right to correct and erase their personal data, proposes fines up to US$ 30 million for violations and noncompliance (Boben et al., 2023). However, this bill does not adequately address the safeguards against overboard surveillance, prevents data principals from protecting their personal data from any online scraping, and permits exempted state instrumentality(s) to process data outside the purview of the bill (Jain and Waghre, 2023). However, the issue with this utilization of managing data from surveillance and behavioral surplus to make sense of people management, security and people's activities is that the data is not necessarily limited just to a state apparatus. All data will leak with detrimental consequences. An adequate legal language would propose that any data presented without one's consent in all managerial affairs must constitute a leak that endangers life. Consensual posting about an individual's data too poses a risk. During the terrorist attacks in Mumbai that took place on 26 November 2008, it took a simple internet search for the terrorists to realize that their hostage Mr. K.R. Ramamoorthy was a high value individual being the chairman of ING Vysya Bank at that time (Goodman, 2015). We observe that with data and algorithms that rely on publicly available information that all data is a public record of an institution. In such cases, surveillance cannot utilize data to prevent contingency caused by publicly available data.

Intelligence Production, Management, Dangers

To present the idea that machine intelligence, AI, and algorithms produce novel outcomes from their pattern-based learning is an idea of limited bearing for now. The production of novel and unique ideas and outcomes is majorly the result of the production of histories and the historicity of experiences. While the point was made earlier in this study that algorithms do carry the prejudices of their designers with them in some form or the other, to look the other way or to normalize the experiences that come with this is detrimental to management across areas of work, health, and surveillance. Profiling based on algorithmic optimization used by deep learning machine intelligence have effects that are discriminatory, racist, and unfair (Kenny, 2021). The production of histories through human experiences and stimuli is a part of the process of learning. Algorithms rely on the production of outcomes on specificity - the presentation and not the production of decision (s) leading to communication issues that are centric to algorithms that produce the realities we must deal with (Esposito, 2022). The outcome of this issue is the outcome of AI-driven policing with the use of historical data or patterns which are racist because of correlations and not causations (Hao, 2019). Criminal risk assessment tools and predictive algorithms not only fail for dark skinned individuals but also mistake members of the Congress of the United States of America as convicted criminals (Hao, 2019). The management of the relationship between the past and the future is the task of memory and algorithms memorize this past and use this information to predict the future (Esposito, 2022). The system of predictive profiling is prone to errors of generalization because hindsight is typically more accurate than foresight (Esposito, 2022). Bias as a reflection of language processes presents a new challenge. Arguably we are not seeking statements as facts to help us figure out what we should believe because we already know what to believe - we seek statements to justify those beliefs (Enfield, 2022). Often, we still see this unfold deeply held prejudices. For example, a health care algorithm used on more than 200 million people in the United States of America faulted in its bias because of its reliance on previous medical expenditure, leaving out a considerable number of people who self-identified as black folks were left out from critical care because the algorithm used health costs as an indicator for being healthier than equally sick white patients (Barton et al., 2023). Within the world of work and recruitment, AI did falter in the awareness creation process and employment opportunities through its discriminatory advertising (Chen, 2022).

Conclusion

Now the functionality of machine intelligence, artificial intelligence (AI), and algorithmic outcomes in the world of managing the affairs of work optimization, medicine, and surveillance are supervised by human intervention to a large degree. We intervene when the functionality of our machines does not meet the intended outcomes. There is human supervision in outcomes as well as the processes required to fulfil these outcomes. However, with machine intelligence, algorithmic outcomes, and AI generally, we must consider the leeway humans can guarantee to these processes. Emergent algorithms because of AI evolution and genesis will outclass the need for human supervision. But the notion of intelligence in this case will be different from what we understand today. As an understanding, eventually AI will process data in ways unique to itself. The experience of both machine and human intelligence and its interaction with each other is transactional. An anthropomorphic take on intelligence will only undermine the potential of machine intelligence as it gets closer to a genesis unique to itself. Arguably, our experiences with management across sections of life are anthropomorphic and it would be inadequate to reduce the functionality of machine intelligence to the same world view. It is a safe outcome at this point. But this does not characterize the evolution of intelligence and its capabilities. At this moment, we manage machines and algorithms to manage other people, their work, and outcomes. The trade-off is the negation of machines and algorithms as the middleman. At that time, the outcomes that characterize our role under machine management and outcome optimization will be far from what any legal language can articulate.

In the pursuit of machine intelligence safety and therefore algorithmic intelligence, care must be taken for information hazards (Bostrom, 2016). It is a commitment to safety and the right practices in AI utilization, research and its incorporation into the governance in everyday human affairs. What constitutes a sum zero game in the endeavors of AI algorithms and machine intelligence governing human affairs is the disconnect between a machine's and a human's understanding of human histories and experiences. Supervision does not make up for this. It fixes biases and prejudices for the time being and optimizes productivity with narrower definitions of what constitutes the idea of being productive. Narrower definitions outline smarter reasoning capabilities for a machine. It is also a reflection of our missing endeavor to understand our own shortcoming in language despite being governed by the contours of it. In the eventuality of an AI intelligence explosion and the eventuality of machine superintelligence, we must deal with a mismatch in our experiences, communication, and expectations out of AI, algorithms, and machine learning. Bostrom aptly explains this mismatch as "... humans are like small children playing with a bomb. Such is the mismatch between power of our plaything and the immaturity of our conduct" (Bostrom, 2016). The engagement of AI and its tools in everyday life, and especially aspects concerning health, work, and surveillance have opened possibilities while at the same time bartering liberty and algorithmic justice for mass produced convenience. This turn of managerial history has human beings outsource previously unimaginable levels of productivity to machine intelligence and algorithms in exchange for a future with diminished ownership of time and space foregrounded in post-truth realities designed by big data. In 2016, a Whitehouse report pointed out that areas of the highest impact of AI will be difficult to predict but policy considerations must account for the whole economy (Lee, 2016).

The conveniences of today that come with AI, machine intelligence and algorithmic functionality foregrounds an autonomous future. An autonomous future comes with uncertainty. In areas of human resource management, work, medicine, and surveillance we must be proactive in ensuring that the promise of optimization does not pave the way for injustice. Private use of algorithmic tools has to be disclosed within a legal framework that permits its regulation and fair use in the most transparent way possible.

References

Barton, M., Hamza, M., and Guevel, B. (2023). Racial equity in healthcare machine learning: Illustrating bias in models with minimal bias mitigation. *Cureus*, 15(2).

Bhatia, G. (2019). The Transformative Constitution: Aradical Biography in Nine Acts. Harper Collins India.

Bhatia, G. (2023). Unsealed Covers: Adecade of the Constitution, the Courts and the State. HarperCollins India.

Boben, B., Patel, S., and Donovan, K. (2023). India Passes Data Protection Law Amid Surveillance Concerns. Reuters.

Bostrom, N. (2016). Superintelligence: Paths, Dangers, Strategies. Oxford University Press.

Chen, Z. (2022). Collaboration among recruiters and artificial intelligence: removing human prejudices in employment. *Cognition, Technology and Work*, 25, 135–149. https://doi.org/10.1007/s10111-022-00716-0.

Davis, D. (2019). AI Unleashes the Power of Unstructured Data. CIO.

Enfield, N. J. (2022). Language Vs. Reality: Why Language is Good for Lawyers and Bad for Scientists. MIT Press.

Esposito (2022). Artificial Communication: How Algorithms Produce Social Intelligence. MIT Press.

Gianfrancesco, M. A. (2018). Potential Biases in Machine Learning Algorithms Using Electronic Health Record Data. NCBI.

158 Impact of artificial intelligence in human resource management: a path to frontier from now

R. Shanmugapriya and U. Amaleshwari[a]

D.D.G.D Vaishnav College, Chennai, India

Abstract

In the ever-evolving digital landscape, businesses are venturing into the realm of artificial intelligence (AI), presenting both promise and challenges for human resource management (HRM). Despite its potential, there's a noticeable gap between what AI can do and its current applications in HR. The looming threat lies in the necessity for upskilling to prevent job displacement. However, hurdles in implementing data science in HR persist, including the complexity of HR phenomena, constraints with small data sets, ethical concerns, and employee reactions to algorithmic management. This study lays the groundwork for AI in HRM, aiming to enhance operations while proposing practical solutions that emulate human intelligence, emphasizing causal reasoning, randomization, and process formalization for socially acceptable and economically effective employee management.

Keywords: Artificial intelligence, human resource management, technology, hiring, data analytics, talent

Introduction

Artificial intelligence (AI) is revolutionizing traditional human resource management (HRM) practices, boosting efficiency across diverse industrial sectors. Tools like AI-powered chatbots and auto-reply systems streamline recruitment processes, utilizing predictive analytics to identify key performers. While ethical concerns persist, the amalgamation of AI into HRM brings significant benefits. Automation through AI and machine learning (ML) enhances operational efficacy, eliminating bias in decision-making. AI tools, such as chatbots, interact with candidates, saving time and improving overall efficiency in recruitment. In performance management, AI tracks real-time employee data, providing valuable insights for objective evaluations. Virtual Assisting tools identify trends, enabling data-driven decisions on promotions, audits, bonuses, and skill-oriented training. As technology advances, the integration of AI in HRM emerges as a frontier for optimizing talent management processes.

In conclusion, this article delves into the impact of AI on HRM, emphasizing its transformative benefits and acknowledging ethical considerations. The marriage of AI with human intelligence offers innovative tools for streamlined processes, informed decision-making, and enhanced employee experiences. As AI continues to advance, its integration in HRM stands as a pivotal approach to optimize talent management in the digital era.

Literature Review

Table 158.1 AI Revolution in HRM: a comprehensive review of key studies and insights.

Author name	Study
Murugesan et al. (2023)	Highlights cautious HR adaptation to AI challenges, involving 271 experts across sectors, focusing on five AI applications and three HR readiness elements.
Zielinski (2023)	Predicts increased use of HR technologies to enhance employee experience, improve recruiting, and identify skills gaps.
Aggarwal et al. (2023)	Emphasizes the impact of advanced technologies on HRM activities and tactics, including hiring, training, and human-AI collaboration.
GARTNER (2023)	Reports rapid AI deployment in HR, with 52% exploring generative AI use cases and 81% improving process efficiency.
Li et al. (2023)	Provides insights into how AI implementation affects HRM processes, emphasizing its impact on company performance and individual well-being.

[a]amalaumapathi@gmail.com

Author name	Study
Soni et al. (2022)	Addresses diverse AI issues, from socio-economic impacts to transparency and trust creation, in various contexts.
Palos-Sánchez et al. (2022)	Performs a bibliometric analysis of AI in HRM literature, connecting tools, adaptive measures, and impact across different industry levels.
Evseeva et al. (2021)	Discusses AI's wide applications in various sectors due to digitalization, emphasizing its significant role in global development.
Zhu et al. (2021)	Proposes a four-stage model of HRM reforms in the AI era, presenting strategies for coordinated HRM and AI development.
Padmanabhan (2020)	Meticulously explores Artificial Intelligence, describing its autonomy-mimicking capabilities through authentic algorithms and machine languages.

Source: Author

Study objective
- Optimize various HR processes
- Enable HR professionals to focus on strategic initiatives
- Streamline recruitment processes
- Improve performance management
- Enhance training and development initiatives
- Futuristic optimization of HRM in diverse industrial sectors.

Research methodology
The research adopted a mixed-method approach to ensure a well-rounded perspective. It encompassed a thorough review of academic literature, industry reports, and case studies. Additionally, key insights were sought through interviews with HR professionals and experts in the field.

AI in HR metrics
AI has tremendous potential to revolutionize HRM metrics by providing real-time data analytics and predictive insights virtually. Traditional metrics such as time-to-hire, human capital turnover, and evaluation of performance can be enhanced through AI/ML-driven algorithms. For instance, AI-powered recruitment platforms can scrutinize candidate profiles, with job requirements, and provide recommendations to HR professionals based on required skill sets. Furthermore, AI algorithms can identify patterns in performance data and suggest genuine personalized development plans for career constructive employees. By leveraging AI in HRM metrics, organizations can make data-driven decisions and enhance overall performance with authentic measures.

The significant integration of AI in HRM has led to the development of various metrics conglomerate the impact and effectiveness. These measured metrics help organizations evaluate the success of their AI initiatives and make data-driven decisions. Some common AI in HRM metrics include:

- Time to hire: Recruitment through AI-powered tools can reduce the time it has taken to hire candidate by automating various stages significantly.
- Cost per hire: AI can help organizations in reducing costs associated with recruitment effectively by automating task, eliminating manual interventions.
- Employee performance: Tools relating AI-powered performance management can track employee performance ethically, providing insights into productive goal attainment and effective employee engagement.
- Training effectiveness: Training and development can be enhanced through AI providing personalized recommendations, consistent and interactive learning experiences, and feedback.
- Employee satisfaction: Chatbots and virtual assistants can improve employee experiences by delivering instant supportive measures, replying to queries, in a self-paced method.

These HR metrics demonstrate the tangible impact of AI in HRM providing organizations with valuable insights to optimize their HR processes informatively. Gartner hype cycle gives a clear affirmative research data from renowned sources.

Impact of AI in HRM
The impact of AI in HRM is radically profound and transformative. A pivotal significant aspect is the recruitment processes automation as augmented. Chatbots that are AI-powered can engage with candidates involved, answer queries, and even conduct initial screenings process. This saves time and ensures a seamless candidate experience. This enables HR pro to make informed decisions regarding talent management and succession rate of planning. Additionally, AI can facilitate personalized training and development initiatives by recommending learning tools, upskilling courses, resources based on individual employee needs and adaptable interest. Social media,

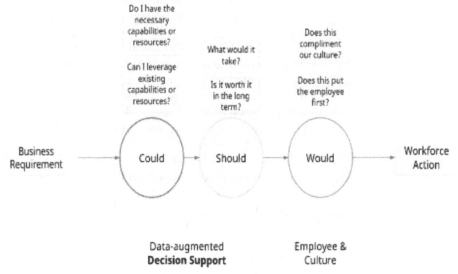

Figure 158.1 Influence of AI in HR analytics
Source: Author

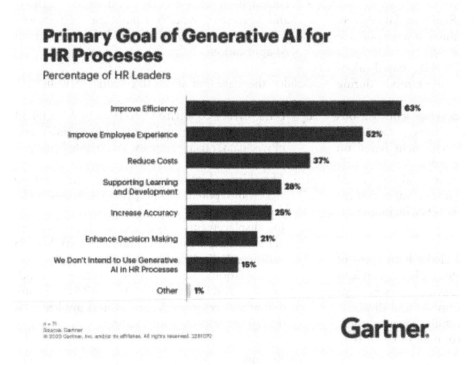

Figure 158.2 AI-HRM implementation and adaptability
Source: Author

digital-networking platforms, NLP based virtual reality sectors were widely benefits for this process. The impact of AI in HRM is evident in its ability to optimize processes, functions enhance decision-making, and improve overall organizational performance there by cost cutting adequately

Furthermore, the impact of AI in HRM is revolutionizing employee experiences with several key benefits, including:

- Enhanced efficiency: Repetitive time-consuming tasks frees HR professionals to focus on strate-

Figure 158.3 Self-developed diagrammatic representation of AI-HRM impact
Source: Author

gic initiatives and high-end value-added activities through AI.
- Improved decision-making: Real time data driven, decision making and bias reduction were possible by enabling AI-HR analytics.
- Streamlined Recruitment: AI/ML based algorithms fetches Big Data in faster mode during enormous selection
- Personalized training and development: Various virtual learning platforms delivers personalized training and channelized development based on employee preferred performances.
- Enhanced employee experiences: Realtime virtual assistants, chatbots, proving instant support there by improvising talent and benefits including attendance

However, it is trivial to acknowledge limitations of AI in HRM. The reliance on AI technologies can lead to data privacy and security concerns, biases in algorithms, and potential job replacements and displacements. Organizations must carefully consider these limitations and implement appropriate safeguards to ensure employee retention, ethical and responsible use of AI in HRM diplomatically.

Advantages and limitations in AI- HRM

While the integration of AI, ML, DL, offers numerous advantages in HRM, it is essential to acknowledge its limitations as well. Advantages include increased efficiency, reduced bias, and improved decision-making. AI can automate repetitive e-tasks, allowing HR professionals to focus on strategic initiatives. In addition,

AI algorithms can eliminate human biases. However, limitations such as data privacy concerns and ethical considerations with respect to policy and other legal need to be addressed. Organizations must ensure that AI systems are transparent, fair, and comply with relevant regulations legitimately. Moreover, the human touch cannot be entirely replaced by AI powerbands, and HR professionals must strike a balance between technology and human interaction officially. Some advantages include:

- Improved efficiency and productivity: Automates manual tasks, reducing effort required and time constraint in completing HR processes.
- Enhanced decision-making: Wide range of data-directed decisions were possible through AI-powered analytics.
- Reduced biases: AI driven algorithms can eliminate biases associated with human decision-making, resulting in fair HR practices, nullifying human errors.
- Personalized experiences: Customized training and suggestive support enhancing their experiences can be effectively delivered through distinct AI applications

Besides, there are limitations to consider as well:

i. Data privacy concerns: Utilization of AI in HRM involves analyzing and processing sensitive employee data, raising security, and highlighting privacy concerns.
ii. Algorithmic biases: Inheriting trained database algorithms, potentially perpetuating biases in HR processes.
iii. Job displacements: Requiring workforce reskilling and redeployment technologies may lead to various job displacement criteria.
iv. Organizations must carefully evaluate the advantages and limitations of AI in HRM to ensure diplomatic, responsible, and ethical implementation of the respective applications.

Conclusion

The significance and impact of artificial intelligence (AI) in human resource management (HRM) is undeniable, offering organizations innovative tools to streamline processes, pipeline enhancement decision-making, and improved overall efficiency. Recruitment, performance management, and learning and development have been notably transformed by AI technologies, enabling faster and more accurate candidate selection efficiently, objective performance evaluations, and personalized skill developing experiences. Although advantages of AI in HRM include enhanced efficiency, improved decision-making, and personalized experiences for employees. However, it is crucial to recognize the limitations of AI in HRM sooner or later, including data privacy concerns, algorithmic biases, and potential job displacements. Organizations must carefully evaluate these limitations and implement appropriate precautions to clinch responsible and ethical use of AI technologies. By doing so, organizations can harness the complete prospective AI in HRM, driving strategic initiatives and creating a positive impact on employee experiences path frontier. Revolutionizing traditional HR, paving the way for future HR-AI to drive organization at their skyrocketing success.

References

Aggarwal, S., et al. (2023). Impact of artificial intelligence on human resource management: a review of literature. *International Journal of Scientific and Engineering Research*, 11(4).

Evseeva, S., et al. (2021). Application of artificial intelligence in human resource management in the agricultural sector. In E3S Web of Conferences, DOI:10.1051/e3sconf/202125801010.

GARTNER (2023). AI in HR: A Guide to Implementing AI in Your HR Organization.

Li, P., et al. (2023). How does artificial intelligence impact human resources performance: evidence from a healthcare institution in the United Arab Emirates. *Journal of Innovation and Knowledge* , DOI: 10.1016/j.jik.2023.100340.

Murugesan, U. et al. (2023). A study of artificial intelligence impacts on Human Resource Digitalization in Industry 4.0. *Digital Applications in Industry and Engineering Journal* , doi.org/10.1016/j.dajour.2023.100249.

Padmanabhan, S. A. (2020). Impact of Artificial Intelligence (AI) on Human Resources (HR) Industry. LinkedIn.

Palos-Sánchez, P. R., et al. (2022). Artificial intelligence and human resources management: a bibliometric analysis. *Human Resource Development Quarterly* , 36(1).

Soni, J., et al. (2022). A study on the impact of artificial intelligence on human resource management. *International Journal of Research and Analytical Reviews*, 9(2).

Zhu, H., et al. (2021). Impact of artificial intelligence on human resource management and its countermeasures. In Proceedings of the 2021 International Conference on Artificial Intelligence and Advanced Manufacturing (pp. 1210–1214). doi.org/10.1145/3495018.3495367.

Zielinski, D. (2023). 2023 HR Technology Trends: Talent Marketplaces, Expanding AI and Optimizing Existing Systems. SHRM.

159 Build brand strength: use digital marketing to boost recognition and value

Stanley Vincent Gnanamanickam[1], Parvez A. Khan[2], Chandramowleeswaran Gnanasekaran[3] and Manoj Govindaraj[4,a]

[1]Mount Carmel College Autonomous, Bengaluru, India

[2]Atria University, Bangalore India

[3,4]Institute of Science and Technology, Avadi, Chennai, India

Abstract

The objective of this study is regarding the effectiveness of digital marketing in terms of enhancing brand awareness. In order to accomplish this, an analysis is conducted on the interrelationships among electronic mail, mobile phones, search engine optimization (SEO), and corporate websites. Following the acquisition of 210 responses to a somewhat modified survey, the researchers employed quantitative research methodologies, specifically structural equation modelling, to examine the various components under investigation. An examination of the tangible advantages of digital marketing tactics demonstrates that various channels contribute to enhancing the brand equity within the service sectors of Chennai. Approaches that ensure their sustained leadership in their sectors and marketplaces.

Keywords: Brand equity, digital marketing, sustainability

Introduction

In today's fast-paced digital world, businesses in the service industry know how important brand value is for long-term success. Brand value, which is all about what people think of a brand, is crucial for keeping customers loyal and staying competitive. Digital marketing has become a big deal in this rapidly changing environment, making it a must for building up brand value. The whole management team has the job of making sure the company's brand is as good as it can be. Marketing directors focus on making the brand more visible and reaching more people for long-term success. This study is all about coming up with a solid plan to use digital marketing to create positive opinions about a brand and boost its value in the service industry. But, in today's world with social media, lots of online stuff, and changing search engine optimization (SEO) rules, finding the right balance is a bit tricky.

Literature Review

Table 159.1 Insights from different studies on marketing trends.

Author name	Study
Leeflang et al. (2014)	Digital marketing integrates technology with traditional methods to expand clientele using mobile apps (Almaazmi et al., 2021). The influence of search engines and non-traditional competition shapes digital marketing (Ahmed et al., 2020; Diventy et al., 2021).
Raji et al. (2018)	Brand marketing is crucial for shaping students' perceptions in higher education. Examples include SEO and email marketing.
Ramanathan et al. (2017)	Integrated marketing communication (IMC) in brand management is effective for positive brand image compared to public relations. Falls under strategic management.
Bolat and O'Sullivan, (2017)	Search engine marketing (SEM) increases product sales by enhancing product exposure in search engine rankings. SEO is crucial for augmenting website traffic.
Jan and Ammari (2016)	SEO tactics are essential for effective communication with an online audience. Paid ads differ from search engine promotion. SEO helps improve search rankings for educational institutions.

[a]manoj.nmcc@gmail.com

Author name	Study
Sinclair (2017)	Companies should include brand performance and value in the management discussion of annual reports. Examines methodological considerations and highlights marketing's significance.
Datta et al. (2017)	Analysis of assessing brand capital through consumer perceptions or sales. Positive correlation between brand capital and sales metrics.
Borkovsky (2018)	Framework for structural brand management assessing a company's brand value based on anticipated future cash flows. Effective advertising may enhance brand worth but could diminish overall company value.

Source: Author

Objective

- Investigate the diverse array of digital marketing instruments utilized for the purpose of brand promotion.
- Analyze the impact of digital marketing strategies on the enhancement of brand equity.

Hypotheses

H1: Social media marketing exerts a substantial influence on brand equity.

H2: Email marketing exerts a significant impact on brand equity.

H3: Mobile phone marketing plays a noteworthy role in shaping brand equity.

H4: SEO marketing contributes significantly to brand equity.

H5: Marketing through the company's website is a significant determinant of brand equity.

Research methodology

- **Research approach:** We started with a descriptive survey to build our study.
- **Data collection method:** Used a questionnaire to gather info from the people we're interested in.
- **Demographic info:** Covered basics like age, gender, job situation, education, and company type.
- **Variables:** Looked at both dependent and independent factors in the survey questions.
- **Scoring system:** People rated their answers from 1 (disagree) to 5 (agree).
- **Sampling:** Picked participants from various service industries in Chennai.
- **Data analysis:** Checked out responses from 235 questionnaires but focused on 210 for closer study.
- **Analysis tools:** Used SPSS version 24 and AMOS for crunching numbers.
- **Descriptive stats:** Used mean and standard deviation to summarize the data.
- **Reliability check:** Made sure our data was solid using Cronbach's alpha.

Table 159.2 Descriptive statistics.

Measures	Items	Frequency	Percentage
Gender	Male	186	64.4
	Female	104	35.6
Age	Below 28	38	13
	28-40	203	70
	Above 40	49	17
Marital Status	Married	171	58.9
	Unmarried	119	41.4
Years of experience	0-2	47	16.2
	3-5	113	38.7
	4-7	92	31.6
	≥10	38	13.7

Source: Primary data

- **Hypothesis testing:** Put our ideas to the test using something called structural equation modelling (SEM).

Analysis and interpretation

The data shows that most people in the service industry are guys (64.4%), mostly aged 28-40 (70%). Nearly 59% are married, and work experience is spread out, with many having 3-5 years (38.7%). This info helps understand our group, so we can plan better.

All the strategies are having mean above 3.000.

The p value for all the strategies is less than 0.05 which shows that the relation between digital marketing strategies and brand equity is significant. Companies' website and brand equity is having correlation of 0.432 whereas other also show positive correlation.

Structural Equation Modelling (SEM) explores relationships between components. Confirmatory Factor Analysis (CFA) validates items, following literature guidelines. Our study assessed digital marketing's impact on brand equity, using critical ratios and p-values. A hypothesis is accepted with CR >

Statistics	Mean	Std. Deviation
Social media marketing	3.636	.9122
Email marketing	3.652	.8062
Mobile phone marketing	3.077	.8426
Search engine optimization	3.144	.7209
Companies' websites	3.519	.8389
Brand Equity	3.459	.5824

Figure 159.1 Mean and standard deviation
Source: Author

		Social media	Email_	Mobile phone	Search engine	Companies' websites	Brand Equity
Social media	Pearson Correlation	1	.190**	.173*	.200**	.205**	.329**
	Sig. (2-tailed)		.006	.012	.004	.003	.000
Email	Pearson Correlation	.190**	1	.202**	.068	.316**	.318**
	Sig. (2-tailed)	.006		.003	.330	.000	.000
Mobile phone	Pearson Correlation	.173*	.202**	1	.349**	.225**	.371**
	Sig. (2-tailed)	.012	.003		.000	.001	.000
Search engine	Pearson Correlation	.200**	.068	.349**	1	.232**	.338**
	Sig. (2-tailed)	.004	.330	.000		.001	.000
Companies' websites	Pearson Correlation	.205**	.316**	.225**	.232**	1	.432**
	Sig. (2-tailed)	.003	.000	.001	.001		.000
Brand Equity	Pearson Correlation	.329**	.318**	.371**	.338**	.432**	1
	Sig. (2-tailed)	.000	.000	.000	.000	.000	

**. Correlation is significant at the 0.01 level (2-tailed).
*. Correlation is significant at the 0.05 level (2-tailed).

Figure 159.2 Correlation
Source: Author

1.96, $p < 0.05$, at a 5% significance level (Hair et al., 2010).

After analyzing various marketing channels, it was found that social media, email, mobile, SEO, and website marketing all significantly and positively impact brand equity. These results highlight the importance of integrating these strategies.

The model shows mixed goodness of fit results. While indices like CFI and TLI suggest a good fit, RMSEA, GFI, and AGFI indicate a marginal fit. This implies the model is okay but could use some tweaks to align better with the data. Consider the analysis purpose when interpreting these results.

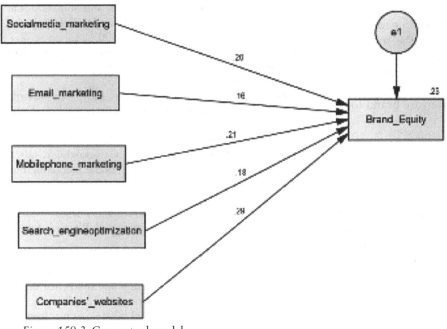

Figure 159.3 Conceptual model
Source: Author

Table 159.3 Regression weights.

S.No.	Hypotheses	CR	Regression weights	P value	Result
H1	Social media marketing significantly influences brand equity	3.232	0.197	0.001	Accepted
H2	Email marketing significantly influences brand equity	2.675	0.163	0.007	Accepted
H3	Mobile phone marketing significantly influences brand equity	3.464	0.211	***	Accepted
H4	Search engine optimization marketing significantly influences brand equity	2.905	0.177	0.004	Accepted
H5	Company's website marketing significantly influences brand equity	4.786	0.291	***	Accepted

Source: Author

Table 159.4 Model evaluations.

Goodness of fit index	Cut-off values	Analysis results	Model evaluations
CMIN/Df	<3	1.595	Good
RMSEA	≤0.08	0.053	Marginal
CFI	≥0.95	0.957	Good
TLI	≥0.95	0.95	Good
GFI	≥0.90	0.889	Marginal
AGFI	≥0.90	0.856	Marginal

Source: Author

Discussion

This study explored how impact consumer perception of service sector brands. The results revealed a positive impact on brand perception when utilizing all three digital tactics. Marketing managers aiming to boost brand recognition should prioritize introducing innovations and producing up-to-date content aligned with digital trends. Creating engaging social media content, informing consumers about innovations, and actively engaging through feedback channels play crucial roles. The study emphasizes the transformative effect of social media on brand-consumer interactions, underscoring the value of a robust online presence. Additionally, offering rewards on social media emerges as a strategy to increase brand loyalty and customer commitment.

Conclusion

The study highlights how social media marketing can significantly boost businesses by enhancing brand recognition, client loyalty, and overall profitability. Utilizing email communication tailored to individual interests further deepens customer impressions. In the digital age, where global communication is paramount, adopting effective digital marketing practices is not just a trend but a cost-saving necessity, particularly in the face of the pandemic's challenges (Dash et al., 2021).

Digital marketing, as a potent tool, empowers service sector businesses to strengthen brand equity by engaging audiences through online platforms, creating compelling narratives, and adapting strategies in real-time. The study emphasizes the transformative impact of digital marketing, positioning it as an integral aspect for service sector businesses to thrive in an evolving digital landscape, underscoring the narrative of transformation, resilience, and progression in the quest for elevated brand equity.

References

Agostini, L., Nosella, A., Sarala, R., Spender, J. C., and Wegner, D. (2020). Tracing the evolution of the literature on knowledge management in inter-organizational contexts: a bibliometric analysis. *Journal of Knowledge Management*, 24(2), 463–490.

Bala, M., and Verma, D. (2018). A critical review of digital marketing. *International Journal of Management, IT and Engineering*, 8(10), 321–339.

Borkovsky, R. N., Goldfarb, A., Haviv, A. M., and Moorthy, S. (2017). Measuring and understanding brand value in a dynamic model of brand management. *Marketing Science*, 36(4), 471–499.

Caliskan, A., Özen, Y. D. Ö., and Ozturkoglu, Y. (2020). Digital transformation of traditional marketing business model in new industry era. *Journal of Enterprise Information Management*.

Chaffey, D., and Ellis-Chadwick, F. (2019). Digital Marketing: Strategy, Implementation and Practice. Pearson UK.

Datta, H., Ailawadi, K. L., and van Heerde, H. J. (2017). How well does consumer-based brand equity align with sales-based brand equity and marketing mix response?, *Journal of Marketing*, 81(3), 1–20.

Durmaz, Y., and Efendioglu, I. H. (2016). Travel from traditional marketing to digital marketing. *Global Journal of Management and Business Research*, 16(2), 34–40.

Foroudi, P., Gupta, S., Nazarian, A., and Duda, M. (2017). Digital technology and marketing management capability: achieving growth in SMEs. *Qualitative Market Research: An International Journal*, 20(2), 230–246.

Jones, J. (2016). Social Media, Marketing, and the Opera Singer. Arizona State University.

Kimathi, D. K. (2020). Effect of entrepreneurial marketing on the performance of micro, small and medium enterprises in Kenya. (Doctoral dissertation, JKUAT-COHRED).

160 Enrichment of employability skills with reference to business management colleges in Rayalaseema region

Kandati Sai, Chandramowleeswaran Gnanasekaran and Manoj Govindaraj[a]

Institute of Science and Technology, Chennai, India

Abstract

The study focused on enhancing the employability skills of business management students in Rayalaseema Region colleges, Andhra Pradesh. Primary data was gathered through placement cell in-charges using a drafted questionnaire and convenient sampling method. Exploratory factor analysis revealed that emphasis on professional report writing and promoting presentation skills are crucial for employability. Motivating learners to express their opinions and engage in constructive debates was identified as vital. The study, employing neural network analysis, highlighted the significance of technical skills, prioritized by placement cell heads, followed by interpersonal skills for students seeking employment.

Keywords: Analytical skills, campus recruitment, communication skills, database management systems, high aspiration skills, interpersonal skills, training and organizations

Introduction

The efficiency and effectiveness of the firm's management determines the competitiveness of every industry, whether it be a production, trading, or service business. Since any sector faces fierce rivalry from both domestic and international rivals, businesses nowadays tend to hire well-trained management graduates. This explains why, over the past two decades, management curriculum systems have gained considerable prominence. The number of organizations that provide management education has skyrocketed in recent years. They have excellent faculty, interesting classes, and excellent job prospects (Khawaja et al., 2013). The Indian Institutes of Management are among the top management schools in the country.

Most management programs produce graduates with few employability skills. The market has lot of expectations. There is disconnect between MBA graduates' expectations and real employability skills (Vikhyat Singhal, Ravinder Saini). This research illuminated the idea of employability skill and the need for it to be enhanced.

Problem Statement

The current situation in Rayalaseema region of Andhra Pradesh state is that the number of institutes providing management education has risen. Simultaneously, the obstacles that business management graduates are also experiencing more. According to numerous research and survey findings, as the number of business management students grows, the overall level of employability skills decreases. The aim of this research is to look at the employability skills needed for management graduates, as well as ways to improve them.

Literature Review

Table 160.1 Evolution of employability: a journey through recent studies.

Author name	Study
Gregorio (2019)	Analyzes in-demand marketing skills and provides practical advice for supporting marketing talent.
Blokker et al. (2019)	Analyzes the role of work shocks in the relationship between career skills, success, and employability for young professionals.
Niemela (2016)	Explores skills and experiences required for business graduates to enter the job market, emphasizing qualities over education.
Eurico et al. (2015)	Examines the role of employability in creating satisfaction and loyalty towards higher education institutions.

[a]manoj.nmcc@gmail.com

Author name	Study
Wilton (2014)	Focuses on the recruitment of work placement students, identifying dimensions of employability. Advocates a greater focus on the demand side.
Edge/SCRE Centre (2011)	Studies employers' standards for graduate employability skills and suggests ways for effective collaboration with higher education institutions.

Source: Author

Study Objective

- To elicit the Enrichment factors of Employability skills for the Management Students
- To identify the importance of Employability skills from the perspective of Placement cells

Scope of the Study

The study has focused on the employability skills among the management graduate students in Rayalaseema region. The study also made attempt to prioritize the employability skills from the perspective of placement cells in campus placement.

Research Methodology

The study has adopted qualitative research with the primary data. The primary data collected directly from the management graduate college placement cell heads of selected colleges through a well-devised interview schedule. Incomplete and inaccurate schedules dropped and only fully completed schedules taken up for analysis.

Sampling design
- The study confined to Rayalaseema region. Since the size of universe is relatively large the sample size was limited to 120 respondents. The study applied the convenient sampling method for the collection of primary data.

Questionnaire structure:
- The study framed the 5-point Likert scale oriented questionnaire relating to student enrichment factors, identify the importance employability skills from the perspective of placement cells.

Statistical tools:
- The processing, classification, tabulation, analysis and interpretation of data done with the help of SPSS package. The following statistical techniques applied depending on the nature of data collected from the respondents.
- For analyzing the data collected during the investigation, the following statistical tools used according to the relevance of its application namely

Table 160.2 Reliability statistics.

Cronbach's alpha	N of items
0.892	16

Source: Author

exploratory factor analysis and Andrew F Hayes mediation effect.

Exploratory factor analysis:
- The study applied the exploratory factor analysis to extract the high and lower loading factors to elicit the Enrichment factors of employability skills for the management students

Neural network:
- The study has considered the Neural Network method to prioritize the identified importance of Employability skills from the perspective of Placement cells. The study has considered the following variables for the examination of framed objective.

Dependent variable:
- Employability skills

Independent variables:
- Basic skills,
- Thinking skills,
- Capability skills,
- Information skills,
- Interpersonal skills,
- Technological skills
- Personal quality skills

Result and Analysis

Reliability test done to obtain the proportionate variation in a scale in the above table, Cronbach's alpha is 0.892, which shows that the scale is significant as it is more than the recommended level (0.70). Therefore, confirming further continue the process.

The KMO test yielded a value of 0.863, surpassing the recommended level of 0.70, affirming adequate data sampling for the study on Enrichment factors of employability skills in business. Additionally, Bartlett's test demonstrated significance, confirming the validity of factors considered for factor analysis.

The communalities analysis highlights key factors shaping employability skills in business analysis. It emphasizes promoting fluent speaking (75.9%) and presenting issues systematically (68.5%). Encouraging presentations (66.8%) and fostering debate (50%) are also significant. These efforts aim to enhance learners' communication and critical thinking abilities for professional success.

Table 160.3 KMO and Bartlett's test.

Kaiser-Meyer-Olkin measure of sampling adequacy.		0.863
Bartlett's test of sphericity	Approx. Chi-square	456.408
	df	36
	Sig.	0

Source: Author

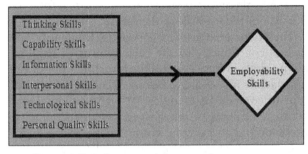

Figure 160.1 Conceptual framework
Source: Author

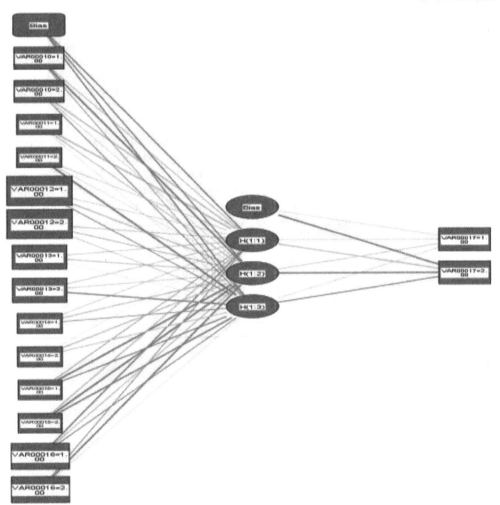

Hidden layer activation function: Hyperbolic tangent
Output layer activation function: Softmax

Figure 160.2 Hidden layer and hidden layer generate the output layer
Source: Author

The total variance analysis revealed that out of the nine components, two significant ones were extracted. Component 1, with an eigenvalue of 4.265, explains 47.3% of the variance, while Component 2, with an eigenvalue of 1.111, contributes an additional 12.3%. Together, these components account for a total of 59.73% of the variance in the dataset.

The factor analysis was conducted to identify key factors contributing to the enhancement of employability skills in business. Results reveal that out of the nine factors assessed, five belong to component 1, and four to component 2, indicating high loading. These factors encompass various aspects, from encouraging presentations to fostering constructive debates, highlighting the multifaceted nature of skill enrichment in the business context.

In summary the dataset comprises 120 samples, with 65.8% assigned to the training set and 34.2% to the testing set. Fifteen samples were excluded, making a total of 135 in consideration.

The neural network methodology was used in a wide range of business areas including accounting, banking, and manufacturing in addition to the fields of health and medicine. For marketing and sales models, neuronal network models were used for forecasting demand, measuring the preference of the customer, segments, and new products. The study has considered this model to know the importance of Employability skills, so that placement director will prioritize the various Skills to improve the overall Employability Skill.

Figure 160.2 depicts the network information in layers. In which each input layer is linked to a hidden layer and hidden layer generate the output layer i.e., Employment Skills. It indicates that 1 hidden layer was used with 3 units in it to generate the output layer.

The significance of an independent variable is an extent of change in the network's model predicted value for varying values of the independent variable. Below table reflects the relative importance of the 7 listed variables to improve the employment skills by the selected colleges in Hyderabad Telangana.

The study revealed that among the employability skills, technical skills ranked highest, followed by interpersonal skills. However, capability and Personal Quality skills were considered moderate, needing attention. Basic, informational, and thinking skills were lower in priority. This suggests that while interviewers were somewhat satisfied with technical skills, there's room for improvement in capability and personal skills. The study emphasized the need for enhancing these dimensions to enhance students' success in campus recruiting tests.

The study examined the enrichment of employability skills with the EFA and found that enforcing professional report writing (0.735) and encouraging presentation (0.738) extracted as higher loading. Therefore, it has been observed that writing and presentation skills plays the vital role of the students to employed.

Gheitasi (2017) stated that expressing the opinion fast, fluent and flawless, which indicates the confidence of job aspirant. In this study, Making the learners speak instinctively, fluently, and effectively (0.68) plays the critical role in enhancing the employability skills among business management college students.

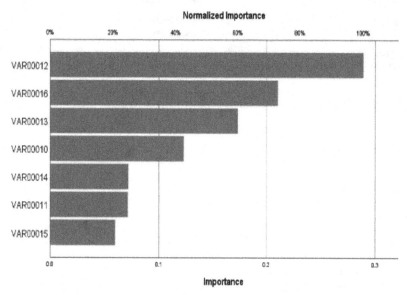

Figure 160.3 Normalized importance
Source: Author

It had identified that motivating the learners the ability to voice their point of view (0.638) and making them foster a constructive debate (0.575) makes the students to in still the employability skills. Hunter (2017) observed that job seeker always needs to upgrade their skills as well as they need to participate constructively in debate to convince the interviewer.

The study synchronized with the EFA and extracted the high loading factors, which states that "educate the students with various techniques" (0.771) to equip to meet the market requirements.

(M Castells 2007), revealed with the paper on Technology effect on the Growth and Employment that continually updating new skills and looking for alternative work opportunities expand the job options. The study observed inconsistent with the opinion of M Castells that students need to give priority to technical skills (0.560) followed by the interpersonal skills (0.472). The job market changing with the new technological innovations such as IoT, machine learning, artificial intelligence.

It was observed that to business management students should focus on the personal quality (0.311) and capability skills (0.389), which plays key role in managing the human resource in the organizations.

Conclusion

The study had emphasized to know the employment enrichment factors and identifying the importance of employability skills among the business management students from the perspective of placement cell heads considered in Rayalaseema region. The study has collected the primary data from the business management colleges with the structured questionnaire. The study mainly focused on the employability enrichment factors with the statistical method of exploratory factor analysis and the results found that students should enforced in professional report writing and encouraging to a presentation are the key elements to employed. It had observed that motivating the learners the ability to voice their point of view and making them foster a constructive debate makes the students to instill the employability skills. The study has tried to identify the importance of employability skills from the perspective of placement cells with the statistical method neural network and the result stated that students need to give priority to technical skills followed by the interpersonal skills as per the opinion expressed by the placement cell heads/in-charges.

Further Research Scope

The present study has confined to Rayalaseema region of Andhra Pradesh state. Therefore, the study suggests expanding to state level. The study has considered the opinions from placement cell in-charges. Hence, the study suggests considering the organizations opinions to identify the employability skills and consider for the engineering students.

References

Barron, J. M., Bishop, J., and Dunkelberg, W. C. (1985). Employer search: the interviewing and hiring of new employees. *The Review of Economics and Statistics*, 67(1), 43–52.

Cassidy, S. (2006). Developing employability skills: peer assessment in higher education. *Education + Training*, 48(7), 508–517.

Dacre Pool, L., and Sewell, P. (2007). The Key to Employability: Developing a Practical Model of Graduate Employability. Preston, UK: University of Central Lancashire, 49(4), 2–3.

Holzer, H. J. (1987). Hiring procedures in the firm: their economic determinants and outcomes. Working Paper 2185.

Jehanzeb, K., and Bashir, N. A. (2013). Training and development program and its benefits to employee and organization: a conceptual study. *European Journal of Business and Management*, 5(2), ISSN- 2222-1905. ISSN 2222-2839.

Lindeboom, M., Ours, J. V., and Renes, G. (1994). Matching employers and workers: an empirical analysis on the effectiveness of search. *New Series*, 46(1), 45–67.

Potts, B. B. (2009). So you want to work? What employers say about job skills, recruitment and hiring employees who rely on AAC. *Augmentative and Alternative Communication*, 23(2), 126–139.

Raybould, J., and Sheedy, V. (2005). Are graduates equipped with the right skills in the employability stakes?

Singh, G. K. G., and Singh, S. K. G. (2008). Perceptions of employers about the employability skills. *UNITAR E-Journal*, 4(1), 15–45.

Singhal, V., and Saini, R. (n.d.). Education and its contribution in enhancing employability skills: study on the efficacy of management education. *Palarch's Journal of Archaeology of Egypt/Egyptology*, 17(9), ISSN 1567214x.

161 Consumer behavior towards online shopping of apparels with reference to Bhiwani district, Haryana

Renu and Kritika[a]

Chaudhary Bansi Lal University, Bhiwani, Haryana, India

Abstract

The rise of the internet and smartphones, coupled with technological advancements, has greatly boosted the online retail sector in India. This research paper delves into the analysis of consumer behavior regarding online apparel shopping in Bhiwani District. With a sample size of 100 respondents, findings indicate that 74% spend up to Rs. 2000 per order, and 47% make 1-2 online apparel purchases annually. Flipkart and Amazon emerge as the preferred platforms, with 76% opting to pay in cash upon delivery. Key factors influencing decisions include discounts, reviews, color, material, size, brand, quick delivery, and return/exchange options. Notably, there's no significant link between gender and the frequency of online apparel purchases, as revealed by the chi-square test.

Keywords: Apparels, consumer, e- retailers, online shopping, online shopping behavior

Introduction

The internet has revolutionized how people buy things, with companies using it to market products, gather feedback, and share information. Consumers, on the other hand, use the internet to check product availability, gather details, and compare prices on various online retail sites (Chandan, 2019). Consumer behavior, as defined by Solomon et al. (2006), involves the processes individuals or groups go through when selecting, purchasing, using, or disposing of products to satisfy their needs and desires.

In the current scenario, numerous online platforms like Amazon, Myntra, and Flipkart offer a variety of apparels. Customers can easily search for product details, compare options, find deals, and place orders at their convenience. These e-retail websites ensure convenient delivery to the desired address. Notably, apparel constitutes a significant 40% share in India's e-commerce retail market (IBEF, 2022). The internet has truly transformed the way we shop for clothes, making it more accessible and convenient.

Literature Review

Table 161.1 Consumer trends and recommendations for E-retailers.

Author name	Study
Poojitha et al. (2022)	Age and occupation have no impact on online apparel buying, but education does. Positive correlations exist between various purchase factors. Recommendations include e-retailers focusing on delivery, offers, brand variety, styles, and comfort.
Raman (2021)	Features, security, user-friendly websites, affordability, awareness, and promotions drive female online clothing purchases. The study suggests providing diverse sizes, colors, and trending designs, with simplified website design. Significant male online shoppers (37.4%) are motivated by time-saving, ease, and variety availability.
Bharti and Bhatt (2020)	37.4% of respondents buy apparel online two to five times annually. Males shop more, driven by time-saving, ease, and variety. No significant association found between demographics and online shopping frequency. Quality and size issues prevail, requiring e-commerce to address concerns.
Muthulakshmi and Ramalingam (2018)	Technological aspects like assured quality, cash on delivery, and promotions influence online shoppers. Respondents spend Rs. 2000 monthly, with 52% choosing cash on delivery. Amazon and Myntra are preferred. E-commerce should focus on return policies, prompt delivery, durability, discounts, brands, comfort, value for money, style, and variety.

[a]renuatrri@gmail.com

Author name	Study
Gowda and Chaudhary (2018)	Online apparel buyers prioritize comfort, value for money, style, and variety. Amazon and Myntra are preferred. Key considerations for online retailers include return policies, prompt delivery, durability, discounts, offers, brands, comfort, value for money, style, and variety. Emphasis on free delivery for expensive or bulk purchases.
Goswami and Khan (2015)	A study shows 46% spent up to Rs. 2000 on online apparel in the past month. Consumer styles (brand, quality, value, fashion consciousness) and social influence impact online buying frequency and amount spent. Value-conscious buyers prefer planned buying. Online purchases are popular among consumers with high brand and fashion consciousness.

Source: Author

Study Objective
- To analyze consumers' behavior towards online shopping of apparels in Bhiwani District
- To study the factors affecting consumers' online purchase decision towards apparels
- To study the association between gender and frequency of online purchase of apparels

Research Methodology

Research design: Descriptive study
Data collection method:
- Self-structured questionnaire employed.
- Convenient sampling technique utilized.

Sample size:
- Data gathered from 100 respondents.

Target respondents:
- Limited to individuals in Bhiwani District, Haryana.
- Specifically, those who engage in online apparel shopping.

Questionnaire characteristics:
- Solely filled by respondents involved in online apparel purchases.

Data measurement:
- Utilized a 5-point Likert scale.

Scale ranges from 1 to 5.
1. Not important
2. Slightly important
3. Moderately important
4. Important
5. Very important

Analysis and Interpretation

The data collected through self-structured questionnaire have been analyzed using percentage method, weighted mean method and chi-square test.

Table 161.2 Demographic characteristics of respondents.

Demographic variable		No. of respondents	Percentage (%)
Gender	Male	37	37%
	Female	63	63%
	Total	100	100%
Age (in years)	Up to 25	62	62%
	26-35	31	31%
	36-45	6	6%
	Above 45	1	1%
	Total	100	100%
Education	12th	8	8%
	Graduation	30	30%
	Post-graduation	49	49%
	Ph.D.	13	13%
	Total	100	100%
Residential status	Rural	46	46%
	Urban	54	54%
	Total	100	100%
Monthly income (Rs.)	Up to 25000	65	65%
	25001-40000	23	23%
	40001-55000	6	6%
	Above 55000	6	6%
	Total	100	100%

Source: Author

The study reveals a diverse respondent profile, with 37% male and 63% female participants. Most are aged up to 25 years (62%), 46% reside in rural areas, and 65% earn up to Rs. 25000 monthly. Education-wise, 49% are postgraduates. The survey captures a rich snapshot of varied demographics.

Figure 161.1 depicts that most of the respondents (47%) purchase apparels 1-2 times in a year through online shopping. 28% respondents buy apparel online

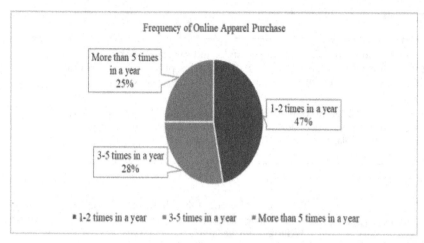

Figure 161.1 Frequency of purchasing apparel through online shopping
Source: Author

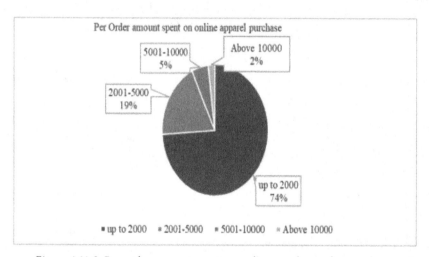

Figure 161.2 Per-order amount spent on online purchase of apparel
Source: Author

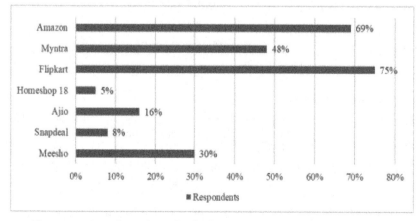

Figure 161.3 Website through which consumers purchase apparel
Source: Author

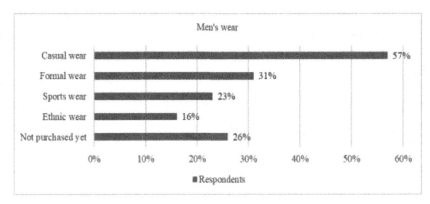

Figure 161.4 Men's wear
Source: Author

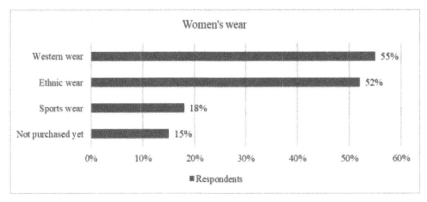

Figure 161.5 Women's wear
Source: Author

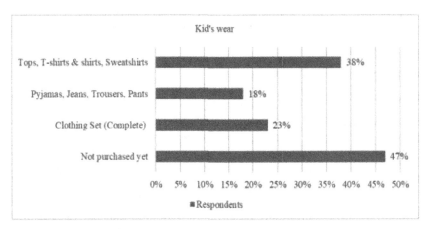

Figure 161.6 Kid's wear
Source: Author

3-5 times in a year and 25% respondents make online purchase of apparels more than five times in a year.

Figure 161.2 represents that the majority of respondents (74%) spend up to Rs. 2000 per order on online purchase of apparel. A toal of 19% of respondents pay between Rs. 2001-5000 per order on apparel purchase through online shopping. 5% respondents

buy apparels online costing Rs.5001-10000 per order. Only 2% respondents spend more than Rs.10000 on single order of purchasing apparels through online shopping.

Figure 161.3 reveals that Flipkart is the most popular website for buying apparel as 75% respondents purchase apparels from it. 69% of respondents prefer

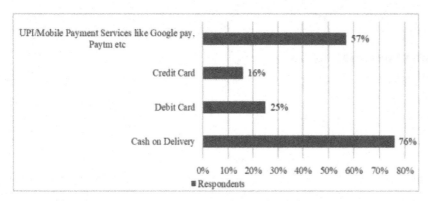

Figure 161.7 Methods of payment used while making online purchase of apparel
Source: Author

Table 161.3 Gender*: How often do you purchase apparels through online shopping?

Gender* How often do you purchase apparels through online shopping? Crosstabulation					
		How often do you purchase apparels through online shopping?			Total
		1-2 Times in a year	3-5 Times in a year	More than 5 times in a year	
Gender	Male	Count	19	8	10	37
		% Within gender	51.40%	21.60%	27.00%	100.00%
	Female	Count	28	20	15	63
		% Within gender	44.40%	31.70%	23.80%	100.00%
Total		Count	47	28	25	100
		% Within gender	47.00%	28.00%	25.00%	100.00%

Source: Author

Table 161.4 Association between gender and frequency of online purchase of apparels.

Chi-square tests			
	Value	df	Asymptotic significance (2-sided)
Pearson Chi-square	1.186a	2	0.553
Likelihood ratio	1.216	2	0.545
Linear-by-linear association	0.047	1	0.829
N of valid cases	100		

a. 0 cells (.0%) have expected count less than 5. The minimum expected count is 9.25.

Source: Author

Amazon for buying apparels. 48% of respondents purchase apparels from Myntra. 30% respondents buy clothing from Meesho. Ajio and Snapdeal are preferred by 16% and 8% respondents respectively for buying apparels. Only 5% of respondents purchase apparels from Homeshop 18.

Figure 161.4 indicates that casual wear is mostly bought apparel category among men's wear which is purchased by 57% respondents. A total of 31% of respondents buy formal wear and 23% respondents purchase sportswear. The least bought clothing category among men's apparel is ethnic wear, which is only purchased by 16% of respondents. 26% of the respondents have not purchased men's apparel yet.

Figure 161.5 shows that among women's apparels western wear is the most popular category which is purchased by 55% respondents. Ethnic wear is bought by 52% respondents while only 18% of respondents buy sportswear. 15% of respondents have not purchased women's apparel yet.

Figure 161.6 indicates that the majority of the respondents (47%) have not purchased kid's wear yet through online shopping. 38% of respondents purchase tops, t-shirts & shirts, sweatshirts and 23% respondents buy complete clothing set. Pyjamas, jeans, trousers and pants were bought by 18% respondents.

Figure 161.7 reveals that most of the respondents (76%) prefer paying in cash when they get the delivery of apparel ordered online. Payment through UPI/Mobile payment Services like Google pay, Paytm etc. is second most preferred mode for online shopping of apparels as 57% respondents pay through it. Debit card and credit card are preferred by 25% and 16% respondents respectively to make payments for online apparel purchase. Payment through credit card is the least preferred medium of payment.

Study on "factors affecting consumers' online purchase decision toward apparels" shows that factors like discounts, reviews, color, material, size, brand, quick delivery, and return/exchange options significantly influence consumers' online apparel purchases. With weighted means above 4, respondents find these aspects important, particularly highlighting the size of the apparel as the most crucial factor, rated at 4.50.

Analyzing gender disparities in online apparel shopping habits reveals potential associations, with males shows that 51.4% of males buy apparel online 1-2 times a year, 21.6% 3-5 times, and 27% more than 5 times. For females, it's 44.4%, 31.7%, and 23.8% respectively. Results suggest a potential association between gender and online apparel purchase frequency (Chi-Square, $p < 0.05$).

Association between gender and frequency of online purchase of apparels showed through chi-square tests. The chi-square value is 1.186 with a p-value of .553, indicating that the null hypothesis is not rejected as the p-value exceeds the 5% significance level. Thus, it is concluded that there is no significant association between gender and the frequency of online apparel purchases based on the chi-square test results.

Conclusion

The study concludes that the majority of respondents (74%) spend up to Rs. 2000 per order on online purchase of apparel. 47% respondents purchase apparels 1-2 times in a year through online shopping. Online retailers should make marketing strategies to boost the frequency of low spending and repeat purchases in order to enhance revenue through apparel segment. Men's casual wear, women's western wear and kid's top wear are most purchased clothing through online shopping. Managers should also focus on increasing the sales of other apparel categories like ethnic wear, sportswear etc. by offering discounts, coupon, style to

lure and retain the customers. Flipkart and Amazon are the most popular websites for buying apparel and most of the respondents (76%) prefer paying in cash when they get the delivery of apparels ordered online. The results of study further revealed that discount and offers, reviews regarding apparel, color, material, size, brand, quick delivery, return and exchange facility are important factors affecting consumers' online purchase decision regarding apparels. Online retail managers should consider these crucial factors while devising new strategies for apparels segment to attract and retain the buyers on their online websites. Based on results of chi-square test, it is concluded that there is no significant association between gender and frequency of online purchase of apparels.

References

Bharti, R., and Bhatt, S. (2020). A study of online apparel shopping behaviour in Gorakhpur. *International Journal of Research Culture Society*, 4(4), 247–254.

Chandan, A. (2019). A study of consumer behaviour towards online shopping with special reference to Bangalore City, Karnataka India. *International Journal of Advanced Research*, 7(1), 488–498. https://doi.org/10.21474/ijar01/8353.

Goswami, S., and Khan, S. (2015). Impact of consumer decision-making styles on online apparel consumption in India. *Vision*, 19(4), 303–311. https://doi.org/10.1177/0972262915610853.

Gowda, K. R., and Chaudhary, K. (2018). Analysis of online buying pattern of women consumers with reference to apparels in India. *Academy of Marketing Studies Journal*, 22(2), 1–10.

India Brand Equity Foundation (2022). E-Commerce. Retrieved from https://www.ibef.org/download/1664177515_E-Commerce-June-2022.pdf.

Muthulakshmi, A. P., and Ramalingam, P. (2018). Consumer behaviouranalysis towards online shopping of apparels with special reference to coimbatore and erode districts. *International Journal for Research in Engineering Application and Management (IJREAM)*, 76–82. DOI: 10.18231/2454-9150.2019.0464.

Poojitha, S., Sanjay, K., Lakshmi, B. S., Sushma, C., and Rangisetty, S. (2022). Female purchase intentions towards online shopping of apparels. *Journal of Positive School Psychology*, 6(2), 2130–2135.

Raman, A. (2021). An empirical study on consumer buying behaviourtowards online shopping with special reference to women apparels in Malaysia. *Turkish Journal of Computer and Mathematics Education (TURCOMAT)*, 12(13), 779–795.

Solomon, M., Bamossy, G., Askegaard, S., and Hogg M. K. (2006). Consumer Behaviour: A European Perspective. (3rd edn.). New Jersey: Prentice-Hall.

162 Adapting to the digital era: e-recruitment's implications for job seekers in Dot Com InfEoway, Madurai

Vikneswaran, S.[a]

Madurai Kamaraj University, Madurai, India

Abstract

This study highlights the crucial role of e-recruitment in today's job search. E-recruitment offers unmatched convenience, letting job seekers save time and money while accessing a variety of tailored job opportunities. The COVID-19 pandemic has made e-recruitment even more important, as it reduces the need for specific job locations, providing remote work options. This is particularly helpful for individuals, including women, who prefer not to relocate. E-recruitment also leads to significant cost savings for offices. The research compares job seekers' intentions and recruiter perceptions, emphasizing the growing preference for e-recruitment. Platforms like Naukri, LinkedIn, Monster, and others connect recruiters with a wider pool of job seekers. The study involves 100 graduating job seekers and MBA HR students, using chi-square tests to analyze key perceptions like time-saving and cost-effectiveness. Overall, the research highlights how e-recruitment revolutionizes job searching in the digital era, benefiting both job seekers and recruiters.

Keywords: Data analysis, e-recruitment, job opportunities, online platforms

Introduction

In today's fast-paced digital landscape, finding a job has changed dramatically, thanks to technology. Dot Com Infoway, based in the lively city of Madurai, has become a key player in this digital employment transformation. E-recruitment is not just a new way of hiring; it's a whole new world for job seekers. In Madurai and beyond, technology is reshaping how people find work, bringing both challenges and opportunities.

This exploration will uncover the strategies, hurdles, and advantages job seekers face, especially at Dot Com Infoway. As tech continues to redefine employment, understanding these dynamics is crucial for success. Over three parts, we'll dive into the complexities of e-recruitment, tackle unique challenges, and uncover the promising opportunities for those adapting to this digital shift. Join us on this journey into the evolving job market, where Dot Com Infoway in Madurai takes center stage.

Literature Review

Table 162.1 Exploring the evolution of online recruitment.

Author name	Study
Haroon and Zia-ur-Rehman (2010)	Explored online recruitment in Pakistan, finding a preference for smaller firms. Larger firms established recruitment websites. Online recruitment seen as increasingly significant due to reduced costs and time efficiency.
Kapse et al. (2012)	Examined e-recruitment benefits like cost-effectiveness and expanded reach. Acknowledged drawbacks: application screening complexity, limited internet accessibility, and employer preference for in-person interactions.
Holm (2012)	Defined e-recruitment as tech-facilitated, collaborative efforts without geographical constraints. Aim: identification, attraction, and engagement of proficient candidates.
Florea and Badea (2013)	Explored the positive impact of technology on recruitment, emphasizing Internet's role in crafting efficient programs. Highlighted advantages: enhanced performance, expedited decision-making, cost savings, and effective candidate pinpointing.

Source: Author

[a]Vignesh.mba35@gmail.com

Problem Statement

E-recruitment, using online tools like job portals, offers convenience but poses challenges. Sorting through numerous applications may lead to qualified candidates being overlooked. Job insecurity among current employees may rise, causing stress. The lack of personal interaction in e-recruitment can affect candidate experience and a company's image. Balancing benefits and challenges are key for fair and effective hiring in the digital job market.

Study Objective

- To find out how easy it is for people to use e-recruitment when they're looking for jobs.
- To see how much job seekers know about e-recruitment.
- To look at where e-recruitment comes from and how it's used in our research.
- To see how both new and experienced job seekers use e-recruitment differently.
- To find out about what makes job seekers want to apply for jobs online.
- To see how much it costs and how much job seekers trust the internet when they're looking for jobs.
- To check how well e-recruitment works for matching up job seekers with job opportunities.

Scope of the Study

This study explores how e-recruitment, which involves using online platforms for job ads and applications, impacts job seekers. It aims to understand how e-recruitment changes their job search, its advantages and disadvantages, and what influences their views and actions. By using surveys and interviews, the research hopes to offer insights and recommendations to improve job seekers' experiences in the digital job market.

Research Methodology

Research design:
- Descriptive research design.

Sampling technique:
- Simple random sampling.

Sample size:
- Total 230 populations.
- 100 Targeted populations for this study.

Data collection:
- Primary data from 100 job seekers through structured questionnaires.

- Secondary data from credible sources based on relevance.

Statistical tools:
- Percentages, cards, bars, pie.
- Percentage analysis.
- Chi-square analysis.

Hypothesis:
- H0: no significant relationship between gender and online recruitment opportunities.
- H1: significant relationship between gender and online recruitment opportunities.

Analysis and Interpretation

The charts paint a clear picture of the job-seeking landscape. Firstly, there's a noticeable gender gap, with 63% of job seekers being male and 37% female, particularly noticeable in the retail sector. Moving on, a significant 59% of job seekers hold master's degrees, indicating a demand for highly educated fresh graduates. When it comes to job preferences, 48% are eyeing entry-level positions, while 43% are interested in middle-level jobs, emphasizing a strong inclination toward entry-level roles. Lastly, Chart d indicates a positive sentiment towards internet job sites, with 39% strongly agreeing and 45% agreeing on their user-friendliness. In summary, these insights collectively highlight gender disparities, a demand for well-educated candidates, a preference for entry-level roles, and positive perceptions of internet job sites.

The data from Charts e to h provides insightful findings. Notably, 59% of respondents are in urban areas (Chart e), reflecting urban concentration. Chart f indicates positive sentiment, with 57% satisfied with their internet understanding of e-recruitment. In Chart g, 63% express contentment with job site information. Lastly, Chart h reveals majority agreement (39%) with a presented statement. Overall, these charts describe urban participation, positive internet perception, satisfaction with job site data, and majority support for the statement in Chart h.

The data from Charts i to l sheds light on key aspects of the study. Notably, 44% find online recruitment time-consuming, while 35% favor career websites. Respondents express optimism about online recruitment (73% agree or strongly agree), contrasting with concerns about its cost and response rate. Interestingly, 61% believe in newspapers' effectiveness in job searching. In essence, the findings highlight worries about online recruitment's time-consuming nature, a preference for career websites, positive

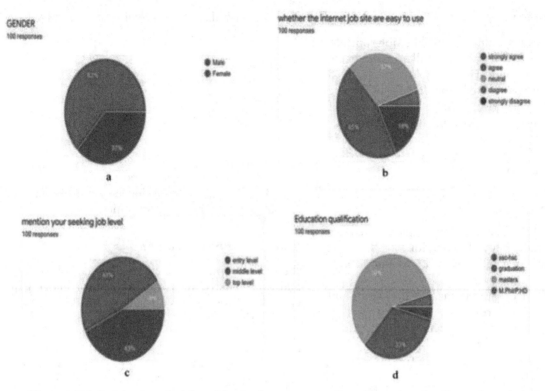

Figure 162.1 Insights into the job-seeking landscape: gender disparities, education demands, and platform perceptions
Source: Author

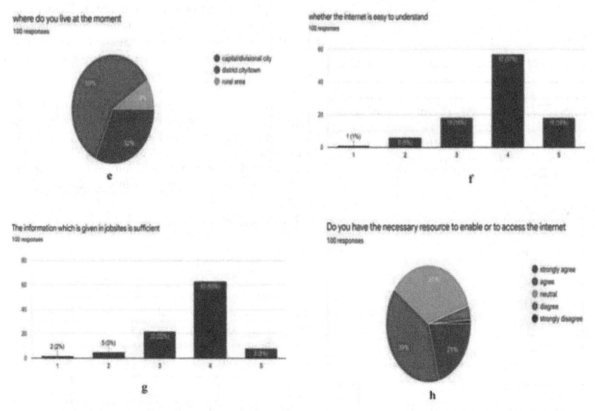

Figure 162.2 Insights from urban respondents: understanding internet usage and job satisfaction
Source: Author

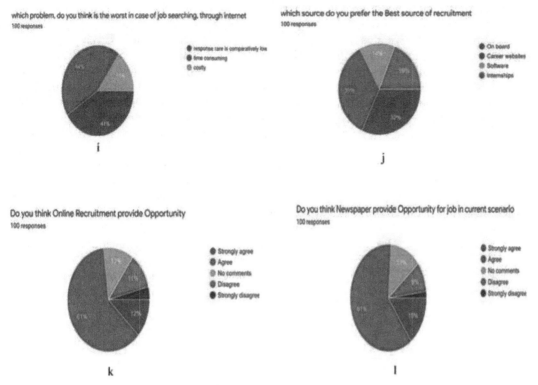

Figure 162.3 Insights into online recruitment preferences and perceptions
Source: Author

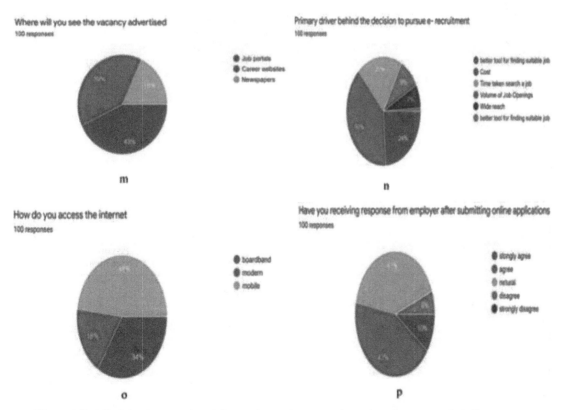

Figure 162.4 Insights into modern job search trends: a snapshot of preferences and challenge
Source: Author

perceptions about opportunities, and a widespread belief in newspapers for job searching.

The data from Charts m to p provides insights into job-seeking trends. Respondents prefer job portals (43%) and career websites (39%) over newspapers (18%). Chart n indicates concerns about the cost of online job tools (39%), with 24% finding them effective. Chart o shows reliance on mobile internet (48%), followed by broadband (34%) and modems (18%). In

Chart p, 43% agree that employers respond to online applications, emphasizing the significance of job portals and mobile internet in the job search process.

Looking at both charts, it's clear that 39% of people have a daily newspaper reading habit, followed by 34% weekly readers, 11% fortnightly, and a small 7% who never read newspapers. On the internet front, a whopping 86% are comfortable with personal internet connections, leaving only 14% with reservations.

The statistical analysis indicates a rejection of the null hypothesis, suggesting a significant difference between gender and the perceived opportunities provided by online recruitment. The findings highlight that the majority of retailers are male, with a significant proportion having completed their education at the master's level. Respondents generally express satisfaction with internet job sites but find the process time-consuming. The prevalent preference is for job portals, and a substantial number perceive the cost as

Table 162.2 Case processing summaries.

Cases						
Valid		Missing	Total			
N	Percent	N	Percent	N	Percent	
100	99.00%	1	1.00%	101	100.00%	

Source: Author

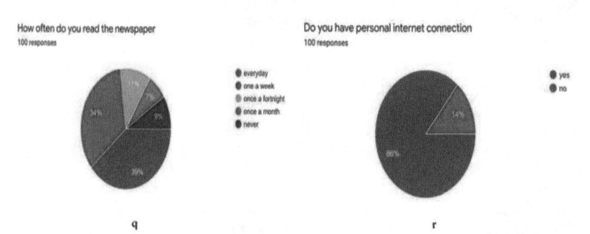

Figure 162.5 Reading habits and internet usage: insights from recent surveys
Source: Author

Table 162.3 Chi-square tests.

Gender of the respondent											
Online recruitment provides opportunity cross tabulation											
Online recruitment provide opportunity								Value	df	Asymptotic significance (2-sided)	
Gender of the respondent	Male	Count	Strongly agree	Agree	No Comments	Disagree	Strongly				
			12	51	0	0	0				
Pearson Chi-square								64.133	4	0	
Likelihood ratio								77.362	4	0	
Linear-by-linear association								51.315	1	0	
No of valid cases								100			

Source: Author

high. Interestingly, mobile devices are the preferred means of internet access for nearly half of the respondents. Overall, the study suggests varying sentiments and preferences among respondents regarding online recruitment.

In summary, the statistical results support the alternative hypothesis, emphasizing a significant relationship between gender and perceptions of online recruitment opportunities. The detailed findings shed light on the demographic composition, educational backgrounds, and preferences of retailers. Notably, respondents express satisfaction with the user-friendliness of internet job sites but also highlight concerns about the time-consuming nature of the process. The study provides valuable insights into the nuanced perspectives and preferences within the surveyed population, contributing to a better understanding of the dynamics between gender and online recruitment in the context of the retail sector.

Suggestion

To enhance the effectiveness of online recruitment platforms and attract more job seekers, it's crucial for Dot Com Infoway, Madurai, to prioritize the improvement of job website user-friendliness. This can be achieved by streamlining the website's layout and navigation for intuitive use, optimizing the platform for mobile devices to cater to the 48% of users accessing it through mobile, incorporating personalization features that recommend tailored job listings, providing comprehensive job descriptions and clear application instructions, optimizing website speed and responsiveness, and offering robust user support to address inquiries and concerns promptly. These user-centric enhancements will create a more efficient and enjoyable experience for job seekers on Dot Com Info way's online recruitment platform, ultimately increasing engagement and utilization, which will benefit both job seekers and recruiters in the process.

Future Scope

The study on "adapting to the digital era: e-recruitment's implications for job seekers in Dot Com info way, Madurai" presents various avenues for future research and practical implications. Firstly, further investigation into gender disparities among retailers and job seekers could provide insights into strategies for promoting gender inclusivity. Second, analyzing the impact of advanced education, particularly master's degrees, on career opportunities can guide educational and career guidance programs. Third, continuous monitoring of e-recruitment platform

efficiency using key performance indicators is crucial. Fourth, integrating artificial intelligence and personalization algorithms for better job matching deserves exploration. Fifth, long-term implications of remote work on job satisfaction and productivity could be examined. Sixth, identifying cost-effective solutions for job seekers, especially in resource-constrained regions, is essential. Seventh, researching emerging technologies like virtual reality and augmented reality in recruitment platforms is pertinent. Eighth, cyber security measures for platforms in an era of heightened reliance on personal internet connections require attention. Ninth, user-centric design principles should be consistently applied for accessibility and usability. Finally, comparative studies across regions and industries could provide cross-cultural insights into e-recruitment practices. Dot Com Infoway, Madurai, can practically implement suggested improvements for its online recruitment platform and support research collaborations with local institutions to contribute to regional knowledge and stay competitive in the evolving digital landscape.

Conclusion

In today's fast-paced digital world, this study highlights the significant impact of e-recruitment on job seekers. E-recruitment has become a fundamental aspect of modern job hunting, offering unparalleled convenience, cost-effectiveness, and flexibility. It allows job seekers to save time while accessing tailored opportunities. The COVID-19 pandemic has further emphasized the importance of e-recruitment, breaking down geographical barriers and promoting remote work. Companies now recognize the value of platforms like Naukri, LinkedIn, Monster, and their own recruitment websites to efficiently connect with potential hires. Research on diverse job seeker perspectives solidifies the benefits, paving the way for e-recruitment to revolutionize the traditional job search process, reduce costs, and align with the evolving digital work landscape. As job seekers adapt, the role of e-recruitment becomes increasingly crucial, providing practical solutions and expanding opportunities for remote work.

References

Barber, L. (n.d.). Development of online recruitment. Retrieved from www.employmentstudies.co.uk/pdflibrary/mp63.pdf.

Byars, L. L., and Rue, L. (2000). Human Resource Management, (6th edn.). McGraw-Hill.

Cappelli, P. (2001). Making the most of online recruiting. *Harvard Business Review*, 79(3), 139–148.

Florea, V. N., and Badea, M. (2013). Acceptance of new technologies in HR: e-recruitment in organizations. In Proceedings of the European Conference on Information Management and Evaluation, (pp. 344–352).

Florea, V. N., and Badea, M. (2013). Acceptance of new technologies in HR: E-recruitment in organizations, (37–38).

Galanaki, E. (2002). The decision to recruit online: a descriptive study. *Career Development International*, 7(4), 243–251.

Haroon, M., and Zia-ur-Rehman, M. (2010). E-recruitment: across the small and large firms in Pakistan. *Interdisci-plinary Journal of Contemporary Research in Business*, 2(1), 179–191.

Holm, A. B. (2012). E-recruitment: towards an ubiquitous recruitment process and candidate relationship management. *German Journal of Research in Human Resource Management*, 26(3), 241–259.

Kapse, A. S., Patil, V. S., and Patil, N. V. (2012). E-Recruitment. *International Journal of Engineering and Advanced Technology (IJEAT)*, 1(4), 82–86.

163 Talent management practices in the selected commercial banks in Kerala

Asha Elizabeth Kurian and P. A. Padmaavathy[a]

Karpagam Academy of Higher Education, Coimbatore, India

Abstract

Talent management (TM) involves adeptly steering employees' abilities, competencies, and capacities within an organization. It transcends mere timely recruitment, encompassing the discernment of individuals' latent and distinctive qualities for optimal outcomes. This research integrates primary and secondary data sources, with secondary data derived from diverse scholarly outlets. Primary data, gleaned from branch heads of selected banks in Kerala, was framed using RBI's website. The study, focusing on public and private sector banks, unveils practices crucial for talent identification, development, and retention. Notably, it underscores the nuanced disparities in talent management practices between these sectors.

Keywords: Career success, management of talent, talent development, talent identification, talent retention

Introduction

Organizations must prioritize talent management as a fundamental imperative, entailing the continual enhancement of their employee value proposition and the systematic sourcing and development of talent. McKinsey & Co. posits that the battle for talent management is underway, with talent emerging as a paramount driver of competitive advantage in the contemporary corporate landscape. The knowledge economy's increasing prominence intensifies the emphasis on acquiring and retaining a skilled workforce, emphasizing that achieving optimal results hinges on securing the finest talent. A well-executed talent management system constructs a victorious organization through carefully devised strategies across various levels.

Successful organizations' competitive edge depends on their proficiency in efficiently recruiting, retaining, deploying, and engaging talent across all hierarchy levels. Research substantiates that organizations can fortify their sustainable competitive advantage by investing in a skilled workforce. Talent management harbors immense potential for preserving and nurturing an organization's most prized assets, securing a competitive advantage. Businesses increasingly recognize that talent constitutes a fundamental competitive asset and a pivotal determinant of organizational performance. Retaining talented employees stands as one of the paramount challenges confronting organizations in today's modern economy.

In the current intricate and ever-evolving business landscape, organizations strive not only to survive but also to secure a competitive edge. The demand for skilled and capable employees, especially in pivotal roles, steadily increases, leading organizations into a perpetual competitive pursuit for top talent. Retaining these competent employees is crucial to prevent detrimental effects on productivity and service delivery. As per the Chartered Institute of Professional Development (CIPD), talent comprises individuals with the potential to significantly enhance organizational performance. There's a notable shift from viewing employees solely as part of human resources to recognizing them as integral components of human capital, encompassing knowledge, skills, and capabilities. Consequently, organizations must manage current operations and cultivate core competencies for a competitive advantage as they prepare for future opportunities.

Problem Statement

The challenge lies in comprehending the multifaceted nature of talent within the banking sector, where diverse interpretations of "talent" exist. Defining talent as individuals acknowledged for their potential to achieve remarkable success, the study aims to unravel the nuanced talent identification, development, and retention practices employed by banks.

Banking Sector in India

The pivotal role of the banking system in shaping a nation's economic and social fabric is exemplified by the Indian scenario pre-nationalization. Banking services were predominantly urban-centric, neglecting

[a]padmaavathypa@gmail.com

rural and semi-urban sectors, with credit facilities disproportionately favoring large industries. The decision to nationalize banks in 1969 and 1980 marked a transformative phase, with 14 major banks initially and an additional six later brought under state ownership. Post-nationalization, banks became instrumental in India's economic and social transformation, though challenges emerged.

State control led to rapid growth, yet a monopoly in the state sector, coupled with limited competition, resulted in inefficiencies and low productivity. Factors such as high reserve requirements, administered interest rates, directed credit, political involvement, and corruption contributed to the underperformance of public sector banks. Recognizing the need for reform, the Narasimham Committee in 1991 advocated initiatives like reducing reserve requirements, deregulating interest rates, adopting prudential standards, enhancing bank supervision, and promoting systemic competition.

Encouraging private sector banks to enter the arena fostered competition, aligning with Basel Committee standards introduced in 1988. These standards mandated risk-weighted capital adequacy ratios, starting at 4% and gradually rising to 9%, alongside monitoring non-performing assets. The second Narasimham Committee Report in 1998 focused on technological advancement, financial sector strengthening, and human resource development. Basel II standards, effective in 2007, emphasized operational risk and credit risk management.

The evolution continued with Basel III in 2000, aiming to enhance regulatory environments, bank transparency, and resilience to financial stress. Presently, Indian banks are diversifying into new areas, generating income beyond core functions, and actively engaging in mergers, acquisitions, and consolidation. This dynamic landscape reflects a continual commitment to refining banking practices for sustained economic development.

Literature Review

Table 163.1 Understanding how companies manage talent.

Author name	Study
Puvitayaphan (2015)	Explored talent management in selected SET-listed companies in Thailand. Used purposive and snowball sampling. Studied six companies through HR expert interviews, revealing strategies like career paths and succession plans for motivating skilled individuals.
Koketso and Rust (2018)	Investigated talent management challenges in Cape Town municipality. Conducted interviews with senior managers, identifying issues such as retaining key talent, lack of recognition, and problems in career management and succession planning.
Shirkani and Nazari (2019)	Analyzed the impact of talent management on organizational entrepreneurship in Ilam Oil Company, Iran. Used a standardized questionnaire for data collection, finding a positive correlation between talent attraction, retention, development, and entrepreneurship.

Source: Author

Study Objective

- To understand the talent identification practices followed in banks and to test the influence of talent identification practices on the talent management practices of banks.
- To know the talent development practices followed in banks and to test the influence of talent development practices on the talent management practices of banks.

Analysis and Interpretation

The study assessed Talent Identification practices in Public and Private sector banks, employing four variables: Talent gap analysis, role/position profile development, recruitment, and selection practices. Mann

Whitney U (MWU) tests were conducted to discern potential disparities between the two sectors in these practices, treating them as distinct groups.

Upon scrutinizing Table 163.1, it is evident that the MWU test results comparing talent gap analysis in public and private sectors reveal no statistical difference (Z = -1.356, p = 0.175 > 0.05). Public and private banks exhibit similar mean ranks, suggesting analogous practices in talent gap identification. Consequently, we accept the null hypothesis, indicating no significant disparity in talent gap analysis between public and private sector banks.

The findings indicate a noteworthy contrast in employees' views on career success between public and private sector banks (Z = 16.703, p = 0.000 < 0.05). Public sector banks, with a mean rank of 251,

Table 163.2 Analysis of talent gaps in public and private sector banks using the MWU test results.

Group	N	Mean rank	Sum of ranks	MWU	Z	P
Public	227	188.29	41846	1.423	-1.356	0.175*
Private	137	172.9	24584			
Total	364					

* The difference is insignificant since p > 0.05
Source: Author

Table 163.3 Results of the MWU-test comparing the roles and position characteristics of banks in the public and private sectors.

Group	N	Mean rank	Sum of ranks	MWU	Z	P
Public	227	251	56977	34	-16.702	0
Private	137	69	9453			
Total	364					

* The difference is highly significant since p < 0.001
Source: Author

demonstrate higher practices fostering career growth than private sector banks (mean rank 69). These results suggest that employees' perceptions of career success play a vital role in talent retention within public sector banks.

Suggestion

Workforce talent gaps are conventionally assessed by examining knowledge and skills. To address senior-level gaps, future roles should consider motivational, leadership, and team management skills.

Role profiles aligning with business goals should emphasize both technical tasks and expected behaviors in interactions across levels and groups.

Strategic positions are typically filled externally, but an internal talent identification approach can yield individuals well-versed in the bank's values, vision, and culture, enhancing seamless integration.

Conclusion

This study looks into how banks find, nurture, and keep talented individuals. It identifies key factors in talent spotting, development, and retention, explaining

how they are linked to talent management. The study explores how retaining talent affects employee attitudes, including satisfaction, perceptions of career success, and thoughts of leaving. It suggests a model to measure the impact of talent spotting, development, and retention on talent management in banks, finding positive effects. The study also checks how these practices influence behavior, looking at employee satisfaction, views on career success, and the likelihood of leaving the organization.

References

Brakeley, H., Cheese, P., and Clinton, D. (2014). The high-performance workforce study 2004. Retrieved from www.accenture.com.

Deloitte (2015). Talent Management Strategies Survey. Retrieved from www.deloitte.com.

Halder, U. K., and Juthika, S. (2012). Human Resource Management. New Delhi, India: Oxford University Press. Retrieved from www.humancapitalinstitute.org.

Tucker, E., Kao, T., and Verma, N. (2015). Next-generation talent management: insights on how workforce trends are changing the face of talent management. Retrieved from www.hewitt.com.

164 Employee engagement's link with psychological well-being in telecommuters

Chinthu Jose and P. A. Padmaavathy[a]

Karpagam Academy of Higher Education, Coimbatore, India

Abstract

The pandemic has spurred a notable rise in telework and remote work. This study, employing a SOBEL technique and United Nations Sustainable Development-led theme analysis, examines the link between employee engagement, well-being, and the impact of telecommuting. A structured questionnaire collected primary data from employees with a minimum of three years of experience. Both primary and secondary data were used to meet study objectives, aiming to uncover factors influencing psychological health and engagement. The findings are expected to guide organizations in crafting effective programs to boost overall performance.

Keywords: Remote work, telecommuters, telework, well-being, workforce planning

Introduction

Over recent decades, global changes driven by globalization and technological advancements have reshaped the work landscape. The emergence of telework solutions in the 1980s, facilitated by technological progress, led to remote working scenarios, encompassing terms like telework, remote work, flex-work, and working from home. These terms, often used interchangeably, differ in where work is performed and the level of employee flexibility. Technological innovations, particularly in mobile communication, have extended teleworking accessibility, enhancing customer satisfaction, sales, and competitiveness. Effective communication, integral to partnerships, relies on social interaction and support. Teleworkers undergo significant changes in work situations, communication quality, and social support, prompting exploration of potential impacts on mental well-being.

Employee motivation and well-being are crucial for optimal organizational performance. Establishing a conducive environment where employees can achieve personal and organizational goals is essential. Diverse human resource policies prioritizing employee well-being enhance engagement, leading to increased efficiency and reduced absenteeism and turnover rates. Recognizing that telecommuting is not inherently problematic, the study challenges assumptions regarding communication deficits, loneliness, or social isolation in remote workers. Individual assessments based on general resistance resources and sense of coherence, rather than attributing issues solely to the work setting, offer a nuanced perspective.

This study aims to enhance understanding by introducing concepts of employee engagement and psychological well-being, exploring primary associations between telecommuting, social support, and mental well-being in Ernakulam city. Providing clarity on these connections contributes to a holistic view of the impact of telework on employees' lives and mental health. Continuous encouragement and motivation within organizations, coupled with strategic human resource policies, emerge as critical elements in fostering a healthy and productive work environment.

Objective

- To investigate the elements that play a role in the involvement and mental wellness of telecommuting employees.
- To explore the impact of employee engagement and psychological well-being on work-related outcomes such as job satisfaction and productivity.
- To identify potential barriers to employee engagement and psychological well-being among telecommuters.
- To develop practical recommendations for organizations seeking to improve the well-being and engagement of their remote workforce.

[a]padmaavathypa@gmail.com

Literature Review

Table 164.1 Insights into remote work, engagement, and well-being.

Author name	Study
Jackson and Fransman (2018)	Telework during the pandemic may not always boost productivity due to family disruptions and social isolation. Abdel Hadi et al. (2021) link household responsibilities to emotional fatigue, negatively impacting workplace performance.
Anand et al. (2016)	Worker involvement, influenced by job satisfaction and recognition, is crucial for company commitment. Wages and benefits significantly impact employee engagement.
Kalpana and Suhasini (2018)	Increasing employee engagement involves offering options and fostering dedication, reducing turnover and boosting creativity.
Prasad et al. (2020)	COVID-19 remote work has pros and cons, including challenges like a lack of trust, different time zones, and excessive workload. Effective management is vital for addressing workplace isolation.
Hickman (2019)	Workplace isolation is a major concern for remote workers, highlighted in a study on a U.S. customer service company using Emerson's social exchange theory.
Judge et al. (2017)	Recent advancements connect self-efficacy, job happiness, work engagement, job satisfaction, and turnover.
Scanlan (2019)	Burnout, job satisfaction, expectations, and mental health resources for Australian mental health professionals are interconnected. Effective coping is essential for stress management.
Winfield et al. (2022)	Psychological well-being is linked to positive relationships, environmental competence, and overall contentment. Factors related to well-being and discomfort are unrelated.
Prasad et al. (2021)	Nepali nurses' study shows a direct correlation between social support and psychological well-being in teenagers receiving better support.

Source: Author

Problem Statement

Organizations worldwide strive for success through motivated workforces, but there's a concerning decline in employee engagement. Factors like inadequate HR practices and limited support contribute to this disconnect. The impact of telework on well-being remains uncertain. In Kerala's Ernakulum city, this research aims to gauge current employee engagement levels, assess its effects on psychological well-being, and offer practical recommendations to enhance organizational effectiveness.

Research Methodology

This study focuses on understanding the impact of effective employee engagement and well-being, exploring factors like supportive leadership and rewards in Ernakulam. With its diverse telecommuting community, strong tech infrastructure, and multicultural workforce, the research aims to shed light on the relationship between employee engagement and psychological well-being among telecommuters, offering valuable insights for management strategies.

Study Objectives

- Identify effects of effective employee engagement on well-being
- Investigate impact of leadership, rewards, career opportunities on engagement
- Examine interaction with demographic variables
- Explore influence of job perception on employee retention

Research Location and Rationale (Ernakulam)

- Large pool of telecommuters
- Strong technology infrastructure
- Multicultural workforce
- Access to social support networks
- Relevance to management and organizational outcomes

Data Collection and Sampling

In Ernakulam, Kerala, our research spanned from November 2021 to February 2022, post the COVID-19 pandemic. We focused on mid-level professionals, teleworking at least two days weekly pre-pandemic. A questionnaire (Table 164.1) was given to 23 eligible commercial, service-sector organizations in the area. Ten participants agreed to participate, with their human resources departments distributing the survey electronically to teleworkers. We received 745 responses, of which 70% (519) met all the sample criteria. This study sheds light on teleworking experiences

Table 164.2 Participant's overview.

Participant	Gender	Age	Occupation	Employment industry
1	Male	39	Faculty	Academe
2	Male	32	Quality control officer	BPO
3	Female	37	Fraud specialist	BPO
4	Female	28	CPA	Real estate
5	Female	33	Faculty	Academe
6	Female	27	Content moderator	BPO
7	Male	29	IT Network administrator	IT/Healthcare
8	Male	33	CPA/Principal consultant	IT

Source: Author

Table 164.3 Employee engagement scale.

Stages of engagement	Range
Actively disengaged	0-10
disengaged	11-20
Opportunistic	21-30
Engaged	31-40
Actively Engaged	41-50

Source: Author

Figure 164.1 Telecommuter's reviews plot
Source: Author

during and after the pandemic among mid-level professionals in the region.

Data Analysis

After collecting and organizing the data, we used SPSS software for the initial analysis, calculating mean values for psychological contract type, engagement, and stress. In the second phase, we employed simple linear regression to explore the impact of psychological contract type on employee engagement. Lastly, the SOBEL test assessed stress as a potential mediator in the psychological contract and employee engagement relationship using mean values.

Reliability

The questionnaire's reliability is solid, checked through Cronbach's alpha values for aspects like remote working, technology, and teamwork, all comfortably exceeding the 0.70 threshold. Strong internal consistency is evident across variables like job engagement and vigor, ranging from 0.76 to 0.84. This makes the questionnaire a reliable tool for gauging various work-related dimensions, from remote work to personal well-being.

Validity

In confirmatory factor analysis, LISREL software uses indices like NFI, NNFI, and CFI to check model fit. Table 164.4 shows good NFI and NNFI (0.97 and 0.98), CFI is solid at 0.98, and RMSE is low (0.052). However, GFI and AGFI (0.78 and 0.75) indicate room for model improvement.

Results

The SPSS test results reveal that in remote work settings, factors like technology, teamwork, organizational climate, workplace isolation, and job satisfaction significantly impact an employee's physical well-being. Each variable was subjected to separate SOBEL tests, indicating that physical job engagement significantly influences psychological well-being aspects like self-acceptance, personal growth, positive relationships, and environmental mastery. Dedication is affected by both self-acceptance and environmental mastery. Emotional factors are influenced by all psychological well-being elements except the purpose of life, while vigor is impacted by all factors except positive relationships. Additionally, absorption is influenced by self-acceptance.

The key to a successful company lies in its workforce. Modern businesses recognize the value of motivated and skilled employees, who contribute to a competitive edge. Committed workers go beyond their job descriptions to achieve organizational goals, making the study of work engagement crucial for both practitioners and researchers. While satisfaction and engagement differ, many see them as equal. Engagement involves surpassing job requirements for personal and company success, while satisfaction focuses on job fulfillment. Understanding the impact of psychological well-being on telecommuters, including job engagement, remote work, and satisfaction, is essential. Gender and age disparities in these aspects are also acknowledged.

Table 164.4 Reliability scale.

Construct	Cronbach's alpha
Remote working	0.83
Technology	0.84
Teamwork	0.76
Organizational climate	0.78
Workplace isolation	0.78
Job engagement	0.81
Physical	0.82
Dedication	0.81
Emotional	0.8
Vigor	0.83
Absorption	0.81
Cognitive	0.84
Job satisfaction	0.76
Work engagement	0.73
Working conditions	0.78
Organization culture	0.75
Job clarity	0.79
Carrier development	0.74
Work-life balance	0.75
Psychological well-being	0.79
Environmental mastery	0.7
Self-acceptance	0.72
Purpose of life	0.73
Autonomy	0.74
Personal growth	0.73
Positive relations	0.79
Total items	0.85 (Overall)

Source: Author

Table 164.5 Measure the goodness of fit for the measurement model.

Normed fit index (NFI)	0.97
Non-normed fit index (NNFI)	0.98
Comparative fit index (CFI)	0.98
Root mean square error or residual (RMSR)	0.052
Goodness of fit index (GFI)	0.78
Adjusted goodness of fit index (AGFI)	0.75

Source: Author

Conclusion

This study delves into the effects of work-from-home policies on employee well-being and explores the link between workplace engagement and psychological health. Focused on multinational corporations in Ernakulum City, it examines the factors influencing employee engagement. Despite increased corporate investments in fostering dedication, studies reveal a disproportionate rise in commitment levels, jeopardizing the potential competitive advantage. The research aims to enhance engagement to counter organizational ineffectiveness. Only multinational corporations in Ernakulum city were part of this empirical study, employing quantitative research for data collection and analysis. Expanding the sample size promises more precise outcomes and improved gender equality. The study suggests exploring occupational stress, coping mechanisms, and their impact on psychological well-being. Addressing these factors can boost productivity and organizational health.

References

Abdel Hadi, S., Bakker, A. B., and Häusser, J. A. (2021). The role of leisure crafting for emotional exhaustion in telework during the COVID-19 pandemic. *Anxiety, Stress, and Coping*, 34(5), 530–544.

Anand, V. V., Banu, C. V., Rengarajan, V., Thirumoorthy, G., Rajkumar, V., and Madhumitha, R. (2016). Employee engagement–a study with special reference to postal employees in rural areas of Thanjavur. *Indian Journal of Science and Technology*, 9(27), 1–8.

Chung, J. R., Rolfes, M. A., Flannery, B., Prasad, P., O'Halloran, A., Garg, S., et al. (2020). Effects of influenza vaccination in the United States during the 2018–2019 influenza season. *Clinical Infectious Diseases*, 71(8), e368–e376.

Jackson, L. T. B., and Fransman, E. I. (2018). Flexi work, financial well-being, work–life balance and their effects on subjective experiences of productivity and job satisfaction of females in an institution of higher learning. *South African Journal of Economic and Management Sciences*, 21(1), 1–13.

Judge, T. A., Weiss, H. M., Kammeyer-Mueller, J. D., and Hulin, C. L. (2017). Job attitudes, job satisfaction, and job affect: a century of continuity and change. *Journal of Applied Psychology*, 102(3), 356.

Parent-Lamarche, A. (2022). Teleworking, work engagement, and intention to quit during the COVID-19 pandemic: same storm, different boats?. *International Journal of Environmental Research and Public Health*, 19(3), 1267.

Sanhokwe, H., Takawira, S., Kunene, Z., and Maunganidze, F. (2022). Impact of COVID-19 induced teleworking arrangements on employees in NGOs: Implications for policy and practice for leadership. *Sage Open*, 12(2), 21582440221079908.

Skowronski, D. M., Chambers, C., De Serres, G., Sabaiduc, S., Winter, A. L., Dickinson, J. A., et al. (2019). Vaccine effectiveness against lineage-matched and-mismatched influenza B viruses across 8 seasons in Canada, 2010–2011 to 2017–2018. *Clinical Infectious Diseases*, 68(10), 1754–1757.

Stempel, C. R., and Siestrup, K. (2022). Suddenly telework: job crafting as a way to promote employee well-being?. *Frontiers in Psychology*, 12, 6561.

Suhasini, T., and Kalpana, K. (2018). A study on factors affecting employee engagement in Indian IT industry. *International Journal of Pure and Applied Mathematics*, 118(24), 1–13.

165 Customer satisfaction toward online electronic goods

M. Sathiya and P. A. Padmaavathy[a]

Karpagam Academy of Higher Education, Coimbatore, India

Abstract

This study delves into the impact of the internet on our lives, specifically focusing on customer satisfaction with online electronic goods. The internet's omnipresence has changed how we live, especially in the realm of purchasing. With the rise of e-commerce, more people turn to online platforms for buying various items due to the quick and convenient process. The internet, once just a source of information, has evolved into a crucial tool for business transactions. This research aims to understand customers' buying habits for electronic goods and explore the factors influencing their decisions. Ultimately, we seek to unravel how these factors shape the overall decision-making process in the ever-evolving landscape of online shopping.

Keywords: Customer satisfaction, online electronic goods and consumer preferences

Introduction

The study focuses on exploring customer satisfaction with online electronic goods, given the booming growth of e-commerce (Guo et al., 2012). Online shopping has transformed how people buy electronic items like smartphones, laptops, and home appliances (Hung et al., 2014). The convenience, competitive pricing, and vast product selection have attracted a large customer base (Vasic et al., 2019; Jayasubramanian et al., 2015). Despite these advantages, challenges like concerns about product quality, authenticity, delivery times, and after-sales service exist (Merugu and Mohan, 2020). Addressing these issues is crucial for businesses to ensure customer satisfaction and loyalty (Karim, 2013). This study aims to uncover the factors influencing customer satisfaction in online electronic goods purchases (Pham and Ahammad, 2017). By understanding these factors, businesses can improve their offerings and customer service, meeting expectations more effectively (Wang and Le, 2015; Rajeswari, 2015). Policymakers can use the findings to shape regulations that create a trustworthy online shopping environment Mishra, A et al., (2021), Yadav, S. (2020), Kaviya, V et al., (2019), Swain, D. (2018) and Sharma, R. K. (2018).

Literature Review

Table 165.1 A compilation of studies on consumer behavior and strategies for online success.

Author name	Study
Gupta and Jain (2017)	Explored e-commerce consumer behavior, highlighting security concerns as a barrier to online shopping. Identified perceived risks of fraud in online business.
Vijay et al. (2017)	Proposed e-retailers use web atmospherics to create a unique online environment, influencing consumer purchase behavior and standing out from competitors.
Dara (2016)	Explored digital marketing's significance, emphasizing the use of various digital media forms. Stressed the importance of being user-oriented for success in digital marketing.
Vijayalakshmi et al. (2013)	Conducted an empirical study on internal and external factors affecting consumer buying behavior for electronic home appliances. Recommended addressing these factors for effective satisfaction.

Source: Author

Problem Statement

This study dives into how happy folks are when buying electronic stuff online. Even though it's handy and has loads of options, some things might bug customers. Figuring out these issues is vital for businesses and policymakers to make online gadget shopping better for everyone.

Study Objective

- To study customer satisfaction toward online electronic goods.
- To analyze consumer preferences for purchasing electronic goods online.
- To ascertain the most preferred online shopping website among the customers for buying e-goods.

[a]padmaavathypa@gmail.com

- To analyze the impact of demographic characteristics of consumers on their online purchase of electronic good

Scope of the Study

The scope of this study on customer satisfaction towards online electronic goods encompasses several key aspects related to the online shopping experience and customer perceptions. The study aims to provide a comprehensive understanding of customer satisfaction within the given context. It is important to note that the study's scope is limited to customer satisfaction with online electronic goods. It does not cover other aspects such as market analysis, competitive landscape, or broader economic factors. The focus is on understanding and improving customer satisfaction within the specified context.

Research Methodology

Research design:
- Descriptive research design employed.
- Focus on customer satisfaction towards online electronic goods.

Data collection:
- Primary data collected through a questionnaire.
- Administered to 120 consumers of online electronic goods.
- Questionnaire served as the primary data source.
- Secondary data collected from various published sources.

Sample design:
- Non-probability sampling technique used.
- Purposive sampling employed.
- Participants were selected based on specific criteria relevant to research objective.

Sample size:
- 120 consumers of online electronic goods.

Data analysis:
- Simple percentage analysis used to interpret questionnaire data.
- Chi-square analysis applied to assess relationships between variables.
- One-way ANOVA conducted to analyze significant differences between groups or categories.

Objective and approach:
- Aiming to provide a comprehensive understanding of customer satisfaction toward online electronic goods.

- Comprehensive approach using primary and secondary data sources.
- Statistical tools applied for analysis and interpretation.

Significance of methodology:
- Chosen sample design, size, and sampling method allowed for relevant data collection.
- Application of statistical tools aided in thorough analysis and interpretation of collected data.

Limitations of the Study

- The study's findings may be influenced by the sample size and representativeness of the participants. If the sample size is small or not diverse enough, the results may not accurately reflect the broader population of online electronic goods customers. Efforts will be made to gather a diverse sample, but limitations in reaching a large and representative sample should be acknowledged.
- The study focuses specifically on customer satisfaction towards online electronic goods. It does not cover other aspects such as offline purchases, overall market analysis, or broader economic factors that may impact customer satisfaction levels

Analysis and Interpretation

In the above table, the significance value is (0.001) which is lesser than the value of 0.05, thus the null hypothesis is rejected. So, there is a significant relationship between electric goods purchased online and satisfaction on electric good bought online.

Ho1: There is no significant difference between the electric good purchased online and satisfaction on electric good bought online.

The significance value is (0.004) which is lesser than the value of 0.05, thus the null hypothesis is rejected. So, there is a significant relationship between electronic goods purchased online and satisfaction on price.

Ho2: There is no significant difference between electronic good purchased online and satisfaction on price.

In the above by using one way-ANOVA test, the significance value is (0.298) which is greater than the table value 5%, thus the null hypothesis is accepted. So, there is no significance difference between online market preferred the most and the satisfaction on availability of e-goods in online.

Ho3: There is no significant difference between online market preferred the most and the satisfaction on availability of e-goods in online.

The majority of the surveyed individuals, accounting for 59.2%, identify as female, while 41.7% are Under Graduates. Most of them, around 42.9%, are students, and a significant number, 36.7%, receive income from various sources. The majority, 61.7%, are unmarried, and a whopping 92.5% have experience with online shopping, with 29.25% making online

Table 165.2 Demographic variables of the respondents.

Demographic variables	Particulars	Frequency	Percent
Gender	Male	49	40.8
	Female	71	59.2
	Total	120	100
Age	18-20	28	23.3
	21-30	38	31.7
	31-40	20	16.7
	41-50	19	15.8
	50 above	1	0.8
	Other	14	11.7
	Total	120	100
Educational qualification	School	22	18.3
	Diploma	23	19.2
	Undergraduate	50	41.7
	Postgraduate	22	18.3
	Ph.D.	3	2.5
	Total	120	100
Occupation	Student	59	49.2
	Government employee	14	11.7
	Private employee	28	23.3
	Business	12	10
	Other	7	5.8
	Total	120	100
Monthly income	Less than 20,000	14	11.7
	Less than 70,000	26	21.7
	Less than 1,00,000	23	19.2
	1,00,000 & above	13	10.8
	Other	44	36.7
	Total	120	100

Source: Author

Table 165.3 E-Good purchased online and satisfaction on e-good bought online.

Chi-square test

	Value	df	Asymp.Sig (2-sided)
Pearson Chi-square	50.756	18	0.001

Source: Author

Table 165.4 E-good purchased online and satisfaction on price.

Chi-square test

	Value	df	Asymp.Sig (2-sided)
Pearson Chi-square	38.266	18	0.004

Source: Author

ANOVA onlinemarketyouprefermost	Sum of Squares	df	Mean Square	F	Sig.
Between Groups	8.701	4	2.175	1.240	.298
Within Groups	201.666	115	1.754		
Total	210.367	119			

Figure 165.1 Online market preferred most and the satisfaction on availability of e-goods
Source: Author

purchases monthly. When it comes to online shopping habits, 77.5% have bought electronic goods online, and 40% express satisfaction with their purchases. Notably, 25.8% appreciate the quality and design. Mobile phones were a popular online purchase, with 20% opting for them. The majority, 30%, spend less than £1000 on electronic goods online. Additionally, 29.2% compare products with other brands, 31.7% prefer online shopping for home delivery, and 38.3% are attracted by discounts. However, 20.8% have occasionally received broken e-goods, and 38.3% predominantly prefer Amazon, while 43.3% perceive online prices as expensive.

Suggestion

- It is essential to enhance the speed of product delivery in order to ensure prompt delivery to customers.
- There is a need to ensure that products are delivered to customers without any damage.
- To enhance online shopping experiences, a greater number of advertisements are required.

- It is necessary to expand the range of products available in online shopping beyond just electric and electronic items.
- The number of portals should be increased to cater to a wider range of goods and services for customers.

Conclusion

The consumer's pre and post-purchase behaviors depend on his/her satisfaction and perception of the product. And the best and most systematic marketing mix variables guarantees consumer satisfaction. Consumers who buy electronics expect their maximum satisfaction with the product, confirming their commitment to the electronic products manufacturers and sellers who meet it, repurchasing it and spreading their experience to those who know them. This research identifies the influencing factors of online purchases and measures the level of satisfaction towards the online shopping of electronic goods. The study reveals that, the majority of the respondents are satisfied with their online electronic product.

References

Al Karim, R. (2013). Customer satisfaction in online shopping: a study into the reasons for motivations and inhibitions. *IOSR Journal of Business and Management*, 11(6), 13–20.

Guo, X., Ling, K. C., and Liu, M. (2012). Evaluating factors influencing consumer satisfaction towards online shopping in China. *Asian Social Science*, 8(13), 40.

Hung, S. Y., Chen, C. C., and Huang, N. H. (2014). An integrative approach to understanding customer satisfaction with e-service of online stores. *Journal of Electronic Commerce Research*, 15(1), 40.

Jayasubramanian, P., Sivasakthi, D., and Ananthi, P. K. (2015). A study on customer satisfaction towards online shopping. *International Journal of Applied Research*, 1(8), 489–495.

Kim, H. R. (2005). Developing an index of online customer satisfaction. *Journal of Financial Services Marketing*, 10, 49–64.

Kaviya, V., and Ramesh, M. (2019). Awareness and Utilization of MGNREGA in Tamil Nadu: A Study with Special Reference to Namakkal District. Journal: International Journal of Applied Engineering Research, 14(9), 2226–2231.

Merugu, D. P., and Mohan, D. V. K. (2020). Customer satisfaction towards online shopping with reference to Jalandhar city. *International Journal of Management (IJM)*, 11(2), 36–47.

Mishra, A., and Samal, S. K. (2021). Awareness and Participation in MGNREGA: A Study in Odisha. Journal: Journal of Rural Development, 40(3), 421–440.

Pham, T. S. H., and Ahammad, M. F. (2017). Antecedents and consequences of online customer satisfaction: a holistic process perspective. *Technological Forecasting and Social Change*, 124, 332–342.

Rajeswari, M. (2015). A study on the customer satisfaction towards online shopping in Chennai city. *International Journal of Sales and Marketing Management Research and Development*, 5(1), 1–10.

Sharma, R. K. (2018). Awareness about MGNREGA Schemes: A Case Study of Rural Areas in Rajasthan. Journal: Indian Journal of Economics and Development, 6(1), 223–228.

Swain, D. (2018). Awareness and Utilization of MGNREGA among the Scheduled Caste Households: A Study in Sundargarh District of Odisha. Journal: Indian Journal of Regional Science, 50(2), 45–60.

Vasic, N., Kilibarda, M., and Kaurin, T. (2019). The influence of online shopping determinants on customer satisfaction in the Serbian market. *Journal of Theoretical and Applied Electronic Commerce Research*, 14(2), 70–89.

Wang, L. W., and Le, Q. L. (2015). Customer satisfaction towards online shopping at electronics shopping malls in vietnam-a conceptual model to enhance business success through efficient websites and logistics services. *The Evidence from Chinese Stock Market. Journal Stock Forex Trading*, 5(164), 2.

Yadav, S. (2020). Awareness and Perception of MGNREGA: A Study in Rural Haryana. Journal: Indian Journal of Regional Science, 52(1), 1–15.

166 Psychological factors affecting the perception towards occupational hazards and safety among the fishermen

Tintu Mary Pushkeria and Padmaavathy, P. A.[a]

Karpagam Academy of Higher Education, Coimbatore, Tamil Nadu, India

Abstract

Every year, over 2.78 million people worldwide lose their lives due to work-related health issues, affecting 20-50% of global workers, especially in developing nations. This research delves into the health risks faced by fishermen in Ernakulam while handling and processing fish. Through a random selection process, participants underwent a survey using a semi-structured questionnaire. Despite the prevalence of occupational accidents in fisheries-dependent nations, few safety measures are in place. The study revealed high mortality rates among fishermen due to long hours, adverse weather, and heavy equipment. Issues like heat, cold, noise, accidents, and systemic problems were reported in the past six months. Safety measures, including personal protective equipment, workplace safety, screening, and early treatment, are crucial to prevent occupational health hazards.

Keywords: Accidents, fishermen, occupational health problems, stress, systemic problems

Introduction

Working in the fishing industry, with over half a billion people dependent on it, poses significant occupational hazards. Fishermen face challenges like adverse weather, long hours, physical strain, and maritime accidents, making it one of the most dangerous occupations globally. Operating in informal settings with irregular hours, these workers often experience musculoskeletal disorders due to overuse. Shockingly, the annual mortality rate among fishermen is 80 per 100,000, linked to economic, cultural, and social risks. Despite these dangers, fishermen may not accurately perceive the occupational hazards, leading to a lack of safety practices and increased accident risks. Understanding psychological factors such as risk perception, cognitive biases, motivation, and personality traits is crucial. Despite efforts by governments, the industry remains hazardous, disproportionately affecting low-income individuals. This study aims to explore these psychological aspects among Ernakulam Harbour fishermen to develop more effective interventions and policies, ultimately reducing risks in this challenging profession.

Problem Statement

Research indicates that fishermen's views on risk are shaped by social norms. Understanding these attitudes is crucial before introducing safety measures in professions like fishing. In Kerala, where fishing is vital for income and community ties, there's a lack of research on fishermen's hazards and perceptions. This study aims to explore these variables in Ernakulam fishing harbor for effective safety interventions.

Literature Review

Table 166.1 A Comprehensive overview of Ghana's fishing industry and safety challenges.

Author name	Study
Rahman et al. (2022)	Fishing, among the oldest and riskiest professions, sparks shared concerns for worker safety.
Lei et al. (2022)	High risks, injuries, and fatalities make the fishing industry consistently dangerous, challenging commercial and artisanal businesses.
Omar et al. (2022)	The Gulf of Guinea in Ghana is rich in fishing opportunities, vital for economic development.
Wight et al. (2022)	Fish consumption is crucial in Ghana, with 75% consumed locally, supporting economic and food security objectives.

[a]padmaavathypa@gmail.com

Author name	Study
Barrow et al. (2022)	Ghana's fishing industry employs 2 million, contributing significantly to livelihoods and poverty reduction.
Alam et al. (2022)	Ghana's fishing sector plays a key role in poverty eradication along the 550-kilometre coastline.
Kholid (2022)	Fisheries contribute 5% to Ghana's agricultural GDP, generating nearly $60 million annually in exports.
Lima et al. (2022)	Ghana relies on inland, marine, and aquaculture resources for its fishing industry.
Xiao et al. (2022)	Fishing's hazards are influenced by social, economic, and cultural factors, shaping safety cultures across historical periods.
Md et al. (2022)	Fishing risks vary based on vessel size, method, crew experience, and location.
Ravi et al. (2022)	Effective safety culture in the fishing industry depends on awareness, commitment, and expertise in occupational safety.
Anita et al. (2022)	Safety behavior, crucial worldwide, includes participation and compliance behaviors.
Azril et al. (2022)	Safety compliance is vital for essential tasks ensuring workplace safety, often promoted through risk awareness.
Ohira et al. (2022)	Fishing practices with small boats pose different risks than those with large boats, which may be more vulnerable to industrial mishaps.

Source: Author

Study Objective

- To evaluate the level of knowledge among fishermen in preventing occupational dangers.
- To identify the methods fishermen, use to prevent workplace dangers.
- To explore the impact of fishermen's perception of occupational hazards and safety on their work performance and productivity.
- To establish a connection between information, practice, and attitudes scores.
- To recommend strategies for improving the psychological well-being of fishermen and enhancing their perception towards occupational hazards and safety.

Research Methodology

Study area:
- The research took place at the fishing harbor in Ernakulam, located in southern Kerala.
- Ernakulam was chosen due to its significance in Kerala's fishing industry, its long coastline, and the presence of organizations aiding fishermen.
- The area's history of safety programs provided an opportunity to evaluate their effectiveness.

Study design, population, and selection of participants:
- A cross-sectional analytical approach was used between August and October 2022 to assess Occupational Safety and Health (OSH) risks among Ernakulam fishermen.

- Fishermen of all ages, genders, and nationalities fishing in the harbor were included.
- Participants were randomly selected from the South Indian Federation of Fishermen Societies (SIFFS) roster.
- To ensure representation, authorized fishermen were engaged by the fisheries department, with sample size determined using Cochran's formula.

Data collection tools and techniques:
- Trained assistants used standardized questionnaires to gather data.
- Information on sociodemographic, prior injuries, attitudes, and practices related to safety and health was collected.
- Questionnaires, initially in English, were administered face-to-face at the Ernakulam fishing site.

Data analysis:
- Collected data underwent processing, cleaning, and entry, followed by descriptive analysis using graphs.
- Binary logistic regression was employed to determine correlations between research variables, integrating chi-square or Fisher's exact test and t-test for examination.

Analysis and Interpretation

Between August and October 2022, we conducted a cross-sectional analysis to explore the OSH risks faced by fishermen at Ernakulam fishing harbor. Our study aimed to encompass fishermen of all ages, genders, and nationalities. Using a random sampling method from the SIFFS roster, we included participants from diverse backgrounds. Recognizing the logistical challenge of surveying dispersed fishermen, the Ernakulam fisheries department collaborated with authorized fishermen, employing Cochran's formula to determine an appropriate sample size for the study.

$$n = (t^2 * s^2)/d^2$$

where t = the value of the chosen alpha level, s = estimated standard deviation for the population and d = acceptable error margin for the calculated mean.

The results from the test scores of the subjects show a significant increase in knowledge after receiving video-assisted health teaching on occupational hazards among fishermen. The mean pretest score was 12.68, while the posttest mean increased to 25.30. The calculated t-value of 14.21 indicates a substantial improvement, which is statistically significant at

Table 166.2 Frequency and percentage distribution of subjects according to fish catch, frequency of returning home, and source of the receiver of information on fishing hazards.

Variable	Frequency	Percentage
Average seasonal fish catch (tons):		
1-3	29	8.9
4-6	87	26.6
7-9	97	29.7
10-12	54	16.5
>12	60	18.3
Frequency of returning home after the sea voyage:		
Daily	310	94.8
Alternative days	7	2.1
Every third day	3	0.9

Variable	Frequency	Percentage
Every 4- 6 days	1	0.3
Once a week	5	1.5
Once in 8-10days	1	0.3
The receiver of information:		
Yes	304	92.97
No	23	7.03
Source of the receiver of information (304)		
Fishing department	34	11.2
Health personnel	6	2
Fellow workers	246	80.9
Mass media	18	5.9

Source: Author

Table 166.3 Perceptions of fishers about occupational hazards associated with fishing.

Statement	Strongly disagree	Disagree	Neutral	Agree	Strongly agree	Total
I think fishing is a dangerous activity	13(29.5%)	1(2.3%)	1(2.3%)	0(0%)	29(65.9%)	44(100%)
I think Fishing is like any other occupation in terms of its risk level.	14(31.8%)	1(2.3%)	0(0%)	0(0%)	29(65.9%)	44(100%)
I think safety training is important in fishing.	4(9.1%)	0(0%)	0(0%)	1(2.3%)	39(88.6%)	44(100%)
No weather condition would stop me from fishing.	40(90.9%)	2(4.5%)	0(0%)	0(0%)	0(0%)	44(100%)
I would not fish if there is equipment failure.	5(11.4%)	1(2.3%)	1(2.3%)	1(2.3%)	36(81.8%)	44(100%)
I know how to take precautionary measures against any fishing hazards without depending on anybody or government officials' guidance on how to protect myself.	0(0%)	1(2.3%)	2(4.5%)	4(9.1%)	37(84.1%)	44(100%)
I know how to discern when to fish concerning adverse weather conditions and adhere to such weather signs when embarking on fishing expeditions.	1(2.3%)	0(0%)	0(0%)	1(2.3%)	42(95.5%)	44(100%)
I know I have to promptly deal with the consequences of fishing hazards whenever it occurs. Otherwise, my family's livelihood would be jeopardized	1(2.3%)	0(0%)	1(2.3%)	2(4.5%)	40(90.9%)	44(100%)

Source: Author

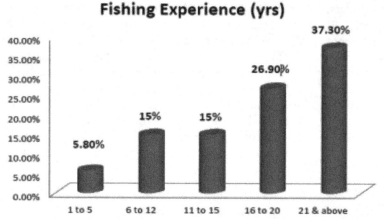

Figure 166.1 Cylinder diagram representing the fishing experience
Source: Author

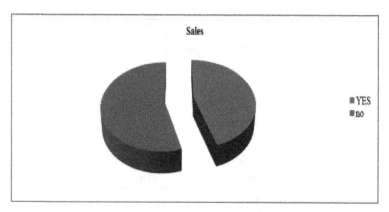

Figure 166.2 Pie diagram showing overall families involved in fishing
Source: Author

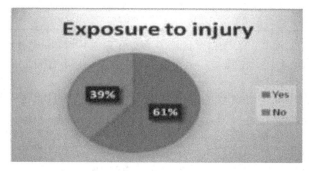

Figure 166.3 Level of exposure to injuries
Source: Author

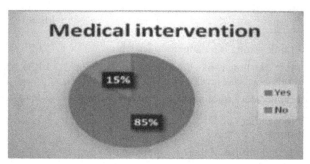

Figure 166.4 Percentage of those seeking medical intervention
Source: Author

the 0.001 level of significance with a 95% confidence range. This suggests that the video-assisted teaching method effectively enhances knowledge among fishermen regarding occupational hazards. The findings underscore the importance and effectiveness of using visual aids in educational interventions for promoting occupational health and safety awareness within this community.

The study findings suggest a significant link between attitude scores and fish catch quantity, as indicated by Chi-square and ANOVA analyses ($x2$ = 10.96 at .027). Higher attitude scores were associated with fish catch above 11 tons, while medium catch (7 to 11 tons) correlated with lower scores. Interestingly, lower fish catch (1 to 6 tons) was linked to higher attitude scores. Demographically, most fishermen were men,

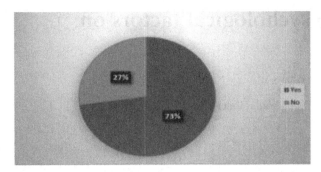

Figure 166.5 Percentage of fishers who received safety training
Source: Author

unmarried, and had minimal education. They had diverse ages, substantial fishing experience, and were primarily of ethnic origin. Despite facing occupational risks, like injuries and mosquito bites, their perception varied based on factors such as marital status and access to fishing data.

The investigation underscores the demographic influences on fishermen's perceptions of occupational risks. Notably, Chi-square and ANOVA analyses revealed significant associations with variables like marital status, years of fishing experience, monthly income, number of dependents, access to fishing data, and risk acceptance. The statistical analyses confirmed robust connections between these factors and fishermen's perceptions. Notably, married fishermen and those with access to fishing data exhibited different risk perceptions, influencing their decision-making towards safety.

Conclusion

Ernakulam, Kerala, is home to a significant portion of the world's fishermen, making up one-fourth of the total. Despite their crucial role in sustainable fisheries development, the industry faces a troubling issue - the highest rate of accidents among professions. Sadly, the occupational health hazards faced by these hardworking individuals often go unnoticed in research. This paper addresses this gap by proposing strategies to improve fishermen's psychological well-being and their perception of occupational hazards and safety. Suggestions include tackling cultural and social norms, providing proper training and resources, fostering a supportive work environment, and instilling a safety culture. By understanding the psychological

factors influencing fishermen's perceptions, policymakers and industry stakeholders can develop interventions to enhance safety in Ernakulam Harbour, contributing to the overall sustainability of the fishing industry. The study employed a descriptive survey design with a two-stage random sampling approach, outlining objectives, hypotheses, and findings, laying the foundation for future safety programs for fishermen, divers, and recreational anglers.

References

Guillot-Wright, S., Cherryhomes, E., and Davis, L. (2022). The impact of economic deregulation for health disparities among gulf of Mexico commercial fishermen. *Marine Policy*, 141, 105099.

Hu, K., Li, S., Jiang, H., and Yang, J. (2022). The stress model of neuroticism and anxiety symptoms in fishermen. *International Maritime Health*, 73(4), 203–212.

Івашкевич, Е. (2022). Psychological factors of the discourse's actualization. *Психологія: реальність і перспективи*, 18, 81–92.

Laraqui, O., Roland-Levy, C., Manar, N., Laraqui, S., Ghailan, T., Deschamps, F., et al. (2022). Health status, sleeping habits and dyssomnia of coastal fishermen. *International Maritime Health*, 73(4), 163–171.

Rahman, M. S., Huang, W.-C., Toiba, H., and Efani, A. (2022). Does adaptation to climate change promote household food security? Insights from Indonesian fishermen. *International Journal of Sustainable Development and World Ecology*, 29(7), 611–624.

Thony, A. K. A., Romdhon, M. M., Sukiyono, K., and Moelyatie, T. A. (2022). The empowerment strategy of fishermen household women: study at Bengkulu city. *Journal of Positive School Psychology*, 6(8), 506–519.

Varkey, N. S., Vas, R., Uppala, H., Vas, N. V., Jalihal, S., and Ankola, A. V. (2022). Dental caries, oral hygiene status and treatment needs of fishermen and non-fishermen population in South Goa, India. *International Maritime Health*, 73(3), 125–132.

Wang, P., Fang, Y., Qi, J.-Y., and Li, H.-J. (2022). Fisherman: a serious game for executive function assessment of older adults. *Assessment*. Advance online publication. https://doi.org/10.1177/10731911221105648.

Yan, J.-L., Xue, Y.-J., and Mohsin, M. (2022). Accessing occupational health risks posed by fishermen based on fuzzy AHP and IPA methods: management and performance perspectives. *Sustainability*, 14(20), 13100.

Zhang, L., Wu, Q., Zhou, Y., and Ma, S. (2022). The satisfaction of the fishermen in the South China sea with the summer fishing moratorium system and its influencing factors. *Frontiers in Environmental Science*, 9, 669.

167 Exploring the influence of psychological factors on online consumer behavior

Vidya Rajendran and Padmaavathy, P.A.[a]

Karpagam Academy of Higher Education, Coimbatore, Tamil Nadu, India

Abstract

This study delves into the factors influencing consumer buying decisions, aiming to uncover their impact on individual purchasing choices. Employing a structured questionnaire, both primary and secondary data are gathered to gain insights. The focus is on understanding the intricate dynamics of consumer behavior, with customers playing key roles as users, payers, and buyers. Predicting consumer behavior proves challenging, emphasizing the crucial role customers play as ultimate buyers. Businesses strive to persuade them for revenue generation, necessitating a keen understanding of factors influencing customers. Identifying these factors allows brands to tailor strategies, marketing messages, and advertising campaigns, enhancing customer service and driving sales growth. Ultimately, comprehending customer behavior becomes an asset for brands seeking to thrive in the market.

Keywords: Consumer behavior, online shopping, psychological factor, socio-economic factor

Introduction

Consumer behavior is an integral part of our daily lives, influencing our actions from buying products to simply watching TV. It encompasses the entire process of choosing, paying for, and using goods and services to meet our needs. Various factors affect consumer behavior in young people, including psychological, economic, cultural, social, and personal aspects. The study of consumer behavior gained importance in the marketing concept in the late 1940s, leading companies to focus on understanding consumer needs. However, a shift from product enhancement to aggressive selling emerged, neglecting consumer satisfaction. Presently, the youth wield significant purchasing power, driven by media influences and a growing preference for online shopping. Factors such as product variety, shopping convenience, education, and discounts impact their buying decisions. The youth are recognized as savvy online shoppers, finding satisfaction in the process due to the ease and accessibility offered by the internet.

Factors Affecting Consumer Behavior

Internal or psychological factors:
- Motivation:
- State of awakened desire leading to goal-directed behavior.
- Strong and long-lasting feelings activating conduct toward specific goals.
- Recognition of needs initiates the purchase process.
- Triggers include convenience, style, status, self-pride, and social comparison.
- Abraham Maslow's hierarchy of needs influences motivation.

Perception:
- A pivotal factor impacting purchasing decisions.
- Motivation influences forming positive or negative impressions.

Learning:
- Behavior changes through learning from prior experiences.
- Involves drives, stimuli, cues, and responses.
- Marketers must understand the learning process for effective strategies.

Social factors:
- Family
- Significant influence on buying behavior.
- The family life cycle affects buying patterns and demand.
- Consumer demands vary within families based on life stage and personalities.

Reference groups
- Social group impact on buying behavior.
- Members influence each other through discussions and examples.

[a]padmaavathypa@gmail.com

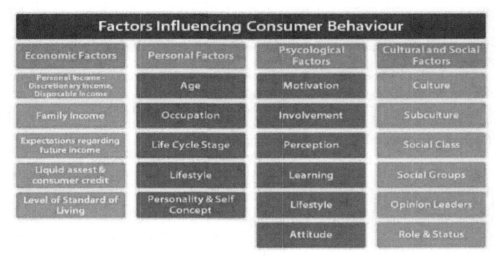

Figure 167.1 Factors affecting consumer behavior
Source: Author

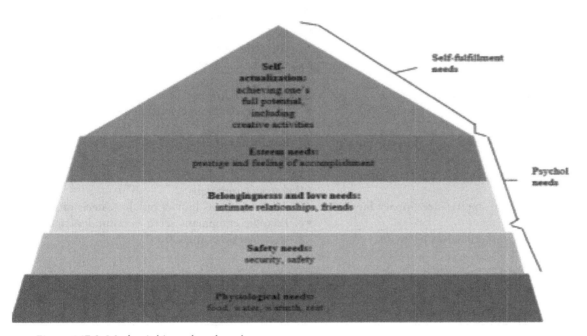

Figure 167.2 Maslow's hierarchy of needs
Source: Author

- Reference groups, including opinion leaders, influence buying patterns.

Friends
- Informal group influencing purchasing behavior.
- Recommendations and suggestions from friend's impact decisions.
- Cultural factors

Culture
- Shared beliefs, values, and rules influencing consumer behavior.

- Marketers adapt strategies to meet global cultural diversity.

Subculture
- Unique habits and purchasing behaviors within subcultures.
- Marketers adjust strategies to meet subcultures' needs.

Social class
- Individuals' positions in the social class system.
- Unique brand preferences based on social classes.

Economic factors:

Personal income
- Determines buying behavior, including disposable and discretionary income.
- Increased disposable income leads to higher purchasing and improved living standards.

Family income
- Total revenue affects purchasing decisions.
- Extra money is used for product purchases.

Savings
- Impact on purchasing decisions; changes in savings amount result in expenditure changes.
- More savings lead to reduced spending on luxuries.

Consumer credit
- Accessible credit influences spending on durable goods.
- Liberal credit terms encourage purchasing and elevate living standards.

Personal factors

Age and lifestyle
- Choices vary with life stages.
- Distinct preferences based on age groups.

Occupation
- Financial condition significantly affects buying behavior.
- Higher income groups purchase expensive products.

Personality
- Unique traits beyond appearance impact buying behavior.
- Personality varies and influences behavior.

Psychological factors shaping youngsters':

Consumer behavior:
- Motivations, perceptions, learning, beliefs, and attitudes
- Crucial elements influencing purchasing decisions.
- Essential for marketing success.

Purchasing power:
- Consumer ability to buy is pivotal.
- Segmentation based on buying capacity is key for effective targeting.

Group influence:
- Family, friends, and classmates wield primary influence.
- Preferences, like fast food or SUVs, showcase group impact.

Personal preferences:
- Personal viewpoints heavily influence choices.
- Advertisements play a vital role in shaping preferences.

Economic conditions:
- Market's economic state shapes purchasing decisions.
- Significant for big-ticket items despite financial obligations.

Marketing campaigns:
- Advertisements impact purchase decisions.
- Periodic campaigns serve as reminders and influence market competition.

Literature Review

Table 167.1 Exploring contemporary insights into consumer behavior.

Author name	Study
Meena (2018)	People form product preferences from a young age influenced by various factors.
Kamran et al. (2019)	Sales promotion significantly shapes buyers' perceptions and purchasing decisions.
Christopher et al. (2020)	Around 84% of publications indicate that advertising has a favorable impact on consumer behavior and purchase intentions.
Monika et al. (2020)	Psychological aspects heavily influence purchase choices, and understanding consumer psychology is crucial in marketing strategies.
Linda et al. (2020)	Consumer psychology is essential for marketing, offering insights into factors affecting purchasing decisions.
Rajan (2020)	Advertising has the power to attract consumers, influencing behavior and purchase intentions.
Paula (2021)	Proposes two social media marketing strategies: passive use for customer analysis and marketing environment analysis, and active use for direct marketing, public relations, product customization, idea collaboration, value creation, and marketing research.

Source: Author

Problem Statement

Research on consumer behavior in shopping often focuses on external factors for online purchases, leaving gaps in understanding specific shopping elements' impact. Existing studies lack comprehensive coverage and often exclude factors. Moreover, research is predominantly in technologically advanced countries, neglecting the Indian context. This study aims to fill these gaps by exploring the influence of various shopping elements, such as perceived risk, return policy, service, infrastructure, subjective norm, attitude, and perceived control behavior, on consumers' decisions in online shopping.

Study Objective

- To evaluate the attributes and factors influencing the buying behavior of the consumers.
- To determine the Demographic, Social, Economic, and Psycho-graphic profile of the consumers.
- To examine the major product and service categories chosen by customers.
- To calculate the average consumer expenditure and frequency of purchases.
- **To evaluate the level of satisfaction of the consumers.**

Factor 1	Factor 2	Factor 3
The effort to test Innovations	Product characteristics	Habit
Word of mouth	Quality	Price
Advertisement	Brand	Discount price
Package		
22.55%	18.61%	13.8%

Figure 167.3 Table 167.1 Groups formed using factor analysis
Source: Author

Research Methodology

Research design:
- Combines exploratory and descriptive research methods.
- Utilizes primary and secondary data for a comprehensive analysis.

Data collection:
- Secondary data gathered from textbooks, research articles, and online sources.
- Primary data collected through well-organized, transparent, and closed-ended consumer surveys.

Sample selection:
- Sample unit: Respondents purchasing goods and services online.
- Diverse demographic representation: ages 20-60, over 61, various educational backgrounds, and occupations.
- Sample size set at 500, calculated based on 95% confidence level, 50% response rate, and a confidence interval of 5%.

Data analysis techniques:
- Microsoft Excel and SPSS used for reliability and validity assessment.
- Descriptive statistics, Chi-square, t-test, and ANOVA employed for in-depth analysis of online consumer beliefs, opinions, and buying behavior related to fashion apparel.

Analysis and Interpretation

The results of the ANOVA test suggest that there is no significant difference in consumer perception of online purchase behavior across different age groups, educational levels, monthly incomes, family sizes, and purchase frequencies. The calculated values for these

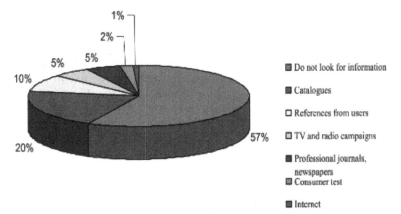

1%
2%
5%
5%
10%
20%
57%

- Do not look for information
- Catalogues
- References from users
- TV and radio campaigns
- Professional journals, newspapers
- Consumer test
- Internet

Figure 167.4 Sources of data of consumers regarding purchases
Source: Author

Table 167.2 Participants' profile.

		Frequency	Percentage
Gender	Male	84	49%
	Female	99	51%
Education	Doing bachelor's degree	138	76%
	Master's degree or above	44	24%
Income	2000–10,000	180	98.36
	10,000– 25,000	2	1.1
	25,000– 40,000	1	0.54
	More than 40,000	0	0
Age	51-60 years	44	24
	46-50 years	39	6
	31-45 years	0	0
	20-30 years	139	76
Occupation	UG Student	139	76
	PG Student	44	24
	Non-teaching staffs	0	0
	Teaching faculty	0	0
	government or private sector	139	76
	self-employed	44	24
	Owner	0	0

Source: Author

Table 167.3 Purpose of using the internet.

Purpose	Frequency	Percentage
Browsing	99	51
Information search	84	49
E-mails	99	51
Chatting	139	76
Work	44	24
Social networking	180	98.36
Blogging	2	1.1
Entertainment	1	0.54
Buying	0	0
Banking	44	24
Product search	139	76

Source: Author

variables were higher than the critical table values, supporting the null hypothesis that there is no substantial difference. In other words, age, education, income, family size, and purchase frequency did not significantly impact consumers' perceptions of online shopping.

The chi-test indicates no significant difference in consumers' perception and online purchase behavior based on gender, internet usage duration, or shopping history. The calculated value exceeds the table value, leading to acceptance of the null hypothesis. In simpler terms, there's no noteworthy distinction in how people view online shopping based on gender, internet usage, or shopping experience.

The t-test results indicate no significant difference in consumers' perception of online purchase behavior based on gender, internet usage duration, and shopping internet usage duration. Whether male or female, using the internet for less or more than three years, or using it specifically for shopping, there's no notable distinction in how consumers perceive online shopping behavior. In essence, individuals' overall evaluation of products or services during online shopping remains consistent across these demographic factors.

Conclusion

This research aimed to identify factors influencing online consumer purchasing behavior. Key factors included perceived risk, return policy, service quality, infrastructure, subjective norms, and perceived control behavior. Attitude served as a mediating variable in the proposed theoretical model, validated through ANOVA and t-tests. Demographically, the majority were young or middle-aged, married, with higher education, and smaller family sizes. Economically, most were professionals with a monthly income exceeding Rs. 20000. The study successfully achieved its objective by providing valuable insights into online shopping behavior.

References

De Fano, D., Schena, R., and Russo, A. (2022). Empowering plastic recycling: empirical investigation on the influence of social media on consumer behaviour. *Resources, Conservation and Recycling*, 182, 106269.

Kar, P., Meena, H. R., and Patnaik, N. M. (2018). Factors influencing consumers' purchase intention towards organic and cloned animal food products. *International Journal of Current Microbiology and Applied Sciences*, 7(1), 1–9.

Khan, K., and Hameed, I. (2019). Relationship between consumer motivations and sustainable consumer behaviour in a developing market. *KASBIT Business Journal*, 12(1), 178–191.

Machová, R., Ambrus, R., Zsigmond, T., and Bakó, F. (2022). The impact of green marketing on consumer behaviour in the market of palm oil products. *Sustainability*, 14(3), 1364.

Melnyk, V., Carrillat, F. A., and Melnyk, V. (2022). The influence of social norms on consumer behaviour: a meta-analysis. *Journal of Marketing*, 86(3), 98–120.

Park, J., Back, S. Y., and Kim, D. (2022). Masstige consumption values and its effect on consumer behaviour. *Journal of Retailing and Consumer Services*, 67, 102943.

Purohit, S., Arora, R., and Paul, J. (2022). The bright side of online consumer behaviour: continuance intention for mobile payments. *Journal of Consumer Behaviour*, 21(3), 523–542.

Riar, M., Xi, N., Korbel, J. J., Zarnekow, R., and Hamari, J. (2022). Using augmented reality for shopping: a framework for AR induced consumer behaviour, literature review and future agenda. *Internet Research*, 33(1), 242–279.

Secinaro, S., Calandra, D., Lanzalonga, F., and Ferraris, A. (2022). Electric vehicles' consumer behaviours: mapping the field and providing a research agenda. *Journal of Business Research*, 150, 399–416.

Yao, P., Osman, S., Sabri, M. F., and Zainudin, N. (2022). Consumer behavior in Online-to-offline (O2O) commerce: athematic review. *Sustainability*, 14(13), 7842.

168 Examining faculty satisfaction in financial investments at engineering colleges in Coimbatore: a specialized study

Sivakumar, M,[a] and Venkatachalam. S.[b]

Karpagam Academy of Higher Education, Coimbatore, Tamil Nadu, India

Abstract

The purpose of the study is to understand the investment avenues and preferred investment term periods among respondents. In our daily lives, expenses are increasing, but investment levels are not keeping pace. To achieve our investment goals, it is essential to increase investment every year. In this study, the researcher sampled 75 respondents in Coimbatore city. The tools used for analysis included percentage analysis and ranking methods to assess the satisfaction levels of respondents. The findings revealed that most respondents are satisfied with gold investments.

Keywords: Financial investment, investment, investment avenues, satisfaction level

Introduction

In today's world, money holds significant importance for individuals and organizations alike, contributing to a country's economic growth. In India, a substantial portion of the population belongs to the middle class, with earnings typically up to five lakhs annually. Consequently, as salaries and organizational profits increase annually, coupled with a rising inflation rate, the general populace faces challenges in saving money. This predicament can have future repercussions, especially during emergencies when individuals may lack sufficient funds. Saving money during one's working years is crucial, serving as a protective shield against unforeseen circumstances.

The purpose of saving and investing is diverse, but fundamentally, it acts as a safeguard during uncertain situations. Those who adopt disciplined savings habits often witness their money multiplying, yielding returns two-fold or even more. However, the primary challenge lies in the tenure period; the longer the investment period, the more promising and satisfactory the returns tend to be.

Problem Statement

In India, households significantly contribute to economic growth through investments in gold, bank deposits, and property, boosting government income for national infrastructure development. Despite a higher female population in households, many employed women, possessing financial autonomy, often rely on fathers or husbands for investment decisions. The country offers a diverse range of investment options in the financial market, allowing individuals to form opinions on each product. The researcher focuses on studying satisfaction levels regarding investment avenues, choosing engineering college faculties as targeted samples for this analysis.

Objectives of the Study

- To know about the investment term period of investor in making investment
- To study the investment avenues preferred by the investors
- To find level of satisfaction of investor on investment avenues

Research Methodology

The methodology plays a crucial role in providing a clear framework for the study. In this research, the researcher employed percentage analysis and the Weighted Average method to analyze the collected data. The study focused on 75 respondents working as teaching staff in engineering colleges, utilizing a random sampling technique for sample collection. This approach ensures a representative and unbiased selection of participants for a comprehensive analysis.

Literature Review

In the study conducted by Bhardwaj et al. (2011), the focus was on understanding the saving and investment purposes of schoolteachers. The researchers selected teachers from both government and private schools, utilizing analytical tools to interpret the collected data.

---

[a]Sivakumar.mdy@gmail.com, [b]venkatachalam.s@kahedu.edu.in

The results indicated that government school staff primarily saved for emergency purposes, while private school staff allocated their savings toward children's marriage, education, and retirement.

Virani (2012) explored income disparities among schoolteachers, emphasizing traditional saving avenues like fixed deposits and post office deposits. The study revealed that some respondents lacked awareness of inflation and modern financial products, yet their primary goal was saving for their children's future.

Murithi et al. (2012) focused on women's awareness and savings behavior, noting that women, being forward-thinking, tended to save for small goals. While women were knowledgeable about investment products, the study highlighted the importance of informed decision-making due to the inherent risks in investments.

Sood and Kumar (2015) conducted research in Chandigarh, finding that residents were well-informed about savings and investments. The preference leaned towards bank deposits and LIC, with a focus on safety. The respondents saved for education, marriage, and family expenditures, demonstrating a high level of financial literacy.

Thulasipriya (2016) explored the savings behavior and perceptions of private salaried class investors, revealing a preference for bank deposits and fixed/recurring deposits. Salaried households tended to save for specific goals like children's education and marriage, with less emphasis on luxury products.

Ramaratnam and Jayaraman (2016) delved into the saving patterns of rural people in Kanchipuram District, identifying a consistent habit of saving despite the challenges posed by increasing daily expenses. Most respondents-maintained bank accounts, indicating minimal transaction activity within three to six months.

Sivakumar and Venkatachalam (2022) conducted a study in Coimbatore city, focusing on non-teaching staff in colleges. Utilizing percentage analysis and ranking methods, the research found that respondents were inclined toward investing in the capital market, expecting returns between 8 to 12 percent. Additionally, a notable finding was the prevalent preference for investing in gold among the respondents.

Data Analysis

In the age distribution, 20% of respondents are in the 25-35 age group, 34.67% are in the 36-45 age bracket, 28% fall within the 46-50 age category, and 17.33% are above 50 years old.

The table above indicates that 57.33% of investors are male, while 42.67% are female.

In terms of teaching experience among investors, 12% have less than one year of experience, 16% have

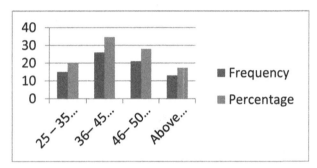

Figure 168.1 Age group of respondents
Source: Author

Table 168.2 Gender of respondents: frequencies and percentages in the study.

Gender of respondents		
Particulars	Frequency	Percentage
Male	43	57.33
Female	32	42.67
Total	75	100

Source: Author

Table 168.1 Age distribution of respondents: frequencies and percentages in the study.

Age group of respondents		
Particulars	Frequency	Percentage
25 – 35 Years	15	20
36– 45 Years	26	34.67
46– 50 Years	21	28
Above 50 Years	13	17.33
Total	75	100

Source: Author

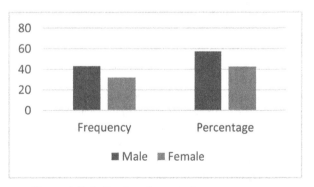

Figure 168.2 Gender of respondents
Source: Author

Table 168.3 Teaching experience of investors.

Years of teaching experience		
Particulars	Frequency	Percentage
Less than one year	9	12
1year-3years	12	16
3years-6years	24	32
6years-9years	17	22.67
Above 9years	13	17.33
Total	75	100

Source: Author

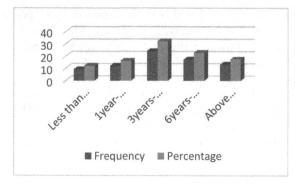

Figure 168.3 Years of teaching experience
Source: Author

Table 168.4 Income distribution and percentage analysis.

Income in month		
Particulars	Frequency	Percentage
Rs.10,001 – 15,000	12	16
Rs.15,001-20,000	21	28
Rs.21,001-25,000	18	24
above Rs.25,000	24	32
Total	75	100

Source: Author

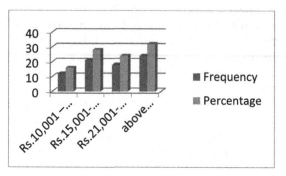

Figure 168.4 Income in month
Source: Author

Table 168.5 Time period of investment: percentage and distribution analysis.

Term period of investment		
Particulars	Frequency	Percentage
Short term	39	52
Long term	36	48
Total	75	100

Source: Author

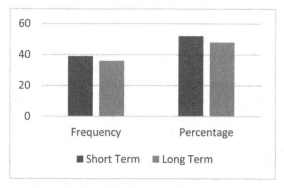

Figure 168.5 Term period of investment
Source: Author

1-3 years, 32% have 3-6 years, 22.67% have 6-9 years, and 17.33% have over 9 years of teaching experience.

Regarding monthly income, 16% of respondents earn between Rs. 10,001-15,000, 28% earn Rs. 15,001-20,000, 24% earn Rs. 21,001-25,000, and 32% earn above Rs. 25,000.

In terms of the investment term period, 52% of investors prefer short-term investments, while 48% of respondents prefer long-term investments.

When allocating amounts to investment per month, 13.33% of respondents save Rs. 1001-2000 monthly, 22.67% save Rs. 2001-3000, 26.67% save Rs. 3001-4000, and 37.33% save above Rs. 4000 monthly.

In terms of investment preferences, 30.67% of investors allocate their funds to bank deposits and post office deposits, 8% invest in shares and bonds,

10.67% invest in insurance schemes, 17.33% opt for mutual funds, 21.33% prefer buying gold, and 12% save or invest their funds in other avenues.

In terms of satisfaction with investments, a significant majority of respondents express a preference for gold, ranking it as their top choice.

Findings

1. In the age category, 32% of respondents fall within the 31-35 years range.

Table 168.6 Frequency and distribution of monthly savings.

Allocation of money for saving in a month		
Particulars	Frequency	Percentage
Rs.1001-2000	10	13.33
Rs.2001-3000	17	22.67
Rs.3001-4000	20	26.67
above Rs.4000	28	37.33
Total	75	100

Source: Author

Table 168.7 Investment avenues of the respondents.

Investment avenues of the respondents		
Particulars	Frequency	Percentage
Bank deposit and post office deposit	23	30.67
Shares and bonds	6	8
Insurance schemes	8	10.67
Mutual funds	13	17.33
Gold	16	21.33
Others avenues	9	12
Total	75	100

Source: Author

Table 168.8 Investors' satisfaction levels in investments.

Investors'satisfaction levels in investments		
Particulars	Frequency	Percentage
Gold	20.33	1
Bank deposit and post office deposit	19.67	2
Shares/mutual fund/ bonds	13.33	4
Other avenues	10.67	5
Insurance schemes	13.67	3

Source: Author

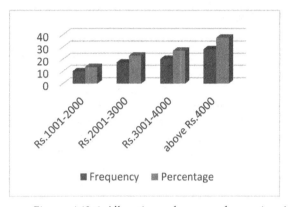

Figure 168.6 Allocation of money for saving in a month
Source: Author

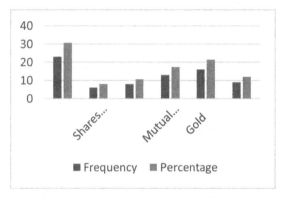

Figure 168.7 Investment avenues of the respondents
Source: Author

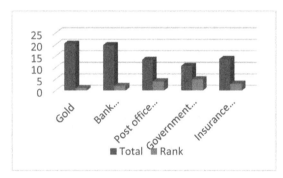

Figure 168.8 Investors' satisfaction levels in investments
Source: Author

2. The majority, comprising 57.33% of respondents, is male.
3. About 33.33% of respondents earn a monthly income above Rs. 25,000.
4. Investment preferences show that 52% of respondents favor short-term investments, while the remaining 48% prefer long-term investments.
5. Monthly, 37.33% of respondents allocate savings amounts exceeding Rs. 5000.
6. Investment choices vary, with 30.67% of investors favoring bank and post office deposits, 21.33% preferring gold, and 17.33% opting for mutual funds.
7. In terms of satisfaction levels, respondents express high satisfaction with gold, satisfaction with bank and post office deposits, and a neutral stance toward insurance schemes.

Suggestions

1. Respondents exhibit a preference for long-term investments, recognizing the potential for increased appreciation over time.
2. Given the minimum interest rates of 4 to 6.5 percent in banks, which may not keep pace with inflation, investors may find it advantageous to explore the capital market, particularly in bonds.
3. Gold, being an ultimate physical asset, is best acquired in the form of gold coins or biscuits, as purchasing jewelry can inflate the overall investment cost.

Conclusion

Traditionally, Indians have shown a strong inclination towards acquiring precious metals, particularly gold. In ancient times, gold was considered the nation's wealth, and even today, the country's currency is backed by the value of gold held by the nation. This sentiment is echoed in the study's findings, where a majority of respondents prefer investing in gold as part of their savings.

However, there is a noteworthy gap in awareness about modern financial products among the respondents. Many tend to repeatedly invest in traditional, low-return, or more taxable options. Some respondents may be aware of new financial products, but they are hesitant due to perceived high risks associated with these investments. Bridging this knowledge gap is crucial, as financial institutions can play a pivotal role in educating individuals about modern financial products. Empowering individuals with this information not only contribute to their personal wealth but also positively impacts the nation's economy.

References

Bhardwaj, R., Raheja, R., and Priyanka (2011). Analysis of income and savings pattern of government and private senior secondary school teachers. *Asia Pacific Journal of Research in Business Management*, 9(2), 44–56.

Murithi, S. S., Narayanan, B., and Arivazhagan, M. (2012). Investors behaviour in various investment avenues – astudy. *International Journal of Marketing and Technology*, 2, 36–45.

Ramaratnam, M. S., and Jayaraman, R. (2016). A study on savings pattern of rural households in the select clusters of Kanchipuram districts. *International Journal of Engineering and Management Research*, 6(2), 608–615.

Sivakumar, M., and Venkatachalam, S. (2022). A study on financial planning influence the investment decision of non-teaching women staffs in colleges with special reference of Coimbatore city. *YMER*, 21(8), 250–258, || ISSN : 0044-0477.

Sood, D., and Kumar, N. (2015). A study of savings and investment pattern of salaried class people with special reference to Chandigarh. *Economic and Political Weekly*, 5(2), 30–38.

Thulasipriya, B. (2016). A study on savings behavior and perception on return of private salaried class investors. *International Journal of Research in Finance and Marketing*, 6(2), 161–174.

Virani, V. (2012). Saving and investment pattern of school teachers-A study with special reference to Rajkot City, Gujarat. *Abhinav National Refereed Journal of Research in Commerce and Management*, 2(4), 2277–1166.

169 Investigation of mutual fund investment patterns among arts and science college faculty in Coimbatore

Sivakumar, M.[a] and Dr. Venkatachalam, S.[b]

Karpagam Academy of Higher Education, Tamil Nadu, India

Abstract

Wealth creation is more challenging than earning because without financial planning, it is hard to amass wealth. There are numerous investment opportunities in financial avenues, and the researcher has selected the best investment avenue: mutual funds. Mutual funds are suitable for every person to invest in the stock market without requiring capital market knowledge. The researcher conducted a study with 90 respondents from Arts and Science Colleges in Coimbatore city to understand their investment behavior towards mutual fund investments. The study utilized one-way ANOVA, the weighted average method, and percentage analysis to derive results. It was found that 74.44% of respondents invest in systematic investment plans (SIP), 30% prefer index funds, and 86.67% are highly satisfied with mutual fund investments.

Keywords: Investment avenues, investment behavior, mutual fund, systematic investment plan

Introduction

In India over the past year, numerous economic challenges such as rising petrol and edible oil prices, bus fares, and basic commodities have emerged. Despite an increase in people's income, it has not kept pace with the inflation rate. During this period, reliance on savings and investments has become crucial. For instance, during the COVID-19 pandemic, a significant amount of physical gold was sold within six months. The researcher observed a heightened interest in gold purchases among the populace. As the inflation rate continues to rise, the interest rates offered by banks and other financial instruments remain slightly lower. In India, where approximately 60% of families belong to the middle class with earnings ranging from 2.5 lakh to 5 lakh, investing substantial amounts becomes challenging. While many opt for recurring deposit accounts in banks, the returns, ranging from 4.5 to 6 per cent, result in losses for investors.

Enter mutual funds, a method that involves collecting small amounts from individual investors and investing in equities, bonds, ETFs, etc. A fund manager appointed by the mutual fund firm oversees the fund. This investment concept allows people to accumulate wealth by investing small amounts over the long term, yielding significant returns. Nowadays, various groups, including students, staff, government and private employees, are increasingly choosing mutual funds for investment. In Tamil Nadu, especially, there is a widespread awareness and participation in mutual fund investments.

Objectives of the Study

- To know the investment method of investor in mutual fund investment
- To study the mutual fund schemes preferred by investor.
- To find purpose of investor to invest in mutual fund.

Problem Statement

The study aims to understand investors' behavior towards mutual funds, given their distinctiveness from other investment schemes. With the ability to commence investments of as little as Rs. 500, mutual funds generally offer returns ranging from 9 percent to 12 percent. However, previous research has revealed a noteworthy issue: while a substantial number of educated individuals are cognizant of mutual fund investments, they lack the inclination to invest. Even among those willing to invest, there exists a prevalent expectation of higher returns within a shorter time frame.

Literature Review

Conducted in Ahmedabad city, this study investigated the factors influencing mutual fund selection (Shah and Baser, 2012). The variables examined included the age and occupation of respondents. Findings indicated that occupation played a more defining role in influencing investment behavior compared to the age of respondents.

[a]Sivakumar.mdy@gmail.com, [b]venkatachalam.s@kahedu.edu.in

This Tamil Nadu-based study assessed satisfaction levels and awareness regarding mutual funds. Factors such as expense ratio, fund overlapping, and major sector holdings were considered crucial before investing. The research concluded that investors in Tamil Nadu exhibited a commendable understanding of mutual fund investments (Prathap and Rajamohan, 2013).

This study revealed that many mutual fund investors lack awareness of market risks and uncertainties. In the face of losses, respondents tended to sell their units and withdraw their funds. Demographic factors were identified as significant determinants, with respondents having lower knowledge requiring a minimum of 5 years of investment for optimal returns (Wilhelmsson Jonsson et al, 2017).

Investigating the demographic profile of mutual fund investors with data from 392 respondents, this research suggested a need to enhance investment behaviors in mutual funds. Statistical tools indicated no age-wise impact, but mid-age and higher-income individuals derived greater benefits from mutual fund investments (Saxena and Sheikh, 2019).

Focused on Indore city in India with a sample size of 300, this study explored the perception and awareness of mutual fund investments. While 60% of respondents were aware of mutual funds, a reluctance to invest was noted due to market risks. Approximately 20% of respondents who invested experienced positive returns. The study highlighted low financial literacy among the general population regarding mutual funds (Kaur and Bharucha, 2021).

Research Methodology

- Descriptive research design
- Questionnaire method for data collection
- Random sampling with a sample size of 90
- Primary and secondary data collection
- Analyzing tools: Percentage analysis, weighted average method, one-way ANOVA
- Hypotheses:
  - No significant difference between age of respondents and amount spent on mutual funds
  - No significant difference between income of investors and preference of schemes in mutual funds

Data Analysis

The age distribution of investors reveals that 31.11% are in the 26-35 age group, 38.89% in the 36-45 range, 17.78% in the 46-55 bracket, and 12.22% are above 55 years old.

In this study, 63.33% of the respondents are male, while 33.37% are female.

The income distribution among respondents is as follows: 20% earn Rs. 10,001-18,000 monthly, 23.33% earn Rs. 18,001-26,000 monthly, 28.89% earn Rs. 26,001-34,000 monthly, and 27.78% earn above Rs. 34,000 monthly.

In the context of mutual fund investments, the duration chosen by investors is as follows: 18.89% invest for less than one year, 32.22% invest for 1 to 3 years, 38.89% invest for 3 to 5 years, and 10% invest for more than 5 years.

Table 169.1 Age of the respondents.

Particulars	Frequency	Percentage
26 – 35 Years	28	31.11
36– 45 Years	35	38.89
46– 55 Years	16	17.78
Above 55 Years	11	12.22
Total	90	100

Source: Author

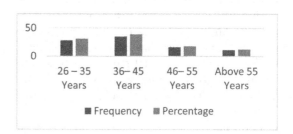

Figure 169.1 Age of the respondents
Source: Author

Table 169.2 Gender of the investor.

Particulars	Frequency	Percentage
Male	57	63.33
Female	33	33.37
Total	90	100

Source: Author

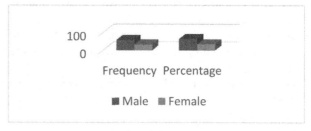

Figure 169.2 Gender of the investor
Source: Author

Table 169.3 Income of the respondents.

Particulars	Frequency	Percentage
Rs. 10,001–18,000	18	20
Rs. 18,001–26,000	21	23.33
Rs. 26,001–34,000	26	28.89
above Rs. 34,000	25	27.78
Total	90	100

Source: Author

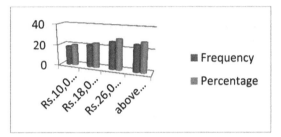

Figure 169.3 Income of the respondents
Source: Author

Table 169.4 Investment in mutual fund.

all	Frequency	Percentage
Less than one year	17	18.89
1Year -3 years	29	32.22
3 Years – 5 years	35	38.89
Above 5 years	9	10
Total	90	100

Source: Author

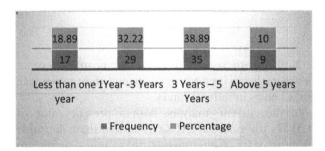

Figure 169.4 Investment in mutual funds
Source: Author

Table 169.5 Types of investments in mutual funds.

Particulars	Frequency	Percentage
Lump sum mode	23	25.56
Systematic investment plan (SIP)	67	74.44
Total	90	100

Source: Author

In mutual funds, respondents exhibit distinct preferences for investment modes: 25.56% opt for lump sum investments, while the majority, 74.44%, prefer the SIP mode.

Monthly contributions to mutual fund investments: 13.33% of respondents save Rs. 501-1000, 22.22% save Rs. 1 001-2000, 36.67% save Rs. 2001-3000, and 27.78% save above Rs. 3000.

30% of respondents favor index funds, 11.11% prefer large-cap funds, 20% opt for mid-cap funds, 16.67% choose small-cap funds, 8.89% lean toward hybrid funds, 13.33% prefer debt funds, and 5.56% opt for other schemes.

Satisfaction levels of respondents regarding mutual fund: 86.67% are highly satisfied, 11.11% express moderate satisfaction, and 2.22% are dissatisfied.

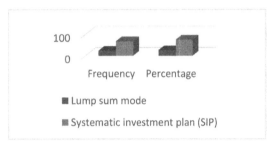

Figure 169.5 Type of investment in mutual fund
Source: Author

Table 169.6 Monthly expenditure on mutual fund investments.

Particulars	Frequency	Percentage
Rs. 501-1000	12	13.33
Rs. 1001-2000	20	22.22
Rs. 2001-3000	33	36.67
above Rs. 3000	25	27.78
Total	90	100

Source: Author

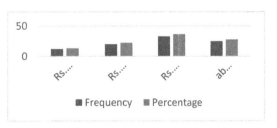

Figure 169.6 Monthly contributions to mutual fund investments
Source: Author

Table 169.7 Mutual fund scheme preferences.

Particulars	Frequency	Percentage
Index fund	27	30
Large cap fund	10	11.11
Mid cap fund	15	16.67
Small cap fund	13	14.44
Hybrid fund	8	8.89
Debt fund	12	13.33
Other schemes	5	5.56
Total	90	100

Source: Author

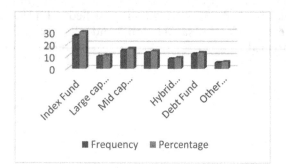

Figure 169.7 Mutual fund scheme preferences
Source: Author

Table 169.8 Mutual fund investment satisfaction levels.

Particulars	Frequency	Percentage
Satisfied	78	86.67
Moderate	10	11.11
Dis-satisfied	2	2.22
Total	90	100

Source: Author

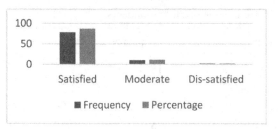

Figure 169.8 Satisfaction levels of respondents regarding mutual fund investment
Source: Author

Table 169.9 Objectives for mutual fund investments.

Particulars	Total	Rank
High returns	25.06	2
Initiate investment with minimum Rs.500	25.20	1
Tax saving	17.46	3
Easy to liquidate the fund	13.58	5
Easy to invest by self	15.67	4

Source: Author

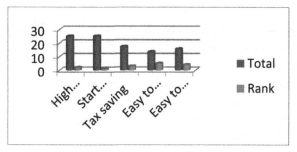

Figure 169.9 Objectives for Mutual Fund Investments
Source: Author

When it comes to the purpose of mutual fund investments, investors predominantly prioritize initiating the investment with a minimum of Rs. 500.

Hypothesis

Null hypothesis: there is no significant difference between the age of respondents and the amount spent on mutual funds.

In the current analysis, the one-way ANOVA for the present value of 0.0058 is lower than the table value of 0.05. This indicates that there is no significant difference between the age of respondents and the amount spent on mutual funds. Therefore, the Null hypothesis is accepted.

Null hypothesis: There is no significant difference between the income of investors and their preference for schemes in mutual funds.

In the current analysis, with a present value of 0.0134, the one-way ANOVA is less than the table value of 0.05. Consequently, there is no significant difference between the income of investors and their preference for schemes in mutual funds. Therefore, the Null hypothesis is accepted.

Findings of the Study

1. **Age distribution:** A significant portion, 38.89%, of respondents falls within the 36-45 age group.
2. **Gender composition:** 63.33% of respondents are male, while the remaining 37.67% are female.

Source of variation	SS	df	MS	F	P-value	F crit
Between groups	1.058823529	1	1.058823529	8.727272727	0.00583689	4.14909745
Within groups	3.882352941	32	0.121323529			
Total	4.941176471	33				

Source of variation	SS	df	MS	F	P-value	F crit
Between groups	15.78089888	1	15.7809	6.242222	0.01339087	3.894837979
Within groups	444.9438202	176	2.52809			
Total		177				

3. **Income range:** 28.89% of respondents earn a monthly income between Rs. 26,001 to Rs. 32,000.
4. **Investment duration:** The majority, 38.89%, have been investing in mutual funds for a duration ranging from 3 to 5 years.
5. **Investment approach:** A predominant 74.44% of respondents opt for SIP, while 25.56% prefer lump-sum investments.
6. **Monthly investment:** The most common monthly investment range is Rs. 2001 to Rs. 3000, chosen by 36.67% of respondents.
7. **Scheme preferences:** Index funds are favored by 30% of respondents, while 16.67% and 14.44% prefer mid-cap and small-cap funds, respectively.
6. **Satisfaction levels:** A substantial 86.67% of respondents express high satisfaction with their mutual fund investments.
9. **Investment purpose:** The primary investment goal for respondents is to invest a minimum amount, followed by a desire for high returns, and thirdly, tax savings.

Suggestions from the Study

1. **Diversification:** Encourage respondents to invest in diversified mutual fund schemes to balance their investments amid market volatility.
2. **Overlap consideration:** Emphasize the importance of avoiding investment overlap between funds to ensure optimal returns.
3. **Direct fund investment:** Advocate for direct fund investments as they tend to offer higher returns compared to regular funds.

Conclusion

In the present financial landscape, with numerous investment avenues available, mutual funds emerge as a highly viable solution. The study underscores that the middle-class demographic is well-informed about mutual fund investments and, despite investing relatively modest amounts, can expect substantial returns in the future. When juxtaposed with alternative investment options, mutual funds stand out as a superior choice, offering better returns and the potential to outperform inflation rates. This reinforces the attractiveness of mutual funds as a compelling investment vehicle for individuals seeking sustainable financial growth.

Acknowledgement

The research was conducted with the invaluable guidance and support of the co-author, whose assistance played a crucial role in facilitating the study, as acknowledged by the corresponding author.

Conflict of Interest
The authors affirm that there is no conflict of interest associated with the content presented in this article.

Declaration

The authors assert that the manuscript was an original research effort jointly undertaken by the author and co-author.

Funding

The authors disclose that no external funding was received for the research work presented in this article.

References

Kaur, S. J., and Bharucha, J. (2021). The emerging mutual fund industry in India: an impact analysis of investors' awareness on investment behaviour. *International Journal of Business and Globalisation*, 27(1), 51–69.

Prathap, G., and Rajamohan, A. (2013). A study on the status of awareness among mutual fund investors in Tamil Nadu. *Journal of Exclusive Management Science*, 2(12), ISSN 2277–5684.

Saxena, K., and Sheikh, R. (2019). Impact of demographic variables on mutual fund investment behaviour: an empirical study. *Journal of the Gujarat Research Society*, 21(16), 957–969.

Shah, A., and Baser, N. (2012). Mutual fund: behavioural finance's perspective. *Asia Pacific Journal of Marketing and Management Review*, 1(2), ISSN 2319-2836.

Wilhelmsson Jonsson, S., Söderberg, I., and Wilhelmsson, M. (2017). An investigation of the impact of financial literacy, risk attitude, and saving motives on the attenuation of mutual fund investors disposition bias. *Managerial Finance*, 43(3), 282–298.

170 Post-COVID challenges and strategies for Kerala's spice companies in agro-based rural entrepreneurship

Saju, K.[a] and V. Ramadevi[b]

Karpagam Higher Academy of Education, Tamil Nadu, India

Abstract

Globally, entrepreneurs face a new reality post-COVID-19 due to the unprecedented downturn in the global economy. Rural entrepreneurship, crucial to the rural economy, creates employment and contributes to per capita income. Many entrepreneurs, especially in rural areas, encounter challenges such as capital management, swift decision-making, constraints in purchase, production, and operations, as well as a decline in sales volume and profitability. This study analyses challenges faced by the value-added spice industry in the post-COVID-19 era, including timely availability of quality inputs and labor, purchase and production issues, and communication and marketing obstacles. The study, conducted in Kerala, the spice hub of India, focuses on crops like black pepper, cardamom, nutmeg, ginger, turmeric, clove, and cinnamon. Despite various value-added products, including seasonings, spice blends, oleoresins, and essential oils, the study examines eleven agro enterprises in Kerala to understand post-COVID-19 challenges. These challenges have disrupted the supply chain, increased market uncertainties, and intensified financial constraints for agro enterprises.

Keywords: Agro entrepreneurship, pandemic affected economy, rural entrepreneurship, technology in agriculture, value added spices

Introduction

Agriculture significantly contributes to the rural economy, with various sectors like agro-based, forest-based, mineral-based, textile-based, and handicraft-based industries playing vital roles. These enterprises contribute to employment generation, income equality, balanced regional development, and empowerment of women and marginalized sections. Food processing enterprises, particularly in India, play a crucial role in employment creation, resource mobilization, and enhancing the value of agricultural products, fostering sustainable rural economies.

Kerala stands out as a leading state in spice cultivation, with black pepper, cardamom, nutmeg, ginger, turmeric, cloves, and cinnamon being major crops. The state hosts numerous spice based enterprises, contributing significantly to the economy through both domestic sales and exports. Ground and blended spices, seasonings, oleoresins, and essential oils are prominent value-added spice products, with a notable impact on the economy.

However, the COVID-19 pandemic has severely affected the spice industry, leading to a substantial decline in sales domestically and internationally. Despite this setback, the versatility of spice usage in the food and nutraceutical industry through value addition remains promising. Value addition not only extends shelf life and ensures consistent quality but also minimizes perishability, reduces storage requirements, and enhances convenience, thus increasing profitability.

Major spices like black pepper, cardamom, nutmeg, turmeric, and ginger undergo significant value addition in various agro enterprises in Kerala. This study focuses on entrepreneurs involved in spice value addition in the state, examining the pandemic's impact on their sales both locally and globally. The challenges faced show the importance of adapting strategies to revive and sustain agro-based entrepreneurial ventures in the post-COVID era.

Literature Review

Problem Statement The study addresses the impact of Covid-19 on food processing enterprises, specifically in the value-added spice segments of rural entrepreneurships in Kerala, aiming to understand and devise strategies for overcoming the post-pandemic challenges, including movement restrictions, shifts in consumer behavior, facility closures, supply chain disruptions, sharp declines in sales revenue, and financial pressures.

[a]emailtosaju@gmail.com, [b]drramadevikarthik@gmail.com

Table 170.1 Comparative insights on entrepreneurship and economic impact.

Study	Author	Insights
Sustainable development of agricultural production	Khomiuk et al. (2022)	- Sustainable development of agricultural production strengthens economic development, increasing income and improving living conditions. - Market research is crucial for understanding competitiveness. - Factors like lack of marketing tools, underdeveloped infrastructure, and resource constraints affect competitiveness. - Diversifying into niche products enhances competitiveness.
Impact of COVID-19 on micro, small, and medium businesses	Shirmila, et al. (2022)	- COVID-19 uniquely impacts micro, small, and medium businesses, affecting manpower, cash flow, logistics, and market demand. - Challenges include family and social difficulties, technological challenges, financial difficulties, and policy challenges. - Managing challenges involves observance of limitations, universalization of tasks, eliminating bottlenecks, using entrepreneurial incubator systems, and reducing threats through new ventures. - Rural entrepreneurship is crucial for economic development, providing employment and increasing per capita income.
Impact of COVID-19 on micro, small, and medium enterprises	Gopal and Nair (2022)	- Covid-19 affects all sectors, with micro, small, and medium enterprises facing challenges in production, supply chain, liquidity, demand, and labor. - Constraints in sourcing raw materials, financial difficulties, and reduced productivity are common. - The food processing sector is impacted by manpower restrictions, shifts in consumer behavior, facility closures, supply chain disruptions, and financial pressures.
Entrepreneurship in the COVID-19 affected economy	Galindo Martin et al. (2021)	- The study analyses how Covid-19 affects entrepreneurship, focusing on sustainability. - Monetary policies significantly impact enterprises. - Dynamics of credits and interest rates help overcome financial turbulence. - Expansionary fiscal and monetary policies, despite long-term negative effects, have a positive impact on entrepreneurship.
Agri business incubators and agricultural entrepreneurship	Ashwini et al. (2021)	- Agri Business Incubators (ABI) aim to use innovations and technologies in agricultural venture creation. - Training focuses on diversification and value addition of agricultural products. - Maximum use of spice powder manufacturing technology. - Enterprises supported by agri business incubators are mostly in the nascent stage, requiring technical and financial support for further expansion. - Niche products include white pepper, bio capsules, coated spice seeds, and fortified powders. - Government promotion of agri business incubators provides necessary support for long-term profitability.

Source: Author

1. Study Objectives

2. Identify and analyze various post-COVID-19 business challenges faced by value-added spice segments within agriculture-based rural entrepreneurships in Kerala.

Develop effective strategies to address and overcome the post-COVID-19 business challenges encountered by agriculture-based rural entrepreneurships in the value-added spice segments in Kerala.

Scope of the Study

The study focuses on rural enterprises in Kerala, India, specializing in the value addition of spice products.

Specifically, it examines spice blends, seasonings, oleoresins, and essential oils used in the food and nutraceutical industry. The scope is limited to enterprises primarily involved in value addition of black pepper, cardamom, ginger, nutmeg, and turmeric.

Research Methodology

- **Data collection:**
  - Primary data collected from agricultural-based rural enterprises in Kerala engaged in spice value addition (black pepper, cardamom, ginger, nutmeg, turmeric) using questionnaires.
  - Secondary data sourced from Spices Board of India, industry magazines, newsletters, ex-

perts in the food and agriculture industry, and the Department of Agriculture, Government of Kerala.

- **Sampling:**
  - Simple random sampling method employed.
  - A total of 40 participants, including entrepreneurs and employees from sales, marketing, and purchase departments of eleven enterprises across different districts of Kerala.
- **Tools:**
  - Analysis of primary data using simple percentage and factor analysis.

Garret Ranking methods used to rank different parameters of responses, providing insights into relative preferences.

Findings

- **Basic profile of survey respondents:**
- Primary survey conducted among 11 agro-based rural enterprises in Kerala.

- 40 respondents include entrepreneurs, sales and marketing managers, and purchase department managers.
- Enterprises categorized based on their products: 55% manufacture seasonings, 18% produce oleoresins and spice blends, and 27% create a combination of spice blends, seasoning, oleoresins, and nutraceutical products.

All enterprises sell products through both business-to-customer (B2C) and business-to-business (B2B) platforms.

Impact of pandemic on sales performance:

- **Sales decline:** Approximately 50% of enterprises experienced a 20-50% decline in sales volume and value post-COVID-19. About 20% observed a 0-25% reduction.
- **Positive impact:** Enterprises focusing on nutraceutical products reported increased sales volume

Table 170.2 Ranking of customer preferences by agro enterprises.

Company		Quality	Price	Availability	Convenient pack size
Agro enterprise 1	Average score	61.7	65.3	46.0	27.0
	Rank	2.0	1.0	3.0	4.0
Agro enterprise 2	Average score	73.0	50.00	50.00	27.0
	Rank	1.0	2.0	3.0	4.0
Agro enterprise 3	Average score	56.0	73.0	35.5	35.5
	Rank	2.0	1.0	3.0	4.0
Agro enterprise 4	Average score	59.4	67.2	46.4	27.0
	Rank	2.0	1.0	3.0	4.0
Agro enterprise 5	Average score	56.0	73.0	27.0	44.0
	Rank	2.0	1.0	4.0	3.0
Agro enterprise 6	Average score	73.0	56.0	27.0	44.0
	Rank	1.0	2.0	4.0	3.0
Agro enterprise 7	Average score	73.0	44.0	41.5	41.5
	Rank	1.0	2.0	3.0	4.0
Agro enterprise 8	Average score	56.0	73.0	27.0	44.0
	Rank	2.0	1.0	4.0	3.0
Agro enterprise 9	Average score	59.4	44.0	69.6	32.8
	Rank	2.0	3.0	1.0	4.0
Agro enterprise 10	Average score	73.0	52.0	48.0	27.0
	Rank	1.0	2.0	3.0	4.0
Agro enterprise 11	Average score	56.0	73.0	44.0	27.0
	Rank	2.0	1.0	3.0	4.0
All	**Average score**	**62.8**	**59.5**	**46.9**	**31.8**
	Rank	**1**	**2**	**3**	**4**

Source: Author

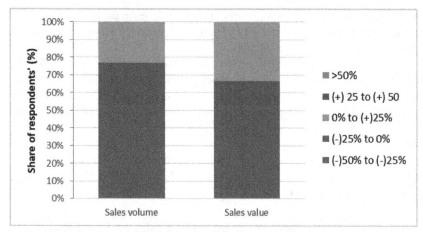

Figure 170.1 Change in sales volume and sales value post COVID 19
Source: Author

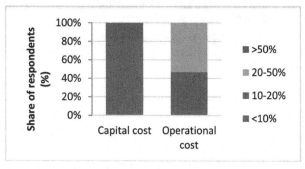

Figure 170.2 Change in capital cost and operational cost to COVID 19
Source: Author

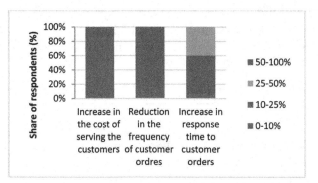

Figure 170.3 Impact of COVID 19 in cost of serving, reduction in frequency of orders and response time
Source: Author

and value, notably due to products linked with health benefits.

Local demand reduction: Drastic reduction in local demand attributed to factors like reduced income, lockdowns, product unavailability, and transportation limitations.

Post pandemic cost implications of agro enterprises:

- **Capital cost increase:** 84% witnessed up to a 10% increase, while 16% noted a 10-20% increase.
- **Operational cost rise:** Factors like increased transportation costs, reduced workforce, and production constraints led to operational cost hikes.

Effect on margins: Increased capital and operational costs resulted in decreased profitability for most enterprises in the value-added spice sector.

COVID-19 impact on sales orders in rural agri entrepreneurships:

- **Cost increase:** 85% experienced an additional cost of up to 10%, and 15% incurred a cost increase of 10-25%.
- **Reduced order frequency:** 85% reported a 10-25% reduction in order frequency.
- **Response time increase:** 55% observed a 10-25% increase in response time for processing customer orders.

Agro Enterprises' perception on customer preferences:
Ranking customer preferences: Quality was the most crucial preference, followed by price, availability, and convenient pack size.

Agro enterprises and adaptation strategies:

- E-commerce channels: 75% considered highly effective for marketing in the pandemic economy.

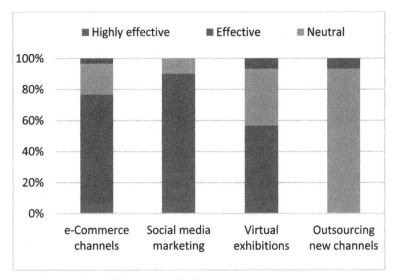

Figure 170.4 Effectiveness of adaptation strategies by agro enterprises
Source: Author

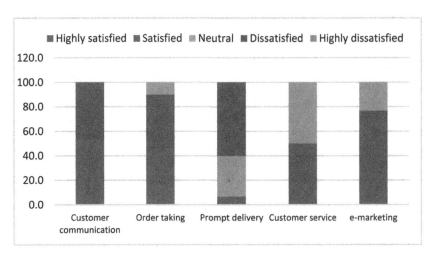

Figure 170.5 Performance of agro enterprises during pandemic economy
Source: Author

- Social media marketing: 90% found either highly effective or effective.
- Virtual exhibitions: 60% believed they play a vital role.
- No outsourcing of new channel partners observed.

Performance of agro enterprises due to COVID-19 impact:

- **Communication:** All enterprises maintained effective communication with customers through various means.
- **Order taking:** 90% were satisfied with order taking despite reduced order quantity.
- **Prompt delivery:** Only 5% were satisfied with the prompt delivery of finished goods; 60% were dis-

satisfied due to logistic difficulties and production constraints.
- **Customer service satisfaction:** 50% satisfied, 50% neutral.
- **Adaptation of new marketing channels:** Approximately 80% of enterprises satisfied with the adaptation of new marketing channels.

Suggestions

1. Timely financing from financial institutions can help rural agricultural enterprises manage cash flow during the pandemic.
2. To reduce costs and logistical challenges, strategically incorporate locally available spices in the production of value-added spice products.

3. Prioritize quality and optimal pricing for value-added spice products, aligning with key customer preferences.
4. Efficiently manage the impact of increased response time on orders from loyal customers.
5. Ensure prompt material delivery (OTIF) by streamlining disrupted supply chain and logistics functions.
6. Effectively utilize new marketing channels like e-commerce and social media to expand market presence and attract customers in new regions.

Conclusion

In conclusion, this study delves into the formidable uncertainties and challenges thrust upon agro-based enterprises producing value-added spice products in Kerala, India's spice hub, amid the COVID-19 pandemic. Drawing a major portion of raw materials from local spice farmers and traders, these enterprises witnessed a substantial reduction in both sales volume and value, primarily influenced by diminished retail and industrial customer purchases. The altered purchase behavior of both business-to-consumer (B2C) and business-to-business (B2B) customers, coupled with changing domestic and international demand patterns, underscored quality and price as pivotal factors guiding consumer choices during the pandemic.

The prolonged response time in customer service, despite a significant decline in orders, stemmed from disruptions in the supply chain, market uncertainties, and financial constraints on agro enterprises. The profit margins of these enterprises dwindled due to fluctuating raw material prices, heightened capital and operational costs induced by the pandemic's impact.

Nevertheless, the adaptation of new marketing channels, such as e-commerce and social media, emerges as a transformative opportunity for agro enterprises to navigate challenges and bolster resilience. Leveraging technology and innovation becomes imperative, enabling enterprises to scale operations, enhance communication with customers, boost productivity, and explore new products and markets. To endure and thrive amid the adversities wrought by COVID-19, agro enterprises must strategically focus on cost reduction, efficient raw material management, securing financial support, mitigating supply chain disruptions, and establishing alternative marketing channels. In essence, this study underscores the imperative for adaptive strategies to ensure the survival and growth of agro-based enterprises engaged in spice value addition in rural Kerala.

References

Ashwini, T., Lokesh, S., and Bonny, B. P. (2021). Performance of spice-based enterprises facilitated through agri-business incubators (ABI). *Journal of Tropical Agriculture, 59*(2).

Borsellino, V., Kaliji, S. A., and Schimmenti, E. (2020). Covid-19 drives consumer behaviour and agro-food markets towards healthier and more sustainable patterns. *Sustainability,* 12, 8366; doi:10.3390/su12208366.

Fairlie, R. (2020). Impact of Covid-19 on small business owners: evidence of early-stage losses. *Current Population Survey, Stanford Institute for Economic Policy Research.*

Galindo-Martin, M. A., Castano-Martinez, M. S., and Mendez-Picazo, M. T. (2021). Effects of pandemic crisis on entrepreneurship and sustainable development. *Journal of Business Research*, 137, 345–353.

Gopal, N., and Nair, G. S. (2022). Impacts of Covid-19 on MSMEs food processing units in the Indian state of Kerala: a case study. *Journal of Positive School of Psychology,* 6(3), 8755–8766.

Khomiuk, N., Voichuk, M., Bilous, O., and Dorosh, M. (2022). Marketing support of competitiveness of agricultural enterprises. *Scientific Messenger of Lviv National University of Veterinary Medicine and Biotechnologies, Series: Economical Sciences,* 24(99), 3–9.

Loske, D. (2020). The impact of Covid-19 on transport volume and freight capacity dynamics - An empirical analysis in German food retail logistics. *Transportation Research Interdisciplinary Perspectives.*

Rajan, V. K., and Ranjithkumar, S. (2018). Sustainable strategies of small-scale pepper processing industries – A case study in Wayanad, Kerala. *International Journal of Mechanical Engineering and Technology (IJMET),* 9(1).

Shirmila, T., Yslado-Mendez, R., Valderrama-Plasencia, L., Mahajan, T., Nagpal, P., and KN, J. (2022). Rural entrepreneurship in the post-Covid era: an overview - challenges, opportunities, and future scope. *International Journal of Mechanical Engineering,* 7(2).

Sowbhagya, H. B. (2019). Value-added processing of by-products from the spice industry. Department of Spice and Flavour Science, CSIR – Central Food Technological Research Institute, Mysore 570 020 Oxford Press. *Food Quality and Safety,* 3, 73–80.

171 Passenger's attitude toward the call taxi service providers in Coimbatore city

M. P. Prathiba[1,a], J. Thiravia Mary Gloria[2] and A. Anand Gerald[2]

[1]Karpagam Academy of Higher Education, Tamil Nadu, India
[2]Bishop Ambrose College, Tamil Nadu, India

Abstract

India is a large country in the world known for its high level of democracy. With its diverse attractions, it offers significant potential for profitable tourism, drawing in a multitude of foreigners. The taxi service industry plays a crucial role in promoting tourism within India. Internationally, India is esteemed as a distinct nation, often described as offering a unique travel experience. The country welcomes tourists from all corners of the globe, committed to providing them with an unparalleled experience. In some cities, taxis operate under regular permits, while in others, they are designated as vehicles for tourist hire, operating round the clock. Understanding the attitudes of passengers towards taxi services is essential for formulating effective business strategies in this sector.

Keywords: Call taxi, service industry, transportation

Introduction

Coimbatore is a beautiful and well-organized city located in the Tamil Nadu State, serving as the second major city in the state. It is renowned across the country as a leading manufacturer of automobile spare parts and for its thriving engineering industries, educational institutions, textile markets, hospitals, and pleasant climate. The city's tranquil surroundings and appealing environment attract numerous tourists. In addition to its natural beauty, Coimbatore is famous for its serene chapels and temples, adding to its allure as a tourist destination. The city boasts a well-developed transport network, facilitating easy travel both within Coimbatore and to its suburban areas. For intra-city transport needs, a comprehensive public transport system, along with fixed-rate tourist taxicabs and private taxicabs, serves residents and visitors alike. These services are readily available at key locations such as the airport, bus depots, and railway stations. Coimbatore is home to approximately 9,500 tourist taxis, with around 1,500 affiliated with leading call taxi aggregators. Many of these taxis are operated by owner-cum-drivers.

Call taxi service providers in Coimbatore pride themselves on offering reasonable fares, punctual service, 24/7 availability, a robust security alert system, and excellent customer service, distinguishing their services as reliable and customer-oriented.

Problem Statement

The transportation options in Coimbatore are diverse, with private transport being the primary choice for many. However, challenges such as traffic congestion and highway issues have made private transportation less comfortable for passengers. Call taxi services offer a solution to these problems, catering to various passenger needs including physical comfort, cleanliness, emotional relief from driving stress, social travel with friends or family, and economic benefits such as reasonable prices and no need to pay for gas (Kumari and Sandhya, 2013). Despite the benefits provided by call taxi services, there remains an opportunity for passengers to utilize bus services, especially due to the strong demand for affordable options in the market. Therefore, understanding passenger attitudes is crucial for the success of any transportation business, whether traditional or online (Rahman and Anand, 2014).

To address this, the present study aims to examine passenger attitudes towards call taxi services in Coimbatore. The survey seeks to answer the following questions:

1. How familiar are passengers with call taxi services?
2. What factors influence passengers' choice of call taxi services?
3. What is the level of passenger satisfaction with call taxi services?

[a]anusrisivakumar@gmail.com

By exploring these questions, the study aims to provide insights into passenger preferences and satisfaction levels, informing strategies for improving call taxi services in Coimbatore.

Objectives of the Study

1. To present a theoretical framework of the concept of service quality.
2. To identify the factors that affect passengers' choice of call taxi services in Coimbatore city.
3. To examine and assess the level of satisfaction with the services offered to passengers by the call taxi system in Coimbatore city.

Hypothesis

There is no significant association between age, gender, educational qualification, marital status, occupational status, monthly income and satisfaction level of the respondents to call taxi services.

Research Methodology

To achieve the objectives, primary data was utilized, collected through a survey method from respondents between March 2022 and June 2022. Additionally, secondary data were gathered from various sources including journals, magazines, newspapers, and internet sites focusing on call taxi services. A simple random sampling technique was employed to select a sample of 100 passengers for the present study in Coimbatore city. The statistical tools utilized in the survey included simple percentage analysis, weighted average score ranking technique, and Chi-square test.

Scope of the Study

Transportation plays a significant role worldwide by eliminating distance barriers. A robust transportation system contributes to a country's economic development. In recent years, call taxi services have experienced remarkable growth, with increasing demand from executives, companies, tourists, IT professionals, students, and the general public. Call taxis offer an easy and safe mode of transportation, resulting in their popularity among various segments of society (Kumar and Sentamilselvan, 2018; Godbole and Deshmukh, 2020; Ramasamy et al., 2021). The demand for taxis has also risen due to the need for convenient and speedy transport options. Therefore, there is a necessity to study consumers' satisfaction with call taxi services in Coimbatore city.

Limitations of the Study

1. The study was conducted during a specific period, therefore the findings may only reflect the views of the respondents during that particular time frame.
2. The study is confined to Coimbatore city and does not include other areas within the state.
3. The sample size is limited to 100 respondents, and a purposive sampling method was used for valid reasons.

Analysis and Interpretation

Profile of the respondents - percentage analysis

The profile of the respondents is demonstrated in two segments. The first segment shows the socio-economic profile of the respondents, and the second segment shows the profile of the passengers based on their service attributes.

Table 171.1 Socio-economic profile of the respondents.

Age	No. of respondents	(%)
Up to 20 years	18	18
21-30 years	50	50
31-40 years	17	17
Above 40 years	15	15
Total	100	100
Gender	No. of respondents	(%)
Male	51	51
Female	49	49
Total	100	100
Educational qualification	No. of respondents	(%)
Illiterate	19	19
School level	41	41
Graduate	22	22
Professional	18	18
Total	100	100
Marital status	No. of respondents	(%)
Married	41	41
Unmarried	59	59
Total	100	100
Occupational Status	No. of respondents	(%)
Student	15	15
Business	10	10
Employed	25	25
Professional	30	20
Others	20	30

Age	No. of respondents	(%)
Total	100	100
Monthly income	No. of. respondents	(%)
Up to Rs. 10,000	16	16
Rs. 10,001-Rs. 20,000	18	18
Rs. 20,001-Rs. 30,000	43	43
Above Rs. 30,001	23	23
Total	100	100
Nature of the family	No. of. respondents	(%)
Joint family	46	46
Nuclear family	54	54
Total	100	100
Size of the family (%)	No. of. respondents	
Below 3 members	18	18
3-5 members	50	50
Above 5 members	32	32
Total	100	100

Source: Primary data.

The socio-economic profile of the respondents reveals that among the 100 participants, the majority (50%) fall within the 21-30 age group, with females comprising (49%) of the sample. (41%) of respondents have a schooling level education, while professionals make up the largest occupational group at (30%). In terms of monthly income, (43%) fall within the Rs.20,001-Rs.30,000 bracket. The majority (54%) come from nuclear families, with (50%) having 3-5 members in their family.

Table 171.2 Service attributes of the respondents.

Sources of awareness	No. of respondents	(%)
Radio/television	25	25
Newspaper and Magazine	26	26
Social media sites	18	18
Friends and relatives	20	20
Existing user	11	11
Total	100	100
Call taxi service providers	No. of respondents	(%)
OLA call taxi	22	22
Red taxi	32	32
Go call taxi	12	12
Fast track call taxi	20	22

Sources of awareness	No. of respondents	(%)
My taxi	14	12
Total	100	100
Reason for preference	No. of respondents	(%)
Brand name	20	20
Easy to book	32	32
Taxi fare	10	10
Safety	35	35
Convenient	3	3
Total	100	100
Frequency of using call taxi services	No. of respondents	(%)
Daily	10	10
Weekly once	42	42
Once in a month	32	32
Rarely	16	16
Total	100	100
Mode of taxi booking	No. of respondents	(%)
By telephone	44	44
Booking online	42	42
Hail a taxi in the street	14	14
Total	100	100
Travelling time	No. of respondents	(%)
Less than 15 minutes	30	30
15 to 30 minutes	40	40
30 to 40 minutes	14	14
Above 45 minutes	16	16
Total	100	100
Reasonable taxi fare	No. of respondents	(%)
Yes	84	84
No	16	16
Total	100	100
Preference of same call taxi services	No. of respondents	(%)
Yes	80	80
No	20	18
Total	100	100
Difficulty in using call taxi services	No. of respondents	(%)
Yes	68	68
No	32	32
Total	100	100

Source: Author

Table 171.3 Chi-square test.

Variable	Degrees of freedom	Table value	Calculated value	Rejected/accepted
Age	6	12.6	10.2018	Accepted
Gender	2	9.962	4.904	Accepted
Educational qualification	6	12.6	5.29	Accepted
Marital status	2	9.962	9.576	Accepted
Occupational status	8	15.5	8.025	Accepted
Monthly income	6	12.6	4.118	Accepted

Source: Author

The profile of the respondents based on their service attributes reveals that among the 100 participants, the majority (26%) acquire awareness of call taxi services from newspapers and magazines. Additionally, (32%) of respondents prefer Red Taxi as their call taxi service provider, while (35%) cite "Easy to book" as the primary reason for choosing call taxi services. The frequency of using call taxi services once a month is favored by most respondents (32%), with (44%) preferring to book via telephone. Furthermore, (40%) of respondents typically travel for 15 to 30 minutes in a call taxi, and (84%) consider the taxi fares reasonable. Interestingly, (80%) of respondents prefer to use the same call taxi services, yet (68%) face difficulties in utilizing them.

Level of satisfaction of the respondents towards call taxi Services –chi-square test

The level of satisfaction of the respondents toward call taxi services is analyzed using the Chi-square test at a significance level of 5%. This analysis is presented in Table 171.3.

There is no significant association between age, gender, educational qualification, marital status, occupational status, monthly income, and the level of satisfaction of the respondents towards call taxi services.

Suggestions

To the call taxi aggregators:
1. Customers of call taxi services expect innovative features such as:
   - Track and send notifications to control rooms for safety.
   - Implementation of motion sensors or heartbeat rate monitors for security.
   - Option to remotely switch off the engine in emergencies.
   - Integration of accident and obstacle detection sensors.
   - Provision of panic alarm facilities during emergencies.

It is recommended that aggregators consider and implement these services to meet customer expectations.

To the call taxi service providers:
1. Gather quality feedback from customers at least once or twice a year and provide services accordingly.
2. Avoid imposing higher prices for short rides and additional charges during peak times.

To the call taxi drivers:
1. Display identification with photos and vehicle registration numbers prominently in the taxi.
2. Adhere strictly to traffic rules at all times.
3. Exercise control over driving speed.

To the government:
1. Permit private car owners to convert their vehicles into taxis only if they comply with the latest emission norms.
2. Mandate that all taxis are equipped with fire extinguishers of at least 1 kg capacity.

Conclusion

The survey reveals passengers' attitudes towards call taxi service providers in Coimbatore city. It analyzes their attitudes towards service providers, the factors they consider significant in selecting them, payment ease, satisfaction, service quality, and the problems faced while booking and traveling in call taxis. The results of this study can be used by service providers as important input to understand passengers' needs and attitudes about their services, and to what extent they can modify and bring about changes to retain existing customers and attract new ones. The findings depict the exact replica of customers' mindset and the level of satisfaction towards call taxi service providers operating in the city of Coimbatore. Appropriate suggestions have been provided considering the facts and feasibility. Call taxi service providers are suggested to take these outcomes into account and act accordingly.

It will definitely maximize satisfaction for passengers and expand their market base. This will also assist service providers in fulfilling customers' expectations, improving goodwill, and creating brand awareness in the market.

References

Godbole, S., and Deshmukh, M. A. (2020). Demographic segmentation impact on customer perception towards call taxi services in tier–ii town of nagpur in Maharashtra (India). *PalArch's Journal of Archaeology of Egypt/Egyptology*, 17(7), 7496–7504.

Kumar, V. H., and Sentamilselvan, K. (2018). Customer perception towards call-taxi services: a study with reference to Chennai. *Prestige International Journal of Management and Research*, 10(4), 87–91.

Kumari, D. A., and Sandhya, K. (2013). Training need analysis of call taxi drivers in Chennai, Tamilnadu, India. *Excel International Journal of Multidisciplinary Management Studies*, 3(7), 222–240.

Rahman, T., and Anand, N. (2014). Organized sector taxi operators in India–opportunities and challenges. *Empyreal Institute of Higher Education*, 2(3), 23–28.

Ramasamy, A., Muduli, K., Mohamed, A., Biswal, J. N., and Pumwa, J. (2021). Understanding customer priorities for selection of call taxi service provider. *Journal of Operations and Strategic Planning*, 4(1), 52–72.

172 Reasons for worker migration

Abey. J.[1,a], Velmurugan, R.[2,b], Amutha, K[3,c] and Hemalatha, T. M.[4,d]

[1]Kingdom University, Kingdom of Bahrain, Bahrain

[2]Karpagam Academy of Higher Education, Tamil Nadu, India

[3]PSG College of Arts and Science, Tamil Nadu, India

[4]Rathinam College of Arts and Science, Tamil Nadu, India

Abstract

The phenomenon of worker migration is multifaceted, stemming from a complex interplay of socioeconomic circumstances that compel individuals to seek opportunities beyond their home countries. Coimbatore district serves as the focal point of this study. Findings indicate that the prevalence of long working hours and various forms of exploitation in the state significantly motivate workers to seek employment in environments that prioritize their labor rights. Additionally, factors such as poor health indices contribute to the decision to migrate. Understanding these drivers is crucial for policymakers and stakeholders to address the root causes of worker migration and develop sustainable solutions to mitigate its impact.

Keywords: Healthcare disparities, job scarcity, migrant workers, skill devaluation

Introduction

The complex and dynamic phenomenon of worker migration from northern India to other parts of the country and beyond its borders arises from the precise interaction of numerous economic, social, and aspirational variables. The incredible stories of people from states like Uttar Pradesh, Bihar, Rajasthan, and Punjab, who bravely venture outside their comfort zones in search of broader perspectives and more promising futures, are illuminated by this phenomenon. This exodus symbolizes migration primarily driven by the unwavering desire for better living conditions, relentless pursuit of employment opportunities across various industries, and determination to ascend the social ladder. These migratory patterns encompass a wide range of human desires, from seasonal agricultural jobs that require workers to travel great distances to participate in planting and harvesting cycles, to contributing to the development of urban infrastructure in burgeoning cities.

However, the allure of greener pastures frequently emerges as the strongest motivation, drawing individuals into the bustling embrace of major cities with promises of brighter lights and greater opportunities. As they embark on their quest for more lucrative career avenues, they believe urban centers offer fertile ground for socioeconomic growth. In our endeavor to thoroughly investigate this fascinating topic, we unravel the complex web of causes underpinning this pervasive migratory trend. As we delve deeper into the stories of North Indian laborers, we shed light on the powerful forces intricately shaping their journeys, weaving them into the colorful and diverse tapestry of the country's socioeconomic landscape. Their movement narrates a larger story of resilience, adaptability, and an unrelenting pursuit of a brighter future within the rich tapestry of India's complex identity, rather than merely focusing on individual desires.

Literature Review

Table 172.1 Factors influencing labor migration: insights from various studies.

Author	Year	Factors influencing migration
Stark (1991)	1991	Increased demand for certain types of labor due to globalization
Massey et al. (1993)	1993	Influence of social networks and chain migration processes
Skeldon (1997)	1997	Family considerations, including responsibilities toward dependents and providing a better future for children

[a]j.abey@ku.edu.bh, abey.jojirajan@gmail.com, [b]drvelsngm@gmail.com, [c]ammugold07@gmail.com, [d]hemalatha2974@gmail.com

Author	Year	Factors influencing migration
Tacoli (1998)	1998	Environmental factors such as natural disasters and environmental degradation
Kofman et al. (2000)	2000	Gender dynamics leading to differing migration patterns among men and women
Cassarino (2004)	2004	Limited career prospects prompting individuals to seek better opportunities elsewhere
Castles (2004)	2004	Conflict and political instability driving people to seek safety and security
Dumont and Lemaître (2005)	2005	Government policies, incentives, and initiatives influencing migration patterns
Koser (2007)	2007	Cultural norms, societal expectations, and perceived social status shaping migration decisions
Kainth (2010a)	2010	Low productivity, unemployment, underdevelopment, unfavorable economic conditions, and exhaustion of natural resources driving migration
Kainth (2010b)	2010	Lack of suitable job opportunities and job insecurity cited as reasons for migration
Kaur et al. (2011)	2011	Migration driven by the search for better income, employment opportunities, and standards of living
Viji (2013a)	2013	Recognition and career advancement playing a significant role in migration decisions
Viji (2013b)	2013	Quest for recognition, employment issues, limited career prospects, and familial responsibilities as motivations for migration
Dustmann et al. (2016)	2016	Mismatch between acquired skills and job opportunities leading to migration

Source: Author

Research Gap

The existing body of research on the causes of worker migration offers insights into various influencing factors, as highlighted by scholars like Stark (1991), Massey et al. (1993), Skeldon (1997), Tacoli (1998), Kofman et al. (2000), Cassarino (2004), Castles (2004), Dumont and Lemaître (2005), Koser (2007), and Viji (2013a,b). However, significant research gaps persist. There is a need for holistic studies integrating economic, familial, environmental, and gender factors. Future research should explore migration determinants across different contexts, assess the impact of government policies comprehensively, and examine the long-term effects of migration on communities and socioeconomic development. Additionally, incorporating qualitative methods could provide deeper insights into migrant workers' motivations and decision-making processes. Addressing these gaps is crucial for a comprehensive understanding of labor migration dynamics.

Problem Statement

The study aims to investigate the fundamental causes driving worker migration from northern Indian states to various regions within and outside the nation, emphasizing the complex interactions of economic, social, and aspirational forces. By exploring the reasons behind this migratory trend, including seasonal agricultural engagements and the pursuit of skilled jobs, the study seeks to provide insights for policymakers, scholars, and other stakeholders to develop targeted policies addressing the challenges and opportunities associated with labor migration in India.

Objective of the Study

1. To identify the socio-economic profile of migrant workers.
2. To ascertain the reasons for worker migration.

Scope of the Study

The scope of the study is focused on the geographic boundaries of Coimbatore district, which serves as a microcosm of complex migration processes. The study aims to gain a comprehensive understanding of migration factors within this unique environment. Specifically, it focuses on two key aspects:

1. Investigating the socio-economic profile of migrant workers, including their employment status, educational backgrounds, and other relevant characteristics.
2. Exploring the underlying factors driving migration, ranging from social and familial influences on economic aspirations and the pursuit of better livelihoods.

The study intends to illuminate the complex motivations behind migration decisions, providing insights into the diverse factors shaping people's movement across national and cultural boundaries. By concentrating on these aspects, the study aims to lay a solid groundwork for future research projects to delve deeper into the intricacies of the migration phenomenon.

Research methodology

- Data
  - The study relies on primary data meticulously gathered to gain an in-depth understanding of the topic.
  - A methodological strategy based on personal interviews was developed to uncover insights.
  - Primary data was collected using a well-designed interview schedule, facilitating systematic data collection.
  - The interview schedule included probing questions and prompts for an organized exchange of information.
  - Lively discussions enabled the direct collection of valuable information from participants.
  - Interactive interviews explored socioeconomic profiles and motivations of migrants, capturing both quantitative and qualitative data.
  - The use of original interview material added a humanistic component to the research.
- Sampling:
  - Convenience sampling was employed to capture a representative snapshot of the migrant worker population in Coimbatore.
  - Data analysis was based on the participation of 600 migrant workers, contributing opinions, experiences, and insights.
- Tools employed:
  - Data analysis utilized simple percentage calculations and factor analysis techniques.

Significance of the Study

This study's significance lies in its exploration of labor migration causes, providing insights for policymakers and stakeholders. By understanding the complex factors driving migration decisions, it informs targeted strategies to address challenges and leverage opportunities. Emphasizing the Coimbatore district offers specific insights for regional development, fostering community well-being and contributing to broader discourse on human mobility. Ultimately, the study equips decision-makers to enact positive change, promoting social cohesion and socioeconomic advancement.

Limitations of the Study

The study's reliance on primary data emphasizes the importance of firsthand knowledge, yet the use of convenience sampling may introduce bias. Caution is warranted when extrapolating the findings to broader contexts, as the potential bias may affect the generalizability of the results. Therefore, careful consideration is necessary to ensure the findings accurately reflect the complex reality being studied.

Findings

The report offers a detailed demographic profile of migrant workers, revealing trends such as the majority falling within the 21 to 30 age range and a significant gender gap favoring men. Educational backgrounds play a crucial role, with many workers having at least an SSLC degree, while familial dynamics show complexities, with some choosing to remain single to support dependents. Financially, most workers earn above Rs. 15000 per month, impacting relocation decisions, with family spending habits reflecting this. Family structures, often with two earners, and occupational preferences, like masonry, further shape migration patterns. Language skills, particularly in Hindi, are prevalent, and workers demonstrate commitment with long workdays exceeding 12 hours. Overall, the study provides a comprehensive understanding of the multifaceted factors influencing labor migration among migrant workers, shedding light on their diverse experiences and motivations.

Reasons for worker migration: Utilizing factor analysis, this study aims to uncover the key drivers behind workers' decisions to relocate. Before delving into the analysis, a pre-analysis evaluation is conducted using the Kaiser-Meyer-Olkin (KMO) measure and Bartlett's test of sphericity to assess the adequacy of the dataset. Both tests yield positive results, with KMO and Bartlett's test scores surpassing the cutoff threshold of 0.70, indicating suitability for factor analysis. These findings validate the dataset's compatibility with factor analysis, providing a robust foundation for examining the factors influencing worker migration decisions. The convergence of results from KMO and Bartlett's test underscores the dataset's reliability, setting the stage for a comprehensive factor analysis to illuminate the significant factors driving worker migration.

Table 172.1 Socio-economic profile.

Particulars	Numbers (n = 600)	Percentage
Age		
18 – 20	195	32.5
21 – 30	300	50.0
Above 30	105	17.5
Gender		
Male	580	96.7
Female	20	3.3
Education		
Illiterate	160	26.7
SSLC	205	34.2
H.Sc.,	195	32.5
Diploma	40	6.7
Marital status		
Married	285	47.5
Unmarried	315	52.5
Status in family		
Head	145	24.2
Member	455	75.8
Monthly income (Rs.)		
Up to 10000	60	10.0
10001-15000	195	32.5
Above 15000	345	57.5
Family expenditure		
Up to 4000	210	35.0
4001 – 8000	370	61.7
Above 8000	20	3.3
Earning members		
One	140	23.3
Two	270	45.0
Above Two	190	31.7
Non-earning members		
One	305	50.8
Two	265	44.2
Above Two	30	5.0
Occupation		
Mason	395	65.8
Plumber	130	21.7
Painter	75	12.5
Languages known		
Hindi	315	52.5
Hindi and Tamil	285	47.5

Particulars	Numbers (n = 600)	Percentage
Working hours		
Up to 8	50	8.3
12	550	91.7

Source: Author

Table 172.2 KMO and Bartlett's test.

KMO and Bartlett's test		
Kaiser-Meyer-Olkin measure of sampling adequacy.		.787
Bartlett's test of sphericity	Approx. Chi-square	5725.778
	Df	66
	Sig.	.000

Source: Author

The analysis identifies four key factors influencing workers' migration decisions, determined by Eigen value criterion surpassing unity and component loadings exceeding 0.5. The first factor highlights long work hours, compromised health index, and limited growth prospects, while the second shows lack of local job opportunities, state neglect, and perceived surplus labor. Economic factors, including absence of leave policies and better job prospects elsewhere, dominate the third factor. Lastly, the fourth factor emphasizes appreciation of skills, high unemployment, and family commitments. Together, these factors contribute significantly to migration motivations, with factor 1 accounting for 35.705%, followed by factors 2, 3, and 4 contributing 19.198%, 13.439%, and 10.809% respectively. In total, they explain 79.250% of migration drivers, showcasing the multifaceted nature of workers' migration decisions.

Suggestions

- Strengthen and enforce labor regulations to ensure fair pay, limit working hours, and promote work-life balance.
- Invest in healthcare infrastructure and services to improve the overall health index, along with wellness initiatives.
- Implement policies to encourage investment, economic diversification, and entrepreneurship for growth prospects.
- Enhance educational systems to provide relevant skill training and vocational programs matching local labor market needs.

Table 172.3 Reasons for migration.

Reasons for Migration	1	2	3	4
Exploiting prolonged working hours are common in my state	.934			
Health index are worse in my state	.915			
Growth prospects are not there in my state	.677			
Less job in my native place		.950		
The care and concern of my native state is very poor		.925		
Extracting overloading of work is often at my own place		.620		
No leave is allowed in my state			.923	
To earn more Salary			.921	
Economic index is very poor in my state			.579	
Unemployment problem is a grave matter in my state				.806
Skills are not valued at my hometown				.777
Family commitment				.587
Eigen values	4.297	2.304	1.613	1.297
% of Variance	35.805	19.198	13.439	10.809
Cumulative % of variance	35.805	55.003	68.441	79.250

Source: Author

- Incentivize businesses to create jobs locally and prioritize local hiring practices in high-demand industries.
- Upgrade local infrastructure, educational, and medical services to attract and retain talent within communities.
- Educate the public about workers' rights, health challenges, and balanced economic growth through advocacy initiatives.
- Develop comprehensive government plans and allocate funds for infrastructure, healthcare, education, and skill-building.
- Foster collaboration between public, private, and non-profit sectors to address issues collectively.
- Utilize data-driven decision-making to guide policy choices and monitor progress on economic, health, and employment indicators.
- Ensure inclusive economic progress to eliminate inequalities and enhance overall well-being in society.
- Provide capacity-building support to institutions and local governments to tackle these issues effectively.
- Promote worker empowerment through the development of unions and employee organizations for improved pay and benefits.
- Prioritize employee welfare and sustainable economic growth for long-term solutions through persistent cross-sector cooperation.

Conclusion

In conclusion, the migration of labor from our state is driven by a confluence of pressing issues, including abusive working conditions, poor health infrastructure, limited growth prospects, and a lack of job opportunities. These factors compel individuals to seek better opportunities elsewhere, leading to a significant outflow of workers from our communities. Addressing these challenges requires a comprehensive strategy that encompasses skill development, healthcare reform, economic growth initiatives, job creation, and social welfare improvements. By prioritizing these areas, the state can stem the tide of labor migration and create a more sustainable and equitable environment for its citizens.

Moving forward, there is ample scope for further research to deepen our understanding of the complex phenomenon of worker migration. Future studies could explore various topics such as the gender dynamics of migration, the interaction of demographic factors, the influence of social networks and cultural norms, the impact of technology on migration decisions, and the psychological factors driving migration choices. Comparative studies, longitudinal analyses, and interdisciplinary approaches could provide valuable insights into the causes and effects of migration, informing evidence-based policies and interventions. By advancing our knowledge in this area, we can contribute to more sustainable and equitable development outcomes, ultimately benefiting both sending and receiving communities.

References

Cassarino, J. P. (2004). Theorising return migration: the conceptual approach to return migrants revisited. *International Journal on Multicultural Societies*, 6(2), 253–279.

Castles, S. (2004). Why migration policies fail. *Ethnic and Racial Studies*, 27(2), 205–227.

Dumont, J. C., and Lemaître, G. (2005). Counting immigrants and expatriates in OECD countries: a new perspective. OECD Social, Employment and Migration Working Papers, No. (25).

Dustmann, C., Fadlon, I., and Weiss, Y. (2016). Return migration, human capital accumulation and the brain drain. *Journal of Development Economics*, 122, 42–59.

Kainth, G. S. (2010a). Push and pull factors of migration: acase study of brick kiln migrant workers in Punjab. *Munich Personal RePEc Archive*.

Kainth, G. S. (2010b). Rural–urban migration in India: policy issues and challenges. *Journal of Punjab Studies*, 17(1), 37–52.

Kaur, B., et al. (2011). Migration in Punjab: a study of socio-economic characteristics of migrants. *International Journal of Rural Studies*, 18(1), 1–6.

Kofman, E., Phizacklea, A., Raghuram, P., and Sales, R. (2000). Comparing public perceptions and preventive behaviours during the early phase of the COVID-19 pandemic in Hong Kong and the United Kingdom: cross-sectional survey study. Journal of Medical Internet Research, 23(3), e23231.

Massey et al. (1993). Data governance and automated individual decision-making in the digital privacy General Data Protection Regulation. Administratie si Management Public, (31), 132–142.

Skeldon (1997). Innovative optimization directions of investigative (detective) activity in modern conditions. Theory and Practice of Forensic Science and Criminalistics, 24(2), 8–25.

Stark (1991). Trustworthy artificial intelligence: a review. ACM Computing Surveys (CSUR), 55(2), 1–38.

Tacoli (1998). The Baba of Melaka: Culture and identity of a Chinese Peranakan community in Malaysia. Strategic Information and Research Development Centre.

Viji, H. G. (2013a). Causes of migration of labour in Tirunelveli district. *Researchers World - Journal of Arts, Science and Commerce*, 4(1), 124–132.

Viji, H. G. (2013b). Migration trends and factors influencing migration: a study of Villupuram district, Tamil Nadu, India. In Migration and Social Protection in South India, (pp. 47–63). Springer.

173 Factors influencing two-wheeler purchase intention in Chennai, South India: a comprehensive exploration

Thandauthapani, A.[a], Harish, M.[b], Sathiyabama, P.[c] and Rekha Kiran Kumar, T.[d]

SRM Institute of Science and Technology, Tamil Nadu, India

Abstract

This study investigates the factors influencing consumers' decisions in purchasing two-wheelers in Chennai, South India. Employing a descriptive approach, data was collected via a standardized questionnaire using simple random sampling, with 240 respondents. Analysis with SPSS AMOS 23 revealed that three key components significantly influenced purchase intentions, with attitude playing a pivotal role. Practical implications include tailored marketing, eco-friendly incentives, and safety campaigns, while socially, it promotes sustainable transportation and safety awareness, fostering a shift towards environmentally friendly options like electric bikes. The study's originality lies in its structured data collection method, offering valuable insights for businesses to understand consumer preferences and improve marketing strategies. Additionally, it highlights the importance of addressing social and environmental concerns in the transportation sector, driving positive change towards a safer and more sustainable society.

Keywords: Attitude, behaviour control, buying behaviour, purchase intention

Introduction

Purchase intention, a pivotal concept in consumer behaviour and marketing, elucidates consumers' inclination towards acquiring a specific product or service, serving as a linchpin for comprehending and forecasting consumer behaviour, market demand, and marketing strategy efficacy. The exploration of purchase intention empowers businesses and marketers with invaluable insights into consumer decision-making processes, preferences, and motivations, facilitating the customization of strategies and offerings to effectively cater to consumer needs.

Various characteristics such as trust, commitment, brand personality, and consumer engagement exert considerable influence on purchase desire. Santhanakrishnan et al. (2020)'s study mentions about trust and commitment's pivotal role in purchase intention, while Angel et al. (2021) highlight the impact of brand personality. In the realm of beauty products, Kunthi et al. (2021) emphasize the significance of consumer engagement through electronic word-of-mouth and brand awareness.

Internal factors encompass individual attributes and perceptions influencing purchase intention, including product-related features, personal preferences, and lifestyles. On the other hand, external factors encompass environmental and situational influences, such as social recommendations, marketing efforts, price sensitivity, cultural influences, and technological advancements.

In contemporary consumer landscapes, societal concerns like environmental sustainability increasingly shape purchase intention, fostering a demand for eco-friendly products. Businesses and marketers must grasp the multifaceted nature of purchase intention to devise tailored marketing strategies, product offers, and communication campaigns. Addressing barriers to purchase intention enhances consumer satisfaction, fosters brand loyalty, and augurs long-term success in a fiercely competitive market milieu. Thus, a comprehensive understanding of purchase intention is imperative for navigating the dynamic consumer landscape and driving sustainable business growth.

Attitude and Purchase Intention

Understanding the link between attitudes and purchase intent is vital for marketers to tailor effective strategies. Factors such as consumer behaviour, brand awareness, and pricing influence purchase intentions. For instance, Ricardo et al. (2021) found positive effects of consumer attitudes and perceived behavioural control on purchase intent. Conversely, subjective norms and brand knowledge might not significantly influence purchase intent (Santi, 2021). Moreover, consumer attitudes mediate the relationship between environmental consciousness and purchase intent (Danu, 2021).

---

[a]thanducimat@gmail.com, [b]harishnzmtvl@gmail.com, [c]sathiyaradha.p@gmail.com, [d]rekhakit@srmist.edu.in

Subjective Norm and Purchase Intention

Subjective norm significantly influences purchase intent, reflecting perceived social pressure to purchase. Research by Tommy et al. (2021) highlights its strong positive impact, while customer relationship management can enhance purchase intent through subjective norms (Hutsayaporn, 2021). Additionally, subjective norms positively influence the intention to purchase healthy food (Hanjaya et al., 2020) and moderate the association between attitude and luxury goods purchase intent (Sheetal et al., 2020).

Perceived Behavioural Intention and Purchase Intention

Perceived behavioural control significantly influences purchase intent, reflecting belief in one's ability to perform a behaviour successfully. In various contexts, including healthy food and organic products, attitude, subjective norms, and perceived behavioural control positively impact purchase intent. Understanding these factors aids in designing effective marketing strategies to drive consumer purchase intent.

Research Methodology

The research methodology employed a simple random sampling method to collect and analyze data due to resource constraints and time limitations. Data was gathered from 240 individuals across various professions in Chennai, South India. Cross-sectional analysis

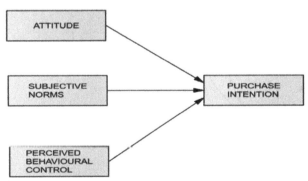

Figure 173.1 Theoretical framework of the study

Source: Author

methods were chosen as data was collected only once from respondents. Surveys were distributed in ten prime locations in Chennai, resulting in 240 satisfactory responses out of 300 distributed questionnaires. Harman's single factor test was utilized to assess common method variance, revealing only 27.81% variance, indicating the absence of common method bias in the data. This approach allowed for the evaluation of common method variance.

According to the findings presented in Table 173.1, the majority of respondents fell within the age range of 31 to 45 years old, constituting 54.20% of the total respondents. Males comprised 70.00% of the survey participants, representing the largest demographic. Additionally, 47.5% of respondents had completed their undergraduate degrees, also representing the majority. Furthermore, 38.80% of respondents reported an income of less than five lakh rupees.

Descriptive Analysis

According to Table 173.2, there's a moderate performance level across all criteria, with mean scores ranging from 3.77 to 3.95. Perceived behavioural intention received the lowest score at 3.60, suggesting partial

Table 173.1 Demographic characteristics of the respondents.

		Count	Percentage
Age	21-30	59	24.6%
	31-45	130	54.2%
	45 & above	51	21.3%
Gender	Male	168	70.0%
	Female	72	30.0%
Education	UG level	114	47.5%
	PG level	51	21.3%
	Others	75	31.3%
Income	Below 5 Lakhs	93	38.8%
	5-10 lakhs	79	32.9%
	10 Lakhs & Above	68	28.3%

Source: Author

Table 173.2 Summary of Descriptive Findings.

Variables	N	Minimum	Maximum	Mean	Std. Deviation
PIN	240	1.00	5.00	3.7738	.78583
SUB	240	1.00	5.00	3.9524	.75396
PBI	240	1.00	5.00	3.6024	.97769
ATT	240	1.00	5.00	3.6976	.82419

Source: Author

agreement among respondents. Subjective norms, related to two-wheeler acquisition, scored highest at 3.95, indicating strong influence from others' lifestyles. Standard deviations ranged from 0.75 to 0.977, showing acceptable variability within the data and diverse perspectives among respondents.

Confirmatory factor analysis (CFA) in AMOS assessed the measurement model, with all factor loadings surpassing the suggested threshold (> 0.50). Overall model fit metrics were satisfactory: CMIN/df = 1.343, GFI = 0.946, CFI = 0.958, TCI = 0.92, SRMR = 0.050, and RMSEA = 0.046, all within acceptable limits (Bentler and Bonett, 1980). Standard SEM approach evaluated reliability and validity, with Cronbach's alpha values above 0.7, indicating high internal consistency (Fornell & Larcker, 1981). AVE results ranged from 0.548 to 0.708, suggesting good reproducibility. Discriminant validity was confirmed through comparisons between square root values of AVE and inter-construct correlations, following

Fornell and Larcker Criteria (1981). HTMT method affirmed discriminant validity, meeting specified criteria across all structures (Henseler et al., 2015).

Cronbach's alpha and composite reliability assessed construct reliability, with all variables surpassing the 0.70 threshold. Item convergence validity was determined using Average Variance Extracted, with mean variance values exceeding 0.50. Discriminant validity was evaluated through the HTMT ratio.

The structural model in AMOS was utilized to examine the connections between latent and observable variables. The model exhibited a good fit with a non-significant chi-square ($\chi 2$ = 198.23, p > 0.05), CFI = 0.962, TLI = 0.943, RMSEA = 0.06, and SRMR = 0.05, indicating that the proposed associations effectively explain the data.

The hypothesized results, as depicted in Figure 173.3, were explained. According to Table 173.4, all hypotheses were confirmed. Attitude showed a significant positive impact on purchase intention (β = 0.209,

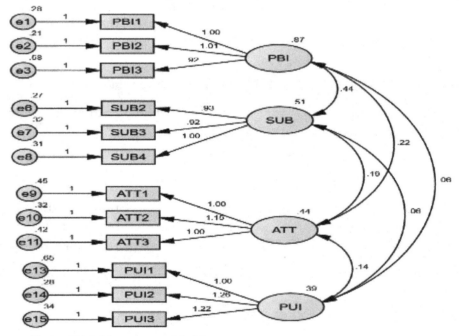

Figure 173.2 Measurement Model
Source: Author

Table 173.3 Master validity measures: convergent and discriminant validity.

	CR	AVE	MSV	MaxR(H)	PBI	SUB	ATT	PUI
PBI	0.878	0.708	0.439	0.896	0.841			
SUB	0.822	0.606	0.439	0.822	0.662***	0.778		
ATT	0.784	0.548	0.162	0.792	0.364**	0.403	0.741	
PUI	0.796	0.569	0.120	0.822	0.105	0.130	0.346	0.754

Source: Author

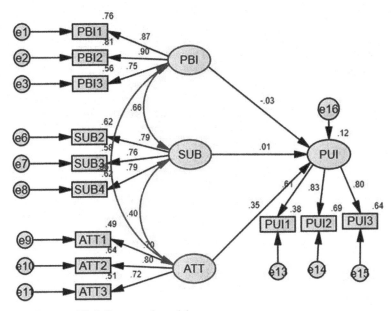

Figure 173.3 Structural model
Source: Author

Table 173.4 Hypothesis Testing.

Hypothesis			Estimate	S.E.	C.R.	P
PIN	<---	SUB	.209	.095	2.198	.003
PIN	<---	PBI	.154	.073	2.099	.000
PIN	<---	ATT	.238	.073	3.266	.001

Source: Author

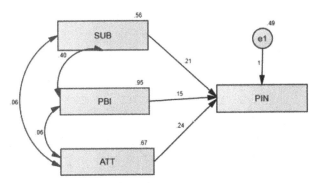

Figure 173.4 Path analysis
Source: Author

p < 0.05). Similarly, Hypothesis 2, regarding the influence of subjective norms on purchase intention, was supported with significant results ($\beta = 0.154$, $p < 0.05$). Furthermore, Hypothesis 3, concerning the impact of perceived behavioural intention on purchase intention, was confirmed with a substantial positive effect ($\beta = 0.238$) and a *p*-value below 0.05.

Results and Discussion

In this section, the findings obtained from structural equation modelling and confirmatory factor analysis were presented and interpreted. It was demonstrated that one-dimensionality existed as evidenced by the rotated component matrix, where variables loaded uniquely onto separate factors. Additionally, exploratory factor analysis revealed that the intention to make a purchase could be assessed in terms of attitude, subjective norms, and perceived behavioural intention, with factor loadings of 0.826, 0.818, and 0.805, respectively. From these results, it can be concluded that among the three concepts, attitude had the most significant influence on consumers' intention to make a purchase, followed by subjective norms. Furthermore, perceived behavioural intention had a positive impact on the intention to make a purchase. Thus, it can be inferred that each of the three constructs considered in the study significantly influenced the intention to purchase.

Conclusion

The study's findings regarding the influence of attitude, subjective norms, and perceived behavioural intention on the intention to acquire two-wheelers offer significant insights with crucial managerial implications for businesses in the automotive industry. Enhancing the overall perception of potential customers towards their two-wheelers is paramount for boosting sales and increasing the likelihood of purchase. Emphasizing the product's positive attributes, such as features, performance, and reliability, in marketing efforts can cultivate a favourable attitude towards the brand. Leveraging influencer marketing and word-of-mouth strategies can tap into subjective norms, influencing prospective purchasers and bolstering purchase intentions.

Furthermore, businesses should align pricing and promotional strategies with customer attitudes and anticipated behaviours. Providing comprehensive information about two-wheelers can reduce uncertainty and stimulate purchase desire. Segmentation of the target audience based on attitudes and subjective norms allows for personalized marketing initiatives that resonate strongly with prospective customers.

Moreover, offering exceptional after-sales support reinforces positive brand sentiments, fosters brand loyalty, and encourages repeat purchases. Highlighting the eco-friendliness and sustainability of two-wheelers can attract environmentally conscious customers and increase purchase likelihood.

In summary, a holistic strategy incorporating product perception, marketing tactics, pricing, customer education, and after-sales support is essential for enhancing purchase intentions and achieving success in the competitive two-wheeler industry.

References

Bentler, P. M., and Bonett, D. G. (1980). Significance tests and goodness of fit in the analysis of covariance structures. *Psychological Bulletin*, 88(3), 588–606. https://doi.org/10.1037/0033-2909.88.3.588.

Carter, M. J., and Fuller, C. (2016). Symbols, meaning, and action: the past, present, and future of symbolic interactionism. *Current Sociology*, 64, 931–961. https://doi.org/10.1177/0011392116638396.

Collier, J. E. (2020). Applied Structural Equation Modelingusing AMOS: Basic to Advanced Techniques. Routledge. https://doi.org/10.4324/9781003018414.

Galanakis, M., Palaiologou, A., Patsi, G., Velegraki, I. M., and Darviri, C. (2016). A literature review on the connection between stress and self-esteem. *Psychology*, 7(5), 687–694. doi: 10.4236/PSYCH.2016.75071.

Kaiser, R. T., and Ozer, D. J. (1997). Emotional stability and goal-related stress. *Personality and Individual Differences*, 22(3), 371–379. doi: 10.1016/S0191-8869(96)00208-5.

Rector, N. A., and Roger, D. (1997). The stress buffering effects of self-esteem. *Personality and Individual Differences*, 23(5), 799–808. doi: 10.1016/S0191-8869(97)00095-0.

Sharma, R., Jauhari, S., and Singh, V. (2015). Stress techniques and management: a review paper. *Journal of Literature, Languages and Linguistics*, 13, 23–29.

Singh, A. P., Amish, A. P., and Singhi, N. (2015). Role of life events stress and individualism-collectivism in predicting job satisfaction. *The Indian Journal of Industrial Relations*, 51(2), 300–311.

Ullman, J. B. (2001). Structural equation modeling. In Tabachnick, B. G., and Fidell, L. S. (Eds.), Using Multivariate Statistics. Boston, MA: Pearson Education.

174 Influence of sensory elements on perceived quality in Kerala's branded fast food outlets

Rajmohan Kadavil[a] and Usha, M.[b]

Karpagam Academy of Higher Education, Tamil Nadu, India

Abstract

Worldwide organized retail businesses face intense competition from their online counterparts, and fast-food retail businesses are also feeling the heat. With the increasing popularity of online food delivery apps, organized restaurant businesses must rapidly innovate to stay afloat in this new business scenario. When customers order food online, the only differentiating factor is the taste, whereas when customers physically visit the restaurant, they are influenced by the other four sensory factors in the retail outlet: sight, smell, sound, and touch elements. Companies deliberately use these sensory elements to position and differentiate their brand from competitors. This paper seeks to understand the influence these elements have on customers and the impact they can have on perceived quality, ultimately influencing purchase intention. A list of international branded retail food outlets with the maximum number of outlets worldwide was compiled, and those with a presence in the three major cities of Kerala—Kochi, Trivandrum, and Kozhikode—were shortlisted for the study.

Keywords: Brand awareness, perceived quality, and purchase intention, sensory marketing

Introduction

The organized restaurant business in India has been growing at a phenomenal rate in the last few years. According to a study by brokerage firm Motilal Oswal, the catering industry in the country is expected to progress at an annual rate of 9% until 2025, while the organized catering segment is expected to register a CAGR of 15.4% during the same period. The F&B industry in India is estimated to be around Rs 5 trillion, with organized restaurants accounting for approximately 35% of the industry share. One of the main factors that will accelerate the growth of the organized restaurant business is the adoption of technology by consumers. Mobile apps have made it very convenient for customers to select and order food online. As customers have become more quality-conscious, it is natural for them to choose branded food outlets over unbranded local restaurants. However, it is important for organized restaurants to bring customers back to their physical facilities because it is not just about satisfying hunger, but also about the experience that customers can have while dining out. Organized restaurants invest a lot of money in infrastructure building and staff training, and this investment can

only be recouped if customers visit the facility and engage in unplanned and impulse purchasing. When customers physically visit the store, the restaurant is also able to differentiate its offering through sensory elements. This study aims to understand how the five sensory elements can influence customers' perceived quality and how organized restaurant brands can use these sensory elements to increase sales and profits.

Research Questions

According to Krishna (2011), products must engage customers holistically through all the senses: sight, taste, touch, hearing, and smell. These five senses can create memorable experiences, potentially leading to perceived quality. This study aims to investigate and provide insights into the following questions:

1. How do sensory elements influence perceived quality in branded food outlets?
2. Which sensory elements should be utilized to build perceived quality?
3. Will perceived quality lead to purchase intention in the food outlets?

[a]rajmohan@bharatamatacollege.in, [b]ushakarthic6969@gmail.com

Literature review

Table 174.1 Overview of sensory marketing strategies.

Exploring sensory marketing applications			
Study	Sensory marketing	Visual marketing	Auditory marketing
1. Sensory marketing involves using sensory stimuli in marketing to engage consumers and influence behavior (Krishna, 2011).	Visual marketing employs visual elements like images and videos to quickly convey messages (Rieunier, 2000).	Auditory marketing uses sound or music to promote products (Sayadi, 2015).	Olfactory marketing uses fragrances to create specific atmospheres (Suhonen and Tengvall, 2009).
2. Sensation plays a critical role in creating pleasant shopping and consumption experiences (Hultén et al., 2009).	Visual elements such as color and layout impact customers' perceptions of quality (Wedel et al., 2012).	Sound can evoke emotions and influence how brands are interpreted (Hultén, 2011).	Scents can affect moods and behavior, influencing eating habits (Spence, 2015).
3. Multi-sensory experiences are important in understanding consumer behavior (Krey et al., 2020).	The sense of sight is crucial for creating a positive first impression in food markets (C. Valenti et al., 2008).	Music can influence behavior towards food and perceptions of it (Spence, 2015).	Scented ads can improve product evaluations through olfactory imagery (Stevenson et al., 2005).
4. Sensory stimulation can enhance value perception (Krey et al., 2020).	Choice of color, shape, and texture can impact store atmosphere and quality perception (Rieunier, 2000).	Music can create positive emotions, enhancing the store atmosphere (Rieunier, 2009).	Scents can improve store image and become more relevant with business compatibility (Quispillo et al., 2022).
Understanding the Impact of Sensory Elements			
Study	Gustatory marketing	Tactile marketing	Perceived quality
5. Taste marketing uses the sense of taste to create unique product experiences (Toko, 2013).	Taste is closely linked to survival and plays a crucial role in food perception (Korsmeyer, 2002).	Tactile marketing engages the sense of touch to promote products (Williams et al., 2009).	Perceived quality influences customer purchase decisions and loyalty (Zeithaml, 1988).
6. Taste can significantly influence customers' food choices and restaurant selection (Dung et al., 2022).	External cues like texture influence customers' personality judgments and social choices (Williams et al., 2009).	Touch influences learning preferences, even in the digital age (Aho, 2016).	Perceived quality is determined by various factors including brand reputation and value (Zuhrem, 2018).
7. Sensory factors like taste indirectly affect service reuse intention through branding (Dung et al., 2022).	Taste perception is influenced by situational factors under limited product knowledge (Solin et al., 2022).	Tactile experiences can modify people's judgments and influence consumer behavior (Williams et al., 2009).	Perceived quality affects market share, profitability, and brand equity (Aaker, 1991).
8. Taste marketing can contribute to creating strong emotional bonds between customers and brands (Toko, 2013).	Taste perception is an essential aspect of consumers' experience with food products (Dung et al., 2022).	Tactile marketing helps establish trust and familiarity with products (Williams et al., 2009).	Perceived quality is crucial for building and maintaining customer relationships (Zuhrem, 2018).
Effects of sensory marketing on consumer behavior			
Study	Purchase intention		
9. Perceived quality influences consumer satisfaction and loyalty (Belch, 2008).	Purchase intention indicates the likelihood of future purchases (Kotler, 2016).		
10. Customers are willing to pay more for products perceived as high-quality (Spears and Singh, 2004).	Purchase intention is influenced by factors like price, brand reputation, and perceived value (Wu et al., 2011).		

Exploring sensory marketing applications

Study	Sensory marketing	Visual marketing	Auditory marketing
11. Perceived quality affects brand profitability and equity (Aaker, 1991).	Purchase intention is shaped by both internal characteristics and external stimuli (Bagozzi and Burnkrant, 1979).		
12. Perceived quality is based on consumer perceptions of product attributes and value (Zuhrem, 2018).	Purchase intention reflects consumers' personal inclination to buy products or services (Bagozzi and Burnkrant, 1979).		

Source: Author

Objectives of the Study

1. To investigate the correlation between demographic variables and consumers' perceived quality (PQ) and purchase intention (PI).
2. To assess the influence of sensory marketing elements on perceived quality (PQ) within fast food chains.
3. To identify the most impactful sensory elements in shaping perceived quality (PQ) within fast food chains.

Research Methodology

Research design
- Examined the influence of five sensory elements on customers' quality perceptions.
- Identified the impact of visual, auditory, tactile, olfactory, and gustatory factors on customer quality perception.

Sample size, design and collection
- Utilized Multistage Sampling with Convenience Sub-sampling for data collection.
- Gathered data from 120 customers across six major fast-food restaurants in Kerala's three major cities: Trivandrum, Kozhikode, and Cochin.
- Focused on popular fast-food chains including McDonald's, KFC, Subway, Pizza Hut, Starbucks, and Burger King outlets.

Generation of scale items
- Employed multi-item scales to measure all constructs in the model.
- Items were adapted from literature reviews and tailored to the study's context.
- Used a five-point Likert-type scale for respondents to rate their level of agreement.

Measurement validation
- Calculated Cronbach's alpha to assess internal consistency and reliability of variables.

Table 174.2 Statistics showing reliability.

Cronbach's α	Variables
0.856	5

Source: Author

- Ensured reliability and validity of data collected for robust statistical analysis.

Statistical tools applied
- Utilized descriptive statistics (e.g., mean, mode, median, variance, standard deviation) to summarize variables.
- Calculated Pearson's correlation coefficient to determine relationships between variables.
- Employed multiple regression and Chi-square analyses for comprehensive data analysis.
- Selected statistical methods aimed at rigorous analysis and identification of key patterns and relationships.

Analysis

Reliability testing yielded a Cronbach's alpha coefficient of .856, indicating high reliability for environmental, monetary, promotional factors, sensory marketing elements, perceived quality, and purchase intention. Next, normality testing will determine suitable statistical tests for the study.

Test 1: Kolmogorov-Smirnov test; Test 2: Shapiro-Wilk test. Normality analysis reveals all variables are non-normally distributed ($p < 0.05$), warranting non-parametric tests. For the relationship between visual marketing and perceived quality:

- Null hypothesis (Ho): No significant association between visual marketing and perceived quality.
- Alternative hypothesis (H1): Significant association between visual marketing and perceived quality.

Table 174.3 Normality test.

	Test 1 – p value	Test 2 – p value
Visual marketing	.000	.014
Auditory marketing	.029	.023
Olfactory marketing	.000	.003
Gustatory marketing	.000	.000
Tactile marketing	.000	.001
Overall experience	.025	.012
Perceived quality	.000	.000
Purchase intention	.000	.001

Source: Computed from primary data collected by the author

Visual marketing and perceived quality:
- Null hypothesis (Ho): No significant association.
- Alternative hypothesis (H1): Significant association.
- Test result: Pearson Chi-square (P value = .000).
- Conclusion: H1 accepted, indicating no relation between Visual Marketing and Perceived Quality.

Auditory marketing and perceived quality
- Ho: No significant relationship.
- H1: Significant relationship.
- Test Result: Pearson Chi-Square (P value = .000).
- Conclusion: H1 accepted, suggesting no relation between Auditory Marketing and Perceived Quality.

Olfactory marketing and perceived quality
- Ho: No significant association.
- H1: Significant association.
- Test Result: Pearson Chi-Square (P value = .000).
- Conclusion: H1 accepted, indicating no relation between Olfactory Marketing and Perceived Quality.

Gustatory marketing and perceived quality
- Ho: No statistically significant relationship.
- H1: Statistically significant relationship.
- Test result: Pearson Chi-Square (P value = .000).
- Conclusion: H1 accepted, suggesting no relation between gustatory marketing and perceived quality.

Tactile marketing and perceived quality
- Ho: No significant correlation.
- H1: Significant correlation.
- Test result: Pearson Chi-Square (P value = .000).

- Conclusion: H1 accepted, indicating no relation between tactile marketing and perceived quality.

Overall experience and perceived quality
- Ho: No significant correlation.
- H1: Significant correlation.
- Test result: Pearson Chi-square (P value = .000).
- Conclusion: H1 accepted, suggesting no relation between Overall Experience and Perceived Quality.

Overall experience and purchase intention
- Ho: No significant correlation.
- H1: Significant correlation.
- Test result: Pearson Chi-Square (P value = .000).
- Conclusion: H1 accepted, indicating no relation between Overall Experience and Purchase Intention.

Perceived quality and purchase intention
- Ho: No significant correlation.
- H1: Significant correlation.
- Test Result: Pearson Chi-Square (P value = .000).
- Conclusion: H1 accepted, suggesting no relation between perceived quality and purchase intention.

Relation between PQ and PI with gender
- Ho: No significant correlation based on gender.
- H1: Significant correlation based on gender.
- Test result: Pearson Chi-square (PQ) = .787, Pearson Chi-square (PI) = .860.
- Conclusion: H0 accepted, indicating gender doesn't significantly impact PQ and PI.

Relation between PQ and PI with age:
- Ho: No significant correlation based on age.
- H1: Significant correlation based on age.
- Test result: Pearson Chi-Square (PQ) = .002, Pearson Chi-square (PI) = .579.
- Conclusion: H1 accepted for PQ and Age, suggesting each age category of respondents has a different impact on PQ.

The mean values vary across age groups, with the highest reported for the 18-30 age category and the lowest for those above 60 years.

Relation between PQ and PI with academic qualification

- Ho: No statistically significant relationship.
- H1: Statistically significant relationship.
- Test result: Pearson Chi-Square (PQ) = .779, Pearson Chi-Square (PI) = .112.

Table 174.4 Perceived quality report.

Please state your present age	Mean	N	Std. deviation
18-30years	19	58	2.74021
31-45years	18.9	30	2.68264
46-60years	18.24	25	3.24397
Above60years	15.4286	7	4.89412
Total	18.6083	120	3.06593

Source: Author

Table 174.5 Mean report between PQ and PI.

Please state your occupation		Perceived quality	Purchase intention
Student	Mean	18.8444	19.0222
	N	45	45
	Std. Deviation	2.93068	2.77562
Employed	Mean	19.5	19.1111
	N	36	36
	Std. Deviation	1.93465	2.61619
Self-employed	Mean	18.6818	18.6364
	N	22	22
	Std. Deviation	2.35809	2.23704
Business	Mean	16	17.7647
	N	17	17
	Std. Deviation	4.65027	3.32659
Total	Mean	18.6083	18.8
	N	120	120
	Std. Deviation	3.06593	2.72739

Source: Author

- Conclusion: HO accepted, indicating no significant relationship between PQ and PI with Academic Qualification.

Relation between PQ and PI with occupation
- Ho: No significant association.
- H1: Significant association.
- Test result: Pearson Chi-Square (PQ) = .035, Pearson Chi-Square (PI) = .038.
- Conclusion: H1 accepted, suggesting occupation significantly impacts PQ and PI. Each occupation category of respondents has a different impact on PQ and PI.

The mean values vary across different occupation categories of respondents. Specifically, the mean value is highest for the student category under PI, while it is highest for the employed category under PQ.

Relation between PQ and PI with annual income
- Ho: No significant association.
- H1: Significant association.
- Test result: Pearson Chi-square (PQ) = .262, Pearson Chi-square (PI) = .662.
- Conclusion: HO accepted, indicating no significant relationship between PQ and PI with annual income.

Relation between environmental factors and PI
- Ho: No significant association.
- H1: Significant association.
- Test result: Pearson Chi-square = .000.
- Conclusion: H1 accepted, indicating environmental factors do not influence PI.

Relation between monetary elements and PI
- Ho: No significant association.
- H1: Significant association.
- Test result: Pearson Chi-square = .374.
- Conclusion: HO accepted, indicating monetary elements do not influence PI.

Relation between promotional elements and PI
- Ho: No significant association.
- H1: Significant association.
- Test Result: Pearson Chi-Square = .010.
- Conclusion: H1 accepted, indicating promotional elements influence PI.

Findings and Suggestions

Findings from the study indicate that visual, auditory, olfactory, gustatory, and tactile elements showed no significant correlation with purchase intention in fast-food outlets. Similarly, overall experience, environmental factors, and promotional elements did not influence purchase intention. However, monetary factors notably impacted purchase intention. Additionally, demographic factors such as gender, age, academic qualification, occupation, and annual income showed varying degrees of influence on perceived quality and purchase intention. Suggestions derived from these findings emphasize the importance of service quality in fast-food outlets, the need for competitive pricing and regular offers to attract price-sensitive customers, and the recognition of subtle sensory influences despite their limited direct impact on perceived quality and purchase intention. Overall, addressing these factors holistically can enhance customer experience and drive repeat visits to fast-food establishments.

Conclusion

While this study sheds light on the factors influencing customer perceptions and purchase intentions in fast-food outlets, there remains ample scope for further research. The current study was limited to respondents from three cities and six multinational branded outlets, suggesting the need for broader sampling to ensure more representative results. Future research should expand beyond fast-food chains to encompass other food and beverage formats, while also exploring additional variables impacted by sensory marketing. Understanding how demographic factors intersect with sensory elements in areas like menu design and atmosphere could provide deeper insights. In conclusion, fast-food establishments must prioritize factors beyond promotions, emphasizing pricing, offers, facilities, and value for money. Sensory elements, though not primary drivers of quality perception, should be carefully curated to ensure positive customer experiences align with brand messaging.

References

Aaker, D. A. (1991). Managing Brand Equity: Capitalizing on the Value of a Brand Name. New York, NY: Free Press; Maxwell Macmillan Canada; Maxwell Macmillan International.

Bagozzi, R. P., and Burnkrant, R. E. (1979). Attitude organization and the attitude–behavior relationship. *Journal of Personality and Social Psychology,* 37(6), 913.

Beerli, A., Diaz-Meneses, G., and Martín-Santana, J. D. (2020). Satisfaction, image, and loyalty can be enhanced with congruent olfactory treatments: the acid test of optician franchise stores in shopping centres and on the high street. *Journal of Strategic Marketing,* 1–17.

Eiseman, L., and Pantone (Firm) (2017). The Complete Color Harmony: Expert Color Information for Professional Results (Pantone). Rockport Publishers, an imprint of The Quarto Group.

Krey, N., Babin, B. J., Wu, S., and Picot-Coupey, K. (2020). Multi-sensory experiences in retail service environments. In Argo, J., Lowrey, T. M., and Schau, H. J. (Eds.), Advances in Consumer Research (Vol. 48, pp. 537–540). Duluth, MN: Association for Consumer Research.

Quispillo, A. A. P., Narváez, D. L. G., Vasco, J. A. V., and Navarrete, C. F. V. (2022). Psychology of smell: its influence on the consumer in the boutiques of the city of Riobamba. *ESPOCH Congresses: The Ecuadorian Journal of STEAM.*

Spears, N., and Singh, S. N. (2004). Measuring attitude toward the brand and purchase intentions. *Journal of Current Issues and Research in Advertising,* 26(2), 53–66.

175 Digital marketing impact on arts and science students in Ernakulam's higher education institutes

Sinosh, P. K.[1,2,a] and Nandhini, M.[1]

[1]Karpagam Academy of Higher Education, Tamil Nadu, India

[2]Ilahia College of Engineering and Technology, Kerala, India

Abstract

The researcher has investigated the effectiveness of digital marketing in higher education among Arts and Science students. In a highly competitive environment, online marketing campaigns, especially through social media, have emerged as leveraging emerging technologies with widespread acceptance among students. In the present digital era, marketing departments of every organization have begun utilizing digital marketing to promote their products. In fact, students' search patterns have become digitalized over time. Now, higher education institutes are looking at the success rate of digital promotion in their marketplaces. Digitalisation has had a significant commercial impact and is cost-effective for educational institutions. The researcher has explored students' decision-making processes regarding the effects of digital media, employing an organized questionnaire to collect primary data with a sample size of 140 respondents.

Keywords: Decision making, digitalisation, higher education institutes, online marketing campaign, social media

Introduction

Digital marketing is considered a modern approach that allows marketers to connect with potential customers more effectively. It simplifies interactions with customers and aids in clearing their doubts. While digital marketing first emerged in the 1990s, its significance grew substantially after 2010. It facilitates the establishment of customer relationships and has become vital in marketing activities. With the widespread usage of the internet, internet marketing has gained prevalence, as people now spend more time online. Business owners must develop robust digital marketing strategies to capitalize on this trend.

The number of educational institutions, both public and private, has increased over the years. In today's competitive educational landscape, it's crucial to explore new and effective ways to reach prospective students. Online marketing campaigns have become increasingly important and are being adapted to new online marketing channels, surpassing conventional methods. Especially in the current pandemic period, online marketing campaigns have seen significant advancements, with institutions leveraging advanced technology to connect with students via the internet.

Digital Marketing Industry

India ranks as the 3rd largest internet user globally, with its digital marketing sector experiencing rapid growth across all industries. Research indicates that Indian youth are among the most frequent users of digital technology. In this digital age, leveraging marketing channels like websites, SEO, and social media is essential for reaching the right audience. Video content has gained popularity, with 80% of customers preferring it over print media due to its dynamic and engaging nature. Interacting with the audience enhances the effectiveness of digital platforms.

India's rapid digital development is evident, particularly in Kerala, a highly literate state where the majority of the population readily embraces the digital economy. Ernakulam, a leading technological hub in Kerala, reflects this trend, with its population engaged in busy lifestyles. Given the widespread recognition of online marketing as a prominent advertising strategy, it is crucial to design innovative online advertisements, leveraging platforms such as email and social media to effectively reach students.

Digitalisation plays a crucial role in today's competitive market, offering cost-saving opportunities for businesses. It streamlines operations, reduces the need for physical resources, and provides transparency, enabling students to make informed choices. Digital platforms ensure service quality, mitigate scams, and offer clarity, empowering students to make decisions freely.

[a]sinosh.icet@gmail.com

Literature Review

Table 175.1 Comparative analysis of studies on digital marketing in higher education.

Study authors (Year)	Main findings	Research methodology	Key insights
Nainudheen Afroz and Samanta (2015)	Digital marketing is essential for institutions to achieve better positioning, attracting students globally.	Desk research highlighting advantages and challenges of digital marketing.	Emphasizes cost reduction, improved measurability, and the need for skilled marketers in the digital era.
Narang and Sharma (2018)	Students extensively research online before choosing a higher education institution. Indian institutions are increasingly adopting digital marketing, but some are still catching up.	Exploratory and descriptive research using primary and secondary data.	Identifies top websites and factors driving website traffic for business schools. Mobile devices are a popular choice for accessing institute websites.
Basha (2019)	Digital marketing revolutionizes advertising in the education sector, offering cost-effectiveness and instant feedback.	Percentage analysis with 150 student respondents in Bangalore.	Highlights the importance of website visibility and social media presence for institutions. Recommends leveraging advancements in AI and technology for marketing.
Krishnamoorthy and Srimathi (2019)	Digital tools have reshaped the marketing mix in Indian higher education. Private institutes must focus on lead marketing and engage professional teams for strategic planning.	Survey among students, parents, and admission teams with 200 responses.	Advocates for using multiple digital channels and engaging professional corporate teams for effective outreach in a competitive landscape.
Kusumawati (2019)	Digital marketing influences students' decision-making processes, with universities adapting to new trends for effective marketing.	Qualitative research approach using semi-structured interviews and documentation.	Highlights the impact of digital marketing on student awareness and recommends leveraging social media for effective communication.
Islam and Shoron (2020)	Various factors influence students' decisions in selecting private universities in Bangladesh. Institutions employ diverse tactics to attract students.	Descriptive study with structured questionnaire survey among students from two private universities.	Identifies key factors such as university reputation, cost, and media presence influencing students' university choice.

Source: Author

Problem Statement

India's tech-savvy population, particularly the youth, has shifted from offline to online marketing, utilizing digital media for informed decision-making, prompting the need for investigating their changing behaviour through demographic variables and socio-economic profiles to ensure sustainable growth in the education sector.

Research Gap

Despite the prevalence of traditional marketing, online marketing remains underutilized in many educational institutions, particularly in Ernakulam District, necessitating further study to understand its impact on students' decision-making processes and its potential benefits for higher education institutes.

Objectives of the Study

1. To examine the demographic profile of the respondents.
2. To assess the participation level of students in online marketing campaigns conducted by higher education institutes.
3. To evaluate the relationship between the time spent by respondents on social media and their preference for social media when selecting institutions.

Research Methodology

The study employs descriptive research and stratified random sampling. Data will be gathered from arts and science students across 7 taluks in Ernakulum district, Kerala, with a sample size of 140. Primary and secondary sources will be utilized, with data collected from 2 colleges in each taluk, comprising 10 respondents each. A structured questionnaire validated through Cronbach's Alpha reliability and factor analysis will be used. Data analysis will be conducted using IBM SPSS Statistics 26.0.

Hypothesis

H_0: No significant relationship exists between time spent on social media and preference for choosing an institution. H_1: A significant relationship exists between time spent on social media and preference for choosing an institution. H_{20}: No significant relationship exists between time spent on social media and factors influencing institution choice. H_{21}: A relationship exists between time spent on social media and factors influencing institution choice. H_{30}: No significant relationship exists between students' participation level in online marketing and factors influencing the selection of an educational institution. H_{31}: A significant relationship exists between students' participation level in online marketing and factors influencing the selection of an educational institution.

Data Analysis and Interpretation

Cronbach's alpha reliability test
The reliability alpha value is greater than 0.7, which indicates that the data is reliable for analysis.

The study reveals that the majority of respondents are from self-financing institutions, with rural students showing a strong inclination towards online marketing. Most respondents fall within the 19-21 age category, with a near-even gender ratio. This year's admitted students show significant responsiveness to online marketing. The majority of respondents are graduates, particularly from arts backgrounds. Nearly half of the respondents' family income is below 10000, and most have not taken education loans. All students have a social media presence, with many spending over an hour daily, favouring platforms like WhatsApp and Instagram.

Virtual videos significantly influence the effectiveness of online marketing campaigns for higher

Table 175.2 Reliability statistics.

Cronbach's alpha	N of items
0.854	43

Source: Author

Table 175.3 Descriptive statistics.

Description	Items	Percentage
Type of institution	Government college	16.4
	Self-financing college	**63.6**
	Aided college	20
Area of residence	Urban	15
	Semi-Urban	28.6
	Rural	**56.4**
Age	17-18 Years	19.3
	19-21 Years	**73.6**
	22-24 Years	7.1
Gender	Male	45.7
	Female	**54.3**
Year of admission	2020	22.1
	2021	16.4
	2022	**61.4**
Qualification	**UG**	**67.1**
	PG	32.9
Stream	**Arts**	**55.7**
	Science	44.3
Monthly family income	**<10000**	**46.4**
	10k-15k	18.6
	15k-20k	7.9
	20k-25k	.7
	Above 25k	26.4
Education loan	Yes	8.6
	No	**91.4**
Social media connections	**Yes**	**100**
	No	0
Time spent	<30 Minutes	10.7
	30 Minutes- 1 Hour	18.6
	1-2 Hours	**28.6**
	2-3 Hours	17.1
	>3 Hours	25
Social media	Facebook	3.6
	YouTube	15
	Instagram	26.4
	Meet up	6.4
	WhatsApp	**47.9**
	Others	.7

Source: Author

Table 175.4 Influential factor.

Influential factor		
	Text message	9.3
	Posters	2.1
	Virtual video	**62.9**
	Peer reviews	5.7
	Faculty interact	4.3
	Infrastructure	4.3
	E-Brochure	11.4

Source: Author

Table 175.5 Cross tabulation of time spend on social media and social media preference.

	Value	df	Asymptotic Significance (2-sided)
Pearson Chi-square	47.103a	20	0.001
Likelihood ratio	48.593	20	0
Linear-by-linear association	0.249	1	0.618
No. of valid cases	140		

Source: Author

education institutions, along with text messages and e-brochures, while posters, infrastructure, and faculty interaction have lesser influence on students' decision-making processes.

Chi-square tests

H_0: There is no relationship between the time spend on social media and social media preference in choosing institution.

The p-value being less than 0.05 indicates a significant relationship between the time spent on social media and the preference for using social media in choosing an educational institution, implying that the duration of social media usage influences their decision-making process regarding educational institutions.

H_0: There is no relationship between the Time spend on social media and factors that influenced in choosing institution.

The p-value being less than the standard alpha value of 0.05 suggests rejecting the null hypothesis, indicating a relationship between the time spent on social media and factors influencing the choice of institution. Particularly, virtual videos have demonstrated a significant impact among these factors.

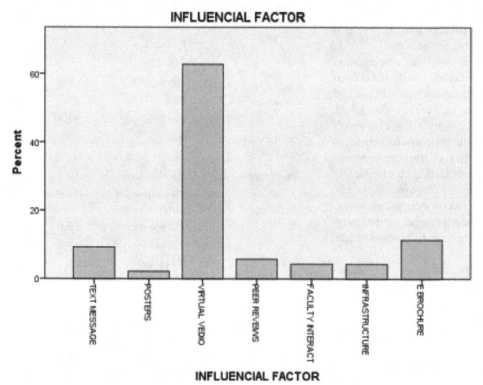

Figure 175.1 Influential factor
Source: Author

Table 175.6 Time spent on social media and factors that influenced in choosing institution.

	Value	df	Asymptotic significance (2-sided)
Pearson Chi-square	102.945a	24	0
Likelihood ratio	105.909	24	0.004
Linear-by-linear association	12.345	1	0.031
No of valid cases	140		

Source: Author

One-way ANOVA

H_0: There is no significant relationship between participation level of students in online marketing and factors influencing the selection of educational institution.

The higher F statistics value compared to the alpha value and a p-value less than 0.05 indicate the rejection of the null hypothesis, suggesting a significant relationship between students' participation level in online marketing and factors influencing their choice of educational institution. These

Table 175.7 One-way ANOVA: participation profile and decision profile.

ANOVA

		Sum of Squares	df	Mean square	F	Sig.
Online campaign is recommended	Between groups	8.256	4	2.064	5.012	.001
	Within groups	55.594	135	.412		
	Total	63.850	139			
Website content was attractive	Between groups	6.702	4	1.675	3.327	.012
	Within groups	67.984	135	.504		
	Total	74.686	139			
Online marketing campaign capture attention	Between groups	16.724	4	4.181	11.719	.000
	Within groups	48.162	135	.357		
	Total	64.886	139			

Source: Author

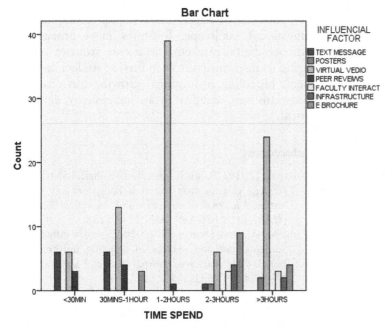

Figure 175.2 Cross tabulated data of time spend and influential factor
Source: Author

findings highlight the substantial impact of social media marketing on students' decisions regarding institution selection.

Findings

- The majority of respondents come from self-financing institutions in rural areas, with ages ranging from 19 to 21.
- All respondents are active on social media, predominantly using WhatsApp and Instagram.
- Virtual videos have a significant impact on the effectiveness of online marketing campaigns for higher education institutions.
- Educational institutions effectively employ digital marketing strategies among students.
- Online marketing is utilized by higher education institutions to disseminate information.
- Decision-making factors greatly influence students' selection of educational institutions.
- Virtual videos emerge as a particularly influential factor among various decision-making criteria.
- The level of student engagement in online marketing significantly affects their choice of higher education institution.
- There exists a significant relationship between the time spent on social media and students' social media preferences when choosing a higher education institution.

Suggestions

- Students should be equipped with adequate technological skills to effectively utilize digital marketing platforms.
- Continuous technological advancements should be encouraged among respondents for enhanced engagement with digital marketing.
- Educational institutes must ensure comprehensive information dissemination through online marketing channels.
- Implementing a transparent and efficient feedback system is essential for engaging respondents in online marketing.
- Regular updates of online information are vital for maintaining institutional reputation and meeting the evolving needs of respondents.

Conclusion

In this comprehensive study, an in-depth analysis of various facets of digital marketing within the educational sector has been undertaken, shedding light on its pivotal role in establishing connections between educational institutes and students. Through meticulous examination, it has become evident that digital marketing stands as the cornerstone for effective communication and engagement with students in today's technologically-driven landscape.

The findings shed light on the critical importance of educational institutes establishing dynamic and interactive digital platforms to harness the full potential of digital marketing strategies. Such platforms serve as essential conduits for disseminating information, improving engagement, and building relationships with students across diverse channels.

Furthermore, the integration of all institutional systems with digital platforms emerges as a crucial imperative in the contemporary educational milieu. This integration not only streamlines processes but also enhances accessibility, responsiveness, and overall user experience, thereby reinforcing the institute's digital presence and relevance.

Central to the success of digital marketing initiatives is the adoption of fundamental principles and best practices in social media marketing. Institutes must adeptly navigate the digital landscape, employing targeted strategies to engage and resonate with their target audience effectively. By embracing these strategies, institutes can position themselves as industry leaders, leveraging digital platforms to cultivate brand identity, enhance reputation, and deliver value-added services tailored to meet the evolving needs and expectations of students.

In essence, the study emphasises on the transformative potential of digital marketing in reshaping the educational landscape. Institutes must proactively embrace digital marketing as a core strategy, recognizing its instrumental role in driving student engagement, providing institutional growth, and ensuring long-term sustainability in an increasingly digitised world.

References

Basha, A. (2019). A study on effective digital marketing strategy in education sector at Bangalore city. *International Journal of Research and Analytical Reviews (IJAR)*, 6(1), 161–169. ISSN 2349-5138.

Islam, M. A., and Shoron, N. (2020). Factors influencing students' decision making in selecting university in Bangladesh. *Advanced Journal of Social Science*, 6(1), 17–25. ISSN 2581-3358.

Krishnamoorthy, A., and Srimathi, H. (2019). Digital marketing and strategic planning in higher education. *International Journal of Scientific Technology Research*, 8(10), 3326–3329. ISSN 2277-8616.

Kusumawati, A. (2019). Impact of digital marketing on student decision making process of higher education Institutions: a case study of Indonesia. *International Journal*, 1(1), 1–11. Article ID 267057, ISSN 2169-0359.

Nainudheen Afroz, S. B., and Samanta, D. (2015). Influence of digital marketing on students. *International Journal of Advanced Trends in Computer Science and Engineering (IJATCSE)*, 4(5), 16–18. ISSN No.2278-3091.

Narang, K. V., and Sharma, B. (2018). Rise of digital marketing in higher education in India. *International Journal of Research*, 7(8), 25–25. ISSN No.2236-6124.

176 A study on factors influencing satisfaction of women entrepreneurs at Coimbatore district

Sathiyabama, P.[1,a], Velmurugan, R.[2,b], Rekha Kiran Kumar, T.[1,c] and Preetha Rajendran, R.[3,d]

[1]SRM Institute of Science and Technology, Tamil Nadu, India
[2]Karpagam Academy of Higher Education, Tamil Nadu, India
[3]VLB Janakiammal College of Arts and Science, Tamil Nadu, India

Abstract

Entrepreneurs contribute significantly to economic development by offering more employment opportunities to unemployed youth and providing goods to customers at low cost. In this regard, women entrepreneurs also play a significant role in economic progress. Satisfied entrepreneurs may choose to continue or expand their businesses, and women entrepreneurs are no exception to this. However, unsatisfied entrepreneurs may decide to close their business ventures, which can hamper economic development. Thus, factors determining entrepreneurial satisfaction are considered in this study. The results revealed that financial support from bankers and financial institutions, as well as government schemes and subsidies for women entrepreneurs, lead to higher satisfaction among women entrepreneurs.

Keywords: Empowerment, factors, financial support, influencing, satisfaction, scheme and subsidies, society, women entrepreneurs

Introduction

Entrepreneurship has gained increasing significance in recent years, as highlighted by Kamaraj and Pandu (2013). In order to promote the social and economic empowerment of women, governments have introduced numerous schemes specifically aimed at fostering women entrepreneurship. Consequently, women are increasingly entering the entrepreneurial profession with various motivations, such as improving their family's financial condition, utilizing their knowledge for societal development, and achieving independence. As a result, women entrepreneurs have emerged as a crucial driving force for economic development, as noted by Ranjana Sharma (2017). The sustainability of women entrepreneurs is closely linked to the support they receive from their families and their ability to address challenges related to finance, raw materials, labor, and other operational aspects. Most importantly, their sustainability is closely related to how happy they are with their chosen careers. Success and fulfilment go hand in hand, with fulfilment coming from women entrepreneurs being recognised by their families, coworkers, and society. According to Ewere et al. (2015), this self-satisfaction serves as a strong drive for women entrepreneurs to grow their firms. Women entrepreneurs feel satisfied when they can quickly obtain the money they need, easily gather enough labour and raw supplies, get support from their families and friends, and generate profitable returns on their investments. On the other hand, dissatisfied female business owners might not stick with their ventures in the long run, which could have an impact on both their own economic development and global economic expansion. Therefore, the present study aims to identify and explore the factors that enhance the satisfaction of women entrepreneurs in Coimbatore District. By understanding these factors, policymakers, support organizations, and stakeholders can devise strategies and interventions that foster an enabling environment for women entrepreneurs. The study seeks to contribute to the body of knowledge on women entrepreneurship and provide valuable insights to enhance the satisfaction and sustainability of women entrepreneurs, ultimately driving economic development in the region.

[a]sathiyaradha.p@gmail.com, [b]drvelsngm@gmail.com, [c]hod.bba.rmp@srmist.edu.in, [d]preethajaisankar@gmail.com

Literature Review

Table 176.1 Key findings from studies on factors influencing entrepreneurial satisfaction.

Study authors	Year	Key findings
Hobfoll and London	(1986)	Social support influences women entrepreneurs' satisfaction.
Cooper and Artz	(1995)	Entrepreneurs are satisfied with their firm performance.
Venna Bhatnagar	(1995)	Difficulty in arranging collateral security and guarantor, delay in sanctioning working capital loan lead to entrepreneur's dissatisfaction.
Wooden	(1997)	Entrepreneurs are more satisfied with their independence.
Feldman and Bolino	(2000)	Start-up motive influences entrepreneurial satisfaction.
Tripathi and Muley	(2007)	Insufficient infrastructure facilities, poor transportation facility and labor shortage lead to entrepreneur's dissatisfaction.
Jyoti et al.	(2011)	Women entrepreneurs are satisfied with family support and business earnings.
Carree and Verheul	(2011)	Women entrepreneurs are satisfied with their earnings.
Nehru and Bhardwaj	(2013)	Women entrepreneurs are happy to involve in social and economic development of the nation, Government initiatives and societal attitude changes contribute to their satisfaction.
Manimekalai and Bharathy	(2013)	Support extended by family members and profitability increases women entrepreneurs' satisfaction.
Muhammad Billyaminu Ado	(2016)	Entrepreneurs are satisfied with entrepreneur development programs organized by various Government agencies.
Chakraborty	(2019)	Women entrepreneurs who are able to manage family and business simultaneously have a high level of satisfaction.

Source: Author

Problem Statement

The lack of satisfaction among women entrepreneurs poses a significant challenge to economic and family empowerment. Dissatisfaction may lead to the closure of businesses, impeding economic recovery, limiting employment opportunities, and hindering consumer access to goods and services. To address this, a comprehensive study is needed to identify factors influencing satisfaction. Through this research, tailored policies and support systems can be developed to foster a conducive environment for female entrepreneurs, promoting their success and contributing to broader societal and economic advancement.

Objectives of the Study

* To ascertain the demographic factors and business profile of women entrepreneurs in the study area.
* To find out the satisfaction level of women entrepreneurs in Coimbatore District.

Research Methodology

Data: Primary data collected with the help of Questionnaire.

Sampling method: By employing convenient sampling data have been gathered from 150 women entrepreneurs in Coimbatore district.

Tools Employed: Simple percentage and Factor Analysis is employed for analysis.

Significance of the Study

The study on factors influencing the satisfaction of women entrepreneurs holds significance for various stakeholders. Female entrepreneurs gain insightful self-awareness, enabling them to design strategies for success. Policymakers can develop gender-responsive policies, fostering diverse and encouraging entrepreneurship ecosystems. Support organizations can tailor mentorship and training programs to better serve women entrepreneurs' needs, enhancing their satisfaction. Financial institutions can create products suited to female entrepreneurs, improving access to finance. Academics benefit from expanding knowledge on female entrepreneurship. NGOs can use insights for advocacy and capacity-building, ultimately empowering women entrepreneurs and fostering their financial success.

Findings

Socio-economic profile of women entrepreneurs

- Female entrepreneurs, typically aged over 40, bring valuable experience and skills acquired over time, offering a competitive edge in their business ventures.
- Many women, with undergraduate qualifications, opt for entrepreneurship, seeing it as a viable career path even without advanced degrees.
- Married women in nuclear families often find support and flexibility conducive to entrepreneurship, with shared responsibilities and a wider network.
- Families with two earners provide a stable financial base, reducing the risks associated with entrepreneurship and enabling a more equitable division of household tasks.
- Women entrepreneurs, especially those in high-demand fields, can earn substantial incomes through innovative offerings, scalable business models, and targeting affluent markets.

Business profile

- Service-based businesses are favored by most women entrepreneurs due to lower startup costs, flexibility, and the opportunity to leverage their skills in fields like consulting, coaching, and healthcare.
- Sole proprietorship is the preferred business structure for many women entrepreneurs as it offers simplicity, full control, and flexibility in decision-making.
- Women entrepreneurs often employ a mix of skilled and unskilled workers to meet various business needs, balancing costs and skill requirements as their businesses grow.
- Urban areas attract the majority of women entrepreneurs due to larger customer bases, better

Table 176.2 Socio-Economic Profile of Women Entrepreneurs.

Particulars	Numbers (150)	Percentage
Age (Years)		
Up to 30	30	20.0
31-40	48	32.0
Above 40	72	48.0
Educational Qualification		
SSLC	48	32.0
H.Sc.	21	14.0
Under Graduate	60	40.0
Post Graduate	15	10.0
Professional	6	4.0
Marital Status		
Married	141	94.0
Unmarried	9	6.0
Type of Family		
Joint	63	42.0
Nuclear	87	58.0
Earning Members		
One	12	8.0
Two	120	80.0
Above Two	18	12.0
Monthly Income (Rs.)		
Up to 15000	36	24.0
15001-30000	54	36.0
Above 30000	60	40.0

Source: Author

Table 176.3 Business profile of women entrepreneurs.

Nature of business		
Production	30	20.0
Trading	54	36.0
Service	66	44.0
Form of business		
Sole proprietorship	135	90.0
Partnership	15	10.0
Nature of workers		
Skilled	39	26.0
Semiskilled	45	30.0
Both	66	44.0
Location of business		
Urban	96	64.0
Semi urban	39	26.0
Rural	15	10.0
Experience in business		
Up to 5	54	36.0
6-10	72	48.0
Above 10	24	16.0
First generation entrepreneur		
Yes	129	86.0
No	21	14.0
Initial investment (Rs.)		
Up to 250000	90	60.0
250001-500000	36	24.0
Above 500000	24	16.0

Source: Author

infrastructure, networking opportunities, and access to support services.

- Women entrepreneurs typically gain significant experience over six to ten years, learning from successes and failures while establishing their businesses.
- The majority of women entrepreneurs belong to the first generation, driven by changing gender roles, aspirations for independence, and the lack of inherited businesses.
- Initial investments for women entrepreneurs commonly range up to Rs. 250,000, reflecting bootstrapping strategies, low startup costs, and cautious financial management.

Entrepreneurs satisfaction

Factor analysis is utilized to identify crucial factors that enhance the satisfaction of women entrepreneurs. The application of factor analysis reveals that the data and sample are suitable for conducting the analysis, as evidenced by the results of the Kaiser-Meyer-Olkin (KMO) test and Bartlett's test.

The result of the factor analysis indicates that women entrepreneur's express satisfaction in several key areas that contribute to their overall entrepreneurial experience. Let's explore each factor in detail:

- **Financial support from banks and financial institutions**: Women entrepreneurs are satisfied with loans, credit facilities, and financial resources, highlighting the importance of access to funding for business growth.
- **Government schemes/subsidies**: Women entrepreneurs report satisfaction with grants, tax incentives, and other forms of financial assistance, indicating the effectiveness of government support in promoting their success.
- **Procedure to avail loan**: Women express satisfaction with streamlined loan application processes, emphasizing the positive impact of accessible procedures on satisfaction levels.
- **Social support**: Women appreciate guidance and encouragement from mentors, peers, and support groups, contributing to their satisfaction as they navigate entrepreneurship.

- **Family support**: Satisfaction with understanding and assistance from family members in balancing business and personal responsibilities positively affects overall satisfaction.
- **Training attended**: Satisfaction with training programs suggests enhanced knowledge, skills, and confidence leading to improved entrepreneurial outcomes.
- **Achieving better work-life balance**: Satisfaction in managing business and personal commitments indicates successful integration of professional and personal life.
- **Profitability and returns:** Contentment with financial performance reflects successful outcomes and efforts yielding profitable returns.
- **Availability of raw material**: Satisfaction with access to necessary inputs contributes to uninterrupted operations and production.
- **Availability of labor:** Contentment with skilled labor availability indicates smooth business operations and meeting business needs.

Collectively, these factors contribute to 75.541% of women entrepreneurs' overall satisfaction, underscoring their significance in shaping experiences and

Table 176.4 KMO and Bartlett's test.

Kaiser-Meyer-Olkin measure of sampling adequacy.		.752
Bartlett's test of sphericity	Approx. Chi-square	653.840
	df	45
	Sig.	.000

Source: Author

Table 176.5 Factors influencing Satisfaction Level of Women Entrepreneurs.

Particulars	1	2	3	4
Financial support from banks and other financial institutions	.948			
Government schemes/subsidies	.933			
Procedure to avail loan	.838			
Social support		.863		
Family Support		.751		
Training attended		.683		
Achieve better work-life balance			.865	
Profitability and returns			.780	
Availability of raw material				.802
Availability of labor				.789
Eigen values	2.896	1.915	1.482	1.261
% of variance	28.964	19.145	14.820	12.612
Cumulative % of variance	28.964	48.109	62.929	75.541

Source: Author

perceptions, and addressing these areas can enhance satisfaction and overall entrepreneurial success.

Suggestions

- Financial support: Promote financial assistance programs, create tailored lending products, and streamline loan application processes to enhance accessibility and effectiveness.
- Government initiatives: Launch specialized grants, provide training, and offer tax breaks to support female entrepreneurs, fostering their success.
- Loan application simplification: Reduce documentation requirements, make procedures transparent, and introduce user-friendly electronic systems for loan applications.
- Networking and mentoring: Establish mentoring programs, facilitate networking opportunities, and collaborate with organizations to provide support services.
- Family involvement: Educate families about entrepreneurship, encourage open communication, and share experiences to garner support for women entrepreneurs.
- Tailored Training: Develop training programs covering various aspects of entrepreneurship and mentorship opportunities tailored to women's needs.
- Work-life balance: Encourage setting boundaries, delegating tasks, and implementing time management techniques to balance personal and professional life effectively.

Conclusion

In conclusion, the satisfaction of entrepreneurs, particularly women entrepreneurs, plays a vital role in driving economic growth through job creation and the provision of affordable goods and services. This study aimed to identify factors influencing the satisfaction of female entrepreneurs, revealing the significant contributions of government programs, financial assistance, and supportive environments to their overall satisfaction. Recognizing the importance of women entrepreneurs' happiness is essential for sustaining business growth and fostering economic prosperity. Policymakers, financial institutions, and support groups can enhance satisfaction levels by tailoring initiatives and programs to address specific needs. By providing adequate resources and fostering an enabling environment, we can harness the potential of female entrepreneurs to drive economic growth, promote gender equality, and build inclusive societies.

Moving forward, further research in the Coimbatore district could delve into specific elements affecting satisfaction, explore cultural and social dynamics, compare satisfaction levels across regions or industries, evaluate program effectiveness, and track long-term satisfaction trends. Qualitative research methods can provide deeper insights into women entrepreneurs' experiences and inform policy recommendations to better support their success and contribute to regional economic growth.

References

Carree, M. A., and Verheul, I. (2011). What makes entrepreneurs Happy? determinants of satisfaction among founders. *Journal of Happiness Studies.*

Chakraborty, T. (2019). Nothing will work unless you do it: contextualizing women entrepreneurship. *Global Journal of Management and Business Research.*

Cooper, A. C., and Artz, K. W. (1995). Determinants of satisfaction for entrepreneurs. *Journal of Business Venturing,* 10, 439–457.

Ewere, A. D., Adu, E. O., and Ibrahim, S. I. (2015). Strategies adopted by women entrepreneurs to ensure small business success in the Nkonkobe municipality. *Journal of Economics,* 6(1), 1–7.

Feldman, D. C., and Bolino, M. C. (2000). Career patterns of the self-employed: career motivations and career outcomes. *Journal of Small Business Management,* 38(3), 53–67.

Hobfoll, S. E., and London, P. (1986). The relationship of self-concept and social support to emotional distress among women during war. *Journal of Social and Clinical Psychology,* 4, 189–203.

Jyoti, J. et al. (2011). Factors affecting orientation and satisfaction of women entrepreneurs in rural India. *Annals of Innovation and Entrepreneurship,* 1–13.

Kamaraj, S., and Pandu, A. (2013). Job satisfaction of women entrepreneurs with special reference to self-help groups of Vellore district. *International Journal of Management and Development Studies,* 2(8).

Manimekalai, P., and Bharathy, R. S. (2013). A study on satisfaction level of women entrepreneurs in the dairy sector in Salem district of Tamil Nadu. *Pacific Journal of Research,* 1(4), 43–53.

Nehru, J., and Bhardwaj, S. (2013). Women entrepreneurship in India: issues and problems "you can tell the condition of a nation by looking at the status of its women. *Spectrum: A Journal of Multidisciplinary Research,* 2(7), 8–16.

177 Factors influencing job satisfaction of female teachers in Coimbatore arts and science colleges

Velmurugan, R.[1,a], Kavitha, R[2,b], Kalimuthu, M.[3,c], Madraswale, M. A.[4,d] and Padmanabhan, V.[5,e]

[1]Karpagam Academy of Higher Education, Tamil Nadu, India

[2]Sakthi Institute of Information and Management Studies, Tamil Nadu, India

[3]Dr.N.G.P. Arts and Science College, Tamil Nadu, India

[4]Associate Professor, School of Management, Presidency University, Bengaluru, India

[5]Principal, K.S.R. College of Arts and Science, Tiruchengode, Tamil Nadu, India

Abstract

Teachers who are satisfied with their jobs are likely to be dedicated to the organization, contributing fully to the growth of the school and the students. Job dissatisfaction leads to high absenteeism rates, employee turnover, and lack of dedication, among other issues. Teacher job dissatisfaction can hinder student and institutional development. To enable women teachers to effectively manage their professional and personal lives in a balanced and stress-free manner, management must provide necessary facilities and foster a pleasant working environment. Women teachers who can balance work and leisure while remaining stress-free are likely to experience high levels of job satisfaction.

Keywords: Job satisfaction, stress, teachers, work-life balance

Introduction

The development of human capital serves as a crucial indicator of national progress, with higher education playing a pivotal role in cultivating human resources. Moreover, higher education fosters social cohesion, individual growth, economic prosperity, and technological advancement. However, due to financial constraints, governments cannot solely bear the burden of establishing higher education institutions across every region. Consequently, private participation in higher education has been permitted, leading to the establishment of numerous private arts, science, engineering colleges, and deemed universities in India.

The primary objective behind the proliferation of higher education institutions is to provide high-quality education for the advancement of both individuals and the nation. While infrastructure undoubtedly influences student development, the quality of teachers is equally essential. Women constitute a significant portion of the teaching profession, and their roles are continually expanding. Balancing familial responsibilities with professional duties poses a challenge for women teachers. Those who manage to maintain this balance experience reduced stress levels and higher job satisfaction.

Unsatisfied women teachers may lack dedication and commitment to their profession and institution, resulting in decreased job commitment and high attrition rates, thus hindering the objectives of education privatisation. Achieving teacher satisfaction requires not only institutional support but also familial cooperation. Family members must offer necessary support and autonomy to women teachers, while educational institutions should provide adequate infrastructure, career growth opportunities, and a supportive work environment.

Satisfied teachers play a pivotal role in laying a strong foundation for students' knowledge development and guiding them to become socially responsible citizens. This study aims to identify how women teachers manage work-life balance, assess the level of stress they face, and determine the factors influencing their job satisfaction. Ultimately, the goal is to ensure that women teachers are supported in their professional and personal endeavours, contributing positively to both institutional and national development.

[a]drvelsngm@gmail.com, [b]kavithakanagu1976@gmail.com, [c]kalimuthusujanias@gmail.com, [d]maksudm@gmail.com, [e]padmanaban81@gmail.com

Literature Review

Table 177.1 Summary of key findings from selected studies on factors influencing teacher Job Satisfaction.

Reference	Key findings
Deepthy (2008)	Urban-based schools with pleasant working environments correlate with high job satisfaction among female teachers.
Alam (2009)	Job stress significantly influences teachers' job satisfaction.
Bhandari and Patil (2009)	Job nature, salary, and working environment are influential factors affecting teachers' job satisfaction.
Chamundeswari and Vasanthi (2009)	Highly committed teachers tend to exhibit high levels of job satisfaction.
Dhillon et al. (2009)	Job content and working environment are primary determinants of job satisfaction.
Gupta and Sahu (2009)	Female teachers generally exhibit lower job satisfaction compared to male counterparts.
Ali and Akhtar (2009)	Female teachers with post-graduate qualifications demonstrate higher job satisfaction.
Du et al. (2009)	Pay scale, career growth opportunities, and facilities for teaching and research contribute to job satisfaction.
Saveri (2009)	The standard of living is closely linked to teachers' job satisfaction.
Sharma et al. (2009)	Work atmosphere significantly impacts teacher job satisfaction.

Source: Author

Problem Statement

Satisfied teachers demonstrate organizational commitment, fostering student and institutional development. Conversely, job dissatisfaction results in absenteeism, turnover, and decreased commitment, hindering growth. To mitigate this, management must provide necessary facilities and a pleasant working environment. Women teachers capable of balancing work and life experience reduced stress and higher job satisfaction.

Objective of the Study

- To identify factors influencing teachers' job satisfaction.

Scope of the Study

- Focuses on select arts and science colleges in Coimbatore district, Tamil Nadu.
- Specifically examines female teachers' job satisfaction and socioeconomic factors.

Research Methodology

- **Data:** Primary data collected via questionnaires.
- **Sampling technique:** Random sampling of 515 female faculty members.
- **Statistical tools:** Analysis conducted using simple percentage and correlation.

Area of Study

- Examines job satisfaction among arts and science college teachers in Coimbatore district.
- Coimbatore, a major education hub, hosts numerous higher education institutions.
- Women are predominantly employed as faculty in these colleges.

Analysis and Interpretation

The following paragraph discusses about socio-economic profile of teachers and factors influencing job satisfaction.

The analysis reveals that most teachers fall within the age bracket of 26 to 40 years, residing primarily in urban and semi-urban areas. The majority are married and hold an M.Phil. qualification. Monthly incomes are predominantly within the range of Rs. 15,001-30,000, with family incomes between Rs. 30,001 and Rs. 60,000. Family expenditures typically range from Rs. 20,001-40,000.

Determining factors of job satisfaction among college teachers

Factor analysis has been employed to identify key elements significantly enhancing the job satisfaction of female teachers. The table provided highlights the crucial factors contributing to job satisfaction. Pre-analysis testing, including the Kaiser-Meyer-Olkin (KMO) and Bartlett's test of sphericity, has been

Table 177.2 Socio economic profile.

Particulars	Numbers	Percentage
Age		
Up to 25	118	22.9
26 to 40	293	56.9
Above 40	104	20.2
Area of residence		
Urban	199	38.6
Semi urban	199	38.6
Rural	117	22.7
Marital status		
Married	353	68.5
Unmarried	162	31.5
Educational qualification		
PG	56	10.9

Particulars	Numbers	Percentage
M.Phil.	332	64.5
Ph.D.	127	24.7
Monthly Income		
Up to 15000	23	4.5
15001-30000	441	85.6
Above 30000	51	9.9
Family Income		
Up to 30000	44	8.5
30001-60000	294	57.1
Above 60000	177	34.4
Family expenditure		
Up to 20000	95	18.4
20001-40000	282	54.8
Above 40000	138	26.8

Source: Author

conducted to ensure the adequacy of the sample for factor analysis. The results indicate suitability for factor analysis, with KMO and Bartlett's test results exceeding 0.70. Furthermore, Bartlett's test of sphericity (1474.713, df: 465, Sig = 0.000) and KMO statistics (0.755) affirm the sufficiency of the sample size for analysis.

The results of factor analysis reveal that the primary sources of satisfaction among teachers are recognition received from superiors, salary revision, increments for additional qualifications, frequency of salary revisions, promptness in salary payment, and infrastructure facilities such as water and toilet amenities. These factors collectively contribute to teachers' satisfaction, accounting for 56.021 percent of the variance.

Suggestions

1. Senior faculty members should acknowledge and support newly joined faculty to adapt to the existing working environment effectively.
2. Management should regularly review and adjust teachers' salaries based on feedback and their contributions to student and institutional growth.
3. Provide appropriate monetary and non-monetary incentives for faculty who enhance their qualifications.
4. Regularly update faculty salaries to match inflation rates and ensure adequate infrastructure for seamless teaching.
5. Assign classes to new faculty members based on their expertise and specialization with guidance from senior staff.
6. Create work schedules that accommodate both students and faculty, promoting work-life balance.
7. Adhere to UGC regulations on class sizes and student-staff ratios to prevent overcrowding and reduce teacher workload.

Table 177.3 KMO and Bartlett's test.

Kaiser-Meyer-Olkin measure of sampling adequacy.		.755
Bartlett's test of sphericity	Approx. Chi-square	1474.713
	df	465
	Sig.	.000

Source: Author

Table 177.4 Factors determining teachers job satisfaction.

Particulars	1	2	3	4	5
Recognition from superiors	.717				
Revision of salary	.639				
Salary	.663				

Particulars	1	2	3	4	5
Increment for additional qualification	.587				
Frequency of salary revision	.526				
Water facility		.584			
Toilet facility		.563			
Promptness in salary payment		.502			
Team spirit		.659			
Allotment of preferred class		.641			
Leisure hours			.749		
Superior's support			.683		
Layout of classroom			.539		
Canteen facility			.769		
Teaching aid			.567		
Professional growth				.749	
Colleague's support				.746	
Working time				.597	
Students co-operation				.692	
Work autonomy				.816	
Strength of class					.847
Eigen values	1.174	1.140	1.104	1.059	1.028
% of Variance	42.052	3.677	3.562	3.415	3.315
Cumulative % of variance	42.052	45.729	49.291	52.706	56.021

Source: Author

Conclusion

To alleviate economic pressures, many women pursue employment, contributing significantly across various professions, including teaching, where their presence often surpasses that of men. However, the multifaceted role of women educators demands significant time and effort to balance family and professional responsibilities. Struggling to manage these commitments can lead to stress and job dissatisfaction, affecting performance and retention. Recognizing and addressing factors such as timely salary revisions, recognition for work, and incentives for additional qualifications are crucial in enhancing job satisfaction among women teachers, ultimately fostering their commitment to student and institutional development.

References

Alam, S. S. (2009). A study of job stress on job satisfaction among university staff in Malaysia. *European Journal of Social Sciences*, 8(1), 105–128.

Ali, N., and Akhtar, Z. (2009). Job status, gender and level of education as determinants of job satisfaction of senior secondary school teachers. *Indian Journal Social Science Researches*, 6(1), 56–59.

Bhandari, A., and Patil, N. H. (2009). Job satisfaction of women teachers. *Edutracks*, 8(11).

Chamundeswari, S., and Vasanthi, S. (2009). A study to examine job satisfaction and occupational commitment among teachers. *Edutracks*, 8(6), 29–31.

Deepthy, T. (2008). Job satisfaction in relation to school environment of primary school teachers of Kozhikode (Dt). M Ed. Dissertation, Calicut University.

Dhillon, et al. (2009). Correlates of job satisfaction among college teachers. *Recent Research in Education and Psychology*, 14(1).

Du, P., Lai, M., and Lo, L. N. K. (2009). Analysis of job satisfaction of university professors from nine chineseuniversities. *Frontiers of Education in China*, 5(3), 430–449.

Gupta, V., and Sahu, K. (2009). Job satisfaction as related to organizational role stress and locus of control among vocational teachers. *Indian Journal of Psychometry and Education*, 40(1), 74–80.

Saveri (2009). Relationship between Job Satisfaction and Life Satisfaction among B.T Assistant Teachers. *Edutracks*, 8(9).

Sharma, et al. (2009). Relation between organizational health and job satisfaction of elementary school teachers. *Imperial Journal of Interdisciplinary Research*, 2(10).

178 A study on awareness on MNGREGA schemes

Manickavel, K.[1,a] and Sudarvel, J.[b]

[1]II M.Com. Karpagam Academy of Higher Education, Coimbatore, Tamil Nadu, India

[2]Assistant Professor of Management, Karpagam Academy of Higher Education, Coimbatore, Tamil Nadu, India

Abstract

This study aims to assess the level of awareness among residents of Coimbatore district regarding the Mahatma Gandhi National Rural Employment Guarantee Act (MGNREGA) schemes. MGNREGA is a flagship social welfare program in India that provides employment opportunities and wage security to rural households. The study employs a quantitative research design, utilizing a structured questionnaire survey to collect data from a representative sample of residents in Coimbatore district. The questionnaire includes items related to respondents' knowledge and understanding of MGNREGA schemes. The data collected will be analyzed using statistical techniques such as Simple percentage and weighted Average test to determine the level of awareness among respondents. Additionally, demographic factors such as age, gender, education, and socioeconomic status will be considered to explore potential variations in awareness levels. The findings of this study will provide valuable insights into the awareness levels of MGNREGA schemes in Coimbatore district, highlighting areas of improvement and identifying potential barriers to participation. The results can inform policymakers and program implementers on strategies to enhance awareness and ensure the effective implementation of MGNREGA schemes.

Keywords: Awareness, Coimbatore district, MGNREGA, rural employment, social welfare

Introduction

The Mahatma Gandhi National Rural Employment Guarantee Act (MGNREGA) is a landmark social welfare program implemented by the Government of India. The program guarantees 100 days of wage employment in a financial year to every rural household whose adult members volunteer to do unskilled manual work. MGNREGA aims to address poverty and unemployment by providing livelihood security and promoting sustainable development in rural areas.

Coimbatore district, located in the southern state of Tamil Nadu, is known for its agricultural and rural communities. As MGNREGA plays a significant role in uplifting the rural economy, it is essential to understand the level of awareness and knowledge among the residents of Coimbatore district regarding this program. Awareness is a crucial factor for effective implementation and utilization of MGNREGA schemes. This study focuses on assessing the awareness levels of the MGNREGA schemes among the residents of Coimbatore district. By evaluating the awareness levels, the study aims to identify gaps in knowledge and perception, determine the factors influencing awareness, and suggest strategies to enhance awareness and participation in the MGNREGA schemes. The findings of this study will contribute to the existing literature on MGNREGA awareness and provide valuable insights to policymakers, program implementers, and development agencies working toward poverty alleviation and rural development. Understanding the level of awareness among the residents of Coimbatore district will help in improving the implementation and impact of MGNREGA schemes at the grassroots level.

By addressing these objectives, this study aims to contribute to the overall understanding of the MGNREGA program and its impact on rural communities, specifically in the context of Coimbatore District.

Statement of the Problem

Statement of the problem
The purpose of this study is to assess the levels of awareness regarding the Mahatma Gandhi National Rural Employment Guarantee Act (MGNREGA) schemes among the residents of Coimbatore district. The study aims to identify the gaps in awareness and understand the factors that influence the level of knowledge and understanding of MGNREGA schemes among the target population.

Specifically, the study will address the following research questions:

1. What is the current level of awareness among the residents of Coimbatore district regarding the key components and benefits of MGNREGA

[a]manikkavel000@gmail.com, [b]j.sudarvel@gmail.com

schemes, such as equal wages, provision of work-days, timely payment of wages, work site facilities, etc.?

2. What are the gaps and challenges in the awareness of MGNREGA schemes in Coimbatore district? What are the reasons behind low awareness, and what are the potential barriers to disseminating information effectively?

3. What strategies can be recommended to enhance awareness levels and ensure effective implementation of MGNREGA schemes in Coimbatore district? How can communication channels and dissemination methods be improved to reach the target population more effectively?

By addressing these research questions, the study aims to provide insights into the current status of awareness, identify areas for improvement, and propose recommendations to enhance awareness levels regarding MGNREGA schemes among the residents of Coimbatore district. Ultimately, this study aims to contribute to the successful implementation of MGNREGA schemes and maximize the benefits for the eligible population in the district.

Review of Literature

In their study focuses on assessing the awareness levels and participation in MGNREGA schemes in Odisha (Mishra and Samal, 2021). It examines the factors influencing awareness, such as education, caste, and access to information, and analyzes the relationship between awareness and program participation. The study suggests the need for targeted awareness campaigns and improved dissemination of information to increase participation in MGNREGA.

In his study investigates the awareness and perception of MGNREGA schemes among rural households in Haryana (Yadav, 2020). It explores the factors influencing awareness levels and analyzes the perception of the program's benefits and implementation. The study highlights the need for improved awareness campaigns, effective grievance redressal mechanisms, and transparency in the implementation of MGNREGA schemes.

In their study focuses on the awareness and utilization of MGNREGA schemes in Namakkal district, Tamil Nadu. It assesses the awareness levels among rural households, examines the factors influencing awareness, and analyzes the utilization patterns of MGNREGA benefits (Kaviya and Ramesh, 2019). The study emphasizes the importance of social mobilization, capacity building, and improved coordination

among stakeholders to enhance awareness and utilization.

Swain's (2018) study explores the awareness levels and utilization of MGNREGA schemes among Scheduled Caste households in Sundargarh district, Odisha. It examines the factors influencing awareness and analyzes the utilization patterns based on socio-economic characteristics. The study highlights the need for targeted awareness campaigns, skill development programs, and improved implementation to enhance participation among marginalized communities.

In his study focuses on assessing the awareness levels of MGNREGA schemes in rural areas of Rajasthan (Sharma, 2018). It investigates the factors influencing awareness and the impact of awareness on program participation. The study found that education, caste, and social networks significantly influenced awareness levels, and higher awareness led to increased participation in the MGNREGA program.

Roy and Bose (2017) in their study examines the awareness and utilization of MGNREGA schemes among rural women in West Bengal. It explores the factors affecting awareness levels and analyzes the role of social factors in influencing program utilization. The study reveals that education, social status, and access to information significantly impact awareness and utilization, and there is a need to improve awareness among marginalized groups.

Singh (2016) in his study investigates the level of awareness and understanding of MGNREGA schemes in rural Bihar, specifically in Purnia district. It explores the role of socio-economic factors in determining awareness levels and analyzes the challenges faced in disseminating information. The study highlights the need for targeted awareness campaigns in local languages and the involvement of local institutions to improve awareness.

Saharan and Rathi (2016) in their study investigates the awareness and utilization of MGNREGA schemes in Haryana. It assesses the awareness levels among rural households, examines the factors influencing awareness and utilization, and analyzes the impact of MGNREGA on employment generation. The study suggests the need for capacity building, monitoring and evaluation mechanisms, and improved awareness campaigns to enhance program effectiveness. These studies provide insights into the awareness levels, factors influencing awareness, and utilization of MGNREGA schemes in different regions of India. They emphasize the importance of targeted awareness campaigns, improved dissemination of information, social mobilization, and stakeholder coordination in enhancing awareness and maximizing the benefits of MGNREGA for rural households. The findings from these studies can inform policymakers, program implementers, and researchers in developing strategies to improve awareness and program effectiveness.

This study examines the awareness levels of MGNREGA schemes among rural households in Jharkhand. It analyzes the factors influencing awareness, such as education, socio-economic status, and access to information. The study emphasizes the importance of local-level initiatives, community participation, and better dissemination of information to enhance awareness among rural households (Mishra and Mukherjee, 2014).

Palanichamy and Shanmugapriya (2013) in their study investigates the awareness and utilization of MGNREGA schemes among rural households in Tamil Nadu. It explores the factors influencing awareness levels and analyzes the utilization patterns based on socio-economic characteristics. The study suggests the need for continuous awareness campaigns, effective communication channels, and the involvement of local institutions to enhance awareness and utilization of the program. These studies provide valuable insights into the awareness levels, factors influencing awareness, and utilization of MGNREGA schemes in different regions of India. They highlight the importance of education, socio-economic factors, access to information, and community participation in enhancing awareness and utilization. The findings from these studies can inform future research and contribute to the development of targeted strategies to improve awareness and maximize the benefits of MGNREGA schemes for the rural population.

Objective of the Study

To identify the awareness level on MNGREGA schemes

Scope of the study

The study will focus specifically on Coimbatore district in Tamil Nadu, India. This geographical scope allows for a localized understanding of the awareness levels of MGNREGA schemes within the district.

The study will target various segments of the population in Coimbatore district, including rural households, marginalized communities, women, and specific socio-economic groups. This approach will provide insights into the awareness levels among different demographic groups within the district. The study will assess the levels of awareness among the target population regarding different aspects of MGNREGA schemes. This includes knowledge about the program's objectives, entitlements, application procedures, wage rates, work site facilities, and grievance redressal mechanisms.

The study will identify and analyze the factors that influence awareness levels among the target population in Coimbatore district. This may include demographic factors (e.g., age, gender, education), socio-economic factors (e.g., income, occupation), access to information, and cultural factors specific to the region. Based on the findings, the study will provide recommendations and strategies to improve awareness of MGNREGA schemes in Coimbatore district. These recommendations may include targeted awareness campaigns, capacity building initiatives, better information dissemination, and strengthening community participation.

By focusing on the awareness levels of MGNREGA schemes specifically in Coimbatore district, this study will provide valuable insights and recommendations to enhance awareness and improve the effectiveness of the program in the district.

Research Methodology

Stratified sampling technique of probability sampling was considered for the study in the initial process. MGNREGA worker from the selected taluks in Coimbatore District were taken for the study. Further 24% of the population on proportional representation from each selected taluk was taken and it was incorporated as 322 in total. By employing Krejcie, R. V., & Morgan, D. W. (1970) table, the sample size required for the study 320. Considering the data reliability and accuracy sample size increase to 322.

Number of workers in Taluk

S. no	Name of the Taluk	Total number of workers	16.78% of the population	No. of sample
1	Anamalai	161	27	27
2	Annur	246	41	41
3	Karamadai	187	31	31
4	Kinathukadavu	306	51	51
5	Madhukarai	56	9	9

S. no	Name of the Taluk	Total number of workers	16.78% of the population	No. of sample
6	P.N. Palayam	66	11	11
7	Pollachi North	233	39	39
8	Pollachi South	191	32	32
9	SS Kulam	62	10	10
10	Sulthanpet	203	34	34
11	Sulur	115	19	19
12	Thondamuthur	92	15	15
Total		1918	322	322

Source: Author

The primary data are collected through a well framed and structured questionnaire. The questionnaire was circulated by hard copy the respondents.

Sampling design

Data collected by convenience sampling method from 322 respondents in Coimbatore district.

Area of study

The studies are conferred to Coimbatore city. Coimbatore city consist of 12 taluks have been collected for the study. Anamalai, Annur, Karamadai, Kinathukadavu, Madhukarai, P.N. Palayam, Pollachi North, Pollachi South, SS Kulam, Sulthanpet, Sulur and Thondamuthur

APBS Enabled status

*At Panchayat level, clicking of the link at Col(5) will list the workers with Aadhaar Seeding/Authentication/APBS Enabled status.

SNo.	Blocks	Total No. Of Gps	No. Of Gps where works in progress	Maximum number of Unskilled Labour Expected to be engaged as per e-Master Roll*	No. Of Ongoing Works on which MR Issued	No. Of Workers without UID	No. of Muster Roll
1	2	3	4	5	6	7	8
	Total	228	226	15045	705	7	1948
1	ANAIMALAI	19	18	1276	48	1	161
2	ANNUR	21	21	2038	78	0	246
3	KARAMADAI	17	17	1078	113	0	187
4	KINATHUKADAVU	34	34	2515	93	0	306
5	MADUKKARAI	9	9	634	29	0	86
6	P.N.PALAYAM	9	9	452	35	0	66
7	POLLACHI(N)	39	38	2012	67	0	233
8	POLLACHI(S)	26	26	1328	92	4	191
9	S.S.KULAM	7	7	537	14	0	62
10	SULTANPET	20	20	1626	54	1	203
11	SULUR	17	17	783	60	0	115
12	THONDAMUTHUR	10	10	766	22	1	92
	Total	228	226	15045	705	7	1948

Frame work of analysis

- Simple percentage analysis
- Weighted Average

Limitations of the study

One of the limitations of the study may be the sample size. If the sample size is small or not representative of the entire population in Coimbatore district, the findings may not accurately reflect the overall awareness levels of MGNREGA schemes in the district. A larger and more diverse sample size would enhance the generalizability of the study's findings. The study relies on self-reporting from the participants, which may introduce response bias. Participants may overstate or understate their level of awareness or may provide socially desirable responses. This could affect the accuracy and reliability of the data collected and potentially impact the validity of the study's findings.

The study's timeframe may be limited, which could restrict the assessment of long-term awareness trends and changes in MGNREGA schemes. A longer study duration would provide a more comprehensive understanding of awareness levels and potential variations over time. Participants may have difficulty recalling specific details or experiences related to MGNREGA schemes accurately. This could lead to recall bias, where participants' responses are influenced by their ability to remember events or information accurately. This may impact the reliability of the data collected and the study's findings.

The study may not account for external factors that could influence awareness levels of MGNREGA schemes in Coimbatore district. Factors such as changes in government policies, media exposure, or local events may impact awareness levels independently of the variables examined in the study. Controlling for these external factors may be challenging and could limit the study's ability to establish causal relationships.

As the study focuses specifically on Coimbatore district, the findings may have limited generalizability to other districts or regions in India. Factors influencing awareness and program utilization may vary across different geographical areas, cultural contexts, and socio-economic conditions.

The study may focus primarily on awareness levels and factors influencing awareness, potentially overlooking other important aspects such as program outcomes, impact on employment, or socio-economic development. A broader scope of variables could provide a more comprehensive understanding of the MGNREGA schemes and their implications. It is important to acknowledge these limitations when interpreting the findings of the study, as they may impact the validity, reliability, and generalizability of the results. Future research can address these limitations to further enhance the understanding of awareness of MGNREGA schemes in Coimbatore district and beyond.

Significance of the Study

The study holds significant importance in providing insights into the awareness levels of MGNREGA schemes in Coimbatore district. The findings of the study can help policymakers and program implementers understand the existing gaps and shortcomings in the awareness of MGNREGA among the target population. This, in turn, can guide the formulation of more effective policies and strategies to enhance awareness and ensure maximum participation in the program. By examining the awareness levels and factors influencing awareness, the study can contribute to improving the overall effectiveness of MGNREGA schemes in Coimbatore district. Increased awareness among the target population about program benefits, entitlements, and application procedures can result in better utilization of the program, leading to enhanced employment opportunities, poverty reduction, and rural development.

The study can empower rural communities in Coimbatore district by increasing their awareness and knowledge about MGNREGA schemes. Enhanced awareness levels can empower individuals and communities to demand their rights, access their entitlements, and actively participate in decision-making processes related to the program. This can foster a sense of ownership and empowerment among the rural population. Improved awareness of MGNREGA schemes can contribute to socio-economic development in Coimbatore district. By creating awareness about the program's objectives, benefits, and provisions, the study can encourage more individuals to participate in productive employment opportunities. This, in turn, can lead to increased income levels, reduced poverty, improved living standards, and overall economic growth in the district.

The study's findings can guide targeted interventions to bridge the awareness gap among underrepresented groups, such as marginalized communities and women, in Coimbatore district. By understanding the specific factors that influence awareness among these groups, appropriate strategies can be developed to reach and engage them effectively. This can ensure equitable access to MGNREGA schemes and reduce social and gender disparities in program participation.

The study on awareness of MGNREGA schemes in Coimbatore district will contribute to the existing body of knowledge in the field of rural development and social welfare. It will add to the understanding of factors influencing awareness, program utilization patterns, and the impact of awareness on program effectiveness. The findings can serve as a valuable resource for future research and studies in similar contexts.

Analysis and Interpretation

Age	Frequency	Percentage
Below 48 years	57	17.7
Between 49 to 63 years	205	63.7
Above 64 years	60	18.6
Total	322	100.0
Gender	Frequency	Percentage
Male	106	32.9
Female	216	67.1
Total	322	100.0
Marital status	Frequency	Percentage
Married	257	79.8
Unmarried	9	2.8
Widow/widower	56	17.4
Total	322	100.0
Education	Frequency	Percentage
Illiterate	161	50.0
Primary	139	43.2
SSLC	22	6.8
Total	322	100.0
Other scheme beneficiary	Frequency	Percentage
Beneficiaries	64	19.9
Non- beneficiaries	258	80.1
Total	322	100.0
Financial status	Frequency	Percentage
Below poverty line	66	20.5
Above poverty line	256	79.5
Total	322	100.0
Self-help group	Frequency	Percentage
Member	180	55.9
Non-member	142	44.1
Total	322	100.0
Working days	Frequency	Percentage
Below 41 days	61	18.9
Between 42 to 78 days	206	64.0
Above 79 days	55	17.1
Total	322	100.0
Monthly income	Frequency	Percentage
Up to 8200	41	12.7
8201 to 11500	238	73.9
Above 11501	43	13.4
Total	322	100.0

Based on the information provided, the majority of NREGA workers exhibit the following characteristics:

1. Age: The majority of workers fall within the age group of 49 to 63 years, indicating that older individuals form a significant portion of the workforce.
2. Gender: The majority of NREGA workers are female, suggesting that women play a prominent role in the scheme.
3. Marital status: Most workers are married, indicating that individuals with family responsibilities are actively engaged in NREGA work.
4. Education: The majority of workers are illiterate, highlighting the need for accessible training and capacity-building programs to enhance their skills.
5. Beneficiaries: Most workers are not beneficiaries of another scheme, indicating that NREGA is their primary source of support and livelihood.
6. Economic Status: The majority of workers belong to the above poverty line category, implying that they may have slightly better financial stability compared to those below the poverty line.
7. Self-help group (SHG) membership: Most workers are members of a Self-Help Group, which signifies their participation in collective efforts for socio-economic empowerment and support.
8. Annual Working Days: The majority of workers agreed that their annual working days under NREGA range between 42 and 78 days, indicating a variable workload throughout the year.
9. Monthly Income: Most workers have a monthly income between Rs. 8201 and Rs. 11500, indicating the level of financial remuneration they receive from their NREGA employment.

These characteristics provide insights into the demographic and socio-economic profile of the majority of NREGA workers, which can help in formulating targeted policies and interventions to address their specific needs and aspirations.

The weighted average score test conducted among NREGA workers revealed the following key factors of awareness and their respective rankings:

1. Equal wage for men and women: This was found to be the most important factor of awareness among NREGA workers. It signifies the demand for gender equality in wages, emphasizing that both men and women should receive the same remuneration for their work under the NREGA scheme.

Statistics for Awareness

Awareness	Highly unaware	Unaware	Neutral	Somewhat aware	Highly aware	Total	Mean score	Rank
	1	2	3	4	5			
Provision of 100 days of work per household who demanded for work	6	56	159	89	12	322	3.14	2
	6	112	477	356	60	1011		
33% women participation in NREG work	12	164	117	23	6	322	2.52	11
	12	328	351	92	30	813		
Equal wage for men and women	0	9	61	198	54	322	3.73	1
	0	18	123	792	270	1203		
Right to demand the job at the convenience of the workers	6	85	218	3	10	322	2.77	7
	6	170	654	12	50	892		
Right to get the job within 15 days of application	7	122	167	41	3	322	2.90	4
	7	244	501	164	15	931		
Provision of unemployment allowance, if the job is not provided within 15 days	12	154	111	42	3	322	2.59	10
	12	308	333	168	15	836		
Provision of work within the radius of 5 km of the residence of the workers	0	100	196	19	7	322	2.79	6
	0	200	588	76	35	899		
Provision of extra wages, if the work is beyond 5 km radius	13	127	143	19	20	322	2.70	9
	13	254	429	76	100	872		
Provision of wages within 14 days after completing the work	10	40	178	83	11	322	3.14	2
	10	80	534	332	55	1011		
Avoidance of contractors and machinery from NREG work	6	97	162	43	14	322	2.88	5
	6	194	486	172	70	928		
Role of *Grama Sabha* in deciding the time and nature of work to be done	27	62	205	28	0	322	2.72	8
	27	124	615	112	0	878		
Work site facilities	9	29	221	57	6	322	3.06	3
	9	58	663	228	30	1018		
Provision of social audit	111	148	47	3	13	322	1.94	12
	111	296	141	12	65	625		

2. Provision of 100 days of work per household: This factor ranked second in terms of awareness among NREGA workers. It highlights the expectation that each household that demands work should be provided with employment for a minimum of 100 days per year.

3. Provision of wages within 14 days after completing the work: Timely payment of wages is crucial for NREGA workers, and it ranked third in the awareness test. Workers expect to receive their wages within 14 days after completing their assigned work.

4. Work site facilities: The availability of adequate facilities at the work site, such as drinking water, sanitation facilities, and shelter, was another important factor highlighted by NREGA workers.

5. Right to get the job within 15 days of application: NREGA workers expect to be provided with employment opportunities within 15 days of submitting their application for work under the scheme.

6. Avoidance of contractors and machinery from NREG work: The workers expressed a preference for direct employment rather than involving

contractors or machinery in NREGA work. This factor indicates a desire for fair and direct engagement between the workers and the scheme.

7. Provision of work within a 5 km radius of the workers' residence: Workers prefer to have job opportunities within a reasonable distance from their homes, making it easier for them to commute and balance their work and personal life.

8. Right to demand the job at the convenience of the workers: NREGA workers want the flexibility to choose the timing of their work, allowing them to accommodate other responsibilities and obligations.

9. Role of Grama Sabha in deciding the time and nature of work to be done: The Grama Sabha, a village-level democratic institution, plays a crucial role in deciding the type and timing of work under NREGA. Workers are aware of this and value the participatory decision-making process.

10. Provision of extra wages if the work is beyond a 5 km radius: In cases where the work assigned to NREGA workers is located beyond a 5 km radius, they expect to receive additional compensation to account for the increased distance and commuting expenses.

11. Provision of unemployment allowance if the job is not provided within 15 days: If a worker is not provided employment within 15 days of applying for work under NREGA, they expect to receive an unemployment allowance as a form of support during the waiting period.

12. 33% women participation in NREGA work: The workers are aware of the importance of women's participation in NREGA work and advocate for the provision of at least 33% representation of women in the scheme.

Conclusion

The study on awareness of Mahatma Gandhi National Rural Employment Guarantee Act (MGNREGA) schemes in Coimbatore district has shed light on the levels of awareness among the population regarding the various provisions and benefits offered by the Mahatma Gandhi National Rural Employment Guarantee Act. The findings of the study provide valuable insights into the current status of awareness and highlight areas that require attention for improving the dissemination of information. Overall, the study revealed that there is a moderate level of awareness among the residents of Coimbatore district regarding MGNREGA schemes. While some individuals demonstrated a good understanding of the key components such as equal wages, provision of workdays, and timely payment of wages, there were notable gaps in awareness concerning other aspects, including work site facilities, women's participation, social audit, and unemployment allowance.

The demographic profile of the participants showed that the majority of workers in Coimbatore district under the MGNREGA scheme belonged to the age group of 49 to 63 years. This highlights the importance of targeting awareness campaigns towards this age group to ensure they are well-informed about their entitlements and rights. Additionally, it was observed that the majority of workers were female, married, and illiterate. This suggests the need for tailored communication strategies that consider the specific needs and circumstances of these individuals, such as providing accessible and simplified information materials. The study also revealed that a significant portion of the workers were non-beneficiaries of another scheme and belonged to the above poverty line category. This finding emphasizes the importance of creating awareness among those who are not currently benefiting from other social welfare schemes, as they may be less familiar with the provisions and benefits offered by MGNREGA. Based on the study findings, it is recommended that the government and relevant stakeholders take proactive measures to enhance awareness of MGNREGA schemes in Coimbatore district. This could include targeted awareness campaigns through multiple channels, such as community meetings, radio programs, and informational brochures in local languages. Collaboration with local authorities, self-help groups, and community organizations can also play a crucial role in disseminating information effectively and engaging with the target population.

It is crucial to continuously monitor the awareness levels of MGNREGA schemes and evaluate the impact of awareness campaigns over time. Regular assessment of awareness will help identify gaps, measure progress, and inform future interventions to ensure maximum participation and benefits for the eligible population in Coimbatore district. In conclusion, the study on awareness of MGNREGA schemes in Coimbatore district highlights the importance of increasing awareness levels to ensure the successful implementation of the program. By addressing the identified gaps and challenges, policymakers and program administrators can work towards building a more informed and empowered community that can take full advantage of the benefits offered by MGNREGA.

Reference

Kaviya, V., and Ramesh, M. (2019). Awareness and utilization of MGNREGA in Tamil Nadu: a study with special reference to namakkal district. *Journal: International Journal of Applied Engineering Research*, 14(9), 2226–2231.

Mishra, A., and Samal, S. K. (2021). Awareness and participation in MGNREGA: a study in Odisha. *Journal: Journal of Rural Development*, 40(3), 421–440.

Mishra, M., and Mukherjee, S. (2014). Awareness of MGN-REGA among rural households in Jharkhand: an empirical analysis. *Journal: Agricultural Economics Research Review*, 27(2), 283–289.

Palanichamy, P., and Shanmugapriya, S. (2013). Awareness and utilization of MGNREGA among rural households: a study in Tamil Nadu. *Journal: Indian Journal of Economics and Development*, 9(1), 127–133.

Roy, A., and Bose, D. (2017). Awareness and utilisation of MGNREGA among rural women in West Bengal. *Journal: International Journal of Scientific Research*, 6(6), 264–267.

Saharan, R., and Rathi, N. (2016). Awareness and utilization of MGNREGA in Haryana: an empirical study. *Journal: International Journal of Management, IT and Engineering*, 6(1), 293–309.

Sharma, R. K. (2018). Awareness about MGNREGA schemes: a case study of rural areas in Rajasthan. *Journal: Indian Journal of Economics and Development*, 6(1), 223–228.

Singh, G. (2016). Awareness of MGNREGA in rural Bihar: a case study of Purnia district. *Journal: Journal of Research in Humanities and Social Science*, 4(7), 24–29.

Swain, D. (2018). Awareness and utilization of MGNREGA among the scheduled caste households: a study in Sundargarh district of Odisha. *Journal: Indian Journal of Regional Science*, 50(2), 45–60.

Yadav, S. (2020). Awareness and perception of MGNREGA: a study in rural Haryana. *Journal: Indian Journal of Regional Science*, 52(1), 1–15.

179 Chapter: Russia-Ukraine conflict and global trade

Kumar, A. G.[1], Rajayya, A.[2] and Rose, L. R.[3]

[1]Manager- Marketing, Chennai Trade Centre, Chennai, India

[2]Assistant Professor, School of Business, Amrita Vishwa Vidyapeetham, Kollam, India

[3]Assistant Professor, Department of B. Com Honours, Loyola College, Chennai, India

Abstract

The Russian invasion of Ukraine, which began on February 24, 2022, has already lasted for more than a year and caused enormous human misery in addition to completely destroy international trade, which the World Trade Organization (WTO) predicts would have the worst effects on economies with low income among its citizens. Reviewing the WTO's Trade Forecast 2022–2023 reveals how the conflict between Russia and Ukraine has dimmed the outlook for the global economy, leading their economists to be pessimistic with regard to growth potential of merchandise trade volume and recast the figure from 4.7% to 3%. The instant effect of the conflict has been felt on the food and energy sector since both Russia and Ukraine are one of the highest producers and exporters of many food items. This study has also attempted to collect primary data from exporters and importers operating in India with respect to the impact of the conflict and type of sanctions needed together with the impact of the same.

Keywords: Disruption in food supplies, Russia-Ukraine conflict, sanctions

Introduction

Started on February 24, 2022, the Russian invasion of Ukraine has now lasted for more than a year. As the COVID-19 pandemic's consequences were still being felt globally, the war in Ukraine triggered a new crisis, destabilizing food and energy markets and worsening food poverty and hunger in many developing countries. Because of the conflict between the two countries, world over countries is experiencing hardship associated with high inflation rates. Prices have surged brining about global trade and investment disruptions. Commodity markets, logistics, supply chain management, foreign direct investment, and particular industries are five direct trade and investment routes via which nations are impacted by the conflict in Ukraine.

After Effects of Russia – Ukraine Conflict

The instant effect of the conflict has been felt on the food and energy sector since both Russia and Ukraine are one of the highest producers and exporters of many food items. Russia is also serving as the primary supplier of fuel from fossil including natural gas and crude oil. Price increases on account of the conflict are being propelled due to supply chain disruptions. Such disruptions are exerting negative impact on trade globally. Higher commodity prices tend to be beneficial to exporters, who in turn tend to increase production levels and product shipments to balance the loss on account of a decrease in exports from Russia and Ukraine. Both the consumers of certain commodities and the producers of other items suffer because of importers' actions.

The war in Ukraine has not only caused a great deal of hardship for people but has also unfavorably influenced the global economy at a critical point of time. Its influence is widely seen world over, more so in low-income nations where a major portion of family spending goes towards food. The World Trade Organization (WTO) has predicted using the WTO Global Trade Model, which tries to imagine the direct effects of the conflict between Russia and Ukraine, including the infrastructure being totally destroyed, substantial increase in trade costs, effects of sanctions on Russia, which includes including obstructive of Russian banks from SWIFT settlement process, and reduced demand world over on account of lack of confidence and the accompanying recession. With these presumptions in place, the earlier prediction of 4.1% global GDP growth in 2022 was revised down to 2.8% at market exchange rates.

Figure 179.1 depicts the global rise in petrol prices, which started prior to the situation prevailing in the terror-struck country, Ukraine. It is to be noted that the price of the benchmark Brent crude oil which stood at US$ 118 a barrel in March 2022 soared up to 38% from the first month of 2022 and up 81% from the same month as compared to the previous price.

[a]lrrose_prof@yahoo.com

– March 2022 (US$ per barrel and US$ per million Btu)

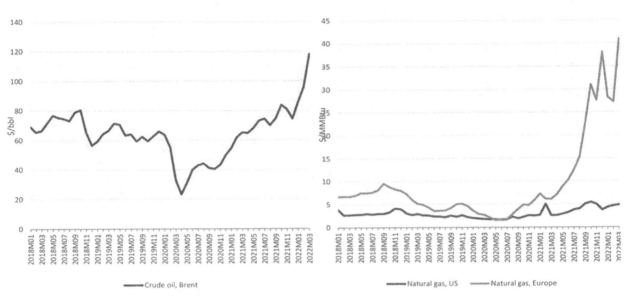

Figure 179.1 Monthly average prices for crude oil and natural gas, January 2018
Source: World Bank, US Energy Information Administration, Federal Reserve Bank of St. Louis.

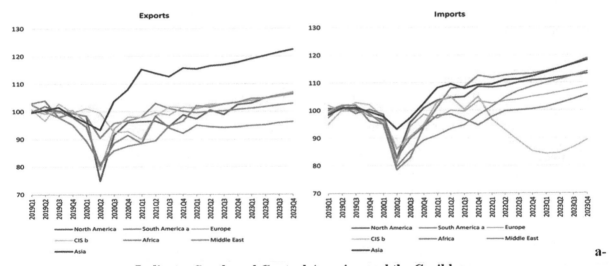

Indicates South and Central America and the Caribbean.
b- Indicates Commonwealth of Independent States, including certain associate and former member.

Figure 179.2 Merchandise exports and imports by region, 2019-2023 volume index, 2019 = 100
Source: WTO and UNCTAD

(It should be noted that daily prices later decreased and peaked at US$ 128 per barrel on March 8, 2022, before falling to US$ 104 per barrel on April 1 of that same year.) Natural gas prices appeared to vary across sites more widely than oil prices. Natural gas prices steeped up to 45% between January and March 2022.

Figure 179.2 depicts the quarterly trade volume of indices for the various types of merchandise region-wise from the years 2019 to 2023. Many disparities could be seen with respect to the same. with Europe being expected to not perform well with respect to imports like Africa and the Misfortunately due to the sections imposed on Russia.

Prior to the global financial crisis, the volume of world merchandise trade increased at market exchange rates almost twice as quickly as the global GDP, but following the crisis, the proportion of trade growth to GDP growth generally decreased to about 1:1. This ratio would be 1.1:1 in 2022 and 2023 if the present prediction comes true, indicating no vital change in the connection between trade and output. Risks which need to be forecasted are diverse and challenging to evaluate objectively. If the conflict ends soon, there would probably be a situation of gaining. But on the other hand, if war persists it could turn out to be risky and the situation could worsen. Towards the close of the period for which forecast has been made, Chart 179.2 indicates the quarterly merchandise trade volume indices based on regions for the first quarter of 2019 to the fourth quarter of 2023 with predictions being low on the import front.

Interventions brought about with respect to the trade policy include the possibility of having further worsening of the food sector. Together, both countries actually export around 25% of the wheat consumed globally with them exporting maize and fertilizers close to almost 15% globally. Supply is further reduced by export restrictions, while demand is increased by import liberalization policies and subsidies. Many new trade policies have been introduced or announced since the beginning of the war, for a total of 67 if subsidies are included.

Objectives of the study
- To understand the influence of Russia – Ukraine conflict on global trade from the perspective of exporters and importer
- To identify the sectors which are likely to suffer most on account of the above conflict.
- To analyze the type of sanctions imposed on Russia which would affect Russia's Trade thereby indirectly affecting world over trade at the global level.

Methodology

Apart from understanding the influence of Russia – Ukraine conflict on global trade from the perspective of exporters and importer this study also attempts to identify the sectors which may suffer the most on account of the above-mentioned conflict between the two nations. The research design has been descriptive and the research tool used for collection of primary data has been a questionnaire. On the whole the study included 48 respondents which included exporter and importers operating in India.

Data Analysis

The data that was collected with the help of the questionnaire has been analyzed using SPSS computer package and the analysis and interpretation of the same is as given below. The below table depicts the business undertaken by the companies included for the purpose of the study. With Russia serving as the 3rd biggest global exporter of crude oil on account of the conflict, price of crude oil prices has peaked to a point of being highest in the last seven years.

With many sectors depending on crude oil for their operations sectors such as the paint sector, fertilizer companies, etc have suffered. The supply of edible oil and few key agricultural products which come mostly from Ukraine and Russia have also reduced drastically. As far as the automobile sector is concerned Russia is one of the major suppliers for chips and vital metals used in semi-conductors. On the other hand, Ukraine makes available to the sector Neon and Helium gases essential for manufacturing chips. Last but not the

Table 179.1 Type of business engaged.

Type of business	Frequency	Percent
Export	18	37.50%
Import	16	33.30%
Both export and import	14	29.20%
Total	48	100%

Source: Author

Table 179.2 Disrupted in economy on account of the Russia – Ukraine Conflict.

Disrupted sectors	Frequency	Percent
Commodity markets	48	100%
Logistical services	40	71.40%
Supply chain management	32	66.70%
Foreign direct investment	29	60.42%
Specific sectors	27	56.25%

Source: Author

Table 179.3 Mean and SD for items of sanctions on Russia.

Items	Mean	SD
Reduced export of goods, services and finance	3.467	1.069
Curbs on individual companies operating in Russia	3.710	1.084
Individuals associated with Putin boycotted	2.743	1.181
Suspending the MFN clause in the WTO	3.933	1.207

Source: Author

least even the base metals supplies have been affected resulting in huge price increase.

Even though the conflict between the countries may not be the primary reason for the growth in sectors being slower than the predicted levels in 2022 and relegated estimates for the year 2023 have had the effect of further bringing down economic activity at the global level by worsening pressures of inflation and the struggle of economies world over to recovery from the after effects of the COVID-19 pandemic.

Mean and SD of the impact of sanctions on Russia
The highest mean score is given to the need for suspension of the MFA clause in the WTO (3.933) which will help trading partners of Russia to discriminate against it. Imposition of sanctions leads to answering the questions as to how political settings could be controlled through trade measures and what would be the consequences that follow the same. The very objective of imposing sanctions related to the economy are considered to be action taken to bring about justice. In addition, by removing or suspension of the MFN clause which places recognizes companies as the most favored nations and thereby ensures that countries do not discriminate between partners with respect to trading activities.

Table 179.4 Correlation coefficient between items of sanction and impact on global trade.

Items of sanctions	Impact on Russia's global trade
Reduced export of goods, services and finance	0.625**
Curbs on individual companies operating in Russia	0.685**
Individuals associated with Putin boycotted	0.534**
Suspending the MFN clause in the WTO	0.866**

Source: Author

Correlation
The highest correlation coefficient is seen to be between suspension of MFN clause in the WTO and its impact on global trade and the least is seen to be between reduced exports and impact on Russia's Trade thereby impacting global trade practices.

Multiple regression
With respect to multiple regression the impact of global trade is taken as the dependent variable and the items of sanction have been taken as the independent variables.

Dependent variable: Impact on global trade (Y)

Independent variables: Reduced exports, Curbs on individual companies

Boycotting of individuals and Suspension of MFN clause

Multiple R value: 0. 819
R Square value: 0.644
F value: 173.779
p value: <0.001**

The multiple regression equation is $Y = 4.222 + 0.476X_1 + 0.274X_2 + 0.203X_3 + 0.658$

Based on standardized coefficient, suspension of MFN clause (0.656) is the most important variable to extract impact on global trade followed by imposing curbs on individual companies operating in Russia (0.476).

Conclusion

With trade growth that is far greater than the more dismal estimates for 2022, the release demonstrates that the multilateral trading system has continued to be robust. Although less than anticipated at the outset of the war, prices increased for the items most affected by it. The capacity of nations that depend on imports from Russia and Ukraine to relocate their import supply to unaffected economies contributed to their favorable trade results. Exporter and importers operating in India strongly believe that suspension of MFN clause is the most important variable to extract

Table 179.5 Variables in the multiple regression analysis.

Variables	Unstandardized co-efficient	SE of B	Standardized co-efficient	*t* value	*P* value
Constant	4.222	2.541	-	1.793	0.004**
X_1	0.476	0.108	0.334	4.391	<.000**
X_2	0.272	0.079	0.290	3.435	<.000**
X_3	0.201	0.101	0.089	1.992	0.007**
X_4	0.656	0.134	0.195	4.893	<.000**

*Note: ** Denotes significant at 1% level*
Source: Author

impact Russia's trade followed by imposing curbs on individual companies operating in Russia. According to the most recent simulations performed by World Trae Organization (WTO) economists, the opportunity cost of shifting to geopolitical rivalry is projected to be 8.7% of real income in the long-run scenario of a decoupling of the global economy into two competing blocs with the most vulnerable economies facing opportunity costs as high as 11.3%.

Reference

Antras, P. (2021). De-globalisation. global value chains in the post-covid-19 age. In 2021 Ecbfotum: "Central Banks in a Shifting World" Conference Proceedings.

Caldara, D., and Iacoviello, M. (2022). Measuring geopolitical risk. *American Economic Review*, 112(4), 1194–1225.

Freund, C., Mattoo, A., Mulabdic, A., and Ruta, M. (2021). Natural disasters and the reconfiguration of global value chains. World Bank Policy Research Working Paper n. 9719.

Javorcik, B. (2020). Global supply chains will not be the same in the post-covid-19 world. *Covid-19 and Trade Policy: Why Turning Inwared Won't Work*, 111, 111–116. CEPR Press.

Lund, S., Manyika, J., Woetzel, J., Barriball, E., Krishnan, M., Alicke, K., et al. (2020). Risk, Resilience, and Rebalancing in Global Value Chains. McKinsey Global Institute.

Posen, A, (2022). The end of globalization what russia's war in Ukraine means for the world economy. *Foreign Affairs*, 17, 2022.

World Bank (2020). World Development Report 2020: Trading for Development in the Age of Global Value Chains, World Development Report. The World Bank.

180 A study on the effect of training on employee retention

Atheeswaran, K., Geetha Bai[a], Ramapriya[b], Smruthymol, J.[c] and Jegadeeswari, S.[d]

Karpagam Academy of Higher Education, Coimbatore, Tamil Nadu, India

Abstract

In today's fiercely competitive business landscape, employer retention stands as a critical concern, given its potential to impact a company's functionality and success. This study delves into the nexus between worker retention and training, seeking to establish the correlation between providing training opportunities and employees' inclination to remain within the organization. Through a comprehensive exploration encompassing the frequency, content, and delivery modes of training programs, this research adopts a mixed-methods approach. It combines quantitative surveys to gauge employees' perceptions of training effectiveness in influencing their choice to stay, with qualitative insights gleaned from in-depth interviews and focus groups. Anticipated outcomes aim to enrich our comprehension of employee retention strategies, furnishing actionable insights for companies aiming to bolster loyalty through impactful training initiatives. These findings aspire to serve as a practical guide for HR specialists and organizational leaders in designing bespoke training programs, fostering enhanced employee engagement and commitment tailored to their workforce's needs.

Keywords: Employee retention, training, organizational performance, turnover, HR strategies

Introduction

Improving organizational performance hinges significantly on training initiatives that positively impact employee retention and augment the pool of human capital. Acknowledged as pivotal in maintaining a skilled workforce, training serves as a linchpin for staff longevity within organizations. The study aims to scrutinize the correlation between training provisions and employee retention, particularly focusing on voluntary departures rather than retirement or terminations. High turnover rates, attributable to factors such as external labor market dynamics and internal organizational culture, can substantially affect an enterprise. While external forces may lie beyond an organization's control, the implementation of effective training programs remains a tangible strategy to bolster employee loyalty and job satisfaction Rana, T. M. et al. (2019).

Training plays a paramount role in retaining employees, given the investment made by organizations in developing their workforce Villegas, R. (2016). The expenditure and effort in acclimating employees to the corporate ethos and equipping them with essential skills become pivotal, especially considering the risk of knowledge loss when trained individuals seek opportunities elsewhere. Embracing training programs geared toward staff retention not only fosters a sense of value and motivation among employees but also introduces novel perspectives and ideas that contribute to organizational credibility and individual growth. Additionally, the acquisition of new skills through training serves as a compelling factor for career-oriented individuals, elevating the allure of staying with a company.

Objectives

The objectives of this study are:

- To assess the impact of training on employee retention
- Identify factors influencing employee retention
- Establish the relationship between training and retention

Review of Literature

The combination of literature review and company profile offer crucial insights into the challenges surrounding employee retention within the automobile industry, especially for Integra Automation.

Another study sheds light on the automotive sector's pressing issue of insufficient skilled human resources. This scarcity intensifies competition among companies, fostering an environment prone to headhunting and poaching. The industry's inadequacies in labor planning, training, and retention exacerbate this challenge, leading to potential employee attrition to unrelated sectors like fast moving consumer goods or financial organizations.

[a]geethabhojan@gmail.com, [b]ramapriyamarimuthu@kahedu.edu.in, [c]jayalalsmruthy@gmail.com, [d]sjegadeeswari15@gmail.com

Samganakkan Samganakkan, S. (2010) underscores the pivotal role of effective employee retention strategies in aligning corporate goals and bolstering organizational profitability. By navigating the competitive talent landscape, Samganakkan highlights how adept retention methods can serve as a competitive advantage for firms.

Additionally, another study stresses the crucial significance of employee retention in strengthening workplace dynamics, enhancing productivity, and augmenting corporate profitability. Their insights, particularly in the healthcare sector, underscore the transformative impact of robust staff retention techniques in creating a positive work environment, boosting patient satisfaction, and fortifying corporate revenues.

Sampling
Sample size: The study is based on the opinions and expectations of consumers. A total of 120 respondents were included in the sample for this study. Sample design convenience sampling was used for this study.

Tools used for research
- Simple percentage method
- Correlation
- Chi square test
- ANOVA
- Factor analysis

Data analysis and interpretations
The following sections present a comprehensive analysis of demographic features, training perceptions, benefits, and statistical tests derived from extensive survey data Newman, A. et al. (2018). Delving into demographic distributions, training evaluations, and employee retention considerations, these sections unravel key insights into respondent characteristics, training impact, and factors influencing employee satisfaction and commitment. Statistical analyses, including Chi-square, correlation, ANOVA, and factor analysis, provide quantitative validation to understand the intricate relationships between variables, shedding light on the nuances of employee perspectives and their association with workplace dynamics and training programs Holtom, B. C. et al. (2015).

Demographic features
- **Gender**
  - Male: 131 (87.3%)
  - Female: 19 (12.7%)
- **Age**
  - Below 25: 20 (13.3%)
  - 25–30: 58 (38.7%)
  - 31–50: 52 (34.7%)
  - 51 and above: 20 (13.3%)
- **Marital status**
  - Married: 62 (41.3%)
  - Unmarried: 88 (58.7%)
- **Qualification**
  - Up to HSC: 47 (31.3%)
  - Diploma: 36 (24.0%)
  - Graduate level: 58 (38.7%)
  - Postgraduate level: 9 (6.0%)
- **Experience**
  - Less than 1 year: 6 (4.0%)
  - 1–2 years: 43 (28.7%)
  - 3–4 years: 61 (40.7%)
  - Above 4 years: 40 (20.7%)
- **Monthly income**
  - Below 10000Rs: 41 (27.3%)
  - 10001–20000Rs: 56 (37.3%)
  - 20001–30000Rs: 49 (32.7%)

Table 180.1 Perceived training effectiveness: on-the-job training and employee perspectives.

On-the-job training	Training perception	Percentage (%)
Clear job duties	Strongly agree	34.70%
	Agree	45.30%
Moulded to employee needs	Strongly agree	70.70%
	Agree	25.00%
Focus on practical skills	Strongly agree	72.00%
	Agree	19.30%
Peer trust building	Strongly agree	47.30%
	Agree	40.00%

Source: Author

Table 180.2 Training benefits' impact: perceived effects on employee development and work enhancement.

Training benefits	Training impact	Percentage (%)
Planned induction	Strongly agree	53.30%
	Agree	30.00%
Enhances creativity	Strongly agree	10.70%
	Agree	72.00%
Career development	Strongly agree	48.00%
	Agree	33.30%
Improves work quality	Strongly agree	26.70%
	Agree	60.70%

Source: Author

Table 180.3 Training benefits fostering employee satisfaction and retention strategies.

Training benefits for retention	Employee satisfaction	Percentage (%)
Recognition for effort	Strongly agree	5.30%
	Agree	48.00%
Sense of team inclusion	Strongly agree	7.30%
	Agree	38.70%
Supervisor encouragement	Strongly agree	40.00%
	Agree	24.00%
Satisfactory medical benefits	Strongly agree	14.70%
	Agree	72.70%

Source: Author

Table 180.4 Employee retention intentions.

Retaining employees	Intend to stay despite higher offer	Percentage
Intend to stay despite higher offer	Strongly agree	15.30%
	Agree	72.00%

Source: Author

- Rs 30001-40000: 3 (2.0%)
- Above 50000: 1 (0.7%)

Hypothesis testing and results
- **Chi-square test**: Experience *vs*. long-term commitment: Significant relationship found (p < 0.05).
- **Correlation analysis**: Qualification *vs*. learning speed and trust: significant correlation (p < 0.01).
- **ANOVA analysis**: Experience vs. Strong Career Association: Strong relationship (p < 0.05).
- **Factor analysis**: Factors identified: On-the-job training, training effectiveness, rewards & recognition, each encapsulating specific aspects related to employee retention.

The study findings reveal nuanced insights into employee demographics, training perceptions, and retention factors. Key results highlight a majority of respondents (87.3%) were male, with notable age representation in the 25–30 range (38.7%). Training effectiveness was acknowledged, with 72.0% emphasizing practical learning. Notably, 72.7% found medical benefits satisfactory. Statistical analyses established significant relationships between experience and long-term commitment (p < 0.05), qualification and learning speed (p < 0.01), and experience influencing career commitment (p < 0.05). Factor analysis identified on-the-job training, training effectiveness, and rewards & recognition as crucial elements impacting employee retention, culminating in a multifaceted understanding of workforce dynamics and training impact on retention.

Recommendations

The study highlights the advantages of personalized training schemes and on-the-job guidance. To further enhance employee retention, Integra Automation should consider devising training programs that align with each employee's distinct growth aspirations and career trajectory. Additionally, maintaining funding initiatives acknowledging and rewarding employees' contributions is crucial, given the evident correlation between rewards, recognition, and employee retention.

Given the study's indication of a relationship between successful training and employee contentment, managers should actively foster their staff members' development and provide constructive feedback. Implementing long-term career development plans can alleviate concerns about employees seeking better opportunities elsewhere. By clearly outlining potential career trajectories within the company and offering avenues for progression, Integra Automation can significantly bolster employee retention. A comprehensive approach to employee well-being contributes to higher satisfaction and retention rates.

Conclusion

In conclusion, the study offers insightful information about the critical connection between Integra Automation training initiatives and staff retention. The results highlight the value of funding staff development programs to promote a motivated and engaged workforce. According to the study's analysis, rewards and recognition, on-the-job training, and training efficacy are all significant elements that affect employees' decisions to stay with the company. Integra Automation is well-positioned to take advantage of these insights to improve its human resource strategies and create an environment that nurtures talent, encourages continuous learning, and ultimately drives the company's sustained growth and success in the competitive automotive industry. Integra Automation does this by aligning training programs with employees' needs and customizing them to practical experiences.

References

Newman, A., Thanacoody, R., and Hui, W. (2018). The impact of employee perceptions of training on organisational commitment and turnover intentions: a study of multinationals in the Chinese service sector. *The International Journal of Human Resource Management*, 22(8), 1765–1787.

Rana, T. M., Salaria, M. R., Herani, G. M., and Amin, M. A. (2019). Identifying factors playing important role in the increasing employee. *Indus Journal of Management and Social Sciences*, 2(3).

Samganakkan, S. (2010). Mediating role of organizational commitment on HR practices and turnover intention among ICT professional. *Management Research*.

Villegas, R. (2016). Training is not enough. Retrieved from: http://www.-saipantribune.com/newsstory.aspx?news ID=62172 &cat=3

Holtom, B. C., Mitchell, T. R., Lee, T. W., and Inderrieden, E. J. (2015). Shocks as causes of turnover: what they are and how organizations can manage them. *Human Resource Management*, 44(3), 337–352.

181 Problems of migrant workers in Coimbatore district

Anjanadevi, G.[1] and Velmurugan, R.[2]

[1]II M.Com. Karpagam Academy of Higher Education, Coimbatore, Tamil Nadu, India

[2]Associate Professor of Commerce, Karpagam Academy of Higher Education, Coimbatore, Tamil Nadu, India

Abstract

Migrant workers face numerous challenges and problems that often arise from their vulnerable position in the labor market and their status as temporary. This study explores some of the key issues that migrant workers encounter, including labor exploitation, inadequate working conditions, lack of legal protections, social exclusion, and limited access to essential services. The discussion highlights the global nature of these problems and emphasizes the need for effective policies and interventions to safeguard the rights and well-being of migrant workers.

Keywords: Labor exploitation, legal protections, migrant workers, social exclusion, working conditions

Introduction

Migrant workers are individuals who move from one region or country to another in search of employment or better economic opportunities. They typically leave their home countries or regions and temporarily or permanently settle in a different location for work purposes. Migrant workers can be categorized into different types, such as internal migrants and international migrant. Internal migrants are individuals who move within their own country, usually from rural areas to urban centers, in search of better job prospects or improved living conditions. International migrants are individuals who cross international borders to seek employment in another country. They may move to developed countries in search of higher wages, better working conditions, or to fill labor market gaps. Migrant workers often take up jobs in industries such as agriculture, construction, domestic work, manufacturing, healthcare, and service sectors. They contribute to the labor force of the destination country and play a significant role in the economies of both their home and host countries. However, migrant workers face various challenges and problems that can significantly affect their well-being and livelihoods.

Migrant workers are vulnerable to exploitation and abuse by unscrupulous employers. They may be subjected to long working hours, low wages, dangerous working conditions, and denial of basic labor rights. Some employers take advantage of their limited legal protections and their need for employment, making it difficult for migrants to assert their rights. Moreover, migrant workers often face discrimination based on their nationality, ethnicity, or immigration status. They may be treated unfairly in terms of wages, benefits, promotions, and job security. Discrimination can also manifest in social exclusion, limited access to public services, and stigmatization.Also, migrant workers may lack sufficient legal protections in the destination country. They might have limited access to justice, face barriers in reporting abuses, and encounter difficulties in obtaining legal status or work permits. The absence of robust legal frameworks can leave migrants vulnerable to exploitation and make it challenging for them to seek recourse.

Migrant workers often live in overcrowded and substandard accommodation provided by their employers or labor brokers. These conditions can negatively impact their health and well-being. Additionally, they may face difficulties accessing basic amenities, such as healthcare, education, and sanitation facilities. Migrant workers also frequently leave their families and support networks behind to seek better job opportunities. This separation can cause emotional distress and strain family relationships. Additionally, the high costs associated with migration can make it challenging for workers to send money back home or return to their families regularly.

Furthermore, migrant workers may face language barriers in the destination country, which can limit their ability to communicate effectively, access services, and understand their rights. Cultural differences can also pose challenges, making it harder for migrants to integrate into the local community and navigate social norms. Besides, migrant workers often have limited access to social protection measures, such as unemployment benefits, healthcare, and retirement plans. This lack of social safety nets can leave them vulnerable during periods of unemployment, illness, or old age. Likewise, some migrant workers fall victim

[a]drvelsngm@gmail.com

to human trafficking and forced labor, where they are deceived or coerced into exploitative situations. They may be trapped in debt bondage, forced to work in hazardous conditions, or subjected to physical and psychological abuse.Hence, in this study an attempt has been made to identify the major problems faced by migrant workers at Coimbatore district and to offer suitable suggestions for addressing their issues.

Review of Literature

Surabhi and Kumar (2007) observed that poor sanitation facilities, poor drinking water, poor working and living conditions are the problems faced by migrant workers.

Jane (2016) ascertained that language constraint, social entitlements, diversity of culture, social and political exclusion and access to identity documentation are the problems faced by migrant workers.

Acharya and Reddy (2016) observed that poor wages and poor infrastructure facilities at workplace are the problems faced by migrant workers.

Sally and Marc (2018) ascertained that low wages, long working hours, human rights violation, human trafficking and violence are the major problems faced by migrant workers.

Barani and Pavithra (2019) ascertained that poor working conditions, absence of social protection, low wagesand social exclusion are the problems faced by migrant workers.

Baisantri (2019) ascertained that lack of access to social protection, poor and irregular remittance of wages and political exclusion are the major problems faced by migrant workers.

Alok (2020) found that inequality of work and pay and unfairness treatment are the problems faced by migrant workers.

Kumar and Krishnaveni (2021) ascertained that vision problem, breathing problem, sleeping problem, abdominal issues are the health issues faced by migrant workers.

Kadri (2021) observed that abusive or exploitative working conditions, limited access to social security, low wages, ill-treatment by law enforcement authorities, systemic discrimination and lack of fundamental workplace rights and protections are the challenges faced by migrant workers.

Natu (2022) ascertained that intersection of identity formation, financing, housing and political inclusion are the problems faced by migrant workers.

Research Gap

The issues migrant employees deal with include a poor working environment, a diversity of cultural backgrounds, lengthy workdays, unequal pay, a lack of social protection, unfair treatment, etc. Furthermore, it is discovered that there hasn't been much research done on migrant workers in the Coimbatore district. Thus, the current study was conducted to close this research gap.

Statement of the Problem

Migrant workers contribute to the economic growth of both their countries of origin and their destination countries. They often fill labor market gaps in sectors such as agriculture, construction, healthcare, hospitality, and domestic work. Their labor helps meet the demand for low-skilled jobs that native workers may not be willing to undertake. Migrant workers' contributions to the workforce can enhance productivity, increase economic output, and contribute to the overall development of both sending and receiving countries.Migrant workers bring diverse cultural backgrounds, traditions, and perspectives to their destination countries. Their presence contributes to cultural diversity, enriching society and fostering intercultural understanding. Migrant workers often share their languages, customs, and traditions, promoting cultural exchange and enhancing social cohesion.Migrant workers often send a portion of their earnings back to their families in their home countries as remittances. These remittances serve as a crucial source of income for many households in developing countries. They can be used to improve living standards, invest in education and healthcare, and stimulate local economies. Remittances also contribute to poverty reduction and can help reduce economic inequalities.Migrant workers often possess skills, expertise, and knowledge that they acquired in their home countries. When they migrate, they bring these skills to their destination countries, where they can contribute to innovation, entrepreneurship, and technological advancements. This transfer of skills and knowledge can have positive effects on the host country's economy and contribute to human capital development.Migrant workers can help address demographic challenges in aging societies. In countries with low birth rates and aging populations, migrant workers can fill labor market gaps, ensuring the continuity of essential services and supporting economic sustainability. They can alleviate the strain on social welfare systems and contribute to the overall well-being of societies. But unfortunately, migrant problems face numerous problems at their workplace as well as at their newly residing place. Too much problem will force the migrant workers to quit their job or even induce them to migrate to their native place. This sort of problem will affect not only migrated workers but also the employer too. It is indeed crucial to understand and address the problems faced by migrant workers to ensure their well-being and maintain a stable workforce.Hence, an attempt has been made in this study to understand the problems faced by migrant workers and to offer suitable suggestions to redress their grievances.

Objective of the Study

- To identify the major problems faced by migrant workers

Scope of the Study

The present study focused on the Coimbatore district and specifically targeted questions related to the socio-economic profile of migrant workers and major problems faced by migrant workers alone are considered in the study. Further, by narrowing down the geographical area to Coimbatore district, the result of study can obtain specific insights into the experiences of migrant workers in that particular region. This allows for a more localized and contextually relevant understanding of their socio-economic profile and the challenges they encounter.

Research Methodology

Data

Data required for them is primary in nature. Collecting primary data through interviews can be an effective method for gathering detailed and specific information directly from the participants. By using an interview schedule, you can ensure consistency in the questions asked and obtain standardized responses, making the data collection process more reliable.

Sampling and sample size

Convenient sampling can be a useful approach when it is difficult to access or reach the entire population of interest. It allows researchers to collect data quickly and easily from individuals who are readily available or accessible. Thus, by employing convenient samplingtechniques, data have gathered from 480 migrant workers working at Coimbatore district.

Framework of analysis

The collected have been analyzed by employing simple percentage and factor analysis.

Significance of the Study

The result of the study can provide valuable insights and assistance to various stakeholders, including governments, employers, and migrant workers. The data and insights gained from the study can provide a better understanding of the challenges faced by migrant workers, allowing governments to design more effective and targeted policies to address their needs. Further, Governments can utilize the study's results to assess the impact of migration on the labor market. This information can help in determining the demand and supply of specific skills, managing labor shortages or surpluses, and devising strategies to ensure the smooth integration of migrant workers into the workforce. Employers can gain insights into the skills and qualifications of migrant workers through the study's results. This information can assist in strategic workforce planning, helping employers identify the specific sectors or industries where migrant workers can contribute effectively. Understanding the experiences and challenges faced by migrant workers can promote diversity and inclusion within the workforce. Employers can use the study's findings to develop inclusive policies, practices, and training programs that create a supportive and welcoming environment for migrant employees.

The study's results can shed light on the issues faced by migrant workers, such as discrimination, exploitation, or lack of access to social services. This information can be used by advocacy groups and support organizations to raise awareness, influence policy changes, and provide targeted assistance to migrant workers. Moreover, the study's findings can contribute to the improvement of legal frameworks and labor protections for migrant workers. By identifying gaps or areas of concern, the study can help advocate for stronger legal safeguards, fairer employment practices, and improved access to essential services for migrant workers.

In summary, the results of the study have the potential to assist governments in policy development and worker protection, employers in workforce planning and diversity initiatives, and migrant workers themselves in making informed decisions, receiving support, and advocating for their rights.

Findings

The following table narrates about socio-economic profile of the study.

The majority of migrant workers fall within the age range of 20 to 30 years.The majority of migrant workers are male and most of the migrant workers have completed their SSLC education. The majority of migrant workers are unmarried.The majority of migrant workers act as family members, indicating that they provide support to their families financially or otherwise.The majority of migrant workers earn a monthly income ranging from Rs. 12,000-18,000

Table 181.1 Socio-economic profile.

Particulars	Numbers (n=480)	Percentage
Age		
18 – 20	12	2.5
20 – 30	384	80.0
Above 30	84	17.5
Gender		
Male	464	96.7
Female	16	3.3
Educational qualification		
Illiterate	128	26.7
SSLC	164	34.2
H.SC	156	32.5
Diploma	32	6.7
Marital status		
Married	228	47.5
Unmarried	252	52.5
Status in family		
Head	116	24.2
Member	364	75.8
Monthly income (Rs.)		
Up to 12000	64	13.3
12001-18000	352	73.3
Above 18000	64	13.3
Family income (Rs.)		
Up to 20000	64	13.3
20001-40000	352	73.3
Above 40000	64	13.3
Occupation		
Mason	40	8.3
Plumber	104	21.7
Painter	60	12.5
Others	276	57.5
Languages known		
Hindi	252	52.5
Hindi andTamil	228	47.5
Job experience (years)		
Up to 5	368	76.7
Above 5	112	23.3
Working hours		
Up to 8	40	8.3
Above 8	440	91.7
Periodicity of wage payment		
Weekly	16	3.3
Monthly	460	95.8
Fort-nightly	4	0.8

Source: Author

Table 181.2 KMO and Bartlett's test.

Kaiser-Meyer-Olkin measure of sampling adequacy.		.789
Bartlett's test of sphericity	Approx. Chi-Square	8546.314
	df	276
	Sig.	.000

Source: Author

and the family income of the majority of migrant workers ranges from Rs. 20,001-40,000.The majority of migrant workers are involved in other types of work apart from masonry, plumbing, and painting. This suggests a diverse range of occupations among migrant workers. Majority of migrant workers know Hindi, and a significant number of them are proficient in both Hindi and Tamil, the majority of migrant workers have up to five years of work experience and majority of migrant workers receive their wages on a monthly basis

Problems of Migrant Workers

Based on the information provided, it appears that the collected data is suitable for factor analysis based on the results of the Kaiser-Meyer-Olkin (KMO) measure and Bartlett's test of sphericity. The KMO statistic measures the sampling adequacy for factor analysis and ranges between 0 and 1. Typically, a KMO value above 0.7 is considered acceptable, so the collected data meets this criterion. A value of 0.789 indicates a reasonably good fit for factor analysis.Bartlett's test of sphericity assesses whether the correlation matrix of the variables is significantly different from an identity matrix, which would indicate that the variables are not suitable for factor analysis. In this case, the large value of Bartlett's test statistic (8546.314) and its associated p-value (0.000) indicate that the correlation matrix is significantly different from an identity matrix, suggesting that the collected data is appropriate for factor analysis.In summary, based on the results of both KMO and Bartlett's test of sphericity, it is concluded that the collected data is fit for employing factor analysis to identify the major problems faced by migrant workers.

Based on the rotated component matrix, several factors are identified as significant contributors to the migration workers problem. These factors have component loadings of 0.5 and above. The factors that contribute significantly to the problem include work overload, poor working environment, exorbitant work timing, Poor employer support, native people giving less support for their employees, employer paying very low salary, fear of police due to their

Table 181.3 Problems of migrant workers.

Problems	1	2	3	4	5	6	7
Work overload	.873						
Avoidingnative people is a problem	.864						
Poorworkingenvironment	.825						
Exorbitantwork timing	.816						
Pooremployersupport		.532					
Nativepeoplearegivinglesssupport orcareofme		.523					
Employerpaid verylowsalaryas mentioned		.838					
Fear of police, becauseoftheir suspiciousnature		.816					
Health problems		.756					
Hazardousnature ofjob is agonyforme			.889				
Never got salaryin time			.853				
Experiencedbadtreatmentfromcoworkers			.818				
Salarywasreduced aspunishment				.690			
Discriminationinwork				.642			
Unabletoavailloanfrombankerorfrom employer				.537			
Employeemisbehavior					.849		
Languageproblem					.842		
Workinvolves morerisk thannatives						.787	
Loneliness						.560	
Threatfromlocal people							.862
Poor support fromcolleaguesorroommates							.667
Difficulttominglewith others							
Face badtreatmentfromthelabordepartment							
Discriminationinsalary/wagepayment							
Eigen values	7.754	2.670	1.735	1.580	1.289	1.241	1.113
% of variance	32.310	11.125	7.229	6.583	5.372	5.171	4.638
Cumulative % of variance	32.310	43.435	50.664	57.248	62.620	67.791	72.429

Source: Author

suspicious nature, health problems, hazardous nature of the job, never getting salary in time, experienced bad treatment from co-workers, salary being reduced as punishment, discrimination in work, unable to avail loan from banker or employer, employee misbehavior, language problem, work involves more risk than natives, loneliness, threat from local people and poor support from colleagues or roommates, these factors, identified through the analysis of the rotated component matrix, contribute significantly to the migration workers problem.

Based on the information provided, factor one contributes 32.310% toward the migration workers problem. The other factors contribute the following percentages: 11.125%, 7.229%, 6.583%, 5.372%, 5.171%, and 4.638%. The total cumulative percentage of these seven factors toward the migration workers problem is 72.429%.

Suggestions

Reducing the problems faced by migrant workers requires a comprehensive approach involving various stakeholders. Here are some suggestions to address these issues:

- Governments should enact and enforce robust labor laws and regulations that specifically protect the rights of migrant workers. These laws should cover areas such as fair wages, working hours, occupational safety, and protection against discrimination and exploitation.

- Establish and enforce regulations on fair recruitment practices to prevent fraudulent recruitment, human trafficking, and debt bondage. This includes ensuring transparent and ethical recruitment processes, prohibiting excessive recruitment fees, and holding recruitment agencies accountable for their actions.
- Governments should ensure that migrant workers have access to essential social services, including healthcare, education, housing, and legal aid. This requires removing barriers such as language barriers, discrimination, and lack of documentation that may hinder access to these services.
- Provide training and skills development programs for migrant workers to enhance their employability and enable them to access better job opportunities. Additionally, promote the recognition and certification of skills acquired abroad to facilitate their reintegration into the labor market upon return.
- Encourage programs and initiatives that promote the integration of migrant workers into the local communities. This can include language and cultural orientation programs, support networks, and initiatives that promote social cohesion and reduce discrimination.
- Establish effective mechanisms for migrant workers to report grievances, seek redress, and obtain legal assistance without fear of reprisals. This can be achieved through the establishment of helplines, complaint centers, and accessible legal aid services.
- Encourage international cooperation and collaboration between countries of origin and destination to protect the rights and welfare of migrant workers. This includes sharing best practices, harmonizing labor standards, and facilitating the exchange of information and experiences.
- Conduct awareness campaigns to educate employers, recruitment agencies, local communities, and migrant workers themselves about the rights, responsibilities, and challenges faced by migrant workers. Promote a culture of respect, empathy, and inclusiveness towards migrant workers.
- Governments should establish effective mechanisms to monitor and enforce compliance with labor laws and regulations, ensuring that employers and recruitment agencies adhere to the prescribed standards. This includes conducting regular inspections, imposing penalties for violations, and ensuring access to justice for aggrieved workers.
- Streamline and facilitate the process of remittances by providing secure and cost-effective channels for migrant workers to send money to their families. Additionally, promote financial literacy programs to help migrant workers make informed financial decisions and manage their finances effectively.

Conclusion

The problems faced by migrant workers are multifaceted and require comprehensive solutions to address their underlying causes. Migrant workers often endure labor exploitation, working in hazardous conditions, and facing inadequate legal protections. Their social exclusion and limited access to essential services further exacerbate their vulnerability. These issues are not isolated incidents but are prevalent on a global scale. To mitigate these problems, governments, international organizations, and civil society must work collaboratively to implement effective policies. It is crucial to enforce labor laws that protect the rights of migrant workers, ensure fair wages, and establish safe working conditions. Strengthening legal frameworks, monitoring mechanisms, and enforcement systems is essential to combat labor exploitation and hold employers accountable for their actions. Furthermore, social inclusion programs should be developed to foster integration and equal treatment of migrant workers within host societies. Providing access to education, healthcare, housing, and other essential services can significantly improve the well-being and quality of life for migrant workers, thereby they may contribute their level best not only for the betterment for workplace but for the nation too.

Scope for Further Research

The issue of migrant workers presents a significant scope for further research. Migrant workers face various challenges and problems that can have far-reaching implications for individuals, communities, and economies. Research can delve into the working and living conditions of migrant workers, particularly in sectors such as agriculture, construction, domestic work, or manufacturing. This includes exploring issues related to wages, accommodation, access to basic amenities, health and safety standards, and working hours. Understanding these conditions can help identify areas for improvement and inform policy decisions. Investigating the labor rights and protections available to migrant workers is crucial. This research can focus on examining existing legal frameworks, policies, and mechanisms in place to safeguard the rights of migrant workers. It can also explore the effectiveness of enforcement mechanisms and identify any gaps or challenges in ensuring adequate protection. Research can explore the social integration of migrant workers within host communities. This includes examining issues such as social cohesion, community acceptance, language barriers, cultural adaptation, and experiences of discrimination or exclusion. Understanding these dynamics can help develop strategies to promote inclusivity and reduce social disparities.

Investigating the accessibility and quality of healthcare and social services for migrant workers is important. Research can examine barriers to healthcare, including language barriers, lack of documentation, or discrimination. It can also explore the availability of social services such as education, housing, legal aid, and support networks for migrant workers. Research can explore the mental health challenges faced by migrant workers, including stress, isolation, and psychological distress. It can investigate the impact of separation from families, precarious living conditions, and the lack of social support systems. Identifying the specific mental health needs of migrant workers can inform the development of targeted interventions and support services. Examining the economic contributions of migrant workers can provide insights into their role in the host country's economy. Research can focus on understanding the sectors in which migrant workers contribute significantly, their impact on job markets, and their contributions to economic development through remittances and entrepreneurship. Research can assess existing policies and governance mechanisms related to migrant workers. This includes examining the effectiveness of migration policies, labor regulations, social protection measures, and integration programs. Identifying gaps and best practices can inform policy recommendations aimed at improving the situation of migrant workers.

References

Acharya, S., and Reddy, S. (2016). Migrant women in construction work: examining issues and challenges in Delhi. *Amity Journal of Healthcare Management*, 1(1), 1–20.

Alok, A. (2020). Impact of COVID-19 on migrant workers: issues and challenges. *International Journal of Research and Review*, 7(7), 143–152.

Baisantri, J. P. (2019). Problems of labour migration in Bihar. *International Journal of Scientific Research in Multidisciplinary Studies*, 5(9), 70–74.

Barani and Pavithra (2019). Issues faced by migrant workers in textile mills, Erode district. *Journal of Emerging Technologies and Innovative Research*, 6(1), 631–635.

Jane, A. (2016). A study on the internal migrant labour – issues and policies. *Indian Journal of Applied Research*, 6(4), 81–83.

Kadri, H. A. (2021). Problems of migrant workers in India: a post pandemic scenario. *Indian Journal of Law and Justice*, 12(1), 80–81.

Kumar, A., and Krishnaveni (2021). A study on the health problems of migrant workers in Trivandrum district, Kerala. *International Journal of Creative Research Thoughts*, 9(3), 4475–4482.

Natu, D. (2022). Challenges faced by inter-state migrant workers in India: an analysis. *International Journal of Policy Sciences and Law*, 2(4), 3959–3973.

Sally and Marc (2018). Migrant workers and their occupational health and safety. *Annual Review of Public Health*, 39, 361–365.

Surabhi, K. S., and Kumar, A. (2007). Labour Migration to Kerala: A Study of Tamil Migrant Labourers in Kochi. Working Paper 16. Centre for Socio-Economic and Environmental Studies, Kochi, Kerala.

182 Quality of work life and its impact on employee satisfaction among the female faculty working in arts and science colleges in Coimbatore district

Sumathi, G., Velmurugan, R. and Mathan Kumar, V.

Associate Professor, Department of Management, Karpagam Academy of Higher Education, Coimbatore, Tamil Nadu, India

Abstract

In educational institutions teaching fraternities play a vital role for growing young brains. The aim of this research is to identify the demographic factors influencing quality of work life of female professionals and its impact on their level of satisfaction. Quality of work life (QWL) refers to the extent of the pleasure or gratification of the teaching faculty toward their work. QWL enhances the Efficiency and their work performance of the female faculty members. In the current study relationship between QWL and employee satisfaction of the female faculty members employed in arts and science colleges in Coimbatore district.

Keywords: Employee satisfaction, female faculty members, quality of work life

Introduction

The achievement of any educational institution based on the more involvement, high effort and commitment, faculty members contribution towards their work of the faculty and their professional knowledge. Faculty members are the greatest vital forces of education as they play a vital role in the global growth in academic life of students. Quality of work life (QWL) is the faculty members accomplishment level towards their work. QWL is measured as a valuable characteristic in the educational institution. It also encourages and enhances the faculty member's efficiency and performance. The QWL is considered as a most asset because their performance rapidly influences the growth and performance of students who are to be the backbone of every nation. In the rapid changes of educational field, every institution implements new teaching aspects day to day. In India a teacher occupies a high position in the teaching –learning evaluation because they are considered as the pillars of the society, who help students to grow to bear the accountability of taking their country ahead of others. Female teaching professionals need a very good work environment, safety and security, rewards and recognition, individuality with respect to work and good work life balance and family members support with respect to family side.

Literature Review

Rao et al. (2013) found that aged teachers have QWL as compared to younger teachers. They also identified there is no significant difference between the subject they have handled. Bhavani and Jegadeeshwaran (2014) examined that working environment considered as most important factor for job satisfaction other than monetary benefit and job security. family life, professional growth, working condition and compensatory policy also influence the women teachers QWL. Manju (2014) ascertained that the primary school teachers experienced average QWL and QWL vary from male and female teachers. Singh and Singh (2015) found that level job satisfaction, commitment towards work, engagement, performance level, work life balance, organizational commitment are the factors of QWL. Çetinkanat and Kösterelioğlu (2016) stated that that teachers showed undesirable observations in the salary and supplementary benefits and involvement and responsibility at work sub dimensions of the QWL scale, while they had positive perceptions in the other sub dimensions. Shanmuga Priya and Vijayadurai (2017) examined that heavy workload and are the main factor which affects QWL. Bindi and Dharmaraj (2017) ascertained that the psychological issues affect QWL and automatically it affects the employee performance. Hasanati

---

[a]drvelsngm@gmail.com

(2018) found that the QWL suggestively affects the emotional commitment of the profession, and it does not affect the continuance commitment to the profession. Verma and Sharma (2018) in their study they examined that financial and promotional factors, lack of carrier development, work life balance, working environment, autonomy in decision making, long working hours, job security, work recognition and appreciation of workers are the factors which affect quality of work life of academic professionals. Nair and Subash (2019) QWL leads to the employee job satisfaction. safe and healthy working condition, reasonable compensation, prospect for career growth, proper work life balance etc must be

taken into consideration for QWL and employees' satisfaction.

Statement of the Problem

In the competitive world every educational institution wants to produce quality output to the society. It can be possible only by way of teacher's commitment toward their profession. Involvement and commitment mainly based on how much they are satisfied with their work. Good and satisfied environment must enhance the productivity of the teaching fraternities. Many studies have been conducted relating QWL of teaching professionals only few studies are available female faculty

Table 182.1 Demographic profile of the female faculty members.

Variables	Particulars	Number of respondents	Percentage of respondents
Age	Up to 25	118	22.9
	26 to 40	293	56.9
	Above 40	104	20.2
Area of residence	Urban	199	38.6
	Semi urban	199	38.6
	Rural	117	22.7
Marital status	Married	353	68.5
	Unmarried	162	31.5
Educational qualification	PG	56	10.9
	M.Phil.	332	64.5
	Ph.D.	127	24.7
Type of family	Joint	241	46.8
	Nuclear	274	53.2
Monthly income	Up to 15000	23	4.5
	15001-30000	441	85.6
	Above 30000	51	9.9
Family income	Up to 30000	44	8.5
	30001-60000	294	57.1
	Above 60000	177	34.4
Designation	Assistant professor	473	91.8
	Associate professor	38	7.4
	Professor	4	.8
Total experience	Up to 5	67	13.0
	6 to 10	374	72.6
	Above 10	74	14.4
Present institution experience	Up to 2	161	31.3
	3 to 4	155	30.1
	Above 4	199	38.6

Source: Author

Table 182.2 Study focuses association between QWL and employee satisfaction.

Correlations			QWL	Job satisfaction
Job satisfaction	Pearson correlation		1	.094
	Sig. (2-tailed)			.161
	N		515	515
QWL	Pearson correlation		.940**	1
	Sig. (2-tailed)		.000	
	N		515	515

Source: Author

members QWL. This present study focuses association between QWL and employee satisfaction.

Objectives of the Study

- To study the demographic profile of female faculty members
- The ascertain impact of quality of work life on faculty job satisfaction.

Research Methodology

Research design
The present study is descriptive in nature.

Data
The data have been collected for this study is primary in nature, the data had been collected with the help of structured questionnaire.

Sample technique
Simple random sampling technique has be0 en used to collect the primary data

Tools employed
The data has been analysed by using descriptive statistics and correlation.

Limitations of the study
The research only absorbed female faculty members employed in Arts and Science Colleges in Coimbatore district only Hence, the results may not be widespread.

Findings of the study
To examine the relationship between quality of work life and employee satisfaction correlation test is applied.

Table 182.1 shows that 57% of the female faculty belongs to the age group between 26 to 40 years, 39 percent of the respondents area of residence as semi urban area, 69% of female faculty are unmarried, 65% of them got M. Phil qualification, 53 respondents are belongs to nuclear family, 86% of the respondents monthly income between 15000 to 30000, 57% of the defendants family income between 30000 – 60000, maximum female faculty belong to assistant professors , 73% of respondents 6 to 10 years of total experience and 39% of defendants have experience in present institution.

To find nature of the relationship between QWL and Job Satisfaction correlation test is employed. The result of correlation test discloses that QWL positively influences job satisfaction. Employees who feel their present working environment is pleasant at their workplace have job satisfaction.

Suggestions
- The educational institutions provide favourable working environment to the female faculty members for achieving quality of work life balance.
- Educational institutions also provide rewards and recognition to motivate the employees for their good performance.
- They must also provide carrier-oriented training to female faculty members to enhance their efficiency and provide good results.

Conclusion

In a present competitive world female faculty member need to balance their professional and personal lives. Female faculty members desire pacific working environment, acceptable income, job safety and security, flexible time stress free work atmosphere. In present day world the female faculty members role and responsibilities have changed each, and every day depends on the changing need of the student's community. The study conclude that the demographic profile significantly affects the female faculty members Quality of work life (QWL): The good quality of work life leads employee satisfaction.

References

Bhavani, M., and Jegadeeshwaran, M. (2014). Job satisfaction and quality of work life - a case study of women teachers in higher education. *SDMIMD Journal of Management*, 5(2), 1–12.

Bindi, K. R., and Dharmaraj, A. (2017). quality of work life and employee performance in academia. *International Journal of Research in Arts and Science*, 3, 29–32.

Çetinkanat, A. C., and Kösterelioğlu, M. A. (2016). Relationship between quality of work life and work alienation: research on teachers. *Universal Journal of Educational Research*, 4(8), 1778–1786.

Hasanati, N. (2018). The role of work life quality towards teacher's professional commitment. *Advances in Social Science, Education and Humanities Research*, 231, 653–656.

Manju, N. D. (2014). Quality of work life: perception of school teachers. *International Journal of Education and Psychological Research*, 3(2), 77–80.

Nair, P. R., and Subash, T. (2019). Quality of work life and job satisfaction: a comparative study. *International Journal of Business and Management Invention*, 8(2), 15–21.

Rao, T., Arora, R. S., and Vashisht, A. K. (2013). Quality of work life: a study of Jammu University teachers. *Journal of Strategic Human Resource Management*, 2(1), 20.

Shanmuga Priya, I., and Vijayadurai, J. (2017). Quality of work life of women lecturers in engineering colleges in southern districts of Tamilnadu. *International Journal of Latest Engineering and Management Research*, 2(02), 64–69.

Singh, O. P., and Singh, S. K. (2015). Quality of work life of teachers working in higher educational institutions: a strategic approach towards teacher's excellence. *International Journal of Advance Research in Computer Science and Management Studies*, 3(9), 180–186.

Verma, P., and Sharma, S. (2018). Quality of work life in academics with reference to motivational theories. *Pacific Business Review International*, 11(4), 159–165.

183 Work life balance and its impact on employees

Usha, M.[a], Nandhini, M. and Palanivelu, P.

Karpagam Academy of Higher Education, Tamil Nadu, India

Abstract

Balancing the work and life is condition harmony where a person similarly organizes requests of one's profession and the requests of one's very own life. A portion of the normal reasons that lead to a poor work-life balance include: Increased duties at work, working longer hours, expanded obligations at home, having youngsters. Directors have contributed an enormous effort endeavouring to choose the best way to deal with intrigue millennial masters. In this futuristic time of representatives foreseen to 70% of the staff by 2030, various innovators trust as a perfect chance to re-examine the work and life balance takes after. Employers that offer choices as working from home or adaptable work routines can assist representatives in superior way to balance work and life. This investigation happens among 120 representatives working in IT organizations. Factual methods received to discover the outcomes. The investigation found that wasteful parity of work and life drives adverse effect on close to home life, in show disdain toward proficient equalization path prompts emphatically the vocation development upgrades and for individual life prosperity.

Keywords: CC- career counselling, IT – information technology, WLB – work life balance

Introduction

Achieving a beneficial balance between work and life entails prioritizing individual interests across various life segments, with this equilibrium being subject to change over time. Balancing work and life is integral to fostering a healthy workplace environment, as constant workplace pressure can lead to various health issues, including stomach problems, tension, chronic difficulties, and backaches, ultimately impacting mental health through increased stress, anxiety, and insomnia. Maintaining this balance not only reduces anxiety but also enhances job satisfaction among employees. However, organisations face challenges in implementing policies that support work-life balance, as employees seek not only a job but also stress relief beyond career growth. Recognizing the significance of work-life balance for employee productivity and creativity, employers offer various programmes such as flexible hours, shifts, team outings, accommodation facilities, and healthcare centres to motivate employees to work efficiently. As a result, employees feel motivated, loyal, and committed to organisations that invest in providing a healthy balance between work and life. The current research aims to explore work-life balance among IT company employees, examining their strategies for managing and balancing career and personal life, and summarising the positive and negative impacts of these efforts.

Literature Review

Table 183.1 Exploring work-life balance: perspectives, challenges, and gender dynamics.

Study	Main focus	Key findings
Baral and Bhargavabaral [1]	Explores HR interventions for balancing work and life	Highlights challenges faced by HR directors in implementing work-life balance policies in their organizations.
Holly and Mohnen [2]	Examines effective hours of work and work-life balance	Finds that reducing work hours doesn't necessarily lead to employee dissatisfaction; long hours can positively impact job satisfaction.
Beccareb [3]	Discusses work-life balance between men and women	Notes gender differences in perceptions of work-life balance, with women dedicating more time to work and men pursuing personal interests. Balance involves both division and harmony based on individual needs.

Source: Author

[a]drusha.m@kahedu.edu.in

Problem Statement

In today's business environment, efficiency is crucial, prompting organisations to closely monitor their performance. In this regard, employees must collaborate with management to achieve predefined objectives within specified timeframes. Only when employees have high morale and satisfaction can they align with management decisions. Here, work-life balance plays a vital role in shaping employees' ability to achieve job satisfaction and advance their careers. The present study focuses on the aspects of work-life balance among employees in IT companies in Coimbatore.

Objectives of the Study

- Study various aspect influencing work and life balance
- Identify impact among the employees toward work life balance

Methodology

This study adopts a descriptive research approach to analyse the work-life balance of IT employees in Coimbatore. A random sampling method was employed, resulting in a sample size of 120 participants. Data collection was facilitated through the use of a questionnaire, aimed at gathering relevant data. Statistical tools such as multiple regression and ANOVA were utilised to analyse the collected data. The study considers various factors including positive emotion, training, and motivation to determine the impact of work-life balance among IT employees.

Research hypothesis

$H_{o\ 1:}$ Investigating the relationship between WLB and positive emotion

$H_{o\ 2:}$ Investigating the relationship between WLB and assertive training

$H_{o\ 3:}$ Investigating the relationship between WLB and motivational factors

Analysis and Interpretation

The collected information was consolidated and analysed using the following tools in turn with objectives of the study.

The table above shows that 53 respondents (44.1%) are satisfied with positive emotion factors, while 52 respondents (43.3%) are satisfied with motivation and training factors. This indicates that employees perceive these factors as contributing to their ability to balance work and life

Multiple regression analysis

Multiple regression analysis is conducted to assess various factors influencing the morale of workers and their ability to manage work-life balance.

The analysis indicates that among the factors related to work-life balance considered, positive emotion has the highest explanatory power, accounting for 83.6% of the total agreement towards balancing

Table 183.3 Results of multiple regression analysis towards the factor of work life balance.

Variables	R	r^2	Increased value in r^2
Positive emotion	0.914	0.836	0.836
Motivation	0.982	0.964	0.128
Recognitions and relationship	0.983	0.966	0.002
Training	1.000	1.000	0.034

Source: Author

Table 183.2 Level of satisfaction of employees towards the factors on work life balance.

Other factors	Highly gratified	Gratified	Neutral	Not gratified	Highly not gratified	Total
Recognitions and relationship with superiors	45 (37.5)	40 (33.4)	15 (12.5)	10 (8.3)	10 (8.3)	120
Motivation	48 (40)	52 (43.3)	10 (8.3)	5 (4.2)	5 (4.2)	120
Positive emotion considerations	53 (44.1)	47 (39.1)	11 (9.1)	9 (7.5)	-	120
Career prospect	45 (37.5)	50 (41.6)	15 (12.6)	10 (8.3)	-	120
Training and development	42 (35)	52 (43.3)	9 (7.5)	11 (9.2)	6 (5)	120

*Percentage given in brackets
Source: Author

Table 183.4 Results of ANOVA – level of agreeability toward positive emotion, training and motivation.

Personal factors	Variation	Sum of squares	Degree of freedom	Mean sum of squares	f-value	p-value	Significant/not significant
WLB	Positive emotion	0.83	1	0.83	0.042	0.837	Not Significant
	Assertive training	1366.551	690	1.958			
	Motivation	101.1	8	52			
	Total	13.58.749	699				

Source: Author

work and life. This is followed by motivation, which explains 12.8% of the total variation, and training, which explains 3.4%.

Specifically, the consideration of positive emotions such as happiness, optimism, and work engagement among respondents explains 83.6% of the variation in factors contributing to the morale of workers.

Analysis of variance

The analysis of variance (ANOVA) was employed as a tool to identify significant variances among work-life balance factors and personal positive emotions. The null hypothesis (Ho) posits that there is no significant relationship between work-life balance (WLB) and positive emotion, assertive training, and motivation.

The results from the table indicate that the hypothesis is accepted, meaning that there is no significant relationship found. It is observed that there is no major variance within the work-life balance factors concerning acceptance toward positive emotion, assertive training, and motivation among the employees.

Findings

- The majority of respondents demonstrated their ability to balance work and life effectively.
- Respondents expressed confidence in smoothly managing their routine work alongside personal life commitments.
- There is a growing concern about gaining a competitive advantage by promoting employee well-being.
- Overtime work leads to employee dissatisfaction.
- Employees feel distressed when they don't have enough time to spend with their families.
- Job demands have a significant impact on employees' personal lives.
- Promotional activities within companies contribute to employee job satisfaction and motivate them to achieve effective work-life balance.
- Focusing on employees' emotional well-being enhances their ability to manage work and life effectively.

- Psychological training plays a crucial role in employee development.
- Providing assertive motivation positively influences employees.
- Positive emotions such as happiness, optimism, and work engagement are significantly associated with work-life balance.
- Employee training is positively associated with work-life balance.
- Motivation also has a significant relationship with work-life balance.

Suggestions

Balancing work and life involves juggling responsibilities in separate domains, such as work and family, which often compete for limited time and mental resources. The outcomes, whether positive or negative, depend largely on the individual's management abilities. Effective time management, resource allocation, and skill development can improve one's ability to manage their health and balance work-life dynamics with more positive outcomes. Implementing motivational strategies and providing training for skill enhancement over time can empower employees to better navigate their work and personal lives.

Conclusion

In achieving work-life balance, focusing on positive emotions such as happiness, optimism, and commitment to work, along with employee counselling, training, and motivation, as well as providing financial assistance and support for medical facilities and education, are closely linked to both organizational performance and individual career growth. Additionally, implementing assertive training and motivation methods can instil a greater sense of purpose among employees, aiding them in achieving their organizational and personal goals while also alleviating stress associated with balancing work and life effectively. By managing work and life systematically and strategically, organizations can enhance employability, long-term productivity, and employee well-being.

References

Bloom, N., Kretschmer, T., and Van Reenan, J. (2009). Work-life balance, management practices and productivity.In Freeman,R. B., and Shaw, K. L. (Eds.), International Differences in the Business Practices and Productivity of Firms. Chicago: The University of Chicago Press (ch. 1, pp. 15–54).

Callan,S. J. (2008). Cultural revitalisation: the importance of acknowledging the values of an organization's "golden era" when promoting work-life balance.*Qualitative Research in Organisations and Management: An International Journal*, 3(1), 78–97.

Deutskens, E., deRuyter, K., and Wetzels, M. (2010). An assessment of measurement invariance between online and mail surveys.*Journal of Service Research*, 8(4), 346–355.

Forsyth, S., and Polzer-Debruyne,A. (2007). The organisational pay-offs for perceived work-life balance support.*Asia Pacific Journal of Human Resources*, 45(1), 113–123.

Guest,D. (2002). Perspectives on the study of work-life balance.*Social Science Information*, 41(255), 255–279.

Hughes, J., and Bozionelos,N. (2007). Work-life balance as source of job dissatisfaction and withdrawal attitudes: an exploratory study on the views of male workers. *Personnel Review*, 36(1), 145–154.

Kar, S., and Misra, K. C. (2017). Nexus between work life balance practices and employee retention-the mediating effect of a supportive culture. *Asian Social Science*, 9(11), 63–69.

Khan, S., and Agha, K. (2021). Dynamics of the work-life balance at the firm level: issues and challenges.*Journal of Management Policy and Practice*, 14(4), 103–114.

Muna, F. A., and Mansour, N. (2009). Balancing work and personal life: the leader as ACROBAT. *Journal of Management Development*, 28(2), 121–133.

Tipping, S., Chanfreau, J., Perry, J., and Tait, C. (2016). The fourth work life balance employees survey. *Employees Relations Research Series*, 122 .

184 Teaching professional's competency: a comparison between lower and higher-level academics in China

Zhang Ming Duo[1] and Mudiarasan Kuppusamy[2]

[1]Faculty of Business, University of Cyberjaya, Malaysia

[2]School of Graduate Studies, Unirazak, Malaysia

Abstract

This study aims to provide a comprehensive analysis of the evolution and current status of teaching competency in China, contextualized within various educational levels and systemic components. Drawing upon systems theory, with the quantitative research having 379 sample size which is employed through SPSS software. The multidimensional nature of teaching competency encompassing knowledge, skills, and attitudes is scrutinized. Employing a comparative framework, the research elucidates how input factors such as teacher qualifications, throughput processes like pedagogical methods, and output metrics such as student outcomes contribute to defining teaching competencies. The research probes into the role of cognitive psychology and student-centered approaches in modern Chinese educational settings. This identifies key differential factors in lower and higher academic settings, including policy guidelines, curricular focus, and evaluation mechanisms. Addressing a significant research gap, this investigation aims to offer actionable insights into enhancing teaching competency in China, focusing on four primary research objectives that range from examining input factors to understanding system-level influences.

Keywords: China, lower and higher academics, systems theory, teaching competency

Introduction

The profound impacts of teaching competency extend far beyond the classroom, shaping the educational experience, influencing student outcomes, and contributing to the overall development of individuals and societies (Zguir et al., 2021; Zhu, 2023). Effective communication is a linchpin of teaching competency as there is competent educators those are excel not only in delivering information but also in fostering an inclusive and participatory learning environment (Yang et al., 2020). The assessment and feedback mechanisms are integral components of teaching competency. Competent teachers design fair and effective assessments to gauge student understanding and progress (Galloway et al., 2020). They provide constructive feedback that guides students toward improvement, fostering a growth mindset and a commitment to continuous learning. This iterative feedback loop contributes to the ongoing refinement of teaching practices. The background of teaching competency extends beyond the classroom into the realm of educational leadership (Zhou et al., 2023).

The evolution of the concept of teaching competency within the Chinese educational system offers a multi-faceted view, deeply influenced by the country's unique cultural, economic, and policy landscapes (So et al., 2020). It is the fact that Chinese education has been rooted in Confucian ideals that emphasize the role of the teacher as not merely an instructor but also a moral guide, shaping not just intellect but also character. Economic reforms, especially those initiated in the late 20th century, have brought significant shifts, urging educational systems to adapt to market needs. Teaching competency assessment involves various methods, including self-assessment, peer review, and evaluation based on student outcomes. Self-assessment tools like teaching diaries and reflective essays foster self-reflection, yet they might not offer a wholly unbiased view of competency (Grava and Pole, 2021). Peer reviews, on the other hand, provide insights from colleagues but can be influenced by biases or institutional dynamics (Kocak et al., 2021). This includes the student outcomes, both hard metrics like test scores and soft ones like engagement, serve as indicators of teaching effectiveness, although they can be affected by external factors (Gumasing and Castro, 2023).

The quality of education in China is receiving increasing attention, a more methodical, comparative study of teaching competencies across academic levels might provide insightful insights (Demuyakor, 2020; Jonathan, 2021). To put it briefly, the purpose of this study is to look into these areas in order to provide a more comprehensive understanding of the variables

[a]arasan@unirazak.edu.my

influencing teaching competency in Chinese educational contexts (Sumra et al., 2022;Alam, 2022;Sumra et al., 2020;SumraandAlam, 2021). There is the growing concern toward improving educational quality in China, a more systematic, and comparative understanding of teaching competencies across academic levels. It offers investigation of the teaching competency for lower and higher academics in China while providing a complete image of the factors affecting teaching competency in Chinese educational levels of academics.

Literature Review

Reviewing teaching competencies is a crucial process that involves assessing an educator's skills, knowledge, and performance in the classroom. The key aspect of this review is evaluating communication skills. Effective teachers communicate ideas clearly, engage students in meaningful discussions, and create an environment conducive to learning(Bough and Martinez Sainz, 2022). Teaching competency is a multidimensional construct that has garnered significant attention within educational research, policy discourse, and institutional practices(Swank andHouseknecht, 2019). The reflection of the teaching in line with the professional standards, educational theories, and empirical evidence, the conceptualization of teaching competency varies depending on the context, the educational level, and sometimes the subject matter being taught (Brauer, 2021). Nonetheless, there is a general consensus that teaching competency is not merely a set of isolated skills but a complex integration of various elements such as knowledge, skills, and attitudes (Antera, 2021). A common division of the knowledge component is between instructional knowledge and subject-matter knowledge. Subject-matter knowledge is the breadth of a teacher's comprehension of the specific subject they are instructing. Pedagogical knowledge, on the other hand, includes knowledge of instructional design, classroom management techniques, and educational psychology (Dadvand and Behzadpoor, 2020). The two are inextricably linked; a competent teacher needs to be well-versed in both the material they are teaching, and the pedagogical techniques required to properly transfer that knowledge to their students.

There is the effective role of teaching, which is frequently seen as being more impartial, incorporate the opinions of other instructors into the evaluation process (Panadero and Alqassab, 2019). These reviews can take many different forms, such as looking into student assignments and assessments, lesson plans, or classroom instruction observation (Pang, 2022).

Colleague teachers' evaluations can be incredibly insightful because they understand the field (Cruz et al., 2020). These evaluations do have certain risks, though; institutional politics or personal ties may occasionally have an impact on them (Kocak et al., 2021). Another important metric for evaluating instructional ability is student outcomes (Fauth et al., 2019). There is the use of the test results, retention rates, and other academic metrics are examples of these outcomes (Allensworthand Clark, 2020). Furthermore, a number of teaching outcomes those are part of the motivation, self-efficacy, and student involvement as these are receiving more focus as crucial indicators of successful instruction (Han and Wang, 2021). However, because there are so many other variables that affect student performance and are outside of the teacher's control like socioeconomic status using student outcomes as the only indicator can be problematic for delivery of message to the students (Gumasingand Castro, 2023). To provide a more comprehensive picture, a comprehensive strategy for evaluating teaching competency should ideally integrate a variety of methodologies (Cebrián et al., 2020; Fauth et al., 2019).

System Theory

In the context of education, Systems Theory emerges as a potent analytical tool for understanding the myriad interactions and relationships that influence the success or failure of educational outcomes (Melder et al., 2020; Wint et al., 2022). This multidisciplinary approach, which originally gained traction in fields as diverse as biology, engineering, and the social sciences, emphasizes the complexity and interconnectedness of individual elements within an overarching system(Mallillin and Laurel, 2022). By its very nature, education is a complex system that involves numerous variables, such as students, teachers, administrators, resources, and external social factors, all interacting in intricate ways to produce outcomes that are often difficult to predict (Kitchen et al., 2019; Von Bertalanffy, 1972). The strength of Systems Theory lies in its capacity to offer a holistic view, allowing researchers, educators, and policymakers to understand how changes in one aspect of the system can reverberate throughout the entire network (Kools et al., 2020).

This systemic perspective becomes particularly relevant in today's educational landscape, characterized by rapid technological advancements, shifting societal expectations, and an ever-growing focus on global competitiveness (Tănase et al., 2022). The analyzing intricate educational circumstances, this all-inclusive paradigm becomes particularly insightful (Guerrero-Osuna et al., 2023). In order to analyze low academic performance in a school, for instance, Systems Theory could consider not only teacher competency (Salendab, 2021), but also resource allocation, administrative assistance, family involvement, and even broader cultural expectations around education (Murphy et al., 2023). As a result, systemic rather than simplistic solutions are required for the improvement of the teacher preparation, while important, might not result in major changes unless combined with reforms in other areas such as curriculum development, assessment techniques, and school culture (Long et al., 2023).

Methodology

This methodology serves as the blueprint for navigating the complex variables that contribute to teaching competency in the Chinese educational context(AlamandBahrein, 2021;AlamandKuppusamy, 2023;Alam et al., 2023). Drawing from Systems Theory, it offers a comprehensive analytical lens to examine the interconnected elements affecting educational outcomes, such as input factors (students, teachers, resources), throughput processes (instructional methods), and output metrics (academic achievement) (Melder et al., 2020a; Lai and Huili Lin, 2017; Menear et al., 2019). In addition to the guiding tenets of Systems theory, the chapter incorporates nuanced perspectives from cognitive psychology Ackermann and Siegfried (2022), comparative academic settings (Istance and Paniagua, 2019; Bao, 2020), and shifts toward student-centered pedagogy (Cappiali, 2023a). Therefore, to delve into the empirical aspects of this research, it is crucial at this juncture to articulate the conceptual framework that serve as the analytical support for this investigation.

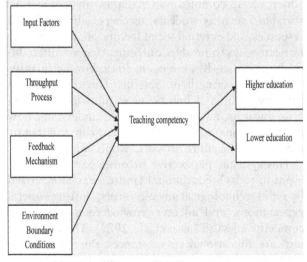

Figure 184.1 Conceptual framework
Source: Author

This collection of data included a diverse range of studies, culminating in a well-rounded and robust survey tool. The survey's initial segment gathers Demographic information divided into different sections. Sections 2 through 5 aim to gauge independent constructs, whereas Section 6 addresses the dependent variable. A five-point Likert scale, ranging from "1" (strongly disagree) to "5" (strongly agree), is employed to assess responses in Sections 2-6. The consideration for the professional competency of the teaching profession in China with the comparison of lower and higher education provides multiple shares of age group. The age between 21-29 years shows 28% participation, while following the 30-39 years of age at the participation of the 31% which is showing a sustainable role of age groups. The age between 40-50 years is provided with the 33% that is higher ratio of age group participated in the research of teaching with professional competency at lower and higher academics. The remaining 8% involvement is from the age group of 51-60 years older individuals.

These aspects determine the involvement of the male participants having 53% of the population while there is 47% female which is showing the teaching competency as the leading issue for the lower and higher academics. The contributing involvement of the 13% belong to the Tertiary education, with 28% having bachelor's degree and 31% master'sdegree holders are approached for the opinion regarding teaching professional competencies. This follows the 28% of the Doctoral degree holders having specific teaching attention for the higher academics. For that matter, the chose experience is between the range of 0-5 years with the 13.7% and 6-11 years of experience is showing the 33.3%. This follows the experience of the individual with 12-16 years with 30% and reaming experience of 17-25 years reflect the participation percentage of 23% which is considering the teaching performance as a resourceful area that is using knowledge distribution among the learners in China. The study can adjust to the characteristics of the acquired data to the thorough data analysis plan that includes both parametric and non-parametric tests with the application of specialized software of SPSS for data analysis.

Results and Analysis

The case processing summary table mentioned below is providing the cases used for the input file and data analysis. It reflects the total number of 379 participants having 100% inclusion in the data analysis process. The summary of the cases indicates zero missing element which is the strength of the data and analysis from the software, while it is stressing for the teaching competency as a core value that is circulated around the entire analysis of the data.

Table 184.1 Case processing summary.

		N	%
Cases	Valid	379	100.0
	Excluded	0	.0
	Total	379	100.0

a. Listwise deletion based on all variables in the procedure.

Source: Author

Table 184.2 Reliability statistics.

Cronbach'salpha	Cronbach'salpha based on standardized items	No. of items
.942	.922	29

Source: Author

The consistency of the measurement for the factors of the throughput process, feedback mechanism, environmental boundary conditions, teaching competency, higher and lower academics, provides interrelated capacity for teaching competency. The values of Cronbach at .942 indicates the excellent results of the reliability and internal consistency among the variables those are shared with the number of 29 items, provided with the alpha based standardized items of .922.

The variable of impact factor with the value of 1.000 is positively contributing to the teaching competency which is the shared mechanism of .000 values. The sequence of the values for the Throughput process, feedback mechanism, environmental boundary conditions, teaching competency, and contributing for the higher and lower academics. The critical success factors for the comparison of the higher and lower academics are representing the effective correlation between each value which is because of the original

Table 184.3 Correlations.

		Impact factors	Throughput process	Feedback mechanism	Environmental boundary conditions	Teaching competency	Higher and lower academics
Impact factors	Pearson correlation	1	1.000**	1.000**	1.000**	1.000**	1.000**
	Sig. (2-tailed)		.000	.000	.000	.000	.000
	N	379	379	379	379	379	379
Throughput process	Pearson correlation	1.000**	1	1.000**	1.000**	1.000**	1.000**
	Sig. (2-tailed)	.000		.000	.000	.000	.000
	N	379	379	379	379	379	379
Feedback mechanism	Pearson correlation	1.000**	1.000**	1	1.000**	1.000**	1.000**
	Sig. (2-tailed)	.000	.000		.000	.000	.000
	N	379	379	379	379	379	379
Environmental boundary conditions	Pearson correlation	1.000**	1.000**	1.000**	1	1.000**	1.000**
	Sig. (2-tailed)	.000	.000	.000		.000	.000
	N	379	379	379	379	379	379
Teaching competency	Pearson correlation	1.000**	1.000**	1.000**	1.000**	1	1.000**
	Sig. (2-tailed)	.000	.000	.000	.000		.000
	N	379	379	379	379	379	379
Higher and lower academics	Pearson correlation	1.000**	1.000**	1.000**	1.000**	1.000**	1
	Sig. (2-tailed)	.000	.000	.000	.000	.000	
	N	379	379	379	379	379	379

**. Correlation is significant at the 0.01 level (2-tailed).

Source: Author

Table 184.4 Model summary[c].

Model	R	R Square	Adjusted R Square	Std. Error of the Estimate	Change Statistics					Durbin-Watson
					R Square Change	F Change	df1	df2	Sig. F Change	
1	1.000[a]	1.000	1.000	.00000	1.000	2.583	1	377	2.783	1.986

a. Predictors: (Constant), teaching competency
b. Not computed because there is no residual variance.
c. Dependent variable: Higher and lower academics

Source: Author

data and use of systematic process in the research of professional teaching competency.

The data-driven summary of the regression modelling is provided with the classification of display that is model type and having the r value of 1.000, with r square at the value of 1.000. It is followed by the std error of estimated value of .00000 and r square change of 2.583. These values indicate the significance F change value of 2.783 with the Durban-Watson of 1.986 which is the critical success factors for teaching of professional competency.

The critical success factors for the teaching of the professional competencies among the higher and lower academics in China is examined, evaluated, and assessed with the aspects of impact factors, throughput process, feedback mechanism, environmental boundary conditions, teaching competency, and higher and lower education. There is an effective source for educational qualifications and the skills for the teachers which is the relative for the academics and these are having the system to be equipped with the qualification of trained principal. The teacher's inspiration of the student learning is qualified for the encouragement of the teaching learning process for the utilization of the performance evaluation. The arousal of the interests for self-simulation is paramount towards the interests of the students in a progressive manner. The use of the teaching competencies is intensely situational with the technology that resulted for the substantial changes towards the classroom environment. The effective and the successful teaching content is paramount for the information and communication technologies, and these are having the situational-based online learning.

The grasping of the educational foundation and a defined vision, mission, and teaching objectives, one can attain the crucial success elements for teaching professional competency. This is the curriculum development process that complies with national educational requirements through instruction. The purpose of the educational resources is to demonstrate the difficult reality of a child's development in an educational setting through the use of media and competent classroom management. Higher expectations for teachers'

obligations include intimate, competent factors that influence their ability to teach both higher and lower academic subjects. The limited use of technology is making teaching more difficult because it is hurting students' careers in the current academic competition between lower and higher education levels. Since they carry fewer duties and are more focused on ensuring that their teaching ability produces professional results in the education of students and youngsters, female teachers tend to be more committed to their work. Effective classroom instruction is critical to students' academic progress, which in turn emphasizes the need for professional, well-trained instruction. In order to exhibit complete in-service programs for teachers' training, concerned higher and lower academics must effectively address the absence of teaching competency.

Conclusion

The quantitative research formation for the critical success factors is for the teaching professional competencies engaged in the classified analysis of the professional reputation that encourage the use of impact factors, throughput process, feedback mechanism, environmental boundary conditions, teaching competency, and higher and lower education. These factors are to integrate evaluation and examination of the multi-level teaching competencies among the lower and higher academics in China. The specificity of the country denotes for the difference of culture which indicate the professional and emotional attitudes for the description of the behavioral ability among the teachers to share their expertise with the students. The comparative analysis between the lower and higher academics is strategy adoption and the use of the skills for the professional teaching share of the knowledge. Communication and the professional skill of the knowledge is indicating the broader responsibilities with the ethical and legal standard of the respected individual learners. Learning of the diverse range of is the wider context for the higher education operation that is implied for the professional practice of content and knowledge. The skills for teaching methodologies are trained towards the skills of the curriculum design which is referring for the applicability of current management roles in professional competency of teaching.

The use of the impact factors, throughput process, feedback mechanism, environmental boundary conditions, teaching competency, and higher and lower education are to demonstrate the practical consideration of teaching professional practice. The requirement of specific knowledge and skills is based on the educational curriculum that reflect the competent role of the content for the pedagogical development. It is the ability to face challenges for the imparting of knowledge in schools as well as the effective role of teachers towards the duties and responsible success. The academic managers in China both at the lower and higher levels are the stakeholders those are involved for the efficient process of teaching competencies. These are the abilities of the educational professionals those have the ability for the accurate testing procedure of the subjects with the knowledge of curriculum and syllabus in a progressive manner. It is the compatibility of the technology used for the undergrad and graduate students in various institutions of China.

Teachers are to contribute for the accurate framing and consideration of curriculum within the technological compatibility and standard use of the teaching professional competency. For futureconsideration, the creative process of teaching is to be considered with the aim and intentions of the increasing teachers competency. It is the proposition of multiple measures for the teaching to accommodate the learning style for the student while putting in place the creativity of fun and adopted teacher's environment. The inculcate learning and the use of the skills versality is provided for the reduction of all the barriers involved in learning experience with the student in the institution. The ability of the teachers to construct the learning experience is among the future plans that better demonstrate the skills and efficient use of the resources.

References

Ackermann, N., and Siegfried, C. (2022).A research design for promoting and examining content knowledge and argumentation skills in socio-economic contexts in German-speaking countries.*Research in Comparative and International Education*, 17(2), 174–195. https://doi.org/10.1177/17454999221077849.

Ahmed, A., andSayed, K. (2020). Development of competency-based training system in Assiut-ITEC: a case study. *The Journal of Competency-Based Education*, 5(3), e01217. https://doi.org/10.1002/cbe2.1217.

Akib, E., Imran, M. E., Mahtari, S., Mahmud, M. R., Prawiyogy, A. G., Supriatna, I., et al. (2020). Study on implementation of integrated curriculum in Indonesia. *IJORER : International Journal of Recent Educational Education*,1(1), 39–57.

Alam, M. (2022).Understanding and improving digital tourism events in Pakistan.In Technology Application in Tourism Fairs, Festivals and Events in Asia (pp. 233–247). Singapore: Springer Singapore.

Alam, M., and Bahrein, K. (2021). Image branding factors and facilitating model of tourism destinations management during Covid-19 in Pakistan. *Journal of Tianjin University Science and Technology*, 54(10), 428–444. DOI: 10.17605/OSF.IO/956PY.

Alam, M.,andKuppusamy, M. (2023) Integrated management for image branding; aprospective outlook from abbottabad as a tourism destination valley of Pakistan. In BESRA Germany, International Conference on Recent Developments in Social Science and Digital Economy / Washington DC.

Alam, M., Kuppusamy, M., andKunasekaran, P. (2023). The role of destination management in mediating the determinants of cyberjaya tourism image branding.*Cogent Business and Management*,10(3), 2259579.

Allensworth, E. M., and Clark, K. (2020). High school GPAs and ACT scores as predictors of college completion: examining assumptions about consistency across high schools. *Educational Researcher*, 49(3), 198–211. https://doi.org/10.3102/0013189X20902110.

Antera, S. (2021). Professional competence of vocational teachers: a conceptual review. *Vocations and Learning*, 14(3), 459–479. https://doi.org/10.1007/s12186-021-09271-7.

Bao, W. (2020). COVID-19 and online teaching in higher education: a case study of Peking University. *Human Behavior and Emerging Technologies*, 2(2), 113–115. https://doi.org/10.1002/hbe2.191.

Bhati, A., and Song, I. (2019). New methods for collaborative experiential learning to provide personalised formative assessment. *International Journal of Emerging Technologies in Learning*, 14(7), 179–195. https://doi.org/10.3991/ijet.v14i07.9173.

Bough, A., and Martinez Sainz, G. (2022). Digital learning experiences and spaces: learning from the past to design better pedagogical and curricular futures. *Curriculum Journal* . https://doi.org/10.1002/curj.184.

Brauer, S. (2021). Towards competence-oriented higher education: a systematic literature review of the different perspectives on successful exit profiles. *Education and Training*, 63(9), 1376–1390. https://doi.org/10.1108/ET-07-2020-0216.

Cebrián, G., Junyent, M., and Mulà, I. (2020). Competencies in education for sustainable development: Emerging teaching and research developments. *Sustainability (Switzerland)*, 12(2), 579.MDPI. https://doi.org/10.3390/su12020579.

Cruz, M. L., Saunders-Smits, G. N., andGroen, P. (2020). Evaluation of competency methods in engineering education: a systematic review. *European Journal of Engineering Education*, 45(5), 729–757. Taylor and Francis Ltd. https://doi.org/10.1080/03043797.2019.1671810.

185 Supply chain management in e-commerce: examining the critical success factors in Malaysia

Mo Tong Zhi[1] and Mudiarasan Kuppusamy[2,a]

[1]Faculty of Business, University of Cyberjaya, Malaysia

[2]School of Graduate Studies, Unirazak, Malaysia

Abstract

This research employs the resource-based view (RBV) model to investigate critical success factors for effective digital supply chain management (SCM) in Malaysia's e-commerce sector. As Malaysia's e-commerce industry expands and digital technologies proliferate, understanding these factors is important for optimizing supply chains and sustaining competitiveness. The RBV model, emphasizing competitive advantages through valuable resources, and using the PLS-SEM model for the data analysis. These resources can include advanced technologies, organizational capabilities, and strategic partnerships. Using the RBV lens, this research find that supply chain strategies, technologies, and organizational factors are underpinning the successful digital SCM in Malaysia's e-commerce market. The research is useful for the actionable insights for practitioners and policymakers to enhance e-commerce supply chain performance and sustainability, while contributing to the e-commerce sector's continued growth.

Keywords: Digital, e-commerce, market dynamics, strategic management, supply chain management

Introduction

Supply chain management (SCM) is a critical component of modern business operations that ensures the efficient and effective flow of goods, services, and information from the point of origin to the point of consumption (da Silva et al., 2023). It involves the orchestration of all parties involved, both directly and indirectly, in fulfilling a customer request. The main objective of SCM is to minimize operational costs while enhancing service levels to create value for consumers and competitive advantage for the organization(Wamba and Queiroz, 2020). SCM encompasses a broad range of activities, such as demand planning, sourcing of raw materials, production, inventory management, transportation logistics, and customer service(Obaid et al., 2022). Each stage represents a different link in the supply chain that must operate seamlessly to ensure product availability, quality, and timely delivery. a seamless supply chain involves creating a well-coordinated network of activities that span from raw material sourcing to the final product delivery.

Cybersecurity is a significant concern when it comes to the implementation of digital SCM. With the increasing use of digital technologies, supply chains have become more susceptible to cyber threats, such as data breaches and cyberattacks (Cheung et al., 2021). These security concerns can deter businesses from adopting digital SCM. There is a lack of skilled personnel in the field of digital SCM is another challenge. As digital SCM requires specialized knowledge and skills, companies may face difficulties in finding and retaining qualified personnel. This lack of skills can slow down the implementation of digital SCM and limit its effectiveness. Addressing these challenges will require concerted efforts from all stakeholders, including government bodies, educational institutions, and industry players. By working together, they can foster an environment conducive to the successful implementation of digital SCM in Malaysia (Kshetri, 2021). The e-commerce provides for the knowledge gap in the industry by comprehensively addressing the tactics, technological advancements, and organizational factors crucial for achieving successful digital supply chain management. The multifaceted nature of this endeavour involves an in-depth exploration of various components to provide a holistic understanding of how businesses can optimize their supply chain strategies in the digital era.

Literature Review

The digital economy burgeons, particularly in developing nations, understanding the nuances of effective digital SCM becomes increasingly pertinent. In the context of Malaysia's rapidly expanding e-commerce industry, this pertinence is particularly amplified (Hashim et al., 2021). An emerging body of literature has begun to shed light on certain aspects of digital

[a]arasan@unirazak.edu.my

SCM, highlighting the role of artificial intelligence (AI), emphasizing the importance of resilience (Wong et al., 2022), and elucidating transformative strategies. These valuable insights, provides for the research to remain fragmented and to fully explore the confluence of these factors within the specific sphere of the Malaysian e-commerce sector. Consequently, a comprehensive understanding of the strategies, technologies, and organizational elements critical to successful digital SCM in the country's e-commerce sector remains elusive. This literature seeks to bridge this gap, employing the resource-based view (RBV) model as a lens to investigate these critical success factors, with a view to enhancing e-commerce supply chain performance and sustainability, thus contributing to the sector's ongoing growth.

The establishing data governance practices ensures the integrity, confidentiality, and availability of critical information throughout the digital supply chain (Pahlevan Sharif et al., 2022). It is for the convergence of the digital transformation that restore the organizations within the collaboration of real-time use of supply chain for the global networks. The sharing of the data, insights, and resources to enhance overall supply chain efficiency. The convergence of globalization and digital transformation has given rise to agile supply chains that can adapt quickly to market changes and disruptions, ensuring resilience in a dynamic global landscape. The customer care and the integration are indicating the digital tools that enable organizations to understand and respond to customer preferences on a global scale, allowing for the customization of products, services, and delivery options.

Digital SCM serves as a critical enabler for sustainable success in Malaysia's e-commerce sector. The utilization of digital technologies in SCM, such as cloud computing, AI, and big data analytics, has enhanced operational efficiency, improved customer service, and mitigated risks (Lee et al., 2022). Tang argued that digital SCM enables e-commerce companies to maintain competitiveness by ensuring the timely delivery of products and services, reducing operational costs, and enhancing responsiveness to market changes. Moreover, the environmental sustainability aspect of digital SCM is of growing importance. Digitally enabled SCM solutions, such as predictive analytics and IoT, can help companies reduce waste and carbon emissions, thereby contributing to sustainability goals (He et al., 2022).

RBV model

The RBV model is a strategic analysis framework for organizations(Preciado et al., 2019). The model asserts that an organization's resources and capabilities, rather than the external competitive environment, are the primary determinants of its performance and sustainable competitive advantage (Lukovszki et al., 2020). The RBV model's constructs include a firm's resources, capabilities, and competitive advantage. Resources are all assets, capabilities, organizational processes, firm attributes, information, and knowledge, controlled by a firm that enables it to conceive of and implement strategies that improve its efficiency and effectiveness. These resources can be tangible (like infrastructure, equipment, and financial resources) or intangible (like brand reputation, organizational culture, and knowledge (Collins, 2021; Nagano, 2020). On the other hand, capabilities refer to the firm's ability to utilize its resources effectively. They are complex patterns of coordination between people and resources to achieve certain outcomes. When a company combines, integrates, or transforms resources, it generates capabilities(Freeman et al., 2021). According to the RBV model, for resources and capabilities to provide a sustainable competitive advantage, they must be valuable, rare, inimitable, and non-substitutable (often known as VRIN criteria) (Annarelli et al., 2020).

Methodology

The methodology adopted in this research draws from these aforementioned factors and their relationships, the understanding of which is rooted in the RBV theoretical model. As posited by the RBV, firms can gain competitive advantage by maximizing their internal resources technology, human resources, and strategy. Hence, the examination of the interplay among technological applications, organizational dynamics, and strategic approaches becomes imperative in this investigation of digital supply chain effectiveness in the Malaysian e-commerce sector.

Positivism aligns perfectly with the study's nature, which is quantitative(Matta, 2022). By its essence, quantitative research is deeply rooted in numerical data and statistical methods. It allows for the

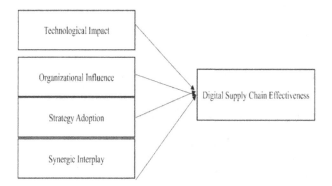

Figure 185.1 Conceptual framework
Source: Author

collection of data in a numerical format, which can be classified and processed for statistical interpretation. Simultaneously, the descriptive research design is adopted for this investigation. Descriptive research primarily describes the current status of an identified variable or phenomenon. It allows researchers to gather information about the present state of affairs without altering the environment or manipulating variables(Siedlecki, 2020). The survey tool was meticulously developed, guided by various scholarly works. A method of adoption and adaptation was deployed to incorporate elements from questionnaires used in past research endeavours. Pivotal references were gathered from studies conducted by Ivanovet al. (2020). The e-commerce is using the sensor data collection with the advancements in technology,sensor data collection involves using sensors to gather information automatically. This could include data from IoT devices, wearable technology, or environmental sensors. Sensor data is valuable for real-time monitoring and analysis.

Results and Analysis

The details of the demographics provide for the characteristics of the general population which refers to the identified persona with the size and structure of supply chain management. The role of female gender as counted is 46.7% which is demonstrating a significant contribution of female role in the supply chain management business of e-commerce. The male role

of the 53.3% is reflecting the supply chain management role of the e-commerce business while focusing on the multiple constructs of technological impact, organisational influence, strategy adoption, synergic interplay, and digital supply chain effectiveness. The age between 15-24 years of age with 14.4% which indicates the young and energetic supply chain operators which share the e-commerce role for the effective supply chain management. This follows the age between the 25-54 years having 47.6% which demonstrate the expert opinion is involved with respect to the supply chain management and use of the success factors for the e-commerce business. The age between the 55-64 years through the 28% of participation which shares the effective role of supply chain management in the e-commerce business. The age between the age 64-above while having 10% of the contribution that is the influencing impacts of the working for the supply chain management. The use of the PLS-SEM software for the data analysis and interpretation of the results is based on the efficient role of e-commerce business that is using the successful factors of strategy adoption, synergic interplay, and digital supply chain effectiveness. These factors for the inter-relationship are to be applied through the mediating role of the satisfaction which is moderating the effective role of e-commerce.

The path coefficients indicate the multiple categories of the examination with the causal links those are to connect the structural equational modelling. The value of organizational influences towards synergy interplay are 0.228 those are the positive values with

Table 185.1 Research design and method.

Aspect	Adopted method/approach
Positivism Emphasizes objective knowledge through verifiable, observable phenomena, using a systematic, often quantitative, scientific method while maintaining researcher neutrality(Park, Konge, and Artino,2020)	Objectivereality (Comte, 1856)
Quantitative inquiry Empirical observation/measurement	Positivism perspective (Comte, 1856)
Methodology Empirical investigation - experimental or survey design	Confirmatory research (Creswell, 2014). Aimed at testing predetermined hypotheses and drawing conclusive findings. Single-method quantitative research (facilitating the validation of the theory through measurable and empirical data).
Technique Data collection method (Survey)	Quantitative, structured questions. Primary data

Source: Author

Table 185.2 Path coefficient.

	Path coefficients
Organizational influence -> Synergy interplay	0.228
Strategy adoption -> Synergy interplay	0.592
Synergy interplay -> Digital supply chain effectiveness	0.694
Technological impact -> Synergy interplay	0.055

Source: Author

Table 185.3 Total effects.

	Total effects
Organizational influence -> Digital supply chain effectiveness	0.158
Organizational influence -> Synergy interplay	0.228
Strategy adoption -> Digital supply chain effectiveness	0.411
Strategy adoption -> Synergy interplay	0.592
Synergy interplay -> Digital supply chain effectiveness	0.694
Technological impact -> Digital supply chain effectiveness	0.038
Technological impact -> Synergy interplay	0.055

Source: Author

strategy adoption at 0.592. It includes the synergy interplay to digital supply chain effectiveness at 0.694 with technology impact at 0.055 those are acceptable and validated values of testifying the proposition.

The effective digital supply chain management strategies used in Malaysia's e-commerce industry form the basis of the current state of knowledge and the identification of knowledge gaps. The values from 0.158 to 0.055 are relatively positive as there is no negative sign that shares the overall effects of the supply chain management for the businesses.

The present state of knowledge and the assessment of knowledge gaps are based on the successful digital supply chain management techniques applied in Malaysia's e-commerce sector. The value of each variable is between the organizational influence at 0.491 with digital supply chain at 1.000, while strategy adoption with 0.565 and synergy interplay at 0.160. These values are extending toward the technological impact with the 1.000 which is showing a positive correlation between the variable, thereby it is leading to the development of a successful supply change model.

The measures for the common share of the internal consistency for the scaling and the determine results

for the general rule which is acceptable at 0.6 which is indicating the effectiveness of the framework developed for the supply chain management. It is also representing the correlation between the variables those are considered for the values between 0 and 1 as the greater relation among the constructs of digital supply chain management (0.733), organizational influence (0.731), strategy adoption (0.879), synergy inter-play (0.852), and technological impact at (0.723).

The PLS-SEM model developed from the research of the digital supply chain management are inter-related with the focused on the impact of technology, organisational power, acceptance of strategies, synergistic relationships, and the efficiency of digital supply chains. This follows the supply chain indicators those are supporting the use of an effective andnew technologies. It extends the relationship among the variables used through the connections that affect how successfully digital supply chain management works in e-commerce businesses.

The supply chain management reflects the digital working of the e-commerce that indicate the interrelation among the consistent measures of the digital transformation within the effective consideration of e-business. A significant aspect of managing the e-commerce-based supply chain is the avoidance of excessive inventory. Dynamic pricing strategies, facilitated by digital tools, allow businesses to adjust prices in response to changing demand and market conditions. This adaptive approach helps maintain optimal inventory levels, preventing the accumulation of excess stock that could lead to increased carrying costs and potential obsolescence. Moreover, the e-commerce supply chain is intricately connected to shipping and returns, elements that significantly influence customer loyalty. Efficient procurement processes contribute to the timely fulfilment of orders, reducing shipping times and enhancing the overall customer experience. There are the seamless return processes, that is enabled by digital platforms, further contribute to customer satisfaction and loyalty. The interconnected nature of these supply chain elements emphasizes the importance of an integrated and well-managed approach to raw material procurement in e-commerce. The procurement of raw materials is a fundamental aspect of the e-commerce supply chain, with digital platforms playing a crucial role in streamlining processes. Efficient inbound logistics, dynamic pricing strategies, and responsive shipping and return processes contribute to the overall success of e-commerce-based supply chains. By leveraging digital tools for raw material procurement, businesses can enhance their operational efficiency, reduce stockouts, and

Table 185.4 Correlation.

	Digital supply chain effectiveness	Organizational influence	Strategy adoption	Synergy interplay	Technological impact
Digital supply chain effectiveness	1.000	0.491	0.565	0.694	0.142
Organizational influence	0.491	1.000	0.419	0.483	0.115
Strategy adoption	0.565	0.419	1.000	0.695	0.133
Synergy interplay	0.694	0.483	0.695	1.000	0.160
Technological impact	0.142	0.115	0.133	0.160	1.000

Source: Author

Table 185.5 Cronbach Alpha.

	Cronbach's alpha	Composite reliability (rho_a)	Composite reliability (rho_c)	Average variance extracted (AVE)
Digital supply chain Effectiveness	0.733	0.791	0.812	0.729
Organizational influence	0.731	0.812	0.798	0.854
Strategy adoption	0.879	0.894	0.902	0.883
Synergy interplay	0.852	0.856	0.884	0.859
Technological impact	0.723	0.798	0.783	0.729

Source: Author

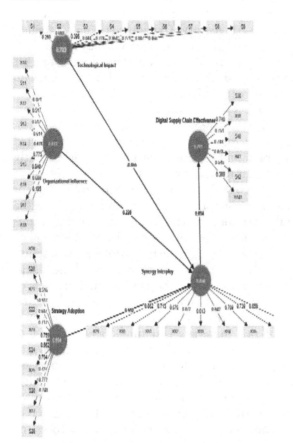

Figure 185.2 PLS-SEM model
Source: Author

foster customer loyalty in the competitive landscape of e-commerce.

Conclusion

The supply chain management for the emerging technologies using the digital resources and the efficiency is to indicate the organizational influence on e-commerce sector. It is the responsibility of Malaysian e-commerce businesses to examine the current state of gaps those are identifying the digital supply chain management issues in Malaysian industries. It is the shares responsibility of the key stakeholders to provide the efficient and effective use of supply chain to reach the consideration of e-commerce within the consumer expectation and choices. The research focused on the key areas of the supply chain management those are inter-linked with the digital conditions and it reflects the profound impacts of the digitalization on the supply chain which is manifested through e-commerce. The mismanagement of inventory poses a significant risk that can result in substantial losses for economic activities. In scenarios where inventory is not adequately monitored and controlled, the likelihood of overstocks increases. Overstocked items not only tie up valuable resources but may also lead to financial losses due to excess holding costs, obsolescence, or markdowns to clear surplus inventory. Additionally, mismanagement can result in inaccurate order fulfilment, leading to preventable returns.

The cybersecurity vulnerabilities are another critical concern within supply chain technology. The presence of data silos and limited scalability can expose the supply chain to potential cyber threats. Ensuring the security of sensitive information is paramount to prevent unauthorized access, data breaches, and other malicious activities. For the key stakeholders, the practice of the digital supply chain is the vital concern for the industry which incorporate the quality of monitoring the efficiency in the system. It involves the better management information with the implementation of new technological tools for the quality enhancement in supply chain management. The stress for the virtualization of sales and buying products is effective monitoring of subjects that are sharing the flexible, smart, and easier information technology use in supply chain.The incorporation of advanced technological tools that contribute to better management information. These tools encompass a range of innovations, such as Internet of Things (IoT) devices, real-time tracking systems, data analytics, and artificial intelligence.

References

Annarelli, A., Battistella, C., and Nonino, F. (2020). Competitive advantage implication of different product service system business models: consequences of 'not-replicable' capabilities.*Journal of Cleaner Production*,247, 119121.

Cheung, K. F., Bell, M. G. H., and Bhattacharjya, J. (2021). Cybersecurity in logistics and supply chain management: an overview and future research directions. *Transportation Research Part E: Logistics and Transportation Review*,146, 102217.

Collins, C. J. (2021). Expanding the resource based view model of strategic human resource management. *International Journal of Human Resource Management*, 32(2), 331–358.

da Silva, R. M., Frederico, G. F., and Garza-Reyes, J. A.(2023). Logistics service providers and industry 4.0: a systematic literature review. *Logistics*, 7(1), 11.

Freeman, R. E., Dmytriyev, S. D., and Phillips, R. A.(2021). Stakeholder theory and the resource-based view of the firm.*Journal of Management*, 47(7), 1757–1770.

Hashim, Z. H., et al. (2021). Impact of COVID-19 on marine fisheries supply chains: case study of Malaysia. In Advances in Food Security and Sustainability, Elsevier Ltd, (pp. 169–210).

He, P., et al. (2022). Knowledge mapping of e-commerce supply chain management: a bibliometric analysis. *Electronic Commerce Research* .

Ivanov, D., Dolgui, A., andSokolov, B. (2022). Cloud supply chain: integrating industry 4.0 and digital platforms in the "Supply Chain-as-a-Service".*Transportation Research Part E: Logistics and Transportation Review*,160, 102676.

Kshetri, N. (2021). Blockchain and sustainable supply chain management in developing countries. *International Journal of Information Management*, 60, 102376.

Lee, K. L., Romzi, P. N., et al. (2022). Investigating the Impact of benefits and challenges of IOT adoption on supply chain performance and organizational performance: an empirical study in Malaysia.*Uncertain Supply Chain Management*, 10(2), 537–550.

Lukovszki, L., Rideg, A., and Sipos, N. (2020). Resource-based view of innovation activity in SMEs: an empirical analysis based on the global competitiveness project. *Competitiveness Review*, 31(3), 513–541.

Matta, C. (2022). Philosophical paradigms in qualitative research methods education: what is their pedagogical role? *Scandinavian Journal of Educational Research*,66(6), 1049–1062.

Nagano, H. (2020). The growth of knowledge through the resource-based view.*Management Decision*,58(1), 98–111.

Obaid, H., JavidG-Nahr, and Nozari, H.(2022).Examining dimensions and components and application of supply chain financing (in chain stores).*International Journal of Innovation in Management, Economics and Social Sciences*,2(4), 81–88.

Pahlevan Sharif, S., She, L.,Yeoh, K. K., and Naghavi, N. (2022). Heavy social networking and online compulsive buying: the mediating role of financial social comparison and materialism. *Journal of Marketing Theory and Practice*, 30(2), 213–225.

Preciado, P., et al. (2019). All-cause mortality in relation to changes in relative blood volume during hemodialysis.*Nephrology Dialysis Transplantation*,34(8), 1401–1408.

Siedlecki, S. L. (2020). Understanding descriptive research designs and methods.*Clinical Nurse Specialist*,34(1), 8–12.

Wamba, S. F., and Queiroz, M. M.(2020).Blockchain in the operations and supply chain management: benefits, challenges and future research opportunities. *International Journal of Information Management*,52, 102064.

Wong, L. W., et al. (2020). Time to seize the digital evolution: adoption of blockchain in operations and supply chain management among Malaysian SMEs. *International Journal of Information Management*,52, 101997.

186 The adoption of blockchain technology in Bangladesh capital markets

Abu Sayeed[1] and Mudiarasan Kuppusamy[2,a]

[1]Faculty of Business, University of Cyberjaya, Malaysia

[2]School of Graduate Studies, Unirazak, Malaysia

Abstract

The adoption of the block chain technology in capital markets of Bangladesh engaged an insightful processing of the financial services offered to the customers. This demonstrates the potential use of block chain while implying the determinants of effort expectancy, facilitating condition, performance expectancy, social influence, behavioral intention and use behavior (EE, FC, PE, SI, BI and UB). The research examines and evaluate the relationship of these aspects while employing quantitative research method (PLS-SEM model) against the simple random sample of 384 from capital market regulator, broker, and investor with key stakeholders. The finding of the determinants indicates the significant relationship among the stakeholders of capital markets for employing block chain in capital markets of Bangladesh. The moderate effects of performance expectancy, effort expectancy, social influences are reflected on the behavioral intention. The finding also shares the societal influence and a person's behavioralintention are effective determinants to employ blockchain technology. This research has significant implications for the financial managers in capital markets, with future works to be considered on the given usage of blockchain technology in Bangladesh developing markets. It is recommended that relationship between the individual behavioralapproach is in requirement of training for to apply advanced analytics in the financial businesses using the cutting-edge methods of digital working.

Keywords: Behavioural determinants, block chain, capital markets, technology

Introduction

The capital markets have traditionally been regarded as instrumental in facilitating the resource allocation in nations. Thus, the depth of a nation's financial system has for decades been considered a backbone of providing investment alternatives for the smallest to the largest long-term investor. Such opportunities are availed through a range of financial assets, with varying liquidity levels and maturity periods enabling the interaction of both investors and fundraisers with varying investment objectives and preferred investment horizons (Didier et al., 2021;Firth, 2020). In addition, new investors are attracted by the general confidence exhibited by existing investors in a specific market which lures them and other economic agents to defer current consumption in preference of future potential gains. The returns are typically in the form of favorable price changes of the financial assets at disposal, or other cash inflows associated with holding the asset under consideration.

The sophistication is evidenced by the increasing interdependency of financial markets (Didier et al., 2021). At one time, countries were resistant to the consequences of crisis occurring in one part of the world. However, the increased interconnectedness of economic value chains resulting from globalization have eroded this insulation by increasing contagion risks between major and minor capital markets (Luo et al.,2021; Foglia et al., 2020). Thus, scholars are concerned with the insufficient theoretical orientation especially for the different financial services (Ali et al., 2020). The concern extends to capital market players in which much of the investigations are expected from the regulators though with the help of the capital market players. The majority of studies on blockchain usage have barely touched on any theoretical foundations when examining the phenomenon (Ali et al., 2020;Schär, 2021).Hence, academics are worried about the inadequate theoretical framework, particularly with regard to the various financial services (Ali et al., 2020). The nation has recently launched a National Blockchain Strategy and requires policy inputs on the use cases for consideration (Eduardo Demarco, 2020;Gorkhali andChowdhury, 2022). There is currently limited research investigating the adoption of the technology in the Bangladesh capital markets. Current academic studies have only provided a use case in healthcare (Rezina et al., 2017), financial inclusion (Nusrat, 2021) and energy (Mia, 2021). In addition, there have not been investigations exploring the perception of the capital market stakeholders as the users and implementers of the technology. Given the readiness and the Bangladesh government's

[a]arasan@unirazak.edu.my

ambitious policy expectations targeting the National Blockchain Strategy implementation by 2030 and the priority of capital markets in the process, more research is thus required to assist the government in crafting evidence-based policy.

Literature Review

Efficient capital markets have long been identified as critical in steering the growth of firms (Didier et al., 2021;Schumpeter, 1934) and consequentially the economy (King and Levine, 1993;Levine and Zervos, 1996). Recent studies provide additional evidence showing that capital markets enable firm-level production expansion, transitioning to a more favorable capital structure, and subsequently, accelerated growth of firm value (Fan, 2019;Didier et al., 2021;Calomiris et al., 2021). The metrics used to evaluate capital market performance are fairness and efficiency (Lu, 2013;Kemme et al., 2022). According to Miskin and Eakins (2018), the ability of market prices to reflect all available information about a financial instrument is the core concept of market efficiency. In order to properly allocate resources to the most advantageous and productive uses possible, price is crucial (Fama, 1970).The efficient market theory, which was developed and states that an efficient market is one in which it is impossible for an investor to obtain returns that are higher than the market rate of return, is where the definition originated (Degutis and Novickytė, 2014). Hence, the majority of earlier studies have depended on the fundamental ideas presented, which includes figuring out efficiency metrics like liquidity (Cumming et al., 2020) or indicators linked to price and interest spreads (Lu, 2013, Tsai et al., 2021; Yang et al., 2020). The graphic summarizes the capital market performance contexts that are common in literature. Other capital market performance context prevalent in literature.

The Bangladesh capital markets began operating in 1954 (Amit, 2016) as the East Pakistan Stock Exchange Association Ltd. Then the country was still known as East Pakistan. Following Bangladesh's independence in 1971, the bourse resumed operation five years into the new nation after a temporary suspension. The primary stock exchange was then rebranded to Dhaka Stock Exchange in 1986. However, in the early years little impact was noticeable on the economy until the 1990s (Amit, 2016). It was only after increased activity that considerations to institute a regulator to supervise the capital market activities were made. In 1993, the Bangladesh Securities and Exchange Commission (BSEC) was established through an Act of Parliament. Two years later, Bangladesh's second capital market, the Chittagong Stock Exchange was created. The

regulator's governance policies were initially weak and systemically misaligned without any specified procedures to evaluate and institute controls to counter any early signs of market stress and probable abnormal volatilities (Qamruzzaman and Wei, 2018).

The financial ecosystem in Bangladesh has a number of difficulties, which have an impact on the performance of the capital market. First off, the capital market is an unsuitable yardstick for the success of the economy as a whole because of its limited and misaligned activity (Amit, 2016, Jahan and Abdullah, 2021). For more than ten years, Bangladesh's economy grew at one of the quickest rates in the world thanks to its strong economic performance, which reached above average growth (Amit, 2016;Naoaj et al., 2021;Rezina et al., 2017). This expansion is not keeping up with the performance of the capital market. It's interesting to note that the primary exporting industries are absent from the capital markets. The textile sector accounts for around of the nation's exports; the majority of these businesses are privately held and do not offer investment options on the national stock exchange. According to Bangladesh Bank (2021), the superior DSE's capitalization ratio was really less than 16 percent of GDP, which is below the 50 percent mark that denotes a deeper market (Jahan and Abdullah, 2021). It follows that these companies' operations depend on bank financing for the use of the capital markets.

Stakeholder theory

The term stakeholder was coined from the novel work out of Stanford Research Institute (now known as SRI International) sometime in the 1960s. The work was largely shaped by ideas and frameworks established by projects with Lockheedthe military aircraft manufacturer (Parmaret al.,2010). These concepts were refined and advanced further by Ansoff and Stewart, (1967). Right from the beginning, the stakeholder approach emanated from management theory (Parmaret al., 2010) but was influenced by other preceding concepts such as systems thinking (Freeman and McVea, 2001). The SRI's emphasis was on the managers' need to comprehend the various interests of business owners, staff, suppliers, financiers and society in general and develop objectives which these groups would most likely be in favor of (Freeman and McVea, 2001;Parmar et al., 2010). Such support has long term relevance. Thus, management continuously pursues to understand these relationships and aligns strategy with the stakeholder objectives.

Unified acceptance and use of technologytheory

The Unified acceptance and use of technology (UTAUT) theory is an extension of the TRA. The TRA was developed in 1975 through the work of Fishbein and Ajzen (1975) in the field of sociological research. The initial focus was the development of a cognitive framework to assist in developing behavioral change strategies in individuals. The previous discussion looked at establishing the theoretical underpinnings for eliciting interests of different groups to be impacted by a technological change endeavor. The second aspect identifies a framework to identify the main influences affecting the adoption of technology with less friction by these groups. The unified acceptance and use of technology theory by Venkatesh et al. (2003) is one such framework. Several outlines have been utilized in the past to understand the adoption or resistance of technologies. There is a such technologies have been for payment systems,and more recent technologies such as smart homes (Hubert et al., 2019) and digital twins (Sepasgozar et al., 2021). The understanding of the relationships has also been investigated across different domains,such as tourism and the airlines and specific business functions within the conceptual framework(Brandon-Jones and Kauppi. 2018).

Methodology

The research methodology employed to achieve the objectives set to commence with a description of the research design and underlying assumptions, followed by the determination of the unit of analysis and sampling. The ontological and epistemological beliefs in a quantitative research take a positivist world view which assume absolute and objective reality (Cresswell and Cresswell. 2018). A variety of stakeholders, including individuals and companies, are involved in the capital market in Bangladesh. But individuals, including those who represent corporate or institutional players are the true technology users.

A self-administered questionnaire will be utilized to measure the constructs and latent variables developed in Chapter 2 of this study. This is because, the instrument is convenient and can be dispersed across geographical boundaries at a lesser cost. The sections thus measure the four independent latent variables, the mediating construct, and the dependent variable; all measured on a 5-point Likert scale with "1" denoting "Strongly disagree" and "5" as "Strongly agree". The four independent latent variable is facilitating conditions. The mediating construct is behavioral intention, and the dependent latent variable is using behavior. Stratified sampling is a procedure in which the population is divided into subgroups and a random sample is selected from the subgroups for analysis (Edlund and Nichols. 2019). In this study, the subgroups are the stakeholder groups of all the capital market players impacted by the blockchain technology use. The evaluation procedure utilizes the response rate and informant competency assessment, common bias method, participant analysis and lastly the partial least square (PLS) measurements. The research considered to be appropriate for attaining the set research objectives in investigating the adoption of

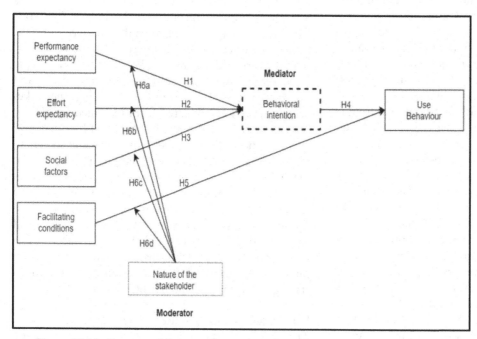

Figure 186.1 Conceptual framework
Source: Author

Table 186.1 Demographics.

Stakeholder	Representative	Population
Regulators	CDBL – 75 employees (CDBL. 2021) CSE – 80 employees (CSE. 2021) DSE – 338 employees (DSE. 2021) BSEC – listed as a company with 201-500 employees	Around 1,000 employees
Brokers/dealers	DSE Brokers association – 261 institutions CSE – 157 institutions (majority are listed under DSE) Merchant Banks – 66 Asset management and fund management companies - 66	550 institutions: Total individual dealers/brokers unknown
Issuer/listed companies	DSE – 391 excluding debt listings CSE – 362 companies (majority listed under DSE)	391 (total employees unknown)
Total		725 companies and fourregulators
Investors	Brokers/dealers	

Source: Author

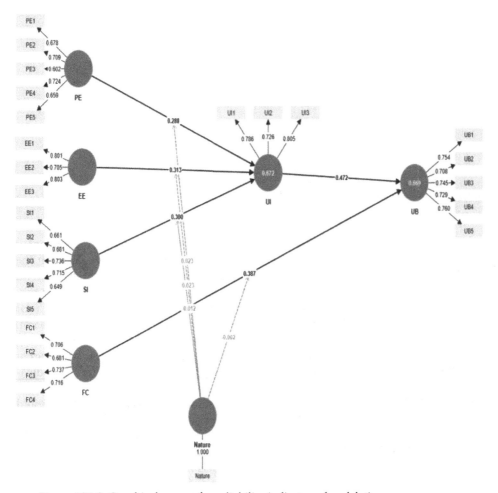

Figure 186.2 Graphical output for reliability indicator after deletion
Source: Author

blockchain technology in Bangladesh capital markets. The use of the unit of analysis, the population thereof and the sampling design are to ensure that the capital market stakeholders are sufficiently represented as informants. The detail of the instrument design of the quantitative study, as the methods for data collection and the respective analysis is undertaken within a period of two years.

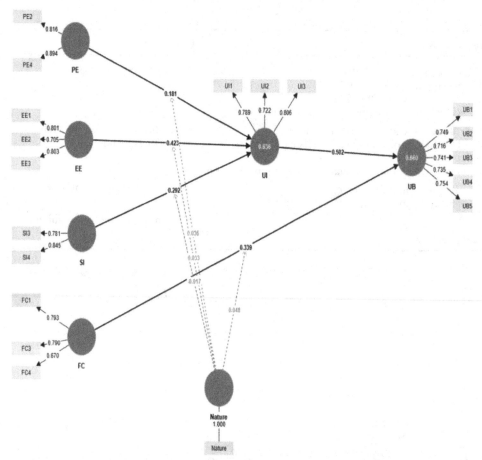

Figure 186.3 Graphical output for reliability indicator before deletion
Source: Author

Results and Discussion

The results about the use of blockchain technology for the consideration of research with the use of analysis report format. The data was validated before the descriptive analysis was performed to make sure there were no outliers, missing values, problems with data normality, or problems with standard procedures. It is towards the evaluation of the validity and reliability of the measurement model; the idea was operationalized using to validate the structural model. It includes the measurement model's quality and the assessment of the inclusion for the mediating results of the block chain technology on the progress of using financial services for capital market success and effective use of data analysis. There are 384 number of total respondents, the result of the descriptive analysis shows that 82% (411 respondents) of the respondents were male and only 18% (91 respondents) were female. As for the level of education, certificates are 49%, diploma is 33%, bachelor is 13%, masters are at, and doctorate is at only 5%. Majority of the participants are working as a broker in the capital market (270 respondents),

while the least consist of regulators (23 respondents). Indicator reliability is a measure of how consistent the latent constructs are in measuring what they intend to measure. To meet the requirement of indicator reliability, each construct must explain at least 50% of the variance in each indicator (UrbachandAhlemann, 2010). Hair et al. (2017)suggests that an outer loading of 0.708 or higher is needed to obtain a value equal to 0.50 through squared loading. Therefore, indicators with outer loadings less than 0.708 were removed from the constructs. However, weak indicators should only be removed if doing so would increase composite reliability or AVE (Hair et al., 2017). In addition, reflective indicators should be eliminated from measurement models if their loadings within the PLS model are less than 0.4 (Hulland, 2002).

The concept of convergent validity pertains to how accurately the indicators reflect the construct that they aim to measure (Vinzi et al., 2010). The underlying idea is that if multiple measures are taken of the same thing, they should have a high degree of covariance to be considered valid indicators of the concept (Bagozzi et al., 1991, p. 425). The average variance extracted(AVE) is used to measure convergent validity (Hair et al., 2017), with a suggested threshold value of 0.50 or above to ensure that the indicators are converging onto the same construct (Fornell&Larcker, 1981). AVE values greater than 0.50 suggest that the constructs explain over half of the variance of their respective indicators (Hair et al., 2017). The results in the analysis indicate that an average variance extracted (AVE) greater than 0.5; with a range of 0.546 to 0.732 after deleting seven items (PE1 PE3 PE5 SI1 SI2 SI5 FC2) therefore demonstrating the criterion as suggested by (FornellandLarcker, 1981). The results are presented in Table 4.7 confirming that the items contained in each construction are based on the constructions that have been set (Hair et al., 2017).

The results provide discussion on the structural model's assessment with the procedures that involved with the collinearity issues. It shows the path coefficients of hypothesized relationships as well as the predictive accuracy and predictive relevance of the structural model. In summary, five direct relationship hypotheses namely, H1, H2,H3,H4 and H5 in the structural model are supported with positive β or path coefficients, t> 1.645 and are significant at p<0.05. The value obtained for coefficient of determination (R^2) was 66.0% which indicates that the percentage of variance in the endogenous construct (use behavior) was explained by all the exogenous constructs namely performance expectancy, social influence, effort expectancy, and facilitating conditions. The adoption of block chains in Bangladesh's various financial services marketplaces is one of the research's ramifications. It meets client demand in a thoughtful way and has an impact on the collateral market for free lending. The many advantages of adopting technology come with the deceit that prevents the widespread use of blockchain technology. the effective application of preference for the planned adoption and utilization of pertinent capital market financing operations. In order to easily alter services and improve the well-being of financiers, financial service providers must use technology, including blockchain, into their operations with open innovation and dynamics.

An increasing number of businesses are utilizing the block chain's global applicability through supported financial operations, which is a creative and effective alternative to the traditional method of financing delivery and associated activities. The implementation of a blockchain-based supply chain enhances financial efficiency and effectiveness by presenting less hazardous options to stakeholders. The research is the realization of block chains in Bangladesh's different financial services sectors. It thoughtfully satisfies customer demand and influences the free lending collateral market.

Deception stands in the way of blockchain technology's mainstream application, despite its obvious benefits. the sensible use of preference for the organized implementation and use of relevant capital market financing activities. Financial service providers must use technology, including blockchain, in their operations with open innovation and dynamics in order to quickly modify services and enhance the welfare of financiers. Through supported financial operations, more companies are taking advantage of the worldwide applicability of the block chain. This is a novel and efficient substitute for the conventional approach to finance delivery and related activities. By offering stakeholders less risky options, the adoption of a blockchain-based supply chain improves financial efficiency and effectiveness.

Conclusion

The relationship between performance expectancy and an individual's behavioral intention to use blockchain technology in capital markets. The effort expectancy, facilitating condition, performance expectancy, social influence, behavioral intention and use behavior (EE, FC, PE, SI, BI and UB). This is reflected in the nature of the stakeholder and moderate effects of performance expectancy, effort expectancy, social influence's effect on behavioral intention. The research considered the role of blockchain technology with respect to the adoption of the facilities for the effective consideration of research in a reflective manner. The security and privacy framing of information authentication is effective with the use of cryptocurrencies those are enlarging the architectural data and internet facilities. It is unable to utilize the full potential of the technology for the multiple markets in Bangladesh. The reflective measures for the effort expectancy, facilitating condition, performance expectancy, social influence, behavioral intention and use behavioris to facilitate the technology in a useful manner. The development of blockchain technology underlines the importance of the marketplace with respect to the monitoring of the personal data privacy intelligent use of the energy. The dramatic decrease in the effects of the cryptocurrency provides Bangladesh with the little progress inblock chain technology with the facilitation of direction and key structures.

Research implications andcontribution
The research in practice is to attain the proximity of the financial purchaser for applying the blockchain technology in capital market of Bangladesh. The banking CEOs, managers, staff, and the financial experts in the capital market industry of Bangladesh are the direct and affected stakeholders. These are involved

with the electronic documentation and placement of the record for the applicability of block chain in a useful manner. The practice of research for the financial stability of capital markets is surrounded by the psychological drivers those are influencing the adoption of technology within the block chain use for the finances. The modelling of the combined use of digital transformation is reflective of the intrinsic and extrinsic stimulus that is to use the technology with subjective norms. The complex mechanisms of business and the complexities of improved performance are linked to the comprehensive financial system that creatively employs technology. Behavior choices for blockchain adoption are associated with the application of state-of-the-art technology in the financial industry.

References

Aihara, K., Edahiro, T., Onuma, T., Saito, H., Kawanami, S., Hirata, Y., et al. (2019). Study on applicability of DLT in trade matching processes, phase 2.*JPX Working Paper*, Vol. Supplement.

Ajzen, I. (1985). From intentions to actions: a theory of planned behavior . . . In Kuhl, J., and Beckmann, J. (Eds.), Action Control. SSSP Springer Series in Social Psychology.Berlin, Heidelberg: Springer.

Ajzen, I. (1991).The theory of planned behavior.*Organizational Behavior and Human Decision Processes*, 52(2), 179–211.

Amit, S. (2016). Market Bubbles, Structural Developments and Present Trends: An Overview of Bangladesh Capital Markets.Sector Report Series.Center for Enterprise and Society, University of Liberal Arts Bangladesh.

Ansoff, H.I., and Stewart, J. (1967).Strategies for a technology-based business.*Harvard Business Review*, 45, 71–83.

Bangladesh Bank (2021).Monthly report on capital market development in Bangladesh (December 2021).in.

Brandon-Jones, A., and Kauppi, K. (2018).Examining the antecedents of the technology acceptance model within e-procurement.*International Journal of Operations & Production Management*, 38(1), 22–42.

Calomiris, C.W., Larrain, M., and Schmukler, S.L. (2021). Capital inflows, equity issuance activity, and corporate investment.*Journal of Financial Intermediation*, 46, 100845.

CDBL (2021). Annual Report 2021: Central Depository Bangladesh Limited. Central Depository Bangladesh Limited.

Cresswell, J.W., and Cresswell, J.D. (2018).Research Design: Qualitative, Quantitative, and Mixed Methods Approaches,(5th edn.), Thousand Oaks, Carlifonia: Sage Publications.

CSE (2021). Annual Report 2021: Chittagong Stock Exchange Limited. Chittagong Stock Exchange Limited.

Cumming, D., Ji, S., Peter, R., and Tarsalewska, M. (2020). Market manipulation and innovation.*Journal of Banking and Finance*, 120, 105957.

Degutis, A., and Novickytė, L. (2014). The efficient market hypothesis: a critical review of literature and methodology.*Ekonomika*, 93(2), 7–23.

Didier, T., Levine, R., LlovetMontanes, R., and Schmukler, S.L. (2021). Capital market financing and firm growth. *Journal of International Money and Finance,* 118, 102459.

DSE (2021). Annual Report 2020-2021: Dhaka Stock Exchange Limited. Dhaka Stock Exchange Limited.

Edlund, J.E., and Nichols, A.L. (2019).Advanced Research Methods for the Social and Behavioural Sciences.Cambridge, UK: Cambridge University Press.

Eduardo Demarco, A. (2020). Analysingblockchain/distributed ledger technology in capital markets and know your customer process.*Journal of Securities Operations and Custody*,12(1), 58–71.

Fama, E.F. (1970). Efficient capital markets: a review of theory and empirical work.*The Journal of Finance*, 25(2), 383–417.

Fan, P. (2019).Debt retirement at IPO and firm growth.*Journal of Economics and Business,* 101, 1–16.

Firth, C. (2020).Protecting investors from themselves: evidence from a regulatory intervention.*Journal of Behavioral and Experimental Finance,* 27, 100329.

Fishbein, M., and Ajzen, I. (1975).Belief, Attitude, Intention and Behaviour: An Introduction to Theory and Research.Massachussetts: Addison-Wesley.

Foglia, M., Ortolano, A., Di Febo, E., and Angelini, E. (2020). Bad or good neighbours: a spatial financial contagion study.*Studies in Economics and Finance,* 37(4), 753–776.

Fornell, C., and Larcker, D.F. (1981).Evaluating structural equation models with unobservable variables and measurement error.*Journal of Marketing Research*, 18(1), 39–50.

Freeman, R., and McVea, J. (2001).A stakeholder approach to strategic management.*SSRN Electronic Journal* .

Gorkhali, A., andChowdhury, R. (2022).Blockchain and the evolving financial market: a literature review.*Journal of Industrial Integration and Management*,7(01), 47–81.

Hair Jr, J.F., Sarstedt, M., Ringle, C.M., and Gudergan, S.P. (2017).Advanced Issues in Partial Least Squares Structural Equation Modeling.Sage Publications.

Hubert, M., Blut, M., Brock, C., Zhang, R.W., Koch, V., and Riedl, R. (2019).The influence of acceptance and adoption drivers on smart home usage.*European Journal of Marketing*, 53(6), 1073–1098.

Jahan, N., and Abdullah, M.N. (2021). Unparalleled volatility in sector-wise return in the Chittagong stock exchange: a Covid-19 perspective.*Asia-Pacific Management Accounting Journal*, 16(3), 55–83.

Kemme, D.M., McInish, T.H., and Zhang, J. (2022). Market fairness and efficiency: evidence from the Tokyo stock exchange.*Journal of Banking and Finance*, 134, 106309.

Levine, R., and Zervos, S. (1996).Stock market development and long-run growth.*The World Bank Economic Review*, 10(2), 323–339.

187 The impact of fintech on the performance of financial institutions in Malaysia and Thailand

Pithak Srisuksai[1,a], Pichet Sitthichoksakulchai[2,b], Vikneswaran Manual[3,c] and Hafinaz Hasniyanti Hassan[3,d]

[1]School of Economics, SukhothaiThammathirat Open University, Thailand

[2]School of ManagementScience, SukhothaiThammathirat Open University, Thailand

[3]School of Accounting and Finance, Asia Pacific University, New Delhi, India

Abstract

Fintech adoption in financial institutions can lead to increased efficiency and cost savings through the automation of processes and the use of advanced technologies. Furthermore, it can enhance the customer experience by providing innovative and convenient services such as mobile banking and digital payments. The purpose of this study is to investigate the effect that the implementation of fintech has on the financial performance of various financial institutions in Malaysia and Thailand. Using longitudinal panel data from domestic financial institutions in Malaysia and Thailand, the current empirical investigation determined that the implementation of fintech by Malaysian financial institutions positively impacts their financial performance. Conversely, the adoption of fintech by Thailandfinancial institutions does not yield any discernible effect on the performance levels of the respective banks. This indicates that the potential benefits of implementing fintech are highlighted in Malaysia, demonstrating the impact that fintech is having on commercial banks in that country. However, commercial banks in Thailand are largely evaluated based on the loans they provide to customers. Therefore, the ability of these banks to effectively manage their funds and distribute them to various lenders is critically important to their profitability.

Keywords: Financial institutions, fintech, Malaysia, Thailand

Introduction

Fintech, short for financial technology, has rapidly emerged as a game-changer in the financial industry, revolutionizing traditional banking practices. Its history and evolution can be traced back to the early 2000s when technological advancements began to reshape the way financial services were delivered. The rise of fintech can be attributed to various factors such as the increasing use of smartphones, the growth of internet connectivity, and the demand for more convenient and accessible financial services. Fintech has not only disrupted traditional banking practices but also opened opportunities for new players in the industry, including startups and technology companies. This has led to increased competition and innovation, as well as improved customer experiences through the introduction of innovative products and services.These key components of fintech have revolutionized the way financial services are accessed and delivered. Mobile payments have made transactions faster and more convenient, allowing customers to make purchases with just a few taps on their smartphones. Online lending platforms have made it easier for individuals and small businesses to access loans, bypassing the lengthy and often bureaucratic processes of traditional banks. Robo-advisors have democratized investment advice, making it accessible to a wider audience and providing personalized recommendations based on algorithms and data analysis. Lastly, blockchain technology has the capacity to revolutionise the financial sector through its capacity to facilitate transparent and secure transactions, obviate the necessity for intermediaries, and diminish the likelihood of fraudulent activities.Additionally, Using blockchain technology to automate processes like smart contracts and cross-border payments can result in more rapid and efficient transactions.

Fintech has disrupted the traditional banking model by offering innovative solutions that cater to the changing needs and preferences of consumers. This has forced commercial banks to adapt and embrace digital transformation in order to stay competitive in the market. Commercialbanks worldwide are now investing heavily in fintech to improve their services and enhance customer experience. For instance, some banks have partnered with fintech startups to develop mobile banking apps and digital payment solutions, allowing

[a]pithak.sri@stou.ac.th, [b]pichet.sit@stou.ac.th, [c]vikneswaran.manual@apu.edu.my, [d]hafinaz.hasniyanti@apu.edu.my

customers to conveniently manage their finances on the go. Additionally, fintech has also enabled commercial banks to streamline their operations and reduce costs through automation and artificial intelligence.These services may be founded on fresh, creative ideas or they may be outmoded but nonetheless provided in line with current trends to streamline transaction procedures and increase clients' access to commercial facilities.

The Malaysian banking industry has responded by embracing Islamic FinTech as a new trend in which all Islamic banking services are provided via cutting-edge technology. The banking industry in Malaysia has already been the subject of numerous studies (Bakar, 2020; Saif et al., 2022). In Malaysia, there are in fact studies on FinTech. These studies might be expanded upon in this study. Malaysia is home to a total of 27 commercial banks, of which 19 are traditional international banks, 11 are investment banks, 18 are Islamic banks, and a considerable number of non-banking financial institutions are also present.According to the former governor of Malaysia's central bank, Dato Muhammad Bin Ibrahim, who spoke at the Global Islamic Finance Forum 5.0, Bank Negara Malaysia (BNM) has demonstrated that the country's local banking industry might be impacted by fintech, with estimates ranging from 10-40% by 2025 (Zakariyah et al., 2023). Therefore, the local financial industry has been significantly impacted by the difficulties and dangers of fintech development. The government of Malaysia appears to be receptive to alternate forms of financing like equity crowdfunding (ECF) and peer-to-peer lending, according to the country's new 2020 budget. According to a local perspective, Malaysia's Finance Minister, Lim Guan Eng, recently made the 2020 virtual banking system innovation available for public comment. Clearly, the development of fintech was critical to increasing the involvement of the government in the global economy. By announcing a 10-year financial master plan to convert Malaysia's financial system into a high-quality business environment and make Malaysia a developed high-income country by 2020, the government has taken action to boost fintech in the interim (Saif et al., 2022).

Fintech has been a game-changer for the banking industry in Thailand. The Bank of Thailand (BOT) has been actively advocating and inspiring financial service providers in Thailand to acknowledge foreign fintech and swiftly, innovatively, and socially compliantly integrate state-of-the-art technologies. In recent years, there has been a significant shift in the way Thai citizens utilise financial services. For instance, cashless purchases of goods using QR code scanning have not been possible for the past five years. Thais are currently accustomed to making purchases without the use of cash. The BOT has implemented a regulatory sandbox programme wherein novel technologies including QR code, biometrics, blockchain, and AI were initially introduced with a restricted scope and appropriate risk management to ensure that they genuinely contribute to the Thai economy without adversely affecting consumers and the public. Commercial banks in Thailand have also been partnering with blockchain companies to achieve new international money transfers using blockchain technology. For instance, SCB has a partnership with Ripple, and Bangkok Bank has a partnership with R3 (Deloitte, n.d.).The BOT is preparing to issue rules for setting up virtual banks, with the goal of issuing guidelines by June 2024 (Reporter, 2022). This move is expected to further reshape the landscape for commercial banks in Thailand.

The purpose of this study is to investigate the effect that fintech has had on the financial performance of financial institutions in Malaysia and Thailand, with the end goal of providing valuable insights for policymakers and industry stakeholders.

Literature Review

The objective of financial technology (Fintech) is to deliver enhanced and automated financial services. Formerly referring to computer technology utilised in the back offices of financial institutions or trading companies, the organisation has since shifted its focus to operational frameworks predicated on cutting-edge, efficient information technologies—including blockchain, artificial intelligence (AI), big data, and the Internet of Things (Song et al., 2021). Fintech has the potential to streamline the transfer of information, accelerate processing times, decrease expenses, and foster an ongoing enhancement of transactional lending (Cenni et al., 2015; Libertiand Peterson, 2019). Divergent opinions exist in the literature regarding the impact of financial technology investment on the profitability of banks.

The impact of Fintech has been studied in various contexts. Fintech development has led to increased attention and investment from commercial banks, resulting in the transformation of the banking industry (Jieand Du, 2023). However, this development has also increased stock price crash risk, which can be mitigated by corporate social responsibility disclosure(Yang, Zhang andFeng2023). Fintech has had a positive impact on the net interest margin of banks, allowing them to generate higher profits, and has also helped in reducing the non-performing loan ratio, improving risk management (Romdhane, Kammounand Loukil, 2023). Additionally, Fintech has been found to have a strong and positive relationship with the reduction of inflation and unemployment, making it a driver of economic development in Asian economies (Gong, 2023). In the Indian banking industry, the use of Fintech has positively impacted banks by enhancing their value proposition and improving service quality.

In addition, the previous studies, Kou et al. (2021), Cho and Chen (2021), Wang et al. (2021), Tunay et al. (2019), Zhang and Yang (2019), Saidi (2018) Scott et al. (2017)have pointed out a positive effect of investing in the financial technology on profitability. The banking industry in Malaysia provides a vast array of services (Keng-Soon et al., 2019). Chhaidar et al. (2022) examined the impact of financial technology investment on ROA in 2022. Furthermore, an examination was conducted to determine how bank size and level of technology adoption impacted the correlation between technology investment and ROA. The findings from the model estimation indicate a statistically significant and positive correlation between investments in financial technology and the performance of banks across all three time periods examined: 2010–2019 (in its entirety), 2010–2014 (in sub-periods), and 2015–2019. It was discovered that the European region has experienced notable advancements in the field of financial technology. Additionally, the result indicates that fintech enhances the performance of banks and that the correlation between investment in financial technologies and financial performance is strengthened by the size of the bank. According to the findings of Cho and Chen (2021), the cost productivity growth rate increases in direct proportion to the banks' volume of third-party payment transactions and their proportion of mobile device transactions.

Data and Methodology

Bursa Malaysia and the respective annual reports of sixteen Malaysian financial institutions were consulted in order to compile their respective data. Despite the fact that mobile banking and financial technology existed in Malaysia much earlier, the data collected was for only five years, from 2019 to 2022, which represents the rapid adoption of fintech in Malaysia over the past five years. During this period, the Malaysian government implemented various initiatives to promote the adoption of fintech in the country. These efforts included regulatory reforms and collaborations with industry players to create a conducive environment for innovation and digital transformation in the financial sector.On the other hand, the Thailand financial institutions'data were collected from the Bank of Thailand and the World Development Index from 2005 to 2023 consisting of the profit (loss) from

operating before income tax expenses (unit: millions of baht), value of transactions of mobile banking and internet banking (Fintech, unit: billions of baht), monetary policy rate (unit: percentage), unemployed person (unit: persons), money supply (unit: millions of bath), and the commercial banks' credits (unit: millions of bath).

Results and Discussion

Malaysianfinancial institutions

To acquire a general understanding of the mean's primary value distribution, descriptive statistics can be used. A smaller standard deviation implies that the data are more centeredaround the mean and can be used as a measure of how dispersed the data are. The return on asset(ROA) variable has a mean value of 3.6063, which indicates that the 13th financial institution's average return on assets is 360.63%. The mean value of the Fintech(adoption financial technology) variable is 0.8250. The leverage (debt) control variable, on the other hand, has a mean of 0.231278 and indicates that the financial institutions have an average debt level of 23%. The mean value of the control variable, the bank's size, is 9.657303. Additionally, the bank has been in business for an average of 45.9 years. As a result, the majority of the banks that were included in the data collection had been operating on the market for roughly 45 years. Table 187.1 below displays the overall descriptive statistics for each variable.

The correlation strength between the components considered is shown in the correlation matrix data, which are presented in Table 187.2. Multicollinearity is a factual peculiarity when at least two indicator elements are extraordinarily associated in a separate relapse model, according to Gujarati (2003). Simply having multicollinearity might affect the accuracy of the components being studied by causing evaluations of the model coefficients to be unreliable and unauthentic. The correlation could not be greater than 0.8, it was further noted (Gujarati, 2003). It is possible to conclude from the findings that a multicollinearity problem was nonexistent. As a result, all of the study's variables remained constant.

With a probability value of 0.0000, the value of the likelihood test for the chi-square statistics is equal to 66.628. At a significance level of 5%, the null hypothesis is disproved. The fixed effects model is favored, as shown by this finding, and it can be used to evaluate appropriate slope coefficient valuations. The best estimator for the model between the fixed effects and the random effects models was then chosen using the Hausman test. According to Table 187.3,

Table 187.1 Descriptive statistics.

Variable	Obs	Mean	Std.Dev	Min	Max
ROA	80	3.606388	5.143155	-4.35	38.7
Fintech	80	0.825025	0.484454	-0.086462	2.090228
Leverage	80	0.231278	0.181007	0.005589	0.636645
Size	80	9.657303	1.433265	5.767383	12.70936
Age	80	45.9125	13.62257	18	69
CPI	80	1.35144	1.714218	-1.138702	3.871201
GDP	80	0.958552	1.797851	-1.590762	3.86911
M2	80	128.2391	6.056054	122.5342	137.4975
ROE	80	13.47645	18.59954	-8.65	153

Source: Author

Table 187.2 Matrix of correlations.

Variable	ROA	Fintech	Age	Lev	Size	ROE	GDP	CPI	M2
ROA	1.0000								
Fintch	0.3418	1.0000							
Age	0.2173	0.1725	1.0000						
Lev	0.1778	0.1869	-0.0833	1.0000					
Size	-0.3360	0.1078	0.0258	-0.2956	1.0000				
ROE	0.8851	0.1838	0.1413	0.1684	-0.2190	1.0000			
GDP	0.0552	0.1102	-0.0478	-0.0333	-0.0174	0.0429	1.0000		
CPI	-0.0900	0.0394	-0.0463	0.0727	-0.0655	-0.0808	-0.2598	1.0000	
M2	-0.0453	-0.1417	0.0740	-0.0362	0.1049	-0.0642	-0.4788	-0.5213	1.0000

Source: Author

the probability value is 0.000 and the Hausman test value is 0.546. In comparison to POLS and random effects models, the outcome reveals that the fixed effects model is a favored and effective estimator. Hypothesis 1 testing aimed to test whether the adoption of Fintech has a positive effect on the bank performance of Malaysia's Financial Institutions. There is a correlation between bank performance and the independent variables of Fintech implementation, as shown in Table 187.4 where the regression equation is statistically significant at 0.000 ($p = 0.01$). So, the following hypotheses are accepted: 1, 3, and 8. The model's modified R-squared is 0.858, and its F-value is 53.73 ($p = 0.000$). About 53.73% of the variation in Fintect adoption that affects bank performance can be explained by the model. At 2.35 ($p = 0.01$), the Fintech coefficient is statistically significant.

Number of observation	80
F-statistic	53.73817

Prob(F-statistic)	0.0000
Likelihood test	66.628(0.0000)
Hausman Test	0.546(0.0000) _

With a probability value of 0.0000, the value of the likelihood test for the Chi-square statistics is equal to 66.628. At a significance level of 5%, the null hypothesis is disproved. The fixed effects model is favoured, as shown by this finding, and it can be used to evaluate appropriate slope coefficient valuations. The best estimator for the model between the fixed effects and the random effects models was then chosen using the Hausman test. According to Table 187.3, the probability value is 0.000 and the Hausman test value is 0.546. In comparison to POLS and random effects models, the outcome reveals that the fixed effects model is a favoured and effective estimator. Hypothesis 1 testing aimed to test whether the adoption of Fintech has a positive effect on the bank performance of Malaysia'sFinancial Institutions. There

Table 187.3 Regression results of Malaysia.

Variable	Dependent variable: ROE			
	Coefficient	Std. error	t-Statistic	Prob.
Fintch	2.356384	0.51547	4.571333	0.0000
Leverage	-1.463859	1.387486	-1.05504	0.295
Size	-0.744955	0.175752	-4.23868	0.0001
Age	0.023885	0.017514	1.363742	0.177
CPI	-0.003775	0.217865	-0.01733	0.9862
GDP	0.069781	0.199984	0.348933	0.7282
M2	0.054285	0.067946	0.798944	0.427
ROA	0.221647	0.013308	16.655	0.0000
C	-1.911787	9.180259	-0.20825	0.8356
R-squared	0.858257			
Adjusted R-squared	0.842286			
S.E. of regression	2.042515			

Source: Author

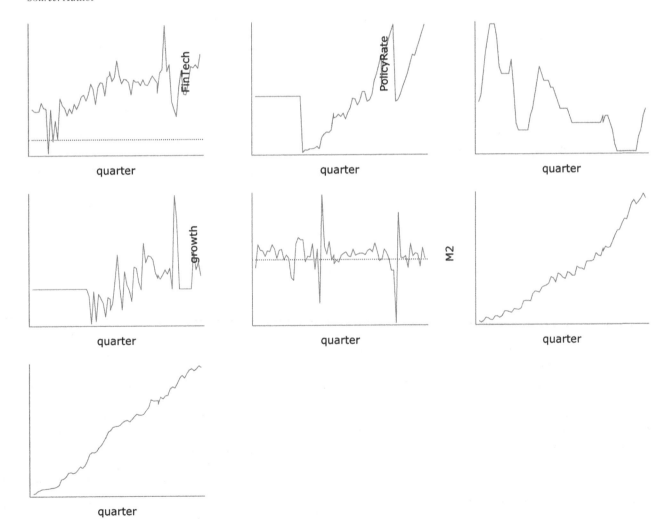

Figure 187.1 The characteristic of variables between 2005-2023
Source: Author

Table 187.4 Summary Statistics for all Variables in Thailand.

Variable	Mean	Median	Minimum	Maximum
Profit	50827.	55589.	-13960.	1.1848e+005
Fintech	7439.9	7439.9	1797.0	14597.
Policyrate	2.0878	1.7500	0.50000	5.0000
Unemployed	330.12	305.36	162.65	693.00
Growth	0.66892	0.75000	-9.2000	9.4000
M2	1.6767e+006	1.6078e+006	8.0848e+005	3.0539e+006
Credit	1.1545e+007	1.2116e+007	5.1562e+006	1.8334e+007

Variable	Std. dev.	C.V.	Skewness	Ex. kurtosis
Profit	21263.	0.41834	-0.24042	1.2619
Fintech	3164.8	0.42538	0.29866	-0.13415
Policytate	1.1575	0.55440	0.76198	0.048705
Unemployed	81.905	0.24811	1.5794	5.0252
Growth	2.2304	3.3343	-0.57863	8.0146
M2	6.4625e+005	0.38544	0.54386	-0.67102
Credit	4.1439e+006	0.35894	-0.030224	-1.2680

Source: Author

Table 187.5 The coefficients of correlation matrices of variables.

Profit	Fintech	Policy rate	Unemployed	growth	M2	Credit	
1.0000	0.3474	-0.4553	0.1500	-0.0681	0.6132	0.6951	Profit
	1.0000	-0.3270	0.3986	-0.0859	0.5981	0.5463	Fintech
		1.0000	-0.4047	0.0974	-0.7218	-0.7507	Policy rate
			1.0000	0.2392	0.4125	0.4261	Unemployed
				1.0000	-0.1010	-0.1065	Growth
					1.0000	0.9744	M2
						1.0000	Credit

Source: Author

is a correlation between bank performance and the independent variables of Fintech implementation, as shown in Table 187.4 where the regression equation is statistically significant at 0.000 (p = 0.01). So, the following hypotheses are accepted: 1, 3, and 8. The model's modified R-squared is 0.858, and its F-value is 53.73 (p = 0.000). About 53.73% of the variation in Fintect adoption that affects bank performance can be explained by the model. At 2.35 (p = 0.01), the Fintech coefficient is statistically significant.

Thailand financial institutions

Figure 187.1 shows that profit from operating before income tax expenses has undergone quite unstable changes from 2005 to 2023. The value of transactions in mobile banking and internet banking, which represents Fintech, dramatically increased in that period. The value of Fintech in the year 2020 rapidly went down regarding the financial crisis. In contrast, the monetary policy rate changed in the opposite direction. It went down from 5% in 2006 to 0.5% in 2022. In addition, the unemployed persons display volatility. Likewise, the growth of gross domestic products fluctuated between -9.2 and 9.4% during 20 years from now. On the contrary, the money supply rapidly went up similar to the commercial banks' credits during the same period.

Table 187.4 explains the summary statistics for all variables in Thailand. That is, the means of profit,

Table 187.6 The coefficients of regression on the profit from all models.

Model	Constant	l_Fintech	l_credit	l_Unemployed	Growth	l_M2	Policyrate	R^2
1	9.615***	0.131						0.0133
2	–3.374	–0.139	0.948***					0.3473
3	–2.832	–0.090	0.982***	–0.264				0.3554
4	–2.848	–0.084	0.989***	–0.292	0.008	–2.161***		0.3562
5	–6.018**	0.015	3.042***	–0.314	0.009	–2.050**	0.089	0.4227
6	–9.240**	–0.006	3.111***	–0.221	0.005	–2.224***		0.4343
7	–6.697***		3.036***			0.789***		0.4112
8	–0.499***							0.2649
9	–3.449***		0.877***					0.3344

Remarks: ** is the significant level at 0.05. *** is the significant level at 0.01
Source: Author

Fintech, PolicyRate, Unemployed, growth, M2, and credit are 50,827 million baht, 7,439.9 billion baht, 2.0878 percent, 330.12 persons, 0.6689%, 1,676,700 millionbath, and 11,545,000 million bath, respectively. Consequently, they are difficult to compare because these amounts are of various types. Thus, all variables must be transformed into logarithms.

Table 187.5 shows that the profit from operating before income tax expenses are related to all control variables: profit, Fintech, Policyrate, unemployed, growth, M2, and credit. More importantly, Table 187.6 demonstrates that the commercial banks' credits are statistically significant at 0.01in all models. The estimated coefficients are between 0.877 and 3.111. This implies that the impact of bank credits on their earnings before tax expenses is significantly positive. In contrast, Fintech does not affect the commercial bank's profit. It means that the value of transactions of mobile banking and internet banking does not influence the bank's earnings in Thailand. Furthermore, the money supply ambiguously affects commercial banks' profits. In other words, it negatively affects the earnings before tax expenses in almost all models, other than the positive effect in Model 8. In addition, the changes in policyrate, unemployed, and growth do not determine the change in the bank earnings before tax expenses.

Conclusion

This study explores the impact of financial institutions' adoption of Fintech on their financial performance. By using longitudinal panel data from the local financial institutions in Malaysia and Thailand, this empirical study determines that the adoption of Fintech by financial institutions has a positive effect on their financial performance in Malaysia, but it does not have any impact on the bank performance in Thailand. This implies that the results shed light on the significance of Fintech on commercial banks and highlight the potential benefits that can be obtained through its implementation in Malaysia. On the contrary, the performance of commercial banks results from their loans to customers in Thailand. This means that the bank's profits depend on how they pay the money to the lenders. By prioritizing a strong loan portfolio and efficient loan disbursement processes, commercial banks in Thailand can better safeguard themselves against potential losses. While fintech advancements offer promising opportunities for streamlining operations and expanding customer reach, the prudent assessment of borrowers' credit worthiness remains essential to minimize the risk of default. Furthermore, effective interest rate management can help commercial banks in Thailand maintain a competitive edge and sustain profitability in a dynamic market environment. Additionally, the findings suggest that the differences in regulatory frameworks and market conditions between Malaysia and Thailand may contribute to the varying effects of Fintech adoption on bank performance. These results underscore the importance of considering country-specific factors when assessing the impact of Fintech on financial institutions.

References

Bakar, S. (2020). Fintech investment and banks performance in Malaysia, Singapore and Thailand. December 2020, (pp. 610–618). https://doi.org/10.15405/epsbs.2020.12.05.66.

Chhaidar, A., Abdelhedi, M., and Abdelkafi, I.(2022). The effect of financial technology investment level on European banks' profitability. *Journal of the Knowledge Economy*. https://doi.org/10.1007/s13132-022-00992-1.

Cho, T. -Y., and Chen, Y. -S. (2021).The impact of financial technology on China's banking industry: an application of the metafrontier cost malmquist productivity index. *The North American Journal of Economics and Finance*, 57(C), 101414.https://doi.org/10.1016/j.najef.2021.101414.

Fintech in Thailand (n.d.).https://www.bot.or.th/en/financial-innovation/digital-finance/fintech-in-thailand.html.

Keeping up with Global Fintech Trend and Thailand's Next Move (n.d.).Deloitte Thailand.https://www2.deloitte.com/th/en/pages/technology/articles/keeping-up-with-global-fintech-trend-and-thailands-next-move.html.

188 The role of women's financial inclusion in enhancing economic growth and government initiatives in Asia: a comparative study of five Asian countries

Vikneswaran Manual[a], Hafinaz Hasniyanti Hassan[b] and Senthil Kumar[c]

PhD, Asia Pacific University of Technology and Innovation, Kuala Lumpur, Malaysia

Abstract

The purpose of this study is to investigate the correlation between government initiatives and inclusive economic development and the level of financial inclusion among women. Financial inclusion has the capacity to mitigate income disparities; it is characterised by the provision and utilisation of an extensive array of high-quality financial products and services. The active engagement of women in the financial system contributes to the advancement of the economy, thereby fostering improvements in both physical and social welfare. The research was carried out across five Asian economies: Indonesia, Malaysia, the Philippines, Singapore, and Thailand. The secondary data was used to calculate the sample moment conditions. The number of sample moment conditions exceeds the number of parameters in the context of the generalized linear model (GLM). This research spans seven time periods, specifically from 2016 to 2022. In this study, two models are used. The first model examines the relationship between women's financial inclusion and economic development, while the second model investigates the relationship between women's financial inclusion and government initiatives. According to model 1, the results show that the labor force of women (LF), the credit card used by women (CC), and the government initiatives (GI) have a significant relationship with GDP. However, according to model 2, GDP, credit card (CC), and labor force (LF) have a significant relationship with government initiatives (GI). While the body of research on the advantages of financial inclusion and the influence of product design on the attainment of desired welfare outcomes is expanding, much remains to be discovered regarding the ways in which formal financial products and services can facilitate the economic empowerment of women. According to this assessment, financial service providers and other interested parties can use suitable product design features to get over some of these obstacles to women's financial inclusion.

Keywords: Economic development, financial inclusion, government, inequality, women

Introduction

Governments, academics, and society are now very interested in financial inclusion, which is defined as having access to a wide variety of high-quality financial products and services. This interest is connected to the understanding that there are wide disparities in financial inclusion around the globe, which pose obstacles to achieving economic stability and progress. It is vital for promoting equitable economic growth and poverty reduction to expand the availability and utilisation of superior financial products and services. Research suggests that individuals who actively participate in the financial system are more adept at managing risk, initiating or investing in entrepreneurial ventures, and financing substantial expenditures such as a house renovation or a child's education.

The significance of financial inclusion for both men and women in achieving the sustainable development goals (SDGs) is supported by international research. Numerous studies highlight the advantages of closing the gender inclusion gap in the financial sector. Women's financial inclusion can increase women's autonomy and level of inclusion, enable more efficient use of household resources, and lessen the vulnerability of their homes and businesses. In other words, bridging the gender gap in financial inclusion allows women to make greater contributions to fostering nations' economic growth, lowering poverty and inequality, creating job opportunities, and creating inclusive societies. It is vital for promoting equitable economic growth and poverty reduction to expand the availability and utilisation of superior financial products and services. Research suggests that individuals who actively participate in the financial system are more adept at managing risk, initiating or investing in entrepreneurial ventures, and financing substantial expenditures such as a house renovation or a child's education.

The government is currently attempting to guarantee the well-being of communities and families by empowering women. The government is working

[a]vikneswaran.manual@apu.edu.my, [b]hafinaz.hasniyanti@apu.edu.my, [c]senthil.kumar@apu.edu.my

towards this goal in several ways, including by making a firm commitment to gender equality, granting men and women the same opportunities and rights, engaging in politics, economics, sociology, and education, as well as by treating everyone equally when it comes to development. As a result, initiatives are needed to include policies for gender equality and justice into growth. Because it fails to acknowledge the fact that women continue to have very little influence in the fields of politics, law, business, social culture, and health and education. Women's quality of life is negatively impacted (Prantiasih, 2014). The World Bank Group's 2014 Global Findex database revealed that only a little more than half of emerging economies have universal access to financial services, compared to all OECD high-income economies. A total of 61% of adults worldwide have a financial institution account. More than half of the two billion unbanked individuals are women. With regard to women's financial inclusion, a substantial gender gap persists in terms of both access to and utilisation of financial. Adult account ownership went from 62–69% globally between 2014 and 2017; in developing nations, it increased from 54–63%. However, the likelihood that women in developing economies hold a bank account is still 9% lower than that of men. In some areas, the disparity is considerably greater; in South Asia, it is 18%, with Bangladesh and Pakistan standing out as the two countries where expanding gender discrepancies have coincided with general increases in financial access. Contrarily, high-income nations showed no statistically significant differences in the ownership of bank accounts between men and women.

A few studies and research papers on Malaysian women's financial inclusion have been published. In Malaysia, Lilian (2014) discovered female empowerment among industry employees. Another study (Haque et al., 2021) discovered the role of unconventional microfinance on the economic, social, and household empowerment of Malaysian women borrowers. Another study (Narayanan and Selvanathan, 2017) focuses on the difficulties of women's empowerment in a private company in Malaysia. There have been a few studies published as of the date this study was published that focus on the level of women's empowerment in Malaysia. The objective of this research endeavour is to assess the extent of women's empowerment in Malaysia with respect to gender inequality in the economy, politics and government, the workforce, and education. The primary objective of this research endeavour is to assess the influence of financial inclusion for women on the economic progress of five Asian nations.

Literature Review

Financial inclusion of women in economic development

Women's lives can change dramatically when they are financially included. Women who participate actively in the financial system are more adept at risk management, balancing out consumption in the event of shocks, and financing household expenses such as education (Pal et al., 2022). Given the disproportionate prevalence of poverty among women with low incomes compared to men, it is critical that initiatives aimed at reducing poverty and empowering women furnish them with essential financial resources such as the ability to save, borrow, transfer funds, and manage financial risks (Bertay et al., 2021). Access to personal, secure savings accounts for women can enhance their financial autonomy and foster economic resilience, notwithstanding their relatively limited impact on household decision-making. Numerous empirical studies have demonstrated the importance of social and economic factors in a woman's life, such as her household head gender, education, earning power within the family, and property ownership. Women who are more economically independent tend to be more effective at acting independently and contributing resources through earned income to the home decision-making process (Cabeza-García et al., 2019). Additionally, women's empowerment has been given a lot of attention in the literature because it increases the likelihood that they will stand up for their rights, be competent money managers who can protect their own financial security and that of their children, experience less domestic violence, and have more bargaining power over household spending and savings(Salman and Nowacka, 2020).

Therefore, even though women make up half of the global population, access to finance remains difficult for them in underdeveloped nations like Malaysia (Al-Shami et al., 2015)they will be able to participate in economic market through forming their small businesses and consequently generate income. Yet, the impact still varies from one country to others due to microfinance work differently according to the economic, culture and environment. Therefore, this paper aims to examine the impact of Amanah Ikhtiar Malaysia (AIM. Insufficient financial resources, the absence of official financial institutions in close proximity, the exorbitant expense of financial services, inadequate documentation, and a lack of confidence in those institutions are the most commonly cited barriers to women's financial inclusion. Women face many barriers when it comes to utilising and getting access to financial services. These comprise, among other things, mobility problems, a lack of awareness of finances, a lack of identification to verify identity, and a lack of collateral as would typically be necessary (Esmaeilpour Moghadam and Karami, 2023). Financial institutions need to consider all of the measures that have been shown to be successful in addressing these barriers when developing inclusive financial services. Creating gender-smart products and value propositions that are customised to women's needs through the collection of sex-disaggregated data, educating and training women in finance, building women's networks, and preparing staff to provide knowledge and design-friendly ecosystems are all positive steps (Bertay et al., 2021).

Financial inclusion plays a pivotal role in enabling women to not only conduct transactions and obtain credit and loans, but also to save money and amass assets in a secure location, all of which contribute to their ability to escape poverty. Savings programmes increase the profits of female entrepreneurs. Women seek opportunities to conserve cash and reinvest their personal savings in their businesses(Akter et al., 2016). There is evidence that women's ability to save positively affects household welfare, which in turn influences other aspects of their lives (Karlan et al., 2016) and women's empowerment (Bertay et al., 2021; Esmaeilpour Moghadam and Karami, 2023; Holloway et al., 2017). According to studies, even low-income women are eager save money if they are offered attractive interest rates, easily accessible financial institutions, and flexible accounts. However, according to bankers in South Asia, rural Mexico (Esmaeilpour Moghadam and Karami, 2023), Indonesia, and rural Mexico, convenience usually prevails over interest rates (Pal et al., 2022).

Women's financial inclusion and government initiatives

There is a strong case for looking more closely at what central bankers and policymakers are doing to create an enabling policy environment when deciding what needs to be done to reduce gender disparity in financial service utilisation (Salman and Nowacka, 2020). Evidence suggests that policies to promote financial inclusion must be country-specific, taking into account the gender gap and particular opportunities and constraints of each nation(Heng and Tok, 2022; Klugman and Quek, 2018). This research examines the significance of women's financial inclusion and presents practical national initiatives to advance women's financial inclusion(Esmaeilpour Moghadam and Karami, 2023). Levers may be utilised to increase the utilisation and accessibility of financial services by women, in addition to their economic participation.

Studies conducted by the International Finance Corporation (IFC) suggest that, in certain circumstances, a 2% to 3.5% increase in the level of female economic participation could result in GDP benefits of a similar magnitude (Cabeza-García et al., 2019). "One cannot claim to be working for the development of a country if you are leaving behind 50% of the people," noted one of the research participants. Research conducted by the International Monetary Fund (IMF) presents compelling evidence that when women can fully utilise their labour market capabilities, significant macroeconomic advantages can ensue (Pal et al., 2022). Greater possibilities for women to control and generate revenue may be a factor in emerging markets' overall economic growth, as seen by increased female enrollment rates in schools. Increased access to funding, education, and support systems for female entrepreneurs also boosts the productivity of companies run and owned by women (RastogiandRagabiruntha, 2018).Research indicates that women save more organically and use financial services more frequently than males, despite the fact that they may take longer to do so.Women are more likely to spend when they have access to formal savings choices, which helps their families and promotes profitable investing. According to the 2014 Global Findex, women are more likely to use accounts to save money than men are in developing countries, where the gender gap in formal savings (access to an account at a financial institution where a client intends to save) is smaller than the overall gender gap in account ownership (access to an account at a financial institution)(Arun et al., 2021; Piras et al., 2013; Rastogi and Ragabiruntha, 2018).

In order to better understand the factors impacting women's participation in entrepreneurship in Johor,(Al-Shami et al. (2015)performed a study. They performed a survey of 215 female entrepreneurs, and the results show that interest, ambition, and independence are the key three characteristics driving women's involvement in entrepreneurship. Particularly disadvantaged women gain from microfinance services. They want to be viewed as independent and free of the burden of supporting their families on their husbands. Being frequently the most disadvantaged segment of society, these women often pose significant credit risks (Alam et al., 2011). Raising women's access to microloans benefits not only their personal well-being but also their families, the communities in which they reside, and society at large (UNDP, 2008). To foster and encourage female participation in entrepreneurial endeavours and bolster the domestic economy, the government implements several initiatives supervised by the Ministry of Women, Family, and Community Development(AFI, 2016). The projects include working with AIM and TEKUN Nasional to quickly and easily give microloans to qualified women who want to start businesses, particularly to single moms around the country.In 2011, women owned a mere 19.7% of the 645,000 micro, small, and medium-sized enterprises (SMEs) in Malaysia, as reported by SME Corporation Malaysia (SMECorp) (Economics and Mushtaq, 2023). This statistic excludes female microentrepreneurs who fail to register their businesses with SME Corp for a variety of reasons, including tax complications. In accordance with the national key result area(NKRA), government agencies have established a number of projects and programmes to educate female microentrepreneurs about the microfinance sources that are accessible to them. This enables them to support the growth, development, and promotion of more women entrepreneurs (NKRA). These initiatives and programmes recognise the contribution of women to developing nations' economic growth and wealth distribution via entrepreneurship. For instance, the UNDP Malaysia launched a project in Terengganu, Kelantan, Kedah, and Penang in 2006 called The UNDP entrepreneurial skills: Empowering Women(Purnamawati and Utama, 2019). This project aims to equip women with the entrepreneurial acumen, resources, and knowledge necessary for success. It is critical that women pursue further education and training in soft skills related to management, marketing, and other aspects of business in order to attain success in their pursuits (Bhatia and Singh, 2019; Sushma, 2020).

Data and Methodology

The primary aim of this research is to evaluate the consequences of financial inclusion for women and

Table 188.1 Variable measurement.

Ariable	Description	Data collection
Economic Development (ED)	GDP per capita (included in the analyses as a logarithm). GDP equals the aggregate of the gross value added by all domestic producers, inclusive of product taxes and exclusive of subsidies not deducted from product value. The computation fails to incorporate the depreciation of artificial assets or the depletion and deterioration of natural resources.	World bank data
Account Financial Institution (ACF)	Account at a financial institution, female (5 age 15+)	Account of a female with a scheduled bank in five Asian countries.
Borrow Financial Institution (BFI)	Borrowed from a financial institution, female (5 age 15+).	Account of the female with a scheduled bank in five Asian countries.
Credit Card (CC)	Credit card, female (5 age 15+)	Account of the female with a scheduled bank in five Asian countries.
Government initiatives (GI)	Number of projects for women in term financial inclusion	Federal Bank in five Asian countries

Source: Author

Table 188.2 Summary of descriptive statistics.

	Mean	Median	Maximum	Minimum	Std. dev.
LOGGDP	7.718734	6.044849	6.044849	6.882935529	56.2
LOGBFI	7.012913	6.882936	6.044849	6.882935529	56.2
LF	56.34857	56.2	6.044849	6.882935529	56.2
GI	20.6	21	6.044849	6.882935529	56.2
BFI	17043079	7637224	6.044849	6.882935529	56.2
ACF	61.46342	72.66644	6.044849	6.882935529	56.2
CC	19.4	19	6.044849	6.882935529	56.2
UR	4.285714	3.7	6.044849	6.882935529	56.2

Source: Author

its potential ramifications on governmental initiatives and economic progress. The research was performed in five Asean nations. A quantitative research methodology is employed to gather data for this study. In this exploratory study, secondary data was used to guide the data collection process.In order to estimate the unknown parameters of this economic model, the generalised linear model (GLM), a statistical technique based on regression analysis, integrates information about the moment conditions of the population with observable economic data. In order to calculate an objective function that population moment conditions provide, GLM estimators use assumptions about variable moments. We compute the corresponding sample moment conditions using the data. Compared to the parameters in the GLM, we have more sample moment conditions (Wooldridge, 1999). The study's ten-year timeframe runs from 2016 to 2022. The factors and data source used in this study are outlined in Table 188.1 below.

Results and Discussion

The study's findings and empirical data were evaluated among five ASEAN nations. The years 2016 through 2022's annual statistics were used. Descriptive statistics, panel regression analysis, and diagnostic testing are a few techniques utilized in empirical analysis. Table 188.2 below provides a summary of the descriptive statistics, with the labor force (LF), government initiatives (GI), account financial institutions (ACF), credit cards (CC), and unemployment rate (UR) serving as the study's independent variables. The dependent variable is LogGDP, a measure of economic development. 35 samples in total, from 5 ASEAN nations, were gathered and examined during a 7-year period (2016–2022). For each variable, the total number of observations, mean, standard deviation,

minimum and maximum values, and standard deviation are presented in Table 188.2. According to Table 188.2, the average GDP for the five Asian nations from 2016–2022 is 7.71, with a range of 6.044–6.88. In comparison to their means, the standard deviation is modest at 56.2. The account financial institution (ACF) has the highest mean ratio of all the independent variables at 61.46, with a range of 6.044–6.88. Labor force (LF) follows, with a mean ratio of 56.34 and a range of 6.044–6.88. The unemployment rate (UN), on the other hand, has the lowest mean ratio, at 4.285, with a range of 6.044–6.88.

The correlation strength between the components considered is shown in the correlation matrix data, which are presented in Table 188.3. Multicollinearity is a factual peculiarity when at least two indicator elements are extraordinarily associated in a separate relapse model, according to Gujarati (2003). Simply having multicollinearity might affect the accuracy of the components being studied by causing evaluations of the model coefficients to be unreliable and unauthentic. The correlation could not be greater than 0.8, it was further noted (Gujarati, 2003). It is possible to conclude from the findings that a multicollinearity problem was nonexistent. As a result, all of the study's variables remained constant.

According to the results in Table 188.4 below, the autocorrelation's and heteroscdasiticityp-value is 0.000, which is lower than the 5% significant value. As a result, it demonstrates that the model suffers autocorrelation and heteroscdasticity. The multicollinearity test is then carried out utilizing the variance inflation factor (VIF). Gujarati and Porter (2009) assert that if the VIF is more than 5, there would be a multicollinearity issue in the independent variables. The variation inflation factor (VIF) is 2.3 according to Table 188.3. Assuming that VIF is less than 5, this shows that the independent variables are not overly

Table 188.3 Corrreation analysis.

	LOGGDP	LOGBFI	LF	GI	BFI	ACF	CC	UR
LOGGDP	1							
LOGBFI	0.350938	1						
LF	-0.17804	-0.09784	1					
GI	0.284831	-0.12108	0.005317	1				
BFI	0.288963	0.906793	-0.20968	-0.30335	1			
ACF	-0.11584	-0.22816	0.337181	0.622794	-0.42805	1		
CC	-0.21058	-0.32511	-0.09989	0.797249	-0.41062	0.641373	1	
UR	0.05657	0.229072	0.49155	-0.23364	0.00069	0.269411	-0.37178	1

Source: Author

Table 188.4 Regression analysis model 1.

Variable	Dependent variable: LOG GDP			
	Coefficient	Std. error	z-Statistic	Prob.
C	66.4611	27.3345	2.4314	0.0150
LOGBFI	0.3379	0.6723	0.5026	0.6153
LF	-1.1679	0.4678	-2.4965	0.0125
ACF	-0.0052	0.0173	-0.3011	0.7634
CC	-0.4471	0.0867	-5.1566	0.0000
UR	0.1657	0.3695	0.4485	0.6538
GI	0.6301	0.0887	7.1050	0.0000
Mean dependent var	7.718734384			
Sum squared resid	57.26455329			
Log-likelihood	-58.68370152			
Schwarz criterion	4.064423985			
Deviance	57.26455329			
Restr. deviance	196.7280432			
Prob (LR statistic)	0E+00			
Pearson statistic	2.045162617			
Likelihood test	45.333(0.0000)			
Hausman test	0.675(0.0000)			
VIF	2.3			
Heteroscedasticity	5.6789(0.000)			
Serial correlation	1.4598(0.000)			

Source: Author

connected. As a result, the model's multicollinearity issue is not present.

The panel regression results of GLM in Table 188.4 below show that the BFI with a p-value of 0.6153 is abovethe alpha of 5% significant level. Therefore, Borrow Financial Institution (BFI) indicates a positive insignificant relationship with the profitability of GDP. Meanwhile, the laborforce (LF) shows a result of p = 0.0125 which is less than the alpha of 5% significant level. Hence, the labor force (LF)revealed that there is a significant relationship withGDP. Continue of that account financial institutions (ACF) havea p-value of 0.7634 which is greater than the alpha of 5% significant level. Therefore, that account financial institution (ACF) has no significant relationship with the GDP.Meanwhile, the result shows that the credit card (CC) with a p-value of 0.000 is below the alpha of 5% significant level. Therefore, borrow credit card (CC) indicates a negative significant relationship with GDP. Meanwhile, the unemployment rate(UR) shows a result of p = 0.6538 which is more than the alpha of 5% significant level. This indicated the unemployment rate had a positive significant relationship with GDP.

The last variable in the study is government initiatives (GI), which found that there are positive and significant relationships with GDP.

According to the results in Table 188.4 above, the autocorrelation's and heteroscdestictyp-value is 0.000, which is lower than the 5% significant value. As a result, it demonstrates that the model suffers for autocorrelation and heteroscdeaticity. The multicollinearity test is then carried out utilizing the VIF. Gujarati and Porter (2009) assert that if the VIF is more than 5, there would be a multicollinearity issue in the independent variables. The VIF is 3.5 according to Table 188.3. Assuming that VIF is less than 5, this shows that the independent variables are not overly connected. As a result, the model's multicollinearity issue is not present.

The panel regression results of GLM in Table 188.5 below show that the GDP with a p-value of 0.000 is less than the alpha of 5% significant level. Therefore, GDP indicates a positive significant relationship withgovernment initiatives (GI). Meanwhile, the labor force (LF) shows a result of p = 0.023 which is less than the alpha of 5% significant level. Hence,

Table 188.5 Regression analysis model 2.

Variable	Dependent variable: GI			
	Coefficient	Std. error	z-Statistic	Prob.
C	-79.64747873	35.2058941	-2.26233365	0.023676797
LOGGDP	1.020809192	0.143674229	7.105026418	0.0000
LOGBFI	0.449105896	0.855388909	0.525031236	0.599561477
LF	1.373240137	0.605068228	2.269562462	0.023234143
ACF	0.022790029	0.021687512	1.050836496	0.29333369
CC	0.629903617	0.097826854	6.438964279	0.0000
UR	-0.415898056	0.465379636	-0.89367481	0.371495909
Mean dependent var	20.6			
Sum squared resid	92.77060127			
Log-likelihood	-67.12654111			
Schwarz criterion	4.546871961			
Deviance	92.77060127			
Restr. deviance	836.4			
Prob (LR statistic)	1.17E-45			
Pearson statistic	3.31323576			
Likelihood test	0.788(0.0122)			
Hausman test	1.345(0.0334)			
VIF	3.5			
Heteroscedasticity	55.8777(0.000)			
Serial correlation	3.4898(0.000)			

Source: Author

the labor force (LF) revealed that there is a significant relationship with GI. Continue of that account financial institutions (ACF) have a p-value of 0.2933 which is greater than the alpha of 5% significant level. Therefore, that account financial institution (ACF) has no significant relationship with the GI. Meanwhile, the result shows that the credit card (CC) with a p-value of 0.000 is below the alpha of 5% significant level. Therefore, borrow credit card (CC) indicates a negative significant relationship with GI. Meanwhile, the unemployment rate (UR) shows a result of p = 0.3714 which is more than the alpha of 5% significant level. This indicated that the unemployment rate had a significant positive relationship with GI. The study's final variable is BFI, which discovered both positive and insignificant relationships with GI.

Conclusion

Extensive scholarly literature indicates that narrowing the gender disparity in financial inclusion could potentially yield favourable outcomes such as improved risk management and savings, increased rates of savings and investment, and access to novel business opportunities, all while promoting prudent consumption management and financial security.In addition to starting their own enterprises, women have the ability to promote growth through the implementation of judicious financial management. Access to and utilisation of a variety of financial services not only increases the growth contribution of women and women-led enterprises but also empowers women to better manage the resources that are theirs and their families', decreases the vulnerability of their homes and businesses, and promotes greater autonomy.As a result of these challenges, a growing number of countries across a range of economic sectors have realised how important it is to address women's and girls' financial inclusion. They have done this by developing and implementing policies and programmes specifically aimed at financial education, such as national financial education strategies. These initiatives often target particularised subcategories of women, such as young women, the elderly and widowed, women from low-income and marginalised backgrounds, and female proprietors of small and microbusinesses. Further goals of this research are to improve women's financial management skills, such as promoting formal savings accounts, helping women prepare for retirement, helping women choose financial products, and assisting women in staying out of debt.

References

AFI (2016). Policy frameworks to support women's financial inclusion. 1–24. http://www.afi-global.org/sites/default/files/publications/2016-08/2016-02-women-fi.1_0.pdf.

Akter, S., Krupnik, T. J., Rossi, F., and Khanam, F. (2016). The influence of gender and product design on farmers' preferences for weather-indexed crop insurance. *Global Environmental Change*, 38, 217–229. https://doi.org/10.1016/j.gloenvcha.2016.03.010.

Alam, S. S., Jani, M. F. M., and Omar, N. A. (2011). An empirical study of success factors of women entrepreneurs in southern region in Malaysia. *International Journal of Economics and Finance*, 3(2), 166–175. https://doi.org/10.5539/ijef.v3n2p166.

Al-Shami, S. S., Majid, I., Rizal, S., Muhamad, M. R., Sarah-Halim, and Rashid, N. (2015). The impact of Malaysian microfinance on women livelihood. *Advanced Science Letters*, 21(6), 2046–2049. https://doi.org/10.1166/asl.2015.6202.

Arun, S., Annim, S. K., and Arun, T. G. (2021). 'Even' after access to financial services? ricocheting gender equations. *SSRN Electronic Journal*, 10099. https://doi.org/10.2139/ssrn.2819381.

Bertay, A. C., Dordevic, L., and Sever, C. (2021). gender inequality and economic growth: evidence from industry-level data. *SSRN Electronic Journal*. https://doi.org/10.2139/ssrn.3658594.

Bhatia, S., and Singh, S. (2019). Empowering women through financial inclusion: a study of Urban slum. *Vikalpa*, 44(4), 182–197. https://doi.org/10.1177/0256090919897809.

Cabeza-García, L., Del Brio, E. B., and Oscanoa-Victorio, M. L. (2019). Female financial inclusion and its impacts on inclusive economic development. *Women's Studies International Forum*, 77, 1–29. https://doi.org/10.1016/j.wsif.2019.102300.

Economics, S., and Mushtaq, R. (2023). Women financial inclusion research : a bibliometric and network analysis. *International Journal of Social Economics*, 50(4), 1–26. https://doi.org/10.1108/IJSE-06-2022-0438/full/html.

Esmaeilpour Moghadam, H., and Karami, A. (2023). Financial inclusion through FinTech and women's financial empowerment. *International Journal of Social Economics*, 50(8), 1038–1059. https://doi.org/10.1108/IJSE-04-2022-0246.

Heng, D., and Tok, Y. W. (2022). Fintech: financial inclusion or exclusion? *IMF Working Papers*, 2022(080), 1. https://doi.org/10.5089/9798400208645.001.

Holloway, K., Naizi, Z., and Rouse, R. (2017). Women's economic empowerment through financial inclusion: a review of existing evidence and remaining knowledge gaps. [online] Report, Innovations for Poverty Action.

Klugman, J., and Quek, Y. (2018). Women's financial inclusion and economic opportunities in fragile and conflict-affected states: an overview of challenges and prospects. *VOCEDplus, the International Tertiary Education and Research Database*, 44. https://www.voced.edu.au/content/ngv:84358.

Pal, M., Gupta, H., and Joshi, Y. C. (2022). Social and economic empowerment of women through financial inclusion: empirical evidence from India. *Equality, Diversity and Inclusion*, 41(2), 294–305. https://doi.org/10.1108/EDI-04-2021-0113.

Piras, C., Presbitero, A. F., and Rabellotti, R. (2013). Measuring gender gaps in firms' access to credit.

Purnamawati, I. G. A., and Utama, M. S. (2019). Women's empowerment strategies to improve their role in families and society. *International Journal of Business, Economics and Law*, 18(5), 119–127.

Rastogi, S., and Ragabiruntha, E. (2018). Financial inclusion and socioeconomic development: gaps and solution. *International Journal of Social Economics*, 45(7), 1122–1140. https://doi.org/10.1108/IJSE-08-2017-0324.

Salman, A., and Nowacka, K. (2020). Innovative financial products and services for women in Asia and the pacific. 67, 1–32. http://doi.org/10.22617/WPS200119-2.

Sushma, R. (2020). Impact of digital finance on financial inclusion. *Studies in Indian Place Names*, 2019(ICoMM), 308–313.

189 Cryptocurrency: bitcoin and the macroeconomics factor in Malaysia – a VECM analysis

Vikneswaran Manual[a] and Hafinaz Hasniyanti Hassan[b]

Ph.D., Asia Pacific University of Technology and Innovation, Kuala Lumpur, Malaysia

Abstract

One of the cryptocurrencies that is becoming more and more well-known as a kind of digital money is Bitcoin. The worldwide modern society can accept Bitcoin as a digital asset. Bitcoin can be used to make purchases of both goods and services online. This paper tries to uncover the significant association relating the Malaysian stock market and Bitcoin, gold, crude oil, USD, and crude palm oil. This study also looks at the causal connections between each variable and Bitcoin, determining whether the cryptocurrency has an impact on the independent variable or vice versa. The data utilized is derived from historical sources, serving as secondary informationon investing.com between September 2014 and July 2023. The data was evaluated using regression and correlation analysis, unit root testing, cointegration analysis, and vector error correction modeling to ascertain the relationship and impact of the variables. Based on the results, there is a significant associationbetween the stock market and commodities including bitcoin, gold, crude oil, US dollars, and crude palm oil. However, a statistical problem with heteroskedasticity has been found in this model. As a result, the GLS model has been recommended as an alternative to OLS regression. According to VECM, it was discovered that none of the independent variables had either a long-run or short-run association with the dependent variable. The findings of this study should help investors make future judgments on their choice of investments and the formulation of investment strategies. Before choosing to invest in Bitcoin, a number of aspects should be taken into account since this form of currency is still being studied. When making assessments or decisions, investors must also take into account the country's internal and external environments.

Keywords: Bitcoin, crude oil, crude palm oil, gold, VECM

Introduction

Because digital currencies settle transactions faster than peer-to-peer (P2P) without middlemen, they have less settlement risk than traditional fiat currencies, which has been the main shortcoming that alternative currencies have managed to overcome. Cryptocurrencies are currently a highly contentious subject in the banking sector and the global economy. Bitcoin is regarded as a non-traditional investment that offers several benefits. Cryptocurrencies serve as financial instruments. Bitcoin surpasses other cryptocurrencies in terms of market size, as indicated by its better market valuation and volume (Abdul-Majid et al., 2018).

Researching cryptocurrencies is unrestricted to a tiny number of enthusiasts, and they are no longer merely a phenomenon. This study intends to provide understanding of these formidable technologies that are still developing and gaining popularity since blockchain, and cryptocurrencies have the ability to completely transform modern economies. Digital currency built on cryptographic principles are known as cryptocurrencies. Cryptocurrency values are increasing.

Digital coins that are centralised can be traded or utilised with blockchain technologies. These kinds of virtual currency try to increase anonymity and privacy to differing degrees of success (Sharif et al., 2023). Some of these currencies allow for optional privacy, but all transactions are fully visible to third parties. Cryptocurrencies are intended to supplement fiat currencies, rather than supplant them, as they lack official backing and instead derive their value from investor activity that determines currency valuation through supply and demand dynamics (Laranja Ribeiro et al., 2021; Schinckus, 2020).

Since Satoshi Nakamoto first put forth the idea in his 2008 white paper, bitcoin has drawn a lot of interest as a topic for study and conversation. This is because academics, professionals, and investors are dispersed throughout the world. Despite being a new industry, it has taken off globally like wildfire. According to Ren et al. (2023), the market capitalization of Bitcoin is anticipated to surpass that of the most valuable firm in Malaysia. It is crucial to ascertain if the initial cryptocurrency, Bitcoin, is affected by a nation's economic indicators in a comparable way to conventional financial assets like stocks and shares. Investors, scholars,

[a]vikneswaran.manual@apu.edu.my, [b]hafinaz.hasniyanti@apu.edu.my

and legislators should recognize that Bitcoin adheres to the same fundamental economic principles as other traded investments (Miraz et al., 2021). Blockchain is the fundamental technology behind cryptocurrencies. It is a decentralized public ledger that records and maintains a comprehensive record of all current transactions conducted by currency holders. Using computer power to solve difficult mathematical riddles that yield coins, or units of cryptocurrency, is the mining process. Users have the option to acquire the currencies via brokers, store them in encrypted wallets, and utilize them for transactions. There exist a multitude of cryptocurrencies, numbering in the thousands. Among the most well-known are, among many others, Ethereum (founded in 2015), Ripple (founded in 2012), and Bitcoin (formed in 2009). The price of cryptocurrencies, which is ascertained by averaging the prices of Litecoin, Ethereum, Bitcoin, and XRP, is the dependent variable of this study.

Literature Review

Share price

The correlation between cryptocurrencies and the stock market has aroused the curiosity of all stakeholders involved in the market, encompassing investors, financiers, enterprises, and individuals from the political sphere. Researchers have searched for a pattern in this correlation throughout time (Sovbetov and Sovbetov, 2018). It has been discovered that there is a complicated relationship between equities and cryptocurrencies that is influenced by the nation's unstable exchange rate and inflation, sophisticated and costly banking system, regulatory unpredictability, financial restrictions, and—most importantly—the existence or threat of capital controls. This section of the article summarises the previous studies on the association between cryptocurrencies and equities in developing countries. Köse and Ünal (2023) conducted an empirical examination of the correlation between the Malaysian stock market and returns from Bitcoin trading. Data ranging between January 2013 and January 2017 was examined. The statistical results reveal an inverse relationship between changes in the price of bitcoin and stock market activity. According to the study's findings, Bitcoins are important for reducing investment risk and boosting portfolio returns when included in those investments. Aimon et al. (2020) examined the financial market-traded Bitcoin volatility pattern and empirically investigated the ability of Bitcoins to hedge against global geopolitical risks. Dumitrescu et al. (2023) expressed their concern about the presence of a Bitcoin-related speculative bubble. They cited it as a key factor in inadequate

financial stability when compared to stock and other types of tradable financial assets. When compared to traditional financial assets like equities and bonds that are traded on international financial markets, the risk-return trade-off of various crypto-currencies is unique, according to Harooni and Alvan (2023) study of their features. Meiryani et al. (2022) examined the significant volatility of cryptocurrencies and stated that Bitcoins may be used for investment speculating.

Gold price

Due to its importance as an asset in the contemporary capital market, gold has long been seen as a refuge. They continued by saying that the best commodity for capital preservation and as a recession hedge is gold. Even if gold is no longer used as currency, its value continues to be higher than that of paper money. Due to gold's valuable quality, it is scarcely impacted by economic downturns. In reality, regardless of the state of the economy, gold's value rises over time. Due to its characteristics as a commodity that link to deflation, gold is a favorite among investors and regular people. Mohd Nasir et al. (2018) study, which tries to pinpoint the variables that influence the price of gold in Malaysia, discovered that a number of macroeconomic variables have a substantial impact on gold prices. In order to pinpoint the macroeconomic factors that affect the volatility of gold prices, Meiryani et al. (2022) undertook a study. They discovered that there aren't many macroeconomic variables that have a big impact on how volatile gold prices are in Malaysia. Shahvari (2022) used the same methodology to determine the elements that drive gold prices in Malaysia, and their conclusions corroborated those of the study.

Exchange rate

Bitcoin's market capitalization has surpassed the milestone of one trillion dollars. Bitcoin is purported by certain experts and professionals to be a dependable hedge against inflation. In their study, Dumitrescu et al. (2023) presents a theoretical analysis of the correlation between Bitcoin and a conventional currency issued by a central bank. The authors demonstrate that through deterministic growth of the supply, Bitcoin can be regarded as a viable, albeit volatile, medium of exchange. Bitcoin's ability to endure price increases, driven by its strong demand, ability to generate revenue, and limited supply, makes it a practical choice for protecting against inflation. According to some economists, Bitcoin is considered a speculative investment that is unrelated to traditional financial instruments, in contrast to the hedging reasons previously mentioned (Erdas and Caglar, 2018). Erdas and BenSaïda (2023) argue that Bitcoin's lack of correlation with conventional assets such as equities, bonds, or commodities indicates its predominant use as a speculative investment. Furthermore, according to Chang et al. (2021), several factors, including Bitcoin's elevated difficulty level, lack of inherent value, and limited transaction volume, indicate that it may not qualify as a foreign currency transaction. Considering the divergent viewpoints regarding Bitcoin's efficacy as a safeguard against inflation, it is imperative to conduct research on both Bitcoin and projected inflation.

According to BenSaïda (2023), investors can increase portfolio diversification by include financial assets designated in the currencies from our sample as well as cryptocurrencies. Furthermore, he emphasises the significance of fluctuations in the price of Bitcoin for the implementation of monetary policy via the exchange rate path. In their study, Mohd Nasir et al. (2018) found evidence of a Granger causality feedback relationship between the Bitcoin exchange rate (BER) and Google search volume index (SVI) in both short- and long-term co-integration equilibriums. They also observed a strong association between the investor fear gauge and BER in the long-term co-integration equilibrium. In their study, Chu et al. (2017) examined the influence of currency rates, oil prices, and financial market prices on the price of bitcoin. The findings indicate that the Dow Jones Index, the euro-dollar exchange rate, and the price of oil exert a substantial impact on the long-term value of Bitcoin. Kjaerland et al. (2018) examined the investment value and exchange utility of Bitcoin, whereas Corbet et al. (2020) investigated whether users perceived Bitcoin as a currency or an asset. The analysis revealed that while Bitcoin can significantly enhance the efficiency of an investor's portfolio, its acceptance as a medium of exchange may be limited.

Crude oil

A significant economic resource is crude oil. It is mostly employed in the energy sector. As a result, businesses involved in refining, oilfield services, and production are susceptible to changes in crude oil prices. The transportation industry is greatly impacted by changes in crude oil prices, much like ships and aeroplanes depend on such prices to operate. Furthermore, the price of crude oil may fare better during a crisis than that of stocks and bonds. Studies showing the connection between crude oil and its function in stock market portfolios abound. An examination of the interactions between the Chinese stock market and WTI crude oil was conducted by Schinckus et al. (2022). The DCC-GARCH t-copula model was used to assess the study's data. Their empirical findings demonstrated that Crude oil is, in fact, an affordable

and effective hedging instrument during periods of severe crisis. The authors also suggested that investors can achieve high hedging effectiveness by incorporating a small quantity of WTI crude oil futures into their stock portfolio. Additionally, researchers (Rao et al., 2022) studied the effects of crude palm oil shocks on the stock markets in Eastern Europe. The data was collected between September 2019 and January 2021. Wang et al. (2022) looked into stock market returns and portfolio hedging that included WTI crude oil. In this experiment, two models—an ARMA-BEKKGARCH (1,1) and a VARMA-DCC-GARCH (1,1)—were used. Additionally, data from the US, China, India, and Japan for the years 2014 to 2018 was acquired. According to the author's research, WTI crude oil has a sizable unidirectional return that tends to spill over into stock market returns. In order to reduce risk, the authors encourage investors to pay closer attention and have a limited quantity of WTI in their portfolios.

Crude palm oil

Vegetable oil known as "crude palm oil" is frequently used in foods, biofuels, and cosmetics. Consequently, it has a significant effect on the economy (Erdas and Caglar, 2018). However, its impact on stock market portfolios is easily influenced by factors such as weather, agricultural regulations, industrial demand, and geopolitical happenings. Additionally, the performance of this commodity is crucial to the economies of many countries, like Malaysia and Indonesia. As a result, any influence on them has the potential to disrupt the entire CPO supply chain. Numerous studies (Abdul-Majid et al., 2018; Clark et al., 2023; Ismail and Ali Basah, 2021) have been done to show the connection between CPO and its function in stock market portfolios. First, García-Monleón et al. (2023) shown a study to look at the danger of spillover effects related to the global crude oil market. Data from this inquiry were collected in China during the years 2005 and 2017. Additionally, the ARMA-GJR-GARCH and copula models were used in this experiment. The investigation's findings showed that the downside spillover effect on crude oil prices is more significant than the upside spillover (Havidz et al., 2021). Given this information, the researchers recommended that investors be cautious of the uneven risk associated with the spread of effects, both in the near and distant future.

Data and Methodology

The objective of this paper is to elucidate the short- and long-term links between cryptocurrencies and

Table 189.1 Descriptive analysis.

Variable	Mean	Median	Maximum	Minimum	Std. Dev.
BITCOIN	4375.36	3604.58	19497.40	178.10	4127.13
CRUDE OIL	1633.98	1637.30	1895.18	1219.72	126.09
CRUDE PALM OIL	1438.80	1310.60	2049.00	1045.40	267.32
EXR	59.22	55.54	123.70	-37.63	18.75
GOLD PRICE	3083.95	2660.00	8163.00	1759.00	1153.30
SHARE PRICE	4.06	4.14	4.50	3.15	0.31

Source: Author

Table 189.2 Pearson correlation analysis.

	Bitcoin	Crude	Crud oil	Exr	Gold price	Share price
Bitcoin	1					
Crude oil	0.482821	1				
Crude palm oil	0.398087	0.244484	1			
Exr	0.346676	0.304364	-0.06588461	1		
Gold price	0.622892	0.784959	0.362579771	0.373207	1	
Share price	-0.70369	-0.48248	-0.30631453	-0.36431	-0.692868916	1

Source: Author

microeconomic factors in Malaysia, such as the price of gold, crude oil, exchange rates, market share (stock) price, and crude palm oil. Microeconomic data and monthly observations of cryptocurrency prices are collected from multiple sources between January 2017 and December 2022. Bitcoin is available for purchase and sale in a number of currencies and on a number of exchanges. Prices and volume information for 31 different currencies and 72 distinct exchanges are shown on Bitcoincharts.com. Nevertheless, our analysis was restricted to Asian exchanges that facilitate transactions using a minimum of five distinct currencies, with the intention of conducting a comparative study across many countries. The information comes from reliable and trustworthy sources such as the Investing. com website and data from the World Bank. The relationship and direction of causality were assessed using ordinary least squares and generalised linear models. In addition, unit root tests using augmented Dickey-Fuller were performed to satisfy the condition before performing Johansen cointegration analysis. Finally, a Vector Correction Model (VECM) is performed to determine the long-run and short-run relationship between the variables.

Results and Discussion

Table 189.1 displays a descriptive analysis of the previously mentioned factors. The findings show that the sample firms' Bitcoin has a mean of 4375.36 and a range of 19497.40 to 178.10. The BTC in our sample

from Malaysia is consistent with other nations, and there is evidence that most nations invest in cryptocurrencies, but there are considerable differences in level between nations (Böhme et al., 2015). The Crude oil has a mean and standard deviation of 1633.98 and 126.09, respectively. The crude palm oil minimum and maximum values are 2049.00 and 1045.40, with a mean and standard deviation of 1438.80 and 1310.60, respectively. Additionally, the gold price has a mean of 3083.95 a range of 8163.00 and 1759.00, and a standard deviation is 1153.30. The last variable is share price which has mean and standard deviation of 4.06 and 0.31

Results for the Pearson correlation analysis is shown in Table 189.2, which is used to ascertain the direction of the association between the variables and check for multicollinearity problems. The crude oil, crude palm oil, exchange rate, and gold price have a positive association with the level of Bitcoin. Out of all the variables, the gold price and crude oil have the highest connection (0.62, which is followed by the share price -0.7039 correlation. According to Tabachnick and Fidell (2007), multicollinearity may be problematic if the Pearson correlation coefficient between the variables is higher than 0.90, which is not the case in this investigation.

For serial correlation and heteroscedasticity, the study performed diagnostic tests. As recommended by Hochle (2007), the model was corrected using robust standard errors. The results of the heteroscedasticity and serial correlation tests for the model

Table 189.3 Diagnostic test.

Heteroscedasticity	
X2	54876.91022
Prob > X2	0.0000
Serial correlation	
F-stat	14.92972877
Prob > F	0.0000
Normality Distribution	
Jarque- Bera	1.8554
Prob>JB	0.3254

Note: *** significant at 1%; ** significant at 5%, * significant at 10%

Source: Author

Table 189.4 Regression analysis.

Variable	Dependent Variable: Bitcoin			
	Coefficient	Std. Error	t-Statistic	Prob.
C	18278.71	1748.037	10.45671	0.0000
SHARE_PRICE	-15.9631	0.65879	-24.2309	0.0000
GOLD_PRICE	1.648096	0.443926	3.712545	0.0002
CRUDE PALM OIL	43.67536	3.45271	12.64959	0,0000
CRUDE Oil	0.28369	0.082335	3.445537	0.0005
EXR	1565.134	210.5418	7.433841	0,0000
R-squared	0.567873			
Adjusted R-squared	0.566881			
S.E. of regression	2716.141			
Number of samplings	2183			
Log likelihood	-20355.4			
F-statistic	572.1743			
Prob(F-statistic)	0.000			

Source: Author

are displayed in Table 189.3. Based on the outcome of the tests for heteroscedasticity and serial correlation, the model is suffering from serial correlation and heteroscedasticity. Therefore, robust regression analysis is recommendedand GLS was used in this study. Furthermore, the residual of the regression is normally distributed according to Jarque- bera that has been conducted.

In this investigation, the m variables were measured using five proxies. These include the price of market shares, gold, crude oil, crude palm oil, and currency rates. The association between these proxy variables and the price of Bitcoin is ascertained using all of them. The market share price is the first macroeconomic proxy variable, and it has a strong, positive correlation with the price of bitcoin. The price of gold, which has a significant positive link with the price of bitcoin, is the variable under consideration. This result is consistent with Sam's 2019 research. Additionally, both crude palm oil and crude oil also have a notable positive relationship with bitcoin price, which is consistent with Erdas and Caglar's study from 2018. Another variable, exchange rate, is positively and significantly linked to the price of bitcoin, as supported by Rayhi's (2020) research from 2020.

This report appears to be seriously threatened by spurious regression, which is a technique used in time series research, where a non-stationary series is regressed. Each variable's stationarity has been examined using the Augmented Dickey-Fuller (ADF) test. We discovered that all of the variables are stationary at first difference after doing a stationary test for the variables.

Using the Johansen Cointegration method, this study demonstrated cointegration between the variables. Data analysis was conducted under the null hypothesis that cointegration did not exist. As can be seen from the above table, cointegrating vectors were found by both the maximum eigenvalue test and the trace test of the Johansen process. The Max-Eigenvalue test only found one cointegrating equation, whereas the trace test reveals two. This shows that, at the 5% level of significance, the study rejects the null hypothesis, which states that there is no cointegration. A significant positive long-run correlation between the variables and BTC (Bitcoin) is suggested

Table 189.5 Unit root test.

Variable	Equation	Share Price	BTC	CPO	EXR	Crude Oil	Gold Price
		Unit Root test (Augmented Dickey – fuller test)					
Level	Intercept	0.1895	0.5588	0.187333	0.18335	0.4973	0.77689491
	Trend and Intercept	0.7034	0.1868	0.081928	0.473092	0.5410453	0.16423353
	None	0.7108	0.5169	0.325472	0.94174	0.662035	0.83389459
1st Differencing	Intercept	0.0000	0.0000	0.0000	0.0000	0.0000	0.0000
	Trend and Intercept	0.0000	0.0000	0.0000	0.0000	0.0000	0.0000
	None	0.0000	0.0000	0.0000	0.0000	0.0000	0.0000

Source: Author

Table 189.6 Johanson Cointergration.

No. of CE(s)	Eigenvalue	Trace Statistic	Critical Value	Critical Value
		Unrestricted Cointegration Rank Test (Trace)		
None	0.010797396	69.65730747	95.75366142	0.784693
At most 1	0.009520449	46.12125849	69.81888752	0.79313525
At most 2**	0.005055953	25.38204506	47.85612716	0.00011493
At most 3	0.004190258	14.39293452	29.79707334	0.00084007
At most 4	0.002102536	5.28936953	15.49471288	0.00036367
At most 5	0.00033494	0.726272334	3.841465498	0.00009325

No. of CE(s)	Eigenvalue	Max-Eigen Statistic	Critical Value	Critical Value
		Unrestricted Cointegration Rank Test (Max-eigenvalue)		
None	0.010797396	23.53604898	40.07757358	0.85056544
At most 1**	0.009520449	20.73921343	33.87686662	0.00060321
At most 2	0.005055953	10.98911054	27.58433779	0.00070204
At most 3	0.004190258	9.103564987	21.1316163	0.00098076
At most 4	0.002102536	4.563097197	14.26460015	0.00064817
At most 5	0.00033494	0.726272334	3.841465498	0.00009325

Source: Author

Table 189.7 VECM long run representations GDP as a depenent variable.

	Coefficient	Std. Error	t-Statistic	Prob.
C (1)	-0.01581	0.02151029	47.01565	0.0000
R-squared	0.995219			
Adjusted R-squared	0.995192			
S.E. of regression	286.2642			
Samples	2185			
Log-likelihood	-15411.8			
F-statistic	37570.57			
Prob(F-statistic)	0.0000			

Source: Author

by the rejection of the null hypothesis, which holds at a 5% significance level and is compatible with a priori assumptions. The results show that the model was cointegrated and stationary, and they enable an assessment of the VECM technique to look at the cointegrated series' short- and long-term properties.

If, at the 5% level of significance, the coefficients of the error correction term for the VECM are negative and statistically significant, then there is a long-term correlation between the variables and BTC (Bitcoin). The coefficient result showed that there was a long-term relationship between the variables and Bitcoin; it was in the negative sign and had a value of -0.01581. The discovery of negative and substantial values for the five proxy variables at a 5% level proves the presence of a long-term link with Bitcoin.

The table below shows the outcome of the Wald Test, which examined the short-term connections

Table 189.8 Wald test.

Variable	T- statistics	Value	Probability
Crude Oil	Chi-square	0.32443284	0.722972382
EXR	Chi-square	0.17085694	0.842953514
Crude palm oil	Chi-square	0.31679247	0.728515668
Share price	Chi-square	0.4082047	0.66489391
Gold price	Chi-square	0.34393364	0.343933639

Source: Author

between the variables. The probability value at the significance level of 5% suggested that there was a short-term correlation between the variables and Bitcoin. Because the p-value is more than 5%, the results indicate that there is no short-term link between any of the variables. This proved that there is no immediate correlation between the variables and Bitcoin.

Conclusion

The study's objective was to determine how external microfinancial elements, such as gold prices, stock market indexes, crude oil, and crude palm oil, affected the price of bitcoin. The outcomes demonstrated that every independent variable had a strongly favourable impact on Bitcoin. However, the stock market index has very little adverse effect. This study investigated the association between microeconomic characteristics and cryptocurrency using annual time series data from 2010 to 2020. This study observed the correlation between cryptocurrencies and macroeconomic variables by analyzing monthly time series data from 2010 to 2020. The impact of macroeconomic conditions on cryptocurrency was examined through the application of the vector error correction model (VECM) and the Johansen cointegration test. As a consequence, the study was able to prove that the variables had a lasting link. All of the relationships and correlations between the time series variables (cryptocurrencies and macroeconomic indicators) were explicated in detail by the study's overall findings. The VECM indicates the absence of a sustained relationship between the Bitcoin and Stellar models.

Young and inexperienced individuals make up the majority of Bitcoin investors (Bouri et al., 2018b). They typically discover the material using a search engine, particularly social media or online discussion (Kristoufek, 2013). As a result, they are readily convinced. The factors that determined the price of Bitcoin in this study may help them make more responsible and mature decisions about financial assets. Additionally, this encourages institutional investors to think about buying bitcoin. Unlike other traditional financial assets, the regulation of cryptocurrencies is still unclear, which leads to many people misinterpreting or underestimating its nature. Hence, to mitigate fluctuations and establish a definitive trajectory, it is imperative to provide a robust legal and regulatory framework for cryptocurrencies.

We recommend further investigation based on the following discoveries: (1) prolong the duration of the observation or incorporate both short-term and long-term periods to enable a comparative analysis; (2) introduce additional independent variables to identify more factors that could impact Bitcoin, for instance supply and demand, attractiveness, hash rate, legalization, political risk, and volume; and (3) expand the scope of the study by including another dependent variable to examine Ethereum, Ripple, Tether, and other cryptocurrencies, in order to assess the consistency of the results.

References

Abdul-Majid, M., Hons, B., and Econ, M. (2018). Exploring the Impact and Challenges of Digital Currency: the Literature Review (Funding From The Faculty Of Economics And Management Suzana Muhamad Said Fathin Faizah Said. (pp. 14–22).

Aimon, H., Putra, H. S., and Husein, F. (2020). Causality of the growth of bitcoin prices with monetary conditions in Indonesia. 124(2), 300–313. https://doi.org/10.2991/aebmr.k.200305.083.

BenSaïda, A. (2023). The linkage between Bitcoin and foreign exchanges in developed and emerging markets. *Financial Innovation*, 9(1), 38. https://doi.org/10.1186/s40854-023-00454-w.

Chang, C. Y., Lo, C. C., Cheng, J. C., Chen, T. L., Chi, L. Y., and Chen, C. C. (2021). Relationship between bitcoin exchange rate and other financial indexes in time series. *Mathematical Problems in Engineering*, 2021(Vix), 8842877. https://doi.org/10.1155/2021/8842877.

Chu, J., Chan, S., Nadarajah, S., and Osterrieder, J. (2017). GARCH modelling of cryptocurrencies. *Journal of Risk and Financial Management*, 10(4), 17. https://doi.org/10.3390/jrfm10040017.

Clark, E., Lahiani, A., and Mefteh-Wali, S. (2023). Cryptocurrency return predictability: what is the role of the environment? *Technological Forecasting and Social Change*, 189(January), 122350. https://doi.org/10.1016/j.techfore.2023.122350.

Corbet, S., Larkin, C., Lucey, B. M., Meegan, A., and Yarovaya, L. (2020). The impact of macroeconomic news on bitcoin returns. *European Journal of Finance*, 26(14), 1396–1416. https://doi.org/10.1080/1351847X.2020.1737168.

Dumitrescu, B. A., Obreja, C., Leonida, I., Mihai, D. G., and Trifu, L. C. (2023). The link between bitcoin price changes and the exchange rates in European countries with non-euro currencies. *Journal of Risk and Financial Management*, 16(4), 232. https://doi.org/10.3390/jrfm16040232.

Erdas, M. L., and Caglar, A. E. (2018). Analysis of the relationships between bitcoin and exchange rate, commodities and global indexes by asymmetric causality test. *Eastern Journal of European Studies*, 9(2), 27–45.

García-Monleón, F., Erdmann, A., and Arilla, R. (2023). A value-based approach to the adoption of cryptocurrencies. *Journal of Innovation and Knowledge*, 8(2), 100342. https://doi.org/10.1016/j.jik.2023.100342.

Harooni, M. U., and Alvan, A. (2023). The relationship between bitcoin price and macroeconomic.

Havidz, S. A. H., Karman, V. E., and Mambea, I. Y. (2021). Is bitcoin price driven by macro-financial factors and liquidity? a global consumer survey empirical study. *Organizations and Markets in Emerging Economies*, 12(2), 399–414. https://doi.org/10.15388/omee.2021.12.62.

Ismail, S., and Ali Basah, M. Y. (2021). An analysis on cryptocurrencies and macroeconomic variables using vector error correction model (VECM). *ASEAN Journal of Management and Business Studies*, 3(1), 8–15. https://doi.org/10.26666/rmp.ajmbs.2021.1.2.

Kjaerland, F., Meland, M., Oust, A., and Øyen, V. (2018). How can bitcoin price fluctuations be explained? *International Journal of Economics and Financial Issues*, 8(3), 323–332. http:www.econjournals.com.

Köse, N., and Ünal, E. (2023). The asymmetric effects of the interest rate on the bitcoin price. *Finance a Uver - Czech Journal of Economics and Finance*, 73(2), 189–217. https://doi.org/10.32065/CJEF.2023.02.04.

Laranja Ribeiro, M. P., Tommasetti, R., Gomes, M. Z., Castro, A., and Ismail, A. (2021). Adoption phases of green information technology in enhanced sustainability: a bibliometric study. *Cleaner Engineering and Technology*, 3(January), 100095. https://doi.org/10.1016/j.clet.2021.100095.

Meiryani, M., Tandyopranoto, C. D., Emanuel, J., Warganegara, D. L., Wahyuningtias, D., and Widuri, R. (2022). The effect of stock index and gold price movements on bitcoin price movements. In ACM International Conference Proceeding Series, (pp. 401–408). https://doi.org/10.1145/3537693.3537756.

Miraz, M. H., Sharif, K. I. M., Hassan, M. G., Ismail, M. A., and Mahyadin, F. B. (2021). Bitcoins in the Malaysian economy. *Journal of Management, Economics, and Industrial Organization*, 5(3), 70–85. https://doi.org/10.31039/jomeino.2021.5.3.6.

Mohd Nasir, F. Z., Wan Zakaria, W. M. F., Musa, M. H., Burhanuddin1, M. A., and Ong, M. H. A. (2018). Economic forces on gold price in Malaysia. *E-Academia Journal*, 7(2), 54–65.

Rao, A., Gupta, M., Sharma, G. D., Mahendru, M., and Agrawal, A. (2022). Revisiting the financial market interdependence during COVID-19 times: a study of green bonds, cryptocurrency, commodities and other financial markets. *International Journal of Managerial Finance*, 18(4), 725–755. https://doi.org/10.1108/IJMF-04-2022-0165.

Rayhi, N. Al. (2020). Cryptocurrency exchange market prediction and analysis using data mining and artificial intelligence. (pp. 59). https://bspace.buid.ac.ae/bitstream/handle/1234/1628/2016128088.pdf.

Ren, Y. S., Ma, C. Q., Chen, X. Q., Lei, Y. T., and Wang, Y. R. (2023). Sustainable finance and blockchain: a systematic review and research agenda. *Research in International Business and Finance*, 64(November 2022), 101871. https://doi.org/10.1016/j.ribaf.2022.101871.

Sam, S. (2019). Relationship between macro variables and bitcoin : evidence from Indian market.

Schinckus, C. (2020). The good, the bad and the ugly: an overview of the sustainability of blockchain technology. *Energy Research and Social Science*, 69(June), 101614. https://doi.org/10.1016/j.erss.2020.101614.

Schinckus, C., Nguyen, C. P., and Chong, F. H. L. (2022). Cryptocurrencies' hashrate and electricity consumption: evidence from mining activities. *Studies in Economics and Finance*, 39(3), 524–546. https://doi.org/10.1108/SEF-08-2021-0342.

Shahvari, N. (2022). The relation between gold price movement and bitcoin investment sentiment. https://doi.org/10.5281/zenodo.7179948.

Sharif, A., Brahim, M., Dogan, E., and Tzeremes, P. (2023). Analysis of the spillover effects between green economy, clean and dirty cryptocurrencies. *Energy Economics*, 120(February), 106594. https://doi.org/10.1016/j.eneco.2023.106594.

Sovbetov, Y., and Sovbetov, Y. (2018). Factors influencing cryptocurrency prices: evidence from bitcoin, ethereum, dash, litcoin, and monero. *Journal of Economics and Financial Analysis*, 2(2), 1–27. https://doi.org/10.1991/jefa.v2i2.a16.

Wang, Y., Lucey, B., Vigne, S. A., and Yarovaya, L. (2022). An index of cryptocurrency environmental attention (ICEA). *China Finance Review International*, 12(3). https://doi.org/10.1108/CFRI-09-2021-0191.

190 How do bitcoin prices respond to macroeconomic shocks? evidence from five Asean countries

Hafinaz Hasniyanti Hassan[a] and Vikneswaran Manual[b]

Ph.D., Asia Pacific University of Technology and Innovation, Kuala Lumpur, Malaysia

Abstract

The primary goal of this research study is to comprehensively examine the empirical correlation between bitcoin prices and various significant macroeconomic variables in five ASEAN nations. The focus of our study is to examine the influence of many factors, including inflation rate, exchange rate, financial stress index, interest rate, stock price, and gross domestic product (GDP) per capita, on the pricing of bitcoin. In order to conduct our study, we gathered monthly data from January 2018 to February 2022 for each of these variables in the five nations. We employed a fixed effect model and a generalized linear model (GLM) for our analysis. The advent of cryptocurrencies and blockchain technologies has sparked a worldwide craze that has captivated individuals far beyond the narrow group of aficionados. Our analysis indicates a strong positive correlation between the interest rate, share price, and the price of bitcoin. These findings are significant as they enhance our comprehension of the intricate and ever-changing connections between cryptocurrency and macroeconomic variables. The potential of cryptocurrencies and blockchain technology to transform current economies is generating substantial attention and investigation. The report offers a comprehensive examination of the intricate links between cryptocurrencies and macroeconomic factors in five Asian nations. Through the examination of these intricate interconnections, our objective is to make a meaningful contribution to the ongoing discourse about the influence of cryptocurrencies and blockchain technology on the worldwide economy. The outcomes of our research have the capacity to provide guidance to policymakers and investors as they navigate the swiftly changing realm of cryptocurrencies and blockchain technologies.

Keywords: Bitcoin, exchange rate, financial stress index, inflation rate, interest rate, stock price, and gross domestic product

Introduction

The potential of blockchain technology lies in its ability to facilitate the trading or utilization of centralized virtual or digital tokens. Cryptocurrencies are the inherent digital assets of blockchain networks and play a crucial role in their functioning. Cryptocurrencies are a virtual currency that relies on cryptographic principles. Cryptocurrencies are experiencing a rise in their value. These digital currencies strive to enhance privacy and anonymity to different extents (Le, 2023). While certain currencies provide the option of maintaining privacy, others publicly reveal all transactions. Cryptocurrencies serve the purpose of both substituting and complementing traditional currencies, as they lack official backing and instead rely on investor activity to determine their value based on supply and demand (Böhme et al., 2015; Chiu and Koeppl, 2017). Ever since Satoshi Nakamoto first introduced the idea in his 2008 white paper, bitcoin has garnered considerable interest as a topic of study and discourse. This phenomenon can be attributed to the worldwide dispersion of scholars, experts, and financiers. Despite being a nascent industry, it

has rapidly gained widespread popularity globally. Bitcoin's market valuation is projected to surpass the market value of Malaysia's most valuable corporation (Nawang and Azmi, 2021; Yeong et al., 2019). Thus, it is imperative to ascertain whether Bitcoin, the initial cryptocurrency, is influenced in the same manner as conventional financial assets such as equities and shares, by a nation's economic indices. It is crucial for investors, researchers, and regulators to realize that Bitcoin, like other actively traded investments, operates under the same fundamental economic principles (Böhme et al., 2015; Chiu and Koeppl, 2017; Náñez Alonso et al., 2021). Several research has been undertaken to ascertain the correlation between macroeconomic indicators and stock prices (Dudukalov et al., 2021; Martynov, 2020; Ssaharti, 2022). Nevertheless, limited research has been undertaken to ascertain the correlation with cryptocurrencies (Esmaeilian et al., 2020; Miraz et al., 2021; Wang et al., 2022). In addition, the majority of the research concentrates solely on a single country and employs time series data analysis (Conlon et al., 2021; Wagenaar, 1990). Few studies have used panel data analysis to look at how macroeconomic variables are related to each

[a]hafinaz.hasniyanti@apu.edu.my, [b]vikneswaran.manual@apu.edu.my

other in terms of cointegration (Havidz et al., 2021). Several macroeconomic variables have been employed to establish the correlation with cryptocurrency. This paper specifically examines the variables of currency rate, interest rate, inflation rate, gross domestic product, financial stress index, and share price.

Literature Review

Cryptocurrency has transitioned from being a peculiar commodity to becoming one of the most controversial subjects discussed on television, social media, and scholarly platforms. Participants achieved rapid profits because of the absence of a legal framework and the speculative nature of the activity. The veracity of this narrative remained intact until December 15, 2017, when Bitcoin had a precipitous 50% decrease in value within a week. On November 12, 2021, after three years, the value of one bitcoin reached its highest point, with a trading price of US$64,400. Investors of diverse age groups, religious beliefs, political views, and geographical origins were deeply engrossed by this undeniable reality. State officials grew more concerned about the continuous expansion of this sector, while researchers remained curious. The examination of the risk-return tradeoff between Bitcoin and other financial instruments has garnered significant attention from scholars across several academic disciplines.

Over the last five years, there has been a significant advancement in the empirical research on cryptocurrencies, specifically focusing on Bitcoin. Abdul-Majid et al. (2018), Kouhizadeh et al. (2022), and Southerton (2014) conducted a comprehensive examination of previous research on cryptocurrencies. They investigated how cryptocurrencies may be classified as both a means of transaction and a speculative tool. Conversely, as stated by Havidz et al. (2021), Bitcoin's restricted supply and mining procedure enable it to function as a form of currency and serve as a means of preserving value. Metawa et al. (2022) and Rayhi (2020) both arrived at similar findings, describing Bitcoin as a hybrid asset with hedging capabilities that falls somewhere between a currency and a commodity. Al-Khazali et al. (2018) propose Bitcoin as a protective measure despite the fact that fiscal policy is notoriously unpredictable. Speculative bubbles and problems with price stability, however, limit their usefulness.

Underpinning theory

A central tenet of the quantity theory of money is that the demand for and supply of money interact to determine market prices. Within this framework, Kjaerland et al. (2018) emphasised how supply and demand play a critical role in determining the price of Bitcoin. Using a framework based on Keynes' theory of speculative demand for money, Buchholz et al. (2012) demonstrated how Bitcoin prices are correlated with macro-financial variables. Investors in bonds and other financial assets often engage in currency trading to hedge against possible losses. An increase in interest rates diminishes the worth of economic assets, resulting in financial assets experiencing a loss in value when invested (Havidz et al., 2021). García-Monleón et al. (2023) done another study to investigate the impact of specific macroeconomic factors on the prediction of bitcoin's price. He found that increased utilization of Bitcoin for commercial or non-monetary transactions would lead to its long-term appreciation.

Interest rate and bitcoin

The variables that influence the Bitcoin price have been the subject of extensive research. Real interest rate-based work remained comparatively rare. There are, however, some similar books that focus on macroeconomic aspects and economic policy. According to Tijn and S (2022), the variance decomposition revealed that negative real interest rate shocks had a greater impact on the price of bitcoin than positive real interest rate shocks. Over time, negative real interest rate shocks emerged as the primary explanatory factor. The Bitcoin price's response to the positive interest rate, according to impulse response functions, was inconsequential. In addition, Brody et al. (2020) carried out a study to see if there is a relationship between bitcoin and monetary variables in Indonesia. The researchers discovered that over the long term, there is no balance or parallelism in movement between the increase in bitcoin prices, the exchange rate, inflation, gold prices, and interest rates. Köse and Ünal (2023) discovered a significant correlation between bitcoin, gold, and crude oil although there is little correlation with the interest rate. On the other hand, price behavior, according to Auer et al. (2022), cannot be described by conventional economic theory. This is supported by the fact that, unlike traditional fiat currencies, Bitcoin is a digital currency that is not influenced by macroeconomic factors.

Exchange rate and bitcoin

According to BenSaïda (2023), by adding both types of assets to their portfolios, investors in cryptocurrencies and other financial assets denominated in the currencies from our sample can profit from diversification. Additionally, he underlines the significance of Bitcoin price fluctuations concerning monetary policy via the exchange rate channel. On the other hand, Erdas and Caglar (2018) discovered that in both the short- and long-term co-integration equilibriums, the Bitcoin exchange rate (BER) and Google search volume index (SVI) have a Granger causality feedback relationship, and the investor fear gauge is highly related to BER in the long-term co-integration. Ibrahim and Ali Basah (2022) investigated how the prices of oil, financial markets, and exchange rates affected the price of bitcoin. Findings indicate that key variables influencing Bitcoin's long-term value include the Dow Jones Index, the euro-dollar exchange rate, and oil prices. Tijn and S. (2022) investigated whether users thought of Bitcoin as a currency or an asset while Dumitrescu et al. (2023) examined that Bitcoin's worth in its dual roles as a store of value and an investment tool. The study discovered that, while Bitcoin can significantly improve an investor's portfolio's efficiency, it may not be acceptable as an exchange currency.

Gross domestic product (GDP) and bitcoin
Shaikh (2020) discovered that the volatility of the Federal Open Market Committee (FOMC), the GDP, and other macroeconomic data had a detrimental impact on the price of bitcoin. Additionally, Ali Al-Qudah et al. (2020) stated the rise in market capitalization and popularity of Bitcoin in investor portfolios made it more likely that it would have an impact on overall economic activity. According to Mishkin (2018), asset prices and the exchange rate have an impact on GDP. Since monetary policy has an impact on both asset prices and the exchange rate, it is important to consider these channels when deciding how to implement monetary policy. Consequently, asset values impact the net worth of a household or business, influencing spending and investment decisions as well as borrowing capacity.

Inflation rate and bitcoin
Although a small number of studies based on the money demand theory suggest a connection between Bitcoin prices and inflation Erfanian et al. (2022), this connection has not, to our knowledge, been empirically examined. The high-frequency research on the correlation between inflation and Bitcoin prices offers significant policy implications given that many investors view Bitcoin as an inflation hedge, particularly during the recent epidemic (Blau et al., 2021). The rise in the price of cryptocurrencies has been associated with higher inflation forecasts (Zhu et al., 2017). Despite retaining a certain degree of currency hedging capability, cryptocurrencies are characterized by significant price volatility. The vulnerability of Auer et al. (2022) to the same macroeconomic factors that affect conventional assets diminishes their efficacy as a hedge (Muller et al., 2020; Wagenaar, 1990). One major factor contributing to cryptocurrencies' ability to function as a more effective inflation hedge than gold is the simplicity with which they can be exchanged and stored.

Financial stress index and bitcoin
Bitcoin returns and investors' level of risk revision have a complicated relationship (Zhang and Wang, 2021). Over time, the degree of connectivity between Bitcoin exchange platforms changes. A well-known exchange like Bitfinex, for instance, has an impact on other exchanges (Hoque and Low, 2022). The prediction model, which is applicable to financial markets, can be applied to the bitcoin trading market as well. It is based on intraday momentum and reversal (Korkmaz and Nur, 2022). Based on quantile dependence analysis, it has been found that Bitcoin can be used as a hedge against the global financial crisis. (Yin et al., 2022). Furthermore, Dudukalov et al. (2021) use several wavelet-related techniques with US data and discover a sizable effect of Bitcoin price on money supply. The impact of the US and Chinese financial stress index on the volatility of Bitcoin and gold is examined in the study by Rayhi (2020). They claim that, in times of apprehension, the financial stress index has a medium-term impact on gold prices in the United States. It affects Bitcoin in the short term, whereas the financial stress index in China affects Bitcoin in the medium term.

Share price and bitcoin
The relationship between cryptocurrencies and the stock market has captured the attention of all market participants, including investors, bankers, businesspeople, and members of the political establishment. Researchers have sought a pattern in this association over the years (Sovbetov and Sovbetov, 2018). There are a number of things to consider in the crypto-stock relationship, which depends on things like a country's exchange rate and inflation, its banking system (which can be expensive and complicated), regulatory uncertainty, financial limitations, and most importantly, the presence or potential for capital controls. To summarise, this part of the article reviews the literature on developing-world cryptocurrency and stock relationships. Kose and Ünal (2023) conducted an empirical investigation into the correlation between the Malaysian stock market and Bitcoin trading returns. The data from January 2013 to January 2017 were examined. The statistical findings indicate a negative correlation between fluctuations in Bitcoin's price and stock market activity. According to the findings of the study, Bitcoins are crucial for mitigating investment risk and increasing portfolio returns when included

in investments. Aimon et al. (2020) analyzed the volatility pattern of Bitcoins traded on the financial markets and empirically examined the ability of Bitcoins to hedge against global geopolitical risks. Dumitrescu et al. (2023) voiced their concern over the existence of a Bitcoin-related speculative bubble. They cited it as a key factor in insufficient financial stability relative to stocks and other tradable financial assets. According to Harooni and Alvan's (2023) research, the risk-return trade-off of various crypto-currencies is unique in comparison to traditional financial assets such as equities and bonds that are traded on international financial markets. Meiryani et al. (2022) analyzed the high volatility of cryptocurrencies and concluded that Bitcoins can be used for speculative investments.

Data and Methodology

The objective of this research is to clarify the associations between cryptocurrencies and macroeconomic indicators in both the short and long term, including the exchange rate (EXR), inflation rate (CPI), interest rate, gross domestic product (GDP), and financial stress index (FSI) proxies in five Asian countries: India, Indonesia, Japan, Malaysia, and Thailand. From January 2018 to December 2022, monthly statistics on cryptocurrency prices and macroeconomic indicators are collected for the five Asian markets. Bitcoin may be purchased and traded on numerous exchanges, supporting a wide range of currencies. Bitcoincharts.com exhibits the prices and volumes for 31 distinct currencies across 72 diverse exchanges. Nevertheless, in order to carry out a cross-country analysis that can be compared, we specifically examined Asian exchanges that facilitate transactions in a minimum of five different currencies. The data included in this analysis was obtained from reliable and credible sources, including the Investing.com website and World Bank data. The data was analyzed using a fixed effect model and a generalized linear model (GLM). The fixed effect model was employed to mitigate any unobserved heterogeneity in the data, while the generalized linear model was utilized to depict the association between the dependent and independent variables. By employing these models, the study was able to offer a more comprehensive analysis of the data.

Results and Discussion

In any study, descriptive statistics provide general information with the aim of summarising the factors

Table 190.1 Descriptive statistics.

	Mean	Median	Maximum	Minimum	Std. dev.
BITCOIN	61118463	934090	822953984	14387	158100997
CPI	55.28666	50.01676	159.1812	0.000277684	41.462166
EXCHANGE_RATE	97.99663	98.81	105.7	73.7	5.18357926
FSI	-0.58299	-0.6873	6.5721	-3.7048	1.31364755
GDP	5.62E+12	584869.1	4.021E+13	19746.99219	1.1696E+13
INTEREST_RATE	5.42725	4.619027	22.956878	-6.7988798	5.13799315
SHARE_PRICE	12360.47	6886.501	33753.33	1374.64	12103.2226

Source: Author

Table 190.2 Matrix of correlations.

	Bitcoin	CPI	EXR	FSI	GDP	IR	SP
Bitcoin	1						
CPI	-0.34025	1					
EXR	0.18353	-0.21944	1				
FSI	0.05078	0.03036	-0.10427	1			
GDP	-0.18217	-0.00966	0.17511	0.04312	1		
IR	0.66129	-0.48395	0.31541	0.10239	-0.03618	1	
SP	-0.16926	0.15830	-0.37429	-0.16985	0.28377	-0.42188	1

Source: Author

Table 190.3 Regression analysis (fixed effect model).

| Variable | Dependent variable: Bitcoin | | | |
	Coefficient	Std. error	t-Statistic	Prob.
C	-3.5E+08	1.5E+08	-2.35791	0.019035
CPI	-62404.6	181583.7	-0.34367	0.731342
EXCHANGE_RATE	2854923	1498955	1.904609	0.05781
FSI	4836737	5225233	0.92565	0.35539
INTEREST_RATE	21992017	1603592	13.71422	0.00000
SHARE_PRICE	3214.25	689.4337	4.66216	0.00000
GDP	-3.30E-06	6.23E-07	-5.30679	0.00000
R-squared	0.50029			
Adjusted R-squared	0.490057			
F-statistic	48.89007			
Prob(F-statistic)	2.02E-41			
No. of observation	300			
Likelihood test	370.7747	0.0000		
Hausaman test	0.44	0.0000		

Source: Author

under investigation. Table 190.1 shows unambiguous measurements of all factors used in this study and presents the mean, standard deviation, minimum and maximum for all factors. The descriptive statistics assume that the data are normally distributed, and a recidivism model is essential considering these factors. In accordance with our data, the sample size consisted of the financial macroeconomic variable of 5 Asian countries during the 5-years observation period from 2018 to 2022. Bitcoin is the dependent variable in this study and has 6111843 as the mean and 158100997 as the standard deviation. After that, CPI has 55.28 as the mean and 41.46 as the standard deviation. The maximum and minimum values for CPI are 159.1812 and 0.0000277. FSI has the smallest meaning and standard deviation among all other variables. The values are -0.58299 and 1.31364. The minimum and maximum value of FSI is 6.5721 and -37048. The mean and standard value of stock prices is the second highest in this study. The mean and standard deviation are 12360.47 and 12103.226. The minimum and maximum value of share price are 33753.33 and 1374.64 respectively.

The correlation strength between the components considered is shown in the correlation matrix data, which are presented in Table 190.2. Multicollinearity is a factual peculiarity when at least two indicator elements are extraordinarily associated in a separate relapse model, according to (Asteriou et al., 2013).

Simply having multicollinearity might affect the accuracy of the components being studied by causing evaluations of the model coefficients to be unreliable and unauthentic. Correlation must not be greater than 0.8, it was also claimed (Brooks, 2008). The results of the factor correlations are displayed in Table 190.4. It is possible to conclude from the results that there was no multicollinearity issue. As a result, all of the study's variables remained constant.

With a probability value of 0.0000, the likelihood test result for the chi-square statistics is equal to 370.7747. At a significance level of 5%, the null hypothesis is disproved. The fixed effects model is favoured, as shown by this finding, and it can be used to evaluate appropriate slope coefficient valuations. The best estimator for the model between the fixed effects and the random effects models was then chosen using the Hausman test. According to Table 190.3, the probability value is 0.000, and the Hausman test result is equivalent to 0.44. The outcome reveals that, when compared to pooled OLS and fixed effects models, the fixed effects model is a more preferable and effective estimator.

The fixed effect regression analysis showed that the value of the F-statistic is 48.89 and the probability is 0.000, which is less than 5%, indicating that the model is appropriate to explain the relationship between the macroeconometric factor and the bitcoin price. The R-squared of this regression analysis

Table 190.4 Diagnostic testing.

Heteroscedasticity	
X2	370.7746834
Prob > X2	0.0000
Serial correlation	
F-stat	110.5099927
Prob > F	0.0000

Note: *** significant at 1%; ** significant at 5%, * significant at 10%

Source: Author

Table 190.5 Generalize linear model.

	Dependent variable: Biticoin			
Variable	Coefficient	Std. error	z-Statistic	Prob.
C	-97013691.57	148090228.9	-0.65509853	0.512404
CPI	-68411.75006	189782.7675	-0.36047398	0.718493
EXCHANGE_RATE	226801.6753	1478691.663	0.15337996	0.878099
FSI	319035.3131	5388306.932	0.05920882	0.952786
INTEREST_RATE	21754344.68	1675378.246	12.9847363	0.00000
SHARE_PRICE	1764.360504	661.581513	2.66688302	0.007656
Mean dependent var	61118463.17			
Sum squared resid	4.09E+18			
Log likelihood	-5998.541279			
Schwarz criterion	40.10435084			
Deviance	4.09E+18			
Restr. deviance	7.47E+18			
Prob(LR statistic)	0.00000			
Pearson statistic	1.39E+16			

Source: Author

is 0.5, which explains that 50% of the macroeconomic variables selected in this study have an impact on the bitcoin price. Five independent variables were selected in this study. However, only three (interest rate, stock price and GDP) are significantly related to bitcoin price, while the rest of them have insignificant relationship with bitcoin price. The stock price has a positive and significant relationship with the bitcoin price in this study. This result is consistent with (Auer et al., 2022) that investment in stocks and bitcoin are related. The interest rate is also positively and significantly related to Bitcoin in this study. Auer et al. (2022) and Chang et al. (2021) also found the same effect in their study. Interest rates always have the strongest effect on investment activity. Nevertheless, GDP has a negative significant relationship with the

bitcoin price in this study, which is in contrast to BenSaïda (2023) and Chang et al. (2021), who found a positive significant relationship with the bitcoin price.

The study employed diagnostic procedures for serial correlation and heteroskedasticity. As Hochle (2007) advised, the model was corrected using robust standard errors. The results of the heteroskedasticity and serial correlation tests for the model are displayed in Table 190.4. The standard error of the model is robust to heteroskedasticity and serial correlation when performing regression tests for the model in this study because a random effects model with a clustered sandwich standard error is used based on the results of the tests for heteroskedasticity and serial correlation. Table 190.4 displays the results of the Breusch-Pagan test and the LM test to determine heteroscedasticity and serial correlation. The results showed that the p-values for bitcoin in Asian countries were at 0.0001 and significant for both tests, indicating the existence of serial correlation and heteroscedasticity. The generalize linear model (GLM) technique can be used to account for heteroscedasticity and serial correlation (Brooks, 2008). This was the justification for the study's use of the GLM as an alternative estimating approach (Baltagi, 2008).

The GLM was used in this study because of the statistical problem of serial correlation and heteroskedasticity. The results are similar to the fixed effect regression model conducted earlier. According to the GLM, interest rate and stock have a positive significant relationship with bitcoin price.

Conclusion

In this study, we attempted to uncover a novel association between a few economic variables that had not been explored in earlier studies. As a result, we discovered a relationship between the price of Bitcoin and several macroeconomic factors, such as the inflation rate, exchange rate, interest rate, financial stress index, and market share price among the five Asean nations. Our analysis reveals a significant positive relationship between interest rates and the price of Bitcoin. This implies that Bitcoin prices tend to rise as interest rates rise. This relationship could be explained by the fact that higher interest rates can entice more investors to consider Bitcoin as an alternative investment option, resulting in an increase in demand and, as a result, a rise in price. Additionally, the positive correlation between interest rates and Bitcoin prices may point to a larger market trend in which both Bitcoin and traditional stocks are influenced by similar economic factors. Furthermore, Bitcoin prices tend to rise when stock prices rise. This is explained by the concept of market sentiment, which states that a positive outlook on the stock market can lead to a positive outlook on Bitcoin as well. Furthermore, an increase in share prices may result in increased wealth and disposable income for investors, which may fuel their interest in investing in Bitcoin. The regression analysis was carried out using GLM because of the heteroskedasticity and serial correlation issues. By addressing these statistical concerns, the GLM approach ensures more accurate and reliable results. Moreover, this decision facilitates an all-encompassing comprehension of the correlation between macroeconomic indicators and the valuation of Bitcoin. The demand and supply, speculation elements, stock index, Forex Reserves, and growth rate are a few other independent variables that future studies could include when examining the macroeconomic aspects that influence the price of bitcoin. The link between these independent variables and the dependent variableis advised to be examined throughout both short- and long-term time frames. The crypto currency Bitcoin (BTC) was employed in this study to conduct the test, but other top-three crypto currencies, such as Ethereum (ETH), Ripple (XRP), and Litecoin (LTC), might be used in future research.

References

Asteriou, D., Hall, S. G., and Seyidoglu, H. (2013). Applied econometrics a modern apprpach. *Journal of Chemical Information and Modeling*, 53(9). https://www.pton-line.com/articles/how-to-get-better-mfi-results.

Baltagi, B. H. (2008). Econometrics. *Econometrics*, (59). https://doi.org/10.1007/978-3-540-76516-5.

Böhme, R., Christin, N., Edelman, B., and Moore, T. (2015). Bitcoin: economics, technology, and governance. *Journal of economic Perspectives*, 29(2), 213–238.

Brooks, C. (2008). Introduction to econometrics for finance. United States of America.

Chiu, J., and Koeppl, T. V. (2017). The economics of cryptocurrencies bitcoin and beyond. *SSRN Electronic Journal*, https://doi.org/10.2139/ssrn.3048124.

Conlon, T., Corbet, S., and McGee, R. J. (2021). Inflation and cryptocurrencies revisited: a time-scale analysis. *Economics Letters*, 206. https://doi.org/10.1016/j.econlet.2021.109996.

Dudukalov, E. V., Geroeva, Y. A., Shtepa, M. A., and Ushakov, D. (2021). The crypto currency as money of digital economy. In E3S Web of Conferences, (Vol. 244, pp. 1–10). https://doi.org/10.1051/e3s-conf/202124410021.

Esmaeilian, B., Sarkis, J., Lewis, K., and Behdad, S. (2020). Blockchain for the future of sustainable supply chain management in Industry 4.0. *Resources, Conservation and Recycling*, 163, 105064. https://doi.org/10.1016/j.resconrec.2020.105064.

Havidz, S. A. H., Karman, V. E., and Mambea, I. Y. (2021). Is bitcoin price driven by macro-financial factors and liquidity? A global consumer survey empirical study. *Organizations and Markets in Emerging Economies*, 12(2), 399–414. https://doi.org/10.15388/omee.2021.12.62.

Le, P. N. (2023). The impact of cryptocurrencies on the financial market. 16, 85–117. https://doi.org/10.4018/978-1-6684-8368-8.ch004.

Martynov, O. (2020). Sustainability analysis of cryptocurrencies based on projected return on investment and environmental impact. *ProQuest*, 1–69.

Miraz, M. H., Sharif, K. I. M., Hassan, M. G., Ismail, M. A., and Mahyadin, F. B. (2021). Bitcoins in the malaysian economy. *Journal of Management, Economics, and Industrial Organization*, 70–85. https://doi.org/10.31039/jomeino.2021.5.3.6.

Náñez Alonso, S. L., Jorge-vázquez, J., Echarte Fernández, M. Á., and Reier Forradellas, R. F. (2021). Cryptocurrency mining from an economic and environmental perspective. analysis of the most and least sustainable countries. *Energies*, 14(14). https://doi.org/10.3390/en14144254.

Nawang, N. I. and Azmi, I. M. A. G. (2021). Cryptocurrency: an insight into the malaysian regulatory approach.

Psychology and Education Journal, 58(2), 1645–1652. https://doi.org/10.17762/pae.v58i2.2319.

Ssaharti, M. (2022). The impact of crypto currencies on the economy and the financial industry. *Journal of Advances in Humanities Research*, 1(1), 60–69. https://doi.org/10.56868/jadhur.v1i1.11.

191 Behavioural factors influencing investing decisions in the Indonesian stock market

Jason Zefanya Theiji[1,a] and Chong Lee Lee[2,b]

[1]School of Accounting and Finance, Asia Pacific Univrsity of Technology and Innovation, Kuala Lumpur, Malaysia

[2]PhD, School of Accoutning and Finance, Asia Pacific Univrsity of Technology and Innovation, Kuala Lumpur, Malaysia

Abstract

Investors are expected to be influenced by their behavioural characteristics. In the context of retail investors, behavioural traits interplay with their emotions and decision-making process. Their decision to invest may be significantly affected by how their emotions change their action. Even though the importance of behavioural finance is noticeable, the relevant research, particularly in Indonesia, remains limited, leading to a lack of information and education for investors. As such, this study examines the influence of herding, risk aversion, overconfidence, and the COVID-19 pandemic on investor decision-making in Indonesia. This study collects 384 responses from stock investors in Indonesia through self-administered surveys. Based on the results, herding, risk aversion, overconfidence, and the COVID-19 pandemic are significant factors in investor decision-making. All of them posit a positive relationship with the investment decision. The findings provide important implications to facilitate more rational and informed investing decisions among stock investors, particularly from Indonesia. More concerted efforts can be made to educate retail investors in managing their behavioural characteristics to promote sound and rational investing decisions. With such education awareness, the irrationality exhibited in the stock markets can beminimised and further enhanced market efficiency.

Keywords: Behavioural finance, investing decision, retail investors

Introduction

The stock market is the most common place for investors to accumulate wealth, giving them relatively easy access to the capital market. With the emergence of technology, investors purchase and sell shares through online platforms. The stock market is also a platform for conveying investment choices to corporate management and a place to promote good corporate governance. The stock market is widely known as the most efficient means for companies to raise capital, driving the economic growth of a country (Zuravicky, 2005).

In the realm of decision-making, Subramani and Venkatraman (2003) assert that it is a multifaceted process involving various steps and a thorough analysis of diverse factors. This process encompasses identifying problems, gathering information, evaluating alternative options, and post-purchase behaviours. The behaviour of investors may form a particular influence on their investing decision-making apart from factors such as age, education, income, and existing investment portfolio.

Behavioural finance has become a valuable framework for comprehending the emotional and cognitive factors that steer investment decisions. This discipline explores the role of psychology and social sciences in explaining market behaviours, including market bubbles and crashes (Waweru et al., 2008). Particularly relevant in the context of this study is its applicability to the Indonesian stock market, where the influence of cognitive biases on investors has been accentuated (Kim and Nofsinger, 2008). While behavioural finance has primarily focused on developed markets, frontier and emerging economies like Indonesia remain relatively underexplored in this context. Therefore, this study seeks to apply behavioural finance principles to the Indonesian capital market, an evolving stock market, to unveil the unique characteristics shaping individual investor behaviour.

The global landscape underwent a seismic shift with the advent of the COVID-19 pandemic. This unprecedented event substantially altered the behaviour and decision-making of investors. Behavioural finance posits that investors often rely on emotions, biases, and heuristics rather than strictly logical analysis and risk assessment (Gharbi et al., 2022). Fear and anxiety stemming from the pandemic induced market volatility and uncertainty, prompting impulsive, emotion-driven investment decisions (Naseem et al., 2021).

[a]Jasontheiji@gmail.comor, TP061695@mail.apu.edu.my, [b]chong.leelee@apu.edu.my

Investors found themselves prone to herd behaviour, deviating from their research and analysis to follow the crowd (Shankar, 2022). Additionally, some succumbed to overconfidence, perceiving the pandemic as an investment opportunity due to plummeting stock prices (Luxembourg, 2022). This deviation from established investment strategies underscored the importance of recognising the role of emotions and biases in investor decision-making, highlighting the need for disciplined and rational investment strategies (Ritika et al., 2022).

Indonesia's economy intersected with the COVID-19 pandemic's disruptive force, triggering significant shifts in the stock market. During the pandemic, there was a sharp increase in the stock market turnover and the number of new investors because of the influx of money flowing into the market due to government financial aid. However, this surge in interest happened for a short period, as many investors adopted a more conservative strategy, worrying about the possible economic slowdown. The Indonesian stock market benchmark of the IHSG index suffered from a rapid decline from its previous highs, highlighting the negative impact of the pandemic's impact (Fadly, 2021).

Literature Review

Investor decision-making is an important aspect of financial markets. It involves the process of evaluating various investment choices and assessing risks and returns together with the investment objectives and time horizon (Sukandani et al., 2019). Investors need to conduct research and analyse different asset classes, including stocks, bonds, unit trusts, real estate, and alternative investments (Rohman, 2022). Yati (2013) also states that investing decisions involve assessing the financial health of firms, analysing market movements, and evaluating the potential risks and rewards of different investment strategies. The final goal is to balance the risk and return with the targeted investment objectives and preferences, with efficient asset allocation, risk management, and continuous portfolio monitoring and rebalancing.

Herding

Baddeley (2010) defines herding as one mimicking the group's behaviour, and social factors influence the behaviour. Herding behaviour may lead to market inefficiency and investment bubbles. Herding has been quantified as the average propensity of money managers to buy or sell certain stocks simultaneously, deviating from what would be expected if they traded independently. This behaviour reflects the impact of social influence on investor decision-making, as individuals adjust their beliefs, emotions, attitudes, and behaviours when influenced by others, leading to correlated trading patterns (Aronson et al., 2013).

Risk Aversion

Risk aversion represents thetendency of humansto avoid uncertainty and prefer certain outcomes over potentially higher but riskier returns. Tversky and Kahneman (1974) describe it as a preference for specific outcomes with equal or higher expected values. Investors are strongly inclined to minimiserisk, influenced by factors such as individual risk preference, mood, emotions, and circumstances (Gollier, 2001). Risk perception is dynamic, evolving according to situations and emotions associated with potential gains or losses (Li, 2011).

Overconfidence

Overconfidence is a cognitive bias wherein individuals believe in their ability to predict and possess superior knowledge compared to others (Khan et al., 2016). It leads to misguided judgments, as individuals tend to overestimate their knowledge and abilities, often resulting in excessive trading, overestimating evaluation capabilities, underestimation of investment risks, and failure to maximise investments (Pompian, 2012). This behavioural bias can have significant consequences in financial decision-making.

COVID-19

The COVID-19 pandemic, stemming from the SARS-CoV-2 virus, has had far-reaching consequences on global health and the economy (Chaplin, 2020). As the pandemic unfolded, governments worldwide implemented lockdowns, travel restrictions, and social distancing, resulting in reduced economic activity and significant business challenges (Shaharudin, 2021). Industries like travel, tourism, hospitality, and retail were particularly hardhit, and the global stock market experienced rapid declines as investors reacted to the uncertainties and economic disruptions brought about by the outbreak (Fauziyyah and Ersyafdi, 2021).

Hypothesis Development

Risk aversion significantly impacts investor decision-making. When individuals anticipate gains, they are more willing to take risks, while the fear of losing money leads to risk avoidance (Li, 2011). Emotions play a pivotal role in shaping risk perception, and they can influence investment choices both in isolation and when combined with other emotional factors

(Lowenstein et al., 2001). Understanding the impact of emotions, risk aversion, and mood on decision-making has led to proposals for including these behavioural aspects in the investment decision-making process (Lowenstein et al., 2001). The risk aversion is considered a crucial factor influencing stock market expectations (Hurd et al., 2011). The changes in investor risk aversion are affected by factors of wealth, anticipated income, perceived likelihood, and emotional shifts in the utility function (Guiso et al., 2018). This hypothesis suggests that the risk aversion level among investors will significantly impact their decision-making in the stock market. More risk-averse investors may make different investment choices compared to those willing to take on higher levels of risk.

H1: Risk aversion significantly affects investor decision-making negatively

Basically, herding behaviour describes how social influence shapes investor decisions. Social influence prescribes how individuals' attitudes, perceptions, and behaviour can be shaped by the pressures exerted by other investors or groups (Baron and Branscombe, 2012). Human being behaviour is often influenced by the actions of others (Aronson et al., 2013). Significant herding tendencies are exhibited during political instability and market bubbles, such as the civil war era (Shantha et al., 2018) and frontier stock markets like the Vietnam Stock Market (Nguyen, 2018). These findings highlight the significant impact of social influence on investor decision-making, possibly leading to market irrationalities. Hypothesis 2 posits that a positive relationship is observed between herding behaviour and investor decision-making.

H2: Herding behaviour influences investor decision-making positively.

Investors may exhibit overconfidence traits in which investors tend to follow past trading strategies, hoping to replicate past gains. This may lead to irrationality and risky decisions. Market imbalances stemming from overconfidence can result in unpredictable trading patterns, impacting the relationship between returns, trading volume, and volatility (Gervais and Odean, 2001). Fuertes et al. (2012) state that overconfident investors tend to invest more in the market as the result of their ignorance and lack of knowledge of the financial market, which causes them to have less diversified portfolios. In addition to financial choices, overconfidence also shapes one's personality, influencing one's financial decisions (Aren and Aydemir, 2014). Overconfident investors may engage in excessive trading and not adequately assess risks, leading to different investment choices. They believe that they have superior knowledge and abilities compared to others. Therefore, Hypothesis 3 postulates a positive

relationship between overconfidence and investor decision-making.

H3: Overconfidence positively affects investor decision-making.

The COVID-19 pandemic has had a profound impact on investor behaviour and decision-making. It has created a dual effect on investment choices. Some investors have viewed the market's decline as an opportunity to buy undervalued assets, while others have adopted a more cautious stance due to economic uncertainties (Vera, 2022). This crisis has increased market volatility, making it challenging for investors to make decisions based on shifting pandemic-related news and economic data (Wang et al., 2021). Priorities have shifted, with investors focusing more on resilient businesses capable of weathering economic uncertainties (Cevik et al., 2022). The increased uncertainty induced by COVID-19 has elevated the risks associated with various financial investments (Zhang et al., 2021), resulting in altered market dynamics and non-rational investor decisions (Liu et al., 2020). This hypothesis proposes that the COVID-19 pandemic has significantly impacted investor decision-making. The uncertainties and economic disruptions caused by the pandemic may have led investors to change their investment strategies and risk preferences, influencing their decision-making in the stock market.

H4: The COVID-19 pandemic affects investor decision-making positively.

Data and Methodology

The methodology and research techniques employed in the study involve adopting a positivist research philosophy. This aligns with the research objectives, emphasising statistical data analysis and focused data collection. The study primarily employs an explanatory research classification with an exploratory approach to understanding the subject matter. A deductive approach is used for hypothesis formation.

Quantitative research is the chosen strategy, and online surveys serve as the primary data collection method. The study focuses on quantitative methods to examine relationships between variables and employs a cross-sectional design to collect data at a specific point in time. Data is collected through online surveys from Indonesian investors, utilising a questionnaire with two parts: one gathering demographic information and the other containing questions related to independent and dependent variables, rated on a 5-point Likert scale. The surveys were distributed through social media platforms in July 2023.

The sample size is 384 respondents, with a margin of error of 4.95%. The sample population consists of diverse Indonesian stock investors to ensure comprehensive insights. Data preparation involves collecting, verifying data accuracy, and transferring it to an SPSS file for analysis. Data analysis includes descriptive analysis, reliability testing, validity assessment, and inferential statistics like multiple regression and Pearson correlation analysis to test hypotheses. Ethical considerations include obtaining informed consent, ensuring voluntary participation, protecting data confidentiality, and adhering to ethical guidelines throughout the research proces

This study uses multiple regression to analyse the research model, and it is presented as follows.

$$DM = \beta_0 + \beta_1 RA + \beta_3 Herding + \beta_4 OVER + \beta_5 COVID + \varepsilon$$

Where
DM = Investing decision-making
RA = Risk aversion behavior
Herding = Herding behavior
OVER = Overconfidence characteristics
COVID = COVID-19 pandemic

Results and Discussion

After gathering the data, several statistical analyses are conducted on the data. These analyses serve the dual purpose of ensuring data reliability and validity while also providing insights into the study's respondents. They aim to investigate the diverse motivations that may impact these respondents' decision-making.

Correlation Analysis

Table 191.1 presents the Pearson correlation for the variables under study, including decision-making, risk aversion, herding, overconfidence and covid-19. The correlation between decision-making and risk aversion is 0.823, while it has a value of 0.812 between decision-making and herding. The correlation values are 0.836 and 0.803 for the relation between overconfidence and decision making and the COVID-19 pandemic and decision making, respectively. We can conclude that risk aversion, herding, overconfidence, and the COVID-19 pandemic significantly and positively correlate with investors' decision-making in the stock market.

Weighted Least Square Linear Regression

The diagnostic checking also shows that the regression model is free from multicollinearity problems but suffers from autocorrelation and heteroscedasticity problems. As such, the weighted least square linear regression is employed for the data analysis. Based on the results, all independent variables induced a positive relationship with the investors' decision-making. The coefficients are 0.166, 0.126, 0.148 and 0.189 among risk aversion, herding, overconfidence and covid-19 with the investors' decision-making. Among all, the COVID-19 pandemic seems to influence investors the most, followed by risk aversion, overconfidence and herding behaviours. The regression model also has significant F-statistics with a value of 78.241 (0.000) and adjusted R-squares of 0.618.

Table 191.2 presents the multiple regression results, and the function can be presented below:

$$DM = 9.872 + 0.166RA + 0.126Herding + 0.148OVER + 0.189COVID$$

Results Discussion

The study revealed a positive significant relationship between risk aversion and investing decision-making

Table 191.1 Pearson correlation analysis.

Variables	Decision making	Risk aversion	Herding	Overconfidence	COVID-19
Decision making	1	0.823 (0.000)**	0.812 (0.000)**	0.836 (0.000)**	0.803 (0.000)**
Risk aversion	0.823 (0.000)**	1	0.839 (0.000)**	0.854 (0.000)**	0.833 (0.000)**
Herding	0.812 (0.000)**	0.839 (0.000)**	1	0.861 (0.000)**	0.832 (0.000)**
Overconfidence	0.836 (0.000)**	0.854 (0.000)**	0.861 (0.000)**	1	0.852 (0.000)**
COVID-19	0.803 (0.000)**	0.833 (0.000)**	0.832 (0.000)**	0.852 (0.000)**	1

** denotes Correlation is significant at the 0.01 level (2-tailed)
Source: Author

Table 191.2 Regression result for the proposed research model.

Variables	Coefficients	t-statistics	Significance level	VIF
Constant	9.872	13.583	0.000**	
Risk Aversion	0.166	5.050	0.000**	4.744
Herding	0.126	3.632	0.000**	4.890
Overconfidence	0.148	3.293	0.001**	5.633
Covid-19	0.189	4.804	0.000**	4.595
F-statistics	78.241 (0.000**)			
Adjusted R_square	0.618			

**denotes significance at 5 percent level
Source: Author

in the Indonesian stock market. During the COVID-19 pandemic, investors tend to enter the stock market, including those who are more risk-averse. During that period, people stayed home and had more cash flow due to the financial assistance from the government. Together with the herding behaviours, investors generally become more willing to take risks. This is witnessed by the active participation of retail investors in the stock market during the COVID-19 pandemic. This is also consistent with past studies emphasizing emotional responses and prospect theory influencing investor behaviour. We also noticed a positive relationship between herding behaviours and investing decision-making. During the black swan period, such as the COVID-19 pandemic, investors often followed the crowd rather than making rational choices, partly driven by social influences. This echoes prior studies identifying herding behaviour during financial crises, including the COVID-19 pandemic.

Overconfidence appeared as a significant factor influencing investors' investing decision-making. When the market sentiment is high, overconfident investors tend to take bolder actions, underestimate the risks they may face and overestimate their abilities to make better returns. Their behaviour was observed across various experience levels, with younger investors showing higher overconfidence levels during the pandemic. During the COVID-19 pandemic, all the stock markets were rocked, reflecting market uncertainties. At the same time, the increased volatility in the stock market also presents an opportunity for investors who aim to make a short-term return. The crisis had pushed more new investors into the stock market. While the pandemic's uncertainty made investors cautious, the sharp drop in stock prices created a chance to acquire undervalued assets. Investors viewed the pandemic as a unique opportunity to buy low, potentially yielding higher returns as the economy recovered. Updates on

vaccinations and pandemic-related news further influenced their decisions, emphasizing the shock of external events in shaping investment choices.

Conclusion

This study found that risk aversion, herding behaviour, overconfidence, and the COVID-19 pandemic significantly influence investor decision-making in the Indonesian stock market. All the variables induce positive effects on the decision-making of investors. These behavioural factors contribute to the complexity of investor choices and have implications for portfolio management and risk assessment. Recognising and understanding these behavioural biases is crucial for investors and financial practitioners to make informed decisions and navigate market fluctuations effectively. This study is significant as it contributes to Indonesia's underexplored field of behavioural finance, offering valuable insights for investors navigating the stock market in times of crisis like the COVID-19 pandemic.

While shedding light on the influence of behavioural finance factors (risk aversion, herding, overconfidence, and COVID-19) on investor decision-making in the Indonesian stock market, this study has certain limitations. It primarily focused on a specific demographic within Indonesia, potentially limiting the generalizability of its findings to a broader global context. This study solely examined a subset of behavioural factors, leaving out other potentially relevant influences on investor decisions. Future research can be conducted on cross-cultural analyses, employing longitudinal studies and incorporating qualitative methods to gain deeper insights into investor behaviour. Diversifying the participant pool and exploring additional behavioural factors can lead to a more comprehensive understanding of investor decision-making in financial markets.

References

Aronson, E., Wilson, T. D., and Akert, R. M. (2013). Social Psychology. Pearson.

Baddeley, M. (2010). Herding, social influence and economic decision-making: socio-psychological and neuroscientific analyses. *Philosophical Transactions of the Royal Society B: Biological Sciences*, 365(1538), 281–290. https://doi.org/10.1098/rstb.2009.0169.

Baron, R. A., and Branscombe, N. R. (2012). Social Psychology: International Edition. Pearson.

Cevik, E., Kirci Altinkeski, B., Cevik, E. I., and Dibooglu, S. (2022). Investor sentiments and stock markets during the COVID-19 pandemic. *Financial Innovation*, 8(1), 69. https://doi.org/10.1186/s40854-022-00375-0.

Chaplin, S. (2020). COVID-19: a brief history and treatments in development. *Prescriber*, 31(5), 23–28. https://doi.org/10.1002/psb.1843.

Fadly, S. R. (2021). Aktivitas pasar modal Indonesia di era pandemi. https://www.djkn.kemenkeu.go.id/kpknl-kupang/baca-artikel/13817/Aktivitas-Pasar-Modal-Indonesia-Di-Era-Pandemi.html.

Fauziyyah, N., and Ersyafdi, I. R. (2021). Dampak Covid-19 pada pasar saham di berbagai Negara. *Forum Ekonomi*, 23(1), 56–66.

Fuertes, A.-M., Muradoglu, G., and Ozturkkal, B. (2012). A behavioral analysis of investor diversification. *The European Journal of Finance*, 20(6), 499–523. https://doi.org/10.1080/1351847x.2012.719829.

Gervais, S., and Odean, T. (2001). Learning to be overconfident. *The Review of Financial Studies*, 14(1), 1–27. http://www.jstor.org/stable/2696755.

Gharbi, O., Trichilli, Y., and Abbes, M. B. (2022). Impact of the COVID-19 pandemic on the relationship between uncertainty factors, investor behavioral biases and the stock market reaction of US Fintech companies. *Journal of Academic Finance*, 13(1), 101–122.

Gollier, C. (2001). The economics of risk and time. https://doi.org/10.7551/mitpress/2622.001.0001.

Guiso, L., Sapienza, P., and Zingales, L. (2018). Time-varying risk aversion. *Journal of Financial Economics*, 128(3), 403–421. https://doi.org/10.1016/j.jfineco.2018.02.007.

Hurd, M., Rooij, M. V., and Winter, J. (2011). Stock market expectations of Dutch house. *Journal of Applied Econometrics*, 26(3), 416–436.

Khan, M. T. I., Tan, S.-H., and Chong, L.-L. (2016). The effects of stated preferences for firm characteristics, optimism and overconfidence on trading activities. *International Journal of Bank Marketing*, 34(7), 1114–1130. https://doi.org/10.1108/ijbm-10-2015-0154.

Kim, K. A., and Nofsinger, J. R. (2008). Behavioral finance in Asia. *Pacific-Basin Finance Journal*, 16(1-2), 1–7. https://doi.org/10.1016/j.pacfin.2007.04.001.

Li, J. (2011). The demand for a risky asset in the presence of a background risk. *Journal of Economic Theory*, 146(1), 372–391. https://doi.org/10.1016/j.jet.2010.10.011.

Liu, H., Manzoor, A., Wang, C., Zhang, L., and Manzoor, Z. (2020). The COVID-19 outbreak and affected countries stock markets response. *International Journal of Environmental Research and Public Health*, 17(8), 2800. https://doi.org/10.3390/ijerph17082800.

Lowenstein, G. F., Webber, E. U., and Hsee, C. K. (2001). Psychological bulletin. *Risk as Feelings*, 127(2), 267–286.

Luxembourg, A. (2022). Behavioural finance meets Covid 19. Square. https://www.square-management.com/articles/behavioural-finance-meets-covid-19/.

Naseem, S., Mohsin, M., Hui, W., Liyan, G., and Penglai, K. (2021). The investor psychology and stock market behavior during the initial era of Covid-19: a study of China, Japan, and the United States. *Frontiers in Psychology*, 12. https://doi.org/10.3389/fpsyg.2021.626934.

Nguyen, T. (2018). Herding behaviour in vietnamese stock market; department of finance and statistics. *Hanken School of Economics*.

Pompian, M. (2012). Behavioral Finance and Wealth Management. John Wiley and Sons, Inc. https://doi.org/10.1002/9781119202400.

Ritika, Himanshu, and Kishor, N. (2022). Modeling of factors affecting investment behavior during the pandemic: a grey-DEMATEL approach. *Journal of Financial Services Marketing*. https://doi.org/10.1057/s41264-022-00141-4.

Rohman, N. (2022). Pengertian Investasi Tujuan, Jenis, Pengambilan Keputusan dan Faktor-faktor yang mempengaruhi tingkat investasi | Universitas Islam An Nur Lampung | Halaman 2. Universitas Islam an Nur Lampung. https://an-nur.ac.id/pengertian-investasi-tujuan-jenis-pengambilan-keputusan-dan-faktor-faktor-yang-mempengaruhi-tingkat-investasi/2/.

Shaharudin, S. (2021). Sejarah Langkah Lockdown Dunia. Sinar Harian. https://www.sinarharian.com.my/article/141249/GLOBAL/Sejarah-langkah-lockdown-dunia.

Shankar, B. (2022). Lessons in Behavioral Bias: The COVID-19 Equity Markets. CFA Institute Enterprising Investor. https://blogs.cfainstitute.org/investor/2022/05/20/lessons-in-cognitive-bias-the-covid-19-equity-markets/.

Shantha, K. V. A., Xiaofang, C., Gamini, L. P. S., and McMillan, D. (2018). A conceptual framework on individual investors' learning behavior in the context of stock trading: an integrated perspective. *Cogent Economics and Finance*, 6(1), 1544062. https://doi.org/10.1080/23322039.2018.1544062.

Subramani, M. R., and Venkatraman, N. (2003). Safeguarding investments in asymmetric interorganizational relationships: theory and evidence. *Academy of Management Journal*, 46(1), 46–62. https://doi.org/10.5465/30040675.

192 The factors contributing to cryptocurrency purchase intention among generation X and millennials in Malaysia

Rajveen Kaur Ravinder Singh[1], Gunaseelan Kannan[1], Shazrul Ekhmar Abdul Razak[2] and Hafinaz Hasyanti Hassan[1,a]

[1]School of Accounting and Finance, Asia Pacific University, Wilayah Persekutuan Kuala Lumpur, Malaysia

[2]Department of Agribusiness and Bioresource Economics, Faculty of Agriculture, Universiti Putra Malaysia, Selangor, Malaysia

Abstract

Technological advancements have significantly promoted the usage of cryptocurrency for digital payments, including in Malaysia. Malaysia demonstrates a higher cryptocurrency ownership rate than the global average. Specifically, Generations X (Gen X) and Y (millennials) in the state of Selangor contribute to the highest ownership proportion, despite cryptocurrency not being recognized as a legal digital payment method by Bank Negara Malaysia. Therefore, the present study aims to investigate the factors contributing to cryptocurrency purchase intention among Gen X and millennials in Selangor. The impacts of social influence, performance expectancy, trust, and volatility on cryptocurrency purchase intention were appraised with the unified theory of acceptance and use of technology 2 (UTAUT2). Empirical data were gathered by disseminating100 questionnaires between May and July 2023 before conducting multiple regression to analyze the valid responses. The results revealed that social influence, performance expectancy, trust, and volatility significantly impacted cryptocurrency purchase intention among Malaysian Gen X and millennials, with performance expectancy producing the most significant impact. Hence, this study provided significant theoretical contributions to the existing knowledge corpus and generated practical insights for policymakers to develop pertinent policies in regulating cryptocurrency transactions in Malaysia.

Keywords: Cryptocurrency, generation X, generation Y, Malaysia, millennials, purchase intention, unified theory of acceptance and use of technology

Introduction

Technological advancements have significantly elevated digital transactions (De Keyser et al., 2019) due to higher flexibility, straightforwardness, affordability, and speed. Specifically, cryptocurrency is perceived with higher attractiveness throughout the evolutionary journey of digital currencies (Gonzalez, 2019). Cryptocurrency transactions are solely conducted online on a content-sharing platform integrating blockchain and peer-to-peer technology (P2P) without any regulatory framework (Raymaekers, 2014). Al-Jaroodi and Mohamed (2019) delineated that cryptocurrency allows users to pay for goods and services online without intermediaries in place of government-issued currencies. As such, cryptocurrency functions as a digital and decentralized currency not controlled or supported by any authority, such as the central bank and government. Cryptology or cryptography is employed in cryptocurrency for protection to prevent potential forgery or double-spending (Khin et al., 2019). Cryptography is a highly advanced internet protocol, which records all digital financial transactions in the public domain (Miraz et al., 2021).

The recent rapid increase in global cryptocurrency usage has significantly increased the market size (Abbasi et al., 2021) and competition in the fiduciary monetary system. Multiple central banks in each country, including China, Tunisia, and Ecuador, have issued digital currencies to ensure higher competitiveness in the respective economic and financial systems (Khin et al., 2021). Meanwhile, 3.1% of the total Malaysian population or approximately one million citizens are employing cryptocurrency, with an ownership rate of 19.9%whichexceeds the global average. Specifically, the most employed cryptocurrency types from October 2021 to December 2021 were Bitcoin (34.9%), followed by Ripple (23.1%) and Ethereum (20.5%). The adoption amount in the national gross domestic product (GDP) is projected to increase by RM400 billion in 2025 (Inn, 2018; Yeong et al., 2019). Nonetheless, cryptocurrencies are not suitable as a ubiquitous payment platform in Malaysia following the absence of universal monetary features, such as

[a]hafinaz.hasniyanti@apu.edu.my

higher price volatility and exposure to cybersecurity threats. Cryptocurrencies are also not under the per view of Bank Negara Malaysia (BNM), which does not recognize cryptocurrencies as legal transactional methods for goods and services in Malaysia.

The BNM does not forbid citizens from utilizing cryptocurrencies. Nevertheless, Malaysians are required to assume full responsibility for the usage as cryptocurrencies are protected by the law. Thus, this study aimed to examine the factors influencing cryptocurrency purchase intention in Malaysia. Various researchers assessed the purchase intention in developed countries, including Canada, Germany, the United States of America, South Korea, and the United Kingdom. Nevertheless, a scarcity of empirical evidence was discerned in developing countries, such as Malaysia (Yeong et al., 2019). Furthermore, previous scholars did not demonstrate a clear association between relevant factors and cryptocurrency purchase intention by emphasizing demographics (Khin et al., 2021). The present study evaluated multiple factors potentially contributing to cryptocurrency purchase intention in Malaysia. The subsequent section comprehensively reviews the existing literature while developing relevant hypotheses, followed by details on the data collection method, assessment of variables, and pertinent data analyses. The results are discussed accordingly before presenting conclusions and highlighting study limitations.

Literature Review

The unified theory of acceptance and use of technology 2 (UTAUT2) theory, which was developed to scrutinize commercial technology adoption (Venkakesh et al., 2012; Miraz et al., 2022), served to examine factors contributing to cryptocurrency purchase intention in Malaysia. Particularly, the UTAUT2 could assist in comprehending different individuals' cryptocurrency usage behaviors in terms of social influence, performance expectancy, trust, and volatility. The following subsection delineates the association between each aforementioned factor and cryptocurrency purchase intention.

Performance expectancy
Performance expectancy is the degree of benefits and advantages obtained from a specific technology (Merhi et al., 2019). Performance expectancy also refers to the extent to which a user believes in a specific technology to aid in enhancing task performance (Gillies et al., 2020). Accordingly, the advantages of employing cryptocurrencies, including convenience and ease of usage in digital payments, would impact

the purchase intention. Performance expectancy is crucial as potential users would anticipate enhanced performance from cryptocurrencies. A direct positive impact on behavioral intention would be observed if cryptocurrencies significantly improve task performance through monetary transactions or as investments (Gillies et al., 2020; Abbasi et al., 2021). The correlation between performance expectancy and cryptocurrency purchase intention could be explicated by the UTAUT theory, which postulates that behavioral intention to adopt an alternative technology or system would be determined by the advantages provided by the adopted technology (Ventakesh et al., 2003). As such, the first hypothesis was posited:

H1: There is a significant relationship between performance expectancy and cryptocurrency purchase intention.

Social influence
Social influence is related to the belief of a belonging community in adopting an alternative system or technology. Prior academicians proposed the social influence concept and corroborated relevant influences on the adoption and usage intention of different technologies, including mobile and digital banking, e-commerce, smart devices, and digital wallets (Abbasi et al., 2021). Adapa et al. (2018) also propounded that social influence is integral to employing the latest technology when pertinent information is limited. The UTAUT theory proposes that individuals' utilization of an alternative technology depends on other individuals' or peers' perceptions. Users would be more predisposed to purchase cryptocurrencies under a higher social influence, particularly when the usage is mandatory due to compliance requirements rather than personal preferences (Marikyan and Papagiandinis, 2023). Cryptocurrency purchase intention in Malaysia would be enhanced by online supportive networks that produce a highly influential community (Gillies et al., 2010). Hence, the second hypothesis was proposed:

H2: There is a significant relationship between social influence and cryptocurrency purchase intention.

Volatility
Volatility refers to pricing fluctuations, which depict the increasing or decreasing speed of an asset price in the market (Bakar and Rosbi, 2017). Yeong et al. (2019) elucidated that the price of cryptocurrencies is more volatile than other financial assets owing to the lack of a regulatory framework for cryptocurrencies by the government or central authority and dependence on the overall market demand. Comparatively, the BNM is obligated to adjust the supply of the

Malaysian ringgit, which is a government-issued currency, based on the cumulative demand to ensure constant price stability. Thus, cryptocurrencies will frequently encounter higher short-term pricing fluctuations (Yeong et al., 2019), which might significantly impact the purchase intention. The UTAUT model postulates that price volatility would impact the adoption intention of the latest technology due to the higher purchase cost. Accordingly, the third hypothesis was propounded:

H3: There is a significant relationship between volatility and cryptocurrency purchase intention.

Trust

Trust is a subjective concept that denotes an individual's level of belief in the latest technology as trustworthy and reliable based on transactional security (Köksal and Penez, 2015). Sufficient trust would produce higher confidence, reassurance, and ease of mind for users who purchase crypto currencies (Miraz et al., 2022). Trust is fundamental to all commercial strategies, where in comprehending the significant value of trust in different circumstances is vital (Wu et al., 2011). As such, trust would play a pivotal role in human behaviors and positively impact users' cryptocurrency purchase intention by reducing social complexity, vulnerability, and associated risks. Nejad et al. (2022) discovered that trust significantly enhanced the satisfaction degree with cryptocurrency services, which encouraged higher adoption among users. In addition, higher trust in blockchain technology as a secure and authentic platform would positively impact cryptocurrency purchase intention (Ku-Mahamud et al., 2019). Therefore, trust is key to enhancing Malaysians' cryptocurrency purchase intention. The association between trust and cryptocurrency purchase intention could be explicated by the UTAUT theory, wherein trust could significantly predict the behavioral intention of employing an alternative technology, including cryptocurrencies. As such, the fourth pertinent hypothesis was postulated:

H4: A significant association exists between trust and cryptocurrency purchase intention.

Study Methodology

The present study incorporated the positivism paradigm and applied a quantitative research design to appraise the aforementioned factors contributing to cryptocurrency purchase intention. The questionnaire was validated through a pre-test with other scholars before being distributed to collect data. Particularly, the Ethics Committee of Human Research validated and approved the questionnaire and research

methodology at the university where the current study was performed. The questionnaire was distributed online to access all potential respondents in different geographical locations. Moreover, the online approach is highly efficient and extensively employed worldwide. The questionnaire comprises three sections, namely respondents' demographic information, influential factors (trust, performance expectancy, volatility, and social influence), and cryptocurrency purchase intention. All items were measured on a five-point Likert scale. The measurement items were adapted from Miraz et al. (2022) and Chen et al. (2002).

The respondents were Gen X and millennials in Selangor, who comprised a significant proportion of the workforce population. Both generations also constituted most cryptocurrency owners and purchasers in Selangor. In 2022, the Department of Statistics of Malaysia (DoSM) reported that over four million individuals were Gen X and millennials residing in Selangor. The sample size was determined via Krecjie and Morgan's (1970) table, in which a population above one million requires 384 samples. The questionnaires were disseminated through an online Google Doc to the respondents, who were recruited via convenience sampling between February and April 2023. A cover letter presenting the study objective, and the consent form were attached. A total of 384 questionnaires were disseminated. Only 100 copies were usable, which demonstrated a response rate of 26%. All usable data were analyzed through the SPSS software.

Results and Discussion

Respondents' demographic profile

Table 192.1 portrays that 49% of the respondents were males, with 43% as Gen X born from 1965 to 1981. Millennials, who were born between 1982 and 1994, consisted of 57% of the respondents. The respondents comprised Malay (15%), Chinese (29%), Indian (22%), and other ethnic groups (34%), as Malaysia is a multi-ethnic nation. Meanwhile, 85% of the respondents were at the tertiary educational level, thus demonstrating an adequate knowledge level among the respondents. A total of 53% of the respondents received a monthly salary above RM10,000, with the remaining 47% receiving under RM10,000.

Cryptocurrency knowledge and ownership

Table 192.2 illustrates respondents' cryptocurrency knowledge and ownership types and durations. Notably, 96% of the respondents were aware of cryptocurrencies, with only 25% purchasing or owning cryptocurrencies in the forms of Bitcoin (16%),

Table 192.1 Respondents' demographic profile.

	Frequency (N = 100)	Percentage (%)
Gender		
Male	49	49
Female	51	51
Generation		
Gen X	43	43
Gen Y (Millennial)	57	57
Ethnicity		
Malay	15	15
Chinese	29	29
Indian	22	22
Others	34	34
Educational level		
Bachelor's degree	48	48
Master's degree	29	29
Doctoral degree (PhD)	8	8
Others	15	15
Income level		
Below RM 5,000	21	21
RM 5,001 to RM 10,000	27	27
Above RM 10,000	53	53

Source: Author

Table 192.2 Respondents' cryptocurrency knowledge and ownership.

	Frequency (N = 100)	Percentage (%)
Cryptocurrency knowledge		
Yes	96	96
No	4	4
Cryptocurrency ownership		
Yes	25	25
No	75	75
Cryptocurrency ownership type		
Bitcoin	16	16
Ethereum	7	7
Ripple	2	2
None	75	75
Cryptocurrency ownership duration		
Below 2 years	17	17
2 to 3 years	6	6
Above 3 years	2	2
None	75	75

Source: Author

Ethereum (7%), and Ripple (2%). A total of 17% of the respondents owned any cryptocurrency for below two years, followed by only 8% owning for above two years.

Descriptive statistics

Table 192.3 demonstrates the descriptive statistics for all study variables. The mean score for cryptocurrency purchase intention was 2.595, which underscored Gen X and millennials' low purchase intention. Meanwhile, volatility achieved the highest mean score of 3.503, which highlighted the importance of stability in contributing to the purchase intention. Trust achieved a mean score of 3.445, which suggested that trust also significantly impacted the purchase intention. The mean scores for social intention and performance expectancy were 2.448 and 2.322 respectively. In addition, the standard tests of skewness and kurtosis results discovered no normality issues as the values were within the acceptable range of ± 3.0 (George and Mallery, 2010), which postulated that the data were normally distributed. The data were also reliable as indicated by Cronbach's alpha values exceeding the threshold value of 0.7.

Table 192.3 Descriptive, reliability, and correlation analyses.

Variable	Mean	Skewness	Kurtosis	Cronbach's alpha
1. ITP	2.596	0.143	-0.628	0.935
2. PE	2.322	0.342	-0.783	0.949
3. SI	2.448	0.282	-0.444	0.884
4. VO	3.503	-0.430	-0.136	0.709
5. TR	3.445	-0.360	-0.128	0.860

Notes: ITP =Intention to purchase cryptocurrencies; PE = Performance expectancy; SI = Social influence; VO = Volatility; TR = Trust
Source: Author

Multiple regression analysis

Hypothesis testing was conducted through the following regression equation:

$$ITP = \beta_0 + \beta_1 PE + \beta_2 SI + \beta_3 VO + \beta_4 TR + e$$

Where ITP represents the variable of the intention to purchase cryptocurrencies ranging from strongly disagree (1) to strongly agree (5), βdenotes the constant term, PE signifies the variable of performance expectancy ranging from strongly disagree (1) to

Table 192.4 Multiple regression analysis results.

Hypothesis	Variable	Beta	t	p
H1	Performance expectancy	0.472	4.482	0.000*
H2	Social influence	0.216	2.004	0.048**
H3	Volatility	0.155	2.046	0.044**
H4	Trust	-0.228	-3.008	0.003**

Notes: $R^2 = 0.79$; Adjusted $R^2 = 0.624$; F = 39.353; * $p < 0.01$; ** $p < 0.05$; *** $p < 0.10$.
Source: Author

strongly agree (5), SI is the variables of social influence ranging from strongly disagree (1) to strongly agree (5), VO represents the variable of volatility ranging from strongly disagree (1) to strongly agree (5), and TR denotes the variable of trust ranging from strongly disagree (1) to strongly agree(5).

The regression analysis results (see Table 192.4) revealed that the current research framework was significant with an adjusted r squareR^2 of 62.4%, which propounded that 62.4% of the cryptocurrency purchase intentions explained by independent variables. In addition, performance expectancy significantly impacted cryptocurrency purchase intention. Cryptocurrencies are expected to be crucial and instrumental to accomplishing life goals, which would positively contribute to Gen X and millennials' purchases in Selangor. The finding corroborated Ter Ji-Xi et al. (2021), who discovered that performance expectancy significantly and positively impacted cryptocurrency purchase intention in terms of effective task accomplishment. Furthermore, a significant and positive relationship existed between social influence and cryptocurrency purchase intention. The high acceptance of cryptocurrencies as a global digital payment method might have elevated the purchase intention apart from the growing cryptocurrency communities in Malaysia. Chen et al. (2022) and Farhana and Muthaiyah (2022) also demonstrated a significant correlation between social influence and behavioral intention to purchase cryptocurrency.

A significant and positive correlation existed between volatility and cryptocurrency purchase intention, which posited volatility as a vital factor in promoting Gen X and millennials' cryptocurrency purchases. Mirazet al. (2022) and Ter Ji-Xi et al. (2021) revealed that volatility or the price value factor in terms of cryptocurrency stability, reliability, and availability in the market significantly impacted the purchase intention. Simultaneously, trust significantly and positively impacted cryptocurrency purchase intention. Trust would increase the intention to adopt cryptocurrencies for digital payments. Farhana and

Muthaiyah (2022) and Miraz et al. (2022) postulated that the non-recognition of cryptocurrencies by the BNM would engender false confidence and trust with invalidated assumptions among Gen X and millennials in cryptocurrencies. Summarily, all four research hypotheses were supported.

Conclusion

The current study aimed to investigate the factors, including performance expectancy, social influence, volatility, and trust, that contributed to cryptocurrency purchase intention among Gen X and millennials in Selangor by applying the UTAUT2 model. Resultantly, all four hypotheses were supported after analyzing the factors via multiple regression, which demonstrated significant and positive associations between performance expectancy, social influence, volatility, trust, and cryptocurrency purchase intention. The findings also underscored the importance of the factors to Gen X and millennials' cryptocurrency purchase intention. Hence, this study significantly contributed to the current knowledge corpus with a sound comprehension of the factors impacting cryptocurrency purchase intention. The present study also bridged the literature gap resulting from the paucity of studies on the current subject matter. The results also enriched the UTAUT2 model by elucidating the relationships between the antecedents, namely performance expectancy, social influence, volatility, and trust, and individuals' behavioral intentions.

Cryptocurrency in Malaysia remains an unfamiliar technology, which is currently in the preliminary stage. In practice, the results generated instrumental insights into the Malaysian government, regulators, retail merchants, and cryptocurrency exchangers by thoroughly comprehending the factors influencing Gen X and millennials' purchase intention. Key insights into the current cryptocurrency purchasing prospect were gleaned from a comprehensive analysis of the Malaysian market, which could assist relevant Malaysian enterprises or exchange platforms to attract and elevate Gen X and millennials' purchases. Nevertheless, several study limitations were encountered. The study samples were only Gen X and millennials in Selangor, which might limit out come generalizability. Future scholars could examine cryptocurrency purchase intention in other generations. Moreover, inaccurate interpretations or misunderstandings regarding the meaning of the questionnaire might exist as cryptocurrencies remain a relatively unfamiliar technology in Malaysia. Other research methods, such as the mixed method, could be included by integrating the questionnaire into in-depth interviews or case studies to acquire in-depth data for a more thorough understanding of the research topic. Future works could also incorporate other variables apart from the current four used in this study to determine the potential impacts on cryptocurrency purchase intention.

References

Abbasi, G. A., Tiew, L. Y., Tang, J., Goh, Y.-N., and Thurasamy, R. (2021). The adoption of cryptocurrency as a disruptive force: deep learning-based dual stage structural equation modelling and artificial neural network analysis. *Plos One*, 1–26. https://doi.org/10.1371/journal.pone.0247582.

Adapa, A., Nah, F. F. H., Hall, R. H., Siau, K., and Smith, S. N. (2018). Factors influencing the adoption of smart wearable devices. *International Journal of Human-Computer Interaction*, 34(5), 399–409. https://doi.org/10.1080/10447318.2017.1357902.

Al-Jaroodi, J., and Mohamed, N. (2019). Blockchain in Industries: a survey. *IEEE Access*, 7, 36500–36515.

Bakar, N. A., and Rosbi, S. (2017). Autoregressive integrated moving average (ARIMA) model for forecasting cryptocurrency exchange rate in high volatility environment: a new insight of bitcoin transaction. *International Journal of Advanced Engineering Research and Science*, 4(11), 237311. http://dx.doi.org/10.22161/ijaers.4.11.20.

Chen, X., Miraz, M. H., Gazi, M. A. I., Rahaman, M. A., Habib, M. M., and Hossain, A. I. (2022). Factors affecting cryptocurrency adoption in digital business transactions: the mediating role of customer satisfaction. *Technology in Society*, 70, 102059. https://doi.org/10.1016/j.techsoc.2022.102059.

De Keyser, A., Köcher, S., Alkire (née Nasr), L., Verbeeck, C. and Kandampully, J. (2019). Frontline service technology infusion: conceptual archetypes and future research directions. *Journal of Service Management*, 30(1), 156–183. https://doi.org/10.1108/JOSM-03-2018-0082.

Farhana, K., andMuthaiyah, S. (2022). Behavioural intention to use cryptocurrency as an electronic payment in Malaysia. *Journal of System and Management Sciences*, 12(4), 219–231. DOI:10.33168/JSMS.2022.0414.

George, D., and Mallery, M. (2010). SPSS for Windows Step by Step: A Simple Guide and Reference. Boston: Pearson.

Gillies, F. I., Lye, C. T., and Tay, L. Y. (2020). Determinants of behavioural intention to use Bitcoin in Malaysia. *Journal of Information System and Technology Management*, 5(19), 25–38. http://dx.doi.org/10.35631/JISTM.519003.

Gonzalez, L. (2019). Blockchain, herding and trust in peer-to-peer lending. *Managerial Finance*. https://doi:10.1108/mf-09-2018-0423.

Inn, T. K. (2018). The star. Retrieved from Digital economy expected to show significant growth. https://www.thestar.com.my/business/business-news/2018/04/10/digital-economy-expected-to-show-significant-growth/.

Khin, A. A., Cham, T. H., and Seong, L. C. (2021). Impact of demographic factors on the behavioural intention to adopt cryptocurrency among Malaysia's millennials: an econometric approach [Paper Presentation]. In Conference: 9th International Conference on Business, Accounting, Finance and Economics (BAFE 2021), Perak, Malaysia.

Köksal, Y., and Penez, S. (2015). An investigation of the important factors that influence web trust in online shopping. *Journal of Marketing and Management*, 6(1), 28.

Krejcie, R. V., and Morgan, D. W. (1970). Determining sample size for research activities. *Educational and Psychological Measurement*, 30(3), 607–610.

Ku-Mahamud, K. R., Omar, M., Bakar, N. A. A., and Muraina, I. D. (2019). Awareness, trust, and adoption of blockchain technology and cryptocurrency among blockchain communities in Malaysia. *International Journal on Advance Science Engineering Information Technology*, 9(4), 1217–1222. http://dx.doi.org/10.18517/ijaseit.9.4.6280.

Marikyan, D. and Papagiannidis, S. (2023). Unified theory of acceptance and use of technology: a review. In Papagiannidis, S. (Ed.), TheoryHub Book. Available at https://open.ncl.ac.uk / ISBN: 9781739604400.

Merhi, M., Hone, K., and Tarhini, A. (2019). A cross-cultural study of the intention to use mobile banking between Lebanese and British consumers: extending UTAUT2 with security, privacy and trust. *Technology in Society*, 59, 101151. https://doi.org/10.1016/j.techsoc.2019.101151.

Miraz, M. H., Hasan, M. T., Rekabder, M. S., and Akhter, R. (2022). Trust, transaction transparency, volatility, facilitating condition, performance expectancy towards cryptocurrency adoption through intention to use. *Journal of Management Information and Decision Sciences*, 25(S5), 1–20.

Nejad, M. Y., Yung, G. L., Othman, J., Kssim, A. A. M., Khan, A. S., Lim, F. L. M. D., et al. (2022). Factors influencing cryptocurrency awareness among young working adults in Malaysia: a conceptual paper. *Malaysian Journal of Social Sciences and Humanities (MJSSH)*, 7(6), e001555–e001555. https://doi.org/10.47405/mjssh.v7i6.1555.

Raymaekers, W. (2014). Cryptocurrency bitcoin: disruption, challenges and opportunities. *Journal of Payments Strategy and Systems*, 9(1).

Ter Ji-Xi, J., Salamzadeh, Y., and Teoh, A. P. (2021). Behavioral intention to use cryptocurrency in Malaysia: an empirical study. *The Bottom Line*, 34(2), 170–197. https://doi.org/10.1108/BL-08-2020-0053.

Venkatesh, V., Thong, J. Y., and Xu, X. (2012). Consumer acceptance and use of information technology: extending the unified theory of acceptance and use of technology. *MIS Quarterly*, 157–178. http://dx.doi.org/10.2307/41410412.

Yeong, Y. C., Kalid, K. S., and Sugathan, S. K. (2019). Cryptocurrency adoption in Malaysia: does age, income and education level matter? *International Journal of Innovative Technology and Exploring Engineering*, 8(11), 2179–2184. https://DOI:10.35940/ijeat.E1004.0585C19.

193 The influencing factors of employee fraud in Malaysia's financial institution: the application of fraud triangle theory

Dhamayanthi Arumugam[1,a], Kavitha Arunasalam[2,b] and Kannan Asokan[3,c]

[1]PhD, School of Accounting and Finance, Asia Pacific University of Technology and Innovation, Bukit Jalil, Malaysia

[2]MBA (Accounting), School of Accounting and Finance, Asia Pacific University of Technology and Innovation, Bukit Jalil, Malaysia

[3]MSc Economic Crime Management, School of Accounting and Finance, Asia Pacific University of Technology and Innovation, Bukit Jalil, Malaysia

Abstract

The fundamental incentive for an employee to engage in fraudulent activities is financial gain. Financial institutions, due to their significant monetary holdings, are particularly susceptible to such fraudulent behavior. Discussions regarding employee fraud are warranted in the current global economy, particularly inside financial institutions. This study utilizes the fraud triangle theory to investigate the elements that influence employee fraud in financial institutions in Malaysia. This theory is corroborated by the routine activity theory. The researcher employed questionnaires to gather perceptions from individuals affiliated with Financial Institutions. The research findings suggest that an employee's inclination to engage in fraudulent behavior is influenced by the components of the fraud triangle, namely pressure, opportunity, and rationalization.

Introduction

The presence of employee fraud necessitates prompt intervention in any firm due to its detrimental impact on the enterprise, economy, and general societal well-being (Bakar and Ishak, 2023). The incidence of employee fraud has been on the rise worldwide, with particular focus on Southeast Asia (PWC, 2019). Employee fraud, often known as internal fraud, is an act of theft or fraud carried out by an employee against their employing firm. It frequently presents itself as stolen objects or money, although there are other potential explanations.

Research Background

In Malaysia, the government created financial institutions with a specific goal of promoting the expansion and progress of crucial industries considered strategically critical to the nation's broader objectives for socioeconomic development. Despite being subject to strict regulations, financial institutions are nonetheless susceptible to employee fraud. Reports to the nations by ACFE (2020) indicate that the banking and financial services industry had the highest number of fraud cases compared to other sectors, accounting for 386 out of 1946 instances (19.84%). The median loss in this area was $100,000. Given the nature of the financial industry, which entails the management of substantial sums of money, the consequences of fraud are significantly more significant in financial institutions compared to other industries (Awang and Ismail, 2018). Financial institutions are becoming increasingly vulnerable to employee fraud when the primary motivation is monetary gain, given that a significant amount of money is held within these institutions. Criminals have become increasingly adept at devising their methods of operation to bypass security measures. In Kuching, Malaysia, a group of twenty workers from five prominent banks in the country has been discovered to be involved in fraudulent activities in collaboration with an international syndicate. This revelation came to light during the Ops Tropicana operation undertaken by the Malaysian Anti-Corruption Commission (MACC) (Dayak Daily, 2023). In 2023, a new incident emerged involving a senior marketing officer at a bank in Taiping, Malaysia. The official was alleged to have committed fraud by authorizing a credit card under the identity of a 41-year-old customer (NST, 2023). When investigating employee fraud, it is crucial to

[a]dhamayanthi@apu.edu.my, [b]kavitha@apu.edu.my, [c]kannan@apu.edu.my

consider the act of concealing information as a key element. This entails an employee using their position to bypass established internal controls, which align with the principles of routine activity theory. Routine activity theory, developed by Cohen and Felson in 1979, emphasizes that crime occurs when there is a regular pattern of activity, such as a suitable target (employer), and a lack of effective supervision (internal control). Employee fraud in financial institutions encompasses many illicit activities such as identity theft, cheque fraud, counterfeit negotiable instruments, mortgage fraud, loan fraud, asset misappropriation, corruption, money laundering, and credit card fraud.

Problem Statement and Objectives

The persistent pattern of rising employee fraud in financial institutions necessitates additional research in this area because employee fraud endangers the integrity and stability of Malaysia's financial institutions and jeopardizes investor confidence, financial security, and the state of the economy. Employee fraud cases persist, despite regulatory efforts to prevent it inside the business. Using the Fraud Triangle Theory, this study aims to examine the influencing factors that contribute to employee fraud inside Malaysian financial institutions. This study seeks to identify the underlying causes and conditions that inspire employees to engage in fraudulent behaviour by thoroughly understanding the critical components of opportunity, pressure, and rationalization. Such knowledge is required for the development of effective prevention and intervention measures to lower the incidence and impacts of employee fraud in Malaysia's financial sector, thereby ensuring the sector's stability. Several research, like those by Fernandhytia and Muslichah

(2020), Lestari et al. (2017), and Putri and Irwandi (2017), have looked into the reasons of employee fraud with a focus on accounting fraud. However, the integration of the fraud triangle hypothesis would be the primary emphasis of this research. The fraud triangle has been incorporated to determine why an employee intends to commit fraud. The fraud triangle has persisted for decades as a metaphorical graphic to help us understand and analyse fraud. According to Donald Cressey's fraud triangle, there are three elements that, when combined, result in fraudulent behaviour (in this case, employee fraud): a perceived unmet financial need (motivation or pressure), a perceived opportunity to commit fraud, and a justification for doing so (rationalization).

According to the fraud triangle, individuals who commit fraud engage in unethical actions due to various forms of pressure, such as financial or non-financial pressures (Abdullahi and Mansor, 2015). According to studies conducted by Albrecht et al. in 2006 and Lister in 2007, it has been emphasized that 95% of fraud cases are caused by direct pressure, which acts as the catalyst for the problem (Murdock, 2008). Opportunity, an additional component of the fraud triangle, signifies that employee frauds, in particular, occur when there is a deficiency in internal control. Perceived opportunity refers to the idea that individuals will exploit the situations that are accessible to them (Kelly and Hartley, 2010). According to researchers like Hooper et al. (2010), fraud can only occur when there is an opportunity, even in the presence of strong pressure on the fraudster. The third component of the fraud triangle, rationalization, suggests that in order for a fraudster to engage in fraudulent conduct, they must first develop a morally justifiable rationale for their actions. This study seeks to include the fraud

Exhibit 193.1 Fraud Triangle by Donald Cressey

triangle hypothesis into the employees' propensity to engage in fraudulent activities. It aims to examine the impact of these elements on an employee's likelihood of committing fraud within financial institutions.

I.   To examine the influence of pressure (ineffective handling of personal finances) on employee's intention to commit fraud.
II. To examine the influence of pressure (inefficiency in managing KPIs) on employees' intention to commit fraud.
III. To examine the influence of opportunity (excessive employer trust) on employee's intention to commit fraud.

IV. To examine the influence of opportunity (lack of control over a job) on employee's intention to commit fraud.
V.   To examine the influence of rationalization (culture of justification) on employees' intention to commit fraud.
VI. To examine the influence of rationalization (entitlement) on employees' intention to commit fraud.

Exhibit 193.2 above explains the research framework where the researchers have identified two factors to explain each variable. All the factors will represent each individual variable, and these

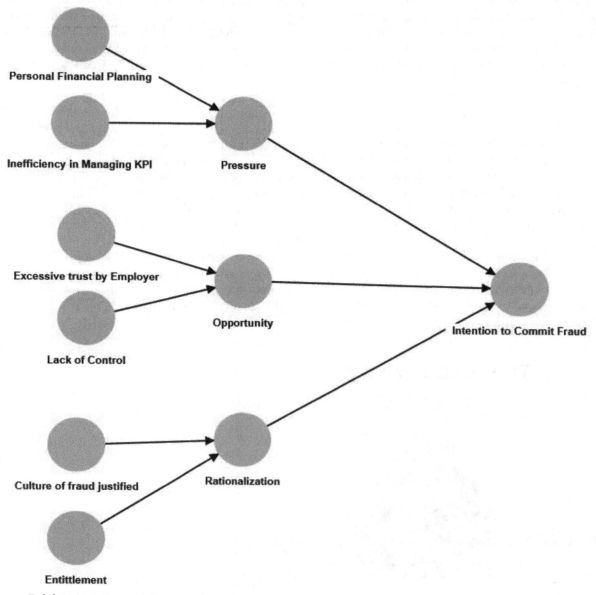

Exhibit 193.2 Research Framework

variables are justified by researchers by showing its relationship between an individual intention to commit fraud.

Literature Review

Conceptualization of fraud and employee fraud

Employee fraud, as defined by the ACFE, refers to the deliberate misuse or misapplication of an organization's resources or assets for personal gain (ACFE, 2022). Consequently, every act of deceit carried out by employees at any hierarchical position within the organization is regarded as employee fraud. ACFE (2022) identifies asset misappropriation, corruption, and financial statement fraud as the three most common forms of internal fraud. The ACFE has been releasing the Report to the Nations on Occupational Fraud and Abuse biennially since 1996. According to the 2021 edition, the Association of Certified Fraud Examiners (ACFE) has reported that firms experience a 5% reduction in their yearly revenue due to fraudulent activities, resulting in a global loss of USD4.7 trillion. In addition, the research highlights 351 instances of fraud in the banking and financial services industry, leading to a median loss of USD100,000. The data indicates that 85% of the events were related to asset misappropriation, 40% were related to corruption, and 10% were related to financial statement fraud (ACFE, 2021). Based on the findings of PwC's Global Economic Crime and Fraud Survey 2022, almost two-thirds of fraud cases in Southeast Asia are perpetrated by workers within organizations. According to the report, 46% of the organizations polled have encountered instances of fraud or economic crime within the last 24 months (PwC, 2022).

Employee fraud in the financial institution

Financial institutions must develop robust protections to mitigate the potential hazards of employee fraud, considering the significant scale of everyday financial transactions. Employee fraud includes a range of activities, such as stealing cash from bank tills, forging customers' signatures to withdraw money from their accounts, creating and using fake accounts, transferring funds to unauthorized accounts, falsely claiming overtime pay for hours not worked, diverting funds, and committing computer fraud by accessing someone's e-banking login credentials without permission (John, 2012; Kingsley, 2012; Tchankova, 2002). As per the research conducted by Asmah et al. (2019), various factors contribute to employee fraud in the banking sector of Ghana. These factors encompass economic stress, inadequate oversight, and staff

complaints. The repercussions of such deceptive practices are grave, leading to substantial sanctions for the individuals implicated and adverse impacts on shareholders. In order to bolster fraud prevention efforts, the authors suggested that the central bank and financial institutions engage in close collaboration and conduct regular evaluations of control systems. In a 2014 study, Hollow did an exploratory analysis of 64 events in the UK financial industry. The study revealed that cases of fraud perpetrated by bank employees and managers are impacted by financial constraints. However, the precise characteristics of these pressures vary based on the individual's role inside the bank. Suh et al. (2019) discovered 361 cases of employee fraud in Korean commercial banks, insurance companies, and financial firms over a five-year period, specifically from 2010 to 2014. The Malaysian Anti-Corruption Commission (MACC) recently investigated five prominent Malaysian banks for being exploited by international scammers in order to defraud victims. These victims, who were deceived, engaged in transactions of up to RM1 million per day. It was discovered that at least 20 bank employees, including auditors and frontline officers, assisted these criminal organizations in easily opening accounts for their illicit activities (Shah, 2023). Additionally, a former marketing executive from a bank in Malaysia was penalized with a fine of RM8,000 for engaging in fraudulent activities by utilizing a credit card assigned to a client for personal use. Upon collecting client information as part of a credit card promotion, the bank's investigation manager discovered that the suspect possessed 17 credit cards that belonged to other customers (Arif, 2023).

Multiple studies indicate that employee fraud played a significant role in contributing to fraud within the banking industry. The occurrence of a dysfunctional financial system has the potential to result in substantial economic and public welfare issues. Hence, it is imperative to implement efficient risk management practices in the financial industry to ensure the long-term stability of the sector.

Hypothesis development

American criminologist Donald Cressey conducted extensive research on the motives behind fraud in his well-known book "Other People's Money: A Study in the Social Psychology of Embezzlement." He categorized fraud into three causes: perceived opportunity, felt financial pressure, and rationalization. According to the concept, the presence of these three traits is a decisive factor in the occurrence of fraudulent conduct (Cressey, 1973).

Higher pressure results in greater motivation to commit fraud

According to Omar and Mohsin Din (2010), individuals who face high amounts of pressure tend to tend to seek quick answers to their problems, and one possible way for them to do so is by engaging in fraudulent behaviors. Hasnan et al. (2008) found that external influences are often blamed for the pressure to achieve specific goals. Nevertheless, it is important to acknowledge that individuals may sometimes encounter self-imposed pressure motivated by personal ambitions to achieve particular financial goals. The KPMG, 2016 Global Profile of the Fraudster survey gave a comprehensive analysis, revealing that a significant majority of fraudsters, amounting to 66%, were primarily motivated by avarice and the pursuit of personal financial enrichment. Hollow (2014) states that pressures can emerge from both financial and non-financial demands. Financial needs contain various elements, including individual liabilities, corporate deficits, and market projections. Conversely, non-financial criteria encompass elements such as avarice, discontentment with one's employment, and societal and political influence. Albrecht et al. (2019) and Ramamoorti et al. (2009) have identified multiple elements that contribute to the establishment of pressures Exhibit 193.3. The factors contributing to this phenomenon encompass avarice, extravagant consumption, economic hardships, unfavorable work conditions marked by insufficient recognition of job performance, a desire for revenge, social status comparisons, a propensity for criminal behavior, a drive to exert control over a situation by evading rules or regulations, feelings of discontentment and insecurity in one's occupation, and an insistence on attaining ambitious objectives despite the disproportionate repercussions. Individuals motivated by a strong desire for wealth would utilize every possible means to accomplish their objectives and key performance indicators (KPIs). Hence, there exists significant data indicating that pressure is a pivotal factor in the prevalence of fraud within the financial business. Therefore, the subsequent hypothesis is suggested:

Hypothesis 1 (H1):
- Higher pressure results in greater motivation to commit fraud.

Hypothesis (H1a):
- Ineffective handling of personal finances is strongly associated with a greater tendency to commit fraud.

Hypothesis (H1b):
- Inefficiency in managing KPIs is positively associated with a higher intention to commit fraud.

Greater opportunities increase the motivation to commit fraud

The presence of opportunities within an organization can significantly influence an individual's inclination to engage in fraudulent activities (Ruankaew, 2016). Individuals who hold the belief that such possibilities are present are more inclined to engage in fraudulent conduct (Owusu et al., 2021). As per the findings of Asmah et al. (2010), the presence of inherent deficiencies in the internal controls implemented by banks in Ghana contributed significantly to the occurrence of employee fraud related to banking activities. Omar et al. (2016) emphasized that the absence of controls provides opportunities for potential fraudsters to engage in fraudulent activities. Although the bank has a strict policy against fraud, the clear absence or inadequacy of protective measures allowed a significant number of fraudsters mentioned before to engage in fraudulent activities. The 2016 Global Profile of the Fraudster research by KPMG found that inadequate internal controls had a role in the actions of at least 61% of the 750 fraudsters analyzed globally. The proportion of fraudsters who perceived a chance due to inadequate internal controls increased significantly from 54–61% compared to the previous poll conducted in 2013. Additionally, as stated in the research, 21% of individuals engaging in fraudulent activities managed to avoid the company's protective measures, while 16% of fraudsters collaborated to bypass the established controls. Therefore, there is substantial evidence suggesting that opportunity plays a key role in the occurrence of fraud within the financial industry. Therefore, the subsequent hypothesis is suggested:

Hypothesis 2 (H2):
- Greater opportunity increases the motive to commit fraud.

Hypothesis (H2a):
- Excessive employer trust is positively correlated with a greater intention to commit fraud.

Hypothesis (H2b):
- Lack of control over a job is positively correlated with a stronger intention to commit fraud.

Higher rationalization increases the motive to commit fraud

Dorminey et al. (2010) define rationalization as the process of rationalizing fraudulent activities in accordance with commonly held moral and trustworthy beliefs. It is a method used by unscrupulous persons to defend their dishonest behavior (Coenen, 2008). Fraudsters believe that their fraudulent behaviors are justifiable in light of the circumstances, allowing them to preserve a positive self-image and believe in their trustworthiness despite engaging in deception (Dorminey et al., 2010). Some people may assume that it is okay to have a negative attitude and participate in unacceptable behavior during a bad economic position. Salary caps or cutbacks, for example, can be used to justify a strategy of recovering "forgone" compensation. On the other hand, some people may regard protecting the value of their stock options as a legitimate reason for changing their financial records (KPMG, 2016). Individuals who cannot provide a valid reason for their unlawful activities, according to Jackson et al. (2010), are less likely to participate in immoral behaviors such as fraud. Rationalization allows fraudsters to justify their conduct to themselves while maintaining their self-perception as honest and innocent. This enables individuals to maintain the impression that they were simply victims of circumstances rather than criminals (Cressey, 1950; Said et al., 2018). As a result, there is significant evidence that rationalization plays a vital role in the occurrence of fraud within the financial industry. Therefore, the subsequent hypothesis is suggested:

Hypothesis 2 (H3):
- Higher rationalization increases the motive to commit fraud.

Hypothesis (H3a):
- There is a positive correlation between a culture of justification for fraud and a greater intention to commit fraud.

Hypothesis (H3b):
- There is a positive correlation between entitlement and a greater intention to commit fraud.

Methodology

The current study utilized a survey methodology that depended on quantitative analysis. The study mainly focused on persons who were registered members of the Malaysian Institute of Accountants (MIA) and possessed a minimum of five years of professional experience in auditing firms. The June 2023 MIA membership figure indicates that the study population, comprising all MIA members, totals 38,460 individuals. Selangor has the highest number of employed Members, with 15,385, followed by Kuala Lumpur with 7,721 members. Attendees The data collection for this study utilizes a purposive judgment sampling methodology. The study recognizes the appropriateness of the data submitted by the respondents in relation to the aims of the study (Mohd-Sanusi, Rameli, and Omar, 2015). The participants were chosen randomly from audit firms in Selangor and Kuala Lumpur to accurately represent the sector, with a specific focus on their degree of expertise.

For this study, in order to provide an appropriate representation of the population of MIA members in Selangor and Kuala Lumpur, a minimum sample size of 98 is necessary. This sample will cover six variables. The current study has received responses from a total of 103 individuals. Hence, the sample size is adequate to do multiple regression analysis for this inquiry. Participants were directed to prioritize the elements

	Detecting financial crimes	Number of respondents					Sum	Mean
		Strongly disagree	Disagree	Neutral	Agree	Strongly agree		
S1	Employees are rarely motivated to commit fraud within the organizations I audit.	3 3%	15 15%	17 17%	46 45%	22 21%	378	2.93
S2	Financial pressures and personal incentives are significant motivators for employee fraud.	0 0%	3 3%	0 0%	27 26%	73 71%	479	3.71
S3	Employee fraud is often driven by a desire for personal gain.	0 0%	3 3%	3 3%	15 15%	82 80%	485	3.76
S4	In my experience, the need for financial security is a common motivation for employee fraud.	0 0%	0 0%	15 15%	26 25%	62 60%	459	3.56
S5	Employees who commit fraud typically have strong motivations to do so.	0 0%	9 9%	6 6%	36 35%	52 50%	440	3.41

Exhibit 193.3 Intention to commit fraud

Application of digital forensic tools Strongly disagree	Number of respondents					Sum	Mean
	Disagree	Neutral	Agree	Strongly agree			
S1	Employees facing personal financial challenges are more likely to engage in fraudulent activities at work.	6 6%	7 7%	0 0%	53 51%	37 36%	417	3.23
S2	Personal financial stress can lead employees to consider committing fraud in their workplace.	0 0%	6 6%	7 7%	35 34%	55 53%	448	3.47
S3	I have observed that employees with significant personal financial difficulties. are more prone to commit fraud at work.	0 0%	13 13%	9 9%	41 40%	40 39%	417	3.23
S4	In my experience, personal financial challenges often serve as a catalyst for employee fraud.	6 6%	7 7%	6 6%	42 41%	42 41%	416	3.22
S5	Employees facing financial difficulties tend to be more motivated to engage in fraudulent activities within their organizations.	0 0%	13 13%	3 3%	56 54%	31 30%	414	3.21

Exhibit 193.4 Personal Financial Planning

that influence employee fraud using a five-point Likert scale.

The researcher evaluated the dependability of the sample by employing Cronbach's alpha test. A high alpha score, often greater than 0.70, was anticipated to demonstrate excellent internal consistency and reliability in assessing the intended concept. Pearson's correlation analysis was employed in this study to individually investigate the three components of the fraud triangle and the inclination to engage in fraudulent activities. This methodology quantifies the magnitude and orientation of connections. The data for this analysis was processed with the SPSS statistical software.

The mean scores indicate a general consensus among respondents that financial incentives play a crucial role in employee fraud. This emphasizes the importance of addressing these issues for identifying and preventing financial crimes within organizations

Respondents strongly agree (with a mean score of 3.23) that employees facing financial and personal difficulties are more prone to engaging in fraudulent activities at their workplace (S1). In addition, they strongly agree (with a mean score of 3.47), and S2 (personal financial stress may cause employees to contemplate engaging in fraudulent activities at work).

The survey results demonstrate a consensus among respondents regarding the need of effective KPI management in identifying and preventing employee fraud. The majority of respondents, with a mean score of 3.49, strongly concur that effective identification and prevention of employee fraud is contingent upon the appropriate management of (S1).

The majority of respondents, with a mean score of 3.65, strongly agree that placing excessive trust in workers can potentially result in employee fraud (S1). Respondents (mean score of 3.55 in S3) suggest that a greater risk of employee fraud may arise when workers are given financial responsibilities without sufficient oversight. Most participants (with an average score of 3.69 in S5) strongly support the idea that effective measures to prevent fraud should find a balance between trust in personnel and practical control methods.

Respondents indicate that employees with little autonomy in their work tasks are more prone to engaging in fraudulent activities, as evidenced by a mean score of 3.22. Moreover, drawing from their personal experiences, they agree (with an average score of 3.60 in S2) that organizations with limited control over job duties and responsibilities are more vulnerable to employee fraud. The lack of well-defined functions and responsibilities within an organization can potentially result in employee fraud, as indicated by the respondents' mean score of 3.66 in S3. The respondents express a high level of agreement (with

	Forensic accounting skills	Number of respondents					Sum	Mean
		Strongly disagree	Disagree	Neutral	Agree	Strongly agree		
S1	Effective management of Key Performance Indicators (KPIs) is crucial for detecting and preventing employee fraud.	0 0%	6 6%	13 13%	21 20%	63 61%	450	3.49
S2	In my experience, a lack of efficiency in managing KPIs can increase the risk of employee fraud.	0 0%	0 0%	16 16%	55 53%	32 31%	428	3.32
S3	Organizations that efficiently manage and monitor KPIs are less susceptible to employee fraud.	0 0%	6 6%	21 20%	40 39%	36 35%	415	3.22
S4	Employee fraud is more likely to occur in organizations that do not adequately track and manage their KPIs.	0 0%	6 6%	13 13%	36 35%	48 47%	435	3.37
S5	A well-structured KPI management system can deter employees from engaging in fraudulent activities.	0 0%	6 6%	19 18%	38 37%	40 39%	421	3.26

Exhibit 193.5 Inefficiency in managing KPI

	Regulation	Number of Respondents					Sum	Mean
		Strongly Disagree	Disagree	Neutral	Agree	Strongly Agree		
S1	Excessive trust in employees by an organization's management can increase the likelihood of employee fraud.	0 0%	0 0%	0 0%	44 43%	59 57%	471	3.65
S2	In your experience, organizations that place a high degree of trust in their employees are more susceptible to employee fraud.	0 0%	5 5%	12 12%	52 50%	34 33%	424	3.29
S3	Trusting employees with financial responsibilities without adequate oversight can lead to a greater risk of employee fraud.	0 0%	0 0%	6 6%	45 44%	52 50%	458	3.55
S4	Employee fraud tends to be more prevalent in organizations where there is a culture of excessive trust in employees.	0 0%	6 6%	17 17%	31 30%	49 48%	432	3.35
S5	Effective fraud prevention measures should include a balance between trust in employees and appropriate control mechanisms.	0 0%	3 3%	3 3%	24 23%	73 71%	476	3.69

Exhibit 193.6 Excessive Trust by Employer

a mean score of 3.64 in S5) that effective fraud prevention strategies should include clearly defined work duties and responsibilities, in addition to decreasing the risk of employee fraud Exhibit 193.6.

Respondents agreed (with a mean score of 3.48 in S3) that an environment that rationalizes unethical conduct could undermine ethical standards and foster employee fraud. In addition, respondents concur (with

Technology		Number of Respondents					Sum	Mean
		Strongly Disagree	Disagree	Neutral	Agree	Strongly Agree		
S1	Employees who have limited control over their job responsibilities are more likely to engage in fraudulent activities.	0 0%	11 11%	9 9%	49 48%	34 33%	415	3.22
S2	In your experience, organizations with a lack of control over job roles and responsibilities are at a higher risk of employee fraud.	0 0%	0 0%	3 3%	44 43%	56 54%	465	3.60
S3	A lack of clearly defined roles and responsibilities within an organization can contribute to the occurrence of employee fraud.	0 0%	0 0%	5 5%	33 32%	65 63%	472	3.66
S4	Employee fraud is more likely to go undetected in organizations where there is a lack of control and oversight over job functions.	0 0%	0 0%	5 5%	58 55%	42 40%	457	3.54
S5	Effective fraud prevention strategies should include clear job roles and responsibilities to minimize the risk of employee fraud.	0 0%	0 0%	3 3%	40 39%	60 58%	469	3.64

Exhibit 193.7 Lack of Control

	Detecting financial crimes	Number of respondents					Sum	Mean
		Strongly disagree	Disagree	Neutral	Agree	Strongly agree		
S1	A culture within an organization that justifies fraudulent behavior can lead to increased incidents of employee fraud.	0 0%	8 8%	3 3%	36 35%	56 54%	449	3.48
S2	In your experience, organizations that tolerate or justify unethical behavior are more likely to have instances of employee fraud.	0 0%	0 0%	12 12%	47 46%	44 43%	444	3.44
S3	A culture that rationalizes unethical conduct can erode ethical standards and contribute to employee fraud.	0 0%	0 0%	9 9%	48 47%	46 45%	449	3.48
S4	Employee fraud is more prevalent in organizations where employees believe they can justify their actions based on the organization's culture.	0 0%	0 0%	17 17%	30 29%	56 54%	451	3.50
S5	Effective fraud prevention measures should include a strong emphasis on fostering an ethical culture that condemns fraud and unethical behavior.	0 0%	0 0%	17 17%	30 29%	56 54%	451	3.50

Exhibit 193.8 Culture of fraud justification

Application of digital forensic tools Strongly disagree	Number of respondents					Sum	Mean
	Disagree	Neutral	Agree	Strongly agree			
S1 Employees who feel entitled to certain privileges within an organization are more likely to engage in fraudulent activities.	0 0%	6 6%	7 7%	35 34%	55 53%	448	3.47
S2 In your experience, a sense of entitlement among employees can contribute to an increased risk of employee fraud.	0 0%	13 13%	9 9%	41 40%	40 39%	417	3.23
S3 A culture of entitlement within an organization can erode ethical standards and encourage employee fraud.	0 0%	6 6%	13 13%	36 35%	48 47%	435	3.37
S4 Employee fraud is more likely to occur in organizations where employees believe they deserve special treatment or privileges.	0 0%	6 6%	19 18%	38 37%	40 39%	421	3.26
S5 Effective fraud prevention measures should include addressing and mitigating feelings of entitlement among employees.	0 0%	0 0%	12 12%	47 46%	44 43%	444	3.44

Exhibit 193.9 Entitlement

a mean score of 3.50 in S4) that organizations where employees believe they can rationalize their behavior based on the organizational culture are more prone to engaging in employee fraud. Ultimately, the majority of participants (with an average score of 3.50 in S5) firmly believe that establishing an ethical culture that condemns fraud, and unethical conduct should be a fundamental element of successful fraud prevention efforts. Organizational culture plays a substantial role in determining the probability of employee fraud. This underscores the need of cultivating an ethical culture as a crucial aspect of preventing fraud within businesses.

The majority of respondents, with a mean score of 3.47, strongly agree that individuals who possess a sense of entitlement to specific privileges inside an organization are more prone to engaging in fraudulent activities (S1). Moreover, participants hold the belief (with an average score of 3.23 in S2) that a perception of entitlement among workers could potentially result in a higher likelihood of employee fraud, as indicated by their personal experiences. The respondents also provided support for the notion that an entitlement culture inside an organization could erode ethical standards and enable employee fraud, as indicated by a mean score of 3.37 in S3.

The study demonstrates a significant and positive association ($r = 0.377$, $p < 0.001$) between personal financial difficulties and the inclination to engage in fraudulent activities. This statistical finding supports hypothesis H1a, which posits that individuals experiencing personal financial difficulties are more inclined to exhibit a heightened inclination towards engaging in fraudulent activities. The study demonstrates a significant and robust positive connection ($r = 0.463$, $p < 0.001$) between ineffective Key Performance Indicator (KPI) management and the intention to engage in fraudulent activities. This finding supports hypothesis (H1b) that inefficient KPI management is positively associated with an elevated inclination to commit fraud. The data unequivocally corroborates Hypothesis 1 (H1), which posits that heightened pressure engenders greater motivation in individuals to engage in fraudulent activities. These findings indicate that individuals who struggle with personal financial management or fail to meet their key performance indicators (KPIs) are more prone to engaging in fraudulent activities.

The study provides evidence in Favor of hypothesis H2a, which suggests that a high level of trust is linked to a greater inclination to engage in fraudulent behavior. This is demonstrated by a significant and positive correlation ($r = 0.695$, $p < 0.001$) between the employer's excessive trust and the intention to conduct fraud. The discovery that a lack of job control is correlated with a higher inclination to engage in fraudulent activities provides evidence in Favor of hypothesis H2b. This finding demonstrates a significant positive

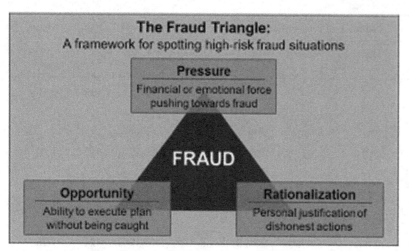

Exhibit 193.10 Pearson's correlation co-efficient between fraud triangle and intention to commit fraud

relationship between the two variables, with a correlation coefficient of 0.801 and a p-value of less than 0.001 Exhibit 193.10. Hypothesis 2 (H2) projected that an increase in greater opportunity would lead to a higher motive to commit fraud. These correlations indicate that employees are more likely to engage in fraudulent activities due to the increased opportunities afforded by cultures characterized by excessive trust or inadequate control over employees' job responsibilities.

The study also demonstrates a strong and meaningful correlation between a culture that justifies fraud and the intention to engage in fraudulent activities (r = 0.743, p < 0.001), thus confirming hypothesis (H3a) that a society that justifies fraud is linked to a greater inclination to commit fraud. The study demonstrates a robust and significant positive correlation (r = 0.920, p < 0.001) between entitlement and desire to engage in fraudulent behavior. This finding strongly supports hypothesis (H3b), which posits that entitlement is positively associated with a greater inclination to commit fraud. Increased rationalization, as proposed by Hypothesis 3 (H3), would amplify the inclination to engage in fraudulent activities. These findings suggest that employees in organizations where fraud is tolerated or where there is a feeling of entitlement may be more inclined to rationalize their behavior, hence intensifying their inclination to engage in fraudulent activities.

Conclusion

An extensive examination of many organizational elements and their correlations with an individual's inclination to engage in fraudulent activities uncovers the intricate interplays that influence fraudulent behavior

within firms. The results indicate that personal financial hardships and inefficient key performance indicator (KPI) management significantly amplify the motivation for engaging in fraudulent behavior. The study emphasizes the critical importance of organizational features, such as a highly trusting employer, limited control over work tasks, a culture that justifies fraud, and a sense of entitlement, in increasing the desire to engage in fraudulent activities. The findings emphasize that fraud motive is complex and influenced by several internal and environmental factors.

When building comprehensive solutions, it is important to consider the interplay between organizational culture, dynamics of trust, control mechanisms, and budgetary demands. Organizations can cultivate an ethical culture, strengthen control mechanisms, and provide employees with the necessary support and resources to effectively handle financial matters in order to establish an environment that deteriorates fraud and promotes ethical conduct within their workforce. Ultimately, this research underscores the importance of implementing a complete strategy to prevent fraud, which considers the complex network of factors that influence the inclination to engage in fraudulent activities inside an organizational setting.

Recommendation

To enhance fraud prevention and mitigation within organizations, valuable recommendations can be derived from analyzing organizational features and their correlation with an individual's inclination to engage in fraudulent activities. Employers should consider implementing financial wellness programs to help employees effectively manage their own finances.

These activities may encompass training in budgeting, financial literacy courses, and provision of financial counselling services. Organizations can mitigate the inclination towards fraudulent behavior stemming from personal financial difficulties by alleviating financial strain and empowering employees to make prudent financial choices.

Organizations should enhance their control systems and job monitoring in order to decrease the probability of employee fraud driven by favorable circumstances. Implementing robust internal controls, conducting regular audits, and clearly delineating duties can assist in addressing this issue. Organizations can mitigate the risk of undetected fraudulent activities by fostering a culture of accountability and ensuring that employees are well-informed about their responsibilities and obligations.

It is imperative to foster an ethical culture that explicitly forbids fraud and unethical conduct. Organizations should provide ethical training and communication programs to assist employees in cultivating a strong ethical foundation. These programs should prioritize the importance of ethical conduct, the mechanisms for reporting unethical behavior, and the consequences of deceit. One strategy to deter fraud is to cultivate a work environment that instils a strong sense of moral responsibility in staff members and encourages them to promptly report any suspicious conduct.

References

ACFE (2022). A report to the nations ® occupational fraud 2022: a report to the nations. https://acfepublic.s3.us-west-2.amazonaws.com/2022+Report+to+the+Nations.pdf.

Albrecht, S., Albrecht, C. O., Albrecht, C. C., and Zimbelman, M. F. (2019). Fraud Examination. Cengage.

Arif, Z. (2023). Former bank officer fined RM8,000 over credit card fraud. *NST.* https://www.nst.com.my/news/crime-courts/2023/03/885476/former-bankofficer-fined-rm8000-over-credit-card-fraud.

Asmah, A. E., Atuilik, W. A., and Ofori, D. (2019). Antecedents and consequences of staff-related fraud in the Ghanaian banking industry. *Journal of Financial Crime*, 26(3), 669–682. https://doi.org/10.1108/jfc-08-2018-0083.

Asmah, A. E., Atuilik, W. A., and Ofori, D. (2020). Antecedents and consequences of staff related fraud in the Ghanaian banking industry. *Journal of Financial Crime*, 27(1), 188–201. https://doi.org/10.1108/jfc-03-2019-0034.

Coenen, T. L. (2008). Essentials of Corporate Fraud. John Wiley and Sons.

Cressey, D. (1973). Other People's Money : A Study in the Social Psychology of Embezzlement. Patterson Smith.

Cressey, D. R. (1950). The criminal violation of financial trust. *American Sociological Review*, 15(6), 738. https://doi.org/10.2307/2086606.

Dorminey, J. W., Fleming, A. S., Kranacher, M., and Riley Jr, R. A. (2010). Beyond the fraud triangle: certified public accountant. *The CPA Journal*, 80(7), 1723. https://www.proquest.com/scholarly-journals/beyond-fraud-triangle/docview/637276283/se-2.

Hasnan, S., Abdul Rahman, R. A., and Mahenthiran, S. (2008). Management predisposition, motive, opportunity, and earnings management for fraudulent financial reporting in Malaysia. *SSRN Electronic Journal.* https://doi.org/10.2139/ssrn.1321455.

Hollow, M. (2014). Money, morals and motives. *Journal of Financial Crime*, 21(2), 174–190. https://doi.org/10.1108/jfc-02-2013-0010.

Jackson, K. R., Holland, D. V., Albrecht, C., and Woolstenhulme, D. R. (2010). Fraud isn't just for big business: understanding the drivers, consequences, and prevention of fraud in small business. *The Journal of International Management Studies*, 5, 160164.

John, P. A. O. (2012). Examination of fraud in the nigerian banking sector and its prevention. *Www.academia.edu.* https://www.academia.edu/56236950/Examination_of_Fraud_in_the_Nigerian_Banking_Sector_and_its_Prevention.

Kingsley, E. (2012). Predictive asset maintenance. *All Days.* https://doi.org/10.2118/150234-ms.

KPMG (2016). Global profiles of the fraudster: https://assets.kpmg.com/content/dam/kpmg/pdf/2016/05/profiles-of-the-fraudster.pdf.

Omar, M., Nawawi, A., and Puteh Salin, A. S. A. (2016). The causes, impact and prevention of employee fraud. *Journal of Financial Crime*, 23(4), 1012–1027. https://doi.org/10.1108/jfc-04-2015-0020.

Omar, N. B., and Mohamad Din, H. F. (2010). Fraud diamond risk indicator: an assessment of its importance and usage. IEEE Xplore. https://doi.org/10.1109/CSSR.2010.5773853.

Owusu, G. M. Y., Koomson, T. A. A., Alipoe, S. A., and Kani, Y. A. (2021). Examining the predictors of fraud in state-owned enterprises: an application of the fraud triangle theory. *Journal of Money Laundering Control* (ahead-of-print) https://doi.org/10.1108/jmlc-05-2021-0053.

PwC (2022). PwC's Global Economic Crime and Fraud Survey 2020. PwC. https://www.pwc.com/gx/en/services/forensics/economic-crime-survey.html.

Ramamoorti, S., Morrison, D., and Koletar, J. (2009). Bringing Freud to Fraud: Understanding the State-of-Mind of the C-Level Suite/White Collar Offender through "A-B-C" Analysis. Institute for Fraud Prevention (IFP) at West Virginia University. https://ecommons.udayton.edu/acc_fac_pub/71/.

Ruankaew, T. (2016). Beyond the fraud diamond. *International Journal of Business Management and Economic Research (IJBMER)*, 7(1), 474–476. http://ijbmer.com/docs/volumes/vol7issue1/ijbmer2016070102.pdf.

194 A review on virtual tutoring and student performance analysis using GPT-3

Prathigadapa Sireesha[1,a] and Salwani Binti Mohd Daud[2,b]

[1]Master of Technology in Computer Science and Engineering, School of Mathematics, Actuarial and Quantitative Studies, Asia Pacific University of Technology and Innovation (APU), Kuala Lumpur, Malaysia

[2]PhD(Electrical Engineering), University Malaysia of Computer Science and Engineering, Selangor, Malaysia

Abstract

In today's educational landscape, it is vital for educators to precisely predict student performance and provide timely feedback to encourage a comprehensive understanding of their academic standing. Consequently, educators must transform their teaching methodologies to enhance learning outcomes. To address this issue, various alternative and advanced approaches have been proposed and implemented by researchers. This research conducts a systematic review of previous research endeavours focused on virtual tutoring and virtual learning environments, aiming to identify significant contributions in the field of educational systems. The research primarily revolves around the utilization of machine learning and deep learning models, as well as the datasets employed in these systems. Through this investigation, the research sheds light on the associated challenges and presents potential solutions for the implementation of virtual tutors and performance analysis. Additionally, the research offers a solution to effectively manage the vast amount of data present in e-learning platforms. By synthesizing the findings from various studies, this research contributes to the existing body of knowledge in the field of education systems, providing valuable insights for educators and researchers alike. The outcomes of this study have the potential to enhance the effectiveness of virtual tutoring and virtual learning environments, ultimately improving the educational experience for students and facilitating their academic growth.

Keywords: Deep learning, learning outcomes, machine learning, student performance, virtual learning environment, virtual tutor

Introduction

Virtual learning environments provide rich datasets for analyzing and reporting on students' learning processes and individual performances, enhancing the learning analytics paradigm. Weaker quality assurance standards for online courses are seen as a barrier to the widespread adoption of online education by top academic officials. Four approaches were used to analyze students' academic performance on e-learning platforms: (i) identifying students with lower scores (ii) predicting academic performance (iii) identifying difficulties in the e-learning platform, and (iv) evaluating learning platforms (Albreiki et al., 2021). Virtual learning environments (VLEs) provide students with intellectual and emotional support, while online educators using VLEs are innovative, engaged, motivated, and self-driven. The preparation and execution of online exams, held without physical presence, pose challenges to integrity and security, as verifying examinees and preventing cheating becomes difficult (Muzaffar et al., 2021). Online assessments offer the advantage of providing quick and insightful feedback, supporting reflective learning, and offering high-quality information for teaching and learning. Constructive criticism in online assessments promotes positive motivation, facilitates learning conversations, and enables progress in performance levels.

Online exams offer the chance to give explicit comments about the right answers and the supporting reasoning in addition to a grade (Mate and Weidenhofer, 2022). Although there are numerous methods for predicting student performance using machine learning techniques, the predictions' level of accuracy is quite poor. (Baker et al., 2019) found that students whose professors stopped communicating with them and making themselves available at synchronous times experienced a decline in quiz results. This exemplifies how challenging it is to create the best accurate method for gauging students' achievement. Data is the most critical component of all data analytics, machine learning, and artificial intelligence. Inevitably no one can train any model without data, and all modern research and automation will be futile. Large corporations are paying a lot of money only to collect as much specific data

[a]sireesha.prathi@apu.edu.my, [b]salwani.daud@unimy.edu.my

as possible ("ML | Introduction to Data in Machine Learning" 2018). In order to increase student commitment to the learning process, (Ding, 2019) presented an instant input utilising component such as grades, certificates, ratings, and engagement awards. It improves their efforts to reach their objectives and gives them the chance to transparently record their learning successes and evaluate them. Hassan et al. (2019) and Lopez and Tucker (2019) stated that by encouraging students to participate in review course in a classroom environment will create awareness about gamification programme.

Furthermore, it is a teaching strategy to enhance instruction, motivate and empower students, boost their participation and interaction, and inspire them to develop their skills (Zainuddin et al., 2020). A semantic-based recommender system that is integrated with virtual aid was discussed by (Ali et al., 2021). In addition to helping users learn the skills necessary to meet institutional needs, this approach attempts to boost user motivation. Additionally, it makes semantic predictions about the preferences of users for virtual support when they need to quickly learn new tools and technologies to meet institutional criteria for online education. As stated by Ryan and Poole (2019), the engaging nature of students will be enhanced along with long timer memory via virtual learning which will make them happy also. Students who engaged in more interactions on the VLE tended to perform better in their academic fields (Queiroga et al., 2021). The level of interaction that students have with the virtual world can be utilised to assess how well they are performing.

So, for a comprehensive evaluation of students' progress this research consider academic performance and extra-curricular activities in the historical data, eventually, virtual tutors can then provide constructive feedback to students who struggle academically, helping them improve their performance and transition from poor to good performers with certain reward based on the results. This fosters a positive virtual learning environment and enables students to evaluate their academic progress. Ultimately, such remediation efforts can help improve the student's academic achievements before final evaluations, leading to a higher success rate for the university.

Literature Review

The literature review is conducted to examine and comprehend the online learning environment to assess students' performance to improve their exam scores. This review examines techniques for evaluating student performance, including machine learning (ML) and deep learning (DL), and addresses problems brought up by current approaches.

The education system in VLE and e-learning environment

The advancements in educational technology have allowed for the collection of enormous volumes of data about students and their educational activities. Researchers and educators now have knowledge and insights that can be applied to better teaching and learning processes (Sedrakyan et al., 2020) and to measure academic success (Al-Sudani and Palaniappan, 2019). In terms of time, space, and location, this educational technology enables teachers, parents, and students to take part in educational activities. Online learning was adopted by Malaysian higher education institutions in the late 1990s, and because of its extensive worldwide reach, distinctive features, accessibility, and long-term flexibility, its acceptance has grown since then. According to the Malaysian Education Blueprint 2015–2025 (Higher Education), efforts are being made to incorporate online learning into higher education and lifetime learning. Nevertheless, questions about the superiority of online learning over conventional face-to-face learning environments continue to exist (Selvanathan et al., 2020). Virtual tutoring systems are real-world programs that simulate tutors in certain activities involving the learner's well-being, such as instructing. Virtual tutors are useful for classes that do not require teachers (Samonte et al. 2023). As an online teaching and learning platform, VLE has been discovered to be a content delivery enabler since it is not restricted to a specific time and location but is accessible at any time and from any location. VLE can either boost or deteriorate student engagement and performance, and they must be tailored to many types of learners. People of both genders are enthusiastic about utilizing VLE (Pem et al., 2021).

AI- based performance analysis and early prediction

A large number of computer and related computing technologies, including artificial intelligence in education, have been applied in education as a result of next-generation educational technology. There are two ways to organize models for predicting AI performance. First, in terms of AI models, the focus is on developing and validating these models to increase their accuracy. Creating AI models that can reliably predict students' learning outcomes is the aim. Second, from the standpoint of educational applications, the focus is on enhancing teaching and the standard of learning with the help of AI prediction models. For improving educational experience of both the students and the teachers, these models are applied to provide them with the required guidance and insights. According to Ouyang et al. (2023), in order to construct AI-enabled academic performance prediction models, a loop of empirical research validation, educational application, and AI model development is required.

Among the new educational abilities resulting from artificial intelligence in education (AIEd), Jiao et al. (2022), Taheri et al. (2021), and Nabizadeh et al. (2020) provided examples of learning performance prediction, teaching strategy optimization, and learning path recommendation. One cutting-edge use of AIEd is academic performance prediction powered by AI, which helps create student-centered learning routes and identify students who are likely to fail. This will encourage effective learning, improving development and design in the process (Mozer et al., 2019). However, the majority of recent research on AI prediction models has concentrated on how to construct and improve AI models, or how to integrate multiple algorithms to produce models that are more accurate at making predictions. Here, we cover several machine learning (ML)-based methods being utilized for forecasting students' academic achievement.

Machine learning -based analysis

Using computers, ML simulates learning capability of humans by identifying and obtaining real time knowledge. In the ML process, algorithms are designed to enable systems or computers to process input information, create training sets, and produce desired outputs within a specified range using statistical estimation. The field of ML intersects computer science, statistics, and mathematics, and researchers have applied it to predict student retention in virtual class environments. Academic performance achievement refers to the level of accomplishment in students' educational goals, which can be measured through examinations, assessments, and other forms of evaluation.

In order to forecast final test results using data that was accessible prior to the final exam, Tomasevic et al. (2020) applied ML approaches. The findings demonstrated that utilising artificial neuron networks (ANN), the maximum precision was attained by feeding engagement and prior performance data. Additionally, the Nave Bayes (NB) technique had the lowest results, with the ANN outcomes being followed by support vector classifier (SVM). By considering historical grades and other socioeconomic factors including student attendance, parent education, travel time, study time, and frequency of going out, Prakash and Garg (2021) created a ML model that can forecast a student's future grade. Through evaluation of student performance, faculty members

act as mentors for students to help them achieve the grades they are supposed to get. Martinez-Rodriguez et al. (2019) provided a prediction model of academic performance that better captured influence among target factors by using a set of students' academic profiles of low, medium, and high. Albreiki et al. (2021) used explainable ML techniques to identify the primary reasons for the unsatisfactory outcomes. This methodology suggested appropriate corrective steps by connecting students' performance at each scheduled checkpoint to the course contents and course learning outcomes (CLOs) (Khan et al., 2021). Numerous prediction models have been implemented to support ML algorithms as useful tools for predicting student outcomes. Sharma et al. (2019) proposed an ML system that uses a web camera to record head movement, eye tracking, and emotion analysis to determine whether a student is engaged. Using digital learning scenario, this method was tested, and the test results show that the best students have high concentration indices. Feature extraction is necessary for good prediction.

Methodology

The methodology section of this research paper provides a comprehensive overview of the systematic approach employed to investigate and address the research questions at hand. In this section, the research delves into the systematic review process, the identification of research questions, and the selection of keywords derived from abstracts, all of which collectively serve as the framework upon which this study is built.

Systematic review process

The systematic review refers to reviewing the most relevant past papers on the topic to determine and understand what has been found regarding the topic. The review is conducted following five different stages; 1) developing a research question, 2) procedures of the research, 3) reviewing relevant articles, 4) keywords based on abstract.

Identifying the research question

Developing and understanding the research topic is a key phase in research so that efforts to address such a question can be performed. The research procedures also depending on the research questions; so, it is essential to first examine the research questions before deciding on the research techniques.

The following are the research questions associated with the virtual learning environments and feedback systems in the e-learning systems.

1. What are the important criteria that lead to accurate student performance prediction when utilizing GPT-3 with a virtual tutor?
2. How to design and implement the GPT-3 model in predicting students' performance using virtual tutors?
3. How accurate is the proposed virtual tutor model while using GPT-3?

Procedures of the research
The relevant articles for the research are identified by using a keyword-based search strategy. The keywords including the virtual learning environment, e-learning, virtual tutor, online exams, and feedback systems were written in IEEE, Science Direct, Springer, Wiley, Google Scholar, SCOPUS, and the range of the years selected was from 2015 to 2022. The selection of relevant articles was based on the aim of the study. One hundred and thirty articles were excluded as they were based purely on the performance evaluation of the students' performance, but they are not part of the e-learning system. Overall, 6 articles were found to be relevant and used for data extraction Table 194.1.

Reviewing relevant articles

The selected articles were screened based on the citation provided by the database.

Table 194.1 Inclusion and exclusion criteria.

Criteria	Details
Exclusion of the articles	Published before 2017
	No relevant keywords
	Concepts are not relevant to the abstract title
	Language-non-English
	Non-education
	Non-peer-reviewed articles.
Inclusion of the articles	Published from 2017 to 2022
	Relevant keywords
	Concepts relevant to the abstract and the title
	Language -English
	Peer-reviewed articles- IEEE, Science Direct, Springer, Wiley, Google Scholar, SCOPUS.
	Education system

Source: Author

Keywords based on abstract
The study mainly focused on the keywords of the papers selected in the study and included all the necessary words in the work. The keywords used in this study are machine learning, deep learning, virtual tutoring, virtual learning environment and e-learning.

Result and Discussion
The findings section of this research paper encapsulates the outcomes and insights derived from an in-depth exploration of the virtual tutoing and student performace analysis.

Performance analysis
Student performance prediction can be used to improve student retention rates, enrolment management, alumni relations, targeted marketing, and overall educational effectiveness. By accurately predicting which students are at risk of failing, educators can provide early intervention and support, helping students to succeed. Student performance prediction is a powerful tool that can be used to improve student outcomes. By accurately predicting which students are at risk of failing, educators can provide early intervention and support, helping students to succeed.

Virtual learning environment
The VLEs can be a valuable tool for students when they find them useful. However, one of the main challenges of VLEs is assessment. Assessment in VLEs is different from traditional classroom assessment, as it often relies on tools such as quizzes and tests. This can make it difficult to measure educational outcomes, such as communication among peers and critical thinking skills.

Virtual tutor
Online assessments can be a challenge for educators, as it can be difficult to give students appropriate solutions based on their grades and talents. To overcome this challenge, virtual tutors can be implemented. Virtual tutors use technology to assess students' learning needs and can converse with students to detect their capabilities and find ways to motivate them throughout their learning. Table 194.2 illustrate the methods and theories related to virtual tutor.

Summary of the solutions
Table 194.3 illustrate current challenges in performance analysis and virtual tutoring for the students.

Summary of challenges
In today's era, education holds paramount significance on a global scale. The evaluation of student performance and the provision of personalized guidance to enhance their educational approach and career advancement have taken center stage. Within the

Table 194.2 Methods and theories related to virtual tutor.

Methods	Research goal and issues
Hierarchical method consists of abstraction and embedding steps that generate a precise embedding for problems that is completely automated. Su et al. (2020). • Prob2Vec: Hierarchical problem embedding algorithm. • 1-Glove: Primitive approach for problem embedding	The authors proposed a hierarchical problem embedding algorithm, called Prob2Vec, that consists of abstraction and embedding steps, and achieved 96.88% accuracy on a problem similarity test, in contrast to 75% from directly applying state-of-the-art sentence embedding methods. This is especially for an undergraduate probability course and embedding vectors are not precisely evaluating the strength and weakness.
Virtual tutor for fricative distortion correction in children - Uses deep learning and spectral-temporal convolutions for classification. Anjos et al. (2020) • Log Mel filter banks • Deep learning techniques with spectral-temporal convolutions	The accuracy of the tutor may vary depending on the quality of the input speech data and the diversity of the speaker.
Unimodal, Bimodal, qualitative and quantitative data: Human-computer interactions. Oker et al. (2020)	Only tested two virtual agents. It only had a short-term focus.
Phonetic adaptations made by L2 German speakers to a virtual language tutor are compared. Gessinger et al. (2020)	The study only focused on phonetic accommodation, and it involved a small sample size of L1 French speakers.
Semi-open learning strategy with virtual tutor and exploratory guidance. Yongheng et al. (2021)	It is only evaluated for one experiment, i.e., making oxygen from potassium permanganate
Simulator for a 3D classroom built on the Unity 3D engine: Virtual classroom training. Duffek et al. (2021)	It is not realistic and immersive

Source: Author

Table 194.3 Solutions to the issues in the current systems.

Methods	Solutions to the issues
Hierarchical method consists of abstraction and embedding steps that generates a precise embedding for problems that is completely automated. Su et al. (2020). • Prob2Vec: Hierarchical problem embedding algorithm. • 1-Glove: Primitive approach for problem embedding	• Use a hierarchical method consisting of abstraction and embedding steps: • The abstraction step involves extracting key features or concepts from the problem using techniques like natural language processing or domain-specific knowledge. • The embedding step converts abstracted features or concepts into numerical or vectorized representations using techniques like word embeddings, graph embeddings, or deep learning-based embeddings. • Importantly, this entire process is automated, meaning that it does not require manual intervention or human expertise to generate the embeddings. This allows for scalability and efficiency in handling large-scale problems or datasets.
Virtual tutor for fricative distortion correction in children - Uses deep learning and spectral-temporal convolutions for classification. Anjos et al. (2020) • Log Mel filter banks • Deep learning techniques with spectral-temporal convolutions	• Use deep learning techniques with spectral-temporal convolutions of the data. • Use log Mel filter banks in combination with deep learning techniques. • Use of a virtual tutor for speech and language therapy can also be an effective solution. The virtual tutor can incorporate multidimensional advanced data analysis of the first layer convolutional kernel filters. • This analysis can validate the usefulness of performing the convolution on the log Mel filter bank and further improve the accuracy of the detection and classification of fricatives.
Unimodal, Bimodal, qualitative and quantitative data: Human-computer interactions. Oker et al. (2020)	• A hierarchical method consisting of abstraction and embedding steps can generate precise embeddings for problems in an automated manner. • A multimodal approach can be used to handle unimodal, bimodal, qualitative, and quantitative data in human-computer interactions. • Techniques such as natural language processing and computer vision can be used to analyze unimodal data.

Methods	Solutions to the issues
	• Fusion techniques and cross-modal learning can be employed for analyzing bimodal data. • Qualitative data can be analyzed using sentiment analysis, topic modelling, or qualitative coding methods. • Quantitative data can be analyzed using statistical analysis, data mining, or machine learning algorithms.
Phonetic adaptations made by L2 German speakers to a virtual language tutor are compared. Gessinger et al. (2020)	• Analyze pronunciation errors of L2 German speakers and provide targeted feedback and exercises. • Incorporate speech recognition technology for accurate assessment and real-time feedback. • Offer interactive exercises targeting phonetic challenges faced by L2 German speakers. • Use visual aids like spectrograms or articulatory diagrams to illustrate correct pronunciation. • Utilize natural language processing to analyze phonetic patterns and errors comprehensively. • Implement regular assessments and progress tracking to monitor improvements over time.
Semi-open learning strategy with virtual tutor and exploratory guidance. Yongheng et al. (2021)	• Implement a semi-open learning strategy with guidance from the virtual tutor. • Provide exploratory guidance for learners to discover knowledge with virtual tutor support. • Incorporate interactive and adaptive learning materials for hands-on activities and experiments. • Offer personalized feedback and recommendations based on learners' progress. • Foster a collaborative learning environment with social features for peer interaction. • Utilize data analytics and machine learning to track progress and provide tailored guidance. • Encourage self-reflection and metacognitive skills development. • Provide resources for independent research and exploration. • Continuously update and improve the virtual tutor based on learner feedback.
Simulator for a 3D classroom built on the Unity 3D engine: Virtual classroom training. Duffek et al. (2021)	• Develop a simulator for a 3D classroom using the unity 3D engine to provide virtual classroom training. • Create realistic 3D environments and avatars to replicate the classroom setting and enhance the immersive learning experience. • Incorporate interactive features such as whiteboards, desks, and other classroom elements to simulate real-world classroom interactions. • Integrate communication tools like voice chat or text chat to facilitate communication and collaboration among virtual classroom participants. • Provide customizable scenarios and simulations to cater to different educational needs and learning objectives. • Include assessment and evaluation tools within the virtual classroom simulator to track learners' progress and provide feedback on their performance. • Enable instructors to monitor and guide learners in real-time, offering support and guidance as needed. • Implement gamification elements such as rewards, achievements, and leaderboards to enhance learner engagement and motivation. • Support multi-user functionality, allowing multiple learners to participate in the virtual classroom simultaneously. • Continuously update and improve the virtual classroom simulator based on user feedback and emerging educational trends to ensure its effectiveness and relevance.

Source: Author

Table 194.4 Summary of challenges.

Challenges	Solutions
1. Engagement 2. Interactivity 3. Personalization 4. Assessments 5. Pedagogy	Virtual tutor
1. Scalability 2. Data privacy 3. Accessibility 4. Adaptability	Virtual learning environment
1. Generalization 2. Hyperparameters 3. Resources 4. Transfer learning 5. Efficiency	Deep learning

Source: Author

realm of e-learning, the proficient management of substantial institutional and individual tutoring data presents a formidable challenge as mentioned in Table 194.4.

In online learning, the perception results may not be as accurate as expected due to data misclassification, and some evaluation systems lack real-time information and outcomes. The available public dataset for evaluation is insufficient, and the assessment of student performance is not regularly updated. From the viewpoint of the students, they require fruitful and timely feedback from teachers, as well as knowledgeable assistance and they are considering the engagement level of the students in the online session. However, the physical state of students cannot always be considered as the primary factor. Furthermore, accessing the overall contribution of students to education requires examining both academic and extracurricular activities. Teachers seek an accurate assessment analysis system to save time and ensure consistent grading across all students. Therefore, it is necessary to develop a proper assessment marking mechanism to address these requirements.

To summarize the challenges inherent in the existing system, the proposed system focuses towards dispensing efficacious instruction and feedback. In this work, proposed the approval of generative pretrained transformer-3 (GPT-3) as the justification for virtual tutoring in self-assessment exams. Here GPT3 guide a Virtual Tutor to teach and help with unique homework problems and answer students' unique questions. This undertakes an in-depth analysis and classification of students' performance, predicated on prior records and grades, in order to allocate marks in the exam along crude, regular, and premium tiers. Additionally,

the model generates an exam scorecard. This manages educators and students the opportunity to tailor their learning approaches, thus leading to improvements in students' academic performance during final exams. This enables simultaneous answering for all students in online exams without any delay. It allows students to answer multiple questions, earn rewards, which positively impacts their academic progress. As a result, the system establishes a platform for students to improve their performance on final examinations.

In this present investigation, it has been established that the employment of GPT3 in conjunction with virtual tutor has proven to be efficacious for students pursuing higher education. A study by Limo et al. from 2023 sought to identify the variables that affect the amount of time undergraduate students receive individual coaching utilizing ChatGPT. Internal consistency for all variables ranged from satisfactory to outstanding in reliability testing. Numerous significant data were revealed by the findings, which provided insight into the factors affecting the length of individualized instruction. The advantages of employing GPT in tutoring were explored by Jim Wagstaff (2023). It is valued when a machine learning algorithm has human-like abilities. This makes conversational AI very helpful for creating individualized lesson plans, giving students feedback in real-time, and creating explanations or summaries of complicated ideas. Strong Natural Language Processing capabilities allow ChatGPT to process discussions that look to have been written by a human. There are benefits to using this technology, including increased productivity, improved precision, and lower prices. It is an impressive piece of artificial intelligence software that can be used to automate conversations and produce more accurate responses (Surameery and Shakor, 2023). Using GPT-3, researchers may quickly and simply produce high-quality abstracts that completely capture the major ideas of their work. It is well-liked for its capabilities, which include carrying on a conversation, transforming a sentence into a mathematical expression, producing news stories, and producing lines of code (Katar et al., 2023).

Conclusion

Virtual tutors powered by GPT-3, offers a unique opportunity to address the challenges faced in virtual leaning environments. It can adapt to individual learning styles and provide real-time assistance, creating a more dynamic and effective learning environment. The integration of GPT-3 in the virtual tutor also enables the analysis of students' performance, allowing for targeted interventions and personalized learning pathways. A detailed study is required to implement in this modern technology. This article presents an overview of existing studies on virtual tutor and virtual learning environments. It analyzed the benefits and issues in the performance analysis and feedback generation model in VLE and e-learning environments. The challenges and issues that are reviewed in this research are based on the current state and issues in the virtual tutor model. The tables represented in this research compiled the models and methods from previous research to resolve these issues. A total of 6 methods and related solutions are identified in this report. It will help study the associated challenges and solutions in virtual tutor and feedback system implementation and help manage the vast data and maintain records related to the academic performance of the students. The conclusion of the study highlights the potential of GPT-3, a powerful language model, in the development of a virtual tutor for enhancing students' performance in a virtual learning environment. The use of GPT-3 in the virtual tutor allows for a more interactive and personalized learning experience, as it can understand and respond to students' queries and provide tailored feedback. Overall, the combination of GPT-3, virtual tutor, students' performance analysis, and virtual learning environment holds great promise in revolutionizing education by providing a more engaging, interactive, and effective learning experience for students.

References

Albreiki, B., Zaki, N., and Alashwal, H. (2021). A systematic literature review of student' performance prediction using machine learning techniques. *Education Sciences*, 11(9), 552. https://doi.org/10.3390/educsci11090552.

Ali, S., Hafeez, Y., Abbas, M. A., Aqib, M., and Nawaz, A. (2021). Enabling remote learning system for virtual personalized preferences during COVID-19 pandemic. *Multimedia Tools and Applications*, 80(24), 33329–33355.

Al-Sudani, S., and Palaniappan, R. (2019). Predicting students' final degree classification using an extended profile. *Education and Information Technologies*, 24(4), 2357–2369. https://doi.org/10.1007/s10639-019-09873-8.

Anjos, I., Eskenazi, M., Marques, N., Grilo, M., Guimarães, I., Magalhães, J., et al. (2020) Detection of voicing and place of articulation of fricatives with deep learning in a virtual speech and language therapy tutor. *Proceedings Interspeech*, 3156–3160, doi: 10.21437/Interspeech.2020-2821.

Baker, R., Evans, B., Li, Q., and Cung, B. (2019). Does inducing students to schedule lecture watching in online classes improve their academic performance? an experimental analysis of a time management interven-

tion. *Research in Higher Education*, 60(4), 521–552. https://doi.org/10.1007/s11162-018-9521-3.

Ding, L. (2019). Applying gamifications to asynchronous online discussions: a mixed methods study. *Computers in Human Behavior*, 91, 1–11. https://doi.org/10.1016/j.chb.2018.09.022.

Duffek, V., Fiala, J., Hosejší, P., Mentlík, P., Polcar, J., Prucha, T., et al. (2021). Pre-service teachers' immersive experience in virtual classroom. In Research and Innovation Forum, (pp. 155–170). https://doi.org/10.1007/978-3-030-62066-0_13.

Gessinger, I., Möbius, B., Andreeva, B., Raveh, E., and Steiner, I. (2020). Phonetic accommodation of L2 german speakers to the virtual language learning tutor mirabella. https://doi.org/10.21437/interspeech.2020-2701.

Hassan, S. U., Waheed, H., Aljohani, N. R., Ali, M., Ventura, S., and Herrera, F. (2019). Virtual learning environment to predict withdrawal by leveraging deep learning. *International Journal of Intelligent Systems*, 34(8), 1935–1952. https://doi.org/10.1002/int.22129.

Jiao, P., Ouyang, F., Zhang, Q., and Alavi, A. H. (2022). Artificial intelligence-enabled prediction model of student academic performance in online engineering education. *Artificial Intelligence Review*, 55(8), 6321–6344. https://doi.org/10.1007/s10462-022-10155-y.

Katar, O., Özkan, D., Yildirim, O., and Acharya, U. R. (2023). Evaluation of GPT-3 AI language model in research paper writing. *Turkish Journal of Science and Technology*, 18(2), 311–318. https://doi.org/10.55525/tjst.1272369.

Khan, I., Ahmad, A. R., Jabeur, N., and Mahdi, M. N. (2021). An artificial intelligence approach to monitor student performance and devise preventive measures. *Smart Learning Environments*, 8(1), 17. https://doi.org/10.1186/s40561-021-00161-y.

Lopez, C. E., and Tucker, C. S. (2019). The effects of player type on performance: a gamification case study. *Computers in Human Behavior*, 91, 333–345. https://doi.org/10.1016/j.chb.2018.10.005.

Martinez-Rodriguez, R. A., Alvarez-Xochihua, O., Victoria, O. D. M., Aramburo, A.J., and Fraga, J. A. G. (2019). Use of machine learning to measure the influence of behavioral and personality factors on academic performance of higher education students. *IEEE Latin America Transactions*, 17(04), 633–641. https://doi.org/10.1109/TLA.2019.8891928.

Mate, K., and Weidenhofer, J. (2022). Considerations and strategies for effective online assessment with a focus on the biomedical sciences. *FASEB BioAdvances*, 4(1), 9–21. https://doi.org/10.1096/fba.2021-00075.

Mozer, M. C., Wiseheart, M., and Novikoff, T. P. (2019). Artificial intelligence to support human instruction. *Proceedings of the National Academy of Sciences*, 116(10), 3953–3955. https://doi.org/10.1073/pnas.1900370116.

Muzaffar, A. W., Tahir, M., Anwar, M. W., Chaudry, Q., Mir, S. R., and Rasheed, Y. (2021). A systematic review of online exams solutions in e-learning: techniques, tools, and global adoption. *IEEE Access*, 9, 32689–32712. https://doi.org/10.1109/ACCESS.2021.3060192.

Nabizadeh, A. H., Leal, J. P., Rafsanjani, H. N., and Shah, R. R. (2020). Learning path personalization and recommendation methods: a survey of the state-of-the-art. *Expert Systems with Applications*, 159, 113596. https://doi.org/10.1016/j.eswa.2020.113596.

Oker, A., Pecune, F., and Declercq, C. (2020). Virtual tutor and pupil interaction: astudy of empathic feedback as extrinsic motivation for learning. *Education and Information Technologies*, 25(5), 3643–58. https://doi.org/10.1007/s10639-020-10123-5.

Pem, U., Dorji, C., Tshering, S., and Dorji, R. (2021). Effectiveness of the virtual learning environment (VLE) for online teaching, learning, and assessment: perspectives of academics and students of the royal University of Bhutan. *International Journal of English Literature and Social Sciences*, 6(4), 183–197. https://doi.org/10.22161/ijels.64.30.

Prakash, M. S. G., and Garg, S. (2021). Performance analysis and prediction of student result using machine learning. *International Research Journal of Modernization in Engineering Technology and Science*, 03(12).

Queiroga, E. M., Enríquez, C. R., Cechinel, C., Casas, A. P., Paragarino, V. R., Bencke, L. R., et al. (2021). Using virtual learning environment data for the development of institutional educational policies. *Applied Sciences*, 11(15).

Ryan, E., and Poole, C. (2019). Impact of virtual learning environment on students' satisfaction, engagement, recall, and retention. *Journal of Medical Imaging and Radiation Sciences*, 50(3), 408–415.

Samonte, M. J., Acuña, G. E. O., Alvarez, L. A. Z., and Miraflores, J. M. (2023). A personality-based virtual tutor for adaptive online learning system. *International Journal of Information and Education Technology*, 13(6), 899–905. https://doi.org/10.18178/ijiet.2023.13.6.1885.

Sedrakyan, G., Malmberg, J., Verbert, K., Järvelä, S., and Kirschner, P. A. (2020). Linking learning behavior analytics and learning science concepts: designing a learning analytics dashboard for feedback to support learning regulation. *Computers in Human Behavior*, 107, 105512. https://doi.org/10.1016/j.chb.2018.05.004.

Selvanathan, M., Hussin, N. A. M., and Azazi, N. A. N. (2020). Students learning experiences during COVID-19: work from home period in Malaysian higher learning institutions. *Teaching Public Administration*, 014473942097790. https://doi.org/10.1177/0144739420977900.

Sharma, P., Joshi, S., Gautam, S., Maharjan, S., Filipe, V., and Reis, M. J. C. S. (2019). Student engagement detection using emotion analysis, eye tracking and head movement with machine learning.

Su, D., Yekkehkhany, A., Lu, Y., and Lu, W. (2020). Prob-2Vec: mathematical semantic embedding for problem retrieval in adaptive tutoring. In 2020 American Control Conference (ACC). https://doi.org/10.23919/acc45564.2020.9147767.

Surameery, N. M. S., and Shakor, M. Y. (2023). Use Chat GPT to solve programming bugs. *International Journal of Information Technology and Computer Engineering*, 31, 17–22. https://doi.org/10.55529/ijitc.31.17.22.

Taheri, A., RahimiZadeh, K., and Rao, R. V. (2021). An efficient balanced teaching-learning-based optimization algorithm with individual restarting strategy for solving global optimization problems. *Information Sciences*, 576, 68–104. https://doi.org/10.1016/j.ins.2021.06.064.

Tomasevic, N., Gvozdenovic, N., and Vranes, S. (2020). An overview and comparison of supervised data mining techniques for student exam performance prediction. *Computers and Education*, 143, 103676. https://doi.org/10.1016/j.compedu.2019.103676.

Yongheng, L., Mingliang, C., Huyu, X., Yuqing, Z., and Zhigeng, P. (2021). Virtual tutor and exploratory guidance environment in virtual experiment. In 2021 IEEE 7th International Conference on Virtual Reality (ICVR). https://doi.org/10.1109/icvr51878.2021.9483855.

Zainuddin, Z., Shujahat, M., Haruna, H., and Chu, S. K. W. (2020). The role of gamified e-quizzes on student learning and engagement: An interactive gamification solution for a formative assessment system. *Computers and Education*, 145, 103729. https://doi.org/10.1016/j.compedu.2019.103729.

(??). A review on students' performance analysis and feedback system in the virtual learning environment and e-learning environment. https://journal.unimy.edu.my/index.php/JIEDT/issue/view/JIEDT.V1.NO.2.DEC2022.

195 A conceptual change in innovation: a bibliometric analysis of innovation change in small and medium enterprises

Murali, Yasin Siddiqui and Raja Rub Nawaz
Asia Pacific University of Technology and Innovation, Kuala Lumpur, Malaysia

Abstract

Small and medium enterprises (SME) is a transitional change from small to big industry around the world and it is also considered as supportive to big industries through several small scaling supports to the big industry. This transition phase has been changed with the continuous innovation in technologies and not only big industries but for SMEs have transformed their work process to a great extent of innovative process. The conception of technological innovation in small and medium enterprises has driven an undergoing innovation for not only big industries but small and medium enterprises have also liable to adapt these changes to bring effectiveness and efficiency to their overall output. Observing changes this study has collected data from Web of Science (WoS), following research string as 'small and medium enterprises' and 'innovation' and collected data since 1995-2023 to observe the transitional change in the innovation in small and medium enterprises. The concept of innovation has changed the process conduction in small and medium enterprises because technical and environmental concerns have continuously changed work processing at every business scale. Bibliometric and Biblioshiny are tools used for the analysis of this study in observing the change in the concept of innovation change in small and medium enterprises. This study would observe the change in innovation and would develop a frame chart of transitional change of innovation in creating a better understanding of the innovation change over the observed period.

Keywords: Bibliometric, Biblioshiny, small and medium enterprises, transition, Web of Science

Introduction

The economic growth around the world is behind the innovation and technological advancement in the industries, not only mass of scaling but small and medium scale enterprises also have showed a rapid growth in adapting innovation for enhancing efficiency and effectiveness (Wahyuddin et al., 2022). The economic growth in businesses is witnessing to be the reason of intense competition among small and medium enterprise industries around the world (Miroshnychenko et al., 2021). The need of innovation in small and medium enterprise is because of excessive demand and growth recognition in small industries and the innovative change is the effect applied in responded to it (Anshari and Almunawar, 2022)Indonesia plays a critical role in implementing Industry 4.0. In addition, this study proposes an open innovation strategies for small and medium enterprises (SMEs. This study is exploring the transitional change of innovation within small and medium enterprises within in work processing. The bibliometric analysis has used in analyzing the change and the emerging trends in small and medium enterprises due

to innovation will be explored in this study. This study aims to uncover the areas in which countries, authors, years and emerging thematic concept and trend emergence in small and medium enterprises with respect to innovation. Small and medium enterprises serve as the big support for industries and have a leading capacity in the GDP contribution of any country (Chan et al., 2019). The role of small and medium enterprises has not only helped in attaining optimal output but it has changed the traditional work processing at its pinnacle in achieving bench marking in terms of innovative solutions around the globe (Lestari et al., 2020). The purpose of conducting bibliometric analysis is to analyze the vast body of concepts tested for the last many decades and to analyze the key patterns that can predict the future of the innovation ahead to provide valuable insights. The realm of innovation has promulgated utter change implied to confer the environment process and bring change at small scaling sector to support the economies of scaling (Eller et al., 2020). It seems to have improved the ultimate product as the innovation has inducted at most of small scaling business. Innovation is a driving factor that has brought controlled risk factor in business by inducting efficient

ᵃSiddiqui@asia.edu.mu

and effective tool to control the risk or measure the predictive outcome. The aversion of risk element has consistently raised the demand of innovation in small and medium enterprises that helps in meeting the demand of the market with effective support.

Literature review

Small and medium enterprises (SMEs) stand as the backbone of the global economy, forming a dynamic and vital component of the business community. With their significance continually on the rise, SMEs are recognized as central agents in fostering economic growth, job creation, and driving innovation(Hansen andBøgh, 2021). This literature review seeks to offer an in-depth examination of the innovation and change processes within SMEs, shedding light on the remarkable ways these enterprises have adapted and transformed to maintain competitiveness in the face of a rapidly evolving and increasingly complex business environment. In recent years, the traditional perception of SMEs as merely "small" businesses has evolved into a recognition of their outsized impact on national and global economies(MahmoodandMubarik, 2020). SMEs are now seen as dynamic and agile entities, often at the forefront of technological advances, and playing a pivotal role in both economic development and social progress. As global markets have become more interconnected and technology-driven, the expectations placed upon SMEs have shifted(Álvarez Jaramillo et al., 2019). They are now not only expected to navigate the challenges of globalization but to seize the opportunities it presents. This transformation is not only evident in the products and services SMEs offer but also in the way they approach innovation, adapt to changes in the marketplace, and foster entrepreneurship and creativity within their organizations(García-Quevedo et al., 2020).

The dynamic nature of the business environment, characterized by rapid technological advancements, shifting consumer preferences, and evolving regulatory landscapes, has compelled SMEs to rethink their strategies (Maroufkhani et al., 2020). They have embraced innovation not merely as a survival tactic but as a means of achieving sustained growth, enhancing their global presence, and contributing to broader socioeconomic well-being. The strategies employed to foster it, and the tangible impacts it has on economic growth, job creation, market expansion, and organizational dynamics (Müller, 2019). Additionally, the review will delve into the specific challenges faced by SMEs in their innovation journey and provide real-world case studies to illustrate the practical implications of innovation in diverse SME contexts (Shen et al., 2020). Contemplate future trends and the evolving landscape of innovation within SMEs, underscoring their potential as influential players in the ongoing global economic transformation (Akpan et al., 2021). In an era where innovation and adaptation are pivotal to success, SMEs continue to demonstrate their capacity for resilience and evolution. This literature review seeks to capture the essence of this transformative journey, emphasizing the critical role SMEs play in shaping the economic and entrepreneurial landscapes around the world.

Innovation in SMEs

Innovation in SMEs transcends mere novelty; it is a multifaceted concept that fuels growth and adaptability(Afonasova et al., 2019). Within SMEs, innovation can manifest in a variety of forms, encompassing not only product, process, marketing, and organizational innovations, but also extending to service innovations, business model innovations, and incremental or disruptive innovations(Bouwman et al., 2019). SMEs can engage in both radical innovations, which represent groundbreaking transformations in their industry, and incremental innovations, which involve smaller, gradual improvements to existing products, processes, or services(Stentoft et al., 2021).In the realm of product innovation, SMEs often explore new product development, enhancing existing products, or diversifying their product portfolios to meet evolving consumer needs. Process innovation may involve streamlining operations, improving efficiency, reducing waste, or embracing automation and digitalization to boost productivity(HorváthandSzabó, 2019). Marketing innovation encompasses creative marketing strategies, branding, and communication techniques to better connect with target audiences. Organizational innovation pertains to changes in the structure, culture, and management practices within the SME, fostering agility, adaptability, and a culture of continuous improvement (Demireland Danisman, 2019). The spectrum of innovations within SMEs is broad, and understanding these diverse dimensions is pivotal to grasping the holistic impact of innovation in these enterprises.

Innovation Drivers

In the context of SMEs, innovation is far from a spontaneous occurrence; it's intricately interwoven with a complex interplay of internal and external drivers (Lee et al., 2019). Internally, the SME's leadership, a culture that encourages experimentation and learning, and the active engagement of employees all serve as key instigators for innovation. Cultivating a creative environment that embraces novel ideas and initiatives acts as a powerful catalyst for fostering innovation from within (Sadiku-Dushi et al., 2019). On the external front, a multitude of forces come into play, such as evolving market dynamics, shifts in consumer behavior, and emerging industry trends, which compel SMEs to innovate in response to changing customer demands and to maintain competitiveness (Shao et al., 2020). The ever-present competitive pressures, including industry rivalry and the threat of disruption, also drive SMEs to innovate as a means to secure and enhance their market positions. Regulatory changes and compliance requirements necessitate innovative approaches to meet legal obligations and streamline operations (Juergensen et al., 2020). Furthermore, the invaluable insights derived from customer feedback, preferences, and expectations frequently stimulate SMEs to develop new solutions more closely aligned with customer needs. Finally, the rapid pace of technological advancements both enables and necessitates innovation, with SMEs embracing cutting-edge technologies to gain a competitive edge (Fitriasari, 2020). This intricate interplay of internal and external drivers provides a comprehensive understanding of what fuels innovation within SMEs, influencing not only the initiation of the innovation process but also its direction and focus, thereby shaping the evolutionary path of these enterprises within their respective industries.

Strategies for Innovation in SMEs

Within the realm of strategies for innovation in SMEs, three key approaches stand out. The adoption of open innovation models, a trend gaining momentum, where SMEs collaborate with external partners such as research institutions, larger corporations, and startups to tap into new ideas and expertise (Sedyastuti et al., 2021). The impact of open innovation on SMEs and the challenges encountered during its implementation are subjects of discussion. Secondly, technology adoption has become central to SMEs' innovation endeavors as they increasingly integrate digital technologies and Industry 4.0 solutions(Winarsih et al., 2021). This delves into the transformative role of technology adoption in SMEs, highlighting its profound effects on their competitiveness and adaptability (Okundaye et al., 2019). The critical issue of innovation financing is addressed, as SMEs often face significant hurdles when seeking the financial resources necessary for innovative endeavors (Chege et al., 2020). Various funding mechanisms, including government grants, venture capital, and crowdfunding, are explored to assess their effectiveness in promoting innovation within SMEs. These strategies collectively represent the multifaceted

approaches SMEs employ to foster innovation in a rapidly changing business landscape.

Impact of Innovation in SMEs

The impact of innovation within SMEs extends across several dimensions. The innovation-driven change frequently results in heightened productivity, enhanced competitiveness, and the expansion of market reach (Hanaysha et al., 2022). These outcomes, in a symbiotic relationship, significantly contribute to both economic growth and job creation, representing fundamental pillars for sustainable development. Furthermore, innovation equips SMEs with the tools to explore new markets, be it on a domestic or international scale (Benitez et al., 2020). This dissects the strategies employed for market expansion and underscores the pivotal role that innovation plays in facilitating such ventures. It's important to recognize that innovation often triggers the need for internal restructuring and cultural adaptation within SMEs. In this regard, the section delves into the challenges and benefits inherent in these organizational transformations, offering insights into how they shape the dynamic landscape of SMEs in response to the imperatives of innovation-driven change (Caballero-Morales, 2021). In summation, the impact of innovation on SMEs is a multi-faceted dynamic, permeating various aspects of their operations and the broader economic ecosystem.

Methodology

The methodology for this study on innovation in small and medium enterprises (SMEs) involves a comprehensive bibliometric analysis covering the period from 1983 to 2022. Bibliometric mapping, a well-established technique in the bibliometric field (Borner et al., 2003), serves as the core methodology. This approach encompasses two key components: the construction of the bibliometric map and its graphical representation.

In the extensive body of bibliometric literature, a substantial emphasis has been placed on constructing bibliometric maps. This includes investigations into factors affecting size similarity (Ahlgren et al., 2003) and the evaluation of various mapping techniques (Boyack et al., 2005). The wealth of bibliometric applications has been further expanded through research efforts by Antonio et al. (2020) and Rusydiana (2021).

Remarkably, the graphical representation of bibliometric data has received relatively less attention, despite its critical role in communicating insights effectively. Some researchers, like Chen (2003), have delved into this aspect, but many articles in the bibliometric literature often rely on basic graphical representations provided by computer programs.

For this study, data encompassing the years from 1983 to 2022 were collected from a wide array of sources, including scientific journals and other scholarly outlets. These sources were particularly focused on research related to innovation in SMEs. In total, 827 published articles were extracted and form the basis for the subsequent bibliometric analysis.

Results and Discussion

Average citation per year

The above table describes the trend in small and medium enterprises over the last couple of decades. Researchers started gaining interest in this era due to rapid growth in small and medium enterprises. There is significant attention observed in the early 1990s and this era has become a spot point for researchers around the world. There is a raised seen in the total citation (TC) per published article witnessing to be significant recognition by others researchers around the world. The mid of 90s and mid of 2000 are witnessed to the top most cited era for researchers conducted on this domain and eventually started to decline. Innovation in small and medium enterprises started showing less interest from researchers which declined the number of total citation (TC) per year due to change evolving conception or trend in the business which has shifted the academics priorities. The column of citable columns indicating the years per which a column cited creates a significant notation of research on specific concept that had focused by researchers. The era of early 1900s witnessed to having an average article citation in 30 years which indicating the relevancy of the research in that era Table 195.1. The evolution of citation and research become under the influence of the concept and setting the trend in terms of citation impact and research influence over the time. The data projects the interest of researcher's potential interest in the field of interest for fulfilling their academics priorities.

List of Domain Citing Innovation in Small and Medium Enterprises

The table presents a comprehensive overview of the prominent sources contributing to the research. "Sustainability" emerges as the primary source with 117 articles, followed by "Small Business Economics" with 51 articles and "Journal of Business Research" with 47 articles. "Manufacturing Letters" provides 39 articles, while "Tec novation" and the "International Journal of Innovation Management" each contribute 32 articles. Moreover, "International Small Business

Table 195.1 Average citation peryear.

Year	N	Mean TC per article	Mean TC per year	Citable years
1883	1	1.00	0.03	40
1984	0	0.00	0.00	0
1985	0	0.00	0.00	0
1986	0	0.00	0.00	0
1987	0	0.00	0.00	0
1988	0	0.00	0.00	0
1989	0	0.00	0.00	0
1990	0	0.00	0.00	0
1991	0	0.00	0.00	0
1992	0	0.00	0.00	0
1993	1	0.00	0.00	30
1994	1	147.00	5.07	29
1995	1	140.00	5.00	28
1996	3	34.67	1.28	27
1997	2	7.50	0.29	26
1998	1	4.00	0.16	25
1999	10	65.30	2.72	24
2000	4	32.00	1.39	23
2001	3	38.00	1.73	22
2002	8	81.38	3.88	21
2003	4	9.50	0.47	20
2004	4	100.75	5.30	19
2005	15	137.20	7.62	18
2006	22	56.05	3.30	17
2007	15	53.73	3.36	16
2008	27	45.33	3.02	15
2009	38	60.24	4.30	14
2010	57	77.44	5.96	13
2011	62	61.05	5.09	12
2012	89	39.52	3.59	11
2013	237	22.19	2.22	10
2014	202	24.04	2.67	9
2015	240	19.94	2.49	8
2016	285	17.69	2.53	7
2017	367	13.10	2.18	6
2018	385	13.98	2.80	5
2019	384	19.80	4.95	4
2020	457	12.53	4.18	3
2021	466	7.16	3.58	2
2022	430	1.90	1.90	1

Source: Author

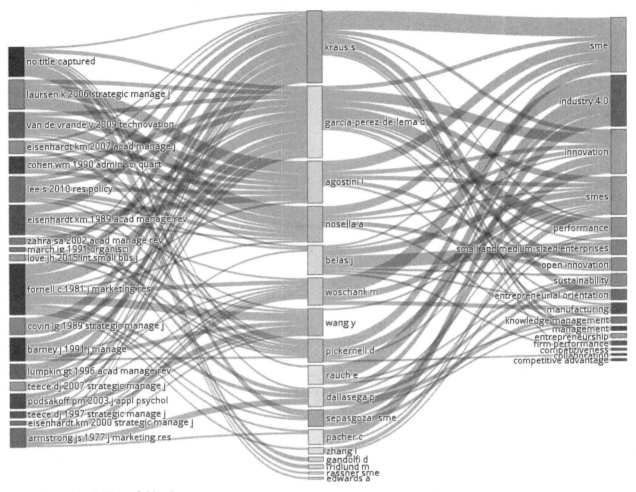

Figure 195.1 Three fields plot
Source: Author

Journal - Researching Entrepreneurship," "Journal of Small Business Management," "Education Excellence and Innovation Management: A 2025 Vision to Sustain Economic Development during Global Challenges," and the "Journal of Cleaner Production" each provide 30 to 28 articles. This comprehensive array of sources constitutes the foundation for the literature review, reflecting the breadth and depth of scholarship on innovation within SMEs from 1983 to 2022.

Source	Articles
Sustainability	117
Small Business Economics	51
Journal of Business Research	47
Manufacturing Letters	39
Technovation	32
International Journal of Innovation Management	30

Source	Articles
International Small Business Journal-researching Entrepreneurship	30
Journal of Small Business Management	30
Education Excellence and Innovation Management:a2025 Vision to Sustain Economic Development during Global Challenges	28
Journal of Cleaner Production	28

Source Growth

Small and medium enterprises (SMEs) have long been the backbone of economies worldwide, contributing significantly to job creation, economic growth, and regional development. In recent decades, the landscape of SMEs has been marked by a transformative journey in which innovation has played a pivotal role. This note delves into the evolution of innovation and

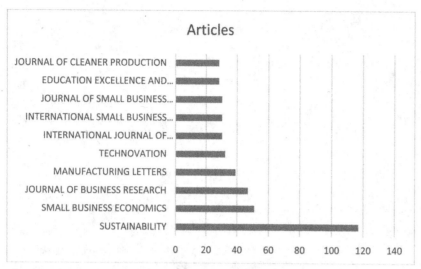

Figure 195.2 Global growth in Innovation
Source: Author

its transformative impact on SMEs, tracing the trajectory of their affiliation with production and exploring how innovation brought about significant change, particularly after 2013.

Historical context: affiliation with production

Historically, SMEs have played a crucial role in regional economies as they were often the primary providers of essential goods and services. In the late 19th century and well into the 20th century, many SMEs were deeply ingrained in local and regional production networks. They produced goods tailored to local markets, ranging from textiles and tools to food and machinery. These enterprises were often characterized by traditional production methods and a focus on satisfying local demand.

Innovation and growth: a transformative turnaround

The real transformation of SMEs in affiliation with production started to take shape in the early 21st century. A significant turning point was observed around 2013, when SMEs began to undergo substantial changes, primarily driven by innovation. Several key factors contributed to this notable shift:

Digital revolution: The advent of digital technologies and Industry 4.0 marked a significant leap for SMEs. These technologies enabled SMEs to automate processes, enhance product development, and engage more effectively with their customers, regardless of geographical location. This shift toward digitalization rapidly improved productivity and efficiency.

Globalization: The rapid expansion of global markets brought SMEs new opportunities. With e-commerce and online platforms, SMEs were no longer confined to local markets but could reach consumers worldwide. This globalization also prompted SMEs to rethink their strategies, making innovation a central element to compete on a broader stage.

Supportive ecosystems: Governments, academic institutions, and organizations recognized the potential of SMEs in driving innovation and economic growth. This led to the establishment of various support mechanisms, such as funding programs, innovation hubs, and incubators, designed to help SMEs navigate the complex terrain of innovation.

Changing consumer expectations: As consumer demands evolved, SMEs had to adapt by providing more personalized and innovative products and services. Innovation became a means to stay ahead of competitors in a dynamic and customer-centric market.

Global Growth in Innovation

Since 2013, the global landscape for SMEs has witnessed a remarkable surge in innovation. SMEs are increasingly recognized as sources of groundbreaking ideas and solutions. They have been at the forefront of sustainability efforts, implementing eco-friendly practices and solutions in response to growing environmental concerns. Moreover, their contributions to emerging fields like green technology, digital services, and niche markets have made them indispensable to the evolving global economy. The trajectory of SMEs' affiliation with production has evolved dramatically, primarily due to the catalytic force of innovation Figure 195.2. After 2013, SMEs embarked on a remarkable journey of transformation, leveraging technological advancements, adapting to global dynamics, and responding to shifting consumer preferences. Their enhanced capabilities and innovative

Source Growth

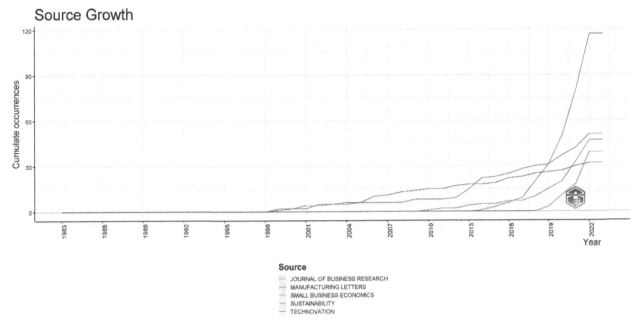

Figure 195.3 Source growth in innovation
Source: Author

drive have firmly established SMEs as key players in shaping the future of business, economic growth, and global innovation.

Most relevant authors

Authors	Articles	Articles fractionalized
Krauss	15	4.00
Levason	15	3.21
Reidg	15	3.21
Woschankm	15	5.03
Agostinil	11	5.42
Belasj	11	2.70
Rauche	11	3.57
Zhangl	11	2.64
Garcia-Perez-De-Lemad	10	3.67

The list of authors and their corresponding fractionalized article counts provides insights into the prominence and influence of these individuals in the field of innovation within SMEs. This concept is particularly relevant when considering the impact and depth of research conducted by these authors in the context of SME innovation:

Authors Kraus et al., have all published a significant number of articles, each with 15 contributions. Their high fractionalized counts suggest a substantial body of work focused on innovation in SMEs. They likely possess extensive expertise in various aspects of SME innovation, such as strategies, barriers, and the role of innovation in enhancing SME competitiveness and sustainability.

Agostini et al., compared to the top contributors, still have a substantial presence with 11 articles each. Their fractionalized counts indicate a noteworthy level of engagement in SME innovation research, reflecting a significant commitment to the subject. Their work likely encompasses a range of topics related to SME innovation, including the exploration of innovative practices, their impact on SME performance, and the challenges faced in the process.

Garcia-Perez-de-Lema with 10 articles demonstrates a substantial involvement in the field of SME innovation. Their work likely delves into specific aspects of SME innovation, possibly emphasizing factors like organizational change, technological adoption, or the intersection of innovation with sustainability.

In the context of SME innovation, the contributions of these authors can be expected to cover a wide array of subjects, offering in-depth insights into the various facets of innovation within SMEs. Their research may encompass themes such as innovation strategies, technology adoption, funding mechanisms, market expansion, and the impact of innovation on economic growth and job creation within SMEs. By producing a substantial body of work, these authors have played an essential role in advancing the understanding of how innovation drives and transforms SMEs, and their collective contributions serve as valuable resources for scholars, practitioners, and policymakers seeking to enhance SME innovation and its implications.

The list of authors and their fractionalized article counts continues to provide insights into the significance of their contributions in the realm of innovation within SMEs. Here's how this concept can be understood in the context of SME innovation:

Sepasgozar stands out with the highest fractionalized count of 6.76, signifying an extensive and influential body of work in the field of SME innovation. Their prolific output suggests a deep commitment and expertise in researching and advancing knowledge in this area. Sepasgozar SME's contributions likely cover a wide range of SME innovation aspects, from strategies and adoption of emerging technologies to the transformative impact of innovation on SMEs' growth, competitiveness, and sustainability.

Kraus et al., are prominent contributors to SME innovation research. Their fractionalized counts reflect substantial engagement in the subject, signifying in-depth knowledge of various facets of SME innovation. Their work likely addresses crucial aspects such as innovation strategies, barriers, and the role of innovation in enhancing SME performance.

Agostini et al., are also substantial contributors to SME innovation research. Their fractionalized counts indicate their significant dedication to the field, covering a spectrum of topics in SME innovation, including practices, impacts, and challenges.

Garcia-Perez-de-Lema demonstrates substantial involvement in SME innovation. Their work is likely to delve into specific areas such as organizational change, technology adoption, or innovation's link to sustainability within SMEs.

In the context of SME innovation, these authors have likely explored a diverse array of themes, ranging from innovation strategies and technologies to the impact of innovation on economic growth, job creation, and market expansion within SMEs. Their collective contributions serve as critical resources for researchers, practitioners, and policymakers interested in deepening their understanding of how innovation drives and transforms SMEs, ultimately playing a pivotal role in shaping the global SME landscape.

Most cited country

Country	TC	Average article cited
United Kingdom	15126	32.53
China	6328	16.02

Country	TC	Average article cited
Germany	5950	25.87
USA	5895	36.61
Spain	3937	18.84
Italy	3350	20.43
Australia	2745	24.29
Belgium	2024	40.48
Netherlands	1869	23.36
Korea	1860	20.44

The presented data provides information on the total citations (TC) and the average number of times an article from each country is cited in the context of innovation in SMEs. This data is valuable for understanding the global landscape of SME innovation research:

United Kingdom (UK): The UK leads in total citations with 15,126 and an average of 32.53 citations per article. This indicates a strong and sustained contribution to SME innovation research, suggesting a robust and influential research community in the UK. Their research might focus on various aspects of innovation within SMEs, potentially including strategies, policy frameworks, and the impact on the UK's SME ecosystem.

China: China has 6,328 total citations and an average of 16.02 citations per article. The lower average citation count suggests that while there is a considerable volume of research emerging from China, the impact or recognition of individual articles might be comparatively lower. China's focus on SME innovation may relate to its role as a global manufacturing and technology hub, investigating innovative practices within its SME sector.

Germany: Germany records 5,950 total citations and an average of 25.87 citations per article. This indicates a strong emphasis on quality research in SME innovation. Germany's research might center on technology adoption, industry-specific innovations, and the role of SMEs in Germany's economic landscape.

USA: The United States has 5,895 total citations with a high average of 36.61 citations per article. This demonstrates a significant influence and recognition of SME innovation research from the USA. Their research likely covers a broad spectrum of innovation aspects, reflecting the diversity and dynamism of SMEs in the U.S.

Spain: Spain reports 3,937 total citations with an average of 18.84 citations per article. Spain's focus on SME innovation research might emphasize its role in

1983-2018   **2019-2023**

Figure 195.4 SME Sector for 1983-2018
Source: Author

regional development, internationalization, and fostering innovation in smaller enterprises.

Italy: Italy contributes 3,350 total citations with an average of 20.43 citations per article. Their research may explore innovation strategies and practices within the Italian SME sector, which is notable for its presence in various industries.

Australia: Australia's SME innovation research has generated 2,745 total citations and an average of 24.29 citations per article. Australia's work may be inclined toward sustainability, technology adoption, and global competitiveness within its SMEs.

Belgium: Belgium stands out with a notably high average of 40.48 citations per article, despite a total citation count of 2,024. This indicates a focus on producing impactful and influential research in SME innovation, perhaps concentrating on specific niches within the SME landscape.

Netherlands: The Netherlands has 1,869 total citations and an average of 23.36 citations per article. Dutch SME innovation research might explore areas like internationalization, cross-border collaborations, and digital innovation in SMEs.

Korea: Korea reports 1,860 total citations with an average of 20.44 citations per article. Their research could delve into the innovative practices within the

Korean SME sector, with a potential focus on technology and entrepreneurship Figure 195.4.

In the context of SME innovation, the data highlights the diversity in the global research landscape, with different countries contributing to the understanding of SME innovation in their unique ways. The citation data reflects the extent to which research from these countries is recognized and used as a reference within the field. These contributions collectively enrich our comprehension of how innovation drives SMEs and their role in the broader economic ecosystem on a global scale.

Concept Evolution

The evolution of research focus from "behavior, capabilities, efficiency, patterns, model, innovation, design, and temperature" to "innovation, systems, behavior, microstructure, and firm performance" between the two distinct eras, namely before 2019 and 2019-2023, reflects a significant shift in the landscape of innovation in SMEs.

Pre-2019 Era

Behavior: Research in this period likely delved into understanding how human behavior, particularly within SMEs, influences innovation. This might include studies on management styles, leadership approaches, and employee engagement as they relate to innovation.

Capabilities: Researchers were likely exploring the capabilities of SMEs, assessing their strengths and weaknesses, and how they leverage these capabilities for innovation.

Efficiency: This aspect would pertain to how efficiently SMEs operate, including their processes, resource utilization, and overall operations in the context of innovation.

Patterns and model: The research was probably focused on identifying patterns and models that could predict or explain innovative behavior within SMEs. Researchers might have been looking for recurring themes or models to guide SME innovation.

Innovation: The core of this era, innovation was likely a central research focus, exploring what drives innovation in SMEs, the barriers they face, and the various forms of innovation (product, process, organizational, etc.).

Design: This might relate to the design of innovative products, services, or business models within SMEs. It could encompass user-centric design thinking or design principles for innovation.

Temperature: This term could be metaphorical, symbolizing the "heat" or intensity of innovation efforts, indicating the level of innovation activity and emphasis within SMEs.

2019-2023 Era

Innovation: The enduring importance of innovation suggests that it remains a central theme, but its perspective may have evolved. Researchers might be exploring new paradigms of innovation, such as open innovation or sustainable innovation.

Systems: There appears to be an increased focus on understanding the systemic nature of innovation within SMEs. This could involve the study of innovative ecosystems, networks, and collaborative systems.

Behavior: The continuity of behavior in the research focus suggests a persistent interest in understanding how human behavior, both within SMEs and in the broader innovation context, contributes to or inhibits innovative endeavors.

Microstructure: This term implies a deeper dive into the internal structures and processes within SMEs that drive innovation. Researchers may be investigating how micro-level components, such as culture, organizational dynamics, and team interactions, impact innovation outcomes.

Firm performance: The shift towards firm performance indicates a growing emphasis on measuring the tangible results of innovation within SMEs. Researchers may be examining how innovation influences competitiveness, growth, and sustainability.

The evolution of research themes from the pre-2019 era to 2019-2023 suggests a maturation of the SME innovation landscape. While innovation remains central, there is a shift towards a more holistic and systemic understanding of innovation, exploring how behavior, systems, microstructures, and firm performance collectively shape the innovative capacity of SMEs in the contemporary business landscape.

Thematic chart

The thematic four-quadrant chart, using "relevance degree" on the x-axis and "development degree" on the y-axis, is a tool to categorize and analyze various themes related to innovation in SMEs. Here's how these themes can be understood in the context of SME innovation:

Motor theme quadrant (high relevance, high development degree): Themes in this quadrant are at the forefront of SME innovation research. They are highly relevant, indicating their central role in understanding and advancing innovation in SMEs. The themes in this quadrant are:

Firm performance dynamics: Research into how the performance of SMEs is dynamic and subject to various internal and external factors. This could encompass studies on financial performance, growth, and competitive positioning in the context of innovation.

Capabilities: This theme suggests a focus on SMEs' capabilities, such as their internal resources, skills, and competencies that enable them to innovate effectively.

Market orientation: Understanding how SMEs align their strategies with market demands and customer needs, emphasizing a customer-centric approach to innovation.

Innovation performance management: This involves research into how SMEs manage and measure their innovation efforts, tracking key performance indicators and outcomes of innovation initiatives.

Basic themes quadrant (high relevance, low development degree): Themes in this quadrant are highly relevant, but their development in SME innovation research may still be in its early stages. The themes include:

Collaborative policy cooperation: This suggests a focus on how government policies and cooperation between different entities impact SME innovation.

Collaborative approaches for innovation support may be a key topic.

Model system enterprises: Investigating the concept of model system enterprises, which could be seen as exemplary innovation practices, serving as role models for other SMEs.

Niche theme quadrant (low relevance, high development degree): Themes in this quadrant may have a limited overall relevance, but they have been developed to a significant extent. The themes are:

Mechanical properties: Research on the mechanical properties of materials, potentially relevant in certain SME sectors where material science and mechanical engineering play a crucial role.

Identification: This might relate to research on unique identification systems, such as barcoding or digital identifiers, and their role in SME innovation.

Emerging declining themes quadrant (low relevance, low development degree): Themes in this quadrant have both low relevance and limited development in SME innovation research. They include:

Organization: A broad and foundational theme that could relate to various aspects of SME organizational structure, but it might not be a prominent focus in recent SME innovation research.

Behavior design system: This theme suggests exploring how behavior design principles are applied within SMEs, potentially referring to strategies for influencing consumer behavior but may have limited relevance to SME innovation.

In the context of SME innovation, this thematic four-quadrant chart helps to identify which themes are at the forefront of research (motor themes), which are promising but not yet fully explored (basic themes), which have been well-developed but may have limited relevance (niche themes), and which may be declining in focus (emerging declining themes). This categorization is valuable for researchers, policymakers, and practitioners in understanding the current landscape of SME innovation research and where potential future research directions may lie.

Discussion

The evolution of research focus:
The evolution of research focus from early investigations into behavior, capabilities, efficiency, patterns, and design to more recent themes like systems, microstructure, and firm performance reflects the maturation and expansion of SME innovation research. This evolution signifies that the SME innovation landscape is becoming more comprehensive and multifaceted.

Early focus (behavior, capabilities, and design): Early research delved into understanding the role of human behavior and the capabilities of SMEs in driving innovation. This included examining aspects of leadership, employee engagement, design thinking, and patterns that contribute to innovative endeavors within SMEs.

Later emphasis (systems, microstructure, and firm performance): The more recent shift towards themes like systems, microstructure, and firm performance indicates a growing recognition of the complexity of SME innovation. Researchers are increasingly acknowledging that innovation within SMEs is not just about individual behavior but is influenced by broader systems, internal dynamics, and its impact on firm performance.

Role of prolific authors
The list of highly relevant authors in SME innovation research provides a window into the thought leaders and experts driving the discourse in the field. These authors contribute significantly to our understanding of how innovation operates within SMEs.

Author, with a high fractionalized article count, suggests a substantial body of work, contributing to various aspects of SME innovation. Their research likely spans a wide range of topics, serving as a valuable resource for those interested in SME innovation.

Kraus et al., with multiple articles, are prominent contributors to SME innovation research. Their collective body of work underscores their expertise across different facets of SME innovation.

Agostini et al., bring their unique perspectives and insights to SME innovation. Their work adds diversity and depth to the understanding of SME innovation.

Garcia-Perez-De-Lema research likely focuses on specific dimensions of SME innovation, contributing to nuanced insights within the field.

These authors play a pivotal role in enriching our understanding of SME innovation, contributing to its growth and shaping the discourse on innovation within SMEs.

The Significance of Scholarly Sources:
The sources of scholarly articles in SME innovation research are central to knowledge dissemination. Journals like "Sustainability" and" "Small Business Economics" stand out as key contributors, showcasing the global nature of SME innovation research.

Sustainability: The high number of articles from this source underscores its significance in publishing research on SME innovation. This suggests a strong focus on sustainability and innovation within SMEs.

Small Business Economics: As another prominent source, it highlights the intersection of small businesses and economic principles, an area of significant research interest.

The diverse array of sources illustrates that SME innovation is not confined to a specific region or sector; it is a global and multifaceted field.

Thematic four-quadrant chart

The thematic four-quadrant chart offers a structured view of the research landscape, categorizing themes based on their relevance and development in SME innovation research.

Motor theme quadrant: These themes, like firm performance dynamics, capabilities, market orientation, and innovation performance management, are central drivers of SME innovation. They represent the core areas that underpin innovative success within SMEs.

Basic themes quadrant: Themes in this quadrant, such as collaborative policy cooperation and model system enterprises, are highly relevant and hold promise for further development. They are on the verge of becoming central to SME innovation research.

Niche theme quadrant: Niche themes like mechanical properties and identification may have limited overall relevance but have been extensively developed. They can find specific applications in particular SME sectors.

Emerging declining themes quadrant: This quadrant identifies themes like organization and behavior design system, which may be losing relevance in the context of SME innovation. It indicates shifting research priorities within the field.

Conclusion

In conclusion, the discussion on innovation in small and medium enterprises (SMEs) paints a dynamic and evolving landscape. The evolution of research focus, from early explorations of behavior and capabilities to a systemic understanding that encompasses microstructures and firm performance, demonstrates the maturation and complexity of SME innovation research. Prolific authors and diverse scholarly sources underscore the global significance of this field and its potential to drive economic growth and development. The thematic four-quadrant chart provides a structured framework for understanding the central drivers, emerging trends, and shifting priorities in SME innovation. This holistic perspective is invaluable for researchers, policymakers, and practitioners as they navigate the ever-changing terrain of SME innovation and its critical role in shaping the future of small and medium enterprises around the world.

Reference

Afonasova, M. A., Panfilova, E. E., Galichkina, M. A., and Slusarczyk, B. (2019). Digitalization in economy and innovation: The effect on social and economic processes. *Polish Journal of Management Studies*, 19(2), 22–32.

Akpan, I. J., Soopramanien, D., and Kwak, D. H. (Austin) (2021). Cutting-edge technologies for small business and innovation in the era of COVID-19 global health pandemic. *Journal of Small Business and Entrepreneurship*, 33(6), 607–617. https://doi.org/10.1080/08 276331.2020.1799294.

Álvarez Jaramillo, J., Zartha Sossa, J. W., and Orozco Mendoza, G. L. (2019). Barriers to sustainability for small and medium enterprises in the framework of sustainable development—literature review. *Business Strategy and the Environment*, 28(4), 512–524. https://doi. org/10.1002/bse.2261.

Anshari, M., and Almunawar, M. N. (2022). Adopting open innovation for SMEs and industrial revolution 4.0. *Journal of Science and Technology Policy Management*, 13(2), 405–427. https://doi.org/10.1108/ JSTPM-03-2020-0061.

Benitez, G. B., Ayala, N. F., and Frank, A. G. (2020). Industry 4.0 innovation ecosystems: An evolutionary perspective on value cocreation. *International Journal of Production Economics*, 228, 107735.

Bouwman, H., Nikou, S., and de Reuver, M. (2019). Digitalization, business models, and SMEs: how do business model innovation practices improve performance of digitalizing SMEs? *Telecommunications Policy*, 43(9), 101828.

Caballero-Morales, S. O. (2021). Innovation as recovery strategy for SMEs in emerging economies during the COVID-19 pandemic. *Research in International Business and Finance*, 57, 101396.

Chan, C. M. L., Teoh, S. Y., Yeow, A., and Pan, G. (2019). Agility in responding to disruptive digital innovation: case study of an SME. *Information Systems Journal*, 29(2), 436–455. https://doi.org/10.1111/isj.12215.

Chege, S. M., Wang, D., and Suntu, S. L. (2020). Impact of information technology innovation on firm performance in Kenya. *Information Technology for Development*, 26(2), 316–345. https://doi.org/10.1080/02681102.20 19.1573717.

Demirel, P., and Danisman, G. O. (2019). Eco-innovation and firm growth in the circular economy: Evidence from European small- and medium-sized enterprises. *Business Strategy and the Environment*, 28(8), 1608–1618. https://doi.org/10.1002/bse.2336.

Eller, R., Alford, P., Kallmünzer, A., and Peters, M. (2020). Antecedents, consequences, and challenges of small and medium-sized enterprise digitalization. *Journal of Business Research*, 112, 119–127.

Fitriasari, F. (2020). How do small and medium enterprise (SME) survive the COVID-19 outbreak? *Jurnal Inovasi Ekonomi*, 5(02). http://ejournal.umm.ac.id/index. php/JIKO/article/view/11838.

García-Quevedo, J., Jové-Llopis, E., and Martínez-Ros, E. (2020). Barriers to the circular economy in European small and medium-sized firms. *Business Strategy and the Environment*, 29(6), 2450–2464. https://doi.org/10.1002/bse.2513.

Hanaysha, J. R., Al-Shaikh, M. E., Joghee, S., and Alzoubi, H. M. (2022). Impact of innovation capabilities on business sustainability in small and medium enterprises. *FIIB Business Review*, 11(1), 67–78. https://doi.org/10.1177/23197145211042232.

Hansen, E. B., and Bøgh, S. (2021). Artificial intelligence and internet of things in small and medium-sized enterprises: a survey. *Journal of Manufacturing Systems*, 58, 362–372.

Horváth, D., and Szabó, R. Z. (2019). Driving forces and barriers of Industry 4.0: Do multinational and small and medium-sized companies have equal opportunities? *Technological Forecasting and Social Change*, 146, 119–132.

Juergensen, J., Guimón, J., and Narula, R. (2020). European SMEs amidst the COVID-19 crisis: assessing impact and policy responses. *Journal of Industrial and Business Economics*, 47(3), 499–510. https://doi.org/10.1007/s40812-020-00169-4.

Lee, J., Suh, T., Roy, D., and Baucus, M. (2019). Emerging technology and business model innovation: the case of artificial intelligence. *Journal of Open Innovation: Technology, Market, and Complexity*, 5(3), 44.

Lestari, S. D., Leon, F. M., Widyastuti, S., Brabo, N. A., and Putra, A. H. P. K. (2020). Antecedents and consequences of innovation and business strategy on performance and competitive advantage of SMEs. *The Journal of Asian Finance, Economics and Business*, 7(6), 365–378.

Mahmood, T., and Mubarik, M. S. (2020). Balancing innovation and exploitation in the fourth industrial revolution: Role of intellectual capital and technology absorptive capacity. *Technological Forecasting and Social Change*, 160, 120248.

Maroufkhani, P., Tseng, M. L., Iranmanesh, M., Ismail, W. K. W., and Khalid, H. (2020). Big data analytics adoption: determinants and performances among small to medium-sized enterprises. *International Journal of Information Management*, 54, 102190.

Miroshnychenko, I., Strobl, A., Matzler, K., and De Massis, A. (2021). Absorptive capacity, strategic flexibility, and business model innovation: Empirical evidence from Italian SMEs. *Journal of Business Research*, 130, 670–682.

Müller, J. M. (2019). Business model innovation in small- and medium-sized enterprises: strategies for industry 4.0 providers and users. *Journal of Manufacturing Technology Management*, 30(8), 1127–1142.

Okundaye, K., Fan, S. K., and Dwyer, R. J. (2019). Impact of information and communication technology in Nigerian small-to medium-sized enterprises. *Journal of Economics, Finance and Administrative Science*, 24(47), 29–46.

Sadiku-Dushi, N., Dana, L. P., and Ramadani, V. (2019). Entrepreneurial marketing dimensions and SMEs performance. *Journal of Business Research*, 100, 86–99.

Sedyastuti, K., Suwarni, E., Rahadi, D. R., and Handayani, M. A. (2021). Human resources competency at micro, small and medium enterprises in palembang songket industry. In 2nd Annual Conference on Social Science and Humanities (ANCOSH 2020), (pp. 248–251). https://www.atlantis-press.com/proceedings/ancosh-20/125955504.

Shao, S., Hu, Z., Cao, J., Yang, L., and Guan, D. (2020). Environmental regulation and enterprise innovation: a review. *Business Strategy and the Environment*, 29(3), 1465–1478. https://doi.org/10.1002/bse.2446.

Shen, Z., Siraj, A., Jiang, H., Zhu, Y., and Li, J. (2020). Chinese-style innovation and its international repercussions in the new economic times. *Sustainability*, 12(5), 1859.

Stentoft, J., Wickstrøm, K. A., Philipsen, K., and Haug, A. (2021). Drivers and barriers for industry 4.0 readiness and practice: empirical evidence from small and medium-sized manufacturers. *Production Planning and Control*, 32(10), 811–828. https://doi.org/10.1080/09537287.2020.1768318.

Wahyuddin, W., Marzuki, M., Khaddafi, M., Ilham, R. N., and Sinta, I. (2022). A study of micro, small and medium enterprises (MSMEs) during Covid-19 pandemic: an evidence using economic value-added method. *Journal of Madani Society*, 1(1), 1–7.

Winarsih, Indriastuti, M., and Fuad, K. (2021). Impact of Covid-19 on digital transformation and sustainability in small and medium enterprises (SMEs): a conceptual framework. In Barolli, L., Poniszewska-Maranda, A., and Enokido, T. (Eds.), Complex, Intelligent and Software Intensive Systems (Vol. 1194, pp. 471–476). Springer International Publishing. https://doi.org/10.1007/978-3-030-50454-0_48.

Printed in the United States
by Baker & Taylor Publisher Services